D1517886

Who's Who in Canadian Sport

Volume 3

by Bob Ferguson

©1999

Canadian Cataloguing in Publication Data

Ferguson, Bob, 1931 -
    Who's who in Canadian sport, volume 3

    3rd ed.
    Includes index.

    ISBN 1-894282-00-0

    1. Athlete—Canada—Biography. 2. Sports—Canada—
Biography. I. Title
GV697.A1F47 1999   796'.092'271   C98-900763-4

Dedication

To Aaron, Alex, Taylor, Jordan and Darien, grandchildren of whom I am extremely proud.

And, to Scott and Shane, sons of whom any father would be proud and daughters-in-law Alison and Lindsey for providing the adhesive that holds it all together.

To those who have encouraged me to proceed despite unexpected setbacks.

And, of course, to the sports personalities whose exploits have made this volume so necessary.

Contents

Introduction

One would have to reside in a vacuum not to be even remotely aware of the athletic exploits of a Wayne Gretzky, Barbara Ann Scott, Gordie Howe, Nancy Greene, Ferguson Jenkins, Gaetan Boucher, Sandra Schmerler, Russ Jackson, Marilyn Bell, Tom Longboat or Paul Henderson. Like eternal flames their magnificent achievements shine perpetually in Canadian sport annals. And, well they should.

But, what of the multitude of athletes, native or otherwise, who have enjoyed their fleeting moments of glory only to fade into obscurity's twilight zone? Does the passage of time diminish their deeds or just their memory?

Volume three of Who's Who is yet another step in an effort to recognize Canada's glorious sports heritage. The efforts and achievements of 4,500 athletes and sports figures, amateur and professional, living and dead and representing virtually every sport, are included.

As is always the case in efforts of this nature there are omissions. In some instances tracing of athletes or their relatives struck a dead end. In other instances exclusion resulted from reluctance on the part of the contacted to reply to requests for information.

It is my hope that you, the reader, will assist in the ongoing search for names, addresses and additional information so that the next such volume will include many more worthy persons who have had an impact on the Canadian sports scene. Any correspondence should be directed to Who's Who in Canadian Sport, 112 Banchory Cresc., Kanata, ON, K2K 2V5.

This volume can never be definitive. It is, however, a major step along the path.

— **Bob Ferguson**

Credits

Editors & Research
Graham Cox
Ron Cox
Ray Lauzon
Business
Brian Burant
Reg McClellan
Bob Parkin
Al Rae
Computer guru
Tim Stewart
Text Layout
Denise Pittuck
Cover design
John Luimes
Reg McClellan
Contributors
Adam Lauzon, Ottawa researcher
Allan Stewart, Canada's Sports Hall of Fame
Allison MacNeill, Ottawa hockey
Al Mann, Wallaceburg Sports Hall of Fame
Allison Neill, Canadian Equestrian Federation
Al Weiss, Canadian Press Toronto
Andre Leclerc, Horseshoe Canada
Andrew Braun, Winnipeg
Ann Deavy, Shooting Federation of Canada
Anne MacRae, Mississauga Sports Hall of Fame
Arleen Noga, Regina, Canadian women's baseball
Barb Wilson, Canadian Figure Skating Association
Bente Jorgensen, Ottawa, a great Dane
Beth Rosen, Ottawa
Betty Bawden Bowen, Edmonton Grads
Bev Miller, Gymnastics Canada
Bill Charlick, Sarnia/Lambton Sports Hall of Fame
Bill Knight, Detroit Red Wings Alumni
Bill McNulty, Athletics, Vancouver, B.C.
Bill Rayner, St. Thomas, baseball historian
Bill Steinburg, RCGA
Bob Gage, London sport historian
Brenda Gorman, Canadian Figure Skating Association
Brian McFalone, Guelph hockey historian
Bruce Murray, Ontario Jockey Club
Bruce Walker, Ontario Jockey Club
Bruce Wylie, Brockville Sports Hall of Fame
Carl Schwende, Quebec Sports Hall of Fame
Caroline Sharp, Volleyball Canada
Cecil Smith, Athletics Canada magazine
Cheri Morrison, Canadian Sportfishing Productions
Cheryl Henhawke, Six Nations of the Grand River
Cheryl Reilly, Canadian Curling Hall of Fame
Christine Brown, International Triathlon Union
Colin Kirk, Canadian Orienteering Federation
David Hart, Water Polo Canada
David Menary, Cambridge Reporter
Dennis "Dee" Murphy, St. John's, Nfld.
Diana Ranken, OFSAA
Diane Imrie, Northwestern Ontario Sports Hall of Fame
Dr. Sidney Soames, Figure Skating historian

Donna Rochon, pistol shooting
Doreen Banville, Ottawa Sports Hall of Fame
Doug Lomberg, Cornwall Sports Hall of Fame
Earl McRae, Ottawa Sun
Ed Grenda, Kingston soccer, snowshoe authority
Elizabeth Dagg, Canadian Football Hall of Fame
Fred Rams, Ontario Aquatic Hall of Fame
Gary LaRose, Ottawa
Greg Mathieu, Canadian Amateur Wrestling Association
Heike Ryan, Dominion of Canada Rifle Association
Henry Bury, Belleville Intelligencer
Howard Starkman, Toronto Blue Jays Baseball Club
Hugh Wilson, Athletics Canada
Ian Kennedy, Vancouver Rugby
Jack Donohue, Basketball, Kanata
Jack Jordan, Football Canada
Jack Wylie, Oshawa Sports Hall of Fame
Jake Dineen, Gloucester
Jane Rodney, Hockey Hall of Fame
Janice Smith, Canadian Football Hall of Fame
Jeff Timpson, Labatt Brier
Jeffrey Reed, London Intercounty baseball
Jennifer Ward, Canadian Equestrian Federation
Jim McAuley, Ottawa sports historian
Jim Shearon, Kanata baseball historian
Joe Foley, Canadian Boxing Hall of Fame
Johanna Earl-Taylor, Ottawa
John Bales, Coaching Association of Canada
John Bulmer, Collingwood Sports Hall of Fame
John Craig, Athletics Ontario
John Gosset, Canadian Basketball Hall of Fame
John Loaring Jr., Windsor-Essex Sports Hall of Fame
John Trager, Canadian 10-Pin Bowling Federation
Judy Carey, Ottawa
Julie Jardine, Campbellton Sports Hall of Fame
June Takahashi, Judo Canada
Karen Hewson, Canadian Golf Hall of Fame
Kathy Ladouceur, Ringette Canada
Kathy Meagher, New Brunswick Sports Hall of Fame
Ken Doucette, Canadian Forces Sports Hall of Fame
Kevin Jepson, Canadian 5-Pin Bowlers' Association
Kim Ali, Tennis Canada
Leane Swales, Canadian Cycling Association
Lefty Reid, Peterborough Sports Hall of Fame
Les Smith, Fort Erie
Linda Petryna, Saskatchewan Sports Hall of Fame
Lisette Stapley, Softball Canada
Liz Shaughnessy, Linda Hiles, Equestrian Sport
Loretto Vella, Tennis Canada
Louise Frogett, Canadian Football Hall of Fame
Lynn Clifford-Ward, Canadian Figure Skating Hall of Fame
Marguerite Grant, Softball Canada
Marilyn Ettinger, Ottawa
Marilyn Haley, Alberta Sports Hall of Fame
Martha Fournier, B.C. Sports Hall of Fame
Martin Cleary, Ottawa Citizen
Matt Charbonneau, Swimming Canada
Matt Thompson, Kanata

Credits, continued

Michelle Lalonde, Calgary Stampeders
Mike Lachapelle, Canadian Lacrosse Association
Merv Bonney, Ottawa
Monique Giroux, Montreal Expos
Morgan Quarry, Ottawa Senators
Nancy Irvin, Water Ski Canada
Natalie Monette, Canadian Canoe Association
Pam Rene, Canadian Olympic Association
Pat Armstrong, B.C. Sports Hall of Fame
Pat Hall, Greater Victoria Sports Hall of Fame
Patti Hutchison, Nova Scotia Sports Hall of Fame
Paul Ramlow, U.S. Trotting Association
Paul Thomas, Basketball, Windsor, Ont.
Peter Vaughn, Dominion of Canada Rifle Association
Phil Pritchard, Hockey Hall of Fame
Rachel Delaney, Canadian Curling Association
Rene Leroux, Embrun broomball, hockey
Rick Brownlee, Manitoba Sports Hall of Fame
Rick Traer, Basketball Canada
Robert Bolduc, Canadian Amateur Speed Skating
    Association
Robin Wilson, Scott Tournament of Hearts
Ron Skronski, Smiths Falls Recreation Hall of Fame
Roy McGregor, National Post

Ruth Krall, Canadian Professional Rodeo Association
Sarah Storey, Canadian Bobsleigh & Luge Association
Sheila Kelly, Saskatchewan Sports Hall of Fame
Sheila Robertson, Canadian Association for the Advance-
    ment of Women and Sport and Physical Activity
Sue Cadieux, Sport North
Sue Hylland, Canadian Olympic Association
Susan Stern, UBC Public Affairs
Sylvie Clark, Badminton Canada
Sylvie Doucette, Canadian Olympic Association
Terry Baker, London
Terry Wheatley-Magee, Field Hockey Canada
Tim Sample, Barrie Sports Hall of Fame
Tom Boreski, Canadian Olympic Association
Tom Casey, Ottawa Citizen
Tom Sweet, Nova Scotia sports historian
Tom West, Calgary Olympic Hall of Fame
Tony Tetchko, Windsor-Essex Sports Hall of Fame
Vaughan Baird, Canadian Aquatic Hall of Fame
Violet Le Blanc, Canadian Table Tennis Association
Wayne Kondro, Ottawa, basketball historian
Wayne Scanlan, Ottawa Citizen
Wendy Vallillee, Lanark Era
William & Margaret Thompson, Burlington

Century Club

Everyone is entitled to an opinion. The following list of Canadian sports personalities, representing the top 10 from each of the 10 decades in the 20th century, were selected by the author based on his assessment. Needless to say you may disagree with some of the choices. They are listed by decade alphabetically. Even I haven't the gall to rate them in order of importance.

1900-09
Dan Bain
Tommy Burns
Walter Ewing
George Gibson
Tom Longboat
George Lyon
George Orton
Harvey Pulford
William Sherring
Cyclone Taylor

1910-19
Cal Bricker
Nig Clarke
Russell Ford
Duncan Gillis
George Goulding
George Hodgson
Newsy Lalonde
Joe Malone
Frank Nighbor
Lester Patrick

1920-29
Ethel Catherwood
King Clancy
Myrtle Cook
Jack Guest
Ada MacKenzie
Bobbie Rosenfeld
Eddie Shore
Jim Trifunov
Huck Welch
Percy Williams

1930-39
Toe Blake
Frank Boucher
Dit Clapper
Lionel Conacher
Lefty Gwynne
Jeff Heath
Aileen Meagher
Howie Morenz
Sandy Somerville
Hilda Strike

1940-49
Syl Apps
Turk Broda
Tony Golab
Ted Kennedy
Joe Krol
Phil Marchildon
Maurice Richard
Goody Rosen
Barbara Ann Scott
Ken Watson

1950-59
Marilyn Bell
Gil Boa
Gordie Howe
Normie Kwong
Gerry Ouellette
Jacques Plante
Terry Sawchuk
Bob Simpson
Marlene Stewart Streit
Lucile Wheeler

1960-69
Jean Beliveau
Bev Boys
Nancy Greene
Bob Hayward
Russ Jackson
Bobby Orr
Sandra Post
Ernie Richardson
Ron Stewart
Elaine Tanner

1970-79
George Chuvalo
Dave Cutler
Phil Esposito
Nancy Garapick
Bobby Hull
Ferguson Jenkins
Guy Lafleur
Frank Mahovlich
Sue Nattrass
Graham Smith

1980-89
Alex Baumann
Sylvie Bernier
Gaetan Boucher
Russ Howard
Silken Laumann
Mario Lemieux
Lennox Lewis
Ian Millar
Linda Thom
Carolyn Waldo

1990-99
Donovan Bailey
Chantal Benoit
Kurt Browning
Wayne Gretzky
Marnie McBean
Sandra Schmerler
Elvis Stojko
Jacques Villeneuve
Larry Walker
Steve Yzerman

A

ABBOTT, Bill Jr. (sailing); b. 21 May 1954, Sarnia, Ont.; m. Joanne Gray; c. Bill, Cam, Chris, Katie; boat builder; with father Bill Sr., brother Larry soling gold '77 Governor's Cup, silver '77 President's Cup, '79 NA, '82 US nationals, '83 Pan-Am Games; 4 CORK bronze; 4 ntl soling class titles; with wife Joanne, Brad Boston won '93 CORK silver; bronze '97 world championships; 2-time Olympian; res. Sarnia, Ont.

ABBOTT, Colin (softball); b. 1 Oct 1970, St. John's, Nfld.; m. Michelle Ghent; Memorial, BA, BCom; salesman; outfielder who wields potent bat; mem. Lloydminster Liners, Rempel Bros, Green Bay All Car; 2 ntl jr. titles with Lloydminster; ntl championships '94 Rempel Bros team, '97 Victoria, '98 Halifax Jaguars; MVP '94 ISC Green Bay world title team; with Green Bay All-Car '95-97, Madison, Wisc. Farm Tavern '98-99; Pan-Am Games gold team '99; ISC MVP, 1st team all-star '94; ASA all-American '94; 2 St. John's athlete of yr awards; res. Portugal Cove, Nfld.

ABBOTT, Joanne (sailing); b. 25 Apr 1955, Sarnia, Ont.; m. Bill Jr.; c. Bill, Cam, Chris, Katie; chartered accountant; began sailing as teenager; sailed with husband several years before taking break to raise her children; formed own crew to compete in '85, '91 world championships; re-teamed with husband and Brad Boston to win '93 CORK silver; bronze '97 world championships; 1st woman to compete in soling class at Olympics '96; res. Sarnia, Ont.

ABBRUZZI, Pat (football); b. 29 Aug 1932, Providence, R.I.; given name: Pasquale; m. Philomena Andreozzi; c. Diane, Debra, Michael, Mary, Julie, Jane; Rhode Island, BSc; teacher, restaurateur; HS all-state '48-49; all-prep Marianapolis '50; all-Yankee conf. '51-54; little all-America '52, '54; all-New England '52-54; 10 R.I., N.E. records including 306yds single game, 99yd TD run; 4yr. college rushing record 3389yds; all-pro Montreal Alouettes '55-58; CFL records 20 TDs single season '52, 182 carries, 1248yds, 17 TDs '56; EFC scoring title '56; coached 7 Warren HS title teams; State team record 32 consecutive victories; pres. R.I. Football Coaches Assn. '72-73; R.I. athlete of '54; R.I. Italian athlete of '53-54; R.I. coach of '75; mem. U of R.I. Hall of Fame; res. Warren, R.I.

ABDO, Reema (swimming); b. 19 May 1963, Aden, South Yemen; Arizona State, UofT, Ont. Provincial Police; backstroke specialist; broke onto ntl scene '81; 14 ntl championship medals, 7 gold, 4 silver, 3 bronze; Cdn record short course 100m, 200m backstroke; represented Canada USSR-Germany-Canada tri-meet, Commonwealth, FISU Games, '84 Olympics; Pan-Pacific championships; FISU games 4x100 medley relay bronze '83; gold France's Diana Invitational '84; Olympic 4x100 medley relay bronze; coached for several yrs at age-group, university levels; active triathlete, long distance runner; Olympic champion award '85; mem. Ont. Aquatic Hall of Fame; res. Caledon, Ont.

ABDOU, Justin (wrestling); b. 18 Jan 1971, Moose Jaw, Sask.; SFU; coach; competing at 85kg won 4 NAIA , '91 US university titles; gold Romanian Open, N.Y. AC open, Sunkist Invitational, Canada Cup, '94 Commonwealth Games, Polish GP, US GP, US Espoir, '87 world cadet; 2 ntl bantam, 2 cadet, 2 jr., 2 espoir, 7 sr. titles; 2 Canada Games gold; mem. Burnaby Mountain Wrestling Club; asst. coach SFU; res. Vancouver, B.C.

ABEL, Sid (hockey); b. 22 Feb 1918, Melville, Sask.; given name: Sidney Gerald; m. Gloria Moranday; c. Gerry, Linda; hockey broadcaster; Flin Flon Man. Sr. League; Detroit Red Wings '38-43, '45-52; team capt. at 24; centred Liniment Line of Don Grosso, Eddie Wares, Production Line of Gordie Howe, Ted Lindsay; Canadian Forces '43-45; playing-coach Chicago Black Hawks '52-54; NHL playing record: 612 scheduled games, 189g, 283a, 97 playoff games, 28g, 30a; mem. 3 Stanley Cup winners; Hart Trophy (MVP) '49; replaced Jimmy Skinner as Detroit coach '57-58; GM '62-71; coach St. Louis Blues '71, GM '72-73; GM Kansas City Scouts '73; NHL coaching record: 382w, 423l, 155t, 9 playoffs, no titles; Red Wings ret. jersey 8; *Hockey News* coach of '53; NHL all-star coach '63; mem. Sask Sports, Hockey halls of fame; res. Farmington, Mich.

ABELSON, Jess (all-around); b. 14 Apr 1892, Cleveland, Ohio; d. 22 Nov 1975, Ottawa, Ont.; m. Mollie; c. Sylvia, Lawrence (d), Stanley, Alan, Bob; flying wing Ottawa Football Club 1910-20; mem. 1913-14 league title teams; mem. 1913 Britannia Cdn war canoe titlists; playing-mgr. Ottawa rugby league team; capt. Ottawa Senators YMCA sr. basketball city title teams '13-14, mem. Cdn champions '14; top-ranked handball player '13-14; track standout early in career; involved with YMCA program 60 yrs; owner, mgr., occasional player Strathconas semipro softball team; sponsored Ottawa Primrose hockey club; founder, pres. Tel Aviv Tennis Club '34; formed 39th Boy Scout Troop; mem. Ottawa Jewish Sports Hall of Fame.

ABENDSCHAN, Jack (football); b. 1942, New Mexico; given name: John Jacob; m. Virginia Lomax; c. Christina, Shelley, John; New Mexico, BA; personnel dir.; offensive guard, defensive end, place kicker; 2nd team AP all-American; pro Sask. Roughriders '65-75; CFL record: 312 converts, 159 field goals, 74 singles, 863 points; sat out 1974 campaign with knee injury; quit Riders 1968 for AFL Denver Broncos trial, when cut rejoined Riders; 7 times WFC all-star, 5 times all-Canadian; 2 WFC, 1 CFL scoring title; res. Abilene, Tex.

ABRAMOWITZ, Moe (basketball); b. 5 Aug 1903, Montreal, Que.; d. 2 Jan 1991, Montreal, Que.; m. Lilian Lessor; c. Mark; company treas.; despite diminutive stature (5'4") veritable court wizard; basketball player, coach, administrator '19-54; record 88 free throws in 101 attempts '22; numerous Montreal area scoring titles, YMHA title teams; coach from '35; 4 Que., 3 Eastern, 3 ntl titles; coached McGill '49-52, Montreal league title, Dodds Cup; with Bob Osborne co-coach '48 Olympic basketball team; former YMHA basketball chair.; charter mem. Que. Board of Referees; 1st athlete inducted into Montreal YM-YWHA Sports Hall of Fame.

ACKLES, Bob (football); b. 16 Sep 1938, Sarnia, Ont.; given name: Robert William; m. Kay; c. Steve, Scott; football exec.; mem. jr. Blue Bombers; joined B.C. Lions organization at '54 inception; water boy, equipment mgr., dir. player personnel, AGM, club historian, GM '75-85; GM Dallas Cowboys '86-92; AGM Arizona Cardinals '93-94; dir. of football operations, Philadelphia Eagles '95; dir. football operations, Miami Dolphins from '96; res. Miami, Fla.

ACOOSE, Paul (t&f); b. 1883 Sakimay Reserve, Sask.; d. 30 Apr 1978, Sakimay Reserve, Sask.; m. Madeleine Osoup; c. 9; band councilor, farmer; began running competitively in late teens at Grenfell area sport days; 3-, 5-mile Sask. road race titles; Western Canada 5-mile track title; won Regina 10.5-mile race '08 beating best Sask. runners by 8 minutes; won '08 Manitoba 5-mile title; turned pro '09; beat England's Fred Appleby in 1st pro race setting world 15-mile record 1:22:22; 2nd Madison Square Garden 20-mile race vs. top international field '10; beat Tom Longboat in 12-mile race at Toronto to close pro career '10; mem. Sask, First Nations Sports halls of fame.

ACTON, Keith (hockey); b. 15 Apr 1958, Stouffville, Ont.; given name: Keith Edward; m. Susan; c. Brooke, Elisa, William, Robert; coach; centre Peterborough (OHA) '76-78, Nova Scotia (AHL) '78-80; claimed in '78 amateur draft by Montreal; played in NHL with Montreal '79-83, Minnesota '83-88, Edmonton '88-89, Philadelphia '89-93, Washington '93, NY Islanders '93-94; NHL record: 15 seasons, 1023 scheduled games, 226g, 358a, 66 playoff games, 12g, 21a; mem. 1 Stanley Cup winner; AHL all-star '80; played in NHL all-star game '82; asst./assoc. coach Philadelphia '94-97; asst. coach NY Rangers from '98; res. Toronto, Ont.

ADAIR, Colin (squash); b. 4 Nov 1942, Montreal, Que.; given name: Colin John; m. Margot Jean Lafleur; c. Jacqueline, Gregor, Dylan; McGill, BA; investment banker; from '60 amassed more than 100 major tournament titles in US, Canada; US singles '68, '71; twice ntl singles champion; 1st Canadian to win US doubles '74; 4 ntl doubles titles; McGill athlete of '64; Squash Canada distinguished service award; res. Montreal, Que.

ADAMS, Diane (curling); b. 7 Jan 1965, Baudette, Minn.; given name: Diane Janet Wolanicki; m. Jim Adams; provincial civil servant; began curling age 10; skipped NWO jr title rink '83; played second for Heather Houston's Cdn. women's title rink '88-89, world champions '89; conducted jr. curling clinics in NWO '91; exec. mem Thunder Bay Major League '88-91; mem. Ont. team of '89; mem. NWO Sports, Cdn Curling halls of fame; res. Thunder Bay, Ont.

ADAMS, Dick (football); b. 13 Feb 1948, Athens, Ohio; given name: Richard Earl; div.; c. Timothy Eugene, Anthony William; m. Catherine Patterson; c. Rachel, Daniel Chelsey; Miami of Ohio, BSc; football coach; all-Southeastern Ohio '63-66, all-Southern Ohio baseball '66; with Miami all-Mid-American Conf. '69-70, best def. back, MVP twice; UPI all-American 2nd team '69-70, athlete of '70; Mid-Am. Conf. defensive player '70; 14 Miami school records; defensive halfback, punter Ottawa Rough Riders '72-75; 4yrs EFC, all-Canadian; led EFC punt returners '72 with 92 for 608yds; mem. '73 Grey Cup winners; coached HS in Ohio '71, asst. coach Carleton, Mount Allison, U Ottawa '76-82; Calgary Stampeders '83, Ottawa Rough Riders '84-86, '95, Saskatchewan Roughriders '87-92, Murray State '92, head coach Bethel College '93-94, asst. Winnipeg Blue Bombers '96-99; res. Winnipeg, Man.

ADAMS, Harry (curling); b. 7 Dec 1932, D'Arcy, Sask.; m. Shirley Goodwin; c. Ken, Connie, Debbie, Lisa; businessman; established reputation in mixed curling winning Salls Trophy, Canadian Branch Lady Gilmour competition, OVCA mixed '75; twice Ont. mixed champion; won Branch Governor-General's, OCA Silver Tankard (double rink); finalist OCA Intermediates; 4 times men's provincial finals; Red Anderson Memorial Trophy '73, Curl 4 TV series '78, City of Ottawa grand aggregate shield '78, Ottawa Masters '78, North Bay Jamaica 'spiel '78, Capital Challenge series '77; res. Nepean, Ont.

ADAMS, Jack (hockey); b. 14 Jun 1895, Ft. William, Ont.; d. 1 May 1968, Detroit, Mich.; given name: John James; m. Helen; hockey exec.; Ft. William, Peterborough, Sarnia amateur; pro centre Toronto Arenas '18; Vancouver 3 seasons; Pacific Coast League scoring title '20 with 24g, 18a in 24 games; Toronto St. Pats '22-26, Ottawa Senators '26-27 Stanley Cup winners; Detroit Red Wings mgr. '27; 18yrs mgr. and/or coach, 12 league titles, 7 in succession, 7 Stanley Cups; coached 1st, 2nd NHL all-star teams once each; innovator of hockey farm system; Central Pro League pres. 1962-68; mem. Hockey, Canada's, Mich., NWO Sports halls of fame.

ADAMS, Jeff (t&f); b. 15 Nov 1970, Brampton, Ont.; motivational speaker; wheelchair track athlete in distances from 100 metres to marathon; silver 800m, 4x400m '92 Paralympics; 800m gold, 400m silver, 4x400m relay bronze '96 Paralympics; competed '92 Olympics but withdrew with 300m remaining due to mechanical difficulties; 2 ntl 10km. marathon titles; '94 Commonwealth Games 800, 1500m gold; IAAF 1500m gold '95; 3 Stoke-Mandeville Games gold, 5 Ian Hume Invitational gold '95, 4 Black Top Invitational gold '96; 5 Canberra Interclub meet gold, 3 silver '96; 1 gold, 3 silver '94 IPC Worlds; res. Don Mills, Ont.

ADAMS, Robert (t&f); b. 20 Dec 1924, Alsask, Sask,; m. Marjorie Pascoe; c. Janice, Murray; UofSask, BA, BEd; retd. HS phys ed supervisor; decathlete '52 Olympics; capt. '54 BEG track team; Fred Rowell Trophy AAU of C outstanding field event athlete 1954; ntl sr. native discus record 148'10" '49; sr. native decathlon record 6636 points '52; t&f team coach '58 Commonwealth, '64 Olympic, '68 Trinidad Games; 5yrs coach Royal Canadian Legion coaching clinic Guelph; head judge pole vaulting '76 Olympics; vertical jumps referee '78 Commonwealth Games, '79 World Cup;

Bob Adams Foundation to assist aspiring t&f athletes initiated by STFA '83; Centennial Medal; mem. Cdn Olympic, Sask., Saskatoon Sports halls of fame; res. Victoria, B.C.

ADELMAN, Louis (football); b. 13 Jan 1905, Devil's Lake, N.D.; d. 3 Jul 1987, Palmdale Calif.; m. Molly Rosenblat; c. David, Howard, Robert, Sheila; HS football to Tammany Tigers (forerunners Winnipeg Blue Bombers); centre 1924-38; 4 Grey Cup finals, 1 winner; capt. '35 team which brought Grey Cup West 1st time; mgr. Winnipeg club '39-45; inducted with '35 team into Manitoba Sports Hall of Fame.

ADKIN, Dennis (builder); b. 6 Jun 1919, Monitor, Alta.; m. Alison Ronalda Fortune; c. Dennis Monte, Laurie Elizabeth, David Roderick; retd. newspaper exec.; during 19yrs as reporter/editor London Free Press instrumental in establishing and development of London Ski Club; club pres. 9yrs, dir. 6yrs; moving to Saskatoon exec. editor Star-Phoenix '65-67, Federated Co-Ops Ltd. in-house publication editor '68-82; key role in development Blackstrap Hill for '71 Saskatoon Winter Games; established, edited Sask. Ski Journal '74-87; pres. Sask. Div. CSA 11yrs; life mem. London Ski Club, Sask. Ski Assn.; mem. Cdn. Skiing, Sask. Sports halls of fame; res. Saskatoon, Sask.

ADLHOCH, Hans (shooting); b. 10 Apr 1935, Heidelberg, Ger.; carpenter; '72, '77 ntl smallbore 3-position champion; '74 ntl smallbore prone title; silver, bronze '78 Benito Juarez International; silver smallbore air rifle team '79 Pan-Am Games; mem. '76 Olympic team; Longueuil athlete of '75; SFC golden anniversary award; distinguished life mem. USNRA; res. Victoria, B.C.

AGER, Barry (basketball); b. 29 Jan 1938, London, Ont.; given name: Barry Laurence; m. Catherine Mutsch; c. David, Robert, Carolyn; UWO BA, McMaster U, BPhE, Ithaca College, MSc.; HS v.-principal; London Dist. HS all-star '56; mem. Western Colts jr. title team '57; UWO Mustangs '58; London Lounge Int. A '59, Tillsonburg Livingstons ntl sr. A champs, Olympic team '60; CIAU all-star McMaster '61; Ottawa Joe Feller's Sr. A team '62; Ottawa ACT basketballer of year; Ottawa Lapointes Sr. A team '63, Bert Marshall Trophy; coached Ridgemont Spartans to Ottawa HS, Valley titles '69; res. Nepean, Ont.

AH YOU, Junior (football); b. 30 Dec 1948, American Samoa; Arizona State; all-around athlete at Arizona State starring in football, basketball, volleyball, t&f; named outstanding lineman Fiesta Bowl, MVP '70 Peach Bowl; sought by NE Patriots but opted for CFL Montreal Alouettes '72-81; def. end; 4 all-East, 2 all-Cdn DE; 5 Grey Cup finals, 2 winners; top def. player '74 Grey Cup; 2 CFL tds; mem. Cdn Football, Ariz. State halls of fame; res. Laie, Hawaii.

AHEARN, Frank (hockey); b. 10 May 1886, Ottawa, Ont.; d. 17 Nov 1962, Ottawa, Ont.; jr., sr. hockey promoter; bought Ottawa Senators from Tommy Gorman '24 and assembled powerful team which included Jack Adams, George Boucher, Alex Connell, Hec Kilrea, Frank Nighbor, Syd Howe, Hooley Smith; won '27 Stanley Cup; depression years forced him to sell his arena, star players in series of deals considered spectacular at time; mem. Ottawa, Hockey halls of fame.

AIRD, Stu (lacrosse/football); b. 14 Apr 1957, Oakville, Ont.; given name: Samuel Stuart; m. Laura Ramsay; c. Emily, Samuel, Neil; UWO BA, U Windsor LL.B, lawyer; mem. UWO Vanier Cup CIAU finalists '77, '79, winner '77; began playing lacrosse age 5; mem. Mississauga Jr A '75-78, Vancouver Burrards '79-80, Owen Sound North Stars '81-90, Buffalo Bandits '93-94; ntl team from '83; mem. 3 Cdn teams at World championships; mem. '83 international championships; 2 Owen Sound North Stars, Mississauga jr A MVP awards; OLA sr., jr league all-star; mem. major indoor league champion Buffalo Bandits '93; 2nd team MILL all-star '94; MILL rookie of '93 and unsung hero '93-95; retd. from competitive ranks '95; res. Ancaster, Ont.

AITCHISON, Gordon (basketball); b. 1909, North Bay, Ont.; d. 6 Jan 1990, Windsor, Ont.; m. Melba Malott; c. Andy, Peggy; Detroit, Assumption College, BA, UofT; retd HS principal; ntl interscholastic pole vault record; mem. UofD, Windsor Alumni, Assumption, Windsor Fords teams; ntl sr. finalist '34, Eastern, Cdn sr. titles '35; mem. silver medal team '36 Olympics; played at UofT '38; player-coach Portage La Prairie while mem. RCAF WW2; coached football, basketball, t&f, CO Cornwall cadet corps '45; mem. Cdn Basketball Hall of Fame.

AITKEN, Don (curling); b. 16 May 1945, Tillsonburg, Ont.; given name: Donald John; m. Terry; c. Bruce; self-employed; mem. 8 Brier rinks; 2nd for Jim Ursel's '77 Que. ntl champions; mem. '75 CBC Classic, '77-79 Kronenbourg Trophy (Switzerland) winning rinks; mem. Cdn Curling Hall of Fame; res. Mount Royal, Que.

AKERVALL, Henry (all-around); b. 24 Aug 1937, Port Arthur, Ont.; m. Lorna Mahan; c. Christopher, Kelli; Mich. Tech, BSc, N.Mich, MEd, N. Colorado EdD; retd. educator; HS jr pole vault record holder; active hockey defenceman '50-72 Port Arthur Jr. A champs, Hamilton Jr. A; 3yrs mem. US ntl college all-star teams, Western Collegiate all-star, NCAA Div. 1 champs, all-American; playing coach Tampere, Finland; capt. '64 Cdn Olympic hockey team; mem. Port Arthur Sr. Bearcats, 3 city titles, 1 MVP award; all-star champion Marquette Iron Rangers; mem. Thunder Bay Twins; utility baseball player '52-64 with champion Port Arthur senior Giants, Red Sox; utility fastball player, '64-75 champion Port Arthur Dairyman, MVP '66, twice all-star 3rd baseman, sr. champ Club 17 team; with Tom Luck Jr. won '72 TB dist. Red Rock pro-am golf title; active curler, skier, bowler, squash player, paddler; HS football, hockey t&f coach; co-ordinator NWO hockey clinics; 2yrs AD Lakehead U; coach GPAC champion Lakehead U hockey team; Lakehead U fastball, paddling, speed skating coach; Port Arthur minor hockey coach, CAHA level 5 instructor; cross-country ski instructor; TB male athlete of yr '63; Celebration '88 fed. govt. medal; mem. North Shore Steelhead Assn., pres. '85-87; bd. mem. Big Thunder ski training centre; mem. Lakehead U Hall of Fame selection comm.; mem. NWO Sports Hall of Fame; res. Thunder Bay, Ont.

ALBERT, Herb (archery); b. 17 Jan 1905, Germany; d. (Circa 1990), Clearbrook, B.C.; m. Marjorie Docherty; c. Edward, Sonja, Elizabeth, Sandra; retd. manufacturer, engraver; emigrated to Canada as youngster; 1st official competition '14 winning distance event with homemade bow, arrows; considered Canada's finest long distance shooter in modern flight archery; from '50 held all Canadian flight records, including 613yds with 50lb light bow; high altitude shooting in California surpassed this mark with 702yds, but not recognized Cdn record; B.E. flight records; helped form Canadian Archery Assn. '51; p-pres. FCA, mem. Alta. Sports Hall of Fame; res. Clearbrook, B.C.

ALBRECHT, J.I. (football/soccer); b. 15 Feb 1931, St. James, N.Y.; m. Anna Maria Johnson; c. Roderick, Hunter, Dean; Georgia Military College, BA, MA, PhD; football exec.; asst. coach Tennessee '50 to '52; teams competed in '50 Cotton Bowl, '51 Sugar Bowl, '52 Cotton Bowl; '51 U S ntl title; coach Southern Cal, Maryland, Wyoming, South Carolina '53-58 with teams participating in Rose, Orange, Sun Bowls; AFL talent consultant '59; mem. Montreal staff '60-62; business mgr., AGM AFL Oakland '63; helped establish Quebec Rifles UFL '64; chief scout San Francisco ''65-67; scout Denver '68-70; rejoined Alouettes '70, GM '72-73; player personnel dir. New England '74; dir. personnel Toronto '75-77; GM Toronto Croatia soccer club 1978; instrumental in Maritimes bid for CFL franchise '79; opinionated broadcaster, newspaper sports columnist; AD Cape Breton 1989-90; special advisor '93 Ottawa , '94 Shreveport Pirates; nicknamed Bird Dog or Super Scout; author "Just J.I.: A Sports Odessey"; res. Halifax, N.S.

ALBRIGHT, Debbie (figure skating); b. 11 Jul 1958, Kamloops, B.C.; given name: Deborah Lee; m. David Islam; c. Mitchell, Rachel; UofT, BSc. MHSc.; exec. dir. Alzheimer Society of Greater Simcoe County; ntl. jr. ladies title '76; bronze Nebelhorn '76, Prague Skate '77, ntl srs. figures Otto Gold Memorial Trophy '79; Ont. Achievement Award, 3 Toronto Cricket, Skating and Curling Club McCordic Memorial awards; rep. Canada internationally through '80; athlete rep. CFSA board '80-86; COA athletes advisory council '81-85; CFSA judge from '78, ISU judge from '95; res. Barrie, Ont.

ALDAG, Roger (football); b. 6 Oct 1953, Gull Lake, Sask.; 4 seasons all-star defensive tackle, centre Regina Rams; Man.-Sask. Junior League outstanding lineman '76; twice Rams MVP; CFL Saskatchewan offensive guard '76-92; 271 games played through '92; 8 all-Western, 5 all-CFL; Schenley outstanding offensive lineman award '86, '88; West Div. Becket-DeMarco Memorial Trophy outstanding offensive lineman award '86, '88; mem. '89 Grey Cup winner; nicknamed Dog; res. Regina, Sask.

ALDRIDGE, Dick (football); b. 19 Jan 1941, Toronto, Ont.; given name: Richard Frederick; m. Elisabeth van Haastrecht; c. Jodi Elisabeth, Richard Todd; Waterloo, BA, BPHe; retd HS teacher; mem. OFSAA basketball champions '59-61; MVP Lakeshore Bears jr. ORFU '62; twice Waterloo football MVP, once basketball, outstanding athlete '66; from '66 Dick Aldridge Trophy awarded annually to Waterloo football MVP; drafted B.C. Lions, traded to Hamilton '64; star linebacker Argos '65-73; Hamilton '74; led Argos punt

returns '65, 7 interceptions '70; career record 19 interceptions 127 scheduled games; head coach York U '76-77, Etobicoke Argonauts '78-79; head boys' physical and health education Banting Memorial HS Alliston, Ont.; mem. OUAA Football Hall of Fame; res. Alliston, Ont.

ALEXANDER, Jeremy (shooting): b. 31 Jan 1948, Liverpool, Eng.; c. Michael; boilermaker; became mem. Calgary Rifle & Pistol Club '58; Calgary jr. smallbore champ '59; Alberta jr. smallbore prone title '64; won Cotteslee Vase Bisley while attending school in England '63; B.C. TR title '90, '96; DCRA Champlain agg. '96; qualified 4 Cdn Bisley teams; res. Victoria, B.C.

ALEXANDER, John (modern pentathlon); b. 18 Nov 1954, South Bend, Ind.; given name: John Ward; Nebraska, Wayne State, BSc; PE instructor; mem. Neb. swim team '73-75, swim, gym instructor '75-77, varsity athlete fencing, cross-country, track, swimming '76-78; trained in modern pentathlon from '70; 6 ntl titles; mem. '76, '80 Olympic teams; Montreal tetrathlon title '81; silver International Texas pentathlon '80, Tucson grand international fencing title '81; Haverhill horse show open hunt class '80; NA triathlon champion '82; res. San Antonio, Tex.

ALEXANDER, Keith (golf); b. 23 Jul 1930, Vulcan, Alta.; given name: Robert Keith; m. Vanessa Ramsay; c. Robert Brent, Marc Christopher, Jonathan Phillip, Susan Jolie Maitland, Andrea Denise, Jennifer Carrie; Colorado, BA, Wharton School of Finance, securities management certificate; investment exec., politician; ntl amateur title '60; 6 Alta. amateur, 2 Alta. open, 2 International Oilmen's titles; mem. 26 Willingdon Cup teams, 4 titles; 4 times Willingdon Cup medalist; 8 Calgary amateur, 5 Calgary open, 2 Edmonton amateur, 1 Edmonton open, 6 Calgary tournament of champions, 2 Alta. Canada Dry Challenge Cup, 6 Lethbridge Chinook Classic, 3 Mayfair GC titles; only Albertan to win prov. titles 4 different decades; mem. 6 World amateur (Eisenhower), 5 Americas Cup, 3 Commonwealth Cup, 1 Humberto de Almeida Brazil Cup, 1 Bogota Colombia International, 1 Paris International, French Amateur teams; Big 7 conf. title '53, low amateur '61 Azalea Open, competed '61 Masters; Colorado College title '56; 2 Guadalajara International titles; twice all-American; officer AGA '68-82, pres. '77; MLA (PC) Edmonton Whitemud from '82; mem. Alta., RCGA halls of fame; res. Edmonton, Alta.

ALEXANDER, Kevin (lacrosse); b. 18 Nov 1955, Victoria, B.C.; real estate agent; began playing age 6; considered "Wayne Gretzky of lacrosse"; mem. Victoria Shamrocks '79-86, Victoria Royal Waxmen '80-86; ntl team '81-90; mem. 7 ntl field, 3 box title teams; '76 Minto Cup, '79, '83 Mann Cup champions; Minto Cup MVP '76; mem. MILL titlist Buffalo Bandits '92-93; selected to all-world team '86; midfielder of '86; in 300 scheduled games amassed 797g, 584a; set or tied 31 box lacrosse records including most game winning goals (40), most hat tricks 1 season (24), most powerplay goals 1 season (30), fastest 3 goals by individual player (13 seconds); coach/player ntl men's field team; asst. coach jr ntl team; coach Syracuse Smash (NLL) '98; nicknamed Spanky; mem. Cdn Lacrosse, Greater Victoria Sports halls of fame; res. Victoria, B.C.

ALEXANDER, Lisa (synchro swim); b. 22 Sep 1968, Toronto, Ont.; UofT; competitive age-level swimmer completing all Red Cross programs to age 12 before entering synchro swimming at age 8; gold solo, figures '92 Scottish Open; team silver, duet (Kathy Glen) bronze '91 worlds; gold solo, duet (Erin Woodley) '94 Commonwealth Games; Helen Vanderburg Cdn top overall swimmer award '91; Ont. female athlete of '96; res. Mississauga, Ont.

ALEXANDER, Ray (football); b. 8 Jan 1962, Miami, Fla.; m. Mariel; c. Cardan, Amber; Florida A&M; wide receiver; drafted Tampa Bay USFL '84; signed Denver NFL '84; Calgary CFL '85-86; Dallas NFL '87-89; B.C. Lions CFL '90-94, '96; Ottawa CFL '95; CFL record 114g, 556recept, 8842yds, 41tds; 4 all-Western, 1 all-Cdn; mem. '94 Grey Cup champions; res. Talahassee, Fla.

ALFREDSSON, Daniel (hockey); 11 Dec 1972, Goteborg, Sweden; right wing Molndal Sweden '91-92, Vastra Frolunda Swedish Elite League '92-95; mem. Swedish ntl team Nissan Cup winners, World championship silver medal team '95; also competed for Sweden '96 World Cup, World championships, '98 Olympics; drafted 5th by Ottawa Senators '94 NHL entry draft; Calder Memorial Trophy '96; NHL all-rookie team '96; 2 NHL all-star teams; NHL record (through '99): 271 scheduled games, 78g, 132a, 22 playoff games, 13g, 6a; res. Partille, Sweden/Ottawa, Ont.

ALIE, Caroll-Ann (boardsailing); b. 7 Jun 1960, Gracefield, Que.; m. Steve Rosenberg; c. Jacob; UofOtt, BSc. (2), Mich., CalState; personal trainer LPGA; mem. Que., ntl women's boardsailing team; dist. 13 windsurfer champion '82-84; 2nd overall Australian windsurfer championships '83; Florida dist. windsurfer overall champion '84; Eastern midwinter windsurfer FS champion '84; ntl boardsailing overall champion '84-91; Western hemisphere windsurfer triangle champion '84; Pan-Am Games gold '95, silver '87, '99; US, Cdn women's titles '91; 3 world Mistral, windsurfer overall titles; Cdn Mistral title '93; mem. '92, '96 Olympic Games teams; Ottawa ACT athlete of '85; 2 CYA, 1 QSF female athlete of yr awards; mem. Cdn. Amateur Sports Hall of Fame; res. Long Beach, Calif./Hull, Que.

ALLAN, Liz (water skiing); b. 24 Nov 1950, Columbia, S.C.; given name: Elizabeth Christine; m. Bruce Reid; c. James Brody; Seminole Jr. Coll.; water ski training centre operator; world overall champion '65-75; 9 world masters titles; 11 US ntl titles; mem. American Water Ski Hall of Fame; res. Alton, Ill.

ALLAN, Maurice (weightlifting); b. 17 Apr 1927, Montreal, Que.; d. 11 Jan 1990, Montreal, Que.; m. Pierrette Laroche; c. Michel, Lucie, Jean; Laval, BA; program-marketing mgr. Air Canada; operated Gymnase Hercule; Que. shot put, hammer throw titles '50; weightlifting coach '50-68; pres. Canadian Weightlifting Fed. '60-70; category I international lifting referee; coach '64 Olympics, mgr. '66 Commonwealth Games team; tech. advisor Canada Winter Games '67, Pan-Am Games '67, Canada Summer Games '69; CdM Mexico Little Olympics '67, asst. CdM '68 Olympics, CdM '72, '76 Olympics; v.-pres IWF '72-80, COA director from '60, sec.-treas. from '77; hon. life pres. CWA '70; pres. AAU of C '70-71; v.-pres. SFC '70-71; '67

Centennial medal, gold medal for 25 years in weightlifting, Foley award sport administrator of '67, Air Canada merit award '67; mem. Order of Canada, Canadian Amateur, Que. Sports halls of fame.

ALLAN, Robert (lacrosse); b. 19 Sep 1934, Orillia, Ont.; m. Patricia Nickels; c. 3 daughters; UofT, mem. 4 Mann Cup title teams; 3 MVP awards; 3 scoring titles while playing Peterborough Jr., Sr. A, Nanaimo Sr. A '53-68; record 89 goals single season '56; coached 6 Ont. title teams; coached ntl team to world field title '78; coached Phildelphia Wings (NL) '74-75, Peterborough '64-72; OLA/ICLL/NLA pro sr. record: 192 scheduled games, 406g, 308a, 101 playoff games, 133g, 124a; Maitland trophy '56; Dennu Huddleston Memorial trophy '57; Bucko McDonald trophy '59; Mike Kelly Memorial medal '64; mem. Cdn, Ont. Lacrosse Hall of Fame; res. Orillia, Ont.

ALLAN, Wanda (archery); b. 24 Jan 1955, Victoria, B.C.; given name: Wanda Marie; m. Bud Sadegur; received bow for 11th birthday and became seriously involved in archery '66; ntl jr. girls' title '69-72; twice runnerup senior nationals; mem. '76, '84 Olympic, 4 all-Americas, 3 worlds teams; 5 BC titles; gold '75, bronze '78 Western Canada Games; bronze target '74 all-Americas Puerto Rico; res. Kamloops, B.C.

ALLBON, Ackie (baseball); b. 8 Nov 1905, Springhill, N.S.; given name: Alfred George; m. Lillian Matthews; retd. town clerk; made sr. baseball debut at 16, pitching 14-inning victory; pitcher, centrefielder Springhill Fencebusters 1922-34; participated in 3 longest games in NS baseball history, 15, 14, 13 innings; registered 21 strikeouts in losing cause '29; mem. 4 NS, 2 Maritime title teams; pres. Springhill Minor Baseball Association; baseball columnist Springhill Citizen; level 1 ntl coaching certificate; award of merit '80; mem. N.S. Sports Hall of Fame; res. Springhill, N.S.

ALLEN, Damon (football); b. 29 Jul 1963, San Diego, Calif.; CalState (Fullerton); m. Desiree; c. Amanda, Alyssa, Ateya; football player; pro quarterback Edmonton '85-88, '93-94; Ottawa '89-91; Hamilton '92-94; Memphis (CFL) Mad Dogs '95; B.C. '96-'98; CFL record: (through '98): 229 games, 66td, 2cvt, 390pts; 1186 carries, 8394yds, 66td; 5434 passes, 2949 completed, 41,730yds, 190int, 231td; 3 Grey Cup finals, 2 winners; offensive star of '87, MVP '93 game awards; 1 Eastern all-star; pitching tryout with Pittsburgh organization '94; brother of NFL star RB Marcus Allen; res. Stone Mountain, Ga.

ALLEN, Keith (builder/hockey); b. 21 Aug 1923, Saskatoon, Sask.; given name: Courtney Keith; m. Joyce; c. Brad, Blake, Traci; played for Cdn navy team; 13 pro seasons AHL Buffalo, Springfield, Syracuse; QHL Sherbrooke; WHL Edmonton, Brandon; parts of 2 with NHL Detroit; mem. '54 Detroit Stanley Cup winner; 10yrs coach/GM/bookkeeper/publicist Seattle Totems (WHL); league title '59; HN minor league exec. of '60; joined Philadelphia '66 as coach; became GM '70 and drafted-traded Flyers into a powerhouse in the '70s and '80s, 1st expansion team to win a Stanley Cup '74; repeated '75; team reached 4 more finals; set pro sports record of staying unbeaten for 35 games '79-80 season; stepped down as GM '83 to become exec. v-pres; HN NHL exec. of '80; Lester Patrick trophy '88; nicknamed: "Bingo"; mem. Flyers, Hockey halls of fame; res. Bryn Mawr, Pa.

ALLETSON, Kim (figure skating); b. 30 Jun 1958, Brockville, Ont.; given name: Patricia Kim; m. Philip Henderson; c. John Charles Philip; UNB, BA, Dalhousie, LLB; lawyer; moved through Minto Skating Club ranks to win Eastern Ontario titles at each level of competition '68-78 before turning pro teaching in Ottawa, Fredericton; ntl jr. champion '74; twice runnerup srs.; Skate Canada '76; mem. '76 Olympic, several worlds teams; attended International Olympic Academy Greece; res. London, Eng.

ALLEYNE, Jeff (boxing); b. 25 Jun 1938, St. Philip, Barbados; given name: Jeffrey O'Neale; m. Carmen Goodridge; c. Derek, Michael; Concordia; telecommunications technician; moved to Canada 1955; Golden Gloves champion '56-60, ntl 156lb title '60; mem. '60 Olympic team; following 4-yr retirement lost split decision in final in bid for '64 team berth; career ring record 83 wins, 4 losses; 1 year sr. football; coached Michel Prevost, Roger Fortin to '76 Olympic team; Prevost won '75 Pan-Am silver, Fortin '78 Commonwealth gold; operator Lafleche Boxing Club; Optimist International service to youth award; active duckpin bowler; res. Greenfield Park, Que.

ALLISON, Ian (basketball); b. 26 Jul 1909, Greenock, Scotland; d. 4 Aug 1990, London, Ont.; given name: Ian Alaistair; m. Jean Reid; c. Heather, Jane; Assumption College, UWO, OCE; retired Walkerville CI athletic dir.; mem. 5 WOSSA soccer champions, 4 WOSSA, Ont. title basketball teams, Eastern Canadian title '28; WOSSA 440 titlist; all-conf. halfback Assumption, mem. Assumption Ont. basketball champions; ORFU football St. Michael's; mem. UofT basketball champions, Windsor Alumni, Ford V8s ntl title; mem. '36 Olympic silver medal team; coached Ont. basketball titlists, WOSSA track, volleyball champions, HS football; Windsor Coaches Assn. award for outstanding contribution to HS athletics; Alpha Kai Omega fraternity award for service in junior sport; National Basketball Assn. of Coaches award for contributions to Canadian basketball; city of Windsor award for outstanding contribution to HS athletics; mem. Cdn Basketball; Windsor-Essex County Sports halls of fame.

ALOMAR, Robbie (baseball); b. 5 Feb. 1968, Ponce, Puerto Rico; given name: Roberto; raised in baseball environment, father Sandy, brother Sandy Jr. both major leaguers; second baseman; launched pro career '85 Charleston (A); '86 Reno (A), Baseball America all-star; '87 Wichita (AA); '88 Las Vegas (AAA); joined San Diego Padres '88; youngest player on ML roster '89 opening day; traded to Toronto Blue Jays '91 becoming integral part of '92-93 World Series champions; through '98 mem. 9 all-star teams; 8 Gold Glove awards; Toronto BBWAA, Labatt's player of year awards '91; signed as free agent by Baltimore '96-98, Cleveland '99; spitting (on umpire) incident '96 led to suspension to start '97 season; MBL record (through '99): 1722 scheduled games, 6611ab, 1117r, 2007h, 371db, 58tr, 151hr, 377sb, 829rbi, .304ba; res. Salinas, PR.

ALOU, Felipe (baseball): b. 12 May 1935, Haina, Dominican Republic; m. Lucie Gagnon; c. Moises, Jose, Valerie, Felipe Jr.; baseball manager; outfielder; represented Dominican Republic '54 Pan-Am Games in baseball, javelin; minor league stints '56-58 with Lake Charles, Cocoa, Minneapolis, Springfield, Phoenix; major leagues '58-74 with San Francisco, Milwaukee, Atlanta, Oakland, NY Yankees, Montreal; ML record: 2082 games, 7339ab, 985r, 2101h, 359db, 49tr, 206hr, 852rbi, 423bob, 705k, 107sb, .286ba; 3 all-star games, '62 World Series; made history '63 appearing in same outfield with younger brothers Jesus and Matty for Giants; 31st player in history to record at least 2000 hits, 200 homers; turned to managing '77 posting 884-751 minor league record with West Palm Beach, Memphis, Denver, Wichita, Indianapolis '77-91; coach Montreal '79-80, '84, '92; mgr. Montreal Expos from '92; established Expos club managerial record with 1127 games, 600 victories '99; hon. citizen Laval; *AP* mgr of '94; res. Laval, Que./Lake Worth, Fla.

ALTMANN, Fred (shooting); b. 13 Feb 1935, Stuttgart, W.Germany; given name: Fred Max; m. Helga Kloster; c. Cindy, Monique; painting contractor; skeet shooting specialist; silver '77-78 Canadian team trials; team gold, individual bronze '80 German grand prix; team gold '82 Commonwealth Games; mem. '78, '82 Commonwealth, '79 Pan-Am Games, 5 world, 6 Benito Juarez championships teams; federal govt. excellence award '83; res. Toronto, Ont.

AMATT, John (mountaineering); b. 19 May 1945, Manchester, Eng.; given name: John Robert; m. Peggy Hagel; c. Jillian; UCal, BEd, U of Durham, Eng. Dip. Ed; pres. One Step Beyond World Wide; lecturer, teacher, management consultant; emigrated to Canada '68; Cdn citizen from '73; more than 30yrs experience climbing, mountain hiking Britain, Norway, France, Italy, Germany, Austria, Greenland, Peru, Mexico, Nepal, China, USA, Canada; mem./principal organizer successful Cdn Mount Everest expedition '82; leader 1st Cdn China mountaineering expedition '81; chair. Alexander Mackenzie Canada Sea-to-Sea bicentennial expeditions '89-93; qualified pro mountain guide, photo journalist; founder Banff Festival of Mountain Films; 2 Alta achievement awards, SFC Cdn sports award; mem. advisory board Banff Centre for Mountain Culture; mem. Alpine Club of Canada, Assn. Cdn Mountain Guides, Meeting Planners Intl, Intl Platform Assn.; Alta. Sports Hall of Fame special award; res. Canmore, Alta.

AMBROSE, John (baseball); b. 20 Jun 1929, Vineland, N.J.; given name: John Francis; m. Beatrice Neale; c. Neal, Philip, Cathy, Nancy, Edward; plumbing contractor; pitcher, infielder, outfielder; pro Boston Braves organization '48-53; twice Quebec City (Provincial League) all-star; amassed variety of all-star, pitching, batting honors St.Thomas, London Sr. IC '54-66; mgr. St. Thomas team; mem. IC title teams '54-55, '58; IC MVP '58; mem. 2 all-Ont. St. Thomas basketball title teams; res. St. Thomas, Ont.

AMEY, Jessica (swimming): b. 15 Nov 1976, Montreal, Que.; butterfly specialist; 7 ntl titles; 6 ntl records; silver 4x100 medley relay '95 world short course championships;

bronze 100m fly '95, 50m FS '93 Pan-Pacific; 2 bronze '94 Commonwealth Games; 2 silver, 1 bronze '96 World Cup III short course; res, Calgary, Alta.

AMUNDRUD, Gail (swimming); b. 6 Apr 1957, Toronto, Ont.; m. Jim Beattie; c. Lauren; Arizona State; software co. applications engineer; began competitive swimming Ottawa Kingfish '67 moving to Vancouver Dolphins '74; 1st ntl age-group (11-12) 100m backstroke title '70; 1st ntl record :54.0 in 100yd FS '73; 1st Canadian girl to swim 100m FS under one minute (:59.8) '73 world championships; two gold, silver, bronze '74 Commonwealth Games; two gold, two silver, bronze '74 Ont. finals; bronze '74, gold, bronze '77 AAU finals; 7 gold '76 ntls; 2 silver, bronze '76 Olympics; two bronze '79 Pan-Am Games; AIWA 100m, 200m FS champion '78-79; 10 ntl FS records during career; mem. '75, '79 Pan-Am, '76 Olympic, '74, '78 Commonwealth Games; 4 yrs. all-American; coached 6yrs; competed as triathlete '88-90; mem. Ottawa Sports, Ariz. State halls of fame; res. Calgary, Alta.

AMYOT, Frank (canoeing); b. 14 Sep 1904, Thornhill, Ont.; d. 21 Nov 1962, Ottawa, Ont.; m. Mary Kelly; civil servant; one of six children of Dr. John Amyot, Canada's first deputy minister of health and pensions; mem. Rideau Aquatic, Britannia Boating Clubs; big man who required custom built racing shell; Canadian Canoe Assn. int. singles '23; 6 ntl sr. singles, 1 double-blade title; capt., mgr., coach Canadian canoe team '36 Olympics; only Canadian ever to win gold in 1000m Canadian singles setting Olympic record 5:32.1; instrumental in saving 3 lives, including footballer Dave Sprague, in Ottawa River boating mishap; helped organize Rideau Canoe Club; mem. Ottawa, Cdn Amateur, Ottawa CSRA, Canada's Sports halls of fame.

ANAKIN, Doug (bobsleigh); b. 6 Nov 1930, Chatham, Ont.; given name: Douglas Thomas; m. Mary Jane Mosher; c. Megan, Bridget; Queen's, BA, SUNY College, MA, OCE; teacher; intercollegiate wrestling, skiing, mountaineering; selected by Vic Emery for number two spot on '64 Olympic bobsled gold medal team; mem. Cdn Winter Olympic, Cdn Amateur, Canada's Sports Hall of Fame; res. Windermere, B.C.

ANDERSEN, Dale (boxing); b. 21 May 1953, Yellowknife, N.W.T.; given name: Dale Irwin; div; derrickman; mem. Rocky Legion boxing club, coached by father Gunner; ntl amateur featherweight, 4 Alta., 1 BC Golden Gloves titles; mem. '71 Pan-Am, '72 Olympic, '74 Commonwealth Games teams; bronze '74 Commonwealth Games; silver '73 Tournament of Europeans East Berlin; 3 silver medals NA championships; boxer of year, runnerup Canadian male athlete of '74; several provincial achievement awards; res. Rocky Mountain House, Alta.

ANDERSEN, Roxy (t&f/builder); b. 26 Jun 1912, Montreal, Que.; given name: Roxanne Atkins; m. Einar Andersen; UofT; City College of San Francisco; track exec.; several Ont. hurdles, relay titles early '30s with Laurel Ladies AC, club she founded; ntl indoor 50yd hurdles, 80m hurdles, 440yd outdoor relay records; US indoor 50yd hurdles, US indoor 440 relay title team '34-36; mem. '36 Olympic, '34 BEG, women's world games teams; pres.-sec. Ont. Women's Amateur Athletic Fed., Ont. Ladies' Hockey League, Queen

City Softball League; US citizen; commissioned by Pacific AAU to organize N. California women's t&f program; during 26-year period did same in Central California, Oregon, Colorado; pioneered ntl age group program; chair. Olympic women's t&f committee '53-57; mgr. US women's t&f team '56 Olympics; 1st woman rep. AAU men's t&f comm.; former pres. Pacific AAU; chair. emeritus Athletic Congress; former chair. AAU women's t&f comm.; author, composer, raconteur; Norman Craig Memorial Trophy Award outstanding Ont. female athlete '34; Bay area distinguished woman award '65; 2000 women of achievement award '74; World's Who's Who of Women, Who's Who in America; mem. US t&f Hall of Fame; res. San Francisco, Calif.

ANDERSON, Andy (softball); b. 25 Oct 1933, Windsor, Ont.; d. 12 Nov 1994, Ottawa, Ont.; given name: Albert Garnet; m. Joyce Hill; c. Andrew, Bonnie Jean, Patricia; retd. RCMP officer, City of Ottawa security dir.; began pitching at 16 with Amherstburg SKD Manufacturing; pitched for Loretto Bros. Wr. Sr. League, Ottawa Wajax, Westmount RCMP, Snowdon, Toronto Beaches Major Fastball Leagues, Oshawa Tony's, Vancouver Sr. League, Gatineau Ambassadors, RCMP National Defence League; league career record 407 wins, 216 losses; mem. 2 all-Cdn World tournament teams; rookie of yr finalist Snowdon League; frequent Most Valuable Pitcher honors Toronto, Ottawa, Montreal leagues; mem. 11 league, playoff champions; 2 Cdn title teams; 19 career no-hitters, 39 1-hitters, competed in 30 tournaments; pitched in 4 games vs. Eddie Feigner's King and His Court; with another pitcher combined for record 15-inning 35 strikeouts (he had 18); retired from game '78.

ANDERSON, Dave (all-around); b. 29 Oct 1932, Winnipeg, Man.; given name: David Frederick; m. Ann Cameron Spencer; c. Ian, Dorothy; UCLA, BSc., MSc., Northern Colorado, EdD; administrator, professor; varsity football, rugby, soccer UCLA; twice all-America soccer goaler; NCAA all-America goaler '54; mem. '53 Rose Bowl, '54 Hula Bowl teams; pro LA Rams '54-55; HS coach '54-63; football coach UCLA '57-59, Manitoba provincial team coach '61-63; mem. National Advisory Council '67-69; chair. Man. sport advisory council '70-73; chair./sect.-treas. Man. boxing, wrestling commission '71-73; former pres. University Athletic Directors Assn.; 16yrs dir. athletic camp; exec. mem. Man. Sports Fed. '74-75; CIAU dir. '73-76; res. Winnipeg, Man.

ANDERSON, Gabby (baseball); b. 29 Nov 1929, Detroit, Mich.; given name: Stanley Robert; m. Lorella Talbot; c. Jeffrey, Richard, Lisa; inspector automobile quality control; pro ball Pony League, '50 rookie of year .335 Peoria, Ill.; Class D Olean, NY '54-55, .355 in '54; quit pro ball, London Majors (Sr.IC) briefly '55; Great Lakes-Niagara League batting title '57 with .403, also MVP; with London rejoined IC '58; runnerup '58 batting race with .398, '59 with .420; won '60 batting crown with .391; IC MVP '59; twice led IC in doubles, once each home runs, runs batted in; 12-year IC average .339; mgr. London '63; v.-pres. Eager Beaver Baseball League (Little League) '65-66, pres. '67-68; helped launch Tyke Div. (9-10 year olds) '68; coached minor, girls hockey from '73; res. London, Ont.

ANDERSON, Gary (swimming): b. 7 Apr 1969, Montreal, Que.; SouthernCal; near drowning age 4 led to swimming lessons; 5 ntl titles; broke John Naber's 13-yr school 200yd backstroke record '90 NCAA's; mem. Ntl team from '87; mem. '88, '92 Olympic, '91 World aquatic, '93 Pan-Pacific, world short course championship teams; gold 200m backstroke, 200m IM, silver 100m backstroke '90 Commonwealth Games; competed '94 Commonwealth, '95 Pan-Am Games; does hospital volunteer work in L.A.; res. Manhattan Beach, Calif.

ANDERSON, George (soccer): b. 23 Jun 1890, Fraserburgh, Aberdeenshire, Scotland; d. 30 May 1985, Winnipeg, Man.; compositor; organized, managed Caledonia junior, juvenile, midget teams; 10yrs mem. Man. Jr. Soccer Assn. exec., 4yrs. exec. Man. Sr. Soccer Assn.; involved in reactivation Dominion Football Assn. '46, exec. capacities '51-68; key role Canada's 1st World Cup entry '57; CFA delegate to '61 Federation Internationale de Football Associations, '66 World Congress; key role Canada's '68 Olympic soccer entry; organizer, mgr. Expo '67 soccer tournament; active in '67 Winnipeg Pan-Am tournament; sect.-treas. Rockwood unit 303 ANAF veterans minor soccer program; mem. Man., Canada's Sports halls of Fame.

ANDERSON, Glenn (hockey): b. 2 Oct 1960, Vancouver, B.C.; given name: Glenn Chris; Denver U; Seattle (WHL) '79-80; mem. Olympic team '80; 3rd Edmonton draft pick, 69th overall '79; pro NHL Edmonton '80-91, '96, Toronto '91-94, NY Rangers '94, St. Louis '95-96; topped 50-goal plateau '83-84, '85-86 with 54 goals each time; NHL record: 1129 scheduled games, 498g, 601a, 225 playoff games, 93g, 121a; played briefly in Germany '94, '96, Finland '94, Switzerland '97; 4 NHL all-star games; mem. Team Canada '84, '95; mem. 6 Stanley Cup winners; res. Vancouver, B.C.

ANDERSON, Jasey Jay (snowboarding): b. 13 Apr 1975, Montreal, Que,; John Abbott Coll.; giant slalom specialist; began snowboarding age 13; gold Sugarloaf GP '96, Snowmass GP '97; silver NA championships '97; bronze FIS World Cup '96; competed '98 Olympics; res. Val Morin, Que.

ANDERSON, Jerry (golf): b. 22 Sep 1955, Montreal, Que.; m. Barbara; c. Chirysse; Texas; pro golfer; turned pro '78; qualified for USPGA tour '89; mem. 2 Dunhill Cup, 2 World Cup teams; won Cdn TPC, Windsor Charity Classic, '87 CPGA title, '84 European Masters, '82-83 Quebec Open, '79 Sask., Ont., Man. Opens; du Maurier Order of Merit '89; competed on US, Europe, Australia/NZ, Asia, South America, South Africa, Cdn PGA tours; res. Scarborough, Ont.

ANDERSON, Kate (t&f): b. 9 Jan 1968, Kingston, Jamaica; given name: Keturah; hurdler; ntl jr 100m, 200m titles '86; competed '87 worlds, '88 (as sprinter), '92, '96 Olympics, '90, '98 Commonwealth, '99 Pan-Am, '93 World University Games, world championships as hurdler; gold '96 Georgia Tech Reebok Invitational, '94 Alabama relays; bronze '98 Commonwealth Games; '99 indoor worlds; 3 ntl titles; res. Toronto, Ont./Tuscaloosa, Ala.

ANDERSON, Les (archery): b. 31 May 1940, Wells, B.C.; given name: Leslie Ernest; m. Lorraine Marie DeLong; senior electrical technical assistant; from '61 won 16 Sask., 3 Alta. titles, 20 invitational tournaments; runnerup field events '73 ntl championships; '73 Championship of Americas field event title; ntl indoor champion '76, outdoor '78; certificate of recognition for outstanding achievement in amateur sport from Western Christian College, Weyburn, Sask, '76; mem. Sask Sports Hall of Fame; res. Prince Albert, Sask.

ANDERSON, Nint (builder/curling): b. 2 Sep 1917, Fredericton, N.B.; d. 28 May 1988, Newcastle, N.B.,; given name: Millicent; m. William Anderson; served curling at club, provincial, ntl administrative levels; instrumental in formation NB mixed curling assn in '60s; 1st and only woman to chair NB men's Ganong Cup '74; NB Ladies' CA v-pres., secty '63-73, pres. '74-76; 1st from NB to receive CLCA appreciation award; hon. mem. Chatham CC; mem. NB Sports Hall of Fame.

ANDERSON, Randy (volleyball): b. 19 Feb 1957, Winnipeg, Man.; given name: Randall Barry; UofM, BPhE.; Man. sports consultant; 17 hockey seasons Winnipeg region; mem. 3 Man. jr. lacrosse champions, 3 ntl Jr. B champions; mem. '77 Canada Games lacrosse; mem. Man. HS volleyball champions '72, '76; ntl jr. titlists '74; mem. Canada Winter Games '75 silver medal team; ntl jr. team '75-76; mem. 4 Great Plains Conf. champions, '78, '80 CIAU champions; ntl men's team '80-81; mem. '80 Canada Games gold medal team; Bill Masterton Trophy for athletic-academic excellence in HS; 3 times Great Plains all-star, twice CIAU all-Canadian; 5 times major tournament all-star; res. Winnipeg, Man.

ANDERSON, Ricky (boxing): b. 28 Oct 1960, Halifax, N.S.; given name: Rick Kenneth; St. Mary's U; ntl jr. light welterweight title '75, int. '76, sr. '80-81; silver '79 world jr. championship; gold Acropolis Greece tournament, 3 European tour competitions '80; bronze Finland Tammer tournament, NZ Games; 8NS titles; mem. '80 Olympic team; athletes rep. Olympic advisory comm.; NS athlete of '80; res. Halifax, N.S.

ANDERSON, Steve (karate): b. 29 Mar 1955, Toledo, O; Southwestern Coll; San Diego State, BSc.; karate instructor; nickname Nasty; began training under World kickboxing champion Chicken Gabriel and earned black belt status '80; US champion '80-87; Cdn titles '88-90; WAKO world titles England '83-84, '85-86, Germany '87-89. Italy '90-92; charter mem. 1st pro karate team '87; NASKA fighter of '80s; Kick Illustrated fighter of '83; selected for 1st issue commemorative karate cards '91; California Karate League competitor of '80-81; NASKA lifetime achievement award '90; active fundraiser for juvenile diabetes; set marathon fighting records; NASKA living legend award '95; record 6 US Capital Classics tournament titles; more than 60 major tournament victories; NA number 1 karate fighter since '80; mem. Fighter Magazine, Black Belt halls of Fame; res. Orleans, Ont.

ANDERSON, Tamara (ringette): b. 12 Sep 1973, Calgary, Alta.; admin. asst.; goal tender '91 Canada Winter Games gold medal team; playing for Team Alberta 7 ntl titles, as mem. Team Canada 3 world titles; 2 1st team, 1 2nd team ntl championship all-star; res. Calgary, Alta.

ANDERSON, Verne (skiing); b. 1937, Rossland, B.C.; d. 30 Sep 1983, Boulder, Colo; given name: Verne Ralph; m. Ardys Klinzing; c. Beverley, Sherri; business consultant; Western Cdn jr. downhill '53; ntl downhill '58-59; mem. '60 Olympic team; top Cdn male competitor '61 European, NA circuits; hampered by injuries competing '62 FIS championships France; men's ntl team coach '62-64; coached Nancy Greene; women's ntl team coach '66-68; mem. Canadian Skiing Hall of Fame.

ANDREOTTI, Jim (football); b. 27 Mar 1938, Chicago, Ill.; given name: James Peter; m. Joan Wray; c. Christopher; Northwestern, BA; stockbroker; co-capt. Northwestern jr. year, all-America linebacker; pro Toronto '60-62, Alouettes '63-67; dealt to Argos '67 but failure to report led to year's suspension; 4 times EFC all-star, twice all-Canadian; COJO liaison officer with US Olympic team '76; res. Montreal, Que.

ANDREW, Trevor (snowboarding); b. 31 Aug 1979, Kentville, N.S.; began snowboarding age 11; halfpipe specialist; 2 ntl titles; 1 WC gold, silver, bronze; competed '98 Olympics; res. Falmouth, N.S.

ANDREWS, Porky (basketball); b. 18 Sep 1917, Victoria, B.C.; given name: George Lloyd; m. Marion Kennedy; c. Wayne Murray, Janet Louise, Scott Alexander;Oregon, BSc.; teacher; 3 Victoria HS track titles; ntl high hurdles record; mem. BC rugby, softball, lacrosse title teams; Royal Colwood Golf Club championship; 2 decades one of nation's top basketballers; mem. ntl title teams '35, '46; player-coach Victoria Dominoes; pro Vancouver Hornets, Alberni Athletics, team he started '49; 2yrs. capt. Oregon team, all-Coast guard, all-American; coach Victoria Hudson Bay Sr. A women's team 2yrs., Victoria HS boys to 3 provincial titles, Victoria HS girls 1 provincial title; governor BC boys HS Basketball Assn.; mem. B.C. Sports Hall of Fame; res. Victoria, B.C.

ANDREYCHUK, Dave (hockey); b. 29 Sep 1963, Hamilton, Ont.; m. Sue; c. Taylor, Caci; left wing Oshawa Generals; mem. Team Canada jr. worlds '83; 1st choice Buffalo '82 draft; Buffalo '82-92; Toronto '92-96; New Jersey '96-99, Boston '99; topped 50-goal plateau 54 '93, 53 '94; eclipsed TML record 49 goals for left winger set by Frank Mahovlich with 53 '94; achieved 500g plateau '97; NHL record: (through '99) 1210 scheduled games, 532g, 608a, 98 playoff games, 35g, 34a; active with American Cancer Society; res. Buffalo, N.Y.

ANDRU, John (fencing); b. 20 Nov 1932, Toronto, Ont; div. Joan Davies; c. Reina; UofT; restaurateur; best overall competitive record by any native-born fencer in Canada; 9 ntl individual, 4 team titles, medalist 34 times, 8 Eastern Cdn, 14 Ont. titles; only husband-wife pair to win ntl individual foils titles same year '63;mem. 2 Olympic, 4 Pan-Am, 4 Commonwealth Games teams; 6 Commonwealth, 3 Pan-Am medals; mgr., capt. '68 Olympic, '70 Commonwealth, '71 Pan-Am Games, world youth teams;

CdM '72 world youth team; international dir., judge '72, '76 Olympics; 1st Canadian qualified Class A pres. of jury by Federation Internationale d'Escrime; AAU of C Central Ont. dir.; established CFA as ntl incorporated body following demise of AAU of C, pres. '67-73; CFA tech., exec. dir. '73-80; COA dir. '67-72, AAU of C '67-71; v.-pres. Commonwealth Fencing Fed. '70-74; Centennial Medal '67; Norton Crowe medal '69; 3 Ont. achievement awards; 6 OFA Don Collinge awards; mem. Canadian Amateur Sports Hall of Fame; res. Toronto, Ont.

ANDRUSYSHYN, Zenon (football/t&f); b. 25 Feb 1947, Gunzburg, Germany; m. Sue Johnson; c. Zoe, Zuriel; UCLA; state dir. Fellowship of Christian Athletes; Cdn jr., men's javelin records; mem '66 Commonwealth Games team; track scholarship UCLA; switched to football, set UCLA punting, field goal records; Sporting News all-American '67, '69; noted as showboat wearing golden kicking boot; pro Toronto Argos '71-77, '80-82, Kansas City Chiefs (NFL) '78, Hamilton Tiger-Cats '79, Edmonton '82, Tampa Bay (USFL) '83-85; shared EFC scoring title with Bernie Ruoff '80; 11-year CFL record 213 converts, 201 field goals, 139 singles, 955 points; 6 times CFL all-star; several Argos club kicking records; mem. Athletes in Action; nicknamed Big Z; res. Tampa, Fla.

ANTHONY, Matt (football/coaching); b. 12 feb 1921, St. Catharines, Ont.; given name: Matt Lloyd; m. Marilyn Feeney; c. Judith, Darryl, Pamela, Valerie; electrical contractor; versatile athlete; capt. Cdn jr. basketball title team; mem. UofOtt, Barrett's Lumber sr. basketball teams; played lacrosse St. Catharines Ont. minor title teams, Ont. sr. league Orillia Tigers, Ottawa St. Anthony, pro Quebec Montagnards; as rower stroke 1st Cdn HS coxless 4s to win NA title at Cdn Henley; mem. St. Catharines sr. baseball/ softball teams; football with Hamilton Wildcats '40, Montreal Alouettes '46, Ottawa Rough Riders '47-48, '51-53, Sask. '49-50; Big Four/Ted Reeves all-Cdn '50; mem. '51 Grey Cup champions; head coach UofOtt 15yrs; asst/ head coach Ottawa Sooners; 4yrs Cdn Navy; recipient Burma Star; res. Nepean, Ont.

ANTON, Ron (curling); b. 7 Aug 1941, Medicine Hat, Alta.; given name: Ronald Michael; m. Sharon Dew; c. Michael, Douglas, Lorna, Margo; UofAlta, BA. educator; pitcher, infielder Medicine Hat baseball teams '53-63, 2 no-hitters; HS football quarterback; HS football coach '65-75, 2 Edmonton city titles; competitive curler '58-76 winning variety of major events; at 19 youngest mem. Brier winner playing 3rd for Hec Gervais; mem. Brier winners '61, '74, runnerup '62; mem. '64-67 Northern Alta. champions; skipped Alta. mixed titlist, ntl runnerup '73; Curl Canada ntl course conductor; mem. Curl Canada certification comm.; all-star Brier 3rd '61, '74; 1st pres. Alta. Assn. of Competitive Curlers; tech. co-ordinator '92 Olympic curling team; mem. Canadian Curling Hall of Fame; res. Spruce Grove, Alta.

APPLEBY, Elizabeth (speed skating); b. 25 Nov 1958, Winnipeg, Man.; m. Gordon Levin; c. Eric; Health Science Centre RN; nurse; Cdn jr. champion '74; mem. ntl team '74-79; set variety of Man., ntl and one world record during 16-yr career; world Jr champ '76; Cdn sr women's title '77-

79; named to world sprint, all-round teams '74-75; mem. '76 Olympic team; mem. Wpg women's sr softball title team '73; mem. gold medal women's cycle team Western Cdn Games '79; mem. Cdn Speed Skating, Man. Sports halls of fame; res. Winnipeg, Man.

APPS, Syl Sr. (hockey/t&f); b. 18 Jan 1915, Paris, Ont.; d. 24 Dec. 1998, Kingston, Ont.; given name: Charles Joseph Sylvanus; m. Mary Josephine Marshall; c. Joanne, Robert, Carol, Sylvanus Jr., Janet; McMaster, BA; retd. brick manufacturer, retired politician; ntl pole vault, '34 BEG titles; mem. '36 Olympic team; capt. McMaster intercollegiate football title team; sr. hockey Hamilton Tigers; pro Toronto '36-48; led NHL in assists, 2nd overall scoring '36-37, '37-38; Calder Trophy rookie of year; Lionel Conacher trophy '37; centred line of Busher Jackson, Gordie Drillon, later Drillon, Bob Davidson; retd. as Leaf capt.; NHL record: 423 scheduled games, 201g, 231a, 69 playoff games, 25g, 29a; Lady Byng Trophy '41-42 with no penalty minutes; twice 1st, 3 times 2nd team all-star; mem. 3 Stanley Cup winners; Ont. Athletic Commissioner '46-48; PC MLA for Kingston and the Islands '63-80; Minister Correctional Services '71-74; jersey 10 retd by Leafs; Paris, Ont. rink, trophy honoring Ont. Athlete of yr bear his name; mem. Order of Canada, Hockey, Copps Coliseum, Royal Canadian Legion, McMaster, Canadian Amateur, Canada's Sports halls of fame.

ApSIMON, John (fencing); b. 5 Aug 1935, England; div. Claire Manning, c. Joanne, Paul, Michele, m. Karen Bergenstein; c. Megan, Noah; Liverpool, BSc, PhD; v-p. research and external affairs Carleton; capt. Liverpool fencing team '57-59; UK ntl universities champion '58; Northwestern Section champion '58; emigrated to Canada and ranked class A fencer in foil, sabre, épée '60-72; 4 times McFarland 3-weapon trophy, Governor-General's épée titlist '69; mem. RA Les Spadassins 3 team gold, 2 silver, 2 bronze in épée, 2 gold, silver, 4 bronze in foil, 5 silver, 2 bronze in sabre; '71 Ont. foil title, Ont. Winter Games foil, team titles; from '60 coach Les Spadassins, Carleton U; guided Carleton to intercollegiate titles '67-68; coached individual OUAA champions '67-69, '74; FIE class B dir. 3 weapons; Don Collinge Trophy OFA '71; pres. RA Les Spadassins, v.-pres CFA '68-73, pres. '73-76, v.-pres. CFA elite '78; mgr. '72 Olympic, '74, '78-79 jr. world title, '75 Ont. Canada Winter Games, '79 Pan-Am Games teams; judge '76 Olympics; competed world sr games Toronto; assists son Paul as U of Ott coach; life mem. Ottawa CSRA; res. Ottawa, Ont.

ARAKGI, Nick (football); b. 9 Aug 1955, Cairo, Egypt; m. Suzanne; c. Nicholas, Michelle; Bishop's; salesman Imperial Tobacco; tight end Montreal '79-85; outstanding blocker; club record 89 receptions for 1062yds, 6tds '82; record 269 receptions, 3590yds, 22tds; EFC all-star '82, '84; Montreal player of '82; Schenley outstanding Canadian award '84; res. Kirkland, Que.

ARBOUR, Al (hockey); b. 1 Nov 1932, Sudbury, Ont.; given name: Alger Joseph; m. Claire Sabourin; c. Joanne, Jay, Julie, Janice; Assumption College; hockey exec; defenceman Windsor jrs; NHL Detroit '53-58, Chicago '58-61, Toronto '61-66, St. Louis '67-71; NHL playing record: 626 scheduled games, 12g, 58a, 86 playoff games, 1g, 8a; mem. 3 Stanley Cup winners; coach/AGM St. Louis '70-

73, scout Atlanta; coach NY Islanders '73-86, '88-94; v.-pres., consultant to GM Islanders from '95; 4 consec. Stanley Cups; NHL coach of yr '78-79; reached NHL milestone 15 Apr '92 coaching 1438th game, passing Dick Irvin; NHL coaching record: ('79-94) 1606 games, 781-577-248; mem. Hockey Hall of Fame; res. Cold Spring Harbor, N.Y.

ARCHIBALD, Joan (fencing); b. 3 Mar 1913, Montreal, Que.; given name: Helen Joan; m. John Riddell; c. John Jr., Joanna, Michael, Edward, Christie; Royal Academy of Music, London, Eng.; variety of provincial, ntl fencing titles prior to '32; mem. '32 Olympic team; turned to horse breeding and produced colt which won Governor-General's, Lt. Governor's Cups Royal Winter Fair; senior horse show judge; res. Mt. Uniacke, N.S.

ARCHIBALD, Nancy (fencing); b. 7 Dec 1911, Montreal, Que.; d. Apr 1996, Vancouver, B.C.; m. Werner Joeck; c. Nancy, Susan, Ian, Neil; social worker; fenced several years MAAA, competing at provincial, ntl levels; Que. champion '34-35; runnerup ntl ladies' foil '37; mem. ntl fencing team '36 Olympics.

ARMITAGE, Rolly (harness racing); b. 8 Feb 1925, South March, Ont.; given name: Roland Montgomery; m. Mary Spearman (d); c. Maxwell Anne, Anne Elizabeth, Blake, James, Don; m. Karen; UofT; veterinarian; pres. Canadian Standardbred Society '73-74; pres. CTA '75-81; pres.-GM Rideau Carleton Raceway '81-90; horse show judge; veterinarian of '82 award; Pontiac County citizen of yr '62; unsuccessful in initial bid in provincial political arena '87; mem. Cdn Horse Racing Hall of Fame; res. Dunrobin, Ont.

ARMSTRONG, Brian (t&f); b. 9 Sep 1948, Toronto, Ont.; given name: Brian Joseph; UofT, BA, LLB; lawyer; from '69-74 represented Canada in international cross-country, marathon races; 2nd Canadian marathon, Olympic trials '72; Detroit Motor City, Western Hemisphere marathons '72; runnerup '73 Canadian, Fukuoka Japan marathons; ranked 3rd among world marathoners '73 by Track & Field News; mem '74 Commonwealth Games team; res. Toronto, Ont.

ARMSTRONG, Charles (coaching); b. 10 Oct 1906, Stratford, Ont.; Assumption College; RC priest; regarded as "Spirit of Assumption"; coach, athletic dir, 1935-72; an innovator he became first Canadian coach to use T-formation popularized by George Halas and Sid Luckman in US; mem. Windsor/Essex County Sports Hall of Fame; res. Windsor, Ont.

ARMSTRONG, George (hockey); b. 6 Jul 1930, Skead, Ont.; given name: George Edward; m. Betty Shannon; c. Brian, Betty Ann, Fred, Lorne; retd hockey coach/scout; nicknamed "Chief"; jr., sr. Toronto Marlboros; Allan Cup winner; Maple Leafs centre '52-71; 13yrs team capt.; NHL record: 1187 scheduled games, 296g, 417a, 110 playoff games, 26g, 34a; 7 all-star games; mem. 4 Stanley Cup winners; coached Marlboros to 2 Memorial Cups; coach Toronto '88-89; scout TML; mem. Hockey Hall of Fame; res. Toronto, Ont.

ARMSTRONG, Jim (curling); b. 30 Jun 1950, Victoria, B.C.; given name: James Peter; m. Carleen; c. Gregory, Jayne, Jody; dentist; mem. BC men's title rinks '73-74, '83-

84, '87, '92; skipped BC mixed title rink '73, BC jr. titlist '71, BC HS titlist '67; all-star 3rd '87 Brier; Ross Harstone award '83, '87; active curling official at numerous ntl championships; mem. Canadian Curling Hall of Fame; res. Richmond, B.C.

ARMSTRONG, Ken (diving); b. 12 Oct 1953, Ingersoll, Ont.; given name: Kenneth Robert; m. Brenda Tifts; c. Jaymi; Texas; diving coach; ntl diving team '73-80; 20 ntl titles; mem. '73, '75 world championships, '78 Pan-Am, '74, '78 Commonwealth Games, '76 Olympic teams; mem. youth camp '72 Olympics, qualified for '80 boycotted Olympics; silver 10m board '78 Commonwealth Games; res.Woodland, Tex.

ARMSTRONG, Lesley (builder); b. 18 Jun 1929, Saint John, N.B.; given name: Lesley Jean Fraser; m. Nigel Armstrong; c. 2 daughters; home economist; competitive figure skater '47-54; childhood bout of polio hampered career; won city title '49; began coaching '55; mem. NB FS exec. '78; dir. CanSkate pgm. '78; mem. National Core comm. '85; formed Sussex Skating Club '56; longest serving dir. NB section CFSA; NB FS volunteer of '86, CFSA award of excellence, Town of Sussex achievement, community service award '86; mem. NB Sports Hall of Fame; res. Sussex, N.B.

ARMSTRONG, Neil (hockey/officiating); b. 29 Dec 1932, Plympton Twp, Ont.; m. Margaret Scott; c. Douglas, Lezleigh; hockey scout; began officiating minor hockey at 15; in early '50s became OHA certified official; became part-time NHL official '57; officiated in NHL 21yrs in 1733 regular season, 208 Stanley Cup playoff (48 finals), 10 all-star games; known as "ironman" for not missing single assignment due to injury in 16 seasons; following retirement became Montreal Canadiens scout; mem. Hockey, Sarnia-Lambton Sports halls of fame; res. Sarnia, Ont.

ARNOLD, Don (rowing); b. 14 Jul 1935, Kelowna, B.C.; given name: Donald John; m. Gwendolyn Mary Amor (d); c. Malcolm, Graham, Andrew; UBC, BPhE., San Francisco State, MSc; Indiana, PhD; exec-dir. Rowing BC; mem. UBC gold medal jr. varsity 8s, '55 Pacific Coast sprint champion; stroke UBC-VRC 4-oared coxless crew '56 unofficial world record 6:05.8 over 2000m course; stroked same crew to '56 Olympic gold; gold coxed 8s, silver coxed 4s '58 Commonwealth Games; '58 Grand Challenge Cup Bedford, Eng. regatta; asst. coach UBC-VRC coxed 8s silver medalists '59 Pan-Am Games; mem. '60 Olympic silver medal 8s; Heather MacDonald Memorial Award, runnerup BC athlete of '58, Robert Gaul Memorial award UBC outstanding graduating student '62, Indiana outstanding graduating student '70, Indiana citation from US Olympic comm.; Ont. contribution to sport citation '74, BC Sports Fed. contribution to sport citation '76, CARA medal of honor for outstanding contribution to rowing 1880-1980; mem. Canadian Amateur, Canada's Sports halls of fame; res. Richmond, B.C.

ARNOLD, Elisabeth (canoeing); b. 15 Jan 1959, Ottawa, Ont.; given name: Elisabeth Solveig; SFU, BA, Queen's, MA; politician; kayak specialist; 5ys ntl team; 2 gold '77 Canada Games; 2 NA jr. gold, 6 ntl golds, 1 Continental

Cup gold, 1 Commonwealth regatta gold; Ottawa city councillor from '94; res. Ottawa, Ont.

ARNOLD, Sherman (shooting); b. 12 Feb 1938, Waters, Ont.; given name: Sherman Stanley; m. Mary Ann Hlewka; c. Sharon, Tim, Sherman Jr.; sheet metal mechanic; handgun specialist; mem. ntl standard pistol team '75-85; Ont. pistol team '76-94; intl. black powder Cdn team '93-99; ntl centrefire team '78-87; 11 ntl, 8 Ont. centrefire titles; 9 ntl standard pistol titles; 1 ntl air pistol title; 2 NY state centrefire, 1 air pistol titles; 2 NRA air pistol , 4 centrefire, 2 standard pistol titles; 5 ntl, Ont. black powder pistol titles; 3 ntl muzzle loading assn. titles; accumulated more than 500 medals and awards; ntl record 592 old style targets centrefire outdoors 25m; ntl muzzle loading team record '96; team gold, individual bronze '97 Pacific zone championships; 6 ntl achievement, 4 Ont. championship awards; res. St. Catharines, Ont.

ARNOTT, Jan (curling); b. 17 Apr 1956, Winnipeg, Man.; given name: Janet Elizabeth Laliberte; m. Douglas Arnott; Red River Community College; accounting co-ordinator; began curling age 11; lead for sister Connie '84, Cdn, World, '92, '95 Cdn champions; participated 3 Man. mixed championships; through '95 mem. 12 major cashspiel winners; mem. 2 Winnipeg Super League titlists; exec. mem. Winnipeg Business Women's League, Women's Competitive Curling Assn.; mem. Man. Sports Hall of Fame; res. Winnipeg, Man.

ARSENAULT, Lise (gymnastics); b. 14 Dec 1954, Cartierville, Que.; given name: Lise Isabelle; m. David Goertz; c. Natalie, Lyne; York, BA, NY State, MEd.; teacher; 4 Que. sr. titles; youngest mem. Cdn team '70 world championships; bronze floor exercises '71 Pan-Am Games; mem. '72, '76 Olympics, '73 FISU; variety of gold, silver, bronze medals Ont., ntl championships; McMaster gym coach '76-78; coach Sparks gym club St. Catharines; HS female athlete of year; Vaudreuil Sports Centre female athlete of '70; res. St. Catharines, Ont.

ARSENAULT, Paul (coaching); b. 8 Aug 1939, Halifax, N.S.; m. Cathi; c. Klay, Holly; UNB, BPhE, Oregon, MSc.; entrepeneur; ex-coach; football, hockey UNB; hockey coach Sir George Williams '63-72, Loyola '72-75, Concordia '75-90; 4th all-time NA college hockey coaches victory list; reached 500 victory plateau '84; 17 league titles; twice CIAU coach of year; 3 Que. hockey coach of year awards; mem. Canadian student team coaching staff '77-78; res. Charlottetown, P.E.I.

ARUSOO, Toomas (swimming); b. 22 Jul 1948, Sweden; div. Angela Coughlan; c. Jessica, Lee, Kate; m. Diane; c. Toomas Jr.; Michigan, BSc.; swim coach, businessman; mem. ntl team '65-71; mem. '66, '70 Commonwealth, '67, '71 Pan-Am, '68 Olympic teams; silver 200m butterfly '67 Pan-Ams; gold 200m, silver 100m butterfly '70 Commonwealth Games; coach ntl team '75 Pan-Ams; Montreal Camo SC '77-78; St. John's Nfld. Aquarama '78-80; Montreal POM '80-81; U of Montreal Champions SC from '82; mem. Canadian Aquatic Hall of Fame; res. Birmingham, Mich.

ASH, Gord (administration/baseball); b. 20 Dec 1951, Toronto, Ont.; York BA; baseball exec.; following 4yrs service with CIBC joined Blue Jays organization as ticket office employee '78; became grounds crew operations supervisor '79; asst. dir. operations '80; administrator player personnel '84; attended Michigan human resource management seminar '88, Queen's industrial relations seminar '90; AGM '89; v-pres baseball/GM '94; v-pres/GM '97; 1 of 4 Cdns to serve as ML GM; mem. Cdn Special Olympics advisory board; res. Toronto, Ont.

ASHCROFT, Christina (shooting); b. 28 Jun 1964, Kitchener, Ont.; given name: Christina Schulze; m. Michael Ashcroft; c. Alexandra; retd. Cdn armed forces; Ont. standard rifle 3-position title '82; mem. '81 Championship of Americas, '82, '86, '90 worlds, Benito Juarez, '83, '87, '91, '95, '99 Pan-Am, '84, '88, '92 Olympic, '94, '98 Commonwealth Games teams; 4 silver, 4 bronze Pan-Am Games; 3 gold, 1 silver, 3 bronze Commonwealth Games; 1 ntl, 1 World Cup gold; 2 SFC female athlete of yr awards; Gil Boa Memorial award '90; 3 Sheila MacQuarrie Memorial awards; mem. Ottawa CSRA Sports Hall of Fame; res. Navan, Ont.

ASHCROFT, Michael (shooting); b. 7 Dec 1964, Leeds, Eng.; given name: Michael James; m. Christina Schulze; c. Alexandra; RMC, BEng.; CF major, aerospace engineer; began shooting as cadet in Hamilton; ntl prone rifle champion '84, '88, '89, '91; team gold '86 Commonwealth, '87 Pan-Am Games, '85, '92 World Cups; team silver '90 Commonwealth Games; individual silver '85, bronze '89 World Cup; 8th '88 Olympics; SFC male athlete of '88, '89; Cdn Forces male athlete of '87; Cdn flagbearer '91 Pan-Am Games; avid cycle road racer; mem. Ottawa CSRA, Cdn Forces Sports halls of fame; res. Navan, Ont.

ASHLEY, John (hockey/officiating); b. 5 Mar 1930, Galt, Ont.; m. June Millman; c. Kristine, Tom; retd. salesman; Jr. A Galt Red Wings, Toronto Marlboros, Guelph Biltmores '46-50; AHL Pittsburgh, Syracuse '50-53; Sr. OHA Stratford '55-58; NHL referee '59-72; mem. Waterloo County, Hockey halls of fame; res. Kitchener, Ont.

ASHTON, Elizabeth (equestrian); b. 16 Mar 1950, Darwen, Eng.; m. Carl Eriksen; UofT, hons. BPHE; Med, Central Mich, MA, Texas(Austin) PhD; pres. Camosun Coll.; mem. ntl jumping team '67-74; gold President's Cup Washington, Rothman's International Toronto, B&W Puissance, McKee International Stakes '72; leading international rider Washington, Royal Horse Show Toronto '72; from '72 mem. Canadian 3-day team event; team gold, individual bronze Bromont mini-Olympics '75; team silver 3-day event '75 Pan-Am Games; alternate mem. '72, '76 Olympic team; mem. '84 Olympic team; ntl 3-day event title '77; team gold 3-day event '78 world championships, '82 Leitchroff Farm trials; bronze Chesterland Horse Trials '79; Canadian horsewoman of '76; Dick Ellis Memorial Trophy '78; res. Victoria, B.C.

ASSELIN, Marie-Claude (skiing); b. 1 Apr 1962, Montreal, Que.; accomplished alpine skier with love of acrobatics; jr. women's Shell Cup FS titles '77-78 sweeping moguls, ballet, aerials, combined; sr. Shell Cup titles '79-80, '82; joined World Cup circuit '81, dominated competition; '81-82 WC grand prix titles, '81-83 WC aerials; won 9 WC events '82-83 season; ntl champion '77-79; NA aerial, combined titles '80; freestyle skier of '79, '81; Julien Trophy French Canadian athlete of '81; Elaine Tanner award '82; federal government achievement award '83; mem. Cdn Ski Hall of Fame; res. Baie James, Que.

ASTRA, Duke (darts); b. 6 Oct 1947, Germany; d. 6 May 1978, Ottawa, Ont.; given name: Vytautas; m. Florence; c. Stephanie, Jennifer; hardware store mgr.; pitched baseball Pembroke 7yrs; mem. HS jr. basketball title team; HS athlete of yr award; began playing darts as lunch-break recreation '72; helped organize, competed in Central Canada DL; with Bob Dupere won '76 ntl doubles title, 5th in worlds; won ntl singles, 4th in worlds '77; Ottawa ACT award '76-77.

ATCHISON, Ron (football); b. 30 Apr 1930, Central Butte, Sask.; given name: Ronald William; m. Monica Manwaring; c. Margaret, Gordon, Kathy; Saskatoon Jr. Hilltops '47-49; middle guard, def. tackle Sask. Roughriders '52-68; noted for toughness, durability; 5 times WFC all-star; honored by fans with "night" '63; Hilltops training field, club house bear his name; mem. Sask. Sports, Cdn Football halls of fame; res. Regina, Sask.

ATHANS, Gary (skiing); b. 12 Jun 1961, Kelowna, B.C.; given name: Gary Wayne; div. Leanne; c. Jesse, Kaylee; ski resort owner, operator; following family tradition excelled on skis both on slopes and water; ntl juve. alpine, waterski champion '75; Western Cdn juve. boys overall waterski titlist '76-77; mem. ntl alpine 8yrs, waterski teams; ntl boys, men's waterski jump records; retd from water skiing '80 to concentrate on alpine World, Europa Cup circuit specializing in slalom, giant slalom; 2nd overall ntl men's alpine championships '80; silver, bronze FIS GS '83; mem. '84 Olympic team; Recurring leg circulatory problem led to retirement from competition '84; res. Kelowna, B.C.

ATHANS, George Jr. (water skiing); b. 6 Jul 1952, Kelowna, B.C.; div. Claire Suzanne Sicotte; c. Shawn Sacha; m. Sandrine Debanne; c. Cassandra; Concordia (SGW campus), BA, McGill; TV producer/dir., pres. Athans Communications; sports commentator CBC 16 yrs; mem. ntl waterski team '66-75; ntl sr. champion '65-75; Western Hemisphere titles '68, '70; world slalom record '69-72; 4 world titles; 33 ntl titles among more than 100 championships; 1st foreign competitor to win US Masters; above average alpine skier; rejected '69 invitation to join ntl alpine team; with father George Sr., 1st father-son combination in Canadian Amateur Sports Hall of Fame; BC athlete of '71; with Bruce Robertson co-holder Norton Crowe award; Que. athlete of '73; 2 BC special merit awards; 2 natl amateur athlete of yr awards; natl sporting goods assn. Athlete of yr award; hon. life mem. CWSA; author "Water Skiing" '75; mem. Order of Canada; mem. Cdn Amateur, BC, Que., Canada's Sports halls of fame; res. Ile des Soeurs, Que.

ATHANS, George Sr. (diving); b. 4 Jan 1921, Vancouver, B.C.; given name: George Demetrie; m. Irene Hartzell; c. George, Greg, Gary; Washington, BA, McGill, MD; retd. physician; 1st of 10 ntl titles, berth on Olympic team '36;

Pacific Coast diving titles '40-44; BEG title '50; bronze '38 BEG; 7th '48 Olympics; diving coach '54 BEG, '60 Olympics; with son George Jr., mem. Canadian Amateur, BC Sports, Canadian Aquatic halls of fame; res. Kelowna, B.C.

ATHANS, Greg (skiing); b. 18 Jun 1955, Kelowna, B.C.; div. Lyn Cowan; c. Carly; m. Peggy Meyers; c. Zoe; UBC; advertising photographer; equally proficient on snow or water skis; only Canadian athlete to win gold both winter, summer Canada Games ('71 alpine slalom, '73 water ski tricks); 8 ntl water ski titles; mem. ntl water ski team '73, '75 world championships; world pro FS alpine champion '76, '80; world pro freestyle mogul, ballet champion '78; world mogul champion '80; author "Ski Free"; res. Vancouver, B.C.

ATKINSON, Bill (baseball); b. 4 Oct 1954, Chatham, Ont.; given name: William Cecil Glenn; m. Marlene Theresa Houle; c. William David; mechanic; a product of Chatham minor baseball program, he also excelled in football, basketball and t&f; signed initial pro baseball contract on his birthday '71; saw minor league service with Jamestown (A), West Palm Beach (A), Quebec (AA), Memphis (AAA), Denver (AAA) before joining Montreal Expos '76-79; joined Chicago White Sox organization '80-83 playing mostly in minors; mem. AAA Denver title teams '76, '83, Appleton A title team '83; ML record: 98 scheduled games, 11-4, 11sv, 99k, 62bob, 3.42era; winning pitcher, scored winning run in 1st Pearson Cup clash between Expos and Blue Jays; '78; coach/mgr. Chatham minor/sr. baseball program '84-98; res. Chatham, Ont.

ATKINSON, Lorne (cycling); b. 8 Jun 1921, Vancouver, B.C.; given name: Lorne Charles; m. Evelyn Mary Speer; c. Daniel Lorne, Janis Marie; retd. bicycle merchant; BC jr. title '39; 4 sr. titles; 4 Pacific Coast 25-mile titles; 4 BC 5-mile track titles; 3 Redmond Derby Pacific Northwest titles; 2 BC 25-mile road titles; ntl 25, 10-mile track titles '49; Que. mile champion '45; mem. '48 Olympic, '50, '54 BEG teams; retd from competition '64; life mem. Vancouver Bicycle Club; res. Vancouver, B.C.

ATKINSON, Ted (horse racing); b. 18 Sep 1916, Toronto, Ont.; retired jockey; raised in NY state; while working at Brooklyn chemical plant as teenager, 98lber encouraged to become jockey; mounted 1st horse taking lessons at Bronx riding academy; worked at Greentree Stables but considered too old (past 20) to be apprentice jockey; struck out on own riding at bush tracks in Midwest; attracted ntl attention in New England at 23; graduated to NY circuit rejoining Greentree as contract jockey; US riding titles '44 (287 wins), '46 (233); rode more than 4000 winners including Tom Fool, '53 horse of year; '49 Preakness, Belmont Stakes with Capot but missed Kentucky Derby; nicknamed "Slasher" by fans, "Professor" by peers; mem. US Jockeys Hall of Fame; res. New York.

ATTFIELD, Roger (horse racing); b. 28 Nov 1939, Newbury, Eng.; m. Tracie; c. John; horse trainer; accomplished show jump and amateur steeplechase rider in Eng., before moving to Canada '70; trained horses for Charles Baker, David Willmot, Earle Mack, Allan Dragone,

Frank Stronach; trained 3 of only 5 Cdn Triple Crown winners (With Approval, Izvestia, Peteski); 7 Queen's Plate winners; 6 Cdn Horse of yr winners; 5 Cdn trainer of yr Sovereign awards; led Kinghaven Farms to 1st place among NA leading owners with earnings in excess of $5M '90; regarded as one of top trainers in NA; mem. Cdn Horse Racing Hall of Fame; res. Toronto, Ont.

AU, On-Kow (lawn bowling); b. 7 Jan 1942, Hong Kong; m. Chung-Pack Au; c. Ernest, Constance; Hong Kong U, BA; broadcaster, journalist; Hong Kong women's singles title '89; moved to BC winning BC Week singles title '92; 2 Indoor Foreman singles titles; V&D singles crown '95; 3 BC fours, 3 singles, 1 pairs silver; mem. ntl team '95-96; Cdn indoor singles bronze '96; bowler of week award '92; res. Vancouver, B.C.

AUBIN, Jack (swimming); b. 29 Jun 1907, Twickenham, Eng.; given name: John Ernest; m. Merion Margaret King; c. Jane Anne; magazine editor; swimming standout in '20s, early '30s; gold 200yd breaststroke '30 BEG; 3 ntl titles; Central YMCA award of merit '27; B.E. Medal '45; International Council of Industrial Editors achievement awards '57, '63; mem. Cdn Aquatic Hall of Fame; res. Islington, Ont.

AUBIN, Marc (harness racing); b. 31 Jul 1933, Quebec City, Que.; retd. RCAF, private detective, steamship agent, night club singer; launched driving career at Connaught Park winning 1st race 1959; ranked among leading West Coast drivers during '70s; shifted to Chicago circuit during '80s; returned briefly to California before settling in Pompano Beach, Fla. '93; guided Magna Bird to season's record for 4yr old trotters '86; through '95 2898 victories with purses exceeding $13M; res. Hollywood, Fla.

AUCH, Susan (speed skating); b. 1 Mar 1966, Winnipeg, Man.; UCal; motivational speaker, TV commentator, coach; began skating age 10; switched to long from short track after '88 Olympics; 3 NA junior titles; 15 ntl titles; 2 Canada Games gold; 2g, 2s, 1b '85 FISU Games; short track world 3000 relay record '86; CR 1000m '97; '88 Olympic bronze 3000 relay (demo) short track; '94 Olympic silver 500m; Canada Cup 500m gold; 3g, 2s Italian World Cup; 3 Cdn sprint titles; Cdn 500m record; beat Bonnie Blair for 3 World Cup 500m gold '95; mem. Winnipeg Speed Skating Club; retd from competition '98 but changed mind and returned to competitive scene '99; turned to coaching, motivational speaking, CBC-TV commentator; '85 sports excellence award, '89 world champion award; CASSA female athlete of year '90, '91; long track female athlete of '90-92, '94-95; Bobbie Rosenfeld trophy '95; mem. Cdn Athletes Assn. Board; mem. Cdn Speed Skating Hall of Fame; res. Calgary, Alta.

AUDETTE, Julien (soaring); b. 6 Jun 1914, Radville, Sask.; d. 28 Oct 1986, Regina, Sask.; given name: Julien Joseph; m. Myrtle Dewsom; c. Ray, Joan, Robert, Douglas, Michelle; pioneered sport in Sask.; founding mem. Regina Gliding and Soaring Club, dir., pres., chief pilot; instrumental in organizing 3 ntl championships in Sask.; originated gliding scholarship program for air cadets; all 8 ntl soaring records, including 6 simultaneously; 7 ntl, 5 international awards; 1st Canadian awarded Federation Aeronatique Internationale Gold C pin with 3 diamonds; Canadian diamond badge; mem. Sask. Sports Hall of Fame.

AUDLEY, Gordon (speedskating); b. 20 Apr 1928, Winnipeg, Man.; m. Grace MacKenzie; c. Karey, Rocky; retd CPR machinist, insurance salesman; first competition Man. Open age 10, won 110, 220yd events in provincial record times; '40-44 competed both speedskating, hockey; '44 Man. jr. speedskating title; '45 Man., Detroit int. titles, 220yd record Sask.; '46 ntl, Man. int. Open, Closed titles; Man. sr. titles '50, '53-57; mem. '48, '52, '56 Olympic, '56 world championships teams; Canadian flag-bearer, bronze 500m '52 Olympics; retd from competition '57; officiated '60 Olympics; mem. Canadian Speed Skating, Man. Sports halls of fame; res. Long Beach, Calif.

AVERY, Earle (harness racing); b. 4 Feb 1894, Knowlesville, N.B.; d. 6 Nov 1977, Woodstock, N.B.; given name: Earle Bradford; m. Elizabeth Kinney; c. Robert, Blair; horseman, potato farmer; active driver, trainer '19-72; 1252 victories, purses totalling more than $3.5 million; American Pacing Classic (Meadow Skipper '64), American Trotting Classic (Porterhouse '63), Cane Pace (Meadow Skipper '63); best time 1:57 4/5 with Meadow Skipper; 21 2:00 or less miles; 7 world record driving performances; US Harness Writers' Clem McCarthy Good Guy award '63; mem. NB Sports, Canadian Horse Racing, US Harness Racing halls of fame.

AVERY, Frank (curling); b. 25 Feb 1902, Austin, Man.; m. Freda (d); c. Brian; retired; Vancouver's Mr. Curling through work in pioneering, promoting game on BC coast; BC title '35, '43; 3rd BC Brier entries '37, '39, '42; skipped BC Brier entry '46; mem. BC entry ntl men's seniors championships '66-67; hon. mem. Canadian Curling Reporters; life mem. Vancouver CC, Pacific Coast CA; mem. Governor-General's CC from '76; mem. Canadian Curling, BC Sports halls of Fame; res. Vancouver, B.C.

AVERY, Jeff (football); b. 28 Mar 1953, Ottawa, Ont.; given name: Jeffrey Clarke; div. Jocelyn Brown; m. Sharon Fitzmaurice; UofOtt, BA, financial consultant; in 4 UofOtt, seasons amassed 1973yds on 110 receptions, 15tds; 3 times OUAA all-star, 2 all-Canadian; Frank Tindall award MVP '75 Central Bowl; 3 times UofOtt most valuable receiver, once leadership award winner; mem. '75 Yates (OUAA), Vanier (CIAU) Cup title teams; pro Ottawa '76-82; 2 Grey Cup finals, 1 winner; EFC all-star '77-78; wide receiver, slotback, reserve punter; CFL record: 169 reception for 2609 yds, 15tds, 102 league games; asst. coach UofOtt '83-84; Rough Riders radio broadcast color commentator '89-96; mem. UofOtt Football Hall of Fame; res. Kanata, Ont.

AWREY, Don (hockey); b. 18 Jul 1943, Kitchener, Ont.; given name: Donald William; bus-tour company owner; defenceman; Niagara Falls Jrs; minor league stints with Minneapolis (CPHL), Hershey, Boston (AHL); NHL with Boston '63-73, St. Louis '73-74, Montreal '74-76, Pittsburgh '76-77, NY Rangers '77-78, Colorado '78-79; Team Canada '72 Summit Series; NHL record: 16 seasons, 979 scheduled games, 31g, 158a, 1065pim, 71 playoff games, 0g, 18a, 150pim; mem. 2 Stanley Cup winners; plays hockey with Boston alumni; nicknamed "Bugsy"; res. Hooksett, N.H.

B

BABBITT, Ethel (tennis); b. 13 Jul 1876, Fredericton, N.B.; d. 20 Aug 1969, Fredericton, N.B.; given name: Ethel Mary Hatt; m. Harold Babbitt; c. Isabel, John David; standout tennis player '08-27; 14 NB championships, 3 Maritime titles in ladies' singles, mixed doubles; ntl honors '10; mem. NB Sports Hall of Fame.

BABBITT, John (tennis); b. 2 Feb 1908, Fredericton, N.B.; d. (circa) 1990, Ottawa, Ont.; given name: John David; m. Dorothy Elizabeth Rooney; c. David, Robert (d), Susan, Cynthia, James, Andrew (d); UNB, Oxford; retired NRC physicist; like mother Ethel and sister Isabel, prominent tennis star in Maritimes; NB singles titles '28-29; Maritime championship '29; Oxford on Rhodes Scholarship; 6yrs. mem. ice hockey team; mem. UNB rugger team, capt. '28; 2 McTier Trophy title teams.

BABITS, Laslo (t&f); b. 17 Apr 1958, Oliver, B.C.; Washington State; javelin specialist; father former European boxing champion, mother former European swimming champion; BC HS champion '76-77; gold '77 Canada Games, '79 BC championships, '81 Modesto Relays, '82 Pac 10 Conf., Can-Ita-Jpn tri meet; '83 Pan-Am Games gold; '82 Commonwealth Games silver; mem. '84 Olympic team; fed. govt. excellence award '84; res. Kalenden, B.C.

BABYCH, Dave (hockey); b. 23 May 1961, Edmonton, Alta.; m. Diana; c. Terence, Ty, Kolton, Jaret, Cal; defence Portland Jr. (WHL) '79-80; 1st pick Winnipeg '80 draft; NHL with Winnipeg '80-85, Hartford '85-91, Vancouver '91-97, Philadelphia '97-98, Los Angeles '99; WHL 1st team all-star; 2 NHL all-star games; NHL record: (through '99) 1195 scheduled games, 142g, 581a, 114 playoff games, 21g. 41a; operates summer hockey school; res. North Vancouver, B.C.

BABYCH, Wayne (hockey); b. 6 Jun 1958, Edmonton, Alta.; given name: Wayne Joseph; golf course owner; jr. Portland Winter Hawks; twice WHL 1st team all-star right wing; 1st pick St. Louis, 3rd overall '78 draft; topped 50-goal plateau with 54 '80-81 season; mem. St. Louis '78-84, Pittsburgh '84-85, Quebec '85, Hartford '86-87; NHL record: 519 scheduled games, 192g, 246a, 41 playoff games, 7g, 9a; res. Winnipeg, Man.

BACK, Len (football); b. 21 Jul 1900, Hamilton, Ont.; d. 16 Mar 1982, Florida; given name: Leonard Percival; m. Lillian (d.); c. Beverly; m. Grace; football exec.; Hamilton Tigers jrs. '18-19 before skull fracture ended playing days; team mgr. '20; mgr. Hamilton Tigers intermediates '21-26; Tiger sr. ORFU team '28-40; joined Brian Timmis as mgr. Hamilton Wildcats, won '43 Grey Cup; rejoined Tigers following WWll, on hand when Tigers and Wildcats combined; mgr. Ticats from '50; honored by Grey Cup comm. '61, City of Hamilton, Ticats FC; mem. Cdn Football, Copps Coliseum halls of fame.

BACKHOUSE-SHARPE, Claire (badminton); b. 13 May 1958, Vancouver, B.C.; m. Douglas Sharpe; c. Megan, Jaime, Kieran; UBC; with variety of partners ranked as one of Canada's top doubles competitors; ntl competitor from '76; 1 ntl single, 6 ladies' doubles, 3 mixed doubles titles; Mexican Open, Eastern, Western, Pan-Am championships, US Open ladies' doubles titles; 2 Pan-Am championships, 2 Pepsi-Cola, 1 US Open mixed doubles titles; '86 Commonwealth Games singles silver; with Johanne Falardeau '82 Commonwealth Games ladies' doubles gold; with Jane Youngberg '78 Commonwealth Games ladies' doubles silver, team silver; mem. '78 Uber Cup, 5 Commonwealth Games, '88 Olympics, 5 All-England, 2 world championships, 2 Scottish International, 2 Sweden Open, 3 Danish Open teams; res. Victoria, B.C.

BACKSTROM, Ralph (hockey); b. 18 Sep 1937, Kirkland Lake, Ont.; given name: Ralph Gerald; m. Fran; c. Martin, Diana, Andrew; hockey executive; capt. Hull-Ottawa Jr. Canadiens Memorial Cup winner; centre Canadiens '58-71; Calder Memorial Trophy NHL rookie of year; Los Angeles '71-72; Chicago '73; WHA Chicago Cougars '73-75, Denver Spurs '76, New England Whalers '77; most sportsmanlike player '74; most popular Cougar award '73-74; WHA all-star centre once; starred with Team Canada '74 in losing series vs USSR; NHL record: 1032 scheduled games, 278g, 361a, 116 playoff games, 27g, 32a; WHA record: 304 games, 100g, 153a; asst. coach Kings; head coach Denver U; coach IHL Phoenix Roadrunners 1990-92; comissioner Roller Hockey International from '93; res. Denver, Colo.

BAERT, Jean-Paul (t&f); b. 6 Oct 1942, Paris, France; guest prof. U of Quebec; mem. French jr. javelin team; moved to Canada '66; throws coach U of Montreal, Que. provincial coach; dir. gen. Que. T&f Federation; CTFA throws coach; master coach; authored "The Throws"; coach pre-Olympic US training camp, Americas team World Cup '77, '79; ntl team coach '74, '78 Commonwealth, '75, '79 Pan-Am, '76, '80 Olympic Games teams; res. Laval, Que.

BAGGULEY, Howard (ski jumping/cross-country); b. 31 May 1909, Ottawa, Ont.; given name: Douglas Howard; m. Maysel Jean Bradley; c. Douglas, David (d); retd fed. govt.; jr., int., sr. jumping, cross-country titles Ottawa, Montreal regions; Que. jumping champion; 2 Ont., 1 ntl jumping titles; Eastern record 227' jump; Eastern US Class B jumping champion; mem. '32 Olympic team; several US pro jumping events; avid 5-pin bowler; perfect 450 string '46, Brunswick award; 426 in '62 earned RA Molson Award; res. Prescott, Ont.

BAGNELL, Norm (softball); b. 11 May 1926, Toronto, Ont.; d. Jun 1987, Toronto, Ont.; given name: Norman James; m. Joan Fraser; c. Ken, Karen, Kim; employee General Motors; pitched 1st of 54 career no-hitters age 11 Essex playground; at 15 sr. Toronto's top team Prince of Wales; noted for ambidextrous pitching; mem. more than 25 title teams, 3 world tournament teams while playing on more than 20 clubs throughout Ont.; averaged 20 strikeouts per game while toiling for Oshawa Pedlars, twice Sr. B titlists; defeated Eddie Feigner's King and His Court; mem. Kincardine OASA Int. titlists '54 posting 510 strikeouts in 35 games and batting .333; Oshawa Tony's 2 Sr. B, 1 Sr. A title, world tournament MVP; '39-72 more than 1000 victories, 26 perfect games among 54 no-hitters, 41 one-hitters, 37 two-hitters, 32 strikeouts in single game, 39 consecutive scoreless innings, 510 strikeouts in 35 games, 17 consecutive wins, back-to-back no-hitters at age 45, lifetime batting average of .300; managed Filtro Perks, Canada's entry in women's world tournament '62; mem. Canadian Softball Hall of Fame.

BAILEY, Ace (hockey); b. 3 Jul 1903, Bracebridge, Ont.; d. 7 Apr 1992, Toronto, Ont.; given name: Irvin Wallace; m. Gladys Rowan; c. Audrey, Joyce, Joanne; salesman; jr. Bracebridge, St. Mary's, Toronto; sr. Peterborough Petes '24-26; pro Maple Leafs 1926-34; Stanley Cup winner '32, scoring title '28-29 for which he was dubbed Ace by sports writers; twice team MVP; career terminated in Boston Dec '33 when he sustained severe head injuries when checked by Eddie Shore; jersey No. 6 was retired by Leafs but at his request was reactivated and given to Ron Ellis; NHL totals: 111g, 82a; mem. Hockey Hall of Fame.

BAILEY, Angela (t&f); b. 28 Feb 1962, Coventry, Eng.; UofT; sprint specialist; '78, '82, '86 Commonwealth Games 4x100 relay silver; 2 Colgate meet records; 2 ntl jr., sr. records; 3 Pacific Conf. Games golds; mem. '80, '84, '88 Olympic, '81 World Cup, '83 world championships, '99 Pan-Am Games teams; 10 4x100 relay, 9 100m, 5 200m, 3 50m, 1 60m titles; mem. 4x100 women's silver relay team '84 Olympics; Elaine Tanner trophy '81; Olympic champions award '85; mem. Mississauga Sports Hall of Fame; res. Mississauga, Ont.

BAILEY, By (football); b. 12 Oct 1930, Omaha, Neb.; d. 18 Jan 1998, Winfield, B.C.; given name: Byron; m. Diana Churchill (d); c. Laura, Lynn; m. Sandra Hyslop; Washington State, BEd; marketing mgr.; all-Pacific Coast honors WSU running back; pro Detroit Lions '52 NFL championship team; Green Bay Packers '53; charter mem. BC Lions '54 scoring 1st TD ever by a Lion and 1st Lions TD ever in a winning cause; all-Cdn halfback '57, MVP, WIFU all-star team; 1st Lion honored by 'night' '60; mem. BC Grey Cup champions '64; 29 CFL tds; exec. mem., trustee, BC Sports Hall of Fame, mem. BC Sports, Canadian Football halls of fame.

BAILEY, Dave (t&f); b. 17 Mar 1945, Toronto, Ont.; given name: David George; m. Barbara Gillespie; c. Karen Joanne, Brian David, Scott Andrew; UofT, BSc., MSc., PhD.; sr. investigator, drug research and development, Smith, Kline, French Canada Ltd.; 4:07.5 mile world record for 17-year-old '62; toured Europe with EYTC '63; 11 Jun '66 became 1st Canadian to crack 4-minute mile barrier with 3:59.1 at San Diego; Canadian mile record 3:57.7 Toronto Police Games '67; bronze '67 Pan-Am Games; gold California relays; silver FISU Games; disappointing '68 Olympic 1500 performance brought retirement; '70 comeback produced 3rd California relays; while preparing for '72 Olympics broke ankle and retired from active competition; coached Saskatoon TC '76-78; res. North York, Ont.

BAILEY, Donovan (t&f); b. 16 Dec 1967, Manchester, Jamaica; marketing consultant; sprint specialist; emigrated to Canada '81; began competing '90; Ont. indoor 60m title, silver 100m Harry Jerome Classic '91; Pan-Am Games 4x100m relay silver '91, '99; ntl indoor 60m title '92; silver 100m '94 Francophone Games; mem. '94 Commonwealth Games gold record 4x100m relay team; world 100m title '95 (9.97); mem. world 4x100 gold medal relay team '95-97; world indoor 50m record 5.56 '96; ntl 100m, 200m records; '96 Olympic gold 100m in world record 9.84, 4x100m relay gold; 2 Norton Crowe trophies; 2 Cdn men's team of yr awards; Ont. athlete of '96, Lionel Conacher, Lou Marsh trophies '96; handily defeated Olympic 200, 400m record-holder Michael Johnson of US in $1.5M 150-metre match race '97; mem. Phoenix TC; rejected suggestion he would pursue CFL career with Argos; res. Oakville, Ont.

BAILEY, Marguerite (basketball); b. 31 Oct 1906, Toronto, Ont.; d. 28 Oct 1992, Vancouver, B.C.; div. Horace Jacobs; retired exec. secty.; mem. famed Edmonton Grads '26-27; mem. Canadian Basketball, Alta. Sports halls of fame.

BAILEY, Marjorie (t&f); b. 21 Nov 1947, Lockeport, N.S.; given name: Marjorie Evalena; m. James Brown; c. Anthony Bobby George; Manitoba Institute of Technology; public health nurse; sprint specialist; ntl team '64-76; mem. '66, '74 Commonwealth, '75 Pan-Am Games teams; bronze 100m (11.42), 4x100m relay '76 Olympics; ntl record 200m 23.06 '76; mem. NS Sports Hall of Fame; res. Lockeport, N.S.

BAILLIE, Charlie (football); b. 14 Feb 1935, Montreal, Que.; given name: Charles Bishop; m. Alyce O'Connor; c. Sharon, Steven, Scott, Peter, Christine; Sir George Williams; mgr. manufacturing Northern Telecom; hockey Jr. Royals '53-54; mem. '53 ntl sr. champion Lakeshore Flyers football team; pro Montreal '54, '56-57, '60-61, '65, Quebec Rifles (UFL) '64, Montreal Beavers (Continental FL) '66; head coach Chomedey (Que. Sr. League) '62; coach TMR Jr. Lions '63; line coach McGill '67-69; offensive co-ordinator SGW '70-71; head football coach McGill from '72; Montreal HS League football MVP '51; OQIFC football coach of '81; res. Dollard des Ormeaux, Que.

BAIN, Dan (all-around); b. 14 Feb 1874, Belleville, Ont.; d. 15 Aug. 1962, Winnipeg, Man.; given name: Donald Henderson; wholesale merchant; excelled in hockey, cycling, gymnastics, figure skating, roller skating, golf, trap and skeet shooting; first athletic medal, Man. 3-mile roller skating title, at 13; last athletic medal figure skating at 56; mem. Winnipeg hockey team winning 9 of 11 matches vs. East 1893; capt. Winnipeg Victorias Stanley Cup champions 1896; retd from topflight hockey '01 after team won 2nd Stanley Cup; ntl trapshooting title Toronto '03; enjoyed wildfowl shooting, owned shoreline of Grant's Lake, one of best goose lakes in Man. flyway, turned property over to Ducks Unlimited; at 70 gave skate waltzing exhibitions with partners half century his junior; mem. Canada's, Man. Sports, Hockey, Man. Hockey halls of fame.

BAIRD, Vaughan (builder); b. 6 Sep 1927, Winnipeg, Man.; UMan., BA, Dalhousie, LL.B, U Paris, diploma, U

Winnipeg, doctorate; lawyer, QC; competed in boxing, diving, swimming but gained prominence for organizational skills; founding dir. Manitoba Sports Federation; founding/present chairman Cdn Aquatic Hall of Fame and Museum; founding pres. Cdn Amateur Diving Assn.; founding dir. Aquatic Fed. of Can.; mem. COA '69-72; v-pres Commonwealth Games Assn.; dir. FINA, ASUA; mem. '67 Pan-Am Games comm.; led crusade to get Pan-Am pool enclosed; life mem. MSF; Air Canada exec. of '71; Silver Jubilee medal '77; CM; authored "A Canadian History of the Art and Sport of Diving"; Bill Schroeder IASMHOF award; mem. Order of Canada; Man. Sports Hall of Fame; res. Winnipeg, Man.

BAJIN, Boris (gymnastics); b. 20 Mar 1933, Yugoslavia; given name: Borislav; m. Natasa; c. Alexandar, Sanja; U of Belgrade, BSc., MPhE.; gymnastics coach; international competitor prior to '60; Yugoslavian ntl coach '60-73; coached competitors in FISU, Balkan, Mediteranean Games, European, world championships, Olympic, Commonwealth Games; Canadian ntl women's coach '74; authored several books, numerous articles on gymnastics; extensive teaching career Europe, Canada; lecturer '76 USGF Congress; head coach '77 ntl coaches' seminar for Australian GF, lecturer NZ ntl gymnastics clinics, also England, Puerto Rico, USA; coach 4 Olympic, 5 European, 6 world championships, 2 FISU, 1 Commonwealth, 1 Pan-Am Games teams; res. Downsview, Ont.

BAKER, Alison (t&f); b. 6 Aug 1964, Ballymena, N. Ireland; McMaster, PhD; environmental engineer; racewalk specialist; came to Canada '68; started competing at 17; Ont. 3km title; silver Pan-Am jr. '82; competed for Canada '82 America's Cup, '85, '89, '93 World Cup, '85 Canada Games, '87, '93 worlds, '85, '89 FISU; '89, '93 World indoor, '90, '94 Commonwealth Games; ntl 10km title '93; bronze Spanish, Czech 10km events '92; Cdn record 44:30.1 for 10km walk '92; res. Kingston/Guelph, Ont.

BAKER, Bill (football); b. 23 Apr 1945, Sheridan, Man.; m. Cathy; c. 3 daughters; Otterbein Coll; jr. Regina Rams '63; off/def tackle, linebacker at Otterbein; twice Ohio Conf. all-star, MVP '67; joined CFL Saskatchewan '68-73, '77-78, BC '75-76; missed '74 season with ankle injury; nicknamed "The Undertaker" for ferocious pass rush; 5 all-West, 4 all-Cdn DE; 2 BC most valuable lineman, most inspirational player awards; Dr. Beattie Martin trophy '76, 2 Norm Fieldgate trophies, Schenley defensive player award '76; mem. 2 Grey Cup winners; CFL pres./CEO '89; mem. Roughriders Plaza of Honor, Cdn Football Hall of Fame; res. Calgary, Alta.

BAKER, Brad (softball); b. 10 May 1965, Oshawa, Ont.; given name: Brad Daniel; m. Jan Simpson; records officer; left-handed pitcher; started sr. softball at 19 with Penn Corp.; played 4yrs USA leagues; played with various Cdn teams from '90; Toronto Gators '94-96, Madison, Wisc. Farm Tavern '97-98, Oshawa Gators '99; during winter months competed in Wellington, N.Z. from '90; 2 ntl, 1 world title; res. Wellington, N.Z./Oshawa, Ont.

BAKER, Charles (equestrian); b. 10 Jun 1920, Toronto, Ont.; m. Susanne Elizabeth Gaby; c. Charles III, Susanne;

Upper Canada College, UofT; sr. exec. officer, board chairman Ontario Jockey Club; mem. ntl equestrian team '47-57; Chef d'equipe Olympic bronze entry, Pan-Am gold medal team, '60 Olympic team; owner individual gold winner Natan '59 Pan-Am Games; res. King, Ont.

BAKER, Joann (swimming); b. 24 Nov 1960, Moose Jaw, Sask.; given name: Joann Elaine; m. Scott Anderson; c. Ryan, Sean, Troy; Arizona State; backstroke, IM specialist; launched career with Thunderbolts SC '72; silver 200m breaststroke, 4x100 medley relay '75 Pan-Am Games; 7 ntl titles; '75 world trials 200m breaststroke, '76 Olympic trials 100m breaststroke; mem. '75, '79 Pan-Am, '76 Olympic Games, Canada-Russia, Canada-West Germany dual meet teams, winning 3 silver, 1 bronze; Man. sr. champion '77; 6 ntl sr., 2 Commonwealth records; competed 2 NCAA championships; retd from competition '80; 2 Thunder Bay athlete of yr awards; mem. NWO Sports, Ont. Aquatic halls of fame; res. Phoenix, Ariz.

BAKER, Mary (baseball/softball); b. 10 Jul 1919, Regina, Sask.; sportscaster; catcher for Blue Sox in P.K. Wrigley's All-American Girls Baseball League '43; proved feminity and top-notch baseball were a solid combination; became league's most publicized player earning nickname "Pretty Bonnie Baker"; 3 times all-star catcher; only full-time woman manager Kalamazoo Lassies '51; returning to Regina led Regina Legion team to provincial, Western Cdn, world women's softball titles; distinction of becoming 1st female sportscaster in Canada with CKRM '64-65; mem. Sask. Sports Hall of Fame; honored by Cooperstown, Cdn Baseball halls of fame; res. Regina, Sask.

BAKER, Norm (basketball); b. 17 Feb. 1923, Victoria, B.C.; d. 23 Apr 1989, Victoria, B.C.; m. Nancy; c. Norman Jr.; policeman; joined sr. ranks at 16; mem. 5 ntl sr. title teams; 38 point single game record; pro Chicago Stags newly-formed Basketball Association of America; with Vancouver Hornets dominated scoring 2yrs setting record 1862 points 70-game schedule; Portland '48 pro playoffs; 1st player written pact with Abe Saperstein of Harlem Globetrotters; toured Europe, North Africa with Stars of World '50; 1 pro season Boston; mem. New Westminster Adanacs Mann Cup lacrosse champs '47; Victoria Shamrocks through '54, coached Shamrocks '59-60 before retiring; CP poll Canadian basketballer of half century '50; Centennial medal '67; mem. Canada's, BC Sports, Cdn Basketball, Greater Victoria Sports halls of fame.

BAKER, Terry (football); b. 8 May 1962, Bridgewater, N.S.; m. Krista; c. Natasha, Ashley, Brianna; Mount Allison; drafted Montreal Concordes '84 CIAU draft; jockeyed around in CFL with Edmonton, Toronto, Montreal '85-86 before seeing first action Saskatchewan '87-89; Ottawa '90-95, Toronto '95, Montreal '96-98; CFL record (through '98): 206gp. 300 fg, 344 cvt, 60s, 1365pts, 1593punts, 67,324tds, 619kickoffs, 36,202 yds; mem. '89 Grey Cup winner; res. Montreal, Que.

BAKONYI, Peter (fencing); b. 10 Jul 1933, Budapest, Hungary; m. Vera; c. Debbie, Ronnie, David; UBC law school; regional real estate manager; 16 BC titles in épée, foil, sabre; 7 ntl titles; bronze épée team '62 BEG; 6th individual épée '63 Pan-Am; silver team épée, 4th individual '66 BEG; 5th '67 Pan-Am; among top 20, highest by Canadian fencer, '68 Olympics; silver '61, '69 Maccabiah Games; bronze épée team, 4th individual '70 BEG; referee '71 Pan-Am, '72, '76 Olympic Games; retd from competition '73; team mgr. '75 Pan-Am Games; ntl jr. development chair. '72-76, ntl jr. Olympic chair. '72-76; v.-pres. CFA 3 terms; res. Vancouver, B.C.

BALA, Ray Sr. (bowling); b. 21 Feb 1931, Windsor, Ont.; m. Marjorie Budolowski; c. Ronald, Jo-Ann, Ray Jr.; U of Windsor; staff inspector Windsor City Police; city school high jump title '44; Border Cities tournament singles title '55; Ont., ntl 10-pin singles titles '55, '58; competed US Masters '55, '58, world tournament '58; res. Windsor, Ont.

BALD, Kathy (swimming); b. 19 Dec 1963, Etobicoke, Ont.; given name: Katherine Ann; m. Kevin Renard; CEO asst 3-D Medical Co.; ntl 12-year-old 100m FS record '76; mem. ntl team '81-84, '85-92; gold 100m breaststroke, silver 200m breaststroke '82 Commonwealth Games; 1 gold, 2 silver, 1 bronze '83 Pan-Am Games; 1 Canada Games, 4 Canada Cup, 2 Swedish Games gold; 1 Commonwealth Games, 5 ntl sr. records; 5 1sts '83 Ont. championships; 5 ntl titles; competed '88 Olympics; 3 fed. govt. excellence awards; Ottawa ACT athlete of '83; mem. Nepean Wall of Fame; res. Mississauga, Ont.

BALDING, Al (golf); b. 29 Apr 1924, Toronto, Ont.; m. Moreen Lyttle; c. Allan, Erin; following overseas stint WWll turned pro '49 as summer starter Toronto Oakdale; asst. pro Burlington GC '50; asst. Islington GC '51-52; head pro Credit Valley '54-56; Ont. Assistants' title '50; won Que. Open '52, 4 Cdn match play titles, CPGA championships '55, '63, '70; 1st Canadian to win PGA tour event '55 Mayfair Open; USPGA tour regular '57; West Palm Beach, Miami Opens, Havana Invitational '57; Mexican Open '63; Alta. Open '73; twice low Cdn in Canadian Open; individual champion and with George Knudson won World Cup team title Rome '68; shoulder operations for tear in rotar cuff curtailed play '65, '70, '77; twice Ont. athlete of year; competes on PGA Srs. circuit; mem. Etobicoke, RCGA, Canada's Sports halls of fame; res. Sebring, Fla./ Mississauga, Ont.

BALDWIN, Bill (shooting); b. 31 Oct 1943, Pincher Creek, Alta.; given name: Wilfred William; div.; c. Linda, Tanya, Billy; welding contractor; competitive shooter from 1977; Alta. muzzle loading pistol, rifle champion 1977; KOCR-MRA club champion 1978-80; 84 match titles through '86; 4 time Bisley qualifier; with Alain Marion won '86 Commonwealth Games pairs gold; won Governor-General's prize '84 DCRA matches; team silver '92 Palma matches; Sask. athlete for Jul '86 award; life mem. DCRA; mem. SPRA, NSR-MRA, SFC; certified shooting coach; res. Gloucester, Ont.

BALDWIN, Frank (coaching/basketball); b. 23 Dec 1920, Halifax, N.S.; d. 30 Apr 1999, Halifax, N.S.; given name: Francis Vincent; development co-ordinator Basketball NS; began coaching '39; coached ntl juve. titlists '50; launched St. Mary's U program; program dir. Cdn Martyrs Parish Centre '63; founding mem. Halifax juve. basketball league; development co-ordinator Basketball NS from '71; coached

NS Canada Games teams '71, '75; played softball 10yrs, involved in summer camp programs 15yrs; conductor numerous basketball clinics throughout NS.; National Assn. Basketball Coaches merit award '76. NS. school Athletic Fed. award '80; mem. Canadian Basketball, Nova Scotia Sports halls of fame.

BALDWIN, Matt (curling); b. 3 May 1926, Blucher, Sask.; given name: Matthew Martyn; m. Betty Jean Hamilton; c. Susan, Sally, Leslie; UofAlta., BSc.; retd petroleum engineer; 8 Northern Alta., 5 Alta titles; 3 Brier titles; '54 Edmonton carspiel; Keen Ice Singles curling TV series 7 of 10 years; dir. Eskimos Football Club 5yrs, club pres.; mem. Governor-General's Curling Club, Alta., Edmonton, UofAlta., Canada's Sports, Canadian Curling halls of fame; res. Edmonton, Alta.

BALDWIN, Ralph (harness racing); b. 25 Feb 1916, Lloydminster, Sask.; m. Jeanette; harness race driver, trainer; apprenticed with father, becoming second trainer, later for Harry Fitzpatrick, before opening public stables; began racing in '30s shifting to US tracks '46 after serving in US army; more than 1100 winners with purses totalling more than $5 million; major victories include 2 Hambletonians (Speedy Scott '63, Flirth '73), 5 Kentucky Futurities, 2 Westbury Futurities, 2 Realization Trots, Messenger Stakes; head trainer Castleton Farms, Lexington, Ky. '60-69; following year's absence returned to racing as head trainer, sometimes driver, Arden Homestead Stables, Goshen, N.Y.; mem. Cdn Horse Racing, USTA Living halls of fame; res. Goshen, N.Y. (summer), Pompano Beach, Fla. (winter).

BALES, John (canoeing/administration); b. 6 Jul 1950, Lachine, Que.; m. Penny Werthner; c. Neill, Elena; McMaster, BA, BPhE, MBA, European Institute Business Administration; pres. Coaching Assn. of Canada; ntl Juvenile boys' singles canoe champion '67; head coach Rideau Canoe Club from '70; Canadian club title '73; CCA ntl team coach '73 world, jr. European championships, '74-75, '77 world championships, '76 Olympics; instrumental in establishing Ntl Sports Centre in Ottawa, Ntl Coaching Institute in Calgary; res. Ottawa, Ont.

BALL, James (t&f); b. May 7 1903, Dauphin, Man.; d. 2 Jul 1988, Victoria, B.C.; m. Violet Laird Parker; c. Jacqueline Allan; UofM; pharmacist; Man., Western Canadian Intercollegiate titles; '27 ntl quarter-mile title, anchored winning mile relay team; '28 Olympic trials 400m in record 48.6 breaking 49.4 standard he had set in heat 1 hour earlier; silver with 48-second run '28 Olympics, team bronze mile relay; Glasgow quarter-mile, Dublin relay, set Irish 200m mark breaking standard set 20 years earlier by Hamilton's Bobby Kerr; mem. relay team which won '29 Madison Square Gardens Millrose Games medley relay; anchored Commonwealth relay team in victory over England; ntl 400yd record stood 37 years; relay bronze '32 Olympics; competed in 1st Maple Leaf Gardens indoor championships, 1st BEG Hamilton; 3 Cdn 300yd, 400m titles; outstanding performer Dublin, Ireland, meet (Tailteam Queen trophy), '33 Canadian amateur athlete of year (Norton Crowe Trophy), Winnipeg Jockey Club sterling silver Grecian urn for contribution to sport; silver medal ntl snowshoe race; mem. Cdn Amateur, Canada's, Man. Sports halls of fame.

BALLANTINE, Bonny (bowling); b. 10 Feb 1939, Regina, Sask.; given name: Bonny Bonnell; m. William Ballantine; c. Drew, Grey, Dawne, Jaye, Brad; secretary; began bowling career as 5-pinner; mixed championship team '55; Western Canadian team championship '61; moved to 10-pin winning Regina mixed doubles; mem. women's championship teams '63, '65; city, provincial women's doubles titles '64, '65, '66; Regina, Sask., Canadian O'Keefe Open singles titles '66; certified AMF 10-pin bowling instructor, began working with youth leagues '67; Regina scratch singles, all-events, ladies' team '68, city, provincial, ntl open singles '69; competed world championship '69; city, provincial all-events, city, provincial open singles '71; Regina Lakeshore Lions sportswoman of '66; mem. Sask. Sports Hall of Fame; res. Regina Beach, Sask.

BALLARD, Harold (entrepreneur); b. 30 Jul 1905; Toronto, Ont.; d. 11 Apr 1990, Toronto, Ont.; given name: Harold Edwin; m. Dorothy Biggs (d); c. William, Harold Garner, Mary Elizabeth; Upper Canada College; pres. Maple Leaf Gardens; champion powerboat racer, speed skater; ntl speedboat record 63mph Rice Lake; Toronto 220, 440, 880yd speed skating titles; following footsteps of skate manufacturing father, became involved with all aspects of hockey at early age; managed Toronto Sea Fleas to Allan Cup, Toronto Nationals to Memorial Cup; principal exec., financial backer Marlboro organization in '30s; Marlies won record 7 Memorial Cups; sr. team '50 Allan Cup; part-owner Toronto Maple Leafs '62-63; principal owner TML '71; owner CFL's Hamilton Tiger-Cats from '77; noted for charitable work; recipient OHA goldstick; newsworthy personality with many detractors; involved with initial Team Canada '72; spent 1yr of 3-yr sentence Millhaven Penitentiary for misappropriation of Leafs funds; mem. Cdn Football, Hockey halls of fame.

BALON, Dave (hockey); b. 2 Aug 1938, Wakaw, Sask.; given name: David Alexander; m. Gwen; c. Jodi, Jeff; tour boat owner; left wing Prince Albert Mintos, Vancouver, Saskatoon (WHL), Trois-Rivieres, Kitchener-Waterloo (EPHL), in NHL '59-73 with Montreal, NY Rangers, Minnesota, Vancouver; NHL record: 776 scheduled games, 192g, 222a, 78 playoff games, 14g, 21a; mem. 2 Stanley Cup winners; rated top 2-way player in NHL '70-71; coached Humboldt Jrs '72-80; diagnosed as having multiple sclerosis '78; res. Prince Albert, Sask.

BANNON, Paul (t&f); b. 22 Mar 1956, Glasgow, Scotland; given name: Paul Patrick; Memphis State, BA; chartered accountant; Scottish schools 1500m champion '71; British jr. 3000m champion '72; 5 times NCAA All-American '73-77, Canadian 5000, 10,000m champion '77; bronze '78 Commonwealth Games marathon; PB: 800m (2:01); 1500m (3:57); mile (4:11); 5000m (13:49); 10,000m (28:36); marathon (2h:16:03); res. Mississauga, Ont.

BANOS, Jean-Marie (fencing); b. 10 Feb 1962, Lavelanet, France; m. Caitlin Bilodeau; c. Justin, Sebastien; U of Montreal; educator; sabre specialist; mem. 1st non-European sabre team to place in top 8 world championships '82; 4 ntl individual, 3 team titles; 2 Governor-General's Cup, Eastern Canadian, London Heroes titles, 1 Heineken, Terre des Hommes title; mem. 2 world youth, 2 world championships,

'81, '83 FISU, '83, '91 Pan-Am, '84, '88, '92 Olympic Games teams; best ever showing by Canadian fencing team 6th '91 World Championships; mem. Montreal team of year '90; res. MacMasterville, Que.

BANOS, Jean-Paul (fencing); b. 27 Jan 1961, Lavelanet, France; U of Montreal; tech. dir. Que. Fencing Federation; sabre specialist; mem. ntl team from '78; 24 ntl titles; best sabre showing by Canadian individual, team 7th '84 Olympics; mem. '84, '88, '92 Olympic, '87, '91 Pan-Am Games teams; individual, team gold '90 Commonwealth championships; 2 ntl individual, team titles; individual gold '87 Pan-Ams; capt. '91 sabre team which posted best Cdn result (6th) at Sr. Worlds; mem. Montreal team of '91; Sport Excellence Award '89; res. Montreal, Que.

BAPTIE, Norval (speed skating); b. 1879, Bethany, Ont.; d. 1966, Baltimore Md.; m. Gladys Lamb; showman; at 14 North Dakota speed champion, at 16 defeated Winnipeg's Jack McCulloch for world title; shattered all speed records as amateur and pro; remained in competition more than 25yrs winning close to 5000 races at distances from 220yds to 5 miles; turned to stunt and figure skating, setting record for barrel jumping; skating backwards, broad jumping, skating on stilts; after WW1 launched touring ice shows; directed first shows featuring Sonja Henie; retired from active skating '39, 1st pro coach Washington, D.C. Figure Skating Club; diabetes led to amputation of both legs by '58; continued to coach in Baltimore, Washington; with Miss Henie became 1st skaters named to US Ice Skating Hall of Fame; mem. Canada's Sports Hall of Fame.

BAPTISTE, Sheridon (bobsled); b. 6 Jan 1964, Georgetown, Guyana; Queen's; standout football player drafted by Ottawa Rough Riders '88 but elected to become competitive sprinter, long jumper and bobsledder; mem. ntl bobsleigh team from '89; brakeman for Chris Lori 4-man team; competed '92, '94, '98 Winter Olympics; 1 silver, 4 World Cup race bronze; CIAU indoor male t&f athlete of yr award; res. Ottawa, Ont.

BARBER, Bill (hockey); b. 11 Jul 1952, Callander, Ont.; given name: William Charles; m. Jenny; c. Kerri, Brooks; hockey coach; jr. Kitchener Rangers; Philadelphia's 1st choice, 7th overall '72 amateur draft; 1 1st team, 2 2nd team all-star left wing; reached 50-goal single season plateau '75-76 season; surpassed 400 NHL career goal plateau '83-84 season; mem. 2 Stanley Cup winners, 6 NHL all-star games; Team Canada '76, NHL all-stars '79 Challenge Cup; retd following '84-85 season; head coach Hershey '84-85, '95-96; asst Philadelphia '94-95, dir. pro scouting '88-96; head coach Philadelphia Phantoms (AHL) from '96; won Calder Cup '98; head coach Planet USA AHL all-stars; 13yr NHL record 420g, 463a in 903 scheduled games, 53g, 55a in 129 playoff games; jersey No. 7 retd. by Flyers; mem. Flyers, Hockey halls of fame; res. Cherry Hill, N.J.

BARBER, Darren (rowing); b. 26 Dec 1968, Victoria, B.C.; UVic; grandson of Hockey Hall of Famer Syl Apps; began rowing age 14; mem. jr. ntl team '86, sr. ntl team from '87; fastest man in Canada on rowing ergometer (which measures strength & stamina) and ranked 2nd in world '92; 6:21 fastest Cdn time ever in pairs '94 worlds; mem. ntl schoolboy 8s gold '85, '92 Olympic gold 8s; 9 Cdn Henley, 5 international, 2 ntl, 1 FISU regatta gold; competed '89 FISU, '92, '96 Olympic Games, '89, '90, '91, '94 worlds; '91 BC Premier's athletic award, '92 CARA centennial medal; mem. Cdn Olympic Hall of Fame; res. Vancouver, B.C.

BARBER, Jack (speed skating); b. 9 Jan 1895, Ottawa, Ont.; d. 4 Jul, 1993, Ottawa, Ont.; given name: Jack Alexander; m. Anna Twedley (d); c. Dorothy; retd. National Capital Commission; too small to pursue hockey career so following WWI launched competitive career at 31; won numerous city, provincial titles; pres., meet dir., fund raiser EOSSA '47-65; pres. OSSA; did much to foster sport among youngsters; Ottawa ACT sportsman of '82; mem. Ottawa Sports, Canadian Speed Skating halls of fame.

BARBER, Sara (swimming); b. 25 Jan 1941, Brantford, Ont.; m. Donald Jenkins; c. David, Robert, Margie; McMaster, BA, BHE; teacher; began swimming Brantford Y at age 9; mem. ntl swim teams '54-62 competing '54, '58, '62 BEG; '55, '59 Pan-Am, '56, '60 Olympic Games; '59 world record 100m backstroke; silver '59 Pan-Am games; silver, bronze in relays '58, '62 BEG; finalist backstroke, butterfly '56 Olympics; 8 ntl backstroke titles; retd from competition '62; Ross Gold trophy; mem. McMaster Sports, Ont. Aquatic halls of Fame, Brantford Area Sports Hall of Recognition; res. Orillia, Ont.

BARBER, Wendy (synchro swim); b. 20 Oct 1962, Mississauga, Ont.; UCal; mem. Calgary Aquabelles; mem. ntl title team '81; with Sue Clarke '83 Spanish, French Open duet titles; 2 Spanish, 1 Swiss, French Open, Pan-Pacific, Eastern div. team titles; '82 Spanish Open figures, '83 French Open solo titles; res. Mississauga, Ont.

BARCLAY, Ann (tennis); b. 31 Jan 1940, Vancouver, B.C.; UBC, BA, BEd.; teacher; began playing tennis age 10; won 1st title in US age 11; claimed BC -13, -15, -18, women's singles, doubles titles; at 15 ranked 5th nationally in singles, won ntl women's doubles; won ntl open/closed -13, -15 ntl titles in singles/doubles; won several Pacific Northwest -13, -15, -18 singles doubles titles; at 15 1st ranked BC women's singles; ranked 2nd nationally women's singles at 20; 3 ntl women's singles titles; competed at Forest Hills, Wimbledon, reaching doubles 1/4 finals; played 2yrs Florida-Caribbean circuit, 2yrs European circuit; won several Ont./Que. titles; injuries sustained in car accident curtailed play in later years; mem. Cdn Tennis Hall of Fame; res. N. Vancouver, B.C.

BARDSLEY, Jim (basketball/tennis); b. 19 Nov 1913, New York, N.Y.; d. Dec 1993, Vancouver, B.C.; given name: James Milton Albert; m. Jean Eckardt; c. James Anthony, Robert Eckardt; UBC, BApSc, BEd.; teacher; mem. 5 ntl title basketball teams '37-48; toured Japan with '39 team; coached sr. men's, HS teams '39-74; teaching tennis pro '46-59; numerous city, provincial, ntl titles; rep. Canada at Wimbledon '70-71, seniors doubles semifinals '70; mem. BC Sports Hall of Fame.

BARIL, Benoit (speed skating); b. 7 Oct 1960, Quebec City, Que.; international competitive debut '77 NA indoor championships; gold world short-track 1000m, all-around

'81; Dick Ellis Memorial Trophy team of '81, CASSA skater of '81; mem. Cdn Speed Skating Hall of Fame; res. Windsor, Que.

BARLOW, Wendy (tennis); b. 7 May 1960, North Bay, Ont.; m. Brad Pattenden; Brigham Young.; tennis pro; 5 ntl age-group singles, 4 doubles titles; gold '77 Canada Games; ntl women's doubles title '77, singles '80; 4th '79 Pan-Am Games; '80 championship of the Americas title; mem. ntl team '74-80, Continental Cup '76-78, Soisbault Cup '78, '80, Federation Cup '77-78, '80, Chiquita Cup teams '80; Cedar Springs Racquet Club pro Burlington '80-81; OTA clinic assessor '81; Moon Mountain School Phoenix athlete of '74; American Legion outstanding student award '74; Victoria athlete of '79, runnerup BC athlete of year; all-American BYU '79; res. Victoria, B.C.

BARNES, Bev (basketball); b. 9 Aug 1951, Ottawa, Ont.; given name: Beverly; UBC; BPhE; teacher; mem. ntl team '71-76; Moscow FISU Games, Bogota World Championships, Mexico City Pan-Am Games, Montreal Olympics; mem. BC entry ntl sr. women's championships '80-81; Div. II soccer; res. Roberts Creek, B.C.

BARNES, Kirsten (rowing); b. 26 Mar 1968, London, Eng.; UVic; began rowing in HS '83; mem. '85 Cdn HS 8 with coxswain championship crew, Ntl team from '87; '87 Pan Am Games pairs without cox gold; competed '88, '92 Olympics; 3 US Ntls, 3 San Diego, 3 Cdn Henley, 2 Augusta, 1 Vienna, 1 Amsterdam titles; '91 world 8s and 4s gold; sport excellence award '89, CARA Centennial medal '91; 2 Dick Ellis Memorial awards; UVic female athlete of year '89-91; Greater Victoria female athlete of '90, university rowing's most valuable rower '87-90; also figure skating coach and judge; mem. Cdn Olympic Hall of Fame; res. Victoria, B.C.

BARNES, Rolph (t&f); b. 16 Jul 1904, Hamilton, Ont., d. 6 Oct 1982, Waterdown, Ont.; given name: William Rolph; m. Charlotte Innes (d.); c. Bill, Rennie, Peter, Bruce; m. Marnie Wilmot Holton; c. Gerry, Margot; Princeton; industrialist; mem. '24 Olympic team; Hamilton and District badminton singles, doubles, mixed doubles champion '32-34; Savanah Club Barbardos Tennis Club title team '72.

BARR, Dave (golf); b. 1 Mar 1952, Kelowna, B.C.; given name: David Allen; m. LuAnn Busch; c. Brent, Teryn; Oral Roberts U.; pro golfer; all-star pitcher Little League, Babe Ruth baseball; defenceman Jr. A Kelowna Buckaneers; runnerup Canadian amateur golf championship '72; '73 Oklahoma State Amateur, 5 college tournament titles, 2nd-team all-American '73; pro '74; 3 BC, Que., 2 Kamloops Opens; Canadian TPC; BCPGA, Alta., Man., Cariboo, Washington State Opens once each; BC.Sun match champion '77; twice runnerup Canadian tournament of champions; CPGA open champion; mem. 4 Dunhill Cup teams; mem. Canadian amateur world team; mem. 9 Canadian world cup pro teams, with Dan Halldorson '85 winner; low individual '83; USPGA tour from '78; won '81 Quad Cities, Victoria Opens, '87 Atlanta Classic; 2 holes-in-one; 4 Canadian Tour Order of Merit titles; '85 CPGA title; runnerup US Open; with Dawn Coe won '89-90 Canadian Airlines International mixed; 2 Canadian tour stroke average awards; 8 SCORE player of year awards; res. Coquitlam, B.C.

BARR, Doris (baseball); b. 26 Aug 1921, Starbuck, Man.; given name: Mary Doris; retd hospital accounting dept; lefthanded pitcher; began career in softball before joining AAGPBL South Bend '43-45, Racine '45-47, Springfield '48, Muskegon '49, Kalamazoo '50; best season 20-8 leading Racine to '46 title; mem. Man. Baseball Hall of Fame; honored by Cooperstown, Cdn Baseball halls of fame; res. Winnipeg, Man.

BARRÉ, Alexandra (canoeing); b. 29 Jan 1958, Budapest, Hungary; given name: Alexandra Sandor; m. Denis; c. Stephanie, Melanie; Laval; mem. Hungarian ntl team '75-79; '76 Hungarian Olympic team, '75 jr. worlds, '78 worlds; mem. Cdn ntl kayak team '80-85; 2 ntl K1 500m titles; 2 gold '83 Pan-Am championships; 3 gold Vichy, 1 Zaandam, Duisburg regatta titles; with Sue Holloway silver 500m K2, bronze 500m K4 '84 Olympics; mem. 3 world championship teams; res. Lac Beauport, Que.

BARRÉ, Denis (canoeing); b. 4 Feb 1948, Lachine, Que.; m. Alexandra Sandor; c. Stephanie, Melanie; TV, film teacher; mem. '72, '76, '80 Olympics; '76 ntl K1 1000m, '80 K2, K4 1000m, K2 500m, Olympic trials, Zaandam regatta K2 500m, 1000m, 10,000m, K4 1000m, 500m, Bydgoszcz regatta K2 1000m, ntl K1 500m; coach Que. Canoe Club; res. Lac Beauport, Que.

BARRÉ, Jean (canoeing); b. 3 Jan 1945, Verdun, Que.; m. Henriette Soucy; c. Carolyne, Jean Francois; Laval, BPhE; fitness consultant; from '59 winner 50 regional canoeing, kayaking titles, 20 times provincial canoeing finalist; twice ntl kayak tandem, 4s titlist; silver '68 NA tandem kayak; ntl canoeing team mem. '68-72; semifinalist kayak tandem, 4s '68, '72 Olympics, Belgrade world championships; silver '62 international school rowing championships; bronze '72 cross-country skiing championships; gold 1st NA roller ski race '72; mem. silver medal Swiss interschool hockey champions '63; TV French network canoeing analyst '68, '72, '76 Olympics; res. Quebec City, Que

BARRETT, Danny (football); b. 18 Dec 1961, Boynton Beach, Fla.; m. Alison; c. Joshua, Zachrey, Whitney; Cincinnati; football coach; pro quarterback CFL Calgary '83-85, '89-91, '96-97, Toronto '85, '87-88, BC '92-93, Ottawa '94-95; USFL New Jersey Generals '86; CFL record: 148g, 33td, 1cvt, 463 carries, 2426yds, 31td, 3029 passes, 1631 completed, 23,134yds, 91int, 132tds, caught 34 passes, 501yds, 2td; 2 Grey Cup finals; set CFL record 601 passing yards single game '93; asst coach Calgary '97; co-capt Cincinnati '82, hon. mention AP all-American; active in Athletes in Action; res. Surrey, B.C.

BARRIE, Rachel (hockey); b. 12 Nov 1982, Arnprior, Ont.; given name: Rachel Elizabeth; goalie; begam playing competitive hockey age 4; became goalie because brother Nathan required target at which to shoot pucks while playing street hockey; competed in minor hockey ranks; Ottawa West team MVP in major atom '92; top goalie award Sudbury Big Nickel tournament '98; drafted by Smiths Falls (CJHL) becoming first girl to play in league; mem. Team

Ont. '99 Canada Games; try out with ntl women's team '97 ranking among top three goalies; res. Arnprior/Ottawa, Ont.

BARRON, Andy (speed skating); b. 2 May 1951, Penrith, Eng.; given name: Andrew James; m. Heather Rendall; UofAlta, BEd.; launched skating career as figure skater; Alta. novice men's, pairs, Prairie juvenile titlist; competed ntl swimming, water polo championships; ntl speed skating team mem. '71-76; ntl 1500m title '73; ntl records for 1500m, 3000m, 5000m, 10,000m distances; won 6 ISU international medals; mem. '72, '76 Olympic teams; ntl jr. team coach '81-82; tech. dir. CASSA '83-91; ntl short track coach from '92; Kinsmen Salute to Youth Award '71; res. Calgary, Alta.

BARROW, John (football); b. 31 Oct 1935, Delray Beach, Fla.; m. Evangelina; c. Gregg, Elaine, Kyle; Georgia Military Academy, Florida; businessman; offensive end Georgia Military Academy; Florida offensive guard, middle guard, team capt. final year; Look all-American, Atlanta TD Club Southeastern Conf. lineman of year, Southeastern Conference AP, UPI, INS all-South 1st team; 3rd draft Detroit (NFL); CFL Hamilton '57-70; 9 Grey Cup finals, 4 winners; EFC all-star 12 times, all-Canadian 11 times; 8 Schenley linemen of year nominations, won '62, runnerup 5 times; CFL lineman of century '67; Hamilton all-star team of pro era '50-67; GM Toronto '71-75; radio colorcaster Hamilton games; mem. Florida, Canadian Football, Florida State Sports halls of fame; res. Missouri, Tex.

BARRY, Cliff (coaching); b. 1 Jun 1946, Montreal, Que.; given name: Clifford Alan; m. Susan Wheeler; c. Carling; Sir George Williams, BA, UWO, BPhed; competitive swim coach; standout water polo player '68-76; mem. ntl Olympic water polo team '72 (capt), '76; mem./capt. '67, '71, '75 Pan Am Games, '71, '75 world championships teams; Canada's outstanding water polo player '68-72; began fulltime coaching '76 in Guelph; Region of Waterloo head swim coach '79; head coach Pointe Claire SC '86; coach Etobicoke SC; among proteges were Victor Davis, Mike West; 3 Cdn swim coach of year awards; coached ntl team titlists '91, ntl women's titlists '90-91; '93 Canada Games coach; swim coach '84, '88 Olympic teams, various Pan-Pac, world, Pan-Am, Commonwealth, Canada Games teams; lectured/coached at Cdn, American coaches clinics, Wilfrid Laurier; coached 8 ntl men's, women's, 7 Ont. title teams; 5 top age group champions; placed 8 swimmers on Olympic, 3 on Pan Am, Pan-Pacific, 6 Canada Games teams; 3 Cdn, Ont. swim coach of yr awards; mem. Ont. Aquatic Hall of Fame; res. Mississauga, Ont.

BARRY, Martin (hockey); b. 8 Dec 1904, St. Gabriel, Que., d. 20 Aug 1969, Halifax, N.S.; pro NY Americans '27-28, Boston '29-35, 5 consecutive 20-goal seasons, Detroit '35-39, Montreal '39-40; mem. '36-37 Stanley Cup winners; Lady Byng Trophy '37, all-star centre '37; NHL record: 195 goals, 192 assists; mem. Hockey Hall of Fame.

BARTLETT, Don (curling); b. 1 Apr 1960, Gander, Nfld.; given name: Donald Brian; m. Shauna Stewart; c. Stewart, Donald; postal clerk; lead for Kevin Martin Alberta rink '91, '92, '95-97 Briers; all-star '91-92; won Briers '91, '97; silver medal '91 Worlds; competed '92 Olympics; mem.

WCT VO Cup title rink '94, FlexiCoil $60,000 'spiel winner '97; res. Spruce Grove, Alta.

BARTLETT, Sue Anne (curling); b. 9 Sep 1943, Grand Falls, Nfld.; given name: Sylvie Anne Byrne; m. John Bartlett (d); c. Joanne, John, Russell; insurance agent; began curling age 23; skipped Nfld. rinks to 11 provincial women's championships giving her distinction of appearing in more ntl championships than any other woman curler in Canada; through '90 her 66 victories in 120 games at the ntl level placed her first in the all-time standings; never won a ntl crown but was a finalist three times; won '71 Nfld. mixed; Nfld sr. women's title '94, '97; mem. Cdn Curling Hall of Fame; res. Labrador City, Nfld.

BARTON, Julie (table tennis); b. 25 Sep 1972, Halifax N.S.; athlete, singer; began representing Canada internationally at 14; noted for fast, powerful, aggressive style of play; mem. ntl team from '87; competed in worlds India '87, Germany '89; 6 ntl junior singles titles; won '88 senior women's title; won Canada Cup title '91; with Caroline Sylvestre silver medal '91 Wiltshire tournament in England; with Michelle Cada '90 ntl jr. girls doubles; won '89 NA jr. singles, doubles; finalist with Lijuan Geng '90 World Cup qualification women's doubles; '91 Pan-Am Games women's, mixed doubles bronze; coached by Mariann Domonkos; twice NS woman athlete of yr; outstanding Black Cultural Centre athlete in NS; twice Ottawa ACT award winner; mem. Nepean Wall of Fame; res. Nepean, Ont.

BARWELL, Gord (football); b. 6 Sep 1944, Saskatoon, Sask.; d. 22 Apr 1988, Toronto, Ont.; given name: Gordon Keith; m. Nancy Phyliss Schoenhals; c. Jay, Jody; Eastern Canadian dir. Athletes in Action; ntl age-group honors HS T&f; 1 season Sask. Hilltops jrs.; Roughriders '64-73; defensive back, offensive flanker; 7 Western Conf. playoffs, 4 Grey Cups; on receiving end of 102yd TD pass from Ron Lancaster Vancouver '65; mem. Roughriders Plaza of Honor.

BARWISE, Bob (shooting); b. 13 Mar 1937, Charlottetown, P.E.I.; given name: Robert Claude; m. Janet; c. Gail, Joanne, Robin, John; Prince of Wales Coll.; retired hotelier, disco, restaurant operator; operates rifle business; former mem. RCMP; 4 Atlantic fullbore titles; pres. PEI Rifle Assn. from '74; 11 times Bisley competitor; commandant '88 team; won Queen's prize 1st stage '80; DCRA Governor-General's silver badge '80, '84; Bisley team adjutant '78; initial winner Burke target rifle award; mem. PEI Sports Hall of Fame; res. Charlottetown, P.E.I.

BARYLUK, Mitch (basketball); b. 20 Jun 1931, Winnipeg, Man.; m. Eileen Brown; c. Marty, Adam; travel agency owner; played, coached varied teams in Winnipeg '43-52, including '50-51 Cdn Jr. champ Stellars; key role rebuilding Thunder Bay men's basketball program; twice pres. TBBA; organized clinics, summer leagues; player-coach Sr. Y Grads '52-55; coached HS, Sr. League teams; won TBBA city men's title with Dinty's Kentuckians '64-68; introduced women's basketball to Thunder Bay; sponsor Thunder Bay Oldtimers; Geraldton tournament titles '81-84, Manitoba Master Hoop Classic '86; TB Oldtimers honor award '86; player/coach/sponsor TB Travel slo-pitch team; mem. NWO Sports Hall of Fame; res. Thunder Bay, Ont.

BASE, John (curling); b. 23 Feb 1963, Oakville, Ont.; sales rep.; twice competed in Canadian junior championships, winning '82 title; won '83 world junior title; 6 time competitor in provincial men's Tankard playdowns; res. Oakville, Ont.

BASS, Danny (football); b. 31 Mar 1958, Lansing, Mich.; Michigan State; owner Hyundai dealership; pro linebacker Toronto '80-81, Calgary '81-83, Edmonton '84-'91; CFL record: 179g, 22 interceptions, 230yds returned, 1td, 19 fumbles recovered, returned 109yds, 2td, 47 QB sacks; 8 WFC all-star; 6 CFL all-star; 3 Norm Fieldgate trophy awards; twice runnerup Schenley defensive player award; led CFL defensive tackles '88; CFL outstanding defensive player '89; 3 Grey Cup finals, 1 winner; mem. Eskimos Wall of Honor; res. Sherwood Park, Alta.

BASSETT, Carling (tennis); b. 9 Oct 1967, Toronto, Ont.; m. Robert Seguso, c. Holden John, Carling, Ridley; tennis player; daughter of sports entrepreneur John F. Bassett; US under-12 clay court title; 1st Canadian Orange Bowl jr. title winner, ntl girls' 18 and under singles; pro at 15; 1st pro victory Ginny of Central Pa. '83; 1st Canadian woman to advance to 4th round Wimbledon '83; at 15 youngest Wimbledon competitor; mem. '83 Federation Cup team; lost to Chris Evert Lloyd Amelia Island final; Osaka Japan tournament title '84; ranked 1st Canada '82-84, 2nd world jr. ranking; highest ranking ever by Cdn in WPTA history moving from 169 to 8 '85; Tennis Magazine '83 pro rookie of year; Canadian female tennis player of '83; 2 Bobbie Rosenfeld trophies; worked as fashion model, movie actress; mem. Cdn Tennis Hall of Fame; res. Toronto, Ont.

BASSETT, John Jr. (entrepreneur); b.1939, Toronto, Ont.; d. 14 May 1986, Toronto, Ont.; m. Sue Carling; c. Carling, John, Vicky, Heidi; Upper Can. College, UNB, UWO; eldest son of media magnate John W. Bassett; mem. UNB hockey title team; quarterback UNB football team; Cdn Open jr. doubles tennis champion at 15; reporter Victoria Times, Toronto Telegram; owned WHA Toronto Toros, WFL Toronto Northmen, later Memphis Southmen and USFL Tampa Bay Bandits; shocked establishment by signing NFL stars Paul Warfield, Larry Csonka, Jim Kiick who had played with Super Bowl champion Miami Dolphins; film producer.

BASTAJA, Nick (football); b. 4 Feb 1953, Hamilton, Ont.; m. Beryl; c. Amorita; SFU; realtor; offensive tackle; tryout Green Bay Packers; CFL Hamilton '75-76, Toronto '77-80, Winnipeg '80-'88; Argos outstanding offensive lineman award candidate '78; CFL all-star '76, WFC all-star '82; last known res. Winnipeg, Man.

BASTET, Evert (sailing); b. 30 May 1950, Maracaibo, Venezuela; Sir George Williams; sailboat mast mfgr., highway engineer; HS pole vaulter, alpine ski instructor, ski jumper, diver; began competing '60; mem. ntl team from '67; skipper jr. pre-Centennial champion '65; crew FD silver '84 Olympics; alternate '68, crewed with Hans Fogh '73-76, Terry McLaughlin from '78; mem. '72, '76, 80, '84, '88, '92 Olympic teams; won '73, '80 world, '74, '79 NA, '79-81 CORK, '71, '76 S.P.O.R.T, '70 US national, '76 European, '80 Hyeres, '81 Can-Am F.D. titles; '73 US laser title; sport excellence award '83, Olympic champion award

'85, with McLaughlin SFC team of year runnerup '80; mem. Cdn Olympic Hall of Fame; res. Brome, Que.

BATES, Mark (triathlon); b. 24 Jun 1968, Penticton, B.C.; m. Hilary Watt; Queen's , BA; triathlete/coach/speaker; mem. Queen's swim, cross-country teams; competitive swimmer Kingston Blue Marlins 7yrs; worked as lifeguard; made triathlon debut in Belleville; winner of numerous major triathlons such as Niagara, Great Lakes, Muskoka; made world debut '89; best world finish 4th '94; 4 ntl triathlon titles; Kingston athlete of '91; res. N. Vancouver, B.C.

BATH, Doc (all-around); b. 9 Mar 1889, Bath, England., d. 19 Sep 1980, Weyburn, Sask.; given name: Leonard Harry; m. Helen; c. Gladys Helen, Valarie Doreen Jean; nurse; Somerset Eng. 440, mile, 6-mile, cross-country championships '08; British army Aldershot command '10 6-mile, '1113 6-mile North and South India champion, emigrated to Canada '25; trainer Weyburn Beaver fastball team 13yrs, also baseball, hockey trainer; coached oldtimers hockey 3yrs; trainer Weyburn Red Wings hockey club '61-75, Comets, Molson's Weyburn Canadians '62-75, Canadian fastball title '72; mem. Sask. Sports Hall of Fame.

BATHGATE, Andy (hockey); b 28 Aug 1932, Winnipeg, Man.; given name: Andrew James; m. Merle Lewis; c. Sandra, Billy; golf driving range operator; capt./rw Guelph Memorial Cup winners '51-52; pro NY Rangers organization '52-53; minor league Vancouver (WHL), Cleveland (AHL); Rangers '54-63, Toronto '63-64, Detroit '65-66, Pittsburgh '67-68, '70-71, Vancouver Canucks (WHL) '68-69, MVP award; played briefly in Switzerland, returned to coach and play briefly with Vancouver Blazers (WHA) '74; early exponent of slapshot; among 1st to develop curved banana blade; his shot which struck Jacques Plante in face 1 Nov. '59 led to history-making introduction of goalie's face mask; capt. Rangers; mem. '54 Stanley Cup winners; Hart Trophy '59; twice 1st, 2nd team all-star; scoring co-champion with Bobby Hull '61-62; NHL record: 1069 scheduled games, 349g, 624a, 54 playoff games, 21g, 14a, 8 all-star games; nicknamed "Tubby"; West Side Trophy, Macbeth Trophy, Frank Boucher Trophy; NHL milestone award '82; prominent golfer; mem. Man. Sports, Hockey, Man. Hockey, Switzerland Ambri-Piotta Hockey Club halls of fame; res. Bramalea, Ont.

BATLEY, Jamie (lacrosse); b. 9 Jan 1967, Peterborough, Ont.; Maryland; '86-87 Peterborough Minto Cup champion all-star; known for offensive prowess; leading scorer Ont. jr A league '86-87, MVP '87; led Kenner Rams to 3 Ont. high school field lacrosse titles; mem. midget all-Cdn title team '83; NCAA Div. 1 all-American '93; mem. ntl team from '89; Peterborough athlete of '87; res. Peterborough, Ont.

BATSTONE, Harry (football); b. 5 Sep 1899, Hamilton, Ont., d. 11 Mar 1972, Kingston, Ont.; Queen's, MD; physician; football, baseball, hockey various school, city leagues; in same backfield with Lionel Conacher led Argos to '20 Interprovincial title, lost Grey Cup final to UofT; won Grey Cup '21; with Pep Leadlay, Red McKelvey helped Queen's win 3 consecutive Intercollegiate titles, 3 Grey

Cups; Queen's coach on 3 occasions; capt. Argos 1921; mem. Queen's, Canadian Football, Canada's Sports halls of fame.

BATTAGLIA, Frankie (boxing); b. 1910, Winnipeg, Man.; d. 1971, California; chance meeting as teenager with Jack Dempsey fashioned life; began amateur ring career '26; mem. '28 Olympic team; pro '30; top world middleweight contender; KO'd number 1 contender Ben Jeby 1st round '32; rematch after Jeby had claimed title resulted in TKO victory for Jeby in 13, result of eye cut; lost world title bid by decision to Freddie Steel '36; retd '38 following 100 amateur, pro bouts; mem. Man. Sports Hall of Fame.

BATTERSBY, Robert (rowing); b. 1 Nov 1948, Vancouver B.C.; given name: Robert Glenn; UBC, BApSc; professional engineer; mem. UBC varsity rowing team '70-72; coxed pairs '71, '75 Pan-Am, '72 Olympic, '74 world championships teams; from '76 coach UBC/VRC women's rowing team; guided 8s to ntl women's, Western sprint titles '79; placed 3 UBC rowers on '81 ntl team; res. Vancouver, B.C.

BATTLE, Greg (football); b. 14 Apr 1964, Long Beach, Calif.; m. Anna; Arizona State; linebacker NFL Denver '86; joined CFL Winnipeg '87-93, '97-98, Las Vegas, Ottawa '94, Memphis '95, Saskatchewan '96; CFL record (through '98): 189gp, 812 def. tackles, 26 qb sacks; 3 Eastern, 2 CFL all-star; 3 James McCaffrey trophies; outstanding CFL defensive player '90, '91, runnerup '89; 3 Grey Cup finals, 1 winner; Grey Cup def. star '90; set CFL record with 14 def. tackles '93 Grey Cup game; def. MVP '85 Holiday Bowl; res. Phoenix, Ariz.

BAUCK, Dean (t&f); b. 19 May 1954, Vancouver, B.C.; given name: Dean Evan; UBC, BSc., MBA; high jump specialist; mem. ntl team '74-81; silver vs. France (indoors), gold vs Britain, Greece, West Germany, Wales '74; bronze '78 Commonwealth Games; ntl jr. record with 1st jump over 7'; gold '81 Pacific Conf. Games; 5th '79 Pan-Am Games; mem. '80 Olympic team; PB: 2.21m outdoors, 2.19m indoors '81; res. Delta, B.C.

BAUER, Bobby (hockey); b. 16 Feb 1915, Waterloo, Ont.; d. 16 Sep 1964, Kitchener, Ont.; given name: Robert Theodore; m. Marguerite Bauer; c. Bobby, Bradley; St. Michael's College, UofT; jr. Kitchener-Waterloo; right winger with Woody Dumart, Milt Schmidt to form Sauerkraut line; trio joined Boston (NHL) '36 season, as Kraut Line helped Boston finish 1st 4 successive seasons, 2 Stanley Cups; coached K-W Dutchmen '56 Olympic bronze; final Boston Gardens appearance '51-52 season scoring goal, assist in special game as Kraut Line honored; among NHL leading scorers 3 times; 4 times NHL all-star, 3 times Lady Byng Trophy; NHL record: 327 scheduled games, 123g, 137a, 48 playoff games, 11g, 8a; mem. Waterloo County, Hockey halls of fame.

BAUER, David (hockey); b. 2 Nov 1924, Waterloo, Ont.; d. 9 Nov 1988, Goderich, Ont.; given name: David William; St. Michael's College, UofT, OCE, Notre Dame U; Basilian priest, teacher; brother Bobby mem. famed Kraut Line; jr. Toronto, Oshawa, Windsor; football, jr., sr. baseball K-W region; managed, coached St. Michael's Majors, won Memorial Cup; coached UBC hockey team; '64 conceived National Team plan which became basic concept for Canadian international hockey participation evolving into Hockey Canada; Hockey Canada director; coached Austrian national team '73 world tournament; assisted with Japanese ntl team development; Officer Order of Canada '67; U of Calgary arena bears his name; mem. Waterloo County, Hockey, Cdn Winter Olympic, UBC, Canada's Sports halls of fame.

BAUER, Lyle (football); b. 22 Aug 1958, Saskatoon, Sask.; Weber State Coll. BA; football exec., relator; 38th overall draft pick Saskatchewan '79; pro guard Winnipeg '82-91; CFL record: 161g; EFC all-star '90; 3 Grey Cup finals, 3 winners; AGM Blue Bombers from '92; res. Winnipeg, Man.

BAUER, Steve (cycling); b. 12 Jun 1959, Grimsby, Ont.; given name: Steven Todd; m. Elayne; c. Kohen; Waterloo; operates Niagara bike tours; ntl pursuit team mem. '77-84; ntl points race titles '79, '81-83; mem. '78, '82 Commonwealth, '79 Pan-Am, '77, '80, '82-83 world championship, '84, '96 Olympic teams; silver sr. road race '82 Commonwealth Games; 190km road race silver '84 Olympics; bronze world pro road race championships '84; 2 30km national Madison, 4 men's 4000 team pursuit titles; 10,000 mass start winner, 2nd 30,000 mass start Barbados '82; 2 Lowenbreau, 1 Tour of Somerville, Tour of Texas, 2 Carlsberg Light, Hull Festival, Zurich, Dienze GP, Grand Prix of Americas road race titles; won 1st stage and retained yellow jersey 5 consec. days '88, led 10 consecutive legs '90 Tour de France; nicknamed "Silent Warrior" on European pro circuit '84-95; acquitted of assault charges brought by Belgian cyclist Claude Criquielion following '88 race crash; mem. 7-Eleven racing team; retd '96; res. Ridgeville, Ont.

BAULD, Donald (all-around); b. 14 Jun 1914, Halifax, N.S.; d. 4 Jul 1996, Halifax, N.S.; m. Evelyn Conrad; c. Donald, Brian; Dalhousie; sporting goods agency owner; versatility encompassed tennis, badminton, basketball, rugby, curling; 2 NS, 3 Halifax County jr. tennis titles; 5 NS, 2 Eastern Cdn men's singles tennis titles; 10 NS #1 rankings, 5th ntl rankings '49; 6 NS, 2 Eastern ntl men's doubles, 1 NS mixed doubles titles; Bermuda men's singles title '59; Ottawa District men's singles '45; 2 NS sr. men's singles titles; twice invited to compete on ntl Davis Cup team but never participated; mem. 2 Gordon Cup teams; with brother Gordon helped Canada claim 1st Gordon Cup in 12 tries '62; 4 Maritime badminton singles, 5 men's doubles, 1 mixed doubles titles, 1 Windsor-Detroit area singles title; capt. Maritime jr. rugby champion Tigers; flying half Wanderers '35-39, 2 Maritime titles; twice capt., leading scorer; mem. Dal Grads, Wanderers Maritime champion basketball teams, team capt., scoring champion; mem. '35 NS champion Grads, 5 consec. city title teams; twice MVP; skip runnersup NS, Maritime jr. title curling rinks; mem. N S entry '58 Brier; winner numerous major bonspiel titles; NS table tennis titlist; mem. NS Sports Hall of Fame.

BAUMANN, Alex (swimming); b. 21 Apr 1964, Prague, Czechoslovakia; given name: Alexander Sasa; m. Tracy Taggart; Indiana, Laurentian; ED Sport Developmennt

Consul, Queensland, Australia; nicknamed "Sasha"; mem. ntl team '78-87; 200m, 400m individual medley, 1500m FS specialist; 34 ntl titles; 32 ntl FS sprint, IM 4 world 200m, 2 world 400m IM, Commonwealth, Olympic 400m IM records; 9 gold Canada Cup meets, 4 gold 4 Nations Cup meet, 3 gold NZ Games, Australian Open meet, CIAU championships, 2 gold FISU, Commonwealth Games; 400m IM gold World Cup; 1st Cdn Olympic swimming gold medal in 72yrs with 400IM WR 4:17.41 Los Angeles 30 Jul '84; added gold 200IM in WR 2:01.42 4 Aug '84; mem. '80, '84 Olympic, '79 Pan-Am, '83 FISU Games teams; 40 Ont., 24 ntl age group records; Viscount Alexander award '84; Lionel Conacher trophy '84; 3 ntl male swimmer of yr awards; 2 CIAU male swimmer of yr; 3 Ont. sports awards; 3 Sudbury athlete of year; '81 Sudbury municipal medallion, award of distinction; with Steve Podborski, Ont. amateur athlete of '81; fed. govt. world record awards '82-84, excellence awards '84-85; flag-bearer '83 FISU, '84 Olympic Games; hon. capt. '94 Commonwealth Games team; 2 Seagram 5 Star awards; Officer Order of Canada '84; mem. Laurentian USports Wall, Cdn., Ont. Aquatic, Cdn Amateur, Canada's Sports halls of fame; res. Brisbane, Australia.

BAUN, Bobby (hockey); b. 9 Sep 1936, Lanigan, Sask.; m. Sallie Krohn; c. Jeffrey, Gregory, Brian, Michele, Patricia; insurance salesman, donut franchise owner, dir. Professional Hockey Alumni; jr. Marlboros, 2 Memorial Cup winners; pro Toronto '56-67, '71-73, Oakland '67-68, Detroit '68-70; mem.4 Stanley Cup winners; pres. NHL Players' Assn; coach Toronto (WHA) '75; NHL record: 964 scheduled games, 37g, 187a, 96 playoff games, 3g, 12a; res. Claremont, Ont.

BAWDEN, Betty (basketball); b. 22 Dec 1917, Edmonton, Alta.; m. Robert Bowen (d); c. Rowena, Robert; retired dept. store buyer, library technician; competitive diver, swimmer ages 10-16; mem. famed Edmonton Grads '39-40; mem. Canadian Basketball, Alta. Sports halls of fame; res. Oakville, Ont.

BAWN, Bev (hockey/baseball); b. 17 Aug 1937, Fredericton, N.B.; given name: Beverly; m. Margaret; safety & training co-ordinator; mem. Eastern Memorial Cup Moncton Beavers '62; with Fredericton Capitals '66 Eastern Cdn Intermediate, '64 NB, '67 Maritime titles; with Campbellton Tigers '72 Hardy Cup; bronze '75 ntl sr. baseball finals; NB titles with Chatham Ironmen, Marysville Royals; coached Mirimichi Gagnon Packers to Hardy Cup title '87; 6 North-South all-star, '71 MVP; governor NB Sports Hall of Fame; mem. NB, Fredericton Sports halls of fame; res. Newcastle, N.B.

BAYDOCK, Donna (volleyball); b. 28 Aug 1957, Winnipeg, Man.; given name: Donna Anne; UMan., BPhE, UBC, MPhE; teacher, coach UMan; volleyball at provincial level '74; mem. ntl jr. team Mexico zone championships; mem. UMan Bisonnettes '75-77, twice capt. MVP; mem. silver medal Man. team '75 Canada Games; all-star mem. Bisonettes ntl jr. champions 1976; 3-year mem. ntl jr. team; sr. team '77-81; Vancouver Old Time Ladies' '80 ntl sr. title team; mem. '79 Pan-Am, '80 Olympic teams; UMan female athlete of '77; CIAU coach of yr award; res. Winnipeg, Man.

BAYER, Jim (administration); b. 1938, Charlottetown, P.E.I.; d. 1985, Wolfville, N.S.; UNB, BPhE, Springfield Coll., MSc.; educator; PE supervisor NS dept. of ed. '65-72; dir. NS dept. of rec. '72-77; AD Acadia U '78-85; p-pres. Atlantic branch CAHPER, AUAA; NS div. Cdn Red Cross Society; p-chair. Interprov. council for sport & rec; board chairman NS Sport Heritage Centre; Cdn Red Cross Society award, Queen's Jubilee medal, Cdn Parks & Rec. Assn. award of merit; hon. life mem. Sport NS, Rec. Assn. of NS.

BAYTOR, Terry (softball); b. 8 Jul 1952, Montreal, Que.; m. Barbara Razniewski; c. Chris, Alexandra; UofT, BA, BEd, MEd; high school principal; Level 5 Softball Canada, Level 3 BC, Elite Calgary coaching credentials; asst. coach ntl sr. men's team '82-89, head coach from '89; has guided ntl team to gold medals in '89 Pan-Am qualifier, '90 Challenge Cup, '91, '95, '99 Pan-Am Games, '92 ISF worlds, silver '96 worlds; res. Brampton, Ont.

BEACH, Ormand (football); b. 28 Oct 1910, Ponca City, Okla., d. 20 Sep 1938, Sarnia, Ont.; m. Marguerite Booth; Kansas, McGill; engineer; all-state fullback '25-28; all-American; described by Dr. James Naismith as "an outstanding anatomical example of the perfect man"' helped Kansas tie Notre Dame 0-0 to give Jayhawkers first Big 6 title, twice team capt.; listed by Grantland Rice as one of all-time defensive greats in US football; as flying wing and defensive linebacker helped Sarnia Imperials win 4 ORFU titles; 3 Grey Cup appearances, 2 winners; all-league, all-Canadian each year he played; Imperial Oil Trophy as ORFU MVP; died in refinery explosion at Sarnia; HS stadium named in his honor; mem. Sarnia-Lambton Sports, Canadian Football halls of fame.

BEACH, Pete (administration); b. 1906, England; d. Mar 1984, Toronto, Ont.; given name: Nathaniel Allworth; UWO.; educator; received early training Toronto West End Y '20-30; standout wrestler, competed in football/t&f at UWO; coached UWO t&f team; chair. P.E. comm. Cdn YMCA; operated summer camps; taught at Albert Coll., Belleville '35-57 (excluding war years); YMCA War Services dir. England, Italy; made major contributions to AAU of C (t&f), CSF (boxing); credited with rebirth of Cdn boxing in post-war period; exec. dir. OFSAA '58-71; guiding force in founding CFSAA; worked with CAHPER/COA; retd "sort of" '71; OFSAA award for educators for services and contributions to young people through school sports bears his name.

BEACOM, Gary (figure skating); b. 23 Feb 1960, Calgary, Alta.; UofT; '77 jr. ntl title; 2nd '83 sr. ntl mem. '84 Olympic team; turned pro '84; Fox Rock & Roll title '94; 1st skater named mem. CFSA skater development comm.; res. Sun Valley, Idaho.

BEAN, Gladys (builder); b. 17 Jun 1918, Montreal, Que.; d. 18 Dec 1986, Montreal, Que.; given name: Mable Gladys; McGill, BA, BPhE; educator; developed, directed McGill's Royal Victoria Coll. aquatic program '60-65; dir. women's athletics from '66; mem. Que. Sports administration council; when McGill's men's, women's athletic programs merged in '76 became asst. AD; CIAU delegate, rep to CIAU women's athletic comm.; recipient CAHPER Tait McKenzie award '78, CIAU Austin-Matthews award '83; award bearing her name given annually to McGill female athlete who has brought most credit to the university; mem. McGill Sports Hall of Fame.

BEATON, Bob (boxing/officiating); b. 19 Jun 1912, Port Hood, Cape Breton, N.S.; m. Bertha MacDonald; c. Graham, John, Anita, Cyril Robert, Bernard; retired insurance co. branch mgr.; lost sight of one eye at 3; award winning runner, jumper, cyclist, boxer, hockey player; with brother Joe pioneered hockey in Britain in mid-'30s; highly regarded hockey coach in Maritimes; competed in Maritime Big Four Sr. HL; 12 pro boxing bouts in mid-'30s, winning all, 9 by KO; ring referee '35-83; officiated 40 ntl, 5 Commonwealth, 1 world title bouts; referee-in-chief NS Boxing Authority from '78; introduced 3-judge system to boxing '54; mem. Cdn Boxing, NS Sports halls of fame; res. Pictou, N.S.

BEATON, Ewan (judo); b. 13 Jul 1969, Winnipeg, Man.; UMan., Concordia.; competing at 60kg won 5 consecutive ntl titles; gold '95, silver '91 Pan-Am Games; Dutch Open gold '93; 3rd degree black belt; competed '92, '96 Olympics; res. Montreal, Que.

BEATTY, Lou (golf); b. 10 Apr 1918, Woodstock, N.B.; given name: Louis Edgar; educator; mem. 3 NB-PEI Willingdon Cup teams; twice runnerup NB-PEI amateur; 5 NB Srs titles; 6 consecutive Maritime Srs. titles '80-85; mem. 12 NB Srs. teams; PEI Srs. title; 30 Woodstock golf club titles; 6 Old Home Week titles; 3 NB Legion titles; set all-time Woodstock GC record '61; Fredericton Open medallist; only golfer to shoot his age (63) at Woodstock Club '81; nicknamed "Sweet Lou"; mem. NB Sports Hall of Fame; res. Woodstock, N.B.

BEAUDRY, Paul (fencing); b. 11 May 1958, Sherbrooke, Que.; Montreal, BSc., McGill, MBA; sabre specialist; ntl jr. titles '75, '77-78; silver '75 Canada Games; won Ottawa Shield '77; 4 times Eastern Canadian Que. titlist; won Governor-General's Cup, Que. Cup, Cornell tournament, Heinneken Cup, Terre des Hommes; mem. silver medal team '78 Commonwealth Games; '77 Que. fencer of year, athlete par excellence Championnats Sportifs Quebecois; res. Sherbrooke, Que.

BEAUPRE, Don (hockey); b. 19 Sep 1961, Waterloo, Ont.; goalie Sudbury (OHA), Nashville, Birmingham, Salt Lake (CHL), Kalamazoo (IHL), Baltimore (AHL), NHL with Minnesota '80-88, Washington '89-94, Ottawa '94-95, Toronto '96; drafted by Minnesota '80; OHA 1st team all-star '80; 2 NHL all-star games; NHL record: 667 scheduled games, 268-277-75, 37,396min, 17so, 70 playoff games, 33-31, 3,923min, 3so; res. Minnesota.

BECK, Ross (all-around); b. 14 Aug 1928, St. Thomas, Ont.; given name: Ross William; m. Annalee Bernice Voaden; c. Judith, Joanne, David, Alan; UWO., hons. BA, PHRE; retd. HS principal; played jr. OBA baseball prov. finals '49; sr. baseball St. Thomas (IC), Nickel Belt League '50-52; tryouts with St. Louis, Brooklyn, Toronto Maple Leaf organizations; standout football/basketball player UWO '48-52; mem. '49 football title team claimed by coach John Metras as "one of best I ever coached"; held ntl rating as basketball official more than 20yrs working all games in '58 ntl sr. men's title series in Ottawa; coached football/basketball at several Ottawa area HS; throughout teaching career played active role in OFSAA as regional rep., prov. principal rep., member of board of dir.; initial recipient Pete Beach award; res. Stittsville, Ont.

BECKETT, Norman (shooting); b. 28 Apr 1909, Hamilton, Ont.; d. Oct 1990, Hamilton, Ont.; m. Alice; c. Susan; accountant; began shooting in teens and developed into one of Canada's top marksmen; anchorman Royal Hamilton Light Infantry Gold team 6 decades; rejected for Overseas duty WW2 for poor eyesight but it was never a problem on the range; qualified 18 Bisley teams, competed 9 times; Bisley Queen's Prize '61; 2nd Bisley grand agg. '59; 2 Bisley Imperial Tobacco Cups; 3 DCRA Governor-General's agg., 1 Macdonald Stewart grand agg.; mem. 2 Kalapore teams; more than 40 individual, unit, team prizes during 60-plus yrs of DCRA competition; received DCRA 60yr badge '89.

BECKMAN, Jim (all-around); b. 13 Aug 1935, Halifax, N.S.; m. Donna Guptell; c. Todd, Daina, Tina; welder; outstanding minor hockey career as right winger; mem. Fairview juvenile Maritime champions; signed by Boston Bruins organization; junior Metro Toronto Lakeshore Bruins 2yrs; all-star 2yrs; all-Ont. title; Estevan Sask. Jr. HL; declined Providence AHL invitation to play Sr. hockey Windsor Maple Leafs, NSHL 6yrs; Sherbrooke Sr. Beavers 4yrs; mem. Bunny Ahearne Trophy winners in Sweden; competed in 5 Allan Cup finals; Grand Falls, Nfld. rec. dir., player-coach Nfld. title team; retired as player at 34; outstanding, versatile baseball player Halifax Cardinals H&D League; player-coach Hantsport Shamrocks, batting champ hitting .340 '60, MVP, league champs; tryout with Atlanta Braves '61; mem. 2 Hantsport Maritime Sr. champs; 1yr Jonquiere, 4yrs Thetford Mines, Que.; played in Grand Falls league '70-74; 2yrs Sr. softball Alberta Brake & Clutch; level 6 softball official; low handicap golfer; res. Calgary, Alta.

BECKSTEAD, Ian (football); b. 7 Sep 1957, Ottawa, Ont.; m. Jean; c. Brandon, Ryan, Laura; Richmond BA, Florida Atlantic MBA; sales mgr.; 2ys jr with Ottawa Sooners; TE Richmond Spiders, best blocker award '80; pro CFL Ottawa '81-83, Toronto '83-93; versatile playing tight end, fullback, guard and centre during pro career; Leo Dandurand EFC outstanding lineman, runnerup Schenley lineman of '88; EFC all-star '87-88, all-Canadian '88; res. Ottawa, Ont.

BÉDARD, Bob (tennis); b. 13 Sep. 1931, St. Hyacinthe, Que.; m. Anne Stacey; c. Mark, Paul, Michael, Peter; Loyola, BA, Sherbrooke, BEd; headmaster, St. Andrews College; semipro hockey, MVP honors Quebec Senior League '55-56; No. 1 Canadian tennis '55-65; mem. '53-61, '67 Davis Cup teams; ntl Open singles champion '55, '57, '58, sharing native record Dr. Jack Wright; 8 Que. Open titles; at least one victory over every No. 1 player from France, Sweden, Denmark, India, US, Mexico, Cuba, Belgium, England, Brazil, Italy '54-59; silver '59 Pan-Am Games, gold '69 Canada Games; with Don Fontana 3 ntl men's doubles; with Mariette Laframboise '59 ntl mixed title; mem. Canada

Fitness Council 2yrs; 3yrs PQLTA v-p., pres., 4 yrs v-p. 2 yrs hon. secty CLTA; with son Peter won 2 ntl father-son titles; mem. Loyola College, Cdn Amateur, Que, Canada's Sports, Cdn Tennis halls of fame; res. Aurora, Ont.

BEDARD, David (diving); b. 23 Oct 1965, Montreal, Que.; began diving age 10; mem. Pointe Claire Diving Club, coached by Don Webb; joined ntl team '83; 29 ntl platform, springboard titles; silver 10m '86, 1m, 10m '90 Commonwealth Games; bronze 10m '87, 3m '95 Pan Am Games; 3m semifinalist '89 FINA Cup; semifinalist 3m, 10m '91 World Cup; gold 10m '88 Swedish Cup; mem. '84, '88, '92, '96 Olympic, '86, '90, '94 Commonwealth, '83, '87, '91, '95 Pan Am Games teams; set Cdn 3m record '89; University Cup 10m, 3m gold '88, Pan Am Invitational '90; res. Pointe Claire, Que.

BÉDARD, Eric (speed skating); b. 17 Dec 1976, Shawinigan, Que.; short track specialist; mem. ntl team from '97; with Marc Gagnon, Derrick Campbell, Francois Drolet '98 Olympic gold in 5000m relay; individual Olympic 1000m bronze; relay silver '97 worlds; 2 ntl championship gold, 1 silver, 3 bronze; competed '97, won gold '98 world team championships; res. Montreal, Que.

BÉDARD, Hélène (table tennis); b. 8 Apr 1968, Ascot Corners, Que.; twice ntl junior champ; undefeated in team match play '89 world championships; mem. women's bronze medal teams '87 Pan-Am, '89 Commonwealth Games; scored major upset beating top-seeded Thanh Mach in '87 Canadian championships; '89 ntl mixed doubles titlist, finalist women's doubles; mem. Canadian team '89 world championships; twice Quebec female table tennis athlete of year; Canadian junior athlete of year '85; res. Sherbrooke, Que.

BÉDARD, Myriam (biathlon); b. 22 Dec 1969, Ancienne-Lorette, Que.; div. Jean Paquet; c. Maude; TV show host; abandoned figure skating as youngster; learned to shoot as Val Cartier cadet; began competing in biathlon at 16; mem. ntl team '87-98; 2 ntl jr., 3 ntl sr., 3 world cup gold; world championship 7.5km title '93; 1st-ever Cdn Olympic biathlon medalist with bronze '92; 2 gold '94 Olympics; competed '98 Olympics; switched to speed skating '98; Biathlon Canada athlete of '90-93; Biathlon Canada female athlete '93-94; Bobbie Rosenfeld, Lou Marsh, Velma Springstead trophies '94; fed. govt. meritorious service award '93; mem. Canada's Sports Hall of Fame; res. Quebec City, Que.

BÉDARD, Nancy (synchro swim); b. 11 Nov 1961, Quebec City, Que.; Champlain Regional College; coach; provincial, ntl, international competitor '73-80; 4 Que. jr. team titles; 1sts figures, solo, duet, team Eastern Div. jr. championships, runnerup figures, solo, duet ntl jrs '74; 4 Que. sr., Eastern Div. team titles; 3 ntl sr. team titles; team bronze '78 world championships, silver World Cup, gold Pan-Pacific; silver '80 American Cup; jr. team coach from '80; all-Cdn coach '81; res. Quebec City, Que.

BEDECKI, Tom (administration); b. 4 May 1929, Glace Bay, N.S.; d. 31 Dec 1993, Ottawa, Ont.; m. Ann McDonald; c. Ginni, Bruce, Dayna, Clint; St. Francis Xavier, BA,

Springfield College, Ohio State, PhD; retd ED Canadian Association for Health, Physical Education and Recreation; mem. McCurdy Cup rugby team, Maritime baseball champions; coached baseball, hockey Colorado College ('57 NCAA champions), hockey Ohio State; HS athletic dir., staff mem. UofOtt, UofFla, Ohio State; mem. SFC exec., Commonwealth Games Assn. of Canada, Canada Sports Awards, International Council for Sport and Physical Education; former dir. Sport Canada, instrumental in initiating, developing international hosting policy, sport exchange programs with USSR, China, Cuba.

BEECROFT, Lynne (field hockey); b. 9 May 1957, Comox, B.C.; UVic, BA MEd; coach UVic, mem. BC HS title team '73; BC jr. team '75-76, '75 ntl title; defence BC sr., ntl team '77-85; 4 times World Cup competitor, silver medal team '83; mem. '84 Olympic team; Cowichan HS athlete of year; Nancy Greene scholarship recipient; BC Premier's athletic award; fed. govt. excellence award '83; accorded Master coach status; 15yrs UVic FH coach earning 8 CIAU gold, 3 silver, 2 bronze; prov. coach '85-92; res. Victoria, B.C.

BEEDELL, John (canoeing); b. 14 Feb 1933, Wellington, N.Z.; given name: John Leslie; m. Ann Borland; c. Michael, Jeffrey, David; Carleton, BA; teacher; ntl jr. K2, C2 champion '56; sr. C2, C4 '57, '59, C2 '61; NA C2, C4 '59; mem. '58 worlds, '60 Olympic teams; res. Ottawa, Ont.

BEERS, John (t&f); b. 17 Aug 1952, Netherlands; given name: John William; m. Angela Elsaesser; UBC, BC Institute of Technology; high jump specialist; ntl team '70-76; ntl, Commonwealth record '73; Viscount Alexander award '72; mem. '72 Olympic, '74 Commonwealth Games teams; silver '75 Pan-Am Games; res. Port Moody, B.C.

BEERS, William George (lacrosse); b. 5 May 1843, Montreal, Que.; d. 26 Dec 1900, Montreal, Que.; Lower Canada College; dentist; outlined 1st laws modern lacrosse; formed National Lacrosse Assn. 1867; toured UK with 1st Canadian lacrosse team to play in Britain 1876, played before Queen Victoria at Windsor; prominent in formation MAAA; several books including Lacrosse, the National Game of Canada (1869); founder Canada Journal of Dental Science (1868), a Canadian 1st; mem. Canadian Lacrosse, Canada's Sports halls of fame.

BEESTON, Paul (administration); b. 20 Jun 1945, Welland, Ont.; m. Kaye Doherty; c. Aimee, David; UWO, BA, CA, Fellow of Inst. of Chartered Accountants of Ont.; baseball exec.; initial employee Toronto Blue Jays '76; progressed up administrative ladder serving as vp. administration, business operations to COO '89, CEO '91; dir. Toronto Sun Publishing, Stratford Festival; selected by Sporting News as 20th most powerful person in sports '94; pres./CEO Toronto Argonauts '94; chief operating officer major league baseball '97; res. Toronto, Ont.

BEGIN, Terry (curling); b. 6 Mar 1938, Port Arthur, Ont.; m. Kathryn Naismith; Carleton, BSc.; curling equipment supplier, patent agent, freelance broadcaster, writer; mem. exec. Ottawa Granite, Navy Curling Clubs, CCA public relations comm., statistician ntl championships; twice

skipped, 3 times winner City of Ottawa Grand Aggregate Shield; competed 5 Ont. Consols; mem. organizing comm. '74 Canadian Schoolboy, '77 Montreal Brier; chairman media comm. '79 Ottawa Brier; senior instructor rating, Curl Canada coaches development program instructing at clinics throughout Ontario, Quebec; Scotty Harper Memorial Award for Radio/TV reports '79; res. Ottawa, Ont.

BEHRENS, Norman (canoeing); b. 20 Dec 1956, Lachine, Que.; m. Kathy Bobula; Concordia, BA; ntl jr. C1 1000m '75-76, C2 1000m, C2 500m '77, C4 1000m '78; gold C1, C2 1000m, C1 500m Sr. America Cup '78, C2 500m Continental Cup '79, C1, C2 1000m, C2 500m '80 Olympic trials, C2 1000m, 500m 1980 Zaandam Holland Invitational regatta, C2, C4 1000m, C2 500m '80-81 ntl championships; ntl sr. record 4:21.1 winning '80 ntl C4 1000m; mem. 2 world championships teams; res. Lery, Que.

BEILER, Egon (wrestling); b. 28 Mar 1953, Linz, Austria; given name: Egon Henry; Waterloo, UWO, BSc, Lakehead, BPHE, DDS; dentist; 3 OFSAA titles; 8 ntl titles classes 136 1/2-149 1/2 lbs; 3 CIAU titles; mem. '72, '76, '80 Olympic, '74, '77-79 world, '74, '78 Commonwealth, '75, '79 Pan-Am teams; gold '74 New Zealand, '78 Commonwealth, '75 Pan-Am Games, '76 Toledo World Cup; bronze '73 European championships; mem. St. Jerome's Kitchener HS soccer title team, 3rd in Ont.; 3 St. Jerome's, 2 Waterloo outstanding wrestler awards; athlete of year St. Jerome's '71, City of Kitchener '73, Waterloo '74, Lakehead U '76; mem. Waterloo County, UWO W-Club, Cdn Amateur Wrestling, Cdn Amateur Sports halls of fame; res. Flesherton, Ont.

BÉLAND, Daniel (figure skating); b. 8 Sep 1960, Montreal, Que.; teaching pro; 1st Quebecer to claim ntl title '75 novice; 3rd ntl jr. '76, 2nd '77-78; jr. world title '77; 2nd Prague Skate '80; 3rd Ennima Challenge Cup '80; began teaching '81; res. Montreal, Que.

BELANGER, Babe (basketball); b. 8 May 1911, Edmonton, Alta.; given name: Noilla; m. Ian MacLean (d); c. Heather, Neil; retd secretary; t&f competitor; mem. famed Edmonton Grads '29-37, 136 games, 1441 points for 10.5 avg.; organized sr. Citizen's honky tonk band; mem. Cdn Basketball, Alta. Sports halls of fame; res. Osoyoos Lake, B.C.

BÉLANGER, Bertrand (harness racing); b. 17 May 1944, St. Michel de Bellechasse, Que.; launched career with Miss Nomer at 17; raced at Quebec Raceway before shifting to Saratoga, N.Y.; a catch-driver for numerous trainers he's rated as a smart tactical driver; Saratoga Harness Horseman of '81; won driving titles at Saratoga, Green Mountain Park, Monticello Raceway; through '95 2566 victories with purses exceeding $5M; res: Sarasota Springs, N.Y.

BELANGER, Frenchy (boxing); b. 17 May 1906, Toronto, Ont.; d. 27 May 1969, Toronto, Ont.; given name: Albert; m. Ivy; c. Gerald, Leilani; pro-fighter, waiter; impressive amateur, early pro record '25-26; beat Frankie Genaro in 10 to win vacant NBA world flyweight title '27; defended successfully against Ernie Jarvis '27, lost to Genaro '28, lost rematch; 2yrs ntl champion losing to Steve Rocco '28;

regained title beating Rocco '29; lost bid for US flyweight title to Izzy Schwartz '29; final pro bout '32, 7th-round KO by Frankie Wolfram; pro record: 52 bouts, 13 won by KO, 24 by decision, 7 draws, 15 lost decisions; 1 by foul, 2 KO's; nicknamed, Canadian Wolverine, Canadian Tadpole; stroke '64 left him paralyzed, speechless but with aid of friend Murphy Blandford spent final years involved with Belanger's Aces softball team; mem. Canada's Sports, Boxing halls of fame.

BELCHER, Val (football); b. 6 Jul 1954, Houston, Tex.; m. Terri Lea; c. Layne, Ashton, Megan; Houston; restaurateur; offensive guard Houston '73-76; tri-capt. '76 Southwest Conf., Cotton Bowl champions; 3rd round pick Dallas (NFL) '77; saw NFL exhibition game action for Patriots vs. Rams; CFL Ottawa '79-82, Winnipeg '83-84; CFL all-Eastern '79-82; all-Cdn '80-82; Schenley outstanding lineman ntl finalist '80-81; named to 2nd unit Southwest Conf. all-decade team of '70s; organized annual Texas Shootout Skins Game golf event at Rideau View Country Club to aid Ottawa Civic Hospital fund-raising; res. Manotick, Ont.

BELCOURT, Tim (curling); b. 4 Jul 1962, Penetanguishene, Ont.; m. Ellen Beck; c. Alicia, Kelly, Nicole; sporting goods store owner; skipped rink Ont. Jr.; mem. Ont. Governor-General's trophy winner '85; second Russ Howard rink 3 Briers; mem. Cdn, world champions '87; mem. 3 Canada Challenge Cups Japan; participated in '87 Olympic trials; runnerup Moncton 100 'spiel; Dick Ellis team award '87; mem. Cdn Curling Hall of Fame; res. Elmvale, Ont.

BÉLEC, Jacques (football); b. 13 Sep 1931, Timmins, Ont.; given name: Joseph Jean Jacques; m. Carolyn; c. Liane, Danielle, Philip; UWO, BA; regional mgr. London Life Ins. Co.; hockey, football UWO; Mustang football MVP '53; pro Montreal '54-56; Grey Cup finalist each year; competitive squash player, golfer; level 3 ski instructor; mountain climber, Mt. Everest, Kalopatai; dir. QGA; capt. Summerlea G&CC; dir. QGA 9yrs, pres. '91; mem. Montreal Badminton & Squash Club; consultant in behavioral science, training, organization, motivation; res. Montreal, Que.

BELFOUR, Ed (hockey); b. 21 Apr 1965, Carman, Man.; m. Rita Marie; c. Dayn, Reaghan; North Dakota; goalie Winkler (MJHL) '85-86; UND '86-87, NCAA title, Saginaw (IHL) '87-89, NHL Chicago '88-97, San Jose '97, Dallas '97-99; IHL rookie of '88; Calder Memorial Trophy '91; Vezina trophy '91, '93; 3 Jennings trophies; Upper Deck all-rookie team; Hockey News rookie of '91, all-star; Trico award for lowest save percentage '91; set NHL record of 11 consecutive playoff victories; mem. '99 Stanley Cup winner; mem. Team Canada '89-90; NHL record: (through '99) 550 scheduled games, 276-174-75, 31,553m, 45so, 91 playoff games, 5486m, 207ga, 6so, 51-35; nicknamed "Eagle"; active with Make-A-Wish Foundation; active triathlete; res. Downers Grove, Ill.

BÉLIVEAU, Jean (hockey); b. 31 Aug 1931, Trois-Rivières, Que.; m. Élise Couture; c. Hélène; Uof Ott, Acadia hon. LLD; retired hockey exec.; jr. Que. Aces; Montreal Canadiens '53-71, team capt. '61-71; NHL record: 1125 scheduled games, 507g, 712a, 162 playoff games, 79g, record 97a; 10 Stanley Cup winners; 6 times 1st, 4 times 2nd team all-star; 25 or more goals in 13 seasons, 80 game-winning goals, 3 4-goal, 18 3-goal games; Art Ross trophy '56; Hart Trophy (MVP) '56, '64; Conn Smythe Trophy playoff MVP '65; record 16 consecutive years in playoffs; French-speaking athlete of '67 (Julien Trophy); Lionel Conacher trophy '56; record 16 assists '70-71 playoffs; sr. v.-pres. corporate affairs Canadiens to '93; nicknamed "Le Gros Bill"; jersey 4 retd by Canadiens; subject of biography "My Life in Hockey"; Canadiens special ambassador rejected appointment as Governor-General '94; Officer Order of Canada '69 upgraded to Companion '98, mem. Canada's, Que. Sports, Hockey halls of fame; res. Longueuil, Que.

BELKIN, Mike (tennis); b. 29 Jun 1945, Montreal, Que.; Miami; teaching pro; with Ron Seifert '57 ntl under-13 doubles; under-15 singles '59, US ntl jr title '60, US boys under-18 nationals (10th place in US tennis ranks), Canadian under-18 singles '62, US Interscholastic singles '63; mem. '67-73 Davis Cup teams; quarterfinalist '68 Australian championships; 3 ntl men's closed singles; top Canadian '71 winning Virginia Slims Masters, semifinalist River Oaks Open, Tanglewood Classic; runnerup Florida championships '72; mem. Cdn Tennis Hall of Fame; res. Miami, Fla.

BELL, Bobby (coaching/administration); b. 13 Aug. 1903, Westmount, Que.; d. 21 Mar 1948, Montreal, Que.; given name: Robert Blagrave; McGill, BA, DDS; dentist; played inter-faculty football; asst. mgr. rugby team, cheerleader; 7yrs McGill hockey; coached McGill hockey '29-37, '42-43, '44-45; 137-58-25 record, 6 Queen's Cup titles, 1 International Intercollegiate title, 2 Que. Sr. HL titles; pres. CIHU, CIRU, Cdn Davis Cup comm., Que. Squash Racquets Assn.; Bobby Bell Memorial trophy awarded annually to Redmen hockey MVP; mem. McGill Sports Hall of Fame.

BELL, George (baseball); b. 21 Oct 1959, San Pedro de Macoris, Dominican Rep.; given name: George Antonia; m. Marie Louisa Beguero; c. Christopher, George Jr., Kevin Antonia; baseball coach; pro Philadelphia organization '78; played in minors at Helena, Spartansburg, Reading, Oklahoma City, Syracuse; drafted by Blue Jays '80; ML debut with Toronto '81; erratic fielder but powerful hitter; in 9 Toronto seasons posted .286 avg with 202hr, 740rbi in 1181 scheduled games; signed as free agent with Chicago Cubs '91; Chicago White Sox '92-93; only player to clear LF roof in 76-yr history of old Comiskey Park, twice in one series '85; Toronto career marked with frequent run-ins with team officials, fans; AL MVP '87; 3 times all-star; set several Toronto records, received numerous awards including AL Silver Slugger; roving hitting instructor Blue Jays '98; mem. Blue Jays Wall of Distinction; res. San Pedro de Macoris, DR.

BELL, Jane (t&f); b. 6 Feb 1910, Toronto, Ont.; d. 1 Jul 1998, Ft. Myers, Fla.; given name: Florence Jane; m. J. Bert Walker (d); c. John, Judith; m. Doane; Margaret Eaton School; retd. PE dir.; standout swimmer, basketball player, hurdler, sprinter; mem. Toronto Ladies, Parkside, Margaret

Eaton championship swim teams; set 100yd hurdles record; mem. '28 Olympic team; with Bobbie Rosenfeld, Ethel Smith, Myrtle Cook won Olympic relay gold; Guelph Country Club golf champion; Myrtle Beach mixed two-ball champion '73; mem. 1st Can-Am women's curling team to tour Scotland '55; competed in women's world curling Scotland '64; mem. Cdn Amateur, Canada's Sports Hall of Fame.

BELL, Marilyn (swimming); b. 19 Oct 1937, Toronto, Ont.; m. Joseph DiLascio; c. Lisa, Michael, Janet, Jodi; Loretto College School, McGill, BA, Rider College, MA; teacher; coached by Gus Ryder, began swimming as sprinter age 9; at 15 standout 26-mile Atlantic City marathon swim; greatest achievement '54 when she became first person to conquer Lake Ontario; swam 32 miles from Youngstown, N.Y. to Toronto in 20:58; 1st woman to conquer Straits of Juan de Fuca '56; youngest to swim English Channel '55, conquered other bodies of water before retirement; Barker Bread trophy '52, Lou Marsh Trophy '54, 2 Bobbie Rosenfeld trophies; award in her honor presented annually at CNE to athlete in water-oriented sport; mem. Canada's Sports, US, Ont. Aquatic halls of fame; res. Willingboro, N.J.

BELL, Max (horse racing); b. 1912, Regina, Sask.; d. 1972, Calgary, Alta.; given name: George Maxwell; m., c. 4; McGill, BComm.; publisher, oilman; purchased 1st horse, Mac Aurelius, from Johnny Longden '36; with Frank McMahon established Golden West Farms; dominant force in NA, European racing circles 36yrs, with victories in Irish Sweeps derby, Queen's Plate, Hollywood Derby; prominent breeder; pres. Balmoral franchise Chicago; dir. Tanforan, Calif.; UMan./Alta. arenas bear his name; mem. Canadian Horse Racing Hall of Fame.

BELLOWS, Brian (hockey); b. 1 Sep 1964, St. Catharines, Ont.; m. Tracey; c. Kieffer; left wing Kitchener Rangers '81-82; OHL 1st team all-star '82; George Parsons award (Memorial Cup most sportsmanlike player) '82; 1st choice Minnesota '82 draft; pro Minesota '82-92, Montreal '92-95, Tampa Bay '95, Anaheim '96, Vancouver '97, Washington '98-99; played in Germany '97-98 before returning to NHL; mem. Spengler Cup title team '97; hit 50-goal plateau with 55 '89-90; NHL 2nd team all-star '90; played 3 NHL all-star games; mem. 1 Stanley Cup winner; Team Canada '84; NHL record: (through '99) 1188 scheduled games, 485g, 537a, 143 playoff games, 51g, 71a; res. Gulf Sport, Fla./Edina, Minn.

BELSHER, Don (touch football); b. 8 Jul 1950, Ottawa, Ont.; given name: Donald Charles; m. Cathy Ritchie; c. Lindsay, Kevin; Algonquin Coll.; truck driver; Jr. A hockey Ottawa 67's '68, M&W Rangers '68-69; MVP CJHL '69; quarterback, defensive back Ottawa Dan Kelly's '73-83, Ottawa Skemers '84, ntl all-star touring team '74; mem. 3 ntl touch title teams; ntl Touch Bowl MVP '75, '80, '83; minor hockey coach; 3 Ottawa ACT awards; res. Ottawa, Ont.

BELYEA, Arthur (rowing/skating); b. 31 Aug 1885, Saint John, N.B.; d. 6 Jan 1968, Albany, N.Y.; given name: Hilton Arthur; provincial, Maritime, ntl, international awards in sculling, skating; starred as single sculler '04-27, skater '05-21; 35 silver cups, trophies, 33 medals; during '24 Olympics

special bronze medal from Olympic committee for good sportsmanship in single sculls; mem. NB Sports Hall of Fame.

BEND, Olive (softball/baseball); b. 7 May 1917, Poplar Point, Man.; d. 2 Feb 1987, Poplar Point, Man.; given name: Olive Elizabeth; m. George Little; c. Roberta, Frances; retd teacher; pitched for Winnipeg sr. women's teams 1937-40; authored numerous no-hitters, averaged 13 strikeouts per game; unique distinction of pitching Man., Sask. teams to provincial titles same year; set personal record 22 strikeouts as mem. Moose Jaw team; pro baseball Rockford, Ill. Peaches of AAGPBL; pitched 4 no-hitters, named to all-American girls' baseball team which played at Wrigley Field, Chicago '42; retired '45; honored Cooperstown, Cdn Baseball halls of fame; mem. Canadian Softball, Man. Sports halls of fame.

BENEDICT, Clint (hockey); b. 1894, Ottawa Ont.; d. 12 Nov 1976, Ottawa, Ont.; given name: Clinton Stevenson; c. Graham; Ottawa Senators (NHA, NHL) '13-24, Montreal Maroons '24-30; habit of flopping on ice to block shot forced rule changes to make action legal; NHL record: 364 scheduled games, allowed 874g, 57so for 2.37 avg., 49 playoff games, 87g, 15so, 1.78 avg.; forced into retirement at 34 after stopping two bullet-like shots from stick of Howie Morenz, 1st shot shattered his nose, 2nd injured his larynx; because of initial shot, vision was impaired and he became one of first goalers to wear face mask; mem. Ottawa Sports, Hockey halls of fame.

BENNETT, Bruce (football); b. 13 Dec 1943, Valdosta, Ga.; given name: Lamar; m. Starling; c. Billy, Bobby, Bradley; Florida, BSc, Valdosta State College, MSc; HS athletic director, football coach; all-American defensive safety UF '65; Saskatchewan '66-72; all-Canadian '69, 6 times WFC all-star; 35 interceptions during 7-year CFL career for 606yds returned; longest single interception return 112yds vs. Calgary at Regina '72; 4 Grey Cup finals, 1 winner; res. Macclenny, Fla,

BENNETT, Dot (lawn bowling); b. 10 Apr 1930, Toronto, Ont.; given name: Dorothy Lillian Hilder; m. Gordon Bennett; c. Tom, Gord, Kathy; retd. cashier; ntl singles gold '91, 4th '95; ntl triples silver '88; ntl doubles bronze '97; res. Bobcaygeon, Ont.

BENNETT, Douglas (canoeing); b. 13 Sep 1918, St. Lambert, Que.; given name: Douglas Haig; m. Edna White; c. Jeanette, Barbara, Elaine, Dryden; retd Bell Canada; '34 intermediate 4s, ntl tandem titles; Eastern div. jr. singles, int. tandem, CCA int. tandem '37; sr 4s '38; ntl intermediate singles '39; qualified for '40 Olympics which were cancelled by war; silver sr. singles, 4th sr. tandem '48 Olympics; ntl 4s '48; mem. St. Lambert HS football title team '35; D'Arcy McGee sr. champions '36; mem. ORFU Montreal Indians, Cubs; St. Lambert HS Mount Royal jr. hockey champions '37-38; class A handicap Beloeil Golf Club '54; Montreal Sportsmen's Assn. sportsman of '47; res. Hudson Heights, Que.

BENNETT, Paul (football); b. 27 Mar 1954, Scarborough, Ont.; Missouri, UWO, Wilfrid Laurier; territorial draft Argos '77; punt return, kickoff return specialist, defensive back;

CIAU, OQIFC all-star '76; CFL Toronto '77-79, '84, Winnipeg '80-84, Edmonton (never played) '84, Hamilton '84-87; CFL punt return yardage record 6073; CFL single season punt return record 965yds rookie season; Argos single game punt return record 185yds on 9 returns '77; 2 EFC, 2 WFC, 3 CFL all-star; Schenley Outstanding Canadian award '83, '85; recipient Dr. Beattie Martin, James McCaffrey, Lew Hayman trophies; 3 Grey Cup finals, 1 winner; Blue Bomber radio broadcaster; mem. Blue Bombers Hall of Fame; res. Winnipeg, Man.

BENNIE, Elsie (basketball); b. 10 May 1908, Sterling, Scotland; given name: Elsie Norrie; m. Donald Robson; c. Margaret Ruth, Beverley Jean; stenographer; mem. famed Edmonton Grads '24-33; mem. Canadian Basketball, Alta. Sports halls of fame; res. Calgary, Alta.

BENOIT, Chantal (wheelchair basketball); b. 1 Oct 1960, Beloeil, Que.; m. Reg McClellan; UofOtt, BA; competitive diver 9yrs; played 8yrs with Kamikazes's wheelchair basketball squad before joining the Royals, Shooters and Ottawa Jazz of Ottawa-Carleton Wheelchair Sports Assn; mem. ntl team from '84; silver '86 Pan-Am Games; competed '84, '88, '92, '96 Paralympics; gold '92, '96 Paralympics, '91 Stoke-Mandeville World Games; Gold Cup gold '94, '98, bronze '90; CWBL gold, MVP with Jazz '92, '95 championships; bronze, all-star '93 CWBL finals; silver, all-star '93-94 CWBL finals; silver with Ottawa Royals '92, '94 NWBT final four; mem. Ottawa Shooters ntl title team '95; MMVP world women's title team '98; Que. Sport Merit award '93; Que, basketball female athlete of '98; Cumberland Council award; res. Orleans, Ont.

BENSON, Heather (field hockey); b. 4 Jun 1961, Victoria, B.C.; given name: Heather Mary Lovell; UVic, UBC,, BPhE., BEd, MEd (specialist in hearing impaired); Jr. HS teacher, counsellor jr. HS; competitive swimmer, soccer player; badminton player, field hockey mem. Victoria Sandpipers, Spartans, Vancouver Meralomas, UVic team '80-81, UBC '83-86, Vancouver Island under 19 team '79-80, sr. '81, BC junior teams '79-81; mem. BC '81 gold medal Canada Games team; BC sr. team '82-83; ntl under 21 team '81-82; mem. ntl gold team Toronto International tournament '82; gold team Scottish 4-country tournament '82; World Cup silver team '83; pre-Olympic training '84; coach prov. age-group teams '85-95, school teams (in varied sports) '79-83, '86-99; CWUAA FH all-star, CIAU tournament eleven '82; media liasion jr. WC ;88; mem. ntl jr. badminton team '75-78; Level 2 coach, Level 1 coach/ co-ordinator; co-chair. BC summer games '88; coach BCIT-UBC player camps; HS outstanding female athlete award; major awards 4 sports at HS level; fed. govt. excellence award '83; Vancouver coach of yr awards '88-89; res. Victoria, B.C.

BENSON, Lorne (all-around); b. 16 Sep 1930, Riverton, Man.; m. Betty Lane; c. Sherry, Bonnie, Lori, Robert, Linda; pipefitter BC railroad; nicknamed "Boom Boom"; Blue Bombers '52 WFC Canadian rookie of year, Dr. Beattie Martin Trophy; CFL record 6 TDs single game '53, matched by clubmate Bob McNamara (since TDs valued at 5 points, is one of 4 sharing 2nd spot to McNamara for single game points with 30), all 6 TDs gained rushing, also CFL record;

hockey defense Winnipeg Maroons '54-55, lacrosse '47-48; Manitoba 100lb boxing title '41; right-handed pitcher Calgary Purity 99ers, Grandview Maroons, 2 games PCL Vancouver Mounties; 3 successive no-hitters Winnipeg jrs.; mem. '67 ntl champion Molson Canadians; coached Churchill, Man. to 28 straight hockey victories, team won 35 of 38 games winning Northern Man. inter. title; mem. curling rink which scored 8-ender in provincial Consols; res. Elkford, B.C.

BENTHAM, Lee (motorsport); b. 27 Jul 1970, Richmond Hill, Ont.; racing driver; began competing at karting level; won 1st race Whitby Kartways '80; race in kart 12yrs winning 19 championships, record 310 podium finishes with 224 wins; competed 5 FIK world championships; NTN Kart series Formula A title '91; ntl sprint grand nationals (kart) title, SKC Challenge Cup, SKC Mondial series Formula A karting titles '92; competed in Cdn Michelin Enduro Grand Sports class '94; advanced to Player's/Toyota Atlantic series ranks '95 placing 3rd in rookie championship; recipient 2 Hard Charger awards; res. Richmond Hill, Ont.

BENTLEY, Doug (hockey); b. 3 Sep 1916, Delisle, Sask.; d. 24 Nov 1972, Saskatoon, Sask.; given name: Douglas Wagner; m. Betty Clark; c. Douglas Jr., Elaine, Patsy, Evelyn; wheat farmer; one of 4 Bentley brothers dominating Prairie hockey '38 at Drumheller, Alta.; NHL Chicago Black Hawks '39-53, NYRangers '53-54; NHL record: 566 scheduled games, 219g, 324a, 23 playoff games, 9g, 8a; with brother Max and Bill Mosienko formed famed Pony Line; NHL scoring title '42-43; 3 times NHL all-star but never on Stanley Cup winner; last minor pro season '61-62; mem. Sask. Sports, Hockey halls of fame.

BENTLEY, Max (hockey); b. 1 Mar 1920, Delisle, Sask.; d. 19 Jan 1984, Saskatoon, Sask.; given name: Maxwell Herbert Lloyd; m. Betty Miller; c. Lynn, Gary; farmer; Chicago Black Hawks '40-48, Toronto '48-53, N Y Rangers '53-54; with brother Doug, Bill Mosienko formed Pony Line; nicknamed "Dipsy-Doodle Dandy" for stickhandling ability; mem. 3 Stanley Cup winners; brief comeback with Saskatoon, finally retired '56; mem. 1st NHL all-star team; NHL record: 646 scheduled games, 245g, 299a, 52 playoff games, 18g, 27a; NHL scoring titles '46, '47; Hart Trophy '46, Lady Byng Trophy '43; tied Busher Jackson's '34 record 4 2nd-period goals '43, tied by Red Berenson '68, Wayne Gretzky '81; mem. Sask. Sports, Hockey halls of fame.

BERENSON, Red (hockey); b. 8 Dec 1939, Regina, Sask.; given name: Gordon Arthur; m. Joy; c. Kelly, Sandy, Gordie, Rusty; Michigan, BSc, MSc.; hockey coach; jr. Regina Pats; all-American, Western Collegiate Hockey Assn. MVP 43 goals in 28-game season Mich; team capt.; led Belleville McFarlands scorers world amateur tournament; pro Montreal organization '61-66; Hull-Ottawa (EPHL), Quebec (AHL) with brief stints with Habs; NY Rangers '66; St. Louis '67-70, Detroit '71-73, St. Louis '74-77; Team Canada '72; NHL record: 987 scheduled games, 261g, 397a, 85 playoff games, 23g, 14a; leader in formation NHL Players' Assn.; nicknamed "Red Baron"; in NHL record book '68 scoring 6 goals in 8-0 St. Louis win over Philadelphia, tying record set '44 by Detroit's Syd Howe vs Rangers; same game tied record 4 goals 2nd period set '34 by Busher Jackson, equalled '43 by Max Bentley, '81 by Wayne Gretzky; NHL Western Division MVP; asst. coach St. Louis '78-79; head coach '79-82; asst. Buffalo Sabres '82-84; coach Michigan State from '84; 4 CCHA titles, NCAA title '96; 9 consec. Great Lakes Invitational titles, 1 College Hockey Showcase title; 23-game undefeated streak '96-97; Jack Adams award winner '81; mem. Mich(U) Hall of Honor, Dekers Club, Mich. Sports halls of fame; named to American Hockey Coaches Assn. all-time favorites list; res. Lansing, Mich.

BEREZOWSKI, Barbara (figure skating); b. 5 Sep 1954, Toronto, Ont.; m. John Ivan; c. Brian, Jarrod; Ryerson; public relations; with partner David Porter ntl jr. dance title '71; sr. ice dance champions '75-76; mem. Skate Canada '73-75 winning silver medal; mem. ntl team 4 world championship competition '73-76; mem. Cdn Olympic team '76; won Lake Placid International Invitational '74; bronze Prestige Cutlery Invitational '75; world pro dance champion '77; Miss Toronto '75; Miss Moscow '75-76; Miss Charm on Ice Munich; runnerup Miss Canada '76; Miss Olympics '76; toured professionally with Stars on Ice USA, Shipstad & Johnson Ice Follies, Toller Cranston Ice Show, Tom Collins World Tour of Champions; chair. Etobicoke Sports Hall of Fame; res. Etobicoke, Ont.

BERGER, Mark (judo); b. 3 Jan 1954, Chernovtsy, Russia; m.; UMan; Soviet master of sport in judo, wrestling, sambo; Western Cdn over-95kg titles '78-80; ntl titles '80-81, '83-84, US open '82; gold '83 Pan-Am Games, '84 Canada Cup; bronze '84 Olympics; competed '81, '85, coach '93 Maccabiah Games; fed. govt. excellence award '84; mem. Man. Sports, Cdn Judo halls of fame; res. Winnipeg, Man.

BERGER, Sam (football); b. 1 Jan 1900, Ottawa, Ont.; d. 24 Jul 1992, Montreal; m. Ilse Marx (div); c. David, Robert, Julia; Osgoode Hall; lawyer; realty co. owner; EFC legal advisor; p.-pres. Ottawa Football Club, CFL; involved as dir. Ottawa 40yrs; purchased Montreal Alouettes '69; involved with 7 Grey Cups winners, 3 in Montreal, 4 in Ottawa; put CFL in big money market signing "Ordinary Superstar" Johnny Rodgers for $1 million-plus; sold Als to Nelson Skalbania '80; brought pro soccer to Montreal; mem. Order of Canada; Cdn. Football, Ottawa Sports halls of fame.

BERGERON, Jean François (boxing); b. 26 Jul 1973, St. Jérome, Que.; store clerk; three ntl 91+ kg titles; gold '94 Copenhagen Cup, '95 Finland Tammer tournament, bronze '96 Bulgaria Strandzata tournament; silver '95 Pan-Am Games; mem. '96 Olympic team; res. St. Jerome, Que.

BERGEY, Kim (wrestling); b. 7 Aug 1972, Regina, Sask.; U Regina; early training in judo helped escalate rise in women's wrestling ranks; competes at 68kg level; won 3 ntl '62kg, 1 ntl 70kg titles; competed 3 world women's championships; 3 Sunkist Invitational gold; res. Regina, Sask.

BERGMAN, Gary (hockey); b. 7 Oct 1938, Kenora, Ont.; given name: Gary Gunnar; mem. champion Kenora Rowing Club junior heavy fours; mem. Tribune Trophy winning United College curling team; played Jr. football, attended Blue Bombers '59 training camp; intermediate hockey

Kenora Thistles, jr. Winnipeg Braves Memorial Cup champions; pro Winnipeg (WHL) '57-60; Buffalo (AHL) '60-61; Cleveland (AHL) '61-63; Springfield '63-64; Memphis (CPHL) '65-66; NHL with Detroit '64-73, '74-75, Minnesota '73-74; WHA Kansas City '75-76; 3 times most valuable defenceman with Detroit; mem. Team Canada '72 series vs. Russia; mem. NWO Sports Hall of Fame; res. Rochester, Mich.

BERMEL, Lynne (triathlon); b. 13 Dec 1960, Trenton, Ont.; div. Joe McAllister; Queen's, BA; marketing, public relations; strong swimmer and runner; winner of numerous 5km, 10km races; made ironman triathlon debut '92 posting 9:53:18 for one of fastest debut times in Cdn ironman history; competed on World Cup circuit '93-95 posting 12 top 5 finishes in 15 races; won Niagara International marathon '95; 3rd world ironman rankings '99; Cdn Ironman of yr, 3 Cdn Forces female athlete of yr, Ottawa ACT multisport awards; mem. Cdn Forces Sports Hall of Fame; res. Ottawa, Ont.

BERNIER, Sylvie (diving); b. 31 Jan 1964, Quebec City, Que.; m. Gilles Cloutier; c. Catherine, Annabelle, Florence; College Andre-Grasset; TV analyst, financial, pharmaceutical cos. spokesperson; mem. ntl team '78-84; 6 gold ntl 3m, 1 gold 1m; bronze 10m '78 ntls; gold 3m Dive Canada, Mex. International, all-American, Rostock International, Can-Am-Mex; silver 3m '82 Commonwealth Games; bronze 3m '83 FISU, Pan-Am Games; mem. '81 FINA WC, '82 world championships, Commonwealth, '83 FISU Games, '83 Pan-Am Games teams; gold 3m Dive Canada, Olympic Games '84; retd from competition '84; Elaine Tanner, Bobbie Rosenfeld trophies '84; fed. govt. champion award '85; FAS ambassador '85 World Youth year; Seagram 5 Star award '84; tech. advisor Diving Canada '85-86; mem. Order of Canada; Cdn Aquatic, Amateur, Que., Laval U, Canada's Sports halls of fame; res. Rosemere, Que.

BERNIER, Trista (t&f); b. 22 Jul 1971, North Bay, Ont.; York, B.Sc., BPE; pole vault specialist; 2 ntl titles; ntl indoor/outdoor record holder; bronze '98 Commonwealth Games; competed '99 Pan-Am Games; res. Toronto, Ont.

BERRETT, Tim (t&f); b. 23 Jan 1965, Tunbridge Wells, Eng.; m. Tara Croxford; UAlta.; educator; came to Canada '87 on Canadian Rhodes Foundation scholarship; racewalk specialist; Cdn record 1:22:27 for 20km walk '96; ntl indoor 5km record 18:47.56 '93; 2 ntl indoor 5km, 1 10km, 3 ntl outdoor 20km titles; US 50km title '90; British Invitational 3km '92; competed '92, '96 Olympic, '93 FISU, '94 Francophone, '94, '98 Commonwealth, '95, '99 Pan-Am Games teams; '91, '93 World championships, '93 World Cup of race walking; silver '94 Commonwealth Games 30km walk; 3 Dr. Fred Tees outstanding university athlete awards; 2 Fred Begley marathon 50km walk awards; res. Stanley Mission, Sask./Edmonton, Alta.

BERRY, Bob (hockey); b. 29 Nov 1943, Montreal, Que.; given name: Robert Victor; m. Lynn Mirach; c. Jina, Cori; Sir George Williams, BA; semipro football; rejected baseball offers Houston Astros; ntl hockey team; pro Montreal organization '68; LA Kings '70-77; NHL record: 541 scheduled games, 159g, 191a, 26 playoff games, 2g, 6a;

coach Springfield Indians (AHL) '77-78, LA Kings '78-80; Montreal '81-84, Pittsburgh '84-87; asst. St. Louis '88-91; AGM Blues '92-93, '96-97; AGM/coach Blues '93-96; asst. coach San Jose '98-99; nicknamed "Crease-Line"; res. San Jose, Calif.

BERRYMAN, Tim (football); b. 21 Dec 1954, Hamilton, Ont.; given name: Timothy James; m. Cynthia Fox Hughes; c. Peter James; Uof Ott, BA; v-pres. Louisiana Icegators (ECHL); all-star middle linebacker UofOtt '74-75; co-capt. undefeated CIAU College Bowl Gee-Gees title team '75; 7 CFL seasons with Edmonton, Hamilton, Ottawa, Toronto; part owner/founder Louisiana Icegators; res. Lafayette, La.

BERTIE, Gordon (wrestling); b. 20 Aug 1948, St. Gabriel de Brandon, Que.; given name: Gordon William; m. Joan Elizabeth Goldfinch; c. 1 son; U of Alta, BSc., BEd., Lakehead U; realtor; 3 CIAU 118-lb titles; 1 ntl 105.5lb FS, 4 114.5lb FS, 1 114.5lb GR titles; silver '74 Commonwealth, bronze '74 worlds, gold '75, silver '76, bronze '74 Toledo World Cup; mem. '71, '75 Pan-Am, '72, '76 Olympic teams; mem. Alta Sports, Cdn Amateur Wrestling halls of fame; res. Edmonton, Alta.

BERTOIA, Reno (baseball); b. 8 Jan 1935, St. Vito, Udina, Italy; given name: Reno Peter; div.; c. Carl, Ruth, Gina; Assumption College, BA; HS history department head; Mic Mac League, Windsor, Class C Detroit Sandlot League; bonus contract Detroit Tigers '53; spring training '56 earned him starting spot 3B, farmed to Charleston later in season; Tigers '57-58, Washington-Minnesota '59-61, Kansas City, Detroit '61-62, Syracuse '63, Japan '64; AL record: 612 games, 27 HRs, 171 RBI, .244 BA; mem. Windsor/Essex County, U Windsor Sports, Cdn Baseball halls of fame; res. Windsor, Ont.

BEST, Bob (shooting); b. 12 Jan 1952, Vancouver, B.C.; given name: Robert Gordon; m. Khirsty Gourlay; UBC, BA; teacher; mem. ntl under-20 fencing team '72 world championships; Western Canada épée title '72; mem. cadet Bisley team '67; 7 times qualified DCRA Bisley team, competed 3; ntl open, closed target titles '82; Canadian Target Rifle Bisley Aggregate titles '82-83; Governor-General's prize Connaught '81; Des Burke Trophy '81; res. Richmond, B.C.

BETKER, Jan (curling); b. 19 Jul 1960, Regina, Sask; m. Frank Macera; c. Steven; admin. asst.; began curling age 13; lead Randy Woytowich '84 ntl mixed title rink; 4 Sask, 3 Scott Tournament of Hearts, 3 world title rinks (3rd for Sandra Peterson Schmirler); gold '98 Olympics; res. Regina, Sask.

BETTY, Trevino (t&f); b. 10 Oct 1971, Portland, Jamaica; UTexas; ntl lj title '96; competed lj '97 FISU Games; 4x100 relay silver '98 Commonwealth, '99 Pan-Am Games; res. Austin, Tex./London, Ont.

BEVAN, Eddie (football); b. 28 Sep 1924, Hamilton, Ont.; d. 29 May 1988, Hamilton, Ont.; given name: Edward Charles; m. Ernestine Pallante; c. Marguerite; truck sales mgr; juvenile to sr. Big Four football Hamilton Tigers '45-48; Wildcats '49; when Tigers, Wildcats amalgamated '50

to become Tiger-Cats, played guard with some offensive duties through '59; capt. '53, '55 teams; 4 Grey Cup finals, 2 winners; asst. coach '60-61; line coach McMaster '62-65; 5 times EFC all-star, 2 East-West Shrine Games; mem. Hamilton's Fabulous Forties team, team of century.

BEVAN, Marv (football); b. 7 Jun 1935, Hamilton, Ont.; m. Cathy Leblanc; c. Leanne, Lisa; Dircom Advt. sales, retd. truck sales mgr; 4yrs jr. Tiger-Cats; pro lineman Rough Riders '56-57, '59-65; K-W Dutchmen '58; dir. Hooked on Kids, organized to take underprivileged kids fishing; with Frank Fraser coached Eastview jr. team; res. Kanata, Ont.

BEVERIDGE, Bill (hockey); b. 1 Jul 1909, Ottawa, Ont.; d. 13 Feb 1995, Toronto, Ont. given name: William Stanley; m. Louise McCabe; c. Judith, Bill, Jenny; real estate broker; goaltender Ottawa jr. Shamrocks; after 5 games promoted to sr. club; after 2yrs shifted to New Edinburgh; while attending Glebe HS served as spare goalie Ottawa Shamrocks, attended Chicago training camp; without knowledge was promoted to full-time pro hockey and dealt to Detroit Cougars who doubled salary to $4,000; mem. Cougars '29-30, Ottawa '30-34; shifted to St. Louis with Senators then dealt to Montreal Maroons '35-38; following '39-41 minors stint closed pro career with NY Rangers '42-43; in 296 NHL games allowed 883 goals, posted 17 shutouts and 2.98 goals-against avg.; in youth catcher Glebe juveniles Ont. champions '26; Ont. basketball champions '27.

BEWS, Tom (rodeo); b. 2 Nov 1944, High River, Alta.; m. Rosemary; c. T.J., Guy, Dusty, Peter; rancher/wrangler/movie industry co-ordinator; saddle bronc, steer wrestling, team roping specialist; qualified in 6 saddle bronc, 4 steer wrestling Cdn finals; 2 saddle bronc ntl final qualifier; Cdn steer wrestling, saddle bronc titles '71; 5 Cdn all-around titles; CPRA rookie of 1964; cowboy of '78 award; Guy Weadick award '76; res. Longview, Alta.

BEYNON, Tom (football); b. 13 Jul 1941, Kitchener, Ont.; div. c. Natasha, Adrian, Michaela; Queen's, UWO; lawyer; mem. Queen's Golden Gaels OUAA champions '63-64; UWO Mustangs ntl CIAU finalists '65; offensive tackle CFL Saskatchewan '66-67, Ottawa '68-70; 4 Grey Cup finals, 3 winners; served as legal counsel for numerous Cdn amateur athletic associations 15yrs; mem. Waterloo County Hall of Fame; res. Waterloo, Ont.

BEZIC, Sandra (figure skating); b. 6 Apr 1956, Toronto, Ont.; given name: Sandra Marie; coach, choreographer, show producer, director; (see brother Val for competitive record) torn ankle ligaments during '75 training forced Sandra to forego '76 Olympics and turn pro; coached by Ellen Burka, Ron Ludington, Bruce Hyland, Brian Foley; coach, choreographer several ntl, international competitors, including Barbara Underhill, Paul Martini, Katarina Witt, Kurt Browning, Brian Boitano, Josée Chouinard; authored "Passion to Skate"; choreographed and/or produced over 20 TV specials for Disney, CBS, NBC, CBC, CTV, HBO including award winning "Carmen on Ice, You Must Remember;" '92, '98 Olympic color commentator; co-producer/dir. Stars on Ice; credited with worldwide artistic clout when named by Globe & Mail as one of 25 most powerful people in sport; included in Maclean's Canadians

Who Made a Difference honor roll; fund-raiser Heart & Stroke Foundation; mem. Etobicoke Sports Hall of Fame; res. Willowdale, Ont.

BEZIC, Val (figure skating); b. 8 Dec 1952, Toronto, Ont.; given name: Val Nickolas; real estate agent; with sister Sandra one of Canada's and world's outstanding pairs skaters; ntl novice title '67; mem. ntl team '69-75; ntl sr. pairs titles '70-74; mem. '72 Olympic, '70-74 worlds teams; injury to Sandra shattered dream of '76 Olympic medal; Zagreb Invitational title '73; pro '75; world pro pairs title '80; res. Oakville, Ont.

BIANCO, Scott (wrestling); b. 9 Nov 1967, Kamloops, B.C.; UBC, SFU; began competing age 16; mem. ntl team '90-96; 82kg gold '91 Challenge Cup, '92 Clark Florez, Mexico; 4 ntl 90kg, 1 100kg titles; 90kg gold '94 Commonwealth Games, '95 Canada Cup; competed '95 Pan-Am, '96 Olympics, '94-95 worlds; outstanding wrestler award '91 Commonwealth championships; res. Burnaby, B.C.

BIASATTI, Hank (baseball/basketball); b. 14 Jan 1922, Beano, Italy; given name: Henry Arcado; Assumption College; baseball, basketball standout Gordon McGregor HS, Assumption HS; first attracted attention as slick-fielding, hard-hitting first-baseman East Windsor Cubs; SrIC London Majors; 10yrs minor pro baseball plus stint with '49 Philadelphia Athletics; pro basketball Toronto Huskies '46; mem.Windsor Alumni, Windsor/Essex County Sports halls of fame; res. Windsor, Ont.

BICKELL, J.P. (builder/hockey); b. 26 Sep 1884, Toronto, Ont.; d. 22 Aug 1951, Toronto, Ont.; given name: John Paris; industrialist/mining exec./financier, public servant; silent partner in Toronto St. Pat's; urged by Conn Smythe transfered interests to Maple Leafs '27; played role in building Maple Leaf Gardens during Depression years; 1st pres., later chair. of Gardens board to his death; memory perpetuated by memorial trophy awarded at discretion of directors to standout Leaf; mem. Hockey Hall of Fame.

BIEBER, Ethel (swimming); b. 6 May 1920, Winnipeg, Man.; d. 1988, Winnipeg, Man.; m. Gordon Bieber; c. 3; began competitive swimming age 10; held juvenile, jr., sr. Women's Amateur SC titles '32-38; ntl jr. 200FS title '34; claimed 2 ntl 200FS, 5 ntl 200, 400FS relay titles setting 4 records in 5yrs; Manitoba 1/2mile title '36; Man. jr. 50, 100, 200FS titles in record times; 3 consec. pier-to-pier Winnipeg Free Press titles '38-40; mem. ntl record setting 400FS relay title team '39, 200FS relay teams '40-42; Man. mile champion '37-41; Western Cdn mile champion '37-40; leaving competitive ranks participated in Synchro Swim; exec. mem. Man. Synchro Swim Assn.; taught/judged Synchro Swim; Royal Life Saving Society champion; mem. Man. Sports Hall of Fame.

BIESENTHAL, Laryssa (rowing); b. 22 Jun 1971, Walkerton, Ont.; UBC; 4th seat on women's quadruple sculls crew; joined crew '95; silver '95 World championships; 4 Cdn, 2 US titles; bronze women's 8s Lucerne '99; mem. '96 Olympic, '99 Pan-Am Games teams; with Jenn Browett '99 PAG double sculls gold; res. Victoria, B.C.

BIGRAS, Adrien (golf); b. 1 Mar 1938, Laval, Que.; m. Claude Moreau; c. Chantal; golf pro; growing up in close proximity to 2 golf clubs it was only natural he would be drawn to the game; began playing while working at the clubs; never played as an amateur; winner of more than 100 tournaments across Canada; 7 Que. pro titles; 2 Canadian club titles; 3 CPGA seniors crowns; 1 CPGA Super Seniors title; authored "Amélior, votre golf"; res. Rosemere, Que.

BIGRAS, Orv (bowling/horseshoes); b. 17 jul 1927, Ottawa, Ont.; given name: Orville Francis Joseph; m. Rose Helen Giroux; c. Steven, Tanya; St. Patrick Coll., BA; retd. cartographer; competed as amateur boxer '39-44; began competitive 5-pin bowling '65, horseshoes '67; competing in final yr of counter pin averaged 275 '65; represented Eastern Canada in ntl competition 3 times singles, 4 times team; led field '71; YBC instructor 4yrs, supervisor 3yrs; competed in Ottawa, Que. TV championships; among 13 400+ singles had best 435; among 10 1000+ crosses had best 1065; 4 father-son tournament titles; high avg. 5 straight sr. league seasons; competing in a variety of horseshoe tournaments in Ont., Que., US, claimed 8 singles, 15 men's doubles (mostly with Leo Gagnon). 3 mixed doubles (with wife Rose) championships; won Ont. sr. games singles '84, men's doubles '87; Silvershoe marathon singles silver '86; numerous tournament MVP awards; high avg. Ottawa mixed league '90; res. Carlsbad Springs, Ont.

BIGRAS, Sylvie (volleyball/administration); b. 14 May 1957, Ottawa, Ont.; m. Andr, Pajot; c. Samuel, Alexandre; Uof Ott, BPHE, MBA; sport administrator; mem. UofOtt varsity volleyball team '75-80; asst. team information officer '84 summer, '88 winter Olympics; '87 PAG; press attache '88 summer Olympics, '90 Commonwealth games; asst. CdM '92 summer Olympics; chief press officer '95 PAG, '98 winter Olympics; Task Force 2000 mem. '87-88; dir. Cdn Sport & Fitness Admin. Centre '86-90; dir. Cdn Sport Council (formerly SFC) '91-96; dir. gen. Volleyball Canada '89-98; dean's honor list UofOtt '77; res. Ottawa, Ont..

BILODEAU, Alain (weightlifting); b. 9 Jun 1966, Ville LaSalle, Que.; teacher; became interested in weightlifting watching '76 Montreal Olympics; coached by brother Jocelyn; competes in 77kg class; mem. ntl team '85-98; competed '90, '94, '98 (2 bronze) Commonwealth Games, '91, '95 Pan-Am Games; won '98 ntl title; res. St. Isidore, Que.

BINNS, Hilda (t&f); b. 20 Oct 1945, Hamilton, Ont.; given name: Hilda May Torok; div. David Binns; dictaphone typist; contracted polio before 10th birthday leaving her a paraplegic; launched athletic career '68 at Ont. Wheelchair trials where she made winning impression in debut; rep. Ont., ntl wheelchair games; led all competitors with 8 medals, 2 world records; 1st Canadian gold medalist (2) International Stokes-Mandeville Games (disabled Olympics); 5 gold, 1 silver, 4 bronze '69 Wheelchair Pan-Ams; 5 gold, 2 silver, 1 bronze '71 Pan-Ams; 1 gold, 2 silver '72 Stokes-Mandeville Games; chair. Ont. Wheelchair Sports Assn.; last known res. Hamilton, Ont.

BIONDA, Jack (lacrosse/hockey); b. 18 Sep 1933, Huntsville, Ont.; d. 3 Nov 1999, London, Ont.; given name:

Jack Arthur James; m. Joanne Mulholland; restaurateur; defence; jr. A Toronto Marlboros '51-53; Sr. A Sault Ste. Marie Greyhounds '54; pro Pittsburgh (AHL) '55, Springfield (AHL) '56-58; Providence (AHL) '59; NHL Toronto '55, Boston '56-59; Victoria Cougars (WHL) '60; Portland Buckaroos (WHL) '61-66; Oldtimers hockey Huntsville from '75; mem. 2 Stanley Cup finalists; mem. 2 WHL title teams; lacrosse Huntsville town league '46-48; Ont. Int. A champions '49-50; Ont. Sr. B champions '51; mem. '52 Minto Cup titlists; '55, '57 Victoria Shamrocks Mann Cup champions; New Westminster Salmonbellies Mann Cup champions '58-59, '62; 7 Mann Cup finals, 5 winners; among Canada's finest box lacrosse players; ended active career Portland '68; Mann Cup record 9 3-goal games; twice Mann Cup MVP; 7 BC Sr. A scoring titles, league, playoff MVP awards; best single season '59 with 70 goals, 74 assists; 4 times 1st team all-star; Max McDonald, Commissioner's Trophy; mem. Canadian Lacrosse, Canada's. B.C. Sports halls of fame.

BIRON, Louis (curling); b. 4 Jun 1958, Thurso, Que.; m. Héléne; c. Marie-Eve, Marc-Antoine; financial consultant; began curling age 12; representing Buckingham CC played lead for Ted Butler '92, Pierre Charette '93, Don Westphal '97 and second Westphal '96 Briers; res. Thurso, Que.

BISHOP, Carole (volleyball); b. 2 Dec 1949, Vancouver, B.C.; UBC, BPhE, MA (2), PhD; clinical psychologist; Vancouver sprint champion '64-65, mem. title relay teams '63-64; BC HS volleyball champions '66; at 16 youngest Cdn to play at international level; 10 times mem. ntl sr. women's title teams; mem. 4 BC jr. champions; ntl team '67-78; mem. 3 Pan-Am, 2 world championship, 1 World Cup, 1 Olympic, 4 NA NORCECA championships teams; NORCECA silver '73; BC HS volleyball MVP '67; all-Balkan '75 tournament MVP, '76 European Cup MVP, '71, '75 Pan-Am Games all-star; ranked 4th setter in world '76; coached 4 city volleyball title teams; '80-81 Vancouver gymnastics titlists; 3 BC govt. academic scholarships; adjunct prof. UBC, assoc. prof SFU, co-ordinator graduate clinical psychology Vancouver General Hospital; mem. BC Sports Hall of Fame; res. Vancouver, B.C.

BISHOP, Jim (lacrosse/hockey); b. 14 May 1929, Toronto, Ont.; d. 7 Sep 1998, Bowmanville, Ont.; given name: James Gerrard; div. Lynn Boothby; c. Joe, Jim Jr., John, Anne, Gael; m. Vonnie Tennant; c. Lynn; St. Michael's College; self- employed; played with St. Vincent's, Scarborough '40-45; coached '46-98, winning 24 Ont. MLA titles; founded/coached Huntsville MLA; organizer/coach/GM Oshawa Green Gaels '63-69, '76-80, '95-97; coached 7 jr. A ntl titles 8 Minto Cup winners; coached both Green Gaels, Detroit Olympics '68, guiding latter to Eastern division, National League finals; coached Windsor Warlocks to consec. President's Cups '70-71; coach/GM Toronto Tomahawks NLL '74, Montreal Quebecois '75; played key role in establishing/building Whitby MLA; guided Whitby Warriors to '97 Minto Cup; with Bruce Norris, Morley Kells helped found NLL; v.-pres. internal administration Detroit Red Wings (NHL) '67-74; career coaching record (all levels) 352-124-3 regular season, 174-55 playoffs; served as exec. Ont., Canada Lacrosse Assns; 1st tech. dir. CLA; L.B. Pearson award for contribution to lacrosse in Canada, Tip

Tether, Merv McKenzie OLA awards; mem. Canadian Lacrosse, Oshawa, Huntsville Sports halls of fame.

BISSETT, David (field hockey); b. 13 May 1954, Vancouver, B.C.; given name: David Robert Russell George; m. Catherine Jean Cookson; c. Russell Douglas; UBC, BComm., LLB.; co-owner development/construction firm; 2 BC ntl title teams; ntl team '73-83; defence '75, '79, silver, '83 gold Pan-Am Games teams; '76, '84 Olympic, '78 World Cup teams; MVP '68 jr. ntl tournament; capt. or v.-capt. ntl team from '77; with more than 110 international matches has competed on international scene more than any other Canadian field hockey player; fed. govt. excellence award '84; res. New Westminster, B.C.

BISSONNETTE, Serge (shooting); b. 12 Apr 1950, St. Jean d'Iberville, Que.; m. Darlene Hagel; c. Céline; RCMP officer; ntl high-power rifle champion '78-79; Des Burke service rifle award; mem. 12 Cdn intl rifle teams; 24 Intl match medals; 63 ntl match medals; 51 ntl team match titles; 14 intl team titles; 28 HPS crosses; 5 bronze crosses; Sask., Que., Lt.-Gov. medals; more than 100 prov. level individual, 50-plus prov. team medals; 1 silver, 3 bronze Gov.-Gen. medals; 3 Ont., 2 Sask. 1 Intl outstanding achievement awards; Jamaican grand agg.; mem. DCRA council from '77, exec. comm. 9yrs; chair. coaching certification comm, service conditions matches, intl team comm., Palma comm.p.-pres. Sask Rifle Assn; exec. NCRRA, NDHQRA; res. Orleans, Ont.

BITKOWSKI, Bruno (football); b. 29 Nov 1929, Windsor, Ont.; d. 1966, Ottawa, Ont.; Assumption College; starred in football, basketball throughout HS, college; selected by Toronto's High News as all-Ont. tackle; pro Ottawa 11yrs; Big Four rookie of year '51; outstanding blocking centre; mem. '51, '60 Grey Cup winners; from '66 award in his name given annually to WSSA most gentlemanly player; mem. Windsor/Essex County Sports Hall of Fame.

BITTEN, Mike (badminton); b. 2 Jun 1962, Senneterre, Que.; m. Doris Piche; c. William Michael; pro Ottawa RA Centre; introduced to sport by father at age 10, began competing age 12; 9 ntl men's doubles titles, 4 with Mike de Belle, 5 with Bryan Blanshard; 16th world doubles ranking; Commonwealth Games team silver '86, '90, doubles bronze '90; mem. '92 Olympic, '86, '90, '94 Commonwealth Games teams; Pan-Am championships men's doubles, mixed doubles gold; Cdn Open mixed (Doris Piché), men's (Blanshard) doubles gold '89; retd from competition '94; res. Ottawa, Ont.

BITZ, Ed (softball); b. 20 Nov 1929, Wilkie, Sask.; m. Helen Lang; c. Leslie, Sheldon, Trent; UofSask, BA, BEd.; teacher; amateur baseball '46-61; coached Saskatoon men's softball team '62; began umpiring '63; Sask. Amateur Softball Assn. zone umpire '66-69, provincial umpire-in-chief '70-74; Softball Canada umpire-in-chief '72; officiated '76, '80 men's world, '78 women's world, '81 world youth championships; instrumental in producing umpiring teaching aids for use throughout Canada; mem. Sask. Sports, Softball Canada halls of fame; res. Saskatoon, Sask.

BJORN, Tyler (sailing); b. 13 Mar 1970, Montreal, Que.; Bishop's, BA; sailing consultant Byte Boats; mem. Bishop's football team '90-94; Que. sailing coach of '94; Que. Laser class rep. '89, '93 Canada Games; training partner '96 Olympics; '96 Finn Class ntl champion; ntl sailing team '97; res. Dorval, Que.

BLACK, David (golf); b. 15 Sep 1883, Troon, Scotland; d. 26 Mar 1974, Vancouver, B.C.; c. Kenneth; golf pro; emigrated to Canada '05; pro Country Club of Montreal '05-09; Rivermead GC Lucerne, Que. through '10-20; 25yrs pro Shaughnessy GC; runnerup Canadian Open '11; 4 CPGA, 2 BC Open titles; '24 Washington State Open title; '29 Pacific North West Open; with Duncan Sutherland defeated great Walter Hagen and partner in '29 exhibition; noted for putting prowess as touring pros came to him with their putting problems; mem. RCGA, BC Sports halls of fame.

BLACK, Elmer (curling); b. 28 Oct 1937, Howick, Que.; m. Brenda Baskin; c. Steve, Kim; MacDonald College; sales mgr.; softball standout 1950s-'70s; Que. schoolboy runnerup '53-55; skipped Que. rink 1964 Brier; curling instructor Montreal Bonaventure Club '63-64; held various admin. roles CBRCCC, including pres.; res. Howick, Que.

BLACK, Fred (football); b. 1 May 1930, Toronto, Ont.; given name: Frederick George; m. Patricia Miller; c. Pat, Chris, Rory, Terry, Laura, Ryan; St. Mike's College; marketing account exec.; mem. Argonauts '49-57, '59-60; CFL record: 132 league, 14 playoff games; mem. '50, '52 Grey Cup title teams; res. Rexdale, Ont.

BLACK, Ken (golf); b. 13 Jul 1912, Vancouver, B.C.; d. Nov 1995, Vancouver, B.C.; given name: Kenneth McKenzie; among Canada's top amateur golfers; national amateur titlist '39, twice runnerup; mem. 11 Willingdon Cup teams; 3 BC amateur titles, Cdn Western Open, BC Closed champion; record closing round 63 at Shaughnessy helped him defeat Byron Nelson, other top US stars in '36 Golden Jubilee tournament; mem. RCGA, BC Sports halls of fame.

BLACKBURN, Frédéric (speed skating); b. 21 Dec 1972, Chicoutimi, Que.; started skating at 7; mem. ntl team from '89; NA short track champion '87; set Cdn jr. 1500, 400m records; NA short track jr. champion '88; Cdn sr. record '91; world short track 5000m silver '90; gold '91 Ottawa short track Friendly Games; Cdn record 5000m relay '91 Albertville international; silver short track 1000m, 5000m relay '92 Olympics; mem. '94 Olympic team; gold '94 worlds; team gold '95-96, 500m bronze '96 worlds; mem. Cdn Speed Skating Hall of Fame; res. Montreal, Que.

BLACKMAN, Craig (t&f); b. 25 Feb 1951, Toronto, Ont.; given name: Craig Augustus; Oregon, BSc.; treatment centre for retarded adults operator; at least 1 gold medal each year nationals '64-72 ('71 except); PB: 22'9" long jump, 47'9" triple jump, 10.7 100m, 20.9 200m, 47.0 400m, 1:51.5 800m; mem. '71 Pan-Am, '69 Pacific Conf., '72 Olympic Games teams; 20.9 split 200m bronze NCAA mile relay; silver '72 NCAA mile relay 45.4 split; gold ntl 400m; 45.5 split in mile relay in which Canada set record 3:04.2 '72 Olympics; res. Scarborough, Ont.

BLACKWELL, Andrea (basketball); b. 23 Nov 1962, Calgary, Alta.; given name: Andrea Jill; m. Richard Bigelow; Bishop's. BA, BSc; teacher/coach; mem. Eastern Regional '78-79, provincial '78, Ont. Canada Games, ntl title teams '79; 2 Ont., ntl titles; 3 CIAU championships; mem. ntl jr. '78, sr. women's team '79-96; '83, '87, '87 FISU, '82, '86, '90, '94 worlds; '87, '91, Pan-Am Games, '84, '96 Olympic teams; mem. '82 Jones Cup title team; bronze '86 worlds; QUAA, CIAU all-star; CIAU female player of '83, CIAU MVP '84; 2 CIAU all-Cdn; Bishop's athlete of yr '83-84; Ottawa ACT basketball award; coach women's basketball Bishop's '84-92; played pro Italy, Belgium, Greece; led club team to '94 Belgian title; mem. Bishop's Athletic Wall of Distinction; res. Kingston, Ont.

BLACKWOOD, Marjorie (tennis); b. 1 May 1957, Karachi, Pakistan; m. Peter Schelling; Millfield School, Somerset, Eng., Texas, UBC; tennis pro, operator Whistler Racquets & Golf Resort; ntl jr. singles, doubles '75; consolation winner '75 Forest Hills Jr.; Rothman's Pacific Coast Open sr. title '75, ntl under-21 title '75; mem. Soisbois Cup team '75-77; 3rd round Wimbledon '82; Canada's No. 1 player '79-81; Ottawa ACT tennis award '73, '75, Ont. Sports Achievement Award '73-75, Texas tennis scholarship '75; mem. Federation Cup team '77-82, non-playing capt. '83; pro. Western Indoor TC Richmond, B.C.; prov. coach BC 2yrs; ntl touring coach 3yrs; mem. Cdn Tennis Hall of Fame; res. Whistler, B.C.

BLAIR, Don (football); b. 6 Apr 1972, Ottawa, Ont.; m. Linda Johnson; UCal; receiver; brilliant career with Calgary Dinosaurs '92-95 culminating with Vanier Cup triumph '95; 138 regular season catches for 2,611yds, 26tds; Hec Crighton, Ted Morris trophies '95; CIAU Howard, Mackie award; drafted by Chicago (NFL) '96, late training camp cut; CFL Edmonton '96-98, BC '99; CFL record (through '98): 43gp, 10td, 1cvt, 62pts, 101recept, 1749yds, 9td; wife Linda mem. '98 Cdn long track speed skating team; res. Edmonton, Alta.

BLAIR, Wren (hockey); b. 2 Oct 1925, Lindsay, Ont.; given name: Wren Alvin; hockey exec.; nicknamed "The Bird"; Ont. Sr. B title Whitby Dunlops; refused Sr. A status by OHA clubs, Blair convinced B league to turn A and challenged for Allan Cup; won league title and beat Kitchener-Waterloo Dutchmen for Ont. crown '57; '58-59 Allan Cup; world title '58 beating USSR 4-2; GM Kingston, '63 EPHL title; Boston (NHL) personnel director, signed Bobby Orr; major role in revival Oshawa Generals OHA jr. A team '62; '65 Memorial Cup; simultaneously GM Clinton Comets (EHL); coached, managed Minnesota (NHL) 8 seasons; GM Pittsburgh (NHL) '75-77; GM Saginaw Gears (IHL) 2 straight Turner Cups; dir. player personnel, farm club operations Los Angeles (NHL) '80-84; GM Kingston Frontenacs OHL '91-96; mem. Oshawa Sports Hall of Fame; res. Oshawa, Ont.

BLAIS, Ginette (trampoline); b. 8 Dec 1956, Cochrane, Ont.; given name: Ginette Marcelle Marie; Waterloo, Queen's.; competitive diver 8yrs; began trampolining '75; runnerup ntl sr. women '76, '78; with Ellen Fullerton '77 ntl jr. women's synchronized trampoline title; Cochrane HS athlete of '73; Ont. sports achievement award '78; res. Cochrane, Ont.

BLAIS, Thérèse (tennis); b. 20 Jun 1932, St. Jèrome, Que.; given name: Thérèse Helie; m. Jacques Blais; c. Richard, Pierre; tennis club pres., teacher; ranked among top 5 Que. players '50-63; 4yrs club pro Ville St.Laurent, 6yrs Laval, from '69 4 Seasons Club Laval, from '70 instructor Brébeuf College; U of Que. instructor '72; Que. Fed. instructor '75-78; authored tennis instruction manuals; conducted TV instruction clinics; TV analyst Jimmy Connors-Ile Nastase match Montreal '77; 1st ranked ntl veterans class; res. Laval, Que.

BLAKE, Rob (hockey); b. 10 Dec 1969, Simcoe, Ont.; m. Brandy Fleming; Bowling Green; defence; NHL LA Kings from '90; mem. Team Canada '91, '94, '97 worlds, '96 World Cup, '98 Olympics; competes in two-man semipro volleyball tournaments in off-season; nicknamed "Blakey"; NHL record (through '99): 531 scheduled games, 103g, 220a, 53 playoff games, 8g, 14a; Norris trophy '98; res. Los Angeles, Calif.

BLAKE, Terry (bowling); b. 6 May 1969, Happy Valley, Labrador; given name: James Gordon; herdman; 4 Nfld bowler of year awards; '92, '95 ntl 5-pin singles titles; res. Corner Brook, Nfld.

BLAKE, Toe (hockey); b. 21 Aug 1912, Victoria Mines, Ont.; d. 17 May 1995, Montreal, Que.; given name: Hector; c. Mary Jane, Joan, Bruce; retd hockey exec.; baseball Nickel Belt, Hamilton leagues, umpired Quebec Provincial League; mem. '32 Memorial Cup winner; on bench as Montreal Maroons won '35 Stanley Cup; Canadiens '36-48; nicknamed "Old Lamplighter"; left wing Punch Line with Elmer Lach, Rocket Richard; NHL record: 572 scheduled games, 235g, 292a, 57 playoff games, 25g, 37a; Hart Trophy '39, Lady Byng Trophy '46, scoring title '39; mem. 2 Stanley Cup winners; 3 times 1st, twice 2nd team all-star; coached Houston to USHL title, Buffalo (AHL), Valleyfield (Provincial) to Alexander Trophy; Canadiens '55-68; 8 Stanley Cups, record 5 in succession '56-60; mem. Order of Canada, Quebec, Canada's Sports, Hockey halls of fame.

BLANCHARD, Leo (football); b. 12 Mar 1955, Edmonton, Alta.; m. Diane; UAlta; despite standout college career in which he played in '77 Can-Am College Bowl and earned WIFL, CIAU all-Cdn status, was never drafted by CFL; joined Edmonton as offensive tackle '79-87, BC '88, Calgary '88-91; noted for durability, had string of 135 consecutive games played; CFL record: 202 games; 6 WFC, 2 all-Canadian all-star ratings; res. Victoria, B.C.

BLANEY, Fred (judo); b. 14 Nov 1955, Sudbury, Ont.; given name: Frederick Murray; m. Mary Winona Christie; NB Dept. Transport; raised in Temprance Vale, N.B.; provincial and/or Atlantic champion '74-80; gold '82, silver '83 Pan-Am Judo championships; 12 international competition medals; 4 ntl titles; mem. '84 Olympic team; mem. NB Sports Hall of Fame; res. Fredericton, N.B.

BLANSHARD, Bryan (badminton); b. 28 Jan 1966, Toronto, Ont.; m. Julie Brouillard; Carleton, BEng.; civil engineer; began playing age 6, competing age 11; ntl jr. singles, men's doubles gold '85; 3 ntl singles, 6 ntl men's doubles titles, 1 with Ian Johnson, 3 with Mike Bitten, 2 ntl

mixed doubles with Denyse Julien; more than 30 open tournament victories; ranked 16 in world men's doubles, 28 singles; '90 Commonwealth Games team silver, men's doubles bronze; mem. '92 Olympic, '90, '94 Commonwealth Games teams; 1 Cdn Open mixed doubles gold; res. Greely, Ont.

BLAXLAND, Jody (field hockey); b. 2 Sep 1963, Vancouver, B.C.; given name: Jody Margaret; m. Ian Fitzpatrick; c. Tyson, Reese, Tanner; Vancouver Community College, UBC, BPhE; BC jr. team '80-82; ntl under-21 team '82; ntl gold medal under-23 team '82; ntl sr. team from '82; mem. '82 World Cup silver medal team; competed '86 World Cup; BC HS, Burnaby community awards, Burnaby outstanding FH player award; 2 CIAU FH all-Cdn; fed. govt. excellence award '83; res. Pitt Meadows, B.C.

BLINN, Moya (weightlifting); b. 28 Sep 1950, Bournemouth, Eng.; given name: Moya Sheila Garlisi; sep.; c. Felice Sheila Jolliffe; Langara Community Coll, Red Deer Community Coll, Algonquin Community Coll.; fitness counsellor, exercise therapist, personal trainer; competed in 52 kg class; pb of 55kg snatch & 75kg clean & jerk; 2 ntl titles; 1 ntl team title; 3 BC championships; 5g, 1s BC Winter Games; 2 Mid-American, Washington State, Sea Festival gold; 1 Port Alberni open, Montreal International Cup gold; competed '87 worlds; 3 best lifter awards; res. Vancouver, B.C./Ottawa, Ont.

BLOUIN, Marc (cycling); b. 13 May 1953, Ste. Foy, Que.; m. Micheline Côté,; sales rep.; Que. novice title '69, jr. '70; mem. ntl team '71, '75 Pan-Am, '72, '76 Olympic, 3 world championships; '74 ntl road racing title team; res. Cap Rouge, Que.

BOA, Andrew (shooting); b. 1851, St. Laurent, Que.; d. 1928, St. Laurent, Que.; m., c. Andrew Stuart, James, Helen, Marion, Margaret; primarily trap and skeet shooter; launched family shooting dynasty; founded competitive rifle, pistol shooting in Quebec.

BOA, Gil (shooting); b. 8 Aug 1924, Montreal, Que.; d. 7 Sep 1973, St.Catharines, Ont.; given name: Gilmour; m. Kay Sillers; c. George, Anne, Victoria; UofT, BSc.; civil engineer; mem. Canadian international smallbore rifle team age 16; military rifle team '49-52, international pistol team '47; King's medal Connaught Ranges Ottawa '49-51; Governor-General's prize '55 (matching father's '48 performance), gold world championships '54; mem. 5 Olympic teams, bronze '56, 4th '52, '64; flag-bearer '64 summer Olympics; gold '66 Commonwealth Games; two silver, bronze '71 Pan-Am Games; 12 ntl smallbore rifle titles; mem. Cdn Amateur, Cdn Forces, Canada's Sports halls of fame.

BOA, James Sr. (shooting); b. 10 Mar 1888, St. Laurent, Que.; d. 1976, Toronto, Ont.; m., c. Gilmour, James Jr.; retd CIL salesman; 2nd generation marksman; Canadian trap champion; mem. 20 Bisley teams '20-53; Governor-General's Prize '48; 1st Canadian shooter to compete in Olympics '20.

BOA, Sandy (shooting); b. 9 Oct 1956, Toronto, Ont.; given name: George Alexander; m. Yvonne Veendaal; c. Andrew

Alexander; Ridley College, UWO, BA; banker; son of Gil Boa; raised in family steeped in shooting tradition; Ont. team '73 Canada Games; Ont., ntl jr. titles '74; Canadian cadet Bisley team '75; Ont. champion '76-77, '82; mem. 4 Benito Juarez, '79 Pan-Am Games, '80 Scandinavian championships teams; 2 gold '79 Western Canada Games; '82 Ont. Olympic prone position title; '82 Palma title team; res. Toronto, Ont.

BOA, Stuart (shooting); b. 1896, St. Laurent, Que.; d. 23 Sep 1944, Montreal, Que.; given name: Andrew Stuart; m. Ethel Louise Beer; c. John Andrew; Westmount Academy; asst. sales mgr. Dominion Ammunitions Div. CIL; 2nd generation marksman; Military Cross WWI; 5 successive ntl trap titles early '20s; initial appearance on Cdn team at Bisley at 18; Governor-General's Trophy DCRA Ottawa matches '24;

BOA, Vicki (shooting); b. 12 Apr 1955, Toronto, Ont.; given name: Victoria; m. Peter Hall; Guelph, BSc.; sales rep.; 4th generation Bisley calibre shooter; mem. 5 Ont. target rifle teams; 2 ntl, 3 Ont. titles; 1st woman to qualify for Canadian Bisley team more than once; with husband won Lake Ont. C5 35 sailing title; res. Toronto, Ont.

BOADWAY, Bob (coaching/swimming); b. 31 May 1938, Port Huron, Mich.; given name: Robert Kenton; m. Donna Lee Roberts; c. Robert Gary, Michael William, Dana Kathleen; Cal State (Long Beach), BA, Chapman Coll; HS all-American Downey CA; 2 US records; 3 US jr. ntl titles, 2 swim, 1 water polo; 3 US sr. men's, 2 NCAA water polo titles; water polo ref. '68 Olympics; swim coach; Level III CNCCP, Elite International ASCA/WSCA, Red Cross instructor/aqua leader, Royal Life Saving Society bronze cross/instructor credentials; active swim coach from '69 Downsview, North York, Burlington, Oakville, Ottawa, Gloucester, Kingston, Scarborough, Pickering, Downey CA, US Naval Base Long Beach, Hacienda Heights, Fontana CA; Ont. tech dir. '77-78, '85-89; CNCCP instructor 10yrs; 8yrs Swim Ont. dir.; 15yrs Ont. swim coaches assn. dir.; 3yrs Cdn swim coaches assn. dir.; coached Team Ont. 4 Canada Games; ntl team '75-76; 9 Ont. age group touring teams; Swim Ont. 20-yr volunteer award; 3 Ont. coach of yr awards; 1 ntl championship team title award; Cdn citizen from '76; res. Port Perry, Ont.

BODASHEFSKY, Larry (softball); b. 9 May 1956, Oshawa, Ont.; given name: Larry James; m. Bev Ross; c. Brock, Blake; Durham Coll.; surveyor; outfielder; began playing age 11 im Oshawa Park League; jr. with Oshawa Falcon TV '76-77; mem. all-star competitive team; Sr. B RH Cabinet '78 Ont. title team; began playing in ISC program '79 with Oshawa Motor Carries; through retirement '91 played for Newmarket, Oshawa, Peterborough, Owen Sound; competed in 7 ISC world tournaments; 4 times all-World; 1st Cdn named to ISC Hall of Fame; res. Oshawa, Ont.

BODOGH, Marilyn (curling); b. 9 Mar 1955, Toronto, Ont.; given name: Marilyn Catherine Bodogh; div. George Darte III; c. Gregory, Christopher; mgr. Bodogh Lumber, motivational speaker; began curling age 10; playing second for sister Christine mem. 4 Southern Ont. jr. title rinks '70-73; Ont. Winter Games winner, runnerup Canadians '71;

mem. 11 women's dist. titlists, 4 SO titlists, 2 Ont. titlists; competed 2nd on '81, skip '86, '96 Scott Tournament of Hearts winners; skip '86 women's world title; winner numerous major bonspiels; noted for loquacious, animated behavior on ice; Edmonton Grads team trophy '96; Ont. team of '86; with sister Christine St. Catharines athlete of '86 award; mem. St. Catharines Sports Hall of Fame; res. St. Catharines, Ont.

BODOGH-JURGENSON, Christine (curling); b. 31 Jul 1953, Toronto, Ont.; given name: Christine Ann Bodogh; m. Enn Jurgenson; account mgr.; nicknamed "Crisper"; as competitive swimmer excelled in backstroke; also standout in HS volleyball, track; began curling age 12; with sister Marilyn and Holly & Heather Graves won 4 SO jr., 1 Ont. Winter Games titles; runnerup Canada Winter Games '71; mem. 10 Ont. women's district, 3 SO, 2 Ont., 1 Alta. title rinks; competed 6 ntl Scott Tournament of Hearts (Lassie), 1 Alta, 2 Ont., 2 BC 1 TC; 2nd '86 women's world title rink; won '96 Saskatoon Ladies Classic, Battle of Sexes charity match (vs. Ed Werenich), several major bonspiel titles from '85; with sister Marilyn St. Catharines athlete of '86 award, Ont. team of '86; mem. St. Catharines Sports Hall of Fame; res. Vancouver, B.C.

BOEHM, Frank (bowling); b. 30 Mar 1934, Regina, Sask.; given name: Frank Michael; m. Annette Weisgerber; c. Frank Jr., Leeanne, Randy, Tracy, Susan; hydraulic technician, machinist; at 24 Regina top avg. 10-pin rookie; ntl title '64; 7th '67 world championships; '68 Canadian World Cup finals, 13th overall world championships; only Canadian to reach World FIQ finals '71; 6 Sask. doubles, 8 team titles, 12 Regina high average titles; mem. Sask. Sports Hall of Fame; res. Regina, Sask.

BOES, Allan (golf); b. 15 Jul 1910, Winnipeg, Man.; m. Nancy Gibson; c. Don, Allan, Brian, Patricia, Michael; ret. Cdn Wheat Board; began career as caddy age 11; never had a golf lesson; won Man. Open, Amateur '41, '43-44, '48, 3 times Man. Amateur runnerup; 8 times Man. Amateur medalist; 4 Winnipeg & Dist. open titles; 2nd low amateur '40 Cdn Open; set Pine Ridge (63), Kildonan Municipal (60) club records; mem. 12 Willingdon Cup teams; Willingdon Cup medalist '47; mem. '50-51 Canada Cup teams; scored Canada's only points Canada Cup singles play '50; Man. Srs. title '68; 15 Southwood club championships, 10 in succession; life mem. Southwood; scored 5 holes-in-one; mem. Man. Sports Hall of Fame; res. Winnipeg, Man.

BOESE, Kurt (wrestling); b. 4 Nov 1929, Bremen, Germany; m. Wilhelmine Lange; c. Christa, Terry; plumbing inspector; North German jr. title '44; emigrated to Canada 1952; 4 ntl, 11 Ont. 154-171lb range titles; 3 Michigan, U of Guelph open titles; 3 bronze Eastern US, AAU championships; bronze '62 Commonwealth, '63 Pan-Am Games; mem. '62 Worlds, '58 Commonwealth, '60 Olympic teams; YMCA coached teams won 6 Ont. titles; 5 times convenor Ont. jr. championships; coach Ont. team 1st Canada Winter Games, ntl team '72 Olympics, 4yrs Waterloo Lutheran, U of Waterloo '71-77; 2 OUAA titles; ntl YMCA leadership award '67; FILA silver star for contribution to Canadian wrestling '76; mem. Waterloo County, Cdn Amateur Wrestling halls of fame; res. Kitchener, Ont.

BOETTGER, Bill (lawn bowling); b. 26 Oct 1941, Kitchener, Ont.; teacher; ntl calibre 5-pin bowler; represented Ont. at ntl competitions; 17 intl lawn bowling appearances; 10 medals including gold men's pairs, bronze men's fours '93 Pacific Bowls, silver men's fours, bronze men's pairs '92 worlds; silver men's pairs '86 Commonwealth Games; also competed '90, '94 Commonwealth Games; res. Kitchener, Ont.

BOGUE, Glenn (t&f); b. 30 Aug 1955, Toronto, Ont.; given name: Glenn Patrick; Villanova, BA hons, MA, LLB; lawyer, property restoration Villanova; bronze mile relay '73 Pacific Conf. Games; Canadian Interscholastic records 21.1 200m, 46.8 400m; bronze mile relay '75 Pan-Am Games; NCAA all-American '75; 400m quarterfinalist '76 Olympics; mem. '76 world indoor dist. medley record team; bronze 400m '78 Commonwealth Games; NCAA mile relay title, all-American '78; NCAA academic all-American '76, '78; Rhodes Scholarship finalist '75; listed Who's Who in American Colleges; services mgr. CTFA; res. Haverford, Pa.

BOHAY, Gary (wrestling); b. 26 Dec 1960, Burnaby, B.C.; Arizona; too small for football he began wrestling at 14; 1st international bout at 23; joined ntl team '83; 6 ntl 62kg freestyle titles; '89 world cup silver; '89 world championships bronze; '87 Yugoslavian Invitational gold; mem. '83 Pan-Ams, '88 Olympic, '90 Goodwill Games teams; Canada's outstanding wrestler award '86, '89; res. Tucson, Ariz.

BOILEAU, Art (t&f); b. 9 Oct 1957, Edmonton, Alta.; m. Ranza Clark; Oregon, BA; mgr. Forerunners; distance runner; 2 ntl marathon titles; competed '83, '93 Worlds, 3 Boston Marathons, 2nd '86 in PB 2:11.15; 3rd '84 National Capital Marathon; twice 10th Fukuoka marathon; mem. '84, '88 Olympic, '86 Commonwealth Games teams; won Los Angeles marathon '87, '89; competes at masters level; res. Vancouver, B.C.

BOILEAU, Myriam (diving); b. 25 Nov 1977, Montreal, Que.; mem. ntl team '92-98; 1m bronze '92 Can-AM-MEX jr. series; 10m bronze '94, silver '98, 3m bronze '98 Commonwealth Games; 1st Cdn to win gold (10m) Rostock GP '99; res. Blainville, Que.

BOIVIN, Leo (hockey); b. 2 Aug 1932, Prescott, Ont.; given name: Leo Joseph; m. Patricia Kirkby; c. Mitch, Paul, Danny; retd. hockey scout; starred with Inkerman Rockets jr. team; mem. Port Arthur West End Bruins; rugged defenceman noted for bodychecking skills; turned pro Pittsburgh (AHL) '51; promoted to Toronto (NHL) for 2 games same season; dealt to Boston '54-66, to Detroit '66-67, Pittsburgh '67-69, Minnesota '68-70; NHL record: 1150 scheduled games, 72g, 250a, 54 playoff games, 3g, 10a; capt. Bruins '63-66; played in 3 all-star games; coached St.Louis '76, '77, Ottawa 67's '72-74; scout St. Louis, Hartford '75-93; mem. Ottawa Sports, Hockey halls of Fame; res. Prescott, Ont.

BOL, René (water polo); b. 5 Jul 1956, Upper Hutt, N.Z.; Carleton; water polo coach; 2nd '74 NZ surf life saving championships; mem. NZ ntl water polo team '74-76; 4 BC invitational title teams; bronze '79, '83 Pan-Am Games;

mem. '77, '79, '81, '83 FISU Games, '84 Olympic teams; 1st '82 ntl championships as mem. BC team; coach UofOtt team '81-84; res. Canberra, Australia

BOLAND, Pat (basketball); b. 13 Apr 1943, Ottawa, Ont.; given name: Patricia Pisnook; m. Kevin Boland; UMan, BA; women's athletic dir. Concordia U; UMan athlete of '63; MVP, all-star '65 Canadian women's basketball championships; team bronze '67 Pan-Am Games; mgr. ntl women's team '73; v.-pres. Quebec Basketball Fed.; mem. National Advisory Council Fitness and Amateur Sport; v.-pres. QUAA, pres. animation research comm.; TV commentator '76 women's Olympic basketball; mem. CWIAU council; chairperson '73 ntl university championships; res. Montreal, Que.

BOLDIREV, Ivan (hockey); b. 15 Aug 1949, Zranjanin, Yugoslavia; left wing Oshawa (OHA) '67-69, Oklahoma City (CHL); claimed in '69 entry draft by Boston; played in NHL with Boston '70-71, California '71-74, Chicago '74-79, Atlanta '79-80, Vancouver '80-83, Detroit '83-85; NHL record: 15 seasons, 1052 scheduled games, 361g, 505a, 48 playoff games, 13g, 20a; res. Detroit, Mich.

BOLDT, Arnold (t&f); b. 16 Sep 1957, Osler, Sask; given name: Arnold William; UMan; teacher; lost leg in grain auger age 3; through determined effort pursued athletic interests in swimming, skiing, volleyball, t&f; gold high jump, long jump '76 Olympiad for Disabled; HJ gold '92 Paralympics; world high jump record for one-legged jumper 1.86m; surpassed it same year K of C Games Saskatoon with 1.94m; progressed steadily boosting world disabled HJ record to 2.04m and LJ to 3.01m Rome '81; Man. indoor HJ record (handicapped and able-bodied) 2.08m; 5 Paralympic championships; unbeaten in disabled meets '76-93; Cdn. flag-bearer '92 Barcelona Paralympics; mem. Canada's, Sask, Terry Fox Sports halls of fame; res. Thompson, Man.

BOLDUC, Alain (boardsailing); b. 3 Aug 1972, Carignan, Que.; U Montreal; began sailing age 4, windsurfing age 14; Eastern Cdn, CYA 23 and under titles '95; silver fleet bronze '94 world championships; mem. '96 Olympic team; Marvin McDill CYA rookie of year award '93; Que. Sailing Fed. athlete of year '93; res. Longueuil, Que.

BOLGER, Pat (wrestling/judo); b. 31 Jan 1948, Alexandria, Ont.; given name: Patrick John; Oklahoma, Waterloo, hons. BA; educator; began wrestling at 14 and never lost a high school bout; won 2 OFSAA titles, Midwestern US title; 7 ntl wrestling titles; OQAA, CIAU, Canadian open wrestling titlist '69; silver '70 Commonwealth, bronze '71 Pan-Am Games; mem. '68, '72 Olympic, '67 Pan-Am, '70-71 World championships, '69, '73 FISU Games teams; coach ntl team Tel Aviv memorial tournament '75; earned judo black belt at 16; 4 Canadian, 1 US jr. judo titles; 2 Oklahoma State titles; '65 NA judo title; judo silver '67 Pan-Am, NA high school, bronze '67 world, '68 US ntl championships; quit judo team when refused permission to represent Canada in both judo, wrestling '72 Olympics after qualifying for both teams; retired '73; 2 Waterloo outstanding athletic career awards; 2 Viscount Alexander Canadian junior athlete of year awards; mem. Canadian Amateur Wrestling Hall of Fame; res. Toronto, Ont.

BOLL, Buzz (hockey); b. 6 Mar 1910, Fillmore, Sask.; d. 23 Jan 1990, Regina, Sask.; given name: Frank Thorman; m. Leona Volbrecht; c. William; Regina Teachers College; retired farmer; mem. '30 Regina Pats Memorial Cup winner; sr. Weyburn Beavers, Toronto Marlboros; pro Syracuse; Toronto '33-38, NY Americans '39-42, Boston '42-44; NHL regular season record 133g, 130a, playoffs 7g, 3a; mem. Sask. Sports Hall of Fame.

BOLL, Rod (shooting); b. 9 Jul 1952, Fillmore, Sask.; trapshooting specialist; mem ntl team from '94; 6 ntl titles in single, double, team trap; world double trap title '94; mem. '96 Olympic Games; res. Fillmore, Sask.

BOND-MILLS, Catherine (t&f); b. 20 Sep 1967, Woodstock, Ont.; given name: Catherine Bond; m. David Mills; UofT; hospital pharmacist; ntl jr. high jump silver; rep. Canada from '85; CIAU indoor, Canada Games multiple medallist; competed '92, '96 Olympics, '90, '94, '98 Commonwealth; 10 ntl heptathlon titles; ntl record 6193 points; achieved PB 6206 points Goetzis, Austria '94; ntl long jump title with PB 6.32 '94; heptathlon bronze '94 Commonwealth Games; CTFA Dr. Fred Tees CIAU athlete of '90 award; UofT Past-Pres. award, athlete of '90; mem. Woodstock TC; res. London, Ont.

BONIFACE, George (baseball); b. 24 Nov 1926, Clifton, N.J.; given name: George Victor; m. Thelma Dwyar; c. Joanne; service mgr.; pro shortstop, 2nd baseman Jamestown (Pony), Johnson City, Tenn, Rochester, Allentown '43-45, '48-49; Sr. IC Stratford, Kitchener-Waterloo '49-64; frequent all-star 2nd baseman; mgr. K-W Dutchmen '58-62; twice all-star mgr.; res. Kitchener, Ont.

BONK, John (football); b. 27 Aug 1950, Hamilton, Ont.; m. Chris; c. Jessie; jr. Burlington Braves '70-71; CFL centre Hamilton '72-73, Winnipeg '73-85; 4 WFC, CFL all-star; 2 Becket-Demarco WFC outstanding lineman awards; Schenley outstanding lineman '84; mem. '84 Grey Cup winner; FB broadcaster '86-91; asst. coach Hamilton '92-93; mem. Blue Bombers Hall of Fame; res. Stoney Creek, Ont.

BONNEAU, Stéphane (tennis); b. 8 Dec 1961, Chicoutimi, Que.; teaching pro; Que. age group titles; ntl under-8 champion; 3 times mem. Galea, Davis Cup teams; semifinalist '79 US Open; mem. Que., Canadian teams '77-92; 2nd ranked Que., 3rd Canada '81; most improved Que. jr. '79; with Caroline Delisle '92 Sun Life mixed doubles; Sun Life ntl singles '84-85; with Martin Dyotte men's ntl doubles '84; mem. '80-85 Davis Cup team; ranked among Quebec's top 10 athletes '79; res. Laval, Que.

BONNELLO, Bonny (equestrian); b. 17 Dec 1950, England; given name: Frances Ann; m. Chesson; began riding age 4, in hunter jumper competitions; at 13 introduced to dressage; campaigned in Europe 1st time '75; with purchase of Satchmo '78 began to impress in international events; mem. '80 Olympic team; res. Sherwood Park, Alta.

BONNEY, Wayne (officiating/hockey); b. 27 May 1953, Ottawa, Ont.; m. Claudette Brophy; c. Allyson; played minor hockey, baseball Ottawa/Nepean; father Merv prominent baseball umpire; began pro hockey officiating in WHA

moving to NHL '79 as linesman; operates off-season officiating school; NHL officiating record (all as linesman): 1309 scheduled games, 202 playoff games; res. Mesa, Ariz.

BONNYCASTLE, Charles (builder); b. 6 Dec 1904, Winnipeg, Man.; d. 13 Nov 1985, Saint John, N.B.; given name: Charles Humphrey; UNB, hon. LLB.; educator; nicknamed "Hum"; largely responsible for Saint John area rowing revival; formed Kennebecasis Rowing Club '71; chair. Renforth Regatta '71-76; CARA dir. '72; helped form NBRA '73, Fredericton Rowing Club '75; posted victories Royal Canadian Henley '77, '81, Redding, Eng. International '81, Cdn Ntls '82; NB rowing champion '79; freeman village of Renforth; mem. NB Sports Hall of Fame.

BOON, Dickie (hockey); b. 14 Feb 1874, Belleville, Ont.; d. 3 May 1961, Outremont, Que.; jr. Montreal Young Crystals; defenceman Monarch HC 1897, Montreal AAA jrs. 1898-1900, srs. '01 helping win Stanley Cup vs. Winnipeg Victorias '02; nicknamed "Little Iron Man"; mgr. Montreal Wanderers '03; 3 Stanley Cups before '16 retirement; never played pro hockey; mem. Hockey Hall of Fame.

BORDELEAU, Alain (t&f); b. 7 Oct 1956, Lachine, Que.; m.; Montreal; distance runner; gold world cross-country trials '81; runnerup National Capital marathon, ntl cross-country '84; mem. '84 Olympic team; res. Laval, Que.

BORODOW, Andy (wrestling); b. 16 Sep 1969, Montreal, Que.; heavyweight; mem. ntl team from '87; 130kg silver FS '92 Pan-Am championships, bronze Greco-Roman '91, 2 bronze '95 Pan-Am Games; 6 ntl FS, 2 GR titles; competed '92, '96 Olympics; 130kg FS gold '94 Commonwealth Games, '85, '89, '93 Maccabiah Games; res. Montreal, Que.

BOROWY, Janet (field hockey); b. 7 Jan 1961, Toronto, Ont.; given name: Janet Elizabeth; Queen's, hons. BA; Ont. jr. '79-80; Ont. team '81 Canada Winter Games; Ont. sr. '81-82; ntl under-21 team '82; silver medal team World Cup '83; fed. govt. excellence award '83; res. Islington, Ont.

BORSHOLT, Lisa (swimming); b. 5 Apr 1962, North Vancouver, B.C.; given name: Lisa Ann; m. Greenwood; Texas; 100m, 200m breaststroke specialist; mem. ntl team '75-84; '76, '84 Olympic, '78, '82 Commonwealth, '83 FISU Games teams; gold 200m '78 Commonwealth Games, world championships; gold 100m, 200m '80-81 winter, summer nationals; res. N. Vancouver, B.C.

BORST, Cathy (curling); b. 3 Sep 1959, Winnipeg, Man.; given name: Cathy King; sep; c. Karston, Travis, Kyle; ntl jr. titles '77-78; prov. mixed titles '88, '94; Alta. women's titles '95, '97-98; skip Scott Tournament of Hearts title '98; nicknamed "Snow White"; res. Edmonton, Alta.

BORTHWICK, Gayle (golf); b. 3 Dec 1943, Regina, Sask.; given name: Patricia Gayle Hitchens; m. Robert John Borthwick; c. Julie; UBC, BEd; teacher; only golfer in Canada to win all four ntl titles, jr. '61, women's amateur '62, mid amateur '92, srs '94-95; won USGA sr. women's title '96; runnerup ntl jr. '60, 4 women's amateurs, 3 Ont. amateurs, 2 BC amateurs, 2 ntl srs. mem. 3 Cdn Commonwealth, 4 Cdn world, 1 Cdn British Amateur teams;

capt. Cdn team '80 British Amateur, 2 world amateur teams; won '70 Australian 2-ball title; 2 BC jr., 2 BC, Ont. amateur, 2 Ont. mid amateur, 2 Ont. sr. titles; mem. 2 BC jr, 7 BC, 13 Ont amateur, 2 Ont. sr. teams; teams chair. OLGA '81-83; Mississauga dist. exec. course rating '78-80; pres. women's intermediate golf assn '89; 4yrs OLGA, CLGA advisory comm.; dir. Ada Mackenzie Memorial Foundation from '85, pres. '92-93; mem. Mississauga Hospital charity tournament comm. '95-96; mem. BC Golf, RCGA, Mississauga Sports halls of fame; res. Mississauga, Ont.

BOSCHMAN, Laurie (hockey); b. 4 Jun 1960, Major, Sask.; given name: Laurie Joseph; m. Nancy Friesen; c. Brent, Mark, Jeffrey; Ottawa. EO dir. Hockey Ministries International, Man. shoe stores partner; centre Brandon (WHL) '76-79, New Brunswick (AHL) '80; 1st pick Toronto '79 entry draft; NHL with Toronto '79-82, Edmonton '82-83, Winnipeg '83-90, New Jersey '90-92, Ottawa '92-93; Ottawa capt.; NHL record: 14 seasons, 1009 scheduled games, 229g, 348a, 57 playoff games, 8g, 13a; WHL all-star '79; res. Stittsville, Ont.

BOSHUCK, Wally (speed skating); b.12 Oct 1928, Saskatoon, Sask.; given name: Walter; m. Dorothy Carrick; c. Lori, Ralph, William, Shawn, Kevin; UofSask BPharm; retd. pharmacist; began speed skating at 16; competed for 7yrs before arthritis forced him to hang up skates; set provincial 220, 440yd records; pres. Saskatoon Lions speed skating club at 18; over the years has served as referee, starter, clerk of course, corner judge, finish line judge, recorder, timer and meet co-ordinator; mem. comm. which wrote modern CASSA constitution; organized clubs in North Battleford, Prince Albert, Moose Jaw; 5yrs dir., 3yrs treas., 1yr vp CASSA; 2 terms pres. SASSA, pres. Saskatoon Lions SSC; developed learn to skate program for youngsters; mgr. Canadian tour for Chinese team; active as coach from '40s; associate life mem. CASSA; '83 Racer award for contribution to sport; CASSA Air Canada official of year nominee twice; Centennial award; CASSA award of merit; mem. Sask. Sports, Cdn Speed Skating halls of fame; res. Moose Jaw, Sask.

BOSS, Leonard (baseball); b. 19 Oct 1919, Springhill, N.S.; m. Colette; c. Joann, Gary; retired miner; regarded as greatest fireballing righthanded pitcher in H&D history; while statistics vague indications are he won 75 per cent of games pitched; authored two no-hitters, several 1-hitters; pitched famed Fence Busters to 4 provincial titles during '40s; mem. Truro Bearcats '47; rejoined Fence Busters '48-49, Halifax Shipyards '50; all-star MVP '50; rejected pro offers from Boston Red Sox, Philadelphia Phillies; mem. NS Sports Hall of Fame; res. Wakefield, RI

BOSSY, Mike (hockey); b. 22 Jan 1957, Montreal, Que.; given name: Michael Dean; m. Lucie Creamer; c. Josiane, Tanya; PR director Humpty Dumpty; jr. Laval Nationals; NY Islanders 1st choice, 15th overall '77 amateur draft; during 4-year jr. career displayed scoring flare with 309 goals; skill carried into NHL as he set '78 rookie scoring record 53 goals; Calder Memorial Trophy; 9 consecutive 50-plus goals seasons; 4 60-plus goal seasons; 1st player to reach 200-goal plateau in 4 seasons; equalled Maurice Richard standard 50 goals in 50 games '80-81; NHL record 35 points 1 playoff year '81; only player in NHL history to

score Stanley Cup series winning goals in consecutive seasons; top Stanley Cup goal scorer '85; set single season hat-tricks record '81; 5 times 1st, 3 2nd team all-star right wing; youngest ever to achieve 500 NHL goal plateau; Conn Smythe Trophy '82; 3 Lady Byng awards; mem. 4 consecutive Stanley Cup winners; chronic back injury forced retirement following '86-87 season; 10yr NHL record: 752 scheduled games, 573g, 553a, 129 playoff games, 85g, 75a; MVP Team Canada '79 Challenge Cup series; competed in '81 (MVP), '84 Canada Cup tournaments; governor Laval Jr.; with Barry Meisel co-authored *"Boss - the Mike Bossy Story"*; Cdn Society of New York achievement award; mem. Hockey, QMJHL hockey halls of fame; res. Laval, Que.

BOTT, Punch (skiing); b. 24 Apr 1917, Montreal, Que.; d. 21 Mar 1994, Pt. Coquitlam, B.C.; given name: Percival Christian; began skiing as elementary school student in Côte des Neiges; one of Canada's skiing standouts in late '30s, early '40s; 11 CASA ntl title medals; holds unique distinction of winning both CASA ntl alpine and nordic titles; began ski jumping '27; tabbed as "schoolboy wonder"; self-coached; won inumerable SCM, City of Montreal, Quebec, Ontario titles; set 160' jump record on now defunct Montreal Ski Hill '38; capt. '36 HS football team; mem. QRFU Westmount Jr. FB title team '37; also played sr. hockey; mem. Cdn Skiing Hall of Fame.

BOTTING, Steve (canoeing); b. 5 Dec 1959, Montreal, Que.; Concordia; '76 ntl juvenile C2 500m; '77 NA jr. C1 500m, ntl juvenile C1, C4 500m; '79 Continental Cup C2 500m; '80 Olympic trials C2 500m, 1000m, Zaandam regatta C2 500m, 1000m; '80-81 ntl C2 500m, 1000m, C4 1000m, '82 C2 500m; ntl sr. record 4:21.1 C4 1000m; mem. '80, '84 Olympic teams; res. Westmount, Que.

BOTTOMS, Lynn (football); b. 2 Jul 1933, Edmonton, Alta.; given name: Lynn Anthony; div; c. John Joseph, Lynn Jr, Michael; Washington, BSc, ME; teacher; catcher, shortstop Sunnybrook sr. softball team '46-50; shortstop Forest Lawn baseball club '50-53; HS football, minor hockey '51-53; Calgary jr. Broncs football '52-53; pro Calgary '54-60, Toronto '60-64; mem. sr. softball Cobourg '64-70; HS football coach from '66; international, regional old timers hockey tournaments from '77; Calgary Broncs outstanding player '53; WFC rookie of '54; provincial award as 1 of top 10 athletes in 1st half century Alta. '55; 3 East-West Shrine Game teams; 4 times Stampeders punt return leader, twice WIFU, Argos; def. right halfback Calgary 50-year dream team '70; regional hockey referee; res. Cobourg, Ont.

BOUCHARD, Butch (hockey); b. 4 Sep 1919, Montreal, Que.; given name: Émile Joseph Calixte; m. Marie Claire MacBeth; c. Pierre, Jean, Émile Jr., Michel, Suzanne; retd. restaurateur; defensive, playmaking standout Montreal Canadiens '41-56; 3 times 1st, twice 2nd team all-star; team capt.; 785 scheduled games, 49g, 144a, 113 playoff games, 11g, 21a; , coach, exec. jr. clubs; dir.-pres. Montreal Royals baseball club; mem. 4 Stanley Cup winners; mem. Que. Sports, Hockey halls of fame; res. Vercheres, Que./Belair, Fla./Montreal, Que.

BOUCHARD, Dan (hockey); b. 12 Dec 1950, Val d'Or, Que.; given name: Daniel Hector; m. Janet Ratcliffe; c.

Jordan, Lindsay; v.-pres SPT Product Development; goaltender; jr. London Knights; pro Hershey (AHL) '70-71, Oklahoma City (CHL) '71-72, Boston (AHL) '71-72, NHL Atlanta, Calgary, Quebec, Winnipeg '72-86; NHL record: 655 scheduled games, 286-232-113, 37,919min, 2061ga, 27s, 43 playoff games, 13-30-0, 2549min, 147ga, 1sho; competed Canada-Russia series '77; played briefly in France; goalie coach Quebec Nordiques 4yrs; father Marcel minor-league player; Hap Holmes (AHL) trophy '72; underwent brain surgery '90; coach Life U title hockey team '97-98; res. Marietta, Ga.

BOUCHARD, Rèmi (golf); b. 31 Jan 1964, Lasalle, Que.; Indiana; pro golfer; Que jr. title '82; won Duke of Kent '84, Que. amateur '87; mem. '87 all Big-10, Willingdon Cup teams; pro from '87; won '89 India Open, CPGA winter tour, '88 Que. PGA, Cdn. Asst. pro, Bic Open; '87 Que. rookie of year, asst. pro of year, Que. pro of year; won Que. Tour La Sauvegarde Cap-Rouge; competed in Asia, US mini-tours; res. Brossard, Que.

BOUCHARD, Sylvain (speed skating); b. 12 Apr 1970, Loretteville, Que.; Laval; began skating age 5; played hockey to age 12; competed in short track to age 16 then switched to long track; power skating teacher; mem. ntl team from '88; 2 ntl juve. long track titles; 3 ntl sprint titles; world record 1000m; competed '94 Olympics; world single distance championship gold '98; 1000m bronze '95, gold '98 world sprints; retd. from competition '98; res. Loretteville. Que.

BOUCHER, Alain (t&f); b. 26 May 1963, North Bay, Ont.; given name: Alain Steve; m. Michelle Louise Cournoyer; c. Nathalie; Danielle; U New Mexico, Uof Ott, BPhE, Uof T, BEd; teacher; steeplechase, road running specialist; Ont. HS cross-country, 2000m steeplechase titles '82; Pan-Am jr. SC, ntl jr. 2000m SC titles '82; OFSAA 2000m SC record 5:37; ntl scholastic 2000m SC record; held ntl jr. 2000m SC record; 1 gold, 5 silver, 2 bronze ntl 3000m SC championships; SC gold '82 Pan-Am championships; competed '82 world jr., '88 world sr. XC, '84 Pan-Pacific SC, '89 FISU, Francophone Games, '90 Commonwealth Games, '91 Ekiden Japan road race; 9 Ont. SC titles; 3 Fergie Dowdal outstanding track athletes awards; '82 North Bay athlete of yr.; dominant road racer '94-98 winning 63 races; 4 NCRA, 3 Ottawa Lions road racer of yr awards; Ottawa ACT road racer of '98 award; mem. North Bay Sports Hall of Fame; res. Kanata, Ont.

BOUCHER, Bill (hockey); b. 10 Nov 1899, Ottawa, Ont.; d. 10 Nov 1958, Ottawa, Ont.; m. Thérèsa Payette; c. Bob, Bill, June; civil servant; pro Canadiens '21-26; top scorer when Habs won '24 Stanley Cup; Boston '26-27, NY Americans '27-28; with Habs right wing on line with Howie Morenz, Aurel Joliat; career total 90g, 34a.

BOUCHER, Bob (hockey); b. 23 Mar 1938, Ottawa, Ont.; given name: Robert Joseph; m. Anne Marie O'Niell; c. Trisha, Kerri Marie, Robbie; UofOtt, Carleton, St.Mary's; scoring leader Ottawa-Hull Jr. Canadiens '57-58 Memorial Cup team; pro Hull-Ottawa (EPHL); coach St. Mary's 13 years, 7 consecutive conference titles; twice CIAU hockey coach of year; asst. coach Philadelphia (NHL) '80-83; coach Windsor (OHL) '83-84; res. River Bourgeois, N.S.

BOUCHER, Frank (hockey); b. 7 Oct 1901, Ottawa, Ont.; d. 12 Dec 1977, Kemptville, Ont.; m. Agnes Sylvester; c. Earl; hockey executive, farmer; early prominence Ottawa's New Edinburgh region starring in hockey, baseball, football; pro hockey Ottawa Senators '21, Vancouver Maroons '22-26, NY Rangers '26-38, '43-44, coach NY Rovers (EAHL) '38-39, Rangers '39-48; GM Rangers '48-55; centred line of Bill, Bun Cook with Rangers; Lady Byng Trophy 7 times in 8 years gave him permanent possession original trophy; led US div. NHL scorers '34 with 14g, 30a; pro career record 219g, 298a; Western Canada Jr. Hockey commissioner 10 years, deposed over rules dispute; mem. Ottawa, Kingston, Madison Square Gardens, Canada's Sports, Hockey halls of fame.

BOUCHER, Frank (hockey); b. 3 Mar 1918, Ottawa, Ont.; given name: Frank George; m. Marguerite Carruthers; c. Diane; accountant; Ottawa midget champions '31; 2 EOSSA jr. titles Lisgar HS; NY Rovers '37-39, league, US titles '38; AHL Providence, Philadelphia; mem. '42 Eastern Canadian finalist Ottawa RCAF Flyers; coach '48 Olympic, world champion RCAF Flyers; playing-mgr. Wembley Lions '49-53, English ntl title '52; coach Belleville srs. '54; playing-coach RCAF teams '55-68; business mgr. Ottawa-based Team Canada '69; son of Hall of Famer Buck Boucher; mem. Olympic Club Canada, Canadian Forces Sports Hall of Fame; res. Mountain, Ont.

BOUCHER, Gaétan (speed skating); b. 10 May 1958, Charlesbourg, Que.; m. Karin Fliege; c. 2;Montreal, UCal; sprinted into ntl prominence at 15 winning indoor, outdoor titles; jr. ntl all-around titles '74, '77; world indoor 1000m, 500m, all-around '77; NA all-around, swept ntl team trials '79; ntl indoor 3000m, world indoor 1000m, 1500m, 3000m, all-around, ntl 3000m, 500m, 1500m, 5000m, all-around '80; world record 1:13.39 1000m, 148,785 all-around points '81 Swiss International; world short track 3000m '81; world outdoor 500m, runnerup world sprint all-around, world short track all-around '82; ntl 3000m record 4:27.01; competed '80, '84, '88 Olympics; silver 1000m '80, gold 1000m, 1500m, bronze 500m '84 Olympics; 1st Canadian Winter Olympic triple medalist '84; world sprint title '84; Que. athlete of '77, 3 times French Canadian athlete of year; Viscount Alexander award '77; 4 SFC athlete of month awards; Dick Ellis Memorial Trophy team mem. '81; CASSA skater of '80; Thompson Trophy fastest Canadian 500m '76-82; Canadian Superstars title '80; fed. govt. sport excellence award '82, champions award '84; flag bearer '84 winter Olympics; Lou Marsh, Norton Crowe trophies '84; Seagram 5 Star award '84; named Que. athlete of '80s; 1st Cdn recipient ISU Jacques Favart trophy; honorary Montreal Canadien; PR attach, Dairy Bureau of Canada; Officer Order of Canada '83; mem. Cdn Amateur, Cdn Winter Olympic, Cdn Speed Skating, Que., Canada's Sports halls of fame; res. Rosemere, Que.

BOUCHER, George (hockey); b. 12 Aug 1895, Ottawa, Ont.; d 17 Oct 1960, Ottawa, Ont.; m. Mabel Olsen; c. Earl (d), Frank; hockey coach, farmer; eldest of famed Boucher brothers, nicknamed "Buck"; halfback '15-'18 Rough Riders; pro hockey Ottawa Senators '15-27, 4 Stanley Cup victories; Montreal Maroons '28-29, Chicago '30-34; 122 career goals; coach Chicago, Ottawa, Boston, St. Louis, Springfield, Noranda, Quebec; coached '49 Ottawa Allan

Cup winner; helped select, train '48 Ottawa RCAF Olympic, world champions coached by son Frank; mem. Ottawa Sports, Hockey halls of fame.

BOUCHER, Kelly (basketball); b. 13 Jan 1968, Calgary, Alta.; UVic, UCal; forward/guard; began playing Grade 7; mem. ntl team '88-97; jr ntl team '86-87; temporarily retd '91-92; competed in '89, '93 COPABA world qualification tournament, '94 Goodwill Games, '94 World championship tournament teams; mem. COPABA gold medal team '95; played pro Italy, Switzerland, Luxembourg, Hungary '92-97; 5 CIAU all-conference, 1 all-Canadian awards; 1st Cdn woman signed to play in WNBA with Charlotte Sting '98; Calgary HS female athlete of '85; participant in COA Adopt-an-athlete program; res. Charlotte, N.C./Calgary, Alta.

BOURASSA, Jocelyne (golf); b. 30 May 1947, Shawinigan, Que.; Montreal, BA, Wisc, BSc; retd pro golfer, promotions, PR Houston Group; nicknamed "Frenchy"; U of Montreal basketball, volleyball, skiing, track star; Que. jr. title '63-65, ladies' amateur '63, '69-71; ntl ladies amateur title '65, '71; Ont. title '71; Scottish girls title '67; low amateur Supertest championship '69; mem. winning World Cup team '70; NZ amateur '71; ntl women's match title '65; LPGA rookie of '72; La Canadienne LPGA tournament title in playoff '73; twice among top 20 LPGA money winners; LPGA most colorful player award '72; Canadian National Advisory Council '73-74; Bobbie Rosenfeld trophy '72, twice French Canadian athlete of year; LPGA treasurer '74-75; 2yr stint as sports writer; golf coach Arizona State '80; mem. Simpson-Sears sports advisory council '75-78; PR with Houston Group from '80; ED du Maurier Classic from '80; Score magazine lifetime achievment award; mem. Order of Canada, RCGA, Que. Sports halls of fame; res. Montreal, Que.

BOURDEAU, Yvan (t&f); b. 6 Sep 1959, Beauport, Que.; social worker; blind sprint, long, triple jump specialist; gold '80 Olympic LJ; ntl titles LJ '81-83, TJ '82-83, 200m, 4x200 relay, 60m '82, 100m '83; res. Quebec City, Que.

BOURGEOIS, Joel (t&f); b. 25 Apr 1971, Grand-Digue, N.B.; c. Naomi; Moncton, B.Mus; steeplechase specialist; top Cdn finisher '92 world cross-country; CIAU X-C gold '94; competed '94, '98 Commonwealth, '95, '99 Pan-Am, '96 Olympic, '91, '93, '95, '97, /99 FISU Games; 4 ntl titles; won '96 Penn Relays; set PB 8:20.08 '99; 3000mSC silver '95, bronze '99 FISU Games; SC gold '99 PAG; res. Grand-Digue, N.B.

BOURNE, Munroe (swimming); b. 26 Jun 1910, Victoria, B.C.; d. 11 Jul 1992, Rothesay, N.B.; given name: Frederick Munroe; m. Margaret Fairweather; c. Robert, Richard, Mary; McGill, BA, MD, Oxford, BA, MA; physician; mem. '28, '32, '36 Olympic teams; team capt. '36; bronze 4x200m '28; 3 gold '30 BE Games; 50m '33 international student games; 100m backstroke, relay Dublin Tailteann '28; mem. McGill, Oxford swimming, water polo teams; pres. Oxford SC '34-35; mem. Montreal AAA; mem. London Otters SC, ntl team race title '34-35; represented Oxford Langlauf skiing '34-35, McGill, MAAA, Oxford in T&F; capt. 3 McGill teams leading them to 2 swimming, 4 t&f, 2 water polo titles; 5 intercollegiate, 2 ntl records; coach McGill swim team '38-40; Rhodes Scholar; Commander Order of St. John '75; mem. Cdn Aquatic, Amateur, McGill Sports halls of fame.

BOURNE, Shae-Lynn (figure skating); b. 24 Jan 1976, Chatham, Ont.; began skating age 7; mem. ntl team from '92; teamed with Victor Kraatz to become top Cdn ice dance duo; 7 ntl, 5 Skate Canada titles; 2 NKH trophy silver; 3 world bronze; gold, silver Championship Series; Nebelhorn Trophy, Grand Prix International gold; competed '94, '98 Olympics; res. Lake Placid, N.Y.

BOURQUE, Ray (hockey); b. 28 Dec 1960, Montreal, Que.; given name: Raymond Jean; m. Christiane; c. Melissa, Christopher, Ryan; defence, Sorel, Verdun (QMJHL) '76-79; drafted by Boston '79; team capt.from '85-86; Calder Trophy '80; 5 Norris trophies; King Clancy trophy '92; 12 1st, 5 2nd all-star teams; played in 15 NHL all-star games; '96 all-star game MVP; became Bruins' all-time leading scorer Feb '97; Canada Cup '81, '84, '87; mem. '98 Olympic team; NHL record (through '99): 1453 scheduled games, 385g, 1083a, 180 playoff games, 36g, 125a; does extensive work for children's charities; res. Boxford, Mass.

BOWDEN, Norris (figure skating); b. 13 Aug 1926, Toronto, Ont.; d. 9 Apr 1991, North York, Ont.; given name: Robert Norris; m. Joan; c. David, Kathy, Danny; UofT, BSc, MBA; chartered life underwriter; '47 ntl men's singles title; with Frances Dafoe ntl pairs '52-55, dance '52, NA pairs '53-56, world pairs '54-55; silver '56 Olympics; international skating judge; flag-bearer '56 winter Olympics; mem. Cdn, US Figure Skating, Cdn Amateur, Cdn Winter Olympic, Canada's Sports halls of fame.

BOWEN, Stacy (t&f); b. 17 Dec 1969, Montego Bay, Jamaica; Alabama; social worker; sprint specialist; ntl jr. 200m title '88; Canada Games record 200m, also 100m gold '89; 3 ntl 200m, 1 400m titles; competed in '90, '94 Commonwealth, '91 Pan-Am, '92 Olympic, '93 FISU, Worlds; 2 gold '94 Francophone Games; bronze 4x400 '94 Commonwealth Games; PB: 11.45 100m, 23.16 200m, 52.28 400m; mem. Phoenix TC; res. Downsview, Ont./ Tuscaloosa, Ala.

BOWER, Johnny (hockey); b. 8 Nov 1924, Prince Albert, Sask; given name: John William; m. Nancy Brain; c. John Jr., Cynthia; hockey scout; jr. Prince Albert; Providence, Cleveland (AHL) '45-56, brief stint NY Rangers, Vancouver (WHL) mid-50s; Maple Leafs '58-70; NHL record: 534 scheduled games, 37so, 2.53 goals-against avg., 72 playoff games, 5so, 2.58 avg.; once 1st team all-star; Vezina Trophy '61, with Terry Sawchuk '65; 3 times Bickell Trophy (most valuable Leaf); 5 times AHL all-star, 3 times Hap Holmes Memorial Trophy AHL MVP, 3 times Leslie Cunningham Trophy; leading goaler award Vancouver '55; following playing career remained with Leafs organization as scout, head scout, asst coach; mem. Canada's, Etobicoke, Sask Sports, Hockey halls of fame; res. Toronto, Ont.

BOWES, Sharon (shooting); b. 17 Sep 1966, Windsor, Ont.; Waterloo; facility co-ordinator Kitchener Minor Soccer Assn; smallbore specialist; began competing at club level '78; mem. ntl team '83-98; competed '86, '90, '94, '98

Commonwealth, '87, '91, '95, '99 Pan-Am, '84, '88, '92 Olympic Games, 6 world championships; 1 Pan-Am, 4 Commonwealth Games air rifle gold, 3 Pan-Am. 3 CG silver, 1 PA, 1 CG, 1 World Cup bronze; ntl air rifle title '90; 2 sports excellence awards; 3 Shooting Fed. athlete of yr awards; res. Waterloo, Ont.

BOWIE, Mary Jane (luge); b. 3 Mar 1948, Ottawa, Ont.; given name: Mary Jane Dyment Finlayson; m. Paul Bowie; c. David, James, Laura; UofOtt, BSc, McGill; retd. fitness consultant; mem. intercollegiate badminton, t&f, cross-country, alpine ski teams; 2 ntl luge titles; twice runnerup NA championships; mem. ntl team 5yrs; mem. '74 European championships, 6 worlds, '76 Olympic teams; '71 Zardini Memorial Avila Que. title; '72 Que. champion; bronze International Grenzhandrennan (Austria) '77; 4th Gosser Preis der Stadt (Innsbruck) '77; intl luge judge; trained Calgary Olympic officials; Level 3 FIS judge; res. Ottawa, Ont.

BOWIE, Russell (hockey); b. 24 Aug 1880, Montreal, Que.; d. 8 Apr 1959, Montreal, Que.; weighed only 112lbs when he joined Winnipeg Victorias 1898; remained amateur (CAHL, ECAHA) throughout career; 234 goals in 80 games over 10-year span; one of few to score 10 goals in single game; 38 in 10 games '07, including 8 one game; led league scorers 5 times; perennial all-star; broken collarbone ended career, became referee; mem. Hockey Hall of Fame.

BOWLAN, David (golf); b. 3 Oct 1962, Charlottetown, P.E.I.; Southeastern Louisiana.; pro golfer; Louisiana Collegiate title '85; All-Star conference title '85; PEI amateur '83; pro '87; won '87 PEI Open; mem. 5 Willingdon Cup teams; Junior college all-American; competed on USTPA, US mini-tours; res. Bunbury, P.E.I.

BOWMAN, Gary (shooting); b. 24 Jun 1957, Hamilton, Ont.; given name: Gary Robert; m. Nancy McLean; c. Connor Russell Brian, Dana Catherine; Mohawk Coll, McMaster, BA; systems planning mgr. Bell Mobility; began shooting as cadet '72; 2 cadet Bisley teams; 2 Ont. grand aggregate titles; qualified 7 Bisley teams, competed once; mem. 3 Palma teams, team silver '92; mem. '94 Commonwealth Games team; res. Mississauga, Ont.

BOWMAN, Scotty (hockey); b. 20 Jun 1911, Winnipeg, Man.; d. 22 Oct 1990, Winnipeg, Man.; given name: Ralph; played defence 7 NHL seasons '34-40 with Ottawa, St. Louis, Detroit; gained fame by scoring 1st penalty shot goal in NHL history 14 Nov 1934 vs. Montreal Maroons; NHL record: 274 scheduled games, 8g, 17a, 22 playoff games, 2g, 2a; mem. 2 Stanley Cup winners; mem. Man. Hockey Hall of Fame.

BOWMAN, Scotty (coaching/hockey); b. 18 Sep 1933, Montreal, Que.; given name: William Scott; m. Suella; c. Alicia, David, Stanley, Nancy, Bob; hockey coach.; playing career cut short by head injury '51-52 Jr. A season when allegedly struck by J.G. Talbot's stick; asst. to Sam Pollock as mgr.-coach Hull-Ottawa, 1 Memorial Cup winner; coached Peterborough Petes, Montreal Jr. Canadiens (OHA); 3 seasons Eastern Canadian scout for Habs; coach/GM expansion St. Louis (NHL) '66-71, Stanley Cup finals 3

times; coach Habs '71-79, 5 Stanley Cup, 6 Prince of Wales, 2 Clarence Campbell titles, 4 in succession; coached Team Canada '76, '81 Canada Cup series; coach/GM Buffalo '79-87; dir. hockey operations Pittsburgh '87-91, following death of Bob Johnson took over as coach '91-93, 1 Stanley Cup win; coach Detroit from '93; 2 Stanley Cup wins; NHL coaching record: (through '98) regular season 1057-484-277, playoffs 194-111; set NHL all-time coaching victory record '84-85 season; 900th NHL coaching victory '95, 1000th victory '97; tied Toe Blake for most Stanley Cup wins, 9, '98; NHL coach of '77, '96, *Sporting News* executive of '80; Hockey News exec. of '84; subject of Douglas Hunter book "*Scotty Bowman - A Life in Hockey*"; mem. Hockey Night in Canada team '87-90; mem. Hockey Hall of Fame; res. Buffalo, N.Y.

BOWNESS, Rick (hockey); b. 25 Jan 1955, Moncton, N.B.; given name: Richard Gary; m. Judy Egan; c. Ricky, Ryan, Kristen; ex-hockey coach, scout, player personnel exec. Nashville Predators; following path set by father Robert, a minor league hockey standout, he first tested his talents with Sydney, NS school team; mem. Halifax jr. Blazers, Montreal in QMJHL; drafted by Atlanta Flames '75; Tulsa (CHL) '76; defensive forward NHL Atlanta, Detroit, St. Louis, Winnipeg '75-82; NHL record: 173 scheduled games, 18g, 37a, 5 playoff games,turned to coaching Sherbrooke (AHL) '82-83; asst. Winnipeg '83-86; head coach Moncton (AHL) '87-89; Maine Mariners '89-91; head coach Boston (NHL) '92; expansion Ottawa '93-95; asst. NY Islanders '95-97, head coach '97-98; asst. Phoenix '99; ESPN color commentator '98; mem. NS Sports Hall of Fame; res. Kanata, Ont.

BOWSFIELD, Ted (baseball); b. 10 Jan 1935, Vernon, B.C.; given name: Edward Oliver; m. Marilyn Holden; c. Edward Oliver "Ted" Jr., Bradley McDonald; retd. dir. Seattle Kingdome; BC basketball all-star '54; pro baseball '54 moving through minors to Boston Red Sox '58-60; 3 of first 4 AL victories vs NY earned him "Yankee-Killer" title; Little World Series finalist '59 as mem. Minneapolis Millers; Cleveland '60; California '61-62, Kansas City '63-65; Vancouver (PCL) '65 where arm troubles forced retirement; 37-39 ML won-lost record; American Assn. all-star '58; several yrs stadium mgr with LA Angels, Seattle Mariners; mem. BC Sports Hall of Fame; res. Monroe, Wash.

BOX, Ab (football); b. 8 Mar 1909, Toronto, Ont.; m. Dorothy Sowerby (d), Phyllis Malpass; c. Linda, Donald, Gary, Donald, Marilyn; retired; Malvern Grads '28-29; protege of Ted Reeve, Balmy Beach '30-31, ORFU, Eastern, Grey Cup titles '30; Argos punter '32-34, '35-38, Grey Cup '33; frequent all-star; Jeff Russel Memorial Trophy '34; mem. ntl baseball, softball title teams; operated Markham children's day camp; mem. Canadian Football, Balmy Beach, Canada's Sports halls of fame; res. Toronto, Ont.

BOX, Charlie (all-around); b. 26 Dec 1911, Toronto, Ont.; d. 21 Mar 1993, London, Ont.; given name: Charles Venning; m. Catherine Norsworthy; c. David, Ellen Foster, Charles M., Martha Ann; UWO, BA, OCE; retired educator; mem. TSSAA jr. rugby titlist '28, sr. rugby '29-30, capt. '30 team; mem. Jr. ORFU Malvern Grads '32 titlists; 4yrs all-star end (outside right), quarterback, punt returner UWO, capt. '37 team; with brother Ab mem. '38 Balmy Beach team; field lacrosse '27-32; box lacrosse '32-33; 3 intercollegiate lightweight (135lbs) boxing titles; '35 Silver Gloves div. title, Southwestern, Central Ont. titles; organized WWII Canadian Forces boxing shows Reykavik; coached jr. lacrosse, football Upper Canada Coll. league '33; coached Toronto Malvern CI rugby, hockey titlists; mem. UWO W-Club Sports Hall of Fame.

BOYCE, Jim (tennis); b. 22 Jun 1951, Toronto, Ont.; given name: James Niell; div. Dale Bilodeau; c. Katherine; m. Jody McCormack; Mississippi State, BSc; exec. dir. Ont. Tennis Assn., ex-real estate agent; 5 age-group titles; 5 ntl singles titles, including 3 under-18 crowns; 3 times all-South Eastern Conf. team; won 105 of 120 college matches; only Cdn jr. to win both ntl and open titles same year ('68); twice ntl men's doubles champion; ranked in Ont. top 8 from jr. days, in ntl top 15 from '71; twice Davis Cup team mem.; touring pro '77-78, pro mgr. Ottawa All Seasons Racquets Club '77-79, club pro Toronto LTC '80-89; chair. '80 Davis Cup tie vs. Mexico; tennis consultant '77-81; dir. ntl tennis camps; NCTA coach '77-79, Eastern Cdn coach '78-80; ntl 45+ singles title '97; pres. JNB Sports Inc.; Pepsi award '67 outstanding Cdn jr, 4 Ont. sport achievement awards; res. Toronto, Ont.

BOYCE, Walter (motorsport); b. 25 Oct 1946, Ottawa, Ont.; m. Leslie Bradbeer; c. Jennifer, Jamie; Colorado, UofOtt; businessman, entrepreneur; with Doug Woods navigating, ntl open rally titles '70-74; only Canadian to hold FIA top seed international rating, having won such events as Press on Regardless Rally for '73 world title, Rally of Rideau Lakes, Canadian Winter Rally; with co-driver Robin Edwards Cdn Production A titlist '79, '81-82; with Jim Brandt '86 NA, Sports Car Club of Americas Group A FIA title; res. Ottawa, Ont.

BOYCHUK, Andy (t&f); b. 17 May 1941, Orono, Ont.; given name: Andrew Harry; m. Darlene Ann MacDonald; U of Waterloo, BSc; professional engineer; 10th Commonwealth Games marathon '66; gold '67 Pan-Am Games; 10th '68 Olympics, '70 Commonwealth Games; 4 national marathon titles; marathon PB: 2:16.13 '75; outstanding harrier and track athlete of '67; Sarnia Observer citizen of '67; Sarnia area's outstanding man of '67; mem. Cdn Road Racing Hall of Fame; res. Sarnia, Ont.

BOYD, Barry (t&f); b. 12 Jan 1952, Calgary, Alta.; given name: Barry Allan; UAlta, BComm; administrator Commonwealth Games Foundation; long jump specialist; who won every indoor, outdoor ntl age-group title from age 17; '69-79 never out of medals in ntl sr. indoor, outdoor competition; ntl jr. indoor long jump record 7.41m; sr. indoor record 7.71m; 9th '75 Pan-Am Games; PB: 7.77m (wind assisted); ntl outdoor title '74, indoor '75; retired following bronze '79 nationals; res. Edmonton, Alta.

BOYD, Mike (curling); b. 13 Jul 1947, Ottawa, Ont.; given name: John Michael; div; c. Marcia, Patrick; Waterloo Lutheran; building service contractor; skipped Ont. Schoolboy champions '66; 3rd NO '72 Brier entry, 2nd '75 Ont. Brier entry, 2nd '76 Ont. mixed champions, all-star ranking each time; 1st player to represent Ont., NO in Brier; co-recipient Sault Ste. Marie sportsman of '72 award; Sault

Ste. Marie Order of Merit '72; scored eight-ender '71; res. Kanata, Ont.

BOYD, Rob (skiing); b. 15 Feb 1966, Vernon, B.C.; started skiing at 3, competing at 11; mem. ntl development group '84-85, ntl Alpine B team '85-87, ntl A team '87-97; 27 ntl titles; competed world jrs '84; Olympics '88, '92; world cup circuit '84-97; 1st Cdn to win WC race in Canada with '84 Whistler downhill victory; tied for 1st Nor-Am downhill standings '86, 2nd '87; 27 top 10 finishes in 84 WC races; tied 3rd '88 WC downhill standings; WC circuit record 3-1-2; Fleishmann Cup title '84; *Ski Racing* magazine Cdn Alpine Skier of year '88; BC Premier's athletic awards '87-88; BC Sports honor roll '86-87; sports excellence awards '87, '89; res. Whistler, B.C.

BOYES, Dave (rowing); b. 26 Aug 1964, St. Catharines, Ont.; m. Cathy; c. Dillon, MacKenzie, Sidney; tool & die maker GM; began rowing age 15; mem ntl team from '85; gold 4 lw 8s, 1 straight pairs, 1 straight 4s US championships; gold lw 8s '93 world championships; with Jeff Lay, Gavin Hassett, Brian Peaker, silver lw 4s '96 Olympics; silver lw 8s Lucerne '99; res. St. Catharines, Ont.

BOYLE, Sheryl (canoeing); b. 13 Nov 1965, Renfrew, Ont.; Carleton ; high performance dir., asst. ntl team coach CCA; former National Gallery projects officer, architect; began competing age 19; mem. ntl team from '86; ntl whitewater titles '93-94; only Cdn female to win world whitewater medals, bronze '93, silver '92; competed '92, '96 Olympics; won Olympic art prizes '92, '94; turned to coaching '97; wrote athlete's marketing guide for Cdn Sport & Fitness Centre; design thesis award Carleton. '90; res. Bonnechere/Ottawa, Ont.

BOYLEN, Christilot (equestrian); b. 12 Apr 1947, Djakarta, Indonesia; given name: Christilot Hansen; m. James A. Boylen; c. Christa-Dora, Billie Jeanne; Branksome Hall; writer; 9 ntl dressage titles; at 17 youngest competitor Olympic Grand Prix dressage '64; 5 gold, 1 silver, 1 bronze in Pan-Am Games competitions;; best showing ever by Cdn individual dressage 7th '76 Olympics; mem. '64, '68, '72, '76, '80, '84, '92 Olympic teams; 2 US ntl titles; 3 1sts '70 Ohio Dressage Derby; twice ntl EFC horsewoman of year; authored Canadian Entry and Basic Dressage for North America; tech. advisor Canadian Dressage Owners and Riders Assn. (CADORA); former v.-pres. International Equestrian Sport Services (IESS) Ltd.; res. Rottingen, Germany.

BOYS, Bev (diving); b. 4 Jul 1951, Toronto, Ont.; m. Stephen Jones; c. Lorin, Suzanne; UMan, UofT; sporting goods business owner '85-93; exec. dir. BC Diving Assn.; 34 ntl sr. titles '66-77; mem. '66, '70, '74, '78 Commonwealth, '67, '71, '75 Pan-Am, '68, '72, '76 Olympic Games teams; 3 gold, silver, 1 bronze Commonwealth, 2 silver, 1 bronze Pan-Am Games; US, Russian, Italian, Hungarian, British championships; brief pro diving career; rep. Speedo Canada; BC chair. Cdn Officials program; 2 Bobbie Rosenfeld trophies; Cdn athlete of decade award; FINA international diving judge; mem. Cdn Amateur, Cdn, Ont. Aquatic, Canada's Sports halls of fame; res. Surrey, B.C.

BRABENEC, Hana (tennis); b. 21 Jun 1928, Prague, Czechoslovakia; given name: Hana Veverka; m. Josef Brabenec; c. Josef Jr.; tennis coach; from 12-27 ranked among top 10 Czech women tennis players; twice runnerup Czech ntl singles; 4 times Czech ntl doubles titlist; '77 coach-mgr. BC tennis team Canada Summer Games, 2 gold, 1 silver, bronze; head coach Vancouver Jericho TC '75-93; res. Vancouver, B.C

BRABENEC, Josef Jr. (tennis); b. 24 Apr 1957, Ostrava, Czechoslovakia; with John Picken all-Cdn jr. under-16, under-18, under-21 doubles titles, 2 indoor sr. doubles titles; ntl indoor singles '79; mem. '78-79, '82-83 Davis Cup teams; 4th mixed doubles '79 Pan-Am Games; silver '77 Canada Summer Games; competed French Open, Wimbledon; mem. Jericho TC; res. Surrey, B.C.

BRABENEC, Josef Sr. (tennis); b. 29 Jan 1929, Prague, Czechoslovakia; m. Hana Veverka; c. Josef Jr.; tennis coach; among top Czech jrs.; Belgian jr. title '47; with wife Hana founded Prague youth tennis school '63; capt. Czech ntl teams '64-69; coach Czech ntl jr. team Florida Cup, Orange Bowl '67; head coach Jericho TC Vancouver '70-75; ntl tennis coach '75-84; coached BC team to 2 gold, 2 bronze '73 Canada Summer Games; introduced uniform teaching program throughout Canada; Davis Cup team capt. '77-82, Federation Cup capt. '77-82; with Ken Sinclair ntl over-35 doubles '78, over-45 doubles '80, Monte Carlo international veterans title '78; authored four tennis books; international secty. Czech LTA '63-69; mem. management comm. ILTF '69-71; dir. ITF Continental Training Centre from '93; res. Vancouver, B.C.

BRACK, Bill (motorsport); b. 26 Dec 1935, Toronto, Ont.; given name: William Andrew; automotive dealer; Players' Challenge Series, ntl championships '73-75; drove in 2 Canadian GP Formula 1 events posting highest finish to that time — 8th '69; strong Formula 5000 series contender '69-72; 1st ntl title at 37; won 3 Formula Atlantic races; operates Bill Brack Racing Enterprises and sought to build racing stable '76; included in fold was Jacques Villeneuve '79; Wayne Kelly Trophy '75 for driver best combining sportsmanship with ability; mem. Cdn Motorsport Hall of Fame; res. Toronto, Ont.

BRADLEY, Eric (parachuting); b. 9 Jul 1953, Fredericton, N.B.; UNB BSc; commercial pilot; 2nd ntl 8-way '76; won 8-way '80; more than 2100 jumps; res. Fredericton, N.B.

BRADLEY-KAMELI, Sue (t&f); b. 17 Sep 1956, Toronto, Ont.; given name: Susan Elaine Bradley; m. Freidoun Kameli; c. Taraneh Christine; UofT, BPHE, San Diego State, UWO., BEd; teacher; hurdles specialist; ntl jr. 100m hurdles record 13.5; juve. 80m record 11.1; 3 ntl 100m outdoor, 5 50m indoor titles; mem. '75, '83 Pan-Am, '76, '80 Olympic, '79, '83 FISU, '81 Pacific Conf., '82 Commonwealth Games teams; bronze 100m hurdles with PB 13.1 '82 Commonwealth Games; SDSU most valuable track athlete '80; res. London, Ont.

BRAFIELD, Leslie (swimming); b. 7 Feb 1960, Toronto, Ont.; given name: Leslie Ann; Arizona State, UofT; 4th 800m FS '79 Pan-Am Games; 800m FS title, 2nd 400m FS

'80 Canada-West Germany meet; 1st 200m FS, 2nd 200m butterfly, 400m FS '80 CIAU championships; won 400m, 800m FS '80 Japan nationals; mem. '80 Olympic team; res. Bramalea, Ont.

BRAGAGNOLO, Mark (football); b. 20 Oct 1955, Timmins, Ont; UofT; OQIFC all-star running back '74-76; 3 consec. OQIFC rushing titles; OQIFC career record 369 carries, 2281yds, 20tds, 7 receptions, 286yds, 4tds; CFL territorial draft Toronto '77-79, Winnipeg '80-81, Hamilton '81-84; Canadian Club TD award '78; res. East York, Ont.

BRAIN, Marilyn (rowing); b. 14 Apr 1959, Halifax, N.S.; m. Howard Campbell; c. Luke, Jefferson; UVic BEd; teacher/coach; with husband operates West Coast Rowing; sweep 2 Canadian Henley, 1 ntl, 3 Head of the Charles, 3 CIAU coxed 8s titles; 1 CIAU coxed 4s title; mem. silver coxed 4s crew '84 Olympics; mem. 6 world championships teams; retd. from competition '86; res. Victoria, B.C.

BRAKNIS, Robert (swimming); b. 8 Jan 1973, Montreal, Que.; 50m, 100m freestyle, 100m, 200m backstroke specialist; mem. ntl team from '93; bronze 4x100 FS relay '93 Pan-Pacific championship; silver 4x100 medley relay '94 Commonwealth Games; silver 100m back '90 Eight Nations youth meet; gold 100m FS, 100m back, silver 200m back, bronze 50m FS '96 Olympic trials; gold 100m back, 50m FS (tie), silver 100m FS, 200m back '96 Canada Cup; silver 200m back '96 US Grand Prix; competed '96 Olympics; res. Mississauga, Ont.

BRANCATO, George (football); b. 27 May 1931, Brooklyn, N.Y.; m. Barbara Thomson; c. Cindi, Wendy, George Jr., Alicia; Louisiana State, BSc, CalState, MA; offensive, defensive halfback Chicago Cardinals (NFL) '53-54; CFL Alouettes '55, Rough Riders '56-62; led EFC pass interceptions '57; EFC all-star '61; defensive asst. to Jack Gotta '70; head coach Ottawa '74-84; asst. Saskatchewan '85-89; head coach Cape Breton '90; asst. coach Carleton U '92; coaching consultant Rough Riders '93, asst. coach Shreveport Pirates '94; coach Arena Football Charlotte, Las Vegas; mem. 4 Grey Cup finalists, 3 winners, 1 as player; Annis Stukus Trophy CFL coach of '75; International Italian of year in football '76; res. Nepean, Ont.

BRANCH, Cecilia (t&f); b. 14 Jan 1957, Halifax, N.S.; m. Mark Hayes; c. Jessie, Bridget; Dalhousie, Nevada, BSc; HS teacher; HS basketball MVP '73; bronze 100m '73 ntl championships; pentathlon silver '73 Canada Games; hurdles specialist; mem. '79 Pan-Am, '80 Olympic teams; bronze '79 AIAW championships, all-American; most outstanding athlete, t&f athlete St. Patrick's HS '75; most outstanding t&f performer Nevada '77, '79; dean's list '77; Cdn Masters 400m hurdles record '92; res. Nepean, Ont.

BRANCH, David (administration/hockey); b. 27 Nov 1948, Bathurst, N.B.; hockey exec.; pres. CHL; secty-mgr. OHA '73-77; exec.dir. CAHA '77-79; commissioner OMJHL, now OHL, '79-98; pres. CHL '96-98; res. Toronto, Ont.

BRANCHAUD, Mike (softball/hockey); b. 30 Aug 1965, Cornwall, Ont.; given name: Michael Joseph Lorenzo William; m. Nancy Ann Pearce; UofOtt BSS; Canadian

Adult Recreational Hockey Assn. program co-ordinator; mem.Stittsville 56ers jr/sr teams, Turpin Pontiacs, Fingal; silver '93 ntl championships; played as mem. famed Eddie Feigner King and His Court 4-man exhibition team '93-98; mem. King of Diamonds fast pitch organization specializing in player development '99; played Jr. B hockey CharLan, Morrisburg; assumed CARHA post '98; res. Cornwall, Ont.

BRASSARD, Jean-Luc (skiing); b. 24 Aug 1972, Valleyfield, Que.; freestyle moguls specialist; mem. Cdn skiing "Air Force"; began skiing age 7, competing age 13; mem. ntl team from '90; through '97 15 world cup gold; won '93 overall world championship; competed '92, '94, '98 Olympics; moguls gold '94 Olympics; 2 World moguls titles; with sister Anne-Marie saved 16-year-old from drowning at Valleyfield, Que. '93; FIS freestyle rookie of '91; 1st Cdn to win Blackcomb WC event '98; co-winner (with Kate Pace) John Semmelink award '94; flag-bearer '98 Olympics; res. Grande-Ile, Que.

BRASSEUR, Isabelle (figure skating); b. 28 Jul 1970, Kingsbury, Que.; m. Rocco Marval; began skating at 6, competing at 7; mem. ntl team '85-94; with partner Pascal Courchesne '82-86, won ntl. jr. pairs title '85; hooked up with Lloyd Eisler '87 scoring '89 Skate Electric, '88, '90 Skate Canada victories; 5 ntl sr. pairs titles (with Lloyd Eisler); 4 world silver; bronze '92, '94 Olympics; competed '88, '92, '94 Olympics; pro '94; Cdn pro pairs title '97; Cdn Meritorious Service award; mem. Cdn Winter Olympic, Canada's Sports, Cdn Figure Skating halls of fame; res. Boucherville, Que.

BRATTY, Gary (weightlifting); b. 15 Jun 1956, Hamilton, Ont.; given name: Gary Ross; McMaster; Hamilton & District, CANUSA Games trials titles '71; silver '71 CANUSA Games; ntl Jr. Olympics 67.5kg title '75; all ntl jr. records, Commonwealth jr. snatch 59.9kg '76; 23 class records Ont. jr., sr., ntl Commonwealth jr.; gold Can-US '76 meet; ntl jr. snatch, clean & jerk records 67.5kg class '76; Ont., ntl sr. lightweight title '77; mem. '78 Commonwealth Games team; PB: 262.5kg total lift '77; best lifter major meet awards '73, '76; res. Halifax, N.S.

BRAUNSTEIN, Terry (curling); b. 18 Apr 1939, Winnipeg, Man.; m. Andrea Greenberg; c. Lisa, Danny; UMan, BComm clothing wholesaler; at 18 won Man. Consols to become youngest Brier skip, forced playoff before bowing to Matt Baldwin 10-6; forced rules revision which prohibited schoolboys from competing for Canadian men's title; rep. Man. '65 Brier; 3 Man. bonspiel grand aggregate titles; 3 carspiel titles; mem. Winnipeg Granite Club, Man., Cdn Curling halls of fame; res. Winnipeg, Man.

BRAY, Shirley (curling); b. 12 Sept 1929, Brandon, Man.; given name: Shirley Elizabeth Walker; m. Richard Merton Bray; c. Reginald, Sandra; all-star 3rd '68 Macdonald Lassie; 3rd Man. Seagram Mixed champion '75; skip Man. entry '85 sr women's nationals; CLCA delegate '77-82; Curl Canada Level II instructor, Level III umpire; pres. MLCA '80-81, hon. life mem. MLCA from '83; 1st woman recipient Gordon McGunigal Memorial Medal for contribution, dedication to game; Curl Canada Herb Millham Award '83; CLCA Appreciation award '85; twice Westman Sportsman of year award nominee; YMCA Woman of Distinction award '90; Brandon Sportsman of year '90; served in executive capacity for varied ntl championships and at club, provincial level; mem. Man., Cdn Curling halls of fame; res. Brandon, Man.

BRAZLEY, Carl (football); b. 5 Sep 1957, Louisville, Ky; m. Jan; c. Sunni Rose, Nicholas; Western Kentucky; football player, film business exec.; defensive back; pro Montreal '80-81, Ottawa '81-82, Toronto '83-86, from '88, San Diego, Minnesota '87; 5 times EFC all-star; CFL all-star '83; 2 Grey Cup finals, 1 winner; defensive award '83 Grey Cup final; res. Louisville, Ky.

BRECK, Ian (football/coaching); b. 11 Aug 1947, Renfrew, Ont.; given name: Ian Ewart; m. Kathryn Barnard; c. Erika, Bridget, Elizabeth; Springfield Coll. BSc, Queen's BEd; football coach; joined Bishop's coaching staff as asst. '84; head coach from '88; through '96 coaching record shows 56-22-4, 5 regular season titles, 3 playoff championships, appearances in 3 ntl College Bowl championships; OQIFC, CIAU coach of '92; res. Lennoxville, Que.

BREEN, Joe (football); b. 23 Apr 1897, Toronto, Ont.; d. 13 Oct 1978, Montreal, Que.; given name: Joseph Melville; m. Winnifred Westman; c. Melwyn Joseph; UofT BSc; civil engineer; capt. UofT '19-20, Grey Cup winner '20; capt. Toronto Argos, Parkdale Canoe Club '21, '24; coach UWO football '29-34; 1 Intercollegiate title; mem. UofT, UWO W-Club, Canadian Football, Canada's Sports halls of fame.

BREMNER, Janice (synchro swim); b. 15 Jul 1974, Burlington, Ont.; introduced to synchro swim by mother; began competing age 9; mem. ntl team from '90; team gold '96 French Open; team silver '95 Pan-Am, '96 Olympic Games, '94 World Aquatic championships; Petro-Canada Cup team gold '92. 2 ntl jr team gold, one duet gold; Petro-Canada Olympic Torch scholarship '94; res. N. Vancouver, B.C.

BRENNER, Veronica (skiing); b. 18 Oct 1974, Scarborough, Ont.; freestyle aerials specialist; ntl title '97-98; worlds bronze '97; ranked 2nd '95, 1st '97 World Cup standings; 8 WC race gold, 5 silver, 1 bronze; mem. ntl team from '94; competed '98 Olympics; res. Sharon, Ont.

BRETON, Skip (broomball); b. 18 Apr 1964, Mattice, Ont.; given name: Yvan Eugene; m. Julie Ryan; c. Ryanne Hailey, Olivia Michelle; carpenter; competed for Embrun Plumbing 9 time ntl champion; mem. '91 world title team; 6 ntl championship MVP awards; 3 Ottawa ACT broomball, ball hockey awards; 2 Ont., ntl ball hockey championships; ntl silver, bronze; centre 3 ntl all-star teams; res. Kanata, Ont.

BREWER, Carl (hockey); b. 21 Oct 1938, Toronto, Ont.; given name: Carl Thomas; m. Marilyn Rea; c. Christopher, Michael, Anna-Lisa; McMaster, UofT, BA; businessman; Weston Jr. B; Marlboros Jr. A; '56 Memorial Cup, MVP '57-58; pro Toronto '57-65, '79-80; twice NHL penalty leader; mem. 3 Stanley Cup winners; quit following dispute with Punch Imlach '65; regained amateur status '66; mem. ntl team '66-67; outstanding defenceman '67 world tournament; player-coach Muskegon (IAHL) '67-68, Finland '68-69; TML sold rights to Detroit but refused to play before '69-70 season; St.Louis '70-72; left retirement

'79-80 for limited duty TML; once 1st, twice 2nd team all-star; NHL record: 604 scheduled games, 25g, 198a, 72 playoff games, 3g, 17a; 5 all-star games; TV color commentator WHA games; gained legal ownership of name Toronto Maple Leafs '83; key figure in retired player successful legal action against NHL over pension funds; res. Toronto, Ont.

BREWSTER, Ken (field hockey/soccer); b. 14 Jul 1935, Barbados, W.I.; Carleton, BComm, UofOtt, MBA; teacher; Barbados ntl soccer team '59-60; mem. Barbados and W.I. ntl FH teams '57-62; mem. exec. Ottawa Field Hockey Club '70-76; coached Ottawa team to silver medal ntl jr. field hockey championships '75; development co-ordinator Outaouais FHC '72-75; avid sailor; res. Orleans, Ont.

BRICKER, Cal (t&f); b. 1884; d. 24 Apr 1963, Grenfell, Sask.; given name: Calvin David; UofT, DDS; dentist; all-around champion UofT and individual intercollegiate champion '05-06; specialist running broad jump (long jump), hop, step and jump (triple jump); won both events '08 Olympic trials setting long jump record 24'1.5" which held 27 years; bronze LJ, 4th TJ '08 Olympics; LJ silver '12 Olympics; officer in charge of Cdn athletes '19 Paris Games for service personnel; mem. UofT; Cdn Amateur, Sask., Canada's Sports halls of Fame.

BRIDLE, Wezer (volleyball); b. 29 Jul 1926, Winnipeg, Man.; m. Joyce; c. Charles, Jim, Clancy, Jeff, Jan, Cal; retd. CNR; excelled in all aspects of volleyball as player, coach, official and administrator; founded Man. Volleyball Assn., 1st pres.; founded Central Y Kids program to develop game as sport of choice for youngsters; promoted. coached them to Manitoba's 1st jr. ntl championship '65; formed Manitoba's age class development system; coached U Winnipeg to 1st CIAU title '68; prov., ntl volleyball officials 20-plus yrs, officiating in CIAU, ntl, Pan-Am, Olympic, NORCECA championships; instrumental in forming Man. Volleyball Officials Assn.; mem. Man. Sports Hall of Fame; res. Winnipeg, Man.

BRIEN, Alvin (canoeing); b. 12 Jul 1956, Halifax, N.S.; d. 3 Feb 1982, Caribbean Ocean; Dalhousie, BPhE; teacher; 3000m-3-mile distance runner Maritime indoor, outdoor meets '72-79; kayak specialist; ntl junior K2 500m; Continental Cup K4 500m '79; Commonwealth '80 Olympic team; ntl K4 1000m title '80; died in sailing accident.

BRIEN, Don (canoeing); b. 1 Sep 1959, Halifax, N.S.; given name: Donald Michael; Dalhousie, BPhE, UBC; provincial, ntl cross-country runner; kayak specialist; NA jr. K2, K4 titles '76; mem. ntl team from '77; NA jr. K1, K2, K4 10,000m titles, ntl juve. jr. K1, K2 titles, gold K1, silver K2, K4 Canada Summer Games '77; ntl jr. K2 500m, sr. C15 titles '78; ntl sr. K4, C15 titles, gold K4 500m Continental Cup '79; gold K1, K2, K4 1000m,K4 500m '83 Pan-Am championships; with Colin Shaw bronze 1000m K2 '85 world championships; mem. '80, '84 Olympic teams; res. Calgary, Alta.

BRIGDEN, William (canoeing); b. 11 Apr 1916, Winnipeg, Man.; m. Marion Patton; c. Robert, Anne, Paul; canoe manufacturer; with partner Jim Nickle dominated 2-man

competition '51 Olympic trials; mem. '52 Olympic team; with Don Starkell twice won pro Flin Flon canoe derby; competed in 6 Le Voyageur Winnipeg to Lockport races winning '70; at 63 2nd 15-mile Kenora race; mem. Man. Sports Hall of Fame; res. St. Vital, Man.

BRIGHT, Johnny (football); b. 11 Jun 1931, Fort Wayne, Ind.; d. 14 Dec 1983, Edmonton, Alta.; div.; c. Darrell Michael, Deanie LaDette, Shaughna Darcine, Kandis Denita; Drake, BSc, UAlta, BEd; Jr. HS principal; HS all-state football, track, basketball; pitched Des Moines, Iowa, to state titles; set 20 Drake football, basketball, track records; led all US college ground gainers, all-American; 1st draft '51 Philadelphia Eagles (NFL); CFL Calgary '52-54, Edmonton '54-64; 7 times WFC all-star, 4 times all-Cdn; Schenley Outstanding Player '59; CFL record: 71td, 10,909yds on 1969 carries for 5.5 avg.; 4 times CFL rushing leader; 5 times surpassed 1000yd plateau single season; 3 times led CFL total carries, 5 times surpassed 200-per-season; 4 Grey Cup finals, 3 winners; Drake football player of century; Indiana silver anniversary basketball team; pro basketball Harlem Globetrotters; pitched perfect game Iowa State tournament; 74-27 record as HS football coach, 304-46 basketball; coach Edmonton Monarchs pro fastball team, '72 coach of year; Edmonton athlete of '59; mem. Alta., Edmonton, Iowa, Eskimos, Canadian Football halls of fame.

BRILL, Debbie (t&f); b. 10 Mar 1953, Mission, B.C.; m. Doug Coleman; c. Neil Bogart Ray, Katie, Jake; UBC; high jump coach; originator reverse jumping style known as Brill Bend; mem. 5 Olympic, 3 Pan-Am, 3 Commonwealth Games, 2 World Cup teams; gold '70, '82 Commonwealth, '71 Pan-Am, '79 WC, International Cup, '82 Millrose Games; 8 ntl titles, 28 international meet titles; 1st Canadian, NA woman to clear 6' barrier '71; numerous Canadian records; world indoor 1.99m '82, Commonwealth record 1.96m '79, US outdoor record 1.95m '82; more than decade ranked among world's best female jumpers; 2 Jack W. Davies, 3 Fred Rowell, '67 Myrtle Cook, 9 Dr. Calvin Bricker Memorial Trophies; with Debbie Van Kiekebelt co-winner Rosenfeld female athlete of '71; BC athlete of decade '80, BCTFA outstanding female athlete of '80; fed. govt. sport excellence award; Officer Order of Canada '83; mem. Cdn Amateur, BC Sports, Ridge Meadows halls of fame; res. Burnaby, B.C.

BRIND'AMOUR, Rod (hockey); b. 9 Aug 1970, Ottawa, Ont.; m. Kelle; c. Briley Olivia; Notre Dame Coll, Michigan State; centre/lw; CCHA freshman of '88-89; drafted from Notre Dame Jr.A by St. Louis; NHL St. Louis '89-91, Philadelphia from '91; NHL all-rookie team '90; Bobby Clarke trophy '92; mem. Team Canada '92-94 worlds, '97 World Cup, '98 Olympics; NHL record (through '99): 778 scheduled games, 273g, 430a, 87 playoff games, 33g, 40a; res. Marlton, N.J.

BRISSON, Thérèse (hockey/ringette); b. 5 Oct 1966, Dollard-des-Ormeaux, Que.; Concordia; prof. Kinesiology UNB; Concordia female rookie of '87, female athlete of '88, '89; defensive MVP Ferland 4-Glaces Que. champs '93; mem. Team Quebec '94, '95 women's sr. ntl champs; defensive MVP '95; mem. NB Maritime Sports Blades ntl bronze team '96; mem. Team Canada from '93; 3 world, 1 Pacific Rim, 1 3-Nations Cup titles; silver '98 Olympics;

competed in '90 world ringette championships; NCCP ringette course conductor; mem. ringette ntl coaching comm.; res. Fredericton, N.B.

BRITTON, Bill (football); b. 15 Dec 1935, Kirkland Lake, Ont.; given name: William Leonard; m. Linda Susan Menzies; c. Christopher, Angela, Daniel, Jane; UWO, BA, UBC, LLB; lawyer; 3 times all-star, sr. year MVP UWO; 1st pick BC '58 CFL college draft; fullback, linebacker, punt returner Lions '58-61, Calgary '62-65; 4yrs commentator Calgary football radio broadcasts; 7yrs dir. Stampeders, pres. '83-84; UWO W-Club Sports Hall of Fame; res. Calgary, Alta.

BROADBENT, Punch (hockey); b. 13 Jul 1893, Ottawa, Ont.; d. 6 Mar 1971, Ottawa, Ont.; given name: Harold Lawton; m. Leda; c. Sally Ann; RCAF officer; amateur New Edinburgh, Cliffsides; pro Senators '10-15, '18-23, '27-28, Montreal Maroons '24-27, NY Americans '28-29; 110 NHL goals; 3 Stanley Cup winners Ottawa, 1 Montreal; '21-22 goal scoring leader with 32; scored 1 or more goals 16 consecutive games (record still stands) '21-22; mem. Ottawa, Canadian Forces, Hockey halls of fame.

BROCHU, Claude (administration); b. 29 Oct 1944, Quebec City; given name: Claude Renaud; m. Michelle; UofOtt, BA, McMaster, MBA; pres./general partner Montreal Expos; exec. v-p. Seagram, Adams Distillers prior to suceeding John McHale as CEO of Expos '86; mem. ML exec. council, ML Baseball Enterprises Inc., Baseball Operations, Professional Baseball Agreement, ML restructuring comm.; Canada's Baseball Man of Year '90; mem. Order of Canada; res. Montreal, Que.

BROCK, Dieter (football); b. 12 Feb 1951, Alabama; given name: Ralph Dieter; m. Kathy; c. 5; Auburn, Jacksonville State; football coach; NFL tryouts with Bufalo, Green Bay, Cleveland; pro Winnipeg (CFL) '74-83, Hamilton '83-84; erased Sam Etcheverry's 25-year-old record with 4796yds passing (topped by Warren Moon) '82; single season pass attempt record 566 '81, 41 single game completions vs. Ottawa '81; 4 times WFC passing leader; all-Canadian '81; Jeff Nicklin Trophy, Schenley Outstanding Player '80-81; contract dispute led to trade to Hamilton for Tom Clements '83; Grey Cup finalist '84; LA (NFL) '85-87; asst. UAlabama-Birmingham 4yrs; asst. Hamilton '95, Ottawa '96, Edmonton '99; asst. Alabama State '97; HS coach/AD '98; mem. Cdn, Blue Bombers Football halls of fame; res. Selma, Ala.

BROCK, Henry (administration); b. 14 May 1859, Oakville, Ont., d. 26 Aug 1933, Toronto, Ont.; given name: Henry Thompson; standout equestrian, shooter, cricketeer, football player; mem. Argonaut Rowing Club; bravery award for rescue near-drowning victim; 1st secty AAU of C 1883, v-pres. 1887-88, pres. 1889, 1900; mem. Cdn Amateur Sports Hall of Fame.

BROCKWAY, Dot (all-around); b. 28 Nov 1901, Milltown, N.B., d. 10 Sep 1981, Milltown, N.B.; given name: Dorothy; 6 gold, 1 bronze 1st Maritime ladies track meet '26; mem. NB sr. ladies' basketball title team '25-26; St. Croix golf league Dr. Gray trophy ladies title '48, '51-52, '56; prov.,

international club tennis competition titles '28-29; mem. NB Sports Hall of Fame.

BRODA, Turk (hockey); b. 15 May 1914, Brandon, Man.; d. 17 Oct 1972, Toronto, Ont.; given name: Walter; m. Betty Williams; c. Barbara, Bonny, Betty; hockey player, coach; Brandon juves, jrs, Winnipeg Monarchs jrs '33-34; IHL champion Detroit Olympics '34-35; sold to Toronto for then record $8,000; pro career spanned 16 seasons, 2 out for WW2 service; Vezina Trophy '41, '48, shared '51 with Al Rollins; 62 regular season shutouts, 13 in playoffs; considered money player, excelled in playoff action posting 1.99 goals-against avg. 101 games; mem. 5 Stanley Cup winners; coached Toronto Marlboros to 3 league titles, 2 Memorial Cups in 11 seasons; coached London Nationals, Moncton N.B. jrs, Quebec Aces; mem. Man. Sports, Man, Cdn Hockey, Royal Cdn Legion halls of fame.

BRODERICK, Kathleen (field hockey); b. 16 Jan 1947, Calgary, Alta.; given name: Kathleen Evann; UMan, BPhE, UAlta, MA; coach Mt. Allison '68-69, UAlta '73-78, Alta jrs '78; asst coach York U from '79, associate coach ntl team from '78; mem. '69 Canada Games silver medal team, 3 ntl title teams; mem. ntl team '76-77; asst. coach '78 World Cup, '79 world championships, '81 World Cup, '83 silver medal World Cup, silver '91, bronze '87, '95 Pan-Am Games teams; coached in '84, '88, '92 Olympics; 3M coach of '89; res. Toronto, Ont.

BRODEUR, Martin (hockey); b. 6 May 1972, Montreal, Que.; m. Melanie; c. Anthony, William, Jeremy; followed in footsteps of photographer father Denis who played goal on Canada's '56 Olympic bronze medal team; moved from Montreal midget to St. Hyacinthe jrs; minor pro Utica '92-93; NHL with New Jersey from '92; Calder Trophy, NHL all-rookie team '93-94; William Jennings trophy '97, '98; mem. Team Canada '98 Olympics; competed '96 World Cup; 1 Stanley Cup winner; NHL record (through '99): 375 scheduled games, 201-105-57, 21,626min, 789ga, 36so, 61 playoff games, 34-27, 3875min, 126ga, 6so; hosts Montreal charity golf tournament annually; ESPY award '95; competed 2 NHL all-star games; scored goal vs. Montreal '97 playoffs; res. Montreal, Que.

BRODIE, Scott (rowing); b. 13 Jul 1971, St. Catharines, Ont.; Temple; began rowing in high school, 4yrs at university; mem. men's coxed 8's crew ntl team from '94; mem. '96 Olympic Games; res. St. Catharines, Ont.

BRONFMAN, Charles (builder/baseball); b. 27 Jun 1931, Montreal, Que.; given name: Charles Rosner; m. Andrea Morrison; c. Stephen Rosner, Ellen Jane; co-chair. Seagram Distillery; key figure as principal shareholder in bringing NL baseball to Canada with inception of Montreal Expos; board chair. '69-90; served vital roles on various ML committees; although he played a hands-off role with club management he enjoyed suiting up in his uniform 83 (a big Seagram brand) at spring training; deeply involved with cultural and philanthropic life in Canada through CRB Foundation; mem. Order of Canada, Cdn Baseball Hall of Fame; res. Montreal, Que.

BRONSON, Pat (all-around); b. 22 Oct 1947, Peterborough, Ont.; given name: Patricia Pauline; although not large in stature, speed, agility, natural athletic talent enabled her to play leading role in several sports, particularly hockey, softball, basketball; 3 HS t&f titles; founding mem. Ont. Women's HA '75; mem. '83 Ont. Sr. D title hockey team, ntl. C titlists; coach '90 Ont. Sr. B team; mem. '92 Ont. Sr. A title team; mem. 5 Peterborough city softball title teams '64-68; PWSA Int. B title '66, 4 Int. A title teams; Ont. Tier II titlists '80; leading batter award; mem. Ont./Eastern Cdn basketball title team '68; MVP Peterborough Women's Basketball Assn. '69-70; mem. 5 consec. Peterborough title teams; mem. 3 slo-pitch title teams; most dedicated player award '87; Peterborough female athlete of '76; YMCA woman of '80; hockey sportsmanship/citizenship award '84-85; basketball dedication award; pres. PWBA '71-93; mem. Peterborough Sports Hall of Fame; res. Peterborough, Ont.

BROOK, Tom (builder); b. 27 Jan 1908, Pelham, N.Y.; d. 2 Aug 1981, Calgary, Alta.; moved to Calgary '41 and reorganized Stampeders organization; pres. Stampeders '48-51; club dir. '56-58; hired Les Lear as coach '48 and, personally guaranteeing players' salaries, brought in stars like Woody Strode and Chuck "Sugarfoot" Anderson; team went on to win Grey Cup with undefeated season then won first 10 the following year; booster of interlocking schedule but staunch supporter of single championship game rather than home and home series; mem. Cdn Football Hall of Fame.

BROOKER, Todd (skiing); b. 24 Nov 1959, Waterloo, Ont.; m. Lisa Uffelman; ski lodge operator; father mem. '56 Olympic hockey team; 1st downhill, 2nd slalom, 3rd GS '75 ntl junior; European Cup circuit '78-79, '81; World Cup tour '78-79, '81-84; 3rd downhill '81 NZ championships; broke into winners' circle WC tour Kitzbuhel Austria, Aspen Colorado '83, Furano Japan '85; WC record 3-3-1; fed. govt. excellence award '85; mem. '84 Olympic team; injuries forced retirement from competition '87; CBS TV skiing color commentator; mem. Cdn Skiing Hall of Fame; res. Collingwood, Ont.

BROOKS, Lela (speed skating); b. 7 Feb 1908, Toronto, Ont.; d. 11 Sep 1990, Owen Sound; given name: Lela Alene; m. Russ Campbell (d); c. Art, Carol, Donna, Dorothy; m. Clifford Bleich; began collecting Ont., ntl titles, records '21; by end '25 had broken 6 world records; won 3 of 4 races and overall women's title '26 world competition; continued to add to ntl, NA honors, several world records including 1/2-mile indoor, outdoor, 3/4-mile outdoor; mile record Detroit Mardi Gras Festival '28; NA indoor title '35; qualified '36 Olympics but opted for retirement; 1st woman admitted to Old Orchard Skating Club Toronto; from outset of career to retirement won all titles available to women speed skaters, Ont. indoor, outdoor, all-Canadian, international and world; mem. Cdn Speed Skating, Canada's Sports halls of fame.

BROSSEAU, Eugene (boxing); b. 1895, Montreal, Que.; d. 1968, Montreal, Que.; post office employee; ntl amateur welterweight titles '15-16, US welter title '16, middleweight '17; fought series of San Francisco exhibitions on behalf of Red Cross '17; blow to neck in '19 bout with George Chip caused left arm paralysis; brief comeback '20; pro record: 27 bouts, won 17 by KO, 7 by decision, 1 no-contest, lost decision to Jack Bloomfield and was KO'd by Mike

McTigue; instructor '24 Olympic team; only Canadian to win 2 US amateur ring crowns and be selected to halls of fame in both amateur, pro ranks; mem. Cdn Amateur, Canada's Sports, Cdn Boxing halls of fame.

BROTHERS, Tanya (t&f); b. 2 Jul 1963, Thunder Bay, Ont.; UMan; sprint specialist; ntl jr. 50m indoor title '80; jr. outdoor 100, 200m '81; Canada Games 100, 200m titles; ntl indoor 200m '82; 3 CIAU titles; mem. '83 FISU, Pan-Am Games teams; silver 4x100m relay '83 FISU Games; bronze 4x100m relay '83 Pan-Am Games; PB: 100m 11.70, 200m 23.45; CIAU female indoor t&f athlete of yr award; res. Winnipeg, Man.

BROUILLARD, Lou (boxing); b. 23 May 1911, Eugene, Que.; dog breeder; 4 successful amateur years; beat Jack Thompson for world pro welterweight title '31; lost crown to Jackie Fields '32; KO'd Ben Jeby in 7th '33 to win NY Commission middleweight title; lost title to Vince Dundee '33; lost 2 title bids on fouls to Marcel Thil; barred from ring 1 year, mgr. received life suspension; won 60 of 1st 64 bouts, 44 by KO; pro record: 140 bouts, won 66 by KO, 43 on decision, 1 on foul, 3 draws, lost 24 decisions, 2 on fouls, once KO'd (Tiger Jack Fox); mem. Canada's Sports, Canadian Boxing halls of fame; res. South Hanson, Mass.

BROWN, Cara (ringette); b. 15 Sep 1965, Edmonton, Alta.; consulting economist; 8 ntl championship gold, 3 silver, 2 bronze '80-97; 2 world championship gold; 6 time ntl championship all-star centre; res. Calgary, Alta.

BROWN, Clayton (rowing/football); b. 16 Sep 1940, St. Catharines, Ont.; given name: Clayton Wayne; m. Lynn Crozier; c. David, Matthew, Susan; Guelph, hons BSc; teacher; mem. 3 SOSSA football title teams; all-Ont. tackle '60; tackle, punter Guelph '63-65; rejected Montreal pro bid; HS coach from '69; Ont. heavyweight jr. 8 rowing title team, NA Intermediate heavy 8s '59; mem. 3 Cdn Henley heavy 8s title teams; NA sr. 8s title; mem. '60, '68 Olympic teams; HS rowing coach '69-76; mem. Ont. Coaches Assn., rowing, football; res. St. Catharines, Ont.

BROWN, Colin (shooting); b. 28 Jul 1924, Ancaster, Ont.; m. Shirley Bray; c. Charles, Susan, Becky; major (retd) Cdn Forces; employed Hamilton Golf & Country Club; began shooting as cadet '39; competed as "Canloan" officer 2Bn Argyll & Sutherland Highlanders WW2; mem. 2 Cdn Forces Bisley teams; '56, '58 Cdn Forces service rifle champion; mem. '62, '65 DCRA Bisley teams, adjutant '66, commandant '73; Bisley Alexander match title '59, 3rd grand aggregate '60; mem. 2 Palma teams; 4 top DCRA F-Class competitor awards; 2 terms exec. v-pres. DCRA; deputy chair. DCRA council; DCRA 60-year badge '98; res. Ancaster, Ont..

BROWN, D. Wes (football); b. 1894, Ottawa, Ont.; d. Apr 1962, Ottawa, Ont.; began 37yr association with football as ticket manager for Rough Riders '25; held various exec. roles with that club; secty IRFU '41-42, '45, '47-61; appointed permanent secty of what would become Eastern div. of CFL '48; CFL outstanding service award; mem. Ottawa Sports, Cdn Football halls of fame.

BROWN, Dale (boxing); b. 15 Dec 1971, Calgary, Alta.; dock laborer; light heavyweight; mem. Bow Waters Amateur BC, coached by father Bob Brown; mem. ntl team from '87; 3 ntl titles; Puerto Rico Invitational tournament '89; silver '90 Commonwealth Games; bronze '91 Worlds, Pan-Am Games, Canada Cup; 81kg gold '94 Commonwealth Games; mem. '92 Olympic team; res. Calgary, Alta.

BROWN, Dick (football); b. 9 May 1925, Cleveland, Ohio; given name: Richard Anthony; m. Anne Peetsalu; c. Mark Anthony, Melanie Louise; UofT, BA; asst. football coach, athletics facilities supervisor Guelph; all-city HS end, punter; CIAU all-star tailback; pro Hamilton '50-54, Toronto '55-57, Montreal '57; mem. '54 Grey Cup winner; punt return specialist; '53 Eastern all-star halfback, all-pro safety; '56 all-star; cornerback Ticat Fabulous Fifties stars ('50-60), Ticat dream team ('50-70), punt returner ('45-73) all-Argos team; coached Burlington Braves, Oakville ORFU Black Knights, Hamilton Hurricanes, U of Guelph; res. Guelph, Ont.

BROWN, Doug (harness racing); b. 11 Sep 1955, Oshawa, Ont.; harness race driver; began driving at 18, winning just 3 races in initial season; reached 7,000 career victories plateau '98; dominated '90 Greenwood/Mohawk circuit; set world record with Town Pro; Cane Pace, Prix d'Ete, Stewart Fraser Memorial with Topnotcher; swept '97 Toronto Pacing series with Riyadh, Cam Fella Pacing Series with Tillys Sam; single season record 443 victories; 1st in OJC history to reach $5M single season winnings; lifetime earnings exceed $66M; 19 consec. yrs among NA top 20 in races won; 18 consec. seasons $1M+ in winnings; 8 O'Brien driver of yr, 1 HTA Messenger awards; res. Bowmanville, Ont.

BROWN, George (rowing); b. 1839, Herring Cove, N.S.; d. 8 Jul 1875, Halifax, N.S.; fisherman; Cogswell Belt race title 1864-68, permanent possession of belt; 1871 competed Halifax 4s, single sculls vs. Scottish, British, US rowers; challenges issued world pro champion Joseph Sadler were avoided but Brown turned pro 1873; defeated Robert Fulton of famed Paris Crew, US champion John Biglin 1873, US singles champion Bill Scharff 1874; Brown bet entire life savings on himself against Scharff and won by six seconds; defeated Evan Morris of US 1874; while preparing for 1875 match with Sadler suffered fatal stroke; mem. NS, Canada's Sports halls of fame.

BROWN, Gord (curling); b. 27 Jul 1918, Manor, Sask.; m. Jean Busby; c. Michael, Denise, Frances; retired civil servant; Sask. jr. tennis title '34; pres. Sask. Tennis Assn. '61-62; 3 Sask., 2 Cdn Legion, 2 Regina Grand Aggregate curling titles; pres. Regina Caledonian Club '61-62; exec. mem. Sask CA '61-64; skipped Ottawa entry to 3rd place '66 Ont. Consols; Canadian Branch Governor-General's double rink winner '66, '72; rep. Ottawa Curling Club Ont. Consols playdowns 7 times 8yrs; competed Ont. Srs.; mem. BCsrs. champions '79, runnerup nationals; res. Red Deer, Alta.

BROWN, Hal (t&f/coaching); b. 2 Dec 1917, Meaford, Ont.; given name: William Harold; m. Mildred Eleanor Hoskin; c. Gerry, Susan; Victoria Coll/Coll of Education, BA, teacher's degree, MA; retd HS teacher; set Cdn HS javelin record '35; Ont. HS LJ champ '36; gold LJ, Commonwealth record '38 BE Games; Intercollegiate 100, 220, javelin gold '39; Maritime LJ record '43; set British Army LJ record , won interservices LJ gold '45; ntl LJ, TJ, javelin titles '46; Jack Davies outstanding athlete of '46 award; pitcher Meaford OABA intermediate baseball champs '37; mem. UofT intercollegiate intermediate basketball title team '39-40; UofT t&f coach '48-70; mem. '59 Pan-Am Games coaching staff; coach ntl team '60 Olympics; OFSAA 50yr (at North Toronto CI) coaching (basketball/t&f) award; with twin brother Wally elected into UofT athletic Hall of Fame; res. Toronto/Clifford, Ont.

BROWN, Larry (t&f); b. 14 Feb 1952, Sudbury, Ont.; given name: Larry James; Texas, BSc, MEd; underground mine sampler; long distance specialist; twice all-Ont. indoor 2-mile champion; '73 2-mile indoor Houston Astrodome, WAC cross-country; '75 WAC 6-mile title, El Paso international marathon; mem. NCAA outdoor track title team '75; American Statesman 10k title '80, 9th in 12,000 field Bloomsday race Spokane Wash.; mem. world cross-country team Limerick, Ireland; res. Elliot Lake, Ont.

BROWN, Lisa (ringette); b. 24 Feb 1967, Edmonton, Alta.; performance.marketing consultant; participated in 15 of 16 ntl championships '82-97 winning 8 gold, 4 silver, 2 bronze; 3 world title teams; 7 times ntl championship all-star centre; sister Cara also ntl team mem.; res. Calgary, Alta.

BROWN, Louise (tennis); b. 19 Nov 1922, Dunnville, Ont.; m. Ross Brown; c. David, Chareen; insurance agent; '57 ntl women's singles title, with Hilda Doleschell doubles; with Ann Barclay '62 ntl women's doubles; ntl women's sr. singles '70-71; capt. Canada's 1st Federation Cup team '63, player '64, non-playing capt. '66-67, '69; gold '69 Canada Games; 27 consecutive years among nation's top 10; women's rep. Players' Assn.; mem. Cdn Tennis, Mississauga Sports halls of fame; res. Mississauga, Ont.

BROWN, Mae (basketball); b. 15 Aug 1903, Minnedosa, Man.; m. Bruce Webb; c. Gary Bruce, Margaret Jane; Alta. Coll.; retired secretary; mem. famed Edmonton Grads '27-31; mem. varied Vancouver teams; mem. Canadian Basketball, Alta. Sports halls of fame; res. Edmonton, Alta.

BROWN, Robert (baseball); b. 5 July 1876, Scranton, Pa.; d. 1962, Vancouver, B.C.; Notre Dame; following brilliant career at Notre Dame turned pro Spokane Indians and led club to PCL title; moved to Vancouver and over 45-year period earned title "Mr. Baseball;" instrumental in leading Vancouver to numerous pennants; key role in bringing modern PCL baseball to Vancouver; twice saw stadiums he had built burn down; promoted construction Capilano Stadium; mem. Cdn Baseball, BC Sports halls of fame.

BROWN, Sophie (basketball); b. 21 Sep 1916, London, Eng.; d. 5 Jul 1986, Victoria, B.C.; m. Frank Drake (d); c. Barbara, Bill; accountant; mem. famed Edmonton Grads '35-40, 103 games, 551 points, 5.1 avg.; competitive softball player; mem. Canadian Basketball, Alta. Sports halls of fame.

BROWN, Ted (curling); b. 4 Oct 1937, Kingston, Ont.; given name: Edward James; m. Kathy Deroche; c. Jeff, Tim,

Mike; self employed furniture upholsterer; Ont. Governor-General's, Whitby Dunlop titles '69; Toronto Royals carspiel '71; 3 times competed Ont. Consols, twice as skip; 3rd Dr. Alex Scott-skipped Ont. Consols winner '75; competed Fredericton Brier; skipped Ont. ntl mixed championships '76; invented Brownie broom; res. Kingston, Ont.

BROWN, Tom (football); b. 5 Dec 1936, Albert Lea, Minn.; div.; c. Susan, Tracy, Steven; UMinn; all-American interior lineman; Knute Rockne Award US Coaches' top lineman '61; runnerup to Navy's Joe Bellino Heisman Trophy; mem. Rose Bowl, Hula Bowl, 1st American Football Coaches All-American Game teams; pro BC Lions '62-67; 3 times WFC all-star, twice all-Canadian; 2 Schenley lineman of year awards; Jeff Nicklin Trophy '64; neck injury in '65 game led to retirement '67; mem. 2 Grey Cup finalists, 1 winner; mem. Cdn Football, B.C. Sports halls of fame; res. Coquitlam, B.C.

BROWN, Wally (t&f/coaching); b. 2 Dec 1917, Meaford, Ont.; d. 26 Feb 1971, Haliburton, Ont.; given name: George Wallace; m. Patricia Doreen Gilday; c. Gary, Robert, Virginia, Kathryn; Victoria Coll/Coll of education, BA, teacher's degree; teacher; Ont. midget LJ title '32; Intercollegiate LJ title '36; set Commonwealth records, competed in '38 BEG; Intercollegiate champ '38-39 setting records in LJ/shotput; Interservices gold LJ, TJ, Shot, Discus, 2 relay teams; ntl LJ, TJ champion, competed '48 Olympic trials; outfielder Meaford Intermediate OABA title team '37; fullback Victoria Coll. intramural UofT football champs '39; coached t&f/ football Parkdale and Bloor CI '46-71; with twin brother Hal mem. UofT Athletic Hall of Fame.

BROWNE, Cec (all-around); b. 13 Feb 1894, Winnipeg, Man.; d. 13 Aug 1985, Winnipeg, Man.; teenage hockey, track, soccer, swimming sensation; at 22 coached Man. juvenile hockey title team, played on jr. title team same year; with Flying Corps WW1 claimed t&f medals, starred in English rugger league; mem. 3 Allan Cup finalists; Sask. all-around t&f champion; football Regina Roughriders '22; starred for Dick Irvin's Dominion Express baseball team; charter mem. Chicago Black Hawks '26; dealt to Seattle (PCL), 2 scoring crowns; dealt to Boston '30 but retired; coach Elmwood juniors Western Canadian finalists '36; Man. Athlete of Century (1870-1970); mem. Man. Hockey, Sports halls of fame.

BROWNE, Less (football); b. 7 Dec 1959, East Liverpool, Ohio; Colorado State.; defensive back drafted by Pittsburgh Maulers (USFL) '84; joined CFL with Hamilton '84-88, Edmonton, Winnipeg '89, Ottawa '92, BC '93-94; 5 all-Eastern; 5 all-Canadian; 3yrs CFL interception leader; CFL record most interception return yds 14 for 273yds '90; CFL record most interceptions and return yds '92; CFL record: 174g, 7tds, 1 2pt cvt., 87 interceptions for 1,508yds, 4tds; mem. 3 Grey Crey Cup finalists, 2 winners; asst. coach Hamilton '97; TV football analyst since '96; res. Vancouver, B.C.

BROWNING, Kurt (figure skating); b. 18 Jun 1966, Rocky Mountain House, Alta.; m. Sonja Rodriguez; novice ntl singles title '83, ntl jr title '85, won '88 Skate Electric, Skate

Canada, '89-91 ntl, world championships; '90 Goodwill Games, Skate Canada, Nation's Cup, Lalique Trophy France titles; 8th '88, 6th '92, 5th '94 Olympics; plagued by back injury prior to '92 Olympics; 1st skater to execute quadruple toe loop in competition ('88 worlds); 1st Canadian to win three consecutive world titles; 4 time world champion; Lou Marsh trophy '90; 2 Lionel Conacher, 4 Norton Crowe trophies; Cdn Sports Council athlete of '93; ISU Jacques Favart award '97; pro from '94; world '95, Cdn '95, '97 pro titles; flag-bearer '94 winter Olympics; mem. Order of Canada, Cdn Amateur (Olympic), Canada's, Alta Sports, Cdn Figure Skating halls of fame; res. Caroline, Alta.

BRUCE, Ian (sailing); b. 7 Jun 1933, Jamaica, BWI; m. Barbara Brittain; c. Tracy, Tobi; McGill, Syracuse, BID; industrial designer, company pres.; capt. Trinity College hockey team '50-51; McGill squash team '51-53; mem. Olympic yachting team '60 Finn Class, '72 Star Class; team capt. '67-68 International 14ft dinghy world team championships titlists; Canadian International 14ft dinghy titles '67, '75, US title '58; major role in design, development high performance Tasar lightweight dinghy; mem. Royal St. Lawrence Yacht Club; res. Dorval, Que.

BRUCE, Lou (football); b. 16 Jul 1933, Toronto, Ont.; d. 16 Jan 1985, Ottawa, Ont; given name: Lou Alexander; div.; c. Heather, Wendy, Jennifer; Queen's, BA; plastics manufacturer; Toronto all-star football, basketball '50-52; mem. Queen's Golden Gaels, CIAU all-star '54-55; pro Ottawa '56-61; 3 times all-star defensive end; mem. Queen's Sports Hall of Fame.

BRUCE, Winston (rodeo); b. 27 Oct 1937, Stettler, Alta.; div.; c, Christie, Laurence; rodeo mgr. Calgary Stampede; learned the rodeo business from the ground floor following in footsteps of father Laurence who produced rodeos from '20-58 including 1st ever indoor rodeo in Camrose '46; produced his 1st pro rodeo at age 12; spent 15yrs as pro rodeo athlete claiming 2 ntl novice saddle bronc titles; 2 pro saddle bronc titles; Calgary Stampede championship, rookie of '59 award; earned world rookie of year award '59, world championship '61; asst. arena dir. at Stampede '69; rodeo mgr. from '70; mem. US, Cdn Rodeo, Alta. Sports halls of fame; res. Calgary, Alta.

BRUNET, Caroline (canoeing); b. 20 Mar 1969, Quebec City, Que.; Laval; kayak specialist; began competing '84; mem. ntl team from '88; competed '88, '92, '96 Olympics, 9 world championships; 10 ntl K1, 5 K2, 5 K4, 3 International K1, 2 K4 gold; silver K1 '96 Olympics; 1 gold, 2 silver '95 world championships; 1st Cdn to win 3 world K1 gold, 1000, 500, 300m '97, repeat '99; 1st Cdn woman ever to win world K1 title; K1 200m, 500m gold, 1000m silver '98 worlds; 4 gold '99 Duisburg regatta; Edmonton Grads team award '95; res. Dollard des Ormeux, Que.

BRUNETEAU, Mud (hockey); b. 28 Nov 1914, St. Boniface, Man.; d. 26 May 1982, Omaha, Neb.; given name: Modere; right wing; jr. Winnipeg K of C; pro Detroit Olympics (IHL) '34-35; Red Wings '35-36; scored lone goal as Wings defeated Montreal Maroons 1-0 in longest game in NHL history '36; except for brief stint with Pittsburgh (AHL) '37-38 remained with Detroit '45-46; best season

'43-44, 35g in 39 games; NHL record 139g, 138a; 3 Stanley Cup winners; after leaving NHL, playe for Indianapolis (AHL), Omaha (USHL); mem. Man. Hockey Hall of Fame.

BRUNO, Al (football/coaching); b. 28 Mar 1927, West Chester, Pa.; given name: Alberto Pavalone; m. Marie Giosio; c. Mike, Maria, Lisa; Kentucky, BA; football coach; end Bear Bryant's Kentucky football teams '47-50, forward Adolph Rupp's Kentucky NCAA basketball title teams '48-49; '50 Orange Bowl, '51 Sugar Bowl; US record 10 TD passes, 4 in single game from Babe Parilli '50; mem. 1st Kentucky Southeastern Conf. title team '50; all-conf., 3rd team all-American '50; Philadelphia Eagles draft; Toronto '52-54, Winnipeg '55-56; mem. '52 Grey Cup winner; coaching from '57; guided Toronto De La Salle CI to football, basketball titles; player-coach London Lords '58-60, ORFU title '60; taught, coached Pennsylvania HS '61-66; asst. Ottawa '66-67, Hamilton '68-70, '82, Harvard '71-81, Ivy League titles '74-75; head coach Hamilton '83-90; Grey Cup finalist '84-85, winner '86; head coach McMaster '94-96; res. Florida/Hamilton, Ont.

BRYDSON, Gordie (hockey/golf); b. 3 Jan 1907, Toronto, Ont.; m. Dorothy Beamish; retd golf pro; flying wing, kicker Toronto Argos '22-23; pro hockey right winger Toronto, Chicago, Detroit '24-38; golf pro from '30; 2 Ont. Open, Millar Trophy, CPGA, Rivermead Cup; 1 CPGA Srs., Que. Open titles; runnerup Canadian Open; 4 Ont. PGA Srs titles; club pro Mississauga Golf and Country Club '31-72; pres. OPGA, CPGA; CPGA life mem.; mem. RCGA, Mississauga Sports halls of Fame; res. Mississauga, Ont.

BUBBS, John (curling); b. 19 Feb 1953, Winnipeg, Man.; m. Shirley; c. Cheryl; electrical contractor; competed Man. Labatt Tankard 6 times, finalist '83; skip Man. entry '85 Brier; grand aggregate winner MCA 'spiel '84; res. Winnipeg, Man.

BUCHAN, Ken (curling); b. 9 Apr 1940, Harriston, Ont.; given name: Kenneth Donald; m. Deanne Catharine Girodat; c. Christine, Margaret; Waterloo Lutheran, BA, Waterloo, BPhE; teacher; 3rd for Bob Mann 3 Ont. Consols, 2 Briers; skipped own rink 7 Ont. Consols playdowns; skipped Ont. entry '69 Brier; Ont. Silver Tankard '72; skipped rink in 3 Ont. mixed championships, '81 ntl mixed Ont. entry; '93, '96 Ont. Srs; active Curl Canada coaching program; res. Kilworth, Ont.

BUCHBERGER, Kerri Ann (volleyball); b. 23 Jun 1970, Russell, Man.; U Regina; middle blocker; mem. ntl team from '91; competed '93 FISU, '91, '95 Pan-Am, '96 Olympic Games, '91, '95 World Cup; gold '96 Continental Cup; bronze '95 Pan-Am Games; Canada Cup game star award; 3 GPAC all-star awards; played in Belgium '92; res. Langenburg, Sask./Winnipeg, Man.

BUCKBORO, Dean (swimming); b. 3 Sep 1953, Grande Prairie, Alta.; given name: Deane Kelvie; m. Carole Wade; c. Vikki Lynn; Foothills Jr. College; truck driver; ntl team '68-73; Alberta 200, 400, 800, 1500m FS; 200, 400, 800, 1650yds FS records; ntl 200, 400m FS records; silver 400m FS, 800m FS relay '69 Canada Games; shoulder injury

forced him to miss '71 Pan-Am Games; mem. '72 Olympic, '73 world championships teams; res. Calgary, Alta.

BUCKINGHAM, Michelle (judo); b. 1 Sep 1968, Los Angeles, Calif.; Concordia; moved to Canada '71; began competing age 9; mem. ntl team from '89; 1 ntl -52kg, 2 -61kg titles; 61kg title '97 Pan-Am judo championships; silver '94 Francophone Games, '95 Pan-Am Games; gold '93 Dutch Open; 3rd degree black belt; competed '92, '96 Olympics; achieved PB placing 5th '97 worlds; Ottawa ACT judo award '97; res. Ottawa, Ont./Montreal, Que.

BUCKNA, Mike (hockey); b. 5 Sep 1913, Trail, B.C.; d. 6 Jan 1996, Trail, B.C.; given name: Mike Matthew; m. Aloise (Lola) Frolik (d); c. Mike Joseph; hotelman; 42 medals, numerous 1st, 2nd place trophies HS t&f; mem. 2 BC title jr. hockey teams; Trail Smoke Eaters '32-35, '46, '49; player-coach Prague Lawn & Tennis Club hockey team '36; coach Czech ntl team to '39; considered father of modern Czechoslovakian hockey; guided Czech nationals to European, world titles '47, 1st European team to claim that honor; mem. '50 Western Canadian Intermediate title team; coach Rossland Warriors '54 BC finals; Trail sportsman of '78; honored by Czech, Swedish governments for contribution to European hockey; mem. BC Sports Hall of Fame.

BUCYK, John (hockey); b. 12 May 1935, Edmonton, Alta; given name: John Paul; m. Anne Smith; c. 3; hockey exec.; jr. Edmonton; pro Edmonton (WHL); rookie scoring record, rookie of year award; Detroit '55-57, Boston '57-78; NHL record: 1540 scheduled games, 556g, 813a, 124 playoff games, 41g, 62a; mem. 2 Stanley Cup winners; once 1st, 2nd team all-star left wing; surpassed Dit Clapper's 20-season same club record, Milt Schmidt's club career point mark; 1st Bruin to achieve 250 goal plateau; NHL's 7th 500-plus goal scorer '75; joined select circle of 50-goal scorers with 51 '70-71; twice Lady Byng, Dufresne (Bruins MVP) awards; Conacher, Lester Patrick trophies; remained with Bruins in exec. capacity; did some broadcasting; dir. Bruins alumni assn.; chair. Massachusetts State Heart Fund more than decade; jersey 9 retd. by Bruins; nicknamed "Chief"; mem. Hockey, Alta Sports halls of fame; res. Boxford, Mass./B.C.

BUDAY, Attila (canoeing); b. 28 Jun 1974, Budapest, Hungary; brilliant junior career winning C2 1000 gold, C1 1000 bronze '92 Junior Worlds; ntl team mem. from '91; gold C2 1000, C4 500 '92 jr World Cup; C1 500, C2 1000 silver '95, '99 Pan-Am Games; brother Tamas also ntl team mem., father Tamas Sr. is coach; res. Missisauga, Ont.

BUDAY, Tamas Jr. (canoeing); b. 23 Apr 1976, Budapest, Hungary; mem. ntl canoe team from '93; 2 gold, 1 silver in C1 events '94 Junior Worlds; C4 500 jr World Cup gold; Pan-Am Games '95, '99 C2 1000 silver; brother Attila, father Tamas Sr. also involved with ntl team; Viscount Alexander award '94; res. Mississauga. Ont.

BUDDO, Don (all-around); b. 6 Oct 1886, Montreal, Que.; d. 27 Jul 1965, London, Ont.; mem. Montreal Wanderers, Wolverines hockey clubs; standout baseball, lacrosse player early 1900s; football Edmonton Western Football League; ran 400m, 800m '08 Olympics; provincial, ntl t&f 100yds, 3-mile, all field event titles except hammer and shot; mem. '08 Emerald Snowshoe Club which set world 1/4, 1/2-mile records; Golden Swastika award for work in Boy Scout movement; mem. Cdn Amateur Sports Hall of Fame.

BUDER, Jeff (golf); b. 10 May 1964, Arnprior, Ont.; Austin Peay State.; pro golfer; '87-88 all-Tenn. State, all-Ohio Valley Conf. teams; '86 Ottawa golfer of year; won 3 college tournaments; mem. Que. Willingdon Cup team; pro from '89; won Emerald Coast mini-tour titles '89, '91, 7 pro-am events; competed US mini, South Africa tours; res. Cornwall, Ont.

BUDGE, Ervin (snooker); b. 15 Jan 1940, Maniwaki, Que.; m. Corinne Lépine; c. Larry, Tracie, Jon; retd snooker executive; 9 KofC snooker titles; US Open title '78; Cdn team capt. '74-91 winning 6 gold, 4 silver in Bermuda, England, USA, Canada; 2 individual international snooker league titles; 4 ACT snooker awards; won more than 50 tournaments 1959-91; founding dir. Cdn Snooker Control Council '74; PR director CSCC '75-84; founding dir. International Snooker League '74; organized Cdn championships '74-80; organized first seniors snooker Olympics '77; organized senior citizen's snooker league for Ottawa, Nepean, Vanier, Kanata, National Capital area; founding dir. Elvis Sighting Society; founder Ottawa Snowsuit Fund gala dinner; res. Aylmer, Que.

BUDGE, Susan (orienteering); b. 2 Jun 1961, Montreal, Que.; given name: Susan Jane; m. Ian Lowe-Wylde; c. Jamie, Briar; Waterloo, BA., Queen's MA; exercise consultant; ntl under-14 title '72; jr. '73-74; NA jr. '75; ntl sr. '76-79, '83; NA sr. '77; 2nd Danish international 3-day '75; 3rd sr. Canadian international 6-day '78; 2nd jr. Canadian international 5-day '76; mem. 5 consecutive world championships teams; at 15 youngest ever world championship competitor; retd '84; won '80 Karrimor international mountain marathon Switzerland; mem.Waterloo cross-country running, ski teams; Class A Laurentian Zone alpine ski racer; Mérite Sportif Québècois, Ont. sports achievement award; res. Terra Cotta, Ont.

BULAU, Horst (ski jumping); b. 14 Aug 1962, Ottawa, Ont.; given name: Horst Hardy; m. Kerry Lennard-White; auto leasing mgr.; alpine skier age 6-14; entered 1st major competition at 12; ntl jr. 90m title at 16; joined Ont. team '78; 1st Canadian gold medalist at world level '79 70m world jr. title; 13 WC victories; 3rd overall WC standings '81-82, runnerup '83; ntl 70m, US 70m, 90m titles '81, ntl 70m, 90m '83-84; mem. '80, '84, '88, '92 Olympic teams; twice Ottawa ACT athlete of year; Ont. athlete of '83; fed. govt. excellence awards '82-84; John Semmelink Memorial award '79, '83; retd. to coaching '88; brief comeback '90; CTV color commentator '94 Olympics; mem. Cdn Amateur Sports, Cdn Skiing, Ottawa Sports halls of fame; res. Sharon, Ont.

BULINA, Bruce (golf); b. 29 Dec 1966, Vancouver, B.C.; S. Carolina; pro golfer; top Ont. jr. '85; mvp USC, all-Metro Conf. teams '86; all-conf. team mem. '89; pro '89; Canadian tour rookie of year '90; competed Asia, US mini-tours; res. Mississauga, Ont.

BULLARD, Mike (hockey); b. 10 Mar 1961, Ottawa, Ont.; m. Linda; c. Kaylie; centre Brantford OHA '78-81; drafted by Pittsburgh '80; remained with Penguins to '86; traded to Calgary '86-88, St. Louis '88, Philadelphia '89-90, Toronto '91-92; played 2 yrs Switzerland, 3 Germany; scoring champion German league '97; NHL record: 727 scheduled games, 329g, 345a, 40 playoff games, 11g, 18a; reached 50-goal plateau with 51 '84; OHA 2nd team all-star '80; res. Landshut, Ger.

BULLOCH, Jim (basketball); b. 23 Feb 1920, Winnipeg, Man.; d. 21 Apr 1991, Winnipeg, Man.; m. Fran Blower; c. Judy, Jim Jr., Dan, Garry; real estate broker; Man. sr. fastball league all-star catcher; coach Western Canadian title winning Legion 141 fastball team; coach St. Andrew's Jr. men, UMan Bisons basketball; '48-55 coach Winnipeg Paulins, '54 ntl champions, world tournament competitors; St. Andrew's Sr. men's coach '59-64, '68-69, 3 ntl titles; Glenlawn CHS 3 consecutive provincial titles; coach '79 ntl champions, '81 Nicolett Inn Sr. men ntl finalists; founder 9-team McGregor Armouries jr. men's league; organized basketball for disabled athletes; instrumental in founding Winnipeg Paraplegic Sports League, Golden Ramblers Wheelchair team; key role in Pan-Am Paraplegic Games '67; Manitoba HS coach of '78; 8 times Winnipeg Sr. men's coach of year; mem. Man. Sports Hall of Fame.

BULLOCK, Bruce (shooting); b. 10 Oct 1969, Burlington, Ont.; given name: Bruce Larsen; Carleton, hons. BA; following footsteps of father Jim and grandfather Don began earning full-bore shooting reputation qualifying for Bisley cadet team '86; mem. 1 Palma world team; 3 under-25 ntl teams; mem. 4 men's Bisley teams; res. Cheltenham, Ont.

BULLOCK, Jim (shooting); b. 15 Feb 1944, Victoria, B.C.; given name: James Charles; m. Carol Larson; c. Jason, Bruce; Sir George Williams; pres. Independent Life Brokers of Canada; began shooting age 10; .22 rifle as cadet; full bore from age 15; Caribbean championship Barbados '78; competed Bisley 10 times; Bisley Grand Aggregate award '84; proficient pistol shooter; father Don ranked among nation's top long range marksmen; res. Mississauga, Ont.

BULMER, Eryn (diving); b. 1 Aug 1976, Edmonton, Alta; Mount Royal Coll.; former gymnast who took up diving after suffering knee injury; competed in both sports '85-89; coached by Hui Tong Dive Calgary club; mem. ntl team '95-98; springboard specialist; 3m gold '96 Olympic trials, '97 FINA World Cup; 1m, 3m gold '98 FINA Grand Prix; 4 ntl 1m, 3 ntl 3m titles; competed '96 Olympics, '94 Goodwill Games; 3m gold, 1m bronze '98 Commonwealth Games; 3m gold '99 Pan-Am Games; res. Calgary, Alta.

BUNBURY, Alex (soccer); b. 16 Jun 1967, Plaisance, Guyana; given name: Alexander; m.; c. Kylie, Teal; pro athlete; began play age 12 St. Léonard Bourassa Montreal; striker Hamilton Steelers '87-90, Toronto Blizzard '90, Montreal Supra '91, West Ham United (English 1st div.) '92-93, FC Maritimo Portugal from '93; mem. ntl -16, -19, Olympic A, B teams; mem. ntl team from '86; scored 3 goals vs. Bermuda in 4-2 Cdn '92 World Cup qualifier victory; twice Cdn player of yr; 55 international caps; res. Portugal/Montreal, Que.

BUNKOWSKY, Barbara (golf); b. 13 Oct 1958, Toronto, Ont.; m. Mark Scherbak; Palm Beach Jr. Coll., Florida State; pro golfer; began playing golf age 10; '81 Ont. match, amateur titles; 2nd ranked ntl amateur '80-82; mem. ntl team '80 world team championships, '82 UK tour; mem. Ont. ntl team champions '80-82; AIAW ntl title '81; pro from '83; tied 4th '84 Freedom Orlando Classic while posting 1st career low 65 (matched '90); Chrysler-Plymouth Charity Classic title '84; 3rd Mazda LPGA championship '93, Sprint Classic '94; best earning season $167,039 '94; nicknamed "Buns"; Score Magazine Cdn female pro golfer of '91; featured in '87 Fairway fashion spread; 1 career hole-in-one; res. West Palm Beach, Fla.

BUONO, Wally (football); b. 7 Feb 1950, Potenza, Italy; m. Sande; c. Amy, Dana, Christie, Michael; Idaho State; football coach; CFL linebacker, punter Montreal '72-81; club record 90yd punt; CFL record: 358 punts, 14,510yds, 40.5avg, 12 singles; noted for durability, 152 consecutive games; in 5 Grey Cup finals, 2 winners; def. co-ordinator Jr. Concordes '82; asst. coach Concordes-Alouettes '83-86; asst. Calgary '87-89, GM,/head coach from '90; 3 Annis Stukus CFL coach of yr awards; hon. chair. Cdn Cancer Society '95; active in Children's Cottage Fund program; res. Calgary, Alta.

BURCH, Billy (hockey); b. 20 Nov 1900, Yonkers, N.Y.; d. Dec 1950,; pro Hamilton Tigers '23; centred line of Green brothers, Redvers (Red), Wilfred (Shorty) and carried team to 1st place NHL '25; Hart Trophy '25; transferred with team to NY where he became capt.; '27 Lady Byng Trophy; dealt from NY Americans to Boston '32; with Chicago '33 broke leg and retired; 5 times team scoring leader; 135g, 42a in 390 games; mem. Hockey Hall of Fame.

BURE, Pavel (hockey); b. 31 Mar 1971, Moscow, Russia; right wing; Soviet league rookie award CSKA '89; mem. 3 world jr. title teams; drafted by Vancouver '89; Vancouver '91-99, Florida '99; Calder Memorial Trophy '92; 1st team all-star '94; topped 50-game plateau with 60 '93, '94, 51 '98; played 3 NHL all-star games; NHL record: (through '99) 439 scheduled games, 267g, 227a, 60 playoff games, 34g, 32a; nicknamed "Russian Rocket"; outstanding performance '98 Olympics included 5g in semifinal game; father Vladimir represented Soviet Union as swimmer in '68, '72, '76 Olympics; rock singer; res. Moscow/L.A.

BURELLE, Jacques (administration); b. 8 Jul 1948, Ottawa, Ont.; UofOtt, BA, Ohio, MA; Indiana, PhD; sports administrator; standout football player UofOtt; site and service co-ordinator Montreal Olympics '75-76; deputy GM Montreal Olympic stadium '77; deputy ED Katimavik (Canada's national volunteer youth service program) '77-81; exec. vp/GM Montreal Manic soccer club '81-84; dir. gen. world gymnastic championships '84-85; co-ordinator Que. Society for Crippled Children Telethon '86; dir. gen. Molson (F1) GP '86-87; ntl dir. Molson sports promotions '87-89; v-pres. business development Molstar group '89-90; v-pres event marketing Everest group '91-92; pres. Eventcorp '92-96; commissioner CPGA tour from '97; res. Toronto, Ont.

BURGESS, Blair (harness racing); b. 27 Sep 1961, Toronto, Ont.; began as groom age 11; learned training skills from

Stew Firlotte, Gary Bourgon, Paul Radley before moving out on his own '85; although noted as a trainer he did some catch-driving including guiding Amity Chef to NA record; same horse established training credentials winning 3-yr-old colt of year honors; CTA trainer of '87 award; several horses he trained, like Road Machine, On The Road Again, Driven By Design, American Premier and Road To Broadway produced major victories; res. Milton, Ont.

BURGESS, Tim (baseball); b. 1 Sep 1927, London, Ont.; given name: Thomas Roland; div.; c. Thomas, Cynthia; UWO.; retd. baseball exec.; mem. several Ont. age-group title teams; pro Hamilton '46; left pro to star in outfield, at 1st base Sr. IC London Majors '48-51; resumed pro career '52 spending much of next decade Triple A Rochester, Columbus with brief ML stints St. Louis, Pittsburgh, California before '62 retirement; 3 silver gloves for fielding excellence; pro lifetime .300 BA; Look AAA all-star '53; Sally League MVP '52; Columbus Jets RBI record 96 '59; mgr. London Pontiacs (Sr IC) '63-64; rejoined pros as coach, mgr. '69; won 2 pennants; mgr. of year Modesto (Cal League) '72, Johnson City (Rookie League) '75; ML coach NY Mets '77, Atlanta '78; mgr. Richmond (IL) '79, Charleston (IL) '80, Tulsa (TL) '81-82 (TL title '82), Oklahoma City (AA) '83-84; mem. Cdn Baseball Hall of Fame; res. Sarasota, Fla./Lambeth, Ont.

BURGESS, Tom (football); b. 6 Mar 1964, Newark, N.J.; Colgate; AP all-American hon. mention '85; quarterback; joined CFL Ottawa '86, '92-93; Saskatchewan '87-89, '94-95, Winnipeg '90-91; 2 all-Eastern; CFL record (through '95): 172 scheduled games, 19tds, 2118 completions on 4034 attempts for 30,308yds, 190tds, 528 carries for 2240yds, 19tds; mem. 2 Grey Cup finalists, 1 winner; Grey Cup offensive star award '90; res. Regina, Sask.

BURKA, Ellen (coaching); b. 11 Aug 1921, Amsterdam, The Netherlands; c. Petra; Dutch champion; emigrated to Canada 1950s; became one of Canada's most respected coaches and choreographers; coached 26 Cdn Olympic and World champions and medallists; with Toller Cranston brought new style to figure skating; among students at various stages of their careers were Cranston, Christopher Bowman, Elvis Stojko and daughter Petra; mem. Order of Canada, Etobicoke, Canada's Sports, Cdn Figure Skating halls of fame; res. Toronto, Ont.

BURKA, Petra (figure skating); b. 17 Nov 1946, Amsterdam, The Netherlands; TV commercial producer; coached by mother Ellen; ntl jr. title '61, sr. '63-65; bronze '64 Olympics; gold NA, world '65; pro Holiday on Ice '66-69; consultant Sport Canada '70-74; CBC production co-ordinator '75; Lou Marsh Trophy '65; 2 Bobbie Rosenfeld trophies; hon. mem. Toronto Cricket, Skating Club; mem. Cdn Amateur, Ont. Sports Legends, Canada's Sports, Cdn Figure Skating halls of fame; res. Toronto, Ont.

BURKA, Sylvia (speed skating/cycling); b. 4 May 1954, Winnipeg, Man.; div. Jocelyn Lovell; m. David Hogg; from initial ntl speed skating title '67, dominated competitive scene through '80, winning 5 ntl titles (conflicting world events prevented competition 9 other years); more than 40 ntl records '67-80; mem. '72, '76, '80 Olympic teams; 4th '76 100m; competed 22 world championships, winning '73 jr., '76 senior, '77 sprint; world sprint points records (2x500m, 2x1000m) '73; world record all-around points (500m, 1000m, 1500m, 3000m) '76; 6 times Cdn. skater of year; 5 times Man. sportswoman of year; with Sue Nattrass shared Velma Springstead award '77; Order of Buffalo Hunt '73; Governor-General's award, City of Winnipeg award '73; began competitive cycling '75; 12 ntl sprint, 100m, pursuit, time trial, road race events titles; 3 gold '79 Western Canada Games; stage winner Coors international bike classic '80; 4th 300m pursuit '77 world championships; unofficial world record 1000m time trial '80; competed '96 Chicago marathon; mem. Cdn Speed Skating, Cdn Amateur, Man., Canada's Sports halls of fame; res. Toronto, Ont.

BURKE, Des (shooting); b. 5 Dec 1904, Ottawa, Ont.; d. 11 Apr 1973, Oakville, Ont.; given name: Desmond Thomas; m. Marcella Frances Simpson; c. William Desmond; Queen's, radiologist; childhood illness prevented strenuous sports so aided by father, teacher, became proficient marksman; placed in charge of cadet shooting training; youngest ever to win King's Prize Bisley '24, lost '29 shootoff for same prize; qualified for 23 Bisley teams, able to compete 12 times; amassed more prizes and awards (14 1sts, 11 2nds) than any other Canadian marksman; mem. 5 Kolapore, 3 MacKinnon teams; mem. King's Hundred 7 times; grand aggregate gold cross twice; published A Practical Rifleman's Guide ('32), Canadian Bisley Shooting: An Art and Science ('70); mem. Canadian Forces, Ottawa, Canada's Sports halls of fame.

BURKE, Jack (boxing); b. 8 Nov 1942, Saint John, N.B.; nicknamed Golden Boy; 3 Golden Boy trophy victories; prov., Maritime, ntl bantamweight titles; silver '64 Pan-Am Games; retired undefeated; mem. NB Sports Hall of Fame; res. Saint John, N.B.

BURKE, Larry (weightlifting); b. 15 Jul 1950, Toronto, Ont.; given name: Lawrence David; Dalhousie, UofOtt; plumber; rugby provincially for NS, wrestled at intercollegiate, ntl levels; 82.5kg lifting title '77 Aalborg Cup; 90kg silver '78 nationals, gold '79; bronze '79 Pan-Am Games 90kg; bronze 90kg '80 Pan-American championships, Canadian nationals; res. Vancouver, B.C.

BURKHOLDER, Dave (football); b. 21 Oct 1936, Minneapolis, Minn; m. Audrey Hewitt; c. Heidi, David Matthew; UMinn, BA; international sales rep.; 3 football letters as UMinn tackle, 2nd Big 10 team, hon. mention all-American; '57 Blue-Grey, East-West games; pro Winnipeg '58-64; 3 times WIFU all-star; Bombers most valuable lineman '62; mem. 4 Grey Cup winners; res. Hopkins, Minn.

BURLEY, Kris (gymnastics); b. 29 Jan 1974, Truro, N.S.; York U; all-around competitor; began competing age 5; 1st Nova Scotian named to ntl team '89; 1st Cdn to successfully execute Yurchenko entry vault; ntl jr. all-around title '90; 2 gold, 2 silver, 1 bronze '90 Pan-Am jr.; Cdn jr. elite all-around title '91; competed '91, '95 Pan-Am, '93 FISU, Worlds, '94, '98 Commonwealth, '96 Olympic Games; 1 gold, 3 silver '94, 1 silver, 1 bronze '98 Commonwealth Games; 3 bronze '95 Pan-Am Games, team gold, vault bronze '99 PAG; 6 ntl sr, 4 ntl jr, 1 ntl novice, tyro titles; twice NS athlete of yr; recipient 3 academic scholarships; res. Fredericton, N.B.

BURNHAM, Barrie (rugby); b. 1 Mar 1938, Vancouver, B.C.; div.; c. Diane, Ricky; salesman; West Vancouver Barbarians and Rowing Club; Melorama Club '61-81; adept kicker with both feet; scum-half/off. half ntl team '62-71; UK '62, Wales '71 tours; Japan '70 with BC team; 4 BC title teams; "capped" 4 times in Canada; 26 Feb '66 recorded rare feat by scoring in every possible way in a game (try, convert, dropped goal, penalty goal, goal from a mark) earning listing in Guiness Book of Records; Howie McPhee Trophy, Vancouver rugby's premier individual award; softball player-coach; mem. BC Sports Hall of Fame; res. Vancouver, B.C.

BURNHAM, Faye (basketball); b. 2 Jun 1920, Vancouver B.C.; m. James Ecclestone; c. Glenn, Brian; UBC; retired phys ed teacher; mem. 6 ntl sr. women's basketball teams; Hedlund's BC women's softball title teams; 3rd base '44 Neons world title team; rejected pro offers Chicago Glamour League; centre forward HS, BC women's field hockey teams, Pacific Northwest titles; coached basketball, field hockey, t&f, softball, volleyball Magee HS Vancouver, Hudson Bay track team; former pres. BC branch women's AAU of C, CAHPER; v.-pres. Canadian Camping Assn.; former dir. Vancouver YWCA; mem. National Advisory Council for Fitness, Amateur Sport; mem. BC Sports Hall of Fame; res. Vancouver, B.C.

BURNS, Leo (administration); b. 20 Oct 1884, Montreal, Que.; d. 5 Sep 1965, Montreal, Que.; average athlete basketball, snowshoeing, distance running; mem. St. Pat's AAA; mgr. '36 Olympic boxing team; ring general '36 ntl championships; track official AAU of C competitions; registrar, pres. Que. branch AAU of C; v-pres. AAU of C; pres. St. Pat's AAA, Shamrocks AAA, QAHA; dir. Que. Lacrosse Assn.; CAHA merit award; mem. Cdn Amateur Sports Hall of Fame.

BURNS, Pat (coaching/hockey); b. 4 Apr 1952, St. Henri, Que.; m. Line; hockey coach; ex-policeman; coach Hull Olympiques '83-87, 1 QMJHL title; coach Sherbrooke '87-88; Montreal (NHL) '88-92, 1st place finish rookie year; Toronto '92-96, Boston from '97; asst. Team Canada Canada Cup gold medal team '91, '86 world junior championships; joined Dick Irvin Sr. as only persons to coach both Montreal and Toronto; also with Irvin lone person to coach three of Original Six teams; NHL coaching record: (through '98) 618 scheduled games, 321-211-86, 108 playoff games, 55-53; 1st to win Jack Adams NHL coach of yr award with 3 different teams '89, '93, '98; HN coach of '93; hockey radio/ TV analyst '96-97; res. Lynnfield, Mass.

BURNS, Tommy (boxing); b. 17 Jun 1881, Hanover, Ont.; d. 10 May 1955, Vancouver, B.C.; given name: Noah Brusso; m., c. 1; ordained minister; under Sam Biddle launched ring career Detroit at 19; 7 straight KO's before adopting name Tommy Burns borrowed from jockey friend; 1st loss to Philadelphia Jack O'Brien; when Jim Jeffries retired Marvin Hart claimed vacant world heavyweight crown; Burns, O'Brien filed counter claims; only Canadian to hold world heavyweight title '06; defended successfully 11 times including draw, win over O'Brien; lost title to Jack Johnson '08; ended ring career '20 with 36 KO's, 9 decision wins, 4 decision losses, 8 draws, 1 no-contest, once KO'd; 1 minute 28 second KO victory over Jem Roche '08 shortest heavy title bout on record; at 5'7" shortest ever to hold heavy title; authored Scientific Boxing '08; mem. Canadian, US Boxing, Canada's Sports halls of fame.

BURROWS, Bob (softball); b. 10 Mar 1947, Victoria, B.C.; given name: Robert John; m. Joette Mason; c. Brady, Lanny, Amanda; Spokane Comm. Coll, Seattle Pacific; insurance adjuster; multi-talented athlete excelling in softball, baseball, basketball; mem. '67 Cdn basketball team Pan-Am Games; BC champion, MVP Oak Bay '65; attended Seattle Pacific on dual baseball-basketball scholarship; drafted by NBA Seattle SuperSonics but opted for baseball with Kansas City organization; 5 minor league seasons ended with serious injury in exhibition game '72; playing coach Victoria Scorpions (Data Tech) sr. A basketball team; ntl championship MVP, finalist '76; mem. Victoria Bates (Budgets) 4 successive ntl title softball teams '75-78; 1 MVP, 3 all-star awards; 15hrs in 6 ntl finals and Guiness Book of World Records inclusion for 4 world tournament HRs and 14 rbi; player-coach Victoria ntl title teams '82-83; Greater Victoria male athlete '74, twice runnerup; 3 team of yr awards; competed '76 world tournament which, due to weather, ended with Canada, USA, NZ sharing title; began refereeing basketball '80; Victoria Little League pres.; mem. Cdn, BC Softball, South Hill Vancouver, Greater Victoria Sports halls of fame; res. Victoria, B.C.

BURROWS, Pat (field hockey); b. 5 Nov 1959, Barrie, Ont.; given name: Patrick David; m. Dr. Susan Wood; Miami (Ohio), UofT, BPHE, Queen's BEd; teacher; attended Miami on ice hockey scholarship; mem. ntl field hockey (outdoor) team '80-90, '94; ntl indoor FH team '91-93; competed '86, '90, '98 world outdoor, '91 indoor World Cup, '84, '88 Olympics, '81, '85, '89 Intercontinental Cup, gold '83, '87, silver '89, '95 Pan-Am Games; MVP '89 Intercontinental Cup; team capt. '85-86, '89-90, indoor '91-93; Petro Canada scholarship; retd from competition '98; mem. Nepean Sports Wall of Fame; res. San Francisco, Calif.

BURTNYK, Kerry (curling); b. 24 Nov 1958, Reston, Man.; given name: Kerry Grant; m. Patti; c. Rachel, Laura; Red River Comm. Coll.; account executive; Man. jr title '78; skipped '79 Canada Winter Games gold medal rink; 8 time competitor Man. finals; at 21 youngest ever to skip Brier winner '81, bronze medal Silver Broom '81; skip '95 Brier, Worlds winner; MCA grand aggregate champion '85-86; skipped Man. rink '81, '88, '95 Briers; organized $250,000 Manitoba cashspiel circuit; nicknamed Bubba; res. Winnipeg, Man.

BUSCOMBE, Lisa (archery); b. 15 Dec 1956, Hamilton, Ont.; sep. David Bertoncini; McMaster, hons BComm, UofT, MIR; researcher; world field archery title '84; Olympic team alternate '84; field archery World Games champion '85; 7 Ont., 6 ntl outdoor archery titles; mem. Cdn Amateur Sports Hall of Fame; res. Toronto, Ont.

BUSH, Eddie (hockey); b. 11 Jul 1919, Collingwood, Ont.; d. 31 May 1984, Collingwood, Ont; given name: Edward Webster; m. Mabel Owens; c. Eddie Jr., Sandra Louise; salesman; Jr. A Guelph Biltmores; minor pro seasoning Pittsburgh, Kansas City; joined Detroit(NHL) '41-43; in 3rd game '43 Stanley Cup final scored once, assisted 4 others

while playing defence as Wings beat Toronto 5-2; post-WW2 Cincinnati scoring record for defencemen; player-coach Collingwood '51-53, 3 Ont. Intermediate A finals, 2 titles; coached Collingwood Jr. C consecutive titles '51-53; coached Guelph, Hamilton, Pittsburgh, Memphis, Kitchener, Richmond, NHL Kansas City Scouts '76; coach Hamilton '62 Memorial Cup winner; OHA jr. coaching record: 17yrs, 401-378-114; mem. Collingwood Sports Hall of Fame.

BUTLER, Kathy (t&f); b. 22 Oct 1973, Scotland; Wisc; 5000m runner; moved to Canada age 11; gold 5000m '95 Big-10 championships, '95-96 NCAA 3000m; ntl title '95; Cdn, NCAA cross-country champion '95; mem. '96 Olympic Games; NCAA cross-country runner of year '96; res. Waterloo, Ont./Madison, WI

BUTT, Sabir (squash); b. 20 Apr 1969, Nairobi, Kenya; claimed 5 ntl jr. age group titles; 4 ntl sr. titles; Western Canada, Ont. Closed, Sask. Open titles; selected to 5 ntl world championship teams, competing in 3; ranked #1 in Canada '94; 2 team gold '95 Pan-Am Games; res. Brazil

BUTT, Susan (tennis); b. 19 Mar 1938, Vancouver, B.C.; given name: Dorcas Susan; div; c. Tara Susan, Donal Lee Finn; UBC, BA, MA, UChi, PhD; psychologist, associate prof.; more than decade among Canada's leading tennis players, winning singles, doubles, mixed doubles titles BC, Ont., Que., Can., Western Can., Pacific Northwest, US Intercollegiate; top ranked ntl women's tennis '60-61, '67; 3rd round Wimbledon '61; capt. '70-72 Federation Cup teams; v.-pres. CLTA '71-72; author "A Psychology of Sport", numerous research publications on psychological motivation in sport; clinical psychologist consultant for many athletes, teams, clubs from local to elite levels; res. Vancouver, B.C.

BUTTERFIELD, Jack (builder/hockey); b. 1 Aug 1919, Regina, Sask; days as player cut short by injury so he turned to role as PR exec./trainer for AHL New Haven Eagles owned by uncle Eddie Shore; later business mgr. Fort Worth (USHL), Oakland (WHL); jack-of-all-trades Springfield (AHL) from concessions mgr to GM; became AHL pres. '66; twice rewrote AHL constitution; key role in keeping minor pro hockey alive as NHL went on expansion binge following conflict with WHA; mem. Hockey Hall of Fame; res. Springfield, Mass.

BUTTERFIELD, Joe (rodeo); b. 15 Sep 1961, Calgary, Alta.; farrier, Christmas tree dealer; calf roping, steer wrestling specialist; ntl calf roping title '90; Alta. circuit high point title '93; 2 BC circuit calf roping titles; Skoal pro rodeo circuit CR title '91; owner Cdn CR horse of yr (Vance) '91, (Jake) '95; Dodge, Skoal pro tour, Calgary Stampede SW titles '92; res. Red Deer, Alta.

BUXTON, Noel (curling); b. 26 Aug 1910, Sheffield, Eng; d. 26 Dec 1988, Winnipeg, Man.; given name: Noel Robert; m. Audrey; c. Noel, Beverley; banker; pres. Deer Lodge CC '61-62; mem. MCA council '62-63, pres. '71-72; instrumental in formation Manitoba Curling Hall of Fame; hon. life mem. CCA, MCA, Deer Lodge CC; mem. selection comm. MSHOF; mem. Cdn Curling Hall of Fame.

C

CADA, Petra (table tennis); b. 2 Feb 1979, Prague, Czechoslovakia; at 14 youngest to represent Canada at world championships; simultaneously held ntl U-14, -17, -21 titles '93, only female ever to do so; women's team gold '95 Pan-Am Games; English junior open title '95; singles bronze '93 world youth championships; mem. '96 Olympic team; res. Ottawa, Ont./Halifax, NS.

CAETANO, Errol (table tennis); b. 8 Aug 1953, Georgetown, Guyana; cable engineer; joined ntl team '71; 5 ntl singles, 7 men's doubles, 6 mixed doubles titles; Caribbean singles, men's, mixed doubles '72; Scandanavian Open '75; Eastern Canadian Open '78; mem. '71, '73, '75 world, Commonwealth championships teams; res. Pickering, Ont.

CAFFERY, Jack (t&f); b. 21 May 1879, Hamilton, Ont.; d. 2 Feb 1919, Hamilton, Ont.; given name: John Peter; m. Jane Campbell; c. 3 boys, 3 girls; shoe merchant; Boston Marathon victories 1900-01; Hamilton Around the Bay marathon 1898, 1900; reduced own BM record by 10 minutes '01; retired from racing '03; comeback bid '08 failed to produce big results; forced from Olympic trials by foot injury paid own way to '08 Games, finished 11th; running coach from '09; mem. Cdn Road Running Hall of Fame.

CAHILL, Leo (football); b. 30 Jul 1928, Utica, Ill.; div.; c. Steven, Christy Lee, Terry, Lisa Ann, Betty Lynn; Illinois, BSc,Toledo, MA; football executive; all-state centre HS sr.; mem. Illinois Rose Bowl titlist; all-Midwest guard, hon. mention all-American, Catholic all-American; Blue-Grey Game; coached football Japan, freshman coach Illinois '53; Lewis College line coach '54-55; asst. Toledo '56-57; South Carolina offensive coach '58-59; asst. Alouettes '60-64; head coach Toronto Rifles (Continental League) '65, won div. title, tied for title '66; coach Argos '67-72, '77-78, GM '86; '71 Grey Cup finalist; GM Memphis Southmen (WFL) '74; league official as league folded '75; TV-Radio sports commentator '87-85; v.-pres. Ottawa '96; mem. Etobicoke Sports Hall of Fame; res. Nepean, Ont.

CAIN, Jim (football); b. 30 Jun 1938, Toronto, Ont.; div. Lynn Becker; c. Pam; m. Pam Mountenay; Detroit, BSc; Stats Can. statistician, economist; among 1st Canadian HS grads sent to US college on CFL team recommendation; pro Ottawa '61-69, playing all line positions except centre; launched pro career on offence and finished on defence; def. tackle as Riders won consecutive Grey Cups '68-69; asst. coach UofOtt '70-72; res. Nepean, Ont.

CAIN, Larry (canoeing); b. 9 Jan 1963, Toronto, Ont.; McMaster; teacher/coach/motivational speaker; ntl jr. record 2:08.59 C1 500m '79; 1st Cdn canoeist in 46 years to win at world level claiming 2 golds '81 jr. worlds; '80 Bydgoszcz regatta jr. C1 500m, 1000m; '80 Pan-Am championships C1 1000m; '82 Nottinghamshire regatta C1 1000m; gold C1 1500m '83 Brandenburg regatta, silver C1 500m; gold,

silver '83 Sofia regatta; gold 500m C1, silver 1000m C1 '84 Olympics; ntl titles: 8 C1, 2 C2 500m, 4 C1, 2 C2, 1 C4 1000m; 2 SFC athlete of month awards; runnerup Viscount Alexander Trophy '81; Canadian Sport Manufacturers Assn. award '81; fed. govt. world champion award '82; coach, Burloak Canoe Club; mem. Order of Canada, Cdn Amateur, Canada's Sports halls of Fame; res. Oakville, Ont.

CAITHNESS, Charlie (soccer/builder); b. 7 Nov 1907, Carnoustie, Scotland; d. 19 Aug 1985, Winnipeg, Man.; player. coach, manager, administrator; managed ANAF Scottish '47-65, Tatra '70-82; 16 Man. championships, including unbroken streak of 12; Scottish won 2 ntl titles; coached Winnipeg Blues in Western Canada League; mgr. ntl champion Manitoba Selects '70; keen interest in youth soccer and development of young players; mem. Man. Sports Hall of Fame.

CALDER, Marty (wrestling); b. 25 Jan 1967, St. Catharines, Ont.; Brock; m. Tanya; coach; began competing age 14; freestyle and Greco-Roman; competes at 68, 63kg level; competed '91 (bronze), '95, '99 (bronze) Pan-Am, '92, '96 Olympic, '94 Commonwealth Games, '91 (bronze), '93, '97 Worlds, gold '92 Sunkist International Open, '93 Polish GP, '92 Canada Cup, '90 Clansman International; ntl 62kg title '94; gold 62kg '94 Commonwealth Games; 4 CIAU, 5 ntl sr. titles; CIAU outstanding wrestler award '92 championships; asst. coach Brock , standout lacrosse player; mem. Cdn jr. title team; drafted by pro Buffalo Bandits; res. St. Catharines, Ont.

CALDWELL, Earl (shooting); b. 27 Oct 1912, Heward, Sask.; given name: Earl Grove; m. Edith Nicol; c. Robert, David; pres. Caldwell Industries; mem. 9 BC skeet, 12 BC. trap all-star teams; '53-73 numerous BC. skeet titles in all gauges; mem. ntl team that broke 498x500; ntl record 9 times PITA all-star; BC. record 7 times all-Canada trap team; 11 provincial titles including all-time 6 doubles crowns; 2 consecutive ntl doubles titles; ntl singles with 494x500; more than 300 titles; mem. '56 Olympic team; res. N. Vancouver, B.C.

CALKINS, Michelle (synchro swim); b. 3 Oct 1958, Calgary, Alta.; m. Douglas DeFilippi; c. Anna, Paul; coach; with Helen Vanderburg won world aquatic duet title '78; retired to coaching '78 with Calgary Aquabelles, working with several world, Olympic champions; ntl team asst.coach '89-93, head coach '94-97; 3 ntl title teams; with Vanderburg shared Elaine Tanner award '77; mem. Alta Sports, Cdn Aquatic halls of fame; res. Calgary, Alta.

CALLAGHAN, Helen (baseball); b. 18 Mar 1923, Vancouver, B.C.; d. 8 Dec 1992, Santa Barbara, Calif.; div. Bob Candaele; c. Ricky, Rocky, Kelly, Kerry, Casey; m. Ron St. Aubin; home care supervisor; centre fielder; played in All-American Girls Professional Baseball League with Minneapolis '44, Fort Wayne '45-48, Kenosha '48; sister Marg also played in league; BC. jr. 100yd sprint champion;

played basketball, lacrosse, softball; son Casey played ML baseball; Lompoc. Calif. scholarship bears her name; honored by Cooperstown, Cdn Baseball halls of Fame.

CALLAGHAN, Margaret (baseball); b. 23 Dec 1921, Vancouver, B.C.; div. Merv Maxwell; c. Guy, Dale; care giver; versatile athlete who played for Cdn champion Vancouver Eilers '51 ntl basketball champions; 8 seasons at 3rd base in AAGPBL with Minneapolis '44, Fort Wayne '45-48, South Bend '49, Peoria '50-51, Kalamazoo '51; competed in '43 women's world amateur softball championships; played 3yrs lacrosse; sister Helen also played AAGPBL; mem. Softball City Surrey Walk of Fame, South Memorial Hall of Fame; honored by Cooperstown, Cdn Baseball halls of fame; res. Delta, B.C.

CALLAGHAN, Pius (builder); b. 2 Sep 1914, Charlottetown, P.E.I.; d. 31 Jul 1990, Charlottetown, P.E.I.; m. Winnie; c. 3; St. Dunstan's BA, LLB; journalist, educator; associated with Maritime AHA 20yrs; pres. PEIJHL '68-69; mem. PEI Sports and Racing Commission '82-87; Callaghan Cup awarded annually to Atlantic Canada Jr. A titlists; chair. Charlottetown Gold Cup & Saucer 3yrs; CAHA meritorious award; mem. PEI Sports Hall of Fame.

CALLES, Ada (curling); b. 12 Oct 1920, Lancashire, Eng.; given name: Ada Davies; m. Samuel Calles; c. Dan, Sam; Trail business college; rep. Kootenay Dist. at BC. championships 9 consecutive years; BC., ntl titles '62, runnerup ntl final '63, title '64; defeated men's Brier champion Lyall Dagg in special match; following 7-year break teamed again with Ina Hansen to win BC. title and tie for 1st, losing playoff in ntl final '71; with Hansen at 3rd skipped BC. to 1st ntl srs title '73; mem. BCLCA exec. '60-67 from zone convenor to pres.; CLCA delegate; chaired '76 BC. girls' provincial championship comm.; mem. Canadian Curling Hall of Fame; res. Kimberley, B.C.

CALLURA, Jackie (boxing); b. 1 Jan 1914, Hamilton, Ont.; d. 4 Nov 1993, Hamilton, Ont.; ntl amateur featherweight title '31; '32 Olympic team; pro '36; US National Boxing Assn. featherweight title beating Jackie Wilson in 15 at Providence '43; defended twice before KO loss to Phil Terranova '43 New Orleans; last pro bout Miami '47; fought 100 pro bouts winning 13 by KO, 43 by decision, one on foul, 10 draws, 27 lost decisions, KO'd 6 times; mem. Canada's Sports, Canadian Boxing, Copps Coliseum halls of fame.

CAMERON, Bev (rowing); b. 17 Jun 1953, Ottawa, Ont,; '75 Canadian Henley, ntl championships single sculls; with sister Trice '75 Canadian Henley double sculls, US women's double sculls; with Cheryl Howard 6th double sculls '76 Olympics; closed competitive career with 4th double sculls (with Howard) '77 world championships; res. Toronto, Ont.

CAMERON, Bob (football); b. 18 Jul 1955, Hamilton, Ont.; m. Louise; c. Brett, Shane; Acadia; quarterback, kicker Acadia; Hec Crighton Award '77; 1st round draft, 6th overall Edmonton '77; signed by Winnipeg as free-agent punter '80; all-time Blue Bomber punting leader; CFL record (through '98): 329gp, 4cvts, 119s, 123pts, 2705punts, 116,791yds; 2 Western, 4 Eastern, 4 CFL, 1 Northern all-star; 2 CFL records; 5 Grey Cup finals, 3 winners; plays with Blue Bombers hockey team; mem. Acadia Sports Hall of Fame; res. Winnipeg, Man.

CAMERON, Doug (curling); b. 18 Aug 1933, Charlottetown, P.E.I.; given name: Douglas Allison; m. Barbara Rupert; c. Marilyn, Nancy, Angus, Gordon; Queen's; retd deputy minister, accountant; won provincial titles spanning 6 decades '49-91; played in 2 ntl schoolboy, runnerup '50; 7 Briers, 5 as skip; skipped PEI '73 ntl mixed, 2 ntl srs; runnerup '64 Tournament of champions; competed 3 tournament of champions tournaments; runnerup '64 CBC Curling Classic; skipped '70 City of Ottawa grand aggregate winner; mem. Cdn Curling, PEI Sports halls of fame; res. Charlottetown, P.E.I.

CAMERON, Fred (t&f); b. 11 Nov 1886, Advocate Harbor, N.S.; d. 18 Mar 1953, Vancouver, B.C.; given name. Frederick; m. Blanche Moffat; tire vulcanizer; began competing '07 meeting with quick success despite lack of training; caught attention of prominent trainer Tom T. Trenholm and career took off; set Maritime, Cdn 10, 5 mile records; won 1910 Boston Marathon; 1st Boston Marathon winner honored by Mayor of Boston with luncheon, establishing a tradition; beat Clarence DeMar, Walter Hackett, Cliff Horne in series of 5 and 10 mile challenge races Amherst, N.S.; turned pro 1911; ran for Illinois AC several years; retired '19; amassed over 100 trophies, 60 cups during career; mem. NS Sports, Cdn Road Running halls of fame.

CAMERON, Harry (hockey); b. 6 Feb 1890, Pembroke, Ont.; d. 20 Oct 1953, Vancouver, B.C.; given name: Harold Hugh; among 1st offensive defencemen; believed 1st player to curve a shot without aid of curved stick; scored 171 goals in 312 games over 14yr pro career Blueshirts (NHA) '13-17, Montreal Wanderers (NHA) '17, Toronto Arenas '18, '20-24 (3 Stanley Cups), Ottawa Senators '19, Canadiens '20; left NHL '24, played in Vancouver, Saskatoon, Minneapolis, St. Louis; coach Saskatoon Sheiks Prairie League '32; mem. Hockey Hall of Fame.

CAMERON, Jack (all-around); b. 3 Dec 1902, Ottawa, Ont.; d. 29 Dec 1981, Danville, Va.; m. Margaret Jane Grant; St. Andrews College, McGill.; goaler Toronto Granites Allan Cup champions '21-23; Olympic gold medal '24; rejected pro offer from Montreal Canadiens; NHL referee '32-36; Que. Open golf champion '28; Que. amateur titles '32-33; qualified 9 US amateurs, once quarterfinalist; mem. Ont., Que. Willingdon Cup teams; ntl amateur finalist '32, 3 times semifinalist; cricket wicketkeeper ntl champion Toronto Yorkshire Cricket Club; partnered Jack Purcell England international badminton matches; with Rod Phelan ntl doubles; 4 times Ont. team mem.; with Bill Stewart Ont. doubles; Ont. sports achievement award; mem. Kingston International Hockey Hall of Fame and as mem. Olympic champion Granites Cdn Hockey Hall of Fame Toronto.

CAMERON, Michelle (synchro swim); b. 28 Dec 1962, Calgary, Alta.; m. Al Coulter; c. Alissa, Jacqueline; UCal; teamed with Carolyn Waldo to win '86 Commonwealth, '88 Olympic duet gold, '85-87 world duet titles; also earned duet gold '85 Rome, Spanish Opens, '85, '87 FINA Cup;

Pan-Pacific; Spanish Open team gold '84; ntl duet, team gold, figures bronze; Spanish Open figures silver '85; sport excellence award '86; Dick Ellis award '85; mem. Order of Canada, Alta Sports, Cdn Aquatic, Olympic, Canada's Sports halls of fame; res. Calgary, Alta.

CAMERON, Trice (rowing); b. 23 Feb 1952, Ottawa, Ont.; given name: Patrice Gail; UofOtt; policy analyst; mem. ntl cross-country B ski team '73-74; Olympic rowing teams '76, '80; with sister Bev '75 Cdn Henley, US women's double sculls; ntl single sculls '77; Cdn Henley singles '79; Cdn quad, Henley quad titles '80; mem. women's committee FIS '75-77, '85-95; chair. women's adhoc rowing comm. '81; silver Coureur de Bois ntl ski marathon; partner Old Chelsea seasonal cross-country ski shop; Level II cross-country instructor, Level I coach; res. Gleneagle, Que.

CAMPBELL, Angus (builder/hockey); b. 19 Mar 1884, Stayner, Ont; d. 1976, Toronto, Ont.; given name: Angus Daniel; UofT, BSc; mining engineer; mem. UofT hockey, lacrosse title teams; played hockey Cobalt, Ont '09-14; after playing days ended played key role in amateur hockey development in Northern Ontario; 1st pres. NOHA '19; served as OHA exec.; mem. Hockey Hall of Fame.

CAMPBELL, Cassie (hockey); b. 22 Nov 1973, Brampton, Ont.; Guelph hons. sociology; soccer/basketball/hockey player; OWIAA all-star defence '96; mem. Ont. Canada Winter Games team '91; silver Esso Nationals with North York Aeros '96; mem. ntl team from '94; 2 world, 2 Pacific Rim titles; mem. '98 Olympic team; Guelph sportswoman of '96; spokesperson HIP program smoking prevention for young girls; res. Guelph, Ont.

CAMPBELL, Clarence (administration); b. 7 Jul 1905, Fleming, Sask.; d. 24 Jun 1984, Montreal, Que.; given name: Clarence Sutherland; m. Phyllis Loraine King; UofAlta, BA, LLB, Oxford, MA; hockey exec., lawyer; halfback Edmonton Eskimos Provincial League, eventually owned club; at 17 organized Edmonton District HA; baseball catcher, outfielder; designed, built Renfrew Park Edmonton; at Oxford capt. hockey team; refereed '28 Olympic lacrosse final; Canadian Branch of Royal Caledonian Curling Club event titles; refereed amateur hockey '29-40, NHL '36-40, officiated 155 scheduled, 12 playoff games; Lt.Col. with Canadian War Crimes Investigation unit WW2; NHL pres. '46-77; prominent role in establishing NHL players' pension plan, expansion program; Lester Patrick trophy '72; Centennial Medal '67; NHL created division in his name; MBE, QC; mem. UofAlta., Canada's Sports, Cdn, US Hockey halls of fame.

CAMPBELL, Colin (curling); b. 17 Jan 1901, Shedden, Ont.; d. 25 Dec 1978, Toronto, Ont.; m. Vera Smith; c. 2 sons, 2 daughters; Queen's; engineer, soldier, politician; mem. Ont. rink '51 Macdonald Brier; capt. Cdn Strathcona Cup team Scotland '60, '70, Switzerland '67; mem. Dominion (now Cdn) Curling Assn. from '38, pres. '47-48; chairman International comm. '48-76; Macdonald Brier trustee from '65; Canadian rep. Scotch Cup advisory comm. '64-67; helped organize International Curling Fed. '66; Canadian rep. ICF '67-78, pres. '69-78; life mem. Hamilton Thistle Club, MCA, QCA, OCA, CCA, PCCA, Grand

National CC of NA, German CA, Royal Caledonian CC; mem. Canadian Curling Hall of Fame.

CAMPBELL, David (basketball/lacrosse); b. 11 Sep 1925, Vancouver, B.C.; given name: David Hector; m. Joan Jarvis; c. Margot, Craig; UBC, LLD; county court judge; basketball BC. int. champion Arrows '44; Vimy Camp R.C. Signals '45; UBC Thunderbirds '46-49; mem. '48 ntl champions, Olympic team; mem. '51 ntl champion Cloverleafs; lacrosse BC. juve. A champions '41-42; Sr. A Richmond Farmers '43-50; Ed Bailey Trophy Intercity League outstanding rookie '43; res. Vancouver, B.C.

CAMPBELL, Debbie (t&f); b. 2 Jul 1958, Halifax, N.S.; given name: Deborah Joy; m. Graeme Fell; c. Glory Ann; UVic; early years spent in figure skating; mem. NS t&f team Canada Summer Games '73; Victoria girls city champion 400m, 800m '74; silver 400m Canada Summer Games '78; ntl 800m, indoor 400m titles '78; 400m Portland, Ore., 800m Eugene, Ore. (PB 2:04) '78; bronze 4x400 relay team '78 Commonwealth Games; bronze Ottawa Indoor Games '82; res. Victoria, B.C.

CAMPBELL, Derrick (speed skating); b. 18 Feb 1972, Cambridge, Ont.; former hockey player, figure skater who began speed skating age 12; mem. ntl team from '89; alternate '92, relay team/individual '94, with Marc Gagnon, François Drolet, Éric Bédard relay 5000m gold '98 Olympics; world championship 500m gold '97; 3 world championship silver, 3 bronze; world team championship overall gold '96, '98; res. Calgary, Alta.

CAMPBELL, Dorothy (golf); b. 1883, Edinburgh, Scotland; d. 1946, New York; m. Hurd (d); m. Howe (d); began competitive caree in Scotland with North Berwick '04-09; emigrated to Canada '10 joining Hamilton club '10-12; mem. Merion Cricket Club, NY from '13; British women's title '09, '11; US titles '09-10, '24; Cdn titles '10-12; mem. Cdn Golf Hall of Fame.

CAMPBELL, Garnet (curling); b. 11 Jan 1927, Avonlea, Sask.; given name: William Garnet; m. DeVerne; c. Vern, Cassandra; farmer; rep. Saskatchewan 10 Briers from '47; skipped '55 winner; skipped Sask. ntl mixed finals '76-77; 6 carspiels, 7 Moose Jaw grand aggregates, 5 Regina titles, Weyburn, Ottawa, Vancouver Totem 'spiels once each; Quebec International, Windsor Invitational, Toronto Canada Life, Calgary Masters titles; twice CBC Keen Ice champion; mem. Governor-General's CC, Canadian Curling Hall of Fame; res. Avonlea, Sask.

CAMPBELL, Hugh (football); b. 21 May 1941, Spokane, Wash.; m. Louise; c. Robin, Jill, Rick, Molly; Washington State, BSc, MEd; football executive; all-American end WSU '60-62; drafted San Francisco; Saskatchewan '63-69; CFL record: 321 receptions, 5425yds, 60 TDs; 3 times WFC all-star, twice all-Cdn flanker; shares CFL single season TD receiving record 17 with Terry Evanshen; coached Whitworth College, Edmonton (CFL) '77-82, USFL LA Express '83, NFL Houston Oilers '84-85; GM Eskimos from '86; guided Eskimos to 6 consecutive Grey Cup finals unprecedented 5 wins in succession; NAIA Dist. 1 coach of '72, '75, CFL coach of '79; mem. Sask. Roughriders Plaza of Honor, Edmonton Eskimos Wall of Honor; res. Edmonton, Alta.

CAMPBELL, Jennifer (swimming); b. 26 Apr 1966, Sudbury, Ont.; m. Bruno Michel; c. Kyra, Cassia; Louisiana State BSc, Laurentian, BPhEd; teacher, coach; began career with Copper Cliff SC age 8; joined Laurentian SC at 15; competed annually in Europe from '78; set 1st ntl 50 FS age group record '75; mem. ntl team '81-85; unprecedented 7 gold '81 Canada Games; competed '82 Commonwealth, '85, '87 FISU games; 3 ntl high point trophies; 32 ntl championship individual medals (13 gold, 10 silver, 9 bronze); athletic/scholastic all-American; teaches aquatics, coaches Laurentian women's swim team; competes in masters swimming, triathlon events; mem. Ont. Aquatic Hall of Fame; res. Sudbury, Ont.

CAMPBELL, Jerry (football); b. 14 Jul 1944, Spokane, Wash.; div. Betty Ellis; m. Kim Kneeshaw; Idaho, BSc; bartender Capt. Jack's Pub; nicknamed "Soupy"; Idaho lineman of year; all-Skyline team '65; pro Calgary '66-68, '76, Ottawa '68-'75; offensive guard, outside linebacker; mem. 3 Grey Cup winners; all-Eastern, all-Cdn 7 times; outstanding Washington state HS lineman of year; Washington pro athlete of '72-73; Idaho pro athlete of '72-74; mem. Spokane, Wash., Idaho, Ottawa Sports, Cdn Football halls of fame; res. Toronto, Ont.

CAMPBELL, John (harness racing); b. 4 Aug 1955, London, Ont.; m. Paula; horseman; more than 200 victories Windsor-Detroit tracks; moved to Grand Circuit mid-'70s; 9 times NA leading money winning driver; 1st driver to top $6 million in purses single season '83, $11 million '88; 1st ever to record $100M US in earnings; more than 7500 victories, $155M in purses; drove 7 winners in 8 starts Meadowlands '83; 1st driver to score 5 times in one card on consecutive nights at Meadowlands; more than 2500 sub-2-minute miles; winner 16 $1M races; drove Willow Weeper world record 1:55.1 Freehold '82; 5 Hambletonian (a record), 3 Little Brown Jug, 5 Messenger Stakes, 3 Maple Leaf Trot, 4 Cane Pace, 3 NA Cup, 2 World Trotting Derby, 26 Bluegrass Stakes, 1 Yonkers Trot, 7 Breeders Crown victories; winner of more than 500 major stakes races; with Mack Lobell, OK Bye, Franconia, Nadia Lobel, Stonebridge Skipper, Run the Table, Miss Easy, Save Fuel, Tagliabue, Muscles Yankee and others shattered numerous track, world records; twice guided Mack Lobell to Harness Horse of year awards; also handled Miss Easy, Central Park West, 2yr old filly pacers of year; Peace Corps, 2yr old trotting filly of year; Totally Ruthless, Artsplace, 2yr old pacing colts of year; piloted Pine Chip to Trotter of year honors '93-94; mem. Cdn Horse Racing, Harness Racing Living halls of fame; res. River Vale, N.J./Ailsa Craig, Ont.

CAMPBELL, R.D. (coaching); b. 12 Apr 1892, Ottawa, Ont.; d. 4 Dec 1970, Ottawa, Ont.; given name: Robert Duncan; m. Annie Laurie McLaren (d), m. Minnie Constance Currie (d), m. Helen Mary Docksteader; c. Bruce; McMaster, BA, OCE; educator; intercollegiate HJ record; '30-53 coached 16 sr., 11 jr. Glebe CI basketball title teams; nearly 50 titles at all levels; coached Glebe Grads '38 ntl sr. title; ntl jr., juve. titles; coached Glebe t&f athletes Arthur Currie Trophy honors 8 times '33-48; established physical culture courses Toronto Hart House, Lake Couchiching for Dept. of Education; introduced team eligibility rules, forward pass, downfield blocking in HS football resulting in Canadian football rules changes; rejected coaching offers McMaster, Rough Riders; Ottawa sportsman of year; Ottawa HS stadium bears his name; mem. Ottawa, McMaster Sports halls of fame.

CAMPBELL, Rachelle (t&f); b. 30 Oct 1956, Guelph, Ont.; given name: Rachelle Mary Angela; m. Bill Clausen; c. Erika, Elyse, Shaun; Connestoga Coll.; day care teacher; 400m, 800m specialist; gold 400m Canada Games '73; gold 400m, silver 800m '74 jr. Olympics; ntl jr. record 52.6 for 400m; gold 4x400m relay team '75 Pan-Am Games; mem. '76 Olympic team; bronze 4x400m relay team '78 Commonwealth Games; ntl 400m title '78; competes at masters level; assists Peter Manning as coach Guelph TC; Guelph sports merit award '77; res. Guelph, Ont.

CAMPBELL, Shirley (swimming); b. 21 Sep 1935, Fergus, Ont.; given name: Shirley Marguerite; m. William Richard Campbell; c. Gary, Sandra; real estate agent; ntl 400m record; qualified for '52 Olympics but illness forced her out; ntl mile Ross Gold Trophy; CNE pro 3-mile race title '52-53; twice fell short in bids to beat Marilyn Bell's Lake Ont. swim record; won Egyptian 3-mile swim; competed in Sportsman's Shows swims; res. Mississauga, Ont.

CANTIN, Diane (horseshoes); b. 30 Jul 1947, St. Raymond, Que.; given name: Diane Paré; m. Réal Cantin; c. Nathalie, Caroline; 6 Que. women's doubles titles; 11 Que. women's singles titles; 8 ntl women's singles titles; records for high ringer percentage for complete tournament: ntl 88% '89, Que. 84% '93; shot only perfect game in Cdn championship history 24x24 '89; perfect 36x36 '89 Que. championship; 3 world records '87, 54 consec. ringers, 1023 ringers, 448 doubles for complete tournament; 7 top 5 finishes in world tournaments, 3 times runnerup; mem. Cdn Horseshoe Hall of Fame; res. St. Raymond, Que.

CAPOZZI, Herb (racquetball); b. 24 Apr 1925, Kelowna, B.C.; given name: Harold Peter; div.; c. Paula, Greg, Sandra, Sheena; UBC, BA, BComm., U of Italy, education degree; owner, operator men's athletic, recreation centre; football UBC, rejected offers from NY Giants; CFL Calgary, Montreal; GM BC. Lions '57-66, Grey Cup '64; chairman CFL, WFC GM's comm.; briefly operated NHL Vancouver Canucks; principal owner Vancouver Whitecaps NA Soccer League, league title '79; chair. Soccer Canada; with Bob Pickell '73 ntl Masters doubles racquetball champion; ntl Masters singles title '74; ntl Golden Masters title '81; mem. UBC Sports Hall of Fame; res. Vancouver, B.C.

CARBONNEAU, Guy (hockey); b. 18 Mar 1960, Sept Iles, Que.; m. Line; c. Anne-Marie, Kristina; centre Chicoutimi (QJHL) '76-80, Nova Scotia (AHL) '80-82, NHL Montreal '80-94, St. Louis '94-95, Dallas '95-99; former capt. Canadiens; 3 Frank Selke trophies; 4 Stanley Cup finals, 3 winners; NHL record: (through '99) 1249 scheduled games, 250g, 397a, 208 playoff games, 36g, 51a; res. Irving, Tex./Montreal, Que.

CARDINAL, Marc (weightlifting); b. 9 May 1956, Kingston, Ont.; given name: Donald Jean-Marc; m. Margaret Newton; c. Jacqueline, Andraya, Jennifer,

Michelle, Sarah, Michael, Stephen (d); UofOtt, MD; radiologist; teenage track, football standout; 18 ntl jr., 1 Commonwealth jr. records; only teenager to clean and jerk 400lbs in Commonwealth competition; class titles '74 Ont. Winter Games, '75-76 ntl jrs., '76, '78, '80 ntl srs. titles; gold '78 Commonwealth, 3 silvers '79 Pan-Am Games; bronze '79 world superheavyweight championships; best lifter award '80 nationals; 8 Commonwealth, 9 ntl sr. records; PB: snatch 167.5 kilos, C&J 220 kilos, total lift 387.5 kilos; mem. Ottawa Sports Hall of Fame; res. Blackfoot, Idaho.

CAREY, Jim (bowling); b. 24 Feb 1933, St. John's, Nfld.; m. Beverley Chapman; c. Lisa, Jennifer, Nancy; fish merchant; 5-pin specialist; 13 times bowled 400-plus singles, PB: 448; 16 games 1000-plus triple, PB: 1091; 3 seasons 290-plus average, 298, 293, 291; mem. Nfld. Bowling Hall of Fame; res. St. John's, Nfld.

CARLYLE, Randy (hockey); b. 19 Apr 1956, Sudbury, Ont.; given name: Randy Robert; defence Sudbury jr. '74-76, Dallas (CHL) '76-77; 1st choice Toronto '76 amateur draft; played in NHL with Toronto '76-78, Pittsburgh '78-84, Winnipeg '84-93; NHL record: 17 seasons, 1055 scheduled games, 148g, 499a, 69 playoff games, 9g, 24a; OHA all-star '76; 4 NHL all-star games; James Norris Memorial trophy '81; mem. Man. Hockey Hall of Fame; res. Winnipeg, Man.

CARNEY, Laurie (curling); b. 1 July 1956, Edmonton, Alta.; given name: Laurie Anne; m. Thomas Henry Carney; UBC, BEd; teacher; BC. Dist. 1 title rinks skipped by Lindsay Sparkes '82-83; BC. title rink '84; with skip Linda Moore Cnd, World titles '85, runnerup Cdn championships '86; all-star lead '84, '86 Cdn, '85 World championships; res. N. Vancouver, B.C.

CARNWATH, Jim (badminton); b. 11 Feb 1935, Woodstock, Ont.; given name: James Dalziel; m. Lianne Darou; c. Sarah, David Fowler, Drew; UofT, BA, LLD; Regional Sr. Justice, Central West Region Superior Court of Justice; mem. 4 Thomas Cup teams; ntl mixed doubles titles '63-64; CBA pres. '77-78; 5 ntl 50+, 3 ntl 60+ singles, 55+ mixed doubles '98 titles; res. Toronto, Ont.

CARPENTER, Keith (tennis); b. 3 Aug 1941, England; given name: Alan Keith; m. Judith Dianne; Sir George Williams, BSc; tennis court constructor; with Derek Penner under-18 doubles '58; ntl Open doubles with Mike Carpenter '66; ntl Open mixed doubles with Eleanor Dodge '62, with Vickie Berner '63; Open singles runnerup '63; ntl Closed singles '73, Closed doubles '74; mem. Davis Cup teams '62-68, '71; mem. Cdn Dubler Cup, Fred Perry Cup teams; won 2 ntl over-45 doubles, Martini Masters '93 titles; mem. Cdn Tennis Hall of Fame; res. Mississauga, Ont.

CARPENTER, Ken (football); b. 26 Feb 1926, Carlyle, Wash.; given name: Kenneth Leroy; m. Doris Jacobson; c. Kimberly, Kenneth Jr.; Oregon State, BA; recreation dir.; halfback Cleveland Browns '50-53, Saskatchewan '54-59; versatile runner, passer, kicker, receiver; '55 Sask. single season TD record with 18, WFC MVP, scoring title; 3 times WFC all-star; 6 year CFL total 55 TDs; head coach Sask. '60; US East-West Shrine, college all-star, NFL all-pro, CFL East-West Shrine games; mem. Roughriders Plaza of Honor; res. Indianapolis, Ind.

CARPENTIER, Patrick (motorsport); b. 13 Aug 1971, Joliette, Que., m. Anick Dunn; racing driver; indoor speed skating champion before competing in jr. karting; won Que. jr. 4-stroke karting titles '84-85; Spenard/David F-2000 series title '89; competed in ntl Formula 2000 races '90; ntl Player's Atlantic series title '92; Vancouver Molson Indy Atlantic title '92; steadily moving up through Player's/Toyota Atlantic championship series from '93; record 7 straight victories in '96 series; series champion '96; moved into IndyCar ranks '97; CART rookie of '97; joined Players Racing Team with fellow Cdn Greg Moore, '98; res. Joliette, Que.

CARRIER, Lyna (synchro swim); b. 29 Apr 1961, Quebec City, Que.; secretary; ntl team mem. '77-80; with twin sister Lyne 3 ntl duet titles; 3 ntl team titles; Pan-Pacific team title '79; team bronze '78 worlds, '79 FINA World Cup; Que. Inst. of Sports synchro athlete of '77-80; mem. Canadian Aquatic Hall of Fame; res. Charny, Que.

CARRIER, Lyne (synchro swim); b. 29 Apr 1961, Quebec City, Que.; secretary; ntl team '77-80; Canada Games solo title '75; with twin sister Lyna 3 ntl duet, team titles; team gold '79 Pan-Pacific Games; team bronze '78 worlds, '79 FINA World Cup; Que. Inst. of Sports synchro athlete of '77-80; mem. Canadian Aquatic Hall of Fame; res. Dolbeau, Que.

CARRUTHERS, Bob (curling); b. 5 Aug 1950, Charlottetown, P.E.I.; m. Joan Marie; c. Robin, Katrina; marketing rep.; skipped PEI entry Seagram Mixed '74; all-star 2nd '77 Seagram Mixed; 3rd for Peter MacDonald's PEI entry '81 Brier; 3rd Bryan Wight's NB entry '85 Brier; res. Riverview, N.B.

CARRUTHERS, Liz (diving); b. 14 Sep 1951, Edmonton, Alta.; given name: Elizabeth Ann: m. John Tweedle; Santa Monica College, CalState; real estate sales rep.; ntl 11-12 100yd butterfly record '63; Alta., Sask. novice, jr., sr. gymnastics titles; ntl diving team '67-76; 10 gold, 25 silver, 10 bronze in 1m, 3m springboard, ntl, International 10m tower; mem. '70 Commonwealth, '71, '75 Pan-Am, '72 Olympic teams; twice ntl champion; Russian, Czechoslovakian, South African International competitions titlist; gold 3m '71 Pan-Am, silver 3m '75 Pan-Am Games; as mem. CalState diving team 1st woman in history in any sport chosen all-American; serious '72 auto accident threatened career but made successful comeback '75; radio-TV diving events commentator in both English, French; head diving instructor Klondike Diving Club Edmonton '76-79; mem. Alta. Sports Hall of Fame; res. Edmonton, Alta.

CARSCALLEN, Susan (figure skating); b. 5 Mar 1955, Sudbury, Ont.; div. Tim Fallon; m. Vance Rodewalt; c. Vale, Quinn; skating teacher; cashier; with Eric Gillies ntl jr. ice dance title '74, sr. ice dance '77, Skate Canada bronze '77, 6th '77 world ice dance; competed '75-77 worlds, '75-77 Skate Canada, '76 Olympics; silver ntl sr. dance '75-76; pro 1 season Stars on Ice, 2 Ice Capades; one of torch bearers '88 Olympics; res. Calgary, Alta.

CARSTAIRS, Kent (curling); b. 9 Jun 1947, Toronto, Ont.; m. Helen; c. Lesley, Stephanie; accountant; playing lead for Russ Howard appeared in 4 Briers, winning '87 and adding world title '87; won Brampton cashspiel '85; runnerup Moncton 100; 1 Canada Challenge Cup victory in Japan; participated in numerous clinics, exhibitions in Canada, Europe, Scotland, Japan; participated Calgary Winter Olympic curling trials; mem. Ontario team of year '87; Dick Ellis award '87; mem. Cdn Curling Hall of Fame; res. Victoria Harbour, Ont.

CARTER, Gary (baseball); b. 8 Apr 1954, Culver City, Calif; given name: Gary Edmund; m. Sandy Lahm; c. Christy, Kimberly, D.J.; baseball broadcaster; capt. HS baseball, basketball, football teams; numerous academic, athletic awards; rejected college scholarship offers for pro baseball; Orange County baseball player of year, HS athlete of '72; mem. National Honor Society '68-72; drafted Montreal '72; minor leagues '72-74; Expos catcher '74-84, '92, NY Mets '85-89, SF '90, LA '91; Sporting News rookie of year; 4 times Expos player of year; Topps, Baseball Digest rookie all-star; 8 times NL all-star, MVP '81, '84 games, tied record 2 all-star home runs single game; 4 Golden Glove, 2 Silver Bat awards; NL record 7 consecutive seasons league leader games caught; Gillette Trophy top fan vote getter '82 all-star game; 1000th ML hit '82; mem. '81 NL Division title, championship series team; '86 Mets World Series champions; ML record: 19 seasons, 2296g, 2056 caught, 1025r, 2092h, 371db31tr, 324hr, 1225rbi; jersey #8 retired by Expos; ABC Superstars competitor '80-81; nicknamed "Kid"; '85 Joan Payson, '86 Good Guy, '88 Danny Thompson, '89 Roberto Clemente, Volunteer of year awards; author "A Dream Season"; runs annual Leukemia Society charity golf tournament; Florida Marlin TV analyst '93-96; Expos TV analyst from '97; mem. Expos Hall of Fame; res. Palm Beach Gardens, Fla.

CARTER, Joe (baseball); b. 7 Mar 1960, Oklahoma City, Okla.; given name: Joseph Chris; m. Diana; c. Kia Kionne, Ebony Shante, Jordan Alexander; Wichita State; TV baseball analyst; outfielder All-Missouri Valley Conf.; NCAA all-district 5 1st team, All-American 2nd team '79-80; Sporting News college player of '81; played in minors with Midland, Iowa, '81-84; American Assn. rookie of '83; majors from '84 with Chicago (NL), Cleveland (AL), San Diego (NL), Toronto (AL), Baltimore (AL), San Francisco (NL); 1st Cleveland player to record 30hrs and 30sb in single season '87; mem. 2 World Series champions; his 3-run HR in ninth won '93 title for Toronto; reached 2000 hit plateau '97; *Sporting News* Silver Slugger award '91; 12 consec. seasons 20 or more HRs; 10 of 12, 6 consec., 100 or more RBI seasons; MBL record (through '97): 2063 scheduled games, 8934ab, 1119r, 2083h, 410db, 52tr, 378hr, 1382rbi, 227sb, .259ba; ESPN analyst '98 post-season; Blue Jays TV analyst '99; mem. Blue Jays Wall of Distinction; res. Leawood, Kan.

CARTER, Mo (motorsport); b. 25 May 1924, Winnipeg, Man.; given name: Maurice Charles; m. Lois Tweed; c. Lesley, Susan, Kelly, Steven, Bradley; St. John's College; automobile dealer; began career in rallies, 2nd '64 Shell 4000; moved into racing '69 winning ntl sedan title; only Canadian to win major US races plus many on Canadian tracks; ntl A Production title '71-72; IMSA American Sedan

& GT champion '72-73; CRCA driver of '70; ntl race driver of '71-72; res. Ancaster, Ont.

CARTER, Wendy (badminton); b. 11 Mar 1956, Glasgow, Scotland; given name: Wendy May Clarkson; m. Greg Carter; c. Ryan, Scott, Christie, Curt; UCal; coach/administrator; ntl jr. singles champion '75; with Tracey Vanwassenhove ntl jr. girls' doubles; with Cam Dalgleish mixed doubles; with Lorraine Thorne doubles runnerup; Devlin Cup singles title '80; 5 ntl singles, 4 ladies' doubles, 5 mixed doubles titles; 2 ntl Open titles; all-England quarterfinalist '77, semifinalist '78; team silver, individual bronze '78 Commonwealth Games; Level 4 coach; v.-pres. Badminton Canada; res. Gig Harbor, Wash.

CARTER-ERDMAN, Kelly Ann (cycling); b. 12 May 1964, Edmonton, Alta.; given name: Kelly Ann Carter; m W. Erdman; UCal; dietician; began racing '83; mem. ntl team '85-92; Olympic team alternate '92; set Cdn sr. record 3,000m individual pursuit of 3:47.69 while placing 4th at worlds; 6 ntl gold, 1 silver; 1 Goodwill Games bronze; silver 3,000m IP '87 Pan-Am Games; Alta. achievement award '88; res. Banff, Alta.

CARTWRIGHT, Ethel Mary (builder); b. 1 Oct 1880, Clapham, Eng.; d. 18 Sep 1955, Magog, Que.; educator; appointed instructor McGill's Royal Victoria Coll. '06-27; instrumental in creating McGill school of phys ed '19; devised eligibility, playing rules for women's basketball; organized women's intercollegiate league; coached RVC team; established Bronze Baby trophy '21-22; recipient Tait McKenzie CAHPER award '48; mem. McGill Sports Hall of Fame.

CARTY, Hank (shooting); b. 6 Sep 1925, Birch River, Man.; given name: Henry; retired; began shooting in militia '51; mem. Man. Rifle Assn council from '57, exec. from '58; mem. shooting comm. '67 Pan-Am Games; dir. MPRA centennial prize meeting '72; chair. rifle events SFC nationals '93; exec. v-pres, MPRA '79-83; pres. '84-93; 25yrs DCRA council mem.; MPRA PRO '57-82; Man. v.-pres. DCRA from '84; militia team coach, capt. '53-57; army cadet coach '74-84; Man. Lt. Governor's gold medal '89; ISU certificate of merit '67; hon. life mem., life governor MPRA; outstanding MPRA volunteer award '91; res. Winnipeg, Man.

CARVER, Julie (shooting); b. 7 Aug 1974, Charlottetown, P.E.I.; given name: Julie Lynn; UPEI; began shooting age 13; progressed from small-bore to full-bore competition posting perfect 105 in Inter-maritime shoot becoming 1st junior, 1st female and 4th Islander to accomplish feat; '93 Nova Scotia champion; mem. mini-Palma, Inter-maritime, Atlantic championship, British, provincial, under-25 ntl teams; '93 DCRA small-bore title; 2 Governor General's medals; res. Charlottetown, P.E.I.

CASANOVA, Bruno (baseball/football); b. 28 Mar 1927, Windsor, Ont.; m. Audrey; c. Jayne, Kim, Barbara, Susan, Lynn; arena manager; all-city tackle Lowe VHS '44; softball, baseball Windsor before turning pro St. Louis Cardinals organization '58; hit .301 Lawrenceville, Va. .313 Hamilton (Pony League) '59, all-star 2nd baseman; closed pro career Duluth '60; 5yrs St. Thomas Elgins Sr. IC; mem. '54 IC title team; baseball supervisor Chatham '57-62, 15 OBA titles; mem. Windsor-Essex Sports Hall of Fame selection comm.; res. Amherstburg, Ont.

CASANOVA, Willie (baseball/football); b. 15 Nov 1930, Windsor, Ont.; given name: William Anthony; m. Connie Kerhoulas; c. Patti Rose, Anne Marie; UWO, BA, UCal, BEd; exec.-asst. Alberta Teachers' Assn.; mem. 1 football, 4 basketball, track HS title teams; mem. Windsor Cardinals jr. baseball champions '46, Mic Mac baseball, softball title teams; pro baseball NY Yankee organization '51-53; Sr. IC baseball St. Thomas, London; coached minor baseball Chatham, Ont.; mem. '54 St. Thomas IC champions; mem. UWO Mustangs football teams '54-58 including undefeated '57 title team; drafted by BC. Lions, traded to Calgary '58; cut before season's opener but remained in Calgary to play baseball Western Canada League through '62; coached St. Mary's Boys School football '59-63, 2 titles, only 2 games lost in 4 years, coached track team to 3 consecutive titles; asst. grid coach Mt. Royal Jr. Coll. '60-62, head coach '63, Alta. jr. title '60; asst. coach UCal '65-67; Ont. HS athlete of '47; mem. Windsor/Essex Sports Hall of Fame; res. Calgary, Alta.

CASEY, Tom (football); b. 1924, Ohio; m. Mary Fuller; c. Geraldine, Martin, Thomas; Hamilton Institute Virginia, UMan, MD; v.-pres. company medical dir. General Electric Co.; 1 year pro football NY Yankees all-American Conf.; Hamilton Wildcats '49, Blue Bombers '50-55; nicknamed "Citation" while achieving all-star status 7 times; led WIFU rushers '50; excelled as offensive, defensive back; gained 100yds single play '52 vs. Saskatchewan; same season gained 205yds in pass interception returns, WIFU Single season TD record with 16; Winnipeg citizen of '55; mem. Man. Sports, Cdn, Blue Bombers Football halls of fame; res. Bethel, Conn.

CASHMAN, Wayne (hockey); b. 24 Jun 1945, Kingston, Ont.; m. Lyn; c. Scott, Becky; hockey coach; jr. Oshawa; pro Boston '67-83; left wing; 1 2nd team all-star; career record: 1027 scheduled games, 277g, 516a, 145 playoff games, 31g, 57a; 5 Stanley Cup finals, 2 winners; Team Canada '72; scout NYR '86-87; asst. coach NYR '88-92. Tampa Bay '92-96, San Jose '97; Philadelphia '98; head coach Philadelphia '97-98; asst. coach Team Canada '97 worlds, '98 Olympics; mem. Oshawa Sports Hall of Fame; res. Ocala, Fla.

CASS, Eddie (baseball); b. 12 Jul 1893, Winnipeg, Man.; d. 23 May 1985, Winnipeg, Man.; Georgetown, UMan, LLB; lawyer; college ball Georgetown, Manitoba; all-star 1st baseman; coach '23 Man. jr. titlists, '24-26 intermediates; retired as player when called to bar '26 but continued coaching jr. teams through '50s, several provincial titles; with Shorty Kennedy formed Winnipeg HS football league; with Syd Halter inaugurated annual Catholic field day; Manitoba's Mr. Baseball; noted orator; mem. Man. Sports Hall of Fame.

CASSAN, Gerry (speed skating); b. 5 Dec 1954, Ottawa, Ont.; given name: Gerard; div. Gisele Tasse, m. Wendy Kieran; c. Brian Couvrette, Sean Couvrette; Air Canada

station attendant; 9 Ont. indoor, 22 outdoor, 4 ntl indoor, 7 outdoor, 3 international indoor, 16 outdoor titles, many records; fastest 500m (40.19) by Cdn skater; mem. '72 Olympic team; gold 500m '74 jr. worlds; Kitchener Oktoberfest indoor title '78; 2 gold, 2 bronze Lake Placid srs competition '83; mem. '63-70 Ont. lacrosse title teams; Ont. jr. open cycling title '72; competed '81 National Capital Marathon; speed skater of '71-72; won 50 km Lake Placid speed skating marathon '91; Cdn sr. masters titles '75, '92; set Cdn Masters record; mem. Ntl Capital Runners Assn.; capt. AC Sunseekers Running Club from '84; Daoust Trophy (Ottawa Valley French Canadian amateur athlete of year) '66, '68; at 8 youngest ever Ottawa ACT award winner; 5 Ont., 3 City of Ottawa sports achievement awards; mem. Ottawa Sports, Cdn Speed Skating halls of fame; res. Nepean, Ont.

CASSELMAN, Bruce (softball); b. 11 Sep 1964, Williamsburg, Ont.; m. Janet Crain; costal engineering technician; catcher; played with Ottawa Turpin Pontiacs, Carp Valley Pride, Kemptville Thunder, Stittsville 56ers; mem. ntl title Toronto Gators fastball team '93-95, 1st Cdn team to win ISC world title '93, repeat '95; Pan-Am Games gold '95; defensive standout with reputation of possessing a game-breaking bat; ISC all-world team '93-94; ntl, NA all-star catcher '92; Ottawa ACT fastball player of 1994; res. Ottawa, Ont.

CASSIDY, John (speed skating); b. 7 Jun 1952, Montreal, Que.; given name: John Philip; m. Jocelyne Coutu; Loyola; fireman; ntl indoor titles '68, '72, outdoor '70; mem. '72 Olympic, '70, '73, '75 world championships teams; 2nd Que., 4th ntl championships '80; last known res. Halifax, N.S.

CATHERALL, Robin (rowing); b. 20 Oct 1955, Vancouver, B.C.; given name: Robin William; m. Helen Wilkinson; UBC, BSc, MA; teacher; mem. '77 Western NA Collegiate champion UBC 8s; gold 8s Henley, ntl championships '77; won Western sprints UBC 8s, 3 golds VRC 8s ntl championships; gold VRC 8s '78 Canadian Henley; silver 8s Pan-Am Games, 3 golds VRC 8s ntl championships '79; mem. ntl team '77-80; twice world championship competitor; res. Parks, B.C.

CATHERWOOD, Ethel (t&f); b. 28 Apr 1908, Hannah, N.D.; d. 26 Sep 1987, Grass Valley, Calif.; div. James McLaren; m. Byron Mitchell; raised in Saskatoon; excelled in baseball, t&f; brought to Toronto by mining millionaire Teddy Oke, she was coached by Walter Knox and soon was challenging world high jumping standards; her grace and beauty won her nickname "Saskatoon Lily"; set world record '28; won '28 Olympic gold with leap of 5'2.7"; embittered by treatment of women athletes by Canadian officials she married and moved to US never again to compete; rejected movie contract offers; mem. Sask, Cdn Olympic, Saskatoon, Canada's Sports halls of fame.

CATTARINICH, Joseph (builder/hockey); b. 13 Nov 1881, Levis, Que.; d. 7 Dec 1938, New Orleans, La; excelled in lacrosse/hockey; goaltender Montreal Nationals; a man of few words he was dubbed "the Quiet One"; a selfless athlete he convinced Montreal mgr. to sign Chicoutimi goalie

Georges Vèzina, thus putting himself out of a job; played important, but frequently unnoticed, role in development of NHL; with Leo Dandurand and Louis Létourneau purchased Montreal club and established Flying Frenchmen; under his management the Habs won 3 Stanley Cups; sold franchise '35; mem. Hockey Hall of Fame.

CAVALLIN, Roy (lacrosse); b. 15 Sep 1919, Vancouver, B.C.; given name: Roy Fred; m. Isabell (d); c. Timmie; 16 years sr. lacrosse; mem. 4 Mann Cup finalists, 3 winners; sr. soccer New Westminster Royals; Sr. A basketball Lauries '38; trainer 1st Cdn soccer team World Cup competition; 2yrs lacrosse referee; trainer BC. Lions '58-76; nicknamed "Fritzie", "Rocky"; p.-pres. BC. Athletic Trainers' Assn.; pres. BC. Sports for Retarded; mem. Canadian Lacrosse Hall of Fame; res. N.Burnaby, B.C.

CERESIA, Mike (racquetball); b. 3 Nov 1962, Sarnia, Ont.; UWO, BA; began playing '83; ntl team mem. from '90; world team gold '88, singles silver '94; ntl singles title '92, 5 ntl doubles titles; team silver '95 Pan-Am Games; ranked 2nd world singles '94; gold worlds '96; res. Mississauga, Ont.

CHABOT, Lorne (hockey); b. 5 Oct 1900, Montreal, Que., d. 10 Oct 1946, Montreal, Que.; in era when diminutive goalers were the vogue, Chabot, at 6'1", stood out; helped Port Arthur win Allan Cup then turned pro NY Rangers '26; posted goals-against averages of 1.56, 1.79 in 2 seasons with Rangers; Maple Leafs '28-33, Canadiens '33-34, Black Hawks '34-35, Montreal Maroons '35-36, NY Americans '36-37; helped Rangers win '28 Stanley Cup; '35 Vezina Trophy, 1st team all-star.

CHALLIS, Terry (softball); b. 29 Dec 1963, Toronto,Ont.; m. Lisa Hope; c. Kyler; sheet metal worker; ISC world championships MVP '93; 1st team all-world fielder '93-94; all-Canadian '94; mem. Toronto Gators 2 ntl, 1 world title; Green Bay All-Car '97, Owen Sound '98, Oshawa Gators '99; res. Whitby, Ont.

CHALMERS, Angela (t&f); b. 6 Sep 1963, Brandon, Man.; m. E. Espinoza; middle distance specialist; began competing age 9; 1 ntl 3,000, 4 1,500, 1 800 gold; competed '85 FISU, '87 Pan-Am, '88, '92 Olympic, '90, '94 Commonwealth Games, '94 World Cup teams; '92 Olympic 3,000 bronze; 3 Commonwealth Games gold; 1 World Cup silver; numerous victories in meets throughout world; 1st woman in Commonwealth Games history to win both 1,500 and 3,000 races '90, only woman to successfully defend 3,000 title '94; won Millrose Games mile '95; ntl 3,000m record 8:32.17 '94; retired from competition '97; Cdn flagbearer '94 Commonwealth Games; Phil Edwards CFTA athlete of '90; Man. female athlete of '90; Athletics Canada athlete of yr award '94; ntl Aboriginal achievement award '95; res. Victoria, B.C.

CHALUPKA, Ed (football); b. 23 Feb 1947, Peterborough, Ont.; m. Rosemary; c. Christine, Paul; given name: Edward Stephen; N. Carolina, BA; CFL v.-pres. football operations/ secty-treas from '93; former managing dir./curator Cdn Football Hall of Fame; all-Atlantic Conf., AP all-American; academic all-American; offensive guard Hamilton '70-76;

3 times all-Eastern; 4 time Schenley nominee; mem. '72 Grey Cup winner; pres. CFL Players' Assn. '81-85; res. Stoney Creek, Ont.

CHAMBERS, Carlton (t&f); b. 27 Jun 1975, Brampton, Ont.; Clemson; sprinter; Ont. HS 100m title '92; gold 4x100 '94 Commonwealth Games; ntl jr 100m record 10.30, mem. record-setting jr relay team which won bronze World jr championships '94; running 1st leg in preliminaries helped Cdn men's 4x100 relay team claim gold '96 Olympics; NCAA All-American with Clemson. '95; res. Mississagua, Ont.

CHAMBERS, Dave (coaching); b. 7 May 1940, Toronto, Ont.; m. Irene; c. Lori, Linda; UofT, BPhE, UBC, MPhE, Ohio State, PhD; AD York U; played Jr. A with Guelph Biltmores/ St. Michael's Coll. '56-60; mem. Guelph '57 OHA title team; coach Ohio State '70-72, York '72-77, '84-90, Toronto Marlboros '79-80, Italian ntl team '81-83, Quebec (NHL) '90-92, Team Canada '88; won IIHF B title Italy '81; res. Newmarket, Ont.

CHAMBUL, Borys (t&f); b. 17 Feb 1953, Toronto, Ont.; given name: Borys Michael; m. Trudy Marian; Wash, BA, Canadian Memorial Chiropractic College Toronto; doctor of chiropractic; discus specialist; mem. ntl jr. team '73-74; Pacific 8 discus title '76; NCAA champion; ntl, Commonwealth record 65.40m '76 pre-Olympic meet; NCAA record; mem. '76, '80 Olympic teams; gold '78 Commonwealth Games; ntl title '82; capt. UW track team '73-74; Wash most inspirational award '76; res. Thornhill, Ont.

CHAMPAGNE, Ed (skiing); b. 12 Jul 1927, Ste. Anne, Man.; given name: Edouard; pharmaceutical rep, skiing administrator; from '45 involved in skiing, alpine in particular, with Puffin/Winnipeg SC holding varied administrative roles; pres. Man. Ski Div. 3yrs; played role in launching Mt. Agassiz, Falcon Lake ski areas in Manitoba; managed Yellowstone, Montana ski area 1yr; ntl alpine ski team exec 21yrs; founder/1st pres. Winnipeg Cycling Club; chair. Man. Cycling Assn '64-68; mem. '67 Pan-Am Games organizing comm.; hon. mem. Cdn Ski Assn.; life mem. Winnipeg Ski Club; mem. Cdn Skiing Hall of Fame; res. Ottawa, Ont.

CHAMPION, Tony (football); b. 19 Mar 1963, Humbold, Tenn.; Tennessee-Martin; wide receiver; joined CFL Hamilton '85-92; 2 all-Eastern, 1 all-CFL; Jeff Russell Memorial Trophy '89; runnerup CFL most outstanding player '89; CFL record: 85 scheduled games, 37tds, 340 receptions for 5,498yds; mem. 2 Grey Cup finalists, 1 winner; last known res. Humbold, Tenn.

CHANG, Albert (tennis); b. 27 Feb 1971, Vancouver, B.C.; Harvard; made pro debut '92; had 1st taste of Davis Cup play beating Carlos Drada 6-2, 6-3 as Canada swept Colombia 5-0; won '94 Celle Challenger France; combined with Leander Paes of India to win Manila Challenger; has recorded victories over Michael Stich and Arnaud Boetsch; competed Wimbledon '95-96; res. Calgary, Alta./Boston, Mass.

CHAPMAN, Art (basketball); b. 28 Oct 1912, Victoria, B.C.; d. 4 Feb 1986, Victoria, B.C.; given name: Arthur St. Clair; m. Kathleen; c. Lyn Arthur, Jim; salesman; HS aggregate t&f title '31-32 in 5 events, high jump, long jump, hop, step & jump (triple jump), shot put, 120yd hurdles; mem. '33 BC. softball champions; at 16 batted .399 sr. baseball league; mem. 5 ntl basketball title teams, '36 Olympic silver medal team; mem. '46 Victoria Dominoes (BC. basketball team of half century), ntl title without losing league or playoff game; player-coach-mgr. Vancouver Hornets pro basketball '47-48; helped Canadian army unit win '45 overseas basketball, volleyball, soccer titles; various Little League, Connie Mack baseball exec. positions; '36 team inducted Canada's, '46 team BC. Sports halls of fame; with brother Chuck mem. Cdn Basketball, BC., Greater Victoria Sports halls of fame.

CHAPMAN, Chuck (basketball); b. 21 Apr 1911, Vancouver, B.C.; given name: Charles Winston; m. Eily Margaret; c. Clara Mary, Janet Kathleen, Fern Ruth; Victoria College; retd; mem. BC. sr. A softball, lacrosse, soccer title teams; mem. 6 BC. basketball title teams, capt. 5; mem. '36 Olympic silver medal team; capt. '46 undefeated Victoria Dominoes (BC. team of half century); '36 team Canada's, '46 team BC. Sports halls of fame; mem. Cdn Basketball, BC., Greater Victoria Sports halls of fame; res. Victoria, B.C.

CHAPMAN, Currie (skiing); b. 7 May 1947, Montreal, Que.; div. Judi Leinweber; m. Dale Ryan; c. Christie, Jordan; Notre Dame, BA, T.Cert.; sport administrator; mem. ntl team '64-69; Vail GS, Jackson Hole downhill, slalom titles '68 Can-Am circuit; 8th '68 World Cup Alpine Meadows, Calif.; coached HS volleyball, soccer, basketball '70-78; head coach ntl women's ski team '78-89; pres. Cdn Sports and Fitness Marketing Council '91-94; v.-pres. program operations Alpine Canada from '94; TV skiing color commentator; fed. govt. coach of '86; mem. CPCA from inception, v-pres from '96, acting pres. '98; mem. Cdn Skiing Hall of Fame; res. Calgary, Alta.

CHAPMAN, John (harness racing); b. 25 Nov 1928, Toronto, Ont., d. 2 May 1980, Toronto, Ont.; m. Janice Feldman; c. Cynthia, Wendy, Cheryl, John Jr.; harness driver, trainer; capt. St. Michael's hockey team; 1st harness race win Dufferin Park '47; 3915 career victories, purses totalling more than $21 million; 34 sub-2-minute miles; drove 4-year-old pacing mare Tarport Hap to world record 1:56.3; drove Delmonica Hanover to successive Roosevelt International triumphs '73-74, trained '75 winner, horse of year Savoir; mem. Cdn Horse Racing Hall of Fame.

CHAREST, Isabelle (speed skating); b. 3 Jan 1971, Rimouski, Que.; U Montreal; switched from figure to speed skating; mem. ntl team from '87; silver 3000m short track relay '94 Olympics; mem. '98 Olympic team; 1 Cnd sr., 3 world records; 2 Goodwill Games gold '94; 2 World short track 3000m relay, 1 overall gold; 500m gold, 1000m bronze '96 worlds; overall ntl title '95-96; world team championship bronze '98; switched from short to long track '98; res. Montreal, Que.

CHARETTE, Agnés (curling); b. 6 Jul 1942, Buckingham, Que.; given name: Agnés Charette; m. Jean St. Pierre; c.

Normand, Éric; Hull Teachers' Coll.; teacher; 3 times Outaouais region tennis rep. Quebec Games; National Capital intermediate title '74; skip Outaouais region business girls title rink '81; skip Que. women's title rinks '83-84, '89, '92-94; 5th mem. '91 Que. Tournament of Hearts rep; Cinzano Cup Que. '82; mem. 3 Que. mixed title rinks; Ottawa women's major league title rink '83; skip Que. Srs title rink '96-99, ntl titles '97, '99; avid golfer, several Buckingham club titles; res. Buckingham, Que.

CHARETTE, France (curling); b. 8 Apr 1958, Masson, Que.; m. Pierre Charette; c. Duff, Kim; golf pro shop administrator; began curling age 23; with Agnés Charette, Chantal Osborne representing Buckingham CC won 5 Que. Women's titles, competing in 5 Scott Tournament of Hearts; competed 3 ntl mixed championships; res. Rockland, Ont.

CHARETTE, Pierre (curling/golf); b. 23 Jun 1955, Masson, Que.; m. France; c. Duff, Kim; golf pro; 1st to play every position, including 5th man, in Brier competition; skipped Que. entry '89, '93 Brier, lead for Don Westphal '96 Brier semifinalists, 2nd '97 Brier, 3rd for Guy Hemmings '98, '99 Brier. '98, '99 finalists; all-star 3rd '99; skipped Que. entry '91, '92, 2nd '86 ntl mixed championships; 3rd for Hemmings '97 McCain East title; pro Buckingham GC, Outaouais GC; res. Rockland, Ont.

CHARETTE, Richard (t&f); b. 8 Nov 1967, North Bay, Ont.; given name: Richard Allan; m. Elizabeth Ivany; c. Benjamin Wylie; UofOtt, BEd, BPhE; teacher; cross-county specialist; mem. CIAU X-C title teams '86-87, '90; individual CIAU title '89; 1500m bronze Pan-Am jrs '86, ntl t&f championships '91; ntl X-C titles '91, '92; res. Ottawa, Ont.

CHARLAND, Jacques (ski jumping); b. 6 May 1930, Trois-Rivières, Que.; m. Nicole Ebacher; c. Manon; electrician; 8 ntl, 3 US, several NA championships; mem. '52, '56, '60 Olympic, '54, '58, '62, '66 world teams; coach ntl team '68-70; resumed competition '71-75; won more than 400 trophies, cups, medals; mem. Cdn Skiing Hall of Fame; res. Trois-Rivieres, Que.

CHARLEBOIS, Bob (hockey); b. 27 May 1944, Cornwall, Ont.; given name: Robert Richard; m. Maureen Delaney; c. Rob, Joy; UofOtt, BSc, MA, Harvard Business School, PMD; dir. corporate training centre Algonquin coll.; Montreal jr. '60-64, Omaha, Houston, Memphis CHL '64-68, Minnesota NHL '67-68, Phoenix WHL '68-72, Tulsa CHL '71-72, Ottawa WHA '72-73, New England WHA '73-76; shifted to coaching UofOtt '80-82; Ottawa South Canadian major bantam '91-92, league champion Ottawa Golden Knights major bantam '92-93, Gloucester Rangers Tier II Jr. A '93-95, league title '94; scouted for Hartford NHL, Gloucester CJHL, St. Michael's OHL; owner-teacher hockey school '64-72; taught PE UofOtt '80-82; mem. Ottawa Senators NHL alumni board, Harvard business club Ottawa, Ottawa Board of Trade, American Society for Training and Development; mem. Cornwall Sports Hall of Fame; res. Ottawa, Ont.

CHARLEBOIS, Vera (golf); b. 24 Apr 1930, Smiths Falls, Ont; given name: Vera Anita Donaldson; m. Albert Gilbert Charlebois; c. Owen Arthur, Dennis Joseph Edward; scored

1st win in Ottawa dist. '63; 22 Chaudiére Ladies' club titles; 4 Ottawa Dist. Ladies' titles (Ahearn Trophy); mem. 4 Quebec interprovincial women's teams, 7 Quebec Rose Bowl teams; 5 O&D 4-ball best ball titles; 3 Eastern provinces titles; 4 Allie Jones trophies; 2 Mina Denison Shield teams; 2 Que. seniors titles; 3rd '84 ntl sr women's; 6 O&D sr women's titles; 2 Daytona Beach club titles; winner varied Ottawa Valley invitationals '70-85; set Chaudiére women's club record 72; club pro Emerald Links GC; mem. Russ Taylor OVCA mixed curling title rink; mem. Smiths Falls Recreation Hall of Fame; res. Ottawa, Ont.

CHARLTON, Ken (football); b. 16 Apr 1920, Regina, Sask.; m. Belle; c. Jim, Tom, Catherine; Regina Westend jrs '38; Regina Western champion jr. Dales '39-40; joined Regina Roughriders '41 but WW2 intervened; played with '42 Winnipeg RCAF team reaching Grey Cup final; '43 All-Service Roughriders; declined Cleveland Rams tryout '45 opting to stay in Canada; with Regina briefly before joining Ottawa 3 seasons; rejoined Regina '48-54, 4yrs capt.; 2 Grey Cup finals; reached all-star status as flying wing '41, '45-46, running back '48-49; all-Western halfback '51; standout punter averaging 38.7yds on 182 punts; could fill in at QB if needed; punishing tackler; among top WIFU running backs, punt returners; pres. St. James Winnipeg sr. ntl champs '63; versatile athlete also excelling in baseball/hockey; mem. Sask. Sports, Roughriders Plaza of Honor; Cdn Football halls of fame; res. Burnaby, B.C.

CHARLTON, Nancy (field hockey); b. 8 Oct 1962, Victoria, B.C.; given name: Nancy Margaret; m. Ian Mollennhauer; c. Arden; UVic, BEd PE teacher; mem. UVic team '81-85; mem. BC team '80-84; competed '81 Canada Games; ntl team '82-88; mem. World Cup silver medal team '83; mem. '84, '88 Olympic, '86 World Ccup, '87 Pan-Am Games teams; flag-bearer '87 Pan-Ams; jr. HS athletic, sportsmanship awards; '81 Vancouver Island Women's FH award for ability, leadership; fed. govt. excellence awards '83, '88; UVic female athlete of '83-84; Victoria athlete of '89; 5yrs Vancouver Women's FH League MVP; res. Victoria, B.C.

CHARRON, Al (rugby); b. 27 Jul 1966, Ottawa, Ont.; given name: Alan John; m. Annette Saikaley; Carleton, BA; pro rugby player, ex-civil servant; lock or back row Ottawa Irish RC, 7 league titles; mem. 5 Ont. 7-a-side title teams, 2 McCormick Cup winners; '90-94 earned 28 caps as mem. ntl team; capt. ntl team '96; scored try vs. NZ '91 World Cup; scored decisive try vs. Wales '93; played for British Barbarians vs. French Barbarians in '94 game celebrating 50th anniversary of liberation of Paris; competed '91 World Cup (quarterfinalist), '93 World Cup of Sevens; turned pro with Moseley in UK '96; mem. 3 Ottawa men's basketball title teams; 4 Ottawa ACT rugby awards, '93 Ottawa ACT amateur athlete of yr; Ont. Excellence award; Bristol player of '99 award; v.-capt. ntl world cup '99 team; res. Ottawa, Ont./Bristol, Eng.

CHARRON, Guy (hockey); b. 24 Jan 1949, Verdun, Que.; m. Denyse; c. Renee, Erik; centre NHL '69-81 Montreal, Detroit, Kansas City, Washington; NHL record: 734 scheduled games, 221g, 309a; mem. 3 Cdn teams world championships '77-79, bronze '78; player/coach Arosa

Swiss League '81-82 champs; GM/head coach Que. Remparts '83-85; asst. GM/coach Team Canada 5yrs, 4 Izvestia, 2 Spengler Cups, '88 Olympics; head coach '90 Cdn jr. world title team; asst. Calgary Flames '90-95, NY Islanders from '95; res. Calgary, Alta.

CHARTERS, Harvey (canoeing); b. 8 May 1912, Toronto, Ont.; given name: Harvey Blashford; m. Margaret Helen Whitham; c. Kent, Craig, Douglas, Kimberley, Elaine; UofT; retd engineer; ntl intermediate tandem '31, sr. 4s '34, sr. tandem '35, mile war canoe '30, '37; silver 10,000m tandem, bronze 1000m tandem '36 Olympics; competed International 14' dinghy sailing regattas; res. North Bay, Ont.

CHASE, George (shooting); b. 19 Jan 1941, Saint John, N.B.; given name: George Ernest; m. Carla Roberta; c. George Bradley Paul, Michelle Lynne; retd.; fullbore specialist; won 8 NB Lt. Governors, 7 times runnerup; 9 NB grand agg titles; 2 Cdn Masters gold, 2 silver; 1 DCRA Macdonald Stewart grand agg; 1 Des Burke Trophy; DCRA Governor-General's bronze; qualified 15 Cdn Bisey teams; big game bow hunting guide specializing in moose, deer, black bears; highly respected artist specializing in wildlife, charactures; also noted sculptor; res. Saint John, N.B.

CHATEL, Sigrid (fencing); b. 26 Apr 1940, Frankfurt, Germany; given name: Sigrid Gazzera; m. Gilles Chatel; c. Dominique, Mark; U of Geneva, BA; PR consultant, convention services; moved to Canada '64; twice ntl champion; bronze '67 Pan-Am Games; mem. '67 worlds, '70 Commonwealth, '71 Pan-Am Games teams; lone Cdn female fencer '68 Olympics; asst. CdM '72 Olympics; mem. COA from '76; chief hostess COJO '73-77; deputy CdM Canadian team '80 Winter Olympics; taught PE Bois-de-Boulonge College Montreal '71-72; 3 times Lévesque Trophy winner Montreal's female athlete of year; res. Montreal, Que.

CHEATER, Millie (t&f); b. 20 Nov 1927, Winnipeg, Man.; given name: Millicent; m. Everett Cousins; c. Kim, Shelley, Kerry; school board secretary; inter-HS 50, 100yd sprint titles '43-45; ntl record 75yd sprint title '46; ntl 60m, 100yds, 100m titles '47; quarterfinalist 100, 200m '48 Olympics; 50, 75yds, 400m relay records; mem. Beta Sigma Phi; res. W.Vancouver, B.C.

CHEEVERS, Gerry (hockey); b. 7 Dec 1940, St. Catharines, Ont.; given name: Gerald Michael; m. Betty; c. Craig, Cheryl, Robby; St. Michael's College; hockey scout; jr. A St. Mike's Majors; pro Toronto '61-62; minor pro '62-67; Boston regular goaler '67-72, '75-80; WHA Cleveland Crusaders '73-74; mem. Team Canada '74, '76; twice WHA all-star; Hap Holmes Trophy (AHL top goaler) '65; CPHL top goaler '67; WHA top goaler '73; NHL record: 12 seasons, 26so, 2.89 goals-against average; mem. 2 Stanley Cup winners; coach Bruins '80-84; scout Boston since '85; thoroughbred horse owner; mem. Hockey Hall of Fame; res. North Andover, Mass.

CHENARD, Line (swimming); b. 10 Apr 1957, Quebec City, Que.; gold 100m backstroke, silver 200m backstroke, 400m medley relay '75 Pan-Am Games; retd from competition '80; res. Quebec City, Que.

CHENIER, Georges (snooker); b. 14 Nov 1907, Hull, Que.; d. 16 Nov 1970, Toronto, Ont,; m. Bernadette Corrilla; c. Cecile; NA snooker champion '47-70; twice runnerup to England's Fred Davis world championships; world record match play break 144 vs. Walter Donaldson, England '50; world record 6 century breaks vs. Montreal's Leo Levitt '55 NA title matches; world record run 150 for pocket billiards vs. world champion Irving Crane '63; later duplicated feat; '66 stroke paralyzed left side restricting use of left arm; mem. Ottawa, Canada's Sports halls of fame.

CHERNOFF, Mike (curling); b. 21 Dec 1936, Kamsack, Sask.; m. Dorine Dennison; c. Cathy, Bruce; Queen's, BSc; geologist; began curling as mem. Kamsack CC, 1952; competitor Kingston, Edmonton, Calgary, Medicine Hat, N. Vancouver, Richmond, B.C.; 11 Association zone titles; 7 provincial finals, 3 winners, 2 runners-up; 3rd stone '64, '78, '83 Alta. Brier entries; semifinalist '78 world championship; skip Ont. Jr. Tankard titlist '57; all-star Brier third '78; skipped 12 major 'spiel winners including 2 Kingston, 1 Ottawa city titles; top shooting percentage '78 Silver Broom; played key administrative roles with Calgary CC '67-77, Southern Alberta CA '80-83; mem. '80 Calgary Brier organizing comm.; v.-chair. CCA ICF committee '83-85; Canadian delegate ICF '83-85; v.-pres. Vancouver men's world comm. '87; res. Vancouver, B.C.

CHERRY, Don (hockey); b. 5 Feb 1934, Kingston, Ont.; given name: Donald Stewart; m. Rose (d); c. Cindy, Timothy; m. Luba; hockey TV commentator, restaurateur; defence Jr. Barrie Flyers; pro Boston organization spending much of career in minors with Hershey, Springfield, Rochester (AHL), Trois-Rivieres, K-W, Sudbury (EPHL), Spokane (WHL); 1 playoff game with Boston (NHL) '55; coach Boston Bruins '74-79, Colorado Rockies '79-80; nicknamed "Grapes"; outspoken, often controversial, corlorfully-attired TV commentator on HNIC Coach's Corner; owner Mississauga Ice Dogs OHL franchise; res. Mississauga, Ont.

CHIARELLI, John (all-around); b. 5 May 1938, Ottawa, Ont.; given name: John Ross; m. Diane Gervais; c. Kimberly, Stephanie; St. Patrick's Coll., Rensselaer Polytechnic Institute, BEng; patent examiner; jr. B hockey St. Pat's '53-56, jr. A Ottawa Shamrocks '56-57, USA Tier 1 RPI '58-62, sr. A Ottawa Montagnards '62-65, Hull Mustangs '65-95; midget off. end/def. back Big 4 football St. Pat's '52, St. Pat's HS jrs '53-54, srs '55-56, St. Pat's Coll. '57; touch football Ott. sr. Valiquette Alouettes '68-70; fastball McNab Phillies '49-56, St. Anthony's, Village Sports Club, Hugh Grant '57-65, Hull Volants '66, Ott. sr. Wajax '67-69, Champagne Electric '69-71; player/coach Metro League Turpin Pontiacs '72-78, GM/coach Turpin '79-94; baseball Ott. sr. league '62-64; mem. Ottawa Curling Club from '67; won 2 City of Ottawa bonspiel grand aggregate titles, 2 Kingston Little Canuck, Fisherman's bonspiels, Gord Perry bonspiel, OCA Governor-General's, Ottawa Masters, CofO srs. grand aggregate; runnerup OCA mixed; coached jr. hockey, football; dir. '81 ntl fastball, 3 Ont. men's, 3 ISC Eastern Cdn championships; chair. Ottawa Masters bonspiel 15yrs, chair. Gord Perry bonspiel 2 yrs, dir. OCC 11yrs; Doran trophy St. Pat's HS, Ottawa ACT sportsman of '86, Softball Canada award of merit, Perth Shootout contributor

to game award; Level 2 softball coaching certificate; Ott. RCSSB trustee 6yrs; leading hitter/3b Hull Volants '66; coached teams in 2 ISC world, 2 Cdn men's fastball championships; res. Ottawa, Ont.

CHIBI, Tony (bowling); b. 31 Jan 1936, Punnichy, Sask.; given name: Anthony Joseph; m. Peggee Hillier; c. Tammy Lynne, Carrie Lynn; electrician; 5 Essex County, 5 Ont., 3 ntl 10-pin singles titles; 1st tournament of America's; Molson Masters titles; world invitational tournament '60-61, '63; qualified 3 ABC masters tournaments; mem. Brunswick advisory staff; perfect sanctioned 300 league play 16 Mar '66; runnerup Canadian Bowling Classic Montreal; high avg. 200 Windsor Major Classic League '62-63; mem. McCallum Challenge Cup winner '64; drafted Detroit pro league '61; award of merit Leamington Dist. Chamber of Comm.; Ont. Athletic Commission merit award; mem. Windsor-Essex County, Greater Miami Sports halls of fame; res. Leamington, Ont.

CHICK, John (builder); b. 21 Jan 1892, Windsor, Ont.; d. 1961, Windsor, Ont.; given name: John Digby; construction co. owner; instrumental role in construction of Windsor Arena; sponsored Ontario Baseball Assn. champion Walkerville Chicks '29; exerted strong influence in bringing pro hockey to Windsor; part-owner, GM Windsor Bulldogs, IHL titles '29, '31; WW2 liaison officer between US-Cnd federal authorities for all NHL, AHL players; considered savior of wartime hockey; more than 25yrs executive officer AHL; mem. Windsor-Essex Sports Hall of Fame.

CHILD, John (volleyball); b. 4 May 1967, East York, Ont.; Centennial College; beach volleyball specialist; teamed with Ed Drakich to win '92, '93 Cdn pro beach, '92 Jose Cuervo NA titles; with Mark Heese '95 Cdn pro beach title; 5 bronze FIVB world championship series; voted best defender, MVP '92; mem. '86 Scarborough Solars ntl indoor champions; competed '96 Olympics; res. Toronto, Ont.

CHIPMAN, A.U. (administration); b. 2 Oct 1902, Winnipeg, Man.; d. 14 Dec 1993, Winnipeg, Man.; given name: Arthur Uniake; m. Louise Arnold; c. Arthur U II, Warwick (d); wholesale food co. chairman; pres. Blue Bombers '44-47; had taste of coaching '41 Grey Cup when Reg Threlfall was ill; pres. CRU, WIFU; 1st trustee Schenley Awards; pres. Winnipeg Rangers '43 Memorial Cup winners; pres. Winnipeg Assiniboine Downs Turf Club; v.-pres. '67 Pan-Am Games comm.; dir. Winnipeg Goldeyes baseball club; mem. Cdn Football, Blue Bombers halls of fame.

CHIPPER, Eric (football); b. 29 May 1915, Ottawa, Ont.; d. 18 Jan 1996, Ottawa, Ont.; given name: Eric Trevor; m. Frances Newell; c. Diane, Marnie; sheet metal worker; jr. football Ottawa Strathconas '35; mem. Ottawa Trojans WW2; Rough Riders '38-50; Walker Trophy '47, Jeff Russel Memorial Trophy '48; capt. Rough Riders '48; Eastern all-star tackle, standout kicker; basketball Ottawa Tech, Int. Diamonds, sr. Barrett Sailors, '45 MVP; twice scoring champion Ottawa Falcons soccer team; sr. softball, hockey Ottawa Car; operated swim, ski schools for Ottawa Westboro Kiwanis; coached Kiwanis peewee hockey, Ottawa Seconds int. football; mem. Ottawa Rowing Club; paddled for

Britannia Yacht Club 2 CCA regattas; minor lacrosse Ottawa St. Annes; bowled Kiwanis league.

CHIU, Barbara (table tennis); b. 14 Jul 1964, Canton, China; began playing age 8; regarded as "blocker" who capitalizes on opponent's errors; '92 NA open doubles gold, singles silver, '96 NA women's doubles gold; with Johnny Huang won Canada's 1st Commonwealth championships mixed doubles gold '94, women's team bronze '94; best international showing '89 worlds winning 13 of 14 matches; team, women's doubles gold, singles, mixed doubles bronze '95 Pan-Am Games; partnered with Lijuan Geng won '96 NA women's doubles gold; mem. '96 Olympic team; res. Vancouver, B.C.

CHOMYC, Lance (football); b. 2 Mar 1963, Edmonton, Alta.; m. Rasa; c. Larissa; UofT; teacher; mem. Edmonton Wildcat Jrs '81-82; led OUAA punters, scorers '83, runnerup '84; OUAA 1st team all-star '83; 6th round draft choice Ottawa '85; 21 day trial with Saskatchewan before joining Argos as free agent '85-93; through '91 led Argos scorers 7 straight yrs; 3rd player in CFL history to top 200 points in single season; set Argos single game FG record with 7 twice in '88; set several Argos place kicking records; set CFL convert record with 76 straight; twice EFC all-star, once all-Canadian; res. Alliston, Ont/ Edmonton, Alta.

CHOQUETTE, Jean (gymnastics); b. 2 Apr 1956, Montreal, Que.; Quebec, BA; teacher; mem. ntl team '75-82; 2 Pan-Am, 1 Commonwealth, 3 FISU, 2 world championships teams; 2 silver '79 Pan-Am, gold, bronze '78 Commonwealth, gold, silver '81 NZ Games; twice Que. athlete of month '81; Que. artistic gymnast of '77-78, '80-81; Que. athlete of '80; res. St. Bruno, Que.

CHORNOBRYWY, Lynn (modern pentathlon); b. 16 Sep 1962, Ottawa, Ont.; given name: Janet Lynn; ntl titles '79, '81-83; surpassed 5000 points plateau 1st time '81; '83 women's world title, record 5328 points; '83 Nordic Cup; fed, govt. world champion award '84; Velma Springstead Trophy '83; res. Baie d'Urfe, Que.

CHOUINARD, Guy (hockey); b. 20 Oct 1956, Quebec City, Que.; given name: Guy Camil; jr. Que. Remparts; 1st Atlanta pick '74 amateur draft; CHL rookie of year Omaha '74-75; NHL Atlanta '74-80, Calgary '80-83, St. Louis '83-84; 50-goal plateau '79 season; NHL record: 578 scheduled games, 205g, 370a, 46 playoff games, 9g, 28a; coach Sherbrooke Faucons '94-96; res. St. Louis, Mo.

CHOUINARD, Jean-Marc (fencing); b. 6 Nov 1963, Montreal, Que.; m. Marie-France Lalibert,; c. Vincent, Simon; urban planner; began fencing at 15; épée specialist; silver jr. worlds; silver World University Games; 4th '84 Olympics; mem. '84, '88, '92 Olympic, '87 Pan-Am Games teams; mem. Canada's best-ever team which placed 6th '91 Worlds; best ever individual Canadian performance placing 7th '86 Worlds; 1st Canadian fencer to rank in world's top 8 yrs; res. Montreal, Que.

CHOUINARD, Josée (figure skating); b. 21 Aug 1969, Rosemont, Que.; m. Jean-Michel Bombardier; College Francais; professional skater; began skating age 7; mem.

ntl team from '88; gold '90, bronze '92 Skate Canada; 3 ntl sr. women's titles; competed 3 worlds, '92, '94 Olympics; coached by Louis Stong; turned pro with Stars on Ice '94; Cdn women's pro champ '97; res. Toronto, Ont.

CHRISTIE, Alan (t&f); b. 14 Jun 1905, Hamilton, Ont.; given name: Alan Thomas; m. Kathleen Aggett; c. Janet, Susan, Carol Anne; UofT, BComm.; retd investment consultant; mem. Penn Relays HS mile titlist '22; ntl interscholastic 440yds champion '23; Ont. open indoor 300yds title '23; Ont. open 440yds '23, '25; Ont. open 400m, silver UPenn US interscholastic championships 440yds '24; Cdn intercollegiate 440yd titles '24-27; in qualifying for '24 Olympic team set 400m record; quarterfinalist Olympic 400m, mem. 4th place 1600m relay team; mem. UofT intercollegiate record setting mile relay team '26; mem. '28 Hamilton 1600m AAU of C title, ntl record relay team; res. White Plains, NY/Cotuit, Mass.

CHRISTIE, Steve (football); b. 13 Nov 1967, Oakville, Ont.; given name: Geoffrey Stephen; m. Alison; c. Alexandra Laine; William & Mary; standout HS soccer/football player; mem. ntl jr World Cup soccer team; set numerous W&M placekicking records including most points (279), most FGs (57 of 83), most cvts (108 of 116), longest FG (53yds 3 times), drafted by Tampa Bay (NFL), Edmonton (CFL); standout rookie season with Tampa Bay earned selection to all-Rookie team; set several Tampa Bay records; traded to Buffalo '92; continued amassing NFL records; became most accurate kicker in NFL history with 100 of 124 for 80.65 per cent '95; personal best 59yd FG '93; accomplished painter; major involvement with Buffalo and Erie County Historical Society; res. St. Petersburg, FL.

CHURSKY, Tony (soccer); b. 13 Jun 1953, New Westminster, B.C.; m. Donna; c. Ian; Simon Fraser; soccer player; amateur soccer Vancouver Croatia, Spartans; pro Seattle Sounders '76-78; led NASL goalers with 0.91 goals against average rookie season; California Surf, Chicago Sting '79; Toronto Blizzard from '80; '77 Soccer Bowl finalist; international debut ntl team '72; res. Toronto, Ont.

CHUVALO, George (boxing); 12 Sep 1937, Toronto, Ont.; m. Lynne (d); c. Mitchell, Steven (d), George Jr. (d), Jesse (d), Vanessa; m. Joanne; St. Michael's Coll.; promotions, TV productions; ntl amateur heavyweight title '55; pro '56; beat James J. Parker for ntl heavyweight title '58; defended vs. Yvon Durelle then lost to Bob Cleroux '60; regained it then lost again to Cleroux; reclaimed title beating Jean Claude Roy '68; defended successfully through '79; fought Muhammad Ali, Joe Frazier, Floyd Patterson, Ernie Terrell, George Foreman; never knocked off feet; career total 97 bouts, won 68 by KO, 9 on decision, 2 draws, lost 15 decisions, 1 DQ, 2 TKOs; TV boxing commentator, occasional movie actor; mem. Order of Canada; Cdn Boxing; Rochester Boxing; Canada's, Etobicoke, Ont. Legends Sports halls of fame; res. Weston, Ont.

CHYNOWETH, Ed (hockey/builder); b. 14 Dec 1941, Dodsland, Sask.; given name: James Edward; m. Linda Lindsay; c. Jeff, Dean; pres./owner Edmonton Ice (WHL); 1st full-time pres. WHL '72; organized Cdn Major Junior Hockey League (CHL) '73; pres. '75-96; key role in getting

CHL and CHA to form policy comm. to oversee/operate Canada's world jr. team program; p-pres. Sask MHA; 2 CHL distinguished service awards; fed. Fair Play award; CHA order of merit; mem. Intl Centre of Excellence/hockey development comm. '87; mem. Hockey Hall of Fame selection comm. '90; res. St. Albert, Alta.

CICCARELLI, Dino (hockey); b. 8 Feb 1960, Sarnia, Ont.; m. Lynda; c. Jenna, Kristen, Ashley; right wing London Knights '77-80; OHL 2nd team all-star '78; pro Oklahoma City (CHL) '80-81; Minnesota '80-89, Washington '89-92, Detroit '92-96, Tampa Bay '96-98, Florida '98-99; topped 50-goal plateau with 55 '81-82, 52 '86-87; topped 1,000 point mark '94, 600g plateau '98; NHL record: 1232 scheduled games, 608g, 592a, 141 playoff games, 73g, 45a; played 4 NHL all-star games; co-owner Motor City Mustangs roller hockey team; co-owner Sarnia Sting jrs. (OHL); res. Kalamazoo, Mich.

CLAIR, Frank (football/coaching); b. 12 May 1917, Hamilton, Ohio; m. Pat Bausman; c. Robin, Holly (d); Ohio State, Miami of Ohio, BSc; retd football exec., scout; all-Big 10 end Ohio State '38; drafted Washington Redskins; asst. coach 71st Infantry Div. in Europe WW2; asst. Miami of Ohio '46, Purdue '47; head coach UofBuffalo '48, Argos '50-54; asst. Cincinnati U '55; head coach Rough Riders '56-69; CFL coaching record: 172-125-7, .579 percentage; made playoffs 17 times 18yrs, league finals 12 times; 6 Grey Cups, 5 winners; twice Annis Stukus Trophy CFL coach of year; nicknamed "The Professor"; GM Rough Riders '70-78, Grey Cup champions '73, '76; scout Argos '82-86; Rough Rider advisor '87-90; Ottawa stadium bears his name; mem. Butler County; Ottawa Sports, Cdn Football halls of fame; res. Sarasota, Fla.

CLANCY, King (hockey); b. 25 Feb 1903, Ottawa, Ont.; d. 10 Nov 1986, Toronto, Ont.; given name: Francis Michael; m. Rae (d); c. Terry, Carol, Ann, Judy, Tom; hockey exec.; amateur hockey Ottawa St. Brigid's; pro at 18 Ottawa Senators; reputation as rushing defenceman; sold to Maple Leafs '30 for unprecedented $35,000+two players; led Leafs to 1st Stanley Cup '31-32; twice 1st, 2nd all-star teams; retired following '36-37 season; coached Montreal Maroons half '37-38 season then switched to refereeing; coach Leafs '50, Cleveland, Pittsburgh (AHL); asst. GM, v.-pres.; also v.-pres. HamiltonCFL club; Bickell Cup for contribution to Leafs; 2 'nights' in his honor Maple Leaf Gardens; nicknamed "King"; noted raconteur; mem. Ottawa, Hockey, Canada's Sports halls of fame.

CLAPPER, Dit (hockey); b. 9 Feb 1907, Newmarket, Ont.; d. 20 Jan 1978, Peterborough, Ont.; given name: Aubrey Victor; m. Lorraine Pratt; c. Donald, Marilyn; accountant, office mgr.; jr. Oshawa at 13; Parkdale Canoe Club, CAHL Boston Tigers; Bruins '27-47, 1st NHL player 20 seasons same club; 9yrs right wing, 11 defence; NHL record: 833 scheduled games, 228g, 246a, 86 playoff games, 13g, 17 assists; best season '29-30, 41 goals 44-game schedule; mem. 3 Stanley Cup winners; 3 times 1st, 2nd team all-star; Buffalo (AHL) after leaving NHL; coached Bruins 2 seasons, Buffalo '60; sweater No. 5 retired by Bruins; mem. Hockey, Peterborough, Canada's Sports halls of fame.

CLARE, Lou (football); b. 13 Mar 1953, Mississauga, Ont.; UMinn; standout hockey player Dixie Beehive organization; jr. St. Catharines Black Hawks; although being groomed for NHL with Chicago accepted UMinn athletic scholarship and shone as def. back/linebacker/place kicker; boyhood dream of playing for Toronto vanished when Argos traded his CFL rights to Hamilton '73; def. back/cornerback with Ticats until dealt to Saskatchewan '75; rejoined Hamilton '79-80, Montreal '81; 2 Grey Cup finals; mem. Mississauga Sports Hall of Fame; res. Brampton, Ont.

CLARIDGE, Pat (football); b. 12 Jul 1938, Chilliwack, B.C.; m. Anne Louise Hanna;Wash; stockbroker; mem. 2 Rose Bowl winners; all-Coast split end; receiver BC Lions '61-66; mem. Calgary '68 Grey Cup winner; CFL record: 198 receptions for 2497yds; WFC all-star '64, CFL top Canadian nominee; football broadcast color commentator; res. Edmonton, Alta.

CLARK, Bud (skiing); b. Jul 1910, Ottawa, Ont.; d. 2 Jan 1975, Ottawa, Ont.; St. Pat's Coll.; sporting goods mgr.; standout skier, paddler; mem. New Edinburgh Canoe Club; international intercollegiate all-around ski champion, Lake Placid combined champion '31; mem. '32, '36 Olympic teams; ntl nordic combined, Que. cross-country title '35; built, operated Skiskule Lodge; charter mem. Cdn Amateur Sports Advisory council; dir. COA; 7yrs pres. CASA; initial curator Cdn Ski Museum; mem. Cdn Skiing Hall of Fame.

CLARK, Jim (coaching); b. 22 Mar 1942, St. Thomas, Ont.; given name: James Richard; m. Barbara Jeanne Cook; c. James Robert; Acadia, BA; football scout; asst. coach Acadia '68-69,Tennessee '69-71, Clearwater Fla. HS '71-75; head coach St. Mary's '76-79; asst. coach UofOtt '79-82, head coach '83-84; scout BC. Lions '85-91, Calgary '95-98; asst. coach Ottawa '92-93, Hamilton '94, Birmingham Barracudas '95; res. Ottawa, Ont.

CLARK, Karen (synchro swim); b. 4 Sep 1972, Montreal, Que.; introduced to synchroswim by older sister; mem. ntl team from '88; solo silver '95 Pan-Am, team silver '96 Olympic Games; team gold '96 French Open, '90 Swiss Open, '91 Petro-Canada Cup, '94 Titrex Cup, '93 ntl sr championships; Helen Vanderburg synchroswim award '87; Petro-Canada Olympic Torch scholarship; res. Mississauga, Ont./Calgary, Alta.

CLARK, Ken (football); b. 26 May 1948, Southampton, Eng.; given name: Kenneth Lawrence; div. Grayce Palmisano; c. Devon, Garrett; m. Terri; c. Ryan, Jesse (stepchildren); St. Mary's, BA, George Brown College, Sheridan College; printing co. owner; HS athlete of '68, George Brown athlete of '70, St. Mary's athlete of '74; Ted Morris Memorial award '73; pro punter Portland Storm (WFL) '74-75, Hamilton '75-77, Toronto '78-79, Los Angeles Rams (NFL) '79-80, Saskatchewan '80-83, Ottawa '83-87; 7 times top CFL punter, 2 EFC, 1 WFC, 3 CFL all-star; LA Rams kicker Super Bowl XIV; all-Canadian, all-WFC '82; CFL record: 12 seasons, 1592 punts, 72,520 yds, 45.6 avg (league record), 2 tds, 23 cvts, 10 fg, 90 singles; res. Barrie, Ont.

CLARK, Paul (t&f); b. 13 Dec 1957, Woodstock, Ont.; optometrist; 3 world, 7 ntl, 1 Pan-Am wheelchair records in distances from 100m to 10km; 15 Ont. Games, 9 Canada Games, 5 Regional Games gold; mem. '80, '84 Olympic, '82 Pan-Am Games for Disabled teams; res. Woodstock, Ont.

CLARK, Ranza (t&f); b. 13 Dec 1961, Calgary, Alta.; m. Art Boileau; Oregon BA; employed Chapters, owns greeting card co.; BC. 1500m title '83; gold 1500m, silver 800m '83 Pan-Am Games; silver NCAA '84 championships; mem. '84 Olympic, '90 Commonwealth Games teams; '89 ntl 800m title; fed. govt. excellence award '84; res. Vancouver, B.C.

CLARK, Wendel (hockey); b. 25 Oct 1966, Kelvington, Sask; m. Denise; c. Kylee Lee, Kassidy; left wing Saskatoon Jr. '83-85; WHL East 1st team all-star '85; mem. Cdn gold medal world jr. team '85; drafted by Toronto 1st overall '85; NHL Toronto '85-94, '96-98, Quebec '94-95, Colorado '95, NY Islanders '95-96, Tampa Bay '98, Detroit '99, Chicago '99; NHL all-rookie team '86; *Sporting News* rookie of '86; frequent injuries curtailed much of career; NHL record (through '99) 760 scheduled games, 326g, 232a, 89 playoff games, 36g, 31a; res. Hopewell Junction, N.Y.

CLARKE, Bill (football); b. 25 Nov 1932, Regina, Sask.; m. Geraldine Bloomer; c. Jim, Tara, Debbie, Peter, Rob; UofSask; retd. politician, chartered accountant; pres. Regina Dales; centre, def. tackle Roughriders '51-65; twice all-star; mem. '50 Cdn schoolboy curling title rink; ntl sr. men's curling title '88; pres. Roughriders; chair. interprovincial, Western Canada lotteries; deputy minister Sask. dept. Parks, Recreation and Culture '82-87; mem. Cdn Football, Sask Sports halls of fame; res. Regina, Sask.

CLARKE, Bobby (hockey); b. 13 Aug 1949, Flin Flon, Man.; given name: Robert Earle; m. Sandy; c. Wade, Jody, Lucas, Jakki; hockey exec.; jr. Flin Flon Bombers; Philadelphia's 2nd choice, 17th overall 1969 amateur draft; mem. Flyers '69-84; 2 Stanley Cups; Flyers capt. '72-79, '82-84; at time youngest NHL team capt.; 1000 game plateau 23 Oct '82; twice 1st, 2nd all-star team centre; 9 NHL all-star games; mem. Team Canada '72, '76; Hart Trophy '73, '75-6; Bill Masterton Trophy '72; Lester B. Pearson Award '73; Lionel Conacher, Lou Marsh trophies '75; Lester Patrick award '80; Frank J. Selke Trophy '83; Pa. sports writers athlete of '74, Good Guy award '83, most courageous award '80; 1st to win *Sporting News* rookie, player, executive awards; *Sporting News, Hockey News* exec. of '95; 1st to win HN exec award in consec. yrs with different teams; NHL record: 1144 scheduled games, 358 goals, 852 assists; v.-pres., GM Philadelphia Flyers '84-90, sr. v.-pres. '92-93; GM Minnesota North Stars '91-92; VP/GM Florida Panthers '93-94; pres/GM/partner Philadelphia from '94; GM Team Canada '87 Canada Cup title team, '98 Olympic team; jersey 16 retd by Flyers; Officer Order of Canada '81; mem. Man. Sports, Flyers, Man, Cdn Hockey halls of fame; res. Moorestown, N.J.

CLARKE, Christine (rowing); b. 11 Aug 1960, Scarborough, Ont.; sweep ntl champion coxed 8s '77, coxless pairs '80; Canadian Henley coxed 8s '77, Head of the Charles '83; mem. '84 Olympic Games, 2 world championships teams; sister Heather also ntl team mem.; res. Vancouver, B.C.

CLARKE, Heather (rowing); b. 25 Jul 1958, Stouffville, Ont.; sweep coxed 8s '77, '80-82 Canadian Henley title crews; 2nd coxed 4s '81 English Henley; 2 ntl coxed 8s titles; mem. '84 Olympic team; sister Christine also ntl team mem.; mem. Cdn Athletes Assn. board; res. Victoria, B.C.

CLARKE, Karen (t&f); b. 7 Oct 1971, Montego Bay, Jamaica; sprint specialist; emigrated to Canada '82; began competing '85; ntl jr. 200m title '89; semifinalist world jr. '90; ntl 100, 200m titles '91; competed '91 worlds, Pan-Am Games, '92 Olympics, '94 Commonwealth Games; ntl indoor 60m titles '92, '93, 200m indoor title '92; gold Times-Colonist 100m '94; PB: 11.40 100m, 23.47 200m; res. Calgary, Alta.

CLARKE, Nig (baseball); b. 15 Dec 1882, Amherstburg, Ont.; d. 15 Jun 1949, River Rouge, Mich.; given name: Jay Justin; Assumption Coll; retd Ford Motors; catcher; 8 consecutive homers Jul '02 as Corsicana thumped Texarcana 51-3 in Texas League game; Detroit (AL) '05, Cleveland (AL) '05-10, St. Louis (AL) '11, Philadelphia (NL) '19, Pittsburgh (NL) '20; ML record: 506 scheduled games, .254ba; mem. Cdn Baseball, U Windsor, Windsor-Essex, Canada's Sports halls of Fame.

CLARKE, Richard (sailing); b. 20 Nov 1968, Toronto, Ont.; Trent U. rugby coach; following in footsteps of father Alan who won bronze in '67 Pan-Am Games and who competed in '72 Olympics, he moved from Laser and Flying Dutchman to Finn Class '89; bronze Finn Gold Cup (worlds) '93; CORK gold, NA silver '95, bronze '94; silver '86 IYRU world youth championships; member '96, alternate '92 Olympic teams; Finn gold '99 PAG; CYA male athlete of '93, Ont. sailor of '93; 2 Ont. all-star rugby awards; res. Peterborough, Ont.

CLARKE, Stephen (swimming); b. 21 Jul 1973, Sutton Coldfield, Eng.; Florida; began swimming age 4, racing age 6; butterfly specialist; silver 4x100m FS relay '91 Pan-Am, '98 Commonwealth Games; bronze 4x100m medley relay '92 Olympics; bronze 4x100m FS relay '93 Pan-Pacific championships, 4x100 medley relay '98 Commonwealth Games; gold 100m FS, silver 100m fly, 4x100m medley relay '94 Commonwealth Games; 5 Canada Cup gold, 2 silver '96; 8 ntl titles; with Marcel Gery, Ont. swim athlete of '92; res. Brampton, Ont./Gainsville, Fla.

CLARKSON, Candy (basketball); b. 30 Nov 1958, Hamilton, Ont.; given name: Candace Leah; div. Kevin Lohr; m. David Bruce Jirik; c. Ashleigh Elizabeth, Alexis Victoria, Tyler Phillip Bradley; Guelph, BSc, Brock, BEd; teacher; mem. OFSAA title teams '75-76; ntl jr. title team '76; ntl sr. women's team '77-80, '82-84; ntl title team '85; all-Cdn university 1st team '77-80, '82-83; tournament MVP '77 ntl sr. women's championship; OWIAA single game record 49 points; bronze worlds, FISU, Pan-Am Games; competed '84 Olympics, '79, '83 Pan-Am Games, 2 world championships; Guelph female athlete of '79, Brock co-athlete of yr '82-83; mem. Brock, Guelph Sports halls of fame; res. Unionville, Ont.

CLARKSON, Reg (all-around); b. 19 Aug 1925, Victoria, B.C.; given name: Reginald Louis; m. Peggy McCarthy; c. Mary, Rita, Clare, Joan, Greg, Reg Jr., Peggy, Kevin; UBC, BA, BSW, MSW, Victoria Normal School, TCert.; prison service social worker; mem. BC. HS soccer, basketball title teams; mem. '46 Western Conf. college football champions; pro baseball Vancouver Capilanos '46; contract sold to Brooklyn Dodgers; left field under Walter Alston Ft. Worth batting .337, named all-star; arm problems '48; batted .281 Mobile; semipro Edmonton '49 batting .381, leading league all offensive departments; .327 Vancouver Capilanos '50; pro basketball Vancouver Hornets '46-47; football Edmonton '49-50; traded to Calgary for Normie Kwong '51; Vancouver athlete of '46; mem. BC. Sports Hall of Fame; res. Vancouver, B.C.

CLASS, Harry (builder/diving); b. 1 Mar 1916, Berlin (Kitchener), Ont.; m. Helen Hirons (d); c. Duncan, Philip; pres. frozen food co.; began diving career late '20s; won Western Ont. Jr./Sr. 3m titles '32; 5 Cdn sr/ 3m, 1 1m titles; 3m bronze '34 BEG; won '36 Olympic trials but CASA chose not to add him to team; while serving in army WW2 engaged in English diving exhibitions for Red Cross; served on CASA exec. 10yrs; diving chair. 4yrs; CNE sports comm. 25yrs; chief referee world pro high diving championships '62-63; editor/publisher Canadian Aquatic News '58-59; Swim Ontario Friend of Swimming award; dir. Swim Ontario (Ont. Aquatic) Hall of Fame; master swimmer; French Open gold; mem. Ont. Aquatic Hall of fame as both athlete and builder; res. Kitchener, Ont.

CLAYTON, Harold (lawn bowling); b. 10 Jun 1916, Lang, Sask.; given name: Harold Wright; retd. provincial civil servant; from '45-60 among Saskatchewan's top curlers; 5 Sask., 2 ntl singles lawn bowling titles; mem. '70 BEG team; mem. Sask. Sports Hall of Fame; res. Regina, Sask.

CLAYTON, Juanita (softball); b. 10 Jan 1969, Manitou, Man.; Utah State; social worker; catcher; began playing age 13; ntl jr team '85, '87; competed jr. worlds, '91, '95 Pan-Am Games, '96 Olympics, '94 worlds; 4 yrs NCAA Div. 1 with Utah State, 2 MVP awards; all-star catcher '95 ntl championships; res. Kaleida, Man.

CLEEVELY, Bill (canoeing); b. 23 Oct 1908, Montreal, Que.; d. 26 Nov 1990, Ottawa, Ont; given name: William Gerald; m. Margaret Grace Forbes (d); c. Susan, Lynn, Billy; retired CNR; mem. Otterbrun Boating Club '24-28, both tandem and 4s; ntl sr. tandem title with J.O.Mason '27; coach, capt. OBC '35, '47-48; OBC exec., commodore '37; Eastern Div. CCA flag officer, secty. '43, '53-60; commodore CCA '46, secty.-treas. '58-64; mgr. canoe team '60 Olympics; Voyageur Canadian canoeing award '72.

CLEGHORN, Odie (hockey); b. 1891, Montreal, Que.; d. 13 Jul 1956, Montreal, Que.; given name: Ogilvie; unique distinction of playing major hockey as both forward and goaler, later referee; mem. Canadiens '18-25; 2 seasons Pittsburgh Pirates; 9yr NHL record 96 goals, 29 assists; played 1 game in goal allowing 2 goals; brother Sprague.

CLEGHORN, Sprague (hockey); b. 1890, Montreal, Que.; d. 11 Jul 1956, Montreal, Que.; forward NY Crescents;

Renfrew (NHA) '09-10; teamed with Cyclone Taylor on defence; once scored 5 goals single game; 6 seasons Montreal Wanderers; Ottawa Senators '19-21, briefly Toronto St.Pat's then Canadiens '22-25, Bruins '26; in 17 seasons (missed '18 with broken leg) 163 goals, 296 games; mem. 2 Stanley Cup winners; brother Odie; mem. Hockey Hall of Fame.

CLEMENS, Roger (baseball); b. 4 Aug 1962, Dayton, Ohio; given name: William Roger; m. Debra Lynn Godfrey; c. Koby Aaron, Kory Allen, Kacy Austin, Kody Alec; Texas, San Jacinto JC; righthanded pitcher; helped Legion team win State title '79; all-district football def. end, basketball centre; drafted NY Mets '81 but didn't sign; 3yrs all-American; NCAA world series title '83; 1st Texas baseball player to have number (21) retd.; made pro debut Winter Haven (Fla. St.) '83, New Britain (EL) '83, Pawtucket (EL) '84; Boston (AL) '84-96, Toronto '97-98; New York (AL) '99; nicknamed "Rocket Roger"; competed '86, '99 world series; AL MVP '86; record 5 Cy Young awards; Joe Cronin award '98; three times led AL in strikeouts single season; 5 ERA titles; 2 20k games; MBL record (through '99): 480 scheduled games, 3462.1ip. 247-134w/l, 3316k, 45sho, 1080bob, 2917h, 3.01era; 6 all-star games, recorded 21 victories in initial season with Toronto '97, 20 (15 in succession) in '98; reached 3000 strikeout plateau '98; active in community charity programs in Boston; created K for Kids program; Ont. athlete of '97; res. Houston, Tex.

CLEMENT, Diane (t&f); b. 27 Sep 1936, Moncton, N.B.; given name: Diane Elaine Matheson; m. Doug Clement; c. Jennifer, Rand; Sir George Williams; food consultant, restaurant owner, cookbook author; ntl 100m, 200m records '54-55; mem. '56 Olympic team; bronze 4x100 relay '58 Commonwealth Games; pres. CTFA '74-76; co-founder Richmond Kajaks t&f club; mgr. '84-88 ntl t&f team; mem. NB Sports Hall of Fame; res. Vancouver, B.C.

CLEMENT, Doug (t&f); b. 15 Jul 1933, Montreal, Que.; given name: Douglas Bruce; m. Diane Matheson; c. Jennifer, Rand; Oregon, BSc, UBC, MD; sports physician; 400m, 800m specialist; mem. '52, '56 Olympic, '54, '58 Commonwealth Games teams; silver 4x440yds relay '54; John Davies award '53, Vanier award '69; physician '70 Commonwealth, '71 Pan-Am, '76, '84 Olympic Games; coach '88, '92 Olympic, '86 Commonwealth, '91, '93 (head) world championship teams; co-dir. Allan McGavin sports medicine centre; prof. UBC faculty of medicine; team doctor Vancouver Canucks; mem. Order of Canada '91; UBC Sports Hall of Fame; res. Vancouver, B.C.

CLEMENTS, Tom (football); b. 18 Jun 1953, McKee's Rocks, Pa.; given name: Thomas Albert; m. Kathleen Ann Brady; c. Stephanie Alice, Tom Jr.; Notre Dame; lawyer/ coach; QB coach Notre Dame '92-95, New Orleans Saints from '97; HS basketball all-American (recruited by N.Carolina); ND quarterback, all-American 3 of 4 years; mem. '74 ntl championship team, Sugar Bowl winner; Heisman Trophy nominee sr. year; pro Ottawa '75-78; Saskatchewan, Hamilton '79; NFL Kansas City '80; Hamilton '81-83; traded to Winnipeg for Dieter Brock '83; retired after '87 season; CFL record: 12 seasons, 4657 attempts, 2807 completions, 39041 yds, 60.3 pct, 252 tds,

214 interceptions; Schenley rookie of '75, Grey Cup winner '76, '84; 6 times EFC all-star; CFL all-star '84; '76, '84 Grey Cup MVP; 5 times EFC passing yardage leader; twice Ticats MVP, Jeff Russel Trophy winner '81; runnerup Schenley outstanding player '81; CFL star of year award '84; mem. Blue Bombers, Cdn Football halls of fame; res. New Orleans, La.

CLEMONS, Mike (football); b. 15 Jan 1965, Clearwater, Fla.; m. Diane; c. Rachel; William & Mary; football player, business owner; as collegian amassed 4778 all-purpose yds, 31tds '83-87; NCAA Div 1-AA all-American, Virginia major colleges offensive player of '86; 8th round draft KC Chiefs '87; attended Tampa Bay NFL camp '88; made Argos debut 27 Jul '89; quickly earned nickname "Pinball" for exciting, elusive running style; 1st CFL TD vs. Ottawa 9 Oct '89; shattered own single season pro football record for combined yds with 3840 in '97; EFC, CFL all-star as special teams player; CFL record (through '98): 161gp, 1023 carries,4983yds, 83td, 3cvt, 630recept., 6554yds, 44td; 2 Eastern, 1 CFL all-star; Jeff Russell Memorial award '90, 1 CFL record; '91, '96 Grey Cup winner; CFL outstanding player award '90; active in charitable work in Toronto; mem. Argos basketball team; mem. Athletes in Action; CFL outstanding player '90; Tom Pate Memorial award '94; CFLPA sportsman award; 2 ALS Ironman awards; John Candy Memorial award '95; res. Mississauga, Ont.

CLEVELAND, Jon (swimming); b. 19 Dec 1970, Fresno, Calif.; UCal, began competing age 9; mem. ntl team from '87; breaststroke specialist; 23 ntl titles; mem. 3 4x50, 1 4x100 Cdn record relay teams, 1 4x100 world record team; 1st '88, '92 World Cup breaststroke rankings; CIAU 100, 200, 4x100 medley relay short course records '90; 5 CIAU titles; Commonwealth Games gold 200m, 4x100 medley '90, silver 4x100m medley relay, bronze 100, 200 '94; silver 100m, bronze 4x100 medley relay '95 Pan-Am Games; mem. '88, '92, '96 Olympic teams; 2 CIAU male swimmer of yr; 3 Swimming Canada male athlete of year awards; res. Calgary, Alta.

CLEVELAND, Reggie (baseball); b. 23 May 1948, Swift Current, Sask.; given name: Reginald Leslie; m. Kathleen Kubicki; c. Michelle Annette, Michael David, Todd Joseph, Tim; car salesman; HS athlete of '65 starring in curling, t&f; 2 Alta. javelin records; Babe Ruth League no-hitter '61; pro St. Louis organization '66, Cardinals '69-73, Boston '74-78, Texas '78, Milwaukee '79-81; righthanded starter, reliever; Sporting News NL rookie pitcher of yr, St. Louis chapter BBWA rookie of year; Red Sox Man of '76; 1st Cdn to start ALCS playoff game '75; World Series finalist '75; ML record: 428 scheduled games, 1809ip, 57cg, 930k, 543bob, 105-106, 25sv; 12so, 4.01era; mem. Cdn Baseball Hall of Fame; res. Calgary, Alta/Mansfield, Tex.

CLIFF, Leslie (swimming); b. 11 Mar 1955, Vancouver, B.C.; m. Mark Tindle; c. Scott, Lisa; Arizona State BC (finance); portfolio mgr.; 15 ntl, 4 British, 1 US titles; 3 gold, 2 silver '71 Pan-Am, 2 gold '74 Commonwealth, silver '72 Olympics; specialist 200m, 400m, 800m FS, 200m backstroke, 400m IM; ntl jr. athlete of '72; BC. swimmer of '71-73; hon. capt. '94 Commonwealth Games team; helped initiate Zajac swim camps; Elaine Tanner trophy '72;

Officer Order of Canada '71; mem. Cdn Aquatic, Canada's, BC. Sports halls of fame; res. Vancouver, B.C.

CLIFFORD, Betsy (skiing); b. 15 Oct 1953, Ottawa, Ont.; m. Dale Higgins; c. Blake, Carly, Jolene, Roseanne; Algonquin College; Fleet News publication asst.; began skiing age 3; ntl jr. title age 12, women's crown at 13; 8 ntl slalom, GS titles through '75; at 14 youngest Canadian skier ever in Olympics ('68 Grenoble); at 16 youngest world championship winner with GS gold Val Gardena, Italy '70; at 17 women's special slalom title Val d'Isere, France, slalom Schruns, Austria, 2nd overall WC slalom '71; freak accident resulted in 2 broken heels '72 WC downhill; overall Can-Am team title '73; silver '74 WC downhill St. Moritz, bronze WC downhill Pfronten, Germany; WC record 3-3-4; retired '76; twice Ottawa ACT athlete of year; mem. Ottawa, US, Cdn Skiing, Cdn Amateur, Canada's Sports halls of fame; res. Alcove, Que.

CLIFFORD, Harvey (skiing); b. 18 Sep 1926, Oak Point, N.B.; d. 13 Jan 1982, N. Palm Beach, Fla.; m. Ellen Vera Kaarsberg; c. Christian, Heidi; Queen's; ski resort owner, operator; brother John Clifford; major ski honors included Taschereau Cup, Canadian Kandahar; US downhill '48; 16th place Olympic downhill finish best ever by Cdn skier to '48; coach, capt. ntl ski team '50 worlds; coach '52 Olympic team; ski school instructor Banff, Laurentians, NZ; chief examiner Canadian Ski Instructors Alliance; 8yrs pres. Mount Snow, Vt. ski development; 7yrs pres. Stratton Mountain, Vt.; owner, operator Glen Ellen, Vt. resort to '79 retirement; mem. Cdn Skiing, Ottawa Sports halls of fame.

CLIFFORD, John (skiing); b. 13 Feb 1923, Ottawa, Ont.; m. Margaret Phillips; c. Betsy, Joanne, Stephen (d), Susanne; ski area developer, operator; despite schoolyard accident which left him almost blind in right eye, became alpine, water skiing champion; hitch-hiked to Chile to represent Canada Ski Union of Americas (Pan-Am) meet, won overall title; 3 ntl, 2 Que. titles; '48, '52 Olympic team alternate; mem. ntl team '50 world championships; ntl waterski title '55; 4 Que. titles; 9th world waterski finals '55; involved in development Camp Fortune, Carlington Park, Mt. Ste. Marie, Mt. Tremblant, Mt. Cascades, Calabogie Peaks, Mt. Pakenham ski areas; autobiography "*White Gold, The John Clifford Story*"; mem. Cdn Skiing; Ottawa Sports halls of fame; res. Pakenham, Ont.

CLIFFORD, Shanty (baseball); b. 16 Jan 1924, Clairton, Pa.; d. 4 May 1990, Brantford, Ont.; given name: Luther; m. Lorraine Saunders; retired Brant County Bd. of Ed. supervisor; Pa. state discus, shot put champion '41; catcher-1st baseman Homestead Grays, Indianapolis Clowns Negro National League; mem. '49 Grays pennant winners; Sr. IC Galt, Brantford throughout '50s; batting title '56 with .397; frequent all-star; RBI co-leader '58.

CLIFFORD, William (shooting); b. 1878, Brampton, Ont.; d. 1917, France; cabinet maker; mem. 10th Royal Grenadiers; mem. Cdn Bisley teams '10-11; mem. MacKinnon Cup winning team '10; claimed Bisley King's, Prince of Wales prizes '11 and subsequently honored by Toronto parade on return from England; during WW1 QMS in charge of Ross rifle div.; discovered Ross rifle didn't perform well in battle conditions and urged its withdrawl from service; subsequently got into a dispute with inventor Sir Ross and knowing he had no hope of winning argument switched to Royal Flying Corps where he lost his life on mission over France; built ceremonial chair still in use at DCRA Connaught Range in Nepean.

CLIMIE, Jock (football); b. 28 Sep 1968, Toronto, Ont.; slotback Queen's, LLb; lawyer; led OQIFC receivers '88-89; 1st team all-Canadian '88-89; set CIAU receiving record 1091yds '88; CIAU record: 121 receptions for 2130yds, 18tds; CFL Toronto '90, '95, Ottawa '90-94, Montreal from '96; CFL record (through '98):131gp, 464recept., 7192yds, 47td, 1cvt, 285pts; res. Ottawa, Ont.

CLINE, Paddy (rowing/basketball); b. 2 Feb 1899, Hamilton, Ont.; d. 13 Mar 1993, Hamilton, Ont.; given name: George; m. Alice Isabel McKenzie; Firestone Co. employee; mem. ntl Int. title basketball team '27, Ont. YMCA sr. champions, OBA semifinalists '29; coached Hamilton Y, guided Livingstone Church girls '39 Ont. jr. church title; began rowing '20; stroked Leander Boat Club's lightweight crew '27 ntl title; coached '30-60 producing 40-plus Canadian Henley winners including 4 Hanlan Memorial Cups for sr. heavyweight crews; coached 3 Olympic crews; trophy in his name presented annually by CARA to Canadian Henley lightweight race winners; launched McMaster rowing program; instrumental in founding Eastern Cdn college rowing program; life mem. YMCA; mem. Copps Coliseum Hall of Fame.

CLOUTIER, Guylaine (swimming); b. 1 Oct 1971, Levis, Que.; U Montreal; breaststroke specialist; began competing age 7; mem. ntl team from '85; 17 ntl titles; mem. '88, '92, '96 Olympic, '90, '94 Commonwealth Games, '91, '93 FISU Games teams; through '92 competed in 28 World Cup races winning 3g, 11s, 4b; 7 ntl titles; gold Monte Carlo, Italian, French events; twice 2nd in world breaststroke rankings; silver 100, 200 breaststroke '90 Commonwealth Games; 2 '95 Pan-Am Games silver; 1g, 1s '91 FISU Games; 1 CIAU female swimmer of yr, 3 Swim Canada female athlete of year awards; res. St-Constant, Laprairie, Que.

CLOW, Craig (skiing); b. 27 Aug 1956, Montreal, Que.; men's aerial world cup champion '82; 4 1sts, 4 2nds, 2 3rds in 21 WC freestyle events '80-84; res. Montreal, Que.

CLYDE, Ian (boxing); 15 May 1956, Verdun, Que.; given name: Ian Nathanial; m. Annette Wahl; c. Heather, Amanda; insurance broker; ntl light-flyweight title '72; qualified '72 Olympic team but barred because of age; mem. ntl team 8 years, '76, '80 Olympics, '78 Commonwealth, '79 Pan-Am, 3 NA championship, 1 world teams; quarterfinalist '76 Olympics; silver '78 Commonwealth; bronze '79 Pan-Am Games; 1st Cdn medalist (bronze) Cuban invitational '79; Canadian flyweight title '73-80; 5 Que. Golden Glove, Eastern Canadian titles; pro '80; managed by Angelo Dundee; Continental flyweight title '83; res. Verdun, Que.

COAFFEE, Cyril (t&f); b. 14 Feb 1897, Winnipeg, Man.; d. 3 Jul 1945, Winnipeg, Man.; mem. North End Amateur Athletic Club; ran 11.2 for 100m '20 Olympic trials but

funding allowed for only 9 competitors and he was 10th ranked; Winnipeg supporters paid for his trip to Antwerp where he finished 3rd in qualifying heats but didn't reach semifinals; tied Charlie Paddock's world record 9.6 for 100yd dash '22 ntl championships; resulting ntl record stood more than 25 years; ntl 220yd title, teamed with Laurie Armstrong, Billy Miller, Peavey Heffelfinger for ntl record 1:30 in 4x220yd relay; ran for Illinois AC Chicago '23-24; tied 100yd Olympic record 10.8 to qualify for Paris Games; capt. '24 Olympic team but failed to live up to expectations; following games faced many of world's top sprinters in series of British meets and registered frequent victories; ended career losing to Percy Williams '28 Olympic trials; mem. Cdn Amateur; Man., Canada's Sports halls of fame.

COBEN, Muriel (softball/curling); b. 17 Feb 1921, Gelert, Ont.; d. 8 Jun 1979, Saskatoon, Sask.; given name: Muriel Eleanor; dispatcher; righthanded pitcher; led Tessier Millionaires to undefeated season '36; played for Saskatoon Pats '38-42, '44-45; with Rockford Peaches in AAAGPBL '43; joined Saskatoon Ramblers '46; helped Edmonton Mortons win ntl title '51 posting 2-1 record in final; retd '59; mem. Joyce McKee title curling rink '60; mem. Sask., Saskatoon Sports, Alta. Softball halls of fame; honored by Cooperstown, Cdn Baseball halls of Fame.

COCHAND, Louis (skiing); b. 5 Jan 1917, Ste. Marguerite Station, Que.; given name: Louis Emile; div. c. Josette, Louis Pierre, Heidi, Charles, Antoinette; Lower Canada College; hotelier; Que. Kandahar slalom '36-37, downhill, combined '38; Que., Ont., N O combined, downhill, slalom titles '38; gold Austrian downhill '39; founder Canadian Ski School and Instructors' Alliance; 10yrs pres. CSSIA; authored 1st Canadian Ski School manual; mgr. '48 Olympic team; organized 1st Laurentian midget ski meet '53; installed 1st Eastern Canadian double chairlift Chalet Cochand '59; 9yrs pres. Laurentian Resort Assn.; founder, pres. Canadian Area Lift Assn.; British gold Kandahar pin with pearl, diamond Tremblant ski pin, French Croix de Guerre with star, American Air Medal; active skeet shooter; 2nd 12 gauge C Class world championships; McMartin Skeet trophy Montebello '62; mem. Cdn Skiing, Tremblant Ski halls of fame; res. St. Sauveur des Monts, Que.

COCHRANE, Nigel (sailing); b. 12 Nov 1961, Toronto, Ont.; began sailing age 12; ntl team mem. from '85; with Gord McIlquham enjoyed success in 470 competition '85-88, capped by 4th '88 world championships, 8th '88 Olympics; teamed with Jeff Eckard '89 winning skipper '89 ntl title, '90 Goodwill Games, '91 Pan-Am Games; mem. Royal Canadian Yacht Club; res. Vancouver, B.C.

CODY, Della (synchro swim); b. 4 Apr 1917, Plaster Rock, N.B.; d. 22 Sep 1986, Fredericton, N.B.; given name: Della Howlett MacFarlane; m. Norman Cody; UNB; educator; pioneered synchro swim in NB; taught 1st synchro swim credit course UNB '58; helped form NB branch CASSA, 1st pres. '66; coached NB Canada Winter Games team '67; served varied prov. exec. roles and was sport's historian; judge local, prov., divisional, ntl, int'l levels '66-80; 1st B. accredited ntl level judge '68; NB synchro swim trophy bears her name; mem. NB Sports Hall of Fame.

CODY, Harry (speed skating); b. 6 Sep 1887, Ireland; d. 22 Aug 1936, Toronto, Ont.; given name: Robert Henry; c. 2 sons; NA outdoor champion '16; co-founder, coach Toronto Speed Skating Club; coach Old Orchard Speed Skating Club; mem. Cdn Speed Skating Hall of Fame.

COE-JONES, Dawn (golf); b. 19 Oct 1960, Campbell River, B.C.; m. Jimmy Jones; c. James Richard; Lamar U, BSc; pro golfer; began playing age 12; BC. jr titles '78-79; BC. women's amateur titles '82-83; Cdn amateur tile '83; as collegian won Dick McGuire, Husky invitationals; all-American; pro '83; joined LPGA tour '84 qualifying in 1st attempt; career low round 64; capped steady improvement on tour with victory '92 Kemper Open, '95 Tournament of Champions; with Dave Barr won Cdn Airlines International Mixed team title '89; sponsors jr. tourney at home BC. club; *Score* Magazine Cdn. female golfer of '94; mem. Inaugural Cdn Nations Cup team '99; res. Tampa, Fla.

COFFEY, Paul (hockey); b. 1 Jun 1961, Weston, Ont.; given name: Paul Douglas; m. Stephanie; c. Savannah, Blake; jr. Sault Ste. Marie, Kitchener; twice OHA all-star; Edmonton 1st pick, 6th overall '80 draft; defence Edmonton '80-87, Pittsburgh '87-92, Los Angeles '92-93, Detroit '93-96, Hartford '96, Philadelphia '96-'98; Chicago '98-99, Carolina '99; NHL record (through '99): 1322 scheduled games, 385g, 1102a, 194 playoff games, 59g, 137a; 12th player to reach 1300 point plateau; 1st NHL defenceman to amass 1000 assists; 4 1st, 4 2nd team all-star; gold Team Canada Canada Cup '84, '87, '91, Worlds '90; 3 James Norris trophies; mem. 4 Stanley Cup winners, 14 all-star games; res. Mississauga, Ont.

COFFEY, Tommy-Joe (football); b. 1936, McAdoo, Tex; West Texas State, BSc; employment agency owner; receiver, placement kicker; outstanding lineman '59 Copper Bowl; 8th round draft Baltimore Colts (NFL) '59; Edmonton (CFL) '59-60, '62-66, Hamilton '67-72, Toronto '73; CFL record: 971 points, 65 TDs, 204 converts, 108 field goals, 53 singles, 650 pass receptions, 10,320yds, 63 TDs; CFL single season scoring record (since broken by Dave Cutler) 148 points '69; 3 times WFC, 4 times EFC all-star, 8 times all-Cdn; 3 EFC, 1 WFC scoring titles; WFC record 81 receptions (since broken) '64-5; 3 times runnerup Schenley outstanding player; 3 Grey Cup finals, 2 winners; mem. Eskimos Wall of Honor, Cdn Football Hall of Fame; res. Burlington, Ont.

COGGLES, Susan (ringette/softball); b. 8 Feb 1979, Edmonton, Alta; UAlta, Tennessee; '95 Canada Winter Games gold; 4 ntl championship gold; 3 ntl championship all-star forward awards; mem. ntl ringette team '98 European Summit Series, final game MVP; centrefielder Team Alta. 3 ntl championships, '98 all-star fielder; silver '97 Summer Games team Alta.; competed for Team Canada vs. Japan; mem. ntl team reserves; Softball Alta. player of '98; res. Edmonton, Alta./Chatanooga, Tenn.

COGHILL, Sandi (bowling); b. 2 Oct 1961, Winnipeg, Man.; accounting clerk; began 5-pin bowling age 5; joined competitive ranks '85; 9 ntl open medals, ntl women's singles title, 3 ntl team titles; 6 ntl masters medals, 2 women's team gold; twice ntl tournament all-star; res. Winnipeg, Man.

COHEN, Laurie (t&f); b. 1904 Winnipeg, Man.; d. 27 Nov 1995, Winnipeg, Man.; established sprinting credentials as Winnipeg high schooler claiming title honors '23-28; won Manitoba, Western Canada 100, 220yd titles '23-24 setting records in each instance; competed in ntl championships '26-27; from '23-31 won every race he entered in Man. championships except 1, a loss to Cyril Coaffee; coached with Winnipeg Amateur Athletic Assn. '32-41; 40yrs official with Man. t&f Assn.; mem. Man. Sports Hall of Fame.

COLE, Betty (golf/curling); b. 21 Sep 1937, Calgary, Alta.; given name: Betty Stanhope; m. Gordon Cole; c. Jacqueline, Robert; 5 Alta. jr. golf titles; 20 Edmonton City Opens, 14 Alta. Opens; '56 ntl jr., '57 Canadian Open, '67 Canadian Closed; '64 Eastern Provinces, '66 Saskatoon Open; mem. 22 Alta., 2 Ont., 2 Sask. interprovincial teams; mem. 2 Commonwealth, 3 World teams; top ranked Cdn player '74, '76; from '70 ranked among Canada's top 10 10 times; skipped 3 Alta. curling champions; ntl Lassies runnerup '78; 4 Edmonton city titles, 4 Northern Zone titles; Edmonton's outstanding athlete '57; mem. CLGA ntl exec. '80-83; mem. RCGA, Alta. Sports halls of fame; res. Edmonton, Alta.

COLEMAN, Lovell (football); b. 9 May 1938, Hamtramck, Mich.; m. Maureen Denise; Western Mich.; contractor; lettered as college fullback '57-59; mid-west conf. all-American '58; turned pro CFL Roughriders but never played there, being dealt to Calgary for Jack Gotta; 11 CFL seasons with Calgary, Ottawa, BC.; 3 times rushed for more than 1000yds single season; 3 times more than 200 carries single season; scored 62 CFL career tds, 42 rushing, on 1135 carries for 6566yds; best single season '64 with 260 carries for 1629yds, 10tds; same season had best single game with 238yds vs. Hamilton; 3 CFL rushing titles; Schenley outstanding player, Calgary athlete of '64; mem. Western Mich Hall of Fame; res. Richmond, B.C.

COLEMAN, Mel (rodeo); b. 7 Dec 1955, Islay, Alta.; m. Theresa; c. Jake; feed store owner; mem. Cdn Professional Rodeo Assn from '74; CPRA rookie of '74; 5 ntl AA all-around championships; 7 ntl saddle bronc titles; Bud pro tour sadle bronc champion '91; holds Cdn Finals Rodeo (CFR), Ntl Finals Rodeo (NFL) saddle bronc qualifications records; res. Phoenix, Ariz.

COLISTRO, Peter (t&f/basketball); b. 26 Nov 1952, Vancouver, B.C.; m. Regina Girard; c. Michael, Marianne, Anthony; dispatcher; 1st person to break 6-minute mile in a wheelchair; represented Canada in track, basketball 4 Paralympics; mem. 4 Cdn Gold Cup basketball teams; res. Burnaby, B.C.

COLLINS, Merv (football); b. 10 Aug 1933, Toronto, Ont.; given name: Mervyn Douglas; m. Christine Salvenmoser; c. David, Natalie, Steven; UAlta, BEd, UofOtt, MEd; personnel mgr.; offensive guard, linebacker Balmy Beach ORFU finals vs Sarnia Imperials '52; only rookie to crack starting lineup Grey Cup champion Argos '53, Hamilton '55, Ottawa '56-65, Edmonton '66, retd '67; mem. '60 Grey Cup champions; frequent CFL all-star; founding mem. CFL Players' Pension Fund; res. Markham, Ont.

COLLINS, Steve (ski jumping); b. 13 Mar 1964, Fort William, Ont.; given name: Stephen Clark; ntl team '79-

84; world jr. 90m title '80; Lahti WC 90m, Big Thunder International 70m '80; ntl jr. 70m title '81; world record 99.5m off 70m, 120.5 off 90m Thunder Bay '80, Finnish record 124m Lahti '80; Czech ski flying title '80; mem. '80, '84 Olympic teams; Thunder Bay athlete of '80; SFC athlete of month March '80; Ont. achievement award; Tom Longboat award '79; Viscount Alexander Trophy '80; mem. Cdn Skiing, NWO Sports halls of fame; res. Thunder Bay, Ont.

COLMAN, Ann (figure skating); b. 18 Apr 1936, Toronto, Ont.; given name: Ann Johnston; div. Jeremy Colman; c. Dale Ann, Robin Jeremy, Courtney Susannah; UofT, BA; mem. '56 Olympic, '54-56 world championship teams; taught skating Toronto Cricket and Skating Club, Town of Mount Royal '57-60; regained amateur status and served as judge '72-99; children were all ranked provincially, nationally in squash; res. Don Mills, Ont.

COLMAN, Frank (baseball); b. 2 Mar 1918, London, Ont.; d. 19 Feb 1983, London, Ont.; given name: Frank Lloyd; m. Anne; c. Frank, Jerry; Sr. IC batting title, MVP award '36 with London led to pro offers; southpaw pitcher but sore arm led to switch to 1st base-outfield; ML service Pittsburgh '42-46, NY Yankees '46-47; standout minor league career; batted .363 Willmington, Del. '40, .319 with 18 HRs, 98 RBI Seattle (PCL) '49, .310 Seattle '50; player-coach Toronto (IL) '51-53; owned, operated London franchise Sr. IC '55-57, '59; Great Lakes-Niagara League '58; managed London to IC title '56, Great-Lakes Niagara crown '58; instrumental in formation London's Eager Beaver Baseball Assn., pres. several years; mem. Cdn Baseball hall of fame.

COLVILLE, Neil (hockey); b. 4 Aug 1914, Edmonton, Alta.; d. 26 Dec 1987, Vancouver, B.C.; given name: Neil MacNeil; centred younger brother Mac, Alex Shibicky NY Rangers Bread Line '36-42; capt. RCAF (Ottawa) Flyers Allan Cup champions '42; Rangers '46-49; switched to defence with Frankie Eddolls '48-49; coached '50-51 Rangers, 6yrs Rangers capt.; mem. 1 league champion, 1 Stanley Cup winner; 3 times all-star; mem. Alta Sports, Hockey halls of fame.

COLVILLE, Nelson (shooting); b. 11 Nov 1905, Port Perry, Ont.; d. 1988, Vancouver, B.C.; m. Eunice Voss (d.); c. Louise; optician; Ont. Rifle Assn. tyro title '21; 1st of 63 Connaught Matches Ottawa appearances '21; won Walker Match Connaught 1922, Governor-General's match title 1957; mem. 11 Bisley teams, twice team commandant; twice named to Bisley team after passing age 70; Connaught 60-year award '81; mem. Alta. Sports Hall of Fame.

COMBE, Harvey (golf); b. 1860, Guilford, Eng.; d. 1922, Victoria, B.C.; m. Charlotte Margaret Wray; c. Nora; BC. Supreme Court registrar; first-class tennis player, self-taught golfer; 9 BC. amateur titles; inaugural Seattle open titlist; helped form Victoria GC 1893; co-founder Pacific North West Golf Assn. 1895; held Victoria GC course record 72 many years; wife won 5 BC. women's titles; daughter won 3 Victoria city, 2 Pacific Northwest titles; considered father of BC. golf; secty. Victoria GC 1900, '05-18.

CONACHER, Brian (hockey); b. 31 Aug 1941, Toronto, Ont.; given name: Brian Kennedy; m. Susan Davis; c. Sean; UWO, BA; v-p. building operations Maple Leaf Gardens; Jr. A Toronto Marlboros; UWO hockey; ntl team mem. '64 Olympic, '65 World championships; pro Leafs organization, AHL Calder Cup champion Rochester Americans '66, NHL with Toronto '67 Stanley Cup winners; also played with NHL Detroit, WHA Ottawa; licenced real estate salesman; author "So You Want to Be A Hockey Player"; sports dir. CKLW-TV '70; color commentator '69 World championship, '71 CIAU, '72 Canada-Soviet series, 1st WHA game, '76, '88 Winter Olympics; made coaching debut Cortina '64; GM/coach Mohawk Valley Comets (NAHL) '73-76; GM Indianapolis Racers (WHA) '76-77, Edmonton Oilers (WHA) '77-78; marketing mgr. Edmonton Northlands '79-84, CEO Hamilton Entertainment/ Convention Facilities '85-89, CEO Royal Agricultural Winter Fair '89-92, Maple Leaf Gardens v-p. from '92; NAHL GM of '75; res. Toronto, Ont.

CONACHER, Charlie (hockey); b. 10 Dec 1909, Toronto, Ont.; d. 30 Dec 1967, Toronto, Ont.; given name: Charles William; m. Sonny; c. Peter (Charles William Jr.), Brad, Scott; brother Lionel; began as goaler but shifted to wing; capt. Marlboros '26 Memorial Cup; Toronto Maple Leafs '29-38, Detroit '38-39, NY Americans '39-41; coach Chicago '48-50; scoring titles '34, '35; 3 times 1st, twice 2nd team all-star; originally on line with Joe Primeau, Baldy Cotton, when Busher Jackson replaced Cotton, became known as Kid Line; NHL record: 460 scheduled games, 225g, 173a, 49 playoff games, 17g, 18a; coached Oshawa '44 Memorial Cup winner; annual humanitarian award bears his name; mem. Canada's Sports, Hockey halls of fame.

CONACHER, Lionel Jr. (football); b. 8 Jan 1936, Toronto, Ont.; m. Judith Wilson; c. Lionel III, Duff, Bryce; UWO; Cdn Tire dealer; versatility as high schooler led to numerous awards in football, cross-country running, boxing, hockey, t&f; son of Lionel sr; Cdn water skiing jumping titles '50-54; wrestled, played football at Western; football MVP award '59; 2 seasons CFL with Montreal Alouettes '60-61; in '80s mem. Cdn Hobielsailing team in world championships; avid skier, windsurfer; res. Toronto, Ont.

CONACHER, Lionel Sr. (all-around); b. 24 May 1901, Toronto, Ont.; d. 26 May 1954, Ottawa, Ont.; given name: Lionel Pretoria; m. Dorothy Kennedy; c. Connie, Deanne, Lionel Jr., David, Brian; Duquesne; pro athlete, politician; nicknamed "Big Train"; at 12 Toronto City Rugby League; at 16 Ont. 125lb wrestling title; at 18 middle wing Toronto Central Y Ont. rugby title team; ntl light-heavyweight boxing title '20 in first bout, later fought exhibition with Jack Dempsey; same year senior city rugby, baseball, lacrosse; mem. '26 Toronto Maple Leafs Triple A pro baseball champions; mem. '21 Argos title football team scoring record 15 points in 23-0 Grey Cup victory over Edmonton; NHL defenceman Pittsburgh '25-26, NY Americans '27-30, Montreal Maroons '30-33, '34-37, Black Hawks '33-34; NHL record: 500 scheduled games, 80g, 105a, 35 playoff games, 2g, 2a; mem. 2 Stanley Cup winners; MLA (Lib), MPP (Lib); Ont. Athletic Commissioner; Canada's athlete of half century '50; trophy honoring Canada's outstanding male athlete bears his name; mem. Canada's Sports, Cdn Football, Boxing, Lacrosse, Hockey, Ont. Sports Legends halls of fame.

CONACHER, Pete (hockey); b. 29 Jul 1932, Toronto, Ont.; given name: Charles William Jr.; m. Shirley Ann Randle; investment rep.; jr. Galt '49-51; NHL Chicago '51-54, NY Rangers '54-56; reinstated amateur, mem. '59 World Champion Belleville MacFarlands; minor pro ranks St. Louis, Buffalo (AHL) '65-66; NHL record: 47 goals, 38 assists; res. Etobicoke, Ont.

CONACHER, Roy (hockey); b. 5 Oct 1916, Toronto, Ont.; d. 1984, BC.; m. Fran; c. Roy Jr., Mark, Candace; 1 of 10 siblings in family which included twin brother Bert, brothers Charlie and Lionel; early athletic interest in softball but following older brothers turned attention to hockey, playing Marlboro bantam, midget; mem. '36 Memorial Cup winner West Toronto Nationals; all-star mem. OHA sr. champ Dominion Breweries '37; played sr. NO league then attended Boston Bruins camp at 22; considered most naturally talented of hockey playing Conachers; led NHL with 26 goals '39; played 11 NHL seasons with Boston, Detroit, Chicago; NHL record: 490 scheduled games, 226g, 200a, 42 playoff games, 15g, 15a; 2 Stanley Cup winners; Art Ross trophy '49; following '52 retirement coached Midland to 2 Ont. Jr. C titles; mem. Hockey Hall of Fame.

CONDON, Eddie (tennis/skiing); b. 18 Jul 1901, Ottawa, Ont.; d. 30 May 1985, Ottawa, Ont.; given name: Edmund; UofOtt; federal govt. auditor; cross-country skier, runner specializing in 1500m, mile; 3rd both events '20 Olympic trials; City of Ottawa, Eastern Ont, ntl interscholastic titles both events; ntl, NA Intercollegiate, Eastern US, Ottawa cross-country titles; officiated '32 Olympics, '50 World competitions; chair. US Olympic ski trials, NA championships; 9 Ottawa tennis singles titles, NB, P.E.I. provincial titles; organized 1st ntl jr. tennis championships, 25yrs chair.; co-chair. '38-68 International Kate Smith Trophy ski meet; mem. CLTA jr. development comm. 20yrs; mem. '49 Gordon Trophy team; variety of exec. roles OLTA, CLTA '25-75; CLTA exec.-dir.; editor CLTA manual, record book; founding mem. ntl ski museum; life mem. Rideau LTC, Ottawa Ski Club; Governor's award 75th anniversary Lake Placid Ski Club; Ont. govt. achievement award; mem. Cdn Tennis, Ottawa Sports halls of Fame.

CONDREN, Stephen (harness racing); b. 6 Jul 1957, St. Catharines, Ont.; harness race driver; began driving on OJC circuit '77; won only 12 races in 1st 3yrs; posted 401 wins '87; 200 or more winners 12 consec. seasons '81-92; 21 Dec '87 snapped Ron Waples' '79 single season Greenwood track victory record with 365th win; with Goalie Jeff won '89 NA Cup; '95 Cadillac Breeders Crown with Armbro Officer; '97 Robert Stewart Stakes with Stonebridge First; more than 4500 career victories, $51M in purses; O'Brien driver of '97 award; res. Milton, Ont.

CONDY, Buddy (baseball); b. 21 Nov 1922, Springhill, N.S.; d. 2 Sep 1993, Halifax, N.S.; given name: William; c. Suzanne, Sheilagh, Patricia; Dalhousie, BSc, MD, CM; physician; made sr. baseball debut at 14 with grand slam homer in 1st plate appearance for Springhill Fence Busters

'38; mem. Fence Busters '38-39, '45-46, Halifax Arrows '47, Halifax Capitals '48-51, Saint John Boosters '52, Halifax Cardinals '55; mem. 4 championship teams; recognized premier slugger H&D League; lifetime H&D BA .356; twice batting champion; best season '51 batting .409 but finishing 2nd to Stellarton's Joe Fulgham; led H&D in hits, HR, RBI rookie season '47; MVP award; career BA as Fence Buster .445; regarded by peers as "best player ever to have played in NS"; avid golfer with recorded hole-in-one; Halifax mayor's award '48; Dalhousie award '83; mem. NS Sports Hall of Fame.

CONE, Mac (equestrian); b. 23 Aug 1952, Memphis, Tenn.; m. Brenley Carpenter; c. 2 daughters; Southern Ways stable operator; mem. US ntl team; moved to Canada '82; mem. Cdn ntl team from '82; only rider to compete on both US, Cdn ntl teams; competed 10 Nations' Cups; qualified for '95 Pan-Am Games but injury to horse Elute forced withdrawl; won '94 NY Autumn Classic, Roots Speed Classic, '92 Coup des Ameriques; mem. '96 Olympic team; ntl show jumping title with Elute '98; res. King City, Ont.

CONGALTON, Jim (curling); b. 26 Sep 1879, Guelph, Ont.; d. 9 Oct 1947, Winnipeg, Man.; m. Blanche Hildegarde Dyson; c. Helen, Frances; salesman; at 12 youngest mem. in history of Guelph Curling Club, presented to Governor-General as youngest curler in Canada at the time; skipped '27 Winnipeg Granite rink which lost to Ossie Barkwell of Yellow Grass, Sask. for right to rep. West '27 inaugural Brier; mem. 2 Brier winners, '30 as third, '32 as skip; mem. Cdn, Man. Curling halls of fame.

CONGALTON, William (baseball); b. 24 Jan 1875, Guelph, Ont.; d. 16 Aug 1937, Cleveland, Ohio; given name: William Millar; m. Harriet; public utilities employee; nickname "Bunk"; outfielder Chicago Cubs '02, appeared in 42 games; following minor league stints played with Cleveland (AL) '05-07 before being dealt to Boston '07; ML record: 309 games, 6hr, 95rbi, career .293ba.

CONN, Michelle (field hockey); b. 17 Sep 1963, Edmonton, Alta.; UCal, BSc, Mount Royal Coll, BA, Dean's list; financial analyst; 93 International caps; carded athlete '83-92; ntl team asst. capt '89-92; competed '88, '92 Olympics; PAG bronze '87, silver '91; competed '86 (bronze), '90 World Cup; 2 Champions Trophy, 1 Wembley competition; ntl outdoor championship gold '86, silver ;90, bronze ;84; 3 gold, 1 bronze ntl indoor championships; ntl ball hockey bronze '96, silver ;97; competed '95 ntl triathlon championships; 1 Alta Achievement award; CIAU all-Cdn 1st team '85; 2 Calgary Booster Club, 2 UCal merit awards; athlete of yr nominee; asst. coach UCal '86-89; asst. coach Alta. U-16 women '89, Alta. Sr. men indoor team '95; res. Calgary, Alta.

CONNELL, Alex (hockey); b. 8 Feb 1900, Ottawa, Ont.; d. 10 May 1958, Ottawa, Ont.; m. Kay Muir; c. Bettianne; fireman; mem. '21 Allan Cup Ottawa Cliffsides; pro goalie Senators '24; mem. '27 Stanley Cup winner; retired '33 but made '34 comeback Montreal Maroons Stanley Cup winner; NHL record 6 successive shutouts; retired again and coached St. Patrick's College, Senators (QHL) until illness forced him out '49; noted for black cap he always wore while playing goal; catcher St. Brigid's City, interprovincial baseball teams; lacrosse with brother Charlie '20 Ottawa Senators Eastern Cdn champions; mem. Ottawa Sports, Hockey halls of fame.

CONNELL, Charlie (all-around); b. 4 Dec 1897, Ottawa, Ont.; d. 30 Apr 1980, Ottawa, Ont.; m. Ruth Edmonson; c. Frances, Elaine; photo engraver; mem. '27-28 Mann Cup winners; capt. Woodroffe '22 Ottawa title team; retired from box lacrosse at 35; Val Cartier army camp middleweight boxing crown '15, Canadian Service Corps title Thorncliffe, Eng.; national amateur middleweight title '19-20; 20yrs mem. Rough Riders; mem. 4 Ottawa district basketball title teams; refereed, coached football, lacrosse; mem. Ottawa Sports, Ottawa CSRA Sports, Cdn Lacrosse halls of fame.

CONNELL, Grant (tennis); b. 17 Nov 1965, Regina, Sask.; m. Sarah Cooper; Texas A&M; Tennis Canada consultant; twice all-American; NCAA player of '85; left-hander; ntl U-18 singles,with Glenn Michibata ranked #1 doubles team in world '87-92; ranked #1 Cdn singles 4yrs; ranked #1 IBM/ATP doubles '91 (Michibata), '93 (Patrick Galbraith); mem. Cdn Davis Cup team '84-97; turned pro '86; mem. Cdn Olympic team '88, '96; 22 career doubles titles; Tennis Canada player of '87, '90, '95; Team Canada most improved player '89; with Galbraith world doubles title '95, twice Wimbledon finalists; with Byron Black of Zimbabwe won Italian Open, Wimbledon finalists '96; ATP tour doubles team of yr '93; retd from competition '97; mem. Cdn Tennis Hall of Fame; res. Vancouver, B.C.

CONNELLAN, Peter (coaching); b. 17 Jul 1937, Regina, Sask.; m. Elizabeth Wilson; c. Karen, Heather; UAlta. BPhE, BEd., Oregon MSc; teacher; played hockey UAlta '56-58, '60; HS teacher '61-68; principal '61-76; UCal sr. lecturer, football coach '77, '83-95; 8 conf. titles, 4 Vanier Cup winners; conf. regular season record 70-32-2; prof. emeritus UCal '93; pres. CIAU Coaches Assn. '94-95; 2 Frank Tindal CIAU coach of yr awards; 3M Cdn male coach of '90; CFL, Football Canada award of merit '98; mem. Alta. Sports Hall of Fame; res. Calgary, Alta.

CONNERTY, Doug (bowling); b. 23 Dec 1929, Kemptville, Ont.; given name: Douglas Eric; m. Barbara Eleanor Haddow; c. Jane Patricia, Michael Eric, Kelly Rosemary; retd. Bell Canada; competitor/volunteer in game of 5-pins in Ottawa area more than 32yrs; mem. OVFPBA exec. 18yrs, OFPBA 6yrs; OMBA 20yrs, YBC 25yrs; involved as course conductor for Level I & II technical coaching certification pgms; represented Ottawa in 17 prov. championships '69-95; coached Ont. team to prov. title '88, 4th in ntls; won 2 Smiths Falls Open titles; posting tournament record 3088 pinfall for 10 games; recorded perfect 450 game '89; mem. Ont. title team '72, runnerup ntls; Preston Lanes dedicated service award; Zone MBA delegate of yrs award; life mem. OVFPBA; Ottawa area bowlers appreciation award '91; YBC recognition award '92; Ont. achievement award '94; OFPBA Zone pres. of '96 award; special plaque as founding mem. Ottawa Zone & YBCA '98; res. Nepean, Ont.

CONNOLLY, Edward (boxing); b. 16 Nov 1876, Saint John, N.B., d. 1932, New York, N Y; BE lightweight title

1896; world welterweight title 1900; retd age 24 due to poor health; mem. NB Sports Hall of Fame.

CONROY, Jim (football); b. 18 Oct 1937, Vancouver, B.C.; m. Carol Ann Henry; c. Jennifer, Joan, Julie, Debby; SouthernCal, BSc, Carleton, PEng; small business owner; played football/baseball USC '55-59; football team co-capt. '57; mem. NCAC baseball title team '58; drafted by Buffalo (NFL) '59; pro with Ottawa CFL '60-67, Winnipeg '68; 4 CFL all-star linebacker; asst. coach UofOtt '69-72; res. Ottawa, Ont.

CONYD, Magdy (fencing); b. 22 Jun 1939, Alexandria, Egypt; Aachen U, W. Germany; physical fitness consultant, director; ntl foils titles '64, '71-72; highest foil rating in Canada '68-70, '72-73, '75; Governor-General's international open foils titles '65-70, '72; Ont. titles '64-65, Quebec '66, BC. '68-75; mem. 4 world, 2 Olympic teams; team bronze '70 Commonwealth Games; retd from competition '76-82; res. Vancouver, B.C.

COOK, Bill (hockey); b. 8 Oct 1895, Brantford, Ont.; d. 5 May 1986, Kingston, Ont.; given name: William Osser; early hockey Kingston, Sault Ste. Marie; pro Saskatoon Sheiks '22-26; 3 WCL scoring titles; '24-25 season 31 goals in 30 games; with demise of WCL, he and brother Bun purchased by NY Rangers '26 playing through '37; right wing on line with Bun and Frank Boucher; twice scoring champion; 3 times 1st, once 2nd team all-star; NHL record: 452 scheduled games, 229g, 138 assists, 46 playoff games, 13g, 12 assists; mem. 2 Stanley Cup winners; Rangers Alumni Assn. award '86; mem. Canada's Sports, Hockey, Kingston District halls of fame.

COOK, Bun (hockey); b. 18 Sep 1903, Kingston, Ont.; d. 19 Mar 1988, Kingston, Ont.; given name: Frederick Joseph; m. Mary Rheaume; c. 3 sons, 2 daughters; farmer; jr. Soo Greyhounds; mem. Allan Cup champions; pro Saskatoon Sheiks '22-26, NY Rangers '26-36, Boston '36-37; NHL record: 473 scheduled games, 158g, 144a, 46 playoff games, 15g, 3a; mem. Hockey, Kingston District halls of Fame.

COOK, Murray (administration); b. 6 Dec 1940, Sackville, N.B.; given name: George Earl Murray; m. Jan; c. Cheryl, Brian, David; Ohio, BS; baseball exec.; attended college on basketball scholarship; shortstop Pittsburgh organization Batavia (A) '62, Gastonia (A) '63-64; GM Gastonia '65; joined Pirates front office '66; asst. farm dir. '68; dir. minor leagues, scouting '76; dir. player development NY Yankees '83, GM '83-84; v-p. GM Montreal Expos '84-88; GM Cincinnati '89-90; scout Florida Marlins; res. Florida.

COOK, Myrtle (all-around); b. 5 Jan 1902, Toronto, Ont.; d. 18 Mar 1985, Elora, Ont; given name: Myrtle Alice; m. Lloyd McGowan (d); c. Kenneth, Donald; sportswriter; excelled in t&f, paddling, softball, tennis, ice hockey, speedskating, cycling, basketball, lawn bowling; 400m relay gold '28 Olympics; 100m world record; 100m gold Paris, Philadelphia '28 meets; indoor 60yds winner NY, Chicago, Philadelphia, Montreal; with Brendan Macken international mixed tennis titles, Que. mixed, ladies' doubles; during 40yr journalistic career had major impact on Cdn women's sport;

Governor-General's medal for track, '67 Centennial medal; mem. Cdn Amateur, Que., Canada's, MAAA Sports halls of fame.

COOK, Tommy (hockey); b. 17 May 1907, Ft. William, Ont.; d. 21 Oct 1961, Thunder Bay, Ont.; St. John's College; played junior Ft. William Dominions; college Winnipeg's St. John's College; senior Ft. William Thundering Herd; pro Tulsa Oilers '28; AHA scoring title; NHL Black Hawks, Montreal Maroons '29-38; NHL record: 311 scheduled games, 77g, 98a, 24 playoff games, 2g, 4a; mem. 1 Stanley Cup winner; on retirement coached hockey, baseball in Thunder Bay region; mem. NWO Sports Hall of Fame.

COOKE, Graham (golf); b. 11 Sep 1946, Belleville, Ont.; given name: Leonard Graham; m. Sally; c. Erin, Leigh; Michigan State; landscape architect, golf course architect; Ont. jr., medalist ntl jr. '65; NCAA all-American; quarterfinalist Western Amateur bowing 2 and 1 to Ben Crenshaw; participated twice US Amateur; mem. 18 Willingdon Cup teams, '91 champions; 5 Duke of Kent, 4 Alexander of Tunis, '78 Eastern four-ball; runnerup '79 ntl amateur; 4 Que. amateur, 5 times runnerup; mem. '77 Nations Cup, '78 World Pairs, '80 Morocco Invitation, 2 Eisenhower Cup teams; 4 times Que. golfer of year; res. Hudson, Que.

COOKE, Jack Kent (entrepreneur); b. 25 Oct 1912, Hamilton, Ont.; d. 6 Apr 1997, Upperville, Va.; div. Barbara Jean Carnegie; c. John Kent; div. Jeanne Maxwell Williams; c. Ralph (d); div. Suzanne Martin; c. Jacqueline; m. Marlene Romallo Chalmers; business exec., publisher; mem. Ted Reeve's Malvern CI football title team; acquired substantial piece of Toronto Maple Leafs (IL) baseball team, 4 pennants in 7yrs; Sporting News Minor League exec. of '52; unsuccessful bids to purchase Toronto Argos, Detroit Tigers; chair., chief operating officer Washington Redskins (NFL) from '60, Super Bowl winner '83; pres. California Sports Inc. (LA Lakers, LA Kings) '65-79; pres. Forum of Inglewood, Calif. '66-79; pres. Boxing Forum '72-79; trustee Little League Foundation; dir. National Athletic Institute; with Branch Rickey sought unsuccessfully to launch Continental Baseball League '58; mem. Canadian Baseball Hall of Fame.

COOKE, Stan (all-around); b. 18 Oct 1914, Port Arthur, Ont.; d. 1989, Thunder Bay, Ont.; c. Gordon, William, Stanley Jr., Philip, 1 daughter; real estate agent; jr. hockey Ft. William '32-34; sr. Port Arthur '35-36, St. Moritz, Switzerland '36-38, Ft. William Forts '39-40; mem. jr. title Hornets baseball team '31; rowing gold medalist St. Paul '33, Winnipeg '34, Minneapolis '35; competed in Cdn Henley regatta '35; district men's FS swimming champion '31; 2 holes-in-one, Strathcona GC McGolrick trophy; mem. Westfort Alleymen '45, Northern Engineering Nescoes '46 softball title teams; Ft. William CC curling titles '53-55. 2 sr. zone titles; scored 8-ender '84; Bell-Fast trophy Cdn Elk's bonspiel '84; 1st event winner NWO 60-plus bonspiel; quarterback Ft. William CI jr. football title team '32-33; sr. team '34-35; Dynamiters district sr. champs '36; halfback '37 Flamingoes district sr. champs; Ft. William CI sr. basketball team '34, YMCA Leaders title team '35, Canadian Car AA title team '45; mem. NWO Sports Hall of Fame.

COOMBE, Eldon (curling); b. 8 May 1941, Kingston, Ont.; given name: Eldon James; m. Lynda Ann Jeffrey; c. Jeffrey James, Laurie Lynn; retd. legal survey technologist; 1st of 10 Ont. Consols playdown appearances '63 as lead for Bob Knippleburg; Coombe-skipped quartet (Keith Forgues, Jim Patrick, Barry Provost) won Div. 1 OCA titles 7 successive years; rep. Ont. '72 St. John's, Nfld. Brier after winning Consols in 4-way playoff; 3 Canadian Branch Royal Caledonian Curling Club Royal Victoria Jubilee titles; 7 Red Anderson Memorial Trophy titles; '72 CBC Curling Classic, Whitby Dunlop 'spiel; swept major Branch title honors '66 winning Jubilee, Colts, Governor-General's titles; 3 times Ottawa ACT curler of year; res. Ottawa, Ont.

COOMBES, Cy (lacrosse); b. 24 Oct 1938, Peterborough, Ont.; given name: Cyril Maxwell; mem. '53 Ont. Bantam A hockey titlists; known for speed/scoring ability; 15yrs sr./pro lacrosse player; 1062g, 612a, including playoffs, placed him atop all-time OLA scorers list; Sr. A/major series schedule record 113g '69; in 10yr span among top 10 OLA scorers 9 times; mem. 2 Mann Cup title teams; coached Hastings Minto Cup winner '61, runnerup '62, Mann Cup finalist '83; mem. Cdn Lacrosse, Peterborough Sports halls of fame; res. Peterborough, Ont.

COOPER, Barbara Ann (squash); b. 8 Oct 1949, Brighton, Eng.; began playing age 19; 2 ntl women's doubles, 1 mixed doubles titles; ntl 40+ hardball title '94; won British open/closed singles '86, world 40+ masters singles '92-93; won '93 NA open, Ont closed, '94 Ont. masters 40+, women's, mixed doubles; mem. ntl women's team '94; res. Toronto, Ont.

COOPER, Ralph (football/builder); b. 3 Nov 1908, Hamilton, Ont.; d. 31 Aug 1994, Burlington, Ont.; given name: Ralph William; m. Evelyn Joanna McArthur; c. Kathleen Joanna, Barbara Evelyn, William Press; successfully amalgamated Hamilton Tigers of ORFU and Hamilton Wildcats of IRFU into Hamilton Tiger-Cats '50; pres. '50-52, director to '72, governor '73-77; varied IRFU (Big Four) exec. roles through '50s; helped establish university player draft system; Big Four pres. '55 played key role in developing working agreement with NFL re player movements; chair. newly formed Cdn Football Council '56; v.-pres. CFL '59, pres. '60; devised East-West interlocking schedule; mem. Cdn Football Hall of Fame.

COOPERBAND, Mary (softball/t&f); b. 16 May 1915, Winnipeg, Man.; m. Clifford Rusen (d); c. David Mark, Vivian Carla; UMan. BA; pitcher; mem. New Method Laundry Int. girls title team '29; Sr. Tigerettes '30-32, MVP '32; Ramblers '33-35. all-star '33; primary school 185'11", HS 208', unofficial world 217'6" ball throw records; played university basketball, volleyball; res. Winnipeg, Man.

COPELAND, Royal (football); b. 12 Oct 1924, North Bay, Ont.; given name: Royal Hayward; m. Barbara Ann; c. Nola Jean, Cindy Ann; CalState, BA, Azusa Pacific College, MA; retd. teacher, avacado farmer; mem. Teddy Morris coached RCN team; halfback Argos, Stampeders '45-56; with Joe Krol became Toronto's Gold Dust Twins; won special '49 100yd match race to determine fastest runner in CFL; CFL record: 111 scheduled games, 14 playoff contests, 34 TDs;

EFC scoring leader '45; tied Argos single-game TD record with 4 (all on passes from Krol) vs. Montreal '45, 3 interceptions vs. Hamilton '45; 3 times EFC all-star; Jeff Russel Memorial Trophy '49; mem. 4 Grey Cup winners; mem. Cdn Football Hall of Fame; res. Oxnard, Calif.

COPP, Bobby (hockey); b. 15 Nov 1918, Port Elgin, N.B.; given name: Robert Alonzo; m. Mary MacMillan; c. Judith Ann, Bonnie Lynn; Mount Allison, BA, UofT, DDS; dentist; rugby '36-37, track '38, hockey '34-38 Mount A, '38 Maritime Intercollegiate hockey title; mem. Amherst St. Pat's '37 Maritime jr. champions; UofT intercollegiate titlists '40-41; sr. Marlboros '40-42; pro Maple Leafs '42-43; Canadian Army Dental Corps '43, mem. Maritime title RCAF Flyers Halifax, Ottawa Commandos; coached Ottawa Senators (QHL) 2 months before amateur reinstatement '46; Allan Cup finalist '48, winner '49; excluding 2 games '50 with Leafs, 3 months Smiths Falls Bears '52, mem. Senators '49-55; mem. NB Sports Hall of Fame; res. Ottawa, Ont.

CORAZZA, John (t&f); b. 27 Feb 1954, Quebec City; given name: Giovanni Daniele; m. Adrienne Allard; UofOtt, BA; salesman; javelin specialist; ntl team '77-80; bronze '77 Pacific Conf. Games; silver '77 World Cup trials; gold '79, silver '80 ntl outdoor championships; silver International Cup '80; gold '80 Olympic alternate competitions West Germany, England, Norway, bronze France; PB 84.34m; mem. 2 NB teams ntl team handball championships; mem. UofOtt volleyball team; last known res. Ottawa, Ont.

CORAZZIN, Carlo (soccer); b. 25 Dec 1971, New Westminster, B.C. midfielder Cdn Olympic team '92; pro debut '92 with Winnipeg Fury CSL title team; CSL all-star; Vancouver 86ers '93; Cambridge United '93-94, top team scorer '95-96; mem. ntl team '94-98; 19 international caps; res. New Westminster, B.C.

CORBETT, Ed (softball); b. 25 Jan 1917, Calgary, Alta.; m. Lila Foss; c. Penny, Wendy; played for various Calgary teams including '42 Western Cdn title team; retd as player to become umpire, hockey, baseball official; organized Calgary Softball Umpires Assn, serving in several exec. capacities; founding mem. Calgary District ASA, Alta. ASA, Cdn ASA, serving each in varied exec, capacities; pres. Calgary Minor SA, Minor Sports Assn., Alta. Fastball Assn., Western Canada SA; Alta. Softball commissioner '60-65; v.-pres for NA Intl Softball Fed.; co-chair AASA Hall of Fame comm.; Calgary sportsman of '66; mem. Alta. Sports, Cdn, Alta. Softball halls of fame; res. Calgary, Alta.

CORDUKES, Don (golf); b. 16 Jun 1925, Ottawa, Ont.; given name: Donald John; m. Helen Donna; c. Donna, Norma; Carleton, BComm; retd. Air Force; 5 Ottawa C&D match, 2 medal titles; 2 Chaudiere, 7 Ottawa Hunt club titles; course records Royal Ottawa 66, Outaouais 68; 1 Cdn Forces, 2 RCAF championships; 6 Collie Cup, 3 ODGA best ball, 2 CBOT best ball, 2 OVGA seniors titles; Alexander of Tunis titles '66, '68; Ottawa ACT golfer of '68; mem. 1 Que. Willingdon Cup team, competed '48 Cdn Amateur; res. Ottawa, Ont.

COREY, Ron (administration); b. 13 Dec 1938, Montreal, Que.; m. Danielle Grégoire; c. Stéphanie, Frédérick; hockey exec., former journalist; pres. Montreal Canadiens '82-99; pres. Molson Centre, a structure he was instrumental in making a reality; dir. numerous major corporations; involved in numerous community fund-raising projects; mem. NHL exec. comm.; mem. Order of Canada; res. Montreal, Que.

CORKEY, Joe (baseball/curling); b. 4 Oct 1913, Kingston, Ont.; d. 24 Sep 1994, Kingston, Ont.; given name: Joseph Frederick; m. Stella Irwin; c. Steven Joseph; retired store owner; catcher Collins Bay '32, Kingston Ponies '36; drew 4yr suspension for 'professionalism' (later reduced to 2yrs); played 'outlaw' baseball Quebec 2yr; on reinstatement '38 helped organize Kingston City League; retired from active play at 37; exec. mem. Goodyears sr. hockey club '52-56; OHA sr. B titlists; mem. '60 Ont. Brier entry; sponsored stock car racing '57-77; began golfing at 38; scored hole-in-one Cataraqui.

CORNER, Peter (curling); b. 20 May 1968, Brampton, Ont.; given name: Peter John; Ont. Police Coll.; constable Halton regional police; began curling age 12; finalist '87 Pepsi Jr.; lead for Russ Howard 4 Briers, '93 Cdn, world titlists; all-star lead '93-94 Briers; '93 VO Cup champion; 3 TSN Skins Games; res. Burlington, Ont.

CORNISH, Geoffrey (golf); b. 1914, Winnipeg, Man.; m. Carol Burr Gawthrop; UBC, Mass; golf course architect; designed more than 200 courses including Halifax New Ashburn, Montreal Summerlea, Toronto York Downs; pres. American Society of Golf Course Architects '71; co-author "*The Golf Course*" and "*Architects of Golf*"; Golf Course Superintendents Assn. of America distinguished service award; US National Golf Foundation distinguished service award; mem. RCGA Hall of Fame; res. Amherst, Mass.

CORNISH, Ray (badminton); b. 11 Jan 1932, Stratford, Ont.; given name: Rayfield Philip; m. Ruth Marie Schlotzhauer; c. Janine, Judith, Peter; UofT, BSc Phm.; pharmacist; with Bev Chittick Ont. mixed doubles title '64; with Bill Parkes Michigan open men's doubles '61; Tor. Granite men's singles '58, with Joan Hennessy mixed doubles '59; with Jim Poole '83 Cdn men's 50+ doubles; 2 WO men's singles, 10 men's doubles, 6 mixed doubles; ranked #1 veterans 35+ WO tennis '73; Stratford Sportsman of '80; res. Stratford, Ont.

CORRIGALL, Jim (football); b. 7 May 1946, Barrie, Ont.; m. Marybeth; c. Jimmy, Amy; Kent State; football coach; all-Mid-American Conf. 1st team all-star 3yrs; AP all-American hon. mention; Kent State's most efficient defensive lineman, most valuable sophomore awards; 1st jr. Kent State capt.; NEA all-American '69, first Canadian; competed '69 North-South Shrine Bowl; 2nd round NFL St. Louis Cardinals draft '70; pro Argonauts '70-81; EFC Gruen Trophy '70 rookie of year; James P. McCaffrey Trophy '75 EFC outstanding defensive player; '75 Argos' Shopsy Award; all-EFC defensive end 7 times; 4 times CFL all-star; '75 Schenley outstanding defensive lineman award; played 146 CFL games; defensive line coach Miami of Ohio '83-94, head coach Kent State '95-'97; mem. Canadian Football, Barrie Sports halls of fame; res. Rootstown, Ohio.

CORSIGLIA, Robin (swimming); b. 12 Aug 1962, Kirkland, Ohio; given name: Robin Marie; SouthernCal; breaststroke specialist; youngest mem. '76 Canadian Olympic swim team, bronze 4x100 medley relay; 200m breaststroke, broke own Canadian, Commonwealth record for 100m '76 national championships; national short course 200m medley record 2:05.20 '76; ntl record 100m breaststroke 1:12.60 '77, 200m 2:33.27 '78; gold 100m '78 Commonwealth Games; mem. '79 World championships, Pan-Am Games teams; Governor-General's silver '76; last known res. Santa Monica, Calif.

CORSON, Shayne (hockey); b. 13 Aug 1966, Barrie, Ont.; m. Kelly; c. Shelby, Dylan, Summer; left wing OHL Brantford '83-84, Hamilton '84-86, NHL Montreal '86-92, '96-99, Edmonton '92-95, St. Louis '95-96; mem. Team Canada jr. worlds '85, '86, Canada Cup '91, worlds '93, '94, Olympics '98; 2 world gold, 1 silver medals; competed 2 NHL all-star games; capt. St. Louis '95-96; NHL record (through '99): 872 scheduled games, 233g, 348a, 103 playoff games, 36g, 41a; mem. Barrie Sports Hall of Fame; res.Port Carling, Ont.

CORT, Gail (rowing); b. 5 Aug 1956, St. Catharines, Ont.; given name: Gail Susan; m. Alan Horan; Brock, BPHE, Waterloo; 4 Ont., 2 ntl, 2 Canadian Henley coxed 4s, 1 Ont., 2 ntl, 1 Cdn Henley coxed 8s titles; bronze coxed 8s world championships '78; Swiss, Australian, Amsterdam international regatta titles; 2 NZ coxed 4s, 1 coxed pairs, 1 single sculls, 1 coxed 8s titles; mem. '76, '80, '84 Olympic, 4 world championships teams; St. Catharines oarswoman of '77; last known res. St. Catharines, Ont.

COSENTINO, Frank (football); b. 22 May 1937, Hamilton, Ont.; m. Sheila McHugh; c. Tony, Mary, Teresa, Peter; UWO., BA, McMaster BPhE, UAlta, MA, PhD; retd. educator, dept. head York U.; 4yrs quarterback UWO Mustangs; mem. 2 CIAU title teams; capt. 1st CIAU championship team '59; 10 years CFL, 7 Hamilton (5 Grey Cup finals, 2 winners), 2 Edmonton, 1 Toronto; 5yrs head coach UWO, 2 CIAU titles; head coach York '78, '84; Frank Tindall CIAU coach of '70 award; righthanded pitcher Hamilton Sr. IC team; authored *"Canadian Football: The Grey Cup Years"; "Passing Game"; "Ned Hanlan; "Not Bad, Eh?"; "The Renfrew Millionaires"; "Almonte's Brothers of the Wind."*; with M.L.Howell *"A History of Physical Education in Canada"*; with Glynn Leyshon *"Olympic Gold". "Winter Gold"*; with Don Morrow *"Lionel Conacher"*; mem. UWO W-Club, OUAA Football Legends Sports halls of fame; res. Eganville, Ont.

COSTELLO, Murray (hockey); b. 24 Feb 1934, South Porcupine, Ont.; given name: James Murray; m. Denise Marie Lancop; c. Michelle, Dan, Jennifer, Jim, Elizabeth, Mary;Windsor, BA, UofOtt, LLB; retd hockey administrator; pres. CAHA, retd '98; centre Junior A St. Mike's '50-53; pro '53-58 Chicago, Boston, Detroit in NHL, Hershey (AHL), Edmonton (WHL); 6yrs PR dir. WHL; 4yrs exec. dir. Seattle Totems; 2yrs exec. dir, GM Totems; mem. Ottawa Old Pros; appointed to IIHF exec. council '98; res. Ottawa, Ont.

COSTELLO, Ralph (golf); b. 7 Apr 1923, Saint John, N.B.; m. Frances; journalist, publisher; NB-PEI Golf Assn v.p.

'60-61, pres. '61-62; pres. Riverside GC '65-66; governor RCGA '74, v.p '80, pres. '81; pres. Cdn Golf Foundation '86-89; wrote book "The First Fifty Years"; instrumental in bringing CPGA, 3 ntl amateur tournaments to NB; past chair NB Sports, RCGA halls of fame; Toastmasters' Intl. award '81; NBGA trophy bears his name; hon. gov. RCGA from '85; hon. life mem. NBGA from '88; Sport NB award '89; Rotary Club Paul Harris Fellowship; mem. NB, Saint John Sports halls of fame; res. Rothesay, N.B.

COTÉ, Benoit (harness racing); b. 22 Mar 1934, Quebec City, Que.; m. Pierrette; c. Alain, Marc, Lucie, Éric; horseman; highly rated by peers as catch driver in important stakes races in Montreal; most racing in Montreal area; drove Delmonica Hanover to world record 2:00.1 '72 Que. Grand Circuit Trot; operates public stable; trained, drove for Drummond, Richelieu Farms; through '95 3625 victories, $18 million in purses; mem. Canadian Horse Racing Hall of Fame; res. Anjou, Que.

COTÉ, Gérard (t&f); b. 28 Jul 1913, St. Barnabé, Que.; d. 13 Jun 1993, St. Hyacinthe, Que.; m. Lucille Lemoine; c. 3 girls, 1 boy; advertising salesman; developed running stamina while training to be boxer; champion roller skater; world snowshoe racing record '38; 1st Boston Marathon bid 1936 but overtrained by running course 2 days before race; record 2:28.28 1940 winning first of 4 Boston Marathons; other victories '42-43, '48; 2nd 5 Yonkers Marathons before winning 1st of 3 '40; 3 US AAU marathon titles; career record 264 races, 1st 112, 2nd 56, 3rd 26; leg cramps led to 17th '48 Olympics; mem. '50, '54 B.E.Games teams; retired from running '56; record 46 minutes snowshoeing 8-mile event St. Paul, Minn. '58; Ste. Rosalie recreational facility bears his name; Lionel Conacher, Lou Marsh trophies '40; mem. Order of Canada; Canada's, Que. Sports, Cdn Amateur, Cdn Roadrunning halls of fame.

COTTON, Harry (football/boxing); b. 28 Jul 1909, Vancouver, B.C.; d. 2 May 1989, Ottawa, Ont.; given name: Henry Ferguson; m. Olive Eve Wootton; c. Peter Ross (d), John Miles; Royal Military College; real estate agent, retired soldier; football RMC '28-29; BC. champion Vancouver AC '30-31, Winnipeg Blue Bombers '34-35; English rugby Vancouver Rowing Club '29-31; Garrison Football Club Winnipeg '32-34, Man. all-stars '33-34; runnerup British army middleweight boxing title '37; Canadian army western div. middleweight title '32-33; founded Little League baseball Rivers, Man. '50; district administrator Little League Eastern Ont. '60-64; mem. winning curling rink Royal Victoria Jubilee '63.

COUGHLAN, Angela (swimming); b. 4 Oct 1952, London, Eng.; given name: Angela Denise; div. Toomas Arusoo; c. Jessica, Lee, Kate; registered massage therapist; ntl team '67-72; competed '67 (1 silver, 3 bronze), '71 (1 gold, 3 silver, 1 bronze) Pan-Am, '68 (1 bronze) Olympic, '70 (1 gold, 2 silver, 1 bronze) Commonwealth Games; 24 ntl gold, 2 silver; set 1 world record; coached Oakville Aquatic Club '73-76, Pointe Claire '77-78; head of pre-school aquatics St. John's, Nfld '78-79; Velma Springstead Trophy '70; Canadian female swimmer of '70; mem. Cdn Olympic, Cdn, Ont. Aquatic halls of fame; res. Toronto, Ont.

COULON, Johnny (boxing); b. 12 Feb 1889, Toronto, Ont.; d. 29 Oct 1973, Chicago, Ill.; boxing coach; age 19 won vacant world bantam title, defended 12 times before losing to Kid Williams '14; title matches twice within 3 week period, later 3 times in month; retired following loss to Williams; comeback '16-18; nicknamed "Chicago Spider"; 96 pro bouts, 24 won by KO, 32 by decision, 4 draws, KO'd twice, lost 2 by decision, 32 no-decision bouts; boxing coach to age 73; mem. US, Canadian Boxing, Canada's Sports halls of fame.

COULSON, Evelyn (basketball); b. 28 Jan 1912, Calgary, Alta.; m. Alfred Cameron; c. James, Verna; retired stenographer; mem. legendary Edmonton Grads '31-35; mem. Canadian Basketball, Alta. Sports halls of fame; res. Edmonton, Alta.

COULTER, Art (hockey); b. 31 May 1909, Winnipeg, Man.; d. (circa 1995), Miami, Fla.; given name: Arthur Edmund; m. Gertrude Schneitzer (d); c. Art Jr, Patty; retired; Pilgrim AC '24; pro Philadelphia '29; NHL defenceman Chicago '31-35, NY Rangers '35-42; followed Bill Cook as Rangers capt.; mem. 2 Stanley Cup winners; 4 times 2nd team all-star; NHL record: 11 seasons, 30 goals, 82 assists; nicknamed "Trapper" because of penchant for talking hunting, fishing; mem. Man., Cdn Hockey halls of fame.

COULTER, Bruce (football); b. 19 Nov 1927, Toronto, Ont.; given name: Bruce David; m. Joyce Brown; c. Susan, Bruce Jr., Douglas, John; UofT; retd. Bishop's athletic dir.; HS all-star football, basketball, t&f; pro def. halfback, quarterback Alouettes '48-57; nicknamed "Bones"; head coach McGill Redmen '58-61, Bishop's Gaiters '62-87; Bishop's AD to '91 retirement; CIAU coach of year '87; winningest CIAU coach 137-80-3 (beaten by Tuffy Knight '96); Frank Tindall award '86; p.-pres. Canadian Assn. of University Athletic Directors, QUAA; p.-dir. CIAU; Bishop's Stadium bears his name; mem. Bishop's Wall, Cdn Football Hall of Fame; res. Lennoxville, Que.

COULTER, Tex (football); b. 2 Oct 1924, Smith County, Tex.; given name: Dewitt; m. Ruth; c. David, Ann, Jeff, Dena; West Point, Texas Christian; artist, writer; all-Texas HS honors '40-42; twice West Point all-American; pro NY Giants (NFL) '46-52, 3 times all-pro; Alouettes '53-56; 3 times all-Cdn; Schenley lineman of '55; mem. Texas Football Hall of Fame; res. Austin, Texas.

COULTHARD, Bill (basketball); b. 29 Dec 1923, Buffalo, N.Y.; m. June Frances; c. Carol, Chris, Bruce, Betty, David; Assumption College, BA; personnel mgr.; all-city Windsor HS '41; all-state Detroit Tech '44; mem. Assumption College team '47; mem. ntl champion Tillsonburg Livingstons '51-52; mem. '52 Olympic team; retired following '52-53 season; res. Tillsonburg, Ont.

COURNOYER, Yvan (hockey); b. 22 Nov 1943, Drummondville, Que.; given name: Yvan Serge; m. Ginette; c. Marie-France, Yannick, Melanie; businessman; Montreal Jr. Canadiens; pro Montreal '64-79; NHL record: 968 scheduled games, 428g, 435a, 147 playoff games, 64g, 63a; 40 or more goals 3 successive seasons '71-74; 9 3-goal games; 7 points (5g, 2a) as Montreal beat Chicago 12-3 '75; 4 times 2nd team all-star; Smythe Trophy '72 playoffs; mem. Team Canada '72; mem. 10 Stanley Cup winners; coached Montreal Roadrunners Roller Hockey team; asst coach Canadiens '95-97; Canadiens special ambassador; mem. Hockey Hall of Fame; res. Blainville, Que.

COURTWRIGHT, Jim (t&f); b. 16 Dec 1914, North Bay, Ont.; given name: James Milton; m. Mary Nora Roche; c. Joseph, James, Patricia, Stephen, John, Mary Ellen, Anthony, Frank; UofOtt, BA; Queen's, BSc, Columbia; retired v.-pres. Queen's; excelled in t&f (javelin), basketball, football; mem. '36 Olympic team; gold '38 Commonwealth Games; best individual performance BE vs. US relay and team match London, Eng., '36; 12 competitive basketball seasons; mem. '42 ntl finalist Montreal Oilers; HS, college football; Jenkins Trophy Queen's '41 best combined athlete-student; Ames Trophy Glebe CI '34 best student-athlete; Fink Trophy '37 UofOtt best student-athlete; res. Kingston, Ont.

COUSINEAU, Alain (skiing); b. 28 Jul 1953, Montreal, Que.; m. Helene Ouellette; c. Emelie, Julien; pro skier, restaurateur; Laurentian zone ski team '69-70, Que. team '70-71, ntl team '71-75; pro '75-76 season; 2 Que. Kandahar, ntl GS titles; World Pro Ski circuit '77-81, 7th overall '77, 6th '78; Volvo Cup '78; res. Lachute, Que.

COWAN, Gary (golf); b. 28 Oct 1938, Kitchener, Ont.; m. Elaine Koebel; c. Rob, Todd, Jamie, Suzie; retd insurance exec.; Ont. juve., jr., ntl jr. titles; only Canadian to twice win US Amateur '66, '71; Canadian amateur '61, 5 times runnerup; Ont. Open '68, 3 times runnerup; 9 Ont. amateur titles; NZ Centennial Invitational, Porter Cup, US North-South titles; individual low scorer world amateur '62, low amateur US Masters '64, low amateur Canadian Open '60; mem. 22 Ont. Willingdon Cup teams, 5 winners; mem. 6 America's Cup teams, 8 world amateur teams, 5 Commonwealth teams; qualified for seniors pro tour '90; won 1st seniors pro tour title Dotham, Ala. '94; CTV golf color commentator; mem. Waterloo County, RCGA, Canada's Sports halls of fame; res. Kitchener, Ont.

COWAN, Jack (soccer); b. 6 Jun 1927, Vancouver, B.C.; given name: John Lawrence; m. Margaret; c. Gael Isobel, Lynn Jacqueline; UBC, BSc, St. Andrews College, Scotland; electrical engineer; UBC Big Block '45-49; Vancouver Coast League '48-49, '55-56; BC. all-stars vs. touring Newcastle United team; pro '50 Dundee Scottish League 1st div., twice league cup winners, runnerup '52 Scottish Cup; returned to Canada '55, mem. ntl champion Vancouver Canadians; mem. BC Sports Hall of Fame; res. Burnaby, B.C.

COWDREY, Jim (softball); b. 6 Dec 1957, Toronto, Ont.; given name: James Michael; div. Margaret Reynolds; m. Wendy McDougall; c. Shannon, Amanda, Michael, Erin; private investigator; from '69 one of game's foremost righthanded pitchers and above average hitters; through '83 more than 50 no-hitters; wide array league, tournament most valuable pitcher, player awards; mem. '74 Ont. midget, '77 jr. title teams; rookie of year, MV pitcher Ont. Fastball League '80; mem. '80, '84 silver medal world championships teams, '83 gold medal Pan-Am Games team;

MV pitcher, player '81 national championships, '82 Ont. fastball tournament; perfect game leading Agincourt to '82 Ont. title; remained with Agincourt through '94, with New Jersey Windmillers '95-99; res. Brampton, Ont.

COWLEY, Bill (hockey); b. 12 Jun 1912, Bristol, Que.; d. 31 Dec 1993, Ottawa, Ont.; m. Jessie; c. Jill, Jane, John, Dan; retired hotel owner; mem. Primrose juniors, Shamrocks, Ottawa all-stars '32 European tour; Halifax Wolverines '34; pro centre St. Louis Eagles (NHL) '34, Boston '35-47; NHL scoring title '41, Hart Trophy '41, '43; mem. 3 NHL title, 2 Stanley Cup winners; NHL record: 195 regular season goals, 353 assists, 12 playoff goals, 34 assists; 4 times 1st, once 2nd team all-star; 3yrs pres. Smiths Falls Rideaus; part owner Ottawa 67's jrs. '67-75; mem. Ottawa, Smiths Falls Sports, Hockey halls of fame.

COX, Bobby (baseball/coaching); b. 21 May 1941, Tulsa, Okla.; m. Pam; c. Keisha, Kami, Skyla; Reedley (CA) jr. coll.; manager; 3B; playing career, mostly in minors with Reno, Salem, Panama City, Albuquerque, Salt Lake City, Tacoma, Austin, Richmond, Syracuse, Ft. Lauderdale and 2 seasons NY Yankees extended '60-71 before injury forced retirement; Topps mgr. Ft. Lauderdale '71, West Haven (EL pennant) '72, 4yrs Syracuse (IL Governor's Cup '76); coach Yankees '77; mgr. Atlanta '78-81, '90-99, Toronto '82-85 (AL East title '85); GM Atlanta '85-90; 7 NL East titles; 2 World Series titles; 2 SN mgr of yr awards; 2 AP mgr of yr awards; BBWA mgr of yr award; res. Marietta, Ga.

COX, Doug (wrestling); b. 8 Oct 1957, Fergus, Ont.; carpenter, wrestling coach Guelph U.; Greco-Roman, freestyle competitor at 90kg; mem. ntl team from '85; 4 ntl GR, 2 FS titles; World Cup bronze '80; Commonwealth Games silver '86; Pan-Am Games FS gold, GR bronze '87; competed '88, '96 Olympic Games; res. Guelph, Ont.

COX, Ernie (football); b. 1894, Hamilton, Ont.; d. 26 Feb 1962, Hamilton, Ont.; m. Cecilia Gibbs; c. Donald, Mrs. Ralph Hammel; firefighter; from Hamilton sandlots to Hamilton Tigers; following WW1 rejoined Tigers '19; played 16 seasons; perennial league, Cdn all-star; inaugural winner Jeff Russel Memorial Trophy '28; mem. 3 Grey Cup winners; nicknamed "Iron Fireman"; mem. Canada's Sports, Cdn Football halls of fame.

COX, Kathy (parachuting); b. 27 Jul 1951, Brampton, Ont.; given name: Kathleen; m. Sutton; jumped into ntl sports limelight winning '73 Cdn overall parachuting title; 4 ntl style, overall, accuracy titles; mid-East US women's title; capt. ntl women's sport parachuting team 5th place overall Yugoslavia world championships; accuracy title '79 Rossignol pro para-ski championships; individual world title for precision landing '80; overall China tournament title; 3rd Cdn woman to earn diamond wings with 2000 freefall jumps; mem. CSPA competition, coaching comm.; CBC athlete of '80; Ont. Sports Achievement awards '78-80; mem. Order of Canada; res. Terrace Bay, Ont.

COY, Eric (t&f); b. 16 May 1914, Nottingham, Eng.; d. 28 Oct 1985, Winnipeg, Man; m. Margaret Helen Claudia Hindson; c. John, Rick, Judy; technical services superintendent; NA snowshoe sprint title '33-41 (except

'38); 1st ntl javelin title '35; mem. '38 BEG team; ntl discus, javelin, shot put crowns '38; gold discus, silver shot put '38 BEG; AAU of C athlete of year; mem. '40, '48 Olympic, '50, '54 BEG teams; football Winnipeg Wanderers, Lew Hayman's RCAF Hurricanes; coached t&f, wrestling, hockey; mem. Man., Canadian Amateur, Canada's Sports halls of fame.

COZZARIN, Sharon (shooting); b. 5 Oct 1956, Fergus, Ont.; given name: Sharon Hewitson; m. Leo Cozzarin; c. Kayla; financial planner; launched shooting career '85; handgun specialist; mem. ntl team '89-96; set ntl record winning air pistol '90 Cdn world trials; set world record winning air pistol gold '91 Pan-Am Games; added team silver; competed '92 Olympics; gold '93, silver '94, bronze '92 Crossman air gun championships; sport pistol gold '94 World Cup, also competed '93 World Cup, '96 pre-Olympic World Cup (silver sport pistol); silver air pistol team, bronze individual air pistol '94 Commonwealth Games; sport pistol finalist '95 Pan-Am Games; female shooting athlete of '91 award; res. Fergus, Ont.

CRAIG-EATON, Betty (rowing); b. 26 Sep 1957, Brockville, Ont.; given name: Marion Elizabeth Craig; m. Bruce Eaton; Carleton, BA; insurance adjuster; mem. '76, '80, '84 Olympic teams; ntl titles: 1 coxed 8s, 2 coxless pairs; Canadian Henley titles: 1 coxed 8s, 3 coxless pairs, 1 coxless 4s; silver '78, '81, bronze '82-83 world championships coxless pairs; coxless pairs titles: 3 Rotsee, 2 West German, 1 Bosbaan, 1 Moscow regattas; with Tricia Smith silver women's pairs '84 Olympics; fed. govt. sports excellence awards '82-84; owner, trainer show jumping horses; res. Aldergrove, B.C.

CRAIG, John (t&f); b. 2 Sep 1953, Toronto, Ont.; given name: John Henry; m. Gael Carol Joyce Robertson; c. Noah, Joshua; Texas, BSc; sports administrator OTFA; ntl jr. 800m '73, sr. '74; mem. '78 Commonwealth, '79 Pan-Am, '80 Olympic, '81 World Cup teams; competes in Masters races; ntl outdoor 1500m champion '79-80, indoor 1500m '80-81; PB: 1500m 3:38.6, mile 3:58.05, 800m 1:49.4; twin brother Paul; published track book for juveniles; res. Thornhill, Ont.

CRAIG, Paul (t&f); b. 2 Sep 1953, Toronto, Ont.; given name: Paul Frederick; m. Judith May Johnson; c. Brydon, Lindsay;Texas; teacher; ntl sr. 1500m title '73, '77; US South-West Conf. mile '73-74; ntl record 3:38.0 '76 Olympic 1500m; mem. '78 Commonwealth, '79 World Cup, '80 Olympic teams; competes in Masters events; ntl 3000m record 7:49.6; twin brother John; res. Agincourt, Ont.

CRANE, Cec (bowling); b. 19 Aug 1924, Winnipeg, Man; given name: Cecil Phillip; m. Ilene Harris; c. Tom, Bonnie, Nancy, Danny, Harold, Patsy; machinist; outstanding 5-pin bowler since taking up game '46; 12 times London Trades Major League champion; 3 Inter-City, 4 Ont. Legion titles; ntl singles title '63; *London Free Press* Headpin Highlights singles; PB: 420 single, 1593 5-game string; last known res. Ingersoll, Ont.

CRANHAM, Scott (diving); b. 8 Sep 1954, Toronto, Ont.; Indiana, Texas, BA; family therapist; mem. university,

Pointe Claire diving teams under coach Don Webb; from '71-80 won 30 ntl diving titles (feat surpassed by only Bev Boys); mem. '72, '76, '80 Olympic, '73, '78 Worlds (finalist each time), '74, '79 Commonwealth, '75, '79 Pan-Am Games teams; silver 3m, bronze 10m '74, '78 Commonwealth Games; 1st to record inward 3 1/2 tuck, armstand triple tuck in '78 Berlin world competition; 5th '80, 2nd '81 world professional cliff diving championships; Ont. coach Canadian Amateur Diving Assn. '81; res. Pte. Claire, Que.

CRANSTON, Toller (figure skating); b. 20 Apr 1949, Hamilton, Ont.; Ecole des Beaux Arts Montreal; skater, artist; '64 ntl jr. title; '67 Que. Winter Games; 5 ntl sr. singles titles; '73 Skate Canada; mem. 6 Worlds, '72 Olympic teams, ISU winter, summer tours '71-74; launched own short-lived pro ice show '76; 3 Labatt pro skate titles; performed frequently with ice shows and on TV specials; '84 Olympics TV color commentator; German FSA award of decade; '95 Olympic Order; Norton Crowe trophy '74; mem. Order of Canada, Cdn Amateur, Canada's Sports, Ont. Sport Legends, Cdn Figure Skating halls of fame; res. Mexico.

CRAWFORD, Judy (skiing); b. 22 Dec 1951, Toronto, Ont.; given name: Judith MacPherson; m. Kim Rawley; c. Kristin, Shawn, Leanne, Andrea; UofT, BA; ski coach, examiner; ntl ski team '68-75; ntl titles '71, '73, US title '71, European Cup race France '73; 3rd WC slalom Grindelwald, Switzerland '73; 4th slalom '72 Olympics, '70 world downhill, '74 world combined; John Semmelink Trophy for achievement in skiing, sportsmanship; Cdn ski coach of yr award; Camp Fortune ski coach; examiner Canadian Ski Coaches Federation; mem. Cdn Skiing Hall of Fame; res. Ottawa, Ont.

CRAWFORD, Marc (hockey/coaching); b. 13 Feb 1961, Belleville, Ont.; m. Helene; c. Dylan, Kaitlin; hockey coach, ex-TV analyst; jr. with Cornwall (QMJHL) '79-81; CHL Dallas '81-82; AHL Fredericton '82-86; NHL Vancouver '81-87; NHL playing record: 116 scheduled games, 19g, 31a, 20 playoff games, 1g, 6a; turned to coaching (GM) Cornwall (OHL) '89-91, St. John's (AHL) '91-94, Quebec (NHL) '94-95, Colorado (NHL) '95-98, Vancouver '99; 1 Stanley Cup winner; NHL coaching record (through '98): 294 scheduled games, 165-88-41, 52 playoff games 31-21; 3 div., 2 conf. titles; AHL coach of '92; Jack Adams trophy '95; asst. Team Canada '96; head coach Team Canada '98 Olympics; HNIC analyst '98-99; res. Vancouver, B.C.

CRAWFORD, Rusty (hockey); b. 7 Nov 1884, Cardinal, Ont.; d. 19 Dec 1971; given name; Samuel Russell; amateur 3 seasons Verdun, 2 seasons Prince Albert, Sask., 1 season Saskatoon; Quebec Bulldogs '12-18; mem. Ottawa, Toronto Arenas; 3 Stanley Cup winners; Saskatoon '20, Calgary '21-25, Vancouver '26; closed career at 45 with Minneapolis '29; through 21-yr pro career never missed game due to injury; greatest single game accomplishment was playing entire 112 minutes of Quebec vs. Toronto Stanley Cup final and scoring winning goal; mem. Sask. Sports, Hockey halls of fame.

CRAVEN, Murray (hockey); b. 20 Jul 1964, Medicine Hat, Alta.; m. Sheri; c. Haley, Sara; jr. Medicine Hat '80-84;

NHL with Detroit parts of 2 seasons, Philadelphia '84-91, Hartford '91-93, Vancouver '93-94, Chicago '94-97, San Jose '97-99; NHL record: (through '99) 1052 scheduled games, 266g, 491a, 118 playoff games, 27g, 43a; served as capt. or alternate capt. with Hartford, Chicago, San Jose; Flyers Class Guy award; res. Whitefish, Mont.

CREANEY, Doreen (lawn bowling); b. 20 Nov 1935, Toronto, Ont.; given name: Doreen Ann; c. Sandra; exec. asst.; Ont. singles title, silver medal ntls '92; Ont., Cdn pairs champion '95; ntl singles title '99; res. Toronto, Ont.

CREBER, Bill (curling); b. 30 Nov 1935, Toronto, Ont.; m. Carol Anne Ward; c. Brad, Jill; sales rep.; best known for marathon loss to London's Ken Buchan '69 Ont. Consols; led Ont. Silver Tankard titlists '64-65; skipped '74 Tankard winner; skip 3 Toronto Curling Assn. title rinks, 3 Southern Ont. all-star titlists; skipped winners Whitby, Peterborough, St. Catharines, Orillia, Royals Classic, Avonlea Beef O'Rama, Parkway Open, Canada Life 'spiels; runnerup '67, '77 Ont. Tankard; OCA Intermediates title '81; res. Markham, Ont.

CREELMAN, Sharon (field hockey); b. 27 Apr 1964, Windsor, Ont.; UNB, York; coach Waterloo; mem. NB provincial teams from '80-83; ntl teams '82-92, UNB team '82-83; 3 CIAU FH all-Cdn; 1 CIAU FH coach of yr award; mem. World Cup silver medal team '83; mem. '84 Olympic team; fed. govt. excellence award '83; res. Waterloo, Ont.

CREIGHTON, Dale (baseball/football); b. 12 Jun 1934, London, Ont.; m. Marion Thompson; c. Matthew, Paul, Lyndsey; UWO, BA; retd. sr. v-p. individual marketing London Life; 1st base, catcher, outfielder; mem. 6 Ont. baseball title teams '48-58; capt. 3 title teams; sr. baseball Great Lakes-Niagara, Intercounty League London Majors; '58 2nd team all-star; mem. PS, HS basketball title teams, leading scorer twice, all-city twice; mem. HS, WOSSA, Red Feather tournament title football teams; 3 times all-conf. scoring leader, all-star; standout fullback UWO Mustangs '54-57; twice OUAA all-star; all-star, leading rusher ORFU London Lords '56; team MVP, ORFU all-star inside linebacker K-W Dutchmen '58; mem. UWO W-Club Sports Hall of Fame; res. London, Ont.

CRICHLOW, Renn (canoeing); b. 9 May 1969, Ottawa, Ont.; SFU, BSc (kinesiology), Harvard; kayak specialist; began kayaking at 12 as mem. Rideau Canoe Club; mem. ntl team '85-96; ntl midget K1 500m title '85; solid junior career winning gold or silver in 14 of 16 major events including Paris International where he claimed K1 500 and 1000m titles '87; earned bronze K1 1000m '87 junior worlds; 4 gold '88 Continental Cup; 9 ntl senior titles; gold K1 500m '91 Duisburg International, '93 Paris regattas; 1st Canadian to win world championship at senior level with K1 500m title '91; competed '88, '92, '96 Olympics; mem. Burnaby Canoe & Kayak Club; Harry Jerome award; Ottawa ACT Athlete of Year '91; life mem. Rideau Canoe Club; mem. Nepean Wall, Cdn Olympic Sports Hall of Fame; res. Nepean, Ont./Brookline, Mass.

CRIGHTON, Hec (diving/football); b. 2 Apr 1900, Toronto, Ont.; d. 17 Apr 1967, Toronto, Ont.; given name: Hector

Naismith; c. Ronald; UofT, BA, Wisc, MSc; educator; ntl diving title '20; refereed 16 Grey Cup finals through '50; authored 1st CIAU football rule book; trophy in his honor awarded annually to outstanding football player CIAU; mem. UofT Sports, Cdn Football halls of fame.

CRIPPS, Ken (baseball/bowling/darts); b. 4 Dec 1938, Chatham, N.B.; given name: Kenneth Joseph; m. Joan Kingston; c. Angela, Jacelyn, Ken Jr., Michael, Paula, Stephen, Ralph; ex-barber, school bus driver. Miramichi Ice co. owner; pitcher Chatham Ironmen '54-74; mem. NB sr. title team '67-68; mem. Napan Braves Maritime champions '75; coach Chatham jr. Ironmen '70-84; 2 NB titles; ntl darts singles title '75; Maritimes 5-pin singles bowling title '93; coached jr. bowlers, curlers, baseball players; Town of Chatham achievement award '75; mem. Chatham Sports Wall of Fame, NB Baseball Hall of Fame; res. Miramichi, N.B.

CRISTOFOLI, Ed (hockey); b. 2 Jan 1939, Trail, B.C.; given name: Edmund Luciano; m. Shirley Clark; c. Cheryl, Eddie Jr., Dean, Randy; Cominco foreman; centre, defenceman; Melville, Sask. jrs '57-58; Trail Smoke Eaters '59-63; mem. '61 World, '62 Allan Cup title teams; coaching from '63, guiding juveniles to BC. title; coached peewee teams to 4 provincial titles; level 3 CAHA coach; res. Trail, B.C.

CRITELLI, Chris (basketball); b. 5 Dec 1956, St. Catharines, Ont.; given name: Christine Ann; Winnipeg, Laurentian, Old Dominion , BSc; athletic dir., coach; all-Cdn 3yrs; academic all-American Old Dominion '81; ntl team '74-80; mem. 2 Laurentian ntl titlists, 2 Old Dominion US championship teams; mem. '76 Olympic, '75, '79 Pan-Am, world championships, FISU Games teams; MVP International Cup '79; pro New England Gulls, Chicago Hustle '81-82; women's AD, varsity coach Brock from '83; mem. Cdn Basketball Hall of Fame; res. Thorold, Ont.

CROCKER, Willard (tennis); b. 1898, Quincy, Mass.; d. 1964, Montreal, Que.; Tuft's, McGill; teamed with Jack Wright to form outstanding intercollegiate doubles team; one of first players of his era to work with/encourage juniors; won '25 ntl open singles; mem. Cdn Davis Cup team '23-30; posted only two Cdn victories vs. Cuba '24, sole victory over Japan '28; best performances came on clay courts; with Wright 3 ntl open doubles titles; mem. Cdn Tennis Hall of Fame.

CROMBIE, Jamie (squash); b. 13 Sep 1965, Morrisville, Vt.; began play age 13; won 1st tournament he entered Brae Glen Club; mem. 6 ntl world championships teams; mem. '94 Pan-Am tournament silver medal team, individual gold; Man., Ont., Que., Alta. open titles '94; turned pro '89; team gold '99 Pan-Am Games; res. Calgary, Alta.

CRONIE, Ab (hockey); b. 29 Jan 1915, Calgary, Alta; given name: Thomas Albert; m. Mary Gripich (d), Iva Stefani; c. Mervyn Allan; retired Cominco; mem. Alta. school soccer title team; 4 provincial age group hockey title teams; Trail Smoke Eaters '34-43; playing-coach '38 Allan Cup, '39 world title teams; pro tryouts NY Americans, Rangers, Detroit; MVP, Sportsman awards '50-51; BCAHA

outstanding player award '52; mem. BC Seniors' Curling Assn.; res. Trail, B.C.

CRONIN, Carl (football); b. 18 Oct 1908, Chicago, Ill.; d. 13 Sep 1983, Vancouver, B.C.; given name: Carl Michael; m. Ruth Harmon; c. Michael, Pat (d), Dennis (d), Thomas (d); Notre Dame; retd electrical business; HS football, pole vault, javelin standout; halfback, quarterback Notre Dame '29-31; 1st US import Winnipeg '32 as player-coach; guided Winnipeg to '33 Western title, losing Grey Cup bid to Toronto; Calgary Broncos coach '35-40; mem. Canadian Football Hall of Fame.

CROOK, Jan (field hockey); b. 9 Oct 1956, Edmonton, Alta.; given name: Janice Maureen; UVic, BA, UofSask.; asst registrar UCal; pres. CWUAA; 8yrs competitive age-group swimmer; mem. BC softball team '73 Canada Games; ntl field hockey team '74-81; mem. 4 World Cup tournament teams, twice placing 5th; 3 European tour teams; team capt. '79-81; twice HS athlete of year; HS sportsmanship award; 3 times jr. HS athlete of year; asst. AD UCal '94-95; res. Calgary, Alta.

CROOKALL, Dot (lacrosse); b. 6 Feb 1899, Toronto, Ont.; d. 31 May 1965, Snug Cove, Bowen Island, B.C.; given name: John; outstanding field lacrosse star with Vancouver teams '11-25; mem. 5 Minto Cup winners, 4 in succession with Vancouver AC '11-15; pro '19; several years baseball umpire; mem. Cdn Lacrosse, BC Sports halls of fame.

CROOKS, Charmaine (t&f); b. 8 Aug 1961, Mandeville, Jamaica; m. Anders Thorsen; Texas, BA; child psychologist, sport/media consultant; moved to Canada '66; ntl jr. 400m '79; 11 ntl 400m, 800m titles; ntl jr. 400m record 52.33 '80; gold Pan-Am jr. championships, 2 Francophone Games silver; 4x400m relay gold '82, '86, bronze '94 Commonwealth Games; 1st Cdn woman to break 2min barrier in 800m with ntl sr. record 1:38.52 '90; gold Buchanan Invitational '82, Tokyo International '83, Harry Jerome Classic 400m '94, Seattle 800m gold '94; 400m silver '82 NCAA championships; gold 400m '83, silver 4x400 relay '87 Pan-Am Games; 800m silver, 4x100 relay bronze '94 Commonwealth Games; 4x400 silver '84 Olympics; 4x400 World Cup gold '89, '92, 400m silver '92; mem. '80, '84, '88, '92, '96 Olympic, '83 FISU, '83, '87 Pan-Am Games teams; flag-bearer '96 summer Olympics; retd from competition '98; 4 fed. govt. sport excellence awards; 2 UTEP, 2 BC t&f female athlete of year awards; John F. Bassett Memorial award '91; Olympic champion award '95; Bruce Kidd athletic leadership award '96; Governor general's community service award '92; mem. Cdn Athletes Assn. board; co-host CBC Cycle show '94; mem. IOC ethics committee; res. N.Vancouver, B.C.

CROSBY, Andy (rowing); b. 5 Nov 1965, Bella Coola, B.C.; UVic, Memorial; began rowing at 17; mem. ntl 8s with cox team '85-92, '96; 1 jr, 3 sr Canadian Henley titles; silver '90-91 worlds; gold '90 US Nationals, Amsterdam International; 2 gold Duisburg International regatta '91; gold '92 Olympics; competed '86 Commonwealth, '88, '92, '96 Olympic, '89 FISU Games, 6 world championships; UVic's male rower of year '89; mem. Cdn Olympic Hall of Fame; res. Hamilton, Ont./St. John's, Nfld.

CROSS, Jay (sailing); b. 15 Feb 1953, Toronto, Ont.; engineer; 470 class sailor; 3 ntl, 2 NA, 1 CORK, 1 Hyeres titles; mem. '76, '80, '84 Olympic, '79 Pan-Am, 6 world championships teams; res. Toronto, Ont.

CROTHERS, Bill (t&f); b. 24 Dec 1940, Markham, Ont.; m. Morven; c. Margaret Grace, Andrea Lynn, William Rognvald; UofT, BPharm; retd. pharmacist; OFSSA sr. 440yd, ntl jr. 440 titles '59; '61-68 competed regularly both indoor, outdoor Canadian, US, European meets, leading field 440, 880yd events; at one time held all ntl records from 440 to 1500m; 65 wins in 75 indoor meets; mem. '64, '68 Olympic, '65 FISU, '62, '66 Commonwealth, '67 Pan-Am Games teams; 800m silver '64 Olympics, gold '65 FISU Games; ranked 1st '65, 2nd for decade behind Peter Snell for 800m by Track and Field News; US 880yd title record 1:46.8 '63, same year posted two fastest 880s in world; ntl sr. 440, 880 titles '61-65; Lou Marsh trophy '63; Lionel Conacher trophy '64; mem. National Sports Advisory Council; mem. UofT, Cdn Amateur, Canada's Sports halls of fame; res. Stouffville, Ont.

CROWE, Norton (administration); b. 6 Jul 1877, Ridgeville, Ont.; d. 14 Sep 1929, Toronto, Ont.; given name: Norton Hervey; one of most prominent sports executives Canada has produced; instrumental in stabilizing Canadian amateur sport; AAU of C secretary 19yrs; standout baseball player in youth, mem. Toronto city title teams; 1st secty. OHA; mgr. ntl swim team '11 Festival of Empire Games; mem. '24 Olympic exec. comm.; trophy in his name awarded annually to Canada's top amateur male athlete; mem. Cdn Amateur Sports Hall of Fame.

CROWELL, Eddie (golf); b. 2 Feb 1925, Halifax, N.S.; given name: Edwin Harvey; Dalhousie, BComm.; began golfing age 12; played in NS amateur as jr. '39; won 20 titles '46-56, including 3 Abercrombie, 4 Ashburn, 4 NS amateur, 3 Halifax City & District, 1 Brightwood Goodwill, Halifax Bicentennial, Maritime Amateur, NS Open, Truro Invitational; quarterfinalist Cdn Amateur; served term as pres. NSGA; took hiatus from competitive golf '56-82; won 2 Maritime srs. titles; mem. NS Sports Hall of Fame; res. Halifax, N.S.

CROWLEY, Maureen (t&f); b. 26 May 1953, Brampton, Ont.; given name: Maureen Adele; m. Ted de St. Croix, SFU; teacher; 800m, 1500m specialist; ntl team '71-79; 6th 800m, team bronze 4x400m relay '74 Commonwealth Games; Canadian 400m title '74; silver 150m, 800m NZ Games; injuries removed her from '76 Olympic team contention but recovered to compete in world cross-country '77, '79; 5 Cdn masters cross-country titles; set ntl women's master indoor mile record 4:49.44; res. Sweden.

CRUMMER, Keith (t&f); b. 29 Jun 1911, Wallaceburg, Ont.; d. 20 Jun 1990, Chatham, Ont.; given name: Charles Keith; m. Frances Bevan; c. Richard, Diane, Jane, Joan; Ohio State; Union Gas employee; excelled in pole vault, shot put, javeline, discus; 7 WOSSA records '27-31, 2 sr. overall titles; 3 Ont. Athletic Commission meet records; Kent County pole vault mark 11'8" '29; 15 ntl interscholastic medals while setting 4 records; javelin silver '30 ntl championships; 4th javelin '30 BEG; shared all-around title

Canadian Legion meet Cornwall and tied '32 Olympic gold medalist Duncan McNaughton in high jump '30; 53 T&f medals, 30 silver cups and John McMartin Memorial Cup, 2 WOSSA sr. title shields, 2 Kennedy CI trophies and wide array of ribbons; defence '30-31 OHA finalist Chatham Maroons.

CRUTCHFIELD, Linda (skiing/water-skiing/luge); b. 3 Apr 1942, Shawinigan, Que.; div. Robert Bocock; Sir George Williams, Burke Mountain Academy; ski school director; winner by 11 seconds 1st major ski race Mt. Tremblant Taschereau; invited by Vic Emery '67 to test luge (one-man toboggan), made 4 runs, won ntl title; 10th '68 Olympics; mem. ntl teams in skiing, luge, water skiing; ntl alpine team '60-65, including '64 Olympics; 14 water ski titles, several jump records; 1st Cdn woman to clear 100' water ski jump; mem. 4 world water ski championships teams; ski school, water ski school dir.; twice ntl alpine, luge, once NA luge champion; John Semmelink Memorial Trophy '64; twice Velma Springstead Trophy; mem. Cdn Skiing, Quebec Sports halls of fame; res. St. Sauveur des Monts, Que.

CULLEN, Ronald (coaching); b. 19 Oct 1915, Toronto, Ont.; priest, educator; coached football, hockey, baseball at Windsor Assumption HS for more than 40 years producing numerous athletes who advanced to NHL, NFL, CFL and major league baseball ranks; mem. Windsor/Essex County Sports Hall of Fame; res. Windsor, Ont.

CULVER, Diane (skiing); b. 14 Sep 1952, Montreal, Que.; given name: Diane Mary; m. William John Grey; McGill; ski coach, examiner; Pontiac Cup '69; mem. ntl alpine team '70 world championships, World Cup team '70-72; 8th GS WC final '70; coached women's Can-Am ski team '75-76; instructor Mt. Tremblant, examiner for Canadian Ski Instructor's Alliance; only female selected on 10-member Canadian demonstration ski team Inter-Ski (International reunion of ski schools) Italy '83; res. New Zealand.

CUMMING, George (golf); b. 20 May 1879, Bridge of Weir, Scotland; d. 26 Mar 1950, Toronto, Ont.; golf pro; rose from caddy ranks to pro Dumfries GC; migrated to Canada 1900; pro Toronto GC 50yrs; Cdn Open title '05, 4 times runnerup; tied lowest 18-holes, 8th place '05 US Open; CPGA title '14, 3 times runnerup; pioneered CPGA organization, initial capt., 4yrs v.-capt., 6yrs capt. CPGA; considered Dean of Canadian golf pros; mem. RCGA Hall of Fame.

CUMMINGS, Bruce (football); b. 26 Mar 1927, Ottawa, Ont.; d. 16 Jun 1991, Ottawa, Ont.; given name: Bruce Fredrick; m. Mary Gardner; c. Lynn, David (d); UofT, BSc; engineer; Varsity Blues '47-49; Johnny Copp Memorial Trophy Uof T '47; pro Ottawa '50-53; EFC all-star '51; Ottawa MVP, Hiram Walker Trophy winner '50; EFC Jeff Russel Memorial Trophy winner '51.

CUMMINGS, Dave (wrestling); b. 24 Sep 1948, Ottawa, Ont.; d. 30 Apr 1985, Calgary, Alta; given name: David Harold; m. Susanne Ferrier; construction equipment operator; ntl freestyle titles '73-74, Greco-Roman '69, '74; mem. '74 world championships, '75 Pan-Am, '76 Olympic

Games teams; asst. coach ntl GR team '76 European tour, Olympic Games; coach UCal wrestling club '77-81; killed in ultra-light aircraft accident.

CUNNEYWORTH, Randy (hockey); b. 10 May 1961, Etobicoke, Ont.; given name: Randy William; m. Marie; c. Jenny, Gregory, Cameron; left wing Ottawa 67's (OHL) '79-81; Rochester (AHL) '80-85, Springfield '91; claimed by Buffalo '80 entry draft; played in NHL with Buffalo '80-81, '98, Pittsburgh '85-89, Winnipeg '89, Hartford '90-94, Chicago '94, Ottawa '94-98; NHL record (through '99) 866 scheduled games, 189g, 225a, 45 playoff games, 7g, 7a; mem. Calder Cup winner Rochester '81; capt. Ottawa '96-98; player/coach Rochester '98-99; res. Pittsford, N.Y.

CUNNINGHAM, Cathy (curling); b. 30 Dec 1959, St. John's, Nfld.; m. Geoffrey Wade; c. Jenny, Jessica; mgr.; began curling age 11; 2 Nfld mixed, 7 Nfld women's title rinks; res. St. John's, Nfld.

CUNNINGHAM, Jake (curling); b. 5 Jul 1960, St. John's, Nfld.; given name: Geoffrey Wade; m. Cathy; c. Jenny, Jessica; financial consultant; 3rd '78, skip '79 Nfld. ntl jr. men's; 3rd for Jeff Thomas '84-85 Briers, 5th man '99 Brier; res. St. John's, Nfld.

CUNNINGHAM, Keith (shooting); b. 11 Feb 1950, London, Ont.; given name: Keith Allan; div. Arlene Clancy; c. Jason Wesley, Jesse Robert; Colorado School of Trades; retd. Cdn Forces infantry officer, Chief Operations Officer MilCun Marksmanship Complex; served in US Army '70-72, Cdn Army '75-95; began shooting competitively age 20; mem. 8 Cdn Forces Bisley teams; 11 ntl Bisley teams; 7 combined service/target rifle titles; 8 Cdn Forces target rifle, 5 Ont sniper rifle, 5 Ont sniper pairs, 3 Ont service rifle titles; 1 ntl sniper rifle, 3 ntl sniper rifle pairs titles; Ont. Lt. Governors silver '97; 2 Palma, 8 Commonwealth teams; 2 Des Burke awards; team silver '92 Palma; mem. '94 Commonwealth Games team; coached 4 Cdn Forces Bisley teams, 6 individuals to Queen's medal; Level 3 ntl coach; mem. Cdn Forces Sports Hall of Fame; res. Burnt River, Ont.

CURRAN, Randy (baseball); b. 23 Feb 1967, Kitchener, Ont.; Miami Dade Jr. College; city employee; mem. Kitchener jr. Dodgers; Cdn Olympic team '88; rejected Montreal Expos offers '87; pro ball in Verona, Italy '92-94; mem. Kitchener Panthers Sr. Intercounty team '84-91, from '95; IC rookie of '85, MVP '93, '96, Commissioner's Tophy '96; 1 1st team, 3 2nd team all-star 1B selections; set IC single season HR record 17 '93; 3 league HR, 2 total bases, 2 RBI, 2 runs scored, 1 walks titles; all-time IC HR leader with 85 (through '96); also through '96 260 lifetime RBI, 334 hits, 57 doubles; brother Kevin standout IC LHP with Kitchener; res. Kitchener, Ont.

CURRIE, Andy (football); b. 5 Jun 1911, Brandon, Man.; d. 14 Aug 1990, Winnipeg, Man.; m. Thelma Wright; c. David, Roger; UMan, BA; deputy minister; coached HS, UMan., Regina Pats; refereed 15yrs Winnipeg area; at 17 Sask. Roughriders '28 Grey Cup, week later helped Pats win ntl jr. title; UM '29, '31, Roughriders '28, '30, St.John's Srs '32, Winnipeg football club '33; PE dir. for Winnipeg schools '51; provincial dir. PE & R '57; dir. P & R greater

Winnipeg '61; 20yrs WIFU official, 14yrs supervisor of officials; mem. Canadian Football Hall of Fame.

CURRIE, Gordon (coaching); b. 20 May 1923, Seamans, Sask.; m. Shirley Clarke; c. Bob, Doug, Jim; Notre Dame College, BA, Mt. Allison, BEd; retd. politician; served as Minister of Science & Technology, Telephones, Education & Manpower '82-86; coached Balfour Tech to 8 prov. football, 6 in succession, 3 prov. hockey crowns; 4 Regina Red Sox baseball title teams; coached Regina Rams '65-76 winning 108 of 135 games, 6 ntl, 8 Man.-Sask., 7 Western Jr., 1 Alta. Jr. league titles; ntl amateur coach of '75; CFL, CAFA service to the game awards; mem. Order of Canada, Sask. Sports Hall of Fame; res. Regina, Sask.

CURRIER, Doug (bobsled); b. 25 Aug 1967, Brockville, Ont.; nationally ranked shotputter who switched to bobsleds '89 and became ntl team mem. in rookie year; with Chris Lori, John Graham, Ken Leblanc won 2 ntl 4 man titles, 2 World Cup 4 man races, both at Calgary; finished 1st in world rankings '90, 3rd 4 man, 2 man (with Lori) '91; competed '92 Olympics; res. Prescott, Ont.

CURRY, Floyd (hockey); b. 11 Aug 1925, Chapleau, Ont.; given name: Floyd James; m. June Howie; c. Dawn, Candice; hockey exec.; jr. Oshawa Generals '41-43; '43 Memorial Cup; 2 seasons Montreal Royals (QSHL); mem. '46-47 Alexander Trophy (Allan Cup) champions; pro Buffalo (AHL), Canadiens '47-58; NHL record: 601 scheduled games, 105g, 99a, 91 playoff games, 23g, 17a; mem. 4 Stanley Cup winners; honored by fans with "night" '57; 5 times all-star; playing-coach Montreal Royals (QSHL) '58-59, EPHL coach '59-61, Que. Aces (AHL) '61-64; dir. advertising sales Canadiens from '65; nicknamed "Busher"; res. Montreal, Que.

CURTIS, Crystal (horseshoes); b. 27 Oct 1978, Blairmore, Alta.; nursing assistant Crowsnest Pass health centre; began pitching horseshoes age 9; 4 Alta. jr. girls titles; 6 ntl jr. girls titles; 2 ntl jr. girls records; world jr. girls champion '93; Alta. player of '93; res. Bellevue, Alta.

CURTIS, Ulysses (football); b. 10 May 1926, Albion, Mich.; m. Katherine; c. Carol, Sylvia, Warren; Florida A&M, BA, BPHE, McMaster; HS teacher; Negro all-American '48-49; pro Toronto '50-54; 3 times Argos scoring leader; single season TD record 16 in 12 games '52; 235 CFL points in 5 seasons, 47 TDs; mem. 2 Grey Cup winners; twice EFC all-star; nicknamed "Crazy Legs"; coached 3 Eastern Cdn Toronto jr. title teams; 3yrs backfield coach York U; 5yrs teacher-counsellor, program co-ordinator Ont. Athletic Leadership Camp; last known res. Willowdale, Ont.

CUSTIS, Bernie (football); b. 23 Sep 1929, Philadelphia, Pa.; given name: Bernard Eugene; m. Lorraine DeFoe; Syracuse, BEd, Niagara, MEd; educator; football, baseball on Syracuse scholarship; drafted as quarterback by Cleveland Browns; QB, halfback Hamilton '51-54, Ottawa '55; coach Oakville Black Knights (ORFU) 6yrs; Burlington jrs 8yrs, 3 ntl finals; Sheridan Community College '71-80; McMaster from '81; CIAU coach of '82; scout Argos '89-96; scout/player personnel dir. Hamilton '97; mem. Canadian Football Hall of Fame; res. Burlington, Ont.

CUTHBERT, Linda (diving); b. 20 May 1956, Toronto, Ont.; given name: Linda Joanne; m. Andrej Markes; c. Sonia, Jamie; George Brown College; sports marketing, communication; mem. ntl team '73-80; 4 ntl titles, '77 Canada Cup, overall '79 Canada Cup, springboard '77 European invitational; Commonwealth Games gold, 2 Pan-Am Games bronze, silver jr worlds; mem. '74, '78 Commonwealth, '75, '79 Pan-Am, '80 Olympic teams; suffered serious concussion striking head on board during '80 Olympic trials but recovered to close career with tour of Orient '80; pres. CADA Ont.; '92 Olympics TV commentator; FINA international A judge; mem. Cdn Aquatic Hall of Fame; res. Toronto, Ont.

CUTLER, Dave (football); b. 17 Oct 1945, Biggar, Sask.; given name: David Robert Stuart; m. Barbara Justice; c. Rob, John, Scott; SFU; radio time salesman; NAIA Dist. 1 all-star, hon. mention Little all-American linebacker; 2 team inspiration awards; NFL trial with Green Bay; Edmonton (CFL) '69-84; place kicker; 8 WFC, 7 CFL scoring titles; set CFL single season records (since surpassed) for scoring, most converts, field goals; runnerup '73 Schenley outstanding Canadian; surpassed George Blanda's 2002 all-time pro points record (since topped by Lui Passaglia); CFL record: 16 seasons, 254 scheduled games, 627 of attempted record 650 converts, 464 of attempted record 790 field goals, 218 singles, 2237 points; played record 253 consecutive games; 9 Grey Cup finals, 6 winners, including 5 in succession; mem. Eskimos Wall of Honor, Cdn Football Hall of Fame; res. Ardrossan, Alta.

CUTLER, Wes (football); b. 17 Feb 1911, Toronto, Ont.; d. 10 Jun 1956, Toronto, Ont.; UofT; standout end, tackler, blocker, exceptional receiver who starred with UofT '31-32, Argos '33-38; mem. 3 Grey Cup winners; CP all-star '33-38; Jeff Russel Memorial Trophy '38; Varsity Bronze T; mem. Cdn Football, Canada's Sports halls of fame.

CUTRONE, Angela (speed skating); b. 19 Jan 1969, St. Léonard, Que.; U Montreal; began skating at 11; switched from figure to speed skating; short track specialist; ntl team from '88; 3 ntl, 2 world. 1 NA, 1 Ottawa short track titles; mem. 3000m short track relay team '92 Olympic record, gold; 3 world records; world short track team gold '91, '94, 3000m relay gold '91, '92, '93; res. St. Léonard, Que.

CUTTING, Flo (bowling); b. 26 Dec 1904, Toronto, Ont.; m. Percy Cutting (d); business college; mem. Toronto playground softball, basketball, t&ftitle teams early '20s; mem. Lakeside-Olympia Ont. softball title team; league secty-treas. 12yrs; began bowling 1930; initial pres. Toronto Ladies' Major League '37; charter mem., secty. CBA; secty at inception of union between Ont.-Western Cdn. bowlers and launching of Cdn 5-pin championships '53; secty. Second Mile Srs. league 10yrs; only Easterner made hon. life mem. WCBA; life mem. OBA, CBA; 2 Ont. achievement awards; mem. Ontario Bowling Hall of Fame; res. East York, Ont.

CYNCAR, Marco (football); b. 13 Apr 1958, Edmonton, Alta.; UAlta.; pro football player; played HS, minor football in Edmonton; jr with Edmonton Wildcats; Edmonton territorial exemption; turned pro Eskimos then dealt to

Hamilton '80; reacquired by Edmonton '81; slotback Eskimos '81-90; CFL record: 177 games, 276 receptions, 4167yds, 10tds; 6 Grey Cup finals, 3 winners; res. Edmonton, Alta.

CYR, Alain (judo); b. 21 Sep 1955, Quebec City, Que.; construction inspector; bronze '74 jr. worlds; 4 Que., 4 ntl, 2 Eastern Cdn, 2 Que. Cup, 1 Canada Cup, 1 NY, Que., Dutch Open titles; placed in top 8 '81 world championships, top 6 '83 Pan-Am Games; mem. '80 Olympic team; res. Montreal, Que.

CYR, Louis (weightlifting); b. 1863, St. Cyprien de Napierville, Que.; d. 1912, St. Jean de Matha, Que.; m. Melina; legend that at 17 he pulled loaded wagon from mud by lifting it on his back and decided to become travelling strongman; challenged David Michaud, Canada's strongest of the period, to rock lifting contest; Cyr won lifting 480lb boulder; at 22 joined Montreal Police Force but retired when attacked on beat with an axe; signed by promoter Richard Fox and billed as world's strongest man; accepted all challenges and never lost; toured Europe 23 months becoming household name in Western world; tour highlight 1889 London's Royal Aquarium Theatre when he lifted a 551lb weight with one finger, 4100lbs on platform stretched across his back, 237.25lbs with one hand to shoulder level then above head and with one hand raised 314lb barrel of cement to shoulder; Marquis of Queensbury (father of modern boxing rules) offered him horse if he could hold pair of horses tied to his arms to a standstill, Cyr won horse; most astounding feat 1895 in Boston when he lifted 18 fat men on plank on his back in what is claimed to be the greatest lift ever made by man, 4337lbs; died at 49 of Bright's disease; mem. Canada's Sports Hall of Fame.

CZAJA, Mitch (basketball/curling); b. 4 Aug 1935, Winnipeg, Man.; given name: Mitchell Peter; m. Mary Gail Langdon; c. Clinton, Aaron, Ainsley; UMan; mechanical engineer; provincial schoolboy curling champion; lost ntl title to Bayne Secord on last rock; curled with Norm Houck, Bruce Hudson, reached Man. Consols. lost '56 finals; 2nd Ken Buchan's Ont. Brier entry '69; 4 times Ont. Consols competitor; mem. Ont. Tankard winner, '93 Ont. Srs champs; HS basketball '51-52, ntl jr. finals Winnipeg Light Infantry team '53; sr. Winnipeg Kodiaks, lost '57 ntl final to Montreal; mem. Tillsonburg Livingstons '60; mem. '59 Pan-Am Games team; Ont. Masters title teams '80-81; res. London, Ont.

CZICH, John (badminton); b. 17 Jan 1953, Renfrew, Ont.; given name: John Mironko; m. Daniele Gallichand; c. Emilie, Marie Chantale; Royal Military College; retd. Canadian Forces air engineering officer, computer firm official; RMC light-heavyweight boxing title; Ont. jr. badminton singles '72; finalist national men's closed '76; Boulevard Club doubles '77, singles '80; gold men's doubles '77 Pan-Am championships; mem. '78 silver medal Commonwealth Games team; '78 Scotland Open men's singles, doubles, silver Eastern, Western singles; mem. '79 Thomas Cup, '80 Devlin Cup teams; '80 Pepsi-Cola series singles; retd from competition '83; ntl team coach from '90; RMC outstanding athlete award; mem. Cdn Forces, Ottawa CSRA Sports halls of fame; res. Nepean, Ont.

D'AMICO, John (officiating/hockey); b. 21 Sep 1937, Toronto, Ont.; given name: John David; m. Dorothy Gordon; c. Anthony, Jeffrey, Tina, Angelo; hockey exec.; made NHL officiating debut '64; mostly as linesman but did some refereeing; worked more than 1700 scheduled games, more than 250 playoff games in career which extended through '88; worked more than 20 Stanley Cup finals, 7 all-star games; officiated 4 Canada Cup, '79 Challenge Cup, '87 Rendez-Vous series; NHL officiating coach since retirement; mem. Hockey Hall of Fame; res. Mississauga, Ont.

D'AMOUR, Frenchy (curling); b. 10 Oct 1912, Rossland, B.C.; given name: Theophile; m. Neathlea (Nettie) Templeton; retired; skip runnerup '47 Brier; skip '48 Brier winner; 2nd for Reg Stone '62 Brier; skip '49 winner, '50 finalist Edmonton carspiel; hon. life mem. Trail Curling Club; '48 Brier champs inducted into BC Sports Hall of Fame; res. Trail B.C.

D'AMOUR, Léo (shooting); b. 27 Jul 1929, Rigaud, Que.; m. Monique Bastien; c. Danielle, Lyette, Paul, Jean, Louise; Loyalist Coll.; retd. Cdn Forces, Rolls Royce Can.; mem. 8 Cdn Bisley teams; 2 ntl teams to Australia, 1 Palma team, 1 Ont. Goodwill Bisley team, 1 BC California long range championship team; Lt. Gov. medals Que., NB; won varied Ont., Que., Maritime match titles; Atlantic champion; DCRA grand aggregate title '78; served various exec. roles in DCRA, including pres.; in youth enjoyed tennis success; res. Laval, Que.

DACYSHYN, Anna (diving); b. 10 Jul 1969, Edmonton, Alta.; UofT, BSc; switched from gymnastics to diving age 12; mem. ntl team from '86; 10m gold '88, '90 Winter Ntls, '89 Summer Ntls, Commonwealth trials, '90 Commonwealth Games, '88, '89 University Cup, Mastercard trials, '88 Pan Am Invitational, '90 world trials; semifinalist 10m '89 Fina World Cup; 10m silver '89, 91 Winter Ntls, '89 Vienna Volksbank Intl; res. Toronto, Ont.

DAFOE, Frances (figure skating); b. 17 Dec 1929, Toronto, Ont.; div. Norman Melnick; c. Blake, Adrian; m. Paul Bogin; NYC Parsons School of Design; costume designer CBC-TV, freelance theatrical, dance, film designer; with Norris Bowden ntl pairs titles '52-55, dance title '52, NA pairs '53-56, world pairs '54-55; mem. '52, '56 Olympic teams; silver '56 Olympics; international, world, Olympic FS judge; mem. Order of Canada, Cdn Amateur, Cdn, US Figure Skating, Cdn Winter Olympic, Canada's Sports halls of fame; res. Jupiter, Fla./Toronto, Ont.

DAHLSTROM, Clint (shooting); b. 30 Jul 1925, Saskatchewan; m. Phyllis (d), Patricia Page; c. Bruce, Susan, stepchild Jane; UofSask, MSc, Princeton, PhD; retd geologist; began competitive smallbore rifles career Calgary '54; bronze free rifle, team silver '63 Pan-Am Games; set US smallbore prone record 400 '76; mem. ntl smallbore team '66-78; competed '62 worlds; in fullbore competition mem. 14 Cdn Bisley, 5 Cdn Palma teams; Canada Winter Games team gold; ntl air rifle, 4 ntl gallery rifle, ranked high master in US, Canada; winner numerous club, provincial awards; proficient with crossbow; commissioner Olympic Rifle Club, coach Bisley, Commonwealth Games teams; Lt. Governor awards Sask., BC; res. Victoria, B.C./Sun City West, Ariz.

DAHLSTROM, Patricia (shooting); b. 11 Jul 1931, England; given name: Patricia Page; m. Clinton Dahlstrom; c. Jane, stepchildren Bruce, Susan; retd speech therapist; emigrated to Canada '56; began smallbore shooting Calgary '60; ntl women's sporting rifle title '65; began fullbore shooting '80; mem. Cdn Goodwill team to Australia '88; mem. Ont. Bisley team '94; 1st Cdn woman to reach Bisley Queen's Prize final; adjutant '95 Cdn Bisley team; qualified/ competed '96-97 Bisley teams; mem. '96 Cdn Palma team; Tess Spencer award, Women's pairs title '97 DCRA shoot; avid tennis player; res. Victoria, B.C./Sun City West, Ariz.

DAIGLE, Alexandre (hockey); b. 7 Feb 1975, Montreal, Que.; centre Victoriaville (QMJHL) '91-94; twice QMJHL all-star; CMJHL rookie of '92; 1st Ottawa draft pick '93; signed by Senators for headline-grabbing $12.3M; through '96-97 season had failed to live up to expectations; noted for speed but definite under-achiever; Viscount Alexander award '93; traded to Philadelphia '98, Tampa '99, NY Rangers '99, Hartford (AHL) '99; NHL record (through '99): 401 scheduled games, 92g, 123a, 12 playoff games, 0g, 1a; res. Montreal, Que.

DAIGLE, Nora (boxing); b. 18 Nov 1961, Richibucto Village, N.B.; given name: Nora Marie-Louise; NB Community College, civil engineering technologist dip.; tech. support officer fed. public works; whetted athletic appetite with hockey, broomball, softball in youth then began kickboxing age 23; won NA featherweight, super featherweight titles; turned attention solely to boxing age 32 achieving #2 world ranking by Women's International Boxing Federation; pro record through '97 3-1-1; has competed in such venues as Caesar's Palace, Trump Taj Mahal (Atlantic City), Montreal Forum, Montreal Molson Centre; suffered severe beating in world lightweight title loss to Tracy Boyd of Flint, Mich., '97; res. Ottawa, Ont./ Quebec City, Que.

DAIGLE, Sylvie (speed skating); b. 1 Dec 1962, Sherbrooke, Que.; U Montreal; intending to play hockey she arrived at arena when speed skating was in session and she got hooked at age 9; mem. ntl team from '80; 10 ntl, 2 NA, 3 Canada Games, 7 world titles; world records 3000m (5:32.31), 1000m (1:43.66), 500m (49.54) '83, short track 500m (46.72), 2 Cdn short track records; mem. '80, '84, '88, '92, '94 Olympic teams; gold 1500m, silver 3000m, 1000m '88 Olympics; gold 3000m relay '92 Olympics; world short track gold '83-84, '88-90; Thompson Trophy fastest Cdn 500m '81; 2 Elaine Tanner, 1 Velma Springstead trophies; Que. Sports Institute skater of '79; French Cdn athlete of year (Eugene Lavoix award) '83; fed. govt. world champion awards '83, '89; Thompson Tophy for fastest Cdn 500m '81; CASSA female short track athlete of year '88-89, '91; flag-bearer '92 winter Olympics; mem. Que. women's hockey team; mem. Cdn Amateur, Que. Sports, Cdn Speed Skating halls of fame; res. Outremont, Que.

DAIGNAULT, Michel (speed skating); b. 25 Jun 1966, Montreal, Que.; U Quebec (Montreal); began speed skating at 12; mem. ntl team '84-94; mem. '88, '92 Olympic teams; 2 silver, 2 bronze Olympic short track medals; 5 world short track gold; '85 FISU Games gold; set world record 2:25.25 '88 Olympic 1500m; 4 Cdn senior records; 4 NA championships; Que. athlete of year '89; CASSA male athlete of year '88-89;sport excellence award '85; world champion award '87; brother Laurent also ntl team mem.; mem. Cdn Speed Skating Hall of Fame; res. Montreal, Que.

DAIGNEAULT, Doug (football); b. 4 Aug 1936, Montreal, Que.; given name: Douglas John; m. Jane DeCoste; c. Betsy, Debbie, Lois, Vickie, Julie; Franklin Academy, Clemson, BSc; salesman; former associate athletic dir., basketball coach Concordia; all-state, hon, mention all-American football, basketball sr. year Franklin; mem. league champion baseball, basketball, football teams; leading scorer freshman basketball Clemson; mem. Orange, Sugar, Bluebonnet Bowl teams; coach basketball South Carolina Textile League; mem. Ottawa (CFL) '60-64, '60 Grey Cup champions, Montreal '64-66; coach Concordia basketball 328 wins, including 66 consecutive league games, 178 losses, 9 league titles, participated 7 ntl championships; football coach '71-75, '72 league title; res. Chateauguay, Que.

DAIGNEAULT, Julie (swimming); b. 25 Jun 1965, Montreal, Que.; freestyle specialist; 10 ntl titles, 1 Canada Cup title; mem. '82 Commonwealth, '83 FISU, Pan-Am, '84 Olympic Games teams; bronze 400, 800m FISU, 200, 400, 800m Pan-Am Games; 3 ntl records; res. Pierrefonds, Que.

DAIGNEAULT, Réjean (harness racing); b. 19 Feb 1948, St. Damase, Que.; harness race driver; began career as groom for Hervé Filion at 16; went on his own after 7yrs; began driving 1973; noted for patented rocking style in sulky; best season '86 when he won 312 races including his 2000th victory; through '95 3632 victories and purses in excess of $28M; res. Yonkers, N.Y.

DAINES, Duane (rodeo); b. 15 Oct 1958, Innisfail, Alta; m. Cheryl; c. Jennifer, Bailey, Sydney; auctioneer; specialized in saddle bronc/calf roping; mem. CPRA from '79; 3 ntl all-around (AA) titles; 1 ntl SB title; 2 Copenhagen/ Dodge tour SB titles; 1 Coors Chute-Out series SB title; 1 Calgary Stampede SB title; 2 Brahma Boot tour SB titles; 1 Sask., BC circuit SB titles; 1 Wrangler Jeans Rodeo Showdown SB title; 1 BC/Sask. circuit AA titles; CPRA cowboy of '95 award; paralyzed in Armstrong, BC rodeo accident '95; dir. CPRA; res. Innisfail, Alta.

DALEY, Gail (gymnastics); b. 5 Apr 1946, Saskatoon, Sask.; m. Richard Bakker; c. Brian, Kerri; Southern Illinois, BSc, Montclair State MA, Kean Coll MA; speech language pathologist; spotted by coaches Mike Matich, Chuck Sebestyen during tumbling demonstration age 11 and introduced to gymnastics program; Sask. jr title '59; Alta., Western Canada jr titles '60-61; mem. Cdn World Games team; 4 ntl sr. titles; mem. '63 (team silver, 2 individual bronze) Pan-Am Games, '64 Olympic Games teams; moved to US winning several collegiate titles, 3 all-American honors; turned to coaching, officiating; coached Rutgers, Montclair State; officiated 2 International Special Olympics; volunteer Calgary '88 Olympics; Cdn female athlete of '64; Fed. of International Gymnastics pin; mem. Sask., Saskatoon Sports halls of fame; res. Washington, N.J.

DALEY, Jim (coaching); b. 15 Jul 1954, Ottawa, Ont.; m. Diane Hilko; Carleton, BA, Queen's, BEd; ex-football coach; def. end Ottawa Sooners '70-73, capt. '73 ntl finalists; linebacker Queen's '74-75; level 4 coaching cert.; began coaching St. Pat's HS Ottawa '76, asst. Carleton '79-81, St. Pius HS '78-82; head coach Ottawa Sooners '82-84; UofOtt '85-90; asst. Ottawa (CFL) '91-93, Saskatchewan '94-95. head coach '96-98; CFL coaching record 18-36; led Sooners to '84 ntl jr title; 2 OFC coach of yr, North East Regional Assn. coach of '84; 2 OQIFC coach of yr awards; res. Regina, Sask.

DALLA RIVA, Peter (football); b. 11 Dec 1945, Fanzolo, Treviso, Italy; m. Carol; c. Mark, Lisa; ambassador Molson-O'Keefe; emigrated to Canada age 8; jr. Burlington Braves; sr. ORFU Oakville Knights; entire CFL career as tight-end Montreal '68-81; 3 all-East, 3 all-Cdn tight end; twice nominee Outstanding Cdn, 1 Outstanding player nomination; Alouettes' leading receiver 5yrs; CFL record: 197 games, 450 receptions, 6413yds, 54tds, 340pts; all-star game MVP '73; 6 Grey Cup finals, 3 winners; jersey 74 retd by Alouettes; mem. Cdn Football Hall of Fame; res. Beaconsfield, Que.

DALTON, Chuck (basketball); b. 1 Sep 1927, Windsor, Ont.; given name: Charles Harwood; m. Marcia Lawton; c. Karen Ann, Charles Scott; UWO; sales manager, real estate; outfielder London Majors Sr. IC 3yrs, St. Thomas (IC), Frood (NO) 1yr each; basketball UWO, 2yrs Tillsonburg Livingstons; mem. '52 Olympic team; knee injury ended playing career; coach London Intermediates 1 season; pres. London Curling Club; res. London, Ont.

DAMPHOUSSE, Vincent (hockey); b. 17 Dec 1967, Montreal, Que.; centre Laval (QMJHL) '83-86; 2nd team all-star; played in '84 Memorial Cup; NHL Toronto '86-91, Edmonton '91-92, Montreal '92-99, San Jose '99; played briefly in Germany '94-95; capt. Canadiens; played in 2 NHL all-star games; mem. '93 Stanley Cup winner; NHL record: (through '99) 1005 scheduled games, 347g, 582a, 93 playoff games, 29g, 42a; scored 1st Molson Centre goal; mem. Team Canada '96 World Cup; res. Blainville, Que.

DANIAR, Stephen (wrestling); b. 18 Jul 1955, Ft. William, Ont.; m. Leslie Bell; Laurentian, Lakehead, BEd, MEd; educator; 1 ntl jr., 5 sr. titles; mem. '76, '80 Olympic, '77-78 World Cup teams; gold 197lbs '78 Commonwealth, bronze '79 Pan-Am, '77, '79 Cerra Pelado Cups, '78 World Cup; mem. '78 Mexico world championships team; 4 Thunder Bay achievement awards; most valuable NWO wrestler '78; Thunder Bay male athlete of '79; mem. '81 Northwestern Ont. indoor soccer title team; coached

Lakehead wrestlers '82-85, teams won 4 GPAC titles; named jr. coach of '82, GPAC coach of year '84-85; came out of retirement to win Commonwealth Wrestling Championship gold '85; mem. NWO Sports, Cdn Amateur Wrestling halls, Lakehead U Sports Wall of Fame; res. Thunder Bay, Ont.

DANIEL, Babe (basketball); b. 30 May 1917, Camrose, Alta.; d. 4 Oct 1995, Edmonton, Alta.given name: Muriel; m. George Lineham (d); c. Susan, Marilyn; retired hospital supervisor; competitive golfer, bowler, softball player; mem. famed Edmonton Grads basketball team '37-39; mem. Canadian Basketball, Alta. Sports halls of fame.

DANIELS, Danny (t&f/builder): b. 11 Jan 1929, Greater Yarmouth, Norfolk, Eng.; given name: Edwin Robert; m. Marjorie Joyce Gillings; c. Kristi Jane, Kent Jonathan; UAlta, BEd, PhD; consultant/actor; running specialist; '45-51 won varied UK jr/sr titles 440yds-mile distances; moved to Canada winning variety of road running/race walking/LJ/HJ/pentathlon titles at regional/ntl/world levels; 12 ntl, 4 NA, 1 Pan-American masters titles; Level 3 NCCP coach; Nigerian ntl distance program head coach '73-75; Team Yukon head coach '89-90; meet dir. Pan-Am, NA, Cdn, US International t&f meets; ntl Run Canada comm. '79-96; pres. Cdn Masters Athletic Assn '83-85; pres. Athletics Yukon '86-90; v-p. BC Athletics '95-96, pres. '97-98, BC Seniors Games Society from '96; curator Cdn Road Running Hall of Fame '91-96; 3M coaching award '96; Edinburgh Harriers Outstanding Athlete award '48; mem. Cdn Road Running Hall of Fame; res. Sidney, B.C./Green Valley, Ariz.

DANN, Etta (basketball): b. 9 Mar 1914, Edmonton, Alta.; d. 1978 High River, Alta.; m. Leland Sodererg; c. Eddie, retd. secretary; standout softball player; mem. famed Edmonton Grads women's basketball team; mem. Alta. Sports, Cdn Basketball halls of fame.

DANYCHUK, Bill (football); b. 29 Aug 1940, Timmins, Ont.; given name: William D'Arcy; m. Audrey Ann Dawdy; c. Maria Deanna, William Clayton; Tenn, BA; pres. D'Arcy Enterprises, v-p. Bazaar & Novelty Co.; all-star basketball, football, track, MVP basketball, football Niagara Dist. HS; offensive guard Tennessee '62-64; mem. Tiger-Cats '65-75; 10 times all-star; Ticat MVP '68; mem. Hamilton best team of century; v.-pres. CFL Players' Assn. 7yrs; dir. World Bingo League; mem. Ukranian Sports Hall of Fame; res. Oakville, Ont.

DANYLUK, Terry (volleyball/coaching); b. 1960, Tofield, Alta.; m. Lori; UAlta. volleyball coach; setter ntl team '78, '81-84, UAlta '78-81; competed '82 Worlds, '84 Olympics; mem. UAlta CIAU title team '81; pro Japan's Suntory Club, Japan Cup title '85; Mulhouse, France '86; Leysin, Switzerland '88-91, 4 Swiss Cup titles; 4 Swiss, 1 Japan, 2 CIAU player of yr awards; 1 CIAU, ntl tournament MVP awards; '81 CIAU all-Canadian, UAlta outstanding male athlete of yr awards; began coaching career UAlta '91, CIAU coach of '97; mem. UAlta Sports Wall of Fame; res. Edmonton, Alta.

DARCH, Art (football): b. 15 Oct 1931, Niagara Falls, Ont.; given name: Arthur Clifford; m. Joyce Sharp; c. Kelly, Jay, Shannon, Darcy; insurance co. pres.; standout HS football, basketball, track; athlete of year awards '51-52; rejected Mich track scholarship for pro football Hamilton; 1st string offensive guard '52-58, missed '59 with injury, Toronto '60-62; mem. 4 Grey Cup finalists, 2 winners; Dominion HS t&f titles '50-51; Ont. jr. shot put, discus, OFSSA discus titles '51; pres. Tiger-Cats QB Club '66-72; freelance radio-TV sportscaster from '63; res. Burlington, Ont.

DARLING, Dora (golf); b. 11 Aug 1904, Montreal, Que.; d. 19 Nov 1997, London, Ont.; given name: Dora Jean Virtue; m. Arthur Balfour Darling (d); c. Judy, Mary, Brian; women's Canadian Open, runnerup Closed '36; 3 Quebec women's, 3 ntl sr. women's titles.

DARLING, Judy (golf); b. 6 Oct 1937, Montreal, Que.; given name: Judith Kathleen; div. John Douglas Evans; c. Kathy, Cindy, Tracey, Daphne; McGill, BSc; nurse; Quebec Ladies titles '57-61, '72; ntl jr. '57; ntl women's closed '60; ntl women's open '60-61; res. Boca Raton, Fla.

DARRAGH, Jack (hockey); b. 4 Dec 1890, Ottawa, Ont.; d. 28 Jun 1924, Ottawa, Ont.; given name: John Proctor; m. Elizabeth; c. Aileen, Frances, Marion; accountant, poultry breeder; amateur Fort Coulonge, Ottawa Cliffsides; pro Ottawa '11 Stanley Cup champions; mem. Super Six, capt. several Ottawa teams; mem. 4 Stanley Cup winners; on line with Frank Nighbor, Cy Denneny; shifted to left wing when Punch Broadbent joined line; career total 195 goals including 24 in one 22-game season; mem. Ottawa Sports, Canadian Hockey halls of fame.

DARWIN, Howard (entrepreneur); b. 10 Sep 1931, Ottawa, Ont.; given name: Howard Joseph; m. Constance Goudie; c. Kim, Nancy, Jack, Jeff; retd. jeweller; 30-35 amateur bouts Beaver Boxing Club; switched to refereeing, promoting fights, managing fighters; promotions included wrestling, closed circuit TV boxing matches; invested in jr. A hockey with formation Ottawa 67's, part-owner; purchased London Gardens, London Jr. A hockey team; remained in hockey through '98; brought Triple A baseball Lynx to Ottawa '93; IL exec. of '95; 1 Memorial Cup, 1 IL championship team; Ottawa ACT Earl Bullis Achievement award '98; ex-trustee Ottawa Sports Hall of Fame; mem. Ottawa Sports Hall of Fame; res. Ottawa, Ont.

DASOVIC, Nick (soccer); b. 5 Dec 1968, Vancouver B.C.; midfielder who honed skills in Vancouver minor program; 2ys North York (CSL); '92 CSL all-star; mem. APSL Montreal Impact title team '94; played with Saint-Brieuc (France) '95, FC Treleborgs (Sweden) '96, Vancouver 86ers '96, St. Johnston Scottish 1st div. '96-98, Scottish League finalists '98; made ntl team debut '92; 32 international caps; res. Vancouver, B.C./Perth, Scotland.

DATTILIO, Gerry (football); b. 11 Jun 1953, Chomedy, Que.; Northern Colorado; Verdun jrs.; coll. career record more than 4000yds total offence; pro Montreal '75-81, '84, Calgary '82-83; linebacker, slotback, def. back, receiver before becoming starting quarterback Alouettes '78; 2 Grey Cup finals; Schenley outstanding Canadian award '80; res. Montreal, Que.

DAVID, Tracy (soccer/coaching); b. 21 Jan 1960, Tomslake, B.C.; UAlta, BPhE; soccer coach UAlta; steeped in soccer tradition from childhood she played with Tomslake Strikers girls team at 15; right fullback Ajax under-18 ntl championships team '78; statistician UAlta Golden Bears '78-79; with Heather Rennebohm organized university women's club team (Edmonton Angels) which achieved considerable success claiming 6 ntl club titles in 10yrs, 5 in succession '82-86; team capt. 8yrs; fullback ntl women's team '86-90; began lobbying for UAlta women's soccer program '82; capt. 1st UAlta women's soccer team '83; helped in organization of women's university soccer league; began coaching UAlta '85; 4 conference, 1 ntl CIAU titles; 3 CWUAA, 1 CIAU coach of year awards; joined Edmonton Azzure team as a player in '91; pres. CIAU women's Soccer Coaches Assn '87-95; mem. UAlta Sports Wall of Fame; res. Edmonton, Alta.

DAVIDSON, Bob (hockey); b. 10 Feb 1912, Toronto, Ont.; d. 26 Sep 1996, Toronto, Ont.; given name: Robert Edgar; m. Tanis; c. Bob, Jim, Tom; retd hockey executive; Jr. A Toronto Canoe Club '29-32; sr. Marlboros '32-33, Toronto All-Stars '33-34; pro Maple Leafs '34-46, capt. '45; mem. 2 Stanley Cup winners; coached Leafs' Pittsburgh farm club '47-50; chief Leafs scout '51, dir. player personnel; J.P. Bickell Leafs' outstanding service award '95; soccer several years Toronto East End club.

DAVIDSON, Chris (rowing); b. 24 Oct 1971, Toronto, Ont.; Queen's, BSc Cross-country runner who turned to rowing in high school; won ntl straight pair, 4s titles '95; gold US lightweight 8s '93; bronze lightweight straight 4s '93 world university, straight pair '94 Commonwealth Games; silver straight 4s '95 Pan-Am Games; competed '96 Olympic Games; national team from '93; res. Oakville, Ont/ Victoria, B.C.

DAVIDSON, Scotty (hockey); b. 1892, Kingston, Ont.; d. 6 Jun 1915, France; given name: Allan; learned hockey under game's originator James T. Sutherland in Kingston; led Kingston Frontenacs to OHA title '10-11; pro Toronto Blueshirts (NHA) '12-14; 19 goals 20 games '12-13, 24 goals '13-14 leading Toronto to Stanley Cup; killed in action WW1; mem. Hockey Hall of Fame.

DAVIES, Bill (football); b. 1916, Montreal, Que.; d. 28 May 1990, Montreal, Que.; m. Chris; c. Patricia (Trish); starred in football, hockey, lacrosse, softball, baseball; backfielder Montreal noted for two-way play, toughness; Jeff Russel Trophy '39; softball, baseball MVP awards, batting titles; hockey jr. sr. Royals; defence Sr. Royals '39 Allan Cup finalists; mem. Canadians, Verdun lacrosse league teams; co-founder NDG Maple Leafs jr. football team; 13yrs coach Lakeshore Flyers, Cdn intermediate champions '53.

DAVIES, Jack (administration); b. 1897, Paris, France; d. 22 Jul 1978, Montreal, Que.; m. Winnifred Hurdman; c. John Bruce; businessman, soldier; more than 300 trophies, medals, prizes amassed in t&f, swimming, water polo, badminton, tennis, table tennis, boxing, equestrian, sailing from childhood to '63; 20yrs mem. Cdn t&f comm, officiated '34 BEG; mem., dir., mgr. numerous Commonwealth, Pan-Am, Olympic teams '34-76; 14 times official Canadian delegate B.E., Commonwealth Games Fed.; v-p. Que. Branch AAU of C 17yrs; co-founder, life mem. QTFA; pres., life mem. AAU of C; only Canadian

ever elected to IAAF; 1st Canadian v.-pres. Commonwealth Games Fed. '70-76; pres. Canadian CGA from '53; mem. advisory board, life mem. COA; chairman Commonwealth records comm. from '52; 1st Canadian, charter mem., world t&f Statisticians Assn. from '50; life mem. CTFA, ILTC, QLTF, UKOA, AAU, Canadian Bobsled and Luge Assn., SFC, CAWA; chairman Canadian Amatuer Sports Hall of Fame; honored by numerous provincial, national, world sports bodies; co-founder MAAA mixed badminton club, K of C badminton club, owner, coach Notre Dame de Grace badminton club; Officer Order of Canada '71; mem. Cdn Amateur Sports, Cdn Aquatic, Helms halls of fame.

DAVIES, Jim (cycling); b. 8 Jan 1906, London, Eng.; given name: James Arthur; m. Vera Beatrice Newport; c. Shirley Edith, Diane Estelle; retd sales rep.; BC bicycle champion '25-28, ntl champion '27-28; equalled world record '28 Olympics; Vancouver Province, Colonist Cups; numerous exec. positions BC Track Cycle Assn.; mem. BC Sports Hall of Fame; res. Vancouver, B.C.

DAVIES, Rod (sailing): b. 17 Nov 1969, Ajax, Ont.; York; Only Cdn to win gold at world youth championships; twice Cdn youth titlist; Canada Games gold '89; CORK gold '90; competed Flying Dutchman class '91 Pan-Am Games, 4 world championships; won 6 regatta titles '94 before suffering major back injury which threatened career; through grit, determination battled back to qualify in Laser class for '96 Olympics; brother Ray also Laser sailor; Town of Pickering recognition award '94; 2 Ont., ntl, 1 world achievement awards; res. Pickering, Ont.

DAVIS, Clark (wrestling); b. 15 May 1957, Calgary, Alta.; Concordia; ntl jr. 82kg freestyle, Greco-Roman title '76; ntl jr. GR 90kg '77; Pan-Am jr. 82kg FS, 90kg GR '76; bronze '77 jr. world 82kg FS, silver '79 Pan-Am Games 82kg FS, silver '81 FISU Games 90kg FS; 10 ntl sr. FS titles; '81 82kg FS Skopje tournament; '82 90kg World Cup title; silver 90kg worlds, gold 90kg Commonwealth Games '82; mem. '84 Olympic team; Que. athlete of '82; fed. govt. excellence award '83; mem. Cdn Amateur Wrestling Hall of Fame; res. Montreal, Que.

DAVIS, Pat (coaching); b. 15 Jan 1936, Windsor, Ont.; given name: Patricia Ann; UofT, BPHE, North Carolina, MEd, OCE; retd. phys ed teacher; varsity basketball UofT, softball, basketball in Windsor; dir. women's athletics Waterloo; coach Athena volleyball team; coach Waterloo AA senior women's '75 Ont. title team; Windsor W.F. Herman CI volleyball, basketball, track, gymnastics teams '58-66; CVA coaching comm. chair. '75-78; past coaching chair. Ont. Volleyball Assn.; OWIAA pres. '79-80; chaired comm. which formulated amalgamation of OQWCIA and WIAU to form OWIAA; CIAU constitution comm. chair. '80-81; res. Waterloo, Ont.

DAVIS, Penny (sailing); b. 2 Mar 1968, Carlisle, Eng.; given name: Penny Jane Stamper; m. Scott Davis; UBC; 3 consecutive Cdn youth Laser II titles; Canada Games gold '95; with partner Sarah McLean competed '92 Olympics in 470 class; joined talents with Leigh Pearson '93; gold '95 Pan-Am; competed '96 Olympics; BC sailor of '94; CYA female athlete of '92; res. Vancouver, B.C.

DAVIS, Victor (swimming); b. 10 Feb 1964, Guelph, Ont.; d. 13 Nov 1989, Montreal, Que; splashed onto international aquatic scene at 17 winning '81 NZ gold; 30 ntl titles in 100m, 200m breaststroke, 200m butterfly, 200m, 400m IM; NZ 100m butterfly, 200m breaststroke, 2 US, 2 Canada Cup, 1 Swedish 200m breaststroke, 1 US, Canada Cup 100m breaststroke titles; 7 Cdn, 4 world, 1 Commonwealth Games records; gold '82 worlds, Commonwealth, '84 Olympic Games 200m breaststroke, silver 100m breaststroke '82 Commonwealth, '84 Olympic Games; WR 2:13.34 200m breaststroke '84 Olympics; silver 4x100 medley relay '84, '88 Olympics; 3 Swim Canada athlete of yr awards; Ont. excellence award, fed. govt. world champion award '83; killed in hit and run accident; mem. Order of Canada, Cdn, Ont, International Aquatic, Cdn Amateur, Waterloo County, Canada's Sports halls of fame.

DAWSON, Andre (baseball); b. 10 Jul 1954, Miami, Fla.; given name: Andre Nolan; m. Vanessa Turner; c. Daries, Amber; Florida A&M; drafted Montreal '75; outfield regular Expos '77-88, Chicago Cubs '89-92, Boston '93-94, Florida '95-96; NL rookie of year, Sporting News rookie of year; Expos' all-time run, triples leader, 2nd to Gary Carter home runs; 3 Silver Bat, 4 Gold Glove awards; NL MVP '90, twice runnerup; SN NL player of '81; 3 Expos player of year awards; shared ML record 2 HRs single inning, club record 19-game hitting streak, 3 doubles 1 game, 2 triples 1 game, 6 hits doubleheader; mem. '81 div. title team; hampered by knee surgery following '83 season; uniform #10 retired by Expos (2nd time since same number worn by Rusty Staub also retired); mem. Expos Hall of Fame; res. Miami, Fla.

DAWSON, Bob (football); b. 4 Feb 1932, Windsor, Ont.; m. Louise Bennett; c. Debbie, Lori; consulting firm owner; leading scorer AKO Windsor 3 consecutive years including ntl jr. title '52; Tiger-Cats '53-59, rookie of '53; coached Burlington Braves to jr. league title '60; coached McMaster 4 league titles '61-65; res. Ancaster, Ont.

DAWSON, Earl (administration); b. 17 Dec 1925, St. Boniface, Man.; d. 28 Mar 1987, Winnipeg, Man.; m. Madeline O'Callaghan; c. William, Patrick, Nancy, Donald, Randall; regional rep. Fitness & Amateur Sport; pres. MAHA '59-63; chair. CAHA rules comm. '63-66; v-p. minor hockey CAHA '66-67; v-p.junior hockey CAHA '67-68; pres. CAHA '69-71; chair. Centennial midget hockey championship '67; initiated, chaired 1st ntl referee's clinic '63-64; initiated congress for all levels of hockey in CAHA '69; left international hockey scene '70 to assume duties with Fitness & Amateur Sport; Brandon Sun sportsman of '62; USAHA citation '70; life mem. CAHA; mem. Man. Hockey Hall of Fame.

DAWSON, Eddie (basketball); b. 10 Oct 1907, Alford, Lincolnshire County, Eng.; d. 1968, Windsor, Ont.; Detroit; outstanding guard, floor leader; mem. Cdn champion Windsor Alumni '28, Windsor Ford '36 teams; mem. Cdn Olympic silver medal team '36; coach Windsor Patterson CI 36yrs coaching such standouts as Bill Rogin, Jimmy Farmer, Fred Thomas, Bob Simpson, Tommy Grant and Zeno Karcz; coached Patterson '35 championship track team; mem. Windsor-Essex Sports Hall of Fame.

DAWSON, Jamie (badminton): b. 28 Jul 1969, Geneva, Switzerland; UMan.; won French Open singles '91; '95 ntl singles title; gold singles, bronze doubles '95 Pan-Am Games; mem. '96 Olympic, '95 world championships teams; res. Winnipeg, Man.

DAY, Hap (hockey); b. 14 Jun 1901, Owen Sound, Ont.; d. 17 Feb 1990, St. Thomas, Ont.; given name: Clarence Henry; UofT; pharmacist; jr. Midland, Ont.; sr. Hamilton; pro Toronto St. Pat's '24; 33 years involved with hockey as player, coach, referee, general manager; teamed with King Clancy on Maple Leafs defence; record 4 goals single game by defenceman '29, broken '77 by Leafs' Ian Turnbull; capt. 1st Toronto Stanley Cup winner '32; NHL record: 581 scheduled games, 86g, 116a, 53 playoff games, 4g, 7a; coached West Toronto Nationals '36 Memorial Cup; closed competitive career NY Americans '38; refereed 2 seasons then rejoined Leafs as coach, 5 Stanley Cups, 3 in succession; Toronto mgr. '50-57; mem. Hockey Hall of Fame.

DAY, James (equestrian); b. 7 Jul 1946, Thornhill, Ont.; div.; c. Catherine, Richard; farm manager, horse trainer; operates Day by Day racing stable at Woodbine; mem. ntl team '64-77; individual gold '67, team silver '75 Pan-Am Games; team gold '68 Olympics; tied world puissance record 7'3" NY '66, Toronto '68; mem. winning world Prix des Nations team '70; NA 3-day title '73; '66-68 horseman of year; mem. '68, '72, '76 Olympic teams; turned to horse training working primarily for Sam-Son Farms 20yrs; trained Dance Smartly, Sky Classic to Breeders' Cup, Eclipse awards; 4 US trainer of month awards; 4 Sovereign trainer awards; mem. Cdn Olympic, Canada's Sports halls of fame; res. Everett, Ont.

DAYMOND, Irv (football): b. 9 Oct 1962, St. Thomas, Ont.; m. Connie; c. Michael, Alexandria, Marjorie; UWO; offensive centre; drafted by BC '84 CIAU draft; signed/released Calgary '86; Ottawa '86-96; all-Eastern '91-92; res. Barrhaven, Ont.

de ROUSSAN, Hugues (handball); b. 23 Mar 1955, Montreal, Que.; m. Annie Blanc; c. Vincent; Montreal, BSc; journalist; ntl team '74-80; Que. team '74-80; Latine Cup '75; mem. '76 Olympic, '76, '77, '80 Americas Cup, '78 world championships; coached variety Que. handball teams; mem. Cdn delegation '82 Olympic Academy; res. Montreal, Que.

de ST. CROIX, Ted (orienteering); b. 30 Aug 1957, Vineland, Ont.; m. Maureen Crowley; Trent, BSc, Carleton; computer programmer; boys -14 Ont. title; 2nd NA boys 15-16 '71; Ont. boys 15-16 '72; NA jr. men '73; men's 17-18 Goteborg Sweden '74; Swedish men's 17-18, Ont. elite '75; US elite '76; 18yrs in top 3 in elite category '74-91; 13 ntl elite (11 in succession) '76-87, 4 NA elite titles; competed 9 worlds; best ever finish by non-European 10th worlds '85; 2nd Asia-Pacific championships '84; res. Sweden.

DEACON, Bruce (t&f); b. 5 Dec 1966, Ottawa, Ont.; teacher; long distance runner; represented Canada 10,000m '91 FISU Games; gold '95, silver '92 10,000m ntls; competed '94 Commonwealth, '96 Olympics marathon, '95 world outdoor championships, qualified for '98 Commonwealth Games but withdrew due to injury; res. Nepean, Ont./N. Vancouver, B.C.

DEACON, Tom (all-around); b. 21 Dec 1917, Ottawa, Ont.; d. 20 Jul 1993, Ottawa, Ont.; m. Irene Rich; c. Judy, Tom, Doug; jr. hockey Ottawa; RCAF Flyers '39-43; Service League all-star RCAF Rockcliffe; playing-coach RCAF Uplands '50-52; mem. interior BC, Yukon title teams '52-53; coached RCAF Downsview '54-55; mem. Ottawa Old Stars, Sr. Olympics (over 55) title team '78; from '53 officiated English pro league, ODHA; conducted officiating schools Canada, Europe; mem. RCAF service football title teams '40-41; Ottawa Combined ORFU '43; soccer Corinthians, United Ottawa Sr. City League; highly-rated amateur welterweight boxer '35-39; gold over 55 class '76, over 60 class '80 National Capital marathon.

DEAN, Bob (football); b. 17 Dec 1929, Pittsburgh, Pa.; given name: Robert Wadsworth; m. Shirley Anne Donaldson; c. Geoffrey, Matthew, Clayton; Maryland, BSc, UAlta, BEd, MEd; school administrator; contributed field goal, game-winning convert Edmonton's 26-25 '54 Grey Cup victory over Montreal; Ted Reeve's all-Canadian rating '55; 5yrs mem. Alta. volleyball team; res. Edmonton, Alta.

DEAN, Geordie (lacrosse); b. 8 Dec 1960, New Westminster, B.C.; firefighter; mem. Coquitlam Jr. A '78-81, Richmond Woodies from '82, New Westminster Salmonbellies from '82, ntl team from '85; 2 Mike Kelly Mann Cup MVP awards, 8 league all-stars; 2 Labatt/CP Air awards; 2 Maitland, 1 Huddleston scoring title trophy; 3 Commissioner's trophy Western Lacrosse Assn. MVP, 2 Ellison trophy WLA playoff MVP awards; res. New Westminster, B.C.

DeBENEDETTI, Tania (wrestling); b. 30 Dec 1972, Hamilton, Ont.; McMaster ; certified trainer; competes at 46kg level; 2 ntl sr. titles; gold '96 NYAC open; res. Hamilton, Ont.

DeBLONDE, Clare (curling); b. 8 Jan 1943, Swan Lake, Man.; m. Irene Yackel; prov. govt. accountant; runnerup Man. schoolboy title '59; youngest skip Man. bonspiel winner '66; Man. 'spiel winner '72; skip '76 Man. Consols winner, Brier runnerup; 3rd for Earle Morris '80 Man. Brier entry; coach '84 Brier champion Mike Riley rink; res. West St. Paul, Man.

DeBLONDE, Garry (curling); b. 28 Jun 1940, Swan Lake, Man.; m. Diana Wookey; c. Joel, Riley, Karen; UMan, hons. BSc, MSc, PhD; teacher; mem. 4 Man., 2 ntl mixed title rinks; 2 Man. Brier entries; twice mem. Man. bonspiel title rink; '75 Man. carspiel title; twice mem. Ont. Labatt Tankard playdown rinks; pres. Winnipeg Heather CC '72; 8yrs mem. MCA exec. council; v.-chair. CCA Pepsi Jr. championships '80-81; technical dir. Curl Canada '80-86, '88-90; developed, supervised '88 Olympic curling program '87-88; res. Winnipeg, Man.

DèCARIE, Al (boxing); b. 22 Apr 1916, Montreal, Que.; d. 1996, Montreal, Que.; m. Rita Couture; c. Joan, Dennis; office mgr., purchasing agent; active boxer '28-35; coach

Montcalm Boxing Club '36-41; pro referee '38-51; coach Palestre Nationale '45-51; v-p. QABA '51-60, pres. '61-64; chair. CABA '61-67; dir. COA '61-67; dir. Palestre Nationale, Paul Sauve Centre '55-71; mgr/coach ntl boxing team '63 Pan-Am, '66 Commonwealth, '68 Olympics; media liaison '76 Olympic boxing; v-p. Old Timers Boxing Group Inc; boxing event whip '78 Commonwealth Games; pres. Montreal Region ABA '76-82; AAU of C citation '54; Montreal Sportsmen's Assn. award of merit '57; O'Keefe award, US Navy appreciation certificate '67; BCABA exec. of decade award '70; life mem. BCABA.

DECKERT, Merv (handball); b. 9 Mar 1949, Winnipeg, Man.; m. Shirley (d); c. Kelly, Paul, Christine; m. Colleen; UMan., BSc, BEd; teacher; keen athlete in youth excelling in baseball, volleyball, hockey, basketball, badminton, soccer and golf; turned attention to handball while at UMan; 8 ntl open/closed titles; at 35 won world title; Manitoba male athlete of '84; mem. Man. Sports Hall of Fame; res. Lorette, Man.

DECSI, Laszlo (shooting); b. 22 Dec 1934, Budapest, Hungary; m. Donna; c. Sharon, Cindy, Michael; became an amputee '72; without benefit of a coach began pistol shooting '74; mem. ntl SFC hand gun team '75-99, ntl disabled team from '88; ntl titles, 1 air pistol, 1 standard, 3 centre fire, 1 Cdn 1800 .22 cal., 3 centre fire, 1 grand aggregate titles; 3 Benito Juarez gold; 4 Australian, 1 British, 5 European Masters, 3 Windsor indoor, 5 Cdn masters; twice high visitor US nationals; represented Canada 4 Paralympics; official '76 Montreal Olympics; competed in 1st world air gun championships for disabled '84; sport pistol world record '93 wheelchair worlds; ntl indoor centrefire record 594/600; 2 world amputee records; chair. International Sports Organization for Disabled 8yrs; proficient archer; res. Tweed, Ont.

DEFIAGBON, David (boxing); b. 12 Jun 1971, Nigeria; competes at 91 kg; winner of 186 of 207 bouts; '90 Commonwealth Games gold for Nigeria; '96 Cdn ntl champion; pre-Olympic Atlanta tournament gold '96; competed '92, '96 Olympics; silver '96 Olympics; turned pro '96; res. Halifax, N.S.

DEGLAU, Jessica (swimming); b. 27 May 1980, Vancouver, B.C.; butterfly specialist; mem. ntl team '95-98; competed '96 Olympics, '98 Commonwealth Games, '99 Pan-Am Games; Canada Cup 200m fly gold '96; 100m, 200m fly gold Rio de Janiero '95; silver '95 Summer nationals; 2 gold '98 Winter nationals; World Cup short course 200m fly gold '98; 2 indiv., 2 team bronze '98 Commonwealth Games; 2 individual, 2 relay gold, 2 silver '99 PAG; res. Vancouver, B.C.

DeGRUCHY, John (football); b. 15 Dec 1860, Toronto, Ont.; d. 1940, Toronto, Ont.; involved in exec. capacity with Toronto AC, Toronto Rugby and Athletic Assn.; organized Toronto city football series among Argos, Balmy Beach, Varsity and donated Reg DeGruchy Memorial trophy for the competition; promoted Thanksgiving Day Classic between Sarnia Imperials and Balmy Beach; driving force behind 6-man football which would become popular at senior level during 1940's; served Cdn football in various capacities for 50yrs; charter mem. Cdn Football Hall of Fame.

DEKDEBRUN, Al (football); b. 11 May 1921, Buffalo, N.Y.; given name: Allen Edward; m. Corinne Scoones; c. Gregory, Rick; Cornell, BSc; retd. chair. Niagara Frontier Transportation Authority; all-American quarterback Cornell '45; Coffman award '46 East-West Shrine Game MVP; mem. '46 college all-star team; 3yrs US All-American Conf.; 6rs CFL Toronto, Hamilton, Ottawa; mem. '50 Argos Grey Cup winner; coached Canisius College, U of Buffalo; potentate Ismailia Shrine Temple Buffalo; only man to have won both Coffman, Hollingbery awards; res. Williamsville, N.Y.

DELAHANTY, Megan (rowing); b. 24 Mar 1968, Edmonton, Alta.; UBC; Cdn Henley 4 without cox, 8 with cox gold '90; US Ntl 8 with cox gold '91; world championships 8 with cox gold '91; CARA Centennial medal '91; 2 Dick Ellis Memorial awards; mem. Cdn Olympic Hall of Fame; res. Vancouver, B.C.

DELAHEY, Wally (football/coaching); b. 23 Sep 1932, Toronto, Ont.; given name: Wallace Allan; m. Patricia Ann Fowler; c. Karen, Diane, Jill, Brian; UWO, BPHE, OCE; retd AD Waterloo; entire Humberside CI football career on undefeated team; excelled at basketball, t&f, gymnastics, swimming; 4yrs varsity football, 1yr swimming; 6yrs HS coach; Waterloo coach '64-81, AD '89-94; pres. K-W branch CAHPER '63-64; pres. Canadian Football Coaches Assn. '69; mem. all-Canadian Football Selection Comm. '72-76; vp CIAU '89-90, pres. '90-92; CIAU dir. '90-94; asst. CdM '87 FISU Games, CdM '91; chair. Canadian Red Cross Society water safety services Kitchener branch '64-69; secty.-treas. Twin Cities HSAA '62-66; waterfront dir. Camp Tawingo Huntsville '69-76; v-p. Canadian Universities Football Coaches Assn. '79-81; mem. CAFA rules comm. '77-78; Waterloo honor award; mem. Waterloo Sports Hall of Fame; res. Waterloo, Ont.

DELAMARRE, Victor (weightlifting); b. 1888, Lac St. Jean, Que.; d. 1955, Montreal, Que.; m., c. 4 sons, 6 daughters; pro strongman, wrestler, policeman; following footsteps of idol Louis Cyr joined Montreal Police Force despite size, 5'6", 145lbs; lifted world record 309.5lbs one hand '14; with 1 finger lifted 201lbs; lifted platforms with 60 people weighing 7000lbs; pro wrestler from '31, reported to have had 1500 bouts; mem. Canada's Sports Hall of Fame.

DELANEY, Jack (boxing); b. 18 Mar 1900, St. Francis, Que.; d. 27 Nov 1948, Katanah, N.Y.; given name: Ovila Chapdelaine; pro at 19 adopting name Delaney when ring announcer had difficulty pronouncing Chapdelaine; lost to Paul Berlenbach '25 for world light-heavyweight title; beat Berlenbach for title '26 but never defended; last bout, as heavyweight, '32; in 86 pro bouts won 42 on KO, 27 decision, 1 foul, 3 draws, 7 decisions lost, 3 times KO'd, 2 no decisions, 1 no-contest; beat many top names including Tommy Loughran, Tiger Flowers; mem. Canadian Boxing, Canada's Sports Hall of Fame.

DELASALLE, Philip (gymnastics); b. 18 Jul 1958, Victoria, B.C.; given name: Philip Lawrence; UVic;

instrument technician; began gymnastics career at 6; 1st all-around '73, '76-80 ntl championships; mem. '76, '80 Olympic, '78 Commonwealth Games teams; gold all-around, team '78 Commonwealth Games; 15 gold, 8 silver, 2 bronze ntl, international competitions; Viscount Alexander award '75; Sports BC overall athlete, male athlete of '78; Victoria Transcendental Meditation Society Best Gymnast award '79; with Owen Wastrom operated Prince George gymnastics club '81-85; mem. BC, Greater Victoria Sports halls of fame; res. Victoria, B.C.

DELGADO, Carlos (baseball); b. 25 Jun 1972, Aguadilla, Puerto Rico; given name: Carlos Juan; 1st baseman; turned pro with Toronto organization '89; St. Catharines (NY-P) '89-90, Myrtle Beach (Sally) '91, Syracuse (IL) '91, '94-95, '98, Dunedin (FSL) '92, '98, Knoxville (Sou) '93; Toronto Blue Jays (AL) '93-99; noted for prodigious home run blasts early in career but spent time seasoning in minors until permanent call-up '96; 29th player to clear Tiger Stadium with home run blast; set Jays club records '99 with 44hr, 134rbi; 2 Neil MacCarl Jays player of month awards; 3 Howard Webster Jays' minor league player of yr awards; *USA Today* baseball weekly minor league player of '92; MVP awards in 6 leagues; Southern, AL all-star; mem. ML all-star Japan tour '98; *Baseball America* winter league player of '94; res: Aguadilla, PR.

DELMAGE, Al (curling); b. 16 Jan 1940, Regina, Sask.; m. Dora Scott; c. Gail, Sharon, Sandra, Ron; retd. govt. finance officer; skip NWT entries '80, '84-85, '87, '89, 5th man '93 Briers, '72, '84, '86 ntl mixed, '91 ntl senior men's; 5 ntl Elks championships, '89 winner; participant, organizer Arctic Winter Games '70-96, 3 curling gold medals; exec. mem. NWTCA '68-96; exec. mem. Sport North Fed. '76-82, '85-86, pres. 83-85; NWT curling technical co-ordinator '75-81, '89-96; NWT curling instructor '75-96; NWT government curling co-ordinator '86-96; exec. mem. Ft. Smith CC '66-68; exec. mem. Yellowknife CC '68-96, pres. '88-89; Elks exec. mem. '71-96; 3 times Yellowknife athlete of year; mem. Sport North team of year '85; mem. Cdn Curling Hall of Fame; res. Emerald Park, Sask.

DELVECCHIO, Alex (hockey); b. 4 Dec 1931, Fort William, Ont.; given name: Alexander Peter; m. Teresa De Guiseppe; c. Kenneth, Janice, Corrine, Alex Jr., Leonard; owns Alex Delvecchio Enterprises; jr. Ft. William, Oshawa; pro Detroit '50-73; left wing on line with Gordie Howe, Norm Ullman; NHL record: 1549 scheduled games, 456g, 825a, 121 playoff games, 35g, 69a; team capt. '61-73; coached Wings '73, GM '74-77; twice 2nd team all-star; active with Red Wings alumni; 3 Lady Byng trophies; Lester Patrick award; mem. Michigan, NWO Sports, Canadian Hockey halls of fame; res. Orchard Lake, Mich.

DEMERS, Jacques (coaching/hockey); b. 25 Aug 1944, Montreal, Que.; m. Debbie; c. Mylene, Brandy, Stephanie, Jason; ex-hockey coach; began coaching in Que. jr. ranks; moved into pro ranks with Chicago, Indianapolis, Cincinnati (WHA) '72-79; made NHL debut with Quebec '79-81; coach/GM Fredericton (AHL) '81-83; returned to NHL with St. Louis '83-86, Detroit '86-90, Montreal '92-96, Tampa Bay '97-99; NHL coaching record: (through '98) 923 scheduled games, 390-412-121, 93 playoff games, 55-43;

1 Stanley Cup winner; 1st coach to win back-to-back Adams trophies; AHL coach/exec. of yr awards; res. New Tampa, Fla.

DEMERS, Jacques (weightlifting); b. 27 Jul 1960, Greenfield Park, Que.; Oceania championships 75kg title '81; 4 ntl sr. titles; 1 Ont. title; bronze '82 Commonwealth Games; gold C&J, silver total, bronze snatch '83 Pan-Am Games; silver 75kg '84 Olympics; 6 ntl sr., 8 Commonwealth records; French, Austrian titles '84; played Wagubu tribesman movie Quest for Fire; fed. govt. excellence award '84; res. Brossard, Que.

DEMONTE, Denise (orienteering); b. 4 Dec 1954, Toronto, Ont.; given name: Denise Maria; m. Ron Lowry; c. Stephen, Eric; McMaster, BPhE, UWO., MA cross-country skier; 30km Muskoka Loppet, silver 55km '80 Riviere Rouge Loppet, bronze 160km Canadian Ski Marathon; ntl team '79-87; Canadian champion '81, US, New England titles '79; competed in 4 world championships; 18th '85 worlds, best finish by Cnd woman in world competition; res. Hamilton, Ont.

DENG, Si-An (badminton); b. 25 Jun 1963, Shanghai, China; m. Yong Jaing Liu; c. Joshua; began playing at 12, competing at 17; mem. Chinese ntl team; moved to Canada '88; '93 ntl single, doubles titles; represented Canada '94 Commonwealth Games, silver women's singles, bronze (with Denyse Julien) women's doubles; doubles gold (with Julien) '95 Pan-Am Games; mem. '96 Olympic team; res. Richmond, B.C.

DENNENY, Cy (hockey); b. 23 Dec 1891, Farran's Point, Ont.; d. 10 Sep 1970, Ottawa, Ont.; given name: Cyril Joseph; m. Malvina K. Eastman (d), m. Isobel Clark; c. Kathlyn, Janet, Alma (d); civil servant; early hockey Cornwall County League, Russell, Ont. '12, O'Brien Mine team; pro Toronto Shamrocks '14-15, Ottawa Senators '16-28; on line with Frank Nighbor, Punch Broadbent; mem. 5 Stanley Cup winners; coach, asst. mgr. 1yr Boston Bruins; refereed 1yr NHL; coach jr., sr. amateur teams Ottawa '31-32; coach Senators '32-33; NHL record: 12 seasons, 246 goals, 20 3-goal games, 5 4-goal games, 1 6-goal game; 12 consecutive game goal-scoring streak '17-18; exponent of curved stick; mem. Ottawa, Cornwall Sports, Canadian Hockey halls of fame.

DENONCOURT, Sonia (soccer/officiating); b. 25 Jun 1964, Sherbrooke, Que.; Sherbrooke, BPhE, UofOtt, MSA; merchant, educator; began soccer officiating at 13; refereed in ntl women's championships '81; lineswoman CSL '87-92; officiates Canada Games '93, APSL from '93, CIAU men's championships '94, women's ntl, world, Chiquita Cup championships from '83, men's CONCACAF championships '94; appointed 1 of 12 referee for '95 FIFA women's worlds; 1st woman to referee an Olympic game; 1st female referee in Brazilian pro soccer; CSA Ray Morgan Memorial award; res. Montreal, Que.

DEPIERO, Mary (diving); b. 14 May 1968, Thunder Bay, Ont.; Lakehead U; began diving career at 14; mem. ntl team from '88; '91 5th place finish 1M best-ever for Cdn at Worlds; 4g, 3b ntl 3m, 4g, 1s, 1m championships; 1m gold

'90, bronze '94 Commonwealth Games; res. Thunder Bay, Ont.

DESABRAIS, Paul (softball); b. 24 Sep 1924, Hull, Que.; given name: Joseph Paul Ernest; sep.; c. Guy, Andre; retd. construction engineer superintendant; perfected pitching skills with RCAF '43; introduced windmill delivery to Ottawa area but played outfield until pitch legalized '49; through '50s, '60s National Capital region's premier pitcher; 12 consecutive seasons Oscar-Lambert Hull Commercial League; retd. from competition '78; in 35-year career 255 wins, 57 losses; in '55 appeared in 73 games in 4 leagues; pitched 4 complete games, 1 5-inning match single day '51; 11 consecutive victories, including 7 shutouts '58; 2 perfect games among 12 career no-hitters; 3 times Gil O. Julien, twice Ottawa ACT Trophy candidates; mem. Softball Canada, Ottawa Sports halls of fame; res. Vanier, Ont.

DESCHAMPS, Claude (softball); b. 7 Aug 1934, Ottawa, Ont.; d. 22 Sep 1983, Ottawa, Ont.; m. Dolorese Seguin; c. Marc, Lucie, Louise; LaSalle Academy; exec. dir. Softball Canada; 2nd baseman Hull; helped organize Hull Volants team '71, Atlantic Seaboard Major Fastball League, '73 ntl men's sr. softball championships Hull; major role sr. fastball Ottawa area with organization Metro Major League; 6yrs secty.-general Hull International Softball tournament; Softball Canada exec.-dir. '75-83; key role in formation Softball Canada Hall of Fame; mem. Softball Canada, Ottawa Sports halls of fame.

DESCHATELETS, Richard (wrestling); b. 4 Apr 1954, Sturgeon Falls, Ont.; m. Suzanne Rochon; Guelph, BA; AD Brock; '73 ntl jr. 82kg FS title; bronze 74kg '73 jr. worlds; 5 ntl sr. FS, 1GR titles; CIAU 82kg FS title '79; Cerro Pelado 82kg '78, 90kg '80, '84; gold 82kg '78 Commonwealth Games; bronze 90kg '79 Pan-Am Games, '77, '80 World Cup, 100kg '82 World Cup; silver 82kg '75, 100kg '83 Pan-Am Games; gold 100kg '82 Commonwealth Games; scored upset victory over USSR Olympic gold medalist at World championships; mem. '76 Olympic team; Sturgeon Falls HS athlete of '72; Guelph athlete of '76-77; established Azilda wrestling club where he coaches; coach Brock; 2 CIAU, 1 OUAA coach of yr awards; fed. govt. excellence award '83; mem. Guelph, Cdn Wrestling halls of fame; res. St. Catharines, Ont.

DESCLOUDS, Rick (coaching); b. 3 Apr 1951, Montreal, Que.; c. Danny, Dwain; St. Pat's Coll BA, Ottawa Teachers Coll; teacher; coached community hockey 8yrs winning 2 Ntl Capital titles with Westboro Kiwanis; 31yrs minor baseball coach, 25 as major div. tournament coach; reached prov finals 8 times, winning 3 consec titles; twice ntl championship finalists; coached 81 Ottawa Board title teams in 8 different sports including 12 basketball titles in 15yrs, 20 volleyball crowns in 22yrs; coached Glashan Spikers volleyball team to 13 Ont. titles, 7 elementary, 6 bantam; 2 Ottawa ACT Little League team awards; ACT sportsman of '88; Hudson Sargeant Ottawa School Board award '93; Pinecrest baseball diamond bears his name; res. Stittsville, Ont.

DESJARDINS, Éric (hockey); b. 14 Jun 1969, Rouyn, Que.; m. Manon Bouthiller; c. Jakob; defence Granby

(QMJHL) '86-88, Sherbrooke (AHL) '88, NHL Montreal '88-94, Philadelphia from '95; QMJHL Butch Bouchard trophy; 3 Barry Ashbee trophies; mem. Team Canada '88-89 world jr., '91 Canada Cup. '96 worlds, '98 Olympics; mem. 1 Stanley Cup winner; Hockey News 2nd team all-star '95; 1 NHL all-star game; NHL record: (through '99) 746 scheduled games, 88g, 290a, 128 playoff games, 17g, 41a; res. St-Adolphe-D'Howard, Que.

DESJARDINS, Gerry (hockey); b. 22 Jul 1944, Sudbury, Ont.; given name: Gerard Ferdinand; m. Michelle Parenteau; c. Daniel; sales rep./part owner Canada Steel; jr. Toronto Marlboros; minor pro '65-68; NHL Los Angeles, Chicago, NY Islanders, Buffalo '68-78, excluding '74-75 Baltimore (WHA); 10yr major pro record 331 games, 12 shutouts, 3.29 goals against average; goaltending consultant Buffalo; Red Garrett Memorial Trophy with Cleveland (AHL) '68; res. London, Ont.

DESJARDINS, Larry (all-around/builder); b. 15 Mar 1923, St. Boniface, Man.; given name: Laurent Louis; St. Boniface Coll, St. Paul's Coll, UMan.; retd politician; baseball LHP, 1B St. Boniface juves, St. Paul's Coll, Norwood srs, RCN, St. Boniface Native Sons, semipro Cincinnati, Winnipeg Rods (ManDak League); football 2-way tackle St. Paul's, UMan, Blue Bombers; coached Isaac Newton HS, St. Paul's Coll., Winnipeg Rods; exec. mem. Blue Bombers; hockey defenceman St. Boniface jrs, Esquires; pres./GM St. Boniface jr. Canadians; area scout for Montreal Canadiens; among 1st to scout European talent '68 Olympics; entered political arena '50 holding numerous portfolios through '87 retirement; ED Man. Health Organizations '87-90; 1st pres. Man. Sports Fed.; mem. Man. Sports, Man. Hockey halls of fame; res. Winnipeg, Man.

DESJARDINS, Paul (football); b. 12 Sep 1943, Ottawa, Ont.; given name: Paul Robert; m. Vona Elizabeth Freeman; c. Michelle, Steven, Jason; UofOtt, BSc, UMan, MSc, PhD; v-p. GM Biovail Corp.; mem. UofOtt Gee-Gees '60-65; pro Winnipeg '65-70, Toronto '71-73; CFL all-star centre (East) '71-73, all-Cdn '73; '68 Winnipeg MVP; best all-around athlete UofOtt '63-64; top volleyball player UofOtt '64-65; Gil O. Julien Trophy French Canadian athlete of '65; mem. UofOtt Football Hall of Fame; res. Toronto, Ont.

DESJARLAIS, Robert (fencing); b. 26 Aug 1907, St. David Yamaska, Que.; d. (circa 1993), Westmount, Que.; m. Laurette Douvet; c. Mirielle, Lorraine, France; St. Laurent Coll., St. Paul's Academy; mem. '48 Olympic, '50, '54 BEG, '58 World championships teams; fencing secty., prov. pres.; fencing chairman AAU of C; Baron de Coubertin award '78; mem. Que. Sports Hall of Fame.

DESLAURIERS, Mario (equestrian); b. 23 Feb 1965, Venise-en, Que.; div.; c. Sari; 5th generation show horse rider; outstanding foreign, international rider Madison Square Garden '83; 2nd Spruce Meadow '83; spare '83 Pan-Am Games team; gold aboard Aramis '84 World Cup; mem. '84, '88 Olympic teams; fed. govt. world champion award '84; won Bryhar Futures Stakes aboard Fiezal '95; ntl show jumping title aboard Amistad '97; res. Kingston, N.H.

DESMARTEAU, Étienne (t&f); b. 1877, Montreal, Que.; d. 1905 Montreal, Que.; policeman; at 6'1", 225lbs smallest

of 5 brothers; with brother Zacharie competed annually Toronto, NY, Montreal, Boston Police Games; specialized in 56lb weight toss, like today's hammer throw; sponsored by MAAA became 1st Canadian Olympic gold medalist '04 winning weight toss; event discontinued following '20 games; world record 15'9" height and 36'6.5" distance; '76 Olympic facility named in his honor; mem. Cdn Amateur, Que., Canada's Sports Hall of Fame.

DESPATIE, Alexandre (diving); b. 8 Jun 1985, Montreal, Que.; began swimming/diving age 5; coached by Michel Larouche; holds ntl jr. records on all 3 boards; won ntl 10m title '98; electrified international diving followers by earning '98 Commonwealth Games 10m gold at 13; mem. CAMO club; res. Laval, Que.

DESSUREAULT, Michel (fencing); b. 11 Mar 1957, Bouchette, Que.; given name: Michel Daniel; m. Anne Marie Viau; c. Marie-Michel; Carleton BA.; dir. Caron Training Centre, French teacher, coach, operator Gatineau fencing club, fencing equipment co. owner; began fencing at 13; ntl status fencer '75-94, épée, foil specialist; mem. '75, '79, '83, '87 Pan-Ams, '76, '84, '88 Olympic, '77, '79, '81 FISU, '78, '82 Commonwealth Championships teams; 7 ntl jr. titles, 4 épée, 3 foil; ntl sr. épée title '80, foil '81; mem. 3 RA ntl foil title teams; 4 Governor-General's foil, 2 épée titles; team foil bronze '78, silver '82 Commonwealth championships, épée gold '86 Commonwealth Games; épée team gold, individual silver '83 Pan-Am Games; best Cdn Olympic fencing showing 10th '84; mem. COA advisory council; mem. '91 Sports Canada task force on policy review; mem. Ottawa CSRA Sports Hall of Fame; res. Gatineau, Que.

DEVAL, Gordon (fishing); b. 18 Jan 1930, Winnipeg, Man.; m. Britta; c. Ronald, Randall, Connie, Wendy; UofT, Shaw Business School; insurance agent; all ntl distance casting records from '55; all-around champion from '55; 1st represented Canada world championships '57 and annually from '75; world title runnerup '75; Commonwealth champion '77-80; NA salmon fly title '79; 2-hand spinning distance title '80; world record anglers' fly distance 174', 1-ounce spin distance and 3/8-ounce unrestricted bait distance 531' and 384' respectively; from '75 established more than 40 records; res. Scarborough, Ont.

DeVENNEY, Sandra (all-around); b. 7 Mar 1946, Fredericton Junction, N.B.; given name: Sandra Lea Davenport; m.; admin. officer prov. govt.; competing in wheelchair t&f, table tennis, basketball, swimming won 24 gold, 24 silver, 8 bronze medals, 6 records Cdn wheelchair games '71-78; founding mem. NB Wheelchair Assn; competed 2 Stoke-Mandeville Games (3 silver, 2 bronze), 2 Olympiads for Disabled, '75 Pan-Am Wheelchair Games (1 gold, 1 silver, 3 bronze); mem. ntl women's wheelchair basketball team '76-77, 6 NB wheelchair basketball teams; 2 best female athlete awards; Fredericton athletic achievement awards '73-78; mem. NB Sports Hall of Fame; res. Fredericton Junction, N.B.

DEVINE, Jack (administration); b. 22 Feb 1919, Toronto, Ont.; d. 28 Apr 1989, Belleville, Ont.; given name: William John; m. Minnie Woodman; c. Bruce, Nancy, Stephen; sports broadcaster; pres. OHA '67-69, CAHA '73-75; dir. IIHF

'75-78; pres. Ont. Sports Writers, Sportscasters Assn.; commander Bay of Quinte Power Squadron; life mem. OHA, CAHA, Prince Edward Power Boat Racing Club; hon. mem. Metro Toronto HL; OHA Gold Stick award; SFC broadcasting award '67; CBF award of decade '70-80; City of Belleville award '76; mem. Belleville Sports Hall of Fame.

DEVLIN, Alex (basketball); b. 12 Dec 1949, Edmonton, Alta.; given name: Alexander Joseph; m. Dianne Linda Gillies; c. Jeremy, Kelly Anne; SFU, BA; HS coach, ex-lumber salesman; centre, forward SFU '69-73; hon. mention all-American NAIA '73; mem. ntl team '72-76; missed '72 Olympics due to injury; mem. '76 Olympic, '74 world, '75 Pan-Am, '73 FISU, '74 America vs. world teams; res. Port Moody, B.C.

DEVLIN, Paul (curling); b. 16 Sep 1946, Winnipeg, Man.; given name: Paul Ernest; m. Marnie; c. Renee, Courtenay; salesman; runnerup Man. men's championships '69; twice runnerup Alta. men's championships; skip Alta. '79 Brier, BC '85 Brier; res. Vancouver, B.C.

DEVONISH, Nicole (t&f); b. 24 Aug 1973, Toronto, Ont.; Texas; gold LJ, silver 200m '92 ntl jr championships; silver LJ '92 world jr.; mem. '93 FISU, '94 Commonwealth, '96 Olympic teams; LJ gold '95-96 SWC championships; silver LJ Penn Relays, NCAA championships '96; Cdn LJ record 6.66m '96; Cal Bricker Memorial Trophy '92; Myrtle Cook trophy '89; res. Newtonville, Ont.

DEWAR, Phyllis (swimming); b. 5 Mar 1916, Moose Jaw, Sask.; d. 8 Apr 1961, Toronto, Ont.; m. Murray Lowery (d); c. Judith, Joanne, Wayne, Frank; 3 Sask., 1 ntl 1-mile titles; gold 100yd, 400yd FS, 300yd medley, 400yd relay '34 BEG; set 5 ntl records '35; qualified '36 Olympic team but flu bout produced poor performance; gold 400yd FS '38 BEG; Bobbie Rosenfeld Trophy '34; mem. Canadian Aquatic, Amateur, Sask., Canada's Sports halls of fame.

DeWARE, Mabel (curling); b. 9 Aug 1926, Moncton, N.B.; given name: Mabel Keiver; m. Ralph Baxter DeWare; c. Kimberly, Peter, Michael, Joanne; politician; skip ntl women's '63 title team; p.-pres. Moncton YM-YWCA, Beaver Curling Club, NB Ladies Curling Assn; mem., minister NB Legislature '78-87; summoned to Cdn Senate '90; mem. NB Sports, Cdn Curling halls of fame; res. Shediac, N.B.

DEWIS, Karen (tennis); b. 19 Sep 1962, London, Ont.; UCLA BA magna cum laude, UofT, LLB, Georgetown, LLM; law firm partner; held ntl age group singles, doubles titles from -12 through -18; twice runnerup ntl women's singles; mem. AIAW ntl title team; Que. Open Alcan singles '81; Ont. singles, doubles (Sue Black) '82; mem. 1 jr. Wimbledon, 2 jr. Italian Open, 1 Soisbault Cup teams; played some events on women's pro circuit; retd. from competition '88; res. Washington, D.C.

deWIT, Willie (boxing); b. 13 Jun 1961, Three Hills, Alta.; given name: William Theodore; m. Suzan Ayers; c. Ashley, Sarah, Len, Caitlyn; UAlta LLB; lawyer; sought as quarterback by UAlta; became hooked on boxing with initial

bout which he won in 20 seconds; Alta. 81kg heavyweight titles '79-80; BC Golden Gloves 81kg title '80, Alta. Golden Gloves 91kg title '81; ntl 91kg title '81, '83, super heavyweight '82, Alta. 91kg title '81; '80 Mayor's Cup; 91kg gold '81 NZ Games; 1st Cdn to win NA 91kg title '82, repeat '83; 91kg gold '82 Commonwealth Games, '83-84 world championship challenge; silver '84 Olympics; Alta. Golden Boy award 1981; Canada's "best prospect" '81; outstanding service to Canadian amateur boxing award '80; fed. govt. world champion award '83; Calgary athlete of '83; turned pro '84; won Cdn heavyweight title '86; retd. from ring '88; mem. Alta Sports Hall of Fame; res. Calgary, Alta.

DEWITTE, Marcel (curling); b. 27 Nov 1927, Belgium; given name: Marcel George Maurice; div. Joan Ann Newell; retd. arena, parks mgr., refrigeration engineer; ice maker Simcoe Curling Club '58-60, Sarnia G&CC '61-62; ice superintendent 16-sheet Ivanhoe CC London '63-76; Ont. Legion Zone A rep. '68; rated as one of Canada's most competent curling ice makers; conducted clinics under OCA auspices; mem. '74 London Brier, '81 Silver Broom steering committees; chief ice maker '74, '86, '91-95 Briers, '78 Cdn Lassie, '86 Tournament of Hearts; '80 men's jr. worlds; '81 Silver Broom, '82-83 Ont. Labatt Tankard; '93-94 Worlds; CCA '95 achievement award; res. Norwich, Ont.

DEXTER, Glen (sailing); b. 1 Nov 1952, Lunenburg, N.S.; given name: Glen Vincent; m. Jane Filbee; Dalhousie, BSc, LLB; lawyer; with Andreas Josenhans, Sandy MacMillan Olympic class world soling champion '77, '80; prov. titles '74-76; youngest soling crew '76 Olympics; 1st Maritime Olympic sailors; NS achievement award, Moosehead sports award; mem. NS, Canada's Sports halls of fame; res. Tantallon, N.S.

DIACHUN, Jennifer (gymnastics); b. 14 Aug 1953, Toronto, Ont.; given name: Jennifer Marie; m. Peter Palmer; c. Michael; UofT, UBC, BSc; physiotherapist, assists husband in marketing business; ntl sr. title '69-72, '74; Canadian Intercollegiate title '73, '76; mem. '68, '72 Olympic, '70, '74 world tournament, '73 FISU Games teams; 2 bronze '71 Pan-Am games; coach Phoenix Gym Club '77-78, Thompson GC '79-80; Ont. Gymnastics Fed. outstanding person in gymnastics '75; res. Oakville, Ont.

DIBBEN, Hugh (all-around); b. 13 Jun 1930, Peterborough, Ont.; given name: Hugh Ernest; played cricket Peterborough Whitaker CC '48-67; mem. Matthews Cup Ont. title team '48; excelled as tennis doubles player with Quaker Park TC; with Don Little '68, Tony Bigg '73 Kawartha League title; singles title '72; mem. 2 Quaker title teams; competed 35yrs in volleyball; mem. all-Ont. Int. title team '61; 20yr basketball career included HS, Ont. Int. B title teams; Peterborough table tennis title '53; mem. Peterborough Sports Hall of Fame; res. Peterborough, Ont.

DICKESON, Jean (golf); b. 19 Sep 1922, Baker Brook, N.B.; given name: Jean May; m. Hugh Dickeson; administrative skills led to 9yrs NB Ladies Golf Association jr. development chair, v-p., secty-treas '63-71; 10yrs ntl executive from '71 becoming ntl pres. '78-79; CLGA delegate to World Council '78, Commonwealth Council '79;

2yrs v.-pres. Great Britain Ladies Golf Union; NB Ladies Curling Assn. dir./pres. '84-'88 Sport NB Volunteer of '90; Jubilee medal '77; mem. NB, Edmundston Sports halls of fame; res. Edmundston, N.B.

DICKIE, Bill (hockey); b. 20 Feb 1916, Campbellton, N.B.; d. 23 Dec 1997, Ste. Jolie, Que; given name: William Rufus; c, Brian; Mount Allison; retd. chemical co. mgr.; mem. '32 NB, Maritime HS title teams; '34 NB Sr. B, Maritime titles, NB, Maritime intercollegiate titles with Mount A. '35; capt, coach, goalie Mount A NB undefeated title team '36-37; with John Beavers '38-39 Sydney Millionaires '40-41 Maritime Sr. A titles; Montreal Pats '41-42; 1 game Chicago Blackhawks '42; Hockey News most-popular amateur player '42; Valleyfield outstanding citizen plaque '74; mem. NB, Campbellton Sports Hall/Wall of Fame.

DICKINSON, William (lacrosse); b. 22 Sep 1918, Vancouver, B.C.; d. 31 May 1979, Vancouver, B.C.; during 17yr box lacrosse career scored 611 goals, 330 assists in 398 games; mem. 1 Mann Cup, 4 provincial winners; league MVP '46 Salmonbellies; 5yrs referee; 6yrs league commissioner; 2yrs coach; mem. Canadian Lacrosse, BC Sports halls of fame.

DICKSON, Gordon (t&f); b. 2 Jan 1932, Calgary, Alta.; m. Sheilah MacKenzie; c. Kevin, Craig; Drake, BA, NYU, MA; accountant; ntl 10,000m title '58; ntl cross-country '57-59; ntl marathon titles '57-60, '64; mem. '58, '62 Commonwealth, '59 Pan-Am, '60 Olympic Games teams; bronze '59 Pan-Am marathon; 3 times in top 10 Boston Marathon, 3rd '59; won 5 Around the Bay races; pres. Hamilton Athletic Club; Norton Crowe award '59; mem. Cdn Roadrunning Hall of Fame; res. Burlington, Ont.

DIDUCK, Judy (hockey/ringette): b. 21 Apr 1966, Edmonton, Alta.; owner specialty advertising sales co.; competed in every ntl women's championship with Edmonton Chimos from '85; '92 ntl title; defensive MVP '94; played '90-91 season in Switzerland; defence 4 Team Canada world, 2 Pacific Rim, 1 3-Nations Cup titles; mem. '98 Olympic team; mem. Team Alberta '90 world ringette champions; brother Gerald plays in NHL; res. Edmonton, Alta.

DIETIKER, Judy (speed skating/cycling); b. 5 Mar 1956, Manchester, Eng.; m. Peter Davison; c. Chris, Jenny, Natalie, Paul, Anthony; fitness consultant; began speed skating age 8; 2 Ont. Bantam titles; 6 Ont. sr titles; Lake Placid Diamond Trophy; ntl team '70-94 competing in European, China tours, Olympic trials, world championships; 2 silver, 1 bronze '71 Canada Winter Games; set numerous ntl rcords; competed 1st-ever ntl women's cycling track/road championships; claiming track gold '72, '74, road gold '73, '75; mem. ntl team '74 worlds; Ont. track title '80; broke women's 1000m world record '80; represented Canada numerous US events '81; 1st woman president in 108-yr Ottawa Bicycle Club history '85; competing at Masters level claimed gold Ont. championships '91, Canada's Capital and ntl Masters '94; coach in speed skating, cycling; CASSA roll of honor; mem. Ottawa Sports Hall of Fame; res. Manotick, Ont.

DILIO, Frank (administration); b. 12 Apr 1912, Montreal, Que.; d. 26 Jan 1997, Montreal, Que.; m. Lillian Desmarais; c. Frederick, Elizabeth, Patricia, Francis; retired city clerk; '31-38 secty. St. Anne's Young Men's HL, league title; secty. '39-41 QJAHA, pres. '41-44; registrar, secty QAHA '44-63; pres. QMJHL '69-71; Montreal Sportsman of '43; CAHA merit award '63; division of QMJHL bears his name; mem. Canadian Hockey Hall of Fame.

DIMITROFF, Tom (football); b. 6 Jun 1936, Barberton, Ohio; d. 20 Jan 1996, Strongsville, Ohio; m. Helen; c. Randy, Sharon, Tom; Miami of Ohio; football exec.; quarterback Ottawa (CFL) '57-58, Boston Patriots (AFC); HS coach Barberton; asst. coach Miami of Ohio '69-72, Kansas State '73, Ottawa '74-77, '84-86; head coach Hamilton '78, Guelph U '79-83, Rough Riders '84, scout Cleveland (NFL) '87-96; mem. Guelph U Sports Hall of Fame.

DINEEN, Bill (hockey); b. 18 Sep 1932, Arvida, Que.; given name: William Patrick; m. Patricia Sheedy; c. Shawn, Peter, Rose, Gordon, Kevin, Jerry; St. Michael's Coll; hockey scout; '53-58 in NHL with Detroit, Chicago; mem. 2 Stanley Cup winners with Detroit; NHL record: 323 scheduled games, 51g, 44a, 37 playoff games, 1g, 1a; minor league stints '58-70 with Buffalo, Cleveland, Rochester, Quebec, Seattle, Denver; coached Houston WHA '72-78, 2 Avco Cups; coached Adirondack AHL '83-90, 2 Calder Cups; GM Adirondack; several coach of yr honors WHA, AHL; coach Philadelphia NHL '91-93, 60-60-20 record; mem. Ottawa Sports Hall of Fame; res. Lake George, N.Y.

DINEEN, Kevin (hockey); b. 28 Oct 1963, Quebec City, Que.; m. Ann; c. Hannah, Emma; U Denver; rw St. Michael's Jr. B; U Denver '81-83; Team Canada '83-87; mem. '84 Olympic, '85, '89, '93 Worlds, Canada Cup, Rendez-Vous '87 teams; drafted by Hartford; brief minor league stints with Birmingham, Houston; NHL Hartford '84-91, '95-97, Philadelphia '91-95, Carolina '97-99, Ottawa '99; capt. Hurricanes 2yrs; reached 1000 game plateau Ottawa '99; NHL record (through '99) 992 scheduled games, 338g, 382a; 53 playoff games, 23g, 18a; 2 NHL all-star games; *SN* 2nd all-star team '87; True Grit award, 3-Star award of excellence, Mark Kravitz , Hartford Booster Club MVP awards, Bud Light/NHL man of '91 award, Philadelphia Media Class Guy award '92; res. Ottawa, Ont.

DINSLEY, Tom (diving); b. 25 Jun 1941, Regina, Sask.; given name: Thomas Edward; m. Patricia Venini; c. Sean; Indiana, BSc, UBC, LlB.; lawyer; dominated BC diving scene '58-65 winning 7 consecutive titles; ntl champion '62-65; 3m silver '62 Commonwealth, gold '63 Pan-Am Games; mem. '64 Olympic team; CIAU title '68; mem. top ranked Indiana aquatic team 4yrs; '62 Indiana state champion; throughout career never lower than 2nd ntl championships; mem. BC Sports, Ridge Meadows, Cdn Aquatic halls of fame; res. Pitt Meadows, B.C.

DION, Michel (shooting); b. 30 Jun 1959, Pont Rouge, Que.; m. Anita; c. Anna Maria, 1 son; Laval; teacher; rifle specialist; began shooting '70; ntl team '80-98; team silver small bore prone, big bore 3-positions '83 Pan-Am Games; competed '92, '96 Olympics, '83, '91, '95 Pan-Am, '86,

'94, '98 Commonwealth Games; team silver '86 Commonwealth Games; gold ind. smallbore '86, 3-position pairs (with Wayne Sorensen) '86, '98; Games record '86; bronze ind. smallbore rifle prone '94 Commonwealth Games; world cup prone gold '92; SFC athlete of '95; res. Paris, France.

DIONNE, Marcel (hockey); b. 3 Aug 1951, Drummondville, Que.; given name: Marcel Elphege; m. Carol Gaudet; c. Lisa Lee, Garrett; retd realtor/dry cleaning/plumbing business owner; jr. A Drummondville, St. Catharines; twice led OHA jr. scorers; Detroit's 1st pick, 2nd overall '71 amateur draft; NHL rookie record to that time 28 goals, 49 assists, 77 points '71-72; Detroit '71-75, Los Angeles '75-87, NY Rangers '87-89; 6 50-plus goal seasons, 5 in succession; 1 Art Ross, 2 Lady Byng, 2 Lester B. Pearson awards; 2 1st, 2nd team all-star centre; mem. Team Canada '76, '81, '82, Canada Cup '76; NHL record: 1348 scheduled games, 731g, 1040a, 49 playoff games, 21g, 24a; Drummondville arena bears his name; ex-partner/pres. Carolina Stingrays (ECHL); plays OT hockey; mem. Greatest Legends of Hockey touring team; mem. Hockey, Canada's Sports halls of fame; res. Buffalo, N.Y.

DiPIETRO, Rocky (football); b. 30 Jan 1956, Sault Ste. Marie, Ont.; m. Patty Stamps; c. Joseph, Daniel; UofOtt, BA; HS teacher; wide receiver, slotback, all-Cdn UofOtt; mem. '75 Vanier Cup winner; number one protected player Hamilton '77 draft; played entire CFL career with Hamilton '78-91; all-time leading Tiger-Cat, CFL receiver with 706 receptions; career total 9762 reception yds; Schenley outstanding Canadian award '82; EFC all-star; 4 Grey Cup finals, '86 winner; mem. UofOtt, Cdn Football halls of Fame; res. Ridgeville, Ont.

DIXON, George (boxing); b. 29 Jul 1870, Halifax, N.S.; d. 6 Jan 1909, New York, N.Y.; nicknamed "Little Chocolate"; at 16 KO'd Young Johnson; claimed vacant world bantam title 1888; defended twice; beat Cal McCarthy in 22 rounds 1891 to win featherweight title; defended 3 times before losing to Solly Smith 20 rounds 1897; regained crown beating Dave Sullivan in 10 1898; lost to Terry McGovern 1900 then, when McGovern couldn't make weight, fought Abe Attel for title losing in 15 '01; final fight '06; pro record 158 bouts (estimated he fought some 800 times including barnstorming), won 30 by KO, 55 by decision, 1 on foul, 38 draws, 21 decisions lost, 4 times KO'd, 9 no decisions; longest fight 70 round draw with McCarthy; mem. US, Canadian Boxing, NS, Canada's Sports halls of Fame.

DIXON, George (football); b. 19 Oct 1933, New Haven, Conn.; d. 6 Aug 1990, Montreal, Que.; m. Carol Grant; c. Kirk, Eric; U of Bridgeport; promotions; Green Bay (NFL) draft; pro Montreal '59-65; 7yr CFL record 59 TDs, including 18 '60 season, 896 carries for 5615yds, 6.3 avg.; best single season '62 216 carries for 1520yds, 7.0 avg., 11 TDs; with Willie Fleming shared CFL mark longest single play gain 109yds '63; '62 Schenley outstanding player, Jeff Russel Memorial Trophy; Lord Calvert Trophy; frequent EFC, all-Cdn all-star halfback; mem. Cdn Football Hall of Fame.

DOCHERTY, Alexander (t&f); b. 6 May 1904, Scotland; d. 3 Nov 1973, Montreal, Que.; m. Gwendolyn Mullins; c.

Doreen, Gilbert; McGill; Northern Electric installation superintendant; middle distance runner; mem. Montreal AAA; ntl 1500m record; ntl mile champion; mem. '28 Olympic team; scored several victories on pre, post Olympic UK tour; Montreal Forum indoor meet title; rejected invitation to attend Notre Dame.

DOCKERILL, Sylvia (swimming); b. 17 Sep 1951, Vancouver, B.C.; given name: Sylvia Elizabeth; div. Christopher Dodd; m. Preston; UBC, BHE; home economics teacher; mem. ntl team '69-72; '70 Commonwealth, '71 Pan-Am, '72 Olympic teams; gold 100m breast stroke '71 Pan-Am, 7th medley relay '72 Olympic Games; res. Victoria, B.C.

DODGE, Ann (canoeing); b. 26 Mar 1958, Halifax, N.S.; given name: Ann Marie; div. Frederick Cooper; m. Mark Smith; c. Jasmine; Dalhousie, BPhE, Miss Murphy's Business College; kinesiology teacher Acadia; 3 gold '73 Canada Games; mem. ntl team '74-79; mem. '75 jr. worlds, '74, '77-78 worlds, '76 Olympic teams; specialized in singles, K2 (with Sue Holloway); mem. Dalhousie volleyball team '77; NS athlete of '73; mem. NS Sports Hall of Fame; res. Coldbrook, N.S.

DOEY, Jennifer (rowing); b. 9 Jan 1965, Scarborough, Ont.; m. Richard Doey; teacher; started rowing in HS '80; mem. Ntl team from '83; 2 Cdn 4s w/c, 1 8s w/c titles; 3 Head of the Charles 8s w/c; '86 Commonwealth Games gold 4s with cox; 2 Amsterdam International 8s w/c; 1 US Nationals 4s w/c, 2 8s w/c, 2 4s without cox; '89 FISU Games 4s without cox silver; '90 Vienna International pairs without cox gold; '91 world 4s without cox, 8s w/c gold; sport excellence award, '91 CARA Centennial Medal, Dick Ellis Memorial senior team of year '91 trophy; res. Lambeth, Ont.

DOHERTY, James (harness racing): b. 27 Sep 1940, Saint John, N.B.; trainer/driver/owner; drove 1st race and won '56; worked Milton Downey stable '60s; raced at Montreal, New England tracks; on NE circuit '66-76 winning NA driving title '72; one of only four drivers to win a race at Meadowlands each year since it opened in '76; best season 270 wins '76; through '97 4319 career victories, over $32M in purses; guided Green With Envy to aged pacing mare of year honors '84-85; with Sunbird Groovey set world record for aged trotting mare on half-mile track; wins include Alexander Memorial, New Jersey Classic, American National; mem. NE Harness Writers, NB, Saint John Sports halls of fame; res. Saint John N.B./Clifton, N.J.

DOHERTY, Kevin (judo); b. 6 Nov 1958, Toronto, Ont.; Concordia; ntl team '76-84; 1 ntl 71kg, 3 78kg titles; 1 US, Ont. Canada Cup 71kg title; 2 Canada Cup, International German, 1 Hungarian, Dutch 78kg titles; mem. '79, '83 Pan-Am Games, '77, '82 Pan-Am championships, '81 world championships, '84 Olympic teams; gold 71kg '77, silver 78kg '82 Pan-Am championships; silver 71kg '79 Pan-Am Games; bronze 78kg '81 worlds; fed. govt. excellence awards '82; mem. Cdn Judo Hall of Fame; res. Notre Dame de Grace, Que.

DOJACK, Paul (football); b. 24 Apr 1917, Winnipeg, Man.; given name: Paul Stanley; m. Ellen Annie Dawson; retd boys' school director; co-founder Dales Athletic Club;

softball pitcher, quarterback city juve. football title team; coached Dales 4 consecutive Western Canadian football titles, '38 ntl jr. title; WIFU official, supervisor '47-73; officiated 546 games, including 15 Grey Cups, 9 as head referee; syndicated sports column on football rules; chair. '67 ntl jr. championships, Regina Centennial bantam football tournament; 36yrs youth correctional services; v-p. Sask. Sports Hall of Fame '81, chair. selection comm. '76; mem. Cdn Football, Canada's, Sask. Sports halls of fame; res. Regina, Sask.

DOLAN, Kim (curling): b. 4 Dec 1958, Charlottetown, P.E.I.; given name: Kim MacLeod; m. Liam Dolan; c. Marc, Sinead; self-employed Restaurants & Pubs; began curling at 13; 3 PEI jr., 3 PEI mixed, 7 PEI women's title rinks; res. Charlottetown, P.E.I.

DOLAN, Paul (soccer): b. 16 Apr 1966, Ottawa, Ont.; promotion mgr. Umbro Canada; goaltender Vancouver Whitecaps NASL, Hamilton Steelers CSL, Vancouver 86ers A League; '88 CSL all-star; keeper for ntl -20 team '85 World Cup; youngest keeper to compete in World Cup game; participant 4 World Cup campaigns; mem. ntl team from '84; competed in '86 World Cup; 48 international caps; res. Vancouver, B.C.

DOLEGIEWICZ, Bishop (t&f); b. 8 Jul 1953, Toronto, Ont.; Texas; discus, shot put specialist; 1 ntl jr., Commonwealth discus, sr. shot put records; 8 ntl shot put titles; gold shot put '75 FISU Games, silver shot put '75, '79 Pan-Am Games, bronze shot put '78, discus '82 Commonwealth Games; mem. '76, '80, '84 Olympic, '79, '81 World Cup teams; res. Saskatoon, Sask.

DOMBROSKI, Ben (shooting); b. 31 Mar 1959, Orsainville, Que.; car dealership employee; fullbore rifle specialist; won Ont. grand aggregate; 2 Ont. Lt. Governor's awards; qualified 8 Bisley teams; DCRA Governor-General's, Macdonald-Stewart Grand Aggregate, Bisley Aggregate titles '98; res. Angus, Ont.

DOMIK, Bernard (roller skating); b. 27 Sep 1933, Montreal, Que.; m. Rosemary Byard; c. Virginia Suzanne, Kenneth Bernard; cartage co. owner; ntl novice 4s champion '55; Eastern regional 4s titles '55, '57; ntl intermediate 4s '59; 2nd NA 4s '59; represented Canada in Roller Skating Rinks of America; retired '59; res. Toronto, Ont.

DOMIK, Bob (softball); b. 8 Jun 1942, Duparquet, Que.; m. Ann Purdy; c. Dawn Darlene, Sunday Rozalee; Davita Dorothy; partner cartage business; mem. '72 world title team, pitched no-hitter, voted world's best pitcher with 0.00 ERA; 7 ntl championships from '68, 2 titles; 14 consecutive strikeouts, 18 of 21 outs one '75 7-inning game; designed pitching program available through Softball Canada; pres.-founder Canadian International Softball Ambassadors; res. Cameron, Ont.

DOMONKOS, Mariann (table tennis); b. 12 Feb 1958, Budapest, Hungary; m. Adam Sharara; Concordia, UofOtt; coach; 9 Que. singles, 11 women's doubles, 7 mixed doubles titles; 10 ntl singles titles (in succession); mem. ntl team from '72; 4 ntl jr. girls, 1 NA jr. girls titles; NA women's doubles '72; gold medal sweep, singles, women's, mixed

doubles, team '79 Pan-Am Games; with Gloria Hsu gold '85, with Joe Ng silver '91 Commonwealth championships doubles; competed '88 Olympics; competed as amateur in West German pro league '81-82 ranking 3rd overall; '82 ntl Open women's singles titles (1st Canadian); certified Que., Cdn. table tennis coach; Que. team athlete of '78; Southwest Que. athlete of '78, '80; ntl team coach '88-98; mem. Que. Sports Hall of Fame; res. Ottawa, Ont.

DONAGHEY, Sam (soccer/administration); b. 2 Feb 1922, Londonderry Co., Northern Ireland; m. Margaret Henderson; c. Alison Yvonne, Glynis Margaret, Samuel, Motra Elaine, Kery, Derryn; retd. policeman, cartographer; excelled in soccer, boxing, coached t&f in youth; emigrated to Canada '52; founder/player/mgr. Edmonton Police Soccer Team; coached youth soccer; anchor Edmonton Police Tug-O-War team '53-55; exec. Edmonton Dist. SA, ASA from '55; wrote 1st Alta soccer handbook; founder/editor Alberta Soccer Bulletin; Cdn Soccer News; upgraded soccer officiating in Alta.; Edmonton District HA exec '60-61; founder/exec. Western Canada SL, CSA; ntl team mgr. '67 PAG, '68 Olympics; clubhouse chair./assoc. dir. Edmonton International Speedway; key role in '78 Edmonton Commonwealth Games; liasion dir. '73 Brier; Intl ambassador '83 FISU Games; founder/pres. CSA Alumni Assn. from '97; ASA outstanding contribution award; Carling award '60; Edmonton sport leadership award; Edmonton Sportsman of '69; 2 United Way sportsman awards; hon. Chief 7 Cree, 1 Blackfoot, Ojibawa, Metis bands; life mem. Club Stardust Edmonton; recipient 1 of 7 Royal Bank jr. Olympic ring; Klondike Days silver tankard award; Royal Irish award; Northern Ireland sports council award; Edmonton mayor's award; 3 Alta awards; Commonwealth Games award; CSA Aubrey Sanford award; Kidney Foundation award; Editor's Choice award for poetry; Defence of Britain medal; War Service medal; Centennial medal '67; Cdn 125 medal '92; Cdn, Alta police long service medals; Masonic medal of merit; mem. Order of Canada, Edmonton Sports, Historical halls of fame; res. Edmonton, Alta.

DONAHUE, Jake (t&f): b. 6 Apr 1940, St. Stephen, N.B.; given name: John Edward; m. Theresa; wheelchair t&f, table tennis; won 6 gold, 16 silver, 12 bronze in ntl wheelchair competitions '73-83; 3 silver, 5 bronze in 4 Pan-Am Wheelchair Games; ntl shotput record 6.14m '84; bronze '76, '80, silver, bronze '84 Olympics for Physically Disabled; St. Stephen's athlete of '76; NB merit award '76; NB outstanding athlete '78, CWSA most improved athlete '78; Bill Greenough Sports Person of '79; 2 St. Stephen's Courier athlete of yr awards; mem. NB Sports Hall of Fame; res. St. Stephen, N.B.

DONALDSON, Ron (boxing): b. 6 Sep 1970, St. Catharines, Jamaica; shipper; middleweight; won 75kg title Canada vs. USA '93; coached by Russ Anber; gold 75kg '94 Commonwealth Games; res. Chateauguay, Que.

DONATELLI, Eden (speed skating); b. 19 Jul 1970, Mission, B.C.; McGill; began skating at 4; mem. ntl team from '86; set Cdn short track midget 300m record '83; 1st overall '86 Cdn jr. championships; mem. '86 world record short track 3000m relay team; set Cdn long track junior 5000m record; 8 world short track gold medals; '88 Olympic

500m silver, 3000m relay bronze; set Cdn sr. record placing 6th '88 Olympics 1000m; 2 Cdn junior, 1 Cdn intermediate, 6 Cdn senior records; 2 Pacific Rim team short track titles; world champion award '87, '89; BC jr. athlete of '87; mem. Athletes motivating excellence group; res. Mission, B.C.

DONISON, Butch (wrestling); b. 29 Sep 1938, Avonlea, Sask; given name: Sebastien; m. Patricia Greenaway; c. Mike, Diana; Denver, BSc; engineer; youngest of three wrestling brothers; 15yr wrestling career during which he competed in every weight class at provincial level winning titles in all but one; 3yrs all-Rocky Mountain Conf.; 13 provincial titles '53-67; 3 ntl titles; Commonwealth Games middleweight silver '66; coach Regina WC '65-67, U of Regina wrestling team '68-69; mem. Sask. Sports Hall of Fame; res. Regina, Sask.

DONISON, Danny (wrestling); b. 12 Aug 1932, Avonlea, Sask.; m. Marilyn Sedman; c. Lori, Lisa; U of Regina; administrator; 6 Sask. light, welter, middleweight titles '53-68, 5 times runnerup; ntl lightweight title '55; Man. lightweight title '58; coach Regina WC '54-65; chair. wrestling comm. Sask. branch AAU of C '55-60; 2yrs secty. Regina Caps hockey club; secty.-treas. Regina Boxing & Wrestling Club '55-68; Man. outstanding wrestler award '58; mem. Sask. Sports Hall of Fame; res. Regina, Sask.

DONISON, Lee (wrestling/boxing); b. 9 Mar 1928, Avonlea, Sask.; m. Joan Peterson; c. Brian Lee, Garan-Loren, Ross Normand, Joanne Betty; Purdue; insurance exec.; Sask. heavyweight wrestling titles '53-56; Sask. light heavyweight boxing title '52, '63, heavyweight '53-57; ntl light heavy boxing title '63; alternate '54 BEG team; only Canadian athlete to win provincial, ntl boxing, wrestling titles 4 successive years '53-56; chairman Sask. boxing & wrestling '53-54, boxing '55-58, '62-63; Sask. championship outstanding wrestler award '54; mem. Sask. Sports Hall of Fame; res. Regina, Sask.

DONNELLY, Sharon (triathlon); b. 29 Jul 1967, Scarborough, Ont.; given name: Sharon Lynn; m. David Rudnicki; Royal Military College, B Comm; triathlete, reserve officer; specialist in Olympic distances; began competitive career as swimmer; competed in '84 Olympic trials; mem. '84 ntl record 4x100 medley relay team; held ntl, prov. 100m fly records; mem. Cdn Forces running team '90-95, CF winter biathlon team '94-95; launched, coached Petawawa running club '93-95, swim coach; ntl triathlon title '97; competed on WC circuit from '97; Cdn female WC triathlete of '97; CF female athlete of '95; 2 Ont. achievement awards; Ottawa ACT triathlete of '96-97; World Military Games fair play award '95; 2 Ont. international elite female triathletre awards; 10th in world rankings '96; honored by city of Gloucester '98; gold '99 Pan-Am Games; mem. 2000 Olympic team; mem. Cdn Forces Sports Hall of Fame; res. Kingston, Ont.

DONOHUE, Jack (basketball/coaching); b. 4 Jun 1931, New York, N.Y.; m. Mary Jane Choffin; c. Carol, John Joe, Kathy, Mary Beth, Bryan, Maura; Fordham, BA, NYU, MA; consultant Vancouver Grizzlies; began coaching St. Nicholas of Tolentine NYC '54, shifted to Power Memorial NYC; HS coaching record 250-46 including 71 consecutive victories due largely to efforts of Lew Alcindor (Kareem Abdul Jabbar); coach Holy Cross '65-71 compiling 106-65 record; Eastern region coach of '70; Cdn ntl team coach '72-90; guided team to 4th '76 Olympics; gold '83 FISU Games; qualified team for '80, '84, '88 Olympics; noted raconteur, TV commentator, business consultant; conceived popular Donohue's Legends TV series; CIAU championship tourney MVP award bears his name; spokesman for year of the coach in Canada; Cdn Coaching Assn. Geoff Gowan award; King Clancy award for work with disabled; mem. Cdn Basketball; Ottawa, Cdn Amateur (Olympic) Sports, NYC Coaches, Cdn Assn. of Public Speakers halls of fame; res. Kanata, Ont.

DORATY, Ken (hockey); b. 23 Jun 1906, Stittsville, Ont.; d. 4 May 1981, Moose Jaw, Sask.; given name: Kenneth Edward; m. Dorothy; c. Saundra, Curtis; billiard parlor chain owner; raised in Rouleau, Sask.; mem. '25 Regina Pats Memorial Cup winners; diminutive size earned him variety of nicknames "Mighty Atom, Little Poison, Mighty Mite, Midget, Mighty Molecule" and one which stuck "Cagey"; brief stint Chicago '26-27; Toronto '33-35; gained reputation as money player with knack for scoring "big" goals like one at 4:46 of 6th overtime period as Toronto nipped Boston 1-0 in 5th game best-of-five '33 Stanley Cup semifinal; '34 accounted for fastest 3 goals in regulation play as Toronro beat Ottawa 7-4; frequently at odds with Conn Smythe, he closed NHL career with Detroit '37-38; coached Moose Jaw Canucks to '46 Memorial Cup finals; key role in Metro Prystai signing with Chicago; mem. Goulbourn Wall, Sask. Sports Hall of Fame.

DORSCH, Henry (football); b. 11 Nov 1940, Weyburn, Sask.; m. Helen Patricia Kalb; c. Douglas, Natalie, Debra; Tulsa, BSc; annuity broker; 2yrs Regina Rams before starring at fullback Tulsa; defensive back, backup fullback Saskatchewan '64-73; 4 Grey Cup finals, 1 winner; mem. Roughriders management comm. '75-80; GM Roughriders '78-80; res. Regina, Sask.

DORSEY, Dean (football); b. 13 May 1957, Toronto. Ont.; m. Lee McArthur; c. Paul, Thomas, Matt; UofT BPhE; v-p. Impac Golf, retd. football coach; punter, place kicking specialist; played jr Scarborough Rams '77; Jr A hockey Sault Ste. Marie '76-77; special teams award UofT; pro CFL Toronto '82; USFL Washington Federals '83; CFL Ottawa '84-87, '89-90; NFL Philadelphia '88; CFL Edmonton '91 tied Mark Mosley's all-pro record 23 consecutive field goals '87; all-Eastern '87; head coach Jr. Riders '97-98, QMJFL '98 champions; res. Kanata, Ont.

DOTY, Frederick (football); b. 25 Oct 1924, Toronto, Ont.; m. Beverley Brown; c. Cole, Tobin; UofT, BSc; retd civil engineer, pres. Dufferin Concrete Products; jr. Calgary '44; basketball Calgary RCAF '43-44; pro football Toronto '45-49; played both Argos, Varsity '46; 3 Grey Cup champions; mem. Mississauga Sports Hall of Fame; res. Mississauga, Ont.

DOUCET, Everard (builder/hockey); b. 29 Dec 1911, Bathurst, N.B.; d. 2 Oct 1971, Bathurst, N.B.; m. Betty; coached all levels juve. through sr.; 3 Maritime titles; coached Bathurst Papermakers to North Shore titles '49-52; inagurated Bathurst minor hockey, baseball programs; Centennial medal; mem. NB, Bathurst Sports halls of fame.

DOUCET, Paul (boxing); b. 9 Oct 1917, Bathurst, N.B.; d. 8 Oct 1939, Bathurst, N.B.; nicknamed "Kid Lulu"; following standout amateur career turned pro '35; held Maritime lightweight title '38, Cdn jr. welterweight '39, Eastern Cdn lightweight '40; from '36-38 fought 37 times posting 30 wins, 5 losses, 2 draws, 15 KOs; ranked 3rd contender for Cdn lightweight title; fought Maurice Arnault (French welter champion), Dave Castilloux (Cdn lightweight titlist); killed in auto accident; mem. NB Sports Hall of Fame.

DOUCETTE, Gerry (football); b. 18 Sep 1933, Toronto, Ont.; given name: Gerald David; m. Mildred Ruth Grosse; c. Mike, Steve, Jill, Sue; salesman; led Etobicoke Rams to TDIAA title; Balmy Beach ORFU '53; Argos '54-59; backup quarterback, punter, place kicking specialist; CFL record: 75 scheduled games, 366 passes, 180 completions, 14 tds, 158 kickoffs, including 62 '56 season, 8458yds, 180 punts, 6691yds; dir. Argos ticket sales '78-79; res. Oakville, Ont.

DOUGLAS, Jim (lacrosse); b. 12 Mar 1919, New Westminster, B.C.; considered one of best box lacrosse players in his era; mem. 2 Mann Cup winners, 5 league champions; league MVP '39; 466 career goals, 182 assists, 218 games in 11 years with New Westminster; mem. Canadian Lacrosse, BC Sports halls of fame; res. Burnaby, B.C.

DOUTHWRIGHT, Joyce (basketball/field hockey); b. 25 Apr 1950, Moncton, N.B.; given name: Joyce Anne; m. Dick Slipp; c. Shanda, Tyler; UNB, BPhE, BA; teacher, coach, coaching co-ordinator NBFHA; mem. ntl women's basketball team '69-76, NB team from '71; NB ntl title team '80, player-coach; 4 times ntl tournament all-star; mem. NB field hockey team '69-74; MVP UNB field hockey team '70-71; coached basketball, field hockey UNB; 2 CIAU FH coach of yr awards; tech. dir. NBABA '74-76; mem. '76 Olympic team; coach NB team '79 Canada Games; coached NB women's basketball Francophone Games bronze medal team '97; 2 CIAU FH coach of yr awards; mem. UNB phys ed dept. '76-80; selector ntl field hockey team; UNB athlete of '73-74; CIAU FH rookie of yr trophy bears her name; mem. NB Sports Hall of Fame; res. Fredericton, N.B.

DOWDING, John (figure skating); b. 27 Apr 1957, Oakville, Ont.; given name: John Stuart; m. Diane Doris; pro skater; with sister Debbie ntl jr. dance title '74; teamed with Lorna Wighton from '75; ntl titles '76-79; mem. '80 Olympic, world teams; only Cdn Oberstdorf title winners; 1st Cdn dance team to join Ice Capades; pro dance title '83; res. Fresno, Calif.

DOWDS, Maureen (t&f); b. 3 Jul 1948, Whitehorse, Yukon; given name: Maureen Joan; UMan, UWO.; E-D Manitoba Special Olympics, ex-HS phys ed teacher; shot put specialist; twice top HS, UMan female athlete; Red River shot put title '64; ntl jr. '67; bronze, ntl jr. record 47'1" '67 Pan-Am Games; ntl title '68; CWIAA title '72; runnerup ntl championships '74-75; 4th '75 Pan-Am Games with PB 16.46m to tie record; injury forced her from '76 Olympics into retirement; mem. Man. Sports Hall of Fame selection comm.; mem. Man. Sports Hall of Fame; res. Winnipeg, Man.

DOWELL, Hanson (administration); b. 14 Sep 1906, Stewiacke, N.S.; given name: Hanson Taylor; m. Marjorie Alice Mosher; c. Charles Hanson, Roy Francis Mosher, Judith Helen, Edgar Douglass, Janet Marjorie; Dalhousie, LLB; retired judge; Central Valley HL officer '35-36; pres. Maritime AHA '36-40; v-p. CAHA '40-45, pres. '45-47; pres. CVHL '52-53; treas. MAHA '68-74, NSHA '74-81; USAHA citation '50; CAHA merit award '62; life mem. CAHA, Middleton CC; mem. NS Sports Hall of Fame; res. Middleton, N.S.

DOWNEY, Raymond (boxing); b. 23 Sep 1968, Halifax, N.S.; c. Tyler Flint, Raya Flint; pro boxer; son of Dave Downey former Cdn middleweight champion; became Cdn jr featherweight champ at 14; at 17 won Cdn intermediate light middleweight title; at 18 became Cdn senior light middleweight king; mem. Citadel Amateur Boxing Club coached by Taylor Gordon; bronze '88 Olympics; silver '90 World Cup, Commonwealth Games; gold '89 Canada Games, '90 President's Cup in Indonesia; SFC Viscount Alexander trophy '89; Olympic champion award '89; turned pro '93; pro record: 13-1-1, 9kos; res. Philadelphia, Pa.

DOWNS, Darcy (skiing); b. 26 Aug 1968, Regina, Sask.; m. Jane Mather; freestyle specialist; Nor-Am aerials champion '91-92; 10 WC medals; 4 straight ntl combined titles '92-94; ntl ballet title '95; world combined gold '97; ntl aerials silver '98; Ottawa ACT FS skier of '97; res. Vancouver, B.C.

DOYLE, Jimmy (golf); b. 28 Feb 1933, Winnipeg, Man.; d. 6 Apr 1991, Sandy Hook, Man.; given name: James Arthur; m. Beverly Byron; c. Drew, Byron, Pat, Maureen; Man. jr. title '51; mem. ntl jr. basketball champion Winnipeg Light Infantry team '51; Sask. Open title '61; runnerup Man. Open '57; ND State Open, Thunder Bay Open titles; won '75 Man. Amateur; 2 Man. Srs titles; '88 age group sr. A title; '89 medalist sr. interprovincial team championships, 3rd individual; 11 Man. Willingdon Cup teams; Cdn amateur title, low medalist '68; mem. '68 Eisenhower Cup team; Man. athlete of '68; mem. Man. Sports Hall of Fame.

DRAFFIN, Ernie (soccer); b. 21 Sep 1909, Winnipeg, Man., d. 19 Dec 1982, Winnipeg, Man.; m. Louise; c. Arlene; politician; goaler '23-24 Welton Cup HS team, '25-26 Man. HS title team, '27, '30 Man. jr. title teams, '31 Westbrook John Queen Cup winner, '33 2nd div. United Weston team; '34 Man. title team; assisted in formation National League; Man. FA pres. '55-61; tech. dir. soccer '67 Pan-Am Games; MFA registrar; founding dir., hon. life mem. Man. Sports Fed.; life mem. MSA; CCF MLA Assiniboia; mem. Man. Sports Hall of Fame.

DRAKE, Clare (coaching); b. 9 Oct 1928, Yorkton, Sask.; m. Dolly Carlson; c. Debbie, Jamie; UBC, BPhE, UAlta, BEd, Washington, MSc, Oregon, EdD; prof., hockey coach; jr. A hockey Regina, Medicine Hat, sr. Yorkton; semipro baseball; basketball, football, hockey UBC, hockey team capt. sr. year, hockey UAlta; began coaching minor hockey, football, basketball, t&f '51, football, baseball '55; coach German ntl HL '54-55; UAlta head hockey coach from '58 (excluding '69-70, '75-76, '79-80); coach Edmonton Oilers (WHA) '75-76; asst. coach Winnipeg (NHL) '88-91; special assignments coach San Jose from '92; UAlta head football coach '62, '67-68; rare feat of guiding UAlta to Vanier Cup football title '67, CIAU hockey title '67-68; winningest univ. hockey coach NA history, 1st Cdn univ. hockey coach to record 500 victories; through '87 guided UAlta to 622 wins, 16 conference, 6 ntl titles; coached Lacombe Rockets '65 Ahearne Cup; ntl team '72, '81, '87 FISU Games, gold '81; co-coach '80 Olympic team; coached first-ever Cdn team Spengler Cup winner '84; ntl novice singles racquetball title '71; Edmonton sportsman of year '67, '75; hon. life mem. Alta. Football Coaches Assn.; 2 CIAU hockey coach of yr awards; active administrative role football, hockey; authored numerous hockey articles; UAlta arena bears his name; mem. UAlta Sports Wall, Canada's, Alta. Sports halls of fame; res. Edmonton, Alta.

DRAKICH, Ed (volleyball); b. 30 Sep 1962, Windsor, Ont.; UofT; 2 CIAU all-Cdn; represented Canada in 120 international indoor matches '85-88; pro with Munich '88-89; played beach volleyball from '85 winning 4 ntl titles; sister, mother both played on ntl teams; with Jose Cuervo NA champion '92; competed 6 world beach championships; res. Toronto, Ont.

DRAXINGER, Kevin (swimming); b. 16 Mar 1967, Vancouver, B.C.; UBC; backstroke specialist; mem. ntl team from '87; 2 Canada Games gold; 9 ntl titles; 4 CIAU titles; 6 World Cup competitions gold medals; bronze '90, silver '94 Commonwealth 200m backstroke; mem. '91 FISU, '92 Olympic team; ntl 200m record holder; 1 CIAU male swimmer of yr award; res. Richmond, B.C.

DRAYTON, Jerome (t&f); b. 10 Jan 1945, Kolbermoor, W.Germany; given name: Peter Buniak; McMaster, BA; govt. fitness consultant; 1st of 4 ntl 10,000m titles '68; ntl record for distance 28:25.8 '70; ntl 5000m title '70; ntl marathon champion '72; 3 Fukuoka Japan marathon titles; Boston marathon '77; world record indoor 3-mile 13:06.0 '75, 10-mile track record 46:37.6 '73; mem. 3 Commonwealth, '76 Olympic teams; silver '78 Commonwealth Games; '79 National Capital, '80 Maryland International marathon titles; retired from competition '84; Norton Crowe trophy '77; mem. Cdn Roadrunners, Etobicoke, Canada's Sports halls of fame; res. Toronto, Ont.

DRILLON, Gord (hockey); b. 23 Oct 1913, Moncton, N.B.; d. 23 Sep 1986, Saint John, N.B.; given name: Gordon Arthur; m. Barbara Alice Lee; NB govt. consultant; jr. Moncton Athletics, Wheelers, Toronto Young Rangers, Lions, sr. Pittsburgh '35; pro Maple Leafs '36-42, Canadiens '42-43; NHL record: 155g, 139a, playoffs 26g, 15a; twice 1st, 2nd team all-star; NHL scoring title, Lady Byng Trophy '37-38; chosen by fans as most popular NHL player '39; with Bob Davidson, Syl Apps Sr. formed Leafs' DAD line; southpaw softball pitcher Toronto Danforth Aces, Maritime CNR; competed Eastern Cdn tennis championships; honored by City of Saint John; mem. Canada's, NB Sports, Canadian Hockey halls of fame.

DRINKWATER, Graham (hockey); b. 22 Feb 1875, Montreal, Que.; d. 26 Sep 1946, Montreal, Que.; given name: Charles Graham; McGill; jr. MAAA 1892-93 title team; McGill jr. football, int. hockey champions; Montreal Victorias 4 Stanley Cup winners, team capt. 1898-99; never turned pro; mem. Hockey Hall of Fame.

DRISCOLL, Mary Ellen (golf); b. 30 Dec 1937, Saint John, N.B.; ed. dir. St. Joseph's Hospital; 6 NB, 3 Maritime jr. titles '53-58; lost ntl jr. title in playoff '57; 25 NB women's amateur, 6 NS ladies, 10 (consec.) NB sr. Ladies titles through '97; mem. 38 NB ladies amateur teams; runner-up Cdn amateur '65; 27 Riverside Club titles; nominated as alternate to 3 Commonwealth teams; dubbed "Queen of NB Golf"; twice broke 70 barrier; mem. NB, Saint John Sports halls of fame; res. Rothesay, N.B.

DROLET, François (speed skating); b. 16 Jul 1972, Ste-Foy, Que; short track specialist; 2 bronze '95 Universiade; 2 world championship relay silver; 2 world team championship gold '96; with Marc Gagnon, Derrick Campbell, Éric Bedard gold '98 Olympic 5000m relay; gold '98 world team championships; res. Montreal, Que.

DROLET, Nancy (hockey); b. 2 Sep 1973, Drummondville, Que.; orthotherapist/massotherapist; standout softball player mem. ntl team '90-91; Pan-Am Games silver '91; competed '89 Canada Summer Games in softball, '91 Canada Winter Games in hockey; began playing hockey age 5; mem. Jofa-Titan 8 Que., 3 ntl title teams; Team Que. 3 ntl title teams; forward 3 world, 1 Pacific Rim, 1 3-Nations Cup title teams; mem. '98 Olympic team; Elaine Tanner Trophy '92; res. Repentigny, Que.

DRYDEN, Dave (hockey); b. 5 Sep 1941, Hamilton, Ont.; given name: David Murray; m. Sandra Bailey; c. Debra, Greg; Waterloo, Wilfrid Laurier, BA, York, (hons) BA, Niagara Falls, MA; retd. PS principal; goaltender Galt Jrs.; 9 NHL seasons with NY Rangers '61-62, Chicago '65-69, Buffalo '70-73, Edmonton '79-80; WHA with Chicago '74-75, Edmonton '75-70; minor league stints with Rochester, Buffalo (AHL), St. Louis (CPHL), Dallas (CHL), Salt Lake (WHL); NHL record: 203 scheduled games, 48-57-24, 10,424min, 9so, 555ga, 3 playoff games, 0-2, 137min, 9ga; WHA record: 242 scheduled games, 13,920min, 8so, 808ga, 19 playoff games, 958min, 63ga; asst. coach Edmonton '79; mgr./coach Peterborough OHL '79-81, goalie coach Detroit '85-91, goalie consultant Nippon Paper Crane, Japan from '96; WHA MVP award '79; res. Oakville, Ont.

DRYDEN, Ken (hockey); b. 8 Aug 1947, Hamilton, Ont.; given name: Kenneth Wayne; m. Lynda; c. Sarah, Michael; Cornell, UMan, McGill, LLB., hon LLD, Windsor, UBC, York; hockey executive, lawyer, author; jr. B Etobicoke; Boston 3rd choice, 14 overall '64 amateur draft; opted for Cornell; 3 times all-American, ECAA tournament MVP; Boston U outstanding opponent award '69; ntl team; pro Montreal Voyageurs '70-71; Canadiens '71-79; sat out '73-74 to complete law studies; Calder Memorial Trophy, 5 Vezina Trophies, 1 Conn Smythe Trophy; 5 1st team, once 2nd team all-star goaler; mem. Team Canada '72, '76; NHL record: 397 scheduled games, 46so, 2.24 avg., 112 playoff games, 10 so, 2.40 avg., 338-89-74 win-loss-tie record; mem. 6 Stanley Cup winners; authored *The Game*, with Roy MacGregor *Home Game*, 2 other books; Ont. Youth commissioner '84-86, Yukon youth consultant '87; pres./ CEO/GM Maple Leafs from '97; ABC-TV color commentator 3 winter Olympics; initiated Ken Dryden scholarships; mem. Etobicoke, Canada's Sports, Hockey halls of fame; res. Toronto, Ont.

DRYDEN, Nikki (swimming): b. 4 May 1975, Calgary, Alta.; backstroke, FS specialist; began competing age 10; 16 ntl titles; mem. ntl team from '91; 3 silver '91 Pan-Am, bronze '94 Commonwealth Games; mem. '92, '96 Olympic Games teams; competed '93 Pan-Pacific championships; Victoria jr athlete of '91; res. Gainesville, Fla.

DUBE, Ajay (field hockey): b. 10 Oct 1960, Paris, France; Humber College, York; owns sports apparel co.; emigrated to Canada age 11; goalkeeper Ont., Cdn under-21, senior teams; retd from ntl outdoor team '89 but returned '94; mem. Outaouais, Ookpik clubs; mem. '87 gold medal Pan-Am Games team; mem. '88 Olympic team; competes in both outdoor, indoor competitions; varied exec. roles with Ookpik, FH Ont.; competed '93 Ottawa marathon; mem. Big Brothers organization; res. Toronto, Ont.

DUBÉ, Danielle (hockey): b. 10 Mar 1976, Vancouver, B.C.; pro hockey player; played 13yrs Grandview MHA; Jr. B with BC champion Grandview Steelers '94, Abbotsford Pilots '95; Jr. A Penticton Panthers '94; goaltender Central Texas Stampede Western Pro League '96-97; plays roller hockey with Vancouver Voodoos; mem. Team Canada from '93; 1 world, 2 Pacific Rim, 1 3-Nations Cup titles; res. Vancouver, B.C.

DUBLINSKI, Tom (football): b. 8 Aug 1930, Chicago, Ill.; m. Jo Ann Hurley; c. Michael, Karen, William, Mary Jo, Richard; Utah, BSc retd. insurance exec.; pro Detroit '52-54, Toronto '55-57, '62, NY Giants '58, Hamilton '59, '61, Denver '60; all-conf. HS baseball, football, college football; offensive player of week US college ranks, hon, mention all-American quarterback; 4th in US total offence sr. year, 2yrs conf. offensive leader; mem. Detroit NFL title teams '52-53, div. champs '54; only pro quarterback to play entire college all-star game offensively and defensively '54; mem. '58 Giants' div. champs; completed CFL record 16 of 18 passes for Argos vs Ticats '55 season opener; mem. '59, '61 EFC Hamilton title teams; played in inaugural Cdn East-West all-star game; res. Fountain Hills, Ariz.

DUBNICOFF, Tanya (cycling): b. 7 Nov 1969, Winnipeg, Man.; UMan.; marketing; started racing '90; won 1st ntl sprint crown same yr; gold sprint '91, '95, '99, 500m time trial '99 Pan-Am, '94, '98 Commonwealth games; '93 world championship, '94 World Cup; 8 ntl titles; 1 Pan-Am Games, 1 world record; 3 World Cup race victories; ITT 500m silver, sprint bronze '98 worlds; competed '92, '96 Olympics; flag-bearer '99 Pan-Am Games; also excelled in hockey, ringette; res. Calgary, Alta.

DUBOIS, Luc (skiing): b. 19 Jun 1946, Ste. Agathe, Que.; m. Line Marcoux; c. Olivier, Elise, Magalie;Montreal, BA, UofOtt, BPhE; ski event producer; distributor health supplements; ex-hotellier; broken leg during '65 ntl jr. championships ended promising competitive career; coaching '66-76; Level IV CSIA certificate; Que. team coach '70-71; asst. coach men's WC team '71-72; asst. program dir. CSA '72-73; program dir. '73-76; p.-pres. Canadian Ski Coaches Fed.; v-p. CSIA; mem. ntl tech.

comm. CSCF, CSIA; demonstrator '79 Interski; jr. college athlete of '64; competitive water skier '60-64, Que. champion, masters champion; res. St. Jovite, Que.

DUBOIS, Theo (rowing); b. 19 May 1911, Brussels, Belgium; given name: Theo Alfred; UMan, BArch; retd. architect, Wpg planning examiner; ntl jr. singles '38, CAAO singles, sr. doubles '39; qualified for cancelled '40 Olympics; NAAO sr. doubles with Albert Riley '40; US singles '40-41, '47; ntl singles '41-42; Eastern Rowing Assn. singles '42; ntl doubles '47; failed to qualify '48 Olympics despite posting time faster than Olympic winner; retired from major competition '48; veteran's trophy '76-77 North Western Rowing Assn. regatta; outstanding cyclist; twice defeated US champion Adolph Velthuysen '34; representing Ottawa YMCA won EO light heavyweight boxing title '43; Lou Marsh Trophy, Canadian athlete of '41; mem. Man. Sports Hall of Fame; res. Winnipeg, Man.

DUCEY, John (baseball); b. 31 Aug 1908, Buffalo, N.Y.; d. 12 Sep 1983, Edmonton, Alta.; m. Grace Jay Mungull; c. Brant, Duane; real estate broker; batboy Edmonton Western pro league '21; 1st base Edmonton Yeomen jrs.; umpire Calif., N.E. '31-45; co-founder Intercity Big 4 League Alta. '46; mgr. class A Western International league '53-54, Eskimos semipro club (WCL) '55-61; mgr. ntl team National Baseball Congress global world series runnerup '57; formed Edmonton Oldtimers BA '64; hon. dir. Edmonton Trappers AAA club; trustee Carling-O'Keefe award of merit; mem. Edmonton, Alta. Sports, Canadian Baseball halls of fame.

DUCHESNAY, Isabelle (figure skating); b. 18 Dec 1963, Hull, Que.; div. Christopher Dean; UofOtt; pro skater; with brother Paul formed ice dance team which earned ntl jr. silver '82, bronze Cdn sr. championships '84-95; feeling they were being ignored by Cdn skating officials took advantage of dual Canadian-French citizenship to compete for France where they claimed ntl titles '85-92; world bronze '89, silver '90, gold '91; competed '88, '92 Olympics winning silver '92; 1 silver, 2 bronze European championships; turned pro and toured with varied ice shows from '90; appeared in TV/film productions; did some TV/radio announcing in France, Germany, Canada; organized/managed own skating tours in Europe; conducted leadership/stress seminars; hon. pres. Pavillon du Parc Foundation '96; hon. pres. Star 97 ballroom and competitive dancing '96; back injury to Paul led to retirement from competition '97; thwarted by CFSA in getting coaching certification left Canada again to teach with Kerry Leitch at JP Igloo Ice & Inline Sports Complex; rinks in France, Aylmer, Que. bear their name, also street in Aylmer; awarded French Legion of Honor; res. Ellenton, Fla.

DUCHESNAY, Paul (figure skating); b. 31 Jul 1961, Hull, Que.; Uof Ott, BSc; pro figure skater; dual Canadian-French citizenship; with sister Isabelle formed ice dance team which won world championship; (see Isabelle for competitive record); back injury led to retirement from competition '97; thwarted by CFSA in getting coaching certification left Canada again to teach with Kerry Leitch at JP Igloo Ice & Inline Sports Complex; rinks in France, Aylmer, Que. bear their name, also street in Aylmer; awarded French Legion of Honor; res. Ellenton, Fla.

DUCHESNE, Gaétan (hockey): b. 11 Jul 1962, Les Saulles, Que.; left wing Quebec (QJHL) '79-81, Hershey (AHL) '83, NHL Washington '81-87, Quebec '87-89, Minnesota '89-93, San Jose '93-95, Florida '95; NHL record: 1028 scheduled games, 179g, 254a, 84 playoff games, 14g, 13a; res. Montreal, Que.

DUDLEY, George (builder/hockey): b. 19 Apr 1894, Midland, Ont.; d. 8 May 1960, Midland, Ont.; UofT, LLD; lawyer; played hockey in Midland; after earning law degree turned to executive roles; mem. CAHA exec. '25, pres. '40-42, secty '45, secty-mgr.; major role in early visits to Canada by Russian teams; treas. OHA; pres. IIHF; head hockey section '60 Olympic Games at time of death; mem. Hockey Hall of Fame.

DUFF, Alexander (coaching): b. 12 Apr 1887, Scotland; d. 16 Dec 1952, Toronto, Ont.; given name: Alexander Robert; UofT, BSc; chemical engineer; hon. coach High Park Club; formed Dolphinets SC teaching aquatic skills for girls and women; guided Jean Kirkpatrick 1st Cdn woman to medal in US competition; coached Dorothy Prior 1st Cdn female swimmer to compete in Olympics '28; coached Cdn swimming/diving team '34 BEG; asst coach '36 Olympics; Toronto pool bears his name; mem. Ont. Aquatic Hall of Fame.

DUFF, Dick (hockey): b. 18 Feb 1936, Kirkland Lake, Ont.; given name: Richard Terrance; St. Michael's College, Assumption College, BA; retd hockey scout; jr. St. Mike's; pro Toronto '54-63; left wing line with Tod Sloan, George Armstrong; NY Rangers '64, Montreal '65-69, Los Angeles '70, Buffalo '71-72; asst coach Leafs '79-81, scout '81-93; NHL record: 1030 scheduled games, 283g, 289a, 114 playoff games, 30g, 49a; mem. 6 Stanley Cup winners; res. Mississauga, Ont.

DUFF, Mike (motorsport): b. 13 Dec 1939, Toronto, Ont.; given name: Michael Alan; m. Carol Sullivan; c. Christopher, Jacqueline, Tony; mechanical technician; launched Cdn motorcycle racing career '55; European circuit road racer '60; 5th 350cc class, 3rd 250cc class '63 worlds; 2nd 250cc '65 worlds; 9th person in world to lap Isle of Man at 100 mph avg.; 1st to lap Belgian GP course on 250cc at 125 mph avg.; Belgian GP title '64, Dutch TT 125, Finnish GP 250cc '65; 2nd Isle of Man '65; major injury sustained '65 led to '68 retirement following US, Cdn circuit races; changed name to Michelle following sex change operation '85; mem. Cdn Motorsport Hall of Fame; res. Brampton, Ont.

DUFFY, James (t&f): b. 1 May 1890, Sligo County, Ireland; d. 23 Apr 1915, Ypres, Belgium; stone cutter; emigrated to Canada '11; 5th marathon '12 Olympics; Ward marathon, Hamilton Around-the-Bay marathon titles '12; Boston marathon '14; pro with limited success '14; killed overseas WW1.

DUFRESNE, Christian (tennis): b. 29 Apr 1950, Montreal, Que.; m. Marie-Josée Bonin; c. Julie, Caroline; UofOtt, Montreal, BPhE; tech. dir. Tennis Canada; Royal Lifesaving Society bronze medal; certified scuba diver; tennis instructor Laval '69-73; Four Seasons TC '73-78; administrative dir.

QTF '75-79; tech. dir. QTF '79-80; tech. dir. CTA '81-90; last known res. Laval, Que.

DUFRESNE, Coleen (basketball): b. 15 Feb 1953, Halifax, N.S.; UofOtt, BPhE, McGill; teacher; NS, Que. shot put, javelin, triple jump records; led OUAA basketball scorers 4yrs; ntl team '74-76; mem. '75 world, Pan-Am Games, '76 Olympic teams; mem. Que. team '71, '75 Canada Winter Games teams; all-Cdn '75; Ottawa region basketball athlete of '74-75; coached sr. basketball Que., NB, Que. provincial jr. team; asst. coach '79 Canada Games gold medal team; taught HS phys ed Pte. Claire '76-79; mem. UNB phys ed staff '80-84; UMan basketball coach from '84; 2 CIAU coach of yr awards; res. Winnipeg, Man.

DUGAN, Arnie (lacrosse/hockey): b. 9 Jan 1928, Windsor, Ont.; given name: Arnold; played jr. hockey Lakefield, Peterborough, Stratford, Toronto Young Rangers; pro Washington (AHL), Akron (IHL), Lake Placid (EL), Milwaukee (IHL), Detroit (IHL), Peterborough Srs.; played baseball, football with jr. teams; lacrosse Ont. Sr. B champs '47-48; mem. 3 Mann Cup titlists; twice 1st team all-star; mem. Cdn Lacrosse, Peterborough Sports halls of fame; res. Peterborough, Ont.

DUGAN, Jackie (boxing): b. 28 Apr 1926, Peterborough, Ont.; given name: John Edwin; won 95 of 105 amateur bouts; lost only 2 of 46 pro bouts; armed forces middleweight title '44-45; Cdn middleweight title '47; retd. as unbeaten title holder; dir. Toronto St. Alban's Boys Club; mem. Peterborough Sports, Cdn Boxing halls of fame; res. Peterborough, Ont.

DUGGAN, Herrick (sailing): b. 1862, Toronto, Ont; d. 1946,; given name: George Herrick; Upper Canada College, UofT; construction engineer; assisted in formation Toronto Yacht Club 1880, Lake Yacht Racing Assn.; as mem. Royal St. Lawrence YC Montreal 1896 challenged for Seawanhaka Cup; designed 5 of 18 challengers and skippered Glencairn I to cup victory; defended successfully vs. US, UK challengers; designed unusual yacht Dominion, claimed as single hulled with two waterlines although rivals said it was double-hulled catamaran; in his time considered best designer of small boats in world; designed, built total of 142 boats; mem. Canada's Sports Hall of Fame.

DUGGAN, Keltie (swimming): b. 7 Sep 1970, Edmonton, Alta.; UAlta; began swimming age 8; breaststroke specialist; mem. ntl team from '87; 8 Ntl, 5 CIAU, 1 Pan Pacific titles; '87 Pan Am Games gold 100m breaststroke, silver 4x100 medley relay; '90 Commonwealth Games gold 100m breaststroke, bronze 4x100 medley relay; '90 worlds 50m bronze; Swimming Canada's female athlete of year '89; 2 CIAU female swimmer of yr; UAlta Bakewell trophy female athlete of year '89-90; sport excellence award; res. Edmonton, Alta.

DUGRE, Lou (curling): b. 9 Apr 1945, Moncton, N.B.; given name: Louis Joseph Marcel; div.; c. Jean Paul; DND; mem. 4 NB, 1 Ont., 2 Canadian Legion championship rinks; mem. '73 NB Brier entry; skipped '76 Whitby Sun Life winner; Ont. Challenge Round '76; tied 3rd '76 Ont. Consols; competed '84 Que. Labatt Tankard; res. Orleans, Ont.

DUGUID, Don (curling); b. 21 Oct 1935, Winnipeg, Man.; div.; c. Terry, Dale, Dean, Randy, Kevin, Jill Staub; CBC curling commentator; 6yrs mem. Terry Braunstein rink; mem. Howie Wood Jr. '57 Man. Brier entry; third for Braunstein '65 Brier winner; skipped Brier, Silver Broom winners '70-71; 3 times Man. bonspiel grand aggregate winner; popularized youth curling schools, use of microphones on curlers for live broadcasts; from '72 CBC curling commentator working '94 Commonwealth, '92, '98 Olympic Games; chair. '98 Brier; mem. Canada's, Man. Sports, Cdn, Man. Curling halls of fame; res. Winnipeg, Man.

DUHAIME, Greg (t&f); b. 11 Aug 1953, Espanola, Ont.; d. 28 Oct 1992, Port Elgin, Ont.; distance runner; ntl 3000m steeplechase record 8:36.3 '79; ntl indoor 3000m title '80; 3 ntl steeplechase, 1 5000m titles; Pacific Conf. Games steeplechase title '81; bronze steeplechase '82 Commonwealth, '83 Pan-Am Games; ntl steeplechase, cross-country records; mem. '79 Pan-Am, '84 Olympic Games teams; mem. North Bay Sports Hall of Fame.

DUHAMEL, Miguel (motorsport); b. 26 May 1967, Lasalle, Que.; with brother Mario raced mini-bikes before graduating to bigger machines; turned road race pro '88; raced for Honda FIM Endurace Cup, Team Suzuki Cdn Superbike series '89; won 1st AMA Superbike race for Yoshimura Suzuki '90; won Daytona 200, 7 600cc SuperSport races; AMA title '91; won FIM world endurance team title with Team Kawasaki '92; won 2nd 600cc SuperSport series title with 7 race wins '93; rode Harley-Davidson debut of VR 1000 Superbike '94; 1st Cdn to win AMA SuperBike crown '95; won 6 SuperSport finals for Honda '96; won 5th pro Honda Oils 600cc SuperSport title '97; AMA pro athlete of '95 award; res. Los Angeles, Calif./Sarasota, Fla./Montreal, Que.

DUHAMEL, Yvon (motorsport); b. 17 Oct 1939, Montreal, Que.; m. Sofia Cecchino; c. Mario, Jina, Miguel; businessman; 7 times White Trophy winner, highest award in Cdn motorcycling; '67-68 Daytona Classic 250cc class; ntl '81 GP 750cc; 1st rider to lap Daytona at more than 150mph; '71-72 AMA ntl titles at Tallegada, Ala., AMA 125 miler at Atlanta; '73 250 mile Ontario, Calif. title; top point scorer English match race series; 10th stock car grand ntl '73; world 750cc title '73; European 750cc title '74; world snowmobile title '70; only winner 500-mile Winnipeg-St. Paul snowmobile race title '72; ntl speed records both motorcycles, snowmobiles; '77 ntl GP 250cc title; retd '77 but returned to racing '82 to add to legend; mem. Que. Sports Hall of Fame; res. LaSalle, Que.

DUKESHIRE, Kelly (basketball); b. 23 Feb 1960, Kimberley, B.C.; UVic; policeman; mem. 4 time CIAU champion Vikings; ntl team from '80; forward gold medal '83 FISU Games team; ankle injury kept him from '84 Olympic team; CIAU Jack Donohue MVP trophy; fed. govt. excellence award '84; res. Victoria, B.C.

DUMART, Woody (hockey); b. 23 Dec 1916, Kitchener, Ont.; given name: Woodrow Wilson Clarence; mem. OHA champion Kitchener jrs. '34-35; brief minor pro stint then became Boston (NHL) regular '37-54 (excluding '42-45

service in RCAF); with Milt Schmidt, Bobby Bauer formed famed Kraut Line; NHL record: 771 scheduled games, 211g, 218a, 82 playoff games, 12g, 15a; mem. 2 Stanley Cup winners; mem. Waterloo County, Hockey halls of fame; res. Needham, Mass.

DUMELIE, Larry (football); b. 7 Dec 1936, Lafleche, Sask.; given name: Lawrence; m. Karen Marie Mitton; c. Michele, Bobby, Sherrie, Doug, James; Arizona, BA, BSc; Cdn GM Computer Systems Corp.; defensive back Saskatchewan '60-68; 3 times led Sask. in interceptions; 2 Grey Cup finals, 1 winner; coach Saskatoon Hilltop jrs '69; pres. Saskatoon Handball Assn., doubles champion '69; minor hockey coach London, Ont. '73-74; active in Oldtimers hockey; res. Osgoode, Ont.

DuMOULIN, Seppi (football); b. 1878, Montreal, Que.; d. 25 Mar 1963, Hamilton, Ont.; given name: Septimus; exceptional kicker, backfielder; mem. 6 ntl title teams; mem. Hamilton Tigers '94-06; instrumental in formation Saskatchewan FL, Western Canada RFU; hon. coach Tigers '10, Winnipeg '19; only man to hold chief offices in 3 major football unions, IRFU, WCRFU, ORFU; pres., life mem. Tigers; CFL outstanding service award; charter mem. Cdn Football Hall of Fame.

DUNBAR, William (curling); b. 3 Aug 1895, Kinmount, Ont.; d. 14 May 1974, Vancouver, B.C.; m. Gladys Dougan; c. Verna Doreen; UofSask; farmer; honed curling skills in US; skipped Sask. Brier entry '40; won '54 Saskatoon carspiel; Sask. football club '21; Saskatoon prov. rugby champions '23; Sask. high jump, broad jump, shot put, 100yd dash, discus titles '22; baseball Western Cdn pro league; mem. Sask. Sports Hall of Fame.

DUNCAN, Cecil (administration); b. 1 Feb 1893, Ottawa, Ont.; d. 25 Dec 1979, Ottawa, Ont.; c. Beryl; public servant; lacrosse, baseball player, boxer in youth '10-20; key role in formation Ottawa sr. city hockey league; managed Ottawa all-stars on successful European tour '32-32; governor/v-p. AAU of C '34-36; pres. CAHA '36-38; 1st Cdn rep./v-p. Ligue internationale de hockey sur glace; championed hockey at all international levels; managed Sudbury Wolves on world title-winning tour of Europe '38; managed Ottawa Tigers sr. ORFU team '45-46; v-pres Quebec Rugby Union; secty-treas/registrar ODHA 51yrs; secty Eastern Ont. Baseball Assn., Ottawa jr. Football league; US Amateur Hockey Assn citation of honor/gold shield '50/life mem.; Ont. Sport Achievement Award '75, special Ont. citation '76.

DUNCANSON, Albert (hockey); b. 2 Oct 1911, Winnipeg, Man.; given name: Albert Gordon; m. Violet Burr; c. Judith, Mary Jane; retired oil co. administrator; mem. Elmwood Millionaires '31 Memorial Cup winner; mem. '32 Olympic gold medal team; mem. '37 Ont. senior champion Dominion Brewery team Toronto; res. Knowlton, Que.

DUNDERDALE, Tommy (hockey); b. 6 May 1887, Benelia, Australia; d. 15 Dec 1960 Winnipeg, Man.; centre; 5yrs sr., pro Winnipeg '05-09; Montreal Shamrocks (NHA) '10; Que. Bulldogs '11; Victoria, Portland (PCHA) '12-23; Saskatoon, Edmonton (WCHL) '24; twice scoring champion; during 12 PCHA seasons scored more goals than any other player in league; scored in each of Victoria's 15 games '14; league all-star centre; career total 225 goals in 290 league games plus 6 goals in 12 playoff games; coached, managed teams in Los Angeles, Edmonton, Winnipeg; mem. Man., Cdn Hockey halls of fame.

DUNHAM, Steve (rodeo); b. 18 Jul 1956, High River, Alta; horse trainer; bareback/calf roping specialist; CPRA mem. from '76; 2 ntl AA titles; 5 ntl BB titles; 1 ntl high point title; 2 Calgary Stampede BB titles; 1 Cowboy of yr award; 1 Coors Chute-out BB title; 2 Alta. circuit AA titles; 1 Alta., 2 BC circuit BB titles; 1 Skoal pro rodeo tour BB title; 1 Dodge pro rodeo tour BB title; res. Turner Valley, Alta.

DUNIGAN, Matt (football); b. 6 Dec 1960, Lakewood, Ohio; m. Kathy; c. Dane, Dolan, Madison; Louisiana Tech; TV color commentator; ex-coach; retd. quarterback; broke Terry Bradshaw's LTU record with 7010 career yards offence; all-Southern Conf. 1st team '82, 2nd team '81; state MVP, Kodak/AP all-American; pro Edmonton '83-87, BC '88-89, Toronto '90-91, Winnipeg '92-94, Birmingham '95, Hamilton '96; CFL record: 194 scheduled games, 850 carries, 5031yds, 77tds, 2cvts, 5476 passes, 3057 completions, 43,857yds, 306tds, 211int, 14 playoff games, 3tds, 50 carries for 324yds, 4tds, 321 pass attempts, 175 completions, 2679yds, 16tds, CFL record 713 passing yds 1 game '94; set/tied 3 CFL records; 2nd only to Ron Lancaster in career passing yds; 2 all-WFC, 2 all-EFC, 1 all-Southern, 4 all-Cdn; 3 times most outstanding player nominee, ntl runnerup '93; Tom Pate Memorial Award '89; Jeff Russel award '93; 5 Grey Cup finals, 2 winners; 12 concussions in 14yr CFL career led to retirement; Valdosta State off. co-ordinator '97-98; TSN football commentator '99; res. Birmingham, Ala.

DUNLAP, Frank (football/hockey); b. 10 Aug 1924, Ottawa, Ont.; d. 26 Sep 1993, Ottawa, Ont.; given name: Frank Egan; m. Mary Kathryn Heney; c. David, Michael, Patrick, Daniel; St. Patrick's College, BComm, Osgoode Hall, LLB; county court judge; hockey St. Mike's Majors '42-44, brief '43 stint Toronto Maple Leafs; Ottawa Commandos (QSHL) '44, Hull Volants (QSHL) '45, Ottawa Senators (QSHL) '36, Pembroke Lumber Kings '47; football Ottawa Trojans '42, Ottawa Combines '43, pro Ottawa(CFL) '44-47, '50-51, Toronto '48-49; all-Cdn quarterback '46; mem. '51 Ottawa Grey Cup champions; mem. Canada Fitness Council '67-69.

DUNLAP, Jake (football); b. 18 Aug 1926, Ottawa, Ont.; given name: John; m. Dena Morrison; c. John, Joanne; UofOtt, Osgoode Hall LLB; lawyer, prov. govt. appointee; lineman Ottawa '43-48, '51, '53-54, Toronto '49-50, Hamilton '52; hockey Ottawa Senators '45-46; football radio color commentator; dir. Rough Riders; GM '78-82; Ont. agent-general to US; gifted raconteur, master of ceremonies; mem. Ottawa Sports Hall of Fame; res. Ottawa, Ont.

DUNLAP, Moffatt (equestrian); b. 31 Mar 1941, Toronto, Ont.; div. c. Louise, John; UWO, BA; real estate broker; mem. Canadian Equestrian team '58-76; bronze medal Nations' Cup team '67 Pan-Am Games; gold team '70 world championships; dir. Canadian Equestrian Team; v.-chair.,

administrative comm. Royal Winter Fair; past dir. Canadian Pony Club, Canadian Horse Shows Assn. Canadian Horse Council and Horseman's Benevolent and Protective Assn. (Ont. region); res. King, Ont.

DUNN, James (builder/hockey); b. 24 Mar 1898, Winnipeg, Man; d. 7 Jan 1979, Winnipeg, Man.; became involved with hockey on return from WW1 where he received Military Medal for bravery; local league secty/convenor/timekeeper; when his league was taken over by MAHA '27 he turned his talents to that organization; MAHA v-pres. '42; served 6yrs as pres MAHA; v-pres./pres. CAHA; convenor '67-68 world tournaments; also held exec. offices in baseball, softball, football, lacrosse, speed skating, basketball, boxing, t&f; mem. Hockey Hall of Fame.

DUNN, Marc (volleyball); b. 9 Sep 1965, North Bay, Ont.; m. Kristine Drakich; UofT; fireman; CIAU indoor volleyball standout winning all-Canadian, MVP awards; mem. ntl indoor team 3yrs; turned to beach volleyball as partner with brother-in-law Ed Drakich '95; mem. '96 Olympic team; res. Toronto, Ont.

DUNN, Mary (basketball); b. 6 Mar 1902, Hamilton, Scotland; d. 4 Aug 1996, Calgary, Alta.; m. Robert Dickson; c. Mary, Bruce, Joan, Jean; secretary; mem. legendary Edmonton Grads '22-26; mem. Canadian Basketball, Alta. Sports halls of Fame.

DUNSMORE, Fred (all-around); b. 30 Mar 1929,; m. Margaret; c. Jeff, John, Danny; chartered accountant; all-star HS quarterback age 15; 2 seasons Streatham English hockey league, rookie of yr; at 17 mem. Brandon Wheat Kings jrs.; star forward, capt. Winnipeg Maroons Red Wreckers Allan Cup champions '64; appeared in 5 ntl finals; mem. ntl team '65 world championships; serious eye injury tarnished his ability but did not detract from it; pitcher, 3B Rosedales, St. Boniface Natives '45-54; rejected Philadelphia Athletics pro offers; trial with Winnipeg Goldeyes '54 but opted to retain amateur status; finalist for Man. athlete of century '70; mem. Man. Hockey, Man. Sports halls of fame; res. Winnipeg, Man.

DUPREY, Donalda (t&f); b. 1 Mar 1967, Fredericton, N.B.; Lousiana State; teacher; hurdler; began competing age 11; 2 ntl jr. 400m, 1 100m hurdle titles; mem. 4x400m jr. record relay team; gold 400m, 100mH '94 Harry Jerome Classic, 400mH '94 Francophone Games; ntl 100m, 400mH titles '94; Texas Relays 100mH, ntl indoor 400m titles '93; mem. '86, '90, '94 Commonwealth, '92 Olympic, '94 Francophone, '95 Pan-Am, 3 world championships teams; silver 400mH '86 Commonwealth Games; bronze 4x400 '94 Commonwealth Games; silver 100mH '95 Pan-Am Games; Athletics Canada athlete of '94; res. Port Elgin, Ont./ Baton Rouge, La.

DURELLE, Yvon (boxing); b. 14 Oct 1929, Baie Ste. Anne, N.B.; m. Thérèsa; c. Geneva, Yvon Jr., Paul, Françine; fisherman, club owner, museum operator; nicknamed "Doux"; first recorded bout '47; national middleweight title 4 May '53 (KO'd George Ross in 12th), light heavyweight title 9 Sep '53 (12-round decision over Gordon Wallace), lost crown 17 Nov '53 to Doug Harper in 12, regained it 7

Jul '54, defended twice; BE light heavyweight title '57 stopping Wallace in two; defended once; challenged Archie Moore for world light heavyweight title '58, losing on KO in 11; KO'd in 3rd '59 rematch; challenged George Chuvalo '59 for ntl heavyweight crown but was KO'd in 12; retired to try wrestling '61; brief boxing comeback '63; pro boxing record 105 bouts, 44 won by KO, 38 by decision, 10 lost on decision, 3 on fouls, 9 by KO, 1 no contest; cleared on manslaughter charge evolving from fight with bar patron; mem. NB, Canada's Sports, Cdn Boxing halls of fame; res. Baie Ste. Anne, N.B.

DURNAN, Bill (hockey); b. 22 Jan 1915, Toronto, Ont.; d. 31 Oct 1972, Toronto, Ont.; m. Amanda; c. Deanna, Brenda; goaler Sudbury jrs '33-35 OHA finalists; 3 seasons NOHA contenders; Kirkland Lake Allan Cup winners '40; ambidextrous brilliance attracted Montreal scouts; Vezina Trophy '43-44 rookie season; 7 seasons with Habs 6 Vezina Trophies; 1st team all-star 6 times; mem. 4 league champions, 2 Stanley Cup winners; '48-49 established modern NHL record 4 consecutive shutouts, playing 309 minutes 21 seconds shutout hockey; career 2.36 goals against avg. in 383 scheduled games, 34 shutouts; standout softball pitcher with at least 14 no-hitters; once fanned 24 in 9-inning game; pitched Montreal to 4 successive provincial titles; mem. Canada's Sports, Hockey halls of fame.

DUSSAULT, Jacques (coaching/football); b. 4 May 1950, Montreal, Que.; div.; c. François, Jean-Michel; McGill, BPhE, Miami of Ohio, MPhE; football coach; asst. coach Albany State '80-81, Montreal (CFL) '82-85; from '97, Acadia '87-88; head coach Mount Allison '89-90; Montreal Machine (WFL) '91-92; asst. McGill '92, St. Leonard, Que./ Eastern Cdn jr. champs '94-95; head coach Que. elite team which won Cdn title '93-94, Cannes Iron Masks (WFL) '96; has served as guest coach with NFL Buffalo, Philadelphia, NY Giants, NY Jets, Pittsburgh, New England, WFL Frankfurt Galaxy, also Boston U, Michigan State; TV football analyst, RDS; res. Montreal, Que.

DUTHIE, George (administration); b. 25 Oct 1901, Fraserburgh, Scotland; d. 9 Mar 1968, Toronto, Ont.; c. Lorne, Donald, Carole Anne; CNE staff mem.; marathon swim organizer; mem. National Advisory Council Fitness, Amateur Sport; responsible for RCAF sports, entertainment WW2; M.B.E.; mem. Cdn Amateur, Canada's Sports halls of fame.

DUTTON, Mervyn Red (hockey); b. 23 Jul 1897, Russell, Man.; d. 15 Mar 1987, Calgary, Alta.; given name: Norman Alexander; m. Mary McDonald; c. Joseph, Alexander, Norman, Beryl; St. John's College; retd construction exec.; intercollegiate Winnipeg '14-15, overseas '15-19; hockey Winnipeg '20-22; pro Calgary '23-26, Montreal Maroons '26-30, NY Americans '30-37, player-coach '36-37; coach, mgr. Americans '36-42; succeeded Frank Calder NHL president '43-46; pres. Calgary Stampeder Football Club '56-58; NHL playing record as defenceman 29 goals, 67 assists; mem. Order of Canada; mem. Cdn, Man. Hockey, Man. Sports halls of fame.

DVORAK, Tom (equestrian); b. 25 Jul 1965, Braunschwieg, Germany; m. Ellen Rumball; c. Alexandra; began riding friend's pony and acquired 1st horse age 12; turned attention to dressage age 14; moved to Canada '82; mem. ntl team from '90; 15 Grand Prix victories; won '94 Cdn League Volvo World Cup aboard Asanti; team gold '93 NA regional challenge; competed '90 world equestrian games, '96 Olympics; res. Keswick, Ont.

DWYER, John (boxing); b. 15 Aug 1847, St. John's, Nfld.; d. 19 Mar 1882, Brooklyn, N.Y.; county court clerk; raised in Brooklyn; at 5'9 1/2", 163lbs small for heavyweight but packed powerful punch; beat Jim Elliott in 12 rounds 9 May 1879, Long Point, Ont., to claim world heavyweight title; retired undefeated.

DYE, Babe (hockey); b. 13 May 1898, Hamilton, Ont.; d. 3 Jan 1962, Chicago, Ill.; given name: Cecil Henry; foreman contract paving firm; halfback Toronto Argos, baseball Toronto; jr. hockey Ont. champion Aura Lee '17; Toronto St. Pat's '19-26, Chicago (NHL) '26, missed '27 with broken leg, NY Americans '28, 4 times NHL scoring champion; twice scored 5 goals single game; 2^{ce} 11-game scoring streaks; mem. 1 Stanley Cup winner; highest goals-per-game record in NHL with 200 in 225 games; coached Chicago Shamrocks (AA), refereed 5 NHL seasons; mem. Hockey Hall of Fame.

E

EAGLE, Don (gymnastics); b. 23 Mar 1944, Halifax, N.S.; given name: Donald Gordon; m. Jean Adams; c. Heather, Doug; UNB professor, asst. AD; Atlantic Intercollegiate all-around champion '65-66; coach, official, administrator from '67; founded Fredericton Eagles gym club '68; founded NB gymnastics assn. '67; chair. NBGA '72-74; served various roles at provincial, ntl, intl, levels; officiated at '75, '87 Pan-Am, '78, '82, '90 Commonwealth, '92 Olympic Games; mgr. Cdn gym team '88 Olympics; has earned highest rating possible for gymnastics official; life mem. Cdn Gymnastics Fed.; mem. NB, Fredericton Sports Hall of Fame; res. Fredericton, N.B.

EAGLESON, Alan (administration/hockey); b. 24 Apr 1933, St. Catharines, Ont.; given name: Robert Alan; m. Nancy Elizabeth Fisk; c. Trevor Allan, Jill Anne; UofT, BA, LLB; disbarred lawyer, player agent; ex-dir. Hockey Canada; arranged '72 Summit series; organized 5 Canada Cup series; exec. dir. NHL Players' Assn. '67-91; twice Etobicoke outstanding young man award; Vanier award 1 of Canada's 5 outstanding young men '68; University College bronze award, Arts Trophy for athletics '57; following FBI investigation, US grand jury issued indictment on 32 counts of fraud, embezzlement, racketeering, receiving kickbacks and obstruction of justice '94; subsequent RCMP investigation led to criminal charges; guilty pleas in US, Canada and plea bargaining result in minimal 18 month prison sentence '98; paroled after serving just 6 months of sentence; criminal activities resulted in expulsion from Canada's Sports, Hockey halls of fame, also stripped of the Order of Canada he had received in '89; res. Toronto, Ont.

EATHORNE, A.J. (golf); b. 12 Jul 1976, Calgary, Alta.; given name: Anna-Jane; New Mexico State; began playing golf at 13; B.C. women's amateur titles '95-97; Cdn women's amateur title '97; mem. 5th ranked New Mexico State U team '88; Diet Coke Roadrunner invitational medalist, NGCA 1st team all-American '97-98; turned pro '98; won 2 Futures tour events; earned LPGA tour card and exempt status as co-medalist '98 final qualifying tournament; 3 top 10 finishes in rookie '99 season; res. Penticton, B.C.

EAVES, John (skiing); b. 8 Apr 1953, Montreal, Que.; given name: John Ironside; m. Brigitte Callory; Bishop's College; pro skier, promoter; son of former ski champion Rhoda Wurtele; freestyle specialist; 3 world combined FS titles; 3 world aerials titles; won Challenge of Sexes Superstars rowing competition, 5th overall '79; Challenge of Sexes, Challenge of Superskiers titles '80; Australian FS titles '79-80; movie stuntman *For Your Eyes Only, The Soldier*; composed, recorded music in Nashville for ballet skiing; Laurentian zone alpine skier; advanced wind surfer; mem. Cdn Skiing Hall of Fame; res. Calgary, Alta.

EBBELS, Bill (tennis); b. 20 Jul 1922, Saskatoon, Sask.; given name: William Dennis; m. Ruth Hutchison; c. Harold,

John, James, William, Virginia, Andrea; U of Sask, BComm; investment dealer; Sask. -13 title '35; UofSask singles '41; jr. A hockey Saskatoon Chiefs; basketball UofSask. Huskies; hockey UofSask '46-47; Halifax Naval College tennis title '42; 8 Sask. men's singles (record); 7 Sask. men's doubles; 4 Regina singles, doubles titles; Regina Civil Service TC champion; 9 Sask. veterans singles, 7 veterans men's doubles title; only player provincial men's, veteran's singles same year '67; at 49 oldest competitor '69 Canada Summer Games posting 7-5 singles record; Regina squash champion '67-68; hip replacement operations ended competitive career '80; 2 terms pres. SLTA; Regina B'nai B'rith Sportsman's Award '72; mem. Sask., UofSask Sports halls of fame; res. Regina, Sask.

EBEN, Mike (football); b. 29 Jan 1946, Zatec, Czechoslovakia; given name: Michael Christopher; m. Nancy Marsden; c. Lhara, Christopher; UofT, BA, MA, PhD; housemaster, teacher Upper Canada Coll; ex-prof. York U; initial winner Hec Crighton Trophy; 4yrs all-star, OUAA MVP, led UofT to inaugural Vanier Cup triumph; pro Toronto '68-69, '71-77, Edmonton '70, Hamilton '77, Ottawa '77; CFL record: 341 receptions, 4752yds, 24tds; WFC, EFC all-star; Schenley outstanding Cdn nominee; 37 consecutive pass catching games; 1 Grey Cup final; asst. coach York U '84; mem. UotT Sports, OUAA Football Legends halls of fame; res. Toronto, Ont.

ECKARD, Jeff (sailing); b. 18 Dec 1965, Pietermaritzburg, S.A.; sailmaker; skipper 470 crew; teamed with Nigel Cochrane won ntl championships '89-91; gold Goodwill Games '90, Pan-Am Games '91; mem. Royal Victoria YC; res. Victoria, B.C.

ECKEL, Shirley (t&f); b. 3 Feb 1932, Toronto, Ont.; given name: Shirley Gretchen; m. Dr. William H. Kerr (d); c. Gretchen, Christopher, Elizabeth, Thomas; UofT, BA; ranked 4th internationally 50m hurdles age 12; gold '45-46 jr. Olympics; at 20 ntl 80m hurdles title, record, ranked 8th in world; mem. '52 Olympic, '54 BEG teams; ntl 80m titles '52-53, '55; throughout career NA champion; res. Islington, Ont.

ECUYER, Al (football); b. 1937, New Orleans, La.; Notre Dame; stockbroker; capt. ND, twice all-American guard; drafted NY Giants (NFL); Edmonton (CFL) '59-65, co-capt. '64, Toronto '66, Montreal '67-68; twice nominated outstanding player, outstanding lineman; twice coaches all-Canadian (2nd team); Vancouver Sun all-star interior linebacker; twice Blue Bombers' all-opponents team; res. New Orleans, La.

EDDIE, Arden (baseball); b. 4 Aug 1947, Wallaceburg, Ont.; m. Shelley; c. Ashley; realtor/home renovator; honed early skills in Wallaceburg before joining London Diamonds juniors; knee injury playing as sea cadet in Nova Scotia reduced his pro prospects but didn't dampen his enthusiasm for game; mem. '68 Cdn jr. champion London Diamonds;

mem. London Sr. Intercounty team from '67; became London Majors club owner '76; mem. '75 Intercounty champs, 5 div. winners; 2 IC exec. of yr, 1 Commissioners Trophy awards; 1 1st team, 6 2nd team all-star selections; led IC in triples twice, stolen bases 3 times, walks 4 times; set numerous IC records '67-97 including 832 games, 31 seasons, 764h, 179sb, 382rbi, 645bob; instrumental in keeping sr amateur baseball alive in London; signed Fergie Jenkins for '84-85 seasons; his team has played key role in community affairs and has led league in attendance since '67; has served Majors as pres./GM/mgr./player; mem. Wallaceburg Sports Hall of Fame; res. London, Ont.

EDEH, Rosey (t&f): b. 16 Aug 1966, London, Eng.; Rice; c. Lisha; TV sports reporter; emigrated to Canada '69; began competing age 13; hurdles, sprint specialist; 1 ntl jr., 6 ntl sr. records; 3 jr. ntl, 4 sr, ntl, 1 Que., 10 international invitational meet gold; competed '88, '92, '96 Olympic, '89 Francophone, FISU, '90 Commonwealth, '95 Pan-Am Games, '91 world indoor, '92 World Cup, '93 world outdoor teams; top Que. female athletic prospect award '88; res. La Salle, Que.

EDEY, Marjorie (golf); b. 8 Dec 1913, Winnipeg, Man.; d. 27 Mar 1981, Winnipeg, Man.; given name: Marjorie Isobel; m. William Edey; mem. St. Charles G&CC; world record 36 club titles; won Man. women's amateur '46-51, Winnipeg & Dist. titles '48-51, Man. Srs. titles '62-65; mem. 20 interprovincial teams, 3 Srs. teams; gained permanent possession Alcrest Cup emblem of St. Charles club title; Edey Cup became replacement; mem. Man. Sports Hall of Fame.

EDGE, Ken (bowling); b. 16 Jun 1927, Hamilton, Ont.; given name: Kenneth Mills; m. Phyllis Veronica Stewart; c. Patricia, Linda; electrical contractor, politician; co-founder Hamilton Bowlers' Assoc. '63; helped establish O'Keefe Bowler of Month tournament; pres. Ont. Bowlers' Congress; founded Crippled Children's bowling tournament Hamilton; Builders of Bowling Industry award; chairman Hamilton Parks & Rec.; mem. Ont. 5-Pin Bowling Hall of Fame; res. Hamilton, Ont.

EDWARDS, Betty (swimming); b. 22 Feb 1911, Toronto, Ont.; given name: Elizabeth Alberta; m. Frank Tancock (d); c. Brian Frank, Beverley Elizabeth; UofT, BA; post grad work Toronto Hospital for Sick Children; retd. asst. to chair. dept. philosophy York U; FS, backstroke specialist, ornamental (synchronized) swimmer; mem. '32 Olympic, '30, '34 BEG teams; won '30 Detroit River swim; 2 ntl titles; 2 ntl records; 6 Ont. titles, 1 record; 1 Que.title; won '29 1/2 mile Dominion Day, Brule Lake, CNE titles, '34 Hamilton Bay swim; 2 CNE 1 mile titles; 1 Toronto HS 100yd FS title; 3 Granite Club long plunge titles, 3 ornamental titles; UotT jr./sr. T awards; special gold medal for 440yd FS ntl record '27; Gale trophy '39; starred in two Associated Screen News films; mem. UofT Sports, Ont. Aquatic halls of fame; res. Islington, Ont.

EDWARDS, Jake (curling); b. 7 May 1921, Kingston, Ont.; d. 6 Aug 1978, Kingston, Ont.; given name: Jack Leisk; m. Lois Smith (d); c. Sandra, Tracy; m. Joan Whalen; auto dealer; knuckleball pitcher with various Kingston area baseball teams; rejected pro contract Jersey City Giants; mem. Canadian Army overseas baseball titlists WW2; twice Amherstview Club golf champion, twice srs champion; Alcan Srs title '76; OCA Governor-General's, Silver Tankard titles, twice Burden, Globe & Mail trophies; 6 times Ont. Consols competitor; rep. Ont. '60 Brier; 2 Ont. Srs titles; 10 consecutive wins 2 straight years City of Ottawa bonspiel, 1 grand aggregate title; mem. National Fitness Council '64-67; mem. Kingston Dist. Sports Hall of Fame.

EDWARDS, John (canoeing); b. 1 Jul 1954, Almonte, Ont.; m. Susan Gifford; c. Bliss, Chantry; UBC, Simon Fraser, Architectural Assn. School, Carleton, BArch; architect; competitive paddler '67-78 collecting variety of gold, silver, bronze medals in ntl, international competitions; mem. ntl team '72-78; mem. '72, '76 Olympic, '75 Pan-Am, '75, '78 world championship teams; gold 1000m, 500m C1, 1000m C2, silver 500m C2 '75 Pan-Am regatta; commodore CPCC '88-93; consultant Pantages Theatre restoration; Canada 125 medal; res. Carleton Place, Ont.

EDWARDS, Phil (t&f); b. 13 Sep 1907, Georgetown, British Guiana; d. 6 Sep 1971, Montreal, Que.; given name. Philip Aron; NYU, McGill, MD; physician; capt. track teams NYU, McGill; ntl middle-distance titles Canada, US, Ireland, Poland, Latvia; 4th 800m, relay bronze '28 Olympics, bronze 800m, 1500m, 4x400 relay '32 Olympics, capt., 800m bronze, beat world record but finished 5th 1500m '36 Olympics; 880yd gold representing British Guiana '34 BEG; led McGill to 6 consec t&f titles, 5 as capt.; part-time coach McGill track team; sole 4-time winner American indoor ntls 600yd titlrs; held 13 ntl records; initial winner Lou Marsh Trophy '36; Lionel Conacher trophy '36; AAU of C top athlete '36; trophy bearing his name awarded annually to Canada's outstanding t&f athlete; mem. Cdn Amateur, McGill, Canada's Sports halls of fame.

EDWARDS, Ted (football/basketball); b. 20 Dec 1915, Ottawa, Ont.; given name: Frederick; m. Doris Margaret Irvine; c. Ted Jr., Peggy, Pat, Penny; UofOtt, Queen's; retd. civil servant; halfback Rough Riders '37, '39-40; mem. 2 Grey Cup finalists, 1 winner; guard ntl finalist Glebe Grads basketball team '37; coached jr. football Queen's '38; quarterbacked Montreal Bulldogs '41; all-star halfback intermediate service league '42; playing coach, all-star halfback QRFU finalist Verdun '43; halfback, capt. Ottawa Trojans ORFU '44-46; coach UofOtt football '45-54; fastball Snowden Junction League '41-42; guard Montreal Oilers basketball team '42-43, capt. '43, ntl finalists '42; guard, capt. UofOtt ntl intermediate finalists '44; sr. city basketball '44-46; basketball coach, college, city league clubs '47-55; coached 3 NORFU league titlists Sudbury '55-57; mem. Ottawa CSRA Sports Hall of Fame; res. Ottawa, Ont.

EGERTON, Stan (t&f); b. 2 Oct 1925, Toronto, Ont.; given name: Stanley Harris; m. Dollie Olphert; c. George, Carolyn, Stan Jr., James; fire dept. capt.; Toronto city pole vault title '39-40; Cdn army 2nd Div. 100, 220yd spring title '43; pole vault silver '50 BEG; joined Masters program '74; pole vault bronze '75, gold '77, '79 World Masters Games; Ont., Cdn pole vault, 100, 200m masters titles '80-85; Cdn, world 60m record for 60-year-olds '86; res. Toronto, Ont.

EHRLICK, Allan (equestrian); b. 4 Apr 1946, Toronto, Ont.; given name: Allan Howard Lincoln; m. Linda Lowe; UofT; farm manager; 3-day event specialist; mem. ntl team '66-76; 3 ntl 3-day event titles; '73 NA title; mem. '67, '71 Pan-Am, '68, '72, '76 Olympic Games teams; polo player Toronto Polo Club; res. Campbellville, Ont.

EIRIKSON, Tom (rodeo); b. 5 Feb 1954, Innisfail, Alta; m. Candy; c. Wyatt, Josh, Rebecca-Jo; movie stuntman; saddle bronc, calf roping, steer wrestling, team roping; qualified for 7 ntl finals; 4 ntl all-around championships; 3 Linderman awards; res. Okotoks, Alta.

EISLER, Laurie (volleyball/coaching); b. 3 Sep 1964, Regina, Sask.; given name: Laurie Baber; m. Terry Eisler; c. Clayton; U Sask, BEd, MSc; coach UAlta; concentrated on volleyball at university after successful HS career in t&f, basketball, volleyball; setter Sask. Huskiettes '82-87; 4 CWUAA all-star awards, CIAU 2nd team '87; switched to coaching assisting Mark Tennant '87-91, 1yr stint as head coach; shifted to UAlta as head coach '91-92; 5 ntl CIAU championship appearances, 12-3 record; 3 CIAU women's volleyball titles; 4 CWUAA, 1 CIAU coach of yr awards; 3M coach of '96 award; coached ntl women's beach volleyball team '96 Olympics; res. Edmonton, Alta.

EISLER, Lloyd Jr. (figure skating); b. 28 Apr 1963, Seaforth, Ont.; given name: Lloyd Edgar; McMaster; nicknamed "Herbie"; Western Ont. sectional juve. men's title '75; partner Lorri Baier '73-82, Katherina Matousek '82-86; Isabelle Brasseur '87-94; Ont. Winter Games pairs gold '76; ntl novice pairs '77; ntl jr. pairs '79; bronze '79 jr. worlds pairs; ntl novice singles '80; runnerup jr. world pairs '80; 5 ntl pairs titles; 2 Skate Canada gold; 4 worlds silver; '92, '94 Olympic pairs bronze; mem. '84, '88, '92, '94 Olympic teams; turned pro '94; Cdn pro pairs title '97; Cdn meritorious service award '95; mem. Canada's Sports, Cdn Figure Skating halls of fame; res. Hamilton, Ont.

ELDER, Jim (equestrian); b. 27 Jul 1934, Toronto, Ont.; m. Marianne; c. Michael, Mark, Elizabeth, Erin; Upper Canada College, UofT, BA; company pres.; mem. ntl team '50-84, individual international champion Royal Winter Fair 3 times; 4 Eastern Canadian titles; team development series champion '65-66; mem. 8 Olympic '56-84, 7 Pan-Am Games '59-83; jumping team gold '68 Olympics, '80 Olympic alternate, '59, '71 Pan-Ams, '70 worlds; individual, team silver '83 Pan-Ams; team bronze '56 Olympic, '67 Pan-Am Games; mem. '82 Nation's Cup team; Rothman's Montreal Grand Prix title '82; Officer Order of Canada '83; mem. Cdn Amateur, Canada's Sports halls of fame; res. Aurora, Ont.

ELFORD, Gear (football); b. 4 Apr 1902, Hamilton, Ont.; d. (circa 1990), Hamilton, Ont.; given name: Harold Norman; m. Alice; c. Estelle; retd; mem. CRU int. champion Hamilton Tigers '21; outstanding lineman '22-30 Tigers ORFU, IPRU; '23 ORFU title Hamilton Rowing Club; 5 IPRU titles, 2 Grey Cups; basketball Hamilton city, church leagues; recorded Hamilton's 1st perfect 450 in 5-pin bowling '37; lineman best-of-century Tiger team '67.

ELGAARD, Ray (football); b. 29 Aug 1959, Edmonton, Alta.; m. Gina; c. Linnea, Myles; Utah (criminology); financial planner; drafted 2nd round '83 Sask.; retd '96; CFL record: 220 scheduled games, 78tds, 2 2pt conversions, 830 receptions for 13,198yds; 6 all-Western, 4 all-CFL all-star; 3 Dr. Beattie Martin trophies; 3 outstanding Cdn; set/tied 3 CFL receiving records; mem. 1 Grey Cup winner; nicknamed "Harley"; active in Sask. chapter Children's Wish Foundation; res. Las Vegas, Nev.

ELIOWITZ, Abe (football); b. 15 Nov 1910, New York, N.Y.; d. 19 Nov 1981, Livonia, Mich.; m. Ida Lachman (d); c. Susan, Linda, Samuel; Michigan State, BSc; teacher; all-American MSU '32-33; southpaw passer, punter Ottawa (CFL) '33-35, Montreal '36-37; baseball Ottawa Crains St. Lawrence League; fullback, halfback, flying wing; Big Four scoring leader '35; 4 times all-star; Jeff Russel Trophy '35; coached football, baseball, cross-country running Detroit Cooley, Redford HS; 2 city football, 3 baseball titles; mem. Canadian Football Hall of Fame.

ELLEFSON, Steve (all-around); b. 16 Oct 1954, Edmonton, Alta.; given name: Stephen John; Lethbridge U; relator; partial paraplegic; excelled in skiing, basketball, tennis, road racing; mem. ntl disabled ski team; world combined champion '86-88; forced to quit skiing due to back injury; '88 Paralympic downhill bronze '88; began wheelchair track, road racing '89; Alta. 10km title '91; Alta. tennis title '89-91; gold '92 Calgary Police 1/2 marathon, Mother's Day 10km, Calgary Stampede marathon, Oz Day Masters 10km '96; silver Vancouver Sun 10km, Alta. 36.7mile marathon '92; competed '96 Paralympics; mem. Calgary Grizzlies basketball team, '89 ntl wheelchair titlists; Toronto Spitfires tournament all-star '91; res. Calgary, Alta.

ELLETT, Dave (hockey); b. 30 Mar 1964, Cleveland, Ohio; given name: David John George; m. Annie; c. Sierra; Bowling Green; defenceman; played minor hockey in Ottawa; father Bob played in AHL and coached in OHA; CCHA all-star, NCAA all-tournament team as BGU won NCAA championship '84; drafted by Winnipeg '82 entry draft; played in NHL with Winnipeg '84-90, Toronto '90-97, New Jersey '97, Boston '97-99, St. Louis '99; NHL record: 1077 scheduled games, 151g, 407a, 109 playoff games, 11g, 45a; played 2 all-star games; with Garry Galley owns All-Star Saloon in Almonte, Ont.; res. Kingston, Ont.

ELLIFF, Jim (lawn bowling); b. 30 Nov 1935, Toronto, Ont.; m. Julia Price; c. David (d), Laura; UofT; sales agent; skipped '77 Ont. Colts triple title team; won Ont. men's singles '80, '98; vice Ont. fours title teams '89, '97; skipped US Open trebles title team '93, singles '94, '95, pairs '95; ntl silver medals singles '80, fours '89; 2 bowler of week awards; mem. ntl team '80-83; mgr. ntl team '98 Commonwealth Games; res. Aurora, Ont.

ELLINGSON, James (football); b. 18 May 1963, Calgary, Alta.; m. Kathleen; c. Alexanne, Rachel; office equipment co. mgr., part-time sports broadcaster; nicknamed "Duke"; slotback Richmond Raiders Jrs; CFL Sask. '86-90, Ottawa '90-96; CFL record: 169g, 19tds, 1cvt, 255recept., 3502yds, 8 playoff games, 14recept., 201yds, 1td; mem. 1 Grey Cup winner; res. Kanata, Ont.

ELLIOTT, Allen (administration); b. 6 Feb 1922, Manitoba; m. Dagmar; c. Terry, Joann, James; retd sales mgr.; from

'64 dir. Babe Ruth Baseball International; pres. Baseball BC '72-90; 5yrs dir. Sport BC; pres. Baseball Canada '90-92; life mem. Western Canada Baseball; life mem. BC Babe Ruth Baseball; mem. BC Baseball honor roll BC Sports Hall of Fame; res. Surrey, B.C.

ELLIOTT, Bob (all-around); b. 29 Mar 1910, Kingston, Ont.; d. 21 May 1970, Kingston, Ont.; given name: Robert Fawcette; m. Sarah Delia "Deed" Whitney; c. Robert Whitney, Elizabeth Mae; Queen's, BA; purchaser aluminum co.; son of Hockey Hall of Famer Chaucer Elliott; halfback, offensive end, corner linebacker Queen's; mem. 2 intercollegiate title teams; 5 athletic letters; lost eye playing football '34; sr. ORFU football Balmy Beach '35; football coach Garrison, RMC, Queen's WW2, guided Garrison Ont. Int. title '40; 5yrs intercollegiate official; mem. '29 Queen's intercollegiate, 2 Kingston YMCA Ont. Int. basketball title teams; semipro baseball Brockville, Smiths Falls, Delora Srs, Creighton Mines, Kingston Ponies '24-38; coached 3 Kingston jr., juve. title teams, '67 OBA title team; mem. 3 OCA Governor-General's Trophy, 2 Silver Tankard curling rinks; mem. '60 Ont. Brier rink; life mem. Kingston Curling Club; honored by peers with appreciation day '68; Wally Elmer Memorial Trophy (Kingston sportsman of year); Kingston distinguished achievement award; Ont. achievement award; mem. Queen's, Kingston Dist. Sports halls of fame.

ELLIOTT, Chaucer (hockey/football); b. 1879, Kingston, Ont.; d. 13 Mar 1913, Kingston, Ont.; given name: Edwin Smith; m. Elizabeth Montague; c. Robert Fawcette; played point, capt. Queen's; capt. 1899 Granites ntl title football team; Toronto baseball team '03; coach Toronto Argos football team, '06 Hamilton Tigers title team; mem. Montreal AAA; organized semipro baseball league; owned, organized, managed St. Thomas Canadian Baseball League; hockey referee '03-13; mem. Hockey Hall of Fame.

ELLIOTT, Geoff (t&f); b. 7 Apr 1931, Ilford, Eng.; given name: Geoffrey Michael; m. Pamela Seaborne; c. Ann, Carol, Yvonne; U of London, BSc, U of California, MA; retd. asst. dean PE UAlta.; rugby player in England; mem. English international T&F team '50-59; pole vault gold '54, '58 Commonwealth Games; mem. England's '52 Olympic team; mem. RAF Fighter Command basketball team; Canadian citizen '70; chair. sports div., venues co-ordinator '78 Commonwealth Games; authored several articles on gymnastics, kinesiology, t&f, 5 books; CBC color commentator; dir. SFC; trustee O'Keefe Sports Foundation; CTFA dir.-gen. '78-81; part-time consultant UCal; res. Calgary, Alta.

ELLIS, Craig (football); b. 26 Jan 1961, Los Angeles, Calif.; m. Linda; c. Brittany, Jasmyne; San Diego State.; pro receiver San Francisco (NFL) '82, Winnipeg (CFL) '82, Calgary '83, Saskatchewan '84-85, Toronto '86, '93, Miami '86, LA Raiders '87, Dallas (NFL) '88, Edmonton (CFL) '89-92; 3 times leading CFL receiver; 3 all-WFC, 2 CFL all-star; Jeff Nicklin award 90; runnerup CFL outstanding player '90; set CFL record 8yrs catching passes all games; 1 Grey Cup final; CFL record: 121 scheduled games, 88tds, 493 carries for 2,095yds, 30tds, 580 receptions for 7,757yds, 58tds; res. California.

ELLIS, Phyllis (field hockey); b. 11 Nov 1959, Oakville, Ont.; m. Stewart Gavin; c. Max, Taylor; UofT; mem. Ont. team '75-84, ntl -21 team '80, -23 team '82, ntl team '80-84; defence World Cup silver medal team '83; mem. '84 Olympic team; fed. govt. excellence award '83; mem. UofT Sports Hall of Fame; res. Toronto, Ont.

ELLIS, Ron (hockey); b. 8 Jan 1945, Lindsay, Ont.; given name: Ronald John Edward; m. Janis Eveline; c. Ron Jr., Kathleen; York U; resort owner; influenced by father Randy, mem. '48 RCAF Flyers Olympic champions, peewee North Bay, Ottawa Cradle League; Weston Dukes Jr. B at 15; Jr. A Marlboros; mem. '64 Memorial Cup winner; pro Maple Leafs '64-81; NHL record: 1034 scheduled games, 332g, 308a, 70 playoff games, 18g, 8a; began Leafs career wearing No. 8 but at Ace Bailey's request wore No. 6 which had been retired with Bailey '34; mem. 1 Stanley Cup winner; Team Canada '72, '77; mem. Lindsay Sports Hall of Fame; res. Collingwood, Ont.

ELMER, Ken (t&f); b. 24 Apr 1948, Vancouver, B.C.; given name: Kenneth Mark; m. Janet Neufeld; c. Jonathon, Shannon; UBC, BA; teacher; mem. UBC soccer team '67-71; middle distance specialist; mem. '72 Olympic, '73 Pan-Pacific, '74 Commonwealth, '75 Pan-Am Games teams; 5th 800m '75 Pan-Ams; PB: 3:58.5 mile, 3:40.5 1500m, 1:48.2 800m; major role BC Elementary School participation championship program; Bobby Gaul UBC outstanding athlete award '73; organized Henry Jerome Classic, Vancouver Sunkist meets; mem. UBC Sports Hall of Fame; res. New Westminster, B.C.

ELMER, Wally (hockey/coaching); b. 1898, Kingston, Ont.; d. 28 Aug 1978, Kingston, Ont.; given name: Wallace Druce; m. Inez Tucker; service station, dry cleaning operator; standout jr. with Kingston Frontenacs '18; St. Paul Minn. '22; pro Saskatoon Shieks '23-24; Victoria Cougars '25 Stanley Cup champions; also played with teams in Windsor, Philadelphia, New Haven before returning to Kingston to coach Queen's hockey team '29; coached Kingston Jr. B, Sr. B OHA titlists; original mem. International Hockey Hall of Fame comm; Kingston Ponies baseball club dir.; Central Ontario baseball league dir.; Kingston youth centre named in his honor; name inscribed in Kingston Book of Honorable Achievement; trophy bearing his name awarded annually to Kingston sportsman of year.

ELRICK, Elizabeth (basketball); b. 15 Jan 1901, Glasgow, Scotland; d. 29 Jun 1984, Winnipeg, Man.; m. Rex Murray; c. Maureen, Rhoda; mem. famed Edmonton Grads '22-23; mem. Canadian Basketball, Alta. Sports halls of fame.

ELSBY, Ted (football); b. 3 Jan 1932, Galt, Ont.; d. 1985, Beaconsfield, Que.; given name: Edward Ernest; m. Pauline Patricia Pepper; c. Elaine, Paul, Steven, Gary; salesman; jr. Brantford Indians; pro defensive tackle Alouettes '54-65; mem. '56-57 East-West Shrine Game teams; EFC all-star '64; 1st-ballot nominee '64 3 Schenley Awards, best Canadian, best lineman, best player, winning none; football coach U of Montreal 4yrs, Sir George Williams 1yr, Beaconsfield HS 2yrs; mem. Waterloo County Hall of Fame.

EMERSON, Eddie (football); b. 11 Mar 1892, Cordeil, Ga.; d. 27 Jan 1970, Ottawa, Ont.; m. Heasley Parker; c. Marilyn; automobile salesman; flying wing on offence, inside wing on defence '09-37, unpaid, with Ottawa; 3 Grey Cup finals, 2 winners; twice club pres., '30 while playing, '47-50; Big Four pres. '48-49; noted auto racer; Ottawa area pool champion; city league hockey; mem. Canada's, Ottawa Sports, Canadian Football halls of fame.

EMERY, John (bobsleigh); b. 4 Jan 1932, Montreal, Que.; m. Debbie; c. Allison, John David; Trinity College School, Queen's, MD; plastic surgeon; Stubb's Trophy RCN(R) best all-around athlete; with brother Victor formed Laurentian Bobsledding Assoc. '57; with Victor, Doug Anakin, Peter Kirby '64 Olympic gold; won over-190lb 13-mile California mountain race (Double Dipsea) '70; swam across Golden Gate Bridge entrance '75; triathlon ('80 Hawaii Ironman), marathon ('79 Boston) competitor; Centennial Medal; mem. Cdn Winter Olympic; Cdn Amateur, Canada's Sports halls of fame; res. San Francisco, Calif.

EMERY, Victor (bobsleigh); b. 28 Jun 1933, Montreal, Que.; m. Jenifer Wontner; c. Vanessa, Samantha, Alistair; Trinity College School, UWO, BA, L'Alliance Française, Harvard, MBA; dir. Savoy Hotels chain; competed internationally Olympic Finn Class sailing, class A 4-way skiing; pilot '64 Olympic, '65 world championship gold medal bobsled teams; mem. COA, chef de mission-adjoint '68 winter Olympic team; from '70 TV commentator bobsleigh, luge, cross-country skiing during world, Olympic competitions; helped in Cdn bid '88 Calgary Winter Olympics; '80 Olympic fund-raiser; active cross-country skier; mem. Cdn Winter Olympic, Cdn Amateur, Canada's Sports halls of fame; res. London, Eng.

EMMS, Hap (hockey); b. 16 Jan 1905, Barrie, Ont.; d. 23 Oct 1988, Niagara Falls, Ont.; given name: Leighton; c. Paul; standout baseball pitcher, soccer, hockey player; rejected pro baseball offers; scoring leader OHA Jr. B Barrie Colts; mem. Allandale CNR Apprentice League champs, Ont. Jr. finalist Midland, Brantford intermediates; pro Montreal Maroons '26; farmed to Stratford (CanPro), 1 title in 2 seasons; 2yrs Windsor (IL); acquired by NY Americans '30; Detroit '32-34; Americans '34-37; Boston '38; NHL record: 320 scheduled games, 36g, 53a, 14 playoff games, 0g, 0a; gained reputation as rugged defender, tenacious checker; 2yrs Pittsburgh, playing-coach Omaha Knights, 1 American Assn. title; coached Barrie Colts, Juveniles; coach St. Louis '45-46; Barrie Flyers Jr. A '47-61; Niagara Falls Flyers '61-74; jr. coaching record 15yrs, 362-355-67; 5 OHA, 4 Eastern Cdn titles, 4 Memorial Cups; OHL division named in his honor; founded Barrie Flyers Minor Hockey Assn.; mem. Barrie Sports Hall of Fame.

EMPRINGHAM, David (motorsport); b. 28 Dec 1964, Toronto, Ont.; m. Sue; UWO, BEc; began racing at 22 when parents presented him with Spenard/David Racing School course as graduation gift; competed in Player's/GM series, Firestone Firehawk Endurance series (GS class), Porsche Turbo Cup series before stepping up to Atlantic series machines; claimed Toyota Atlantic series titles '93-94, runnerup '95; advanced to Indy Lights '96 claiming 3 poles and 3 victories; series rookie of yr award; Gilles Villeneuve

award; '96 series title; joined Stewart team '98 as coach; res. Toronto, Ont.

EMSLIE, Bob (baseball); b. 27 Jan 1859, Guelph, Ont.; d. 26 Apr 1943, St. Thomas, Ont.; given name: Robert Daniel; umpire; amateur pitcher Waterville Kansas, London, Harriston, St. Thomas; pro Camden N.J.; ML Baltimore (AA) 1883-85, Philadelphia (AA) 1885; ML record: 44-44w-l record, 3.19era; best season 1884, 32 victories; 1st Cdn to pitch ML shutout; injured arm barnstorming; turned to umpiring 1887, back in ML 1890 Amer. Assn.; Western League 1891, National League 1891-1924; WL advisory board on retirement; nicknamed "Blind Bob" by John McGraw for involvement in famed Fred Merkle boner play (failure to touch 2nd base); mem. Baseball Hall of Fame honor roll of umpires, Cdn Baseball Hall of Fame.

ENNIS, Peter (basketball/coaching); b. 6 Apr 1946, Sudbury, Ont.; d. 14 Jan 1997, Sudbury, Ont.; given name: Peter Lawrence; m. Gail Ainslie; c. Liam, Kelly; Laurentian, BA; educator, basketball coach; coached Lady Vees '79-96, posting 248-48 record, including 189-14 in regular season play; 2 CIAU titles, 2 CIAU silver, 3 bronze medals; 7 OWIAA titles; 4 OWIAA coach of yr awards; twice CIAU coach of yr; his Lady Vees qualified for ntl tournament 17 consecutive yrs; 7 yrs chair Interuniversity Athletics at Laurentian; asst. coach ntl women's team '89-94, head coach ntl women's team '96 Olympics; coach '95 Canada Games gold medal team; women's team coach '93 FISU Games; mem. Laurentian Sports Wall of Fame.

ENOS, Ed (football); b. 30 Jun 1934, Boston, Mass.; given name: Edmund Francis; m. Janice McCluskey; c. Edmund III, Michael, Laurie; Connecticut, BSc, Boston, MEd, PhD, U of Munich, German College (Leipzig), Swiss Research Institute; retd. chair. Bio-PE dept., athletic dir., Concordia.; Connecticut football '53-57; pro linebacker NY Giants '57, '59, BC Lions '57-59; coach HS '60, Norwich U '61-62, Montreal Alouettes '63-64; AD Loyola College '65-74; '74-90 Bio-PE dept. chairman, AD Concordia; from '79 supervisor Montreal Expos conditioning program; founder Bio-PE dept., International Institute Comparative PE, Sports; dir. Lakeshore General Hospital Sports Medicine symposium, Olympic PE, Sports symposium; NY Rangers research, fitness consultant; Tau Kappa Epsilon fraternity alumnus of year; US Sports Academy distinguished service award; mem. Loyola College Senate, Connecticut, Alouettes Alumni Assn. Sports halls of fame; res. Baie D'Urf,, Que.

ENRIGHT, Jim (wheelchair basketball, t&f); b. 28 Apr 1964, Gatineau, Que.; civil servant; mem. Ottawa-Carleton Wheelchair Sports, Cdn Amputee Sports Assns. from '79; ntl high jump record 1.66m; Ont. javelin 40m record; Stoke Mandeville World Games gold '89, '91; mem. Ottawa Royals NWBT silver medal team '92, bronze '94; CWBL gold with Royals '89; ntl championship MVP '94; 2yrs sports administrative liaison officer '92 Cdn Winter Games for disabled; competed '92, '96 Paralympics; v-p OCWSA '85-87, '91-92; res. Gatineau, Que.

EON, Suzanne (synchro swim); b. 19 Feb 1924, Montreal, Que.; d. 23 Jan 1994, Lac St. Charles, Que.; St. Mary's Academy, Bart's Business School; synchronized swimming coach '50-78 guiding competitors to 124 ntl open, closed titles; coached 5 Pan-Am entries '55-75, 4 international invitationals '57-76, 3 worlds '73-78, 2 Pan-Pacific Games, 3 Canada Games; international coaching record '55-78: 10 gold, 18 silver, 7 bronze medals; Dick Ellis trophy team '75, Swedish Best Nation in World trophy team '76; coached Sylvie Fortier to ntl jr. athlete of '75 award; Quebec City media coach of '63, Confederation medal '67; mem. Order of Canada; CASSA distinguished service award, Canadian council for co-operation in aquatics award, Que. coach of year, Sports and Fitness coach of month award '74, Standard Brands award '75; runnerup Air Canada amateur coach of '73; mem. Order of Canada.

ERDMAN, Wayne (judo); b. 3 Feb 1952, Kitchener, Ont.; given name: Wayne John; judo instructor; Ont. 160lb title '67; Eastern Cdn. jr. 154lb title '68; ntl 70k '71, '73, '75, '76; 78k '80; ranked world's top 16 holding '72 Olympic gold medalist, '73 world champion Nomura of Japan to points draw '73 worlds; Pan-Am 70k gold '74; Pan-Am Games 70k gold, ranked world's top 8 '75; mem. '76 Olympic team; Canada Cup 78k bronze '80; runnerup ntl amateur athlete of '74; res. Don Mills, Ont.

ERVASTI, Ed (golf); b. 13 Jan 1914, Minneapolis, Minn.; given name: Edward Walker; m. Jane Bradshaw; c. Thomas, John, David; Wayne State; retired general manager; finalist '43 Salt Lake City, Utah amateurs; '47 Michigan amateur, St. Louis district titles; only Michigan qualifier '53 US Amateur; twice low amateur Erie, Pa., Open; London District title '66; 3 Sunningdale, 1 London Hunt club titles; 6 ntl srs titles; Rankin Memorial Trophy winner once; 2 Ont. srs titles; 2 US srs titles; res. London, Ont.

ESMIE, Robert (t&f); 5 Jul 1972, Kingston, Jamaica; sprinter; emigrated to Canada '84; began competing at 16; gold 100, 200m Canada vs. Ireland '92; silver 100m '94 Harry Jerome Classic; bronze 100m '94 NY Games; silver 100m, gold 200m '94 ntl championships; PB: 10.18 100m, 20.70 200m; mem. 4x100 gold relay team '95-97 world outdoor championships, '96 Olympic Games; mem. '94 Commonwealth, '96 Olympic Games teams; 2 Cdn men's team of yr awards; resigned from relay team '97 citing personality conflicts; mem. Adenac AC; res. Sudbury, Ont.

ESPOSITO, Phil (hockey); b. 20 Feb 1942, Sault Ste. Marie, Ont.; given name: Philip Anthony; div. Donna; c. Laurie, Carrie, Cherise; Fox hockey analyst, ex-hockey exec.; Sarnia Jr. B, St. Catharines Jr. A; pro Sault Ste. Marie, St. Louis; NHL winger Chicago '63-67, centre Boston '67-75, NY Rangers '75-81; NHL record: 1282 scheduled games, 717g, 873a, 130 playoff games, 61g, 76a; 1st player NHL history 100 or more points single season; 1st player more than 70 goals single season with 76 '70-71; tied Frank Mahovlich most Stanley Cup playoff points single season with 27; 50 or more goals 5 consec. seasons; 5 consec. 100-plus point seasons; 1st player 150 or more points (152) '70-71; 27 3-goal, 5 4-goal games; 3rd in career goals, points; standout with Team Canada '72, '76; mem. 2 Stanley Cup winners, 6 1st, 2 2nd all-star teams; 5 Ross, 2 Hart, 2 Lester Patrick, 2 Lester Pearson, 1 Lou Marsh, 2 Lionel Conacher trophies; founder Phil Esposito Foundation, Masters of Hockey OT game; NHL milestone award; jersey No. 7 retired by Bruins; TV color commentator; VP/GM NY

Rangers '86-90; instrumental in organizing successful Tampa Lightning NHL franchise expansion bid for '92-93 season; pres./GM Lightning '92-98, fired mid-season '98; Officer Order of Canada '72; mem. Canada's Sports, Hockey, SSM Hockey halls of fame; res. Tampa, Fla.

ESPOSITO, Tony (hockey); b. 23 Apr 1943, Sault Ste. Marie, Ont.; given name: Anthony James; m. Marilyn; c. Mark, Jason; Michigan Tech, BSc; ex-hockey exec.; pro Vancouver (WHL) '67, Houston (CHL) '68; NHL goaler Montreal '68-69, Chicago '69-84; NHL record: 886 scheduled games, 52,585 min. 2563 goals, 76so, 2.92 avg.; 3 1st team, 2 2nd team all-star; 6 NHL all-star games; Calder Memorial Trophy '70; mem. 1 Stanley Cup winner; won/shared 3 Vezina Trophies; US citizen; mem. Team Canada '72, Team USA '81 Canada Cup series; pres. NHLPA; VP/GM Pittsburgh '88-90; dir. hockey dev./scout Tampa Bay Lightning '95-98, fired mid-season '98; jersey No. 35 retd. by Blackhawks; mem. Hockey, Sault Ste. Marie Hockey halls of fame; res. St. Petersburg Beach, Fla.

ESTWICK, Leslie (t&f); b. 20 Dec 1960, Goderich, Ont.; computer consultant; mem. Athletics Canada bd dir.; ntl HJ title, runnerup heptathlon '87; 5 gold HJ Jesse Owens Invitational; bronze HJ, silver 60mH '87 CIAU championships; silver 60mH Belgium, 100mH, HJ Italy '88; bronze HJ '89 Francophone Games; 3 ntl HJ titles; gold 100mH '92 Provo Invitational; gold heptathlon '93 Ohio Relays; competed '90, '94 Commonwealth, '91 Pan-Am Games, world championships; mem. Ottawa Lions TC; mem. Ottawa Athletic Club racing team '99; 1 gold, 3 silver '97, 2 gold '99 world masters; 3 gold '98 Caribbean Masters; res. Gloucester, Ont.

ETCHEGARY, Gus (soccer); b. 28 May 1924, St. Lawrence, Nfld.; given name: Augustine Alexander; m. Kay Diab; c. Glenn, Grant; retd exec. v-p Fishery Products International, chair. Fisheries Council of Canada '81-82; mem. 3 St. Lawrence soccer title teams; pres. BN Peninsula, St. John's, Nfld. soccer assn.; v-p CSA; soccer referee; St. Pierre Miquelon service to soccer award; mem. Nfld. Sports, Soccer, St. Lawrence, St. John's Soccer halls of fame; res. Paradise, Nfld.

ETCHEVERRY, Sam (football); b. 20 May 1930, Carlsbad, N.M.; m. Juanita Louise Mulcahy; c. Steve (d), Mike, Jim, Nancy, Jennifer; Denver, BA; stockbroker; quarterback '50 Pineapple Bowl; pro Montreal (CFL) '52-59, St. Louis Cardinals (NFL) '60-61; nicknamed "The Rifle"; CFL record '54 (when league began keeping records) to '59: 1630 completions on 2829 pass attempts for 25,582yds, 163int, 174tds; single season EFC passing yardage record 4723yds '56; shares CFL record longest completed pass 109yds to Hal Patterson '56; 3 Grey Cup finals; traded to Hamilton '60 but opted for NFL; coach Que. Rifles (UFL), Alouettes '70 Grey Cup winner; 6 times EFC all-star; Schenley outstanding player '54; Jeff Russel Memorial Trophy '54, '58; pres. Montreal Concordes '82-83; mem. Que. Sports, Cdn Football, MAAA halls of fame; res. Montreal, Que.

EVANS, Art (football); b. 29 Jul 1915, Toronto, Ont.; m. Dorothy Rule; c. Sandra Louise; retired packing house G-M.; HS, jr. lacrosse '30s; tackle, end, middle linebacker Toronto '35-39; mem. '37-38 Grey Cup winners; capt. '38

Argos; mem. '42 RCAF Hurricanes Grey Cup winner; v-p Stampeders '75-76, pres. '77-78, mem. 4-man exec. committee; last known res. Calgary, Alta.

EVANS, Clay (swimming); b. 28 Oct 1953, El Bagre, Colombia; given name: Thomas Clayton; UCLA; butterfly, backstroke specialist; mem. '72, '76 Olympic, '79 Pan-Am Games teams; 100m butterfly bronze '79 Pan-Ams; ntl 100m backstroke, 200m IM titles '72, 100m butterfly '76; silver 100m butterfly, bronze 50m FS '80 Four Nation Cup; retd. '80; ntl 200m IM record '72; mem. UCLA water polo team; Governor-General's medal '76; res. Huntington Beach, Calif.

EVANS, Eddie (rugby); b. 15 Sep 1964, Terrace, B.C.; UBC; IBM business planner Japan; jr. football Victoria, Vancouver; prop Cdn jr. rugby team, ntl sr team '85-98; competed 3 World Cups; Canada's most capped player; earned 1st of 48 caps vs. USA '86; mem. IBM Tokyo team; res. Tokyo, Japan.

EVANS, Jodi (basketball); b. 16 Aug 1968, Calgary, Alta.; UCal, BComm, Oxford (Rhodes Scholarship); guard HS provincial title team '86; mem. UCal team that went 69-0 and won '88-89 CIAU titles; mem. jr. ntl team '87, sr. team '88-96; mem. '91 FISU Games bronze medal team; competed '90, '94 world, Goodwill Games, '91 Pan-Am, '96 Olympic Games; COPABA gold '95, bronze '93; played on Oxford men's '93 title team; pro with English, German, Greek teams; CIAU all-Cdn '90-91; Nan Copp player of '91 award; HS female athlete of '86 award; res. Norway.

EVANS, Mark (rowing); b. 16 Aug 1957, Toronto, Ont.; Oxford; gold coxed 4s, coxless pairs Nottingham International; coxed, coxless 4s, coxless pairs Canadian Henley, ntl championships; mem. coxed 8s gold crew '84 Olympics; Dick Ellis award '84; twin brother Michael; res. Toronto, Ont.

EVANS, Michael (rowing); b. 16 Aug 1957, Toronto, Ont.; given name: John Michael; Princeton, AB, Oxford; ntl, Ont. pairs, 4s, 8s champion '75-83; bronze FISA world youth championships '75; stroke '77 coxed 8s, '79, '81, '83 coxless pairs world championships; gold Nottingham International coxed 4s, coxless pair; mem. gold coxed 8s crew '84 Olympics; 9 Canadian Henley titles; finalist English Royal Henley, mem. '80, '84 Olympic teams; stroke Princeton IRA regatta freshman champions '76; stroke varsity heavy 8s '77-81; capt. varsity heavyweight program '79-81; Dick Ellis award '84; res. London, Eng.

EVANSHEN, Terry (football); b. 13 Jun 1944, Montreal, Que.; given name: Terrance Anthony; m. Lorraine Galarneau; c. Tracy Lee, Tara, Jennifer; Utah State; ex-sales mgr.; Portland Seahawks (Atlantic Coast Conference) '64; halfback-receiver Alouettes '65, '70-74, EFC rookie of yr; Calgary '66-69, Hamilton '74-77, Toronto '78; twice Schenley top Canadian; twice EFC, 4 times WFC all-star, once all-Cdn; 600 CFL career receptions for 9697yds, 80tds, only 3 fumbles; shares longest pass reception record with Hal Patterson 109yds from Jerry Keeling '66; twice led EFC, WFC receivers single season; with Hugh Campbell shares single season TD pass receptions with 17; CFL record most

games catching passes 181; 3 times 1000-plus reception yards single season; CFL record 10 consecutive games catching TD passes; 61 games catching TD passes; caught 4td passes vs. Ottawa 7 Sep 1975; mem. 3 Grey Cup finalists, 1 winner; CBC-TV football color commentator 2yrs; awarded $1.6M in damages from '88 auto accident which severely affected his memory; conducts speaking tours; mem. Cdn Football Hall of Fame; res. Toronto, Ont.

EVILLE, Vern (t&f); b. 21 Dec 1910, Brandon, Man.; d. 9 Nov 1973, Halifax, N.S.; given name: Vernon Drew Millidge; m. Joyce Whitney Favin; c. Drew; Acadia; standout basketball, rugby, track & field performer; mem. Acadia Axemen ntl sr. cage finalists; standout on half line for Acadia in English rugby league; Maritime jr. discus, long jump titlist '28; led Ken Wo squad to team title '29 winning 440, 880 dashes, high jump, 120yd high hurdles; named to Cdn team for '30 Empire Games but polio terminated career; mem. NS Sports Hall of Fame.

EVON, Russ (all-around); b. 15 Aug 1917, Windsor, Ont.; d. 9 Nov 1998, St. Thomas, Ont.; given name: Russell Phillip; m. Hellen; c. Donna, Ron; retd. owner laundry, dry cleaning business; as teenager among 5 best fastballers in Canada; Border Cities Softball Federation '38; fanned record 25 consecutive batters, several no-hitters; 3 world tournaments, coached 4th, winning one; 18 Sr. IC baseball seasons London, St. Thomas '43-60; career .345 batting avg., twice batting champion; led each league in which he played at least once, including strong Detroit Class A League '39; mem. 3 Ont. basketball title teams; OHA Int., International HL; outstanding player award IHL '40-41; 35yrs hockey referee; strong swimmer; involved in more than 30 rescues of potential drowning victims; top-ranked 10-pin bowler; mem. Windsor-Essex Sports Hall of Fame.

EWERT, Elmer (archery); b. 19 Sep 1934, St. Catharines, Ont.; m. Beverely Smith; c. Lorraine, Kevin, Trevor; Notre Dame U (BC), Waterloo; laboratory technologist; '67 ntl champion; mem. Ambassador's Cup, world championships teams, '72 Olympic team; '74 Ont. champion; res. Wellesley, Ont.

EWING, Walter (shooting); b. 11 Feb 1878, Montreal, Que.; d. 1927, given name: Walter Hamilton; m. Ethel Raeburn McIntyre; c. Morris, Marguerite, Walter James, David Russell; pres. Lackawanna Coal Co.; began trapshooting '05; won '08 Olympic gold with score of 72 of possible 80; declined invitation to defend title '12 Olympics; won Clarendon Cup in 1st annual Canadian Indians tournament in Montreal '06; won ntl championship, Grand Canadian Handicap, Brewers and Malsters Cup, provincial individual titles; also competed in DCRA rifle events winning 8-man Dominion, 10-man provincial, 5-man international, 6-man provincial and 5-man Lansdowne Cup team titles in same year; mem. Cdn Olympic, Canada's Sports halls of fame.

EXELBY, Clare (football); b. 5 Nov 1937, Toronto, Ont.; given name: Clare Douglas; m. Maureen Girvin; c. Julie Lynn, Randy Allan; UofT, BA; teacher Erindale Coll; mem. ntl finalist Parkdale Jr. Lions '56, ntl title '57; pro Toronto '58-59, '61-63, Calgary '60, Montreal '64-65; WFC all-star defensive back, league interception leader; all-Canadian def. back '64; coached 5 Toronto city HS title teams; def. coach York U '68-72; def. co-ordinator jr. Argos '78-79; res. Toronto, Ont.

EYNON, Bob (swimming); b. 16 Aug 1935, North Bay, Ont.; given name: Robert Barrie; m. Mary Ellen Thompson (d); c. Susan, Robert, Patrick; UWO, BA, Illinois, MSc; retd. associate prof., swimming coach; successful competitive career led to coaching ntl women's swim team '67 Pan-Am Games, UK touring team '73-74; CIAU swim coach of '66, '75; treas. CASA '60-72; chair. Ont. Swimming Coaches Assn. '66-73; chair. CIAU Swimming Coaches Assn. '73-75; Ont. merit award '70; Cdn Red Cross Society merit award '71; works Buck Dawson summer camp; res. London, Ont.

EZINICKI, Bill (hockey/golf); b. 11 Mar 1924, Winnipeg, Man.; nicknamed "Wild Bill" for his love of body contact; a free-wheeler, he was noted for violent body checks which frequently put opponents out of game; carried insurance policy which paid him per stitch taken in on-ice battles; jr. 1yr Winnipeg Rangers, mem. Oshawa Generals Memorial Cup team '44; pro '44-55 with Toronto, Boston, NY Rangers; played in 2 NHL all-star games; mem. 3 Stanley Cup winners; NHL record: 368 scheduled games, 79g,105a, 40 playoff games, 5g, 8a; retd '55 to pursue career as pro golfer; spent some time on PGA tour; mem. Man. Hockey Hall of Fame; res. Boston, Mass.

FABRE, Édouard (t&f); b. 21 Aug 1885, Ste. Geneviéve, Que.; d. 1 Jul 1939, Montreal, Que.; m. Blanche; c. Marcelle, Marie-Blanche, Édouard; construction worker; in 30 years of competition ran 315 match races, won hundreds of trophies, medals; in one 24-hour event was pitted against horse to see who could run furthest, Fabre won; competed '06 Athens marathon, '12 Stockholm Olympics; entered 1st Boston marathon '11; won on 5th try '15; won 200-mile, 6-day snowshoe marathon Quebec to Montreal, averaging just under 6 mph; mem. Canada's Sports Hall of Fame.

FABRIS, Lucio (badminton); b. 7 Nov 1957, Sudbury, Ont.; given name: Lucio Mario; m. Judy Humphry; UofT, BPharm; pharmacist; from '73-81 dominant force on Ont., ntl badminton scene; ntl jr. men's doubles '73-74; swept Ont., ntl jr. singles, men's, mixed doubles '75; ntl mixed doubles '76; silver '78 Commonwealth Games; OUAA men's singles, doubles '79; Ont., municipal sport achievement awards; res. Creighton Mine/Sudbury, Ont.

FABRO, Sam (builder); b. 8 Dec 1920, Udine, Italy; m. Anne Marie Temple; c. James; UWO; retd. board chair. W.G. McMahon Ltd.; accomplished hockey, baseball, football player; mem. Winnipeg Rangers Memorial Cup champs '41; sr. Reo Flyers; chair. baseball competition '67 Pan-Am Games; pres. Man. Baseball Assn. '68-69; chair. Man. Games '74-78; among founders Man. Hockey Players Assn., chair. '66-80; mem./chair. Winnipeg Enterprises '67-83; launched Man. marathon and canoeathon; chair. of same; chair. Man. Hockey Hall of Fame; chair. Man. Sports Hall of Fame; v-chair. Man. Wildlife Foundation; day declared in his honor in Winnipeg; mem. Order of Canada; Man. Order of the Buffalo; Man. Sports, Hockey halls of fame; res. Winnipeg, Man

FAIRBANKS, Lloyd (football); b. 28 Apr 1953, Raymond, Alta.; m. Jackie; c. Kelly, Todd, Kathy; Brigham Young; offensive lineman Calgary '75-82, '89-92; Montreal '83-86, Hamilton '87-89; 3 times WFC, 3 EFC, 2 CFL all-star; Schenley offensive lineman finalist '82; Beckett-DeMarco (outstanding WFC lineman) award '82; mem. Stampeders Wall of Fame; res. Raymond, Alta.

FAIRHOLM, Jeff (football); b. 7 Nov 1965, Montreal, Que.; Arizona; slotback; 1st round pick Sask '88-93, Toronto '94-96; Jackie Parker rookie trophy '88, runnerup CFL rookie '88; Dr. Beattie Martin trophy '89; twice runnerup CFL outstanding Cdn; 1 all-Western all-star; mem. 1 Grey Cup winner; res. Toronto, Ont.

FAIRS, Jack (football/baseball/tennis); b. 22 Aug 1923, Toronto, Ont.; given name: John Russell; m. Peggy Duncan; c. Nancy, Kimberly, John; UWO, BSc, Columbia, MA; prof.; football UWO '42-46; backfield coach UWO '48-62; catcher minor pro baseball '39-54, London Sr. IC, Welland Atlas Steel; '48 Sandlot World Series title; part-time scout NY Yankees; coached 5 Ont. Bantam A title teams; tennis coach '48-62; UWO squash coach '59-96; US

Intercollegiate squash titles '77, '80; UWO no lower than 2nd CIAU squash from '72; Squash Canada distinguished service award; 3M 50yr coaching award; mem. UWO W-Club Sports Hall of Fame; res. London, Ont.

FALARDEAU, Johanne (badminton); b. 2 Mar 1961, Montreal, Que.; given name: Marie Johanne Lucille; Laval; coach, Que. Badminton Fed.; 2 Que. singles, 1 doubles titles; 2 ntl singles, 3 doubles, 2 mixed doubles titles; 3 singles, 4 doubles, 2 mixed doubles Pan-Am championships titles; 1 French doubles, mixed doubles titles, 1 US doubles title; team silver '78, '82, doubles gold '82 Commonwealth Games; fed. govt. excellence award '83; res. Quebec City.

FALONEY, Bernie (football); b. 15 Jun 1932, Carnegie, Pa.; d.14 Jun 1999, Hamilton, Ont.; m. Janet Wallace; c. Bernie Jr., Wally; Maryland, BSc; pres. construction machinery, industrial products company; football, baseball, basketball Maryland '50-53; rejected pro baseball offers; all-American, Atlantic Coast Conf. player of year, all-American Scholastic team; quarterbacked, co-capt. Maryland undefeated season, ntl title '53; '52 Sugar Bowl, '53 Orange Bowl; SF 49ers 1st draft '53; pro Edmonton '54; Bolling AFB Generals 2 service titles '55-56; Hamilton '57-64, 1st QB to lead both Eastern, Western team to Grey Cup victories ('54, '57); Montreal '65-66, BC '67; CFL record: completed 1493 of 2876 passes for 24,264yds, 151td, 201 interceptions, .519 percentage; CBC color commentator '68; 9 Grey Cup finals, 4 winners; Dapper Dan award Washington DC Touchdown Club '53; CFL Schenley outstanding player '61, Jeff Russel '65; Maryland man of '71/distinguished sports alumnus award '72; twice Ted Reeve all-Cdn team; coached '73 CFL all-stars over Grey Cup champions; mem. Cdn Football, Canada's Sports, Copps Coliseum halls of fame.

FALOON, Joanna (canoeing): b. 1 Jun 1955, Ottawa, Ont.; given name: Joanna Patricia; m. Wally Kaczkowski; c. Kenneth; UAlta., Illinois Coll. of Podiatric Medicine; Podiatrist; top athlete Notre Dame HS '72; mem. UAlta water polo team '75-76; mem. Rideau canoe Club '71-73; ntl jr. K4 title; ntl women's C2 title '85; world, US C2 women's title '91; world, ntl C1 women's title '92; competed '91-97 Hawaii outrigger world championships; 5 gold NA marathon canoe racing championships '97; 2 gold, 1 silver US marathon canoe/kayak championships '98; retained NA C1 marathon title '99; built reputation as one of world's top marathon canoe/kayak paddlers; also competes in triathlon, running events; mem. Nepean Sports Wall of Fame; res. Merrickville, Ont.

FANNING, Jim (baseball); b. 14 Sep 1927, Chicago, Ill.; given name: William James; m. Marie; c. 2; Buena Vista College, BPhE, Illinois, MA; baseball exec.; pro ball at 22 catcher Chicago Cubs organization; 64 ML games Cubs '54-57; mgr. Tulsa (TL) '58, Dallas (AA) '59-60, Eau Claire, Wisc. '61, field and GM; Braves' special assignment scout '63-64; AGM '64-66; dir. scouting, farm operations '67;

dir. ML scouting bureau commissioner's office '68; mem. numerous baseball organizational comm.; Montreal Expos at '68 inception; GM through '76; v-p from '73; dir. player development '77-81, from '83; field mgr. '81-82, '84, advisor to GM, broadcaster; scout Colorado Rockies from '92; charter mem. Buena Vista sports hall of fame; '72 Buena Vista Alumni Assn. outstanding service award; Hartley Iowa baseball park named in his honor; res. Henryville, Que.

FARLEY, Phil (golf); b. 27 Mar 1912, Toronto, Ont.; d. 10 Apr 1974, Toronto, Ont.; m. Ruth; c. Maureen, Michael, Diane, Philip Edward; stockbroker; Ont. jr. title '30; 6 Ont. amateurs, 2 Ont. Opens, 1 Que. amateur; runnerup 3 ntl amateurs; low amateur 5 Cdn Opens; 3 times Cdn amateur finalist; with Phil Brownlee '61 Ont. best ball; mem. 12 Ont., 3 Que. Willingdon Cup teams; 6 G.S. Lyons team titles; 1 Duke of Kent, 3 Ont. srs, 2 RCGA srs, 2 CSGA titles; pres. OGA '49; RCGA governor '50-74; RCGA pres. '67; mem. RCGA Hall of Fame.

FARMER, Jim (football); b. 28 Nov 1916, Glasgow, Scotland; d. 5 Jan 1988, London, Ont.; given name: James Gordon; m. Joan; c. Brian, Peter, Sarah; Assumption College, UWO, OCE; salesman; undefeated distance swimmer 4yrs; all-star HS football, basketball; sr. individual t&f honors '34; Windsor Patterson CI all-time all-around athlete; mem. '35 jr. A baseball champions; pitched sr. A softball; with Assumption mem. ntl basketball finalists '36; capt. CIAU '37-38 basketball champions; OQAA all-star fullback '38; pro Toronto Argos '39; dir. Windsor Rockets (ORFU) '47; mem. CIAU football rules comm. '59-75; 7yrs referee-in-chief OQAA, 10yrs editor, rules interpreter OQAA, OUAA, CIAU; mem. Windsor-Essex County, UWO W-Club Sports halls of fame.

FARMER, Ken (hockey); b. 26 Jul 1912, Westmount, Que.; m. Larayne Strachan; c. Howard, Ian, Cynthia, Pamela; McGill, BComm; retd chartered accountant; hockey McGill '31-34; mem. '36 Olympic silver medal team; CIAU tennis doubles champion; pres. COA '53-61; chair. Ntl Advisory Council on Fitness, Amateur Sport '62-65; pres. Commonwealth Games Assn. of Canada '78-84; dir. Montreal Olympic organizing comm.; mem. Order of Canada, Cdn Amateur Sports Hall of Fame; res. Montreal, Que.

FARNSWORTH, Terry (judo); b. 27 Aug 1942, Portland, Me.; given name: Terry Allen; m. Heather Higgins; c. Lanisa Dawn, Joshua George; Sophia U (Tokyo), BEc; manufacturing co. pres.; ntl 93k titles '72-73; gold '69, double silver '73 Maccabiah Games; mem. ntl team '71-73; competed '72 Olympics, '73 Pan Am Games, '71-73 worlds; mem. selection comm., judo chairman Canadian Maccabiah Games Comm.; res. Bois des Filion, Que.

FARRELL, Neil (t&f); b. 13 Feb 1915, Arthur, Ont.; given name: Neil John; m. Isabel Couper; retd Ont. govt.; average distance runner; chair. ntl t&f comm. '56-60; secty. AAU of C '61-66; mem. ntl records comm. '56-67; mem. AAU of C Hall of Fame Comm. '61-67; t&f rep., dir. COA '57-60; mem.-at-large COA '61-64; p.-pres., secty Southwestern Ont. branch AAU of C, Hamilton Olympic Comm.; mgr. Canadian BEG t&f team '58, Olympic t&f team '60; asst.

mgr. Canadian Commonwealth Games teams '66, '74; mgr. '70, GM '78 Commonwealth Games teams; hon. secty. CCGA from '63; mem. SFC citations comm. '65-67; deputy ref. '76 Olympic marathon; v-p America Zone Commonwealth Games Fed.; Ont. sport achievement award '68; mem. Cdn Amateur Sports Hall of Fame; res. Hamilton, Ont.

FARROW, Brad (judo); b. 5 Oct 1956, Vancouver, B.C.; given name: Brad William; m. Laurel King; c. Taylor, Kristen; Concordia, BSc, UWO, MBA; management consultant; began judo career age 11; 5th degree black belt; 11 Canadian 63kg and/or 65kg titles; gold 63kg '75, 65kg '79 Pan-Am Games; mem. '76, '80, '84 Olympic teams; gold '79, '81 Dutch Open, '80 German Open, '83-84 Canada Cup; silver '79 Hungarian Cup; bronze '77 British Open, '80 Pacific Rim, Cuban Open, '81 Pacific Rim, German Open; mem. ntl team '75, '79, '81 world championships; bronze '83 FISU Games; mem. Cdn Judo Hall of Fame; res. Calgary, Alta.

FAUL, Adam (boxing); b. 18 Apr 1929, Regina, Sask.; m. Marjorie Evelyn Shaw; c. Kevin Darrell, Cheryl Lynn, Mark Perry, Gregory Shaw; municipal secty-treas.; '45-47 Sask. light heavyweight title; ntl light heavyweight title '47; Western Diamond Belt, 1 Sask., 2 ntl heavyweight titles, Olympic trials '48; mem. '48 Olympic team; ring record 60-4; football Regina Eastend jr. Bombers, Sask. Roughriders '44; mem. Sask. Sports Hall of Fame; res. Spy Hill, Sask.

FAULKNER, Alex (hockey); b. 21 May 1936, Bishop's Falls, Nfld.; given name: Selm Alexander; m. Doris May Reid; c. Shawn, Alexandra, Tammy Sue; owner, operator sr. citizen's home; mem. Nfld. title teams all levels; 6 times all-Nfld. sr.; NHL Detroit '62-64; twice Stanley Cup finalist; Allan Cup semifinalist Galt '72-73; mem. Newfoundland Sports Hall of Fame; res. Bishop's Falls, Nfld.

FAULKNER, John (swimming); b. 12 Dec 1923, Kingston, Ont.; given name: John Arthur; m. Margaret Isabelle Rowntree; c. Laura Megan, Melanie Anne; Queen's, BA, BPhE, Michigan, MSc, PhD; professor, director UofM Institute of Gerontology; intercollegiate football '46-50, basketball '46-47; football, basketball coach Ottawa Glebe CI '52-56; coached Ottawa Ski Club ntl jr. title team '53; coach UWO swim team '56-60, OQAA titles '59-60; coached swimming, diving teams '60 Olympics; active American College of Sports Medicine from '60, trustee '63-75, pres. '71-72; published myriad papers on research on physiological responses to sport; twice competed National Ski Marathon; UofM Burke Aaron Hinsdale scholar award '62, American College of Sports Medicine citation '78; res. Ann Arbor, Mich.

FAUQUIER, Harry (tennis); b. 28 Aug 1942, Toronto, Ont.; given name: Henry Edmund; m. Lindsay Smith; c. Sarah; Michigan, BA; partner tennis court construction co.; ntl jr. title '59-60; Big 10 title '61-62; capt. Michigan team '63-64; mem. '63 Pan-Am Games team; mem. 10 Davis Cup teams, twice capt.; with John Sharpe ntl Open men's doubles '68; among Canada's top 5 10yrs; 5yrs No. 1 Ont.; won international tournaments North, South America, Europe;

competed at Forest Hills, Wimbledon; assisted Ken Sinclair in organizing ntl Open tournaments Toronto, Montreal; mem. Cdn Dubler Cup, Fred Perry Cup teams; 4 ntl srs doubles titles; mem. Cdn Tennis Hall of Fame; res. Aurora, Ont.

FAWCETT, Mark (snowboarding); b. 17 Jan 1972, Saint John, N.B.; ardent windsurfer who has excelled on World Cup pro snowboarding circuit; began snowboarding age 12; 2 WC gold, 2 bronze; 2 ISF World Series gold, 2 ISF Masters gold; ntl slalom title '98; competed '97 world championships, '98 Olympics; equipment breakdown ruined Olympic slalom hopes at Nagano; ISF surfboarder of '95; nicknamed Fuzzy; res. East Riverside, N.B./Hood River, Ore.

FEAGAN, Ron (harness racing); b. 10 Mar 1942, Goderich, Ont.; d. 12 Jan 1979, Dundas, Ont.; m. Susan; c. Blair; 1st Cdn to drive 200 winners single season; Cdn co-horseman of '65; youngest driver to reach 1000 victory plateau '68; Canada's leading race winner '66, '69-70; top Cdn money winner '68, '70; Golden Horseshoe Circuit dash, money leader '72-76; 3000 win plateau '78; purses exceeded $6M; drove H.A. Meadowland '66 Queen City Pacing Stakes, Canadian Pacing Derby, Canadian Harness Horse of year honors; mem. Cdn Horse Racing Hall of Fame.

FEAR, Cap (football); b. 11 Jun 1901, Old Sailbury, Eng.; d. 12 Feb 1978, St. Catharines, Ont.; given name: Alfred Henry John; m. Gertrude Lilian Farr; construction superintendent; outside wing Toronto Argos '20-27, 3 league titles, 1 Grey Cup; mem. team which lost only one game '21-22 seasons; Hamilton Tigers '28-32, 2 league titles, 2 Grey Cups; hockey Aura Lee sr. OHA, Ont. Hydro Toronto Mercantile League; runnerup NA welterweight boxing title; stroke Argonaut Rowing Club lightweight 8s, 4s same day Canadian Henley victors; Lachine, Detroit, Dominion Day regatta titles; mem. Hamilton best-of-century (1867-1949) amateur era all-star football team; mem. Canada's Sports, Cdn Football halls of fame.

FEDERKO, Bernie (hockey); b. 12 May 1956, Foam Lake, Sask.; given name: Bernard Allan; m. Bernadette; c. Jordan, Dustin, Drew; hockey broadcaster; centre Saskatoon (WHL) '73-76, Kansas City (CHL) '76-77; 1st pick St. Louis '76 amateur draft; played in NHL with St. Louis '77-89, Detroit '89-90; jersey #24 retd. by Blues; NHL record: 14 seasons, 1000 scheduled games, 369g, 76a, 91 playoff games, 35g, 66a; WHL all-star '76; WHL MVP '76; played in 2 NHL all-star games; GM/head coach St, Louis Vipers roller hockey team '93-95, club pres. '95-98; res. St. Louis, Mo.

FEDORUK, Sylvia (all-around); b. 5 May 1927, Canora, Sask.; UofSask, BA, MA, FCCPM; retd. physicist, prof. ex-Lt. Governor Sask.; 2 gold, 1 silver, 1 bronze, T.Eaton Trophy top individual performer '47 Dominion t&f championships; mem. Saskatoon Ramblers '48 provincial women's, '54 Regina Gorins, '55 Saskatoon Ramblers Western Canada softball champions; 12 intervarsity title teams (5 basketball, 2 t&f, 3 volleyball, 2 golf) '46-51; intervarsity individual golf title '51; Governor-General's gold medal UofSask '49; Queen's Jubilee medal '77; coached university volleyball, curling teams 2yrs; 3rd for Joyce McKee 3 provincial, 2 ntl curling championships; pres. CLCA '71-72; pres. SLCA '59; pres. Women's Athletic Board UofSask '49; dir., mem. Order of Canada, Cdn Curling, Sask. Sports Halls, UofSask Sports Wall of Fame; res. Regina, Sask.

FEDOSA, Bob (curling); b. 14 Dec 1945, Saskatoon, Sask.; given name: Robert William; m. Sandra Jean; York, BA; retd. educator; 7 times Ont. men's finalist; skip Ont. entry '79 Brier; skip 2 Ont. Silver Tankard winners; res. Brampton, Ont.

FEE, Earl (t&f); b. 22 Mar 1929, Elstow, Sask.; given name: Earl William; div.; c. Tyler, Curtis, Melanie Suttar; UofT, BSc, MSc; retd. nuclear engineer; early track exposure '46-53 then took 33yr hiatus from sport '53-86; began training North York TC '86 then shifted to Saugeen TC and Credit Valley Marathon Club; from '86-98 broke more than 25 age group world records in 300, 400m hurdles, 400, 800, 1500, mile runs; through '98 held 17 existing world masters, 7 Cdn masters track records; 6 ntl cross country age group titles; 4 Cdn Masters athlete of meet awards; 4 Ont. Masters male t&f athlete of yr awards; 3 Mississauga Master athlete of yr awards; authored *Secrets of a World Masters Champion - How to be a Champion*; res. Mississauga, Ont.

FEKETE, Tim (fencing); b. 31 Jan 1957, Ottawa, Ont.; given name: Lehel Imre Rudolf; 5 Ont. foil, sabre titles; 2 ntl foil titles; mem. 2 ntl sabre title teams; Ottawa shield winner; mem. '74 Commonwealth, '75 Pan-Am, '76, '80 Olympic, 7 world championship tournament teams; last known res. Ottawa, Ont.

FELL, Graeme (t&f); b. 19 Mar 1959, Romford, Eng.; m. Debbie Campbell; c. Cori-Ann Jill, Taylor John; athletic consultant; 3,000m steeplechase, 3000m specialist; began competing age 11; as mem. GB ntl team won '82 Commonwealth Games silver; emigrated to Canada '84; 6 ntl titles; 2 Cdn sr. records; competed '82, '86, '90, '94 Commonwealth, '88, '92 Olympic Games; CG gold '86, bronze '94; World Cup bronze '85; 2 CIAU all-Cdn; Tribute to Champions award '87, Athletics Canada athlete of '94; BC male athlete of '85; res. Vancouver, B.C.

FELL, Jeffrey (horse racing); b. 20 Jun 1956, Hamilton, Ont.; jockey; riding Winter's Tale became 1st winner Suburban, Brooklyn, Marlboro Cup, NY state's 3 richest handicap races single season; Hialeah, Gulfstream, Belmont riding titles; shares NY state record 6 consec. race victories '80; with Norcliffe '76 Prince of Wales, Queen's Plate; '79 Whitney Stakes, '81 Wood Memorial; through '83 victories exceed 2300, earnings exceed $30M; mem. Cdn Horse Racing, Copps Coliseum halls of fame; res. Hallandale, Fla.

FELLOWS, Ron (motorsport); b. 28 Sep 1959, Windsor, Ont.; given name: Ronald Charles; m. Lynda Stewart; c. Lindsay, Samuel, Patrick; pro racer; received racing license '78; raced on Ont./Que. region club circuit; competed in Formula 1600 series; competed in Players-GM series from mid '80s winning series title '89; drove in SCCA Trans-Am series '91-96 posting 19 victories at Watkin's Glen; won Chev Mfgrs title '95; became 2nd Cdn driver (Earl Ross was 1st) to claim a NASCAR title winning Parts America

150 truck race with record performance Watkin's Glen '98; same season, teamed with Rob Morgan to drive world Ferrari to victory at Watkin's Glen; became 1st non-American to win Busch Grand National Lysol 200 race '98; made Winston Cup debut '98; Bud Pole award NASCAR Busch series '99; res. Mississauga, Ont.

FENNELL, Dave (football); b. 4 Feb 1953, Edmonton, Alta.; N. Dakota, UAlta, LLD; lawyer; jr. Edmonton Wildcats; def. tackle Edmonton Eskimos '73-83; nicknamed "Dr. Death"; mem. 9 Grey Cup finals, 6 winners, 5 in succession; outstanding Cdn, def. player '82 Grey Cup final; top def. player '83 all-star game; 5 times all-WFC, all-Cdn; Schenley outstanding Cdn award '79, runnerup '80; Schenley best defensive player award '78; Norm Fieldgate Trophy '78-79; Dr. Beattie Martin Trophy '78-80; mem. Cdn Football, Alta Sports Halls, Eskimos Wall of Fame; res. Edmonton, Alta.

FENNELL, Pat (boxing); b. 7 Jun 1957, Toronto, Ont.; given name: Patrick William; UofT; Ont. 81kg, Golden Gloves titles '77, '79; ntl amateur 81kg '77, '79-80; NY State Golden Gloves '79; bronze '79 US Golden Gloves; gold '78, bronze '79 Tammer Turnaus international; gold '79 AAU championships; gold '79 Tour of France; bronze '79 Pan-Am Games; 2yrs jr. hockey; mem. volleyball team Ont. Winter Games '75; mem. '80 Olympic team; res. Toronto, Ont.

FERBEY, Randy (curling); b. 30 May 1959, Edmonton, Alta; m. Wendy Bain; c. Cody, Spencer, Taylor; customer service printing industry; skip '85-86 ntl mixed; all-star '86; competed 3 Briers, 2 winners; 3rd for Pat Ryan '88-89 Brier, '89 world title rinks; all-star '88, world all-star '89; 2 Alta Achievement awards; runnerup '87 Olympic trials; Dick Ellis Memorial trophy '89; mem. Cdn Curling Hall of Fame; res. Sherwood Park, Alta.

FERGUS, Bert (badminton); b. 1 Nov 1932, Trail, B.C.; given name: Robert Miles; m. Cordiet Veritege; BC Normal School teaching cert., UBC BEd, Special Ed., Western Wash. MEd; retd. school administrator; semifinalist in 1st ntl jr. champiionships '50; with Daryl Thompson ntl men's doubles title '55; mixed doubles gold, and with Dave McTaggart men's doubles silver '57 Mexican Open; with world champion Eddy Choong of Malaysia took US Open men's doubles silver '59; with Wayne Macdonnell ntl men's doubles title '63; 15 gold medals in singles, men's, mixed doubles in ntl masters championships; world masters '86 bronze men's singles, doubles, '94, '98 men's singles, doubles silver, '98 team silver, mixed doubles bronze; numerous BC jr, sr, masters titles; mem. Thomas Cup teams '58-64, team mgr. '67; Vancouver achievement award '66; Queen's Jubilee medal; life mem. Badminton BC, Vancouver Racquets Club; res. Richmond, B.C.

FERGUSON, Arnold (lacrosse); b. 28 Jul 1922, Anyox, B.C.; d. 27 Jan 1981, Victoria, B.C.; given name: Cecil Arnold; m. Floss Ray; c. Diana, Dale, Barbara; BC Liquor Control Board; active role lacrosse, soccer; mem. '43 New Westminster, '55 Victoria Mann Cup champions; Vancouver Adanacs; R.L.Maitland Sportsmanship award '50, Sid

Thomas Memorial Trophy '51; initial recipient Laurie Dillabough Trophy as mem. Shamrocks; refereed lacrosse several years; mem. Cdn Lacrosse Hall of Fame.

FERGUSON, Bruce (shooting); b. 10 Apr 1958, Charlottetown, P.E.I.; given name: Athol Bruce; UPEI, BSc; computer technician; began smallbore shooting as a cadet; moved into fullbore ranks '88; won DCRA Gooderham match '92; mem. variety of mini-Palma, provincial, Maritime teams; mem. '93 Cdn Bisley team; cadet shooting instructor from '83; res. Charlottetown, P.E.I.

FERGUSON, Dorothy (baseball); b. 17 Feb 1923, Virden, Man.; given name: Dorothy Blanche; m. Donald Key; c. Douglas, Dona; set 220/mile records as speed skater with Winnipeg club 6yrs; 2B St. Vital Tigerettes intermediate softball champs '41-42; helped St. Vital win sr. women's titles '43-44; blessed with strong arm, good legs, became outfielder Rockford Peaches in AAGPBL '45-54, helping that team win titles '45, '48-50; mem. Man. Baseball Hall of Fame; honored by Cooperstown, Cdn Baseball halls of fame; res. Rockford, Ill.

FERGUSON, John (hockey); b. 5 Sep 1938, Vancouver, B.C.; given name: John Bowie; m. Joan; c. Christina, Catherine, John Jr., Joanne; hockey exec.; stick boy Vancouver Canucks (WHL); jr. Melville Sask., sr. Ft. Wayne; pro Cleveland Barons (AHL); left wing Montreal Canadiens '63-71; team's "policeman;" NHL record: 500 scheduled games, 145g, 158a, 85 playoff games, 20g, 18a; mem. 5 Stanley Cup winners; asst. coach Team Canada '72, GM '81; GM WHA all-stars who beat Russians 3 straight games '79; coach, GM NY Rangers '75-79; GM Winnipeg Jets WHA Avco Cup winners '79; GM Jets (NHL) '79-87; GM Cdn world silver medallist '89; dir. player personnel Ottawa Senators '92-95; pro scout San Jose '97-99; twice *Sporting News, Hockey News* exec. of yr; pres. Windsor Raceway 3yrs; operated Montreal Québècois Pro Lacrosse League; mem. BC Sports Hall of Fame; res. Amherstberg, Ont.

FERGUSON, Ken (shooting); b. 24 May 1952, Springhill, N.S.; given name: Kenneth Earl; m. Elizabeth Yvonne D'Orsay; c. Alan, David, Edward; correctional services officer; rifle specialist; 4 NS district titles; 5 Maritime titles; 6 DND Queen's medals; Des Burke, Helmer aggregate awards; 5 ntl service rifle, regional, 8 CSC institutional titles; 5 NS service rifle titles; represented Cdn Forces at 11 international competitions in England, Scotland, US, Australia; res. Springhill, N.S.

FERGUSON, Larry (lacrosse); b. 4 Jan 1939, Peterborough, Ont.; given name: Larry Sidney Gordon; div. Denise Forbes; c. Warrren, Kent, Brad; m. Lynda Moore; owner Home Brew Wine store; graduate of Peterborough minor lacrosse, hockey ranks winning Ont. titles at peewee, bantam, midget levels; mem. Brampton Minto Cup winner '57; as jr. won sr. OLA scoring title '58; also scoring title '65; mem. 3 Mann Cup champions; 63 points scored in 34 Mann Cup games; noted for accurate underhand shot; in 18 seasons played 544 games scoring 750g, 718a; played/coached pro lacrosse with Philadelphia Wings, Boston Bolts; coached

Peterborough Lakers '87 after which he retd. from game; mem. Cdn Lacrosse, Peterborough Sports halls of fame; res. Peterborough, Ont.

FERGUSON, Lorne (hockey); b. 26 May 1930, Palmerston, Ont,; given name: Lorne Robert; m. Irene Johnson; c. Lorne Jr., Robert, Kimberlee, Lori, Timothy; retd. Labatt's sales rep.; sr. baseball, jr. B hockey Kingston; jr. A Guelph Biltmores; NY Rovers; Tulsa USHL; NHL Boston '49-55, Detroit '55-57, Chicago '57-59; NHL record: 422 scheduled games, 82g, 80a; led '53-54 Hershey Bears, AHL in goals with 45; on line with Red Sullivan, Dunc Fisher which set AHL points record for one line; minor hockey coach Kingston; mem. Kingston Dist. Sports Hall of Fame; res. Kingston, Ont.

FERGUSON, Merv (administration); b. 1 Jul 1909, London, Ont.; m. May; notary public; polio terminated promising versatile athletic career; directed efforts to administration; secty. BC Lacrosse Assn.; 8yrs mem., chairman Vancouver Athletic Commission; governor Pacific National Exhibition Sports Comm.; mem. BC branch AAU of C '48; 10yrs BC amateur boxing commission; 9yrs treas. amateur sports council; chairman BC Sports Hall of Fame; pres. AAU of C '63-65; secty-treas AAU of C ntl boxing comm.; 10yrs exec. mem. Pan-Am Games Assoc.; mem.-at-large British Commonwealth Games Assn.; 3yrs pres. Canadian Amateur Sports Federation; asst. mgr. '67, mgr. '71 Pan-Am Games teams; mem. Canada Games council; chairman technical advisory board Canada Summer Games '73; mem. COA; pres. BCLA '43-58, CLA '62-63; CLA liaison officer to International Amateur Lacrosse Federation '67-72; mem. BC Sports Advisory Council; BC Sportsman award '67-68, Air Canada amateur sports exec. of year; mem. Cdn Amateur, BC Sports, Cdn Lacrosse halls of fame; res. Galiano, B.C.

FERGUSON, Reid (curling); b. 16 May 1953, Toronto, Ont.; given name: William Reid; Wilfrid Laurier, BA; restaurateur; Toronto HS hockey all-star; Laurier golf team; East York Ont. junior baseball champions; lead with Paul Savage '77 Ont. champion rink, competing in Brier; Thunder Bay cashspiel winner '76; res. Vancouver, B.C.

FERGUSON, Rich (t&f); b. 3 Aug 1931, Calgary, Alta.; d. 24 May 1986, Rancho Mirage, Calif.; div. Kathleen Mavis McNamee; c. David, Jeanne, John; Iowa, BSc, BComm., UWO, MBA; businessman; 3rd to Roger Bannister, John Landy '54 BEG miracle mile Vancouver in 4:04.6; equalled that time '55 NCAA championships; Lionel Conacher trophy '54; former pres. Spalding Canada.

FERGUSON, Skit (baseball); b. 16 Oct 1925, Reserve Mines, N.S.; given name: Philip; m. Helen Charlton; c. Karla, Stephen, Elaine, Brenda; St.FX, BSc., Tech. U of NS, BSc (mech. eng.); retd. engineer, operations mgr. Imperial Oil; lefthanded pitcher, 1st baseman, outfielder; mem. '44 Maritime jr. champion Dominion Hawks (struck out 19 in title final); '45 Cape Breton sr. league champion Dominion Hawks; posted 18-1 w-l record, won Halifax & District League batting title with .468 as mem. '46 Truro Bearcats; mem. '45-46 St. FX intercollegiate title teams; mem. semipro Drummondville Cubs (Que. Prov. League) '47; mem. HDL Halifax Shipyards team '48-49; coached

minor baseball '55-60, Maritime midget titlists '57; returned to active play Dartmouth Arrows, Halifax Mets '62-66; mem. 2 Maritime sr. title teams; overall sr. pitching record 50-5; rejected pro offers; jr. hockey Cape Breton '43; 2 intercollegiate scoring titles, 1 Halifax Industrial HL scoring crown; twice skipped rink to NS consols playdowns; mem. '63 NS mixed title rink; skipped 2 Atlantic Oilmen's 'spiel winners; mem. St. FX, NS Sports halls of fame; res. Dartmouth, N.S.

FERGUSON, Tracey (t&f/wheelchair basketball): b. 7 Sep 1974, Richmond Hill, Ont.; Illinois; motivational speaker; standout wheelchair basketball, track athlete; basketball gold '92, '96 Paralympic Games; '94 world championship gold medal basketball team; Ada MacKenzie Memorial Foundation bursary twice; res. Champaign, Ill.

FERGUSON, Vince (baseball/hockey); b. 11 Feb 1906, Halifax, N.S.; d. 29 Aug 1984, Halifax, N.S.; given name: Vincent de Paul; m. Gertrude Butler; c. Carol, Sheila, Paul; electrical inspector; excelled in baseball, hockey, rugby, soccer, t&f; participated in baseball as player, coach 1919-45; sometime pitcher but mostly infielder, outfielder; jr. baseball Halifax Socials '24-26; mem. NS, Maritime champion St. Agnes team '30; noted as clutch hitter and person capable of coming up with big play under pressure; 1931-39 with Willow Park, Casinos, Halifax Capitals, Cardinals, frequently leading teams to provincial finals with his bat and baserunning speed; batted left, won 5 batting titles, one with .449 average; playing coach Halifax Shipyards team during WW2; played senior hockey '27-35 with Crescents, Wolverines; mem. 2 NS title teams, '35 Allan Cup champion Wolverines; noted as playmaker, he won two league scoring titles; rejected pro offers from Montreal Maroons; honored by NS Amateur Baseball Assn., City of Halifax; mem. NS Sports Hall of Fame.

FERGUSSON, Layton (baseball); b. 5 Sep 1908, Port Morien, N.S.; given name: Neil Layton; retd. lawyer; early association with baseball Port Morien jr., int. sr. leagues; pitched for Reserve Miner Boys in Cape Breton Colliery League, 1st Cape Breton team to reach NS finals; mem. Sydney sr. amateur team 1yr; pro Glace Bay Miners, '36 Cape Breton Collier League finalists; pres. Cape Breton jr. league; secty-treas. Colliery sr. league several years; mem. NS Sports Hall of Fame; res. Glace Bay, N.S.

FERNANDEZ, Tony (baseball); b. 30 Jun 1962, San Pedro de Macoris, DR; given name: Octavio Antonio; m. Clara; c. Joel Octavio, Jonathan David, Abraham Antonio; essentially a shortstop but can play second or third base; broke into pro ranks with Kinston (Carolina) '80; Syracuse (AAA) '81-83, '84; Toronto (AL) '83-'90, '93, '98-99, San Diego (NL) '91-'92, NY (NL) '93, Cincinnati (NL) '94, NY (AL) '95, Cleveland (AL) '97; in World Series with Toronto '93, Cleveland '97; 4 all-star games; 4 Gold Glove awards; reached 2000 hit plateau '98; MBL record (through '99): 2082 scheduled games, 7788ab, 1046r, 2240h, 410db, 92tr, 92hr, 829rbi, 245sb, .288ba; DR Little League bears his name; res. Boca Raton, Fla.

FERRARO, John (football/basketball); b. 18 Dec 1910, Buffalo, N.Y.; d. 28 Sep 1981, Bridgewater, N.J.; given name: John James; m. Edna Winifred Letts; c. John Jr.,

Robert Letts, Linda Joan; Cornell, BSc; oil co. sales supervisor; all-NY state basketball team '28-29; mem. undefeated Cook Academy '29-30 Eastern States basketball title team; mem. US all-star basketball team which introduced sport to Venezuela '30; capt. '33 Cornell football team; all-American '31-33; capt. Cornell basketball '33-34, Ivy League scoring title, Eastern Intercollegiate all-star; playing-coach Hamilton Tigers '34-35; Orm Beach trophy '34; Grey Cup finalist '35; Montreal '36-40; 7 times all-Cdn; quarterback Hamilton best-of-century (1867-1949) amateur era team; Lew Hayman's best-of-'30s dream team; Cornell 30-year ('12-42) all-intercollegiate team; Eastern Intercollegiate 50-year ('01-51) all-star team; mgr.-player, scoring leader Dominion Douglas '36-37 Eastern Canadian basketball title team; coach Queen's basketball '37-38; player, leading scorer McGill Grads '39-40 ntl title basketball team; mgr.-player-coach ntl finalist Oilers basketball team '41-42; mem. Cornell Athletic, Cdn Football halls of fame.

FERRONE, Dan (football); b. 3 Apr 1958, Oakville, Ont.; m. Barbara; c. Matthew, Marco, Danielle; SFU; operates Ferrone Ventures Inc., football exec.; NAIA Div. 1 all-star guard; pro Toronto '81-88, '90-92, Calgary '89; 5 all-EFC, 1 all-WFC, 3 all-Cdn selections; twice runnerup Schenley outstanding offensive lineman award; Leo Dandurand outstanding EFC offensive lineman award twice; 5 Grey Cup finals, 2 winners; nicknamed "mayor of Oakville"; pres. CFLPA from '94; res. Oakville, Ont.

FIELDGATE, Norm (football); b. 12 Jan 1932, Regina, Sask.; given name: William Norman; m. Doreen Caughlin; c. Carey, Lesley, Janine; automotive parts distributor; from Sask. junior ranks, joined original BC Lions team '53; last of originals to retire '66; co-capt. Lions several seasons; offensive, defensive end, corner linebacker; 37 career interceptions; 3 time WFC all-star, once all-Cdn; 3 times Lions' MVP; most popular Lion '65; one of two Lions (with By Bailey) honored by fans with 'day' '62; mem. BC Sports, Cdn Football halls of fame; res. North Vancouver, B.C.

FILANE, Domenic (boxing); b. 17 Mar 1969, Schreiber, Ont.; given name: Domenic Figliomeni; sport wear designer; began competing '83; Schreiber '88 Olympic torch athlete of yr; 3 Detroit Golden Gloves titles; ntl 48kg champion '90-96; bronze '90, '94 Commonwealth Games; competed '92, '96 Olympic, '95 Pan-Am Games; bronze '94 Copenhagen Cup; gold '96 Stockholm Box Open; bronze '96 Multi-Nation Liverpool tournament; res. Oakville, Ont.

FILCHOCK, Frank (football); b. 10 Aug 1916, Crucible, Pa.; Indiana; retd.; all-around HS athlete capable of sprinting 100yds in 10 sec. flat; pro Pittsburgh (NFL), Washington, NY Giants; suspended over gambling charge; subsequently cleared but chose Cdn football with Hamilton, Montreal; coached, quarterbacked Hamilton Tigers to '48 final vs. Ottawa but lost when he broke wrist early in game; led Alouettes to Grey Cup '49; outstanding player of year award; Imperial Trophy ORFU MVP; head coach Edmonton '52 guiding them to WIFU title but Grey Cup loss; coach Saskatchewan '53-57, reached playoffs 4 consec. years; Lionel Conacher trophy '49; res. Portland, Ore.

FILION, Henri (harness racing); b. 22 May 1941, Angers, Que.; d. 9 Apr 1997, Aylmer, Que.; m. Ginette Martel; c. Henri Jr., Andr,e, Alain, Chantal; one of 8 racing Filion brothers; drove Blue Bonnets track at 19; US circuit mid-'60s; while campaigning at Foxboro '72 swamp fever claimed 11 of his horses; joined brother Hervé, in NY; 7 consecutive $1 million seasons; 3318 victories, $21 million in purses; classic victories include Sheppard Pace, Westchester Trot, Reynolds Memorial, Goshen Cup; died in track accident in Aylmer, Que.

FILION, Hervé, (harness racing); b. 1 Feb 1940, Angers, Que.; m. Barbara Ann; c. 4; harness race driver; standardbred racing's most prolific race winner with 14,783 career wins; 1st driver in world with more than 400 (407) wins single season '68; boosted own record to 605 '72 then 637 '74, 798 '88, 814 '89 (broken '92 by Walter Case Jr.); 15 USTA driving titles; 7 times season leading money winner; through '95 14,783 victories with purses exceeding $85M; won 101 major stakes races including 2 Little Brown Jugs, 2 Cane Pace, 2 Breeders Crowns; world champion '70; international drivers' stakes winner Australia '71; 8 winners one day Hinsdale N H '78; 5 winners clocked at 1:59.4 or less one day Brandywine '70; twice French Canadian athlete of year (Julien Trophy); '71 Lou Marsh Trophy; Hickok pro athlete of month Nov '71; Proximity Award '73; 10 Harness Tracks of America driver of year awards; charged with race fixing '95; Officer Order of Canada '71; mem. Canada's, Ottawa Sports, Cdn Horse Racing, Living Horsemen's halls of fame; res. Oldbridge, N.J.

FILION, Yves (harness racing); b. 23 Dec 1946, Angers, Que.; given name: Yves Lëo; harness race driver; campaigned on small Cdn tracks to '66 when he launched into faster company at Montreal, NY tracks; worked for a time with brother Hervé before branching out on his own; from '75 has based activities at Blue Bonnets; through '95 3554 victories, $18M in purses; drove Runnymede Lobell to '88 Cane Pace, Prix d'Ete, NA Cup, Confederation Cup victories; leading Blue Bonnets driver '76, '85, '88; res. Lachute, Que.

FILTEAU, Nancy (judo); b. 3 Apr 1962, Swift Current, Sask.; given name: Nancy Jewitt; m. Ron Filteau; c. Tyler, Justin; meat inspector; began judo career '73 earning '83 Pan-Am Games silver, '86 Commonwealth Games gold; retd '87 to raise family; returned to competition '94; bronze '95 Pan-Am Games; silver '94 CNE, US Open; competed '96 Olympics; res. Moose Jaw, Sask.

FINDLAY, Dave (canoeing); b. 13 Nov 1927, Almonte, Ont.; m. Betty Asselline; c. David, Janet, Steven, Laura, Allison; UofT, BSc; retd. engineer; coach Ottawa Valley clubs '56-80; commodore ntl assn. '63; mgr, ntl team '74-78, Olympic team '76; Carleton Place Citizen of '80; res. Carleton Place, Ont.

FINDLAY, Dick (boxing); b. 23 Mar 1945, Vancouver, B.C.; div; c. Ricky; Molson's Brewery employee; moved through weight-class ranks from 85lb-139lb '57-66 claiming 2 Emerald, 6 Golden Gloves titles; ntl amateur 139lb title '66-68; mem. ntl team '66 BEG, '67 US Nationals, Pan-Am

Games, '68 Olympics; 2 BC Golden Boy, 1 Diamond Boy awards; BC outstanding boxer '68; refereed 5yrs; res. Vancouver, B.C.

FINDLEY, John (harness racing); b. 2 Sep 1924, Braeside, Ont.; m. Mary Jane Chateauvert; Ont. Veterinary College; retd veterinarian, horse breeder, driver, trainer; 8 consec. Ont. Golden Horseshoe Circuit driving titles; leading NA driver '69, runnerup '70; leading NA percentage driver 200-300 drives category '75; 13 individual driving titles; more than 1500 career victories, $2 million in purses won; among outstanding horses he has bred, trained and/or raced are Dalyce Blue (only Cdn sired filly to win open stake race in US, 1st Canadian-bred 3-yr-old trotter to better 2:05 mile), Peaches Atom (champion Canadian-bred trotting mare '63-65), Autumn Frost, Crimson Duchess (2-year-old Canadian trotter of year), The Black Douglas, Canny Choice, Moon Magic (1:58 fastest mile by Findley-bred pacer); mem. Cdn Horseracing Hall of Fame; res. Arnprior, Ont.

FINE, Jack (bowling); b. 28 Jul 1925, Toronto, Ont.; m. Valerie Simmonds (d); c. Janet, Harry, Joanne, Walter; UofT, BA; bowling exec.; founder Bowling Proprietors' Assn. of Ont. '54, serving as pres, treas, dir. 25yrs; co-founder BPA of Canada, serving in varied exec. roles, including pres.; dir. BPA of America; mem., promotion chair Multi-unit Bowling Information Group; founder Builders of Bowling Industry annual awards dinner '73; founder, pres. Bowlerama Ltd., Canada's largest bowling chain with 17 Southern Ont. centres; pres. Bowling Sales of Canada; mem. Ont. interprovincial squash team; veterans class club squash champion '66; recipient Ont. govt. recognition certificate, Ont. corporate sports citation; mem. Ont. 5-pin bowling Hall of Fame, builders' div., Greater Toronto 10-pin Hall of Fame; res. Toronto, Ont.

FINK, Hardy (builder); b. 8 May 1947, Hof, Germany; given name: Hartmut Walter; m. Cynthia Fay Bonesky; c. Heidi Marion, Jennifer May; Hamilton Teacher's Coll., McMaster BPhE, BA, UAlta. MSc, UBC, MPhE; gymnastics consultant; began competing age 16; mem. Ont. jr. team '66-67, sr. '69-71; Alta. sr title '74; capt. McMaster team '69-73; head coach Hamilton Germania Gym Club '68-74; part-time coach Bounder gym club Edmonton '73-75; gym instructor McMaster '72-73, UBC '83-98; ntl men's FISU Games team '70; Ont. coaching chair. '72; mem. ntl coaching certification pgm '75-84; part-time coach Port Alberni Parks '76; established, owned, operated Port Alberni Gymnastics Academy '76-83, accumulating 143 BC, 4 ntl, 38 Western Cdn titles; conducted coaching clinics throughout NA, coached Cdn girls team on European tours '82-83; established UBC gym club '84; held various exec. roles locally, provincially, nationally; 6 times ntl team CdM; at 21 youngest international judge; judged at Olympic, Worlds, Pan-Ams, Commonwealth Games '74-87; conducted numerous judging courses; chaired variety of ntl, prov. judging comms.; ntl high performance coach '88-98; authored numerous gymnastics publications, CBC-TV gymnastics analyst; CGF builder of '78; IOC recognition award '80; BCGA coach of '80; CIAU coach of '85; res. Vancouver, B.C.

FINLAY, Robert (t&f); b. 3 Aug 1943, London, Eng.; m. Eleanor Young; c. Katherine Anne, Jennifer Margaret;

Waterloo; tech/account rep computer services; OFSAA x-country title team '61, OQAA 1, 3 mile titles '66, OQAA 3mile '67, OQAA x-c titles '66-67; competed in Pan Am Games '67, Commonwealth Games '70, Olympics '68, '72, Pan-Pacific '69; Inter. x-c champ '69; Victoria Australia 10mile road champ '71; mem. Toronto Olympic Club; Waterloo athlete of year '66-67; ntl indoor records 2mi, 3mi, 5000m, outdoor 2000m, 3000m, 5000m, 2mi; res. Scarborough, Ont.

FINN, Ron (officiating/hockey); b. 1 Dec 1940, Toronto, Ont.; m. Sheilagh Roach (d); c. Sean, Shannon, Tara, Theresa; NHL linesman '69-96; worked 2 NHL all-star games, Rendez-Vous '87, Canada, Challenge Cup series; officiated 1st Montreal vs. Chicago exhibition in London, Eng,; set NHL record working 252nd career playoff game '91; worked 1980 scheduled games, 291 playoff games; worked final NHL game at 55; instructor various Ont. hockey officiating schools; with David Boyd authored "*On the Lines*"; res. Brampton, Ont.

FINNAMORE, Arthur (baseball); b. 13 Dec 1882, Fredericton, N.B.; d. 23 Feb 1978, Saint John, N.B.; m. Althea Sallaws MacLean; UNB; dept. of agriculture; nicknamed "Flying Frederictonian" for performances in 100, 220yd track events; at 14 received $5 per game to play baseball for Doaktown, Boisetown teams thereby becoming pro; officially joined pro ranks at 23 catching for Glace Bay in Cape Breton League; later played in Western Canada; captained, coached Glace Bay to league title '13; became highly respected umpire; university rugby star; as mountain climber scaled Bald Mountain, Mount Carleton; mem. NB Sports Hall of Fame.

FIRBY, Howard (coaching); b. 18 Sep 1924, Montgomery, Ala.; d. 30 Mar 1991, Vancouver, B.C.; given name: Howard Baldwin; div.; c. Louise, Grant, Joanne; Vancouver school of art; freelance commercial artist, pro swimming coach; HS track champion; afflicted by polio '45; coach Vancouver SC '47-56; founding coach Canadian Dolphins SC '56-67; coach Winnipeg Cardinal SC '67-69; tech. dir. '70-72; coach Coho SC Victoria '73-80; asst. coach '55 Pan-Am Games; starter '54 BEG; ntl team coach '58 BEG, '64 Olympic Games; coach-mgr. ntl team South Africa tour '67, Russia tour '69; coached swimmers, including Helen Hunt, to 11 world records, Games' gold in all strokes, more than 100 individual ntl sr. titles, more than 300 ntl sr. records; 6 ntl team titlists; Centennial medal '67; mem. BC, Canada's Sports, Cdn Aquatic, International Swimming halls of fame.

FIREMAN, Jack (builder); b. 9 Feb 1939, Toronto, Ont.; div.; c. Belinda, James; UofT, BA, Osgoode Hall LB, NYU, LLM; lawyer, QC; a litigation lawyer with a great passion for fastpitch softball, he financed and founded Toronto Gators team '93; in initial season won ntl men's sr. title, became 1st Cdn team to win ICS World championship '94, repeat '95; gold medal Pan-Am Games qualifier; res. Toronto, Ont.

FIRLOTTE, Stewart (harness racing); b. 1 Jul 1940, Noranda, Que.; m. Joanne; c. 2; following above average junior hockey career pursued pro aspirations with Quebec Aces in AHL; after falling short in NHL bid moved to Moncton NB to play sr. hockey and work for industrial finance firm; promotion led to Toronto but sport desires still prevailed; having invested in a horse while playing hockey he reasoned he could enjoy life better in the equine environs than a business office; went to work with Ben White stables in Florida as groom 1970; returned to Canada '76 to open public stable and invest in horses including triple crown winner Ralph Hanover; gained national attention campaigning Town Pro '89 winning Breeders Crown at Pompano, Fla.; strong showings with Digger Almahurst, Historic and Headline Hanover secured his place among NA's top trainers; res. Orlando, Fla.

FIRTH, Sharon (skiing); b. 31 Dec 1953, Aklavik, N.W.T.; given name: Sharon Anne; civil servant; with twin sister Shirley one of Canada's premier cross-country skiers; ntl jr. champion '68-9; mem. ntl team from '70; mem. '72, '80, '84 Olympic teams; 4 ntl 3x5km relay, 2 5km, 1 each 10km, 17km, 20km titles; 2 NA 10km, 1 each 3x5km relay, 5km titles; gold 3x5km relay '80, 5k '81 Gitchi Gami Games, 20km '81 Dannon series; 29th '81-82, 35th '82-83 World Cup circuit; John Semmelink Memorial award '72; mem. Order of Canada, Cdn Skiing Hall of Fame; res. Yellowknife, N.W.T.

FIRTH, Shirley (skiing); b. 31 Dec 1953, Aklavik, N.W.T.; given name: Shirley Anne; m. Jan Larson; PR officer; with sister Sharon among Canada's premier cross-country skiers; '69 junior 5km title; mem. ntl team from '70; mem. '72, '76, '80, '84 Olympic teams; 5 consecutive ntl 10km, 4 5km, 3 20km, 2 3x5km relay titles; 2 NA 3x5km relay, 1 5km titles; 10km gold '76 Canada Cup, '76, '80, '81, 3x5km relay '80 Gitchi Gami Games; 5km, 10km, 20km gold '80 Dannon series; best WC finish ever by Canadian placing 4th 10km Czechoslovakia '81; 11th '81-82, 25th '82-83 World Cup circuit; John Semmelink Memorial award '72; mem. Order of Canada, Cdn Skiing Hall of Fame; res. St-Etienne de Crossey, France.

FISHER, Darlene (baton twirling); b. 8 May 1959, Nanaimo, B.C.; given name: Darlene Corbett; m. Jim Fisher; registered nurse; competitive twirler '66-80; 7 prov. grand championships, 6 international regional titles, 5 placements top 3 US Grand National Open; coach Batons West Twirling Team, 4 prov. titles; chair. BC Baton Twirling Assn.; res. Nanaimo, B.C.

FISHER, Frank (football/hockey); b. 1 Jan 1901, Barlieboro, Ont.; d. 23 Apr 1983, Toronto, Ont.; given name: Franklin; m. Dorothy Smith; c. Franklin Stewart, Ellenora; RMC, Osgoode Hall, BA, LLB; lawyer Q.C.; mem. '20-21 Varsity Blues intercollegiate football champions, '20 Grey Cup winner; mem. Varsity Grads Allan Cup hockey titlists '27, Olympic gold medalists '28; life mem. Royal Canadian Yacht Club, Toronto University Club; mem. Toronto Golf Club.

FISHER, Hugh (canoeing); b. 1 Oct 1955, New Zealand; SFU, MD; physician; kayak specialist; mem. '76, '80, '84 Olympic, '77, '79, '82, '83 world championships teams, silver K2 1000m '82, bronze K2 500m '83 worlds; 7 ntl K2, 4 K4, 1 C4 titles; 3 Zaandam K2, 2 K4 titles; Vichy K1, Bydgoszcz Poland K1, K2, Tata K2 titles; silver K2 1000m Moscow, Brandenburg '83; with Alwyn Morris gold 1000m, bronze 500m K2 '84 Olympics; coach BC team '81 Canada

Games; world outrigger champion '79-80; fed. govt. excellence awards '83-84; mem. Order of Canada, Cdn Olympic, BC Sports halls of fame; res. Penticton, B.C.

FISHER, Joan (t&f); b. 26 Sep 1949, Ottawa, Ont.; given name: Barbara Joan; m. T.G.F. Fenton; Carleton, UofOtt, BSc (hons); compensation analyst Treasury Board; '65 ntl midget records 60yds (7.0), 100yds (10.9), 220yds (25.0); '67 juve. records 100yds (10.8), 220yds (24.6); mem. '67 Pan-Am 4x100m relay team; ntl jr. 220yd record (23.9) '68; ntl 200m, 400m titles '68 Olympic trials; 400m semifinalist '68 Olympics; last known res. Ottawa, Ont.

FITCH, Ed (shooting); b. 28 Mar 1949, Montreal, Que.; given name: Edward; m. Sharon Paul; c. Rena, Leora; RMC, BSc; CF Command and Staff Coll.; Dir. Military Engineering/Cdn Military Engineer Branch Advisor; marksmanship training began with archery and evolved into smallbore rifles with Queen's Own Rifles and HS cadets; mem. RMC rifle/pistol teams; competed frequently in BCRA, PQRA, DCRA matches; CFSAC pistol tyro title '81; mem. 2 Cdn Forces Bisley teams; major interest ISU pistol but plays active role in Long Range Black Powder competition from '78; liaison officer BCRA '78-81, v-p PQRA '83-84; mem. DCRA council '83-84; dir. DCRA Black Powder pgm, '88-93; DCRA council/exec. comm from '88; mem. 2 Cdn Maccabiah Games ISU pistol teams, 1 silver, 5 bronze; instrumental in involving CF in CISM-Pistol; mem. Cdn team 1st World Military Olympics (CISM) '95; res. Ottawa, Ont.

FITZGERALD, Billy (lacrosse); b. 1888, St. Catharines, Ont.; d. 1926, at 19 mem. Sr. Athletic Lacrosse Club St. Catharines, Globe Shield '05-12; mem. undefeated '07-08 teams; mem. Conn Jones team Vancouver, Minto Cup; Toronto Lacrosse Club; following WW1 played briefly in Vancouver; helped organize St. Catharines team Ont. semipro league; coached Hobart College of Geneva, N.Y., Swathmore College, West Point; refereed OALA sr. division; mem. Canada's Sports, Lacrosse halls of fame.

FITZGERALD, Marie (speed skating); b. 12 Apr 1946, St. Paul, Alta.; given name: Marie Louise Phyllis; ntl outdoor mass start champion '64; ntl outdoor mass start records 220, 880yds, 3/4 miles, 1 mile; ntl indoor mass start champion '63-70; ntl indoor mass start records 440, 880yds, 3/4, 1 mile; ntl open indoor title '65; mem. Alta. outdoor team inaugural Canada Winter Games; ranked among best indoor skaters ever developed in Canada; mem. Cdn Speed Skating Hall of Fame; res. Rocky Mountain House, Alta.

FITZGERALD, Mel (t&f); b. 20 Jul 1953, Trepassey, Nfld.; m. Jane; printer; wheelchair athletics; ntl 1500m, 800m titles '78-79, 10,000m title '83; Pan-Am gold 1500m '78, 800m '78, '82, 5000, '82, silver 100m '78, 1500m, 400m '82; Olympic gold 800m, silver 1500m '80; Rome invitational gold 1500m '81; 800m world record '82; Norton Crowe award '80; mem. Order of Canada; res. St. John's, Nfld.

FITZPATRICK, Allan (soccer/badminton); b. 29 Jun 1909, Montreal, Que.; d. 12 Oct 1990, Pierrefonds, Que.; given name: Daniel Allan; m. Edna Heazel (d); Sir George William; asst. purchasing agent; mem. ntl title soccer teams

'34-35; frequent all-star; 2yrs Stelco team coach; 2yrs dir. Que. FA; helped launch Murray Badminton League; held varied exec. roles over 35-year period; coached, played major role in promoting badminton nationally; known throughout Que. as "Mr. Badminton"; active in game's administration provincially, nationally; CBA pres.'71-72; ntl team mgr. '66, '70, asst. GM '74, '78, GM '82 Commonwealth Games; CBA rep. Canadian Commonwealth Games Assn. '66-70, treas. '70-86, hon. v-p from '87; past sports dir. MAAA; CCGA rep. on Sports Fed. of Canada; mem. Canadian Amateur Sports Hall of Fame selection comm. '71-80; Queen's Jubilee medal '77; H.I. Evans Memorial award for contributions to Canadian badminton; QBA awards '64, '78; New England BA award '71.

FLACK, Herb (speed skating); b. 29 Jun 1913, Penetang, Ont.; given name: Herbert Samuel; m. Norma Heagle; c. Victor, Elinor; DeLaSalle College; retd; Toronto, Ontario, NA indoor, outdoor, ntl outdoor champion '29; Diamond Trophy international outdoor title '29; ntl int. outdoor titles '30-31; NA sr. indoor champion '35; mem. '32 Olympic team; res. Stroud, Ont.

FLAMAN, Fern (hockey); b. 25 Jan 1927, Dysart, Sask.; given name: Ferdinand Charles; hockey scout; defenceman; mem. Boston Olympics (EL); Bruins (NHL) '44-51, '54-61, Maple Leafs '51-54, Providence (AHL) '61-64; player/coach/GM Rhode Island Reds '63-64; smooth-skating, hard-hitting player who broke into pro ranks as teenager during WW2; won league titles in AHL, WHL, CHL as coach; coached Northeastern Huskies '70-89 winning several championships including 4 Beanpot trophies, Hockey East title '89; US college coach of '82; more than 250 career collegiate victories; NHL record: 17 seasons, 910 scheduled games, 34g, 174a, 63 playoff games, 4g, 8a; scout NJ '90-99; mem. 1 Stanley Cup winner; 3 2nd team all-star; mem. Rhode Island, Sask. Sports, Hockey halls of fame; res. Westwood, Mass.

FLANAGAN, Flin (football); b. 27 Sep 1897, Thorne, Que.; d. 12 Mar 1994, Ste-Anne-de-Bellevue, Que.; given name: James Cyril; McGill, DDS; dentist; surviving serious WWI battlefield wounds he starred for McGill football/hockey teams '19-23; mem. Yates Cup champion '19 team; capt. hockey team '22-23; noted for stick-handling, prolific scoring skills; declined Montreal Canadiens pro overtures; coached McGill '28 title team; mem. McGill Sports Hall of Fame.

FLANAGAN, Pat (wrestling); b. 31 Aug 1918, Toronto, Ont.; d. 10 Jun 1985, Toronto, Ont.; given name: Winnett Wallingford Watson; m. Evelyn; c. Warren, Dennis; prominent in jr. football with jr. Argos, Balmy Beach, wrestling in high school; launched pro career in England adopting name of Flanagan to avoid confusion with Whipper Billy Watson; active competitor until he reached mid-50s then turned to refereeing in 1970s; active in community activities; highly respected by peers, fans.

FLEMING, Vic (harness racing); b. 1887, Dundas, Ont.; d. 1955, Lexington, Ky.; m., c. Bill, Charlie, Jim; horseman; 35 year racing career; recorded 1st 2-minute mile '20 with Louie Grattan; 3 $25,000 events single week '28 with Grattan Bars, 2 in identical 1:59.5 mile clockings; drove Billy Direct to fastest mile (to that time) in 1:55 '38; same day steered The Widower to 1:59.5 mile; during career drove 8 pacers, 4 trotters to sub 2-minute miles; injured in Delaware, Ohio, spill, retired to work as racing official Saratoga, N.Y.; mem. Hall of Fame of the Trotter, Canadian Horse Racing Hall of Fame.

FLEMING, Willie (football); b. 2 Feb 1939, Detroit, Mich.; m. Arlene McDaniels; c. Eric, Anthony; Iowa; sales manager; all-city HS halfback '56; AP all-Big 10 '57, tied single season 11 TD record; starred '59 Rose Bowl; pro BC '59-66; nicknamed "Willie-the-Wisp"; twice surpassed 1000yd rushing mark single season; twice teamed with Joe Kapp for 106yd TD pass; shares CFL single play record 109yds; CFL record: 86td, 1 convert, 517 points, rushing 6125yds, 868 carries, 7.1 avg, 37td, 231 receptions, 4480yds; single season yardage record 2027 - 1234 rushing, 639 on pass receptions, 154 on kickoff returns '63; scored decisive TD '64 BC Grey Cup victory over Hamilton; 3 times most popular Lion, WFC all-star; once all-Cdn; mem. BC Sports, Cdn Football halls of fame; res. Detroit, Mich.

FLEMONS, Wade (swimming); b. 26 Aug 1960, Regina, Sask.; m. Michelle Bogaard; Stanford, BSc, IE, UWO, MBA; corporate finance; backstroke specialist; Canada Cup 100m gold; 4 Nation Cup 100m, 200m, 4x100 medley relay gold; Japanese nationals 100m, 200m gold; mem. '78, '82 Commonwealth, '79, '83 Pan-Am, '80 Olympic, '83 FISU, '78, '82 world teams; bronze 100m '82 Commonwealth Games; NCAA 200m breaststroke gold, 100m silver '81; BC achievement award; res. Vancouver, B.C.

FLETCHER, Bill (curling); b. 16 May 1954, Kingston, Ont.; given name: William Stanley; m. Pamela; c. Kate, Jess, Maddy; biology researcher; mem. Ont. entry '71-72 ntl schoolboy; all-star lead Earle Morris Ont. rink '85 Brier; 2nd '95 Ont. Intermediate title rink; res. Ottawa, Ont.

FLETCHER, Cliff (hockey/administration); b. 16 Aug 1935, Montreal, Que.; div; c. Chuck, Christie; hockey exec; began hockey career with Junior Canadiens serving 10yrs as scout; Eastern Cdn scout St. Louis (NHL) '67; AGM St. Louis '69-72, 3 Stanley Cup finals, 2 West div titles; joined Flames in Atlanta as GM '72; organized franchise shift to Calgary '80; in 11 seasons under his guidance Flames won 1 Stanley Cup, 2 President's trophies, 2 Campbell Conference, 3 Smythe div. titles; pres/CEO/GM Maple Leafs '91-97; advisor to GM Tampa Bay '98; res. Toronto, Ont.

FLETCHER, Douglas (all-around); b. 18 Nov 1892, Leicester, Eng.; d. 6 Aug 1976, Victoria, B.C.; m. Ethel Maud; c. Dorothy, Joan; hotel, meat market proprietor; 9yrs Albion Cricket Club scoring numerous centuries; active to age 50; pres. Greater Victoria League '42-68; organized minor lacrosse '44; coached and/or managed 35 provincial champions; pres. BCLA '48; v-p CLA '57; active player to age 40; refereed several years; with late Ivan Temple organized Victoria MHA '43; pres. Vancouver Island Sr. HL; 12 consecutive pitching victories Sons of England '34 softball league champions; 2 holes-in-one during golf career which began '29; 5yrs Uplands GC pres.; BCAHA Diamond Stick award '64, Sid Thomas Memorial Trophy '52, Memorial Arena plaque '60, Centennial Medal '67, Victoria Sportsman of '68, Sport Magazine plaque '68; life mem. Greater Victoria LA; mem. Cdn Lacrosse, BC Sports halls of fame.

FLETCHER, Pat (golf); b. 18 Jun 1916, Clacton-on-Sea, Eng.; d. 21 Jul 1985, Victoria, B.C.; m. Dorothy Fraser; c. Patricia Ann, Allan Hugh, Edward Michael; golf pro; 3 Sask. Open titles; CPGA title '52; low Canadian '53 Canadian Open; 1st Canadian since '14 to win Canadian Open '54; former golf pro Saskatoon G&CC, Royal Montreal; Que. Spring Open title '56-57; mem. 4 Hopkins Trophy match teams; CPGA pres. '62-65; mem. RCGA, Sask., Canada's Sports halls of fame.

FLEURY, Lionel (hockey); b. 25 Dec 1912, Quebec City, Que.; m. Raymonde Doyon; c. Louise, Jacques, Denyse, Alice, Marc, Charles; retd. personnel advisor; active golfer, hockey player; referee, coach, mgr. jr. A hockey, baseball; regional, provincial, ntl hockey pres.; IIHF executive mem.; life mem. QAHA, CAHA; involved in conception of Canada Games; founder Que. region minor hockey organization; coach, mgr., secty, pres. Jr. A hockey league simultaneously; US AAHA citation, Centennial Medal, Laval U Sportsmanship award; res. Ste. Foy, Que.

FLEURY, Theoren (hockey); b. 29 Jun 1968, Oxbow, Sask.; m. Veronica; c. Josh, Theoren, Veronica, Beaux; centre/rw; mem. '87-88 world jr title teams; Turner Cup (IHL) winner '88; at 5-5 smallest player in NHL in '90s; jr. Moose Jaw (WHL) '84-88; 201 jr. goals; 9th draft choice Calgary '87 entry draft; pro Salt Lake (IHL) '88-89, Calgary (NHL) '89-99, Colorado '99, NY Rangers '99; 51 goals in 79 games '90-91; *Hockey News* jr player of '88; mem. Team Canada '90-91 worlds, silver '91, Canada Cup '91, world cup '96; mem. '98 Olympic team; shared Alka Seltzer plus award with Marty McSorley '91; 1st team NHL all-star '95; played in 5 NHL all-star games; NHL record: (through '99) 806 scheduled games, 374g, 480a, 77 playoff games, 34g, 45a; became all-time Flames scoring leader '99; Juvenile Diabetes NA man of yr '92; res. Calgary, Alta.

FLEWWELLING, Larry (diving); b. 8 Sep 1965, Kentville, N.S.; UAlta; coached by father Herb won 3 ntl 1-metre, 1 3-metre titles; mem. '88 Olympic, '87 Pan-Am, '90 Commonwealth Games teams; 3-metre silver '90 Commonwealth Games; competed FINA World Cup '89, world aquatic championships '91; res. Edmonton, Alta.

FLOOD, Lisa (swimming); b. 1 Aug 1971, Scarborough, Ont.; Villanova, BA (psychology); membership services Ont. Coll of Teachers; breaststroke specialist; began swimming age 1 in YMCA infant swim program; 2 gold, 1 silver '95 Pan-Am, 2 bronze '91 Pan-Am, 2 bronze '94 Commonwealth Games; competed '92, '96 Olympic, '93, '95 Pan-Pacific championships; ntl 4x100 medley relay record '95; '91 Villanova female athlete of yr; '91-92 all-American, Big East outstanding female athlete; Eastern women's swimming athlete as outstanding swimmer '91 Princeton meet; NCAA top 8 award '94; res. Pickering, Ont.

FLOREAL, Edrick (t&f); b. 5 Oct 1966, Gonaives, Haiti; m. LaVonna Martin; c. Edrick Jr., Mikaielle Gisele; Georgia; coach; emigrated to Canada age 8; 1st athlete to win 3 consec. NCAA, 10 consec. ntl triple jump titles; 1st Canadian to exceed 17m in triple jump both indoor/outdoor; 20 ntl, 5 NCAA triple, long jump titles; 7 times all-American; ntl TJ/LJ records jr. and sr.; mem. '88, '92 Olympic, '86, '90, '94 Commonwealth Games, 3 world championship teams; bronze TJ '90 Commonwealth Games; 8.20m ntl LJ, 17.29 TJ records; coach HS, Nebraska, Georgia Tech, Kentucky; to '98 coached 20 NCAA all-Americans, 6 runners up, 6 Olympians, 4 Olympic medalists, 1 Paralympic gold medalist; res. Atlanta, Ga.

FLUTIE, Darren (football); b. 18 Nov 1966, Manchester, Md.; m. Terri; c. Taylor Amanda, Troy; Boston College; wide receiver; B Coll. single season record 111 catches for 1731yds, 8tds '84; career leader B Coll. 134 recept. for 2000yds, 14tds; pro NFL San Diego '88-89, Phoenix '90, CFL BC '91-95, Edmonton '96-97, Hamilton '98; CFL record (through '98): 125gp, 665recept, 9949yds, 45td. 1cvt, 274pts; 3 Grey Cup finals, 1 winner; 4 all-Western, 2 CFL all-Cdn; also used as punt, kickoff returner; 5yrs 1000yd plus receiving; shared league record 4 games 100+yds receiving single season; plays guitar in Flutie Brothers band; res. Franklin, Mass.

FLUTIE, Doug (football); b. 23 Oct 1962, Manchester, Md.; m. Laurie; c. Alexa, Doug Jr.; Boston College, BSc; quarterback; gained fame for 50yd Hail Mary TD pass in last minute of BCU 47-45 win over Miami '84; Heisman Trophy '84; all-American, UPI, Sporting News, Kodak, ECAC player of '84; all-time NCAA passing leader at graduation; selected/signed by USFL New Jersey Generals '85; spent '85 season on NFL Rams development squad; traded to Chicago '86, New England '87-89; joined CFL BC Lions '90-91, Calgary '92-95, Toronto '96-97, Buffalo (NFL) '98; named to '98 Pro Bowl team; CFL record: 117 scheduled games, 61tds, 612 carries for 4118yds, 2545 completions on 4854 attempts for 41,355yds, 270tds, 131int; 4 Jeff Nicklin, 1 Jeff Russel, 6 CFL outstanding player, 2 Grey Cup MVP, 4 all-Western, 1 all-Eastern, 5 all-CFL all-star, 1 Terry Evanshen awards; set/tied 2 CFL passing records; mem. 3 Grey Cup finals, 2 winners; brother Darren mem. Eskimos/Tiger-Cats; street (Flutie Pass) in Natick, Mass. bears his name; avid musician (drummer), he and Darren (guitar) have touring group known as the Flutie Brothers, released CD entitled *Catch This* '96; cereal ("Flutie Flakes"), candy bar bearing his name introduced '98; res. Natick, Mass.

FLYNN, Chris (football); b. 17 Nov 1966, Buckingham, Que.; m. Sandy Brassard; c. Chelsea; St. Mary's.; teacher, coach; led SMU Huskies to 4 straight AUAA titles while amassing 83-8 record; set CIAU career record 87td passes; played in 2 Vanier Cup finals; the most acclaimed quarterback in Canadian college history, he was named recipient of Hec Crighton Trophy unprecedented three times; despite brilliant college career was only token CFL draft by Ottawa; opted for WLAF Montreal Machine but saw little action behind undistinguished American players; played semipro Montreal Voyageurs, Ottawa Bootleggers of Empire

League, Empire League player of '92; coach Montreal CEGEP, Philemon Wright HS; semipro team in France; 3 time Ottawa ACT football award winner; ACT athlete of year '91; 4 Buckingham athlete of year awards; made '94 headlines with rescue of drowning woman from river in France; res. Buckingham, Que.

FLYNN, Clarke (bobsled/weightlifting); b. 8 Jul 1959, Jever, Germany; m. Laurie Graham; c. Kylie Grace, Taylor Michela; UofOtt, BAdmin; marketing; v-p Bobsleigh Canada; mem. ntl bobsleigh team '80-88; competed 6 world championships, '84 Olympics; competitive Olympic-style weight lifter '79-84; competed in ntl weightlifting championships '82-84; WC bobsleigh commentator TSN Winter Speed, US Prime Sports, '94, '98 Olympics, '97 worlds; res. Nepean, Ont.

FOGH, Hans (sailing); b. 8 Mar 1938, Copenhagen, Denmark; m. Kirsten Andersen; c. Morten, Thomas; gardener, sailmaker; Danish Pirate class title at 19; European Flying Dutchman title '60; FD silver '60 Olympics; FD world title '62; Kiel Week FD title, 4th '64 Olympics; Danish 505 titles '65-66; Scandinavian FD titles '65, '67; emigrated to Canada '69, Canadian citizen '75; US nationals FD '70, soling '81-82; crewed for Paul Elvstrom world soling title '74; skippered soling bronze '84 Olympics; British Open FD, NA FD, soling, Great Lakes, Atlantic Coast soling titles; mem. 7 Olympic teams; 4 CORK soling titles; ranked among world's top 10 competitive sailors; author Sailor's Manual; mem. Order of Canada, Etobicoke, Cdn Amateur Sports, Canada's Sports halls of fame; res. Etobicoke, Ont.

FOLEY, Jim (football); b. 27 Oct 1947, Ottawa, Ont; m. Lesley Cheryl Scharf; c. Rodney James, Tara; UPEI, BA; human resources officer Regional Municipality of Ottawa-Carleton; pro running back, wide receiver Montreal '71-72, Ottawa '73-77; EFC rookie of year; Hiram Walker Trophy '74 as players' player; Schenley top Canadian award '75, Lew Hayman trophy '75; mem. 2 Grey Cup winners; asst. coach Carleton '79, UofOtt '90; res. Ottawa, Ont.

FOLEY, Joe (boxing); b. 19 Jul 1938, Badger, Nfld; m. Lorraine Amos; c. Raymond Carl, Dwayne Joseph; retd. Cdn Forces; light middleweight; fought competitively '57-66; nicknamed "Punchey"; NB area light middle title '58-59, Eastern Cdn, CF titles '59; Cdn Infantry Brigade Group titles '59-61, '63-65; Eastern command, tri-services titles, runnerup CF title '60; tri-services title '63; mem. Black Watch boxing team '62-65; competitive record 49 bouts, 46 wins (35 by KO), 3 losses; established Oromocto BC '78; coach Oromocto Pioneer BC '88; 3 Mr. Boxing Canada awards; played key role in bringing Cdn Boxing Hall of Fame to Oromocto; Royal Cdn Legion appreciation award; Oromocto recognition award; mem. Cdn, Rochester Boxing halls of fame; res. Oromocto, N.B.

FOLIGNO, Mike (hockey); b. 29 Jan 1959, Sudbury, Ont.; given name: Mike Anthony; m. Janis; c. Cara, Lisa. Nicholas, Marcus; coach; right wing Sudbury (OHA) '75-79; 1st team all-star '79; 1st pick Detroit '79 entry draft; played in NHL with Detroit '79-81, Buffalo '81-90, Toronto '90-93, Florida '93-94; NHL record: 15 seasons, 1018 scheduled games, 355g, 372a, 57 playoff games, 15g, 17a;

launched coaching career in Toronto organization '95-96 as asst. St. John's (AHL), Toronto; pro scout Leafs '96; asst. coach Colorado '97-98; head coach Hershey Bears (AHL) '99; res. Hershey, Pa.

FOLK, Rick (curling/golf); b. 5 Mar 1950, Saskatoon, Sask.; given name: Richard Dale Basil; m. Elizabeth Short; c. Kevin, Andrea; UofSask; sporting goods store owner; skipped '68 Sask. HS champions, runnerup nationals; skip Sask, jr. title rink '71; Western Canada university champion '70; 5 Sask. mixed titles; '74, '83 ntl mixed titles, twice runnerup; skipped Sask. 3 Briers, '80 title, twice runnerup; BC 4 Briers, twice runnerup, '94 winner; '80, '94 world champion; mem. Sask. jr. golf team '66-68; Sask. jr. golf title '67-68; mem. 6 Sask. Willingdon Cup teams; Sask. men's champion '71-72; asst. golf pro '74-75; elected to Sask. provincial govt. '82-86; Minister Culture & Recreation '83-86; Dick Ellis trophy '80; mem. Cdn Curling and with '80 rink Sask Sports, with '94 rink BC Sports halls of fame; res. Kelowna, B.C.

FONSECA, Peter (t&f); b. 5 Oct 1966, Lisbon, Portugal; Oregon, BA, Windsor (teaching cert.); owner import business; marathon specialist; moved to Toronto '68; made marathon debut '90 with bronze LA; Pac-10 10,000m titlist '90; cross-country all-American '90; silver Rheims, Houston Tenneco, Toronto marathons '94; gold '95 Houston, Toronto marathons, Kelowna half-marathon '96; competed '94 Commonwealth, '96 Olympic Games; CTFA Fred Begley Memorial trophy '90; res. Toronto, Ont./Lisbon, Portugal.

FONTAINE, Lucien (harness racing); b. 4 Dec 1939, Pointe Aux Trembles, Que.; nicknamed "Loosh"; received early training working for Keith Waples, Clint Hodgins; Big Apple driving titles '68, '77-78; best year '77 with 245 victories; Messenger Stakes with Valiant Bret '73; more than 3300 victories, $20 million in purses; res. Tarrytown, N.Y.

FONTAINE, Nicolas (skiing); b. 5 Oct 1970, Magog, Que.; freestyle specialist; mem. ntl team from '90; 4 ntl aerials titles; competed '92 (demonstration), '94, '98 winter Olympics; world championship gold '97; World Cup aerials gold '96-99; 6 World Cup race gold, 2 silver, 1 bronze; res. Magog, Que.

FONTANA, Don (tennis); b. 18 Jun 1931, Toronto, Ont.; given name: Donald Anthony; UCLA; tennis consultant; 2 Ont. Open singles titles; with Bob Bedard Que. Open doubles, 3 ntl men's doubles; finalist '56 ntl men's singles; mem. 10 Davis Cup teams, 3 non-playing capt.; played Wimbledon twice, Forest Hills 11 times, French Open once; organized ntl championships for CLTA; chief consultant Rothmans Cdn Grand Prix tournaments; TV tennis color commentator; res. Toronto, Ont.

FONTEYNE, Karen (synchro swim); b. 29 Jan 1969, Calgary, Alta.; given name: Karen Denise; UCal, BComm, UWO, MBA; economic analyst Amoco Canada; switched from gymnastics to synchro with Calgary Aquabelles at age 11; mem. ntl team '87-96; with Cari Read won '93 ntl duet championship; known for innovative style; team gold '96 French Open; team silver '95 Pan-Am, '96 Olympic Games, '94 Worlds, French, German Opens; team gold '94 Titrex

Cup, '90 Swiss Open; Petro-Canada Olympic Torch scholarships '90-92; res. Calgary, Alta.

FONTINATO, Lou (hockey); b. 20 Jan 1932, Guelph, Ont.; c. Nancy, Louie, Roger; farmer; jr. Guelph Biltmores; pro '52-53 Vancouver, Saskatoon (WHL); NHL defenceman NY Rangers '54-63; career terminated by neck injury; NHL record: 535 games, 26 goals, 78 assists, 1247 penalty minutes; reputation as 'policeman', one of league's tough guys; res. Guelph, Ont.

FOOT, Fred (t&f); b. 28 Oct 1916, Folkestone, Kent, Eng; given name: Frederick Albert; m. Mary Betty Reid; c. Angela, Deborah; ret'd Metro Toronto police; from late '40s one of Canada's top track coaches; coached East York TC, UofT, '56 Olympic, '62 Commonwealth Games teams; 3 CIAU cross-country coach of yr awards; prominent athletes coached included Bill Crothers, Dave Bailey, George Shepherd, Jackie McDonald, Bruce Kidd, Sue Bradley; res. East York, Ont.

FOOTE, Adam (hockey); b. 10 Jul 1971, Toronto, Ont.; m. Jennifer Cook; defence Whitby (OMHA), Sault Ste. Marie (OHL) '88-91, Halifax (AHL) '91-92, NHL Quebec '91-95, Colorado '95-99; OHL 1st team all-star '91; mem. '96 Stanley Cup winner; mem. Team Canada '96 World Cup, '98 Olympics; NHL record (through '99): 499 scheduled games, 23g, 90a, 77 playoff games, 3g, 12a; also plays a good game of lacrosse; res. Newcastle, Ont./Colorado.

FORBES, Pansy (synchro swim); b. 8 Mar 1898, England; d. 16 Sep 1989, Peterborough, Ont.; given name: Pansy Evelyn Louise; c. Iris Mary; led Peterborough Ornamental Swim Club to world fame as coach throughout '40s, '50s, '60s; recognized world leader in her sport, a pioneer in training methods and innovative procedures; Peterborough Citizen of '53; Cdn Centennial Medal; Ont. Citizenship medal '73; Ont. Synchronized Swimming Assn. Achievement award; mem. Cdn Aquatic, Peterborough Sports halls of fame.

FORD, Alan (football); b. 2 Jul 1943, Regina, Sask.; given name: Robert Alan; m. Sally Ann; c. Tracy, Robert, Jill; U of Pacific, BA; retd. football exec.; accepted UP basketball scholarship then switched to football; pro split end, halfback, flanker, cornerback, def. back, tight end, punter. Roughriders '65-76; set Sask. record 207 consecutive games played (regular season and playoffs); handled bulk of Sask. punting over 12 seasons kicking ball 1041 times for 41,880yds, 40.23yd avg., 23 singles, 6647 career receiving/rushing yds; twice Canadian Schenley award nominee; Grey Cup record 87yd punt '67; 4 Grey Cup finals, '66 winner; ass't coach, admin dir, AGM, GM, CEO. Roughriders '79-99; mem. Roughriders Plaza of Honor; res. Regina, Sask.

FORD, Albert (swimming); b. 21 Dec 1904, Redding, Eng.; d. 24 Nov 1988, Winnipeg, Man.; m. Ruth Kosar; c. Betty, Carol, Leon; UMan, PEng; standout swimmer '24-36; freestyle specialist; 3 Cdn, 11 YMCA, 18 Man., 1 Sask. titles in distances from 50yds-3 miles; held Man. records in all but 50yd FS; named to '36 Olympic team but work/family committments kept him off team; pres. Man. section CASA '42-44, '51-52; ntl pres. '53-54; meet referee BE & Commonwealth Games '54;; chair. '67 Pan-Am Games aquatic committee; Man. swimmer of half century; life mem. Winnipeg Winter Club, Winnipeg Canoe Club; mem. Man. Sports, Cdn Aquatic halls of fame.

FORD, Bruce (rowing); b. 18 Sep 1954, Victoria, B.C.; given name: Bruce Singleton; UVic, UBC, BSc; fisheries technician, BC Fish & Wildlife Branch; mem. UVic varsity 8s '72-73, jr. varsity, varsity 8s '73-74; began sculling as mem. Victoria City RC '76; Canadian Henley jr. single sculls '77; sr. single, double sculls '77-78, '82, quadruple sculls '77-78; gold double sculls '79 Pan-Am Games, bronze coxless quad sculls '84 Olympics; 3 ntl single, double sculls, 1 quadruple sculls titles; Royal Henley double sculls challenge cup '80; mem. '80, '84 Olympic teams; co-winner Victoria athlete of year award, BC team of year award '79; res. Richmond, B.C.

FORD, David (canoeing); b. 23 Mar 1967, Edmonton, Alta.; one of top kayakers in world; ntl team mem. from '83. 7 ntl titles; competed '92, '96 Olympics; won Canada's first-ever gold medal World Cup '92; res. Edmonton, Alta.

FORD, Russ (baseball); b. 25 Apr 1883, Brandon, Man.; d. 24 Jan 1960, Rockingham, N.C.; given name: Russell William; hotel mgr, draftsman, banker, mill shipper; followed older brother Gene (who played briefly with Detroit 1905) to majors with NY Highlanders 1910; spitball pitcher who became author of emery ball in Southern Assn. '08; 26-6 record '10, 1.65era, 1 1-hitter, 1 2-hitter, 3 3-hitters; 22-11 in '11 then slipped to 13-21 in '12; asked to take pay cut from $5,500 to $3,500 so jumped to Buffalo, Federal League where he posted 21-6 record '14; with emery ball pitch outlawed '15 his career ended shortly thereafter; ML record 99-71, 2.59era; mem. Cdn Baseball Hall of Fame.

FORDER, Anna (figure skating); b. 25 May 1951, Oshawa, Ont.; given name: Anna Louise; m. Murray McLaughlin; c. Brooke Kimberly; Durham College; figure skating coach; teamed with Richard Stephens in pairs competition '63-68; mem. '68 Olympics, '69 Worlds teams; from '70 taught and coached all levels from novice through world, Olympic calibre; mem. Oshawa Sports Hall of Fame; res. Blackstock, Ont.

FORGERON, Mike (rowing); b. 24 Jan 1966, Main-A-Dieu, N.S.; made debut on ntl team '91 Pan-Am Games winning silver men's coxless pairs, bronze men's 8s; '92 Olympic gold men's 8s; FISU Games double sculls silver '93; gold straight 4s '94 Amsterdam International; with Todd Hallett double sculls '96 Olympics; mem. Cdn Olympic Hall of Fame; res. Victoria, B.C.

FORGUES, Keith (curling); b. 17 Sep 1942, Vulcan, Alta.; m. Carole Pender; c. Lisa, Michael; UAlta, BSc; chemist; 3rd '63 Edmonton zone Consols winner; 7 consec. years Ottawa Dist. Consols titlist '68-74, skip '71; 3rd Eldon Coombe '72 Ont. Brier rink; 4 Canadian Branch Royal Victoria Jubilee titles, 1 as skip; 2 Branch Governor-General's trophies, 1 as skip; 2nd for Terry Begin City of Ottawa grand aggregate title '71-72; CBC cross-country curling series winner '72, runnerup '73; Whitby invitational '72; Northern Ont. CA bonspiel title '75; Branch Colts '66; 7 Red Anderson Memorial Trophies; res. Ottawa, Ont.

FORHAN, Bob (hockey); b. 27 Mar 1936, Newmarket, Ont.; m. Sandra O'Rourke; c. Bobby, Michael, Scott, Joe; UBC, BPhE; teacher, politician; OHA jr. B champion Weston Dukes '52-53; leading scorer jr. A Guelph Biltmores '53-56; sr. A Sudbury Wolves; mem. Kitchener-Waterloo Dutchmen '60 Olympic silver medal team; Trail Smoke Eaters '64 world tournament team, ntl team '64 Olympics, '65 world tournament; res. Newmarket, Ont.

FORREST, Craig (soccer); b. 20 Sep 1967, Vancouver, B.C.; goalkeeper; began play age 12 Bel Aire City, Coquitlam '79; mem. BC -16 ntl title team; mem. ntl -20 B, World Cup teams, 37 international caps; mem. ntl team from '88; pro Ipswich '88-97, Chelsea '97, West Ham United '97-98; English 1st div. champions '92; Cdn player of '94 award; TV analyst '98 World Cup; res. Ipswich, Eng./ Vancouver, B.C.

FORREST, Robin (lawn bowling/field hockey); b. 10 Mar 1946, Vancouver, B.C.; given name: Robin Mary Stewart; m. Steve; c. Christopher, Jennifer; civil servant; active participant/official field hockey from teens; selected to Vancouver Island ladies' FH rep list '79-81; 1st Cdn woman to qualify to umpire men's FH matches '77; co-founder Victoria Rebels Sports Club '71, Vancouver Island jr. boys FH league '73; competes for Rebels Renegades VILFHA Div. 3; coach BC under-16 girls FH champions '86; life men. VILFHA; began lawn bowling '87; BC women's pairs champion '92; mem. ntl team '95-96; ntl women's singles title '96; res. Victoria, B.C.

FORRESTER, Ron (jiu-jitsu); b. 3 Jun 1927, Durham, Eng.; m. Ethel Moore; mgr. technical services, welder; 8th degree black belt jiu-jitsu, 2nd degree black belt karate; martial arts prof.; founder-pres. Canadian Jiu-Jitsu Assoc. Inc.; black belt of '68 award CJA; coach ntl team, title winners international tournaments Hawaii '77, Toronto '78; American JI distinguished service award '75; Ont. special achievement award '78; mem. Black Belt Hall of Fame; res. Oakville, Ont.

FORSHAW, Sheila (field hockey); b. 28 Jun 1958, Toronto, Ont.; York, BSc; communications officer; former E.D. OWIAA; mem. Ont. jr. team '74-77, Ont. sr. team from '76, York team '77-82, Nomads club from '77, ntl team from '78; mem. '83 World Cup silver medal team, '84 Olympic team; York athlete of '80; fed. govt. excellence award '83; OWIAA communications officer; mem. Mississauga Sports Hall of Fame; res. Willowdale, Ont.

FORSYTH, David (soccer); b. 15 Dec 1852, Perthshire, Scotland; d. 13 Sep 1936, Beamsville, Ont.; m. Augusta Miglius (d); c. Otto; UofT; HS principal; considered father of Canadian soccer; raised in Berlin (Kitchener); capt. Berlin Lacrosse Club; mem. Berlin Cricket Club; canoeist, lawn bowler, cyclist; centre UotT football (soccer) team; organized Western Football Assoc., NA's 1st league 1880, remained involved through 1919, 5yrs secty.; hon. life pres. Dominion FA; secty.-treas. OFA 5yrs; King's Silver Jubilee medal '35; UotT math silver medal; chairman Berlin Board of Health; mem. Waterloo County Hall of Fame.

FORTIER, Sylvie (synchro swim); b. 31 Aug 1958, Quebec City, Que.; BA, public relations; 24 gold, 4 silver, 2 bronze

at ntl level '73-76; 12 Que. titles; 2 silver Pan-Pacific Games '74; 8 golds mid-Canada regionals '75-76; solo silver '75 Pan-Am Games; 3 silver '75 world championships; 2 gold, 1 silver '76 international championships; 2 golds, 1 silver '76 Pan-Pacific Games; world champion '76; Elaine Tanner Trophy '76; mem. Cdn Aquatic, Canada's Sports halls of fame; res. Quebec City, Que.

FOSTER, Red (administration); b. 1 Mar 1905, Toronto, Ont.; d. 18 Jan 1985, Toronto, Ont.; given name: Harry; m. Kathryn; Ridley College; advertising exec., humanitariam; hockey Toronto Canoe Club jrs., St. Mary's, Marlboros srs.; organized, coached, played for Sr. OHA Sea Fleas; halfback jr. Argos, capt. Ont. title team; Argos srs.; Sr. ORFU Balmy Beach '28-30, Grey Cup '30; lacrosse Maitlands Sr.OALA; shortstop Toronto Garrison Officers' League Machine Gunners softball team; won 1st official outdoor hydroplane (sea flea) outboard race in Canada; runnerup world international championships, earning reputation as one of NA's most daring and capable drivers; pioneered sports broadcasting; established charitable foundation for mentally challenged; chair., CEO Canadian Special Olympics; chair. Canada's Sports Hall of Fame; mem. Lou Marsh Trophy selection comm., CNE Sports Comm.; Ont. special achievement award; many community awards for charitable works; mem. Order of Canada, Canada's Sports Hall of Fame.

FOULDS, William C (football); b. 1888, Toronto, Ont.; d. 1954, Toronto, Ont.; UofT; QB Toronto Varsity '09 Grey Cup win; coached Argos '11, '14-15; won Grey Cup '14; held various exec. posts with Argos, CRU; pres. CRU '21, '37; chair. rules comm.; referee-in-chief IRFU; instrumental in establishing East-West Grey Cup final '21; personally financed Eskimos travel costs to assure ntl final would be held; charter mem. Cdn Football Hall of Fame.

FOURNIER, Lionel (t&f); b. 19 Mar 1917, Pincher Creek, Alta.; d. 3 Sep 1993, Canmore, Alta.; given name: Lionel Joseph; m. Rita May Lorden; c. Robert, Ellen, Paul, Anne; UBC, BA, BComm, McGill, BSc, UAlta, MA; prof.; 2nd high jump, long jump '37 BEG trials; 3 track, 2 football letters UBC; capt. McGill t&f team '47-48; intercollegiate discus record; Canada's 1st international decathlon competitor '48 Olympics; t&f coach UAlta; among initiators of sports competitions for Canada's handicapped athletes '67; ntl team coach '67 Pan-Am Games for wheelchair athletes, '68 paralympics, Alta. team '69 ntl wheelchair championships; co-ordinator '68 ntl wheelchair championships; founder Canadian Wheelchair Sports Assn., Edmonton Paralympics Assn.; mgr. ntl wheelchair team '69 Pan-Ams; administrator-coach ntl t&f training centre for Canadian Legion Edmonton '68-69; chair. rec. div. CAHPER '67-69; initiated, developed t&f, football, basketball, volleyball programs Quebec's Saguenay region '47-62; chair. 1st playground Olympics for greater Montreal '52; Paralympic award winner; mem. Alta Sports Hall of Fame.

FOWLER, Dick (baseball); b. 30 Mar 1921, Toronto, Ont.; d. 22 May 1972, Oneonta, N.Y.; given name: Richard John; m. Joyce Howard; c. Tom (d); rhp, began pro career Cornwall, Batavia, Oneonta in Can-Am League; moved to Toronto (IL) '41; 10 seasons with Philadelphia Athletics

(NL) amassing 66-79 record, 4.11era, 221games, 1303ip, 382k, 578bob, 11sho; pitched 1-0 no-hitter for Connie Mack's Athletics vs. St. Louis Browns 9 Sep 1945, his lone win that season following return from WW2 service; returned to minors with Charleston '53-54; mem. Cdn Baseball Hall of Fame.

FOWLIE, Jim (swimming); b. 26 Jul 1956, Prince George, B.C.; given name: James Kenneth; m. Lynn Bengston; c. Carrie Ann, Johnathan; swimming coach; 400IM silver, 200m butterfly bronze '73 Canada Games; bronze 4x200 FS relay '74 Commonwealth Games; ntl 400IM record '74; 400IM gold, Commonwealth record '75 world trials; mem. '75 worlds team; 400IM gold Pan-Am Games trials '75; gold, ntl record 4:26.25 (fastest in world that year) '76; failed to qualify for '76 Olympic team; retd to coaching Prince George SC '77, Lions Gate SC '78, UCal '79-80; coached Alberta '81 Canada Games; coach Manta Aquatic Club Winnipeg, North York Aquatic Club; mem. CASA apprentice coaching program; coached men's team '81 long course western nationals; mem. ntl coaching staff '81 youth championships Sweden; numerous ntl team appointments '81-91; asst. coach '90 Commonwealth Games; sr. coach AIS from '92; coached Australian teams 3 world short course championships, '96 Olympics, 2 World Cups; res. Belconnen, Australia.

FOX, Fred (t&f/hockey); b. 18 Jan 1914, Lunenburg, N.S.; given name: Fred Gordon Stephen; m. Jacqueline; c. Michael, Patricia, Pamela; Mount Allison; retired firefighter, public servant; NS 220yd sprint title '30, Maritime titles 100, 200yd dashes '31; 100yd record stood 28 years; Maritime sprint champion jr. '33, sr. '34-35; Highland Games sprint titles '34-35; competed '32, '36 Olympic, '34, '38 BEG trials; mem. '37 Coronation, '40 Armed Forces track teams; mem. 15 Maritime Firemen title track teams; mem. Lunenburg Falcons, Chester Ravens hockey teams '30s-'50s, 6 league titles, 1 scoring title; mem. Berwick Apple Kings; top scorer Mount A Maritime intercollegiate title teams '32-33; mem. NS finalist Lunenburg HS baseball team '31; mem. 3 NS finalist Lunenburg Bluenosers softball teams; following WW2 turned to hockey's administrative branch; pres. South Shore HL '48-51; pres. MAHA '59-61, '70-74; pres. NSHA '74-79, '81-84; mem. NSFAS advisory council 5yrs; dir. Sport NS to '83; mem. NS Sports Hall of Fame selection comm.; NS sport exec. of '83; Royal Canadian Legion meritorious award, King's Coronation, Queen's Coronation, Jubilee medals, Centennial medal, CAHA outstanding, meritorious service awards, Toronto Metro, NOHA, OMHA, NS Metro Valley plaques, MAHA long service pin; Lunenburg honored him with Fred Fox Day '80; 1st life mem. NSHA; life mem. Royal Cdn Legion Lunenburg branch; life mem. national POW Assoc.; hon. life mem. Lunenburg Fire Dept.; mem. NS Sports Hall of Fame; res. Lunenburg, N.S.

FOX, Rick (basketball); b. 24 Jul 1969, Toronto, Ont.; given name: Ulrich Alexander; m. Vanessa L. Williams; North Carolina; basketball player/actor; moved with family to Bahamas at age 2; moved to Warsaw, Indiana, at 14; from '87-91 appeared in 140 North Carolina Tarheels scheduled games scoring 1703 points; *Sporting News* 3rd team all-American '91; Boston Celtics 1st round NBA draft pick

(24th overall) '91; small forward 6-7, 231; NBA all-rookie 2nd team '92; played with Boston '91-97, LA Lakers '97-99; NBA record: ('91-98) 483g; playoffs 12g, 46p; mem. Team Canada '89, '94 world championships; had cameo role in movie "*He Got Game*"; mother Dianne Gerace high jumper Cdn team '64 Olympics; res. Salem, Mass.

FOX, Terry (t&f); b. 28 Jul 1958, Port Coquitlam, B.C.; d. 28 Jun 1981, New Westminster, B.C.; given name: Terrence Stanley; SFU; active HS basketball player; lost right leg to cancer at 18; indomitable spirit provided inspiration to entire nation as he sought to run across Canada to raise funds for cancer research; Marathon of Hope raised $23.5 million; launched run 12 Apr '80 in Newfoundland; covered 5342km before illness in Thunder Bay (cancer had spread to lungs) forced him to quit 2 Sep '80; ntl day of mourning declared on his death; subject of '83 movie; '80 Lou Marsh Trophy; Companion of Order of Canada '80; Order of Dogwood, CP man of year '80; SFU established gold medal in his memory and communities throughout country named parks, sports facilities, streets, halls of fame in his honor; hon. mem. Canada's Sports Hall of Fame.

FOXCROFT, Bob (fencing); b. 17 Aug 1934, London, Ont.; given name: Robert Samuel; salesman; 12 times Ont. foil, épée, sabre champion; 5 ntl sabre titles; mem. '59, '67, '71 Pan-Am Games teams; bronze team foil '59, team sabre '67; mem. '62, '66, '70 Commonwealth Games teams; bronze team sabre '66; mem. '74 Commonwealth fencing championships sabre team silver medalists; mem. '64, '72 Olympic, '58, '67 world championships teams; retired after 25 competitive seasons '79; fencing coach Seneca College, London Sword Club, UWO, Toronto Jewish Community Centre; v-p AAU of C at its dissolution; pres. Ont. Fencing Assn.; Ont. special achievement award '65, '71; res. North York, Ont.

FOXCROFT, Ron (officiating/basketball); b. 5 Nov 1945, Hamilton, Ont.; given name: Ronald Lewis; m. Marie Louise Grant; c. Steven, David, Ronnie; pres. Fluke Transport, Fox 40 International Inc.; under tutelage of Kitch MacPherson launched 35yr basketball officiating career '63 at high school level, 29 consec. yrs CIAU referee; achieved international and NCAA Div. 1 status officiating in more than 30 countries including the '76 Olympics gold medal game and NCAA Sweet 16 '98; lone Cdn to referee in NCAA from '80; 1st Cdn elected to NASO, 2 terms as chair.; refereed 6 Ont. HS title, 7 CIAU title, 15 OUAA West title games; worked OUAA West playoffs 23yrs, 10 NIT, 4 NCAA tournaments, title finals Sun Belt, Atlantic 10, Metro Atlantic Conference; OUAA West officials panel supervisor from '93; international events included Olympic, Pan-Am, World, FISU, Continental Cup, Goodwill Games, Japan Classic; inventor of award winning Fox 40 pealess whistle now used by sports officials throughout world; dir. Hamilton Tiger-Cats from '93; chair. '94 World championship of basketball Hamilton organizing comm.; co-chair '96 Hamilton Grey Cup; pres./CEO Hamilton-Brantford 2001 Canada Summer Games bid comm.; chair. '98 CIAU basketball championship bid comm.; plays active role in community affairs serving on boards of numerous organizations; pres. Hamilton Chamber of Commerce '95; named by *Profit* magazine among top 10 Cdn entrepreneurs of decade;

Stoney Creek Citizen of '91; B'Nai Brith Canada award of merit '95; Hamilton Distinguished Citizen of '97 award; mem. Cdn Basketball Hall of Fame; res. Burlington, Ont.

FOYSTON, Frank (hockey); b. 2 Feb 1891, Minesing, Ont.; d. 24 Jan 1966, Seattle, Wash.; mem. '11-12 OHA sr. title Toronto Eaton team; pro '12 Toronto (NHA); centre '13-14 Stanley Cup winners; Seattle '15-24; guided 1st US Stanley Cup winners '16-17; Victoria '24-26; mem. '25 Stanley Cup winner; Detroit '26-28; 6 Stanley Cup finals, 3 winners; mem. Hockey Hall of Fame.

FRACAS, Gino (football); b. 28 Apr 1930, Windsor, Ont.; given name: Gino Mark; m. Leona Deck; c. Mark, Michael, Gina, Paul, Donna; UWO, BA, UAlta, BEd, Michigan, MA; retd. prof., football coach; 4 seasons fullback, linebacker UWO '51-54, 3 times all-star, twice OQAA scoring champion, '55 MVP; pro fullback, linebacker Edmonton (CFL) '55-62; co-capt. def. signal caller '61-62; 3 Grey Cup finals, 2 winners; head coach UAlta '63-66, 3 league titles, '63 Golden Bowl, beginning of ntl College Bowl play; met UotT 1st official College Bowl '65; head coach Windsor Lancers '68-86; '69 western div. CCIFC titlists, '75 OUAA west div. champions; head coach CIAU all-stars '79 Can-Am Bowl; 2 OUAA West coach of yr awards; v-p Canadian Football Coaches Assn. '69-70; mem. CAFA ntl working comm. for football certification; life mem. Alta. FCA; ntl wrestling drawmaster '67-78, '76 Olympics, '78 Commonwealth Games, Worlds; FILA award of merit; authored "*Basic Football Fundamentals*"; CIAU trophy awarded annually to top assist. football coach bears his name; Football Canada-CFL award of merit '87; retd from teaching '95; coaches HS football; dir. Windsor-Essex Sports Hall of Fame; mem. UWO W-Club, Windsor-Essex Sports, Windsor Alumni, OUAA Football Legends halls of fame; res. Windsor, Ont.

FRANCIS, Emile (hockey); b. 13 Sep 1926, North Battleford, Sask.; given name: Emile Percy; m. Em; c. Rick, Bobby; retd hockey exec.; 14 pro seasons with 12 clubs including parts of 6 as goaler NHL Black Hawks, NY Rangers; nicknamed "The Cat"; retd '60, managed Western Canada baseball clubs; coach Guelph jr. A '61; GM, 3 stints as coach Rangers '61-76; exec. v-p GM St. Louis '76-83; pres., GM Hartford '83-89; NHL playing record: 3.74 goals per game avg., in 95 games; coaching record: won 393, lost 273, tied 112 regular season, won 40, lost 53 in playoffs; *Sporting, Hockey News* hockey exec. of year awards; Lester Patrick Trophy '82; mem. Hockey Hall of Fame selection comm.; mem. Hockey, Sask., North Battleford Sports halls of fame; res. Palm Beach, Fla./Glastonbury, Conn.

FRANCIS, Ron (hockey); b. 1 Mar 1963, Sault Ste Marie, Ont.; m. Mary Lou; c. Kaitlyn, Michael, Connor; centre SSM jr. '80-82; 1st Hartford draft pick '81; NHL Hartford '81-91, Pittsburgh '91-98, Carolina '98-99; reached 1000a plateau '98; Selke, Alka-Seltzer plus award '95; 2 Lady Byng trophies, 4 Whalers MVP awards; 4 NHL all-star games; mem. 2 Stanley Cup winners; NHL record: (through '99) 1329 scheduled games, 449g, 1037a, 133 playoff games, 40g, 83a; reached 1500 point plateau '99; res. Pittsburgh, Pa.

FRANK, Bill (football); b. 13 Apr 1938, Denver, Colo; m. Barbara; c. Jeffrey, Kari-Lynn; San Diego Jr. College, Colorado; businessman; award winning college wrestler; West Coast and jr. college all-American; mem. Colorado all-time all-star team; pro BC '63-64, Toronto '65-68; following tryout Denver (NFL) joined Winnipeg '69-76; 7 times all-Cdn offensive tackle; Blue Bombers lineman of '70-75; Dr. Bert Oja award '70; 6 times Schenley Award nominee; mem. Argos quarter-century team '74, Winnipeg all-time dream team; mem. Athletes in Action; player rep. Canadian Football Players' Assn.; mem. Blue Bombers Hall of Fame; res. Winnipeg, Man.

FRANK, Chris (bobsleigh); b. 6 Feb 1949, Banger, N. Wales; m. Nancy Keyes; c. Elizabeth, Graham; Carleton, BComm; broadcasting consultant; mem. ntl team '74-78, Diamond Trophy race winner; competed '75, '77, '78 world championships, '76 Olympics; 2nd '78 NA championships; best world title finish 12th 4-man sled '78; active canoeist, '80 Olympic team alternate; res. Ottawa, Ont.

FRASER, Alexa Stirling (golf); b. 5 Sep 1897, Atlanta, Ga.; d. 15 Apr 1977, Ottawa, Ont.; m. Dr. Wilbert A Fraser; c. Sandra, Alin Robert, Richard Douglas; women's southern championships '15-16, '19; US women's amateur '14, '19-20, 3 times runnerup, semifinalist twice; Cdn women's amateur '20, '34, twice runnerup; 8 Ottawa City & District women's titles; teamed with Bobby Jones on '18 Red Cross fund-raising tour; mem. Ottawa, RCGA halls of fame.

FRASER, Anna (skiing); b. 25 Jul 1963, Ottawa, Ont.; m. Rob Sproule; c. Kate; marketing, communications consultant; freestyle specialist; daughter of former House of Commons Speaker John Fraser; began skiing at 3; member Ont. team before joining ntl team '84-88; won 5 World Cup series gold medals; 4th in aerials '88 Olympics; had best year '86 winning ntl ballet, aerials titles, 4 of 8 aerials events on WC circuit; 37 individual WC medals on Grand Prix circuit; World Cup aerial GP title '86; retd. from competition following '88 Olympics; *TSN Women in Sport* interviewer; CBC '92, '98 Olympic FS color commentator; motivational speaker FAME; mem. Ottawa Sports, Cdn Skiing halls of fame; res. Toronto, Ont.

FRASER, Bud (basketball/t&f); b. 16 Oct 1923, Bridgewater, N.S.; given name: Arthur; m. Ella Thomson; c. Geoffrey, Robin, Judy, Terry, Jill, Scott; McGill, BSc, Minnesota, MA; retired educator; NS high jump title '40; Armed Forces high jump title '42-43; Southeast Asia Armed Forces champion 6 events '45; CIAU basketball all-star '48-50; Montreal city basketball all-star '48-50; capt. McGill basketball team; silver award McGill Athletic Council, 3 track letters; coached Maritime int. champion Brookfield Elks '50-51, Western Canada Intercollegiate basketball champion UMan '54-57, Minnesota freshman basketball team; Winnipeg basketball coach of '53-54; sr. consultant Sport Canada; athletic dir. UofT; last known res. Florida.

FRASER, Cam (football); b. 16 Feb 1932, Hamilton, Ont.; given name: Cameron Donald; m. Betty Robertson; c. Donna Sandra; retd. steel company employee, businessman; kicking specialist; Tiger-Cats '52-62, '69; career total 101 singles;

10yr totals (CFL records only kept from '54) 987 punts, 44,287yds, 44.9 avg.; CFL record most punting yds single season 7222yds on 157 punts '57; quit 7yr retirement to fill in for injured Joe Zuger '69; from '73 coached champion Ancaster girls' softball team; punter Tiger-Cats pro era ('50-67) team; res. Mississauga, Ont.

FRASER, Frank (football); b. 26 Oct 1935, Montreal, Que.; m. Janet Beers; c. Gregory, Natalie, Nathan, Wawnita; Ohio State, Tennessee A&I; retd. mechanical engineer; jr. A hockey Que. Frontenacs, Jonquiére; jr. baseball Laval Ahuntsic Montreal league; Montreal HS, US college football; CFL halfback '56-63 with Montreal, Ottawa, Regina, Edmonton, Winnipeg; led Canadian pass receivers '59-60; with Marv Bevan coach Eastview jr. team; res. Kanata, Ont.

FRASER, George (football); b. 2 Feb 1911, Stanley, Scotland; d. 9 Dec 1992, Ottawa, Ont; given name: George Henry; m. Violet May Jay; c. Andy; retd Canada Post; Ottawa Gladstone jrs '31; flying wing, end, guard, kicker Rough Riders '32-47; until '39 had never kicked a football, when regular kicker was injured he filled in and booted 3 field goals; interim coach '46; asst. coach '47; 3 Grey Cup finals, 1 winner; Jeff Russel Trophy '45; 6 times all-star; highly durable player missing only one game in entire CFL career; mem. Ottawa CSRA Hall of Fame.

FRASER, Gord (cycling); b. 19 Nov 1968, Ottawa, Ont.; m. Caryn Isom; pro cyclist; began racing '86; specialized in track several years before switching to road racing; broke kneecap during '91 Canada Cup race; competed '90, '94 Commonwealth, '96 Olympic Games; competed in Canada with Control Data Systems; amateur in Europe with ASPTT team, winning 18 races '94, including Tour of Basque Country title, Robert Gauthier trophy, Paris-Troyes; exceptional sprinter; pro Motorola Cycle team '94-96, Mutuelle de Seine-et-Marne team '97, Mercury Cycle team '98, competing mostly in NA; won 4th stage '97 French GP du Midi Libre; competed, failed to complete 1st Tour de France '97; won 1st stage Spain's Tour of Austurias '98; 3 medals '98 Fresno races; '99 Pan-Am Games road race silver; nicknamed "Flash Gordon"; with Linda Jackson co-winner '95 Ottawa ACT athlete of yr; mem. Nepean Sports Wall of Fame; res. Tucson, Ariz.

FRASER, Hugh (t&f); b. 10 Jul 1952, Kingston, Jamaica; given name: Hugh Lloyd; div. Ann Kennedy; c. Robin, Curtis, Mark; m. Alexandra Reid; Queen's, BA, UofOtt, LLB; lawyer, prov. court judge; sprinter; ntl team '71-78; mem. '75 Pan-Ams, '76 Olympics, '78 Commonwealth Games teams; ntl 100m, 200m title holder; ntl indoor 300yd record 31.0; ntl automatic timing 200m 20.86 '75 Pan-Am Games beating Harry Jerome's '68 Olympic 21.22; 15th world '75; mem. 4x100 bronze relay team '75 Pan-Am Games setting Cdn record 38.86; football UofOtt '76, drafted by Toronto (CFL) but did not play; Bobby Kerr Memorial Trophy '71; dir. CTFA '81-83; CdM inaugural world athletics championships '83; pres. Sports Federation of Canada '85-90; v-p '90-94, pres. '92-94 Commonwealth Games Assn.; chair. Dubin sports advisory council '88-90; chair. Cdn Human Rights Commission; mediator varied sports disputes '90-93; guest lecturer on sports and the law

Carleton, Concordia '76-93; mem. international court of arbitration for sports from '95; arbitrator '96 Olympics, '98 Commonwealth Games; res. Ottawa, Ont.

FRASER, Iain (soccer); b. 3 Apr 1964, Gedburgh, Scotland; pro soccer player; honed skills in Scotland; defender Hamilton Steelers, Toronto Blizzard, Montreal Supra (CSL) '87-90; 13 CSL goals; Colorado Foxes (APSL) '93-94; Knights (CISL) '95; New England Revolution (MLS) '95-97; indoor Milwaukee (NPSL) '98; Cdn ntl team '94-97; 20 international caps; res. Burlington, Ont.

FRASER, Kerry (officiating/hockey); b. 30 May 1952, Sarnia, Ont.; given name: Kerry Hilton; div Mattie Spencer; m. Kathy McVeigh; c. Marcie, Ryan, Jessica, Matthew, Ian, Jaime, Kara; NHL referee/PR for financial institution; played minor hockey; attended NHL officiating school '72; refereed 8 Stanley Cup finals, World Cup series, '98 Olympics; NHL record as referee through '98: 1106 scheduled, 166 playoff games; works with amateur hockey officials groups in off-season; avid sailor; res. Voorhees, NJ.

FRASER, Martin (canoeing); b. 14 Apr 1959, Deep River, Ont.; given name: Martin Roy; m. Jane Sues; UofT, BSc; accountant; with Steve Wilson ntl juve. tandem canoe titles '74-76; ntl juve. singles '74-76; ntl jr. 500m, 1000m singles '78; 3rd 500m singles, tandem, 1000m tandem '78 NA championships; with Ivan Charalambij 2nd 500m, 1000m tandem Mexico Cup '78; 2nd 1000m tandem, 3rd 500m singles (top NA finisher in each) '79 Canada Cup; jr. ntl C2 500m title '79; C1 500m, 1000m titles '81 Continental Cup; C4 1000m ntl title '82; ntl canoe team mem. from '76; mem. '80 Olympic team; PS, HS outstanding student awards, Ont. scholar; res. Mississauga, Ont.

FRASER, Sherry (curling); b. 26 Jun 1967, Lethbridge, Alta; data co. administrator; began curling age 11; 2nd Kelley Law (Owen) BC women's title rink '95, '97; 4 times runnerup; bronze '97 Olympic trials; BC mixed title finalist '93; mem. '93 Richmond 'spiel, '96 Saskatoon Ladies Classic title rinks; winner STOH Ford Hot Shots competition '97; res. Vancouver, B.C.

FRAZER, Gerry (shooting); b. 18 Jun 1939, Edmonton, Alta.; given name: Gerald; m. Lili Kopala; c. Richard, Lynn, Tracy, stepchildren Dorothy, Rachel; UBC, BSc; retired mechanical engineer; began shooting competitively age 9; fullbore rifle specialist; 2 BC Lt. Governor's titles; qualified 6, competed 4 Cdn Bisley teams; mem. '88 Palma team; v-pres BCRA, mem. DCRA exec. council; res. Halifax, N.S.

FRÉCHETTE, Sylvie (synchro swim); b. 26 Jun 1967, Montreal, Que.; Montreal; performer/trainer Cirque du Soleil water show '97; learned to swim age 7; switched to synchro at 8; swept Cdn jr titles '81-82; mem. Ntl B team '82, Ntl A team '83-96; Canada Games solo gold '86; won ntl solo, duet (with Nathalie Guay); world aquatic championship solo gold '91 with highest score (201.013) ever recorded at worlds, awarded 7 10s; 2 world, 4 ntl solo titles; assisted figure skaters Isabelle Brasseur-Lloyd Eisler with pairs routine '92 Olympics; scoring error by Brazilian judge resulted in Olympic solo silver '92 but appeal launched by IOC exec. v-p Dick Pound finally resulted in change to gold in special ceremony '93; team silver '96 Olympics; sport excellence award '86; world champion award '87; Elaine Tanner Trophy '86; Aquatic Federation of Canada female athlete of year '89-90; Grace Under Pressure award '94; pool at Montreal's Claude Robillard Centre named in her honor; Luso Fraternities trophy from Intl. Assn. for Non-Violent Sports; fed. govt. meritorious service award '93; mem. Cdn Aquatic, Canada's, Que. Sports halls of fame; res. Las Vegas, Nev.

FREDRICKSON, Frank (hockey); b. 11 Jun 1895, Winnipeg, Man.; d. 28 May 1979, Toronto, Ont.; UMan; insurance agent; capt. UMan team; mem. Allan Cup, '20 Olympic champion Winnipeg Falcons; scored both goals in 2-0 gold medal victory over US; Victoria Aristocrats, later Cougars; 2 Stanley Cup winners; half season Detroit, Boston '27-30; twice led PCL, WCL scorers; 1st NHL player-coach-mgr. Pittsburgh '30; knee injury ended playing career '31; coach hockey, lacrosse Winnipeg '31-32, hockey Princeton '33-35, UBC 7yrs; 1st player to write instructional articles on hockey for newspaper (*Toronto Star*) '32; mem. BC, Man. Sports, Cdn, Man. Hockey halls of fame.

FRENCH, Joan (softball); b. 11 Dec 1935, Calgary, Alta; given name: Joan Grace Irene Jorginson; m. Bernie French (d); c. Jeffrey Warren, Bernie Grant (d); Calgary Business Coll.; realtor; participated in t&f, basketball, curling, softball; 3rd base Hillhurst Sunnyside Sr. A Alta. champions '56-62; named to Cdn team for world championships in Australia '63 but trip cancelled due to lack of funding; mem. Calgary Comets Sr. A team '63-68; 4 provincial titles; coach Calgary Timac Tires Sr. A '69-74, 4 provincial titles, Canada Games silver '69; coached Cdn Sr. A championships '69-74, 2 silver medals; Western Cdn Masters gold '87; pres., dir. Sport Alta. 8yrs; Calgary Booster Club leadership award '79; mem. Alta. Sport, Cdn Softball halls of fame; res. Calgary, Alta.

FRIESEN, Ron (diving); b. 13 Feb 1949, Saskatoon, Sask.; given name: Ronald George; UofSask, BPHE, UVic, LLB; lawyer; CIAU 3m title '69, 1m, 3m '70-71; bronze 3m '70 Commonwealth Games; ntl 1m, 3m, 10m tower titles '71, 3m, 10m tower '72; mem. '69 FISU, '71 Pan-Am, '72 Olympic teams; most distinguished US phys ed. graduate '71; rec. dir. Oak Bay, B.C. '75-78; res. Vancouver, B.C.

FRITZ, Bill (t&f); b. 14 Aug 1914, Ferry Bank, Alta.; given name: William Duncan; m. Kathleen Nickell; c. David, Jim, Barbara; Queen's, BSc; retired engineer; WOSSA int. 1/4-mile, broad jump, mile relay champion, sr. 220, 1/4-mile setting Windsor, WOSSA records; intercollegiate 1/4-mile, 220 titles; 4th '34 BEG 1/4-mile; ran for Toronto Beaches, West End Y; mem. '36 Olympic, '38 BEG teams; Glasgow 1/4-mile, Munich 400m titles; silver 1/4-mile, gold relay '38 BEG; Victoria State record 47.4 winning Melbourne Australia 1/4-mile handicap race '38; Millrose, Boston indoor 600m titles '38; Queen's Jenkins Trophy for athletic-scholastic excellence; mem. Windsor-Essex Sports Hall of Fame; res. London, Ont.

FRITZ, Bob (football); b. 29 Jul 1909, International Falls, Minn.; d. (circa 1990), Fargo, N.D.; given name: Robert Francis; m. Phyllis Marcille; Concordia College, BA,

Minnesota; retd sporting goods business; all-conf. fullback '31-34; UPI all-American '34; head coach-quarterback-fullback Winnipeg Rugby Club '35-37, '42; all-Cdn QB; player-coach Bombers '37; player-coach Edmonton Eskimos '38-40; mem. '42 Grey Cup finalist Western Canada Air Force team; 3 Grey Cups, 1 winner; life mem. Blue Bomber Alumni Assn.; Blue Bomber certificate of merit '70.

FRITZ, Bud (harness racing); b. 15 Jul 1935, Walkerton, Ont.; given name: William; made driving debut at Elmira Raceway at 14; enjoyed great success with Apaches Fame '90-91 winning NA Cup, Prix d'été, and several other major stakes races; with 1:51.4 mile Apaches Fame became fastest Canadian sired horse of all time; Cdn Horseman of '86; leading driver/trainer in Ont. Sires Stakes '86; through '95 1816 driving victories and purses exceeding $8M; res. Walkerton, Ont.

FROBEL, Doug (baseball); b. 6 Jun 1959, Nepean, Ont.; given name: Douglas Steven; m. Barbara Ann Ambrose; self employed; moved through Ottawa Nepean Canadians system to pro ranks with Pittsburgh organization '77; saw minor league action at A level with Charleston, Shelby, Auburn, Salem, AA with Buffalo, AAA with Portland, Hawaii, Indianapolis, Vancouver; ML with Pittsburgh '82-85, Montreal '85-86, Cleveland '87; pinch runner for Willie Stargell in his final major league game; ended pro career with White Sox farm in Vancouver Triple-A '89; teacher of youth baseball, lecturerer on sports mental excellence; mem. Ottawa, Nepean Sports hall/walls of fame; res. Nepean, Ont.

FROST, Barclay (t&f); b. 6 Jun 1941, Pembroke, Ont.; given name: Barclay William; m. Janet Small; c. Kendra, Kevin, Kirk; Carleton, BA; teacher; mem. '60 HS football champions; HS HJ, LG records; Ottawa HS boys' singles badminton title '61; outstanding HS athlete award '61; active basketball, softball, hockey player; coach Ottawa Harriers pole vaulters; twice competed ntl t&f championships, 3rd '62 long jump; coach 8 consecutive cross-country t&f PS title teams; jumping events official Olympics, Pan-Am Games, Ottawa Citizen Indoor Games, Canada Games; co-chairman Ont. t&f oficials council '80-81; mem. Goulbourn Sports Wall of Fame; res. Munster, Ont.

FROST, Stan (shooting); b. 2 Sep 1939, Montreal, Que.; given name: Stanley Edward; m. Anne; Queen's, BSc; health physicist, v-p environment & safety Cameco; began shooting '53; ntl smallbore team '65-83; gold master's badge '70 world English match rifle championships; team bronze '73 300m free rifle Benito Juarez (World Cup); 3-position Ont. indoor title '73, prone title '74; silver master badge English match '74 worlds; fullbore gold '88 worlds; DCRA 2 Ottawa Regiment, Gooderham, 1 Des Burke, Gibson match titles; several Ont. smallbore prone, standard rifle titles; competed '75 Pan-Am Games, 2 ISU Worlds; won Ont. Lt. Governor '87, Sask. Lt. Governor, Sask. grand agg., PPRA grand agg. '91; 2 ntl 556/.222 titles; 2 Pershing trophy team titles; SFC exec. mem. '68-69, v.-chair. match rifle section '70-75; mem. 10 Bisley teams; DCRA exec. v-p '96-98; res. Saskatoon, Sask.

FROSTAD, Mark (horse racing); b. 19 Jan 1949, Brantford, Ont.; m. Pam; c. Kate, Justine; Princeton, BA, UWO, MBA;

horse trainer; began working summers at father George's Bo-Teek Farm; ran own bloodstock business for several yrs before becoming a trainer '90; guided Bruce's Mill to Sovereign Award champion 3-yr old male '94; principal client Sam-Son Farms; trained Cdn 3-yr old male champion Victor Cooley, Chief Bearhart to Cdn turf male titles '96; Sovereign Award top trainer finalist '96; won '96 Queen's Plate with Victor Cooley, Breeders' Stakes with Chief Bearhart; with Cryptocloser won Prince of Wales Stakes '97; served term as pres. Cdn Thoroughbred Horse Society; trustee OJC; res. Toronto, Ont.

FRY, Barry (curling); b. 21 Dec 1939, Winnipeg, Man.; given name: Barry William; m. Judith Marjorie; c. Ryan Bennet; sales agent; skipped 2 Man. 1 ntl mixed, 1 Man title rinks; skipped '79 Macdonald Brier (last under their sponsorship); 3 Man. senior men's title rinks; 4 carspiel titles; mem. Man. Curling Hall of Fame; res. Winnipeg, Man.

FRY, Gladys (basketball); b. 26 Feb 1907, Kitscoty, Alta.; d. 17 Mar 1991, Calgary, Alta.; given name: Gladys Alberta; m. William Jackson Douglas; c. Robert John, James Gordon; UAlta; lab technician; 4yrs UAlta team; mem. Tipton Tigers, Narsconas; mem. legendary Edmonton Grads '27-36; part of Grads team which played exhibitions in conjunction with '28, '32, '36 Olympics; 161 games, 1679 points, 10.4 avg.; HS t&f champion; twice Edna Bakewell Trophy for highest t&f points UAlta; mem. Canadian Basketball, Alta. Sports Halls, U Alta Sports Wall of Fame.

FRY, Harry (rowing); b. 13 Sep 1905, Dundas, Ont.; d. 1985, Dundas, Ont.; given name: Harry Brittain; m. Elsie Mason; c. Stephanie, Gary, Brian (d); Park Business College; Union Gas employee; began rowing '30 Leander Boat Club; 3rd seat bronze medal crew '30 BEG; 8-oared crew bronze '32 Olympics; retired following '36 Olympics; Hamilton YMCA handball champion '41, '43-45.

FRY, Jay (football); b. 23 Mar 1929, Hamilton, Ohio; given name: Jay Charles; m. Phyllis Anne Burna; c. Jay T, Elizabeth, Julie; Miami, BA, MA; coach; played football, wrestled Miami 50-52; competed Salad (now Fiesta) Bowl title team; mem. MAC title team, all-MAC; coached Celina HS 52-53; player/coach K-W Dutchmen 53-55, all-ORFU 3yrs; coached OAC (now Guelph U) 3yrs; college football/wrestling titles; head wrestling/asst football coach Miami '56-62; guided 1 MAC wrestling, 2 MAC football title teams, Tangerine (now Citrus) Bowl winner; asst football/wrestling coach York '62-63; head wrestling/asst. football coach Indiana only Indiana team to compete in Rose Bowl '68, Big 10 title '67; asst. coach Ottawa (CFL) '70-73, Grey Cup title '73; coach Memphis Southmen (WFL) '74-75, won division title; asst. NY Giants (NFL) '76-78; initiated, operated Can-Am sports camps near Oxford, Ohio many years; mem. Guelph, Miami, Indiana Football, Butler County Sports halls of fame; res. Oxford, Ohio.

FRYATT, Dave (soccer); b. 24 Jul 1921, Chilliwack, B.C.; given name: David Mark; m. Verona Lucille Nicholson; c. Richard, Marcia; accountant; active competitor 21yrs; from '52 administrator provincial, ntl, international levels; BC Soccer Commission secty '52-54, chair. '55-61, '75-81, treas. '52-67; Cdn Soccer Assn. dir. 25yrs, v-p '62, pres. '63-64, p.-pres. '65-67, treas. '69-71; Pacific Coast SL v.-

pres-treas. '57-58, auditor '59-62; secty-treas BC youth soccer 34yrs; CSA exec. '57 World Cup team; founding mem. Vancouver Sun tournament of champions '52; founding mem./dir. West Coast Soccer Society from '86; mem. '73 Canada Summer Games comm., Soccer Canada World Cup comm. '76-77, '79-81; v-p/treas. CSA Alumni Assn '87-98; life mem. BC Youth Soccer Assn., CSA; PCSL appreciation award; 2 Aubrey Sanford meritorious service awards; Kaizen lifetime achievement award; CSA president's outstanding service award; Sport BC dedication to sport award; Centennial medal; mem. BC Sports Hall of Fame; res. Burnaby, B.C.

FRYER, Brian (football); b. 16 Jul 1953, Edmonton, Alta.; m. Barbara Brady; c. Colin, Jason; UAlta BPhE; exec. dir. Football Alta.; set city, Alta. long jump, triple jump records, Cdn hurdles record; receiver, mem. Western Jr. champion Edmonton Huskies '71; 3 times all-conf., all-Cdn, '75 Hec Crighton Trophy winner Alta. Golden Bears; mem. College Bowl champions '72; Eskimos territorial draft '76; 1st Cdn collegian to be drafted by and play for NFL team; only rookie to make Washington NFL lineup '76; 10 games before returning to Canada and CFL; mem. Eskimos '78-85; 5 Grey Cup titles; mem. UAlta Sports Wall of Fame; res. Edmonton, Alta.

FUHR, Grant (hockey); b. 28 Sep 1962, Spruce Grove, Alta.; div. Corrine, Jill; c. Janine, Rachelle, R.J.; m. Candice; c. Kendy; hockey goaltender; jr. Victoria (WHL) '79-81; twice all-star, '80 rookie of year; 1st choice Edmonton '81 entry draft; NHL's 1st black goalie; Edmonton (NHL) '81-91 with brief minor stints in Moncton, Cape Breton; traded to Toronto '91, LA '95, St. Louis '95-99, Calgary '99; 6 NHL all-star games; twice NHL all-star; backstopped Oilers to 5 Stanley Cups; Vezina Trophy '88; shared Jennings trophy '94; NHL record most games by goalie single season 75 ('87-88); twice mem. Team Canada, mem. Team NHL Rendez-Vous '87; served 55 game suspension for cocaine use start '90-91 season; NHL record (through '99): 845 scheduled games, 398-282-112, 47,740min, 25so; 142 playoff games, 8416min, 89-46, 4so; above average golfer; res. Ladue, Mo.

FUHR, Heather (triathlon); b. 19 Jan 1968, Edmonton, Alta.; given name: Heather Sherry; m. Roch John Frey; triathlete; UAlta, BComm; track, cross-country runner UAlta; competed in initial triathlon '89; raced professionally from '91; 3 consec. Japan ironman triathlon titles '95-97; Alabama, Brazil, Cdn powerman titles; won '97 Pacific Grove triathlon; won world ironman triathlon title '97; won '99 Isuzu Ironman women's title; Cdn triathlete of '97; *Triathlete Magazine* long distance triathlete of '97; performance of '97 competitors award; res. San Diego, Calif.

FULLER, Debbie (diving); b. 24 Jun 1966, Montreal, Que.; given name: Debbie Lynne; Ohio State.; gold 3m, 5m, silver 1m '80 Norway Cup; 2 ntl 10m, 1 3m, 1m titles; gold 10m, 3m '86 Commonwealth Games; bronze 3m '87 Pan-Am Games; mem. '80, '84, '88 Olympic, '82, '86 Commonwealth, '83, '87 Pan-Am, '86 worlds, '85 FISU, NZ Games, Australian Open teams; '87 sport excellence award; mem. Cdn Aquatic Hall of Fame; res. Pte. Claire, Que.

FULLER, Rose (softball); b. 17 Mar 1954, Vancouver, B.C.; given name: Rosemary Ann; UVic, MEd; Nikken distributor, therapist, ex-teacher; began playing organized softball at 14; at 16 mem. Victoria Vicettes Sr. B team; with catcher Joanne Mick developed series of intricate hand codes to communicate; righthanded pitcher whose fastball was clocked at 120 km/h; mem. silver medal Canada Games team; joined Sr. A Green & Louis team (later Doc's Blues/Alpha Sports) '74; played key role 10 consecutive provincial, 6 ntl championships; competed '77 Tokyo Friendship Games; mem. silver medal '78 world championships team; during '78 season posted spectacular 52-1-2 record; mem. 6 intl. tours teams; named one of top 3 female pitchers in world; frequent MVP, top pitcher, all-star awards; rejected US pro offers; retd. from competition '83 but continued conducting free pitching, coaching clinics; Victoria female athlete of '75; mem. BC Sports, BC, Vancouver, Cdn Softball halls of fame; res. Cobble Hill, B.C.

FULLER, Wendy (diving); b. 8 Jan 1965, Montreal, Que.; given name: Wendy Marie; m. Scott Reich; Miami; 3yrs competitive gymnast; mem. ntl diving team '79-88; sister Debbie also on team; 10m gold, 1m, 3m silver Germany, 10m gold, 3m silver Switzerland '80 European tour; silver 10m Dive Canada '81; silver '87 Pan-Am Games; mem. '81 NZ Games, '83 Commonwealth Games teams, '85 FISU Games, '87 FINA World Cup, Pan-Am Games teams; mem. '88 Olympic team; res. Miami, Fla.

FULTON, Greg (administration); b. 8 Dec 1919, Winnipeg, Man.; m. Angela Bombardier (d); c. Robert, Byrne, Rebecca; UAlta, BComm.; hon. CFL secty-treas; developed play-by-play summaries as student newspaper reporter; statistician Stampeders '50-66; compiled 1st CFL official record manual '66; mem. CFL rules comm. from '64; editor Official CFL Playing Rules from '67; CFL hon. secty-treas. from '67; helped organize CFLPA pension plan '67; 1st recipient Commissioner's Award '90; mem. Cdn Football Hall of Fame; res. Toronto, Ont.

FULTON, Jack (lacrosse); b. 30 Jul 1926, New Westminster, B.C.; m. Jean Kemp; c. Craig, Jackie; Marine College; retd. deputy fire chief; mgr. New Westminster Salmonbellies '56-66; exec.-mem. Cdn Lacrosse Assn. '67-74, pres. '71-72; GM ntl team '74 world championships; governor Cdn Lacrosse Hall of Fame '67-73, chair. '74-81; treas. jr. Salmonbellies '75-78; mem. Cdn Lacrosse Hall of Fame; res. New Westminster, B.C.

FULTON, Ken (golf); b. 8 Dec 1943, Prince Rupert, B.C.; given name: Kenneth William; m. Sheila Ross Fairty; c. Stacey, Kari, Erin, Katherine, Jennifer; Ariz. State, BSc; golf centre owner/operator; Arizona State amateur title '65; played on PGA tour '68-73; 2 ntl club pro titles; CPGA Seniors title '96; mem. European Seniors tour '97; res. Port Hope, Ont.

FUNG, Lori (rhythmic gymnastics); b. 21 Feb 1963, Vancouver, B.C.; m. J.D. Jackson; ntl all-around titles '82-83; mem. 4-Continent club title team '82; gold all-around '84 Olympics as sport became part of Olympic program 1st time; turned to coaching following '88 retirement; mem.

Order of Canada, Cdn Amateur, BC Sports halls of fame; res. Vancouver, B.C.

FURLONG, Jim (football); b. 13 Apr 1940, Lethbridge, Alta.; Tulsa; teacher; play with Calgary junior Bronks earned Tulsa athletic scholarship; offensive end, punter, Missouri Valley Conference all-star '62; linebacker, punter Calgary '62-73; CFL career record: 707 punts, 28,898yds, 40.9 avg., 37 singles; WFC all-star '65; res. Lahr, W. Germany.

FUZESI, Mary (rhythmic gymnastics); b. 21 Feb 1974, Budapest, Hungary; moved to Canada age 3; began rhythmics at 9; mem. ntl team from '86; spurred by success of Lori Fung, scored first international victory in Greece '89; Cdn elite title '90; 3 gold, 1 silver, 1 bronze '90 Commonwealth Games; gold, silver, bronze medals in '90 French competitions; 3 bronze medals in Bulgaria '90, 3 gold Four Continents competition Japan, bronze world cup Belgium; 2 gold, 2 silver, 2nd overall '91 Pan-Am Games; '88 Elaine Tanner trophy; res. Thornhill, Ont.

G

GABLER, Wally (football); b. 9 Jun 1944, Royal Oak, Mich.; given name: Wallace Gabler III; m. Jacqueline Bescoby; c. Wallace IV, Tamara, Melissa; New Mexico Military Institute, Michigan, BA; investment dealer, v-p Nesbitt Burns; HS all-state defensive back; jr. college all-American NMMI; Michigan QB '65 Rose Bowl champions; pro Toronto '66-68, '72, Winnipeg '69-70, Hamilton '71; CFL career record: 854 completions, 1690 attempts, 13,080yds, 61tds; res. Burlington, Ont.

GABRIEL, Brian (shooting); b. 5 Aug 1956, Kitchener, Ont.; given name: Brian Bruce; licensed electrician; skeet specialist; ntl team '79-89; mem. '80 Olympic, '82 Commonwealth, '83 Pan-Am Games; ntl title '82; team gold '82 Commonwealth Games; silver Pan-Am Games '83; 50th anniversary all-Cdn title '82; Cambridge athlete of '80; fed. govt. excellence award '83; res. Kitchener, Ont.

GABRIEL, Tony (football); b. 11 Dec 1948, Hamilton, Ont.; given name: Tony Peter; m. Diane Ellen Gaudaur; c. Benjamin Daniel, Laura Daniele, Shane Bradley; Syracuse, BSc; stockbroker; split end, broke most of Syracuse major pass receiving records; NCAA record 2 TDs in just over 2 minutes; pro Hamilton '71-74; 3 last minute catches set up Hamilton 13-10 Grey Cup victory '72; CFL playoff record 15 receptions vs. Ottawa '74 semifinals; Ottawa '75-81; 3 Grey Cup finals, 2 winners; 5 times EFC leading receiver; 5 times 1000-plus yards in receptions single season; caught passes in 161 games including pro record 138 consecutive games; CFL record 8 seasons catching passes every game; CFL career record: 614 receptions for 9841yds, 69tds; 11 times EFC all-star, 8 times all-Cdn; 4 Schenley Canadian player of year awards; Jeff Russel Memorial Trophy '78; Schenley Outstanding Player award '78; 3 Lew Hayman EFC outstanding Canadian awards; Canadian player of game '76 Grey Cup; caught Grey Cup winning TD pass from Tom Clements; Shopsy award '76; Canadian Superstars TV series winner '76; mem. Ottawa, Canada's Sports, Cdn Football halls of fame; res. Burlington, Ont.

GADSBY, Bill (hockey); b. 8 Aug 1927, Calgary, Alta.; given name: William Alexander; m. Edna Anne Marie; c. Brenda, Judy, Donna, Sandy; retd. P.R., sales rental crane co.; golf range dir.; jr. hockey Edmonton; pro Kansas City (USHL), Chicago '46-54, NY Rangers '54-61, Detroit '61-66; coach Detroit '68-69; 3 times 1st, 4 times 2nd team all-star defenceman; collected close to 600 stitches during 20yr NHL career; never on Stanley Cup winner; while Chicago capt. '52 stricken by polio but returned to become 3rd player in NHL history to play 20 seasons; with Pierre Pilote shared record most assists by defenceman single season and led NHL defencemen 437 lifetime assists (both later topped by Bobby Orr); NHL record: 1248 scheduled games, 130g, 437a, 1539pim, 67 playoff games, 4g, 23a, 92pim; 2yrs coach Edmonton Oil Kings, '67 league title; mem. Red Wing Oldtimers team; mem. Alta Sports, Hockey halls of fame; res. Southfield, Mich.

GAGE, Bob (builder); b. 1 Jan 1920, Smithville, Ont.; UWO (Assumption Coll.), BA, UofT, BSW; retd sports writer; played active role in promotion of amateur sport at high school, university levels; key role in compiling history of HS sport in London; Fred Sgambati media award; Doug Gilbert media award; Cdn Sports Advisory Council award; initial recipient CIAU media award; OFSAA outstanding contribution to t&f award; CIAU Football Coaches Assn. award; Cdn Amateur Wrestling Assn. media award; Ont. Achievement award; Ntl. Assn., Basketball Coaches merit award; federal govt. Tribute to Champions award; hon. life mem. CIAU Information Directors; life mem. Basketball Hall of Fame; mem. UWO W Club, OUAA Football Legends halls of fame; res. London, Ont.

GAGNÉ, Maurice (cycling/speed skating); b. 2 Dec 1936, Amqui, Que; competitive cyclist '58-67; mem. '58, '62 Commonwealth Games, '58 world championships teams; competitive speed skater '58-72; ntl indoor mass start champion '70-71; ntl indoor mass start records; NA, ntl outdoor titles '66; Canada Games title '67; Que. skater of year award; honored by CASSA for participation in development of sport in Que.; mem. Canadian Speed Skating Hall of Fame; res. Charlesbourg, Que.

GAGNIER, Ed (gymnastics); b. 1 Feb 1936, Windsor, Ont.; m. Carolyn; c. Bonnie, Becky; Michigan, BSc, MA; retd. gymnastics coach; Canadian jr. athlete of '54; mem. '56 Olympic team; Big 10 all-around champion '57; Mich Yost honor award '57-58; Iowa State gymnastics coach '63-85; 3 times NCAA coach of year; coach US FISU games team '70, 10 Big-8 conf. champions, 3 NCAA ntl title teams; gymnasts he coached won 16 individual NCAA, 71 Big 8 titles, 53 all-America honors; mem. US Olympic gymnastics comm., chair. NCAA Gymnastics rules comm.; mem. US Gymnastics Foreign Relations Comm.; pres. National Assn. College Gymnastics Coaches; varied ISU athletic dept. admin. roles; mem. US Gymnastics, ISU Sports halls of fame; res. Ames, Iowa.

GAGNON, Marc (speed skating); b. 24 May 1975, Chicoutimi, Que.; began skating age 6; following on heels of brother Sylvain and coaching parents; is regarded as "the Wayne Gretzky" of the short track speed skating world; mem. ntl team from '91; overall gold '90 Canada Winter Games, NA short track championships '92, Lake Placid International '92; 8 gold, 6 silver, 1 bronze world short track championships; overall, relay gold '95, '98 world team, 1500m, 3000m, overall world individual '98 championships; 4 '95, 2 '94 Bormio Cup gold; 1000m bronze '94 Olympics; with Derrick Campbell, François Drolet, Éric Bédard '98 Olympic 5000m relay gold; serious back injury in '93 competition but rebounded to winning form; 2 gold, 1 silver '96 China Challenge; set world 1000, tied 500m world short track records; res. Montreal, Que.

GAGNON, Sylvain (speed skating); b. 30 May 1970, Dolbeau, Que.; began speed skating to improve hockey skills; numerous ntl, NA age-group titles; mem. ntl team '89-98; 2 Cdn senior 5000m relay records; silver short track 5000m relay '89 worlds, '92 Olympics; 2 gold world team championships '95; 3 gold, 1 silver '95 Bormino Cup; Korea Challenge match relay gold '93; world short track 1500m gold '93; 2 Cdn International Challenge gold; res. Montreal, Que.

GAIN, Bob (football); b. 21 Jun 1929, Akron, Ohio; m. Mary Katherine Bastin; c. Jenny Lynn, Janis, Judy Ann; Kentucky, BA; retd.; earned all-State honors in West Virginia high school days; twice All-American at Kentucky; Outland Trophy as top college lineman in US; 1st pick Green Bay (NFL) '51 draft; dealt to Cleveland but opted for season in CFL with Ottawa before joining Browns '52; CFL all-Cdn '51; def. tackle, middle linebacker, def. end with Browns; placement kicker; competed in Orange, Sugar, Senior Bowls, College all-star game and only Great Lakes Bowl; played on several pro all-star teams, 5 Pro-Bowl games; in 13 pro seasons scored 1td on 22yd pass interception '60; Southeastern Conf. player of quarter century '50-75; mem. Upper Ohio Valley Dapper Dan Club, West Va., City of Cleveland, Akron-Summit County, National Football Foundation College, King's Island, Kentucky Athletic, Cleveland Sports halls of fame; res. Timberlake Village, Ohio.

GAINES, Gene (football); b. 26 Jun 1938, Los Angeles, Calif.; given name: Eugene Carver; m. Marion Backstrom; c. Ellen Courtney, Eugene Jr., Elaine Carla; UCLA, BSc; football coach; pro Montreal '61, Ottawa '62-69, Montreal (player-coach) '70-76; outstanding def. back; 42 career interceptions returned 683yds; returned kickoff 128yds in playoff vs. Hamilton '64; Jeff Russel Memorial Trophy '66; 6 Grey Cup finals as player, 4 winners; 5 all-EFC, 3 all-CFL; asst. coach Montreal '76-80, '96-98, Edmonton '81-82, Los Angeles (USFL) '83, Houston (NFL) '84-85; Winnipeg '86-90, BC '91-95; mem. Cdn Football Hall of Fame; res. California.

GAINEY, Bob (hockey); b. 13 Dec 1953, Peterborough, Ont.; given name: Robert Michael; m. Cathy (d); c. Anna, Stephen, Laura, Colleen; hockey exec.; hon. degree Trent U; jr. Peterborough Petes; 1st Montreal pick, 8th overall '73 amateur draft; defensive forward; Team Canada '76, '81; NHL playing record: 1160 scheduled games, 239g, 262a, 182 playoff games, 25g, 48a; NHL coaching record: 376 scheduled games, 154-171-51, 44 playoff games, 23-21; 8yrs team capt. Canadiens; coach Epinol France '89-90; Minnesota North Stars, Dallas Stars '89-96, GM from '92; mem. 6 Stanley Cup winners; 4 Frank Selke Trophies; 1 Conn Smythe Trophy; Cdn Society of NY achievement award; AGM Team Canada '96 World, '98 Olympic teams; mem. Canada's, Peterborough Sports, Hockey halls of fame; res. Coppell, Tex.

GAIRDNER, Bill (t&f); b. 19 Oct 1940, Oakville, Ont.; given name: William Douglas; m. Jean Donalda Sparling; c. Christine, Emilie, Ruthann, Billy, Franklin; Colorado, BA, Stanford, MA, PhD; former pres. Fitness Institute; decathlete; mem. '63 Pan-Am, '64 Olympic, '66, '70 Commonwealth Games teams; decathlon silver '63 Pan-Am; PB: 7147 decathlon points '64 Olympics, 14.2 in 110 hurdles, 51.3 in 400 hurdles, 10.9 100m, 22' long jump,

49'2" shot put, 5'10" high jump, 48.8 400m, 156' discus, 12'6" pole vault, 196'8" javelin, 4:24.5 1500m; ran PB 400 hurdles age 32; varied exec. roles municipal, provincial, ntl t&f, skiing associations; pres. Canadian Masters Cross-Country Ski Assn.; 4th ntl Masters 30k cross-country '80; 1st degree judo black belt; TV color commentator '76 Olympics, '77, '79 t&f World Cup, '78 Commonwealth Games; res. King City, Ont.

GAIT, Gary (lacrosse); b. 4 Apr 1967, Victoria, B.C.; Syracuse; pro coach/player; began playing age 4; with twin brother Paul helped Syracuse win 3 NCAA titles '88-90; mem. ntl team from '89; mem. Mount Washington Wolfpack '92-93, Philadelphia Wings, Detroit Turbos '93-97, Baltimore Thunder from '98; 7yr pro career (through '97) 209g, 160a in 61 scheduled games; 2 Enners awards as NCAA Div. 1 player of yr; 2 McLaughlin awards as NCAA Div. 1 midfielder of yr; 3 1st team all-American; Brine Award NCAA Div. 1 title game MVP '90; 2 NCAA playoff scoring titles; set US intercollegiate Lacrosse Assn. season goal scoring record; mem. 4 Cdn, 1 US field lacrosse teams, 2 major indoor league titles, 1 Minto, 1 Mann Cup title teams; mem. '94 World Cup team; res. Syracuse, N.Y.

GAIT, Paul (lacrosse); b. 4 Apr 1967, Victoria, B.C.; Syracuse; promotional rep.; began playing age 4; with twin brother Gary helped Syracuse win 3 NCAA titles '88-90; mem. ntl team '89-98; competed '90 North-South game; mem. NCAA 25th anniversary team; mem. ntl team 3 World games; mem. Detroit Turbos, Mt. Washington Wolfpack, Rochester, Philadelphia Wings, Syracuse Smash teams; also played on OLA, WLA teams; '89 Brine award; 1 NCAA playoff scoring title; 3 1st team all-American; mem. 4 Cdn, 1 US field titles, 2 major indoor, 1 Minto, 1 Mann Cup titles; 3 major indoor league, 2 Minto Cup, 1 Mann Cup MVP awards; 2nd team NLL all-star '98; 1 MILL scoring title; mem. '94 World Cup team; res. Syracuse, N.Y.

GALBRAITH, Clint (harness racing); b. 22 Jul 1937, Tara, Ont.; c. Don; campaigned on Buffalo/Batavia circuit from '57; dominated NY Sire Stakes with Nick Kash, Top Freight, Bye Bye T, Pastabyrd; time-trialed trotter ABC Freight in 1:57.1 as 2-year-old; campaigned legendary Niatross, harness horse of '79-80, winning Woodrow Wilson Pace, Kentucky Pacing Derby '79, Little Brown Jug, Messenger Stakes, Meadowlands Pace, Prix D'été, Oliver W. Holmes, Gaines Memorial, Cane Pace, Dancer Memorial, Battle of Brandywine; set world records with Niatross, Call For Rain; more than 2700 winners, $17 million in purses; res. Scottsville, N.Y.

GALBRAITH, Sheldon (figure skating); b. 24 May 1922, Teulon, Man.; given name: Sheldon William; m. Jeanne Schulte; c. Jeannie, Brian, Kathy, Barbara Jane, Mary Louise; figure skating teacher; California Pacific Coast jr., sr. champion '37-40; US ntl titles '39-40; pro Ice Follies '40-43; pro Ottawa Minto Club '46-47, Seattle '48-49, Toronto skating club '49-97; Olympic team coach '48, '56, '60; pupils include world champions Barbara Ann Scott, Frances Dafoe, Norris Bowden, Barbara Wagner, Bob Paul, Donald Jackson; key role in founding Cdn. Pro Skaters Assn.; mem. Cdn Figure Skating, Cdn Olympic, Canada's Sports halls of fame; res. Aurora, Ont.

GALE, Bill (harness racing); b. 18 Oct 1948, Toronto, Ont.; m. Janice Johnston; c. Jason, Jennifer; introduced to driving by Morris MacDonald; dominated dashwinning, UDR titles Windsor Raceway; Wolverine, Hazel Park throughout '80s; became a key figure on OJC circuit in '90s; through '97 won 74 major stakes races including '86 Breeders Crown with Sunset Warrior, Maple Leaf Trot with Program Speed; more than 6200 career victories, $39M in purses; res. Eden Mills, Ont.

GALLANT, Georgie (t&f); b. 4 Dec 1928, Shediac, N.B.; given name: Georges Joseph; 5 Boston Marathon runs, top Cdn '52 placing 20th overall; successive Dartmouth Natal Day 6-mile race victories '56-62; 5 8-mile Halifax Natal Day race titles; 3 New Glasgow 5-mile race titles; res. Cap Pele, N.B.

GALLANT, Peter (curling); b. 20 Dec 1958, Charlottetown, P.E.I.; m. Leanne; c. Brett, Christopher; salesman; began curling age 13; skipped PEI 4 ntl mixed championships winning Cdn title '87; 2nd for Peter Jenkins '82 Brier; 3rd '91, '93, '95, '97, '99 PEI Brier representatives; res. Charlottetown, P.E.I.

GALLEN, Winnie (basketball); b. 4 Jul 1917, Mawer, Sask.; d. 5 Feb 1996, Sherwood Park, Alta.; m. William John Reid; c. Ian, Suellen, Melanie; mem. HS basketball title team; mem. famed Edmonton Grads '36-37, '39-40; 6 prov. shot put, discus medals; mem. 3 prov. title softball teams; 1yr pro softball Chicago; mem. Muttart Lumber hockey team; 4 Northern Alta. zone curling titles, '71 Alta sr. ladies' titlist; mem. Canadian Basketball, Alta. Sports halls of fame.

GALLEY, Garry (hockey); b. 16 Apr 1963, Montreal, Que.; m. Terry-Lynn Callaghan; c. Shaylynn, Wyatt; Bowling Green (communications major); played minor hockey in Ottawa; CJHL Gloucester; defenceman; BGU CCHA '83-85 div., '84 NCAA champs; 2 1st team CCHA all-star, NCAA all-American '84; drafted by Los Angeles '83; brief AHL stint in New Haven; played NHL Los Angeles '84-87, '97-99, Washington '87-88, Boston '88-92, Philadelphia '92-95, Buffalo '95-97; NHL record: 1023 scheduled games, 110g, 440a, 85 playoff games, 7g, 23a; topped 1000 career penalty minute mark '97; 2 Barry Ashbee top Flyers defenceman, 1 Punch Imlach awards; competed 1 Stanley Cup final, 2 all-star games; mem. Team Canada '93, '97 (silver) worlds; with Dave Ellett owns All-Star Saloon in Almonte; res. Almonte, Ont.

GALLINGER, Stephen (boxing); b. 10 Jun 1974, Port Colborne, Ont.; stockboy; heavyweight; gold Canada vs. USA 91kg; '94 Commonwealth Games silver 91kg; res. St. Catharines, Ont.

GAMBLE, Dick (hockey); b. 16 Nov 1928, Moncton, N.B.; given name: Richard Frank; mem. Moncton Bruins Maritime Jr. champions '45, Que. sr. all-star team '51; NHL Montreal '51-53, '55-56, Chicago '54-55, Toronto '65-67; mem. '52 Stanley Cup winner; 11 AHL seasons Buffalo, Rochester; 4 AHL all-star teams; mem. 3 Calder Cup champions; coach Rochester Americans '68-71; NHL record: 195 scheduled games, 41g, 41a, 14 playoff games, 1g, 2a; AHL MVP '66; AHL record 4 seasons 40-plus goals, 11 seasons 30-plus goals, most goals (131) 3 consecutive

seasons '64-67; mem. Rochester Americans, NB Sports halls of fame; res. Leroy, N.Y.

GARAPICK, Nancy (swimming); b. 24 Sep 1961, Halifax, N.S.; given name: Nancy Ellen; UAlta, Dalhousie.; teacher; mem. ntl team '74-83; 14 ntl gold, 15 silver, 13 bronze; 1 world championship silver, bronze; 2 Canada Cup gold, 1 silver, 2 bronze; 1 4-Nations Cup gold, bronze; 1 Japanese nationals gold; 1 Australian nationals bronze; 1 Pan-Am silver, 3 bronze; 2 Olympic bronze; 3 CIAU gold plus a wide array of gold, silver and bronze won in numerous ntl, international competitions; world record 2:16.33 200m backstroke '75, 100m backstroke 1:03.28 (during heat) '76 Olympics; 5 ntl records; mem. '76, '80 Olympic, '79 Pan-Am, '78 Commonwealth Games teams; Bobbie Rosenfeld Trophy '75; with Diane Jones (Konihowski) shares '75 Velma Springstead award; seriously injured cycling accident '83; Governor-General's silver medal '76, AUAA swimmer of '82; mem. Cdn Amateur, NS Sports halls of fame; res. Halifax, N.S.

GARDINER, Charlie (hockey); b. 31 Dec 1904, Edinburgh, Scotland; d. 13 Jun 1934, St. Boniface, Man.; given name: Charles Robert; emigrated to Canada age 7; excelled in baseball, rugby, hockey; goaltender Selkirk intermediates at 14; with Winnipeg Maroons APHL '26-27; Chicago (NHL) '27-34; NHL record: 316 scheduled games, 112 victories, 2.02 GA avg; 21 playoff games, 1.37 GA avg.; 47 career shutouts; Vezina trophy '32, '34; 3 1st team, 1 2nd team all-star; 1 Stanley Cup winner; mem. Man. Sports, Man., Cdn Hockey halls of fame.

GARDINER, Herb (hockey); b. 8 May 1891, Winnipeg, Man.; d. 11 Jan 1972, Winnipeg, Man.; given name: Herbert Martin; played with Winnipeg Victorias '08-09, Bankers League '10-11; served Cdn Army overseas '15-18; Calgary Tigers '19-26; joined NHL at 35 with Montreal '26-29; player/coach Chicago '29 returning to Canadiens for playoffs; dealt to Boston then Philadelphia Arrows of Can-Am league; mem. Man. Hockey Hall of Fame.

GARDINER, Tyrone (boxing); b. 2 Apr 1939, Sydney, N.S.; m. Floria MacKeigan; c. Jamie; correctional officer; began boxing '54; Maritime lightweight, Eastern Cdn titles '61; Cdn lightweight title '63; retd undefeated '66; mem. Cdn Professional Boxing Assn., Cape Breton Boxing Comm.; pres. Venetian Gardens Boxing club; mem. NS Sports, Cdn Boxing halls of fame; res. Cape Breton, N.S.

GARDNER, Cal (hockey); b. 30 Oct 1924, Transcona, Man.; given name: Calvin Pearly; m. Mary Malone; c. David, Paul; retd account exec., Telemedia; centre CUAC, Winnipeg Esquires; Winnipeg Rangers '43 Memorial Cup champions; leading scorer, MVP NY Rovers (EHL); NY Rangers '45-48, Toronto '48-52; Stanley Cup winning goal '49; mem. '51 Stanley Cup winner; Chicago '52-53; Boston '53-57; NHL record: 696 scheduled games, 154g, 238a, 61 playoff games, 7g, 10a; playing-coach, MVP Springfield (AHL); leading scorer Providence; playing-coach Kingston (EPHL); leading scorer Cleveland Barons (AHL); both sons played in NHL; color commentator 3yrs Bruins, later Leafs network; son Paul (ass't coach Nashville Predators) had 10-yr NHL career; Man. Hockey Hall of Fame; res. Toronto, Ont.

GARE, Danny (hockey); b. 14 May 1954, Nelson, B.C.; given name: Daniel Mirl; sports broadcaster, ex-coach; jr. Calgary Centennials; 2nd Buffalo choice '74 amateur draft; Buffalo '74-81, Detroit '81-86, Edmonton '86-87; twice attained 50-goal plateau, 50 '76, 56 '80; 2nd team all-star right wing '80; Team Canada '76, '81; NHL record: 827 scheduled games, 354g, 331a, 64 playoff games, 25g, 21a; color commentator Tampa Bay '92-93; asst. coach Tampa Bay '93-96; Sabres broadcaster '89-92, '97-98; res. Nelson, B.C./Buffalo, NY.

GAREAU, Jacqueline (t&f); b. 10 Mar 1953, L'Annonciation, Que.; m. Gilles; c.Yannick; respiratory technician, operates sporting goods store; marathon specialist; l'Ile d'Orleans, Montreal International, Skylon, National Capital, Los Angeles marathon titles; competed 5 Boston marathons winning '80 race after Rosie Ruiz sham discovered; ntl 10km road race, 10,000m titles '85; 5th '83 world championships; 2 ntl sr. records; mem. '84 Olympic team; mem. Que. Sports, Cdn Road Running halls of fame; res. Boulder, Colo.

GARLAND, Lynda (baton twirling); b. 10 May 1948, Hamilton, Ont.; given name: Lynda Van Sickle; m. Wayne Garland; McMaster; assoc. registrar Mohawk Coll.; secty. WBTF '81-83; chair. WBTF amateur rules commission, international clinics commission '80-83; founder, pres. Twirl Canada; Cdn rep. WBTF '79-83; chairman Ont. chapter '72-75, '79-82; pres. WBTF from '94; ntl, international judge; coached ntl sr. women's gold medalists '81-82; res. Hamilton, Ont.

GARNEAU, Louis (cycling); b. 9 Aug 1958, Quebec City, Que.; m. Monique Arsenault; c. William, Edouard, Victoria; Laval , B.A.; pres./ designer sport apparel mfgr. co.; 4 ntl titles, 3 road race, 1 time trial; 1 Que., Hamilton GP, GP du Carretour, Montreal GP, Beauport GP titles; mem. '84 Olympic, '78, '82 Commonwealth, '83 FISU, '82-83 world championships teams; res. St-Augustine de Desmaires, Que.

GARROW, Alex (basketball); b. 3 Jan 1937, St. Regis, Que.; d. 6 Aug 1997, Fort Erie, Ont.; given name: Alexander Edwin; m. Carol Harris; c. Terrence, Kathryn, Patrick; Alabama, Algonquin College; nickname "Chief"; all-Catholic Buffalo HS basketball; Alabama on basketball scholarship '57-58; Tillsonburg Livingstons '60-61; mem. national title team '60; plan to turn pro Elmer Ripley's Washington ABA team scrapped through injury which sidelined him '62 season; mem. '63 Yvon Coutu team Montreal, sr. league MVP '63-64; capt. 1st Que. team '67 Canada Winter Games; coached Nepean bantam basketball.

GARSIDE, Bert (bowling); b. 16 Aug 1931, Toronto, Ont.; given name: Bert Kenneth; m. Hester MacDonald; c. Brian, Tracy, Caron, Michael; retd.managing dir. Ontario 5-Pin Bowler's Assn.; bantamweight who backed boasts with actions; standout pool player, bowler; once tied Russian chess master while still in HS; 4 perfect 450 games; lifetime 255 average; record 15 consecutive TV appearance victories; won every major tournament except O'Connor Open during competitive days; mem. Scarborough record-setting ntl championship men's team; moved into bowling administration '59; dir. Canadian Bowling Congress '62-66; exec. dir. CBC, OBC from '66; instrumental formation

1st Toronto bowlers' assn., Master Bowlers' Assn.; founder, pres. Scarborough Proprietors', Scarborough Bowlers' Assn.; created bowling equipment (shoes); syndicated newspaper instruction column, several instruction manuals; invented instant average calculator; collated, rewrote 5-pin rule book; key role establishing bowling as recognized sport on Ont., ntl scene; helped unify East-West, standard scoring system, equipment standards; Scarborough Sports and Recreation Assn. award; Builders of Bowling Industry award '79; mem. Ont. 5-Pin Bowling Hall of Fame; res. Pickering, Ont./Florida.

GARTNER, Mike (hockey); b. 29 Oct 1959, Ottawa, Ont.; given name: Michael Alfred; m. Colleen; c. Joshua, Natalie, Dylan; pro hockey player; jr. Niagara Falls '76-78; OHA rookie of year '76-77, all-star '78; mem. Team Canada world jr. team '78; Washington 1st pick, 4th overall '79 draft; pro Cincinnati WHA '78-79, RW Washington NHL '79-89, Minnesota '89-90, NY Rangers '90-94, Toronto '94-96, Phoenix '96-98; NHL record: 1432 scheduled games, 708g, 627a, 122 playoff games, 43g, 50a; reached 50-goal plateau with 50 '85; 30 or more goals 15 consecutive seasons; with 611th career goal 9 Mar '94 moved into 5th place on all-time list; achieved 700g plateau '97; 7 NHL all-star games; mem. Team Canada for 4 Canada Cup, 2 World tournaments; 2 NHL fastest skater awards; ESPN TV analyst; pres. NHLPA; active in varied charitable organizations; res. Toronto, Ont.

GARVIE, Clarence (coaching); b. 1912, Saskatoon, Sask.; d. 23 Jan 1993, Saskatoon, Sask.; given name: Clarence Harry; m. Vi Woods; c. Marion, Gordon (d), Neil, David; UofSask, BA, BSc; HS principal; standout swimmer, football, hockey player at college, mem. 8 title teams; coached football, t&f, swimming various levels in Sask.; established Saskatoon, Riverdale TC; established SHSAA '50, pres. '52-53; pres. Saskatoon Hilltop jr. football club '68; wrestling chairman '71 Canada Games; officiated pole vault event '76 Olympics; mem. Sask., Saskatoon, Uof Sask. Sports halls of fame.

GARVIE, Gord (wrestling); b. 25 Oct 1944, Saskatoon, Sask.; d. 7 Aug 1988, Saskatoon, Sask.; given name: Gordon Taylor; m. Joan Katherine Willness; c. Trona Lee, Lana Katherine, Carla Vi, Barton Minor; UofSask, BA, BEd, MSc, UAlta, PhD; asst. professor, wrestling, football coach; football Nutana Blues '59-61, Saskatoon Hilltops '62-65, Saskatchewan Huskies '66-69, 7 times all-star, MVP Blues, Hilltops; Western Canada Hec Crighton award nominee '69; hockey to jr. A level; CIAU wrestling titles '67-69, ntl amateur title '69; UofSask. athlete of '66-69; mem. '68 Olympic, '69 world championships teams; player-coach Thunder Bay Mustangs football club '70-71; Lakehead U wrestling coach '70-75; coached 5 ntl open titlists; mgr. '73 FISU Games team, asst. coach Toledo World Cup team; coach '74 Commonwealth, '74-76 World Cup, '76 Olympic teams; mem. Cdn Wrestling, Sask., Saskatoon, Lakehead U, Uof Sask. Sports halls of fame.

GASSIEN, Reg (harness racing); b. 11 Aug 1949, Lindsay, Ont.; began competitive driving career at 16 and paid his dues racing on fairground circuit before graduating to OJC circuit '81; equalled Greenwood track record with 6 consecutive race victories on one card; involved in 2 triple dead heats; believed to be only driver to have participated in a pair of triple ties; through '97 won 2,700 races and totalled more than $13M in purses; several Kawartha Downs driving titles; among most frequent winners were Jo Car Lyn, Treecoscious, Cathedra, Our Jude and Lantern Light; res. Lindsay, Ont.

GASTON, Cito (baseball); b. 17 Mar 1944, San Antonio, Tex.; given name: Clarence Edward; m. Denise; c. Adrian, Carly; baseball exec.; outfielder minors with Binghamton, Greenville, West Palm Beach, Batavia, Austin, Richmond ('64-68) Santo Domingo, Leon Mexico ('79-80); major leagues '67-78 with Atlanta, San Diego, Pittsburgh (NL); ML playing record 1026 scheduled games, 3120ab, 314r, 799h, 106 2b, 30 3b, 91hr, 387rbi, .256ba; turned to coaching Atlanta '81, Toronto '82-89; mgr. Blue Jays '89-97; 2 World Series winners; Jays batting coach 2000; ML managerial record 681-635; 1st Afro-American to manage WS winner; Canada's baseball man of '89; mem. Blue Jays Wall of Distinction; res. Dunedin, Fla.

GATE, George (swimming/coaching); b. 11 Dec 1924, Carlisle, Cumberland, Eng.; given name: George Frederick; div.; c. Richard, Diane, William, Brenda; aquatic dir. Pointe Claire; coach Ocean Falls, B.C. '50-63, Pte. Claire from '65; coached '54 Commonwealth, '63 Pan-Am, '68 Olympic, '73 world championships, '77, '81 Maccabiah Games; Swim Canada special recognition award; dir. Swim Canada; mem. Cdn Aquatic, Que., BC, Canada's Sports halls of fame; res. Pointe Claire, Que.

GATLEY, Lyle (rowing); b. 22 Sep 1945, Vancouver, B.C.; given name: Lyle Daryle; m. Donna Hoffman; c. Kevin, Alisa; UBC, BEd, MA; teacher; mem. ntl jr. record-setting 4x440 relay track team; UBC varsity 8s '67; pairs with Jack Ulinder; mem. '68 Olympic team; res. Delta, B.C.

GAUDAUR, Jake Jr. (football/administration); b. 5 Oct 1920, Orillia, Ont.; given name: Jacob Gill Jr.; m. Isobel Grace Scott; c. Jacqueline Gaye, Diane Ellen, Janice Arlene; retd. football exec.; son of former world pro rowing champion; '38 NA schoolboy rowing singles, ntl jr. singles; ntl sr. mile rowing title '41; mem. '39 ntl jr. lacrosse champion Orillia Terriers; 1st pro football at 19 Hamilton; Toronto '41; mem. '42 Grey Cup champion RCAF Hurricanes; mem. 8-player group who purchased, operated ORFU Toronto Indians '45-46; simultaneously played pro lacrosse Hamilton Tigers; co-capt. '47 Montreal Alouettes, lacrosse Que. Montagnards; capt. '48-49 ORFU champion Hamilton Tigers; capt. '50-51 Tiger-Cats; retd to become Hamilton club dir.; reactivated '53 to centre Hamilton to Grey Cup victory; club pres. '54; pres.-GM '56-68; EFC pres. '59; CFL pres. '62; dir. Canadian Football Hall of Fame '63-84, mem. selection comm. '68-84, chair. '78-84; CFL commissioner '68-84; chair. CFL players pension advisory board, rules comm.; chair. CFL management council '81-84; governor Canada's Sports Hall of Fame; Officer Order of Canada; mem. Cdn Football, Canada's, Orillia, Copps Coliseum Sports halls of fame; res. Burlington, Ont.

GAUDAUR, Jake Sr. (rowing); b. 3 Apr 1858, Orillia, Ont.;d. 11 Oct 1937, Orillia, Ont.; given name: Jacob Gill; m. Cora Coons (d); Ida Harris (d); Alice Grace Hemming (d); c. 6 sons, 6 daughters; pro oarsman, boat livery, fishing guide; 1st race at 17; 3rd to Ned Hanlan, James Riley; 1st significant race in shell 1879 Barrie regatta; challenged Hanlan's conqueror, William Beach, losing by length; 1887-97 set records nearly every time he rowed; from 1892 world's best oarsman; 3-mile record 19:6 Austin, Tex., 1893; lowered mark 1894 to 19:1.5 (still stands); beat Jim Stanury for world's pro title 1896, defended 1898 vs. Robert Johnson of Vancouver; retired following loss to Australia's George Towns 1901; mem. Canada's, Orillia Sports halls of fame.

GAUDET, Oscar (hockey); b. 27 Oct 1941, Moncton, N,B,; m. Peggy; Labatt's sales rep.; helped Moncton Bears '75 and Moncton Hawks '79 win Hardy Cup; pro with Chicago (NHL) organization; league titles with Buffalo AHL '64, Dallas CHL '69, Portland WHL '71; CHL scoring title '67-68; never fewer than 20 goals in a season during pro career; 482 points in 447 pro games; Dallas MVP '68-70; Maritime sr. league assist record '62-63 with 110; AHL rookie of '64 award; mem. Moncton, NS, NB Sports halls of fame; res. Moncton, N.B.

GAUTHIER, Gèrard (officiating/hockey); b. 5 Sep 1948, Montreal, Que.; m. Shirley Williams; c. Michael, David; 2trs officiating at jr. level; attended 1st NHL training camp '71; made NHL debut as linesman 16 Oct '71; reached 2000 game plateau '98; worked 2 NHL all-star games, 2 Canada Cup series, 7 Stanley Cup finals; '98 Olympics; NHL record (through '98): 2009 scheduled games, 239 playoff games; res. Dollard des Ormeaux, Que.

GAUTHIER, Pierre (administration/hockey); b. 28 May 1953, Montreal, Que.; m. Manon Roberge; c. Catherine, Vincent; Syracuse, BSc, Minn, MSc; hockey exec.; scout Quebec Nordiques '83-85, asst. dir. scouting '86-88, chief scout '89-93; AGM Anaheim '93-95, GM Baltimore Bandits (AHL); GM Ottawa Senators '95-98; President/GM Anaheim from '98; GM Team Canada world championship silver medal team '96; with Bob Clarke, Bob Gainey helped assemble '97 world championship gold medal, '98 Olympic teams; res. Irvine, Calif.

GAVILLUCCI, Angelo (t&f/wheelchair basketball); b. 3 Jul 1960, Melbourne, Australia; office clerk; shot put, discus, javelin specialist; wheelchair basketball player; mem. Ottawa Lions TFC; world shot put record; ntl shot put, discus records; Ont. , EO shot put, discus, javelin records; mem. ntl team from '90; competed '94 worlds; '98 Paralympics sledge hockey team; Ottawa Lion's TFC President's award '94; res. Ottawa, Ont.

GAY, Mary (golf); b. 16 Sep 1931, Toronto, Ont.; retd supervisor payroll and records; Ont. Open '52, 3 times runnerup; 5 times runnerup Canadian Open, 3 times runnerup Cdn Closed; mem. Cdn ladies' team 2 UK tours, 3 Ont., 2 Alta. interprovincial teams; skip '62-63 Ont. Business Girls curling champions; mem. Waterloo County Hall of Fame; res. Waterloo, Ont.

GAYFORD, Tom (equestrian); b. 21 Nov 1928, Toronto, Ont.; m. Martha West; c. Margaret, Mary, Janet, Virginia, Elizabeth; UofT; retd stockbroker. co. dir.; began riding age 2, competing age 8; with father, Major Gordon Gayford, first father-son combination to compete internationally; mem. '59, '67, '71 Pan-Am Games, '70 world, '52, '60,

'68 Olympic teams; coached ntl equestrian teams '72, '80 Olympic, '78 world, '79, '83 Pan-Am Games teams; mem. '59 3-day gold team, capt. '71 Pan-Am Games; mem. '68 Olympic gold Prix des Nations team; Rothman modified GP, ntl horse show jumping titles '72; US Horse Show, NY puissance titles 3 successive years; set NA puissance record '63; when horse Big Dee mysteriously beaten in stall retd from competition '72; CdE Cdn ntl jumping team 5 Nations Cup gold, 2 Pan-Am silver; designed Montreal '76 Olympic jumping course; international team coach '78-96; Cdn horseman of '62; founding dir. Toronto Polo Club; competed in polo; licensed owner-trainer OJC steeplechase circuit; helped reorganize Ntl Hunt & Steeplechase Assn '50; branched into thoroughbred training through '84; dir., exec. Cdn Hunter Society; bred War Life Governor General's Cup winner RWF '57; ntl dir. Cdn Pony Club 5yrs; chair. equestrian div. Coaching Assn.; ntl chair. Level 3 jumping program; founding dir. CEF '77. exec. through '98; qualified intl jumper judge, course designer; founding dir. OEF, dir. best ever program; mem. Cdn Amateur, Canada's Sports halls of fame; res. Stouffville, Ont.

GEE, Gordon (curling/motorsport); b. 2 Sep 1931, Virden, Man.; given name: Gordon Edward; m. Elaine Carol Olsen; c. Timothy Hardy, Leslie Fay; retd. racing team crew chief; goalie jr. B hockey Lenore, Man.; jr. curler Man.; 3rd '79 Fairbanks Alaska International bonspiel champions; twice 3rd Whitehorse International 'spiel champions; 3rd '80 Yukon, '81 Territories Brier entries, 2nd '82 Territories Seagram mixed entry; raced stock, sprint cars throughout Yukon, Alaska, '75-76 championships; last known res. Whitehorse, Yukon.

GEIGER, Marla (curling); b. 19 Dec 1970, Nanaimo, B.C.; began curling age 8; Industry Canada co-ordinator; BC HS girls, prov., ntl jr. title rinks '87; world jr. title rink '88; BC jr. champion, runnerup ntls '89, BC mixed fnalist '92; 3rd 2 Kelley Law (Owen) BC STOH title rinks, 2 runnerup; won Saskatoon Ladies Classic '96; bronze '97 Olympic trials; res. Vancouver, B.C.

GELINEAU, Jack (hockey); b. 11 Nov 1924, Toronto, Ont.; d. 12 Nov 1998, St. Bruno, Que.; McGill , BComm; retd. seniors home mgr.; goalie RCAF team during WW2; played with Jr. Canadiens '44-45, McGill '45-49 posting 48-21-2 record; intermediate basketball, football, varsity baseball; tryout with Boston (AL); capt. McGill '46 Queen's Cup title; while still attending university was called up to Boston (NHL); Calder Trophy '50; dealt to Chicago following salary squabble with Jack Adams; NHL record: 143 scheduled games, 46-64-33, 8580min, 447ga, 7so, 4 playoff games, 1-2, 7ga, 1so; retd '54; hon. pres. Redmen hockey team; McGill male athlete of '48; British Empire Medal for wartime bravery; mem. McGill Sports Hall of Fame.

GELLARD, Kim (curling); b. 6 Nov 1974, Toronto, Ont.; UWO, BA; admin. asst. Scotia McLeod; skip ntl jr. title rink '93, world jr. '94; 3rd for Marilyn Bodogh '96 STOH, world title rink; competed as Team Canada mem. '97 STOH; competed '97 Olympic trials; skipped Ont. '99 STOH; Cdn female team of '96 award; res. Markham, Ont.

GENDRON, Francine (t&f); b. 16 Nov 1955, Montreal, Que.; U of Quebec Montreal; teacher; ntl jr. 800m, 500m titles '75; sr. 800m '77, 1500m '79; sr. 400m hurdles '75, '77; ntl outdoor 1000m record 2:36.9, 400m hurdles 58.23, indoor 600m 1:30.8, 1000m 2:45.3; ntl sr. indoor 800m, 1500m titles '78; gold 800m Canada vs, Italy '78; mem. '77 FISU, '78 Commonwealth, '79 Pan-Am, FISU, World Cup, 1980 Olympic teams; '81 Que. university 600m, 1000m, 300m, ntl 800m titles; res. Laval, Que.

GENDRON, Gilles (harness racing); b. 20 Jan 1945, Quebec City, Que.; sep; promising hockey player; turned to pro driving '67; trained by Marcel Dostie; NA record 232 victories Blue Bonnets '72; twice Cdn rep. world driving championships, 3rd '79; 13 consecutive 200+ victory seasons racing almost exclusively Blue Bonnets until he was expelled from track in '85 for reasons never explained; continued racing exclusively in US; among top 10 NA 7 times; winner 10 Blue Bonnets driving titles; became 9th NA driver to surpass 4000 victory plateau 1985; res. Hudson, Que.

GENEREUX, George (shooting); b. 1 Mar 1935, Saskatoon, Sask.; d. 10 Apr 1989, Saskatoon, Sask.; given name: George Patrick; m. Lee; c. Andrea, George; Uof Sask, BA, McGill, MD; diagnostic radiologist; trap specialist; at 13 1st major competition title; 3 successive Man.-Sask. jr. titles; NA jr. championship, Sask. title, tied 2nd world finals, gold '52 Olympics; Lou Marsh trophy '52; ntl jr. athlete of year; rheumatoid arthritis ended sporting career at age 20; Saskatoon citizen of year; mem. Saskatoon, Cdn Amateur, Canada's, Sask. Sports halls of fame.

GENG, Lijuan (table tennis); b. 15 Jan 1963, Hebel, China; m. Horatio Pintea; c. James Ross; Carleton; pizza business owner; began playing age 8; won '85 world doubles, silver in singles, while representing China, under name He Zhili; mixed doubles world gold '87; double gold Czech Open, 1st ever for Cdn table tennis athlete; '89 English Open, '90 German, Hungarian, '91 Czech, '92 French, Italian Open, '95 US, '95-96 NA singles titles; with Julie Barton finalist women's doubles '90 worlds; undefeated during '89-90 Canada Cup season; 5 gold '95 Pan-Am Games. mem. '96 Olympic team; 5 ntl title sweeps; 1st Cdn woman to win World Cup medal with bronze '97; 1st ranked female player Canada, NA, 10th world; with husband played professionally in Germany '90-94; Ottawa ACT table tennis award '97; res. Ottawa, Ont.

GENGE, Ronald (archery); b. 4 Aug 1922, Camaru, New Zealand; m. Rose; c. Lois Daphne, Colin Leslie, Christopher Ian, Gregory Floyd; retd. cabinet maker; made own bow, other equipment and launched archery career '36; 15 competitive years all branches of sport, target, field, hunting, flight; moved to Canada '57; made, repaired archery equipment, conducted instruction classes; mem. organizing comm. ntl coaching program; ntl level archery coaching co-ordinator '66-79; '72 Olympic coach, archery official '76 Olympics; conducted 1st ntl training camp '72; international judge candidate to world governing body (FITA) '72-76; Canada's technical lecturer to Olympic solidarity seminars '77, '80; mem. Alta. advisory comm. ntl coaching development program; lecturer IOC coaching seminar '78; hon. life mem. Federation of Canadian Archers; Scoula Centrale Dello Sport of Rome award, Queen's jubilee medal, Australian Archery Assoc. award; level 4 coaching status; res. Edmonton, Alta.

GENOIS, Rèjean (tennis); b. 30 Dec 1952, Quebec City, Que.; given name: Joseph George Rèjean; m. Marie Falardeau; c. Annie, Maxime; Florida State.; tennis pro, accountant; '71 jr. Davis Cup title; pro tour '75; leading player '76 Rothman Grand Prix tour; mem. 7 Davis Cup teams; top seed Canada '76-78; 84th world rankings '78; ntl indoor title '81; led 3-2 Davis Cup qualifying round victory over Colombia '83; Quebec City athlete of '73; pres. Quebec Tennis Fed. '89-98; mem. Que. Sports Hall of Fame; res. Loretteville, Que.

GEOFFRION, Bernie (hockey); b. 14 Feb 1931, Montreal, Que.; m. Marlene Morenz; c. Linda, Robert, Danny; business exec.; nicknamed "Boom Boom"; pro debut '50-51 Montreal; Calder Memorial Trophy rookie of year '51-52; 2nd player to score 50 goals single season '60-61; retd '64; coached Quebec City 2 consecutive pennants; drafted by NY Rangers '66-68; retd due to ulcers; Rangers coach briefly, coach Atlanta '72-75, Canadiens briefly '79; NHL record: 883 scheduled games, 393g, 429a, 132 playoff games, 58g, 60a; Atlanta TV color commentator, publicity dir.; 2 Ross, 1 Hart trophies; mem. 7 Prince of Wales Trophy, 6 Stanley Cup winners; mem. Canada's Sports, Hockey halls of fame; res. Marietta, Ga.

GEORGE, Ed (shooting); b. 27 Jul 1904, Miami, Man.; d. 29 Mar 1988, Winnipeg, Man.; given name: William Edison; m. Aurora Johnson; c. Ronald, Rae, Beverly, Linda; UMan, dairy dip.; retd Cominco sales mgr.; internationally renowned target rifle shooter, coach; with son Ron dominated Sask. shooting scene '51-71; St. George's Cross (top 25 in Commonwealth); 15 prov. titles, 15 Governor-General's silver medals; mem. 1st Cdn team to win all international team prizes '69 Bisley matches; qualified 6 Bisley teams, competed 5; '58 Bisley grand aggregate, City of Ottawa match; hon. life mem, Sask., Man. rifle, fish & game assoc.; secty. SPRA '57-64; mem. Sask. Sports Hall of Fame.

GEORGE, Ron (shooting); b. 1 Oct 1937, Winnipeg, Man.; given name: Ronald Edison; m. Leni Mayer; c. Mark, Shari, Scott; UofSask, MEng, MSc, Waterloo, PhD; consultant, ex-pres. ACTC Technologies Inc.; with father Ed dominated Sask. shooting scene '51-71; St. George's Cross, 15 prov. titles, 15 Governor-General's Silver medals; mem. 18 ntl, 20 prov. teams; mem. 1st team to win all international team prizes '69 Bisley; Queen's gold badge (3rd) Bisley; pres. SPRA '64-71; exec. mem. Alta. football assn., Sport Alta.; mem. Sask. Sports Hall of Fame; res. Calgary, Alta.

GERARD, Eddie (hockey); b. 22 Feb 1890, Ottawa, Ont.; d. 7 Aug 1937, Ottawa, Ont.; given name: Edward George; m. Lillian Mackenzie; c. Ailsa, Margaret; printer; active hockey, baseball, cricket, canoeing as teenager; with Don Mackenzie Dominion canoe tandem title at 15; backfielder Rough Riders '09-13; defenceman Senators '13-24; team capt. '20-21; mem. 4 Stanley Cup winners, 1 on loan to Toronto St. Pat's; coached Montreal Maroons to '26 Stanley Cup; managed NY Americans '30-32; rejoined Maroons '33; St. Louis Eagles '34 but illness forced him to retire mid-

season; mem. Canada's, Ottawa Sports, Hockey halls of fame.

GERELA, Ted (football); b. 12 Mar 1944, Powell River, B.C.; Washington State; played soccer as youth but was conventional style place kicker Washington State; discovered Gogolak brothers NFL success with soccer-style kicking so altered own style; pro running back, placement kicker BC Lions '67-73; Dr. Beattie Martin Trophy; twice 5 field goals single game; CFL record: 132 converts, 123 field goals, 69 singles, 570 points; CFL scoring leader '68; res. Powell River, B.C.

GERIS, Harry (wrestling); b. 22 Nov 1947, Netherlands; given name: Harry Ted; m. Jo-Anne Kathleen Knight; c. Jason Scott, Shawn Joseph, Ryan Alexander; Oklahoma State, BSc; insurance broker; Ont. HS titles '66-67; 5 ntl Open FS, 3 GR unlimited class titles; US ntl jr. college heavyweight title '68; heavyweight silver '72 AAU, USWF championships; bronze '75 Pan-Am Games; AAU heavyweight title '76; mem. '66 Commonwealth, '73 FISU, '72 NCAA, '72, '76 Olympic teams; pres. Ont. Olympic Wrestling Federation '77-79; pres. London Wrestling Club; mem. Cdn Wrestling, Ntl Junior College Wrestling halls of fame; res. London, Ont.

GERVAIS, Hec (curling); b. 4 Nov 1933, St. Albert, Alta; d. 19 Jul 1997, St. Albert, Alta.; given name: Hector Joseph; m. Helen Bowman (d); c. Janet, Sandy, Hector Jr., Stanley, Kim; farmer; football Edmonton Wildcats, '53 tryout with Eskimos; 9 times Northern Alta. provincial curling playdown rep, 4 titles; 2 Brier titles, '61 world title; Toronto Tournament of Champions, 2 Calgary Masters titles; known for push shot; freelance broadcaster at major curling events; mem. '87 Edmonton Brier comm.; Curl Canada Brier MVP award bears his name; mem. Cdn Curling, Alta. Sports halls of fame.

GERY, Marcel (swimming); b. 15 Mar 1965, Smolenice, Czechoslovakia; m. Michaela; c. Nathaniel, Nolan; Seneca College; real estate broker; began swimming age 8; mem. Czech ntl team; defected to Canada '86; mem. Cdn ntl team '87-94; freestyle, butterfly specialist; 20 ntl titles; Cdn records 100, 200 FS, 100 fly; held world short course 100 fly record '90-94; 1 Commonwealth record; 2 Rome Seven Hills, 1 France International, 11 World Cup races, 2 Fina Cup, 1 Quebec Cup, 1 Monte Carlo gold medals; '90 Commonwealth Games 4x100 medley relay gold, 100m fly silver, 4x100m FS relay bronze; Olympic 4x100 medley relay bronze '92; ranked 1st World Cup butterfly '90-91; Ont. athlete of '91; mem. Ont. Aquatic Hall of Fame; res. Aurora, Ont.

GETLIFFE, Ray (hockey/golf); b. 3 Apr 1914, Galt, Ont.; m. Lorna; c. John, Lorna; retd. textile co. executive; pro hockey Boston '36-39, Montreal '39-45; mem. 2 Stanley Cup winners; 5 goals for Habs vs. Bruins '43; NHL record: 393 scheduled games, 136g, 137a, 45 playoff games, 9g, 10a; mem. Ont. Willingdon Cup winner '38; pres. QGA, '60, RCGA '69; governor RCGA '61-75; hon. life gov. '78; mem. Canadian Srs GA, American Srs GA, US Eastern GA, Southern Srs GA; res. London, Ont.

GETTY, Don (football); b. 30 Aug 1933, Westmount, Que.; given name: Donald Ross; m. Margaret Inez Mitchell; c. Dale, David, Darin, Derek; UWO, BA; retd. politician, investment firm owner; teamed with Jackie Parker, Johnny Bright, Normie Kwong in Edmonton backfield '54; quarterbacked Eskimos to '56 Grey Cup victory over Montreal; topped WIFU in yds-per-completion '59, runnerup to Russ Jackson Cdn player of year; WIFU passing leader '61; 10yr CFL completion avg. .536; dir. Eskimos football club; Alta. MLA '67-80, 2 ministerial portfolios; Premier Alta. '85-92; past dir. Derrick Golf and Winter Club; officer Order of Canada '99; mem. Eskimos Wall of Honor, UWO W-Club, OUAA Football Legends halls of fame; res. Edmonton, Alta.

GIACOMIN, Ed (hockey); b. 6 Jun 1939, Sudbury, Ont.; ex-goaltender; after failing to stick with Jr A, Detroit Red Wings clubs returned to Sudbury to play 2 seasons Midnight Industrial League; joined EHL Washington Presidents '69, advanced to Providence AHL; spent 7 seasons in minors before joining NHL NY Rangers '65-75; 9 shutouts in 2nd season led Rangers to playoffs; 5 time all-star; traded to Detroit '75-78; NHL record: 289w, 54so, 2.82 goals against avg.; jersey #1 retd by NY; mem. Hockey Hall of Fame; res. Ft. Myers, Fla.

GIARDINO, Wayne (football); b. 7 Nov 1943, Peterborough, Ont.; given name: Wayne Maurice; m. Nancy Von Fielitzsch; c. Nicole, David; Florida State, BA; retd football exec.; capt. FSU, all-state running back; rejected Dodgers baseball invitation for football scholarship; college baseball world series '65; linebacker, occasional fullback Ottawa '67-76; Gruen Trophy (EFC rookie of year) '67; Hiram Walker Trophy; Schenley outstanding Canadian nominee '71; frequent all-star; dir. personnel Ottawa '83-87; asst. coach '84; asst. coach UofOtt '90; coach Ottawa Sooners '94; asst coach, media consultant Hamilton '95-96; ass't coach, Orlando, AFL '97; res. Almonte, Ont.

GIBBONS, Pops (softball); b. 24 Aug 1916, Nevis, St. Kitts; d. 2 Jul 1998, Scarborough, Ont.; given name: Percy Walston; m. Irene MgGregor; c. Ginger, Nancy, Percy Jr., Shane, Lori, Scott; employed Champion Team Ware; active player in youth; interest in coaching and training remained throughout his life; exceptional coach of young players; had a great love for children and was known as "Pops" to all; served as usher Maple Leaf Gardens more than 25yrs; trainer NA Fastpitch Assn. World Series champion Scarborough Royals '96; trainer Toronto Gators '93 ISC world title team; subject of YTV special '97; a familiar figure at tournaments throughout Ontario and country working with wide array of teams; to his death he reported daily for duty at Champion Team Ware.

GIBEAU, Marie-Josée (canoeing); b. 2 Nov 1972, Lachine, Que.; m. Ouimet; mem. ntl team '88-90, '93-96; bronze '89 Junior Worlds; gold K-4 500, silver K-2 500 '95, K2, K4 gold '99 Pan-Am Games; world K-2 200m, K-4 200m champion '95; gold K-2 '98 worlds; competed '96 Olympics; Edmonton Grads team award; res. Lachine, Que.

GIBSON, Bryan (boxing); b. 10 Nov 1947, Kentville, N.S.; given name: Bryan Richard; m. Teresa Ann Dorey; c. Curtis, Chad; stationary engineer; Montreal Expos tryout camp '69;

Que. Golden Gloves middleweight champion '71-76; Eastern, ntl titles '74-75; NA light heavyweight title '75; middleweight bronze '74 East German championships; '76 Eastern ntl middleweight title; mem. '75 Pan-Am, '76 Olympic teams; res. Kentville, Kings Co., N.S.

GIBSON, Cheryl (swimming); b. 28 Jul 1959, Edmonton, Alta.; given name: Cheryl Ann; m. Ralph Brokop; c. Andrew, Lindsay; Arizona State, BSc, CA; lawyer, accountant; mem. ntl swim team '74-82, '76, '80 Olympic, '75, '79 Pan-Am, '78, '82 Commonwealth Games teams; silver 200m butterfly, 400m IM, bronze 200m backstroke, 200m IM '75 Pan-Ams, silver 100m, 200m backstroke, 400m medley relay '79 Pan-Ams, silver 400m IM with PB ntl record 4:48.10 '76 Olympics, gold 200m backstroke, bronze 100m backstroke, 400m IM '78 Commonwealth Games; 4 1sts, 1 2nd '77 Canada Cup meet; 2 silvers '78 worlds, setting Commonwealth record 2:14.23 200m backstroke; 2 1sts US ntls '76; 3 1sts, 1 2nd '81 US Intercollegiate; 4 1sts '81 ntls; gold 4x100 medley relay, silver 200m IM '82 Commonwealth Games; 11yrs dir. Swimming Canada; 4yrs Alta. Sport Council Tech Comm.; mem. sponsor comm. '96 World Figure Skating championship; co-chair Swimming World Cup Society; chair. unsuccessful bid by Edmonton to hold '99 World Swimming championship; Alta. Premier's award '77, Velma Springstead Trophy '76, Governor-General's silver medal '76, Edmonton athlete of '77, Arizona State female athlete of '81, female swimmer of '76, '78; Edmonton YWCA woman of distinction award '98; mem. Cdn Aquatic, Alta. , Ariz. State Sports halls of fame; res. Edmonton, Alta.

GIBSON, Doug (hockey/softball); b. 28 Sep 1953, Peterborough, Ont.; given name: Douglas John; 3yrs Peterborough Jr.A, breaking Mickey Redmond's goal-scoring mark; Memorial Cup finalist '72; centre AHL Rochester Americans '73-80 with NHL stints with Boston Bruins, Washington; mem. Garmisch-Partenkirchen '81 German title team; twice AHL MVP, 1st team all-star; '75 AHL scoring champion; Hockey News minor league player of '75; softball standout at 2nd base and pitching; Peterborough player of '78; mem. Rochester Americans, Peterborough Sports halls of fame; res. Peterborough, Ont.

GIBSON, George (baseball); b. 22 Jul 1880, London, Ont.; d. 25 Jan 1967, London, Ont.; m. Margaret McMurphy; c. Marguerite, George Jr., William; pro baseball player, bricklayer; round face earned him nickname "Mooney"; moved from semi-pro to pro ranks Eastern (later IL) League Buffalo, Montreal; catcher Pittsburgh (NL) '05-16, NY Giants '17-18; ML career record: 1203 games, .236ba, 15hr, 331rbi; best season '14 batting .285 in 102 games; considered among game's best handlers of pitchers; strong arm made him one of few catchers with 200 assists in single season; 1st player to catch 150 games single season '09; mgr. Pirates '20-22, '32-34, Chicago Cubs '25; coach Washington '23, Toronto (IL) '34; World Series winner '09, finalist '17; Canada's baseball player of half century '50; all-time all-star catcher with Pirates; mem. Canada's Sports, Baseball halls of fame.

GIBSON, Jack (builder/hockey); b. 10 Sep 1880, Berlin (Kitchener), Ont.; d. 7 Oct 1955, Calgary, Alta.; Detroit Medical School; dentist; outstanding player with OHA intermediate champs 1897; instrumental in organizing Portage Lake team '02, capt., leading scorer; recognized for organizing 1st pro league in world, the International League '04 with teams from Houghton, Calumet, Sault Ste. Marie, Mich., and Pittsburgh and Sault Ste. Marie, Ont.; Portage Lakes team, considered one of finest ever assembled challenged Ottawa Silver Seven and Montreal to championship series but were refused; when star players were lured back to Canada he set up dental practice in Calgary; mem. Hockey Hall of Fame.

GIBSON, Jack (builder); b. 27 May 1931, Peterborough, Ont.; given name: John William; served as coach, manager, convenor, pres. PCCHL '61-62; 9yrs mgr. Peterborough Jr. B team; with Neil Thompson operated Peterborough softball teams '61-66; mgr. Mann Cup title teams '66, '73; helped organize semipro league '68, won title '69; mgr. Maryland Arrows in pro league '74-75; 1st team to play in Landover Cap Centre; mgr. Canada's field lacrosse team '67 world championships; mem. Peterborough Sports Hall of Fame; res. Peterborough, Ont.

GIFFORD, Heather (water polo); b. 24 Mar 1956, Ottawa, Ont., m. Shaun Seaman; c. Eben, Logan, Hannah; Queen's, BPhE; goaltender; introduced to water polo Canterbury HS '72; mem. Team Ont. '74-82; mem. Ottawa Water Polo team '73-82; ntl team '77-82; key role in Canada's world championship title '81; made major contribution to sport coaching City of Ottawa jr. women '80-82; v-p Ont. Water Polo Assn. '81-82; player rep. Ont. Water Polo Coaches Comm. '77-81; v-p, dir. responsible for ntl women's team development Water Polo Canada '83-85; commissioner Cdn Water Polo League '83; mem. Ont. Aquatic Hall of Fame; res. Kanata, Ont.

GIGUERE, Nathalie (swimming); b. 16 Jan 1973, Quebec City, Que.; freestyle, breaststroke specialist; 6 ntl titles; competed '89, '91, '93 Pan-Pacific championships, '91 world, '92 Olympic, '90, '94 Commonwealth Games; gold 200m breaststroke '90 Commonwealth Games; res. Charlesbourg, Que.

GILBERT, Don (curling); b. 28 Jun 1930, St. Thomas, Ont.; d. 4 Oct 1998, St. Thomas, Ont.; given name: Donald Alexander; m. Patricia Marie Anderson; c. Michael, David, Stephen, Jeffrey; UofT, DDS; dentist; 2nd on Ont. Colts title rink '59; skipped Dunker Trophy winner '63 OCA Colts competition; 3rd '61 OCA Governor-General's trophy winner; 2 OCA Silver Tankard winners; skip '68 Ont. Brier entry, 6-4 record Kelowna; hon. life mem. St. Thomas CC.

GILBERT, Don (football/coaching); b. 6 Oct 1943, Buffalo, N.Y.; given name: Don Alan; m. Patricia Gale Tananbaum; c. Eric Jonathon, Kara Ann; Buffalo, BEd, MEd; real estate agent; 12 major HS athletic letters, various community awards, 6 major college letters while starring in football, basketball, baseball; Dom Grossi Award (outstanding Buffalo U athlete) '65, Penn State Award (outstanding student-athlete) '65; defensive back, reserve QB Ottawa (CFL) '66-67, Winnipeg '68; head football coach UofOtt '71-75, 5 consecutive conference titles, Canadian College Bowl title '75; CIAU football coach of '75; coach Rough Riders '74 CFL all-star game victory; TV color commentator

Buffalo Bills '80; mem. UofOtt Football Hall of Fame; res. East Amherst, N.Y.

GILBERT, Glenroy (t&f/bobsled); b. 31 Aug 1968, Port of Spain, Trinidad; Louisiana State; moved to Canada '76; began competing long and triple jump 15; won TJ silver '85 jr. ntls; LJ gold, TJ silver '86; shifted attention to sprints winning Pan-Am Games 100m gold '95; 2nd to Donovan Bailey's sub-10 second 100 '95 LSU Invitational; 4x100 relay gold '94 Commonwealth, '96 Olympic Games, '95-97 worlds; '93 world championship silver; 100m PB 10.04 '95, 20.37 in 200 '93; competed '88, '92, '96 summer Olympics, '90, '94 Commonwealth, '95, '99 Pan-Am, '89, '94 Francophone, '93 FISU Games; '99 PAG 4x100 relay silver; mem. 4-man bobsleigh team '94 Olympics; 2 Cdn sr. records; 2 Dick Ellis team awards; Ottawa ACT athlete of '96, athletics award '97; res. Ottawa, Ont.

GILBERT, Rod (hockey); b. 1 Jul 1941, Montreal, Que.; given name: Rodrigue Gabriel; m. Arunee Leeaphorn; hockey exec.; jr. A Guelph; OHA scoring leader, Red Tilson Memorial Trophy; pro NY Rangers farm system; Rangers regular '62-78; 1st, 2nd team all-star once each; Team Canada '72; NHL career record:1065 scheduled games, 406g, 615a, 79 playoff games, 34g, 33a; West Side Assoc. Trophy Rangers' MVP; Bill Masterton Memorial Trophy '76; NHL milestone award '82; mem. Hockey Hall of Fame; Lester Patrick trophy '91; NY mgr. community relations; youth hockey clinic instructor; jersey #7 retd by NY; res. New York, N.Y.

GILBEY, Janice (water polo); b. b. 10 Oct 1957, Ottawa, Ont.; d. 7 Feb 1984, Toronto, Ont.; Algonquin Coll.; launched competitive career Canterbury HS '72; joined Ottawa league '73; Team Ont. '75-79, ntl team '79-82; world championships gold '81; mem./asst. coach Toronto Golden Jets '83; v-p women's development Ont. Water Polo Assn. '83; diagnosed with leukemia '83; mem. Ont. Aquatic Hall of Fame.

GILCHRIST, Jack (weightlifting); b. 16 Mar 1938, Brantford, Ont.; m. Lois Audrey Clifford; c. Paul Timothy Clifford, Sharon Roselyn; traffic mgr.; began lifting Woodstock club age 13; served in various exec. roles Woodstock club '56-71; launched Lambeth Athletic Club '64; began coaching '60; became level 2 IWF referee '67; exec. roles in Ont., Cdn Assns.; instrumental in preparing rule manuals; pres. OWA '71-77; Ont. rep. CWF, IWF rep.; varied admin. duties at ntl, intl levels; tech. official '76 Olympics; team mgr. '78 Commonwealth Games; conducted numerous officials, coaching clinics; Ont. distinguished service award '71; CWA outstanding contribution award '76; last known res. Lambeth, Ont.

GILES, Peter (canoeing); b. 18 Apr 1970, London, Ont.; mem. ntl team from '88; '91 Pan-Am Games bronze K-1, K-2, K-4 1000; gold K-4 500, silver K-4 200 Milano World Cup '96; competed '96 Olympics; res. Lake Echo, N.S.

GILES, Steve (canoeing); b. 4 Jul 1972, St. Andrews, N.B.; mem. ntl team from '89; mem. '92, '96 Olympic teams; silver C-2 1000, C-1 500, 200 '96 Milano World Cup; competed 7 World championships earning bronze C-1 500m

'93, gold C-1 1000m '98; C-1 1000m gold, 500m silver '99 Pan-Am Games; '99 Duisburg regatta C-1 1000m gold; res. Lake Echo, N.S.

GILL, Nicolas (judo); b. 24 Apr 1972, Montreal, Que.; Quebec; began competing age 6; mem. ntl team from '89; 10 ntl titles; 86kg bronze '92 Olympics, gold '94 US Open, '95, '99 Pan-Am Games, Hungarian Open '95, Belgian Open '96; competed '89 Francophone, '90 Commonwealth, '91, '95, '99 Pan-Am, '92, '96 Olympic Games, '91, '93, '95 worlds; 1st Cdn to win worlds silver '93, bronze '95; 4th degree black belt; Viscount Alexander trophy '92; res. Montreal, Que.

GILLETT, George (softball); b. 21 Feb 1934, Hoyt, Sunbury Co. N.B.; m. Anna; CFB truck driver; coach/mgr./prompter/exec. more than 40yrs; coached 37 provincial, 14 interprovincial title teams; zone dir. Softball NB; organized '84 Eastern Cdn intermediate championships; Joe Garagan award for contribution to greater Fredericton area softball; mem. NB Sports Hall of Fame; res. Hoyt, N.B.

GILLICK, Pat (baseball/administration); b. 22 Aug 1937, Chico, Calif.; m. Doris Sander; c. Kimberley; SouthernCal, BSc; baseball exec.; mem. USC college world series titlists '58; semipro Edmonton '58; 5ys lefthanded pitcher Baltimore farm system, 45-32 record; asst. farm dir., scouting dir. Houston '64-73; co-ordinator player dev., scouting NY Yankees '74-76; v-p player personnel Toronto '76; exec. v-p baseball operations '77-94; GM Baltimore '95-98, Seattle '99; Canada's baseball man of '83; 2 ML baseball exec. of yr awards; mem. Cdn Baseball Hall of Fame; res. Seattle, Wash.

GILLIS, Duncan (t&f); b. 3 Jan 1883, Cape Breton, N.S.; d. 1965, Vancouver, B.C.; policeman; silver 16lb hammer throw '12 Olympics; BC hammer record unsurpassed until '67; ntl heavyweight wrestling title; flag-bearer '12 summer Olympics; mem. Cdn Amateur, BC Sports halls of fame.

GILLIS, Eddie (baseball); b. 6 Oct 1916, New Waterford, N.S.; given name: Eddie Martin; Dalhousie; retd teacher, baseball coach; Triple A rated Cape Breton Colliery pro league at 17; 5'5.5", 135lb second baseman, all-star status rookie season; outstanding player awards '35, '48 all-star games; player-coach Waterford Strands '39, 2 Cape Breton titles; coached New Waterford Maritime bantam champs '70, int. champs '38, NS juvenile champs '60, bantam champs '45; Halifax ntl jr. champs '76, Kentville ntl jr. finalists '62-63, NS ntl jr. finalists '64, NS entry '77 Canada Games; NS juve. title '61, sr. '60, '63, Maritime midget '60, 7 NS HS title teams; Maritime jr. '53, NS sr. '80, runnerup ntl championships '81; pro scout Milwaukee Braves, St. Louis Cardinals; baseball dir. Cooper Sports Camp '70; conducted successful boxing clubs Cape Breton, Kentville, Halifax 20yrs producing numerous amateur, pro titlists at provincial, ntl levels; mem. famed Caledonia rugby team; mem. NS Sports Hall of Fame; res. Kentville, N.S.

GILMOUR, Billy (hockey); b. 21 Mar 1885, Ottawa, Ont.; d. 13 Mar 1959, Montreal, Que.; given name: Hamilton Livingstone; m. Merle Woods; c. Germaine; McGill, engineer; Ottawa Silver Seven '02-06, right wing 3 consecutive Stanley Cup winners; 10 goals 7 games, 5 in 4

playoff contests rookie season; Montreal Victorias Eastern Canada Amateur HA '07; Ottawa Senators '08-09, won Stanley Cup, 11 goals 11 games; retired 6 seasons; tried '15-16 2 game comeback with Senators, scored against George Vezina, then retired; mem. Ottawa, Hockey halls of fame.

GILMOUR, Buddy (harness racing); b. 23 Jul 1932, Lucan, Ont.; given name: William; m. Gwen Harner; c. 4; ret'd harness race driver; drove first race '52 Dufferin Park; first win with Money Maker same year; Batavia Downs fire '61 destroyed almost entire stable; Roosevelt Raceway dash winning record 1:56 '73; through '95 5380 winners with purses totalling more than $444 million; more than 40 sub-2-min. miles; twice Al B. White Trophy Roosevelt dash winner; Roosevelt Futurity with Strike Out '71; as trainer had greatest success with George Campos-owned pacer Myakka Prince '73 tying Roosevelt track record for aged geldings with 1:59 mile, $166,980 in winnings; 2nd driver in history to top $1.8 million single season winnings '73 (other Herve Filion); more than 50 major stakes race victories, including 12 in '84-85 with On The Road Again; mem. Cdn Horse Racing Hall of Fame; res. Westbury, N.Y.

GILMOUR, Doug (hockey); b. 25 Jun 1963, Kingston, Ont.; m. Amy Pavel; c. Jake, Maddison, Tyson; centre Cornwall Jr. '81-83; OHL 1st team all-star '83; drafted by St. Louis '82; NHL with St. Louis '83-88, Calgary '88-91, Toronto '92-97, New Jersey '97-98, Chicago '98-99; Selke trophy '93; 2 NHL all-star games; NHL record (through '99) 1197 scheduled games, 397g, 835a, 152 playoff games, 54g, 117a; cameo appearance in movie *Bogus*; res. Toronto, Ont.

GIRARD, Ken (golf/hockey); b. 18 Dec 1936, Toronto, Ont.; given name: Kenneth John; m. Vivian Spencer; c. Lori Ann, Brian; golf pro London Hunt; won Ont. PGA title '68; 2 Ont. PGA titles; won both jr., sr. div. Bermuda titles; 3yrs jr. hockey Toronto Marlboros; mem. 2 Memorial Cup teams; played 7 NHL games with TML '56-60; res. London, Ont.

GIRLETZ, Wilf (rodeo); b. 28 Sep 1928, Dewinton, Alta; d. 17 May 1995, Hanna, Alta.; given name: Wilfred Gordon; m. Maxine; c. Kevin, Ray, Glenda, Randy; rancher; began rodeo career age 15; 5 ntl bull riding titles; 3 ntl all-around (AA) titles; became stock contractor from '84 raising rodeo bulls at Youngstown, Alta., ranch; died of injuries suffered in riding accident; mem. Cdn Rodeo Hall of Fame.

GISIGER, Michelle (lacrosse); b. 17 Aug 1960, Winnipeg, Man.; given name: Michelle Marie Lynne; UMan, BPhE, BEd; teacher; with Roger Dawes cycled Winnipeg to PEI on tandem bicycle '84; mem. Man., ntl women's FH team '79-84; UMan on FH scholarship '80-85; Man. soccer player '85; div. A sr. women's soccer, basketball player; mem. Man. sr. women's field lacrosse team '85-92; competed with ntl team '89, '93 World Cup, '92 William & Mary tour, Scotland, England, Wales tour; spent summer '91 teaching phys ed Mali as part of CTF special project to help developing countries; res. Winnipeg, Man.

GLADSTONE, Jim (rodeo); b. 18 Nov 1942, Cardston, Alta.; c. 5; Lethbridge Coll., UAlta, LLB; lawyer; grandfather James 1st Alta. native senator; father Fred ntl calf roping champion; competed in 1st rodeo age 11; turned pro '60 establishing reputation on Indian semi-pro circuit; Indian Rodeo Cowboy Assn. calf roping titles '63, '65, added steer wrestling, all-around titles '68; 3 ntl calf roping titles; qualified for 8 ntl rodeo finals, 4 NA finals; scored Canada's 1st world victory in timed event '77; surpassed Kenny McLean's 10yr record for career earnings '61; Indian Rodeo's man of yr '78; mem. Alta. Sports Hall of Fame; res. Alderside, Alta.

GLASSER, Red (bowling); b. 5 Feb 1931, Regina, Sask.; given name: Anton; m. Clotilde Brown; c. Gerald, Barry, Janyce, Anthony, Donald, Douglas, Cathy; retd auto bodyman; 10-pin bowler; 6 Sask. singles, doubles titles; ntl singles '62, doubles '64; perfect 300 game '62; Cdn rep. ABC Masters '62, World Invitational '63, World FIQ tournament '71; instructor, v-p Regina men's 10-pin Assn.; tackle '40 ntl jr. Navy title football team; mem. Sask. Sports Hall of Fame; res. Regina, Sask.

GLASSER, Sully (football); b. 25 Oct. 1922, Regina, Sask.; d. 1 Aug 1986, Regina, Sask.; given name: Sullivan John; m. Terry Hier; c. Donna, Brenda, Sullivan, Jill, Marsha, Grant; chartered life underwriter; backfielder. Roughriders '46-57; WFC all-star 1946; scored TD vs. Ottawa '51 Grey Cup; 6yrs sr. baseball, jr. hockey.

GLAZIER, Lori (snowboarding); b. 19 Sep 1971, Oshawa, Ont.; began snowboarding age 19; 2 ntl championships; placed 5th US Open; mem. '98 Olympic team; res. Courtice, Ont./Whistler, B.C.

GLEN, Kathy (synchro swim); 9 Jan 1966, Madison, Wisc.; introduced to synchro age 10; 1st mem. Vancouver Aquasonics to achieve ntl team status '84; with Christine Larsen '90 Commonwealth Games duet gold; with Lisa Alexander '91 world championship duet bronze; res. Port Moody, B.C.

GLESBY, Tom (boxing); b. 17 Jul 1969, Winnipeg, Man.; mem. Napper's Boxing Club; Cdn amateur heavyweight champion '88, '91; '88 Bulgarian tournament title; '91 Canada Cup champion; mem. '88, '92 Olympic, '91 Pan-Am Games teams; pro record 20-1-1; stripped of Cdn heavyweight title '97 for failure to defend title in 3yrs; res. Welland, Ont.

GLOAG, Norm (basketball); b. 9 Jul 1919, Vancouver, B.C.; d. 11 Jun 1997, Vancouver, B.C.; given name: Norman Grainger; m. Elizabeth Jones; c. John, Mary; retd. airline sales mgr.; sr. men's basketball Vancouver '38-48 excluding '42-45; mem. Cloverleafs Sr. A team Philippines tour, '48 ntl titlists; mgr. ntl team '56 Olympics, '59 '62 world tournament; Cdn basketball rep. '60, '64, '68, '72, '76, '80 Olympics; chair. Van. ABA '51-85, 2 terms pres. CABA '70-74; dir. Basketball Canada; mem. Pan-Am Games committee; dir. COA, Vancouver-Garibaldi Olympic comm.; mem. women's commission FIBA; v-p Central Board FIBA '76-80, mem. Central Board '80; Air Canada Amateur Sports Exec. of '75; mem. Cdn Basketball, Cdn Amateur, BC Sports halls of fame.

GLOVER, Penny (squash); b. 18 Aug 1942, Cardish, Wales; Welsh Inst. of Advanced Technology; labor relations mgr.;

Ont. open title '71; 7 Ont. closed titles; mem. ntl women's squash team Australian tour '75; ntl veterans (40+) '83-84, (45+) titles '89-90; Level A official; Ont. Sports Achievement award '83; res. Ottawa, Ont.

GLYNN, Hugh (administration); b. 26 Jul 1925, Richard, Sask.; m. Joan Penfold; c. Michael, Sheryl, Kelly; retd. sports exec.; refrigeration, heating mechanic, coached baseball, minor hockey and competed in figure skating; served in various executive capacities at club, Ntl levels; exec. mgr. CFSA '66-74; v-p, pres. National Sport & Recreation Centre '74-92; key role in design, establishment of NSRC on Naismith Dr., Gloucester; res. Nepean, Ont.

GMOSER, Hans (skiing/mountaineering); b. 7 Jul 1932, Braunau, Austria; given name: Johann Wolfgang; m. Margaret Grace MacGougan; c. Conrad, Robson; attended Harvard Business School; mountain guide, businessman; 1st ascent in of 16,525ft. Mt. Blackburn, Alaska; 1st ascent Wickersham Wall on Mt. McKinley; 2nd ascent East Ridge Mt. Logan (19,850ft. Canada's highest) developed alpine ski touring Western Canadian mountains, helicopter skiing Bugaboos, Cariboos, Monashees; hon. pres. Association of Cdn Mountain Guides; hon. mem. International Federation of Mountain Guides Association; mem. Order of Canada, Cdn Skiing Hall of Fame; res. Banff, Alta.

GODBOUT, François (tennis); b. 10 Apr 1938, Montreal, Que.; m. Sibylla Hesse; c. Louis, Christian; Sherbrooke, BA, Montreal, LLD; lawyer; Que., ntl jr. titles '56; mem. '59-64, '69 Davis Cup teams; pres. QTF '69-71; secty. Que. Athletic Fed. '72-77; v-p COA from '78; mem. Air Canada Awards selection comm. from '78; v-p Tennis Canada '80; mem. Calgary Olympics comm., '86 soccer World Cup bid comm.; mem. Que. Sports, Cdn Tennis halls of fame; res. Montreal, Que.

GOERMANN, Elfriede (gymnastics/coaching); b. 30 Oct 1937, Rastenburg, Germany; given name: Elfriede Wolff; m. Wolfgang Goermann; c. Monica, Jens; Ntl, Man. team coach '77-86; head coach, program dir. Winnipeg Gymnastics Centre '77-87; chair Man. Coaches Assn. '82-83; chair Man. provincial judges '67-72; served as international gymnastics judge '74-80, including judge at '76 Olympics; mem. high performance judges assembly; judge Western Cdn championships '84-87; life mem. Canadian Gymnastics Federation; Brevet judge of women's gymnastics, top international judging award; mem. Man. Sports Hall of Fame; res. Winnipeg, Man.

GOERMANN, Monica (gymnastics); b. 1 Sep 1964, Winnipeg, Man.; m. Michael Tomlinson; c. Maija Danielle; Man. BPhE; gym teacher, operates dance studio; coached by mother Elfriede; silver all-around '77 junior nationals; all-around silver '78 Commonwealth Games; gold all-around, team, uneven bars, silver floor exercises, bronze beam '79 Pan-Am Games; mem. '80 Olympic team; '79 ntl all-around, beam, floor exercises, uneven bars titles, '80 Swiss invitational team gold, all-around, floor exercise bronze; tied for gold floor exercises '81 UK vs. Canada meet; Vince Leah Memorial award '99; mem. Man. Sports Hall of Fame; res. Winnipeg, Man.

GOFF, Ken (boxing); b. 2 Mar 1910, Portsmouth, Eng.; d. 26 Jan 1993, Regina, Sask.; m. Margaret Dobson; c. Beverly, George, Peggy, Penny; Paragon Business College; accountant; fought as featherweight, lightweight '30-34; Sask. champion, ntl semifinalist '34; began coaching '36 Regina Olympic Club, Regina City Police Club '44-49; asst. coach '48 Olympic, mgr.-coach '56 Olympic teams; trained ntl champions Claude Warwick, Adam Faul; Regina father of '60; pres. Regina Boxing Club '73; Regina B'nai B'rith sports personality of '81; mem. Sask. Sports Hall of Fame.

GOLAB, Tony (football); b. 17 Jan 1919, Windsor, Ont.; given name: Anthony Charles; wid.; c. Michael, Keri-Ann; U of Puget Sound; retired RCAF Wing Cdr., Sport Canada official; basketball Dominion champion Windsor Alumni, Ottawa Glebe Grads; football Sarnia Imperials '38 ORFU champions; fullback Rough Riders '39-41, '45-50; '41 Jeff Russel Trophy (Big Four MVP); '41 CP award Canada's outstanding athlete; 9 times all-Cdn; 4 Grey Cup finals, '40 winner; coached Hamilton ORFU Panthers '52-53, RMC '54-57, 3 successive titles; Atlantic Football Conf. v-p '59; GM Alouettes '68-69; consultant Sport Canada '72-84; nicknamed "Golden Boy"; Lionel Conacher trophy '41; mem. Order of Canada, Ottawa, Cdn Forces, Cdn Football, Canada's, Royal Cdn Legion, Windsor-Essex Sports halls of fame; res. Kanata, Ont.

GOLD, Otto (coaching); b. 18 May 1909, Prague, Czechoslovakia; d. Apr 1977, Toronto, Ont.; Prague novice '19, jr '20 figure skating titles; won 1 novice, 5 jr, 1 sr singles, 1 pairs European titles; retired from competition '30; began teaching in Switzerland '32; taught in Prague '34-35; moved to England '36 joining Coliseum skating show '37; emigrated to Canada '38; professional Minto Skating Club Ottawa '38-46; pioneered summer skating schools in Kitchener '40; taught at Vancouver/New Westminster '446-50; taught in Toronto from '50; helped launch career of Dorothy Hamill at Norwalk, Conn.,; students included: Donald Jackson, Donald Gilchrist, Frances Dafoe, Norris Bowden, Barbara Ann Scott and Mary Rose Thacker; mem. Cdn Figure Skating Hall of Fame.

GOLDHAM, Bob (hockey); b. 12 May 1922, Georgetown, Ont.; d. 6 Sep 1991, Toronto, Ont.; given name: Robert John; m. Elinor Platt; c. Patricia, Susan, Barbara; defence Toronto Marlboros jrs.; pro Hershey, Washington, Pittsburgh (AHL), Maple Leafs '41-46 (excluding '42-45 Navy WW2); Black Hawks '48, Red Wings '51-56; mem. 5 league champion, 5 Stanley Cup winners; 2nd team all-star defenceman; NHL record: 650 scheduled games, 28g, 143a, 66 playoff games, 3g, 14a; coached St. Michael's Majors 3yrs; mem. Minto Cup lacrosse title team Orillia Terriers '41; mem. Hamilton Tigers lacrosse team '41-46.

GOMEZ, Avelino (horse racing); b. Oct 1928, Havana, Cuba; d. 21 Jun 1980, Toronto, Ont.; m. Patricia; c. Avelino Jr., Matthew, Jackie; jockey; several victories in US, Canada through '58, returned to Cuba investing in business, real estate; lost all in Castro revolution; Canadian citizen '64; 6 ntl racing titles; led NA riders with 318 victories '66 with .32 highest percentage ever for NA champ; 1st Cdn. jockey to win 300 races single season; 4 Queen's Plate winners, Lyford Cay '57, Victoria Park '60, Tilted Hero '66, Jumpin'

Joseph '69; flamboyant crowd pleaser nicknamed Go Go Gomez, El Perfecto, Cuban Hawk; defied death threats riding Victoria Park '60 Queen's Plate; at time of death, (of injuries in 3-horse Woodbine spill), ranked 7th among race-winning jockeys on world list with more than 4000 winners; mem. Etobicoke, Canada's Sports; Canadian Horse Racing halls of fame.

GOOD, Norah (t&f); b. 10 Jun 1957, Ottawa, Ont.; m. Brent Broughton; c. Jared, Neal, Matthew; health care worker; visually challenged athlete; 400m, 800m, 1500m, 3000m running titles, 3000m walk title '83 Canadian Games for Physically Disabled; ntl 3000m run record; 3000m run title '84 international Games for Disabled, silver 1500m; mem. East Ottawa Lions TC; participated in '87 Olympic torch run; res. Ottawa, Ont.

GOODFELLOW, Ebbie (hockey); b. 9 Apr 1906, Ottawa. Ont.; d. 10 Sep 1985, Sarasota, Fla.; given name: Ebenezer Ralston; m. Rosalind Sloan (d); c. Ebbie Ramsey, Douglas Margaret; all-star centre Ottawa Montagnards; pro Detroit organization; all-star Olympics International League '28-29; centre, defenceman Red Wings '29-43; coached Wings during '42 Stanley Cup finals vs. Toronto; coach Black Hawks '50-52; Hart Trophy (MVP) '40; twice 1st team, once 2nd team all-star; mem. 3 Stanley Cup winners; NHL record: 575 scheduled games, 134g, 190a, 45 playoff games, 8g, 8a; led American Div. scorers '30-31; mem. Hockey Hall of Fame selection comm.; mem. Ottawa, Michigan, Hockey halls of fame.

GOODMAN, Russell (skiing); b. 5 May 1953, Montreal, Que.; McGill ; chartered accountant; international alpine status '73, best international slalom ranking among Canadians Feb '73-May '75; 10th '74 slalom world championships St. Moritz, best finish to that time by Canadian male skier in Olympic, World Cup or world championship competition; runnerup '72 ntl slalom final, '74-75 GS; '75 Can-Am GS, ntl spring slalom Rossland, B.C., Hunter Mountain Can-Am GS, Waterville Valley Can-Am dual slalom; 3rd Can-Am overall '75; mem. European Cup team '73-74; 4th Andora slalom '73, 7th Caspoggio, Sella Nevea, Czechoslovakia slaloms '73; 6th Sella Nevea GS, 9th slalom '74; pres. Red Birds Ski Club Mt. Tremblant; mem. Canadian Ski Instructors Alliance; res. Pointe Claire, Que.

GOODYEAR, Scott (motorsport); b. 20 Dec 1959, Toronto, Ont.; given name: Donald Scott; m. Leslie; c. Christopher, Michael, Haley; race driver, driving school owner, operator; began kart racing age 9; won 14 Ntl, NA karting titles '69-76; entered Formula Ford circuit '80 winning series title, Cdn Drivers Assn driver of year; Cdn Formula Ford titles '81-82; competed on Formula 2000, Trans Am circuit '83-84; placed 4th '85 Pro Sports 2000 series championships; drove in '86 Rothman's Porsche Turbo Cup series, earned 2nd RDA driver of year title; won 5 of 9 starts, series championship in Formula Atlantic series for Houston-based Tom Mitchell team; passed CART rookie test '87, placed 8th Toronto Molson Indy, earned $119,479 in 7 CART races; 3rd in GTO div. of Daytona 24hrs; won 3 of 8 races and Rothman's Porsche Turbo Cup championship '88; successful '89 Formula Atlantic series led to inclusion on

McDonnell Racing team; joined Budweiser/King team; lack of sponsor left him sidelined '95 season; Walker team '96; joined IRL '97 withTreadway team; '98 Panther Racing team owned by NFL QB Jim Harbaugh; qualified for 1st Indianapolis 500 race '90, runnerup '92, '97; won '92, '94 Michigan 500, '99 Phoenix 200; res. Newmarket, Ont./ Carmel, Ind.

GOPLEN, Henrietta (speed skating); b. 14 Jul 1932, Saskatoon, Sask.; given name: Henrietta Barbara Flora Ann Mackay; m. Bernard Peter Goplen; c. Gary Bernard, Craig Eldon, Gordon Robert, Barbara Lynn (d); UofSask BSc; home economist; participated in basketball, t&f, volleyball; began speed skating age 10; city titles '43-46; Alta indoor/ outdoor title '48; set Sask 3000m record; heavy involvement in community activities; served on UofSask senate '79-84; active role in varied capacities with Saskatoon Lions, Saskatchewan, Cdn Amateur Speed Skating Assn '42-83; Level II coaching certificate; coach Saskatoon Lions '75-83 judge '88 Olympics, '87 world short track championships; active mem. Participaction Saskatoon '73-80; delegate to Participaction conference Sweden '79; mgr. '83, '87, CdM '86 Winter Games; pres. Sask Sports Hall of Fame '88; v-p CASSA '88-92, pres. '94; chair. awards comm. '97-98; hon life mem. Saskatoon Lions SSC; '82 Sask SS coach of yr; Century 100 sports award, CASSA Centennial medal, Dairy Producers merit award; authored *"Saskatchewan's Sportsman Gourmet Guide"* cook book; mem. UofSask Sports Wall, Saskatoon Sports Hall of Fame; res. Saskatoon, Sask.

GORBUS, Glen (baseball); b. 8 Jul 1930, Drumheller, Alta.; d. 12 Jun 1990, Calgary, Alta.; given name: Glen Edward; c. Kriston, Kari, Kandis; sales mgr. catering co.; pro Brooklyn Dodgers organization '49; Class D Medford Ore., Class C Bisbee-Douglas, Class A Pueblo, AA Fort Worth '49-54; drafted by Cincinnati '55, traded to Philadelphia same season; split '56 between Phillies, Triple A Miami; traded to St. Louis '57, spent part of season Triple A Omaha; sold to L.A. Dodgers '58, spent season Triple A Spokane; tired of life in minors, retired '59; began career as 3rd baseman, converted to outfield; world record longest baseball throw 445'10" Omaha '57; mem. Alta Sports Hall of Fame.

GORDON, Frances (basketball); b. 1915, Red Deer, Alta.; given name: Frances Marie; m. Oswin Clifford Mills (d); c. Brian Arthur, Gerry Douglas; Edmonton Normal School; retd teacher; mem. famed Edmonton Grads '36-37; mem. Canadian Basketball, Alta. Sports halls of fame; res. Red Deer, Alta.

GORDON, Jackie (hockey); b. 3 Mar 1928, Winnipeg, Man.; given name: John; retd hockey exec.; 17 yrs player, coach, manager Cleveland (AHL), 4 Calder Cup winners; New Haven (AHL) '49-50, Cincinnati (AHL) '50-51, brief stints NY Rangers '48-51; 4yrs. asst. GM Rangers; coached Minnesota 3 seasons, part of 2 others, some scouting, GM '74-78; AGM Vancouver '79-84, GM '85-86, sr. v-p '87, sr. advisor '87-91; NHL coaching record: 290 league games, 116-124-50 ties, 25 playoff games 11-14 ; mem. Man. Hockey Hall of Fame; res. Vancouver, B.C.

GORDON, Megan (diving); b. 12 Apr 1971, West Vancouver, B.C.; UBC, BComm, French immersion; agent NSB; competitive swimmer '78-82; competitive gymnast '78-84; began competitive diving age 9; mem. jr. ntl team '81-86, sr. ntl team '89-96; 5 sr. ntl 10m silver medals; bronze Volksbank Intl, silver Bolzano Intl '93; 5th '91 Pan-Am, silver '93, 6th '95 FISU games, 5th '94 Goodwill Games; Olympic alternate '92; BC athlete award '85-92; BC govt passport to education scholarship '86-89; Nancy Greene scholarship '89, '92; BC best-ever athlete '88; BC flag bearer Western Canada Games '87; motivational speaker BC Esteem Team; coaching at all levels; res. Vancouver, B.C.

GORDON, Paige (diving); b. 25 Apr 1973, N. Vancouver, B.C.; UBC; gymnast, began diving age 8; mem. ntl jr team; medalled at jr. worlds, jr Can-Am-Mex series; swept 3 Canada Games title '89; mem. ntl sr team '90-96; bronze '90, silver '94 Commonwealth, silver '91 Pan-Am, '93 FISU Games; mem. '92, '96 Olympic, '90, '94 Commonwealth, '91 Pan-Am Games teams; 4 ntl 10m, 3 ntl 3m titles; 4th ranked 3m in world; sole Cdn invited to participate in '94 Goodwill Games; 2 Italian outstanding diver awards; BC jr athlete of '89; Elaine Tanner award '91; BC sr athlete of '93; with sister Megan, mem. BC Esteem Team; res. w. Vancouver, B.C.

GORDON, Taylor (coaching/boxing); b. 16 Sep 1931, Melfort, Sask.; m. Greta Marina Blackmore; c. Dwain Keith, Ann Marina, Wayne Ephraim; boxing coach; retd. as CPO after 25yr RCN career; coached ntl team 5 Olympic, 4 Pan-Am, 5 Commonwealth Games, 4 world championships; head coach and/or mgr. Team Canada 5 NA championships, 1 Goodwill, Australian Games, 5 Canada, 4 President's, 2 King's, 2 World Cups, 13 major international tournaments; asst. tech. dir. '67 Pan Am Games; coaching instructor Colorado Olympic training Centre '82; tech. dir. Olympic qualification tournament '96; field supervisor '96 Olympics; coached Chris Clarke to '75 PAG gold; son Wayne Olympic team capt '84, asst. coach '92 providing 1st father-son combinations in such roles in Cdn Olympic boxing; successful in placing an athlete from his own Citadel Amateur Boxing Club on ntl team in 8 Olympic Games; mem. exec. comm. CABA; res. Lower Sackville, N.S.

GORDON, Wayne (coaching/boxing); b. 30 Mar 1963, Victoria, B.C.; given name: Wayne Ephraim; m. Treva Tucker; c. Ann Kathleen, Rachael Amelia, Taylor Jesse; boxing coach; 4 Cdn amateur boxing titles; competed welterweight class '83 Pan Am, '84 Olympic Games; coach ntl team '88 world jr. championships, '92, '96 Olympics, '98 Commonwealth Games; res. Beaverbank, N.S.

GORING, Alison (curling); B. 15 Nov 1963, Toronto, Ont.; given name: Alison Dawn; automotive accounts clerk; mem. Bayview CC; began curling age 12; skipped '83 Cdn jr. title rink; skipped ntl women's title rink '90; skipped 3 Ont. women's title rinks, 1 Team Canada rink in Scott Tournament of Hearts; Level I official; res. North York, Ont.

GORING, Butch (hockey); b. 22 Oct 1949, St. Boniface, Man.; given name: Robert Thomas; m. Cathy; c. Shannon,

Kelly; hockey coach; jr. Winnipeg Rangers, Jets, Dauphin Kings; mem. ntl team '68; 4th LA pick '69 amateur draft; pro Springfield '69-70, LA '69-80, NY Islanders '80-84, Boston '84-85; mem. 4 Stanley Cup winners '80-83; NHL record: 16 seasons, 1107 scheduled games, 375g, 513a, 134 playoff games, 38g, 50a; playing-asst. NYI '81; coach Bruins '84-86, Spokane (WHL), Capital Dist. Islanders '90-93; IHL Las Vegas Thunder '93-94, Utah Grizzlies '94-98, NY Islanders '99; 2 IHL titles; IHL coach of '96 award; Bill Masterton Trophy '78, Lady Byng Trophy '78, Conn Smythe Trophy '81; mem. Man. Hockey, Sports halls of fame; res. Utah.

GORMAN, Charles (speed skating); b. 6 Jul 1897, Saint John, N.B.; d. 12 Feb 1940, Saint John, N.B.; given name: Charles Ingraham; gas station operator; pitcher, outfielder, led NB baseball league batters .450, MVP '25; rejected NY Yankee pro offers; ntl outdoor titles '24-26; NA indoor titles '26-28; NA outdoor title '24; mem. '24, '28 Olympic teams; beat '24 Olympic champion Clas Thunberg of Finland for '26 world title, retained title breaking 1/6-mile record, shaving second from own 440yd standard '27; 7th 500m 1928 Winter Olympics when another skater fell in his path; denied another heat, left games in protest; NA record 220yd indoor, 400yd indoor, outdoor, 1/6-mile times still stand; once won 16 events in 11 days. mem. Cdn Speed Skating, NB, Cdn Amateur, Canada's, Saint John Sports halls of fame.

GORMAN, T. P. (Tommy) (entrepreneur); b. 9 Jun 1886, Ottawa, Ont.; d. 15 May 1961, Ottawa, Ont.; given name: Thomas Patrick; m. Mary Elizabeth Westwick; c. Betty, Frank, Joe; sportswriter, coach; at 22 youngest mem. '08 Olympic lacrosse gold medal team; 1 of 5 men involved '17 birth of NHL; introduced hockey to NYC with Americans; coach/owner Senators title teams '20-21, '23, Black Hawks '34, Montreal Maroons '35, Canadiens '44, '46; coached and/or managed 7 Stanley Cup winners; left NHL '46 to take over Ottawa Auditorium; Ottawa Senators (QSHL) pres., '49 Allan Cup winners; asst. GM Aqua Caliente race track Mexico '29-32, acquired Connaught Park '40s; introduced harness racing to National Capital area; involved Ottawa entry International baseball league; mem. Ottawa, Hockey, Cdn Horse Racing halls of fame.

GORRELL, Miles (football); b. 16 Oct 1955, Calgary, Alta.; UofOtt; offensive tackle; CFL Calgary '78-82, Ottawa '82, Montreal '82-85, Hamilton '85-91, '96, Winnipeg '92-95, '97-98; 5 all-Eastern, 1 all-CFL all-star; 2 Leo Dandurand trophy; 2 runnerup CFL outstanding offensive lineman awards; 1st CFL position player to play 300 scheduled games; 4 Grey Cup finals, 1 winner; res. Winnipeg, Man.

GOSS, Sandy (swimming); b. 2 Oct 1966, Amherst, N.S.; m. Judy; c. Riley; Florida; stockbroker; began competitive swimming age 8; mem. Ntl team from '83-89; FS, backstroke specialist; 33 ntl championship medals, 8 gold, 8 silver, 17 bronze; 11 intl meet medals; 8 Cdn Sr., 3 Commonwealth records; 200m backstroke gold, 4x100 FS relay silver '86 Commonwealth Games; '84 FS, '88 4x100 medley relay Olympics silver; '87 NCAA 200m back silver; 6 Ntl championships; 2 Olympic champion awards; '87 Sport excellence award; '88 Ont. aquatic athlete of year; mem. Ont. Aquatic Hall of Fame; res. Toronto, Ont.

GOSSELIN, Nathalie (judo); b. 31 Mar 1966, Levis, Que.; competes at 52kg; 3 ntl titles; 2 silver Pan-Am championships, '94 Dutch Open; bronze '95 Pan-Am Games '91 Canada Cup, '94 US Open, '96 Sophia tournament; competed '96 Olympic Games; athlete rep. Judo Canada tech. comm.; 4th degree black belt; res. Ottawa, Ont.

GOTFREDSEN, Leif (rowing); b. 28 Jun 1934, Herning, Denmark; m. Betty Carol Walsh; c. Signe, Erik; George Brown College, Ryerson PTI; retd. electrician; competed Denmark '52-57 winning coxed 4s title, 2nd Nordic coxed 4s championships '53, sr. 8s Great International Berliner regatta title '55; mem. Toronto Argonaut Rowing Club '60-70; ntl sr. double sculls '62, jr. single sculls '63, sr. single sculls '64; mem. '64 Olympic team; silver Pan-Am double sculls '67; orsman, exec., coach Victoria City RC '74-79; director BCRA '74-81, v-p '81; ntl team coach '78-80, jr. team coach '86-87; CARA coach of '78; dir. CARA '81-85; Greater Victoria Sports Council Sportsman of Year; '79-80 CARA Centennial award; res. Victoria, B.C.

GOTTA, Jack (football); b. 14 Nov 1931, Ironwood, Mich.; m. Joan Patterson; c. Jeff, Tony, Jake, Gia; Oregon State; realtor, retired football executive; pass receiver, Oregon State; service football Hamilton AFB; capt. '55 USAF team, all-service all-star, league MVP; caught 44 passes for 8tds; last cut Cleveland (NFL) '56, Calgary (CFL) for final 7 games; '57 Shrine Game; Saskatchewan '60-63; Montreal '64; CFL playing record: 253 receptions, 4317yds, 20tds; WFC all-star; asst. coach Sask. '65-66; asst. Ottawa '67-69, head coach '70-73; Grey Cup '73; twice Annis Stukus Trophy CFL coach of year; coach Birmingham (WFL) '74; GM and/or coach Stampeders '77-79, '82-83; coach Sask. '85-86; 11yr CFL coaching record (including playoffs): 89-87-5; TV football color commentator '84; res. Cochrane, Alta.

GOULDING, Bev (administration); b. 29 Jun 1912, Toronto, Ont.; given name: George Beverley; m. Kathryn Currie; c. George David, Nancy Kathryn; UofT, BA; retd. teacher; coached HS football, basketball winning 6 assn. football, 3 assn., 1 CABA juve. basketball titles; exec.-dir. Ont. Federation of School Athletic Associations '71-77; mem. Peterborough Sports Hall of Fame; res. Peterborough, Ont.

GOULDING, George (t&f); b. 16 Nov 1884, Hull, Eng.; d. 31 Jan. 1966, Toronto Ont.; given name: George Henry; mile walker, marathon runner; mem. '08 Olympic team; 300 career race victories at distances from 1-40 miles; gold '12 Olympics 10,000m race in record 46:28.4; twice world mile records including 6:25.8 Toronto '11; many stunt races; 10 miles against man driving horse and buggy; defeated 4 man US relay team in 4 mile NY walk; 8 1/4 miles 1 hour walk around Toronto Varsity oval; '16 record for 7 miles 50:40 Rutgers U; mem. Cdn Amateur, Canada's Sports halls of fame.

GOULET, Joanne (golf); b. 5 May 1935, Melville, Sask.; U of Regina; administrative officer; 30 Regina, 6 Sask. titles; at 16 youngest golfer ntl women's championships; mem. '64 world championships team; Commonwealth Trophy semifinalist '64 British Open; course records Regina GC, Wascana G&CC, Saskatoon Riverdale GC; numerous provincial teams; national jr. chairman; Regina golf course named in her honor; mem. Sask. Sports Hall of Fame; res. Regina, Sask.

GOULET, Michel (hockey); b. 21 Apr 1960, Peribonka, Que.; m. Andree; c. Dominique, Vincent, Nicolas; hockey exec.; left wing Quebec jr. Remparts'76-78; Birmingham (WHA) '78-79; 1st round pick Quebec '79 draft; NHL Quebec '79-90, Chicago '90-94; topped 50-goal plateau 57 '83, 56 '84, 55 '85, 53 '86; 3 1st, 2 2nd all-star; competed 5 all-star games; mem. Cdn '83 world championship bronze team; Team Canada '84, '87 Canada Cup titlists; NHL record: 1089 scheduled games, 548g, 604a, 92 playoff games, 39g, 39a; jersey #16 retd. by Nordiques; dir. player personnel Colorado Avalanche from '95; mem. Hockey Hall of Fame; res. Lone Tree, Colo.

GOURLAY, Jean (field hockey); b. 29 Sep 1957, Kapuskasing, Ont; m. Steve Major; UofT, BPHE, BEd; teacher; mem. Ont. jr. team '74-76, int. '76-80, sr. '78-83; UofT team competing in tours throughout world; mem. '78, '83 World Cup, '79 world championships teams; World Cup silver '83; ntl team capt. '79, co-capt. '82-83; named to World 2nd all-star team '83; mem. UofT Sports Hall of Fame; res. Burlington, Ont.

GOWAN, Geoff (administration); b. 2 Nov 1929, Ravenglass, Cunbira, Eng.; given name: Geoffrey Russell; m. Rhoda Tyson; c. Susan Elizabeth, Simon Russell; Loughborough Coll. of Ed. Dip. PE, Purdue, MSc, Wisconsin, PhD; retd. pres., tech. co-ordinator Coaching Assn. of Canada; long jump, triple jump specialist college, county levels; rugby footballer college, club levels; major coaching role Royal Canadian Legion t&f clinics, Guelph; coached 4 Olympic track finalists; key role development comprehensive coaching programs for Canadian sport; author numerous articles, lecturer, TV color commentator national, international t&f competitions; mem. Order of Canada; res. Ottawa, Ont.

GOWANLOCK, Ab (curling); b. 14 Dec 1900, Glenboro, Man.; d. 27 Sep 1988, Dauphin, Man.; given name: Albert Adam; m. Esther Kemp (d); c. Gail; began curling as a youngster in Glenboro; skipped Manitoba rinks to Brier titles '38, '53; scored 4 8-enders; ardent golfer; life mem. Manitoba Curling Assn., Dauphin and Glenboro Curling Clubs; mem. Man, Cdn Curling, Man. Sports halls of fame.

GOWSELL, Paul (curling); b. 5 Sep 1957, Squamish, B.C.; given name: Christopher Paul; m. Kathi Ostrom; c. Sam, Sophie; waterworks inspector; skipped 2 world jr. title rinks; '80 Alta. Brier rep.; twice topped $65,000 rink earnings '77-78; official spare '88 Olympics; res. Calgary, Alta.

GOYETTE, Danielle (hockey); b. 30 Jan 1966, Ste-Foy, Que.; began playing hockey at 16; mem. Team Que. '94-96 women's sr. ntls; gold '95, '96 Esso ntls; MV forward '96 ntl championships; leading scorer '92, '94 world championship tournaments, all-star awards; 4 world, 2 Pacific Rim, 1 3-Nations Cup gold; attends Olympic Oval high performance female hockey program; mem. '98 Olympic silver medal team; res. Calgary, Alta.

GRAHAM, Charles (boxing); b. 13 Mar 1896, Carlisle, Eng.; d. circa 1980s, m. Ivy; c. 2 daughters; boxed, coached in England as amateur, pro; coached Edmonton '54-73; guided champions in every division from flyweight to heavyweight except light middleweight; coached Marv Arneson '68 Olympics, '70 Commonwealth Games gold, 5 ntl titles; mem. Alta. Sports Hall of Fame.

GRAHAM, Gail (golf); b. 16 Jan 1964, Vanderhoof, B.C.; m. Terry Graham; Lamar, BSc; golf pro; began playing golf at 13 in Winnipeg; 2 Man. amateur titles; mem. Cdn Commonwealth title team '87; mem Canada's inaugural Nations Cup team '99; low amateur '87 LPGA du Maurier Classic; won LPGA Fieldcrest-Canon Classic '95; won Alpine Australian Ladies' Masters title '97; NCAA academic All-American; 1 career hole-in-one; low career round 66; *Score* magazine Cdn female golfer of '96; res. Kelowna, B.C.

GRAHAM, Hugh (equestrian); b. 10 Feb 1949, Georgetown, Ont.; m. Cindy Firestone; c. Laurel; self-employed; tutored by Olympic gold medallist Jim Day; launched show jumping career in 1970's; mem. ntl team from '82; 7 GP jumping titles; 2 Cdn titles; team gold '87, silver '83 Pan-Am Games; aboard Sirocco won '89 NA title; mem. '84, '96 Olympic, '83, '87, '95 Pan-Am Games teams; competed in world championships, 4 World Cup finals; won 2 Queen Elizabeth II Cup titles; 2 Rothman's equestrian of year awards; res. Schomberg, Ont.

GRAHAM, John (bobsled/t&f); b. 20 Nov 1965, Moose Jaw, Sask.; UCal, BA; real estate developer; competive hurdler who was '88 Olympic semifinalist; 3 Commonwealth Games bronze medals; 7 Cdn titles, 3 in 400m sprints, 4 in 400m hurdles; mem. ntl bobsled team '87-92; with Chris Lori, Ken LeBlanc, Allan Cearns ntl 4-man title '88; with Lori, Leblanc, Doug Currier ntl 4-man crowns '90, '92, world cup gold '91, 1st place WC ranking '90; competed '92 Olympics; res. Seattle, Wash.

GRAHAM, Laurie (skiing); b. 30 Mar 1960, Orangeville, Ont.; given name: Laurie Jean; m. Clarke Flynn; c. Kylie Grace, Taylor Michela; UofT Schools; downhill specialist; mem. Southern Ont. ski team '74-77; ntl ski team '77-87; ntl downhill champion '80, super GS '84; WC '79-86 record 6-4-5; WC super GS France, downhill title Mt. Tremblant '83, downhill Val d'Isere, Banff '85; downhill bronze '82 world championships; NA Ski Trophy series downhill title '83; mem. '80, '84, '88 Olympic teams; retd from ntl team '88; tournament of champions challenge gold NZ '95; won 3 legends of skiing downhill titles; Jeep Eagle tournament of champions title '95; MCI relays gold '96, Sprint world ski challenge as mem. Team NA '98; athletes liaison '94 Olympics; Ski Racing International Journal Cdn alpine female skier of '83 award; Bobbie Rosenfeld award '86; fed. govt female athlete of '86 award; fed. govt. excellence awards '82-87, '89; mem. Order of Canada, Cdn Skiing, Canada's Sports halls of fame; res. Nepean, Ont.

GRAHAM, Milt (football); b. 28 Jul 1934, Watervliet, N.Y.; given name: Milton Russell; m. Gertrude Engle; c. David, Mark, Laurie; Colgate, BA; retd FBI agent, Cape Cod inn owner; played football/basketball in college; hon. mention football all-American; drafted by both NFL, NBA; pro football Ottawa '56-61; mem. '60 Grey Cup champions; CFL all-Canadian '58; mem. Boston Patriots AFL '61-63; '62 Unsung Hero award; res. Yarmouth Port, Mass.

GRAHAM, Phil (rowing); b. 16 Jul 1970, Halifax, N.S.; Trent, BA; began competing in cross-country skiing age 8; attended Canada Games as skier; raced for Nfld team '85-91; spent summers '84-86 canoeing in Northern Ont.; began rowing at Trent; mem. ntl rowing team from '93; 2 Pan-Am Games '95 silver; FISU Games straight pairs gold, quadruple sculls silver '93; 2 ntl straight pair titles; gold straight pair '94 Amsterdam International; competed 2 world championships, '96 Olympics; res. Cornerbrook, Nfld.

GRAHAM, Sally (shooting); b. 12 Oct 1953, Lakefield, Ont.; mem. Lakefield Rifle Club; 8 consec. Cdn Women's small bore titles; Cdn expert class grand aggregate title '72; Masters class grand aggregate '74; mem. 3 Ont. 4-member Cdn title teams; 5yrs mem. ntl team; mem. Peterborough Sports Hall of Fame; res. Peterborough, Ont.

GRAND'MAITRE, Josée (racquetball); b. 28 Jul 1961, Montreal, Que. UofOtt, BSc, Quebec, admin. certificate; 8 Que. titles; 3 ntl doubles, 1 ntl singles titles; 3 world doubles silver; competed '95 Pan-Am Games; coach ntl espoir team from '94; ntl team rep. Racquetball Canada bd. of dir.; mem. COA athletic council; Level 3 coaching cert.; technical course conductor; res. Montreal, Que.

GRANDI, Thomas (skiing); b. 27 Dec 1972, Bolzano, Italy; began skiing in Nancy Greene program age 9; slalom, GS specialist; mem. ntl team from '92; US GS title '93; 5 ntl GS titles; competed '94, '98 Olympics; res. Banff, Alta.

GRANEY, Jack (baseball); b. 10 Jun 1886, St. Thomas, Ont.; d. 20 Apr 1978, Louisana, Mo.; given name: John Gladstone; m. Pauline Perry; c. John (d), Margot; automotive dealer, sportscaster; early baseball as pitcher Western Ont.; minor pro Rochester, Wilkes-Barre, Portland; Cleveland (AL) as outfielder '10-22 amassing .250 lifetime BA 1402 games; mgr. Des Moines (WL) '22; as leadoff 1st batter to face Babe Ruth when he appeared with Boston Red Sox as pitcher '14 (Graney singled); mem. '20 Cleveland World Series champions; 1st player to move to broadcast booth, voice of Indians '33-54; 1st player to wear number on uniform scheduled '16 league game; Cleveland branch SABR bears his name; trophy for outstanding media contribution to Cdn baseball bears his name; mem. Cdn Baseball Hall of Fame.

GRANT, Benny (hockey/golf); b. 14 Jul 1908, Owen Sound, Ont.; d. 30 Jul 1991, Owen Sound, Ont.; given name: Benjamin Cameron; m. Phyllis Dare Pratt; c. Carole Anne, Benny, Robert; Imperial Oil employee; mem. '27 Memorial Cup champion Owen Sound Greys; pro London '28; Toronto '29-34, loaned to NY Americans '30, '34; stints in minors Boston Cubs, Syracuse, Philadelphia, Springfeild, St Paul; sold to Chicago '42, retd; returned to Toronto '43, Boston '44; Charlie Gardiner Trophy top goalie St. Paul '42; 3 times AHL all-star; MVP Syracuse '32, Springfield '37; Owen Sound golf club men's champ '53, 5 srs titles.

GRANT, Bud (football/coaching); b. 20 May 1927, Superior, Wisc.; given name: Harry Peter. m. Pat; c. 5; Minnesota; retired football coach; 2 seasons pro basketball Minneapolis Lakers; pro football Philadelphia Eagles; offensive end Blue Bombers '53-56, topped WFC pass receivers 3 of 4yrs; 3 time WFC all-star; WFC single season 68 reception record; coach Winnipeg '57-66, 112 wins, 66 losses, 3 ties .647 percentage; 8 league finals, 6 Grey Cup finals, 4 winners; nicknamed "The Iceman"; coach Minnesota (NFL) '67-83; NFL coaching record: 151 wins, 87 losses, 5 ties; 4 Super Bowl appearances; Uof Minn athlete of 1/2 century '51; mem. Man. Sports, Cdn, US Football, Blue Bombers halls of fame; res. Kewadon, Minn.

GRANT, Danny (hockey); b. 21 Feb 1946, Fredericton, N.B.; prov. sports consultant, hockey coach; jr. Peterborough Petes '62-66; pro Montreal '66-68, Minnesota '68-74, Detroit '74-78, Los Angeles '78-79; set Minnesota club record for consecutive games (442); 50 goal plateau with Detroit '75; Calder Memorial trophy '69; AHL Golden Skate award '86; won NHL showdown competitions '75-76; scoring titles Original Six Hockey Heroes trounament '84-85; instrumental in acquiring AHL franchise for Fredericton; pres/player/asst coach Fredericton Express; Express jersey 16 and NHL jersey 21 retd; coached Fredericton Capitals to NB intermediate titles '80-81, Eastern Cdn Hardy Cup '80; coached Fredericton Boldons Red Wings to Atlantic midget crown '89; coach UNB '95-97; Halifax Mooseheads (QMJHL) '97; director of scouting operations Halifax from '98; governor Canada's Sports Hall of Fame; NHL record: 736 scheduled games, 263g, 273a, 43 playoff games, 10g, 14a; mem. NB Sports Hall of Fame; res. Nasonworth, N.B.

GRANT, Duncan (parachuting); b. 29 Jul 1950, Whitehorse, Yukon; m. Ginette Vanasse; c. Marc, Nicole; sport administrator; tech. dir. Canadian Sport Parachuting Assn '80-85, Fitness Canada '86, Cdn Archers '86-93, Baseball '93-98; 1st 10-way '74; 2nd 10-way '75-76; 2nd 8-way '77, '79; 3rd 4-way '76, '78-79; instructor examiner, instructor rigger, CAC coach; aerial photographer; more than 3300 jumps, 37 hours free fall time; exec. dir. Baseball Canada; res. Ottawa, Ont.

GRANT, Fred (harness racing); b. 23 Jan 1951, North Sydney, N.S.; while playing junior hockey, was thrust into standardbred scene as a track announcer when regular announcer died; received his driver's license and won the first race, the first time he went behind a gate with a horse; worked for Stanley Dancer, Billy Haughton training the likes of Silent Majority, Handle With Care; branched out on own developing Senor Skipper, Ella Hanover and Major Knight; became leading trainer at Meadowlands '84; trained world record holder Wholesale, free-for-all pacer Cambest; his major impact on sport came as trainer although he drives occasionally winning 323 races and more than $1M in purses; res. East Rutherford, N.J.

GRANT, Martha (swimming/equestrian); b. 22 Oct 1954, Saskatoon, Sask.; given name: Martha Stina Nelson; m. Donald James Grant; Uof Sask, BSc, BEd; competitive swimmer '63-72; 43 provincial records, ntl age-group standards 200m IM; '71 sr. girls 100m backstroke mark; mem. Dolphins SC; men. '72 Olympic team; 1st 200m backstroke, 200m IM '72 Warsaw meet; became involved in equestrian sport attaining B1 National Pony Club standard before age eligibility excluded her; continues to show horses, judge at volunteer level; coach HS volleyball; level 1 t&f coaching certificate; active cross-country skier; mem. Sask., Saskatoon Sports halls of fame; res. Saskatoon, Sask.

GRANT, Mike (hockey); b. 1870s, Montreal, Que.; d. 1961 Montreal, Que.; capt. Montreal Victorias, Stanley Cup 1894, 1896-98; mem. Victorias (CAHL) 1899-1900, '02, Shamrocks '01; retd. to refereeing following '02 season; mem. Hockey Hall of Fame.

GRANT, Tommy (football); b. 9 Jan 1935, Windsor, Ont; m. Ida Gagnon; c. Colette, Lisa, Tommy Jr, Michelle; car salesman; outstanding HS jr. (AKO) football career led to pro ranks Hamilton '56 where he won EFC rookie of year Gruen Trophy; halfback 14 seasons Hamilton, Winnipeg; caught 329 passes for 6542yds, 19.9 avg., 51tds; most productive season '64, 44 passes for 1029yds; 105yd kickoff return vs. Montreal '62; frequent all-star; 1yr pro outfielder Detroit Tigers chain; mem. Cdn Football Hall of Fame; res. Burlington, Ont.

GRASSICK, Greg (football/coaching); b. 1900, Regina, Sask.; d. 4 Apr 1983, Regina, Sask.; m. ; c. Janet, Marion, Jim, Geordie; McGill; halfback under coach Shag Shaughnessey McGill; halfback, coach. Roughriders '27-32, 5 Grey Cup finals; introduced huddle to Western football as coach Regina Dales '33; coached Roughriders '34; helped introduce forward pass to Cdn. game '29 Grey Cup; accomodations mgr. Roughriders '48-50; mem. Sask. Sports Hall of Fame.

GRATTON, Paul (volleyball); b. 8 Nov 1958, Ottawa, Ont; m. France Fouquette; UofOott, BPhE; athlete representative, pres. Sim Gratton Inc.; mem. ntl jr. team '77; ntl sr. team '78-85, capt. '82-85; competed '84 Olympics; pro volleyball Osaka, Japan '84-87; 3 championship MVP awards; 3yrs best hitter, all-star in championships, 2 best server awards, 1 best blocker award; pro Treviso, Italy '91; Frejus, France '87-92; 3 French titles, 3 French Cup; 2 runnerup French championship, 1 silver, bronze European championships; MVP/best hitter several tournaments; pro Bordeaux, France '93; pres. Sport International Management '94; part-time volleyball teacher UofOtt from '95; volleyball consultant conducting clinics for players/coaches from '92; res. Orleans, Ont.

GRAVELLE, Gérard (ski jumping); b. 15 Dec 1934, Hull, Que.; m. Rita Guertin; c. Michel, Rosane; blacksmith; mem. '60 Olympic, '62 world championships, '55-57 Que. Games teams; Gil O Julien trophy as French athlete of '61; Ont. athlete of yr. nominee '62-63; res. Hull, Que.

GRAVELLE, Red (hockey); b. 7 Dec 1927, Aylmer, Que.; d. 18 Jan 1997, Trenton, Ont.; given name: Orval; m. Jeanne Perrier (d), Phyllis Sprowl; c. Suzanne, John, Paul, Phil, Rebecca; superintendant works, engineering Solicitor General of Canada; Jr. B Ottawa '45-47; pro tryout NY Rangers '47; mem. RCAF Flyers Olympic title team '48; Sr. A Ottawa, Smith Falls, Pembroke, Quebec City, Belleville, Trenton, P.E.I.; hockey referee '55-75 working

Allan, Memorial Cup finals; '66 anniversary medallion for Jr. A playoff officiating; retired RCAF '70; active in Old Timers hockey; as mem. '48 Flyers mem. Ottawa Sports Hall of Fame.

GRAVES, Adam (hockey); b. 12 Apr 1968, Toronto, Ont.; m. Violet; c. Madison; centre Windsor (OHL) '85-87, Adirondack (AHL) '87-88; drafted by Detroit '86; NHL with Detroit '87-89, Edmonton '89-91, NY Rangers from '91; 2nd team NHL all-star '94; NHL record (through '99): 830 scheduled games, 276g, 231a, 113 playoff games, 35g, 26a; mem. Stanley Cup winner; hit 50-goal plateau 52 '94; King Clancy Memorial trophy '94; mem. Team Canada '88 World jr. title team; capt. Team Canada '93; played organized soccer 12yrs; celebrity chair. NYC Family Dynamics; 3 Players' Player, 10 NYR club awards; res. Tecumseh, Ont.

GRAVES, Richard (ski jumping); b. 22 Apr 1955, Montreal, Que.; given name: Richard MacFarlane; Guelph; at 14 jr. B alpine racer, mem. Ottawa jr. cross-country team; switched to jumping '70; mem. ntl jumping team '72, jr. titlist '72-73; runnerup US jrs, 3rd srs, 37th world ski flying championships, 20th world jr. '73; 7th Garmisch International '74; 2nd NA plastic jumping championships '75; ntl 70m title '75-76; O'Keefe international '76; res. Ottawa, Ont.

GRAY, Clyde (boxing); b. 10 Mar 1946, Windsor, N.S.; m. Evelyn Coates; c. Tony, Jennifer, Clyde Jr, Jeremy; 30 wins, 2 losses, 32 amateur bouts; 2 NY State Golden Gloves titles; managed by Irv Ungerman, 69 wins, 10 losses, 79 pro bouts; victories included 49 by KO; ntl, Commonwealth welterweight titles simultaneously; unsuccessful 3 world title bids; ntl welter title '71 beating Donato Paduano; '73 Commonwealth title beating Eddie Blay; defended ntl crown 7 times; lost title to Guerra Chavez regained it within 12 months; defended Commonwealth crown 7 times; lost title to Chris Clark '79 regained it within 4 months; only Cdn to retire as reigning ntl, Commonwealth champion; mem. fed. govt. task force to improve safety in boxing '80-81; supervisor Ont. boxing '80; Ont. Athletic Commissioner '81-88; introduced passport system of boxer ID & licencing; fight judge; boxing instructor Regent Park BC from '91; mem. Cdn Boxing, NS Sports halls of fame; res. Scarborough, Ont.

GRAY, George (t&f); b. 1865, Coldwater, Ont.; d. 1933, Sault Ste. Marie, Ont.; at 1885 Canadian Amateur Athletic Assn. meet Toronto put shot 41'5.5" to win title with initial toss in 1st competition, held it 17yrs; acclaimed world champion; eldest brother John twice won 2-oared rowing title of America; 2 cousins were rowers Jake Gaudaur Sr., all-round athlete, track coach Harry Gill; world shot put record 43'11" 1887, held it through '02, broke own record several times; at retirement had won 188 medals, trophies for shot put; mem. Canada's Sports Hall of Fame.

GRAY, Gerry (soccer); b. 20 Jan 1961, Glasgow, Scotland; given name: Gerard; m. Michelle Rafferty; c. Shannon, Daniel, Justine; Business Succession Planning; received initial taste of soccer in Scotland and on moving to Canada pursued his soccer education with Malton minor program; served international apprenticeship with ntl youth team;

played key role in helping Canada win CONCACAF zone title; competed '79 FIFA world championships; pro Vancouver Whitecaps '80-82, Montreal Manic, NY Cosmos, Chicago Sting, San Francisco Golden Bay, Tacoma Stars, Hamilton Steelers; earned 1st international cap in rookie season; competed in 11 Olympic tournament contests including run to '84 Olympic quarter-finals; played 33 full sr. international games; with Whitecaps in indoor play scored 29 goals in 32 games '80-81; Mississauga pro athlete of '80; mem. Mississauga Sports Hall of Fame; res. Tacoma, Wash.

GRAY, Herb (football); b. 12 Jun 1934, Baytown, Tex.; given name: Herbert William; m. Joy; c. James Kevin, Stephen Craig, Bryan David; Texas, B.S.; co. v-p; 3 all-district HS awards, all-Southern, all-American sr. year; Texas all-Southwestern Conference 4 years, lineman of year, all-American sr. year; pro Winnipeg '56-65; all-star guard-end 7 times, frequent all-Cdn; defensive capt. 9yrs; played Sr. Bowl, Can-US Shrine Games; 6 Grey Cup finals, 4 winners; '60 Schenley Award Outstanding lineman (1st def. player); '65 Dr. Bert Oja most valuable Bomber lineman award; Winnipeg defensive player of 1st 1/2 century; mem. Cdn, Blue Bombers Football, Blue Bombers Alumni Alley, Man. Sports halls of fame; res. San Antonio, Tex.

GRAY, Rob (t&f); b. 5 Oct 1956, Toronto, Ont.; given name: Robert John Kelly; Southern Methodist, Osgoode Hall; lawyer; discus specialist; Toronto HS champion '73-75; Ont., ntl jr. title '76; ntl sr. title '79, '83; silver '82, bronze '78 Commonwealth Games; mem. '79 Pan-Am, '80, '84 Olympic, '79, '83 FISU Games teams; steroids use resulted in banishment from '86 Commonwealth Games team, indefinite CTFA suspension; last known res. Downsview, Ont.

GRAY, Steve (rugby); b. 19 Jul 1963, Ottawa, Ont.; given name: Stephen Douglas; Algonquin Coll.; customer acct. rep. BC Hydro; Jr. A hockey Ottawa Senators; wing/centre ntl -19s vs. Japan '82; earned 1st of 47 caps vs. USA '84; ntl record 3 tries vs. USA '87; competed '87, '91, '95 World Cup, '93 World Cup of 7s, 6 Hong Kong 7s tournaments; retd. '97; nicknamed "Kats"; res. Vancouver, B.C.

GREAVES, Joe (baseball/curling); b. 23 Nov 1914, Port Arthur, Ont.; given name: James George; m. Dorothy Benson; c. Elaine, John, Jim, Bernard; retired printer, hall of fame curator; earned nickname "Two-bagger Joe" during standout 28yr baseball career as player, coach, organizer, umpire; organized Port Arthur Little League '52; coached, umpired LL 16yrs; softball organizer, fund-raiser, umpire '33-47; chairman Legion sports comm. '46-50; formed Legion Boxing Club; organized, managed Green Rivers sr. football club '37; mgr. Packers football team '38-40; exec. mem. Port Arthur Mustangs sr. football team '46-47; organized Port Arthur sr. basketball team '39; had key role in Thunder Bay minor hockey program; exec. mem. Port Arthur Curling & Athletic Club; exec. mem. Northwestern Ont. CA 10yrs; key role in promoting youth curling; mem. Port Arthur stadium building comm; mem. Port Arthur Parks & Civic Recreation comm; developer, curator Northwestern Ont. Sports Hall of Fame; mem. NWO Sports Hall of Fame; res. Thunder Bay, Ont.

GREEN, Donald (sailing); b. 8 Oct 1932, Hamilton, Ont.; given name: Donald MacKenzie; m. Marion Alexandra Little; c. Sharon, Stephen; Ryerson PTI, UWO, McMaster; chair., chief exec. officer Tridon Cos.; inherited love of sailing from father Victor; at 12 captained Royal Hamilton Yacht Club's 3rd place entry '46 international jr. regatta Toronto, '47 won same event; at 19 sailed around world aboard Brigantine Yankee skippered by Capt. Irving Johnson; authored book "*White Wings Around the World*"; '78 skippered Evergreen to Canada's Cup victory; yacht destroyed '79 Fastnet disaster; new Evergreen built '81; past-commodore RHYC; governor Olympic Trust of Canada; dir. Cdn National Sportsmen's Shows; chairman True North Syndicate; Burlington young man of '69; 1 of 10 outstanding Ont. young men '69; Ryerson Fellowship '79; mem. Order of Canada; res. Burlington, Ont.

GREEN, Gary (hockey); b. 23 Aug 1953, Tillsonburg, Ont.; given name: Gary Lee; m. Sharon Causyn; c. Jennifer; Guelph, BA; TSN hockey color commentator; minor pro defenceman WHA Vancouver Blazers chain before turning to coaching; chief operating officer Tam O'Shanter Hockey School at 21; 3yrs asst. to Roger Neilson Peterborough Petes; coach Petes at 24, Memorial Cup finals 2 straight years, championship '79; co-authored 3 hockey books; merged Tam O'Shanter, Can-Am hockey schools; launched series of intl pro hockey symposiums; coach Hershey Bears to start '79-80; elevated to Washington 14 Nov '79 becoming youngest coach in NHL history at 26; 5 Nov '81 fired; NHL record: 50-78-29 ties; OMJHL coach of '79; res. Riva, Md.

GREEN, Peter (rowing); b. 15 Feb 1920, South Wellington, B.C.; given name: Peter Valentine; m. Sylvia Pearl Isnor; c. David, Valerie; McNaughton Hall Hamilton; retired DND; stroke oar for Leander club heavy 4s '43, stroke heavy 8s following year; scored several US, Canadian regatta victories; mem. Olympic 8s semifinalists '48; lost to Vancouver crew '52 Olympic trials; res. Victoria, B.C.

GREEN, Ron (curling); b. 11 Apr 1947, Toronto, Ont.; given name: Ronald Lawerence; div. Carol; c. Leslie; m. Linda; c. Lindsay, Robyn; pres. Gratham Industries; with Paul Savage Ont. jr. title '66; with Bill Creber runnerup to Ken Buchan '69 Consols; with Savage Ont. Brier entry '73, '74, '77; won '73-74 Royals carspiel; competed CBC Curling Classic '73-74, won '77-78; won '75 Century Curling Classic Calgary; skipped own rink to Canada Life title Toronto; all-star lead '73-74 Briers; only player from Eastern Canada named to Brier all-time all-star team for 1st 50yrs; res. Toronto, Ont.

GREEN, Shawn (baseball); b.10 Nov 1972, Des Plaines, Ill; given name: Shawn David; outfielder; standout HS career Tustin, Calif. Led to scholarship offer from Stanford U; drafted by Toronto '91; donated portion of signing bonus to Metro Toronto Housing Authority Breakfast Club for needy children; minor league stops in Dunedin, Knoxville, Syracuse (MVP) before joining Blue Jays as regular '95; gold glove fielder with strong arm; lefthanded batter with power; became 1st Blue Jay to post 30hr/30sb in single season '98; belted 42hr, 123rbi, club record 28 game hitting streak '99 earning all-star status; gold glove award '99; traded to LA Dodgers '99; IL rookie of '94, IL, Florida State all-star, IL batting title '94; res. Newport Beach, Calif.

GREEN, Shorty (hockey); b. 17 Jul 1896, Sudbury, Ont.; d. 19 Apr 1960,; given name: Wilfred Thomas; Sudbury Intermediates NOHA '14-15; after WW1 joined Hamilton Tigers, '19 Allan Cup; returned to Sudbury to '23; pro Hamilton Tigers '23, league title '25; as capt. spokesman for players who refused to participate in playoffs unless club paid $200 per player; club owners refused and Toronto-Montreal were forced to meet for title; Hamilton franchise shifted to NY; Green scored 1st goal in Madison Square Garden 19 Dec '25; coached through '33 before retiring; mem. Hockey Hall of Fame.

GREEN, Ted (hockey); b. 23 Mar 1940, Eriksdale, Man.; given name: Edward Joseph; m. Pat; c. 3; hockey exec.; St. Boniface jrs, Winnipeg (WHL) Memorial Cup winners, Kingston (EPHL), NHL Boston 60-72; mem. '72 Stanley Cup winner; steady, stay at home defenceman; NHL record: 620 scheduled games, 48g, 206a, 31 playoff games, 4g, 8a; played in WHA with New England Whalers '72-75, Winnipeg Jets '75-79 winning 4 Avco Cups; playing career and life seriously threatened when his head became target of Wayne Maki stick assault at Ottawa Civic Centre, 3 brain operations followed; returned to pro ranks for 9 more seasons but his aggressive nature was subdued; turned to coaching Carmen Hornets (Man. intermediate champs) '79-80; asst. Team Canada '84 Canada Cup; asst. Edmonton '81-85, '86-89, '97-98, head coach '89-93; ass't to Oilers president '93-'97; 5 Stanley Cup winners; mem. Man. Hockey Hall of Fame; res. Edmonton, Alta.

GREENE, Nancy (skiing); b. 11 May 1943, Ottawa, Ont.; given name: Nancy Catherine; m. Al Raine; c. Charles, William; Cahilty Lodge co-owner; ntl team '59-68; mem. '60, '64, '68 Olympic teams; GS gold, slalom silver '68 Olympics; mem. world championships team '62-66; 7 ntl, 3 US titles; '67-68 World Cup; FIS, WC combined golds '68; WC record 14-2-4; retd following '68 Olympics; Order of Canada silver medal '67, Order of Dogwood, Lou Marsh, Bobbie Rosenfeld trophies '67-68; B'nai B'rith woman of '68; hon. chair. Nancy Greene Ski League; BC female athlete of century; mem. '68-69 fed. Task Force on Sport for Canadians, FIS WC comm.; prominent as sports ambassador; TV color commentator; Toni Sailor summer ski camp; dir. ski racing Blackcomb Mountain; ski dir. Sun Peaks resort; special rep. Rossingnol Skis; active mem. Cdn Ski Team alumni; flag-bearer '68 winter Olympics; Officer Order of Canada '67; named Canada's female athlete of century '99; mem. Cdn, U.S. Skiing, Cdn Amateur (Olympic), Cdn Winter Olympic, Canada's, BC, Ont. Legends Sports halls of fame; Cdn Walk of Fame; res. Sun Peaks, B.C.

GREENFELD, Sherman (racquetball); b. 3 Jun 1962, Winnipeg, Man.; UMan. BEd; racquets pro; began playing age 16; record 10 ntl titles; unbeaten 13 consecutive yrs in Man. tournament play; bronze '79 Canada Winter Games; gold '95 Pan-Am Games qualifier; silver, bronze '95 Pan-Am Games; gold men's singles '94, '98, with Mike Ceresia silver men's doubles '94 world amateur championships; mem. 2 ntl men's title teams; won tournament of Americas title; twice Man. YMHA Jewish athlete of yr; res. Winnipeg, Man.

GREENIDGE, Ricardo (t&f/bobsled); b. 12 Feb 1971, Ottawa, Ont.; Blinn College; 200m specialist; 1st international appearance vs. US '89; silver 100, 200m vs. Ireland '92; ntl jr. 200m title '90; competed world jr. championships '90; ntl indoor 200m title '93, outdoor title '94; competed in '93 world indoor championships, '94 Commonwealth Games; silver 200m '94 Francophone Games; PB: 10.44 100m, 20.87 200m '92; mem. ntl bobsleigh team from '96; as brakeman for Pierre Lueders WC gold '97; competed '98 Olympics; ntl 2-man title '99; mem. Ottawa Lions TC; HS soccer standout; res. Calgary, Alta.

GREENOUGH, Gail (equestrian); b. 7 Mar 1960, Edmonton, Alta.; m. Neil Runions; sc. Jeff, Derek; UAlta. BA; freelance coach; began riding age 11; competed in dressage before shifting to show jumping; won individual dressage bronze Alta summer games; ntl team '83-93; mem. Nations Cup title team '84; riding Mr. T became 1st women/North American to win world title '86; qualified but did not compete 3 World Cup finals; CBC-TV color commentator '88 Olympics, '97 World Cup; honored by Alta. Sports Writers, Metro Toronto Convention Centre Women's Show; TSN female athlete of '86; finalist ntl female athlete of '86; subject of TV special; mem. Order of Canada, Cdn Amateur, Alta Sports halls of fame; res. Calgary, Alta.

GREENWAY, Tom (judo); b. 28 Sep 1956, Lethbridge, Alta.; given name: Thomas Myers: U of Lethbridge; 95kg victories CNE, jr. Olympics '74; 4 provincial, 2 ntl titles; 3 gold Western Canada Games; mem. '76, '80 Olympic, '79 Pan-Am Games, '78, '80 Pan-American championships teams; victories '77 US Youth championships, '80 Takahama Cup, '80 Pan-Am championships, '81 Czechoslovakian, Desert Opens; UMan. title '81; silver '79, bronze '80 US Open; demo bronze '86 Commonwealth Games; res. Lethbridge, Alta.

GRÉGOIRE, Hélène (water skiing); b.10 Mar 1953, Hull, Que.; given name: Hélène Madeleine; div. Robert Langevin; c. Joelle, Michelle; Montreal, DMD; dentist; dominated girls division ntl championships '69-70, gold slalom, jumping, tricks; ntl team '70-77; 10 ntl titles; 6 gold Can-Am competitions; mem. 1 World Cup, Pan-Am Games, 3 world championships teams; Julien Trophy French Canadian amateur athlete of '70; Que. Sports Federation water skiing sports merit award '74; as alpine skier ntl jr. GS gold '69; mem. elite development comm. CAWSA; supervisor Que. Games water skiing '81; mem. Ottawa Sports Hall of Fame; res. Hull, Que..

GRENDA, Ed (snowshoe/soccer/hockey); b. 11 Jan 1942, Vancouver, B.C.; given name: Edward Ronald; m. Helen Elizabeth Andrascik; c. Bradley, Adam; UBC, BA, MA, London School of Economics; university lecturer, social science consultant; competitive snowshoer racing in Canada, USA, France '74-92; won 400m title Lewiston, Me., '81, 8km race walk Ottawa '83, Lewiston '85; ntl 8km race walk titles '83, '85; 3 Ont./West Que. 8km titles; 4 race walker of yr awards; dir. Cdn Snowshoe Assn. '91-97, head coach '91-97, co-chair. International Snowshoe Comm. (France) '92-94; dir. Ont. Soccer Assn. '91-95, v-p '95, pres. '95-97;

dir. Cdn Soccer Assn. '96-98; pres/dir. International Hockey Hall of Fame and Museum Kingston '80-95; secty IIHFM '95-97; res. Kingston, Ont.

GRENIER, Louis (speed skating); b. 20 Jul 1960, Toronto, Ont.; computer technician; ntl indoor all-around titles '72-73, '79; NA indoor title '79; 2nd 500m, 4th 1000m, 3000m world indoor '79; 2nd 1500m, 3000m, all-around '80 world indoor; Caltex Cup Australia '79; world short track 500m, 1000m, 3000m, all-around '83; world record 500m; Norton Crowe Trophy '83; fed. govt. world champion award '83; short track team leader '94 Olympics; mem. Cdn Speed Skating Hall of Fame; res. Lac Beauport, Que.

GRETSINGER, Bert (curling); b. 7 Apr 1951, Winnipeg, Man.; m. Carmel; c. Kristine, Matthew; businessman; 6 Brier appearances, played 3rd for Bernie Sparkes '76, Rick Folk '89, 2nd Folk '93-94, skip '99 Brier; winner '94; mem. '94 world title rink; res. Kelowna, B.C.

GRETZKY, Wayne (hockey); b. 26 Jan 1961, Brantford, Ont.; m. Janet Jones; c. Paulina Mary Jean, Ty Robert, Trevor Douglas; jr. Peterborough, Sault Ste. Marie; OHA rookie of year '77-78; pro WHA Indianapolis '78-79 (rookie of year), Edmonton (WHA, NHL) '79-88, Los Angeles '88-95, St. Louis '95-96, NY Rangers '96-99; nicknamed "Great One"; scoring prowess rewrote record book; at retirement held/shared 61 NHL records; 9 50-plus goal seasons; 4 times topped 200-point single season plateau 212 '81-82, 205 '83-84, 208 '84-85, 215 '85-86; record 92g single 80-game season '81-82; 163a '85-86; youngest player to achieve 1000 point plateau in 424th game '84-85 season; surpassed Gordie Howe's all-time NHL goal record of 801 '94, assist record of 1850 '97; 9 Hart Trophies, 8 in succession, '80-87, '89, 10 Ross Trophies, 7 in succession, '81-87, '90-91, '94; 4 Lady Byng Trophies, 5 Lester B Pearson awards; 2 Conn Smythe trophies, '94 Lester Patrick award; 3 Emery Edge; 3 performer of year awards; 8 1st team, 5 2nd team all-star centre; 4 NHL plus/minus titles; 16 NHL all-star games; 3 NHL all-star game MVP awards; Lou Kaplan WHA rookie of '79 award; mem. '78 jr. worlds, '82 worlds, 4 Canada Cup teams (3 titles), capt. '96 World Cup team, mem. '98 Olympic team; NHL record: 1487 scheduled games, 894g, 1963a, 208 playoff games, 122g, 260a; mem. 4 Stanley Cup winners; 51-game consecutive point scoring streak '83-84; fastest 50 goals 39 games '81; 6 Lionel Conacher, 4 Lou Marsh trophies; *SI* Sportsman of '82, Hickox Pro athlete of '83; 3 successive Seagram's 7 Crowns hockey player of year awards; 4 *Sporting News*, 5 *Hockey News* awards; AP, Ont. athlete of year awards; AP male athlete of decade '89; *Hockey News* Greatest Player of All-time award '98; co-owner, pres. Belleville Bulls Jr.A OHA '82-84; owner Hull Olympiques QMJHL '85-92; co-owner with Bruce McNall, John Candy of CFL Argos '91-93; partner restaurant chain, Windsor Rec. complex; Brantford Rec. complex, Edmonton street bear his name; Officer Order of Canada '84; initial recipient US Hockey Hall of Fame award bearing his name; mem. Hockey Hall of Fame; res. Thousand Oaks, Calif.

GRIBBIN, Chris (administration); b. 20 Aug 1921, Montreal, Que.; given name: Christopher Howard; m. Yvette Gerin-Lajoie; c. Christine, Michael, Philip; Loyola, BA, McGill, Montreal; retd. exec.-dir. Quebec Golf Assn.,

professor Montreal; Cdn Ski Instructors Alliance secty-treas, Level IV examiner '48-63; 12yrs Montreal alpine, nordic ski coach; Intl Assn Golf Administrators pres. '78-79; began QGA association as tournament dir. '54, exec. dir '66-90; instrumental in translation of golf rules to French '60s; established Que. provincial qualifying system; initiated most favorable "Greenbelt" legislation '70s; stimulated prov., district annual golf symposiums; co-ordinated turfgrass referral service subsidized by QGA, bilingual club handbook; developed training program to improve candidates for Willingdon Cup team; promoted modernization QGA constitution; res. Pte. Claire, Que.

GRIFFIN, Audrey (swimming); b. 16 Jun 1902, Burgess Hill, Sussex, Eng.; d. 28 Aug 1995, Victoria, B.C.; given name: Audrey Mildred; m. John Russell Kieran; St. Anne's Academy; ntl, Pacific Northwest titles; never lost a BC women's championship entered '15-30; tireless competitor, swam every distance from 50yds to 3 miles, never losing a 220, 440 or 880yd event; nicknamed "Mike"; 5 ntl championships, twice runnerup; 9 Victoria mixed 3 mile swim titles in 12 attempts, beating both men, women; mem. BC, Greater Victoria Sports halls of fame.

GRIFFIN, Pat (wheelchair basketball); b. 14 Nov 1960, Alberton, P.E.I.; given name: Patrick Emmett; m. Barbara Jean Lalor; c. Craig Patrick; St. Mary's, BComm; senior inquiries agent Revenue Canada Taxation; began playing wheelchair basketball '79; mem. Edmonton Raiders, 4 ntl titles, 4 championship MVP awards; mem. Team Canada from '84, capt. '86-92; co-capt. '92 Paralympic team; gold Stoke-Mandeville Games '89-91; competed '96 Paralympics; high scoring performer; 4th '86 ntl wheelchair 10km road race; mem. ntl bronze medal sledge hockey team '94 Paralympics Norway; res. Edmonton, Alta.

GRIFFING, Dean (football); b. 17 May 1915, St George, Kan.; d. 1998, Sandwich, Ill.; div. Bea Metcalfe; c. Barbara, Doug; m. Ann Dockendorf; c. Christopher, Susan; Kansas State; retd. restaurateur; center Chicago Cardinals '35; helped Regina win '36 WIFU title but CRU ruled club had broken eligibility rules so Grey Cup challenge rights were forfeited; nicknamed "Bad Man"; 5 times all-Cdn center; Sask. player-coach through '43; Toronto Balmy Beach player-line coach '44; owner-coach Stampeders '45-47; mgr.. Roughriders '54-57; operated all-America Bowl Game Tucson '58-59; mgr. Denver (AFL) '59-63; scout Detroit, Chicago to '70; mem. Cdn Football Hall of Fame.

GRIFFIS, Si (hockey); b. 1883, Onaga, Kansas; d. Jul 1950, Kenora, Ont.; given name: Silas Seth; rover, defence Rat Portage (Kenora) Thistles '03-07; retired following '07 season, returned '12-18 Vancouver Millionaires (PCHA); helped Kenora claim league titles 1900-04, Stanley Cup '06; capt. Millionaires Stanley Cup final '15; nicknamed "Sox"; stroked jr. 4s '05 Canadian Henley title; excelled as southpaw golfer, 10-pin bowler; mem. NWO Sports, Hockey halls of fame.

GRIFFITH, Cal (baseball/administration); b. 1 Dec 1911, Montreal, Que.; d. 20 Oct 1999, Melbourne, Fla.; given name: Calvin; Staunton Military Academy, George Washington U; baseball executive; following father's death

'20, he and sister Thelma adopted by uncle Clark; Washington Senators batboy '22; gained baseball club operation experience Chatanooga, Charlotte, AL Senators; on death of uncle '55, co-owner (with sister), pres. Senators; transferred club to Minnesota '60, renamed Twins; under his regime '65 AL pennant, World Series loss to LA Dodgers 4-3, 2 divisional titles ('69-70); sold club '84.

GRIFFITH, Harry (coaching); b. 19 Sep 1878, Hamilton, Ont.; d. 9 Dec 1960, Toronto, Ont.; given name: Henry Crawford; m. Ethel Clare Wright; c. 1 son, 1 daughter; Ridley College, Trinity College, BA, MA; educator; QB varsity football team; coached Trinity '07-10, 2 consecutive Grey Cups; Ridley rugby, cricket coach '11-49; mem. Canada's Sports, Cdn Football Hall of Fame.

GRIFFITHS, Frank (builder/hockey); b. 17 Dec 1916, Burnaby, B.C.; d. 7 Apr 1994, Vancouver, B.C; UBC, FCA; founded/developed Northwest Sports Enterprises '74 and purchased Vancouver hockey club; fostered relations with Vancouver-based club and province; NHL governor '74-94; vice-chair. NHL, mem. audit comm. '79-87; assisted numerous clubs in solidifying finances; mem. Hockey Hall of Fame.

GRIFFITHS, Joe (coaching); b. Mar 1885, Swansea, Wales; d. 22 Jul 1967, Saskatoon, Sask.; m. Mary Elizabeth Byers; c. Betty, Patricia; UofSask, hon. LLD teacher; 32yrs t&f, swimming coach UofSask.; coached each sport in separate Olympics '36, '48; UofSask. swim team unbeaten 11 straight years; organized 1st annual Sask. HS t&f meet; Griffiths's Trophy awarded annually to Western Cdn U swim title team; Regina Stadium named in his honor; life mem. Royal Life Saving Society; CAHPER honor award; Saskatoon Citizen of Year; mem. Sask., Saskatoon Sports halls of fame.

GRIMSLEY, Ross (baseball); b. 7 Jan 1950, Topeka, Kan.; given name: Ross Albert III; m. Byrd Worrell; c. Patrick; Jacksonville State Community Coll.; baseball coach; all-conf., J.C. all-American; drafted by Cincinnati '69; minors with Sioux Falls (A), Indianapolis (AAA); ML lhp with Cincinnati '71-73, Baltimore '73-77, '82, Montreal '78-79, Cleveland '80-81; ML record: 345 games, 124-99, 3.81era, 199 complete games; became 1st 20-game winner in Expos history '78 with 20-11 record, 2.05era, earned all-star status; 2-1 record '72 World Series; minor league pitching coach for Mariners '84-89, '90-93, Braves '89; dir. baseball operations Amarillo Dillas '94-95; pitching coach Rochester (AAA) '96, Reading (AA) from '97; nicknamed "Skuz"; res. Reading, Pa.

GRINER, Wendy (figure skating); b. 16 Apr 1944, Hamilton, Ont.; given name: Wendy Elizabeth; m. Dr. Donald Peter Ballantyne; c. Peter, Rob, Karen; Branksome Hall; registered medical technologist; '59 ntl jr. champion; sr. title '60-63; NA title '63; silver '62 world championships; mem. '60, '64 Olympic teams; res. Thunder Bay, Ont.

GRINNELL, Rae (skiing); b. 24 Apr 1921, Toronto, Ont.; m. Betty Heron; c. Eric, Jane, Douglas, Sheila; UNB, BScF; retd forest economist; zone, provincial, CIAU titles; developed ski clubs several areas in Canada; Ont. zone, div. pres. CASA 12 years, ntl pres. '61-64; 1st Cdn, 2nd NA on FIS Council '63-71; mem. FIS eligibility comm. '62-73; COA dir. '63-73; chairman National Ski Museum; 8yrs exec. mem., v-p Canadian Amateur Sports Federation; mem. Cdn Skiing Hall of Fame; res. Manotick, Ont.

GROFF, Doug (canoeing/skiing); b. 16 Sep 1912, Winnipeg, Man.; d. 1933, Winnipeg, Man.; m. Florence Kieper; c. Judith, Geraldine, Susan, Nancy; retd. wholesale sporting goods; mem. Winnipeg Canoe Club; 6 sr. singles titles; 5 65-mile Les Voyageurs race titles; won Cdn intermediate fours '35, singles '36, tandem '37, Sr. tandem, singles '37; cox Cdn quarter-mile war canoe titlist '38; won American Canoe Assn. 6-mile singles, single blade 4s, double blade 4s, Sr. singles '38; qualified for '40 Olympic team winning 10,000m tandem '39; won Man. Sr. 4s '46; rear commodore WCC '38, vice commodore ACA '38; chair. WCC 85th reunion '78, pres. WCC past commodores assn, hon. commodore WCC '80; mem. 3-man team making 1st ski ascent Mt. Athabasca '40; chief ski mountaineering instructor Cdn army '43-44; chair. Manitoba Zone CASA '48; chair. CASA Central div.; Man. downhill title '35, slalom '35-36, '38-39, jumping '36, '38, cross-country '37-40, Srs. slalom '79; life mem. WSC; won 141 International dinghy sailing title Red River '39; won Labatt's Pro-Am golf title Pine Ridge '62; chair., v-p organizing board '67 Pan-Am Games committee; mem. Man. Order of Buffalo Hunt; honored by Winnipeg Police Commission, Pan-Am Games Assn., Man. Good Citizenship award; mem. Man. Sports Hall of Fame.

GROSS, George Jr. (water polo); b. 8 Mar 1952, Toronto, Ont.; Yale, BSc; UofT, BEd; owner G-Squared Promotion Ltd., G-Squared Productions Ltd.; competitive swimmer, mem. '73 FISU Games team; ntl water polo team '75-87; averaged goal-per-game 170 consec. intl games; defence 2 Olympic, 5 Pan-Am, 2 FISU, 3 world championships teams; bronze '79, '83 Pan-Am Games; competed ntl championships '77-94, 14yrs all-star, MVP '81, '86; 2 UofT MVP awards; men's ntl team coach '87-91, '94-96; founder/coach Toronto Golden Jets '81-91, 2 titles, Phantoms '93-95, 1 title; 5 Eastern WP League (US) all-star awards; International referee; accredited Level 1 clinic conductor; Sport Canada consultant '77-79; pres. Golden Jets, Phantoms, mem. Ont. WP board; deeply involved at administration level of sport; columnist for now defunct *Aquatics* magazine; founded/folded *Inside Water* magazine; son of prominent Toronto sports columnist; mem. Yale Wall, Ont. Aquatic Hall of Fame; res. Thornhill, Ont.

GROUT, Cameron (swimming); b. 23 Oct 1939, Montreal, Que.; m. Marsha Leigh Beaton; c. Christi, Robin; McGill, BSc; investment dealer; 21 ntl titles; medalist '58 BEG, '59 Pan-Am Games; finalist '60 Olympics; coach MAAA '63-64, Que. all-star team '64; dir. CASA Que. section '64-65, NS section '73-75; pres. NS section CASA '70-72; ntl dir. CASA '73-75; 1st pres. Sport NS '70-73; dir. Olympic Club Canada '73-75, pres. '73-74; dir. COA '74; dir. SFC '72-73; chair. NS Kinsmen Special Olympics '73; chair. Oakville Parks, Recreation Commission '76-90; chair. Canadian Council for co-operation in aquatics '77-78; NS award for sport, recreation administration '75; hon. life mem. Sport NS; Canadian swimmer of year '58-59; Montreal athlete of '58-59; outstanding McGill athlete '58; mem. MAAA Hall of Fame; res. Oakville, Ont.

GROUT, Glen (diving); b. 31 May 1952, N.Vancouver; B.C.; SFU; ntl jr. 1m, 3m springboard titles '69; gold 3m winter nationals '72; bronze 2m, silver 10m '73 summer nationals; silver 10m '73 winter nationals; gold 10m '75 winter nationals; mem. '73, '75 worlds, '74 Commonwealth, '76 Olympic teams; res. Vancouver, B.C.

GRUNDY, Art (shooting); b. 1 Dec 1933, Windsor, Ont.; given name: Robert Arthur; m. Sue; c. Gloria, Angela, Arlene; retd. GM supervisor; began competitive shooting '48; ntl smallbore champion '64; mem. '80 Olympic team; qualified 11 Bisley, 4 Palma teams; Ont. Games gold '73; 2 Indiana State prone titles; mem. North Shore, Cedar Springs Rifle Clubs, Livonia Sportsman Club; active hockey, slow-pitch softball player; mem. '70-71 ntl Sr. B lacrosse champion Windsor Warlocks; NRA distinguished marksman award '94; nicknamed "The Grunt"; res. Belle River, Ont.

GUAY, Lucie (canoeing); b. 12 Dec 1958, Montreal, Que.; m. Yvon Robert; c. Francis, Simon; ex-electrical supply co. employee, fitness dir.; kayak specialist; ntl jr. K1 500m record; 5 ntl K4 500m, 2 K2, 1 K1 titles; 12 500m, mostly K4, titles international regattas; mem. bronze 500m K4 crew '84 Olympics; mem. ntl team '79, '81, '82, '83 worlds, '80, '83 Pan-Am championships, '81 Commonwealth Cup, '80, '84 Olympic Games; res. Blainville, Que.

GUDEREIT, Marcia (curling); b. 8 Sep 1965, Moose Jaw, Sask; given name: Marcia Schiml; m. Kerry Gudereit; c. Colin; systems analyst; began curling age 15; lead for Sandra Schmirler's STOH, world title rinks '93-94, '97, gold '98 Olympics; res. Regina, Sask.

GUDWER, Doug (skiing); b. 22 Jun 1956, Prince George, B.C.; given name: Douglas Wade; Ft. Lewis College, Durango, Colo; park ranger; cross-country specialist; 3rd '72 ntl jr. championships; ntl team '72; US jr. title '73; ntl jr. '74; all-American '75-76; spare '76 Olympics; Canadian 50km title; mem. world championships team '78; 3 1sts '80 ntl championships; Mark Warber scholastic award '75; res. Banff, Alta.

GUELLY, Debbie (rodeo); b. 13 Oct 1968, Fort St. John, B.C.; barrel racing specialist; NRA pole bending title '84; 2 NRA steer undecorating titles; NRA cowgirl of '89; joined CPRA ranks '90; Alta LBR Futurity ('91), Derby ('92) titles; Bud pro tour LBR title '95; holds LBR single season money winning record; Wrangler circuit LBR title '96; 2 ntl LBR titles; res. Hudson Hope, B.C.

GUERRERO, Vladimir (baseball); b. 9 Feb 1976, Nizao Bani, Dominican Republic; outfielder; joined pro ranks '93 playing in minors with developmental, rookie, Albany, West Palm Beach (A), Harrisburg (AA) before joining parent Montreal Expos late in '96; established himself as a franchise player with prodigious home runs; set franchise record 42 homers, 131rbi, 84 extra-base hits, .600 slugging percentage, 31 game hitting streak (tops in ML) in '99 season; 1st Expo to top 30hr, 100rbi, 100r 2 consecutive seasons; ML all-star; brother Wilton (infielder) also Montreal teammate; *Baseball America's* AA player of '96, Eastern League MVP, rookie of yr, all-star, Rawlings rookie of yr, *SN* minor league player of '96; EL batting title '96; res. Nizao Bani, DR.

GUEST, Jack (rowing); b. 28 Mar 1906, Montreal, Que.; d. 12 Jun 1972, Toronto, Ont.; given name: John Schofield; m. Mary Macdonald; c. John Jr., Donald; business exec.; jr., assn. singles '27; mem. Argonaut jr. 8s under coach Joe Wright Sr., twice lost Diamond sculls titles to Joe Wright Jr. '28-29; with Joe Jr. silver double sculls '28 Olympics; ntl single sculls title '29; defeated German champion by nearly 200yds to win world diamond sculls '30; retd from competition '30; pres. Don RC '38-52, Dominion Day Regatta Assn. '46-56, CAAO '55-56; dir. COA '60-68; mgr. '56 Olympic rowing team; asst. mgr. BEG rowing teams '62, '66; 1st Cdn elected to world rowing governing body (FISA) '69; mem. Cdn Amateur, Canada's Sports halls of fame..

GUILBAULT, Michele (golf); b. 7 Jan 1960, Montreal, Que.; Florida State; ntl reduction in handicap award '74, dropping from 26 to 9; 3 Que. amateur titles; Que., ntl jr. '78; low amateur '79 Peter Jackson Classic; mem. Que. jr. team '76-78; Que. amateur team '79-81; ntl jr. team '77-78; sr. team '79-80; Commonwealth team '79; FSU team '79-81; 5 intercollegiate victories '79-80; all-American '81, all-state '79-81, all-region '80-81; mem. AIAW title team '81; 8 course records; Canada's top jr. golfer '77; Que. athlete of '78; HS athlete of '77; mem. Canada's 1st Commonwealth title team '79; res. Pte Claire, Que.

GUINN, Tom (shooting); b. 1 Sep 1944, St. Catharines, Ont.; electrician; pistol specialist; mem. ntl team from '74; free pistol gold, air pistol bronze, team bronze '83 Commonwealth Games; free pistol team gold, air pistol silver '86 Commonwealth Games; free pistol gold, team gold '79 PAG; ntl air pistol title '81; Benito Juarez air pistol gold '78; mem. '76, '80, '84 Olympic, '75, '79, '83 PAG, '82, '86 Commonwealth, 9 Benito Juarez, 6 Worlds championships teams; SFC Golden Anniversary Award '82; fed. govt. award '83; res. Fonthill, Ont.

GUNELL, Roy (water polo); b. 28 Aug 1943, Hamilton, Ont.; given name: Roy Richard; m. Patricia; c. Lisa, Joel; UofT, Teachers' College; teacher; competitive swimmer Hamilton Y, Aquatic Club '56-63; mem. 7 ntl title water polo teams '58-72; Ont., ntl referee from '71; v-p Water Polo Canada '74-77; FINA referee, 7 world, 3 Pan-Am, 3 Olympic, 5 FISU Games, more than 125 international events; founded, coached, administered Stoney Creek Water Polo Club '84-94, 3 Ont. titles; chair. coaches comm. OWPA '93; HS coach from '70; mem. exec. comm. International Referees Assn. of Water Polo; mem. Ont. Aquatic Hall of Fame; res. Stoney Creek, Ont.

GUNNLAUGSON, Lloyd (curling); b. 18 Dec 1929, Cypress River, Man.; d. 5 Jun 1988, Winnipeg, Man.; given name: Lloyd Harold; m. Jeanette Collins; c. Darryl, Derrick, Lynette, Alanna; plasterer; began curling Man. jampail ranks; part owner Valour Rd. CC; Man. seniors titles '82-85, Ntl seniors '82-84, runnerup '84; skipped '83 Man. men's title rink, a rare title double; won 4 MCA bonspiel events, 6 Valour Rd. CC club titles; Man. athlete of year nominee '84; p.-pres. Valour Rd. CC; club rep. to MCA; life mem. MCA, Valour Rd. CC; nicknamed "Gunner"; mem. Canadian Curling, Man. Sports halls of fame.

GUNTER, Andy (shooting); b. 5 Sep 1892, Lower Queensbury, N.B.; d. 4 Jul 1986, Saint John, N.B.; given name: Andrew George; m.; c. Doug; educator; mem. Cdn Bisley team '33; adjutant Cdn Bisley team '48; placed in Queen's 100 '48; secty-treas. Saint John Rifle Assn. '28-31, NB Rifle Assn.; City of Ottawa gold medal '32; Bostock trophy '32; Ntl Rifle Assn medal '33; Donegal medal (Bisley) '33; hon. life mem. DCRA; mem. NB Sports Hall of Fame.

GURNEY, Helen (coaching); b. 16 Oct 1918, Whitby, Ont.; UofT; educator; coached Windsor Forster Spartans to 8 WSSA basketball, 8 volleyball, 7 overall t&f titles and 16 divisional track titles '44-58; officiated women's basketball on international level 22yrs; formed 1st women's board of officials Windsor '45-46; editor women's basketball rule book '62-67; founding mem. OFSAA, mem. of OFSAA '52-77; Cdn rep. to American Physical Education Assn.; authored history of girls sports in Ont and history of CAHPER; recognized authority in youth leadership development; Queen's silver jubilee medal '77; Herstory Award; mem. UofT, Windsor Essex Sports halls of fame; res. Windsor, Ont.

GURNEY, Jack (football); b. 9 Apr 1923, Brantford, Ont.; given name: John Thomas; m. Doreen Melba Shaw; c. Diane Charlene, Elisabeth Ann; McMaster, BA; retd Bell Canada; refereed basketball all levels to college '42-73; minor football official '44-52, all leagues through college '52-73; OUAA referee-in-chief '73-89; amateur football case book editor '72-90; secty. Canadian Football Officials Assn. '69-78, rules interpreter '79-90; editor, rules interpreter Canadian rule book for amateur football '76-90; Air Canada amateur official of '86 award; mem. McMaster Sports Hall of Fame; res. Nepean, Ont.

GUROWKA, Joe (curling); b. 28 Apr 1933, The Pas, Man.; m. Shirley Young (d); c. Jim, Kim; UMan, B.C. UWO, MBA; retd. civil engineer, co. pres.; rep. Dixie Curling Club in provincial play 18 years earning nickname "Dixie Joe"; 10 Ont. championships appearances, twice winner; runnerup '66 Brier; mem. 3 Ont., 3 Cdn sr. title rinks; Canada Life bonspiel title '69, '79; pres. OCA '83-84; CCA '88-89; chair. Curl Canada development comm.; chair. Curl Ont.; active provincial, ntl coach; mem. Governor-General's Curling Club; mem. Cdn Curling Hall of Fame; res. Mississauga, Ont.

GURR, Donna-Marie (swimming); b. 18 Feb 1955, Vancouver, B.C.; taxi driver; 5 gold '69 British nationals; mem. '70, '74 Commonwealth, '71 Pan-Am, '72 Olympic teams; 3 Pan-Am gold, 2 Commonwealth, 1 Pan-Am silver, 3 Commonwealth, 1 Olympic bronze medals; ntl backstroke titlist '69-72; 5 Canada Summer Games, 10 ntl titles; mem. Order of Canada; mem. BC Sports, Cdn Aquatic halls of fame; res. Vancouver, B.C.

GURUNLIAN, Varouj (basketball); b. 1 Mar 1955, Alexandria, Egypt; m. Sylvia Stepanian; c. Christopher, Lisa, Christine; Dawson College, Laurentian, St.FX, BSc, BEd; HS teacher; soccer, basketball in Egypt; moved to Montreal age 14; HS basketball, soccer MVP awards '69-73; 3yrs Dawson basketball all-star; top scorer Que. '75 Canada Games gold medal team; mem. Dawson ntl title team, all-Canadian, MVP, college athlete of '76; St.FX rookie of '77; AUAA all-star '78-81; 2nd all-time St.FX scorer; all-Cdn, athlete of '81; St.FX foul shooting percentage record '81; mem. ntl team '76-84; guard '80, '84 (alternate) Olympic, '77, '79, '81 FISU, '83 Pan-Am Games teams, gold '78 Commonwealth championships; coached HS, 3yrs Dawson. ntl gold, silver, bronze, Que. team to gold '85 Canada Games; university level referee; listed in Armenian American Who's Who in Sport; mem. Dawson College Hall of Fame; res. Montreal, Que.

GUTNICK, Paul (shooting); b. 7 Jun 1927, Winnipeg, Man.; given name: Paul Eugene; m. Terrence Elizabeth Nydis; c. Raymond Charles, Bernard Lyndon; office mgr., accountant; began competitive shooting at 16; among finest marksmen in Man. history winning virtually all major match titles over span of more than 40yrs; rep. Man. in DCRA competition 25 consec. yrs; mem. '62 Bisley team; while shooting in '70 Manitoba summer matches won unprecedented six titles including grand aggregate; 1st Manitoban to win Calgary Frost on Pumpkin shoot; mem. 1st militia team to beat Cdn Forces regulars and Americans; active in shooting administration; exec. council mem. MPRA, DCRA; conducted hunter safety programs; Queen's Jubilee medal '78; res. Winnipeg, Man.

GUZZO, Patrick (hockey/softball/baseball); b. 14 Oct 1917, Ottawa, Ont.; d. 19 Jan 1993, Ottawa, Ont; m. Mary; c. Patrick, Barry, Donnie, Meri-Lee; county court officer; sr. softball pitcher at 15; mem. Eastern Ont. title teams; among leading pitchers, hitters 12 seasons '30s-'40s; mem. Ont. baseball title teams, 3 Hull, Que. title teams; mem. 2 int., 2 interscholastic hockey title teams; 3 Allan Cup Eastern Cdn finals; mem. '48 Olympic, RCAF Flyers world title teams; numerous hockey MVP awards; nicknamed "Patsy"; mem. Cdn Forces, Ottawa Sports halls of fame.

GWYNNE, Lefty (boxing); b. 5 Oct 1912, Toronto, Ont.; given name: Horace; m. Henrietta Aisbitt; c. John, Gordon, Larry; retd. Rec. centre employee; 118lb gold '32 Olympics; pro bantamweight boxer '35-39; Canadian pro bantamweight title '38-39; retd. undefeated '39; 26yrs jockey, trainer, jockey's agent; mem. Cdn Amateur, Canada's Sports, Boxing halls of fame; res. Etobicoke, Ont.

H

HACKNER, Al (curling); b. 18 Jul 1954, Nipigon, Ont.; given name: Allan; m. Margaret Nicol; c. Andrew, Graham; railway switchman; skipped Alta. mixed title winner '77; men's NOnt. titles '80-82, '85, '88-89, '92, '95; Brier runnerup '80-81; skipped Rick Lang, Bob Nicol, Bruce Kennedy ('82), Lang, Ian Tetley, Pat Perroud ('85) to Brier, World championships; 5 Thunder Bay, 3 Longlac, 2 Regina, 1 St. John's, Edmonton, Sault Ste. Marie, Saskatoon, Kelowna, Kamloops major cashspiel titles; fed. govt. world champion award '82; mem. Cdn Curling, (team) NWO Sports halls of fame; res. Thunder Bay, Ont.

HADFIELD, Vic (hockey); b. 4 Oct 1940, Oakville, Ont.; given name: Victor Edward; driving range operator; left wing; jr. St. Catharines Teepees; pro AHL Buffalo '60-61, Baltimore '62-63, NHL NY Rangers '61-74, Pittsburgh '74-77; 2nd team all-star '72; mem. Team Canada '72; mem. Rangers' GAG Line; plodding digger with tough guy reputation; reached 50 goal plateau '72 with 50; capt. Rangers '71; scout Rangers '78-79; NHL record: 16 seasons, 1002 scheduled games, 323g, 389a, 73 playoff games, 27g, 21a; res. Burlington, Ont.

HADLOW, Terry (weightlifting); b. 13 Nov 1957, North Bay, Ont.; UofOtt; trainer; gold 67.5kg '75 Canada Games; 90kg '78, '80-81 national championships; gold, national sr. record 90kg '80 Pan-Am championships; bronze 90kg '77 Queen's silver jubilee; silver 90kg '78 Commonwealth Games, '79 Pan-Am Games; mem. '80, '84 Olympic teams; received absolute discharge following conviction for importing anabolic steroids '84; expelled from '84 Olympics for failure to pass steroids test; trainer ntl men's volleyball team '99; res. Winnipeg, Man.

HAFEY, Art (boxing); b. 17 Jan 1951, Stellarton, N.S.; given name: Arthur Douglas; m. Cathy Marie MacKenzie; self employed; former number 1 contender for world featherweight title; lost title bid on TKO to multi-titlist Alexis Arguello '74; split matches vs. Reuben Olivares, winning by TKO, losing by decision; KO'd former world jr. lightweight champion Alfredo Marcano; stopped in 7 by future world featherweight champ Danny Lopez in final pro bout; forced into early retirement by eye injury; turned briefly to coaching in PEI; mem. NS Sports, Canadian Boxing halls of fame; res. Trenton, N.S.

HAHN, Robin (equestrian); b. 19 Jun 1933, Regina, Sask.; m. Maureen; c. Apryl, Amber, Jaysen; UBC; farmer; began showing horses Western Canada age 17; mem. 3-day event team '67, '71 Pan-Am, '68, '72, '76 Olympic Games; 5th '67 Pan-Am 3-day aboard Warden; 9th '68 Olympics aboard Taffy; '70, '72 ntl 3-day titles; capt. '71 Pan-Am gold team; capt. '76 Olympic 3-day team; active in sport's exec. branch provincially, nationally; qualified show judge; mem. Sask. Sports Hall of Fame; res. Lumley, B.C.

HAIG, Cathy (field hockey); b. 22 Feb 1957, Montreal, Que.; John Abbott College, McGill; teacher, fitness instructor; mem. Que. sr. team, ntl team '77-81; mem. bronze medal team European Zone indoor championships '81; Montreal West HS athlete of '70-74; John Abbott College athlete of '76; Que. field hockey player of '77, '81; res. St. Pierre, Que.

HAIGHT, Deedee (skiing); b. 28 Apr 1964, Trail, B.C.; given name: Diana Catherine; m. Thomas Arn; ntl juve. title '78; overall Europa Cup title '81; FIS slalom title '83; 2 top 10 WC finishes through '83-84; mem. '84 Olympic team; ntl downhill title '84; res. Armstrong, B.C.

HAIGHT, Jim (hockey); b. 2 Jun 1913, Humboldt, Sask.; given name: James Oscar; m. Anna Nova Bannantyne (d); c. Barbara Gale, James Wilson; Nutana College; retd Cominco; mem. '30 Saskatoon Wesleys provincial midget, '31 juve., '32 Western Cdn jr. titlists; mem. Nelson Maple Leafs '34; Trail Smoke Eaters '35-40; reputation as hard-rock defenceman; mem. '38 Allan Cup, '39 world champions; grand-daughter Deedee ntl ski team; as mem. '38-39 Smoke Eaters mem. BC Sports Hall of Fame; res. Rossland, B.C.

HAINE, Audrey (baseball); b. 9 May 1927, Winnipeg, Man.; given name: Audrey May; m. Austin Daniels; c. Marilyn, Craig, Cheryl, Kathryn, Scott, Douglas; retd secretary; right handed pitcher; played in AAGPBL at time when fast pitch softball was the vogue, with Minneapolis '44 winning title despite team losing home park; shifted to Ft. Wayne '45, Grand Rapids '46-47. Peoria '47-48, Rockford '51; career record 72-70; 493k, 3.48 ERA; avid bowler, golfer; mem. Man. Baseball Hall of Fame; honored by Cooperstown, Cdn Baseball halls of fame; res. Bay Village, Ohio.

HAINEY, Tom (swimming); b. 11 Jun 1966, Atikokan, Ont.; co-owner Barrier Breakers Outfitting; coach; born with spina bifida he began swimming age 11, racing age 12; gold 100m, 400m FS, 100m breaststroke, 200m IM, silver 100m butterfly '84 Paralympics; gold 400m FS, 100m fly '86 Worlds; 2 silver '88 Paralympics; competed '90 Worlds, '92 Paralympics, '94 Commonwealth Games; 5 ntl, 4 world records; swam entire 97km width of Quetico Provincial Park in tribute to late mother; res. Atikokan, Ont.

HAINSWORTH, George (hockey); b. 26 Jun 1895, Toronto, Ont.; d. 9 Oct 1950; goal Kitchener jrs, Allan Cup '18; pro Saskatoon '23-24, Canadiens '26-33, '37, Maple Leafs '33-37; stopped first-ever NHL penalty shot Nov. 10 '34 Leafs vs. Canadiens; Vezina trophy 1st 3 seasons with Montreal; allowed 43 goals in 44 games '28-29 with 22 shutouts as team won 22 games; traded to Toronto for Lorne Chabot; died in auto accident; NHL record: 2.02 avg., 91so, 465 scheduled games, 2.15 avg., 8so, 52 playoff games; mem. Hockey Hall of Fame.

HAIST, Jane (t&f); b. 1 Mar 1949, St. Catharines, Ont.; York, Tennessee; mem. '74 Commonwealth, '75 Pan-Am,

'76 Olympic teams; gold, Cdn, Commonwealth records shot put, discus '74 Commonwealth Games; bronze discus '75 Pan-Am Games; ntl discus record 61.70m '75 vs. Sweden; best shot performance Cardiff, Wales, '74 16.12m; 11th discus '76 Olympics; gold discus Adelaide International meet, Pacific Conf. Games, Perth International meet '77, Tom Black Classic '79; Rowell Trophy outstanding Cdn amateur athlete in jumping, weight events '74; res. Fenwick, Ont.

HALDER, Wally (hockey/tennis); b. 15 Sep 1925, Toronto, Ont.; d. 27 Oct 1994, Toronto, Ont.; given name: Wallace Edwin; m. Joyce; c. Gregory, Christina, Matthew; UofT, BA, OCE; p-pres. Olympic Trust; capt. UotT hockey team; mem. '48 Olympic gold medal team; swimming, diving instructor Ont. Athletic Commission; coach UotT, Trinity College hockey teams; ntl sr. doubles tennis champion; mem. Gordon Trophy tennis teams; Biggs Trophy UotT; mem. UofT, Ottawa Sports (as mem. 48 Flyers) halls of fame.

HALEY, Andrew (swimming); b. 16 Jan 1974, Moncton, N.B.; Dalhousie; began competing age 15; 6 ntl, 3 world records; bronze 400m FS '92 Paralympics; 5 gold '93 Cdn Foresters championships; gold 100m FS '94 Commonwealth Games; res. Dartmouth, N.S./Ottawa. Ont.

HALL, Chris (lacrosse/coaching); b. 17 Sep 1950, Victoria, B.C.; human resources mgr.; mem. 2 Western Lacrosse Assn. title winners, coached 2 others; mem. '79 Mann Cup winner, coached another '83; player/coach 6 Cdn field lacrosse title teams; mem. '82 bronze, '86 silver lacrosse world cup; played professionally Ntl Lacrosse League Boston Bolts '75; ntl team coach '89-94; coached '90 World Cup silver medallists; coach Victoria lacrosse team; res. Victoria, B.C.

HALL, Glenn (hockey); b. 3 Oct 1931, Humboldt, Sask.; given name: Glenn Henry; m. Pauline Patrick; c. Patrick, Leslie, Tammy, Lindsay; farmer, hockey coach; Windsor Spitfires jrs, MVP; pro Indianapolis AHL '52; Edmonton '53-55 with brief stints at Detroit; 12 shutouts led NHL '56-57; Chicago '57-67, St. Louis '67-71; mem. '61 Stanley Cup winner; 5 times led NHL in shutouts; 3 Vezina trophies; Calder Memorial rookie of year; Conn Smythe Trophy; King Clancy award '93; 7 times 1st team, 4 times 2nd team all-star goaler; NHL record: 891 scheduled games, including 552 in succession, 2239ga, 2.51 avg., 84so, 113 playoff games, 32ga, 2.79 avg. 6so; 13 all-star games, 27 periods, 22ga, .81 avg.; goaltending consultant Calgary; jersey #1 retired by Blackhawks; mem. Sask, Hockey halls of fame; res. Stony Plain, Alta.

HALL, Joe (hockey); b. 3 May 1882, Staffordshire, Eng.; d. 5 Apr 1919, Seattle, Wash; given name: Joseph Henry; mem. Winnipeg Rowing Club, Rat Portage until turning pro '05-06 with Kenora; Que. Bulldogs '10-16, 2 Stanley Cups; finished career Montreal Canadiens winning NHA title '18-19; influenza epidemic ended Stanley Cup series in Seattle and Hall's life; mem. Man., Cdn Hockey halls of fame.

HALL, Peter (sailing); b. 5 Jun 1949, Montreal, Que.; given name: Peter William; m. Margot McFarlane; c. Krista, Nicholas, William; Queen's, BA, McGill., BCL.; business

developer, lawyer; helmsman in soling, lightning competitions; mem. ntl yachting team from '75; mem. '77 World Cup champion soling crew; '89 Lightning world champion; gold '77, '79, silver '76, '78, '80-81, '94 CORK championships; silver '77, bronze '78 Kiel Week competition; bronze '83 NA, '78 European championships; Lightning silver '87 Pan-Am Games; competed '91, '95 Pan Am Games; 3 Que., 1 ntl sailor of yr awards; 1 Que team of yr award; res. Westmount, Que.

HALLAS, Kory (basketball); b. 23 Apr 1969, Ottawa, Ont.; c. Ashley, Chance; Eastern Mich; pro basketball player; mem. OFSAA champion Almonte HS; NCAA all-star; mem. ntl team '91-98; 3 NBA tryouts; 4yrs pro Europe with Italy, Spain, Lebanon; annual Almonte 3 on 3 charity tournament bears his name; res. Almonte, Ont.

HALLDORSON, Dan (golf); b. 2 Apr 1952, Winnipeg, Man.; given name: Daniel Albert; m. Pat; pro golfer; '69 Man. jr.; '71 Man. PGA; 4 Man. Opens; '77 Sask. Open; '80 Que. Open; mem. 5 Cdn World Cup teams, winner (with Jim Nelford) '80, (with Dave Barr '85); twice qualified for pro tour '74, '78, regular from '78; Pensacola Open '80, Colorado Open '82, Deposit Guaranty Classic '86; CPGA title '86; Score magazine outstanding Cdn pro of '82; twice CPGA player of year; Canadian Tour Order of Merit '83; competed on USPGA, Asia, Ben Hogan tours; overcame hand and back ailments which threatened career; res. Cambridge, Ill.

HALLETT, Todd (rowing); b. 12 May 1970, Shelburne, N.S.; Dalhousie; at urging of friend decided to "give rowing a try" with almost instant success; gold singles, doubles '88 jr. ntls; mem. ntl team from '91; US straight 4s title '94; competed '92, '96 Olympics; '94-95 worlds; single sculls bronze '91, silver 8s '95 Pan-Am Games; Rowing Canada junior sculler of '88 award; res. Dartmouth, N.S.

HALLIDAY, Milton (hockey); b. 21 Sep 1906, Ottawa, Ont.; d. 16 Aug 1989, Ottawa, Ont.; m. Hilda Joad; c. Barry Milton, Marion Hilda, Carolyn Mary; body shop owner; mem. Stewarton AC, Gunners Int. Club; pro Ottawa Senators '26-28; mem. '27 Ottawa Stanley Cup winner, backup centre to Frank Nighbor; minor pro London, Hamilton, Boston Cubs, Cleveland; nicknamed "The Blond Flash".

HALPENNY, Rachelle (all-around); b. 9 Nov 1950, Hull, Que.; given name: Rachelle Marengere; m. James Halpenny; c. Charles, Justin; St. Lawrence, Algonquin Coll.; sports consultant; gold slalom, rifle shooting, table tennis, bronze archery, track '78 international games for cerebral palsey; gold table tennis, slalom, silver soccer, bronze club (shot put) '82 CP Games; res. Rockland, Ont.

HALTER, G. Sydney (football/administration); b. 18 Apr 1905, Winnipeg, Man.; d. 24 Oct 1990, Winnipeg, Man.; Uman, BA, LLB; lawyer QC; treas. Winnipeg football club '35, pres. '42; pres. Winnipeg Amateur Athletic Assoc. '30-45; pres. Man. branch AAU of C '35-38, pres. AAU of C '38-46; WIFU commissioner '53-57; initial CFL commissioner '58-66; chair. Man. Horse Racing Commission '65-71, '78-81; Manitoba Sports Hall of Fame honored members gallery bears his name; Officer Order of Canada '77; mem. Cdn Horse Racing, Cdn Amateur, Canada's, Man. Sports, Cdn Football halls of fame.

HALVORSEN, John (t&f); b. 17 Aug 1966, Oslo, Norway; m. Susan Elizabeth Ferguson; UofOtt, BASc, MBA; engineer Nortel; long distance running specialist; 4 Norwegian 10,000m, 2 5000m championships; represented Norway '88, '92 Olympics; competed in world cross-country races from '85 (as junior); landed immigrant Canada '94; 4 CIAU X-C titles; 3 CIAU X-C all-Cdn; competed '87 FISU Games; won OFSAA sr boys X-C title '89; won several ntl X-C, Timex road race titles; Nordion National Capital 10km title '95; 2 Gasparilla Tampa 15km, 1 Orlando Red Lobster 10km, Spokane Bloomsday 12km, Boston 10km milk run, Jacksonville River Run, titles; competed '91 NY Marathon; set several course records; Runners World road racer of '89; 2 UofOtt athlete of yr awards; res. Ottawa, Ont.

HAM, Tracy (football); b. 5 Jan 1964, High Springs, Fla.; m. Valarie; c. Tracy II, Caleb; Georgia Southern (sports management); quarterback; led GSC to 2 Div 1-AA titles; only player in US college history to rush for more than 3000yds and pass for over 5000yds; turned pro CFL Edmonton '87-92, Toronto '93, Baltimore '94-95, Montreal '96-98; CFL record (through '98): 197gp. 4731 passes, 2542 complete, 38,603yds, 161int, 273td, 1015carries, 7832yds, 59td, 354pts.; Jeff Nicklin trophy '89; CFL outstanding player '89; 1 all-Western, 1 all-CFL all-star; set 2 CFL QB rushing records; mem. 3 Grey Cup finals, 1 winner; '95 Grey Cup MVP; nicknamed "Hambone"; active in Athletes in Action; made acting debut in *Raisin in the Sun* '94; res. Statesboro, Ga.

HAMBLY, Fraser (bowling); b. 14 Mar 1943, London, Ont.; m. Hope McBride; York, BA; teacher; began bowling five-pins age 12 quickly stamping himself a natural; won ntl jr. singles, team '57; 2 ntl open singles, 2 Masters team titles; 4 Ont. open singles, 2 open team titles; more than 40 career tournament victories including $10,000 Cdn invitational singles '74, 7 MBA victories; won high tournament average, ntl titles through 5 decades; career avg. 260, 16 perfect 450 games, 2 sanctioned; career high triple 1162, high five 1654, high 10 3087; proficient golfer; coach 2 Toronto slo-pitch softball title teams; bowling coach; Toronto Major Bowling League exec.; mem. Ont. 5-pin Bowling Hall of Fame; res. Toronto, Ont.

HAMBROOK, Sharon (synchro swim); b. 28 Mar 1963, Calgary, Alta.; m. Ben Voreyho (d); c. Kelsey, Micaela; with Kelly Kryczka world duet championship '82; silver solo '83, team gold '83, silver '79 Pan-Am, duet silver as sport introduced to '84 Olympic Games; 1 ntl duet, 3 team titles; duet gold Scandinavian Open, Mazda invitational; team gold Scandinavian Open, America Cup; Pan-Pacific solo, figures, duet, 2 team gold; Aquatic Fed. swimmers of '82; fed. govt. world champion award '83, excellence award '84; mem. Cdn Aquatic, Olympic halls of fame; res. La Jolla, Calif.

HAMILTON, Doug (rowing); b. 19 Aug 1958, Toronto, Ont.; m. Lynn Polson; c. Frederick, Douglas; Queen's, LLB; lawyer; Cdn Henley jr. coxless pairs title '78; Cdn Henley single sculls, 2 double sculls titles; 2 US ntl single sculls

titles; ntl single, double sculls titles; 2 world university single sculls titles; mem. bronze coxless quad sculls crew '84 Olympics; mem. men's gold medal quad '85 worlds (1st Cdn gold at modern world rowing championships); quad sculls bronze '86-87 worlds; quad sculls gold Royal English Henley (course record) '87; mem. '88 Olympic team; v-p high performance Rowing Canada '89-97; COA dir., chair. sports & venues comm. 2008 Toronto Olympic bid; chair. Toronto High Performance Centre; Cdn team of yr award '85; Kingston athlete of '82; Queen's Jenkins Trophy top male graduating student '83; res. Toronto, Ont.

HAMILTON, Douglas (harness racing); b. 20 Mar 1947, Port Elgin, Ont.; followed grandfather Lambert and father Irwin onto county fair circuit but at 17 elected to pursue bigger purses at Windsor Raceway; after stints with Gerry Bookmyer and the late Ron Feagan he went on his own; through '95 had amassed 3321 victories and purses exceeding $18M; operated from Northlfield Park, Ohio before shifting to Chicago area; claimed varied driver titles Sportsman's Park, Balmoral; drove Nite Strike to world record for aged pacing mares '86; res. Beecher, IL.

HAMILTON, Jack (administration); b. 11 Jun 1886, Caledonia, Ont.; d. 5 Aug 1976, Regina, Sask.; given name: John Welch; m. Elsie White Greason; c. Donald, Hugh; GM lumber co.; organized construction 3500 seat hockey rink Saskatoon '18; coached Regina Vics hockey club '20s, later club pres.; SAHA pres. '25-27; CAHA pres. '30; secty Regina Roughriders football club '23-27, pres. WIFU '28; pres. Sask. branch CAAU, ntl pres. '37; COA exec 17yrs; pres. Sask Amateur Basketball Assn. '33-34, AAU of C '37-38; headed Queen City Gardens Co. which raised funds to install artificial ice in Regina hockey rink, operated rink 11 years; headed operation to construct 3500 seat Moose Jaw rink '57; numerous honors from sport, business community, nation; King George VI coronation medal for work on behalf of athletics; Jack Hamilton rink in Regina; Regina Optimist Sportsman of Year; CAHA medal of merit; honorary life mem. SAHA; mem. Sask., Cdn Amateur, Canada's Sports halls of fame.

HAMMOND, Alvin (hockey/t&f); b. 18 Dec 1891, Rolla N.D.; d. 11 Mar 1979, Regina, Sask; given name: Richard Alvin; m. Grace Wood; c. Richard Alvin Jr., Margery; salesman; all-around t&f athlete, Sask. 100, 220, 440yds sprints, running broad jump, hop, step & jump titles; won these events 3 times in Saskatoon, Regina, Moose Jaw, once Swift Current; represented Sask. 3 times in Olympic trials; hockey Victoria club, '14 world amateur title Regina; mem. Sask. Sports Hall of Fame.

HAMMOND, Gord (lacrosse); b. 5 Mar 1926, Toronto, Ont.; m. Yvonne Burnie; c. Bob, Joanne, Abbie, Nola, Steve, Ken; Ryerson PTI; retired buildings mgr.; mem. Mimico OLA midget title team; Sr. A Mimico Brampton '43, Mimico '44, Orillia '46, '52-53; Ont. title '43, Eastern Canada '52; Int. Orillia '47, '49, Midland '48, Alliston '50-55; referee '56-64; varied OLA executive roles '65-67; secty-treas. CLA '67-82; governor Lacrosse Hall of Fame; helped reactivate international competition dormant from '28 with '67 world tournament Toronto; hockey Toronto Navy jrs '43-44, Orillia Terriers Sr. B '47-49; OHA referee '50-60; Alliston lacrosse MVP '50; OLA Mr. Lacrosse award '67; CLA Lester B.

Pearson award '76; mem. Cdn Lacrosse Hall of Fame; res. London, Ont.

HAMPTON, Richard (shooting); b. 12 May 1914, England; d. 23 Dec 1997, Nepean, Ont.; m. Veronica Garvin; c. Ralph; retired Cdn Forces major; qualified for Bisley team 21 times; 5 ntl high powered titles; mem. 4 Cdn Army Bisley teams; gold rifle award; authored regulations, conditions for Cdn Forces rifle competition; top 50 Bisley aggregate DCRA shoot 26 times, top 40 23 times, top 30 21 times, top 20 17 times, top 10 10 times, top 5 5 times; 6 individual DCRA match titles; Bisley Queen's Prize '66; coached Bisley cadet teams; Desmond Burke Trophy; mem. Canadian Forces Sports Hall of Fame.

HANLAN, Ned (rowing); b. 12 Jul 1855, Toronto, Ont.; d. 4 Jan 1908, Toronto, Ont.; m. Margaret Gordon Sutherland; c. 2 sons, 6 daughters; pro oarsman, politician; US Centennial singles 1876; beat Wallace Ross 1877 for Canadian title; beat Eph Morris 1878 for US title; by 1879, "Boy in Blue" nickname referred to rowing outfit, NA rowing king; 1st oarsman to master sliding seat; world rowing title 6yrs before losing to Australian William Beach 1884; retired from racing '01; one end of Toronto Island rechristened Hanlan's Point; town in Australia named in his honor; 20-foot statue erected in his memory CNE '26; lost only 6 of more than 350 career races; Toronto alderman; mem. Canada's Sports Hall of Fame.

HANLEY, Bill (builder/hockey); b. 28 Feb 1915, Balleyeast, Northern Ireland; d. 17 Sep 1990, Toronto, Ont.; given name: William; Ont. Agricultural Coll.; became involved with hockey as timekeeper jr., Maple Leafs games; became asst. to George Panter, OHA business mgr.; became secty-mgr. OHA '74 to his death; mem. Hockey Hall of Fame.

HANNIBAL, Frank (builder); b. 23 Sep 1892, Bristol, Eng.; d. 27 Mar 1959, Winnipeg, Man.; joined Winnipeg football exec. '34; helped build club which in '35 would become 1st Western Canadian club to win Grey Cup; became club pres. '41 and was rewarded with another Grey Cup; held many exec. offices, including pres. WIFU; CFL outstanding contribution award '53; mem. Cdn Football Hall of Fame.

HANSEN, Ina (curling); b. 7 Nov 1920, Boissevaine, Man.; given name: Georgina Rutherford; m. Alvin Hansen; c. Lynn Vernon, Joanne Candace; UofSask; city clerk; represented Kootenays in BC provincial women's play 18 times, 12yrs in succession; 7 provincial, 3 ntl titles; skipped '62, '64 women's title winners; 3rd for Ada Callas '73 Srs title; East Kootenay zone convenor; mem. BCLCA exec. '55-57, pres. '57; jr. delegate '58, sr. delegate '59 to WLCA; BC voice in establishment of Cdn championships; mem. Canadian Curling Hall of Fame; res. Kimberley, B.C.

HANSEN, Lars (basketball); b. 27 Sep 1954, Copenhagen, Denmark; given name: Lars Erik; Washington, BA; businessman; mem. ntl team '72-77; '76 Olympic, '75 Pan-Am, '73, '77 FISU Games teams; drafted NBA Chicago Bulls; played briefly '80 champion Seattle Supersonics; tryout Kansas City; pro basketball Italy, Spain; res. Coquitlam, B.C.

HANSEN, Rick (all-around); b. 26 Aug 1957, Port Alberni, B.C.; given name: Richard Marvin; m. Amanda Reed; c. Emma Kathleen, Rebecca, Alana; UBC, BPhE; disability consultant; truck accident at 15 left him paralyzed both legs; HS most inspirational athlete award; initiated, capt. BC wheelchair volleyball team '76, 3 ntl titles; 7 ntl wheelchair basketball title teams; track sprint, marathon competitor; ntl marathon record, 5 world track records, 1 Pan-Am Games record; 12 track gold BC Games, gold 800m, silver 1500m, bronze 4x100m relay '80 wheelchair Olympics; 6 gold '82 wheelchair Pan-Am Games; 7 marathon victories; BC wheelchair tennis singles titles '81-82, Hawaii Games singles, doubles titles; coached able-bodied volleyball, basketball HS level; Man in Motion 40,000km world tour '87 raised $20M which led to establishment of Rick Hansen Institute at UBC funding research into spinal cord injuries; goodwill ambassador, fund raiser; fed. govt. excellence award '83; BC physically disabled athlete of year awards '79-80, '82; outstanding Canadian athlete award; 3 UBC special achievement awards; BC Sports Hall of Fame W.A.C. Bennett award; '94 Royal Bank award; Canada's man of yr '87; Companion Order of Canada '87; mem. UBC Sports, Terry Fox, Cdn Road Racing halls of fame; res. Vancouver, B.C.

HANSEN, Warren (curling); b. 15 Feb 1943, Edmonton, Alta.; given name: Warren Richard; Northern Alberta Institute of Technology; marketing, public relations; mem. Edmonton Huskies football club 3 consecutive titles '62-64; 2nd Hec Gervais' '74 Brier winner; with Jim Pettapiece launched Silver Broom Curling School '72; 1st tech. dir. Curl Canada '76; responsible for compilation, writing Curl Canada manuals, instructor certification program; CCA, CLCA, Curl Canada dir. marketing, from '80, P.R. '80-90; media attache '92 Olympics; res. Vancouver, B.C.

HANSON, Fritzie (football); b. 13 Jul 1912, Perham, Minn.; d. 14 Feb 1996, Calgary, Alta.; given name: Melvin; m. Maxine; c. Trudy, Marilyn, Paula, Alix; North Dakota State; insurance broker, v-p Reed Stenhouse; brilliant HS career included single game in which he scored 11 TDs, 9 converts; Little all-American NDS; WIFU Winnipeg '35-46, Calgary '47-48; elusive running skills earned him nickname "Twinkle Toes"; 8 Grey Cup finals, 4 winners; vs. Hamilton '35 gained 300-plus yards on punt returns, including 78-yarder for TD, on muddy field; 5 times WIFU all-star halfback; '38 WIFU scoring title, Dave Dryburgh trophy; Lionel Conacher trophy '39; mem. Cdn Football, Man., Canada's Sports halls of fame.

HARDING, Dick (t&f); b. 9 Feb 1934, Chatham, Ont.; given name: Richard; m. Gilliam Bastian; c. Beverley, Wendy, Geoffrey, Timothy, Christopher; UofT, BSc; marketing mgr.; sprint specialist; mem. '54 BEG (440yds), '55 Pan-Am (200m, 400m, relays), '56 Olympic (100m, relay) teams; pres. Que. TFA '62; mgr. t&f team '66 Commonwealth Games; mem. at large COA; Hec Phillips CIAU t&f trophy '54; res. Markham, Ont.

HARDING, Rodney (football); b. 1 Aug 1962, Oklahoma City, Okla.; Oklahoma State, def. tackle Toronto '85-94, Memphis '95, Calgary '96-97; 2 Grey Cup finals, 1 winner; 5 all-Eastern, 2 all-CFL, 1all-Southern, 1 all-Western all-star; res. Oklahoma City, Okla.

HARE, William (shooting); b. 14 May 1935, Ottawa, Ont.; given name: William Edward; m. Frances; Carleton, BA, Queen's , BD; United Church minister; pistol specialist, mem. '62, '70, '74 world, '63, '67, '71 Pan-Am, '64, '68, '72 Olympic, '74 Commonwealth Games teams; team silver '63, '71 Pan-Ams; 4th overall '67 Canada Winter Games; Ont. handgun title '70; competed ntl handgun finals '55-80; gold team standard pistol, silver team air pistol '73 Confederation of Americas shoot; gold rapid fire '74 Commonwealth Games; chair. SFC handgun section '69-72, SFC dir. '73-76, ntl handgun team manager; coach '78 world, Commonwealth Games, '79-80 Karelia matches Finland; res. Namao, Alta.

HARGREAVES, Doug (coaching); b. 20 Dec 1931, Sault Ste. Marie, Ont.; given name: John Walter Douglas; m. Norma Frances; c. Vicki, Gayle, Lynn; Queen's, BA, Dalhousie, UWO, MSc; retd football/basketball coach, retd Cdn Forces; off. guard Queen's; coached at HS level Kingston, Moose Jaw, Sault Ste. Marie, college level Queen's, RMC, US Coast Guard Academy, Dalhousie, Shearwater, N.S.; RCAF flying instructor, HS teacher; AD Dalhousie '72-75; assoc. prof./head coach Queen's '76-94; played major role in running NA style football clinics in Europe; guided Gaels to league semifinals 16 consec seasons, 9 league titles, 3 Vanier Cup finals, 2 winners; became ntl career leader CIAU football games coached '94; key role in establishing Queen's Football Hall of Fame; lifetime CIAU coaching record 128-103-3; mem. Queen's Football Hall of Fame; res. Kingston, Ont.

HARMEN, Wendy (baton twirling); b. 6 Sep 1957, Regina, Sask.; U of Regina, BEd; civil servant; capt. Optimist Buffalo Gals world corps, dance twirl champions '76, '78; 5 ntl twirling titles; former ntl Miss Majorette; 1st world hoopbaton, world duet (Pam Wilson Price) '76; tech. chairman Sask.; coach, judge; res. Regina, Sask.

HARNETT, Curt (cycling); b. 14 May 1965, Toronto, Ont.; competitions co-ordinator IMG; began cycling competitively at 16; track specialist; ntl team '83-96; 1000m silver '84, sprint bronze '92, '96 Olympic Games; gold 1000m, bronze sprint '87 Pan-Am Games; silver sprint '90, '94 Commonwealth Games; gold sprint '90 Goodwill Games; silver '90 World sprints; ntl jr. sprint, points race, team pursuit titles '83; 6 ntl sprint titles; PB: 1:06.06 ('84); mem. '83, '87 Pan-Am, '84, '88, '92, '96 Olympic, '86, '90, '94 Commonwealth Games teams; 1st sub 10-sec. 200m world sprint record 9.865; res. Leaside, Ont.

HARPELL, Winnifred (all-around); b. 3 Oct 1929, Owen Sound, Ont.; given name: Winnifred Marie; m. Richard Bocking; c. 6 sons; moved with family to Port Arthur at age 1; active in figure skating, t&f, tennis; mem. Thunder Bay FS Club '38-48; sr. champion '45; jr., sr. t&f titles '43-49; Port Arthur sr. women's doubles '44-45; jr. women's singles Port Arthur, Duluth '46; 1st Cdn to compete in US women's tennis championships '46; 1st girl to win ntl title after only 2 1/2yrs in game; 1st to win all 3 titles 1 tournament; mem. NWO Sports Hall of Fame; last known res. Montreal, Que.

HARPER, George (shooting); b. 21 Sep 1936, New Glasgow, N.S.; given name: George Ross; m. Azul Annis Nickerson; c. Stephen, Jamie; retd. major, logistics officer DND; high powered rifle specialist; mem. ntl cadet Bisley team '55; 7 times qualified ntl Bisley team, competed 5 times; mem. 2 Palma match teams, 1 Kalapore match winner; top Canadian, 14th overall, Bisley '72; recipient Commandant's Prize; Bisley record 100 14Vs '72 MacKinnon Team match; mem. 3 Bisley Overseas match title teams; Alexander Graham Bell match title team '55; recipient 2 Donnegal medals, 3 Queen's badges at Bisley; ntl Tyro, Connaught match titles; mem. Cdn team Australian match '92; Lt.Gov. gold PEI, 2 bronnze NB; capt. 2 N S, 1 Maritime rugby title teams mid-'50s; also excelled in gymnastics; took up marathon running as conditioner at 35; participated in 15 major marathons in Ottawa, Montreal, Halifax; v-p NCRRA/NDHQRA from '90; mem. Cdn Forces, NS Sports halls of fame; res. Gloucester, Ont.

HARPER, Glenn (football); b. 12 Sep 1962, Edmonton, Alta.; Washington State; punter; drafted by Sask (CFL) '86; played in CFL with Calgary '86-88, Toronto '89-90, Edmonton '91-96; 2 Western all-star; CFL record: 171g, 2cvts, 42s, 1404 punts for 57,641yds, completed 12 of 17 passes for 199yds, 3tds; 13 playoff games, 2 Grey Cup finals, 1 winner; res. Edmonton, Alta.

HARPER, Ted (cycling); b. 14 Jul 1917, Sherbrooke, Que.; d. 9 Jan 1998, Barrie, Ont.; given name: Edward Arthur; m. Margaret Fraser Murray (d), Brenda Deen; c. Edward William, Ross (d), Patricia; sports columnist, advertising salesman; pro 6-day bike racing specialist competing throughout NA during '30s; with WW2 popularity of sport waned and he retired to work in munitions factory; charter-mem. Stroud Optimist Club; p-pres. Barrie Optimists; authored *Six-Days of Madness*

HARPER, Terry (hockey); b. 27 Jan 1940, Regina, Sask.; given name: Terrance Victor; m. Gladys Piluk; c. Terrence Gregory Peter, Jeffrey Todd, Brigitte Dawn; UBC,SFU, Loyola, McGill; real estate broker, hockey coach; '56 Olympic track team tryout; mem. Regina Rams football club '57-60; Sask. Roughriders tryout '60; mem. Regina Pats hockey club '57-60; mem. Memorial Cup finalists; picked for '60 Olympic hockey team but couldn't get release from Pats; pro Montreal Royals '60; Hull-Ottawa Canadiens (EPHL) '61-62, Montreal (NHL) '62-72, LA '72-75, Detroit '75-79, St. Louis '80; mem. 5 Stanley Cup winners; designed, developed 1st plastic hockey skate boots; asst. coach Colorado Rockies '81; GM Sacramento (RHIL) '94-97; NHL record: 1051 scheduled games, 35g, 219a, 112 playoff games, 4g, 13a; res. Birmingham, Mich.

HARRINGTON, Dave (highland games); b. 12 Jan 1945, Fresno, Calif.; div. Janet Hogg; c. Brenna, Joanna, Andrew; m. Margaret Barrie; sc. Nathan, Rachel Barrie; Stanford, BA, BEd; international management consultant; ntl discus title '71; ntl t&f team '73; ntl Highland Games champion '78-84; most travelled Cdn competitor; more than 800 individual competition victories, fewer than 20 losses; all Cdn records, 3 NA records; world sheaf toss record '83; US champion '83; '81-84 ranked among world's top 10; active as games builder; avid art collector; res. Ottawa, Ont.

HARRINGTON, Ed (football); b. 8 Feb 1941, Speer, Okla.; given name: Edison Dean; div.; c. Wendy, Dusti Kia; Langston, BSc; patient advocate North Bay psychiatric hospital; Oklahoma state weightlifting titles '60-62; nicknamed "Hercules"; pro Houston (NFL) '62; Toronto (CFL) as offensive guard '63; EFC all-star '64; Toronto Rifles Continental League '65; rejoined Argos '67-70; 3 times all-eastern, all-Cdn; quarter-horse breeder; plays, writes Bluegrass music; res. Field, Ont.

HARRIS, Lesley (badminton); b. 18 Oct 1954, Kuala Lampur, Malaysia; given name: Lesley Elizabeth; m. R.K. Bercuson; McGill, BA; project, systems analyst; ntl jr. singles, doubles badminton titles '73-74, ntl ladies' singles finalist '75, doubles finalist '76-77; mem. '75 Uber Cup semifinalists; bronze ladies singles '71 Canada Winter Games; with Mila Zaruba Horak '70 girls -18 ntl tennis doubles; res. Town of Mount Royal, Que.

HARRIS, Merelynn (basketball); b. 28 Apr 1969, Toronto, Ont.; given name: Merelynn Lange; m. Harris; c. Deja Sabine, Kassandra Nicole; UNLV; standout centre, winner 2 HS MVP awards; UNLV freshman of '89, leading scorer, rebounder '91-92, all-Conference '92, 2 Big West titles; made Cdn ntl team age 16; mem. '86, '90, '94 world championship, '90 Goodwill, '91 FISU, '85 world junior championship, '96 Olympic teams; bronze '93, gold '95 COPABA championships; pro France, Germany '92-94; WNBA Phoenix Mercury '99; res. Las Vegas, Nev.

HARRIS, Mike (curling/golf); B. 6 Sept 1961, Georgetown, Ont.; golf pro; skip Ont. jr. curling title '86, Ont. mixed '89; skip 3 Ont. Tankard rinks, '92, '93 runnerup; skip 3 Welton Beauchamp titles; defeated Alberta's Kevin Martin 6-5 to earn right to represent Canada in '98 Olympics; after placing 1st in round robin and breezing through semifinal fell victim to flu and a hot Swiss rink to settle for Olympic silver '98; set course record 66 winning '92 Aurora pro-am; former head pro Donalda GC; head golf instructor Pischelsdorf, Austria; res. North York, Ont./Pichelsdorf, Austria.

HARRIS, Wayne (football); b. 4 May 1938, Hampton, Ark,; given name: Carrol Wayne; m. Anne Dearth; c. Wayne Jr., Heather Wynelle, Andrew Cooper; Arkansas; v-p, mgr. field operations drilling, exploration co.; linebacker, guard Eldorado Jr. HS, all-state '52-53; HS all-state '55-56, all-Southern, all-American '56; Arkansas HS all-star game outstanding lineman '56; Arkansas scholarship '57-60; all-Southwest Conference '59-60; all-American '60; Houston Post award outstanding Southwest Conference player; Arkansas, Louisiana, Texas athlete of year '60; '59 Gator, '60 all-American, Cotton Bowls; Arkansas Association Neil Gibson Martin Victory Trophy '60; drafted by Boston Patriots; pro Calgary '61-72; all-Western Conference 11 times, all-Cdn 9 times; 4 times Schenley outstanding lineman, once runnerup; 3 Grey Cup finals, 1 winner; outstanding player '71 Grey Cup; Demarco-Becket Trophy winner; Calgary athlete of '67; 2 most popular player awards; twice Stampeder president's award; sweater #55 retd. by club on Wayne Harris Day '73; roasted by CFL Player's Assn. '76; coached jr. football '73, HS football '75-76; mem. Canadian Football, Alta., Ark. Sports halls of fame; res. Calgary, Alta.

HARRISON, Herm (football); b. 29 Sep 1939, Rocky Mountain, N.C.; given name: Herman Austin; c. Tamara;

Arizona State, BA; sales CKMX/CJAY radio; conf, all-star, hon. mention all-American; pro end Calgary '64-72; CFL record: 443 receptions for 6693yds, 43tds; best season '68 1306yds; best game vs. Sask. 29 Sep '68 12 receptions 237yds; 3 WFL, 2 CFL pass reception titles; 4 TD receptions single game vs. Winnipeg '70; 3 1000-plus yards seasons; 60 consecutive game reception string '68-72; 16 100-plus yards games; 5 times WFC all-star, 4 all-Cdn; 2 most popular player awards; nicknamed "Ham Hands"; Stampeders club dir. '75-81; jersey retd by Duquesne HS; Penn. House of Reps, citation; mem. Cdn Football Hall of Fame; res. Calgary, Alta.

HARRISON, Neil (curling); b. 23 Jan 1949, Peterborough, Ont.; given name: Neil Gordon; m. Jane Clune; c. Amber, Sean; firefighter; began curling age 12; mem. Ed Werenich's Ont., ntl firefighters title rinks '78-80,'82-84; mem. Werenich's Ont. Labatt Tankard title rink '81, '83-84; competed 6 Briers total, 1 winner; mem. Werenich's Ont., ntl, World title rink '83; CCR all-star '83-84, '88; normally plays lead; Dick Ellis team award '83; fed. govt. world champion award '83; mem. Canadian Curling Hall of Fame; res. Pickering, Ont.

HART, Bret (wrestling); b. 2 Jul 1957, Calgary, Alta.; m. Julie; c. Jade, Dallas, Alexandra Sabina, Blade; Mount Royal Coll.; pro wrestler; won city/prov. titles in 3 weight categories; following college became film director but lure of wrestling ring took over; nicknamed "The Hitman"; noted for accurate textbook execution of every manoeuver; signature move The Sharpshooter; developed interest in sport from father Stu, former CFL football player and wrestling gym operator; has made guest appearances as actor in TV series *Lonesome Dove, Mad TV* and animated role in *The Simpsons*; writes column for *Calgary Sun*; accomplished cartoonist; WHL Calgary Hitmen, of which he is former co-owner, named after him; res. Calgary, Alta.

HART, David (water polo); b. 6 Dec 1951, Hamilton, Ont.; given name: David Andrew; m. Francesse Kopczewski; c. Jesse, Kasia; McMaster., BA, BPhE; master coach Water Polo Canada, owner Oyate Native Gallery; as competitive swimmer set 7 Ont., 6 ntl records; mem. ntl jr men's water polo title team '69, runnerup '70; mem. 4 ntl sr. men's title teams, 5 OUAA titles; mem. '72, '76 Olympic, '71, '75 Pan-Am Games, '75 world aquatic championships; coached Hamilton Aquatic Club to ntl sr. men's title '77, jr. men's gold medal team '77 Canada Games; Ivor Wynne Trophy McMaster outstanding athlete of year; 13yrs tech. dir. Water Polo Canada; coach Carleton from '94; OUAA coach of '94; coach ntl men's team from '96; innovator who launched Cdn Water Polo League, Legacy coaching program, Cdn Dream Team '99, men's ntl team alumni; Jimmy Thompson Memorial award; mem. McMaster Sports, Ont. Aquatic halls of fame; res. Osgoode, Ont.

HART, Gaètan (boxing); b. 9 Nov 1953, Buckingham, Que.; div. Line Charboneau; c. Denis, Melanie, Mathieu; m. Ghyslaine; hardware trucker; retired pro boxer; 7 amateur bouts, won all; 91 pro bouts, 60 wins, 27 losses, 4 draws; 26 KOs; 3 times ntl lightweight titlist; beat Cleveland Denny for title '78, defended 3 times; lost title to Nicky Furlano '79, regained it from Furlano '80; stripped of title for failure to defend within designated time; regained title from Michel

Lalonde '81; lost title to Johnny Summerhayes; fought 5 world champions including Aaron Pryor, Claude Noel; Denny died following beating by Hart '80, Ralph Racine in coma several weeks following Hart beating '80; retired from ring '84; made brief, but unsuccessful comeback bid '90-92; Buckingham street named in his honor; subject of NFB film "*Le Steak*"; res. Buckingham, Que.

HART, Nelson (lawn bowling/administration); b. 11 Jun 1888, Opa Twp., Ont.; d. 7 Dec 1959, London, Ont.; pres.UWO.; as young man avid ice boater; mem. Ont. doubles lawn bowling title team '39; pres. OLBA, CLBA; 6yrs lawn bowling umpire; represented UWO on CIAU board; CIAU pres. '50-51; co-founder Western Ont. Secondary School Athletics (WOSSA), 10yrs hon. secty.; hon. secty. COA '38-49; chef de mission Cdn Olympic team '48; 25yrs AAU of C secty; variety of other AAU of C exec. offices, pres. '48; mem. B.E., Commonwealth Games Assoc. of Canada advisory board '49-59; mem. Cdn Amateur Sports Hall of Fame.

HARTL, Gus (shooting); b. 1954, Austria; municipal employee; handgun specialist; began shooting competitively '78; competed in PPC, Bullseye, ntl standard, centrefire, air pistol events claiming a myriad of titles; set ntl PPC record 600 47x '86 then improved on it with 600 50x '95; holds PPC aggregate 1198 97x of possible 1200; 2 NRA, 1 Canton, Detroit regional PPC titles; mem. only 2 Cdn teams to win world PPC titles; mem. Bullseye competition Mayleigh Cup title team '89; 1 ntl standard pistol, 3 ntl 1800 (2700) .22cal, 4 centrefire, 2 .45cal, 3 grand aggregate titles; Ont. Handgun Assn. award; mem. NRA 1490, 2600 clubs; NRA distinguished revolver award; numerous president's 100 medals; res. Toronto, Ont.

HARTLEY, Errol (field hockey); b. 16 Mar 1940, Allahabad, India; given name: Errol Patrick: m. Patrick; m. Patricia Ann; c. Adrian Christopher, Lorraine, Nicole; London, P Eng, MIEE, BSc; engineer; rep. BC 4 consecutive interprovincial title-winning teams '68-71; coached BC '72 interprovincial champions; coached Canada's bronze medal team '71, silver '75 Pan-Am Games; coached ntl team '70-79; 10th '76 Olympics; res. Trinidad.

HARTMAN, Barney (shooting); b. 2 Nov 1916, Swan River, Man.; m. Joahanna Carr; c. Shelley Jo-Anne; retd. sales promotion; considered world's greatest skeet shooter; capt. 10 NSSA all-American skeet team; 4 perfect 100x100 410 gauge; nearly 30 world records in 12, 20, 28, 410 gauge, all-around categories; world record .9875 avg. with 395x400 with 410 gauge '66; world record .9991 avg. with 1049x1050 12 gauge '68 (mark broken '71 by US shooter with perfect 1.000); 28 gauge .9980 record '69 with 499x500, 20 gauge .9983 record avg. '71 with 599x600; '66-73 avg. .99038 all-around category; once broke 2002 clay targets without miss; silver, 4 bronze world international competition '61-63; 9yrs industry pro shooter with highest overall standard 12, 20, 28, 410 gauge; author '67 instruction book "*Hartman on Skeet*"; mem. Order of Canada, Ottawa, Ottawa CSRA, Canadian Forces, US National Skeet Shooting Assn., Canada's Sports halls of fame; res. Orleans, Ont.

HARTSBURG, Craig (hockey); b. 29 Jun 1959, Stratford, Ont.; m. Peggy; c. Chris, Katie; defence Sault Ste. Marie (OHL) '76-78; pro Birmingham (WHA) '78-79; Minnesota (NHL) '79-89; capt. North Stars 6 seasons; NHL playing record: 570 scheduled games, 98g, 315a, 61 playoff games 15g, 27a; competed 3 all-star games; launched coaching career as asst. Minnesota '89-90, Philadelphia '90-94; head coach Guelph (OHL) '94-95, Chicago '95-98, Anaheim '98-99; NHL coaching record: (through '98) regular season 323-306-91, playoffs 21-16; mem. Team Canada 3 world tournaments; Canada Cup gold '87; Canada Cup best defenceman '87; OHL coach of '95 award; mem. North Stars 25th anniversary dream team; res. Anaheim, Calif.

HARTZELL, Irene (swimming); b. 19 Oct 1922, Winnipeg, Man.; div. Dr. George D. Athans; c. George Jr., Greg, Gary; during '40s Man. breaststroke titlist, ntl record holder; 4 consec. Man. synchronized swimming titles; returned to competitive swimming in masters category '88; won prov., ntl titles and established numerous records; mem. BC world record mixed medley relay team '95; silver, 2 breaststroke bronze World Masters, setting ntl records in each instance; res. Kelowna, B.C.

HARVEY, Buster (hockey); b. 2 Apr 1950, Fredericton, N.B.; given name: Frederick John Charles; engine machine shop; began career Halifax jr. Canadiens '67 Maritime title team; NB title Fredericton Jr. Red Wings '68; Hamilton Jr. Red Wings OJHL '68-70; drafted by Minnesota NHL '70-74, Cleveland AHL '71-72, Atlanta NHL '74-75, Kansas City NHL '75-76 CHL '77, Detroit NHL '76-77, Philadelphia AHL '77-78; NHL record: 7 seasons, 407 scheduled games, 90g, 118a, 14 playoff games, 0g, 2a; mem. Kansas City CHL title team '77; OJHL rookie of '69, scoring leader; 2nd team AHL all-star '72; coached Fredericton Jr. Red Wings to NB title '80; mem. NB Sports Hall of Fame; res. Fredericton, N.B.

HARVEY, Doug (hockey); b. 19 Dec 1924, Montreal, Que.; d. 26 Dec 1989, Montreal, Que.; given name: Douglas Norman; m. Ursula; c. 5; employee Connaught Park; mem. Ottawa Border Baseball League team 2 years; led league hitters one season with .351 BA; rejected Boston Braves pro offers; mem. Montreal Royals Allan Cup winner; pro hockey Montreal '47-61, NY Rangers '61-64, Detroit '66-67, St. Louis '68-69; coach Rangers '61-62; mem. 6 Stanley Cup winners; 7 Norris Trophy; 10 1st team, 1 2nd team all-star defenceman; jersey #2 retd by Canadiens; mem. Hockey Hall of Fame.

HARVEY, Nancy (golf); b. 2 May 1962, Swift Current, Sask.; m. Glen "Doc" Harvey; Arizona State; psychologist, pro golfer; began playing at 14; mem. Sask jr. team '77-80; Sask ladies amateur title '80; mem. international jr. team '80; mem. Sask amateur team '81-84; turned pro '88; career low round 67; with husband manages public golf course; mem. Canada's inaugural Nations Cup team '99; res. Mesa, Ariz.

HARVEY, Pierre (cycling/skiing); b. 24 Mar 1957, Rimouski, Que.; m. Mireille Belzile; Laval; engineer; competitive swimmer age 12-15; competitive cyclist at 15;

mem. ntl team '75-80, '84; mem. '76 Summer, '84 Winter, Summer, '88 Winter Olympic teams; competitive cross-country skier at 17; ntl team '80-88; ntl 15km titles '81-83, '85-88, 30km '82, '85-88, 50km '83, '86-88; NA 3x10km relay '81, 15km, 30km '83; Sett Internationale Del Fondo 30km '82; ntl 3x10km relay '82, 25.5km '83; won '87 WC 30km race Sweden; twice 4th WC 15km events; 14 times among WC top 8; mem. Order of Canada, Cdn Skiing, Que. Sports halls of fame; res. St-Ferreol-Les-Neiges, Que.

HARVEY, Scott Jr. (baseball/hockey); b. 17 Apr 1949, Fredericton, N.B.; given name: Laurence Melvin; NB Power Commission; pro baseball with LA Dodgers Ogden, Utah, Pioneer League farm club '67; St. Louis Cardinals' St. Petersburg, Fla. State League, Lewiston, Northwestern League farm clubs '69-70; mem. several NB title teams; mem. NB team '69 Canada Games; record 13 appearances with ntl title teams, 2 jr., 11 sr., winning gold '81, '82, 2 silver, 2 bronze; pitched losing 1-0 decision vs. Cuban world amateur titlists '76; set NBSBL batting avg. record with .552 '77; pro hockey AHL Boston Braves; Fredericton athlete of '65; mem. Fredericton Sports Wall, NB Baseball, NB Sports halls of fame; res. Fredericton, N.B.

HARVEY, Scott Sr. (baseball); b. 30 Mar 1926, Grand Manan, N.B.; m. Joan Estey; c. Scott Jr., Jane; Mt. Allison; retd. exec.-secty. NB Mutual Insurance Assn.; mem. '47-48 NB champion Marysville Royals, Brooklyn Dodgers tryout '48, Black's Harbour Brunswicks '49-54, Marysville Royals '55-64; coached Royals 6yrs; 11yrs mem. NB Federation of Amateur Baseball, 7 as pres.; v-p Baseball Canada 7yrs; res. Fredericton, N.B.

HASLAM, Eleanor (t&f); b. 1939, Saskatoon, Sask.; m. Ole Jensen; c. 4;UofSask, UBC; cancer researcher; mem. Nutana Kiwanis TC under coach Bob Adams; Sask. HS 50, 75yd dash, ntl juve. 100yds, 220yds, sr. 220yds records; mem. '56, '60 Olympic, '58 BEG teams; set Olympic 800, world 60yd indoor records; 3 ntl titles; ntl juve. 220 record 24.5, 5 golds '57 Western Canada championships; twice broke ntl women's 100yd dash record, lowered 220 mark to 24.1; relay team bronze '58 BEG; 1st female winner Dr. Fred Tees Trophy Canada's outstanding university athlete '58; Governor-General's academic medal; mem. Sask., Saskatoon Sports halls of fame; res. Denmark.

HASLAM, Phyllis (swimming); b. 24 May 1913, Dharmsala, India; d. 23 Aug 1991, Toronto, Ont.; given name: Phyllis Georgie; UofSask, BSc, UofT, social work dip., Trinity College, DSLitt; exec.-dir. Elizabeth Fry Society; ntl 100, 220yd breaststroke records '32; world record 1:18.3 100yd breaststroke '32 (unrecognized as standard, again lowered before time registered); BEG 200yd breaststroke mark 2:52.6 in heats; BEG 200yd silver, team gold 3x100yd relay; mem. UofSask. swim team '31-34, UotT swim team '35-36; received Varsity T; volunteer swim coach several years; officer Order of Canada '78; mem. Cdn Aquatic, Cdn Amateur, Sask. Sports halls of fame.

HASSETT, Gavin (rowing); b. 13 Jul 1973, Saint John, N.B.; UVic; began rowing '89; mem. ntl team from '93; competes lightweight men's straight four; gold men's light 8s '93 worlds, straight 4s Amsterdam '94, US

championships '95; bronze straight 4s '93 FISU Games; silver lw 4's '96 Olympics; res. Victoria, B.C.

HATANAKA, Bill (football); b. 3 May 1954, Bathurst, N.B.; given name: William Harry; m. Janet Christine Daly; c. William Robert, Ryan James; York, Hon BA, Harvard Business School; v-p, dir. ntl sales mgr. RBC Dominion Securities; 1st round draft Rough Riders '76; CFL Ottawa '76-78, Hamilton '79; mem. '76 Grey Cup title team; set Grey Cup record longest punt return 79yds; res. Toronto, Ont.

HATCH, John (basketball); b. 23 Feb 1962, Calgary, Alta.; m. Patricia; c. Ryan, Shannon, Jason; St.FX, ntl team '83-87; forward '83 FISU Games gold medal team; mem. '83 Pan-Am, '84 Olympic Games teams; 2 CIAU all-Cdn; fed. govt. excellence award '84; res. Milan, Italy.

HATSKIN, Ben (builder); b. 30 Sep 1917, Winnipeg, Man.; d. 18 Oct 1990, Winnipeg, Man.; given name: Benjamin; m. Cecelia Rashcovsky; Oklahoma; real estate exec.; among first Canadians offered US college football scholarship; pro Winnipeg '36-41; Grey Cup winners '39, '41; jr. hockey Kildonan Stars '36; formed Jets hockey club in WCHL '66; instrumental in formation World Hockey Assn. with Winnipeg Jets as members; signed Bobby Hull to give WHA credibility; maintained jr. entry in WHL; chair. WHA, owner Honolulu franchise WFL '73; involved in International Basketball Assn. for Winnipeg '86; Manitoba Man of Year, *Sporting News* Executive of Year '73; mem. Man. Sports, Hockey halls of fame.

HATTIN, Heather (rowing); b. 15 May 1961, Windsor, Ont.; given name: Heather Carlyle; m. Robert Ridpath; c. Jenna Carlyle; Guelph, BSc, UofT, MSc; rehabilitation specialist; began rowing in HS; joined Don Rowing Club '76; international competitive debut '83 Pan-Am Games winning heavyweight doubles silver; alternate '84, competed '88 Olympics; competed '84-86 worlds; lightweight singles bronze '86 Commonwealth Games; Mississauga female amateur athlete of '87; mem. Athletes Resource Group, Cdn Rowing Athletes' Council, UofT, Guelph Athletes' councils; mem. Mississauga Sports Hall of Fame; res. Guelph, Ont.

HAUCH, Paul (swimming/administration); b. 27 Dec 1903, Tokyo, Japan; d. 21 Mar 1981, Orlando, Florida; m. Marion Louise Bole; c. Guy, Jon, Bill; Northwestern, UWO, MD, Royal College of Physicians, Surgeons, DMR(D); radiologist; capt. UWO football '31; initial recipient G.Howard Ferguson Award UWO outstanding athlete, scholar; capt. UWO basketball '29, swim team '32; runnerup freshman tennis championships Northwestern '25; founder/ swim coach London YMCA Aquatic Club '46-73; pres. Ont. section CASA '45-59, secty. '59-68; v-p ASUA '59; dir.-v-p COA, chairman medical advisory comm. '60-69; mem. COA '69-76; mem. technical swim comm. FINA '56-68, mem. FINA bureau '68-72, hon. secty. FINA '72-76; successfully defended rights of foreign-born Canadians to represent Canada in Olympics; introduced Swim-A-Thons; Air Canada amateur sports exec. of '67; Ont. Athletic Commission award '68; mem. National Fitness Advisory Council '65-66; mgr./physician 3 Olympic teams;

Centennial medal '67; mem. W-Club, Cdn Amateur, Cdn, Ont. Aquatic halls of fame.

HAUCH, Rosemarie (t&f); b. 19 Dec 1957, Carleton Place, Ont.; discus, shot put specialist; bronze shot put '75 jr. nationals; Ont. shot put title '77; ntl indoor shot put '83-84, outdoor '83; 9 silver (1 discus), 7 bronze (1 discus) in ntl, international competitions '75-83; mem. '83 FISU, Pan-Am Games teams; shot put bronze '82 Commonwealth Games; res. Chesterville, Ont.

HAWCO, Sherry (gymnastics); b. 17 Feb 1964, Cambridge, Ont.; d. 26 Oct 1991, Cambridge, Ont.; given name: Sherry Louise; m. Mark Delanty; c. Brandon Hawco; team gold, all-around silver '78 Commonwealth Games; gold team, beam '79 Pan-Am Games; mem. '80 Olympic team; ntl title '81.

HAWERCHUK, Dale (hockey); b. 4 Apr 1963, Toronto, Ont. m. Crystal; c. Alexis, Eric; centre Cornwall Royals '79-81; CMJL, QMJHL player of year '81; Memorial Cup Most Sportsmanlike player '80, MVP '81; 1st overall '81 draft; pro Winnipeg '81-90, Buffalo '90-95, St. Louis '95-96, Philadelphia '96-97; Calder Memorial Trophy '82; mem. Team Canada '87, '91 Canada Cup; MVP, Star of Stars award '91; topped 50-goal plateau with 53 '85; NHL record: 1188 scheduled games, 518g, 891a, 97 playoff games, 30g, 69a; res. St. Albans, Mo./Orangeville, Ont.

HAWKINS, John (t&f); b. 8 Jun 1949, Kelowna, B.C.; given name: Francis John Alexander; UBC, BPhE, MPhE; fitness centre instructor; high jump specialist; BC midget title '64, juve. '65, jr. '67; switched from scissor jump to Fosbury Flop and '71 became 1st Cdn to clear 7'; mem. '70, '74 Commonwealth, '71 Pan-Am, '72 Olympic, '70, '73 FISU Games teams; silver '70 Commonwealth, bronze '73 FISU Games; ntl indoor record '72; WCIAU, Pan-Pacific titles '73; mem. CIAU basketball champions FISU Games team '70, BC men's '77 volleyball titlists; BC athlete of '71; res. Vancouver, B.C.

HAWLEY, Sandy (horse racing); b. 16 Apr 1949, Oshawa, Ont.; given name: Sanford Desmond; div. Sherry; div. Vicky Beck; m. Lisa John; c. Russell, Bradley; PR ambassador OJC, ex-jockey; runnerup Ont. HS 96lb wrestling title; began riding under tutelage of Duke Campbell '68; top NA apprentice '69; NA leading race-winning jockey '70, '72; competed Southern California circuit '79-88; 515 victories '73 eclipsed Bill Shoemaker's '53 mark of 485 (subsequently beaten by Chris McCarran's 547 '74); 4 Queen's Plate, 8 Canadian Oaks titles; at 27 youngest jockey to reach 3000 victory plateau '76; topped 6000 win plateau '92; underwent 2 skin cancer operations '87, lung cancer surgery '93; injured '95 Woodbine spill; LA Kings (NHL) penalty box official; 2 Lou Marsh trophies, George Woolf award, US racing's Eclipse award, Avelino Gomez award, 2 Soverign awards; Joe Palmer award; retd '98; career record: 6449w, 4825p, 4158s, with 31,454 mounts, career earnings $88,666,071; mem. Order of Canada, Ntl Museum of Racing, Canadian Horseracing, Canada's, Oshawa, Mississauga Sports halls of fame; res. Mississauga, Ont.

HAY, Bill (hockey); b. 8 Dec 1935, Saskatoon, Sask.; given name: William Charles; m. Nancy; c. Pam, Penny, Donald;

Colorado College, BSc; hockey exec.; Calgary (WHL) '58-59, Chicago (NHL) '59-67; Calder Memorial Trophy; with Bobby Hull, Murray Balfour formed Chicago's Million Dollar Line; NHL record: 506 scheduled games, 113g, 273a, 70 playoff games, 18g, 37a; mem. '61 Stanley Cup winner; chair. Hockey Canada development comm. chair Saddledome Foundation; v-p Bow Valley Industries, '81-90; created International Hockey Centre of Excellence '85; Centre of Excellence planning advisor for CHA; mem. Hockey Canada International comm. '82-90; mem. Hockey Hall of Fame selection comm, Special Olympics Advisory Board; dir. Hockey Hall of Fame, chair. from '98; pres/ alternate governor Calgary Flames; mem. Sask Sports Hall of Fame; res. Calgary, Alta.

HAY, Charles (builder/hockey); b. 28 Jun 1902, Kingston, Ont.; d. 24 Oct 1973, Calgary, Alta.; c. Bill; UofSask; retd oil exec.; goaltender; finalist '21 Allan Cup with Uof Sask; major role in negotiating first international series involving Canada-Russia '72; helped organize Hockey Canada; HC pres.; key role in formulation of ntl team program; mem. Hockey Hall of Fame.

HAY, Denny (rodeo); b. 6 Nov 1967, Stony Plain, Alta; m. Susan; c. Amber, Rebekka; rancher; saddle bronc, calf roping specialist; ntl novice saddle bronc title '87; CPRA rookie of yr '89; 2 BC circuit SB titles, Coors Chute Out, Skoal pro rodeo titles '91; APRC AA, SB titles '94; CFR SB average leader '96; 2 ntl SB titles; res. Mayerthorpe, Alta.

HAY, George (hockey); b. 10 Jan 1898, Listowel, Ont.; d. 13 Jul 1975, Stratford, Ont.; given name: George William; Winnipeg Jr./Sr. Monarchs 1915-16, Regina Vics 1920-21; pro Regina Caps 1920, 87 goals, 57 assists 4 years; Portland Rosebuds, 18 goals before '26 sale to Chicago; Detroit Cougars 1927-33; NHL career record: 73 goals, 54 assists; left wing coaches' dream team; mem. Man., Cdn Hockey halls of fame.

HAYDENLUCK, Greg (t&f/bobsled); b. 7 Jul 1958, Emerson, N.B.; m.; UofT; South Dakota; teacher; NCAA Div II all-American decathlete; ntl decathlon champion '85, '87; competed as decathlete '82 Commonwealth Games; turned to bobsleigh at 26; mem. ntl team '84-92; 3 ntl 2-man, 4-man titles; competed '88, '92 Olympics; res. Toronto, Ont.

HAYES, Bob (football/coaching); b. 29 Mar 1933, Perth, Ont.; given name: Robert Gerald; m. Heather Robbins; c. Robert, Thomas, Jodan, Holly, Laurel; St.Mary's, BA; retd. athletic dir.; running back Stadacona, Shearwater; 3 MVP awards, 2 scoring titles; 4 Purdy Cup title teams; 1st Maritime Football Union player to top 1000yds rushing single season with 1265 on 133 carries Shearwater '57; coach/AD St. Mary's; introduced single pillar football goalpost to Maritime game '67; mem. St. Mary's Hall of Fame; res. Halifax, N.S.

HAYES, Cheryl (swimming/karate); b. 18 Dec 1958, Saskatoon, Sask.; given name: Cheryl Lynn; deaf from birth; mem. Saskatoon Goldfins SC; mem. '73, '77 World Games for Deaf, '75 Pan-Am Games for Deaf teams; 3 silver, 3 bronze World Games for Deaf, 4 gold, 1 silver Pan-Am Games for Deaf; 50m pool world records 100 butterfly, 100 backstroke, 200 IM; coached by Harry Bailey; Saskatoon Goldfins most valuable swimmer '76; turned skills to karate winning bronze medal, yellow, green belts; res. Saskatoon, Sask.

HAYES, George (hockey); b. 7 Sep 1920, Montreal, Que.; d. 19 Nov 1987, Beachville, Ont.; given name: George William; m. Judy; c. Bill, George Jr., Susan; hockey official, freelance writer; jr. hockey Ingersoll, Woodstock; baseball outfielder, 1st baseman Stratford, Ingersoll, Woodstock, Tillsonburg; football Woodstock provincial jr. champions '36; pushed into hockey refereeing '40 when handed life suspension from amateur sport after brawl in Tillsonburg baseball game; NHL linesman '46-64; 1549 league, 149 playoff games; OHA, AHL referee, worked Memorial Cup finals '46; officiated more than 3000 games all leagues; mem. Hockey Hall of Fame.

HAYES, Jay (equestrian); b. 14 Jun 1957, Hartford, Conn.; m. Shawn Carpenter; c. Lauren, Ainsley, Regan; Connecticutt,. BSc; horseman, North Ridge stables operator; raised on dairy farm; began riding age 12; played intercollegiate polo; Cdn citizen, mem. ntl team from '85; mem. 23 Nations Cup teams, 5 World Cup finals, '90 World championships; mem. '92 Olympic team (leading qualifier); won Tropicana GP '94-'96; res. Cheltenham, Ont.

HAYES, John (soccer); b. 25 Mar 1913, Belfast, N. Ireland; d. 3 Sep 1974, Saskatoon, Sask.; given name: John Fielding; m. Doris Roegele; c. Faye, Brian, Cheryl; railway carman; 40 years active soccer goaler; 6 Saskatoon Shields; faced various visiting UK clubs; indoor soccer to age 59; coached 3 provincial jr., HS, 1 midget, 3 Saskatoon HS title teams; goaler Saskatoon United broomball team '54-73, 7 successive city titles; honored by Saskatoon SA for contribution to game; trophy bearing his name awarded by Saskatoon United to city HS soccer titlists from '75; mem. Sask. Sports Hall of Fame.

HAYHURST, Tom (shooting); b. 1868, England; d. 1948, Toronto, Ont.; emigrated to Canada 1892; while still in England won Prince of Wales prize at Bisley 1889; Pte. 13th Battalion Cdn Light Infantry; became 1st Cdn marksman to win Queen's Prize at Bisley (in shootoff) 1895.

HAYMAN, Lew (football/coaching); b. 30 Sep 1908, Paterson, N.J.; d. 29 Jun 1984, Toronto, Ont.; given name: Lewis Edward; m. Joan; New York Military Academy, Syracuse; football exec.; came to Canada '32 to join Warren Stevens at UotT; considered Canadian Football's greatest architect; coached 5 Grey Cup winners, '33, '37-38 Argos, '42 RCAF Hurricanes, '49 Alouettes; coach Argos '33-40, RCAF Hurricanes '41-45; part-owner, coach, GM Alouettes '46-54; Argos exec. officer from '57; CFL pres. '49-50; responsible for several CFL firsts, televised games, night games, Sunday games, break in color bar; managing dir. Argos '79-81; hon. chair. from '81; mem. Canadian Football Hall of Fame.

HAYMAN, Ron (cycling); b. 31 Aug 1954, Camosie Glen, Scotland; given name: Ronald Leslie; BC Institute of Technology; sales/marketing mgr.; ntl jr. track title '72, team pursuit '72-75, individual pursuit '79, 10-mile title '75-76,

road race title '77, '79; mem. '72, '76 Olympic, '73-75, '77-78 world, '78 Commonwealth Games teams; 3 seasons Belgian pro circuit winning 15 6-day events; '79 Tour of Ireland title; 3 Vancouver Gastown GP titles; pro '79 scoring several major victories; sport dir. 7-Eleven pro team; level 3 coach, level 2 course conductor; TV analyst '96 Olympics; res. Summerland, B.C.

HAYTER, Ron (baseball/boxing/administration); b. 30 Jul 1936, Regina, Sask.; m. Jacqueline Bacon; c. Sparkle, Sandra, Nevin; semi-retd. journalist, politician, mem. ntl parole bd., operates own news & PR firm; worked with a variety of weeklies before becoming a reporter with *Edmonton Journal*, correspondent for *Time Magazine*; promising southpaw boxer in youth and played competitive baseball to age 44; p-pres., life mem., dir. Baseball Alta, CPBF; dir. Baseball Can., founding mem. IBA; past exec. WBA; life mem. WCBA; mem. selection comm. Cdn Baseball Hall of Fame; exec. dir. Edmonton Boxing & Wrestling Commission; chair. Edmonton Intl. Baseball Foundation, organizers of World Youth AAA baseball championships in Edmonton; played key role in baseball acceptance as Olympic sport; founding dir. '78 Commonwealth Games; Edmonton city alderman '71-95; hon. dir. Crystal Kids Youth Centre; p-pres., life mem. Alta. Urban Municipalities Assn.; hon. life mem. Fed. Cdn Municipalities; Vanier award as one of Canada's five outstanding young Cdns '74; life mem. Yellowhead Highway Assn.; AUMA award of excellence, distinguished service award; FCM roll of honor; Alta. achivement award; mem. Alta., Nicaragua, Cdn Boxing, Edmonton Sports halls of fame; res. Edmonton, Alta.

HAYWARD, Bob (speedboat racing); b. 27 Oct 1928, Embro, Ont.; d. 10 Sep 1961, Detroit River, Mich.; mechanic Miss Supertest hydroplane crew '57; as driver '59 St. Clair international trophy; upset Maverick '59 in record 104.098 mph to snap 30-year US hold on Harmsworth Trophy; defended title '60-61; record 116.464 mph '60; killed driving Miss Supertest II Detroit River Silver Cup race; Union of International Motor Boating sport medal of honor '60; mem. Canada's Sports Hall of Fame.

HAZZARD, Elmer (water skiing); b. 18 Mar 1932, North Battleford, Sask.; m. Evelyn; c. Greg, Blaine, Arlene; transmission co. owner; Regina Beach open trick, Stoney Lake overall title '70; Sask. sr. overall title '72-73; national sr. tricks title '73-74; from '72 11 gold veterans class tricks; 3 national veterans records; 8 Western Canada tricks titles; judge, coach; v-p Sask. WSA, Regina WSC; 3 Sask. water skier of year awards; mem. Sask Sports Hall of Fame; res. Regina, Sask.

HEADLAND, Martin (motorsport); b. 7 Jul 1950, Beckenham, Eng.; given name: Martin George; m. Elizabeth Shaughnessy; aeronautical engineer; GM Skyservice Toronto; rally driver; with Jean-Paul Pérusse won ntl, NA co-driver Class A titles '87; with Tim O'Neill won ntl, NA co-driver titles '88-89; with O'Neil only outright win by Production car in US rally '89; with Walter Boyce, Perusse, Taisto Heinonen won several US, Cdn ntl titles; with Jeff Zwart 2nd overall in 25-day Panama to Alaska rally '97; mem. Toyota, Volkswagen, Nissan, Suzuki factory teams;

mem. Suzuki world title class team '87-88 Olympus, Wa. team; avid interest as trainer, participant in equestrian show jumping events; res. Schomberg, Ont.

HEANEY, Brian (basketball/coaching); b. 9 Mar 1946, Brooklyn, N Y; m. Liana Hynes; c. Pamela Jane, Jennifer Christine, Brian Niles; Acadia, BSc; v-p Maritime Life, TV analyst; ex-coach.; 8 all-time Acadia scoring records including 74 points single game, 52 in one half, single season scoring avg. 34.5; pro NBA Baltimore Bullets '69-70, EPBL Sunbury Mercs '70; coach St. Mary's '71-79, UAlta '80-82, UofT '83-88; 3 CIAU titles; 1st person to win CIAU titles as player, coach; 1 CIAU coach of yr award; pres. Natl. Assn. Cdn basketball coaches '78-79; mem. '78 Halifax CABA men's sr. A titlists, coached ntl women's team '75 Pan-Ams, worlds, '76 Olympics; TV color commentator '83 FISU, '84 Olympics, '98 worlds; mem. Acadia , St. Mary's, NS Sports, Canadian Basketball halls of fame; res. Oakville, Ont.

HEANEY, Geraldine (hockey); b. 1 Oct 1967, Weston, Ont.; rec. programmer North Toronto Community Centre; defence '91, '93 Toronto Aeros sr. ntl champions; competed annually in ntl championships '87-99; MVP '92, most valuable defence '93, '97 sr. ntls; 3 MVD Sr AA OWHA titles; mem. 5 Team Canada world champions, '98 Olympic (silver medal) teams; MVD, all-star '92, MVD '94 worlds; silver '97, gold '96 3-Nations Cup teams; gold '96 Pacific Rim; mem. '92 women's world champion roller hockey team, silver '94; only woman featured in HNIC top 10 goals for '89-90 season; res. Weston, Ont.

HEAP, Alan (table tennis); b. 10 Mar 1947, Bolton, Eng.; m. Cathy Roccasalva; Hull, BA, McMaster, MA; teacher; British universities champion '66, '68-69; Lancashire Open '72; mem. Ont. team '74-80; National Capital Open '73, '76; Que. Open, Ont. closed '78; Montreal, Toronto, Ont., Eastern Canada Opens '79; res. Markham, Ont.

HEARN, Eugene (speed skating); b. 8 May 1929, Odessa, Sask.; c. Debbie, Jeff, Kathy; charter mem. Saskatoon SSC '42; competitor/coach '56-66; club pres. '50-52; SASSA pres. '57-59; coach Sask. team 1st Canada Winter Games '67; 1st CASSA ntl coach '67; began officiating '70, first as referee then as starter; starter Cdn indoor '71, 4 ntl championships; chief starter NA, intl championships '80-88; official '88 Winter Olympics; active in Special Olympics program; hon. life mem. Saskatoon Lions SSC; Sask. sport volunteer award; Softball distinguished service award; Dairy Producers Foundation volunteer award; CASSA award of excellence; mem. Sask. Sports, Cdn Amateur Speed Skating halls of fame; res. Saskatoon, Sask.

HEATH, Jeff (baseball); b. 1 Apr 1915, Ft. William, Ont.; d. 9 Dec 1975, Seattle, Wash.; given name: John Geoffrey; m. Ann; became US citizen '36; learned baseball fundamentals in Seattle HS; began pro career Zanesville (Mid-Atlantic) '36, Milwaukee (AA) '37; outfielder Cleveland '36-45, Washington '46, St. Louis '46-47, Boston (NL) '48-49; 3 times topped .300 single season, .343 '38, .340 '41, .319 '48; runnerup to Jimmy Foxx '38 AL batting race; twice all-star team mem.; led AL in triples '41; 3 career grand slams; with Boston Braves mem. .300 outfield '48

World Series finalists, but broken leg kept him out of series; led NL in fielding; led player revolt vs. mgr. Oscar Vitt '40; career record 1383g, 1447h, 887rbi, 777r, 102t, 279d, 194hr, 56sb, .293ba; color commentator Seattle Rainiers telecasts, wrote WS stories for Seattle Post-Intelligencer; mem. NWO Sports, Canadian Baseball halls of fame.

HEBENTON, Andy (hockey); b. 3 Oct 1929, Winnipeg, Man.; given name: Andrew Alex; m. Gael; c. Clayton, Theresa; jr. Winnipeg Canadians '48-49; Montreal sr. Royals; pro Cincinnati (AHL), Victoria Cougars (PCHL, WHL), Portland, missed only 3 of 280 games, 3 PCHL titles; NY Rangers '55-63, Boston '63-64; NHL record 630 consecutive game (broken by Garry Unger); NHL record: 189g, 202a; frequent all-star; played 1000th consec. pro game '66; 26yr pro career comprised 1735 games; twice Fred J. Hume Trophy (WHL most gentlemanly player); runnerup NHL rookie of '56; Lady Byng Trophy '57; Rangers Players' Prize; mem. Man. Hockey Hall of Fame; res. Seattle, Wash.

HÉBERT, Jacques (harness racing); b. 22 Aug 1942, Drummondville, Que.; started career with father Joseph and uncle Cyprien in Trois-Riviéres; worked 3yrs with Jean Jodoin before striking out on his own '66; one of most consistent drivers on Montreal circuit winning 100 or more races each season from '71; through '97 had posted 4570 victories with purses totalling more than $23M; res. Montreal, Que.

HEDBERG, Anders (hockey); b. 25 Feb 1951, Ornskoldsvik, Sweden; m. Gun-Marie; c. Mattias, Johan, Hanna; Stockholm Institute PE teaching diploma; hockey exec.; rw on line with Bobby Hull and fellow countryman Ulf Nilsson, proved a proficient sniper with WHA Winnipeg Jets '74-78 playing 286 scheduled games and amassing 236g, 222a; 50 plus goals in each of 4 seasons, 70 '77, 63 '78, 53 '75, 50 '76; played in NHL with NY Rangers '73-85 posting record of 465 scheduled games, 172g, 226a, 58 playoff games, 22g, 24a; on retirement became 1st European to secure top management position in NHL as AGM NYR '85-86; managed Stockholm AJK team; full-time scout TML '91-96; AGM TML '97-99; res. Toronto, Ont./Stockholm, Sweden.

HEDDLE, Kathleen (rowing); b. 27 Nov 1965, Trail, B.C.; UBC; began rowing '85; gold straight pair '87 Pan-Am, 8s & straight pair '92 Olympic Games, '91 worlds; Cdn Henley 4 gold 8s, 3 coxed 4s, 1 single sculls; International regatta gold 3 straight pairs, 2 8s, 1 straight 4s, double sculls; 1 ntl 8s gold; retd '93 season but came back to take world double sculls (McBean) gold '95, Olympics '96, also bronze quad sculls; retd. '96; Tribute of Champions '89 sport excellence award; CARA '91 centennial award; Dick Ellis Memorial sr. team award '91-92; mem. Canada's Sports Hall of Fame; res, Vancouver, B.C.

HEDGES, Brian (football); b. 2 Aug 19552, Fort Churchill, Man.; given name: Brian Robie; m. Kathryn Elizabeth Eadie; c. Trisha, Andrea; Carleton, hons BComm; chartered accountant, sr. v-p, cfo, Russel Metals; honed football skills with Ottawa Bel-Air Lions city title team '64; mem. Laurentian Lions '66-69, Ott. HS champs '68; mem.

Carleton Ravens '70-74; 2 conf. all-star, 1 all-Canadian awards; Doug Banton '73, Jack Vogan '74 awards; def. tackle Rough Riders '76-80; mem. Grey Cup champions '76; played on last Riders team with winning season record '79; res. Etobicoke, Ont.

HEES, George (football); b. 17 Jun 1910, Toronto, Ont.; d. 12 Jun 1996, Toronto, Ont.; m. Mabel Dunlop; c. Catherine Mabel, Martha Ann, Roslyn Georgia; Royal Military College, UofT, Cambridge; retd. soldier, politician; mem. Argos '34, '38 Grey Cup title team; Progressive Conservative MP '50-62, '65-94; mem. Privy Council; Min. Transport '57-60, Min. Trade & Commerce '60-63; Min. Veteran's Affairs '84-94; dir. Montreal World Fair '64; pres. Mtl., Cdn. stock exchanges; mem. Order of Canada.

HEESE, Mark (volleyball); b. 15 Aug 1969, Toronto, Ont.; McMaster; played indoors with McMaster '88-92; focused talents on beach volleyball '90 competing in Barcelona Olympic exhibition; 4 ntl titles; teamed with John Child '95-98 winning bronze '96 world, gold '97 ntl pro championship series; noted for defensive skills; bronze '96 Olympics; best digger/setter '97 Labatt Blue pro beach tour award; res. Toronto, Ont.

HEGAN, Larry (football); b. 14 Feb 1908, Wetaskwin, Alta.; d. 9 Oct 1994, Calgary, Alta.; given name: Robert John; m. Elga Muriel "Mike" Stayner; c. Dick, Mary, Jim, Roger, Tom; UofSask; retd GM Eatons; 5yrs football Uof Sask, 2yrs team capt., 2yrs university hockey; unable to secure job in engineering in '30s played pro football Roughriders '34-39; mem. '34 Grey Cup finalists; '36 WFC all-star; mem. winning 4s '36 international rowing regatta Ft. William.

HEGGTVEIT, Anne (skiing); b. 11 Jan 1939, Ottawa, Ont.; m. Ross Hamilton; c. Timothy, Christianne; retail stores chain comptroller; father Halvor former cross-country champion, uncles Bud Clark, Bruce Heggtveit former Olympic skiers; age 7 Gatineau Zone sr. women's slalom, combined titles; by '52 had won all Ottawa area major competitions; 1st international success '54 Holmenkollen G.S. Norway, at 15 youngest winner in event's 50-year history; 15th combined '56 Olympics; '59 St.Moritz, Arlberg-Kandahar, Que. Kandahar, ntl alpine titles; '60 US slalom, GS, swept Roch Cup events; Canada's 1st Olympic skiing gold medalist, 1st non-European FIS world alpine combined gold medalist '60; 3.3 second Olympic victory greatest margin by woman in Games history; CP female athlete of '59-60; Lou Marsh Trophy '60, 2 Bobbie Rosenfeld awards; mem. Order of Canada, US Ntl, Cdn Skiing, Ottawa, Cdn Amateur, Ont. Sports Legends, Canada's Sports halls of fame; res. Grand Isle, Vt.

HEGGTVEIT, Halvor (skiing); b. 16 Mar 1907, Leland, N.D.; d. 18 Jan. 1995, Clinton, Ont.; m. Dorothy Clark (d); c. Alexander, Anne; raised in Saskatchewan; began cross-country skiing Ottawa '20s; 4 Lady Willingdon Trophy wins; silver ntl championships '30, '33; won every '34 race entered, including Ottawa, Que., ntl cross-country titles; coached daughter Anne until she'd won ntl jr. ladies' downhill, slalom, combined titles at 13; occupational conflict prevented him from participating '32 Olympics

although named to team; mem. Olympic Club of Canada; life mem. Ottawa Ski Club; mem. Ottawa CSRA Sports Hall of Fame.

HEIKKILA, Bill (t&f); b. 17 Aug 1944, Toronto, Ont.; m. Patricia Hunnakko; c. Kirsti, Kaarina, Liisa, Leila; Oregon, BSc, MPhE; Sport Canada consultant; 5 ntl sr. javelin titles; gold '69 Canada Games; ntl juve., sr. javelin records; mem. '67 Pan-Am Games team; Oregon all-American, 2nd '67 NCAA championships; coached several of Canada's top javelin throwers; res. Nepean, Ont.

HEIMRATH, Ludwig Sr. (motorsport); b. 11 Aug 1934, Munich, Germany; m. Brigitte Wlochowitz; c. Ludwig Jr., Karin; auto dealer; 3 ntl driving titles; 7 Ont. driving titles; began racing career on motorcycles Germany '52; competed 1st Players' 200 race '61 Mosport; more than 200 Mosport victories; represented Canada USAC, USRRC, Can-Am events; runnerup to Trans-Am champion Peter Gregg '74; res. Scarborough, Ont.

HELLARD, Rick (triathlon); b. 23 May 1966, Ottawa, Ont.; sports consultant; in 16yr period competed 241 triathlons; victories in 3 OAC, 4 Mt. Tremblant (course rec.), 3 Sharbot Lake, varied races in France, Switzerland, US; 2nd Nogoya, Japan; 3rd Embrun, France, ironman; competed in Australian Worlds; ntl team mem. 4yrs; raced in France 3yrs; accomplished at all distances; won Kingston 1/2 marathon '98; 3 Ottawa ACT awards; res. Ottawa, Ont.

HELLIWELL, David (rowing); b. 26 Jul 1935, Vancouver, B.C.; d. 30 Dec 1993, Vancouver, B.C.; m. Margaret Adam; c. Kerby, Wendy, Cathy, Marnie, John; UBC, CA; company pres.; mem. UBC jr. varsity crew '55; Olympic silver UBC varsity 8s '56; Commonwealth Games silver UBC varsity 4s '58; coach silver medal '59 Pan-Am Games 8s; pres. Vancouver Rowing Club '62; coach Alta. Canada Games '69; rowing chair. Canada Games '73; v-p Canadian Assn. of Amateur Oarsmen '71; trustee BC Sports Hall of Fame '80; hon. v-p Vancouver RC; mem. Cdn Amateur, BC, Canada's Sports Hall of Fame.

HENDERSON, Gil (shooting); b. 5 Sep 1926, Toronto, Ont.; given name: Gilbert James; m. Molly; mechanical contractor; trapshooting specialist, mem. '60 Olympic, '66, '74 world championships, '71 world moving target championships, '75 championship of Americas teams; pres. Canadian Trapshooting Assn.; v-p Shooting Federation of Canada; coach-mgr. shotgun team '72 Olympics, Commonwealth Games team '74; mgr. shotgun events '76 Olympics; res. St. George, Ont.

HENDERSON, Paul (hockey); b. 28 Jan 1943, Kincardine, Ont.; given name: Paul Garnet; m. Eleanor Alton; c. Heather, Jennifer, Jill; account exec., evangelist; jr. A Hamilton Red Wings '60-63; mem. Memorial Cup titlists '62; 1st all-star team; Max Kaminsky Trophy; Detroit (NHL) '63-68, Toronto '68-74; WHA Toronto Toros '74-76, Birmingham (WHA, CHL) '76-81; briefly returned to NHL Atlanta '79; major pro record: 1067 scheduled games (NHL-WHA), 376 goals, 384 assists, 61 playoff games, 12 goals, 15 assists; mem. '71-72 NHL all-star game teams; mem. Team Canada '72, '74; achieved hockey immortality with goal at 19:26

of final period in deciding game which gave Team Canada 6-5 victory over Soviets 28 Sep '72; series MVP; active in Campus Crusade for Christ; mem. Canada's, Etobicoke, Mississauga Sports halls of fame; res. Mississauga, Ont.

HENDERSON, Paul (sailing); b. 17 Nov 1934, Toronto, Ont.; given name: Paul Franklin; m. Mary Katherine Lynn McLeod; c. John, Martha; UofT. BSc; engineer; 4 Aphrodite Cup junior team race titles; mem. Royal Canadian Yacht Club; jr. club champion, fleet capt. '50; 2 CIAU titles; English, US, Bermuda, world, Alexander of Tunis International 14' dinghy titles; Dutch, US, 2 Canadian Flying Dutchman Olympics Class titles; 2 ntl Finn Olympic Class single-handed titles; US Midwest Tempest Olympic Class keel boat title; US Atlantic Coast Soling Olympic Class keel yacht title; NA Fireball title; mem. '64, '68 Olympic teams; coach '72 Olympic yachting team; founding dir. Water Rat Sailing Club; 3rd world '74 FD; ntl Soling Class title '75; dir. ntl sailing team '70-71; Ont. squash open doubles semifinalist '73; Ont. yachtsman of '74; mem. National Fitness Advisory Council '74-76; dir. CYA, International Yacht Racing Union, Ont. Sailing Assn., Canadian Squash Racquets Assn.; key role in Toronto's failed '96 Olympics bid; organized bid to bring world basketball championships to Toronto; res. Toronto, Ont.

HENDERSON, Scott (skiing); b. 15 Apr 1943, Calgary, Alta.; given name: George Scott Robert; div. Patricia Pitt, m. Barbara Ferries; c. (step) Kathryn, Misty, Mark; independent sports equipment sales; ntl alpine ski team '62-69; 3 ntl, US alpine titles; '67 international race winner Australia; top 10 Europe several times '68-69; turned pro; Lange racing director '70-72; ntl men's alpine coach '72-78, produced World Cup race winners '75-76, mem. Cdn Skiing, Alta Sports halls of fame; res. Nederland, Colo.

HENDRICKSON, Lefty (football); b. 27 Apr 1943, Squamish, B.C.; given name: Lynn Alfred; m. Carol Anne; c. Craig Stephen, Scott Patrick; Oregon, BSc; auto dealer; HS basketball all-star '59-62; jr. football all-star '60-63; Pacific 8 hon. mention tight end '67-68; pro BC Lions '68-73, outside linebacker, receiver; CFL record: 123 receptions for 1669yds, 13.5 avg. 7tds; WFC all-star '73; all-star softball 1st baseman Brandon '76, '78; v-p '79 Canada Winter Games; res. Alexander, Man.

HENDRIE, George (horse racing/administration); b. 10 Jun 1906, Hamilton, Ont.; d. 14 Oct 1988, Toronto, Ont.; given name: George Campbell; m. Elizabeth Olmsted; c. George Muir, Anthony Olmsted; Upper Canada College; cartage co. owner, horseman; followed footsteps of grandfather William, father William Jr., as pres. OJC '63-71; hon. pres. from '71; racing steward OJC '30s; dir. OJC '43-52, managing dir. '53; charter mem. Ont. Racing Commission; mem. Canadian Horse Racing Hall of Fame.

HENDRIE, George (horse racing/administration); b. 28 Jul 1930, Toronto, Ont.; given name: George Muir; m. Elizabeth "Betsy" Bartlett; c. George C II, Geoffrey, Jane; Ridley Coll, UWO, BA; retd family transportation co.; carried on family racing interest tradition begun by great-grandfather William; raced a stable in partnership with father and from '88 has enjoyed moderate success with own racing stable; chair.

Board of Trustees Ontario Jockey Club from '92; magnificent E.P. Taylor turf course opened in '94 and highly successful '96 Breeders' Cup at Woodbine rank high on his list of accomplishments as OJC chair.; res. Toronto, Ont.

HENDRY, Joan (t&f); b. 14 May 1945, Glasgow, Scotland; given name: Joan Lynn; Uof Ott, BA; teacher; long jump, sprint specialist; mem. '67 Pan-Am, '68, '72 Olympic, '69 Pan-Pacific, '70 Commonwealth Games teams; relay silver '69 Pan-Pacific, 2 bronze '70 Commonwealth Games; ntl long jump, relay records; Canada's top sprinter over 100m '72 with 11.4; injury forced withdrawal '72 Olympics; began running again '75; co-holder ntl indoor 50m 6.2; '67-71 ntl women's long jump record holder; formed Ottawa Super P.I.T.S. (participants in track) club '79; res. Ottawa, Ont.

HENLEY, Garney (football); b. 21 Dec 1935, Elgin, N.D.; m. Phyllis Diekmann; c. Pamela, Lori, Jody, Garney Kyle; Huron College, BA; retd. university athletic dir., football exec.; most prolific scorer in history of US college football with 394 points 31-games, 4yr career; drafted Green Bay Packers (NFL), NY (AFL) '60; part of '60 season with Packers before joining Hamilton (CFL); shone defensively, offensively '60-75; 59 interceptions for 5tds, record 916yds; caught 4td passes single game; career total 364 punts returned for 2844yds including 83 in '66 season; 10 times EFC all-star, all-Cdn; 6 times Schenley outstanding player nominee, winner '72; Jeff Russel Memorial Trophy twice; Ticats best-of-century team '67; 7 Grey Cup finals, 4 winners; Ticats asst. coach '76; AD Mount Allison U '77; 10 years basketball coach U of Guelph, '74 CIAU titlists; AD, basketball coach Brock U '78-94; dir. FB operations Rough Riders '95; mem. Guelph U, Cdn Football, US College Football, South Dakota Sports halls of fame; res. Volga, S.D.

HENNESSEY, Walter (harness racing); b. 4 Oct 1956, Charlottetown, P.E.I.; in early stages of career rewrote Maritimes record books posting standards for victories and earnings; made initial foray out of Maritimes '83 winning Canadian Ice Racing Classic; ranked among top drivers at Saratoga, Pompano Park in '90s; piloted America's Pastime to world record-equalling 1:51.4 '92; won 7 New York Sires Stakes at Buffalo Raceway, including track record 6 in succession, '92; piloted My Dolly, Catch As Catch Can to Breeders Crown titles '97; through '97 4341 victories for purses totalling more than $23M; res. Coconut Creek, Fla.

HENNIGAR, Carl (speed skating); b. Feb 1926, Halifax, N.S.; given name: Carl Austin; McGill, B Eng; retd. engineer; mem. KW Sertoma SSC '66-97, club pres. '72-76; pres. Ont. ASSA '75-79; com. mem. training institute for sport administrators '80-81, co-chair. '82-83; active organizational role in club, provincial, ntl, NA events; avid cyclist, cross-country skier, basketball, tennis player in youth; maintains ham radio license and holds private pilot's license; very active in community affairs; mem. Cdn Amateur Speed Skating Hall of Fame; res. Kitchener, Ont.

HENNING, Cam (swimming); b. 24 Nov 1960, Edmonton, Alta.; given name: Cameron John; m. Anastazia Shelenko; c. Oscar Wylie, Laszlo John; Alabama, UAlta,BA; mgr. Loomis; backstroke specialist; ntl team '76-84; 5 ntl titles,

6 ntl, 2 Commonwealth Games records; mem. '78, '82 Commonwealth, '79 FISU, '80, '84 Olympic, '83 Pan-Am Games teams; 200m gold, 100m silver '82 Commonwealth Games; 3 Canada Cup gold, 3 Four Nation Cup gold; Southeastern Conf. 200m backstroke champion '81; gold 400m FS, 100m, 200m backstroke '83 CIAU championships;1 CIAU male swimmer of yr award; bronze 200m backstroke '84 Olympics; fed. govt. excellence award '83; mem. Alta Sports Hall of Fame; res. Calgary, Alta.

HENNYEY, Donna (fencing); b. 10 Apr 1942, New York, N. Y.; given name: Donna Jean Atkinson; m. Alex Richard Hennyey; c. Mark Alexander, Allison Marijke; UofT,BA, MA; nutrition consultant; mem. ntl fencing team '67-77, mem. 4 world, 3 Pan-Am, 2 Olympic teams; team silver '75 Pan-Ams; 5 Italian Martini Rossi, 3 NY Martini Rossi, 1 German international, London De Beaumont Cup, Austrian international titles, 2 Ont. women's titles, 6 times runnerup; 2 Eastern Canadian, 3 ntl, 5 Heroes International, 3 Governor-General's, 4 Harmonie International titles; winner Golden Foil, Dell Open events; mem. 3 Ont., 5 ntl title teams; Norman Craig award Ont. female athlete of '68; res. Toronto, Ont.

HENNYEY, Imre (fencing); b. 14 Jul 1913, Cattaro, Yugoslavia; d. 6 Sep 1989, Toronto, Ont.; m. Ilona Szelecsenyi; c. Alex, Sheilah; Ludovika Academy, UofT, BSc; teacher; world university épée title '39 Vienna; Hungarian épée title '41, '43, '47; mem. Hungarian '48, '52 Olympic teams; coached '53-54 Hungarian modern pentathon fencing team; coached UotT fencing team '61-80; coach '68 Canadian Olympic, '70 Commonwealth Games teams.

HENRY, Camille (hockey); b. 31 Jan 1933, Quebec City, Que.; d. 11 Sep 1997, Quebec City, Que.; given name: Camille Wilfrid; div. Aimée Sylvestre (Quebec actress Dominique Michel); c. Martine, Nathalie; diminutive 5-7, 138lbs; rejected baseball for hockey; stickboy with father's Sherbrooke Saints Que. sr. team; 3yrs Que. Citadel jrs.; pro NY Rangers '53-55, '56-64, '67-68, Chicago '65, St. Louis '68-70; Calder Memorial Trophy '54; nicknamed "The Eel"; hosted Montreal radio show; coached NY Raiders-Golden Blades-Jersey Knights WHA '72-74; Lady Byng Trophy '58; 2nd team all-star left winger '58; NHL record: 817 scheduled games, 279g, 249a, only 88 penalty minutes; 48 playoff games, 6g, 12a; 3 all-star games.

HENRY, Daryl (parachuting); b. 25 Apr 1935, Cranbrook, B.C.; given name: Daryl Arthur; m. Carol Warner; UofT, B.Arch.; screenwriter; 1st jump '58; 4 ntl overall titles, team leader '60 world championships; mem. overall title team world's 1st paraski championships '62; ntl team capt. '62, '64, '66 worlds; 1st world accuracy record ever established in competition '62; 1st overall Massachusetts Governor's Cup '62, Las Vegas international '63; NA record 3 consecutive dead centers in competition; 1st overall California pro championships '65; ntl group of 3 altitude record (22,500') '66; coached US Marine team to gold Brazil '65; Cdn team leader Adriatic Cup Yugoslavia '69; judge, TV commentator, coach, exec. in all phases of sport; several ntl, US, UK records; Confederation Medal; author variety of parachuting articles; res. Santa Barbara, Calif.

HENSELWOOD, Jill (equestrian); b. 1 Nov 1962, Ottawa, Ont.; given name: Jill MacAngus; m. Bob Henselwood; Uof Ott, BPHE; co-operator Juniper Farms; t&f athlete in university; certified t&f coach, level 3 jumper coach; entered grand prix competition '89; mem. ntl team from '91; aboard Canadian Colors mem. '92 Nations Cup title team; 9 grand prix victories; mem. '95, '99 Pan-Am Games teams, team bronze '99; won 3 World Cup qualifiers; earned berth on '96 Olympic team but declined because her mount Aerial was unavailable to travel to Atlanta; won '92 Mexico GP, '95 Seoul GP, '96 Indio, Calif. GP; res. Oxford Mills, Ont.

HENTGEN, Pat (baseball); b. 13 Nov 1968, Detroit, Mich.; given name: Patrick George; m. Darlene; c. Taylor Renee, Hannah; righthanded pitcher; played HS baseball/football; capt. baseball team; rejected scholarship offer Western Mich; originally shortstop; made pro debut St. Catharines (NYP) helping them win A league title '86, Myrtle Beach (SAL) '87, Dunedin (FSL) '88-89; Knoxville (Sou) '90, Syracuse (Int) '91-92, Toronto (AL) '91-99; St. Louis (NL) 2000; ML record: (through '99) 252 scheduled games, 1555.2ip, 1551h, 783r, 557bob, 995k, 105-76w/l; 3 all-star games; mem. '93 World Series winner; 1st Blue Jay to win Cy Young award '96; res. Palm Harbor, Fla./Michigan.

HEPBURN, Doug (weightlifting); b. 16 Sep 1926, Vancouver B.C.; given name: Douglas Ivan; health food/ gym equipment distributor; born with clubbed foot which never healed; went on body building program, put 300lbs on 5'10" frame, earned title of strongest man in history; turned competitive '48 pressing ntl record 300lbs; US jr./sr. ntl titles; world heavyweight title '53 with lift of 1030lbs; '54 BEG gold; at age 70 issued challenge to any man in world, without use of drugs, to match his lifting feats, to date no one has responded; considers himself as poorest best known man in Canada; Lou Marsh, Lionel Conacher trophies '53; BC man of '54; mem. Cdn Amateur, BC, Canada's Sports halls of fame; res. Vancouver, B.C.

HERBERT, Gord (basketball); b. 16 Feb 1959, Penticton, B.C.; Idaho; forward ntl team '82-86; mem. 2nd place Jones Cup team '82, FISU gold team '83; mem. '84 Olympic team; fed. govt. excellence award '84; res. Vancouver, B.C.

HERBERT, Michael (equestrian); b. 4 Oct 1932, Oxford, Eng.; given name: Michael Towner; riding instructor; pro. horseman from age 20; trained horses, riders for 3-day events Great Britain; horse/rider combinations have won 8 gold, 2 silver in national, European, Olympic competition; coached '71 Pan-Am Games team gold, individual silver, '78 world championships team gold; Martini & Rossi Horseman of '78; Fellowship of the British Horse Society '70; res. East Ferry, Ireland.

HERLEN, Ossie (boxing); b. 26 Nov 1918, Star City, Sask.; d. 9 Jun 1944, Europe; given name: Ernest Osborne; mem. Saskatoon Tech '37 title football team; started boxing at 15; used ring name Biff Bapp briefly; lost initial Sask. amateur title bid '36; stopped Sask. lightweight titlist Billy Moore in 2nd round '37; Sask. welterweight title '38; Cdn welterweight title '39; boxed in service winning Toronto Garrison welterweight title; ring record: 33 fights, 12 won by TKO, 12 by decision, 3 TKO, 1 draw, lost 5 by decision;

never KO'd in 9yrs of boxing; v-p Saskatoon Golden Gloves Boxing Club at formation '38; mem. Sask. Sports Hall of Fame.

HERLINVEAUX, Louise (curling); b. 3 Oct 1958, Nanaimo, B.C.; UVic; sr. systems analyst BC ministry of finance; 2nd for Pat Sanders' '87 Scott Tournament of Hearts/World women's titlists; lead Steve Skillings' '85 ntl mixed title rink; mem. BC Sports Hall of Fame; res. Victoria, B.C.

HERMANN, Tiny (curling/football); b. 25 Aug 1906, Halifax, N.S.; d. 30 Nov 1966, Metcalfe, Ont.; given name: Charles Bismark; m. Loretta Hutchingame; c. Phyllis, Carolanne; insurance agent, retd RCMP; from his youth exhibited exceptional strength and athletic ability; mem. NS champion Kings Collegiate HS rugby, prov. champion basketball team; starred for Halifax Wanderers AC in rugby, softball, baseball; BEG discus silver, shot put bronze '30; grand aggregate gold cup Cdn Legion field day Cornwall '33; played 8 seasons with Ottawa Rough Riders earning frequent all-star status as inside wing/place kicker; mem. 5 Big Four champions; competed 2 Grey Cup finals, 1 winner; despite massive size was regarded as one of cleanest players in the game; received only one penalty during his career; honored by MacLean's, Canadian Press '39; retd '40 to serve in navy WW2; mentioned in dispatches for rescues at sea; 1st football coach Carleton; coached Ashbury Coll. srs 10yrs; had 2 consec. undefeated seasons; mem. Ottawa Curling Club, Governor-General's CC; launched schoolboy curling in Ottawa; trophy bearing his name competed for by schoolboy curlers 30yrs; '56 Ottawa curler of yr award; instrumental in formation OVCA, served as 2nd pres.; chair. City of Ottawa bonspiel '60; won grand aggregate title '63; chair. '67 Brier comm.; died in plane crash while on Brier business; Outaouais golf club initiated cup, Ashbury Coll scholarship in his memory; mem. NS, Ottawa Sports halls of fame.

HERMANSON, Myrna (synchro swim); b. 1 May 1963, Montreal, Que.; given name; Myrna Jean; div.; c. Caleb; m. Harry Kruger; sc. Eric, Blaine, Rachel; Southern Alberta Institute of Technology; mem. Calgary YWCA Aquabelles '73-81; mem. ntl jr. gold medal teams '77-78; mem. silver medal team '78 Canada Winter Games; silver team '80 sr. nationals; ntl team mem. '80; team gold Swedish International competition; began modelling '81; Alta. Achievement awards '77-78; res. Cochrane, Alta.

HERN, Riley (hockey); b. 5 Dec 1880, St. Mary's, Ont.; d. 24 Jun 1929, Montreal, Que.; given name: William Milton; c. Al (d); business exec.; goaltender hometown OHA jr. team; London ints., srs; 7 title teams 1st 9yrs; pro Portage Lake team Houghton, Mich., '04; Montreal Wanderers '06-11, 3 Stanley Cups; referee, goal judge several years; twice Rosemere golf club champion; pres. St. Rose Boating Club; mem. Hockey Hall of Fame.

HERSHFIELD, Leible (all-around); b. 30 Aug 1909, Winnipeg, Man.; m. Babe; c, Joel, Susan, Myron; gold '24 Winnipeg HS t&f championships; cf 27 consecutive years Winnipeg softball teams, playing entire career without glove; mem. Western Cdn, Ukraine Cdn, vets title teams;

soccer '24-45; Winnipeg dist. amateur football league gold medal '30; 40yrs Winnipeg recreational 10-pin league; Royal Life Saving Society instructor; PE dir. YMHA '36-42, '52-74; Centennial medal; life mem., governor YMHA; best Jewish athlete of 1/2 century '19-69; author "*The Jewish Athlete, a Nostalgic View*;" mem. Man. Sports Hall of Fame; res. Winnipeg, Man.

HERST, Alison (canoeing); b. 7 Mar 1971, Toronto, Ont.; Laurentian; m. Ivano Lussignoli; mem. Cdn ntl team '90-96, Italian ntl team from '98; competed '92, '96 Olympics; gold K-4 200 '95 Worlds, K-2, K-4 200, silver K-2 500 Milano Italy; Edmonton Grads team award; mem. North Bay Sports Hall of Fame; res. Cremona, Italy.

HETHERINGTON, Jill (tennis); b. 27 Oct 1964, Brampton, Ont.; Florida; tennis coach; 4 time all-American; 5 ntl jr. titles; 2 gold FISU Games; record 9 ntl women's doubles, 1 mixed doubles titles; mem. '81-82 Continental Cup teams, Federation Cup team from '83; ranked among world's best doubles players; best WTA tour ranking (with Patty Fendick) #1 '89; Australian Open finalist '89; 1st Cdn to reach Wimbledon doubles semifinals '86; played World Team Tennis for Tampa Bay '92-93; mem. '84 (demonstration sport), '88, '96 Olympic teams; Tennis Canada player of '88, most improved '89, with Carling Bassett doubles team '86, '88, Helen Kelesi '87, Mandy Wilson '89, Patricia Hy '90-91; With Kathy Rinaldi '92 WTA Tour doubles team of year nominee '92; WTA sportsmanship award '92; TC top female doubles player '93; mem. WTA drug testing comm, WTA Special Olympics comm.; retd. from competition '98; asst. women's coach Washington; 11 TC excellence awards; res. Woodinville, Wash.

HEVENOR, George (golf); b. 4 Aug 1904, Saint John, N.B.; d. 24 Nov 1991, Toronto, Ont.; m. Martha; c. George Jr.; retd. stockbroker; mem. Balmy Beach (ORFU) football team '25-26; canoe racer Island Aquatic Paddling Assn.; mem. Toronto Central Y basketball teams 5 years; 3 Ont. srs, 1 CSGA golf titles; 5 Ont. parent-child titles; golf exec more than 30 years; pres. OGA '59, RCGA '73; life governor each assn.

HEWITSON, Bobby (officiating); b. 23 Jan 1892, Toronto, Ont; d. 9 Jan 1969, Toronto, Ont.; sportswriter, curator; despite diminutive stature became standout lacrosse player, football quarterback, hockey official; mem. 1912 Maitlands Ont. lacrosse, Capitals ntl jr. football champions; sports writer *Toronto Globe*, *Telegram*, retd. as sports editor '57; referee lacrosse, football, hockey; 10yrs officiated NHL; 25yrs secty. CRU; closely associated with horse racing; charter mem. broadcasting Hot Stove League; 1st curator Canada's Sports, Hockey halls of fame; retd. '67; mem. Hockey Hall of Fame.

HEWITT, Foster (hockey); b. 21 Nov 1903, Toronto, Ont; d. 21 Apr 1985, Toronto, Ont; given name: Foster William; m. Joan; c. Wendy, Bill, Elizabeth, Ann; Upper Canada College, UofT; sportscaster; intercollegiate 112, 118lb boxing titles; received Varsity T; editor *Toronto Star* radio page '22; broadcast 1st-ever complete hockey game '23; through career of more than 50 years broadcast numerous sports, feature news events; with father, Hockey Hall of Famer W.A.Hewitt, broadcast '25 King's Plate, world's 1st airing of horse race; accomplished yet another broadcasting 1st '27 combining with father, who wired running results, to dramatize Allan Cup play between UotT Grads and Ft William from Vancouver; MC offical opening Maple Leaf Gardens '31; frequent international hockey game coverage throughout world earned him title "The Voice of Hockey"; Canada's 1st TV commentator in '33 experiment; when TV became viable medium acted as play-by-play man 15 years; author several sports books; dir. numerous companies; Canadian broadcaster of year award; NY Hockey Writers award; CTV-CBS special award for Canada-Russia '72 hockey series coverage; Ont., Toronto achievement awards; B'Nai Brith sportsman of year; Charlie Conacher Research Fund citation, award of merit; Upper Canada College athletic complex named in honor of Foster and Bill Hewitt; officer Order of Canada; mem. Ont. Sports Legends, Hockey, Canada's Sports halls of fame.

HEWITT, W.A. (administration); b. 15 May 1875, Cobourg, Ont.; d. 8 Sep 1966, Toronto, Ont.; given name: William Archibald; retired sports editor; 41yrs newspaper man *Toronto News, Toronto Star* (31yrs sports editor); secty. OHA '03-61; registrar, treas. CAHA 39yrs; mgr. 3 Olympic title teams; helped form Big Four football league '07; served terms as pres., secty. CRU; patrol judge Woodbine racetrack from '05; presiding steward Ont. tracks 14yrs; conceived 1st goal nets; 1st attractions mgr. Maple Leaf Gardens '31; with son Foster participated in hockey, horse racing broadcasting 1sts; mem. Hockey Hall of Fame.

HEWLETT, Karen (field hockey); b. 4 Oct 1959, Toronto, Ont.; given name: Karen Lynn; Sheridan College, UofT; animal technician; mem. Toronto Gopher's FH team from '77, 4 prov. titles; mem. Ont. jr. team '75-79, Ont. under-23 team '78-82; mem. Ont. silver Canada Games team '81, Ont. sr. team '78, '80-82; mem. national team '81-96; World Cup silver team '83; mem. '84 Olympic team; 2 HS athlete of year awards; fed. govt. excellence award '83; res. Mississauga, Ont.

HEWSON, Joanne (skiing); b. 23 Aug 1930, Montreal, Que.; given name: Joanne Selden; div. Robert Dewar Staniforth; c. Mariel Hewson, Lisa Dewar; m. Henry Maynard (Mark) Rees Jr.; McGill, Concordia, BFA; artist; McGill ski team '49-51; top girl '51 Olympic ski trials; top Cdn (8th downhill), (13th slalom) '52 Olympics; Alberg Kandahar pin with 3rd downhill; '53 Que. Kandahar title; broke leg in training prior to '54 world championships; coach McGill women's ski team '58-62; co-founder Ski Jay club for girls 8-17, active with group '58-68; active golfer, ladies' pres. Kanawaki GC '82; publicity chairman, jr. development chairman QLGA; res. Westmount, Que.

HEXTALL, Bryan Sr. (hockey); b. 31 Jul 1913, Grenfell, Sask.; d. 25 Jul 1984, Poplar Point, Man.; given name: Bryan Aldwyn; m. Gertrude Lyon; c. Bryan Jr., Dennis, Richard, Heather, Randy; lumber, hardware business; mem. Poplar Point, Man. juve. titlists; jr. Winnipeg Monarchs, Portage La Prairie; MJHL scoring title; pro Vancouver Lions '34-36, WHL title '36; Philadelphia Ramblers '36; NY Rangers '36-48; NHL record: 449 scheduled games, 187g, 175a, 37

playoff games, 8g, 9a; NHL scoring title '42 with 56 pts.; 20 or more goals 7 of 12 NHL seasons; scored winning overtime goal '40 Stanley Cup final vs Toronto; 3 times 1st, twice 2nd team all-star; mem. Man. Sports, Man., Cdn Hockey halls of fame.

HEXTALL, Ron (hockey); b. 3 May 1964, Brandon, Man.; m. Diane; c. Kristin, Brett, Rebecca, Jeffrey; goalie Brandon Wheat Kings (WHL); 6th pick Philadelphia '82 draft; Brandon '81-84, Hershey (AHL) '84-86, '89, Kalamazoo (IHL) '84-84; Philadelphia (NHL) '86-92, '95-99, Quebec '93, NY Islanders '93-94; scored goal vs. Boston '87, playoff goal vs. Washington '89; NHL record: 608 scheduled games, 296-214-69, 34,750 min, 23so, 93 playoff games, 47-43, 5456min, 276ga, 2so, AHL rookie of '86; Vezina trophy '87; Conn Smythe trophy '87; Bobby Clarke trophy '87; 1 Class Guy award; mem. Team Canada '87; res. Voorhees, N.J.

HEYDENFELDT, Bob (football); b. 17 Sep 1933, Santa Monica, Calif.; given name: Robert Marshall; m. JoAnn Good; c. Linda Jo, Robert Tad, Richard Daniel, Dina Marie; UCLA, BSc; furniture wholesaler & jobber; top college punter in US '54; Rose Bowl, North-South Shrine game as UCLA jr. '54; refusal to play Sunday football led to NFL shunning him in draft; pro Edmonton Eskimos winning WFC punting title '55; mem. Grey Cup winner; kicked single which provided 6-6 tie 1st Cdn East-West all-star game '55; res. Lafayette, Calif.

HIBBERD, Ted (hockey); b. 22 Apr 1926, Ottawa, Ont.; given name: Thomas Edward; m. Anna Armstrong; c. Lesley, Wendy, Nancye, Jeffrey, Laurie; retd. underwriting supervisor; jr. hockey New Edinburgh, Ottawa Montagnards, Hull; intermediate Senators; mem. '48 world, Olympic champion RCAF Flyers; with Flyers team mem. Ottawa Sports Hall of Fame; res. Ottawa, Ont.

HIBBERT, Curtis (gymnastics); b. 9 Feb 1966, St. Andrew, Jamaica; York.; gymnastics instructor; began competing age 7; mem. ntl team '83-92; 1st Cdn gymnast to win medal at world championships with horizontal bars silver '87; 1st Cdn gymnast to make 3 Olympic event finals '88; 5 consecutive ntl all-around titles '88-92; mem. '83 Pan-Am Games, '87 FISU, '85, '87, '89, '91 worlds, '88, '92 Olympic, '90 Commonwealth Games, '90 World Cup teams; ntl sports excellence award '89; 5 Commonwealth Games gold, 1 silver, 1 bronze '90; Pan-Am Games silver '83; res. Toronto, Ont.

HICKOX, Mac (canoeing); b. 2 Sep 1946, Boston, Mass.; m. Adrienne Dunn; c. Marin, Randi; McMaster BA, BPHE, UofT, BEd; HS teacher; family moved to Mississauga when he was an infant; left-wing Jr. B Dixie Beehives, St. Catharines Jr. A Black Hawks, Hamilton Red Wings, CIAU McMaster, Toronto; helped Toronto win '71 CIAU title; with Dean Oldershaw won ntl juve. C2 at 15; won 25 ntl, 2 NA titles; represented both Can. and US in Olympic competition, Can, as alternate '64, coach v76, US in pairs '68; coached Mississauga to 6 ntl titles; coached John Wood to '76 Olympic silver; Cdn coach of '76 award; coached Glenforest HS sr. boys cross-country team to OFSAA gold '88; retd. from coaching '94; earned 11 gold in canoeing/cross-country skiing as master athlete '87; founded Cdn Assn. of Coaches in Canoe & Kayak '94; Port Credit HS athlete of '66, Mississauga most valuable member '88-89, volunteer of '90, 2 civic recognition awards; CCA Gilbert award '96; mem. Mississauga Sports Hall of Fame; res. Mississauga, Ont.

HIELTJES, Ben (lacrosse); b. 12 Apr 1963, New Westminster, B.C.; given name: Bernard John; m. Dawna Nelson; c. Benjamin, Hanna; Whittier Coll.. BA; sales mgr.; mem. Whittier College Poets '85-86, North Shore Indians '85-86, New Westminster Salmonbellies '86-92, '95, Richmond field team from '86; ntl team '89-94; competed 2 world championships; mem. 3 Mann Cup winners; '85 President's Cup titlists, MVP; '89 Mike Kelly Mann Cup MVP award; plays recreational basketball; res. New Westminster, B.C.

HIGGINS, Robina (t&f); b. 28 Apr 1915, Winnipeg, Man; d. 31 Dec 1990, Winnipeg, Man.; m. G.D."Pud" Haight; c. Dee, Dorlene, Fred; T.Eaton Co. employee; dominated Cdn t&f scene '35-40; ntl shot put titles '35-36, javelin '39-40, discus '36, ball throw '36, '39-40; javelin gold '38 BEG; Bobbie Rosenfeld award '37; basketball standout with Man. champion Dominion Business College 10yrs; mem. Western Canada finalists; mem. Man. Basketball, Cdn Amateur, Man. Sports halls of fame.

HIGHBAUGH, Larry (football); b. 14 Jan 1950, Indianapolis, Ind.; given name: Larry Eugene; m. Pat; c. Monica, Angela, Tara; Indiana; sporting goods store operator; t&f all-American; world record 60yd dash (6.8); Dallas Cowboys draft '71; pro BC (CFL) '71-72, Edmonton '72-83; CFL record most career interceptions 66; 770yds on returns; 6 WFC, 4 all-Cdn selections; Eskimos MVP '77 playing def. back, wide receiver; 9 Grey Cup finals, 6 winners, 5 in succession; volleyball star; res. Sherwood Park, Alta.

HIGSON, Allison (swimming); b. 13 Mar 1973, Mississauga, Ont.; Stanford; sports media rep.; mem. Cobra SC age 6; 10yrs mem. Etobicoke SC; breaststroke specialist; 4 gold, 1 record '85 Canada Games; mem. ntl team '85-92; won 1st of 14 ntl titles at age 12; 2 gold, 1 silver '86 Commonwealth Games; at 13 youngest ever to win CG gold; bronze '86, youngest ever to medal in worlds; gold, 2 silver, bronze '87 Pan-Pacific; 1 world, 2 Cdn records '88 Olympic trials; relay bronze '88 Olympics; silver, bronze '89 Pan-Pacific; relay silver '90 Commonwealth Games; competed '92 Olympics; 2 Swim Canada jr., 3 sr. female athlete of yr awards; ntl/prov. achievement awards; lone female to win Esso Cup; Olympic champion medal; Ont., Swim Ont. team of yr awards; mem. Ont. Aquatic Hall of Fame; res. Palo Alto, Calif.

HILDEBRAND, Ike (lacrosse/hockey); b. 27 May 1927, Winnipeg, Man.; given name: Isaac Bruce; m. Barbra Park; c. Isaac Jay, Jody Ann, Daniel, Heidi, Melanie; retd. sporting goods manufacturer's rep.; at 15 mem. '43 New Westminster Salmonbellies Mann Cup winner; 16 seasons sr. lacrosse New Westminster, Mimico, Peterborough; more than 900 goals, 700 assists while playing 7 successive Mann Cup finalist, 5 winners with Peterborough; at 17 youngest player ever to win Mike Kelly Mann Cup MVP award; MVP, twice scoring champion both East, West leagues; sr. hockey at 17

Seattle Ironmen; OHA jr. A Oshawa Generals '45-47; sr. Toronto Marlboros; 9yrs pro, parts of 3 NHL seasons NY Rangers, Chicago; US League scoring champion Kansas City '51, AHL top scorer Cleveland '53; mem. Cleveland AHL Calder Cup champions '52-53; 1st team all-star right wing US League '51, AHL '53; leading scorer Belleville McFarlands Allan Cup, world champions '59-60; pro career record: 185g, 209a; coached Peterborough Mann Cup winner '54; McFarlands '59 Allan Cup, '60 world championship; twice Green MVP Trophy; jr. A hockey coach 6yrs Peterborough, London, Oshawa; sr. hockey 6yrs Pembroke, Belleville, Orillia; Allan Cup Orillia '69; Toronto NHL Oldtimers; mem. Canada's Sports, Canadian Lacrosse halls of fame; res. Tucson, Ariz.

HILL, Craig (motorsport); b. 9 Jan 1934, Hamilton, Ont,; given name: Richard Craig; m. Jean McCallum; c. Michael, Mark; sales marketing co-ordinator; progressed through stock cars, super modifieds, sprint cars; won Canada's 1st pro road race, CRDA 500 in D-type Jaguar Harewood Ont. '59; several times ntl sports car, open wheel champion; CTV color commentator Players' Challenge Series; res. Mississauga, Ont.

HILL, Harvey (weightlifting); b. 16 Dec 1897, Shaw's Lane, Eng.; d. circa 1985; m. Elsie; competitor '25-27 then switched to coaching, officiating, administration; coached Verdun Weightlifting Club '28-42, South-Western YMCA Verdun '42-53; mgr.-coach '47 world championships, '48 Olympics, '50 BEG teams; refereed NA championships '36-58, Fédération Halterophile Canadienne '27-54, variety regional, prov., ntl, international meets '27-58; founded Que. Weightlifters Assoc. '36, secty. '36-58; introduced weightlifting to AAU of C '36; organized secretarial weightlifting contests '36-58; founded CWA, secty. '48-58; AAU of C ntl weightlifting chair. '50-52; chair. at founding of BE Weightlifting Federation, v-p '48; mem. Cdn Amateur Sports Hall of Fame.

HILL, Jim (all-around); b. 26 Jan 1914, Kenora, Ont.; standout in hockey, football, basketball, softball, t&f, soccer, golf; goalie Port Arthur Eskimos '28 Intercity midget champions, '30 Port Arthur Tech HS champs, '36-37 TB-Man. senior champs (MVP); played for Duluth, Minn., '38-39; Western Cdn champion PASCOL team '43-44; pro Omaha, Witchita (AA) '39-40, Portland (PCL), Fort Worth (AHL) '40-41; outfielder/shortstop variety of title softball teams '32-45; halfback/punter Port Arthur Collegiate/ Seniors '31-36, 2 title teams; forward 5 HS basketball title teams '32-36; fullback CNR Regina Sask. title soccer team '39; champion HS pole vault/discus/3-mile runner '31-33; began playing golf in '40s winning 2 Duluth tournaments; coached Navy jr. hockey title team '43; mem. NWO Sports Hall of Fame; res. Duluth, Minn.

HILL, Stewart (football); b. 16 Mar 1962, Seattle, Wash; Washington; defensive end; turned pro Edmonton '84-90, BC '91-92, Saskatchewan '93; CFL record: 164 scheduled games, 6tds, 5 interceptions, 12 fumble recoveries, 126 QB sacks, 231 defensive, special teams tackles; Jackie Parker Trophy '84; Norm Fieldgate Trophy '90; 5 all-Western, 2 all-CFL all-star; CFL top rookie runnerup '84; CFL outstanding defensive player runnerup '90; res. Seattle, Wash.

HILLER, John (baseball); b. 8 Apr 1943, Scarborough, Ont.; given name: John Fredrick; m. Janis Patricia Baldwin; c. Wendy Louise, Joseph Scott, Danielle Patricia; farmer, ex- policeman; southpaw pitcher Toronto minors; pro Detroit organization '62; minors Jamestown, Duluth, Knoxville, Montgomery, Syracuse, Toledo; Detroit Tigers '65-80; relief pitching specialist; career threatened by '71 heart attack but made amazing comeback to extend ML career 8 more years; '73 Hutch Award, AL comeback player of year, ML fireman of year, Tiger of year, King Tiger award, 4th Cy Young, MVP voting; tied AL record for victories by relief pitcher with 17 in '74, ML record 31 decisions for fireman '74 (17-14); missed much of '75 with arm injury, 12-8 won-lost record, 2.38era '76; ML career record: 87-76, 545 games, 125sv, 1036k, 2.83era; ML record most concecutive strikeouts, start of game, 6 '68, AL record most intentional walks season 19 '74, ML record 38 saves '73 (broken '83 by Dan Quisenberry); following 215 consecutive relief appearances made 1st start, hurling 4-hit shutout over Milwaukee; mem. '68 World Series winner, '74 AL all-star team; saved child from drowning in Anaheim pool '73; mem. Canada's Sports, Cdn Baseball halls of fame; res. Felch, Mich.

HILLMAN, Larry (hockey); b. 5 Feb 1937, Kirkland Lake, Ont.; given name: Lawrence Morley; sep. c. Laurie, Valerie, Darryn, Peter; retd hockey coach, businessman; jr. Windsor, Hamilton; NHL Detroit '54-57; Boston '57-60, Toronto '60-68, Minnesota, Montreal '68-69, Philadelphia '69-71, Los Angeles '71, Buffalo '71-73; WHA Cleveland '73-75, Winnipeg '75-76; AHL Eddie Shore Award as top defenceman '60; NHL record: 790 scheduled games, 36g, 196a, 579pim, 74 playoff games, 2g, 9a, 30pim; mem. 6 Stanley Cup, 1 Calder Cup winners; AHL all-star; with Ralph Backstrom, Wilf Paiement operates summer fishing camp; res. Beamsville, Ont.

HILTON, Alex (boxing); b. 20 Dec 1964, Ville LaSalle, Que.; given name: Alexander Stewart; m. Olga Grecco; pro boxer; lost only one of 104 amateur bouts; 7 Que. Golden Gloves titles, 3 ntl amateur, 2 jr. Olympic titles; to '83 unbeaten in pro ranks; ntl middleweight title, Continental champion; ranked 15th in world; Cdn Pro Boxing Council middleweight title '92; out-of-ring behavior led to frequent criminal charges; res. Montreal, Que.

HILTON, Dave Jr. (boxing); b. 9 Dec 1963, Port Credit, Ont.; given name: David Stewart Jr; div. Ann-Marie Gatti; c. Jeannie, Anna-Marie; pro boxer; lost only 2 of 132 amateur bouts; 4 ntl, 3 Jr. Olympic, 9 Que. Golden Gloves, '80 Winter Games titles; pro at 17; pro record (through '99) 37-1-3, 25kos; ntl welterweight title '84, stripped of same '85 for failure to defend in specified time; ranked 16th in world; ntl middleweight title '98-99; out-of-ring behavior led to frequent criminal charges; res. Montreal, Que.

HILTON, Dave Sr. (boxing); b. 29 Aug 1940, Edmunston, N.B.; given name: David Stewart; m. Jean Mills; c. Jo-Ann, David Jr., Alex, Matthew, Stewart, Jimmy; boxing trainer; won all 72 amateur bouts; '66 Tennessee Golden Gloves, '67 Texas Golden Gloves, '68 Kentucky Golden Gloves titles; 138 pro bouts, lost 15; ntl featherweight title 10yrs, jr. middleweight crown; retired undefeated; boxing coach; 9 ntl titles in family; res. Montreal, Que.

HILTON, Geordie (golf); b. 17 Jan 1952, Ottawa, Ont.; d. 18 Sep 1990, Oakville, Ont.; given name: George Richard; UWO, hons. BA; exec. dir. RCGA; standout amateur golfer Ottawa area; 3 athletic letters UWO; asst. amateur tournament co-ordinator RCGA '74-75; Canadian Open co-ordinator RCGA '76-77; asst. exec. dir. RCGA '77-78, exec. dir. '78-90; exec. dir. Canadian Golf Foundation '79-81; dir. American Golf Sponsors '80-90; mem. handicap procedure comm. USGA '81-90; board chair. Glen Abbey GC '81-90; treas. CGF '81-90.

HILTON, Matthew (boxing); b. 27 Dec 1965, Cooksville, Ont.; middleweight; won all 106 amateur bouts, 97 by KO; 4 ntl, 1 Jr. Olympics, 8 Que. Golden Gloves titles; to '84 won all 12 pro bouts, 10 by KO; 4th ranked in Canada; out-of-ring behavior led to frequent criminal charges; res. Montreal, Que.

HILZINGER, Karl (football/skiing); b. 7 Sep 1932, Montreal, Que.; d. 15 Dec 1988, Seattle, Wash.; given name: Karl Hans; Sir George Williams, BA, UCLA; manufacturer, sports consultant War Amps Canada; halfback Montreal Alouettes '52, Sask. '53-54, '59, Ottawa '55-58; pro ski instructor Canadian Ski Alliance 20yrs; level 4 rating; pro skin diver 10yrs; lost both legs 20 Jun '64 auto accident; active in teaching skiing, golf, other sports to handicapped youngsters.

HIND, Terry (builder); b. 23 Jul 1920, Winnipeg, Man.; given name: Terrance John; m. Evelyn Carey; c. Richard; retd Red Cross; pitched for jr. Rosedales, sr. CUAC Blues, St. Boniface Native Sons, Carman; pitched several 1-hitters; in one tournament pitched 27 innings in single day allowing 1 run; in 27yrs in amateur-pro hockey was mgr. juve. Winnipeg Monarchs, exec. mgr. Man. Jr. hockey league, helped build Winnipeg Maroons '64 Allan Cup winner, helped Ben Hatskin launch Winnipeg Jets and WHA, helped Ed Rutherford start Man. Major Jr. HL, mgr. Charleswood Hawks; significant 5yr role in football evolution, business mgr. Blue Bombers '65-66, GM '67, promotions mgr. '68-69; involved with baseball 36yrs as player, GM Winnipeg Goldeyes '54-65, GM AAA Winnipeg Whips '71-72, active role in formation of group seeking return of Triple A baseball to Winnipeg '86; mem. Man. Hockey, Sports halls of fame; res. Winnipeg, Man.

HINDMARCH, Robert (hockey); b. 27 May 1930, Nanaimo, B.C.; given name: Robert George; m. Jean; c. Robert Bruce, David Stephen; UBC, BPhE, Oregon, MSc, DEd; prof.; dir. UBC external relations; college football, hockey player; Dr. Gordon Burke football award UBC '52; Bobby Gaul trophy UBC outstanding athlete '53; asst. coach UBC football '55-62; UBC hockey coach from '65; mgr. '64 Olympic hockey team; chair. Hockey Development Council ; dir. CAHA; asst. dir. COA; CdM '84 Winter Olympics; v-p COA; 1 CIAU Austin-Matthews award; res. Vancouver, B.C.

HINDS, Sterling (t&f/football); b. 31 Oct 1961, Toronto, Ont.; m. Antoria Henry; c. Chanelle Antoria Joyce; Washington BA; Re/Max real estate broker, Rogers cable services; sprint specialist; silver 4x100m relay '83 FISU Games, bronze '84 Olympics; with brothers Doug, Jerry ntl t&f team mem.; mem. Washington Huskies '83 Rose

Bowl, 2 Aloha Bowl Games football teams; running back Argos '84; career curtailed by knee injury; mem. Mississauga Sports Hall of Fame; res. Mississauga, Ont.

HINTON, Tom (football); b. 19 Mar 1936, Ruston, La.; given name: William Thomas; m. Patsy Nelson; c. Steve, Janet, Terry; Louisiana Tech, BA; general mgr.; all-state t&f (shot put, discus), football; all-American HS football; 3yrs college all-Conf. guard 3; Gulf State Conf. athlete of year; 1st from conf. to play North-South game, all-American; drafted NFL Chicago Cardinals; pro BC '58-66; WFC all-star guard 5 times, all-Cdn twice; several times Lions' fans most popular; several times Lions Schenley nominee; 6yrs Lions' dir.; res. N. Vancouver, B.C.

HIROSE, Tim (judo); b. 27 Apr 1956, Vancouver, B.C.; teacher; Western Cdn 78kg title '75, 2 ntl 78kg, 1 open, 1 95kg titles; BC open 95kg title '81; mem. '79, '83 Pan-Am Games teams; res. Richmond, B.C.

HIRST, Elgin (football); b. 7 Mar 1929, Cornwall, Ont.; m. Carol Black; c. Edward, Robert James; asst. plant controller, York Board of Education; mem. '50 int. champion Parkdale Lions; mem. '53 ORFU champion Balmy Beach; lost to Winnipeg '53 Grey Cup challenge game; pro Toronto Argos '54-56; pres. Argonaut Alumni Club; last known res. Weston, Ont.

HISTED, Jack (t&f); b. 9 May 1903, Hamilton, Ont.; d. 14 Jun 1988, Hamilton, Ont.; given name: John Henry; m. Ora Eileen Myles; c. John Allan, Betty Ora; retd sales mgr. Domtar, 10yrs Wood Gundy; football 3yrs jr. Tigers; 4 Ont. running HJ titles; runnerup ntl championships; US ntl jr. champion '24; pres. Hamilton Olympic Club; pres. Southwestern Ont. Branch AAU of C; pres. AAU of C '59-60; COA mem.-at-large 10yrs; t&f team mgr. '52 Olympics; chair. constitution, by-laws comm. Pan-Am Games; BE, Commonwealth Games Assn. mem.-at-large 6yrs; v-p ntl sports advisory council 2yrs; chair. PE comm. National Council YMCA '58-64; mem. YMCA ntl exec. comm. '58-64; dir. Greater Hamilton Downtown YMCA '63-64, chair. PE comm. '44-58; Ont. Achievement Award; Hamilton Downtown YMCA citation.

HITCHCOCK, Dean (volleyball); b. 13 May 1956, Plaster Rock, N.B.; m. Deborah Lee Phillips; UCal; distributor Richard McDonald Corp; power hitter; sister Monica was mem. women's ntl team; mem. '79, '81, '83 FISU Games, '77, '80-83 Canada Cup, '79, '83 Pan-Am Games, '78, '82 world championships teams; gold team '80, '82 Canada Cup, '81 Commonwealth championships; retd '85; mem. Saint John Sports Hall of Fame; res. Calgary, Alta.

HITCHCOCK, Ken (coaching/hockey); b. 17 Dec 1951, Edmonton, Alta.; m. Nancy; c. Emily, Alex, Noah; UAlta.; hockey coach; coached Sherwood Park midget AAA team 10yrs amassing 575-69 record; 2 Alta. MHA coach of yr awards; head coach WHL Kamloops Blazers amassing 291-125-15 record; 2 WHL, 1 CHL coach of yr awards; asst. coach Team Canada '87 world champions; asst. coach NHL Philadelphia '90-93; head coach IHL Kalamazoo '93-95, 1 div. title; head coach NHL Dallas '96-99; Stanley Cup '99; head coach world all-stars '98; twice NHL, IHL all-star team

coach; *Sporting News, Hockey News* coach of yr awards; res. Coppell, Tex.

HITCHCOCK, Monica (volleyball); b. 26 Feb 1958, Plaster Rock, N.B.; given name: Monica Joan; m. Claude Moore; UNB, York., Memorial, BPhE; sales rep. Valley Graphics; mem. ntl jr. title team '74-75; power hitter; mem. '75 Canada Winter Games, '77, '81, '83 FISU Games, '77 Canada Cup, '79, '83 Pan-Am, '84 Olympic Games, '81 CIAU championships teams; retd '85 but returned to game '86 playing Sr. A club team which won 9 NB, 1 Eastern Cdn titles; brother Dean was mem. men's ntl volleyball team; mem. NB, Saint John Sports halls of fame; res. Saint John, N.B.

HOBKIRK, Alan (field hockey); b. 7 Nov 1952, Vancouver, B.C.; given name: Alan Arthur; m.; UBC, BA; LLB, Oxford, MA; lawyer; Rhodes scholar; mem. BC jr. team '66-70, 2yrs capt., 1 v.-capt.; BC srs '70-73; 5 ntl title teams; capt. Oxford '75-76; capt. Folkstone International Festival winner '76; mem. ntl team '71-79, 55 caps; bronze '71, silver '75 Pan-Am Games; res. Vancouver, B.C.

HODGE, Ken (hockey); b. 25 Jun 1944, Birmingham, Eng.; rw St. Catharines jrs; pro Buffalo '64-65, Chicago '64-67, Boston '67-76, NY Rangers '76-78; NHL record: 881 scheduled games, 328g, 472a, 97 playoff games, 34g, 47a; 2 Stanley Cup winners; reached 50-goal season plateau with 50 '74; res. Lynnfield, Mass.

HODGES, Bob (speed skating); b. 30 Dec 1943, Saskatoon, Sask.; USask, BSc, UAlta, PhD, Rockefeller U; educator UAlta; began competitive skating in elementary school; competed 15yrs; won ntl bantam, 2 intermediate, 5 sr. titles '53-69; competed internationally '65-72; mem. '68, '72 Olympic Games, '68, '70-71 world championship teams; 2 bronze 1st Canada Winter Games; coached ntl team level '73-76; mem. Olympic development comm. '73-76; CASSA dir., v-p '76-83; mgr '80 Olympic team; recipient of numerous academic awards; mem. Saskatoon Sports Hall of Fame; res. Edmonton, Alta.

HODGINS, Clint (harness racing); b. 18 Jun 1907, Clandeboye, Ont.; d. 21 Oct 1980, London, Ont.; driver, trainer, breeder; drove more than 2000 winning races US, Canada; led US dash winners '49 with 128, money winners with $184,108; 42 sub 2-min. miles; won Little Brown Jug, Messenger Pace, Kentucky Futurity, Cane Pace (twice); drove Adios Butler to 1:59.2 mile, 1st sub 2-min. clocking in Little Brown Jug history '59; co-holder world record 11 victories single program Dufferin Park '39; among best he bred, trained, drove were Bye Bye Byrd (horse of '59), Elaine Rodney, Skipper Thorpe, Sing Away Herbert, Pat's Bye Bye, Terry Parker, Acrasia, Proximity; mem. Cdn Horse Racing, Horseman's halls of fame.

HODGSON, George (swimming); b. 12 Oct 1893, Montreal, Que.; d. 1 May 1983, Montreal, Que.; given name: George Ritchie; m. Edyte Harrower (d); c. George H., Thomas; m. Hilda Birch; McGill.; investment counsel; competed in swimming, water polo at McGill; Festival of Empire Games London '11, defeated world mile record holder Sid Battersby of Britain; only Cdn to win individual

Olympic swimming gold 400m, 1500m FS events in record times '12; also 1000m, mile records, all broken by Johnny Weismuller; competed '20 Olympics; mem. Que., Cdn Amateur, International, Cdn Aquatic, Canada's, McGill Sports halls of fame.

HODGSON, Paul (baseball); b. 14 Apr 1960, Montreal, Que.; given name: Paul Joseph Denis; m. Kimberley; CBC sportscaster; began baseball career Marysville age 12; at 16 joined sr. Marysville Royals; all-star left fielder Cdn sr. championships '76; turned pro Blue Jays '77; minor league stints in Utica, Dunedin, Knoxville, Kingston, N.C.; briefly on Jays' ML roster '80-81; injuries forced retirement '84; mem. '84 Marysville Royals NB sr. title team; trial with Montreal Expos '85; mem. Fredericton Cardinals, Moncton Mets Atlantic Sr. champions; all-star third baseman; associate scout for Blue Jays; mem. NB Baseball, Fredericton Walls, NB Sports halls of fame; res. Fredericton, N.B.

HOFFMAN, Abby (t&f); b. 11 Feb 1947, Toronto, Ont.; given name: Abigail; UofT, BA, MA; dir. gen. Women's Health Bureau; dir. Sport Canada '81-91; at 11 defence Toronto boys' team peewee hockey tournament; represented Canada internationally '62-76 competing 4 Olympic, 4 Pan-Am, 2 Commonwealth, 3 FISU, 1 Maccabiah Games; 8 ntl 800m titles; ntl record holder 800m '62-75 cutting time from 2:10.8 to 2:00.2, 440yd '63-76 with 54.4, indoor 1500m 4:13.3; gold '66 Commonwealth 880yds, '63, '71 Pan-Am 800m, '69 Maccabiah 400m, 800m; silver '75 Pan-Am Games 800m, '67 FISU 800m, bronze '67 Pan-Am 800m, '75 Pan-Am 1500m, '65 FISU 800m; finalist 800m '68, '72 Olympics, Commonwealth record 2:00.2 in latter; flag-bearer '76 summer Olympics; mem. IAAF council from '95; City of Toronto Civic Award of Merit '76, Ont. Award of Merit '75; Herstorical Award '92; mem. Canada's all-time women's outdoor t&f team; Officer Order of Canada; mem. Cdn Olympic Hall of Fame; res. Ottawa, Ont.

HOGG, Wendy (swimming); b. 15 Sep 1956, Vancouver, B.C.; given name: Wendy Elizabeth Cook; m. Douglas Hogg; c. Melissa, Sarah; UBC, UAlta, BPhE; teacher; backstroke specialist; mem. ntl team '71-78; mem. 2 Olympic, 1 Commonwealth, 2 world championship teams; gold 100m, 200m back, 4x100m medley relay '74 Commonwealth Games; world record 1:04.78 4x100m medley relay; 200yd US short course, 200m long course titles '74; bronze 4x100 medley, 4th 100m back '76 Olympics; 5 1sts '76 nationals; ntl records '76 400m FS relay 3:52,98, 200m medley relay 1:59.16, 400m medley relay 4:18.80; BC jr. athlete of '73; BC, Bobbie Rosenfeld, Velma Springstead awards '74; Governor-General's silver medal '76; coach Edmonton Southside SC '76-78, Cranbrook Triton SC '80-82; mem. BC Sports, Cdn Aquatic halls of fame; res. Cranbrook, B.C.

HOHL, David (wrestling); b. 25 Mar 1966, Winnipeg, Man.; UMan.; began wrestling age 14; mem. ntl team from '86; 3 CIAU titles; 2 CIAU Wrestler of Year Awards; competes freestyle at 74kg; 1 jr, 3 sr ntl titles; silver '95, bronze '91 Pan-Am Games; gold '94 Commonwealth Games; competed '92, '96 Olympic Games; gold '87 Challenge Cup, '92 Czech Grand Prix, '95 Trophco Milone

GP; UMan. athlete of '90; res. Winnipeg, Man./St. Catharines, Ont.

HOHL, Elmer (horseshoes); b. 16 Jan 1919, Wellesley, Ont.; d. 5 Sep 1987, Wellesley, Ont.; m. Hilda Seyler; c. Sandra, Susan, Richard, Karen, Steve; carpenter; from '56 held 15 ntl, 19 Ont., 6 world titles; 1 of 2 in World Horseshoe Pitching Assn. history (formed '03) to pitch perfect game of 30 consecutive ringers in competition; pitched 69 consecutive ringers, 3 short of world mark held by Ted Allen, Boulder, Colo., with whom he shares perfect game record; best performance '68 world tournament scoring 572 of maximum 600 to break world record 571 set by Harold Reno, Sabrina, Ohio; ringer percentage of 88.5 broke '69 standard 87.5 set by Casey Jones, Waukesha, Wisc.; 5-pin bowler with 260 avg.; Ont 4-game men's record 1376 posted '71; frequent ntl 5-pin championship competitor; mem. Waterloo County, Intl., Cdn Horseshoe halls of fame.

HOHL, Steve (horseshoes); b. 21 Nov 1962, Kitchener, Ont.; div.; construction estimator/project mgr.; son of world champion Elmer Hohl; 5 Ont. jr. men's titles; 5 Ont. men's singles titles; 4 ntl jr. men's titles; '83 ntl men's title; world jr. men's title '78; competed 3 men's world championships; 2 ntl, 1 world record; res. Kitchener, Ont.

HOLLIMON, Joe (football); b. 5 Nov 1952, Truman, Ark.; given name: Joseph Julius; m. Glenda; c. Terry, Tony, Trenton; Arkansas State; all-Southland Conf. '74; Minnesota draft '75; pro Edmonton from '76; cornerback, punt return specialist; led WFC 9 interceptions '82; 3 all-WFC, 1 all-Cdn selections; numerous team records; CFL Players' Assn. top def. back award; mem. 6 Grey Cup finalists, 5 consec. winners; res. Sherwood Park, Alta.

HOLLOWAY, Condredge (football); b. 25 Jan 1954, Huntsville, Ala.; c. Jasmine; Tennessee; asst. AD Tenn.; rejected baseball offers from Montreal Expos; 12th round NE Patriots NFL draft; pro quarterback Rough Riders '75-80, Argos '81-86, Lions '87; Jeff Russell Memorial Trophy '82; EFC all-star '78, '82; all-Cdn '82; Carlsberg player of '82; Schenley outstanding player '82; 3 Grey Cup finals, 2 winners; former exec CHL Huntsville Channel Cats; mem. Cdn Football Hall of Fame; res. Huntsville, Ala.

HOLLOWAY, Sue (canoeing/x-c skiing); b. 19 May 1955, Halifax, N.S.; m. Greg Joy; c. Sarah, Alexandra; SFU, UBC, BPhE; Cdn Olympic Assn.; ntl jr. cross-country ski title '72; qualified for both skiing, canoeing ntl teams '73; through '83 1 ntl jr. K1, 6 sr. K1, K2, 3 sr. K4, 1 war canoe title; 2 NA K1, K2, 1 K4, 1 K1 6,000m titles; 9 times world championship competitor; 3 golds Canada Cup, Continental Cup, 4 golds Continental championships; 5 1sts '80 European tour; gold K2, K4 500m '83, bronze K1 500m '75 Pan-Am championships; with Alexandra Barr, silver 500m K2, bronze 500m K4 '84 Olympics; gold K2, K4 '83 Vichy regatta; represented Canada cross-country skiing Winter Olympics, K1, K2 Summer Olympics '76; 1st woman to participate in previously all-male Molokai-Oahu outrigger race Hawaii '79, placed 3rd; 4th '81 Hawaii women's race; mem. '76, '80, '84 Olympic teams; named flag-bearer for boycotted '80 summer Olympics; cross-country ski coach; mem. UBC cross-country track teams;

retd. from competiton '84; '94 Olympic team liaison; twice Ottawa ACT amateur athlete of year; nominated for Velma Springstead, Elaine Tanner trophies; mem. Cdn Amateur, Ottawa Sports halls of fame; res. Gloucester, Ont.

HOLMES, Derek (hockey); b. 15 Aug 1939, Ottawa, Ont.; m. Louise Cornu; c. Sean, Katherine; St. Michael's College, Carleton, BA; European players agent; jr. hockey St. Mike's, Ottawa Montagnards; college hockey Carleton; capt. Eastern Ntl Team '67-70; player-coach teams in Austria, Switzerland; ntl coach Finland '61-62; Olympic, ntl coach Switzerland '72-74; GM Team Canada '77 World championships; exec. dir., treas. Hockey Canada; mem. Hockey Club Ambri-Piotta Switzerland Hall of Fame; res. Ottawa, Ont.

HOLMES, Hap (hockey); b. 1889, Aurora, Ont.; d. 1940, Florida; given name: Harry; star goaler National HA, Pacific Coast HA, Western Canadian HL, Western HL, NHL; pro '12-13 Toronto, 15 seasons Toronto, Seattle, Victoria, Detroit during which he posted a 2.90 goals-against avg. 409 games; mem. 7 league title teams, 4 Stanley Cup winners; Holmes Memorial Trophy presented annually to best goaltender AHL; mem. Hockey Hall of Fame.

HOLNESS, Bob (softball); b. 4 Nov 1952, Victoria, B.C.; m. Susan Crowther; c. Jennifer, Rebecca; civic employee; shortstop Victoria Bates BC, Western Cdn title team '69; 10 BC title teams; '76 world champion, '79 Pan-Am Games teams; ntl championships MVP, 4 BC MVP awards; 2nd world championships batting '76; coach sr. softball; res. Victoria, B.C.

HOLZSCHEITER, Herb (golf); b. 8 Jan 1946, West Hill, Ont.; given name: Herbert; m. Mary Scheepers; c. Kelly, Christi; CPGA business school; golf professional; TDIAA HS title '64; Scarborough GC caddy champion '63; worked part-time for Bob Gray Scarborough GC '63-65, asst. pro '65-67; playing pro Thunderbird GC '68-76; asst. '78-86, head pro Weston Golf Club from '87; conducted April golf school for GM employees '73-76; BIC Open '70; runnerup Nfld. Open '72; third Alta. Open '69, Ont. Open '73-74; won Molson-Spec Invitational '73-74; Ont. PGA '75, '78, '80, '82; Hunt Trophy OPGA scoring avg. 67.3 '75; course record 66 Spruce Needles Timmins '69, 66 Brockville '74, 64 Thunderbird (old) '72, (new) '74, 63 Board of Trade CC '76; tournament player's rep. Peter Jackson golf tour; Peter Jackson golf tour tournament dir. '77-78; competed '79 US Open; Ont. Assistants title '82; mem. Ont.-Que. matches team '80, '89; runnerup Srs CPGA title '96; dir. CPGA '75-76; res. Mississauga, Ont.

HOMENUIK, Wilf (golf); b. 30 Dec 1937, Kamsack, Sask.; div. Jean Young; c. Gwen, Scott, Jason; golf pro, teacher; Sask. jr. '54; Sask. amateur '53; Man. amateur '56-57; mem. Man. Willingdon Cup team; pro '58; US tour '66; Man. Open '61, '72, Alberta Open '61, '65, CPGA '65, '71, Peru Open '65, Panama Open '66, Millar Trophy '67, '68, East Ridge '71, Labatt Invitational '73, Lake Michigan Classic '73; Dauphin pro-am '75; mem. Canada's World Cup team '71, '74; head pro London Highlands '76-78; mem. Yorkton Sports Hall of Fame; res. Toronto, Ont.

HOMER-DIXON, Marjorie (canoeing); b. 10 Aug 1945, Indochina; McMaster, BPhE; supervisor women's fitness center, kayak coach; ntl K2 title '67-68, bronze '67 Pan-Am Games; ntl record K1 '68; mem. '68, '72 Olympic teams; silver K2 NA championships '69; mem. 1st Cdn girls K4 NA gold team '69; semifinalist '71 worlds; turned to coaching '72; guided 4 paddlers to age group ntl titles, 2 to jr. world competition; Mississauga Jaycees most outstanding young person award '72; TV color commentator '76 Olympics; mem. Mississauga Sports Hall of Fame; res. Surrey, B.C.

HONG, Al (bowling); b. 14 Dec 1940, Winnipeg, Man.; div. Sharon Potts; c. Kelly, Robert; m. Cathy Munro; exec-dir. Ont. 5-pin Bowling Assn.; began competitive bowling Saskatoon '62; highest season avg. 278 in Saskatoon '72; rolled perfect 450 game '72; mem. '76 Calgary ntl champion men's team; ntl championship all-star; won '69 Man. Open singles; began coaching high school teams '66; Calgary city champion '75; coach ntl women's team Manila worlds '80; won Cornwall open singles '88; res. Pickering, Ont.

HOOD, Graham (t&f); b. 2 Apr 1972, Winnipeg, Man.; Arkansas; exercise psychologist; middle distance specialist; ntl jr. 1500 title '91; US cross-country ntl jr. title '91; competed '90 world jr., world cross country ; '92, '96 Olympics, '94 Commonwealth Games; NCAA 1500 silver '92. indoor mile '95; Pan-Am jr. 1500 gold, 800m bronze '91; won Millrose Games mile '95; won Harry Jerome Classic 1500m '96; 1500m gold '99 Pan-Am Games; Cdn sr 1500m record 3:33.94, 1000m record 2:16.88, mile record 3:51.55; 1500m gold '98 Robin Tait Classic NZ, Sydney GP, Waikiki mile; ntl 1500m titles '91, '97; mem. Burlington Legion Optimist TC; res. Burlington, Ont.

HOOGEWERF, Simon (t&f); b. 11 May 1963, Beaver Lodge, Alta.; given name: Simon Edward Charles; m. Sasah Chritchley; UBC, BSc, MD; physician; 800, 1000m specialist; BC HS 800m champion '80-81; mem. ntl jr. team '81; ntl sr. team '82-91; UBC team '81-86; 3 CIAU 100m, 1 600m indoor titles; ntl 800m titles '83-88; set CIAU, ntl 800/1000m records; competed '84, '88 Olympics, '87 Pan Am, '86, '90 Commonwealth Games, '83, '87, '91 worlds; indoor 800m bronze '91 worlds; Bobby Gaul trophy; mem. UBC Sports Hall of Fame; res. Ottawa, Ont.

HOOPER, Charmaine (soccer); b. 15 Jan 1968, Georgetown, Guyana; North Carolina State BSc; pro soccer striker; began play age 12 with Nepean Hotspurs; moved to Lynwood Spirits; NCAA finalist; 3 time all-American; 1st ntl appearance CONCACAF championships Haiti '91; mem. ntl team '86-99; all-CONCACAF qualifying tournament team '98; led ntl team in scoring '94; played with club teams Norway, Italy; pro with Tokyo Shidox, Chicago; named to intl. all-star team for '99 women's World Cup; CSA female soccer player of '94-95; MVP Chicago Cobras '98; to Jun '99 58 caps, 34 goals; res. Chicago, Ill.

HOOPER, Lyndon (soccer); b. 30 May 1966, Georgetown, Guyana; m. Jennifer Beckford; Wilfrid Laurier, BA; began play age 10 in Zambia; minor soccer Nepean; pro National Capital Pioneers '87, Montreal Supra '88, Toronto Blizzard '89-93, Birmingham City 2yrs, Cinci Silverbacks (NPSL),

Montreal Impact A League champs '95-98; men. ntl -20 team; mem. '92 Olympic team; 61 international caps; res. Willowdale, Ont.

HOOPER, Tom (hockey); b. 24 Nov 1883, Rat Portage (now Kenora), Ont.; d. 23 Mar 1960, Thunder Bay, Ont.; given name: Charles Thomas; with Tommy Phillips helped Kenora Thistles win '01 Man., Northwestern League titles; Thistles challenged for Stanley Cup '03, '05, '07 achieving success latter year but 2 months later lost Cup to Montreal Wanderers; played final season with Wanderers '07-08 again winning Stanley Cup; mem. NWO, Hockey halls of fame.

HOPE, Gord (wrestling/goal ball); b. 12 Aug 1954, Red Deer, Alta.; given name: Gordon Fred Kellock Luke; m. Erin Anne Kelly; c. Michelle, Kathleen, Christina; UofOtt, BA, MA, Carleton, PhD; human & management consulting services; class B1 blind wrestler; silver 57kg '84 world games for blind; ntl wrestling records '76-77, '84; long jump record '78; mem. Ont. ntl goal ball title team '80; mem. ntl goal ball team '78; US ntl blind wrestling title '85; co-ordinator ntl indoor games for blind '79, Cdn marathon for blind '84, Cdn goal ball championships '85; inaugurated annual National Capital invitational goal ball tournament '86; res. Brantford, Ont.

HORGAN, Fred (basketball); b. 22 Jan 1942, Saint John, N.B.; given name: Frederick Gerard; m. Barbara Shideler; c. Kimberly, Cheryl, Lee, Michelle; St.FX, BA, UNB, BEd; retd. teacher; mem. NB basketball officials assn. '67-99; founding mem. CABO '74; 3 time nominee Air Canada exec. award; CABO council of interpreters '74-99; co-edited CABO-FIBA rules casebook; author/editor CABO officials handbook; mem. CABO board of evaluators '80-99; mem. IAABO (NB Branch) '69-99; IAABO exec. '83-94, pres '93, only non-American to hold this post; IAABO approved clinician; tech. advisor FIBA rules instructional films; co-clinician FIBA certification/recertification clinics; one of 10 clinicians worldwide certified to certify/recertify international officials '92-99; COPABA, FIBA technical commissions '98-99; Ted Early Memorial Award; Basketball NB exec. of '85 award; hon. life mem. Basketball NB, IAABO; mem. NB, Saint John, Cdn Basketball halls of fame; res. Saint John, N.B.

HORN, Alf (fencing); b. 6 Jan 1913, Spjelkavik, Norway; d. 1991, St. Laurent, Que.; m. Lavinia; c. Carl, Allan (d); retired Montreal Star; Que. épée champion '38-40, '48-49, foil '40, sabre '40; ntl épée title '48-49; pres. Que. Fencing Assoc.; chair. AAU of C Fencing Comm.; mem. COA Fencing Comm.; BE & C Games Fencing Comm.; coached fencing Central YMCA; mem. '48 Olympic team; mgr. BE & CGames fencing team '54; qualified, but unable to attend '50 BE & C Games; Que. Branch AAU of C plaque for contribution to fencing.

HORNE, Stan (golf); b. 4 Jan 1912, Ripon, Eng.; d. 1995, Nun's Island, Que.; given name: Stanley; m. Suzanne Marcoux; Nun's Island golf dir., pro; CPGA champion '36-38; low Cdn Canadian Open '37, '39; 8 Que. Open titles; 1st Cdn to go on complete US pro golf tour '39-40; low Cdn $10,000 PGA Open Islesmere '45; 4th Miami Open '37; 2nd Lake Placid Open '38; competed Masters '37, '38 (finished stroke ahead of Bobby Jones in latter); 5th

Pinehurst Open, Thomasville Open '40; 3rd St. Petersburg Open '40; won Ont. Millar Trophy twice; Que. Spring Open title '60; CPGA Srs title '62; Que. PGA match play champion 10 times; played in 1st Canada Cup matches; partnered with Jules Huot to beat Ben Hogan, Lawson Little in Miami International 4-ball match; playing with Ed Furgol, Jules Huot at Dubsdread in Orlando '46 set 9-hole record 26 with 7 birdies, 1 eagle, 1 par; 8 holes-in-one; 29yrs Islesmere Golf Club pro; mem. QGA Hall of Fame.

HORNER, Red (hockey); b. 28 May 1909, Lynden, Ont; given name; George Reginald; defence Toronto Marlboros, Brokers' League before joining Maple leafs '28-40; led NHL in penalty minutes 8 successive seasons; record 167 penalty minutes in 43 games during '35-36 season stood 20 years; career total 1254 penalty minutes; capt. Leafs '37-38; NHL record: 42g, 110a; mem. Hockey Hall of Fame; res. Toronto, Ont.

HORTON, Tim (hockey); b. 12 Jan 1930, Cochrane, Ont., d. 21 Feb 1974, Toronto, Ont.; given name: Myles Gilbert; m. Dolores Michalek; c. Jeri-Lyn, Kim, Kelly, Tracey; St. Michael's College; hockey player, franchise donut chain owner; jr. A St. Mike's Majors where he was OHA penalty leader 1st year; pro Maple Leafs '49, spent much of next 3yrs Pittsburgh Hornets AHL, won Calder Cup, all-star defensive berth; Toronro regular '52-70; NY Rangers '70-71, Pittsburgh '71-72, Buffalo '72-74; twice 1st, 3 times 2nd team all-star; mem. 5 Stanley Cup winners; NHL record: 1446 scheduled games, 115g, 403a, 1611pim, 126 playoff games, 11g, 39a, 183pim; killed in single car accident; jersey #2 retd by Sabres in his memory; J.P. Bickell trophy TML MVP '69. mem. Hockey Hall of Fame.

HORVATH, Bronco (hockey); b. 12 Mar 1930, Port Colborne, Ont.; given name: Bronco Joseph; m. Dolly Tonelli; c. Mark, Barbara; retd. hockey exec.; made NHL debut at 25 with Vic Stasiuk and Johnny Bucyk to form Boston's fames Uke Line; missed NHL scoring title '60 by single point to Bobby Hull; NHL '55-68 with NY Rangers, Montreal, Boston, Chicago, Toronto, Minnesota; stints in minors with Rochester, Tulsa; NHL record: 434 scheduled games, 141g, 185a, 36 playoff games, 12g, 9a; played in 2 all-star games; coached London Knights (OHA), Cape Cod Cubs; res. South Yarmouth, Mass.

HORWOOD, Don (basketball/coaching); b. 30 Aug 1946, Carbonear, Nfld.; m. Jill Chipman; c. Chris, Kelly; Memorial. BPhE, BEd, UAlta MA; basketball coach UAlta; small forward Memorial '63-68, capt. '68; coached Victoria Oak Bay HS '69-78; 3 BC titles; asst coach UAlta '78-79, head coach Victoria Spectrum HS '79-83, UAlta '83-99; 2 CIAU titles; CBC-TV basketball color commentator '96 Olympics; 2 CIAU coach of yr awards; res. Edmonton, Alta.

HOUCK, Norm (curling); b. 4 Feb 1934, Winnipeg, Man.; given name: James Norman; UMan, BSc, BEd; retd; skipped Man. entry '62 Brier, losing title in playoff to Richardson rink; 3 ntl Srs. titles, one as skip, 2 as 3rd for Jim Ursel; mem. Man. Curling Hall of Fame; res. Winnipeg, Man.

HOULD-MARCHAND, Valerie (synchro swim); b. 29 May 1980, Riviere-du-Loup, Que; followed lead of synchroswim coach mother Chantal Hould and became involved in sport age 5; at 15 youngest to become ntl A team member; team silver '96 Olympics, team gold '95 jr worlds, '96 French Open; '98 Commonwealth Games solo gold; res. Quebec City, Que./Edmonton, Alta.

HOULDEN, Jim (shooting); b. 15 Feb 1904, Hamilton, Ont.; d. 19 Nov 1994, Milton, Ont.; given name: James Walter; m. Rita Andrea; c. Anne; Queen's, BSc; ballistic engineer; began smallbore shooting as cadet '19 progressing through HS ranks to military rifles on outdoor ranges; ballistician CIL ammo div.; chief ballistician CIL Defence Services WW2; Western sales mgr. CIL, mem. pro shooting staff following WW2; competed at Ottawa's Connaught ranges when opened in '21 and received 60 year award for annual competition (excluding war years) '81; 15 times Bisley team mem., commandant '65; declared best shot in Cdn Armed Forces '32-34; King's silver Bisley '32; in addition to high powered rifle also ranking shooter in pistol, smallbore, trap and skeet; life mem. GBNRA; life gov. DCRA; mem. Man. Sports Hall of Fame.

HOULE, Réjean (hockey); b. 25 Oct 1949, Rouyn, Que.; m. Micheline Côtes; c. Sylvain, Jean-François, Annie; hockey exec.; l/r wing Montreal Jr. Canadiens; 1st overall draft pick by Canadiens '69; played in NHL with Montreal '69-73, '76-83; in WHA Quebec '73-76; mem. 5 Stanley Cup winners; NHL record: 635 scheduled games, 161g, 247a, 90 playoff games, 14g, 34a; PR dir. Molson Breweries '86-95; v-p/GM Canadiens from '95; res. Ville Lasalle, Que.

HOULT, Billy (bowling); b. 18 Jun 1932, Toronto, Ont.; given name : William George; m. Shirley Baker; c. William Jr., David (from 1st marriage), Karen, Vicki, Debbie, Sherry; Dominion Business Coll.; trophy mfgr.; youngest bowler ever to win Cdn Bowling Congress all-events tournament by winning singles, doubles, mixed doubles at 14 (in rubber boots); Eastern, ntl singles '65; only triple Eastern singles champ '70; won 1st Master Bowlers tourney on TV '64; Master Bowlers mixed triples '66; Ont., ntl MB of '67-68; MB 10 percent tourney '70; MB CNE tourney '74; MB pro bowling tourney; mem. '66 Ont. men's title team that placed 2nd to Winnipeg as both teams topped national pinfall record; mem. Ont. mixed title team '73; rolled sanctioned perfect 450 game in major league play Spadina Bowl; mem. numerous tourney title teams; competitive career average 260; mem. Ont. 5-Pin Bowling Hall of Fame; res. Agincourt, Ont.

HOUSTON, Heather (curling); b. 4 Feb 1959, Red Rock, Ont.; Lakehead, HBA; visual artist; Northwestern Ont. jr. champion '74, '76; Ont. Winter Games participant '76; NO mixed champion '84; NWO women's champion '86; Scott Tournament of Hearts titles '88-89; world champion '89; skipped inaugural JVC TSN women's skins game '96; Velma Springstead award '89; Tim Ryan course scholarship Lakehead '83; Dean's drawing medal '84; mem. NWO Sports, Cdn Curling halls of fame; res. Thunder Bay, Ont.

HOUSTON, Neil (curling); b. 19 Jan 1957, Calgary, Alta.; given name: Neil William; m. Beverley Karen Bakka; c. Katherine, Andrew; SAIT, hotel/restaurant admin, UCal, BPhE, Concordia, sports admin.; CCA dir. championship services & special programs; ntl badminton, soccer, 3rd Paul Gowsell Schoolboy curling titles '75; world jr. curling title '76; mem. 4 Alta. men's curling title teams; 2nd for Ed Lukowich '86 Brier, Worlds championships; '88 Olympic bronze medalist; Calgary athlete of '76; res. Orleans, Ont.

HOWARD, Glenn (curling); b. 17 Jul 1962, Midland, Ont.; given name: Glenn William; m. Judy; c. Scott, Carly; mgr. Brewer's Retail; began curling at 11; skip 3 Ont. Pepsi jr. competitions; 3rd for brother Russ, won Governor-General's Ont. title '85; competed 7 Briers, 2 winners; world titles '87, '93; 4 TSN Skins Game titles; 1 VO Cup title; attended '87 Olympic trials; 3 Canada Challenge Cups in Japan; Ont. team of '87; participated in numerous clinics, exhibitions in Canada, Europe, Japan; Dick Ellis team award '87; mem. Cdn Curling Hall of Fame; res. Midland, Ont.

HOWARD, Julie (swimming); b. 23 Oct 1976, Brantford, Ont.; freestyle, backstroke specialist; 6 ntl titles; 5 Cdn records; mem. ntl team from '92; competed '92, '96 Olympics, '94 Commonwealth Games; 3 gold, 3 bronze '96 Canada Cup; 3 World Cup silver, 4 bronze; 1 CIAU female swimmer of yr; 1 CIAU Sprinter's Cup; 2 CIAU records; res. Brantford, Ont.

HOWARD, Kid (boxing); b. 9 Oct 1928, Terrace Bay, N.S.; d. 4 Jan 1975, Halifax, N.S.; given name: Richard; c. 1 daughter (d), 1 son; plumber, liquor store clerk; 1st pro bout at 15; of 108 bouts during 7 year span won 77, lost 26, drew 5; never knocked out; in only 4 did he fail to go distance; Maritime lightweight title '49; ntl title '54-60; campaigned internationally as featherweight; ranked 6th in world by Ring Magazine; at 5'2" considered short even for featherweight; noted for aggressive style and considered "crowd pleaser", met some of ring's top contenders including Kenny Lane, Teddy "Red Top" Davis, Willie Toweel, Orlando Zulueta, Ray Famechon; fought Toweel for BE crown but lost decision; health deteriorated following death of daughter and marriage breakup; mem. Canadian Boxing, NS, Canada's Sports halls of fame.

HOWARD, Russ (curling); b. 19 Feb 1956, Midland, Ont.; m. Wendy; c. Steven, Ashley; dir. golf & real estate Royal Oaks GC; began curling at 13; won '76 Ont. Colts; competed 9 Briers, 2 winners; with brother Glenn, Tim Belcourt, Kent Carstairs won '87 Brier, worlds; with brother Glenn, Wayne Middaugh, Peter Corner won '93 Brier, worlds; Ont. team of '87; 4 TSN Skins Games titles; 1 VO Cup title; attended '87 Olympic trials; 3 Canada Challenge Cup titles in Japan; '85 Ont. Governor-General's title; skipped Ont., NB in Brier play; 2 8-enders; played key role in free guard zone rule, other innovations; at frequent odds with CCA over sponsorship rules; participated in numerous clinics in Canada, Europe, Japan; Dick Ellis team award '87; mem. Cdn Curling Hall of Fame; res. Moncton, N.B.

HOWARD, Tom (t&f); b. 20 Sep 1948, Vancouver, B.C.; given name: Thomas George; div. Cheryl Lynne Spowage; UBC; transit operator; mem. '73 FISU, '75, '79 Pan-Am, '76 Olympic teams; ntl marathon title, 2nd ntl outdoor 10,000m '74; 4th '75 Boston Marathon 2:13.24; bronze '75 Pan-Ams marathon; 30th '76 Olympics marathon; 3 Seattle marathon titles; mem. Cdn Road Running Hall of Fame; res. Surrey, B.C.

HOWE, Bruce (rugby); b. 13 Mar 1941, Palm North, N.Z.; given name: Bruce Leslie; m. Janice Marilyn Franklin; c. Carolyn Anne, Jonathan Bruce; Dunedin Teachers College, PE dip., Oregon, BSc, MSc, PhD; dean faculty of Ed.UVic; played cricket, boxed, competed in track, rugby at NZ HS, college levels; cricket at club level; rugby club, college levels; represented NZ provincially in rugby; toured UK with Oregon team '66; capt. BC '72 vs All Blacks; coached rugby HS, college level, asst. coach NZ provincial team '75; coached Vancouver Island Reps '75-78; 2 McKechnie Cups; coached BC team on '78 Samoa, Fiji tour, won ntl title, beat Australian State Champion Queensland; ntl rugby team coach '79-82; UVic rugby coach; res. Victoria, B.C.

HOWE, Dan (canoeing); b. 31 Dec 1970, Kingston, Ont.; Queen's; engineer; mem. ntl team '89-98; C-4 gold Duisburg Regatta '93; C-2 500 gold, C-1 1000 bronze '95 Pan-Am Games; C-2 1000 silver Milano '96; C-4 200 silver Szeged '96; gold (with Steve Giles) C-2 1000, C-2 500 Hemispheric '96 Olympic qualifier regatta; competed '94, '95, '97 worlds, '96 Olympics; res. North Bay, Ont.

HOWE, Gordie (hockey); b. 31 Mar 1928, Floral, Sask.; given name: Gordon; m. Colleen Joffa; c. Marty, Mark, Murray, Cathleen; hon. LLD Regina; hockey exec., restaurateur; 1st pro contract '45 Omaha Knights (USHL); 32 seasons major hockey; 26 NHL, Detroit '46-71, Hartford '79-80, 6 WHA Houston Aeros '73-76, New England Whalers '77-79; regarded as one of game's greatest right wingers; NHL record: 1767 scheduled games, 801g, 1049a, 157 playoff games, 68g, 42a; major trophies: 6 Hart (MVP); 6 Art Ross (scoring); 1 Lester Patrick, 1 2nd team all-star, all-star selectee 15 consecutive years; played in 22 all-star games scoring 10 goals, 8 assists; co-holder all-star points in single-game mark of 4 '65; following '71 retirement 2yrs Red Wings v-p before joining sons Marty, Mark with Houston '73-74; despite age, 45, WHA MVP '74; helped Aeros win 2 Avco Cups, all-star each season; major hockey's 1st playing club pres. '75-76; WHA record: 419 scheduled games, 174g, 334a, 78 playoff games, 28g, 43a; at 69 with 40 sec. cameo shift for Detroit Vipers (IHL) 3 Oct '97 became only athlete to play pro hockey over six decades; jersey #9 retd by Red Wings, Whalers; Lionel Conacher Trophy '63; Sport Magazine hockey player of quarter century '71; dir. player development Hartford Whalers; Hartford advisory board; Officer Order of Canada; mem. Whalers, Hockey, Canada's, Sask. Sports halls of fame; res. Traverse City, Mich.

HOWE, Syd (hockey); b. 28 Sep 1911, Ottawa, Ont.; d. 20 May 1976, Ottawa, Ont.; given name: Sydney Harris; m. Frances; c. Shirley; civil servant; mem. 1st Ottawa Memorial Cup finalist losing '28 to Regina; pro Ottawa Senators (NHL) '29-30, '32-34, Philadelphia Quakers '30-31, St. Louis '34; Detroit '35-46; NHL record: 237g, 291a; modern record '44 scoring 6 goals in game vs Rangers, mark since equalled by Red Berenson, Darryl Sittler; on ice when Mud Bruneteau scored goal that ended Stanley Cup's longest game; mem. 3 league champions, 3 Stanley Cup winners; mem. Ottawa Sport, Ottawa CSRA Sports, Hockey halls of fame.

HOWELL, Harry (hockey); b. 28 Dec 1932, Hamilton, Ont.; given name: Henry Vernon; m. Marilyn Gorrie; c.

Danny (d), Cheryl; hockey exec.; jr. Guelph Biltmores; pro NY Rangers '52-69; Ranger record more than 1000 games; Oakland '69-70, L.A. '71; WHA NY Raiders (then Golden Blades), Jersey Knights, San Diego Mariners, player-coach '74-75; AGM Cleveland Barons (NHL) '76, GM '76-77; coach Minnesota '77-78; scout Minn., Edm.; NHL record: 21 seasons, 1411 scheduled games, 94g, 324a, 38 playoff games, 3g, 3a; James Norris Memorial Trophy '66-67; 1st team all-star once; NHL milestone award '82; mem. Hockey, AHL halls of fame; res. Hamilton, Ont.

HOWELL, Ron (football/hockey); b. 4 Dec 1935, Hamilton, Ont.; given name: Ronald John; m. Ruth Jean Moore; c. Robin, Lisa, Cathy, Tracey; retired furrier; Guelph Biltmores OHA jr. A, Tilson Award '55-56; sr. Kitchener-Waterloo; pro Rochester AHL; minors Vancouver (WHL), Long Island (EHL), retired '64; pro football Hamilton '54-62, BC '62, Toronto '64-65, Montreal '66; CFL record: 13 seasons, returned 458 punts for 2742yds, 6.0 avg., 5tds; 4 Grey Cup finals, 1 winner; Gruen EFC rookie of '54; Schenley outstanding Canadian '58; res. Ancaster, Ont.

HOWES, Bob (football); b. 4 Jan 1943, Kirkland Lake, Ont.; given name: Robert Alexander; m. Mary Padden; c. Chris, Beau; Queen's, Waterloo, UAlta; football coach, teacher; mem. basketball, football teams Queen's, football Waterloo; drafted '66 by Calgary; pro BC '69-72, Edmonton '72-81; CFL all-star centre '74; also offensive tackle; capt. Eskimos '75-77; mem. 8 Grey Cup finalists, 5 winners; asst. coach Queen's '84-95, head coach since '96; OQIFC coach of '96; res. Kingston, Ont.

HOWIE, Al (t&f); b. 16 Sep 1945, West Kilbride Ayershire, Scotland; given name: Allan; div.; c. Gabe, Dana; Androssan Academy; stonemason; began racing '79; averages 15-20 marathons, 5-10 ultra marathons annually; NA 24-hour race record; ran 350-mile race '79; world record longest non-stop race 187.5 miles in 37h;57min.; noted for quick recovery ability, ran 150 mile 24-hour race and 6 days later won 50-mile race '82; cross-Canada 72-day record run '91; res. Victoria, B.C.

HOWKINS, Mark (shooting); b. 17 Jun 1953, Brisbane, Australia; given name: Patrick; m. Danielle Perrot; c. Christine, David; self employed; handgun specialist; mem. ntl team '79-95; 7 ntl rapid fire titles; competed '84, '88 Olympics, '87, '91 Pan-Am Games, '86, '90, '94 Commonwealth Games, '85, '89 Championship of Americas, '86, '90 worlds; numerous World Cup competitions; 2 bronze '86, silver '90 Commonwealth Games; gold, silver '85 Championship of Americas; res. Calgary, Alta.

HOWSON, Barry (basketball); b. 17 Jun 1939, London, Ont.; given name: Barry Franklin; div.; c. Micheline, David, Bryan; UWO, BA, Wayne State, MEd; HS teacher, PE department head; mem. all-Ont. HS champions '57-58, OQAA champions Western '60; Tillsonburg Livingstons-London Fredricks Eastern Cdn sr. A titlists '61; Montreal Yvan Coutu Huskies Eastern Cdn titlist '62; London 5B Sports '63; mem. '64 Olympic team, Toronto Dow Kings sr. A champions; Sarnia Drawbridge '66-68, Ont. sr. title '68; gold '66 Canada Winter Games; mem. '67 Pan-Am Games team; London Host-Rent-A-Car team '69-70;

national team world championships '71; Ont. sr. A champion London Celtics '72-73; Sarnia Trader Bryan int. A Bullets '75; Sarnia Northgate Bowl int. '76; twice MVP Windsor Masters (40+) tournament; 3 35+ Sarnia Tennis Club titles; coach St. Patrick's HS basketball, football, track, tennis, Lambton College basketball; mem. Sarnia-Lambton Sports Hall of Fame; res. Sarnia, Ont.

HRITZUK, Eugene (curling); b. 12 Oct 1949, St. Walburg, Sask.; m. Joanne Seltenrich; c. Trina, Valene; UofSask, BA, BEd, MEd; farmer, PE teacher, salesman; standout HS athlete; competed in 19 university sports; coached Sask. basketball, t&f finalists; played sr. baseball Sask., Man., Alta; 3 time Sask softball finalist; Northern Sask. HS curling finalist '66-67; tied for runnerup ntl firefighters '80; amassed more than $100,000 in cashspiels '83-86 seasons; top money winner cashspiel circuit '85-86 with $60,000; won Calgary carspiel '85, Saskatoon Nutana Pot of Gold unprecedented 3 consec. yrs.; twice won Saskatoon Super League; 3 time prov. tankard finalist; posted undefeated record winning Sask. Tankard '85; skip semifinalist '85 Brier, 5th man, coach '86 Brier rink; Saskatoon athlete of year nominee '86; res. Loreburn, Sask.

HRUDEY, Kelly (hockey); b. 13 Jan 1961, Edmonton, Alta.; given name: Kevin Stephen; m. Donna; c. Jessica, Megan, Kaitlin; broadacster; began skating age 4; goalie Medicine Hat (WHL) '78-81; NY Islanders 2nd pick '80 draft; Indianapolis (CHL) '81-84; mem. Team Canada '84; Islanders '84-89; Los Angeles '89-96, San Jose '96-98; shared 2 Terry Sawchuk (CHL top goalie) trophies; Tommy Ivan (CHL MVP) trophy '83; NHL record: 677 scheduled games, 271-265-88, 38,084min, 17so, 85 playoff games, 5163min, 283ga, 36-46; HNIC color analyst; res. Redondo Beach, Calif./Calgary, Alta.

HSU, Gloria (table tennis); b. 7 Oct 1956, South Africa; asst. animator Atkinson Film-Arts; 2 ntl woman's closed doubles' titles; mem. ntl team from '75; national Top 12 title '80; CNE Open women's singles, doubles, mixed doubles, Ont. closed singles title '81; mem. Ont. title team, woman's singles finalist Cdn. closed championships '80; gold women's doubles world student championships '80, team silver '80, '82; team silver '82 Commonwealths; team bronze '83 Pan-Am Games; ntl, US Open team semifinalist '81; mem. '79-83 Commonwealth, worlds teams; res. Toronto, Ont.

HUANG, Johnny (table tennis); b. 5 Oct 1962, Canton, China; m.; coach; began competing age 9; mem. Chinese ntl team winning '85 singles, '86 doubles, '85 Scandinavian open titles; emigrated to Canada '87; undefeated in NA Feb '90-Mar '91; 1st Cdn to win medal (bronze) at World Cup '93; gold, 2 bronze '91, triple gold '94 Commonwealth championships; competed '96 Olympic Games; 2 ntl singles, 1 doubles, 1 team titles; 2 Japan Open, 3 US Open, 5 CNE International, 4 Commonwealth championships, 4 NA titles; ntl jr. team coach from '90; pro Germany '92-93, France '93-95, Japan from '95; res. Toronto, Ont.

HUARD, Camille (boxing); b. 29 Oct 1951, St. Francois de Pabos, Que.; div. Connie Murray; c. Nicolas; m. Suzanne Dernier; c. Christine Marie, Marie-Pier, Noemie; Laval, BA; youth consultant/educator; Que., Eastern Cdn featherweight

(57kg) titles '70, '73-76; Que. Open class bronze '71; Que. lightweight (60kg) title, silver Eastern Cdn.; Eastern Cdn. 57kg title '73; lost '74 NA final to Wilfredo Benitez, later world pro champ; mem. ntl team '74 world championships; silver '75, gold '76 ntl championships; mem. '76 Olympic team losing split decision to Poland's Lazlek Kosedowski; coach Que. team '79 Canada Games, ntl team Finnish International tournament; coach Grande-Riviere boxing club '80-82; res. Gaspe, Que.

HUBAND, Deb (all-around); b. 5 Sep 1956, Ottawa, Ont.; given name: Deborah Ellen; John Abbott College, Concordia, Bishop's., hons. BA, UBC,MSc; coach, speech-language pathologist; mem. Oakville Jays softball team '69-72; Oakville swim club '68-72, Oakville HS swimming, track, volleyball, basketball teams '69-72, Beaconsfield HS basketball, volleyball teams '72-76, Que. softball, basketball teams '74-75, college basketball '76-80, field hockey '76-77; co-capt. ntl women's basketball team '78-84; basketball all-Que. '77-80, all-Cdn '78-80, softball all-Que., all-Cdn '74-75; MVP, all-star awards CIAU championships '77-80; guard '80 Jones Cup gold team; shares CIAU women's single game 50 points record with Carol Turney; mem. '84 Olympic team, 2 world championship bronze; 7 school athlete of year awards; Softball Canada jr. catcher of yr award; Concordia rookie of '76-77; Hon. Howard Ferguson academic award Bishop's '77-79; asst. women's basketball coach UBC '88-91, head coach '95-99; asst. coach women's ntl team '99; coached BC regional girls team '95 BC summer games; mem. Nepean, Bishop's Walls, Cdn Basketball, Ottawa Sports halls of fame; res. Nepean, Ont./Vancouver, B.C.

HUDDY, Charlie (hockey); b. 2 Jun 1959, Oshawa, Ont.; m. Karen; c. Amanda, Ryan; hockey coach; defence Oshawa (OHA) '77-79, Houston (CHL) '79-80, Wichita (CHL) '80-82, NHL with Edmonton '80-91, Los Angeles '91-94, Buffalo '94-96, '97, St. Louis '96; NHL plus/minus leader '83; Team Canada '84; NHL record: 1017 scheduled games, 99g, 354a, 183 playoff games, 19g, 66a; player/asst coach Rochester (AHL) '96; res. East Amherst, N.Y.

HUDON, Joe Jr. (harness racing); b. 30 May 1951, Teulon, Man.; m. Shirley; c. John, Patrick, Phillip; premier driver Cloverdale B.C. track 15yrs; ntl UDR title '80; 4th '78 world driving championships; moved to OJC circuit '91; Cdn horseman of '94; through '97 scored 3579 victories with purses topping $11 million; res. Rockwood, Ont.

HUDSON, Bruce (curling); b. 13 Nov 1928, Winnipeg, Man.; m. Verla Scott; c. Diane, Gordon, Elaine, Scott; UMan; retd. Manitoba Queen's Printer; 11 men's provincial championships, finalist 4 yrs in succession '64-67 matching Ken Watson record; Man. rep. '64, '67 Brier, '81 Seniors; Man. bonspiel title '61; hon. life mem. Manitoba Curling Assn.; res. Winnipeg, Man.

HUDSON, Gordon (curling); b. 5 Jan 1894, Kenora, Ont.; d. 10 July 1959, Winnipeg, Man.; m. Flora MacLean; c. Bruce, Margaret; manufacturers agent; catcher sr. baseball; 5 Man. Bonspiel titles; skipped Brier winners '28-29, winning 28 of 20 games played; pres. Strathcona CC '25-27, later secty; pres., hon. life mem. Man., Dominion Curling Associations; mem. Man. Sports, Cdn Curling halls of fame.

HUDSON, John (t&f); b. 15 May 1936, Belfast, N. Ireland; div. Melissa Louise Harvey; c. Saundra Lynn, Lisa Marie; m. Linda Diane Smith; Dubuque, BSc; sports TV consultant; all-Ireland youth cross-country champion '54; Iowa Conf. cross-country titles '57, '59-60, 1-mile champion '59, 2-mile champion '58-59; 1st ntl t&f coach '69; exec. dir. Coaching Assn. of Canada '71-75; dir. CBC Sports, '78-80; dir. media properties Labatt breweries `79-82; exec. producer Blue Jays baseball `81-96; with Ken Twigg co-founder Maple Leaf Indoor Games Toronto '63; res. Mississauga, Ont.

HUFNAGEL, John (football); b. 13 Sep 1951, Corapolis, Pa.; m. Peni; c. Neely, Lindsay, Cole; Penn State; football coach, real estate broker; all-American quarterback Penn State; competed in Cotton Bowl, Sugar Bowl, Hula Bowl; pro Denver (NFL) 3 seasons; CFL Calgary '76-79, Saskatchewan '80-83, '87, Winnipeg '84-86; player/coach Saskatchewan '87; assisted UCal 2 seasons; offensive co-ordinator/quarterbacks coach Calgary '90-97; head coach/ GM New Jersey Red Dogs (Arena FL) '97-98; asst. BC '98, Cleveland Browns '99; mem. 1 Grey Cup winner; res. Vancouver, B.C.

HUGHES, Billy (all-around); b. Jul 1888, Durham, Eng.; d. 14 Nov 1975, St. Anne's, Man.; m. Marjorie; c. Vivian, Pat, John; athletic trainer; outstanding boxer losing only 9 of 189 bouts over 14yrs; held Cdn feather, bantam, lightweight titles; retd from ring '24; began coaching Montreal Westmount HS, interscholastic title; coached Montreal Winged Wheelers '19-22, Queen's '22-26 (26 consec. victories), Hamilton Tigers '32-33, Rough Riders '35-36, RCAF Manning Pool, WW2; 4 Grey Cup titlists, Queen's '22-24, Hamilton '32; coached IRFU title winners with Ottawa, Manning Pool; trainer Cdn t&f, boxing teams '24 Olympics; numerous pro, amateur hockey teams including Chicago; Winnipeg, Calgary, Regina football clubs; trainer/coach numerous amateur football, rugby, boxing, track teams; coached/trained world speed skating titlist Everett McGowan; YMCA AD/instructor/health unit dir. '42-57; life mem. YMCA, Blue Bombers; mem. Cdn. Football, Man. Sports halls of fame.

HUGHES, Clara (cycling); b. 27 Sep 1972, Winnipeg, Man.; competitive speed skater from '88; began cycle racing at 17; 3000m individual pursuit specialist; 10 ntl titles; competed '91, '95 Pan-Am, '94 Commonwealth, '96 Olympic Games, '93, '94 worlds; 2 Pan-Am Games silver, 2 bronze, 1 Commonwealth Games silver; 2 bronze '96 Olympics; Tour de L'Aude silver '93; world championship Road Individual Time Trial silver '95; Sea Otter Classic '98 gold; Canada Games '93 speed skating 3000m gold; YTV Youth Achievement Award '92; res. Hamilton, Ont.

HUGHES, George (football); b. 19 Aug 1925, Norfolk, Va.; given name; George Samuel; m. Kate Parker; c. George Jr., Kathy, Susan; William and Mary, BSc, MA; retd. football coach, hardware store owner; centre, guard in college appearing in '48 Dixie, '49 Delta bowls; all-state, all-Southern, all-American; participant Blue-Grey, College all-star games; 5yrs pro Pittsburgh , twice all-Pro; 4yrs HS coach, 12yrs coach Norfolk Neptunes Continental, Atlantic Coast Football League; Rough Rider line coach '74-80; mem. Virginia Sports Hall of Fame; res. Norfolk, Va.

HULL, Bobby (hockey); b. 3 Jan 1939, Pointe Anne, Ont.; given name: Robert Marvin; div. Judy Learie; c. Terry; div. Joanne McKay; c. Bobby Jr., Blake, Brett, Bart, Michelle; retired hockey player, cattle farmer; jr. B Hespeler, Woodstock, Galt; jr. A St. Catharines Black Hawks '55-57; pro Chicago (NHL) '57-72, Winnipeg Jets (WHA) '72-79; Team Canada '76; NHL record: 1036 scheduled games, 604g, 549a, 116 playoff games, 62g, 67a; WHA record: 411 scheduled games, 303g, 335a, 60 playoff games, 43g, 37a; 5 50-plus goal seasons Chicago; 1st team all-star NHL 10 times, WHA 5 times; 2nd team NHL twice; 3 Art Ross, 2 Hart, 1 Lady Byng, Lester Patrick Award; 2 Gary Davidson Trophies (WHA MVP); nicknamed "Golden Jet"; sweater #9 retd. by Chicago, Winnipeg; fastest left-handed slap shot 118.3 mph, fastest skater 29.7 mph; 2 Lionel Conacher awards; TV hockey commentator; wrote 2 hockey books; owner grand champion hereford bull '94 Royal Winter Fair; Officer Order of Canada; mem. Canada's Sports, Hockey halls of fame; res. Naples, Fla.

HULL, Brett (hockey); b. 9 Aug 1964, Belleville, Ont.; m. Allison; c. Jude, Jayde, Crosby; UMinn(Duluth); son of Hockey Hall of Famer Bobby Hull; played with Minn.-Duluth WCHA '84-86, freshman of yr award; drafted by Calgary '84; Moncton AHL '86-87; WCHA 1st team all-star '86, AHL 1st team all-star '87; Red Garrett Memorial trophy '87; NHL Calgary '86-87, St. Louis '88-98, Dallas '98-99; 50 goal plateau '90 72, '91 86, '92 70, '93 54, '94 57; achieved 500g plateau '96; NHL record (through '99): 861 scheduled games, 586g, 459a, 130 playoff games, 77g, 58a; 3 1st team all-star; 1 Lady Byng, 2 Dodge Ram, 1 Hart, 1 Pearson, 1 ProSet Player of year awards; played 7 NHL all-star games; *Hockey News* minor league player of yr award; scored '99 Stanley Cup final winner in 3rd overtime of game 6 vs. Buffalo; mem. Team USA '86 Worlds; mem. Team USA '98 Olympics; res. Duluth, Minn.

HULL, Dennis (hockey); b. 19 Nov 1944, Pointe Anne, Ont.; given name: Dennis William; m. Mary Sue; c. Martha, John; Brock, BA; retd. athletic dir. Illinois Institute of Technology; jr. St. Catharines; left wing Chicago '64-77, Detroit '77-78; Team Canada '72; NHL record: 959 scheduled games, 303 goals, 351 assists, 104 playoff games, 33 goals, 34 assists; 2nd team all-star '73; 1 40-goal, 3 30-goal seasons; noted raconteur; res. Welland, Ont.

HUMBER, Bruce (t&f); b. 11 Oct 1913, Victoria, B.C.; d. 18 Aug 1988, Vancouver, B.C.; m. Anne Barry; c. Richard, Lezlie Anne; Washington, BA; sales manager; all-time Seattle prep school records of 9.9, 21.8 in 100, 220yds; at university ran 9.6 and 20.8; mem. 4th place Cdn. Olympic relay team '36; coach '50 BEG track team, '52 Olympic team; mem. Washington, BC Sports halls of fame.

HUME, Fred (lacrosse/hockey/soccer); b. 2 May 1892, Sapperton, B.C.; d. 17 Feb 1967, Vancouver, B.C.; given name: Frederick; player, later pres. New Westminster Salmonbellies; pres. 3-time ntl champion New Westminster Royals soccer team; helped form Western Hockey League; owned, operated New Westminster Royals, later Vancouver Canucks in WHL; major role in bringing BEG to Vancouver '54; mem. BC Sports, Hockey, Lacrosse halls of fame.

HUME, Ian (t&f); b. 20 Aug 1914, Foster, Que.; given name: Ian Knowlton; m. Melita Jean Fraser; c. Edward, Margaret, Heather, Laurel, Vicki; Bishop's; BA; Macdonald College; retired teacher; 1st t&f gold medal '29; competed prov., ntl level 4 jumping events, 110m high hurdles, javelin, relay through '55; numerous Cdn sr. HJ, javelin titles; mem. '54 BE&C Games team; mem. prov. finalists baseball team '40s, prov. Sr. B titlist; 8 gold, 8 silver, 4 bronze world Masters t&f competitions '75-81; world record for 65-69 age group in HJ, pentathlon, decathlon, TJ; t&f coach from '37; coach '66, mgr. '70, referee '78 Commonwealth Games; field coach '59 Pan-Am Games; pres. CTFA '68-71; former mem. COA, rep. several IAAF Congresses; mem. IAAF Comm. for women's athletics from '72; technical official field events from '42; developed new procedures for '76 Olympic decathlon; pres. FAQ, Que. Basketball Assoc.; chair. tech. comm. World Veterans Assoc.; various offical capacities '76 Olympics, '78 Commonwealth, '79 World Cup, '79 Russia-US.-Canada meet, '80 Pan-Am jr. championships; Lt. Gov. Medal for French specialists studies '40; mem. Order of Canada, Bishop's Wall, Cdn Amateur Sports Hall of Fame; res. Melbourne, Que.

HUMPHRY, Jay (figure skating); b. 28 Jul 1948, Vancouver, B.C.; m. Cheryl Frost; v-p operations & bookings VEE Corp.; ntl jr. men's singles title '63; sr. men's '68-69; world competitor '65-69; silver '69 NA; 7th '68 Olympics; 7yrs Ice Follies; operated NY Babes in Toyland 1yr; mgr. Sesame St. road show 10yrs; res. Ham Lake, Minn.

HUNGERFORD, George (rowing); b. 2 Jan 1944, Vancouver, B.C.; given name: George William; m. Jane Knott; c. Geordie, Michael, Andrew, Jane; UBC, BA, LLB; lawyer; with Roger Jackson coxless pairs gold '64 Olympics; Lou Marsh Trophy winner with Jackson '64; dir., v-p Olympic Club Canada; trustee, pres-chair. BC Sports Hall of Fame; mem. Vancouver Athletic Commission; mem. COA Pan-Am Games comm.; BC Jr. athlete of '64; gov. Olympic Trust; Officer Order of Canada; mem. Cdn Amateur, Canada's, BC Sports halls of fame; res. Vancouver, B.C.

HUNT, Claudia (canoeing); b. 12 Mar 1950, Montreal, Que.; m. Sebastian Cardarelli; UofOtt, BSc, MSc; flat water kayak specialist; mem. ntl team '66-75; mem. '67 Pan-Am, '68, '72 Olympic teams; ntl K1 title '69-70, K4 '68-69, '73-75; NA K4 title '70; res. Navan, Ont.

HUNT, Helen (volleyball/swimming); b. 28 Dec 1938, Vancouver, B.C.; given name: Helen Stewart; m. Ted Hunt; c. Shelley; UBC, BEd, MEd; teacher; silver '54 Commonwealth Games, 4x100 medley relay; 100m freestyle gold, 2 relay silver '55, silver 4x100 FS relay '59 Pan-Am Games; competed '56 Olympics; held world 100yd FS record 3 weeks '56; Canada's outstanding female swimmer '55-56; BC athlete of '55; mem. ntl women's volleyball team '67-73, BC ntl championship team '64-74, '77; mem. '67, '71 Pan-Am Games teams; mem. Cdn Aquatic, BC Sports halls of fame; res. Vancouver, B.C.

HUNT, Lynda Adams (diving); b. 4 Jun 1920, Vancouver, B.C.; d. 26 Feb 1997, Halfmoon Bay, B.C.; m. Harold Hunt (d); c. Brian; Western Washington Coll.; at 14 youngest performer '34 BEG; overcame acrophobia (fear of heights) to excel in tower, springboard diving events; mem. '36 Olympic, '34, '38, '50 BEG teams; 2 silver '38, springboard bronze '50; ntl high tower titles '34, '39; coach Vancouver Amateur SC 20yrs, UBCSC 5yrs; judge '54, chaperone '58 BEG; exec. mem. Cdn Diving Assn.; mem. BC Sports Hall of Fame.

HUNT, Ted (all-around); b. 15 Mar 1933, Vancouver, B.C.; given name: Edmund Arthur; m. Helen Stewart; c. Shelly; UBC, BPhE, MPhE, EdD, Washington, MA; school administrator; capt. BC in rugby victories over Australia '58, Japan '61; mem. British Lions '67 McKechnie Trophy winner; mem. Burrards Mann Cup lacrosse team '61, '64; BC Lions' halfback '57-58; Lions' rookie of '57, candidate for CFL top Canadian award '58; mem. '52 Olympic ski jumping team, '54 FIS team, 8th '54 Swedish ntl championships; UBC light heavyweight boxing title 4yrs; BC athlete of '57; Bob Gaul Memorial Award '58; Howie McPhee Memorial Award '61; mem. BC Sports Hall of Fame; res. Vancouver, B.C.

HUNTER, Dale (hockey); b. 31 Jul 1960, Petrolia, Ont.; m. Karynka; c. Dylan, Shalen, Tucker; hockey exec.; lw/ctr Kitchener, Sudbury (OHA) '77-80, drafted by Quebec '79; NHL with Quebec '80-87, Washington '87-99, Colorado '99; Washington team capt. '94-99; only player in NHL history to log 300g, 3000pim; reached 1000 point plateau '98; NHL record: 1407 scheduled games, 323g, 697a, 186 playoff games, 42g, 76a; played in 1 NHL all-star game; joined Washington front office '99; res. Annapolis, Md./ Petrolia, Ont.

HUNTER, Gord (orienteering); b. 20 Jan 1946, Montreal, Que.; div. Anne Marie Cartile; c. Dierdre, Philip; Dalhousie, BA; teacher, politician; mem. '70 Ottawa Sooners (Sr. ORFU); Ottawa Indians rugby team '69-73, '79-81; orienteering competitor from '70; Ont. elite title '75, Que. '76, ntl '72-74; twice 2nd, once 3rd NA championships; 8 Ntl titles, 3 elite, 3 masters (35-40), 2 masters (40-45); represented Canada 6 world championships; gold (45-49) '94, gold, silver (50-54) '98, bronze men's 40-54 golf '98 World Masters Games; editor Orienteering Canada '76-80; dir. COF from '77; mem. international Orienteering Federation Council '80; mem. Nepean Wall of Fame; res. Nepean, Ont.

HUNTER, Jim (skiing); b. 30 May 1953, Shaunavon, Sask.; given name: James Mark; m. Gail Jespersen; c. Anna, Heidi, Maria, Gail, Sterling; motivational speaker; nicknamed "Jungle Jim"; mem. ntl team '70-77; mem. '72, '76 Olympic teams, bronze combined '72; 6 ntl GS titles; US GS title '72; WC record 0-1-1; pro circuit '77-81; 3rd in world pro ranks '77-78, 4th '78-79; author, film script writer; subject of NFB film "The Sword of the Lord;" with Marshall Shelley wrote *Man Against the Mountain*"; TV color commentator '84 Winter Olympics; mem. Cdn, US Ski halls of fame; res. Calgary, Alta.

HUNTER, Malcolm (skiing); b. 23 May 1950, London, Eng.; given name: Malcolm Wesley; m. Theo Palmer; c. Shawn, Chelsea; Carleton, BA; chartered accountant; sports exec.; cross-country specialist; ntl jr. title '68; sr. 15km '69-

70, 30km '71; mem. '70 world Nordic ski championships, '72 Olympic teams; dir. Ont. ski council '84; coach Ont., NWT '73-76; chair. Ont. Cross-Country '90-95; exec. dir. Cross-Country Canada '84-90, from '95; Ont. Special Achievement award; res. Manotick, Ont.

HUNTER, Rod (curling); b. 24 Aug 1943, Norwich, N.Y.; given name: Roderick George McLean; m. Patricia Gail Karman; c. Onalee, Charlene; UWpg, BSc; corporate secretary; 3rd for Don Duguid '70-71 Man. Consols, Brier, Silver Broom title rink; 3rd on '73, skip '75 Man. Brier entry; CBC-TV curling series winner '70-72, runnerup '76; '70 Heather carspiel, International Crystal Trophy Zurich, Switzerland; Man. bonspiel grand aggregate '70, '75; Man. Open '78; 4 times Man. bonspiel Birks Trophy winner; mem. Man. Sports, Canadian Curling Hall of Fame; res. Winnipeg, Man.

HUNTLEY, Gordon (horse racing); b. 6 Nov 1919, Queensville, Ont.; d. 25 Jul 1998, Toronto, Ont.; m. Phyllis; c. Lynn; horse trainer; became interested in horses '44 moving to California to hone his skills; returned to Toronto late '40s and went on to carve an enviable career as one of the nation's top thoroughbred trainers over 6 generations; working at tracks around NA produced more than 1000 race winners including Ramblin Road which dominated Ont. racing scene '63-64 winning Grey, Vandal, Bison City, Seaway Stakes and Silver Ship winner of Victoria, Bison City, Friar Rock, Queenston Stakes during '50s; mem. Cdn Horse Racing Hall of Fame.

HUOT, Jean-Pierre (shooting); b. 21 Oct 1951, Thetford-Mines, Que.; m. Johanne Beaulieu; c. Stephanie, Cyndia, Amèlie; Thetford-Mines Coll, BA (psychology); florist; handgun specialist; shot recreationally several years before going competitive at 35; mem. ntl team '85-99; 3 ntl free pistol, 5 ntl men's air pistol, 3 Crossman ntl indoor titles; competed 5 world championships, 15 World Cups, 2 Championship of Americas; air pistol gold, air pistol pairs (with John Rochon) silver '94, 2 bronze '98 Commonwealth Games; free team gold '91, team air bronze '95 Pan-Am Games; ntl air pistol record 581; Que. Shooting Fed. athlete of '95; special ambassador Thetford-Mines 100th anniversary; res. Pontbriand, Que.

HUOT, Jules (golf); b. 7 Jan 1908, Boischatel, Que.; d 2 Feb 1999, Montreal, Que.; m. Simone Bolduc; c. Louise, Jeannine, Lucie, Robert; 1st Canadian to win USPGA sanctioned tournament '37 General Brock Open Fonthill, Ont.; among Canada's premier tournament golfers '30s-50s; 3 CPGA titles, 4 times runnerup; 5 QPGA, 3 Que. Open titles; twice top Canadian Cdn. Open; played inaugural Masters Tournament, 2 others; mem. 4 ntl Hopkins Cup teams; club pro Lake St. Joseph, Kent, Laval sur le Lac clubs; pres. CPGA '39, '46; pres. QPGA '67-68; wrote book "*Le Golf*"; mem. RCGA, Canada's Sports halls of fame.

HURD, Alex (speed skating); b. 21 Jul 1910, Montreal, Que.; d. 28 May 1982, Tampa, Fla.; m. Maxine Lieberstein (d); c. Alexis, Pamela; business exec.; Ont. title '26; ntl 1 mile outdoor titles '29-30; NA 5 mile titles '30-31, 3 indoor titles; world record 10,000m. silver 1500m, bronze 500m '32 Olympics; mid-Atlantic Joseph Donaghue 3 mile trophy

'33; 2 St. Louis silver skate titles; international outdoor title '34; world indoor 2 mile record '35; world 500m backwards race record 55.3; pro International Ice Follies '38-40, NY Radio City Music Hall ice show '41-43; mem. Canadian Speed Skating Hall of Fame.

HURDIS, John (speed skating); b. 27 Apr 1927, Birmingham, Eng.; m. Mary Kathleen Powell; c. Lynda, Janette, John; retd. asst. dir. professional development services; club skater '43 Eng., South Africa '47; secty. National Ice Racing League of National Skating Assn. of Great Britain; GBNSA judge '49-50; instrumental in formation Grenadier Toronto, Sertoma Kitchener clubs; sec.-tres. Ont. Amateur Speed Skating Assn. '61-64; v-p Cdn. Amateur Speed Skating Assn. '62-64, exec.-sec. '64-67, pres. '64-69, '72-76, dir. '69-70, '72-78, '80-82; co-ordinator several Cdn indoor, outdoor title meets, Barrie Winter Carnival '60-65; mem. COA '72-78, governor National Sports, Recreation Centre '74-76, Sports Ont. dir. '69-71; major role in upgrading, organizing sport; mem. ISU short track tech. comm. '77-80, chair. '80-84; editor *The Racer*, Canada's official speed skating publication; editor Ont. Skater's Edge journal; author variety of articles, books on speed skating; Centennial Medal '67, Queen's Silver Jubilee Medal '78; life mem. Birmingham Ice Racing Club, US amateur Skating Union; hon. mem. ISU; historian, chair. CASSA Hall of Fame committee '79-82; managing editor, production mgr. *The Short Trackers*, international short track speed skating newspaper; mem. Cdn Amateur Speed Skating Hall of Fame; res. Mississauga, Ont.

HUSER, Cathy (skiing); b. 7 May 1963, Trail, B.C.; given name: Catherine Helen; HS 3-mile road race title '79-80; volleyball all-star West Kootenay '80; ntl jr. ski champ '79; 2nd overall ntl championships '80; 2nd '81 Pontiac Cup, 2 downhill victories; mem. ntl ski team '81; HS athlete of '78; res. Salmo, B.C.

HUSHAGEN, Earle (curling); b. 27 Jan 1928, Lampman, Sask.; given name: Donald Earle; m. Wyn Elliott; c. Sandra, Christine, Signe; retd. mgr. Humber Highland CC; 2nd Andy Grant's Ont. Brier entry '55; skipped Ont. entry ntl mixed '67, '70, Ont. entry ntl srs '84, '86; ntl srs. title '86; 2 Ont. Masters titles; major bonspiel titles include Toronto Royals, Whitby, Canada Life; active in administration OCA; hon. life mem. OCA; res. Peterborough, Ont.

HUSHAGEN, Sandra (curling); b. 15 Jul 1953, Toronto, Ont.; m. Randy Baker; c. Eric; Guelph, Wilfrid Laurier, MBA; mgr. business dev. London Health Sciences Centre; gained early repute in track as hurdler; 2nd 100m hurdles Eastern Cdn championships '72; competed Ont dressage championships '81-82; skipped Ont. Jr. women's title rinks '72-73; Ont. business women's SOLCA title rink '82; competed at provincial level in women's, mixed events; made Ont. curling history as first female skip at provincial mixed championships '86, placed 3rd; skipped rink '90 Ont. STOH championships; renewed interest in equestrian sport '97; res. Sparta, Ont.

HUTCHISON, Jim (speedboat racing); b. 10 May 1909, England; d. 1 Jan 1995, Vancouver, B.C.; given name: James Hay; amassed enviable competitive record over 2 decades;

racing his Teasers, broke every record, regularly out-performing European, US rivals '46-64; set 3 Cdn 1-mile class records '52-54; 1st Cdn to design, build, race 3-point hydroplane; instrumental in popularizing hydroplane racing in BC; won 4 consecutive Pacific Northwest Gold Cups, '55 Challenge Cup, Western Canada high point awards '55-56; retired from competition '64 but continued to design/build hydroplanes; designed, built legendary "War Canoe" which won '70 US ntl power boat title; mem. BC Sports Hall of Fame.

HUTCHISON, Patti (basketball); b. 11 Oct 1958, Lockeport, N.S.; given name: Patti Lynne Langille; m. Archibald Hutchison; c. Wendy Elaine; Acadia, Dalhousie, BPhE, Public Administration; Miss Murphy's Business Coll, hons medical secty. diploma; Sports History dev. co-ordinator NS Sport Hall of Fame & Museum; 2 NS AA HS basketball, soccer titles; 3 Lockeport HS female athlete of yr awards; 2 AUAA all-conf. all-star; Acadia basketball MVP '77; capt. NS Canada Games bronze medal team; CIAU silver with Dalhousie; capt. NS Red Fox ntl women's title team '81; played sr. women's basketball '81-96; mem. Dalhousie women's team '96-97 setting 3 AUAA records; mem. 9 NS touch football title teams; 4 MVP awards; 2 Sport NS football player of yr awards; mem. NS jr. field hockey teams '73-75, NS sr. team at ntls '76, NS masters at ntls '97; played HS softball '73-76, NS champions '74-75; Amherst NS slow pitch title team '94; res. Halifax, N.S.

HUTTON, Bouse (hockey/football/lacrosse); b. 24 Oct. 1877, Ottawa, Ont.; d. 27 Oct 1962, Ottawa, Ont.; given name: John Bower; goaltender hockey, lacrosse, fullback football; mem. 3 ntl title teams '07 (Minto Cup, Grey Cup, Stanley Cup); lacrosse Ottawa Capitals, won Minto Cup, toured Eng.; fullback Rough Riders, goaltender Silver Seven; Ottawa int. hockey champions 1898-99; Silver Seven 6 seasons posting 2.90 goals-against avg. in 36 games; registered league's only 2 shutouts '01-02 season; allowed 28 goals 12 playoff games; helped Silver Seven win 2 Stanley Cups; coach jr., sr. hockey Ottawa several years; mem. Ottawa Sports, Hockey halls of fame.

HUTTON, Ralph (swimming); b. 6 Mar 1948, Ocean Falls, B.C.; div. Karen Morison; c. Kyle, Courtney; m. Robin Russell; Colorado State, Foothills College; policeman; nicknamed "Iron Man"; freestyle, backstroke specialist; 11 ntl records, world mark 4:06.5 700m FS; mem. '64, '68, '72 Olympic, '63, '67, '71 Pan-Am, '66, '70 Commonwealth Games teams; won medals in all but '64, '72 Olympics, record 12 Commonwealth Games medals; best showing '66 Commonwealth Games 1 gold, 5 silver, 2 bronze; '67 Pan-Am Games 1 gold, 5 silver; silver 400m FS '68 Olympics; mem. '72 Olympic 800m FS relay team which placed 6th, Cdn record; mem. International, BC Swimming, Cdn Aquatic, Cdn Amateur, BC, Canada's Sports halls of fame; res. Lion's Bay, B.C.

HY, Patricia (tennis); b. 22 Aug 1965, Phnom Penh, Kampuchea; m. Yves Boulais; Bradenton Academy, UCLA; all-American; began playing age 8; mem. Hong Kong Federation Cup team '81-82, '85, '87; ranked #1 Hong Kong '87-88, Canada '92-96; best WTA ranking 28th '93; Cdn citizen from '91; ended Helen Kelesi's 4yr Cdn title reign

'91; 4 Tennis Canada female player of yr awards, comeback player of '91; mem. Cdn Fed. Cup team from '91; led Canada to Fed. Cup victory over Italy '95; recorded victories over Jennifer Capriati, Helena Sukova, Jana Novotna, Magdalena Makeeva, Katerina Maleeva, Helen Kelesi; Wimbledon jr. doubles title (with Patty Fendick) '83; 4 ntl singles titles; mem. WTA Special Olympics comm.; mem. '92, '96 Olympic teams; res. Richmond Hill, Ont./Hilton Head, S.C.

HYLAND, Bruce (figure skating/coaching); b. 7 Jun 1926, Toronto, Ont.; given name: Bruce Leonard; m. Margaret Wilson Roberts; c. Jacquelyn, Douglas, Michael; coach, rink owner; competitive swimmer; roller skating champion; with partners Margaret Roberts, Joyce Perkins won ntl sr. ice dance, 2nd in pairs; produced numerous roller, ice skating shows; weekly Hyland and Sports TV show in Toronto; introduced power skating for hockey players at Tam O'Shanter hockey school; started Professional Skating Assn. of Canada with Sheldon Galbraith, Helmut May, Osborne Coulson; coached Cdn skaters like Maria/Otto Jelinek, Debbi Wilkes/Guy Revell to Olympic/world honors 18yrs; broadcast international skating competitions for Cdn radio; joined Ice Capades organization San Diego as coach '77; remained 7yrs before purchasing rink in Clearwater, Fla. where he and his wife teach skating; mem. Cdn Figure Skating Hall of Fame; res. Clearwater, Fla.

HYLAND, Harry (hockey); b. 2 Jan 1889, Montreal, Que.; d. 8 Aug 1969, Montreal, Que.; early hockey Montreal Gaelics, St. Ann's, Shamrocks; pro with latter '08-09 although still jr. age; scored twice 1st pro game; joined Wanderers in time to play rw on Stanley Cup winner; New Westminster (PCHL) '11-12 16 goals 12 games as team won league title; rejoined Wanderers '13 scoring 8 goals in game vs Que. 28 for season; joined Ottawa '18; mem. Hockey Hall of Fame.

HYLAND, Margaret (figure skating/coaching); b. 21 Mar 1923, Toronto; given name: Margaret Wilson Roberts; m. Bruce Leonard Hyland; c. Jacquelyn, Douglas, Michael; coach, rink owner; with Peter Killam runnerup ntl jr. pairs; with Bruce Hyland runnerup ntl sr. pairs, won ntl sr. ice dance '47; over 18yr span coached the likes of Maria/Otto Jelinek, Debbi Wilkes/Guy Revell and numerous other skaters to world/Olympic honors; joined Ice Capades in San Diego as coach 7yrs before purchasing rink in Clearwater; with husband Bruce mem. Cdn Figure Skating Hall of Fame; res. Clearwater, Fla.

HYNDUIK, Ollie (bowling); b. 8 Nov 1928, Winnipeg, Man.; as teenager gained prominence as CUAC senior women's softball catcher; switched attention to 5-pin bowling; won ntl women's singles crowns '55, '58; from '54-64 won 5 City of Winnipeg women's singles titles; '53-62 held top women's average 8 seasons capped by 256 avg '58-59; rolled perfect 450 game '52; coached Winnipeg to world women's team title '73; 10yrs head bowling pro Winnipeg Winter Club; Man. Order of Buffalo award '73; mem. Man. 5-Pin, Man. Sports halls of fame; res. Dundas, Ont.

I

IACOVELLI, Orlando (wrestling); b. 7 Dec 1939, Ithaca, N.Y.; m. Helen Okros; c. Sheila, David; Ithaca Coll. BSc, MSc, Iowa State; self-employed/landlord; asst. coach Ithaca HS '87-88, head coach '88-91; supervisor men's intercollegiate athletics, wrestling coach '65-86 Guelph; asst. football coach Guelph; coached Guelph to 12 OUAA wrestling titles; dir. Ont. Wrestling School '71-82, 3 ntl titles; ntl team coach 4 world championships, '76 Olympics; v-p CAWA '72-74, acting pres. '72-73; meet dir. 2 CIAU X-Country championships; instituted ntl wrestling coaches clinics; mem. OAWF '68-72; 2 OUAA coach of yr, ntl wrestling title '69; CIAU coach of '76; wrestling all-American '64; mem. Ithaca Coll, Guelph, Cdn Amateur Wrestling, NY State Section IV Athletic halls of fame; res. Ithaca, N.Y.

IGOROV, Metodi (shooting); b. 11 Mar 1959, Sofia, Bulgaria; m. Kamelia Igorova; c. Christina; Quebec BSc, Coll. Edouard Montpetit; rapid fire pistol specialist; 3 Bulgarian, 1 Balkans Games, 1 French Cup, 7 Quebec, 3 Cdn championships; 2 Cap-de-la-Madeleine grand aggregate titles; 1 Bouche-du-Rhône, 1 Côte d'Azur France titles; set Cdn record '96; won gold medal and set rapid fire record '98 Commonwealth Games; also added CG silver in centrefire pairs with John Rochon; res. St. Laurent, Que.

IKEDA, Richard (gymnastics): b. 26 Nov 1974, Kamloops, B.C.; Fraser Valley Coll.; began competing age 9; both parents were ntl level gymnasts; all-around competitor; competed '96 Olympics, '91, '95 Pan-Am, '94, '98 Commonwealth; '93 FISU Games, '93 Worlds, '93 world gymnastics challenge; 1 ntl jr, 4 ntl sr titles; 1 gold, 1 silver, 2 bronze '94, 2 silver, 1 bronze '98 Commonwealth Games; 2 bronze '95 Pan-Am Games; Gymnastics Fed. athlete of '93; father Mits ntl team coach; res. Abbotsford, B.C.

ILESIC, Hank (football); b. 17 Sep 1959, Edmonton, Alta.; given name: Henry; m. Jeri Fedunec; advertising/printing business; punter Eskimos while still high school student '77-81, Argos '82-93; Ti-Cats '95; signed by San Diego, Los Angeles (NFL) '90 but released before playing any league games; 8 all-CFL, 4 all-WFC, 4 all-EFC; 6 CFL punting average titles; 9 Grey Cup finals, 7 winners; CFL record 9 singles on kickoffs, Argos team scoring record 159 points '84; 22 Argos records; CFL record: 256g, 98cvts, 59fg, 183s, 2049 punts, 91,753yds, 44.8 avg; res. Islington, Ont.

IMLACH, Punch (hockey); b. 15 Mar 1918, Toronto, Ont.; d. 1 Dec 1987, Toronto, Ont.; given name: George; m. Dorothy; c. Brent, Marlene; hockey executive; Young Rangers Jrs, Toronto Marlboros, Toronto Goodyears srs.; earned name "Punch" with Goodyears when he was knocked out in a game and swung punches at his team trainer; led army team scorers 1 season as centre; brief trial Detroit (NHL) following WW2; 11yrs player, coach, mgr., eventually part-owner, Que. Aces; joined Bruins organization 1yr mgr.-coach Springfield Indians; mgr.-coach Maple Leafs '58-69, 4 Stanley Cups; sports columnist 5

seasons *Toronto Telegram, Toronto Sun*; coach/ GM Buffalo '70-78; GM Toronto '80-81; mem. Hockey Hall of Fame.

INGARFIELD, Earl (hockey); b. 25 Oct 1934, Lethbridge, Alta; given name: Earl Thompson; m. Grace Nelson; c. Rae-Ann, Jean Marie, Earl Jr.; hockey scout; centre Lethbridge jrs; NHL NY Rangers '58-67, Pittsburgh '67-68, Oakland '68-70, California '70-71; NHL record: 746 scheduled games, 179g, 226a, 21 playoff games, 9g, 8a; coached Regina Pats Jr. 1yr; interim coach NY Islanders '72-73 (record: 30 games, 6-22-2); owner/AGM/coach Lethbridge Broncos 3yrs; Western scout Islanders '72-75, from '82; res. Lethbridge, Alta.

INNES, Cam (coaching); b. 30 Sep 1946, Windsor, Ont.; given name: William Campbell; m. Lynda Quinton; c. James; Queen's, BA, BPHE, Windsor, MPhE, UWO, MBA; dir. people management RLG International; twice OUAA all-conf. center, once all-Cdn; 1st round draft Edmonton Eskimos; 5 seasons, 4 head coach, St.FX, head coach UofOtt '78-81; asst. coach UWO '82-83, 2 conference titlist, 1 OQIFC, Atlantic Bowl champion, 1 College Bowl finalist; Atlantic Conference coach of '77, OQIFC coach of '79-80, CIAU coach of '80; mem. CFL-CIAU liaison comm.; mem. CAFA rules comm.; pres. CIAU Football Coaches Assn. '81-82; ex-marketing dir.UCal; Churchill Bowl chair. '95; res. Burnaby, B.C.

INNES, Marjorie (sailing); b. 11 Jan 1947, Hamilton, Ont.; given name: Marjorie Newton; m. Derek Innes; c. Greg, Sandra; UWO, BPHE, Queen's Teachers College, Fanshawe College; respiratory therapist; lone women competing in male field won 4 ntl Hobie Cat titles; 1st woman to qualify for Hobie Cat world championships '75; also competed '79, '81, '86 worlds placing 3rd in field of 36 in '81; with son Greg, Sue Slocum won 3 consecutive ntl Dart 18 catamaran titles; won 3 solo Dart 18 titles; crewed for husband Derek for '95 ntl Dart title; athlete of yr honors in both public/ high school, competing in badminton, curling, tennis; taught phys ed '66-69 Dorchester HS; res. London, Ont.

INNIS, Jessie (basketball); b. 16 Jan 1911, Edmonton, Alta.; d. Aug 1987, Edmonton, Alta.; m. Edward Maloney (d); c. William Edward; stenographer; mem. Edmonton Gradettes, famed Edmonton Grads '32-35; prov. runnerup silver div. golf; mem. Toddies baseball team; Calgary league bowler; mem. Canadian Basketball, Alta. Sports halls of fame.

ION, Mickey (hockey/lacrosse); b. 25 Feb 1886, Paris, Ont.; d. 26 Oct 1964, Seattle, Wash.; given name: Frederick; standout lacrosse, baseball player in youth; pro lacrosse Toronto Tecumsehs, Vancouver, New Westminster; refereed amateur hockey, attracted attention of Frank Patrick who moved him into pro ranks '13; top official Pacific Coast League, NHL; refereed Howie Morenz Memorial game Montreal Forum '37; retired '41; mem. Hockey Hall of Fame.

IRELAND, Sean (speed skating): b. 14 Nov 1969, Mississauga, Ont.; UCal; coach; began skating age 8; mem. ntl team '88-94; competed '92, '94 Olympics; 2 ntl jr. records; 3 ntl. jr. long track titles; 1 sr long track, 2 sprint titles; mem. ntl team coaching staff; res. Calgary, Alta.

IRVIN, Dick Sr. (hockey/coaching): b. 19 Jul 1892, Limestone Ridge, Ont.; d. 16 May 1957, Montreal, Que.; given name: James Dickenson; m. Bertha Helen Bain; c. Dick Jr., Fay; Winnipeg Strathcona jrs., int. Monarchs; scored all 9 goals vs. Toronto in 9-1 Winnipeg victory, won 5 Man. scoring titles; mem. '15 Allan Cup winner; pro Portland Rosebuds (PCHL) '15-16; reinstated amateur Regina Vics after WW1; turned pro again Regina Caps (WCHL), Portland; when club became Chicago Black Hawks '26 went with them at age 34; in initial NHL season finished point behind Rangers' Bill Cook in scoring race; retired as player after skull fracture '27 season; coach Chicago '30-31; Toronto '32-40, Montreal '41-55; coaching innovator, 1st to rotate 3 intact lines, employ goalie shuttle system; coach 4 Stanley Cup winners; mem. Man., Cdn Hockey halls of fame.

IRVING, Wendy (equestrian): b. 11 Nov 1951, Ottawa, Ont,; m. George Dell; riding instructor; 3-day team event specialist; team gold '71 Pan-Am Games, 44th of 75 competitors '72 Olympics; res. Queensville, Ont.

IRWIN, Al (football): b. 16 Mar 1943, Toronto, Ont.; given name: Alan Lyness; div.; c. Thomas Alan, Jane Anne; McMaster, BA, UAlta, LLB; lawyer, real estate developer; mem. Richview CI TDIAA football titlist, Ont. t&f champions; football, varsity basketball McMaster; pro football 1st draft choice Alouettes, EFC rookie of '64; Toronto '66-68, Edmonton '69, Hamilton '70; end, defensive back; scoring leader Toronto touch football champions '76; res. Willowdale, Ont.

IRWIN, Art (baseball): b. 14 Feb 1858, Toronto, Ont.; d. 16 Jul 1921, Atlantic Ocean,; given name: Arthur Albert; married; simultaneously had wives in Boston, New York, a fact revealed following his mysterious drowning death; shortstop Aetna 1873-74, Amateurs of Boston 1875-79; pro Worcester 1880-82, Providence 1883-85, Philadelphia 1886-89, 1894, Washington 1889, Boston 1890-91; 1010 ML games, .241 lifetime avg.; shortstop 1st "World Series" between Providence and New York Metropolitans 1884; playing mgr. Washington 1889, Boston 1891, Philadelphia 1894; non-playing mgr. Washington 1892, 1898-99, Philadelphia 1895, NY 1896; ML mgr. record: 416-47; inventor of infielder's glove 1885; soccer team mgr. 1894; owner Toronto IL team; scout Highlanders '08-12; brother John also played inf/of in majors; nicknamed "Doc, Sandy, Cut Rate".

IRWIN, Bert (skiing): b. 1 Oct 1917, Princeton, B.C.; given name: Albert Keith; m. Leila Margaret; c. Bert, Marsha, Tom; ret. realtor; during '30s, '40s Class A competitor jumping, cross-country, downhill, slalom; Western Cdn., Pacific Northwestern downhill, slalom titles; '47 Que. Kandahar, Cdn slalom; mem. '48 Olympic ski team; coach '50 women's World Cup team; awarded DFC WW2; res. Kelowna, B.C.

IRWIN, Cathy Lee (figure skating): b. 4 Sep 1952, Vancouver B.C.; m. Jacobs; Seneca College; figure skating teacher; ntl jr. singles '66; gold '67 Que. Winter Games; ladies' singles St.Gervais, France, Grand Prix '70; mem. '72 Olympic team; '72 Moscow Skate; competed '73 world pro with Holiday on Ice; Centennial medal '67; res. Toronto, Ont.

IRWIN, Dave (skiing): b. 12 Jul 1954, Thunder Bay, Ont.; SFU; pres/owner Mountain Image Distributors; ntl team '71-80; World Cup downhill victory Dec. '75 Schladming, Austria; 8th '76, 11th '80 Olympics; US ntl title '80; WC record 1-0-1; Thunder Bay athlete of '73, '75; Ont. athlete of '75; runnerup Cdn athlete of '75; flag-bearer '76 winter Olympics; certified Level 4 CSIA, Level 3 CSCF coach; dir. Masters ski camps; competed Golden Gate Productions ski events '97; dir. Fels Cdn Ski Co.; mem. Cdn Skiing Hall of Fame; res. Vernon, B.C.

ISBISTER, Robert Jr. (football): b. 27 Oct 1914, Hamilton, Ont.; d. 19 Aug 1971, Hamilton, Ont.; m. Hazel Kroeber; c. Betty, Janet, Susan; UofT; noted for booming punts as kicking backfielder Delta CI, Toronto Varsity; mem. Argos '37-38; Eastern all-star '38; punted for 1167yds vs Ottawa 27 Nov '37, averaging 55.6 yds per punt.

ISBISTER, Robert Sr. (football): b. 9 Jun 1885, Hamilton, Ont.; d. 29 Apr 1963, Hamilton, Ont.; m. Madlan Grace Darling (d); c. Robert Jr. (d), Allan (d), Phillip, Donald; flying wing, various line positions Hamilton Tigers '05-19; cited for all-around ability '19; refereed intercollegiate ranks several years; pres. Big 4 '20; mem. Hamilton club board of governors '33; mem. Canada's Sports, Canadian Football halls of fame.

ISHOY, Mark (equestrian): b. 1 Apr 1955, Toronto, Ont.; m. Penny Tulk; c. Claire, Matthew; Guelph, hons. BSc; CEO MGI Packers, partner Maple Freezers, Banner Rendering; gained riding experience foxhunting in Caledon Hills; began showing horses at 18; mem. gold medal team FISU Games, NA jr. 3-day title team '75; open int. 3-day Eastern Canada title '77; Cdn international 3-day title, gold world 3-day '78; capt. 3-day event team '80 Olympics; coached Alta to NA young riders title '88; mem. Cdn Equestrian Team selection comm. '86-92; chair. 3-day event team '92-94; recipient '79 Dick Ellis Memorial Trophy; brother equestrian Neil Ishoy; res. Rockwood, Ont.

ISSAJENKO, Angella (t&f): b. 28 Sep 1958, Jamaica; m. Tony Issajenko; c. Sacha, Natasha, Dimitri, Sophia; York; fitness trainer; mem. Scarborough Optimists TC; sprint specialist; '79 ntl 100m, 200m outdoor champion; Colgate Games meet record 400m (52.20) '80; 5th 100m, 200m WC '79, 4th '81; 12 ntl sr. records with best 100m (11.00), 200m (22.19), 4x100m relay (43.01); Cdn open 50m (6.18); silver 200m, bronze 100m '79 Pan-Am Games; gold 100m, 4x400m relay, silver 4x100m relay, bronze 200m '82, gold 200, silver 4x100, bronze 100 '86 Commonwealth Games; silver 4x100 relay '84 Olympics; mem. '78 Commonwealth, '80, '84, '88 Olympic, '83 Pan-Am Games teams; ntl outdoor 100m, 200m champion '79-82, 100 '88; indoor 50m '80-81, 200m '83; Ont. athlete of '80; SFC female athlete of year; CIAU female athlete of '81; 2 CIAU indoor records;

outstanding female athlete '82 ntl sr. championships; 2 Velma Springstead trophies; Ont., fed. govt. excellence awards '83; mem. Order of Canada; res. Toronto, Ont.

IUS, Chris (boxing); b. 14 Jan 1954, Vancouver, B.C.; given name: Christopher Anthony; m. Patricia Scanlon; c. Natalie; carpenter; competitive boxer '61-76 at weights from 50lb-119lb; Emerald Gloves titles '62-66, '68-70; Wash. State Jr. Golden Gloves title '65; BC Tournament of champions titles '67, '69; Pacific Northwestern title '67; Pacific Coast Jr. title '69; Western Cdn jr. titles '67, '70; Silver Gloves champion '68-69; national sr. titles '70-73, '76; BC '71, Vancouver '72, Tacoma '71, Portland '76 Golden Gloves titles; BC Winter Games title '71; BC senior titles '71-72; Western Cdn. titles '71, '75-76; silver '71 NA championships; bronze '71 Scandanavian Tour; silver '72 Holland International; silver '73 European championships; silver '75 AAU Internationals; mem. '72 ,'76 Olympic teams; Emerald Award '68-70; Jimmy Syme Memorial Award '70-72; North Vancouver amateur athlete of '73; res. Maple Ridge, B.C.

IVAN, Tommy (hockey/coaching); b. 31 Jan 1911, Toronto, Ont.; d. 24 Jun, 1999, Lake Forest, Ill; m. Dorothy (d); retd. hockey exec; coach Omaha Knights (USHL) '45-46, Indianapolis (AHL) '46-47, Detroit Red Wings '47-54; guided Wings to 6 consecutive NHL titles (Prince of Wales Trophy), 3 Stanley Cups in 7 seasons; GM Black Hawks '54-77, credited with building Hawks into strong club through farm system; under his management Hawks won 1 Stanley Cup, 6 division titles; responsible for many NHL rule changes; pioneered in tapping college ranks for talent; co-mgr. team USA '76 Canada Cup series; v-p, asst. to pres., v-p/alternate governor Black Hawks '77-98; NHL coaching record: 610 scheduled games, 302 wins, 196 losses, 112 ties, .587 percentage, 67 playoff games, 36w, 31l, .537 percentage; Lester Patrick Award '75; *Hockey News*/Itech King Clancy Memorial award '94; chair. US Hockey Hall of Fame; mem. Hockey Hall of Fame selection comm.; mem. Hockey Hall of Fame.

IVES, Charles (squash); b. 10 Nov 1915, London, Eng.; given name: Charles William; m. Mollie Irene Beard; c. Barbara; squash pro; began career as ball boy at Queen's Club, London; jr. pro age 18; moved to Canada '33 as teaching pro Winnipeg Winter Club; Carleton Club pro from '77; Cdn Queen's Jubilee medal; hon. citizen of Winnipeg '84; Manitoba Squash Assn bronze plaque; Cdn Squash Racquets Assn distinguished service award; mem. Man. Sports Hall of Fame; res. Winnipeg, Man.

J

JACKART, Dan (rugby); b. 4 May 1960, Natal, B.C.; m. Trudy Hopman; Langara Coll.; firefighter; mem. UBC Old Boys RC; made intl debut '91 vs. Japan; standout tight head '91 World Cup; mem. '92 Cdn team in CANZ series; retd. '96; res. New Westminster, B,C,

JACKES, Arthur (t&f); b. 26 Jun 1924, Toronto, Ont. given name: Arthur Mortimer; m. Charlotte Haultain; c. Norman, Rosemary, Malcolm, Hugh; UofT, BSc; retd.; high jump champion '48-49; mem. '48 Olympic (6th), '50 BEG teams; US citizen '56; res. Greenbank, Wash.

JACKS, Sam (ringette); b. 23 Apr 1915, Scotland; d. 14 May 1975, North Bay, Ont.; given name: Samuel Perry; m. Agnes McKrell; c. Barry, Bruce, Brian; NB rec. dir.; an innovator who began recreation career in Toronto '35; organized Toronto Boys' Club; 1st North Bay rec. dir. '48; developed game of floor hockey and wrote initial rules '36; developed 1st NO playground HA; coached ntl jr. Olympic floor hockey bronze medal team; asst. dir. Toronto West End YMCA '34-40; conceived game of ringette '63 and refined rules '65; presented Sam Jacks Trophy to winning Tween A champion West Ferris in 1st Ladies Recreational Ringette tournament; pres. Ont. society municipal rec. directors '63; Ont. achievement award '71; outstanding contribution and dedication to recreation citation; fellowship American Institute of Park exec., Ont. Society Municipal rec. dirs.; mem. North Bay, Ringette Canada halls of fame.

JACKSON, Busher (hockey); b. 19 Jan 1911, Toronto, Ont.; d. 25 Jun 1966, Toronto, Ont. given name; Harvey; Toronto Marlboros jrs., pro Maple Leafs '30-39; with Charlie Conacher, Joe Primeau formed original Kid Line; mem. 3 league champions, 1 Stanley Cup winner; 4 times 1st, once 2nd team all-star; NHL scoring leader '32-33; NY '39-42, Boston '42-44; NHL record: 633 scheduled games, 241 goals, 234 assists, 72 playoff games, 18 goals, 12 assists; mem. Canada's Sports, Hockey halls of fame.

JACKSON, Don (archery); b. 25 Oct 1932, Lindsay, Ont.; given name: Donald Arthur; m. Rose Ann Coulas; archery business operator; self-taught archer, began shooting '65, ntl field archery title '66; runnerup field, target grand aggregate '67; ntl, Ont. indoor, 9th world target '67; Ont. indoor, ntl target, field, aggregate '68-69, 6th world field, 9th target; ntl target, runnerup field '70; Ont. indoor '70-71; 6th '72 Olympics; numerous ntl records; pro '73-80; reinstated amateur, '80 ntl field, Ont. target, field titles; '81 Ont. indoor, '82 Ont., ntl indoor; res. Lindsay, Ont.

JACKSON, Donald (figure skating); b. 2 Apr 1940, Oshawa, Ont; div. Joanne Diercks; c. Donald Jr., Derek, Michael, Jeannine, Stephanie; exec.-dir. Minto Skating Club; 5 ntl, 2 NA, 1 world title '55-62; bronze '60 Olympics; 1st skater ever to perform triple lutz in competition Prague '62; pro Ice Follies '62-68; world pro champion '70; 1st to execute arms-folded triple salchow ('77), a feat filmed for UK TV show *Record Breakers*; from '78 has marketed Jackson skating products; Minto Club rink bears his name;

Lou Marsh Trophy '62; mem. Order of Canada, US Figure Skating, Cdn Amateur, Canada's Sports halls of fame; res. Ottawa, Ont.

JACKSON, Glen (football); b. 5 Apr 1954, Vancouver, B.C.; m. Barbara; c. Tessa, Marguax; SFU, BA; Dist. 1, all-Northwest all-star '73-75; ranked as one of finest SFU products ever; territorial protection BC; linebacker Lions from '76; noted for durability, never missing game; ranked high among CFL interception ranks; 4 times WFC all-star; res. Vancouver, B.C.

JACKSON, Linda (cycling): b. 13 Nov 1958, Montreal, Que.; UWO, hons BA, Stanford, MBA; competitive swimmer in youth before dropping out of sport for 15yrs during which she carved out a highly lucrative business career as v-p investment banking; despite an opportunity for highly-paid job she opted to pursue her dream of becoming a top-flight competitive cyclist at 32; bronze medals in Cdn road race championships '92-93 led to inclusion on ntl team, gold '95, '97; competed on '93 European tour; standout on '94 European tour including 5th women's Tour de France; 3rd overall California Tour of Redlands, tour of NZ; silver 93.6km women's road race '94, 28km road race '98 Commonwealth Games; competed '95 Pan-Am, '96 Olympic Games; won '97 Tour de L'Aude, ntl time trial, road racing titles; 3rd '97 women's Tour de France; runnerup Tour of Italy '97-98; won Hewlett-Packard International women's challenge '98; with Gord Fraser co-winner '95 Ottawa ACT athlete of yr; NA, ACT cyclist award '97; Cdn female cyclist of '97; mem. Nepean Sports Wall of Fame; res. Los Angeles, Calif.

JACKSON, Roger (rowing/administration); b. 14 Jan 1942, Toronto, Ont.; given name: Roger Charles; m. Linda; c. Christopher, Alex, Geoffry; UWO BA, UBC, MPhE, Wisconsin, PhD; dean faculty of PE UCal; mem. '60-63 university ntl rowing 8s champions; with George Hungerford gold coxless pairs '64 Olympics; with R. Fieldwalter '65 Scandinavian coxless pairs; flag-bearer, finalist single sculls '68 Olympics; mem. '72 Olympic team; dir. Sport Canada '76-78, co-ordinated '76 Olympics Game Plan; v-p COA '81-82, pres. '82-90; chairman advisory board Calgary Olympic Development Assoc.; gov. Olympic Trust; with Hungerford, Lou Marsh Trophy '64; Officer Order of Canada '84; mem. Cdn Olympic, Cdn Amateur, Canada's Sports halls of fame; res. Calgary, Alta.

JACKSON, Rose Ann (archery); b. 15 Jun 1952, Barry's Bay, Ont; given name: Rose Ann Coulas; m. Don Jackson; medical laboratory tech.; ntl indoor women's amateur champion '79-82; outdoor women's amateur unlimited target field, aggregate champion '79-81; 19 open, 14 closed ntl amateur women's records; tied professional men's 60m, 30m, records, men's amateur unlimited hunter record; 1st woman in Canada to break 1300 of possible 1440 points barrier in FITA round; PB: 1322; topped 1300 plateau 3 times; res. Lindsay, Ont.

JACKSON, Russ (football); b. 28 Jul 1936, Hamilton, Ont.; given name: Russell Stanley; m. Lois Hendershot; c. Kevin, Suzanne, Nancy; McMaster, BSc; retd HS principal/ educational consultant; Sr. IC baseball Hamilton; pro football Ottawa '58-69, starting quarterback from '63; CFL record: completed 1341 of 2511 passes for 23,341yds, 125 intercepted, 184tds; led EFC passers 6 times; carried 738 times for 5045yds, 6.6 avg., scored 55tds, 330 pts; 4 Grey Cup finals, 3 winners; 3 Schenley outstanding player awards, 4 top Canadian; 2 Jeff Russel Memorial Trophy; Lou Marsh Trophy '69; 2 Lionel Conacher awards; coached Toronto '75-76; TV color commentator several seasons; CIAU student-athlete annual award bears his name; educational consultant Missisauga Ice Dogs '98; Officer Order of Canada; mem. Ottawa, McMaster, Ont. Sports Legends; Canada's Sports, Cdn Football halls of fame; res. Mississauga, Ont.

JACOBS, Dave (skiing); b. 1 Oct 1933, Montreal, Que.; given name: David Lloyd; div.; c. Bernard, William, Kelly, Tracey; m. Susan Hellie; c. Lara; St. Lawrence, B S., MIT; corporate exec.; jr, B hockey player; won Que. Kandahar '56; ntl downhill champion '57; mem. ntl team '57-61; Val David ski school dir. '62-63; designer/mgr. Talisman ski area '63; head coach ntl alpine team '64-67; sr. mem. Cdn. Ski Instructors Assn; mem. National Coaches Assn.; 2nd '80 veterans super 40 World Cup slalom, GS, downhill, combined; mem. Cdn Skiing Hall of Fame; res. Boulder, Colo.

JACOBS, Jack (football); b. 1920, Holdenville, Okla.; d. 12 Jan 1974, North Greensboro, N.C.; Oklahoma; nicknamed "Indian Jack"; NFL Cleveland Rams, Washington, Green Bay; led NFL punters with Packers '47; quarterback Winnipeg '50-54; CFL record: 709 of 1330 passes for 11,094yds, 41.0 avg, 57 singles; prolific passer, completed 31 of 48 vs. Hamilton '53; 6 TD passes vs. Calgary '52; scout Bombers '55; coach London Lords (ORFU) 2 seasons; asst. Hamilton, Montreal, Edmonton; Jeff Nicklin Memorial Trophy (MVP) '52; twice Grey Cup finalist; twice all-star; mem. Canadian Football Hall of Fame.

JACOBSEN, George (equestrian/skiing); b. 20 Sep 1912, Vienna, Austria; d. 28 Sep 1994, Montreal, Que.; m. Peggy McCulloch; McGill, DSc, Zurich, PEng, Clermont (France); arctic consultant; jr. ski jump, downhill competitor '28-33; equestrian jumping, dressage competitor '28-50; CdM '56 Olympic team; joint master Lake of Two Mountains Hunt '58-94; pres. Cdn Horse Show Assn, which became Cdn. Equestrian Fed. '63-76; chair. CEF '77-84, hon. chair. to death; international equestrian dressage, jumping judge; mem. executive FEI; dir. COA, American Equestrian Federation; dir. Sir Edmund Hillary Foundation; mem. Order of Canada; recipient Royal Swedish Olympic Medal; CEF gold medal; CEF Equestrian of yr trophy bears his name.

JAMES, Angela (hockey); b. 22 Dec 1964, Thornhill, Ont.; rec. co-ordinator Seneca Coll; mem. '91, '93 sr ntl champion Toronto Aeros; 3 COWHL all-star, MVP '91, 3 scoring titles; mem. 4 Team Canada world champions; 3 world all-star; top player award '94; Pacific Rim, 3-Nations Cup gold; Level IV official, intermediate hockey coach; participated

world roller hockey championships winning gold '93, silver '94; res. Thornhill, Ont.

JAMES, Eddie (football); b. 30 Sep 1907, Winnipeg, Man.; d. 26 Dec 1958, Winnipeg, Man.; given name: Edwin; m. Moria Kathleen FitzGerald; c. Don, Gerry; nicknamed "Dynamite"; offensive, defensive halfback Winnipeg, Regina Pats, Winnipeg St. John's, Regina Roughriders through '20s, early '30s; trophy in his honor awarded annually to WFC leading rusher; charter mem. Canadian Football Hall of Fame.

JAMES, Gerry (football/hockey); b. 22 Oct 1934, Regina, Sask; given name: Gerald Edwin; m. Margaret Petrie; c. Debra, Tracy, Tara, Kelly, Brady; retd. hockey exec., hotelier, storekeeper, property mgr; HS football to youngest in CFL at 17; CFL Winnipeg, Sask. '52-64; 63tds, 143cvts, 40fg, 21s for 645pts; 995 carries for 5554yds (5.6yd avg), 57tds; twice rushed for 1000+ yds single season; record for TDs scored rushing with 18 '57; scored 1 other on pass same season to tie Pat Abbruzzi; twice Dave Dryburgh Trophy as WFC scoring leader, once runnerup; twice WFC all-star; twice Schenley top Canadian award; offered contract by NY Giants (NFL); at 16 mem. Winnipeg Monarchs '51 Memorial Cup finalists; Toronto Marlboros '55 Memorial Cup champions; right wing Maple Leafs '54-59; 149 scheduled games, 14g, 26a, 15 playoff games, 1g; competed in 2 major ntl finals within 6 months '59 Grey Cup, '60 Stanley Cup; mem. 6 Grey Cup finalists, 4 winners; coached in Switzerland '63-64; owner/coach/player Yorkton Terriers, Sask. Jr. HL (Tier 2) '66-69, 4 consec. Sask. titles; coached 3 all-star teams; 2 coach of year awards; coached SJHL, WHL teams 19yrs; 2 Sask. titles; 7 all-star coach awards; organized/coached Weyburn Special Olympics floor hockey team; nickmaned "Kid Dynamite"; election to Canadian Football Hall of Fame provided grid shrine with (Eddie "Dynamite" James) 1st father-son combination; mem. Cdn Football, Man., Blue Bombers, Sask, Yorkton Sports halls of fame; res. Nanoose Bay, B.C.

JAMES, Jeff (harness racing); b. 17 Jan 1952, Brantford, Ont.; Guelph; while studying to become veterinarian decided to pursue racing from sulky seat '75; driving debut with 2nd place in Matron Stakes; one of most consistent drivers on Michigan main circuit from '80 winning 4466 races for purses totalling $18M through '97; posted 11-race win streak with Jerry's Cadet '95; res. Farmington Hills, MI.

JANI, Louis (judo): b. 6 Dec 1957, Montreal, Que.; m.; Sport Canada consultant; 6 ntl 86kg titles; Pan-Am Games gold '79, '83; 3 Que. Open gold; gold Pan-Am championships, Canada Cup, East Coast; silver US Open, Pacific Rim, Kano Cup, German, Paris championships; 16 ntl, intl bronze; competed '80, '84, '88 Olympics, '79, '83 Pan-Am Games, '82, '84 FISU Games, '79, '83, '85 worlds; fed. govt. sport excellence award '84; res. Ottawa, Ont.

JANS, Edward (shooting); b. 17 Aug 1946, Medicine Hat, Alta.; m. Irene Roso; draftsman; began shooting as hobby '67; handgun specialist; mem. ntl team from '69; mem. '70, '80 worlds, '71, '75, '79 Pan-Am Games, '72, '80 Olympics, '78 Commonwealth Games teams; bronze team free pistol '75, '78 Benito Juarez International; silver team standard fire '78 Benito Juarez; silver centre fire, gold team free pistol '79 Pan-Am Games; res. Calgary, Alta.

JANS, Melanie (squash); b. 3 Jul 1973, Montreal, Que.; UofT, BPHE; pro squash player; began play age 11; 5 ntl jr. titles; mem. 4 ntl women's teams; competed 2 jr. , '92, '94 worlds; won '94 Barrie Pro-Am, Hi-Tec Curzons Classic; mem. '94 Pan-Am championships 2 silver medal team; 2 gold '95, '99 Pan-Am Games; Petro-Can Olympic Torch scholarship '94; res. Georgetown, Ont.

JANSE, Roy (sailing): b. 4 Jun 1971, Edmonton, Alta.; Tornado class sailor; crew for skipper Marc Peers; former ntl judo team mem.; hooked up with Peers in HS; NA, Cdn championships '93; SPORT gold '96; competed '96 Olympic Games; Edmonton City salute to excellence award '94; res. Edmonton, Alta.

JANSSENS, Sandy (horseshoes); b. 9 Jul 1971, Wallaceburg, Ont.; given name: Sandy McLachlin; m. Dale Janssens; certified general accountant; 6 Ont. women's singles titles; runnerup ntl championships '87; several perfect games; set world record (since surpassed) for complete world tournament average 88.2% '87; world jr. women's title '86; only Cdn to win world women's title '87, 3 times runnerup; played at White House inauguration of George Bush Horseshoe Court '89; res. Wallaceburg, Ont.

JANUSKOVA, Eva (tennis); b. 27 May 1978, Tabor, Czechoslovakia; emigrated to Canada age 5; began playing tennis age 8; through '95 won 15 ntl indoor, outdoor, singles, doubles titles; ranked No. 1 Ont. -14 '90; mem. World Youth Cup under-16 team '92; played Virginia satellite circuit '94; ntl -18 title '95; mem. Nepean Sports Wall of Fame; res. Nepean, Ont./Montreal, Que.

JANZEN, Henry (football); b. 7 Jun 1940, Winnipeg, Man,; m. Judy Munro; c. Dean, Joanne; North Dakota, BSc, Northern Colorado, MA, PhD; dean of men, AD UMan.; Blue Bombers '59-65; Dr. Beattie Martin Trophy as WFC rookie of year; outstanding Canadian Winnipeg '62, '65; all-Cdn '65; led WFC in punt return yards 394, best avg. runback 7.3yds; coached UMan. Bisons to College Bowl championship '69-70; CIAU coach of '69; res. Winnipeg, Man.

JARDIN, Anne (swimming); b. 26 Jul 1959, Montreal, Que.; given name: Anne Elizabeth; m. Jim Alexander; c. Kevin, Ian, Claire; Houston, BPhE, BSc; tech. program co-ordinator CASA '82-89; freestyle (FS), butterfly specialist; ntl team '74-81; gold 4x100 FS relay '74 Commonwealth Games; silver 4x100 FS relay, bronze 200m FS '75 Pan-Am Games; bronze 4x100 FS relay '75 world championships; bronze 4x100 FS, 4x100 medley relays '76 Olympics; silver 4x100 FS relay '79 Pan-Am Games; mem. '80 Olympic team; asst. mgr. '84 Olympic swim team; PB: 100m FS 56.75, 200m FS 2:02.5, 400m FS 4:20; mem. Houston swim team; Governor-General's silver medal '76; mem. Que. Swimming, Sports halls of fame; res. Ottawa, Ont.

JARVIS, Doug (hockey); b. 24 Mar 1955, Peterborough, Ont,; m. Linda; c. Laura, Landry; hockey coach; centre

Peterborough jrs; drafted by Toronto '75 then dealt to Montreal where he played '75-82; Washington '82-85, Hartford '85-87; NHL record: 964 scheduled games, 139g, 264a, 105 playoff games, 14g, 27a; mem. 4 Stanley Cup winners; Selke trophy '84, Masterton trophy '87; established NHL record of playing 962 consec. regular season games; player/asst./head coach Binghamton (AHL) '87-88; asst. coach Minnesota, Dallas from '88; res. Dallas, Tex.

JASIAK, Andrew (shooting); b. 4 Jul 1962, Ottawa, Ont.; OPP officer; mem. numerous Ont. smallbore teams '81-86; '78 cadet Bisley team; '84, '96 Cdn Bisley teams; coach '85-86 cadet Bisley teams; runnerup DCRA grand agg. '95; mem. '85 Palma team; res. Smiths Falls, Ont.

JAUCH, Ray (football); b. 11 Feb 1938, Mendota, Ill.; m. Sarah; c. 4 sons; Iowa, BSc; football executive; mem. '59 Iowa Rose Bowl team; pro Winnipeg '60; turned to coaching after leg injury '61; coach Winnipeg jr. Rods '62, Sask.

JELINEK, Maria (figure skating); b. 16 Nov 1942, Prague, Czechoslovakia; m. Paul Harrington; c. Mark, Michael, Matthew; Michigan; teamed with brother Otto in pairs competion (see Otto Jelinek for record); pro skater '63-69 Ice Capades; mem. Cdn Amateur, Cdn Figure Skating, Canada's Sports halls of fame; res. Toronto, Ont.

JELINEK, Otto (figure skating); b. 20 May 1940, Prague, Czechoslovakia; m. Leata; c. Misha, Jamie; Appelby College, Swiss Alpine Business College; pres. Jelinek International; retd. politician, real estate broker, sporting goods mfgr.; with sister Maria '55 ntl jr. pairs title; 3rd '57-58 world, 4th '59, 2nd '60; 4th '60 Olympic pairs; '61 NA, ntl pairs titles, '62 ntl senior, world pairs; pro skater Ice Capades '63-69; Lake Placid pro pairs title '64; MP (PC) for Halton '72-93; cabinet min. PC govt.; TV color analyst '84 Winter Olympics; dir. Sparta Prague hockey team; mem. Czech Olympic Assn; mem. Cdn Amateur, Cdn Figure Skating, Canada's Sports halls of fame; res. Prague.

JENKINS, Bill (curling); b. 19 Feb 1957, Charlottetown, P.E.I.; given name: William Kenneth; m. Sheila Dianne Matheson; c. Lindsay Dianne; Dalhousie, UPEI, BA; asst. v-p W.F.Moreau & Associates; skip 3 prov. junior titles; ntl jr. title '76; ntl jr. player of '76; prov. Legion title '78; world jr. title '77, highest percentage ever in international competition final; Dick Ellis team award '77; mem. PEI Sports Hall of Fame; res. St. John's, Nfld.

JENKINS, Fergie (baseball); b. 13 Dec 1943, Chatham, Ont.; given name: Ferguson Arthur; div. Katherine Henson; c. Kelly, Delores, Kimberley; m. Maryanne (d); c. Samantha (d), Raymond; pitching coach; righthanded pitcher; 1st pro contract '62 Philadelphia Phillies organization; 4 seasons in minors 43-26 record; Phillies '65-66, Chicago Cubs '66-73, '82-83, Texas '74-75, '78-81, Boston '76-77; ML record 284-226, 49sho, 3192k (6th all-time); 7 20-plus victory seasons, 6 in succession Cubs '67-72, 1 with Texas '74; only pitcher with more than 3000k, less than 1000bob; 4th pitcher in history with 100 or more victories in each league; 3 NL all-star teams; led ML pitchers in putouts with 363; NL Cy Young Award (24-13) Cubs '71; AL comeback player of '74 Texas (25-12); led NL 3 times, AL once complete games; tied ML record with 5 1-0 losses '68 season; 4 Lionel Conacher awards; Lou Marsh Trophy '74; 2yrs pitching coach Oklahoma City AAA, roving instructor Cincinnati organization '93-94, pitching coach Cubs '95-96; hon. capt. NL all-star gane team '95; granted absolute discharge following drug charge conviction '80; pitched London Sr. IC '84; made unsuccessful bid for Ont. legislature seat; 1st Canadian elected to BBHOF; mem. Order of Canada, Cdn, Major League Baseball, Chicago, Ont. Legends, Canada's Sports halls of fame; res. Guthrie, Okla.

JENKINS, Peter (curling); b. 19 Dec 1959, Charlottetown, P.E.I.; skip '77-79 PEI jr. title rinks; 2nd '80-81 PEI mixed title rinks; skip Alpine Super League, Charlottetown title rinks '81-82; mem. runnerup rink ntl mixed '80; skip '82 PEI Brier entry; res. Charlottetown, P.E.I.

JENKINS, Shorty (curling); b. 27 Sep 1935, Hanna, Alta.; given name: Clarence William; m. Johanna Elisabeth Geertje-Willemsen; c. Kitty, Kiet; golf course superintendent/ice maker, retd. Cdn Forces; initial experience in golf club maintenance at Cold Lake, Alta., '59-62; greens keeper Trenton Golf/Curling Club '68-76, Bay of Quinte Golf/Country Club '76-90, Kingston Cataraqui Golf/Country Club from '91; 28yrs mem. Cdn, 18yrs America, 19yrs Ont. Golf Course Superintents Assn.; 5yrs mem. Ottawa Valley, 6yrs Ont. Turfgrass Assn.; began making curling ice '68; through '97-98 icemaker/consultant 3 Briers, 3 Scott Tournament of Hearts, 4 Worlds, 1 ntl juniors, 1 ntl mixed, 1 Olympic trials, 2 WCT VO Cups, 12 TSN Skins Games, 30 Ont. men's/women's/mixed/jr championships; icemaker Swiss tournament of champions, Las Vegas Desert 'spiel, Scottish jr., 9 Ottawa Classic/Welton Beauchamp and various other major bonspiels; Level III ice technician, Level I technical coach, 23yrs coaching various teams; has conducted ice-making clinics throughout Canada/Scotland; served on exec.comm. for several OCA/ OLCA competitions; life mem. Bay of Quinte GCC, Ennismore CC; 10 Labatt, 1 Ont., Las Vegas, Bay of Quinte GCC, OCA, Scott Paper Appreciation Awards; CCA Achievement Award; Ont. Tankard Sportsmanship trophy bears his name; highly regarded by host of Cdn curlers; res. Kingston, Ont.

JENSEN, Al (golf); b. 24 Jan 1938, Montreal, Que.; given name: Allan Howard; div.; c. Allan Jr., Jim; m. Ann Darbyshire; c. Andrew Scott, Erin; retd. golf pro, Cdn Forces; runnerup ntl asst. championships '75; won 4 pro tournaments '76, Earl Stimpson Shield for best overall tournament performance among Ottawa Valley pros '76, '78, '84; 3 competitive course records: 59 Poplar Grove, 70 Petawawa, 64 Hylands South course; Ottawa zone CPGA champion '78; 2 zone asst. titles; runnerup '88 ntl CPGA Seniors; 3 holes-in-1; son Allan Jr. Que. juve. champion '78, Jim mem. Ont. jr. title curling rink '83; res. Ottawa, Ont.

JERANT, Martina (basketball); b. 30 Jan 1974, Windsor, Ont.; Brown, BA; centre Ivy League titlists '92-94; mem. ntl jr team '92, sr team from '93; bronze '93, gold '95 COPABA tournaments; competed '94 Goodwill, '94-95 Jones Cup, '95 FISU, '96 Olympic Games; pro Zagreb, Croatia; Brown freshman athlete of '92, Ivy League rookie

of '92, IL player of '93; competed '94 NCAA tournament; res. Grosse Point, Mich.

JEROME, Harry (t&f); b. 30 Sep 1940, Prince Albert, Sask.; d. 7 Dec 1982, Vancouver, B.C.; given name: Henry Winston; div.; Oregon, BSc, MA; sports consultant; shared world record 10 seconds for 100m dash '60 with Germany's Armin Hary; tied world 100yd sprint record 9.3 Corvallis, Ore., '61; tied Bob Hayes' world record 9.1 Edmonton '66; '62 NCAA 220yd title in 20.8; anchored Oregon team that equalled world 440yd relay record of 40.00 on course with 2 turns; mem. '60, '64, '68 Olympic teams; bronze medal 100m in 10.1 '64; repeated time '68 but finished 7th; gold 100m '67 Winnipeg Pan-Am Games in 10.2; held 6 world sprint records; for several years Sport Canada consultant; Officer Order of Canada; mem. BC, Cdn Amateur, Sask., Canada's Sports halls of fame.

JEROME, Valerie (t&f); b. 28 Apr 1944, St. Boniface, Man.; given name: Valerie Jerome; div. Ronald Parker; c. Stuart; UBC; teacher; ntl sr. 60m, 100m, long jump titles, mem. BC champion 4x100 relay team '59; relay bronze '59 Pan-Am Games; mem. '60 Olympic, '66 Commonwealth Games; chief judge '76 Olympics; distance jumps referee '78 Commonwealth Games; PB: 100m 11.6 '68, 200m 24.2 '68, high jump 1.55m '71, long jump 5.64m '67, 100m hurdles 15.3 '73; res. Vancouver, B.C.

JESPERSEN, Eric (sailing); b. 18 Oct 1961, Port Alberni, B.C.; m; c. Emma Elizabeth, Ross Campbell; boat builder; began sailing at 6, competing at 12; mem. ntl team from '91; with Ross MacDonald became 1st all-Cdn team to win Star Worlds in 83yr history of class '94; Star class Olympic bronze '92; competed '96 Olympics; ntl titles '93-94; with MacDonald CYA male athlete of '94, Rolex Canadian sailor of '92; sister Julie mem. ntl rowing team; res. Sidney, B.C.

JESPERSEN, Julie (rowing); b. 18 Sep 1969, Sidney, B.C.; UVic, BSc; began rowing in HS; mem. ntl team from '88; 5 ntl, 2 US, 4 International regatta titles; gold straight 4s, silver straight pairs '91 Pan-Am Games; spare '92 Olympic Games; World straight 4s bronze '93; brother Eric Olympic yachtsman; res. Sidney, B.C.

JMAEFF, Peter (shooting); b. 31 Aug 1937, Regina, Sask.; m. Gladys; c. Leslie, Karen, Lisa; UofSask. BSc, MSc; mechanical engineer, systems dir. Sask. Medical Care Insurance Branch; fullbore specialist; mem. 5 Cdn Bisley teams; adjutant '83, team commandant '87, vice-commandant '90; SPRA Lt. Governor's title '75, grand aggregate '75, '92; SPRA pres. '75-85, smallbore pres. '88-92; Sask Sports Federation pres. '85; SFC dir. '82-92; chef de mission SFC Benito Juarez '90, Los Angeles '91; ISU International B official; jury mem. 2 world cups; res. Regina, Sask.

JOBIN, Marcel (t&f); b. 3 Jan 1942, Parent, Abitibi, Que.; m.; race walker; 13 ntl 20km, 1 30km titles; silver 30km '82 Commonwealth Games; gold 30km, silver 50km Marcel Jobin International races; mem. '71, '75, '79, '83 Pan-Am, '76, '80, '84 Olympic, '78, '82 Commonwealth, '81 World Cup, '83 world championships teams; world indoor mile walk record 5:55.8 '79, NA, ntl 20km, ntl 5km, 10km records; ntl, Commonwealth 30km records; QTFF male athlete of '83; retired from competition '84; mem. Que. Sports Hall of Fame; res. St. Boniface, Que.

JOE, Peter (table tennis); b. 15 Dec 1959, Vancouver, B.C.; given name: Peter Gordon; UBC; ntl jr. title '76-77; BC champion '78-80; ranked ntl top 5 from '78; 3rd ntl men's singles '78-79, '81; extensive international experience with ntl team; res. Vancouver, B.C.

JOHL, Yogi (wrestling); b. 3 Jan 1970, Vancouver, B.C.; competes at 125kg level; wrestled internationally from '89; 2 ntl sr. Greco Roman, 1 sr. freestyle titles; competed '94 Francophone, '96 Olympic Games, '95 World championships; mem. Burnaby Mountain Wrestling Club; res. Vancouver, B.C.

JOHNSON, Ben (t&f); b. 30 Dec 1961, Jamaica; Centennial College; personal trainer; sprint specialist; 4 ntl 50m, 1 4x200m relay titles; mem. '82, '86 Commonwealth, '83 Pan-Am, FISU, '84 Olympic Games teams; 2 gold, 1 bronze '86, 2 silver '82 Commonwealth, silver 4x100 relay '83 FISU Games, bronze 100m, 4x100m relay team '84 Olympics; ntl indoor 4x200m, ntl sr. 50m, 100m records; world indoor 60m record; earned world's fastest human title beating triple Olympic gold medalist Carl Lewis, world record holder Calvin Smith in '86 Zurich race; PB 9.95 for 100m '86 in Moscow; won '85 World Cup 100m title; won '88 Olympic gold in Seoul with 9.79 run but failed steroid test and was stripped of Olympic gold and world record; suspended from competition 2 years and actions sparked Dubin Inquiry into drug use in sports, subsequent failed drug test led to lifetime suspension from t&f; turned attention briefly to soccer; became personal trainer for soccer star Diego Maradonna '97; 3 Norton Crowe, 2 Lionel Conacher, Lou Marsh trophies; mem. Order of Canada, Cdn Amateur Sports Hall of Fame; res. Toronto, Ont.

JOHNSON, Ching (hockey); b. 7 Dec 1897, Winnipeg, Man.; d. 17 Jun 1979, Tacoma Park, Md.; given name: Ivan Wilfred; defenceman Winnipeg Monarchs '19; 3yrs Eveleth, Minn., Miners; 3yrs Minneapolis Millers; NY Rangers '26-37, 2 Stanley Cups; NY Americans '37-38; continued to play in minors to age 46; player-coach Hollywood Wolves; Helms Award; NHL record: 463 scheduled games, 38g, 48a, 60 playoff games, 5g, 2a; represented Rangers 1st NHL all-star game '34; 3 times 1st team, twice 2nd team all-star; mem. Man., Cdn Hockey halls of fame.

JOHNSON, Chris (boxing); b. 8 Aug 1971, Manchester, Jamaica; middleweight; came to Canada '80; mem. Jamestown Amateur AC, coached by Arnie Boehm; mem. ntl team from '89; brother Greg also boxer; gold '89, '91 Canada Cup, '90 Commonwealth Games, '89, '90, '91 ntl championships; silver '91 Pan-Am Games; bronze '90 Goodwill Games; mem. '92 Olympic team; res. Kitchener, Ont.

JOHNSON, Daisy (basketball); b. 16 Mar 1902, Jumping Pound, Alta.; d. 1979, Edmonton, Alta.; given name: Margaret; Camrose Normal School; teacher; mem. famed Edmonton Grads '20-27; competed 1st ntl, international

championships; sister Dorothy also mem. Grads; until death involved in compiling history, memorabilia of Grads; mem. Canadian Basketball, Alta. Sports halls of fame.

JOHNSON, Danny (harness racing); b. 11 Jan 1950, Windsor, Ont.; Windsor, BSc; broke into sport as groom with Wright stables; won trainer titles at Hazel Park, Wolverine '76; shifted to Meadowlands adding trainer titles '77-79; won driving titles at Hazel Park, Windsor Raceway; driving Stir Fry won '88 US Pacing championship; through '97 3753 victories with purses exceeding $17M; res. Windsor, Ont.

JOHNSON, Dave (swimming); b. 2 Aug 1951, Montreal, Que.; given name: David Michael; m. Wendy Quirk; c. Michael, Rosemary; swim coach; freestyler '70 FISU, '71 Pan-Am Games; asst. coach '75 Pan-Am, '76 Olympic teams; head coach women's swim team '78 Commonwealth Games, world championships; head coach men's team '79 Pan-Am Games, '80 Olympic team; head coach Pointe Claire SC '76-78, Edmonton SC from '78; 2 CIAU swim coach of yr awards; res. Calgary, Alta.

JOHNSON, Don (t&f/skiing); b. 17 Aug 1942, Petrolia, Ont.; given name: Donald Hugh; m. Carole Cunningham; c. Michael, Christopher, Paul; Queen's, MD, FRCS (C), FACS; orthopedic surgeon, dir. Carleton sports medicine clinic; Jr. B hockey; competitor 30 marathons, 6 ultra marathons, 12 ntl ski marathons, '82 Hawaii Ironman, Western States 100 mile run '83; 5 Rideau Lakes cycle tours; 4 Liévre canoe marathons, 5 Colonel By triathlons; team physician Carleton, Sooners, Rough Riders football 10yrs, Senators hockey, ntl cross-country ski, t&f team; medical officer '76 winter, summer Olympics; attempted Mt. Everest climb '81; initiated Don Johnson Fitness Awards; res. Nepean, Ont.

JOHNSON, Don (administration); b. 25 Mar 1930, Halifax, N.S.; given name: Donald Stewart; m. Florence Helen Harris; c. Peter, Michael, Cathy; St. Mary's College; retd. civil servant; pres. '75-77, life mem. CAHA; pres. NAHA; commissioner Southern Shore HL; treas. Softball Nfld.; prov. delegate CASA; pres. St. John's Sr. SL; chair. carnival comm. St. John's Figure Skating Club; governor ntl YBC; commodore Terra Nova Yacht Club; dir. SFC; treas. Nfld., & Lab. Amateur Sports Fed.; hon. life mem. Softball Nfld.; dir. NSRC; chair. interprov. S&R Council; mem. Canada Games council; dir. Hockey Canada; hon. life mem. SFC; ADM Nfld. Parks, Rec. & Youth, dept. of culture, Rec. & Youth; mem. Nfld. & Lab. Sports Hall of Fame; res. St. John's, Nfld.

JOHNSON, Donnie (baseball); b. 8 Apr 1926, Marysville, N.B.; given name: Donald Walter; m. Mae; retd.; Marysville Maroons NB jr. titlists '43; NB sr. titles Marysville Royals '47-48, '55; NB batting titles .443 '52, .415 '57; twice NBSBL all-star 3rd baseman; pro trial Brooklyn Dodgers Vero Beach camp '49; playing coach Marysville Royals '59; turned to umpiring '60; officiated NB sr finals '66, Canada Summer Games '69; coached Marysville bantams to Fredericton city crowns '78-79; mem. NB Baseball (charter), NB Sports halls of fame; res. Fredericton, N.B.

JOHNSON, Dorothy (basketball); b. 22 Jan 1906, Jumping Pound, Alta.; m. Ronald Sherlock; c. Elizabeth Ann; at 15 youngest mem. famed Edmonton Grads '21-27; mem. 1st ntl, international, world title teams; organized women's, mixed bowling leagues Vancouver; sister Daisy also mem. Grads; mem. Canadian Basketball, Alta. Sports halls of fame; res. Vancouver, B.C.

JOHNSON, Greg (boxing); b. 18 Oct 1967, Montreal, Que.; welterweight; gold '90, '91 ntl championships, '90 Indonesia President's Cup; silver '90 Commonwealth Games; res. Montreal, Que.

JOHNSON, Julia (table tennis); b. 28 Aug 1963, Montreal, Que.; given name: Julia Carol; Carleton.; from '74 amassed string of title victories in age group competitions including Montreal Open '75-76, Que. Open '76, '81, Toronto Open '77-78, '80, Ont. Open '77-78, '81, Ont. Closed '77-78; ntl jr. '77, '79-81; Eastern US Open -15, -17 singles, doubles; gold medal team Canada vs US jr. tournament '79; jr. miss singles CNE '80; most improved jr. award '81; mem. ntl team from '81; res. Brampton, Ont.

JOHNSON, Marian (swimming); b. 6 Dec 1954, Montreal, Que.; given name: Marian Lee Stuart; m.Thomas Francis Johnson; c. Matthew, Hailey, Mark, Tracy; McGill, Bed; swim coach; Olympic trials gold in 100m, 200m breaststroke resulted in participation in '72 Olympics; also '73, '75 worlds; gold 4x100 medley relay, silver 100m breaststroke '74, gold 4x100 MR, bronze 100m breaststroke '78 Commonwealth Games; bronze 100m breaststroke '75 Pan-Am Games; gold 100m breaststroke '77 FISU Games; res. Delta, B.C.

JOHNSON, Maureen (baton twirling); b. 28 Mar 1939, Regina, Sask.; given name: Maureen Martin; div.; c. Jeff; dance teacher, coach, judge; 31yrs baton twirling coach; students have won 2 world titles, 80 grand ntl titles; Cdn coach '82-83 WBTF championships, judge '81; dir. Regina Optimist Buffalo Gals; res. Regina, Sask.

JOHNSON, Moose (hockey); b. 1886 Montreal, Que.; d. 25 Mar 1963, White Rock, B.C.; given name: Ernest; lw, defence Montreal MAAA '02-03; pro Montreal Wanderers; mem. 4 Stanley Cup winners; New Westminster Royals '12; 11yrs PCL with Portland, Victoria Maroons, Los Angeles, 123 goals, 270 games; all-star 10 consecutive years; PCL staged special Moose Johnson night in his honor; mem. Hockey Hall of Fame.

JOHNSON, Tom (hockey); b. 18 Feb 1928, Baldur, Man.; given name: Thomas Christian; m. Doris; c. Tom, Julie; hockey exec.; Winnipeg jr. Monarchs '45, Montreal sr. Royals '47; '48-50 Buffalo (AHL); def. Montreal Canadiens '50-63; Boston Bruins '63-65; NHL record: 978 scheduled games, 51 goals, 213 assists, 111 playoff games, 8 goals, 15 assists; mem. 6 Stanley Cup winners; 1st team all-star '59, 2nd team '56; Norris Trophy (top NHL defenceman) '59; coached Boston to 1st Prince of Wales trophy in 30 years '70-71, repeated '71-72 winning Stanley Cup; asst. GM/v-p '73-89; v-p from '89; mem. Cdn Hockey, Man. Sports, Hockey halls of fame; res. Concord, Mass.

JOHNSON, Tom (swimming/coaching); b. 2 Aug 1951, Montreal, Que.; given name: Thomas Francis; m. Marian Lee Stuart; c. Matthew, Haylee, Mark, Tracy; McGill B.Comm; swim coach Pacific Dolphins, UBC; Olympic coach '80, '84, '88, '92, '96; Commonwealth Games coach '78, '82, '86, '90, '94, '98; Pan-Am Games swim coach '75, '79, '83, '87; coached 4 world championships; BC swim coach of yr awards '92-98; 5 CIAU coach of yr awards; Omega coach of yr '97; res. Delta, B.C.

JOHNSON, William (football); b. 4 Dec 1964, Munroe, La.; Northeast Louisiana; drafted by Chicago (NFL) '87-88, New Orleans '89, Calgary from '89; 5 Western, CFL, 1 Northern all-star, Norm Fieldgate trophy '91; led CFL QB sacks '91 with 16; CFL record: (through '95) 115g, 251 def. tackles, 90 QB sacks; mem. 3 Grey Cup finals, 1 winner; res. Calgary, Alta.

JOHNSTON, Bob (rowing); b. 6 Apr 1868, Charlottetown, P.E.I.; d. 9 Aug 1951, Vancouver, B.C.; considered greatest sculler Vancouver Rowing Club, Pacific Northwest ever had; moved west 1888, began rowing '89; dominated rowing scene winning BC, Pacific Coast, ntl sculling titles; as pro '98 lost world title to Jake Gaudaur Sr.; coached by legendary Ned Hanlon; turned to coaching mid-'20s, developed dynasty of excellent oarsmen; coached Ned Pratt, Noel de Mille to '32 Olympic bronze pairs medal; always coached from rowing float, never coach boat; several years VRC dir.; hon. v-p. VRC; mem. BC Sports halls of fame.

JOHNSTON, Cynthia (basketball): b. 11 Oct 1968, Calgary, Alta.; Bishop's, BA, SAIT (photo journalism); forward Bishop's '86-91, 2 CIAU ntl championship tournament appearances; mem. NB silver medal team '94 Francophone Games; bronze medal team '85 Canada Games; mem. ntl jr team '85-86, sr team '87-99; competed '87, '91 FISU, '90 Goodwill, '91 Pan-Am, '94 World, '96 Olympic Games; COPABA bronze '93, gold '95; pro Belgium '92-96, Switzerland '97; HS athlete of '86; Bishop's female athlete of '88-91; Que. university female athlete of yr twice; won -14 NB tennis singles title; res. Calgary, Alta.

JOHNSTON, Ed (hockey); b. 24 Nov 1935, Montreal, Que.; given name: Edward Joseph; m. Diane; c. Michele, E.J. Jr., Joseph; hockey exec.; goaltender Johnstown Jets (EHL) '56-57; minor pro Winnipeg, Edmonton, Spokane, Shawinigan, Los Angeles, Hull-Ottawa '57-62; NHL Boston '62-73, Toronto '73-74, St. Louis '74-77, Chicago '77-78; NHL playing record: 592 scheduled games, 234-257-81, 34,216min, 1855ga, 32so, 18 playoff games, 7-10-0, 1023min, 57ga, 1so; last NHL goalie to play every minute of a season, 70games '63-64; mem. 2 Stanley Cup winners; made coaching debut New Brunswick (AHL) '78-79; head coach Chicago (NHL) '79-80, 1 div. title; head coach Pittsburgh '80-83, '93-97; GM Pittsburgh '83-88, AGM '88-89, '97-99; GM Hartford '89-92; EPHL leading goalie award, record 11so '60-61 season; res. South Hills (Pittsburgh), Pa.

JOHNSTON, John (golf); b. 19 May 1925, Vancouver, B.C.; m. Elizabeth; c. Gregory, John, David; retd. real estate salesman; '53 New Westminster, '59 Canadian amateur beating Gary Cowan one up; Mexican amateur, Penticton Open, BC Open '67; mem. '67 Commonwealth team; 6 times BC Willingdon Cup team mem.; 4 times America's Cup team; mem. BC Sports Hall of Fame; res. Vancouver, B.C.

JOHNSTON, Percy (speed skating); b. 21 Feb 1903, Orillia, Ont.; d. 24 Jul 1988, Oshawa, Ont.; given name: Henry Percy; m. Kathleen; c. Carl, Aileen; maintenance engineer; began collecting massive array of medals '16 at Kitchener Winter carnival; 4 Ont. indoor, 1 outdoor titles; ntl outdoor title '28; NA '29; NA indoor 3/4 mile, 3 mile, 5 mile US records; mem. Cdn Speed Skating Hall of Fame.

JOHNSTONE, Charlie (all-around); b. 10 Aug 1873, Montreal, Que.; d. 25 Jan 1945, Winnipeg, Man. first reach prominence in lacrosse; cover point for 90th Lacrosse Club 1891-95; named to all-Winnipeg team which played world champion Montreal Shamrocks 1895; hockey rover 1897-1902 Winnipeg Victorias; '02 Stanley Cup winner; rowing crew mem. 1896 Minneapolis International regatta; singles champion American, Cdn ntl regattas; won singles, doubles 1897 American ntl regatta; 1901-03 mem. victorious crews US ntl regattas; capt./coach Winnipeg Rowing Club '03-07; coached sr crews in '30s; won 7 American sweep oar championships, feat equalled only by Conrad Riley; accomplished curler, gymnast; mem. Man. Sports Hall of Fame.

JOHNSTONE, Chris (football); b. 12 Dec 1963, Kingston, Jamaica; Bakersfield Jr. Coll.; running back, joined CFL as free agent Edmonton '86-92, Winnipeg '93-95; 1 Eastern all-star; mem. 4 Grey Cup finalists, 1 winner; res. Winnipeg, Man.

JOLIAT, Aurel (hockey); b. 29 Aug 1901, Ottawa, Ont.; d. 2 Jun 1986, Ottawa, Ont.; given name: Aurel Emile; m. Berthe (d), m. Yvette; railway employee; kicking fullback New Edinburgh (Ottawa), Rough Riders, Regina Wascana Boat Club before turning to hockey; mem. New Edinburgh, Iroquois Falls, Saskatoon Shieks; acquired by Canadiens for Newsy Lalonde '22; lw for Canadiens to '38 retirement; nicknamed "Mighty Atom", "Little Giant"; 270 goals over 16 NHL seasons; mem. 3 Stanley Cup winners; Hart trophy '34; 1st all-star team once, 2nd team 3 times; active mem. Ottawa Old Pros '80-85; mem. Ottawa, Canada's Sports, Hockey halls of fame.

JOLIN, Yvon Jr. (barrel jumping); b. 30 Apr 1958, Montreal; Hydro-Quebec employee; world indoor champion '80-86, '88-91; Canadian champion '80-86, '88-'90; 2 world records: clearing 18 barrels and distance of 28'6"; listed in Guiness Book of Records; instrumental in bid to make barrel jumping an Olympic sport; mem. US National Winter Sports Hall of Fame; res. Le Guardeur, Que.

JONAS, Don (football); b. 3 Dec 1938, Scranton, Pa.; given name: Donald Walter; m. Rosemary Eisman; c. Jaudon, Jennifer; Penn State, BSc; football coach; all-American; pro running back Philadelphia (NFL) '62; cut after 1st game; Atlantic Coast League MVP; Newark Bears, Orlando Panthers Continental League, MVP 3 consecutive seasons; led Panthers to 4 pennants, 2 league titles; Continental single-game record 63 pass attempts, 25 completions; single season record 41 TD passes, kicked 56 straight converts '68-69; CFL Toronto '70, Winnipeg '71-74, Hamilton '74; CFL record: 1930 passes, 997 completions, 15,064yds, 98 interceptions, 98tds; Jeff Nicklin (WFC MVP), Dave Dryburgh (WFC scoring), Schenley (CFL outstanding player) awards '71; twice WFC all-star, once all-Canadian; PR dir. city of Orlando '76-79; football coach Central Florida from '79; mem. Scranton Sports Hall of Fame; res. Casselberry, Fla.

JONES, Candy (figure skating); b. 20 Mar 1955, Kingston, Ont.; given name: Candace Lynne; m. Donald Fraser; McGill, BSc; medical student; ntl gold medals freestyle, figures at 13; added gold in dance, pairs; US gold figures, FS; began pairs skating with Don Fraser '73; ntl sr. pairs titles '75-76; mem. worlds '75-76, Olympic teams '76; pro '76, toured with Toller Cranston's Ice Show; appeared at Broadway's Palace Theater; world pro pairs titles '77-79; made appearances on TV in Stars on Ice, Battle of the Ice Stars, Challenge of the Sexes, Headline Hunters; coaches in Laval; res. Harrowsmith, Ont.

JONES, Chris (softball); b. 19 Apr 1967, Oshawa, Ont.; given name: Christopher; Durham Coll.; law clerk; mem. ntl fastball team from '94; Pan-Am Games gold '95; gold '91 Ont, silver '91 ntl championships, '91, '94 ISC worlds; bronze '92, '94 ntl championships; all-Canadian shortstop '93-94; res. Oshawa, Ont.

JONES, Colleen (curling); b. 16 Dec 1959, Halifax, N.S.; given name: Colleen Patricia; m. Scott Saunders; c. Zach, Luke; CBC sports/weather announcer; began curling age 15; mem. 2 NS jr., 7 NS mixed, 14 NS women's title rinks; 3rd husband Scott's ntl mixed title team '93, Paul Flemming's ntl mixed title rink '99; skipped '82, '99 Scott Tournament of Hearts title rink; mem. Cdn Curling Hall of Fame; res. Halifax, N.S.

JONES, Debbie (curling); b. 23 Mar 1953, Winnipeg, Man.; given name: Deborah Anne; m. Stan Walker; legal secty; all-star lead Man., Cdn. mixed title rinks '77; 2nd BC women's title rink '84; all-star 2nd BC women's, Cdn, world title rinks '85; mem. 1st women's carspiel winning rink Kelowna '85; 2nd Team Canada, runnerup '86 Scott Tournament of Hearts; from '77-90 competed 5 prov. mixed, 8 prov. women's championships; 3rd for Janet Harvey '97 STOH; fed. govt. champions award '85; 2nd '88 Olympic gold medal team; mem. '88 TSN Skins title rink; v-p special events '88 men's world curling championships; mem. '85 BC team of year; hon. life mem. North Shore Winter Club; mem. BC Sports, Canadian Curling halls of fame; res. Winnipeg, Man.

JONES, Jim (softball); b. 15 Nov 1959, Conquest, Sask.; given name: James William; m. Lynne Ledingham; c. Cory Benjamin, Jordy Jonathon; USIU San Diego, Kelsey Inst., Camrose Lutheran Coll; exec. dir. Softball Alberta; ex-recreation dir.; played Jr. A hockey Humboldt '78-80; hockey scholarships USIU San Diego, Camrose Lutheran; mem. ntl men's softball team '82-88; Pan-Am Games gold '83, '87; world championship silver medal '84; ntl title team '87; ntl championships all-star '82, '83, '84; Saskatoon athlete of year '83; mem. Cdn Softball, Saskatoon Sports halls of fame; res. Delisle, Sask.

JONES, John (motorsport); b. 19 Oct 1965, Thunder Bay, Ont.; given name: John Bradley; Henry Ford U; at 15 worked as bull cook at arctic gold mine to raise money for 1st race car; racing career began as birthday present when he attended Mosport Racing School; competed in go-kart racing at 14; won Western ice racing title at 16; 1st Cdn and youngest racer ever to win IMSA GTO title at 19; 7 wins included 24-hour Daytona, 12-hour Sebring; lone North American on European Formula 3000 circuit '86-87 seasons; 7 top 10 finishes earned him IndyCar series rookie of year title; res. Thunder Bay, Ont.

JONES, Tom (motorsport); b. 13 Sep 1941, Belfast, N. Ireland; c. John; construction co. owner; emigrated to Port Arthur age 7; began auto racing age 16; turned pro at 19 racing '57 Corvette or '63 Jaguar; in '60s began driving Cdn rally circuits; strong showings led to ranking as Canada's 1st FIA-graded rally driver; dominated International ice racing circuit '73-78; Prairie regional road racing GT-2 class champion '79-80; Sports Car Club of America, Cdn Auto Sports Club titles, 6 track records '80; 1st Cdn to win both GT1, GT2 Western Cdn Sports Car championships same day '80; several top finishes GT3 class '81; US Nationals title '81; signed as #1 Ford driver in Canada; retired from racing '84; Thunder Bay Jaycees NWO outstanding young person award '80; Thunder Bay athlete of '81; mem. NWO Sports Hall of Fame; res. Thunder Bay, Ont.

JONES, Tyrone (football); b. 3 Aug 1961, St. Mary's, Ga.; Southern; linebacker; turned pro CFL Winnipeg '83-87, '89-91, Saskatchewan '92, BC '93; NFL Phoenix Cardinals '88; 3 all-Western, 4 all-CFL, 2 all-Eastern all-star; Norm Fieldgate trophy '85; Schenley outstanding defensive player '85; CFL record: 151 scheduled games, 3tds, 15 interceptions, 15 playoff games; mem. 2 Grey Cup winners; res. Georgia.

JONKER, Karel (rowing); b. 5 Jul 1949, Amsterdam, Netherlands; given name: Karel Anton Johan: m. Karen Farstad; c. Erik; UBC, BA; district sales mgr. GMC; UBC-VRC intercollegiate Western Sprints '70-73; ntl team '70-73; mem. 8-oared crew which won Hanlon Cup '70 St. Catharines; coxed 4, pairs, 8s '70 ntl trials; bronze '71 Pan-Am Games; competed European championships '72-73, English Henley '72, world championships '70; mem. '72 Olympic team; UBC Big Block Club, Olympic Club of Canada; res. Surrey, B.C.

JOSENHANS, Andreas (sailing); b. 12 Sep 1950, Germany; m. Kathryn Ritchie; Dalhousie; sports administrator, sailmaker; with Glen Dexter, Sandy MacMillan won NS soling titles '74-76; mem. '76, '84 Olympic teams; world soling titles '77, '80; also won world Star class title; NS achievement award, Moosehead sports award; mem. NS, Canada's Sports halls of fame; res. Milford, Conn.

JOSEPH, Curtis (hockey); b. 29 Apr 1967, Keswick, Ont.; m. Nancy; c. Tristan, Taylor, Madison; goaltender Notre Dame Coll. (SJHL) '87-88, Wisconsin (WCHA) '88-89, Peoria (IHL) '89-90, Las Vegas '95-96, NHL St. Louis '90-95, Edmonton '95-98, Toronto '98-99; WCHA 1st team all-star '89; competed '94 NHL all-star game; Team Canada

gold '96 World Cup, silver '96 worlds; mem. '98 Olympic team; NHL record (through '99): 524 scheduled games, 248-196-61, 30,170min, 1473ga, 22so, 75 playoff games, 35-38. 5353min, 207ga, 8so; 1st yr Oiler Chrysler Canada award; Oiler MVP, Most Popular player, Molson Cup awards '97; res. Edmonton, Alta.

JOY, Greg (t&f); b. 23 Apr 1956, Portland, Ore.; given name: Gregory Andrew; m. Sue Holloway; c. Sarah, Alexandra; Texas, UofT; ex-food bank exec-director; high jump specialist; ntl Interscholastic record 2.12m; ntl team '73-82; silver '76 Olympics with 2.23m; PB: 2.26m '76; world indoor record 2.31m College Park, Md., '78; gold '78 Oslo Games (2.24m); silver '78 Commonwealth Games; gold '79 Muhammad Ali Games; 4 ntl titles; OUAA, CIAU titles '83; Governor-General's silver medal '76; Lou Marsh, Norton Crowe trophies '76; made unsuccessful bid for PC MLA seat '95; mem. Cdn Amateur, BC Sports halls of fame; res. Gloucester, Ont.

JUCKES, Gordon (hockey); b. 20 Jun 1914, Watrous, Sask.; d. 1 Oct 1994, London, Ont.; given name: Gordon Wainwright; m. Clara Thompson; hockey exec.; mem. Sask. AHA '48-60; pres. CAHA '59-60; exec. dir. CAHA '60-78; life mem. IIHF, CAHA, SAHA; CAHA trust established in his memory; mem. Order of British Empire (MBE), Order of Canada (OM), Canada decoration (CD), Sask., Canada's Sports, Hockey halls of fame.

JUDD, Oscar (baseball); b. 14 Feb 1908, Rebecca, Ont.; d. 27 Dec 1995, Ingersoll, Ont.; given name: Thomas William Oscar; lefthanded pitcher; played amateur Ingersoll, Guelph; minor pro Springfield, Columbus, Ohio, Columbus, Ga., Rochester, Sacramento, Decatur, Iowa, Toronto; ML pitching Boston (AL) '41-45, Philadelphia (NL) '45-48; ML record: 161 games, 99cg, 771ip, 744h, 399r, 334er, 25hr, 304k, 397bob, 40-51, 4so, 7sv, 3.90era; better than average hitter he frequently saw service in pinch hitting role; hit inside-the-park homer Ebbetts Field '46; ML batting record: 206 games, 317ab, 83h, 11d, 5t, 3hr, 36r, 19rbi, 37k, 27bob, .262ba; won 20 games in each ML; at 37 pitched finest ML game for Philadelphia blanking NY Giants 2-0 in 11 innings allowing just 1 hit through 10 innings and 3 for game; pitched Yankee Stadium season opener '42; mem. '43 All-Star team; mem. Cdn Baseball Hall of Fame.

JULIEN, Denyse (badminton); b. 22 Jul 1960, Rouyn, Que.; began competing age 14; mem. ntl team from '81; ntl jr doubles title '79; 8 ntl singles, 5 women's doubles, 5 mixed doubles gold; through '96 competed 13 Cdn Open, 6 worlds, 6 US Opens, 4 Commonwealth, 1 Olympic, 2 Pan-Am Games, 2 Pan-Am championships, various international opens; 3 Commonwealth Games silver, 3 bronze; has represented Canada in Uber, Sudirman Cup team competitions; turned in brilliant performance in '95 Pan-Am games winning singles, women's doubles (with Si-An Deng) and mixed doubles (Darryl Yung); Wimbledon Open, Welsh Open singles titles; mixed doubles (Iain Sydie) gold, women's doubles (Charmaine Reid) silver '99 PAG; accomplished golfer; res. Calgary, Alta.

JUNOR, Daisy (all-around); b. 10 Jul 1920, Regina, Sask.; given name: Daisy Knezovich; m. David Junor; retd. secty;

among top Regina t&f athletes '30-35; mem. Regina all-star basketball squad who played vs. famed Edmonton Grads; mem. Sask. champion Regina Caps women's softball team '45; power-hitting outfielder with South Bend '46-49, Fort Wayne '49 in AAGPBL; competed in 3 ntl 5-pin bowling championships; 5 club, 2 Regina, 1 Sask. sr. golf titles; mem. 5 Sask. interprovincial golf teams; served various administrative roles in Sask. Ladies' Golf Assn., particularly jr. development; honored by Cooperstown, Cdn Baseball halls of fame; mem. North Battleford Baseball, Sask. Sports halls of fame; res. Regina, Sask.

JURASIN, Bobby (football); b. 26 Aug 1964, Wakefield, Mich.; Northern Mich; defensive end; signed as free agent by Sask; in CFL '86-97, Toronto '98; 181 games, 360 tackles, 132 QB sacks, 3tds, 2 on pass receptions; 5 Western, 3 CFL all-star awards; 7 playoff games; 5 Hardest Hitter awards; CFL Hardest Hitter of '90; mem. '89 Grey Cup champions; res. Regina, Sask.

KABAT, Greg (football); b. 21 May 1911, Wisconsin; d. 1985, Weisir, Idaho; m. Faye Besant; Wisconsin, BSc; teacher, coach; football, track, hockey star at Wisconsin; pro Winnipeg '33-40; quarterback, guard, flying wing, fullback; Bomber line coach initial season; expert place kicker, blocker; mem. 2 Grey Cup finalists; key role 1st-ever Grey Cup victory by western team '35; entire '38 Grey Cup game with broken toe; playing coach Vancouver Grizzlies '41; taught, coached football LA area following retirement; coached St. Paul's HS, St. Paul's jrs while playing for Winnipeg; mem. Canadian Football Hall of Fame.

KABEL, Todd (horse racing); b. 7 Dec 1965, McCreary, Man.; as a teenager honed his skills riding young steers/ quarter-horses; under tutelage of trainer Clifford Grey launched career as jockey '84; top Cdn apprentice jockey '86; moved to OJC circuit '90 and career took off; 2 outstanding jockey Sovereign awards; rode Regal Discovery to '95 Queen's Plate; through '96 recorded 1,793 victories; leg injury '96 deprived him of consecutive top jockey awards; res. Toronto, Ont.

KADATZ, Dennis (football); b. 1 Nov 1938, Edmonton, Alta.; given name: Dennis Melvin; m. Denise Esper; c. Karen, Kim, Kurt; UAlta, BPhE, MA,Oregon; former assoc. prof., assoc. dean faculty of PE UCal; mem. Edmonton jr. Huskies '56-56, UAlta Golden Bears '59-60; coach Strathcona HS 3yrs; head coach Huskies '61-63, ntl jr. title '62-63; head coach UCal '64-68; UCal athletic dir. '66-85; asst. FB coach '69-77; Alta. jr. football all-star player, coach; v-p Stampeders '86-88; GM CODA '88-99; Alta. Football Coaches Assn. coach of year; res. Calgary, Alta.

KAILL, Bob (orienteering); b. 12 Dec 1942, Liverpool, N.S.; given name: Robert Douglas; m. Kristina Eriksson; c. Erik; Waterloo, BA, U of Gothenburg, Sweden; coach, criminology reseacher; top Cdn. ntl championships '71; never beaten by North American in major competition; top Cdn. world championships '72, '74; former editor *National Orienteering*; coach Atlantic Youth orienteering team; coached in Australia, Sweden; res. Sweden.

KALAILIEFF, Bette Jean (softball); b. 11 May 1932, Welland, Ont; given name: Bette Jean Hannell; m. Edward Kalailieff; c. Dawn Eileen, Edward Joseph; Welland Business Coll.; newspaper editor/film librarian; founded Port Colborne Comettes Ladies Fastball Club '58 serving as player/coach/mgr through '97; 4 Ont. titles; Ont. Women's Softball Assn treas. '62-70, v-p. '71-75, pres. '75-88, dir. from '88; Ont. softball commissioner '77-85; mem. Softball Ont. exec. council '68-96; Softball Canada v-p. '85-87; dir. Softball Canada from '87; only woman to serve on Port Colborne rec. comm.; player/mgr Port Colborne ladies basketball club '57-78, leading scorer at 45; obtained city grant to start minor girls softball program '62; coached as many as 3 teams simultaneously while still playing; won Ont. squirt '73, bantam '71, midget '72 titles; business mgr.

Port Colborne Operatic Society from '51; Sports Council builder of sport award; Ont. achievement award; Ont. Corps d'Elite award; YWCA Niagara Region Sports Woman of '88; mem. Cdn Softball Hall of Fame; res. Port Colborne, Ont.

KALLOS, Garry (wrestling); b. 5 Mar 1956, Budapest, Hungary; Concordia, insurance agent; 3 ntl FS, 2 GR titles; gold FS '77, '81, GR '81 Maccabiah Games; gold FS '78 CIAU championships; gold 90kg Sambo '83 Pan-Am Games; mem. '80, '84 Olympic teams; res. Montreal, Que.

KANCHANARAPHI, Raphi (badminton); b. 6 Nov 1936, Bangkok, Thailand; m. Suda; c. Rangsiman, Baisri; badminton pro; 4 Thailand ntl titles; mem. 4 Thomas Cup teams; undefeated over 3 years Thomas Cup play; moved to Canada '69; 4 times Ont., Cdn. champion; won Cdn Open twice, mixed doubles, men's doubles once each; res. Willowdale, Ont.

KANE, Frank (hockey/baseball); b. 4 Aug 1932, Chatham, N.B.; m. Carole; St. Thomas U; public utilities board; mem. Chatham All-Stars '49 NB juvenile hockey champs; St. Thomas NB-PEI intercollegiate title '50-51; Miramichi Braves Maritime sr. champs '54-55; Chatham Ironmen NB intermediate champs '60-61; baseball with Chatham Ironmen 17yrs; coached minor hockey/baseball many yrs, winning NB midget title; mem. Chatham Sports Wall of Fame; res. Chatham, N.B.

KANE, Lorie (golf); b. 19 Dec 1964, Charlottetown, P.E.I.; Acadia; pro golfer; began playing age 5; mem. Cdn international team '89-92; Commonwealth team '91; world amateur team '92; Mexican amateur title '91; turned pro '93; participated Central Fla. challenge tour, du Maurier series titles '94-95; competed in 9 LPGA events '96 earning $28,585; recorded career low 69 Youngstown-Warren LPGA Classic '96; gained exempt status '97; 8 top 10 finishes '97, 11 in '98 tour; lost '97 LPGA championship title to Annika Sorenstam in playoff; lost 2 tour events in playoffs '99; posted best ever money earnings on tour by Cdn with $475,249 '98; 4 consec Cdn LPGA titles; Bobbie Rosenfeld Trophy '97; LPGA Heather Farr award '98; mem. Canada's inaugural Nations Cup team '99; res. Charlottetown, P.E.I.

KANGAS, Katherine (parachuting); b. 18 Mar 1944, Finland; Illinois, MSc; UWO, hons. BA; part owner, mgr. Kangas Sauna Ltd.; mem. Finnish, Cdn. t&f teams early '60s; mem. Eastern College volleyball title teams '63-67; ntl parachuting team mem. '70-80; competed 6 world championships; only person in world to compete in 6 worlds and be ntl team mem. 11 years; for 10yrs ranked ntl top 4, worlds top 21; coached US college gymnastics champion '71; pres. UWO gymnastics club '63-67; asst. dir. athletics Lakehead U '68-70; asst. prof. Buffalo State U '70-71; sports dir. CBC Radio Thunder Bay '79; UWO athlete of '67, Thunder Bay athlete of '70, distinguished citizen award '80; res. Thunder Bay, Ont.

KANJEE, Hashmuk (field hockey); b. 27 Dec 1950, Salisbury, Zimbabwe; UAlta, BPhE; coach; outdoor store buyer; mem. Zimbabwe prov. schoolboys team '67-69; ntl schoolboy team '69; prov. sr. t&f team (long jump) '68-71; Zimbabwe armed forces field hockey team '71-72; UAlta t&f team '72-76; Alta. field hockey team '72-77, capt. '77; ntl team mem. '77-94; mem. '79 Pan-Am Games team; coach UBC women's team; res. Vancouver, B.C.

KANT, Hari (field hockey); b. 23 Aug 1969, Ottawa, Ont.; Carleton, BSc; software engineer; goalkeeper; bronze '88 jr. Pan-Am Games; competed '93 Inter-continental Cup, '98 Commonwealth Games; silver '95, gold '99 Pan-Am Games, Australian Cup, '95 Indo-Pan-American Gold Cup; mem. ntl team '87-98; competed in English premier league '98-99; res. Gloucester, Ont.

KAPP, Joe (football); b. 19 Mar 1939, Stockton, Calif.; given name: Robert Joseph; m. Marcia; c. J.J.; Calif. (Berkeley); football exec., actor; HS football, baseball, basketball standout; Berkley on football, basketball scholarship; quarterbacked '59 Rose Bowl loss to Iowa, MVP award; in Hula Bowl; drafted by Washington but opted for CFL Calgary '60-61; following knee surgery dealt to BC '62-67; guided Lions WFC titles '63-64, Grey Cup victory '64; CFL record: completed 1476 of 2709 pass attempts for 22,725 yds, 137tds; twice all-Cdn., '64 Grey Cup MVP, runnerup '63 Schenley Outstanding Player Award; following salary impasse dealt to Minnesota (NFL) '67-70; led Vikings to '67 div. title, '70 Super Bowl; tied NFL record with 7td passes as Vikes drubbed Colt's 52-14 28 Sep '69; Boston Patriots '70-71; acted in several movies, TV shows; coach Berkeley '82-86; PAC-10 coach of '82; Dec '69 Hickok pro athlete of month award, '69 Vince Lombardi dedication award; '63 Bob Bourne Memorial Trophy Lions most popular player; nicknamed "Injun Joe"; founder TD! Inc.; pres./GM Lions '89-90; mem. Cdn Football Hall of Fame; res. Las Gatos, Calif.

KARCH, Karla (basketball); b. 26 Aug 1964, Vancouver, B.C.; div. Jeff Gailus; UCal, UVic; guard '86 bronze medal world championship, '87 Pan-Am, '91 FISU Games, '93 COPABA world qualification teams; mem, CIAU title team '86-87; competed '94 Goodwill Games, world championships; gold '95 COPABA Olympic qualifing tournament; pro Germany, Hungary; mem. Hungarian Cup title, '96 Olympic teams; CIAU all-Canadian '87-88; 2 HS athletic awards; active in COA Adopt-an-athlete program; res. Vancouver, B.C.

KARCZ, Zeno (football); b. 16 Mar 1935, Toronto, Ont.; given name: Zenon Peter; m. Ethel Cullen; Michigan, BA; sales mgr; baseball Detroit Federation League; 2 seasons Windsor AKO; football scholarship Michigan; pro Hamilton '56, became regular '58; equally adept as halfback, end, corner linebacker; EFC all-star 3 times; *Globe & Mail* all-Cdn. defensive linebacker 5 times; Schenley Cdn. Award '65; 8 Grey Cup games, 3 winners; coach Windsor minor hockey, AKO football, Hamilton minor hockey, football; res. Burlington, Ont.

KARIYA, Paul (hockey): b. 16 Oct 1974, Vancouver, B.C.; given name: Paul Tetsuhiko; Maine; lw Penticton (BCJHL '90-92), Maine '92-94; Team Canada Jr. '91-93; Team

Canada '94 (silver), '98 Olympics, 3 World championships; NHL Anaheim '94-99; recorded 50 goals '95-96 season; team capt. from '96; 2 Lady Byng trophies; 2 1st team NHL all-star; Hobey Baker (NCAA outstanding player); Hockey East rookie, player of yr awards; father mem. Ntl. Rugby team on several tours; NHL record (through '99): 283 scheduled games, 168g, 210a, 14 playoff games, 8g, 9a; res. Orange County, Calif./Vancouver, B.C.

KARPUK, Pete (football/baseball); b. 1927, d. 4 Mar 1985, Toronto, Ont.; played pro baseball Toronto (IL), Ottawa (Border), Galt (Sr IC); pro football defensive back Ottawa, Hamilton, Montreal '48-56; CFL record: 12tds, 8 interceptions; caught key TD pass to help Ottawa win '51 Grey Cup; best remembered for coming off bench to tackle Ulysses Curtis to prevent TD following interception in season's final game '51; also noted for dropping lateral pass and giving up on it after thinking he heard officials' whistles before Woody Strode scooped up ball and set up winning TD by Calgary '48 Grey Cup final; mem. 3 Grey Cup finalists, 1 winner.

KARRYS, Steve (football); b. 20 Jun 1924, Montreal, Que.; m. Helen Bazos; c. Anita Elaine, Steven James; UofT; wholesale distributor; mem. Argos '45-46, '51-52, UotT '47, Rough Riders '48-50; 4 Grey Cup finals, 3 winners; defensive back, Argos modern era all-stars ('45-73); res. Willowdale, Ont.

KASTING, Robert (swimming); b. 28 Aug 1950, Ottawa, Ont.; Yale, BA, Stockholm, Dip. Social Science, McGill, LLD; lawyer; all-Ivy honors Yale swim team '70-72; all-American '70, '72; capt. Yale '72; ntl team '67-75; silver 400m FS, 800m FS relays '67 Pan-Am Games; capt., bronze 400m medley relay '72 Olympic team; silver 400m FS, 800m FS relay '66, '70 Commonwealth Games; gold 400m medley relay '70 Commonwealth Games; bronze 100m FS, silver 400m FS, 800m FS, 400m medley relays '71 Pan-Am Games; dir. Olympic Club of Canada; res. Yellowknife, NWT.

KAUFMANIS, Eric (golf); b. 29 Sep 1960, Toronto, Ont.; m. Lisa Colby; c. Sophie, Julianna; Indiana, UofOtt; lawyer; outstanding HS t&f, basketball star; all-Ottawa Valley honors; Que. Golf Assn. boys 10-12, 12-14 titles; Glenlea men's title '74; quarterfinalist East Aurora, N.Y., jr. invitational '75, winner '76; Que. juve. title '75-76; runnerup ntl juve. '75-76; winner '77; Ottawa Dist. jr. '75-76; Ottawa Dist. men's '76; competed Miami Orange Bowl jr. invitational '76; all-Big 10 Conference team '79-80; res. Richmond, B.C.

KAUL, Anil (badminton): b. 25 Dec 1964, Amritsar, India; coach; began playing age 13; moved to Canada '73; mem. ntl team from '87; 2 men's doubles, 3 mixed doubles ntl titles; competed '92, '96 Olympics; gold men's doubles, silver mixed doubles '95 Pan-Am, men's, mixed doubles gold, team silver '94 Commonwealth Games; competed '91, '93 Worlds; 2 Grand Prix men's, mixed doubles bronze; res. Victoria, B.C.

KAWAJA, John (curling); b. 27 Apr 1961, Chandler, Que.; given name: John Warren; m. Laura; c. Kristyn; York, BA; Adidas business unit mgr.; mem. ntl jr. championship runnerup rink '80; 2nd Ed Werenich '83-84 Ont. title rinks, winner '83, '90 (3rd) Labatt Brier, world title winners; all-star 2nd '83 Brier; competed 5 Briers, 2 winners; fed. govt. world champion award '83; Dick Ellis team award '83; mem. Cdn Curling Hall of Fame; res. Agincourt, Ont.

KAWASAKI, Mitch (judo/wrestling); b. 4 Mar 1950, Hamilton, Ont.; given name: Mitchell Akira; div. Darlene Spencer; c. Stephanie, Becky, Katie; Lakehead, hons. BPHE, McGill.; company v-p; twice ntl 193lb judo champion; world competion '71. '73; 4th Pan-Am judo championships; 5th degree black belt; 4 ntl wrestling titles; 4th '75 Pan-Am Games; 2nd Hungarian Freedom Cup; 6th '76 Olympics; gold '74 Commonwealth Games; knee injuries forced him from freestyle to Greco-Roman style wrestling '75; mem. '76 Olympic team; judo teacher Onteora Japanese Community Center; chief instructor Kawasaki Rendokan; mem. Ont. grading board; gead coach Judo Ont.; also successful gymnast; Thunder Bay, Lakehead U male athlete of year awards; Hamilton Civic Diamond Ring award; res. Hamilton, Ont.

KAY, Jack Jr (golf); b. 14 Jul 1964, Montreal, Que.; m. Christie; Furman, BAdm; followed father's footsteps into pro golf ranks; Ont, Jr., New Eng. Jr., Cdn. Jr. titles '82; capt. Furman golf team, 3 college titles, all-American status; semifinalist US Amateur; 2nd '86 Cdn. Amateur; mem. '86 world amateur title team; low amateur BC Open; played in '86 Masters, Cdn. Open; pro '87; competed on Cdn., USPGA, Australian, Asian, US mini-tours; won '91 Singapore Open; res. Markham, Ont.

KAYSMITH, Henry (rowing); b. 3 Nov 1904, London, Eng.; d. circa 1990, Toronto, Ont.; given name: Henry Ernest; m. Jean McGill; c. Beverley; rowed from '23-33 both sculls, sweep oar; capt., coach Argo rowing club '47-56; 2 ntl lightweight titles; coach Olympic rowing team '52; when Canadian boats were wrecked in storm, Canadian crews rented Stockholm RC shells and 8-oared crew set record with 1st photo finish in Olympic history by tieing Swedish crew; pres. Argo Rowing Club.

KAZANOWSKI, Gerald (basketball); b. 12 Oct 1960, Nanaimo, B.C.; m. Claudia Solorzano; c. Sarah; UVic, BA; certified financial planner; forward 4 UVic CIAU title teams; mem. BC HS title team '78; ntl. team '81-92; mem. Cdn world jr. team '79; gold team '83 FISU Games; ntl team runnerup '82 Jones Cup; mem. 4 FISU Games, 3 World championships, '83 Pan-Am, '84, '88 Olympic Games teams; 7th round draft NBA Utah Jazz '83; pro stops in Spain, Sweden, Finland, Switzerland, Argentina , Mexico '83-92; Leon, Spain, all-star '87-88; 1 CIAU all-Cdn; fed. govt. excellence award '84; BC HS player of '78; res. Sidney, B.C.

KAZIENKO, Linda (archery); b. 29 May 1955, Grimsby, Ont.; veterinarian; FITA star tournament target title '78; Arizona State target title '82; 3 ntl target titles; mem. ntl team '79, '83 Pan-Am, '82 Commonwealth Games, '79, '81, '83 world championships, '84 Olympic Games; Pan-Am team silver '79, '83; mem. Guelph U Sports Hall of Fame; res. Burlington, Ont.

KEAST, Brian (cycling); b. 27 Nov 1953, Vancouver, B.C.; given name: Brian Scott; salesman; ntl team pursuit titles '72-73, '75; ntl 10 mile title '72; BC road race '75, track titles '75, '78; ntl 180km road race title '75; '75, '78 Gastown GP, '75 ntl road race title, '73 Tour de l'Est Que., '78 Stage 5 Dolux, N.Z.; mem. '72 Olympic, '74 Commonwealth Games, '73-75 World championship teams; res. Vancouver, B.C.

KEATING, Jack (baseball/hockey); b. 12 Feb 1908, Newcastle, N.B.; d. 5 Jun 1985, Saint John, N.B.; given name: John Richard; surveyor; led NB sr. league in batting with .389 '27; hockey Hawkins Academy, Chatham Ironmen, Saint John Fusilers; pro New York Americans, Buffalo, Providence, Syracuse, St. Paul; coached St. John Beavers to Maritime sr. title '46; nicknamed "Miramichi Flash"; mem. NB, Saint John Sports halls of fame.

KEATING, Murray (t&f); b. 28 May 1952, Manning, Alta.; given name: Kenneth Murray; m. Sheila Punshon; c. Ryan, Allison; SFU, BA; pres/CEO International Parkside Products Inc.; hammer throw specialist; BC HS, ntl juve. titles '70; 2nd ntl jr. '71; ntl jr. title with record 59.22m (194'3"), 2nd NAIA nationals '72; ntl sr. record 64.30m, NAIA title, mem. '73 FISU Games team; ntl title with 67.46m record, 4th '75 Pan-Ams; ntl record 68.30m mem. '76 Olympic team; retd. from competition '78; res. South Surrey, B.C.

KEATS, Duke (hockey); b. 1 Mar 1895, Montreal, Que.; d. 16 Jan 1972, given name: Gordon Blanchard; standout baseball player; at 17 pro Toronto (NHA); returned to amateur briefly with Peterborough then rejoined Toronto; amateur with Edmonton, pro '19-20 with Patricks; led WCL scorers '22-23; sold to Boston (NHL), transferred to Detroit midway through season, joined Chicago '27; scoring champion Tulsa American Assn.; remained in hockey several more seasons with various WCL teams; scored 119 goals in 128 games prior to playing in NHL where he added 30 goals in 2 seasons; mem. Hockey Hall of Fame.

KEELING, Butch (hockey); b. 10 Aug 1905, Owen Sound, Ont.; d. 12 Nov 1984, Toronto, Ont.; given name: Melville Sidney; m. Winfield Hulse (d); UWO; sales rep.; mem. Owen Sound Greys '21-25, Memorial Cup champs '24; London Srs '25-26; Toronto St. Pat's '26; pro Maple Leafs '27-28, NY Rangers '28-38; mem.'33 Stanley Cup winners; NHL record: 157g, 63a plus 11g, 11a, 47 playoff games; asst. coach Philadelphia Ramblers '39-40; mgr.-playing coach Kansas City (AHL) '40-41; refereed AHL '41-46, 3 seasons NHL; thoroughbred horse owner '31-37.

KEELING, Jerry (football); b. 2 Aug 1939, Enid, Okla.; m. Vella; c. Tina, Terry, Tucker; Tulsa; football coach; twice all-Missouri Valley quarterback; CFL Calgary '61-72, Ottawa '73-75; defensive standout early in pro career; CFL record fumble return 102yds '64; CFL career record: 2477 pass attempts, 1302 completions, 18,239yds, 158 interceptions, 119tds; 4 Grey Cup finals, 2 winners; 5 all-Western, 3 all-Cdn selections; Hiram Walker Trophy '73; shares CFL record 109yd TD pass (to Terry Evanshen '66); twice Calgary MVP, most popular player; began coaching

Northwestern Oklahoma State '80; asst. Ottawa '81, '95, Calgary '82-83, Saskatchewan '84; mem. Cdn Football Hall of Fame; res. Enid, Okla.

KEENAN, Bill (skiing); b. 10 Oct 1957, Thunder Bay, Ont.; UCal, BComm; commercial real estate developer; solid grounding in alpine competition led to membership on ntl jr. freestyle team; considered Canada's outstanding moguls skier; accomplished gymnast, water skier; 2nd mogul grand prix, freestyle rookie of year World Cup circuit '80; 5th WC GP '81, 3rd '82; gold, silver Australian international championships '82; world moguls title '83; res. Calgary, Alta.

KEENAN, Mike (hockey/coaching): b. 21 Oct 1949, Bowmanville, Ont.; given name: Michael Edward; div. Rita; c. Gayla; m. Nola; c. Grant, Reed; St. Lawrence, BSc; UofT, MEd; hockey coach, TV hockey color commentator; began coaching at jr B level winning back-to-back Metro Toronto league titles; Peterborough Memorial Cup winner '80, Rochester (AHL) Calder Cup '83, UofT '84 CIAU title; coached 3 NHL all-star games; coached ntl jr. team '80; 3 Team Canada, 2 Canada Cup winners; head coach Philadelphia '84-88, Chicago 88-91 (GM '89-92), coach NY Rangers '93-94, Stanley Cup '94; coach/GM St. Louis '94-96; coach Vancouver '97-99; 6 div. titles; 3 president's trophies; *Hockey News* coach of '91; NHL Jack Adams coach of year trophy '85; res. Vancouver, B.C.

KEENAN, Roy (boxing); b. 26 Aug 1930, Montreal, Que.; m. Irma Joan Draycott; c. Wayne, Glenn; Sir George Williams.; buyer, supervisor; golden gloves 135lb title '49-50; Montreal open 135lb title, ntl title '50; golden gloves 139lb title '52; ntl 139lb title '52; competed '52 Olympics, lost only bout & retired from ring; ring record (all amateur): 58 bouts, won 39, 7 by KO, 15 by TKO, 17 by decision, lost 19, 1 by TKO, 18 by decision; res. Montreal, Que.

KEEPER, Joe (t&f); b. 17 Jan 1886, Walker Lake, Man., d. 29 Sep 1971, Winnipeg, Man.; c. 4 sons, 3 daughters; carpenter, Hudson's Bay Co.; mem. Norway House Cree band; 2nd in 1st race '09 Brandon indoor mile; joined Winnipeg North End AC, won 7 mile road races '10-11; set Cdn 10 mile record 54:50 Ft. William '11; top Cdn placing 2nd ntl 3 mile race Montreal '11; 2nd 5,000, 10,000m heats '12 Olympics, 4th 10,000m final, didn't compete in 5,000m final due to foot injury; competed in exhibition races vs. Tom Longboat in Europe during WWI; Joe Keeper Memorial Run staged annually by Man. Runners' Assn.; recipient Military Medal; mem. Man. Sports, Cdn Road Running halls of fame.

KEHOE, Rick (hockey): b. 15 Jul 1951, Windsor, Ont.; given name: Rick Thomas; m. Peg; c. Karrie; hockey scout; right wing; London Knights, Hamilton Red Wings Jrs.; pro Tulsa CHL '71-72; NHL Maple Leafs '71-74, Penguins '74-85; NHL record: 14 seasons, 906 scheduled games, 371g, 396a, 39 playoff games, 4g, 17a; attained 50-goal plateau with 55 '81; Lady Byng trophy '81; played in 2 all-star games; scout Pittsburgh '85-86, '95-99; asst. coach Pittsburgh '87-95; mem. Penguins, Western Pa. halls of fame; res. Pittsburgh, Pa.

KEITH, Harold (curling); b. 30 Sep 1939, Moncton, N.B.; given name: Harold Chester: m. Sylvia Irene McEwen; c. Rick, Derrick, Kelly, Abbey; company pres.; mem. NB rink '57 ntl Schoolboy championships, '60, '62, '64, '69-70 Briers; above average performer t&f, baseball, softball; res. Riverview, N.B.

KEITH, Vicki (swimming); b. 26 Feb 1961, Winnipeg, Man.; m. John Munro; s-c.Bruce, Cory; Queen's; motivational speaker, creator Reach for your Dreams workshops; strength and endurance placed her among most successful marathon swimmers in history; swam butterfly stroke for 12 miles setting 1 of 17 world records; among remarkable achievements are 129 hours, 45 minutes continuous swimming '86; 1st double crossing Lake Ont. '87; 1st to swim all of the Great Lakes '88; crossing Juan de Fuca in 14 hours doing butterfly stroke; greatest number of Lake Ont. crossings; covered 43.067 miles in 24hrs '90; among other bodies of water conquered: Lake Winnipeg, Catalina Channel, English Channel, Sydney Harbor; has worked as lifeguard, coach both swimming, gymnastics; dir. Ont. Place '89-91, Sport Ont. '93-94; mem. Ont. Sports awards selection comm '96, Terry Fox Hall of Fame induction comm. '97-98; raised hundreds of thousands of dollars for charity, particularly disabled children; has written several children's books; 2 Kiwanis athlete of yr, Kingston athlete of yr, Ont. , Man., Cdn achievement awards; Gus Ryder, King Clancy, Dr. Robert Jackson, Vanier, Trillium, Rosemary George, Heart, Women who make a difference awards; honored by cities of Toronto, Kingston, Winnipeg, Ottawa, Los Angeles, Goderich, Ont., Harbor Beach, Mich., state of Mich.; Ont., International Variety Clubs; B'Nai Brith woman of '89; mem. Order of Canada, Ontario; mem. Terry Fox, Ontario Aquatic halls of fame; res. Scarborough, Ont.

KELEMEN, Kathy (diving); b. 27 Jun 1966, Czechoslovakia; 2 national, 2 Alta., 1 Austrian title; 1st diver to sweep 1m, 3m, 10m events Canada Games '81; bronze 10m '82 Commonwealth Games; mem. '84 Olympic team; res. Calgary, Alta.

KELESI, Helen (tennis): b. 15 Nov 1969, Victoria, B.C.; nicknamed "Hurricane Helen"; turned pro at 15; mem. Cdn Federation Cup teams '86-94; twice French Open quarterfinalist; best WTA ranking 13 in '89; 2 Bobbie Rosenfeld awards; with Monica Seles won '90 Italian Open doubles; unprecedented 4 straight Cdn women's singles titles '87-90; 3 TC player of yr, TC most improved '85; 2 Cdn doubles team of yr awards; mem. '88 Olympic team; brain tumor operations '95, '97; returned to tour briefly '97; res. Vancouver, B.C.

KELLAND, Kelly (softball): b. 1 Nov 1962, London, Ont.; Ohio State. BSc; child care worker; mem. ntl team 10yrs; 1st base '90, '94 worlds, '87, '95 Pan-Am, '96 Olympic Games; 2 silver, 1 bronze ntl championships; bronze '87 Pan-Am Games; MVP, top batter Vancouver sr. women's league '92; res. Kamloops, B.C.

KELLS, Morley (lacrosse); b. 26 Jan 1936, Midland, Ont.; given name: Morley Cecil; m. Gloria Pellegrin; c. Christine, Bradley, Terrence, Louise; from '81, MPP Humber Riding,

Etobicoke, Ont.; mem. Long Branch Monarchs '55 Minto Cup winners; coached Brantford Warriors to '71 Mann Cup; coach, GM Rochester Griffins winning '74 Nations Cup; with Jim Bishop, Bruce Norris, helped create National Lacrosse League '73; CLA Lester B. Pearson Award for contribution to game '73; mem. Cdn Lacrosse Hall of Fame; res. Etobicoke, Ont.

KELLY, Brian (football); b. 27 Mar 1956, Los Angeles, Calif.; m. Kim; c. Ryan, Katelyn, Alanna; Washington State; all-Pac 10 wide receiver '77; CFL Edmonton '79-87; 6 WFC, CFL all-star selections; Schenley CFL rookie of year '79; mem. 5 Grey Cup winners; CFL record 575 receptions, 11,169yds, 97tds, 586pts; led WFC pass receptions 104 in '83; 5 times surpassed 1000yds plateau single season; 18td catches set CFL record '84; nicknamed "Howdy Doody"; res. Edmonton, Alta.

KELLY, Con (football/speed skating); b. 15 Jan 1934, Edmonton, Alta.; m. Marlene McDermott; c. Con Jr., Vincent, Nancy Lee; plumber; nicknamed "Shipwreck Kelly"; all-star HS basketball '51; Sask., Alta. jr. speed skating titles '46-47; jr. football Edmonton Wildcats '52 Little Grey Cup finalists; fullback Eskimos '55-56 Grey Cup finals; res. Edmonton, Alta.

KELLY, Ellison (football): b. 17 May 1936, Lake City, Fla.; m. Sheila; c. Jude, Jerry, Catherine; Mich. State; retd. corrections officer; solid lineman drafted by NY Giants (NFL) '60; to CFL Hamilton '60-70, Toronto '71-72; usually guard/tackle but versatility enabled him to play defensive end/linebacker; played 175 consec. regular season games; 4 all-East guard; 4 all-East tackle; 1 all-Cdn guard; 2 all-Cdn tackle; mem. 7 Grey Cup finals, 3 winners; CFL stars-of-week panel of judges; mem. Cdn Football Hall of Fame; res. Hamilton, Ont.

KELLY, Henry (builder/softball); b. 18 Jan 1922, Stilesville, N.B.; given name: Henry Burton; m. Pearl; from 1938 softball player, coach, official, administrator; played 35yrs Moncton District Softball League, coached 29 of those 35yrs; led teams to 1 Jr., 2 Sr. A Maritime titles; pres. Moncton City League 12yrs; exec. NBSA 18yrs; commissioner CASA '68-77; coach NB all-stars '73, '77 Canada Games; coached Moncton Rebels to 15 NB women's titles, 8 ntl appearances and '75 silver medal; active umpire 12yrs; helped form NB Softball Umpires Assn.; chair. 2 ntl women's championships; refereed/coached amateur hockey; mgr. Moncton Hawks '78 Hardy Cup winner; Moncton softball field bears his name; named City of Moncton ambassador; nicknamed "Hawk"; mem. Moncton Wall, NB Sports Hall of Fame; res. Moncton, N.B.

KELLY, Janis (volleyball): b. 20 Mar 1971, Winnipeg, Man.; UWpg.; twice Canada Cup all-star; gold '93 CIAU championships; CIAU nationals all-star '93; twice GPAC all-star; silver '93 Canada Cup; competed '91, '93 FISU, '96 Olympic Games; bronze '95 Pan-Am Games; gold, MVP '96 Continental Cup; silver '93 Canada Cup; UWpg female athlete of '92; res. Winnipeg, Man.

KELLY, Jim (motorsport); b. 1929, Hamilton, Ont.; d. 5 Oct 1997, Hamilton, Ont. given name: James Edward; m.

Muriel; accountant Revenue Canada; began riding age 20; despite diminutive 5-6, 130lb frame developed effective, if unorthodox, driving techniques; became highly proficient as road racer, hill climber, speedway, trial, enduro, motocross, ice racer; 4 ntl ice racing titles; set cross-country record on Yamaha 650, Sydney, N.S., to Vancouver in 92h22m '72; helped establish Canada as force at international 6-day enduro championships; rated by *Off Road News* as Canada's No. 1 motorcyclist.

KELLY, Patrick (speed skating): b. 23 Jun 1962, Toronto, Ont.; McGill; consultant; son of NHL Hall of Famer Red Kelly and former NA speed skating titlist Andrea McLaughlin; sister Kitty Ice Capades soloist; played hockey McGill '81-83, Toronto Metro Jr. B champions '81; career threatened by leg fracture '84 but rebounded to begin racing '85 and join ntl team '88; long track specialist; competed '92, '94 Olympics; ntl overall, sprint titles '93; res. Calgary, Alta.

KELLY, Pete (hockey): b. 22 May 1912, St. Vital, Man.; given name: Peter Cameron; retd educator; NHL St. Louis Eagles '34-35, Detroit '35-39, NY Americans '40-41, Brooklyn Americans '41-42; mem. 2 Detroit Stanley Cup winners; AHL scoring record '41-42 season; AD UNB 25yrs; mem. NB Sports Hall of Fame; res. Fredericton, N.B.

KELLY, Red (hockey): b. 19 Jul 1927, Simcoe, Ont.; given name: Leonard Patrick; m. Andra McLaughlin; c. Andra Catherine (Casey), Leonard Patrick Jr., Conn Lawrence, Christina Frances (Kitty); St. Michael's College; pres. C.A.M.P. Systems Canada Ltd., pres., board chair. McLaughlin Enterprises Ltd., NYC, pres. Leonard P. Kelly Ltd.; St. Michael's midget champions '43-44; Jr. B champions '44-45; Jr. A Memorial Cup finalists '45-47; Detroit '47-59, Toronto '59-67; retired to coach Los Angeles '68-70; Pittsburgh '70-73, Toronto '73-77; NHL record: 1316 scheduled games, 281g, 542a, 164 playoff games, 33g, 59a; mem. 9 Prince of Wales Trophy, 8 Stanley Cup winners; 4 Lady Byng, 1 Norris Trophy; 6 times 1st team, twice 2nd team all-star; *Hockey News* NHL coach of '70; MP (Lib) York-West '62-65; *Encyclopaedia Britannica* Achievement in Life award '80; manufacturer of ankle bracelets for Ont. govt. to monitor convicts; mem. Canada's Sports, Hockey halls of fame; res. Toronto, Ont.

KELLY, Steven (shooting): b. 24 Aug 1952, Ottawa, Ont.; given name: Steven Thomas; Algonquin Coll., Dip Chem. Tech., Carleton, BSc; chemist; hand gun specialist; Ont., Que. titles; ntl -21 champion '72; ntl team '71-85; bronze standard pistol '74 nationals; gold team air pistol, rapid fire pistol '77-78, free pistol '78, silver individual rapid fire pistol '78-79, bronze air pistol '81 nationals; mem. '74, '78 world championships, '75-77 Benito Juarez, '76 Olympics, '75, '79 PAG, '77 Shooting Championships of Americas teams; team silver standard pistol '76, team bronze rapid fire pistol '76-77; team silver centerfire pistol '79 Pan-Ams; Civil Service RA athlete of '76-77; Ottawa ACT shooting award '75; res. Ottawa, Ont.

KELSALL, Karen (gymnastics): b. 11 Dec 1962, Nanaimo, B.C.; given name: Karen Barbara; California; teacher; ntl jr. champion '76; 3 sr. titles; 13th '75 Pan-Am, 27th '76

Olympics, 4th '78 Commonwealth, 10th '78 Worlds; all-around Coca-Cola International, Elite Zone, Bulgaria-Canada Invitational, Pacific Rim '78; mem. US championships title team '80; Columbian athlete of year award '76-77; BC jr. athlete of '77; res. New York, N.Y.

KELSEY, Howard (basketball); b. 8 Aug 1957, Vancouver, B.C.; Oregon; sales; guard ntl team '78 Commonwealth Cup gold, '82 Jones Cup silver, worlds fair gold '82, FISU gold '83; mem. '80, '84 Olympic team; fed. govt. excellence award '84; res. Mexico.

KEMKAREN, Heather (figure skating); b. 2 Aug 1958, Winnipeg, Man.; UofT; '75 Vienna Trophy; 3rd '76 Richmond Trophy; 2nd ntl championships, 3rd Skate Canada '77; ntl women's singles titles '78, '80, runnerup '79; mem. '80 Olympic team; boardroom decision which bypassed her for world competiton led to retirement; res. Guelph, Ont.

KEMP, Nigel (swimming); b. 8 Jul 1944, Southampton, Eng.; m. Pauline Quixley; c. Carolyn, Stuart; Loughbrough, DLC, Oregon, BSc, MSc; asst. prof. Dalhousie.; competitive swimmer in England; head coach Halifax Trojan Aquatic Club '71-80; ntl teams coach; guided teams in world, Commonwealth, Olympic, FISU competition; dir. Cdn. Swimming Coaches Assn.; chair. CIAU SCA; tech. advisor CASA Ed. Services Div.; mem. National Coaching Development Comm.; most famous protegee Nancy Garapick; ntl swim coach of '75; CIAU swim coach of '74, '80; head swim coach Dalhousie.; res. Halifax, N.S.

KEMP, Sally (coaching); b. 15 Sep 1939, Montreal, Que.; given name: Sally Elizabeth; MacDonald College, Sir George Willams, BA, SUNY (Cortland), MSc; phys ed teacher, asst AD Waterloo; mem. MacDonald basketball team 2 years, MVP soccer, hockey; basketball YMCA Blues '64-68, Harmony, Jackson 5 teams Kitchener winning frequent city titles; coach women's volleyball, basketball, badminton SGW '65-68, basketball '68-82, field hockey '68-77, Waterloo, basketball, volleyball YM-YWCA Leadership camps, Camp Cuyaga; pres. Montreal Women's Basketball League '66-68, East-West Conference Intercollegiate athletics '67-68; pres. Ont. Women's Intercollegiate Athletic Assn.; mem. exec. comm. OLBA '72-74, pres. '74-75; v-p. Waterloo regional sports council from '74; res. Waterloo, Ont.

KEMPSTER, Ray (lawn bowling/curling); b. 21 Aug 1909, Winnipeg, Man.; d. 16 Jul 1995, Ottawa, Ont.; given name: Raymond Francis Edward; m. Astrid Victoria Olsen; RCAF staff college; retired W/C RCAF; HS rugger, track; badminton, tennis, golf, lawn bowling, curling RCAF Saskatoon; RCAF Trenton badminton singles champion '36, RCAF Saskatoon pairs title '43; 2nd Ont. gold medal team '73 Canada Games lawn bowling rinks competition; pres. PLBA of Ont. '78; pres. Rockcliffe CC '54; mem. Ottawa Valley Curling Assoc. exec.; mem. Governor-General's Curling Club.

KENNEDY, Bill (swimming); b. 26 Oct 1952, London, Ont.; given name: William Ray; div. Deborah Stock; c. Richard, Heather; m. Patricia Peters; c. Janelle, Nicklaus;

Michigan, UWO, BA, UofOtt, LLB; lawyer; backstroke specialist; at 14 youngest mem. '67 Pan-Am Games team placing 7th 100m backstroke; 3 gold Canada Games '69; 2 gold '70 Commonwealth Games; bronze 100m backstroke '71 Pan-Am Games; mem. '72 Olympic team; 3 CIAU titles; mem. Cdn Aquatic Hall of Fame; res. Grand Bend, Ont

KENNEDY, Bruce (curling); b. 23 Jun 1948, Port Arthur, Ont.; m. Tracy Lynn Wark; c. Lisa; CP rail engineer; lead Al Hackner's '82 Brier, Silver Broom title winner; mem. 3 NO Brier entries; '79-80 Thunder Bay GP, '80 World Open, '81 Sault Ste. Marie cashspiel champions; fed. govt. world champion award '82; res. Thunder Bay, Ont.

KENNEDY, Corrina (canoeing): b. 30 Nov 1970, Saskatoon, Sask.; UofSask; engineer; 1st woman from Saskatchewan to qualify for ntl canoe team; 2 gold, 1 silver '91 Pan-Am Games; gold K-2, K-4 200 '95 World championships; gold K-4 500 Pre-Olympic regatta '95; 3 gold, 1 silver Szeged '96; gold K-4 200 Milano '96; gold K-2 500 '96 Olympic team trials; Edmonton Grads team award; res. Saskatoon, Sask.

KENNEDY, Louise (swimming); b. 16 Aug 1949, London, Ont.; given name: Helen Louise; div. James Glen Cross; c. Cameron James, Graham, John Conway Kennedy, Karlie Jean Kennedy; m. Bruce Casler; UWO, BA; ntl team '64-67; mem. '64 Olympic team; mem. world record 440yd freestyle relay team Commonwealth Games '66; mem. Cdn Aquatic Hall of Fame; res. London, Ont.

KENNEDY, Sheldon (hockey); b. 15 Jun 1969, Elkhorn, Man.; m. Janna Coakwell; c. Ryan; jr. Swift Current (WHL) playing 159 scheduled games, 134g, 153a; mem. '89 Memorial Cup winner, named tournament all-star; mem. Team Canada '88 world jr. title team; drafted Detroit '88; dealt to Winnipeg '94; claimed by Calgary on waivers '95; signed as free agent by Boston '96; saw AHL action with Adirondack Calder Cup team '92; NHL record: 56 scheduled games, 8g, 10a; sent shock waves through hockey world by charging veteran coach Graham James with sexual assault over a period of 6yrs; resulting investigation put James in prison after pleading guilty to 300 counts; established Sheldon Kennedy Foundation to assist victims of child abuse; following path of Terry Fox, Rick Hansen did cross-Canada fund-raising tour on roller blades '98; launched hockey comeback with Man. Moose (IHL) '98; joined German league '99; res. Calgary, Alta.

KENNEDY, Ted (hockey); b. 12 Dec 1925, Humberstone, Ont.; given name: Theodore; m. Doreen Belfort; c. Mark Ayre; retd. Ft. Erie race track security official; nicknamed "Teeder"; juve., sr. Port Colborne Ont.; joined Maple Leafs at 17, capt. at 22; 5 Stanley Cup victories; Hart Trophy '54-55 season; led Leafs scorers '46-47 with 28g, 32a, 60pts in 60 games; NHL record: 696 scheduled games, 231g, 329a, 74 playoff games, 28g, 28a; centered Leafs' 2nd Kid Line, later known as KLM Line, of Vic Lynn, Howie Meeker; retd '55, returned briefly '57 to help injury-riddled Leafs; coach Upper Canada College, Peterborough Petes(OHL); twice J.P. Bickell Memorial Trophy as Leaf's MVP; jersey #9 honored by Leafs; mem. Hockey Hall of Fame; res. Port Colborne, Ont.

KENNEDY, Tracy (curling): b. 4 Nov 1963, Thunder Bay, Ont.; given name: Tracy Lynn Wark; m. Bruce Kennedy; c. Lisa; competed 4 STOH tournaments, 2 winners; played lead for Heather Houston's '88 Ont., '88-89 Cdn title rinks, '89 world champion, '88 world runnerup; mem. Ont. team of '89; mem. NWO Sports, Cdn Curling halls of fame; res. Thunder Bay, Ont.

KENNERD, Trevor (football): b. 23 Dec 1955, Edmonton, Alta.; m. Caroline; UAlta; placement kicker; CFL Winnipeg '80-91; shared CFL record 7 FG 1 game; tied CFL single game convert record with 9 vs Ottawa '84; set single season CFL scoring record (since eclipsed) with 198 '85; 2 all-CFL, 3 all-WFC; 2 CFL scoring titles; twice led CFL in field goals; CFL record: 188g; 509cvts, 394fg, 149s, 1840 points; 3 Grey Cup winners; res. Winnipeg, Man.

KENNY, Clayton (boxing): b. 21 Dec 1928, Ottawa Ont.; given name: Clayton Orten; m. Helene Anna Dunlop; c. Jamie, John, Bill; retd civil servant; Que. Golden Gloves lightweight title '46; several years Ont. lightweight titlist; ntl lightweight title '52; mem. '52 Olympic team; capt. ntl boxing team '54 BEG; in 103 bouts won 89, drew 4, lost 9; Ottawa outstanding athlete award; Ottawa Boys Club example to youth award; mem. Ottawa CSRA, Ottawa Sports, Canadian Boxing halls of fame; res. Carleton Place, Ont.

KENT, Chris (skiing): b. 12 Oct 1961, Calgary Alta; given name: George Christopher; UCal; fence builder; '77 ntl juvenile downhill, giant slalom titlist; '79 jr. downhill; mem. ntl team from '80; Mt. Hutt, NZ, FIS downhill '80; 4th World Cup downhill Val D'Isere, France, '81; silver '83 FIS GS, ntl super GS '84; Alta. achievement awards '77, '79; res. Calgary, Alta.

KEON, Dave (hockey): b. 22 Mar 1940, Noranda, Que.; given name: David Michael; div. Lola; c. David, Anne, Marie, Kathleen, Tim; m. Jane Bloomer; c. Holly, Jody; business executive; Noranda Mines juveniles; tryout at 15 with Detroit; 3 years Toronto St. Mikes; Maple Leafs '60-75; Minnesota, Indianapolis, New England WHA '75-79; returned to NHL with Hartford '79-82; Calder Memorial Trophy; twice Lady Byng Trophy; Conn Smythe Trophy '67 playoffs; twice 2nd team all-star center; NHL record: 1296 scheduled games, 396g, 590a, 92 playoff games, 32g, 36a; WHA record: 301 scheduled games, 102g, 189a, 36 playoff games, 13g, 23a; mem. Team Canada '77; Rouyn-Noranda arena bears his name; mem. Whalers, Hockey halls of fame; res. West Palm Beach, Florida.

KEPLEY, Dan (football): b. 24 Sep 1953, Albemarle, N.C.; given name: Danny Ray; m. Terry Lynn; East Carolina.; TV football color commentator; MVP freshman college year, all-conf., all-state 3yrs, all-American honorable mention twice, *AP, NEA* all-American '74; MVP as sr.; pro Dallas '75; linebacker Edmonton '75-84; Eskimos' linebacker coach '85-95; 7 Grey Cup finals, 6 winners; 5 all-WFC, all-CFL awards; Schenley defensive player '77, '80-81; CBC, ESPN color commentator; 1 CFLPA western conf. top linebacker, top def. player, 3 Norm Fieldgate awards; mem. Cdn Football Hall of Fame; res. Sherwood Park, Alta.

KER, Michael (swimming): b. 21 Jul 1957, Vancouver, B.C.; given name: Michael Gordon; m. Paula Joan Whisenand; c. Jessica, Justin; pres. Web Plan Inc.; 4 gold, 1 silver '73 Canada Games; ntl sr. records 400m, 800m, 1500m, 500yd, 1650yd FS events; ntl 1500m titles '73, '75; mem. '73, '75 world championships, '76 Olympic teams; 4 gold, 1 bronze '75 Western Canada Games; 4th 400m FS '77 FISU Games; res. Stittsville, Ont.

KERCKHOFF, Hermann (canoeing): b. 27 Dec 1937, Berlin, Germany; given name: Hermann Walter; m. Christa Ottenberg; c. Claudia, Annette, Ina; camp dir.; 4 ntl kayaking titles '69-73; mem. Olympic team '72; from '73 owner-operator Madawaska Kanu Camp; launched Ottawa Whitewater Leaders (OWL) rafting division of school '81; res. Don Mills, Ont.

KERN, Ben (golf): b. 11 Aug 1946, Rolandia, Brazil; m. Janet; c. Shandy, Tobin, Jordan; New Mexico Col.; golf pro; runnerup '65 Ont. amateur, '67 Ont. Open; '68-69 New Mexico intercollegiate, '69 New Mexico college invitational titles; 1st Cdn named 1st team all-American '68; won New Mexico Open '68, '74; pro '69; 4th San Antonio Open; low Canadian '74 Cdn. Open; New Mexico PGA '74, Ont. PGA '77, Cdn Shrine tournament '79; tied 2nd Sun City Open, 6th Sea Pines Open on satellite tour; twice mem. Canadian World Cup team; head pro National Club Woodbridge; *Score* Magazine Cdn club professional of year '91; mem. Mississauga Sports Hall of Fame; res. Brampton, Ont.

KERN, Laurie (t&f): b. 6 Feb 1957, Vancouver, B.C.; UBC, BA; teacher; javelin specialist; ntl jr. titles '73, '75; sr. outdoors '79-80; mem. ntl team '74-81; mem. '75, '79 Pan-Am, '78 Commonwealth, '79 FISU, '80 Olympic, '81 Pan-Pacific Games teams; ntl bantam, midget, jr., sr. records; bronze '78 Commonwealth Games; gold '79 FISU, '80 Colgate Games, '80 Philadelphia Olympic alternative with Canadian record 57.44m; res, Richmond, B.C.

KERN, Stan (softball): b. 17 Apr 1942, Edmonton, Alta.; given name; Stanice Frederick; m. Joan Roth; c. Trevor, Michelle, Rhonda; mem. Alta. jr. champions '61; Edmonton Playboys '65-67; Edmonton Beta-Well Riggers '68-69; Edmonton Sun Life Red Sox '70-72; Victoria Bate '73-77; mem. title winning teams Hull, Calgary, Montana, Edmonton Klondike, Yakima, Victoria, Seattle tournaments; mem. 7 league, 3 Northern Alta., 3 Alta, 6 BC title teams; mem. 10 ntl championships teams; mem. ntl champion Victoria Bate teams '75-78; 9 top pitcher, 5 Most Valuable Pitcher, 5 MVP, 1 all-star pitcher awards; mem. '76 Victoria Bate team, co-holders World Softball championships; 4 BC Sports Council, 2 city of Victoria, 1 CFAX awards; on retirement from game 9 Jun '79 honored with plaques from Victoria Bate, Victoria Budget teams, for contribution to softball in Edmonton, by Edmonton teammates, opponents, fans; nicknamed "The Colonel"; coached '80 BC peewee A softball champions; mem. Cdn Softball hall of Fame; res. Victoria, B.C.

KERNAGHAN, Marty (softball): b. 9 Aug 1958, Grafton, Ont.; given name: Martin Arthur; m. Beverley Macklin; c. Jennie, Abby; corporate pilot/hockey exec.; third baseman; Oshawa Tonys, Camrose, Alta, Calgary Dome Petroleum,

Alta Brake & Clutch, Sioux City; mem. 4 Cdn, 4 US, 4 world title teams; mem. Team Canada Pan-Am Games '83, ISF '92 title teams; 8 times all-world, MVP '86 worlds; won ISC worlds with Sioux City Penn Corp '88-89, National Health Care Discount '91-92; retd '95; v-p/dir. hockey operations Sioux City Musketeers (USHL); res. Sioux City, Iowa.

KERR, Barbara (equestrian); b. 20 Jul 1947, Winnipeg, Man.; given name: Barbara Mary Simpson; m. Dr. Barney Kerr; c. Tara, Kelly, Barbara, Patrick Jackson; UAlta., BPhE; UBC, teacher's cert.; business mgr.; competitive figure skater to age 17; 1st woman on Western Canada ski patrol '66; 1st equestrian breakthrough '69 winning Aachen Stake Trophy in Germany; 1st, 2nd place ribbons Dublin Ladies' championships; 1st Harrisburg GP '70; mem. bronze medal team '71 Pan-Am Games; mem. '72 Olympic team; leading rider (foreign) NY National Horse Show '72; bronze Ladies' world championships '74; '75-78 concentrated on training young horses, raising family; returned to ntl competition '79; mem. winning Western Team Rothmans East-West Challenge Cup; res. Langley, B.C.

KERR, Bill (golf); b. 14 Jan 1911, Belfast, Ireland; d. 27 Jan 1997, Pointe Claire, Que.; given name: William Henry; m. Constance Daniels; c. William Daniels, Robert John; golf pro; twice PGA champion ('45, '60); 5 times CPGA match play champion; 4 times Que. Open winner; 2nd Canada Cup matches; 5th '55 Greater Greensboro Open; competed '60 Mexican Open, '61 Masters, Caribbean tour; won initial pro tournament Mid Ocean GC, Bermuda; 9 holes-in-one; twice ntl Srs winner; hon. mem. Beaconsfield (Pointe Claire), Palm Beach National Golf Clubs (Lake Worth, Fla.).

KERR, Bobby (t&f); b. 1882, Ireland, d. 1963, Hamilton, Ont.; won 100yd, 440yd, 880yd races Hamilton Coronation Games 1902; '02 & '04 for 1902 & 1904, ntl 100yd titles; mem. 1904, '08 Olympic teams; ntl 100yd, 220yd titles '07; ntl 100yd (9.4), 50yd records; gold 200m, bronze 100m '08 Olympics; '08 British Stamford Bridge meet 100yd, 220yd titles, Harvey Gold Cup as meet's outstanding athlete; defended both titles '09 Dublin, became Irish champion; selected for '12 Olympics but chose retirement; during competitive career won nearly 400 awards, trophies, set 6 Cdn records; mem. Canada's Sports, Canadian Amateur Sports halls of fame.

KERR, Cay (swimming); b. 25 Jan 1921, Edinburgh, Scotland; given name: Catherine Ross Gordon; m. Donald Kerr; c. Gordon, David, Donald, Deborah, Andrea, Laura; began swimming early '30s; won first provincial age group title '33; 1st ntl title '35, 1st Cdn record '37; set 2 Cdn, 5 Man. records, won 4 ntl titles '39; 5 ntl titles, 3 Cdn records '40, Cdn female athlete of year nominee; continued to compete at ntl level through '58; devoted attention solely to synchronized swimming '59; set 5 ntl, 11 Manitoba records; won 13 Cdn, 4 Western Canadian, 56 Manitoba titles; 5 Manitoba solo synchronized swim titles; early competitive career spanned '33-'59; returned to pool in masters competition 17 provincial titles, including 5 consecutive solo, 2 duet titles '59-63; 16 provincial Masters age group records; 1 gold, 4 silver, 2 bronze medals World Masters championships '84; more than 35yrs in

synchronized swimming as competitor, coach, judge, administrator; helped organize Canadian Aquatic Hall of Fame; served term as pres. Winnipeg Synchro Swim Club, founding pres. Man. section CASSA; Ntl pres. CASSA '57-60; mgr. synchro swim team '59 Pan-Am Games; meet official '54 Empire, '59 Pan-Am Games; master meet official for swimming, diving, synchro swim judge, coach; pres. Ladies Aquatic Hall of Fame; mem. Red Cross water safety advisory board; Royal life saving instructor, examiner; mem. Man. Sports Hall of Fame, Order of Canada; res. Winnipeg, Man.

KERR, Dave (t&f); b. 1 Jun 1946, Toronto, Ont.; m. Anne Sauasvous; Ball State, Miami of Ohio, BSc; teacher; middle distance specialist; all-American cross-country college champion '67; mem. all-American track team '68, all-American indoor track team '69; runnerup 1500m Olympic trials '68; NCAA 1500m, record holder '68; represented Canada '74 European tour; res. Scarborough, Ont.

KERR, Jane (swimming); b. 12 May 1968, Mississauga, Ont.; Florida, BAdm; employee Anderson Consulting; team capt.Fla., 5 Southeast Conf. titles, 24 all-American awards; FS sprint specialist; launched competitive career age 8; 8yrs ntl team; 32 ntl titles; 4 ntl championship high point titles; ntl 200FS record; 3 silver '83 Pan-Am, 2 gold, 2 silver, 2 bronze '86 Commonwealth Games, silver, 2 bronze '87 Pan-Pacific championships; mem. '84, '88 Olympic teams; 4x100 medley relay bronze '88 Olympics; 3 Mississauga fenale athlete of yr awards; Ont., Swim Ont. team of yr awards; mem. Mississauga Sports, Ont. Aquatic halls of fame; res. Mississauga, Ont.

KERR, John (sailing); b. 9 Aug 1951, Toronto, Ont.; m. Heather McNevin; Upper Canada College, UWO, BSc; v-p. marketing Kerrwil Publications; ntl soling class titles '73-78; European soling title '78; NA, US title '77, '82; CORK title '81-82; 3rd worlds '78; 5th worlds '79; French World Cup title '78; Kiel Week '78; 3rd NA '80; mem. ntl sailing team; mem. '84 Olympic soling bronze crew; gold, silver Duke of Edinburgh awards; res, Mississauga, Ont.

KERR, Terry (harness racing): b. 23 Dec 1953, Kitchener, Ont.; became entranced with standardbred racing age 11 when father Palmer purchased first horse; learned driving techniques from the late Ron Feagan; shifted base of operations from OJC circuit to California, BC and Pompano Park.Fla.; with trotter Dapper Dillon represented Canada in Roosevelt International '77, placing 3rd; guided pacer Quite A Sensation to world record '86; regularly drove Red Bow Tie '96 season; through '97 5406 victories with purses exceeding $15M; res. Coconut Creek, Fla.

KERR, Tim (hockey): b. 5 Jan 1960, Windsor, Ont.; m. Kathy Hafer (d); c: Kayleigh, Kimberley; m. Margaret Wilson; c. Garret, Wesley, Tanner; owner real estate, insurance, construction cos; rw Windsor Spitfires '76-77, Kingston Canadians '77-80, Maine Mariners '79-80; not drafted but joined NHL Philadelphia '80-91, NY Rangers '91-92, Hartford '92-93; topped 50-goal plateau 54 '84, '85, 58 '86, '87; set NHL powerplay single season record with 34 '85-86; Bill Masterton Trophy '89; NHL record: 655 scheduled games, 370g, 304a, 81 playoff games, 40g, 31a;

p-pres. Flyers Alumni Assn.; mem. Windsor/Essex County Sports, Flyers hockey halls of fame; res. Avalon, N.J.

KERR, Randy (harness racing): b. 9 Jun 1956, Kitchener, Ont.; worked for father Palmer, brother Terry as teenager; began driving Western Fair Raceway at 18 then moved to Windsor with Terry; branched out on own '80 winning driving titles Windsor, Leamington; topped century victory mark 16 consecutive years; through '97 2860 victories and purses exceeding $10M; res. Amherstburg, Ont.

KERRIGAN, Mike (football): b. 27 Apr 1960, Chicago, Ill.; Northwestern; quarterback; signed as free agent by New England (NFL) '82; joined Toronto CFL '84; Hamilton '86-91, '95-96, Toronto '92-94; 2 Eastern all-star; set CFL playoff game passing record with 35 vs. Toronto '86; CFL record: 154 games, 5tds, 305yds on 134 carries, completed 1534 of 2870 passes for 21,714yds, 126tds, 163int; 6 playoff games, 2 Grey Cup finals, 1 winner; Grey Cup offensive star '86; res. Hamilton, Ont.

KERWIN, Gale (boxing): b. 9 Jan 1935, Ottawa, Ont.; given name: Gale Allen; m. Joyce Payne; c. Allen, Kathleen, Shawn, Christine; politician, real estate broker; competed as amateur '47-53 attaining finals twice in Olympic trials; pro '54; KOed Bobo Fiddler in 12th for ntl welterweight title '58; lost world lightweight title bid to Joe Brown '59; lost middleweight title bid to Ralph Dupas '60; lost jr. welter title bid to Dulio Loi '61; British Empire welterweight title, ranked 10th world welterweight divison; retd. from ring following 1st round TKO of Frank Marvin '62; pro record: 47 bouts, won 12 by KO, 21 by decision, 3 draws, lost 3 by TKO, 8 by decision; launched Gale Kerwin Boxing Club '97; mem. Ottawa Sports, Canadian Boxing halls of fame; res. Ottawa, Ont.

KERWOOD, Tony (harness racing): b. 26 May 1958, Scarborough, Ont.; given name: Anthony; with urging of father Frank began dabbling in sport age 11; began to impress as driver age 17; spends some time training horses at father's farm near Bowmanville; one of leading drivers on OJC circuit winning 5 UDR titles; drove Pacific Rocket to USTA/USHWA Older Horse Pacer of '95 title; through '95 2355 victories and purses exceeding $20M; res. Campbellville, Ont.

KESLER, Reg (rodeo): b. 16 Oct 1919, Lethbridge, Alta; m. Elizabeth (Liz); c. Greg, Mark (d), Pat, Janet, Leanne, Jeanie; rancher, retd. stock contractor; bucking horse specialist; 3 ntl all-around (AA) titles; 2 Cdn all-around awards Calgary Stampede; produced 1st rodeo Cranbrook, B.C., '51; with Harry Vold supplied much of the rodeo stock in Alta. in the '50 and '60s; mem. Cdn Rodeo Hall of Fame; res. Missoula, Mont./Rosemary, Alta.

KEYES, Carole (luge): b. 2 Sept 1952, Woodstock, N.B.; given name: Carole Maxine; asst. spa co-ordinator Grey Rocks Inn; mem. ntl luge team '74-84; 3 ntl, 2 NA, 1 Empire State singles titles; mem. '76, '80, '84 Olympic teams; competed world championships '77, '79; head coach ntl team '84-87; chief athletic therapist ntl women's basketball team '80-84; Cdn Athletic Therapists Assn. service award; mem. NB Sports Hall of Fame; res. St. Jovite, Que.

KEYS, Eagle (football): b. 4 Dec 1923, Turkey Neck Bend, Ky.; m. Joyce White; c. Betty, Buddy, Dale, Janice, Karen; Western Kentucky State College, BSc, Kentucky, MA; retd. International Steel & Pipe exec., football coach; pro centre Alouettes '49-51; Eskimos '52-54; all-Western '52-54; following '54 Eskimos Grey Cup win retd to coaching; head coach Eskimos '59-63, guiding them to Grey Cup final '60; Saskatchewan asst. '64, head coach '65-70, Grey Cup victory '66, finals '67, '69; head coach BC '71-75; Annis Stukus Trophy CFL coach of '68; mem. Canadian Football Hall of Fame; res. Burnaby, B.C.

KEYTE, Lawrence (modern pentathlon): b. 11 Sep 1963, Boston, Mass. given name: Lawrence Edgar; Queen's; teacher; ntl tetrathlon champion '78, '80-81 (shooting, running, swimming, riding); ntl junior champion '82; 1st individually '79, capt. 1st place Canadian team '79 US tetrathlon championships; 1st overall '80, champion jr. '81 West Point Academy triathlon (delete riding); mem. modern pentathlon (add fencing to tetrathlon) team jr. worlds '80-83; shared Bell HS athlete award '80-81; Ottawa ACT awards '79-80; PB: 4963 points world jr. '83; res. Ottawa, Ont.

KHAN, Sharif (squash): b. 10 Nov 1945, Peshawar, Pakistan; m. Jacqueline Taylor; Millfield School, Eng.; squash pro; Somerset county champion at 13; British jr. champion Drysdale Cup at 16; 12 NA open titles from '69; 9 NA pro, 5 Boston Open, 4 Boodles Gin Open, 4 MAAA Open titles; twice world invitational racquets champion; Mennan Cup world invitational title '79; mem. world-renowned Khan family of squash champions; NA Open Trophy dating back to '54 won by Khan family members 22 times, retd to Sharif's permanent possession '81; Squash Canada distinguished service award; res. Toronto, Ont.

KIDD, Bruce (t&f): b. 26 Jul 1943, Ottawa, Ont.; m. Phyllis Berck; UofT, BA, Chicago, MA; assoc. prof. UofT athletic dir.; Commonwealth 6 mile title '62; ntl 1 mile '61, '63, 3 mile '61, '62, '64, 6 mile '62, '64, cross-country '60, '61, '63; US 3 mile indoor '61-62, 6 mile '62, cross-country '61, '63; British 2 mile indoor '64; mem. '64 Olympic, '62 Commonwealth Games teams; Lou Marsh Trophy '61; Lionel Conacher trophy '61-62; authored '83 study on athletes rights in Canada; '93 Bryce Taylor award for contribution to amateur sport; mem. advisory bd. women's sport intl.; mem. UofT, Cdn Amateur, Canada's Sports halls of fame; res. Toronto, Ont.

KIDD, James (sailing): b. 28 Jul 1953, London, Eng.; given name: James Michael; UofT, hons. BSc; chartered accountant; mem. Royal Cdn Yacht Club jr. sailing program to age 16; ntl, international titles in Albacore, International 14, Fireball classes; mem. ntl team; Flying Dutchman silver '75 Pan-Am Games; 6th FD world championships '76; mem. '76 Olympic team; world International 14 class champion '77; ntl FD titlist, 4th worlds '78; throughout career teamed with younger brother Hugh; res. Toronto, Ont.

KIEFER, Eniko (diving): b. 12 Aug 1960, Montreal, Que.; McGill; 3 US International 1m, 3m titles; 7 ntl age-group 1m, 3m, one 10m titles; '71 world age-group 3m title; 5 ntl sr. 1m titles; 2 Can-Am-Mex jr. titles; CIAU 1m, 3m titles

'81; mem. '76, '80 Olympic, '78 Commonwealth, World teams; 3m bronze '78 Commonwealth Games; outstanding female diver '81 CIAU championships; res. Dollard des Ormeaux, Que.

KIHN, Richard (gymnastics); b. 15 Aug 1935, Alzenau, West Germany; m. Tina; c. Markus, Britta; accountant, hospital controller; ntl men's champion '59, '61, '63-64; qualified for worlds '62, Pan-Ams '63 but was ineligible on citizenship grounds; treasurer Ont., Cdn. Gymnastics Federations, World Cup '80; meet dir. annual Ont. Milk Meet; judge men's gymnastics; rhythmics team mgr.; Ont. special achievement award; res. Etobicoke, Ont.

KILBURN, Joey (bobsleigh); b. 27 Apr 1949, Ottawa, Ont; given name: Joseph William; Sheridan College; coach; began bobsledding '74 as brakeman 4-man sled; 2nd ntl 2-man, NA 4-man '74; NA 4-man title '75; driver 2-man sled '76, '80 Olympics; drove ntl 2-man title sled '77-79, 4-man '79; mem. '79 world championships team; retd '81 but came back to compete in 2-, 4-man events '82; coach/tech. dir. Bobsleigh Can '85-90; development coach '90-92; coached '92 Olympic team; coached US program '93-95; FIBT international coach from '96; res. Ottawa, Ont.

KILLINGBECK, Molly (t&f); b. 3 Feb 1959, Jamaica; given name: Molly Elizabeth; m. Liam O'Connor; York, BA; coach York; ntl indoor 200m title '80, 400m '80-81; 16 gold, 13 silver, 7 bronze medals at both 200m & 400m distances in international competitions; mem. 4x400m gold, 4x100m silver medal relay teams '82 Commonwealth Games, 4x400 silver relay team '84 Olympics; mem. ntl sr. record 4x100m relay '82, 600m record, 4x400 relay '83; CIAU 600, 300, 60m gold '85; gold, silver, bronze '81 Pacific Conference Games; 3 silver '83, 1 silver '85 FISU games; mem. '80 (boycotted) '84, '88 Olympic Games teams; retd. from competition '89; 1 CIAU indoor t&f female athlete of yr; 1 CIAU indoor record; coach Phoenix TC, Windsor Legion TC, Windsor U, York; guest coach People's Republic of China '90; head track coach '93 world deaf games; sprint coach '93 indoor worlds, FISU Games, '94 Commonwealth, '96 Olympic Games (men's 4x100m gold medal relay); OTFA sprint coach '90-95; head coach/GM Windsor Legion T&FC '93-95; 3 OWIAA, 1 OUAA, 1 CAC, 1 Wittnauer coaching excellence awards; Athletics Canada ntl relay co-ordinator, chair ntl women's sprint development prgm, mem. board Toronto 2008 Olympic bids comm.; 10 Ont. sport excellence awards, 3 fed. govt sport excellence awards, 2 York female athlete of yr awards; Harry Jerome award '84; res. Toronto, Ont.

KILREA, Brian (hockey/coaching); b. 21 Oct 1934, Ottawa, Ont.; given name: Brian Blair; m. Judy Ringer; c. William, Dianne, Linda; hockey exec.; nicknamed "Killer"; Ottawa minor ranks to Troy Sr. Bruins; pro Edmonton (WHL) '57-58; Vancouver (WHL), Rochester, Springfield (AHL), Tulsa (CHL) through '68-69 season; brief NHL appearances with Detroit '57, LA '67, 3 goals, 5 assists; 9 seasons Springfield (AHL), 3 Calder Cups; coach-mgr. Ottawa 67's '73-84, '87-94, '95-99, GM only '94; OHA title '77; division title '82, '84; Memorial Cup '84, '99; became winningest Cdn jr coach 17 Jan '97 with 742nd victory; achieved 800 victory plateau 25 Sep '98; 4 OHL coach of yr awards; coach ntl jr. team '83; asst. coach NY

Islanders '84-86; Ottawa declared day in his honor; trustee Ottawa Sports Hall of Fame; names CHL all-time team coach '99; Ottawa arena bears his name; mem. Ottawa Sports, Springfield Hockey halls of fame; res: Ottawa, Ont.

KILREA, Hec (hockey); b. 11 Jun 1907, Navan, Ont., d. 1969, Detroit, Mich.; given name: Hector Joseph; m. Lois Shannon; Detroit Ford; pro Ottawa Senators '25-31, '32-33, Detroit '31-32, '35-39, Toronto '33-35; ranked among fastest skaters in NHL; beat Howie Morenz in match race at Montreal; assisted on Mud Bruneteau goal which ended longest game in NHL history; mem. 3 Stanley Cup champions; NHL record: 176g, 129a; in US Army WW2 received Distinguished Service Cross, Croix de Guerre, 3 Purple Hearts.

KIMBALL, Norm (football/administration); b. 29 Jun 1930, Edmonton, Alta.; m. Sharon; c. Douglas, Brian, Robert; football executive; joined Eskimos organization '61 as minor football co-ordinator; moved through organization serving as office mgr., asst. GM, to GM '64; exec. mgr. '76-85; instrumental in developing Eskimos dynasty which resulted in 9 Grey Cup appearances in 10yrs and 6 successive titles; developed superior scouting system; strong impact on CFL growth with work on various committees; Edmonton Sportsman of year; pres./CEO Alouettes '86, he folded team on eve of '87 season; res. Edmonton, Alta.

KING, Dave (hockey): b. 22 Dec 1947, North Battleford, Sask.; m. Linda; c. Jennifer, Scott, Andrew; UofSask, BAPE, BEd; hockey scout; mem. UofSask Huskies 4yrs; coached 2 Sask.jr. B titlists; asst coach Huskies '72-73, head coach Billings, Mont., WHL '77-79, UofSask. '79-83, CIAU title '83; ntl jrs '81-83, world gold '82; asst Team Canada bronze '82, head coach '83-92; head coach '84, '88, '92 (silver) Olympic teams, Izvestia silver '86, gold '87; coached ntl jr team to world gold '82, bronze '83; coached Japan '98 Olympics; coached Calgary (NHL) '92-95 (109-76-31); asst. Montreal '97-99; European pro scout for Montreal '99; CIAU title '83; 3 world silvers; Dunc McCallum Memorial Trophy '78; WHL coach of '78; CIAU coach of '80, 3 Canada West coach of year, Cdn Coaching Assn. coach of '92 award; *Hockey News* International Sportsman of '91; 3 Colb McEown UofSask awards; consultant Japanese IHF mem. Order of Canada, Cdn Olympic Hall, UofSask Wall of Fame; res. Calgary, Alta.

KING, Don (football/officiating): b. 23 Mar 1919, Regina, Sask.; d. 28 Jun 1986, Regina, Sask.; accomplished in softball, hockey and particularly football; 3yrs Regina intercollegiate ranks before joining Regina Jr. Dales; Western Cdn champions ;39; encouraged by Piffles Taylor played key role in keeping Roughriders alive during '40s as lineman, secty-treas, mgr, asst. coach; began officiating '46; worked more than 1100 games from peewee through pro; pres. Regina football officials assn. 7yrs; instrumental in organizing similar groups throughout country; officiated 4 Grey Cup finals, 2 all-star games, 3 jr finals; 25yrs on-field, 11yrs officiating supervisor; mem. Sask. Sports Hall of Fame.

KING, Donald (cricket); b. 18 Oct 1916, Naramata, B.C., d. 2 Oct 1977, Toronto, Ont.; Pannal Ash Coll. Harrogate, Eng.; achieved rare English schoolboy double academic head boy, athletics capt.; school colors in cricket, racquet sports, track; 440yd, 1-mile, rugby records; earned cap as schoolboy international in rugby; helped organize school teams in France; secty. Ont. Cricket Assn. '47-52; instrumental in restructuring OCA, reorganizing Cdn. CA; re-established international series between US-Canada; Cdn. rep. International Cricket Conference; authored several articles on cricket in domestic, international publications; hon. life mem. Mid-Ulster Cricket group; hon. life mem. Emu Club New South Wales; hon. Old Boy Upper Canada Coll.; hon. v-p. U.K. Assn. of Cricket Umpires; dir. Sports Federation of Canada; MBE.

KING, Mike (football): b. 13 May 1925, Toronto, Ont.; m. Allisen Allan; c. Glen, Gary; company mgr.; Toronto Indians Beaches '44-49; fullback, defensive guard Eskimos '50-57; 201 carries for 910yds '51, WFC all-star fullback '50-51; East-West Shrine game '55; mem. 3 Grey Cup winners; res. West Vancouver, B.C.

KING, Peter (rowing): b. 25 Oct 1940, Glasgow, Scotland; given name: Peter Charles; McGill, BEng, UWO, MBA; dir. office of Auditor General; served in Royal Navy '57-74, achieved rank of Lt.Cmdr., Cnd naval reserve '75-82; dir. CARA from '67, ORC '68-94, pres. '95; life mem. Ntl Assn. Amateur Oarsmen, ORC; mem. Assn. Professional Engineers of Ont., Royal Cdn Military Institute; authored "*Art and a Century of Canadian Rowing*"; authored numerous briefs, articles pertaining to rowing; holds international rowing umpire's license. Level II coaching certificate; coached at local, regional, provincial, national levels; managed university fencing teams; chaired NCD cross-country skiing; mgr. officials '76 Olympics; ME *Catch* magazine; as student won Que., Ont. sabre, foils titles, various rowing crowns; bronze Cdn. Ski Marathon; silver Masters singles '83 Ntl rowing championships; City of London, Ottawa, ORA, CARA Centennial, President's awards; SFC Doug Gilbert award '80; Air Canada Sports Executive of '80; Ottawa ACT Sportsman of '84; mem. Cdn Forces Hall of Fame; res. Ottawa, Ont.

KING, Tim (baton twirling): b. 26 Oct 1958, Kitchener, Ont.; Waterloo, BSc; quality control mgr.; Ont., ntl, world title holder; NA, ntl titles '76, retired undefeated; Twirl Canada judge, coach; chair. Twirl Canada males in twirling comm.; v-chair. Ont. chapter Twirl Canada; ranked among top 100 Ont. racquetball; res. Kitchener, Ont.

KING, Vivian (swimming): b. 4 Apr 1931, Winnipeg, Man.; m. Alex Thompson; c. Wayne, Lorne; Winnipeg juve. titlist '41; Man. Jr. 1/2 mile title '44; Man. 50, 100, 220yds, l/2 mile FS, 50, 100yds backstroke titles '45; swept all Man. jr titles, added Cdn jr. 100yd FS title '46; 23 Man., 4 Western Cdn, 5 Cdn, 10 Ont., 4 Watertown, N.Y., titles '47-51; ntl mile (Ross Gold Cup) champion '49-51; Cdn record 400m FS '48; mem. '48 Olympic team; turned pro '52; won world pro 3 mile title, 4th 26 mile Atlantic City race, swam Lake Winnipeg (18 miles) in record 8:30:00; mem. Man. Sports Hall of Fame; res. Winnipeg, Man.

KINGSMITH, Ray (curling): b. 28 Jun 1927, Queenstown, Alta.; d. 3 May 1988, Calgary, Alta.; m. Nancy Holoboff; c. Marlene, Doug, Joan, Don; Calgary business coll.; sales mgr.

Cominco; pres. Glencoe CC '62; pres. SACA '66-67, secty-treas. '70-79; CCA exec. from '79, pres. '83-84; v-p. Canadian Curling Reporters; baseball player, umpire; organizer, commissioner Calgary Little League; assoc. dir. Calgary Stampeder Football Club; Calgary Sportsman of '80; mem. Canadian Curling, Alta. Sports halls of fame.

KINISKI, Gene (wrestling/football): b. 23 Nov 1928, Edmonton, Alta.; given name: Eugene Nicholas; m. Marion Kay Weller (d); c. Kelly Eugene, Nicholas Clayton; Arizona; retd. bar owner; played football/wrestled Arizona; Alta heavyweight wrestling champion '48-50; AAU champion '51; drafted by LA Rams '52 but better offer brought him home for 3 CFL seasons as Eskimos lineman; 41yrs pro wrestling; def. Lou Thesz for world heavyweight title; held title '66-69; res. Blaine, Wash.

KINNEY, Margaret (basketball): b. 1 Feb 1912, Edmonton, Alta.; d. 9 Sep 1995, Montreal, Que.; m. Fred Howes; UAlta, BA; retired supervisor public affairs Que. region CBC (English); mem. UAlta women's basketball, track teams '28-29, '30-32; mem. famed Edmonton Commercial Grads '28-30; mem. Canadian Basketball, Alta. Sports halls of fame.

KINSELLA, J.J. (builder): b. 12 Apr 1908, Regina, Sask.; given name: John Joseph; m. Joyce Gwynneth Mathie; c. Bruce Michael Stephen, John Dermott Andrew; St. Pat's Coll., Carleton; fed. govt. management analyst; 4-letter HS athlete starring in baseball, football, hockey, boxing; mem. Ottawa Montagnard Jr., Montcalm hockey clubs winning Ott. Dist. Int. title '31; mem. Banker's HL; Ott. Dist. featherweight boxing title '31; organized minor baseball, football, hockey programs; conceived, built Silver Stick hockey tournaments into international event which have flourished from 1957; Ottawa ACT sportsman of '69; res. Ottawa, Ont.

KINSELLA, Ray (builder): b. 27 Jan 1911, Ottawa, Ont. d. 29 Apr 1996, Ottawa, Ont. m. Callista Ryan (d); c. Stephen; played briefly in NHL with Ottawa Senators; Eastern Cdn. welterweight boxing champion; boxing instructor Ottawa Boys Club; founding mem. Civil Service RA, major fund raiser for massive all-purpose complex; 3 terms pres. Ottawa RA Centre; RA Centre arena bears his name; life mem. Ottawa CSRA; mem. Ottawa CSRA, Ottawa Sports halls of fame.

KIRBY, Bruce (sailing): b. 2 Jan 1929, Ottawa, Ont., m. Margo Dancey; c. Janice, Kelly; yacht designer; mem. '56,'64 Finn Class, '68 Star Class Olympic teams; International 14 titles '63-64; mem. 3-boat world International 14 Class team titlists '58, '61; '78-79 NA Tempest Class champion; designed own craft for Admiral's Cup, Fastnet races Eng.; designed Laser, world's most popular sailboat, '69; designer Canada I, Canada's 1st America's Cup challenger since 1800s; mem. Ottawa Sports Hall of Fame; res. Rowayton, Conn.

KIRBY, Peter (bobsleigh/skiing): b. 17 Dec 1931, Montreal, Que.; given name: Peter Murray; m. Lynnette Castonguay; c. Gillian, Martha; Dartmouth College,. BA, McGill; pres. Northsport Ltd.; ntl jr. alpine ski title '53; mem. ntl FIS team '54; capt. Dartmouth ski team '56; bobsled competitor

'61-66; mem. '64 Olympic gold 4-man team, 4th 2-man team; mem. '65 world title 4-man team; mem. Cdn Amateur, Canada's Sports halls of fame; res. Beaconsfield, Que.

KIRKCONNELL, Herb (badminton); b. 6 Sep 1925, Toronto, Ont.; div. Lois, m. Peggy; UofT; retd.; 7 ntl, 8 Ont. sr. men's doubles, 3 Ont. men's doubles titles; mem. Thomas Cup team '61; pres. Ont. Badminton Assn. '76-78; pres. Cdn. Badminton Assn. '79-81; mgr. Cdn team '74, '78, '82, '86 Commonwealth Games; res. Whitby, Ont.

KIRZINGER, Dave (football); b. 1 Mar 1956, Victoria, B.C.; m. Pam; c. Erin Elizabeth; SFU, UBC; sales rep.; HS athlete of '73; BC 1st team HS basketball all-star; starred in basketball SFU 1 season; football starting offensive guard UBC, top lineman '77; 1st draft pick '78; CFL Calgary '78-86; Stampeders player rep.; res. Calgary, Alta.

KISSICK, Myrna (horseshoes); b. 9 Dec 1936, Stauffer, Alta.; given name: Myrna Taylor; m. Jim Kissick (d), Wilf Donald; s- c. Kenneth; retd. farmer/rancher; began horseshoe pitching '72; earned bronze Alta. Summer Games '72; 12 Alta. women's titles; 4 ntl women's titles; competed 8 world championships; Alta high ringer record; with Sylvianne Moisan involved in best game ever thrown by women (126 shoes) '95 ntl championships; 2 Alta. achievement awards; mem. Alta. HPA, Horseshoe Canada halls of fame; res. Caroline, Alta.

KLETTL, Loni (skiing); b. 8 Sep 1959, Lamont, Alta.; given name: Loni Elaine; cocktail waitress, bartender; mem. Alta. Canada Winter Games team '71; 4 Alta. Cup series overall titles; ntl juvenile, Pontiac Cup overall titles '75; mem. ntl team '76-80; NA GS title '78; ntl downhill '79; mem. '80 Olympic team; 5 Alta achievement awards; res. Jasper, Alta.

KLIMPEL, Carol (swimming); b. 30 Mar 1963, Toronto, Ont.; given name: Carol Henny; m.; Texas; freestyle specialist; bronze 100m FS '77 Canada Games; gold 100m FS, 4x100 FS relay, 400 IM '78 Commonwealth Games; gold 4x100 FS relay '79 Canada-Russia dual meet; 2 bronze '79 Canada Cup; ntl 50m 100m, 200m, 4x100 FS relay records; 100m FS gold World Cup '80-81; Speedo world sprint award '80; 21 ntl championship medals; 9 ntl, 4 4-nation, 1 Swedish, 1 Japanese titles; 4 ntl, 2 Commonwealth Games, 1 Commonwealth records; silver 4x100 FS relay '79, '83 Pan-Am Games; mem. '80, '84 Olympic teams; active masters swimmer; mem. Ont. Aquatic Hall of Fame; res. West Hill, Ont./Nashville, Tenn.

KNIGHT, Lee (football); b. 8 Feb 1965, Wallesey, Eng.; m. Lisa; c. Kathy Lee, Sam, Connor; correctional officer; fullback/slotback Burlington jr Tiger-Cats (Braves); signed as free agent Hamilton '87; selected by Montreal '96 equalization draft; claimed on waivers by Ottawa '96; traded to Hamilton '96; 1 Grey Cup final; res. Burlington, Ont.

KNIGHT, Pete (rodeo); b. 1904, Philadelphia, Pa.; d. May 1937, Hayward, Calif.; shared championship honors 1st Calgary Stampede '24; world rodeo championships '26, '35-36; '30 reserve championship American Rodeo Assn; thrown, killed defending title '37; mem. Alta. Sports Hall of Fame.

KNIGHT, Tuffy (coaching); b. 17 May 1936, Clarksburg, W.Va.; given name: David; m. Connie Rose Audia; c. Timothy Allen, Brian David; Fairmont State Coll., BA, West Virginia, MA; football coach; 5ys head football, track, 3yrs basketball coach Crooksville, Ohio, HS; Class A Ohio state HS grid title '63; AD/head football coach Wilfrid Laurier '65-83; OIAA football titles '66, '68; OUAA titles '72-73, '78, '97; CIAU College Bowl finalist '66, '68, '72; CIAU coaching record (through '96) 138-80-5; overtook Bruce Coulter as CIAU winningest coach in '96 season; 3 CIAU Frank Tindall coach of yr awards; OUAA coach of '79, '80; Southeastern Ohio FB coach of '62-63; dir. player personnel Argos '84-88; head FB coach Waterloo '88-97; res. Waterloo, Ont.

KNOX, Swede (officiating/hockey); b. 2 Mar 1948, Edmonton, Alta.; m. Maureen Baldwin; c. Ryan, Brett; Athabaska, BBA, Alya. Inst. Tech.; NHL linesman; played jr. hockey Alta. jr. league; joined NHL '71 appearing in initial game 14 Oct '72; worked 1500th game '91; 1 NHL all-star game, 5 Stanley Cup finals; NHL record (through '98) 1917 scheduled games, 200 playoff games; res. Edmonton, Alta.

KNOX, Walter (t&f); b. 1878, Listowel, Ont.; d. 3 Mar 1951, St. Petersburg, Fla.; Beloit Coll., Illinois; athlete, coach; 1896-1933 recorded 359 1sts, 90 2nds, 52 3rds in formal competition; '07 won 5 ntl titles in single meet beating Cdn world class athletes Ed Archibald (pole vault), Dr. Cal Bricker (broad jump), Bobby Kerr ('08 Olympic sprint champion) in their own specialties while each was at his peak; ntl records 100yd dash (tieing 9.8 world record), 22.8 for 220yd, 46'5" shot put, 12'6" pole vault, 24'2" running broad jump, 10'7.5" standing broad jump; 128' discus; British tour '11 won 57 1sts, 23 2nds, 31 3rds; coach Olympic team Stockholm Games; American all-pro '13 defeating US champ John A. MacDonald in match contest Hanlan's Pt. Toronto; competed vs. BE champion F.R. Cramb for world all-around title '14 winning 6 of 8 events; coach '16 British Olympic but WWI cancelled games; coach '20 Olympic Games; chief coach Ont. Athletic Commission several years; mem. Canada's Sports Hall of Fame.

KNUDSON, George (golf); b. 28 Jun 1937, Winnipeg, Man.; d. 24 Jan 1989, Toronto, Ont.; given name: George Alfred Christian; m. Shirley; c. Kevin, Paul, Dean; golf pro; Man. jr. title '54-55, ntl jr. '55; mem. Man. Willingdon Cup teams '56-57; Man. Open '58-60, Ont. Open '60-61, '78, Atlantic Open '76; 5 CPGA titles; 12 PGA tour titles '61-72; individual low, International Trophy '66 World Cup; with Al Balding won '68 World Cup; tied 2nd US Masters '69; won Australian Wills Masters '69, runnerup '70; winner in playoff with Stan Leonard Shell Wonderful World of Golf '63-64, in playoff with Balding '64-65, runnerup to Gene Littler '65-66, Al Geiberger '67-68; Peter Jackson Cup '76; mem. Order of Canada, RCGA, Ont. Sports Legends, Canada's Sports halls of fame.

KOHARSKI, Don (officiating/hockey); b. 2 Dec 1955, Halifax, N.S.; given name: Donald Nicholas; m. Susan Anderson; c. Jamie, Kevin; hired as WHA official at 18; joined NHL as linesman '77 becoming referee after 163 games; gained international experience in Canada Cup '87, '91; worked 15 consec. conf. finals, 7 Stanley Cup finals, 1 NHL all-star game; NHL record (as linesman/referee) through '98: 1132 scheduled, 158 playoffs games; res. St. Louis, Mo.

KOLAR, Stan (golf): b. 1 Nov 1922, Czechoslovakia; m. Ethel Marie Barlow; c. Terence, Lynn, Tracey; retd. golf pro; runnerup Man. jr. '29; won Thunder Bay amateur '41; Lachute Open twice, Rawdon Open, Que. Open; runnerup CPGA Seniors twice; Canada's 3rd master pro '77; res. Aylmer, Que.

KOMONEN, Dave (t&f); b. 16 Dec 1898, Kakisalmi, Finland; d. 19 Apr 1978, Helsinki, Finland; given name: Taavi; div. c. Patti, Unto; m. Elsa Hamalamen; c. Elia; carpenter; emigrated to Canada '29; ntl, US marathon titles, 2nd Boston Marathon '33; mem. Sudbury Frood Mines AC; unsuccessful bid Finnish Olympic team '32; won '34 Boston Marathon; failed to qualify '34 BEG team; returned to Finland '51; Lionel Conacher award '33.

KONANTZ, Gordon (skiing/sailing): b. 12 Oct 1932, Winnipeg, Man.; given name: Gordon Edward; m. Gail Macdonald; c. Leslie, Donald, Erin; UWpg, Queen's, BComm; GM North American Lumber; competed nationally alpine, cross-country championships; Norwegian Birkenbeiner '77, '79, US Birkenbeiner '75, Cdn masters cross-country '80-81; pres. Loch Lomond Ski Club, Thunder Bay '56; pres. Puffin SC '61-62; chair. Man. div. CSA '67-68; with Gary Coopland formed Man. jr. Jackrabbit program '57; pres. Man. Cross-Country Ski Assn. from '76; chair. ntl ski team comm., dir. cross-country Canada '80-81; commodore Royal Lake of Woods Yacht Club '65, '71; pres. Man. Sailing Assn. dir. CYA '74-76; mem. Winnipeg Pan-Am Games comm. '67; pres. Winnipeg Squash Racquet Club '73-74; dir. Man. Sports Fed. '81-83; chair. Man. Foundation for Sports; level 2 cross-country ski instructor; instructor examiner CYA; mem. Man. Sports Hall of Fame; res. Winnipeg, Man.

KONCHALSKI, Steve (basketball): b. 11 Apr 1945, New York, N.Y; given name: Stephen; m. Charlene MacFarlane; Acadia, BA, Dalhousie, LLB; basketball coach St.FX; mem. Acadia Axemen team '62-66; twice all-conf.; 4 scoring records leading team to ntl title '65; title tournament MVP; Acadia career record 1479pts; coached St. FX to 2 CIAU title tournament appearances; AUAA regular season title '80, '84, AUAA championships '81, '84; ntl team asst. coach '73-94, head coach '95-98; mem. Cdn Basketball Hall of Fame; res. Antigonish, N.S.

KONIHOWSKI, Diane (t&f); b. 7 Mar 1951, Vancouver, B.C.; given name: Diane Helen Jones; m. John Konihowski; c. Janna Lee, Alana; UofSask, BE; mgr. Calgary ntl sports centre; ntl pentathlon champion '69, '72-78; jr. titlist '70; ntl sr. indoor LJ title '74; mem. '70, '74, '78 Commonwealth, '73 FISU, '72, '76, '80 Olympic, '75, '79, '83 (coach) Pan-Am Games teams; pentathlon gold '75 Pan-Am, bronze '73 FISU, '78 Commonwealth Games; Polish, Czechoslovakian pentathlon titles '74; world indoor record 4540pts '75 ntl championships; PB (outdoor) 4673 winning '75 Pan-Am Games; ntl records indoor 50m hurdles 7.1m, LJ 6.37m, shot put 16.23m; ranked 3rd world pentathlon '77-78; team leader Olympic services '94; co-holder Velma Springstead trophy '75 (Nancy Garapick), '78 (Cathy Sherk); 2 Bobbie

Rosenfeld awards; '78 ntl LJ title; CBC radio commentator; COA v-p; mem. Canada's Sports Hall of Fame selection comm.; CdM 2000 Olympics; mem. Order of Canada, Cdn Olympic, Sask. Sports Halls, UofSask Sports Wall of Fame; res. Calgary, Alta.

KONIHOWSKI, John (football): b. 6 Jan 1950, Moose Jaw, Sask.; given name: John William; m. Diane Jones; c. Janna Lee, Alana; Brigham Young, UofSask; operates sports surface co.; 5 ntl age class TJ titles; Sask. HS LJ, TJ, high hurdles records; ntl indoor TJ record 49'10"; won '72 Olympic trials 400m hurdles; ntl record 300m (34.7) '72; football UofSask '71, '73; all-CIAU wide receiver '73; drafted Stampeders '72; mem. Eskimos '74-80; Edmonton nominee '75 rookie of year; mem. 5 Grey Cup finalists, 4 winners; active mem. Prairie Golden Canadian TC; mem. UofSask Sports Wall of Fame; res. Calgary, Alta.

KOOTNEKOFF, John (basketball): b. 10 Aug 1935, Canora, Sask.; given name: John Lee; m. Mary Katherine Farrell; c. J.C., Kurtis, Karolyn Marie; Seattle, BEd, Washington, MSc; facilitator of positive information; mem. Seattle NCAA finalist team '58; mem. '60 Olympic team; player/coach 7 Sr. A ntl title teams; coached several ntl team players during '70s; named 1 of 100 most physically fit over-40 Canadians '76; film dir. radio, TC personality; authored "*From Kooty with Love*"; pres. dir. Horizon Positive Self Image Institute; listed American Coll. Who's Who for academic, athletic achievements; res. Burnaby, B.C.

KOPAS, Jack (harness racing): b. 16 Oct 1928, Lumsden, Sask.; m. Alice; c. John, Roger; horseman; developed racing interest working for Jim Kealey farm; became Gibbs brothers trainer; active driver from '64; Cdn horseman of '69, '76; protegee of Clint Hodgins; among top horses Super Wave, Jade Prince, Shadow Star, Nat Lobell, Super Clint, Areba, Armbro Bramble; 21 classic race victories including 6 Reynolds Memorial, 2 Sheppard Pace, 1 Cane Pace; mem. Harness Racing Hall of Fame; res. Ilderton, Ont.

KOPAS, Ron (baton twirling): b. 2 Oct 1941, Toronto, Ont.; m. Heather Rand; c. Paul, Steven; twirling coach; 5 ntl men's titles; world duet (Isabel Wright) title '59; led ntl champion Ticat corps; WBTF clinic co-ordinator throughout world; WBTF judge; coach Ont., ntl, world corps champions '79-82; tech. chair. Twirl Canada, tech. v.-chair WBTF; res. Bramalea, Ont.

KORN, Alison (rowing): b. 22 Nov 1970, Ottawa, Ont.; Carleton, MJourn., UWO; mem. ntl team from '95; Head of Charles coxed 4's gold '95; silver women's 8's '96 Olympics; coxless pairs gold (with Emma Robinson), silver 8's '97, pairs gold '98, bronze women's 8's worlds; made coaching debut UWO; Ottawa ACT rowing award '97; mem. Nepean Sports Wall of Fame; res. Nepean, Ont./London, Ont.

KOSANOVIC, Zoran (table tennis): b. 1956, Yugoslavia; d. 4 Feb 1998, Toronto, Ont.; m. Darinka Jovanov; c. Tanya, Sasha; mem. Yugoslavian ntl team placing 2nd in world play at 18; emigrated to Canada '79; 5 Yugoslavian, 5 Cdn ntl men's singles titles; at one stage of career ranked 7 in world; coached Cdn ntl, Ont. provincial teams several yrs.

KOSMOS, Mark (football): b. 28 Oct 1945, Baltimore, Md.; given name: Markus Michael; m. Nikki Marie Zaharis; c. Markus Michael Jr., Nicole; Oklahoma, BA; restaurateur; all-league football Eastern Oklahoma Jr. Coll; twice all-league; mem.'69 Pottstown Firebirds (ACFL) title team; pro Montreal '70-71, Hamilton '72, Ottawa '73-77; all-Cdn., Eastern Schenley lineman of yr. nominee '71; all-Eastern '75-76; mem. 4 Grey Cup champions, 3 different teams; radio football show host; mem. Rough Riders advisory board; mem. CFL all-time all-stars; res. Nepean, Ont.

KOUZMANIS, Tom (soccer): b. 22 Apr 1973, North York, Ont. midfielder; 1st draft expansion Nova Scotia Clippers '91; mem. Canada's Olympic -23 team; 1st Cdn player in 110yrs to score pair of goals in 1st 2 intl games for Canada; played with Nova Scotia Clippers, Montreal Supra CSL; mem. Montreal Impact A League '96, Toronto Shooting Stars indoor league; res. North York, Ont.

KOVITS, Herman (rowing): b. 20 Jan 1933, Lashburn, Sask.; given name: Joseph Herman; m. Brenda; c. Carolyn Andres, Eric.; UBC, BA, McGill, DDS; dentist; UBC Big Block award for rowing; mem. '54 BEG gold medal 8-oared crew; mem. Class B BC fastball champions '56; mem. BC Sports Hall of Fame; res. Chilliwack, B.C.

KOZAK, Chelan (equestrian): b. 16 Jan 1969, Revelstoke, B.C.; began competitive career at 14; mem. ntl team from '91; youngest mem. Canada's three-day event team '94 World Equestrian Games; rides Soweto; competed '96 Olympics; res. Clayburn, B.C.

KRAATZ, Victor (figure skating): b. 7 Apr 1971, Berlin, Germany; began skating age 9; mem. ntl team from '92; with Shae-Lynn Bourne formed outstanding Cdn ice dance duo from '91; 7 ntl, 5 Skate Canada titles; 2 NHK trophy silver; 3 Worlds bronze; Championship series gold, silver; Neblehorn trophy gold; competed '94, '98 Olympics; res. Lake Placid, N.Y.

KRAEMER, Bob (football): b. 31 May 1950, Winnipeg, Man.; m. Beverly; c. Robbie, Danny; Uman, BPhE; ntl dir. Athletes in Action; conference all-star quarterback, twice conference MVP; guided UMan to College Bowl titles '69-70; outstanding player '69 College Bowl; 1st round draft Blue Bombers, WFC rookie of '71 as wide receiver; caught 43 passes '73 while setting single game Bombers record with 11 catches; retd '75; res. Abbotsford, B.C.

KRAUSE, Willi (coaching): b. 11 Dec 1909, Pasewalk, Germany; m. Eva Jordan; c. Christa, Axel; retd master pattern maker; limited success as broad jump, javelin competitor; instrumental in developing Erika Fish as German champion, top international competitor; major role in developing Trail T&FC into one of Canada's best; supervised Trail indoor track construction; coached BC track team ntl championships, '64 Olympic trials; within 1st decade in Trail his athletes had won numerous ntl titles, set 6 Cdn, 1 world record while harvesting silver, bronze medals at Pan-Am, Commonwealth Games; several of his trainees earned US university scholarships; Jim Morris award Trail sportsman of '77; Trail citizen of '79; National Recreation Assn award '84; BC certificate of merit '81; mem. BC Sports Hall of Fame; res. Trail, B.C.

KREINER, Kathy (skiing): b. 4 May, 1957, Timmins, Ont.; m. Dave Phillips; c. Nelson Phillip, Liam, Michaela; Utah, BA, UofOtt, MA; sport psychology consultant; home schooler; at 12 youngest ever to win Mt. Tremblant Taschereau downhill; at 14 joined older sister Laurie on ntl World Cup team; mem. '72 Olympic team; gold WC GS Pfronten, W.Germany '74; 6 ntl titles, 4 times runnerup '74-81; gold GS '76 Olympics, 4th combined '80 Olympics; 2 WC silver, 1 bronze medals; 2 Pontiac Cup bronze; FIS gold GS '75; downhill silver '81; 4th overall WC GS '76-77; WC record 1-1-3; raced '80-81 as independant; Bobbie Rosenfeld award, Ont. athlete of '76; with freestyle skiing husband Dave operated ski program Blackcomb Mt., B.C.; mem. Cdn Skiing, Canada's Sports halls of fame; res. N. Vancouver, B.C.

KREINER, Laurie (skiing): b. 30 Jun 1954, Timmins, Ont.; given name: Lauren Margaret; m. Ron Vaillancourt; c. David William, Angela, Russell; municipal employee; ex-ski resort mgr., owner; ntl downhill title '69; mem. '70 FIS, '72, '76 Olympic, '69-76 ntl teams; US ntl GS title '71; 4th GS '72 Olympics; '75 Roch Cup title; overall downhill title '75 Can-Am series; ntl sport tech. advisor alpine skiing from '94; minor soccer administrator; director Timmins Ski Racers; active in Cdn Special Olympics; Ont. Achievement award, Timmins Sportswoman of '72; res. South Porcupine, Ont.

KRISTMANSON, Alan (basketball): b. 5 Nov 1961, Vancouver, B.C.; m. Danielle Cosens; SFU.; golf pro; basketball coach; 3rd team Cdn HS all-star '79; forward ntl team '87-92; WBL '90-91 scoring leader; mem. '87 Pan-Am, FISU, '88 Olympic teams; pro New Zealand '86, avg. 42pts per game; asst. coach SFU; played golf as jr.; turned pro '93; res. Whistler, B.C.

KROEKER, Tim (t&f): b. 25 May 1971, Chilliwack, B.C.; SFU; hurdler; ntl jr. 110mH title '89; 5 ntl titles; bronze '94 Francophone Games; mem. ntl team from '90; competed '91 Pan-Am, '91, '93 FISU, '94 Commonwealth, '96 Olympic Games, '93, '95 worlds; gold '95 Harry Jerome, Fresno relays, '94 Flagstaff, '93 Provo, Utah, relays; bronze '95 Nurnberg Grand Prix; BC athlete of '93; Sr. male athlete of '93; res. Surrey, B.C.

KROL, Joe (football): b. 20 Feb 1919, Hamilton, Ont.; m. Pat (d); c. Richard, Peter; UWO, BA; retd. insurance exec., govt. consultant; nicknamed "King"; runner, passer, kicker; helped UWO win '39 intercollegiate title, Hamilton Wildcats ntl finals '43; with Argos '45-52; mem. 6 Grey Cup winners; with Royal Copeland formed Gold Dust Twins; Jeff Russel trophy '46; Lionel Conacher trophy '46-47; Lou Marsh trophy '46; Grey Cup record 30 points; named to All-Time Argos team '96; mem. UWO W-Club, Ont. Sports Legends, Cdn Football, Canada's Sports halls of fame; res. Toronto, Ont.

KROLL, Horst (motorsport): b. 16 May 1936, Germany; m. Hildegard Schmelzle; c. Birgit; operates auto service business; ntl under-2 litre title '67-68; ntl driving title '68; Germany's Algemeiner Deutscher Automobil Club gold medal with diamonds for distinguished service to international autosport '68; raced in Formula 5000 series in Canada, US; twice runnerup to ntl champion Eppie Sietzes

Sr.; 3 ntl Formula Vee titles; mem. Cdn Motorsport Hall of Fame; res. Scarborough, Ont.

KROMM, Bobby (hockey): b. 8 Jun 1929, Calgary, Alta.; given name: Robert David; m. Geraldine Louise DeRosa; c. David, Robin, Richard, Michelle; manufacturing rep.; amateur hockey Kimberly Dynamiters, North Sydney Victorias, Trail Smoke Eaters; mem. '61 world champion, '62 Allan Cup champion Smoke Eaters; coached Smoke Eaters 4yrs, Nelson Maple Leafs 2yrs; pro coaching ranks Seattle (WHL) 1yr, St. Louis Braves (CHL) 1yr, Dallas Black Hawks (CHL) 9yrs, Winnipeg Jets (WHA) 2yrs, Detroit (NHL) 3yrs; coached 3 CHL champions, 1 Avco Cup WHA champion; CHL, WHA, NHL coach of year awards; res. Livonia, Mich.

KROUSE, Bob (football): b. 21 Feb 1943, Hamilton, Ont.; given name: Frank Robert; m. Marjorie Hughes; c. Robert Joseph, Paul Edgar, John Henry; McMaster, BA, BPhE, Buffalo, MA; HS phys ed teacher; twice all-city HS fullback, defensive back; mem. 1st Cdn HS mile relay team to post sub-3:30 indoor mile (3:27.9); pro Hamilton '63-75; defensive back, fullback, corner linebacker; capt. Ticats '73, player-coach '75; EFC all-star '67; defensive co-ordinator McMaster '80; head coach Sheridan College from '82; Cdn scout Tiger-Cats; res. Grimsby, Ont.

KRUGER, Harry (football); b. 11 Mar 1954, Calgary, Alta.; div. c. Eric, Blaine, Rachel; m. Myrna Hermanson; s-c. Caleb; UCal, BComm; Paintball field owner, Calgary indoor arena, Cochrane outdoor field; CIAU all-Canadian '77; defensive back in CFL with Calgary, Winnipeg, Ottawa '78-84; res. Cochrane, Alta.

KRUPP, Charlie (builder): b. 1906, Winnipeg, Man.; d. 21 Jan 1958, Winnipeg, Man.; YMHA baseball, softball catcher with strong defensive skills; soccer standout; also participated in basketball, football, hockey, lacrosse, 10-pin bowling, curling; while his athletic skills were considerable his major impact came as a builder serving as a coach, executive, sponsor and liberal contributor to many sporting organizations; coached several outstanding sr. men's softball teams '40s-'50s; exec Winnipeg Blue Bombers, Esquires jr. hockey club, Maple Leaf curling club; operated Winnipeg Monarchs jr. hockey club, horse racing stable; sponsored numerous teams including Winnipeg Dominoes women's basketball team; Teeni-League baseball, women's softball, Man. Olympic basketball players all benefitted from his generosity and support; softball park bears his name; mem. Man. Sports Hall of Fame.

KRYCZKA, Joe (administration): b. 4 Jun 1935, Coleman, Alta.; d. 11 Jan 1991, Calgary, Alta.; UAlta. BL; lawyer, judge; mem. '49-50 Alta midget champs; capt. Alta. juveniles; defence with UAlta Golden Bears '53-56; 3 Western Canada Intercollegiate titles; shoulder injury ended playing career; turned to coaching/refereeing' elected to AAHA exec. '63; pres. CAHA '72; instrumental in organizing 1st Canada-Russia series; dir./vp Calgary Olympic Development Assn. '79; nicknamed "Justice Joe"; life mem. AAHA, CAHA, CODA; Canada's Sports Exec. of '72; Alta. outstanding sport achievement award '72; mem. AAHA, Alta, Canada's Sports halls of fame.

KRYCZKA, Kelly (synchro swim): b. 8 Jul 1961, Calgary, Alta.; given name: Kelly Marie; m. William Irwin; c. Stephanie, Kristine, Scott (d), Jennifer, Nicole; UCal, BPhE; mem. Calgary YWCA Aquabelles; ntl jr. solo title, figures, duet, team aggregate '76; ntl sr. team title '77, '81, '83; ntl sr. duet title '79, '82, solo '80-83, figures '80-82; mem. '84 Olympic; '79, '83 Pan-Am, '79, '81 Pan Pacific, '79, '82 World championships team; duet gold '79, '82 World Cup, '79 Pan-Am Games, '80 Scandinavian Open, Mazda Invitational; solo gold '80 Mazda, Swiss Open; solo silver, duet, team gold '82 Worlds, '83 Pan-Am Games; figures bronze '83 Pan-Am Games; duet silver as sport introduced to Olympics '84; teamed with Sharon Hambrook for most duet victories; 5 Alta. achievement awards; Calgary Booster Club outstanding athletic performance award; with Hambrook Aquatic Fed. top swimmers '82; fed. govt world champions award '83, excellence award '84; coach in masters program; mem. Alta. Sports, Cdn Olympic, Cdn Aquatic halls of fame; res. Calgary, Alta.

KUEBER, Philip (rowing): b. 17 Nov 1934, Galahad, Alta.; given name: Philip Thomas; m. Eleanor Kepper; c. Kathryn, Philip Jr., Heidi, John; UBC, BComm, LLB; barrister & solicitor, QC; mem. UBC rowing crew '54-57; gold crew '54 BEG; silver Royal Henley '55, Olympics '56; gold Western sprint championships '55; gov. Olympic Trust; mem. Alta Sports Hall of Fame; last known res. Calgary, Alta.

KULAI, Dan (soccer): b. 10 Nov 1907, Ladysmith, B.C.; d. 22 Aug 1980, Vancouver, B.C.; m. Margaret; c. 1 son, 1 daughter; fire chief; mem. New Westminster Royals ntl soccer title teams '27-28; forward, later keeper with BC Select teams several seasons; refereed 25yrs; officiated in World Cup, Pan-Am Games, most of world's top soccer matches; several years Vancouver city handball singles, doubles champion; mem. BC Sports Hall of Fame.

KULEZA, Kasia (synchro swim): b. 29 Aug 1976, Warsaw, Poland; Vanier Coll.; immigrated to Canada age 7; became involved with synchroswim age 10; team gold '96 French Open, '93 jr worlds, '92 jr ntls; silver '96 Olympic, '95 Pan-Am Games, World Aquatic championships; ntl senior solo, duet (with Stephanie Bissonnette), figures gold 1993; Helen Vanderburg synchroswim award 1993; res. Laval, Que.

KULKA, Glenn (football): b. 3 Mar 1964, Edmonton, Alta.; Bakersfield Coll.; defensive end; signed as free agent Edmonton '86 but released and joined Montreal '86; Toronto '87-89, Ottawa '90-94, Sask. '95-96; 1 Eastern all-star; mem. '87 Grey Cup finalist; turned to pro wrestling '97; last known res. Regina, Sask.

KURRI, Jari (hockey): b. 18 May 1960, Helsinki, Finland; m. Tina; c. Joonas, Ville; rw; Jokerit, Finnish league '77-80, '94; drafted by Edmonton '80-90, Milan Italy '90-91; Los Angeles '91-95; Anaheim '96; Colorado '97-98; 2 1st team, 3 2nd team all-star; Lady Byng Trophy '85; traded to Philadelphia then to Los Angeles same day '91; topped 50-goal plateau with 71 '84-85 and followed up with 68 and 54 in subsequent years; NHL record: 1251 scheduled games, 601g, 797a, 200 playoff games, 106g, 127a; achieved 600g plateau '97; played 7 NHL all-star games; mem. 5 Stanley Cup winners; won Bermuda Cup tennis tournaments in Helsinki '83-85; 2 Kings outstanding defensive player awards; '91 World championships 1st team all-star; competed for Finland '98 Olympics; res. Calabasas, Calif./ Helsinki, Finland.

KUTROWSKI, Linda (wheelchair basketball): b. 20 Jun 1958, Deep River, Ont.; given name: Linda Denovan; m. Ed Kutrowski; Carleton (computer science), Ryerson (chemical technology); civil servant; regarded as one of the most patient and methodical players in Cdn wheelchair basketball annals; mem. 2 ntl title teams with Ottawa Jazz; also competed nationally with Ottawa Royals; mem. '92, '96 Paralympic, '94 World gold medal teams; res. Ottawa, Ont.

KUZMICH, Heather (golf): b. 18 Jul 1968, Port Arthur, Ont.; Georgia; 4 Ont., 4 ntl jr. titles; mem. 4 ntl jr. title teams; 1st international section jr. worlds; longest driving champion '83 women's Western US jr. championships; 3 successive Barcoven club titles; mem. 4 Ont. title teams; 5 course records; ranked #1 Cdn jr. '81-84; *Score* magazine Cdn jr. golfer of '83; res. Trenton, Ont.

KWASNYCIA, Don (shooting): b. 30 Apr 1952, Toronto, Ont.; self employed; mem. ntl team '77-98; ntl skeet record 382/400 '77; ntl skeet titles '77-78; won '81 ntl team trials, '80 Olympic trials; sr. record 434 winning team gold Grand Prix Von Lippe; mem. '78, '86, '94 Commonwealth Games, '77-78, '81, '85 '90, '93 Worlds, '79, '87, '91 Pan-Am Games, '88 Olympic Games; '79-82, '85, '87 Benito Juarez International teams; record 394/400 '79 US nationals; Cdn grand prix gold '92; res. Downsview, Ont.

KWONG, Normie (football): b. 24 Oct 1929, Calgary, Alta.; given name: Norman Lim Kwong; m. Mary; c. Gregory, Bradley, Martin, Randy; Mount Royal College; real estate broker, sports exec.; nicknamed "China Clipper"; Calgary North Hill Blizzard Jrs; 13yrs fullback Calgary, Edmonton; in 10yrs recorded statistics (from '51) 74tds, 9022yds rushing, 5.2yds per carry; Eddie James Memorial trophy as WFC leading rusher 3 times; mem. 4 Grey Cup title teams including 3 consecutive with Edmonton '54-56; 5 times all-star; twice Schenley outstanding Cdn award '55-56; at '60 retirement held over 30 CFL records, including 134 playoff games; Lionel Conacher trophy '55; pres./GM Calgary '88-92; GM BC '96; noted raconteur; prominent in ntl, regional affairs; part owner NHL Calgary Flames; mem. Alta., Canada's Sports, Football halls of fame; res. Calgary, Alta.

KYLE, Doug (t&f): b. 22 Jul 1932, Toronto, Ont.; given name: Douglas Haig; m. Carol Hemmings; c. Suzanne, Bobby; UBC, BA, Michigan, MA; economist; 4 ntl 3-mile, 6 6-mile titles; 1 10-mile, marathon, 3 ntl cross-country titles; 10 ntl records in distances from 2-15 miles, 3000-25,000 metres; 9 Alta. records from 1-10 miles, US 6-mile record; mem. '54 BEG, '56, '60 Olympic, '59, '63 Pan-Am Games teams; silver 10,000m, bronze 5000m '59 Pan-Am Games; silver 7000m Sao Paulo Brazil '59; Fred Tees award outstanding coll. athlete '54; Jack Davies award outstanding

track athlete '56, '59; Norton Crowe award outstanding amateur athlete '56; ntl track team coach '67 Pan-Am, '68 Olympic Games; Calgary athlete of '68; mem. Cdn Roadrunners Hall of Fame selection comm.; mem. Alta., Cdn Amateur Sports halls of fame; res. Calgary, Alta

KYVELOS, Hercules (boxing): b. 25 Feb 1975, Montreal, Que.; competes at 67 kg.; 1 ntl title; '95 Pan-Am Games bronze; competed '96 Olympics; res. Montreal, Que.

L

LABIGNAN, Italo (fishing); b. 26 Dec 1956, Yugoslavia; m. Rhonda Armstrong; c. Amanda, John, Jessica, Patricia; Sir Sanford Fleming Coll.; fish/wildlife technician; TV personality/producer; pro fisherman from age 28; won *Fish & Stream* 64th annual fishing contest '74, Labatt Loyalist smallmouth bass tournament '84; Garcia fishing award '74, Fenwick Master Angler award '78; co-host *Canadian Sport Fishing* TSN series; writer/partner ntl fishing magazine *Canadian Sport Fishing*; authored more than 10 books on fishing; res. Freelton, Ont.

LABLANCHE, George (boxing); b. 17 Dec 1856, Point Levi, Que., d. 10 May 1918, Lawrence, Mass.; KO'd in 13 by Jack (Nonpareil) Dempsey in middleweight title bid 1886; 1889 rematch saw Dempsey disqualified for illegal punch despite 32nd round KO; Lablanche title claim disallowed; record: 69 bouts, won 17 by KO, 18 by decision, 6 draws, 10 decisions lost, 14 times KO'd, 2 lost on foul, 1 no decision, 1 no-contest.

LACELLE, Ron (boxing): b. 7 Apr 1929, Ottawa, Ont.; m. Yvonne Emily Cust; c. Ronald, Harvey, Robert, Coleen, Laura; retd. RCAF; began boxing Ottawa Boys Club age 9; followed Mel Swartzman to newly founded Beaver Boxing Club; won 112lb Golden Gloves '42; 118lb Cdn bantamweight champion '46; 126lb Olympic trials finalist '48 vs. Eddie Haddad; mem. Ottawa Sports Hall of Fame; res. Smiths Falls, Ont.

LACH, Elmer (hockey); b. 22 Jan 1918, Nokomis, Sask.; given name: Elmer James; m. Kathleen Louise Fletcher; c. Ronald James; dir. ntl accounts Maislin Transport; jr. Regina Abbotts, sr. Weyburn Beavers, Moose Jaw Millers; pro '40-55 Canadiens; missed '41-42 season when broken arm, 1st of several major injuries, which earned him nickname "Elmer the Unlucky", sidelined him; teamed with Maurice Richard, Toe Blake on wings to form Punch Line; NHL record: 646 scheduled games, 215g, 408a, 76 playoff games, 19g, 45a; 3 time 1st, twice 2nd team all-star; mem. 3 Stanley Cup winners, 4 league champions; Hart trophy '45; Ross trophy '45, '48; coach Loyola Jr. Canadiens, Montreal Royals (QHL); mem. Sask. Sports, Hockey halls of fame; res. Pte. Claire, Que.

LACHANCE, Michel (harness racing): b. 16 Dec 1950, St. Augustine, Que.; followed brothers Gilles, Pierre and Andre into business; was winning country fair races age 12; won 1st pari-mutuel race age 18; won leading driver awards at Blue Bonnets, Brandywine, Batavia, Foxboro, Yonkers, Roosevelt; driving night and day eclipsed Hervé Filion's single season victory record with 770 wins '86, later surpassed by Filion; led all NA drivers 4yrs; through '97 7986 victories, including 279 major stakes races, for purses exceeding $100M; drove 4 Little Brown Jug, 2 Cane Pace, 2 Messengers Stakes, 2 Prix d'Ete, 1 Canadian Trotting Classic; 1 World Trotting Derby, 3 Yonkers Trot, 1 US Pacing Championship, 4 Matron Stakes, 1 Kentucky Futurity, 1 NA Cup, 4 Hambletonian winners; drove Matt's

Scooter to Harness Horse of '89 title, setting Cdn, world records; drove Western Dreamer to Little Brown Jug record 1:51 1/5 '97 and harness racing's triple crown; mem. Cdn Horse Racing, Living halls of fame; res. Wyckoff, N.J.

LACY, Irene (gymnastics): b. 30 Aug 1946, Nipawin, Sask.; given name: Dorothy Irene Haworth; m. William Gerald Lacy; c. William Guy, William Greg; Southern Illinois, BSc; retd teacher; Cdn all-around title '66; NCAA all-around title '66; mem. Cdn Olympic team '64; mem. '61, '65 World Games team; silver balance beam '63 Pan-Am Games; *Sports Illustrated* award of merit '66; mem. Southern Illinois, Saskatchewan, Saskatoon Sports halls of fame; res. Quesnel, B.C.

LADIK, Oleg (wrestling): b. 18 Sep 1971, Kiev, USSR; 100kg freestyle; moved to Canada '92; competes at 125kg level; mem. ntl team from '95; 3 sr. ntl 100kg titles; gold '93 World Cup, '93, '97 Maccabiah, '94 Francophone Games; competed '96 Olympic Games, 3 Cerro Pelado, 2 Canada Cup, 2 world championship tournaments; 3 USSR jr, 2 sr. titles; res. Montreal, Que.

LAFERTE, Lucien (ski jumping): b. 10 Mar 1919, Trois-Rivieres, Que.; m. Denise Trepanier; c. Sylvie, Luc, Marilie; tool dealer; twice ntl, Eastern states champion; mem. '48, '52 Olympic teams; res. Trois-Rivieres, Que.

LAFLEUR, Guy (hockey): b. 20 Sep 1951, Thurso, Que.; given name: Guy Damien; m. Lise Barre; c. Martin, Mark; Canadiens team ambassador; 233 goals with Que. Remparts juniors; 130g, 79a in final season; Montreal 1st choice, 1st overall '71 amateur draft; right wing Canadiens '71-84, NY Rangers '88-89, Quebec '89-91; 6 consecutive seasons 50 or more goals; reached 500 goal plateau 20 Dec '83; became Canadiens' all-time scoring leader 9 Feb '84; NHL record: 1126 scheduled games, 560g, 793a, 128 playoff games, 58g, 76a; mem. 5 Stanley Cup winners; 6 times 1st team all-star; Art Ross Trophy '76-78; Lester B. Pearson Trophy '77; Hart Trophy '77-78; Conn Smythe Trophy '77; Lou Marsh, Lionel Conacher trophies '77; jersey #10 retd. by Canadiens; mem. Team Canada '76, '81; *Sport Magazine* playoff MVP award '77; named to CHL all-time team '99; Officer Order of Canada '80; mem. Canada's, Que. Sports, Hockey halls of fame; res. Montreal, Que.

LAIDLAW, Robert (parachuting); b. 7 Oct 1953, Winnipeg, Man.; UMan, BA; skydiving school dir.; more than 4000 jumps; Sr. B instructor, instructor rigger; 3rd ntl 8-way '77; 1st 8-way, 3rd 4-way '78-79; 2nd 8-way France '79; res. Deland, Fla.

LAING, George (all-around): b. 20 Oct 1892, Windsor, Ont.; d. 23 Oct. 1963, Windsor, Ont.; given name: George Frederick; m. Agness Dewar; c. Joyce Edith Benson, George Dewar, Charles Alexander; Trinity Coll, McGill, MD, CM; surgeon; versatile athlete who shone in football, cricket, hockey, tennis, badminton, golf; capt., outside wing, centre half McGill Redmen whose skills prompted coach Frank Shaughnessy to call him "the finest athlete I ever had anything to do with, the fastest, easiest runner I had ever seen"; intercollegiate tennis singles/doubles titles, Que. singles '14; Detroit singles finalist '15; Mich. open badminton doubles title '30; while in England during WW1 took up golf and went on to win 7 Essex G&CC titles, 1 international, 5 Cdn Srs titles; Devonshire, Triangular Cup matches; mem. Windsor/Essex County, McGill U Sports halls of fame.

LAING, John (cricket); b. 1874, Toronto, Ont, d. 1 Nov 1947, Toronto, Ont.; lawyer; fast bowler, capable batsman; 9 international matches vs US, avg. 10.83, best effort to time by Cdn; considered world class by peers; NA record 313 runs '03; registered Canada's 1st international hat-trick.

LAIRD, Stu (football): b. 8 Jul 1960, Assiniboia, Sask.; UCal, BA; def. lineman; played 4yrs with Dinosaurs; signed as free agent by Sask. '83; released and joined Montreal Concordes; again released and signed with Calgary; mem. Stampeders '85-96; CFL record: 170 games, 219 tackles, 72 QB sacks; 13 playoff games, 3 Grey Cup finals, 1 winner; 1 Western all-star; Calgary Lord Beaverbrook HS outstanding male athlete '78; v-pres CFLPA; res. Calgary, Alta.

LALIBERTE, Connie (curling): b. 21 Oct 1960, Winnipeg, Man.;given name: Connie Augustine; UMan. BA; computer analyst programmer; excelled in t&f, volleyball, basketball, hockey, bowling, broomball, baseball, field hockey, handball, curling in teens; mem. GPAC field hockey title teams, -23 Western Canada Games title field hockey team; named to ntl FH team '81; competed '81 American Cup; capt. UMan. FH team; holds Level II FH umpiring, Level I coaching certificates; mem. Man, jr, women's title rink '76-77; lead Man, women's title rink '80; began skipping '81 meting with considerable early success; Level 1 Curl Canada instructor's cert.; 3 Man. women's titles; skipped ntl women's title rink '84, '92, '95, Worlds '84, '95; mem. Man. Sports Hall of Fame; res. Winipeg, Man.

LALLY, Joe (lacrosse); b. 1868, Cornwall, Ont., d. 1956, Cornwall, Ont.; given name: Patrick Joseph; player, referee, equipment manufacturer; instrumental in establishing Canadian Lacrosse Assn. '25; donated Lally Perpetual Trophy '30 to be awarded annually to teams representing Canada & US; mem. Cornwall, Canada's Sports, Lacrosse halls of fame.

LALONDE, Bernie (skiing/canoeing); b. 14 Dec 1945, Ottawa, Ont.; given name: Bernard Georges; UofOtt, MD; sports medicine physician; cross-country skier Cdn ski marathons; ntl masters kayak titlist '81, 6th ntl srs '83; asst. coach '72-76, head coach '76-78 ntl women's alpine ski team; head ntl alpine ski team medical group from '78; coach whitewater slalom '81-85; ntl whitewater kayaking slalom team '83 world championships; asst. coach '92 Olympics; medical officer 7 Olympics; res. Ottawa, Ont.

LALONDE, Lally (hockey/football/lacrosse); b. 13 Nov 1926, Ottawa, Ont.; given name: Jean Paul; m. Marjory Rocheleau; c. Tina Tracey; UofOtt; retd. postal employee;

CFL Rough Riders '48-50, Alouettes '51-52; various sr., minor pro teams over 22yr span; lacrosse 25yrs; mem. '51 Mann Cup champion Peterborough Timbermen; coached sr., jr. A hockey 10yrs; coached Hull Beavers to Eastern Cdn jr.A title '69; QJHL coach of '69; PR dir. Rough Riders '69-71; frequent radio sports show host, guest; mem. Gloucester Wall, Ottawa Sports Hall of Fame; res. Ottawa, Ont.

LALONDE, Newsy (hockey/lacrosse); b. 1888, Cornwall, Ont., d. 21 Nov 1971; given name: Edouard; reporter, printer; from 16-28 travelled country with various lacrosse clubs; pro hockey at 18 Sault Ste. Marie, International League; 38 goals in 11 games Renfrew Millionaries '10-11; mem. Canadiens '13-22; 4 times scoring champion; mem. 2 Stanley Cup winners; 4 years player-mgr. WHL Saskatoon Shieks; concluded career '26 in Vancouver; career total 441g, 365 games; coached NY Americans, Montreal Canadiens, Ottawa Senators; mem. Cornwall, Canada's Sports, Lacrosse, Hockey halls of fame.

LAMAZE, Eric (equestrian): b. 17 Apr 1968, Montreal, Que.; Torrey Pines stables operator; overcame upbringing in rough districts of Montreal to emerge as one of Canada's leading show jumpers; successful jr., hunter rider; natural eye for distance has enhanced effectiveness since entering grand prix ring '92; mem. ntl team from '93; 2nd Cdn World Cup League standings '94; won '95 Shell Cup Derby, ntl show jumping title; mem. champion Cdn Nations' Cup team; only show jumper to qualify two horses (Rio Grande, Cagney) for '96 Olympics; failure to pass drug test cost him Olympic Games shot and led to 4yr ban; expulsion rescinded and he returned to competition '97; team bronze '99 Pan-Am Games; res. Schomberg, Ont.

LAMB, Joe (hockey); b. 18 Jun 1906, Sussex, N.B., d. 21 Aug 1982, Ottawa, Ont.; given name: Joseph Gordon; m. Marguerite Gillis (d); c. Joann Isobel, Margot Elizabeth; retd. Lt. Col.; Sussex Dairy Kings sr. '22-25, winning NB, PEI championships, Maritime title '24; Montreal Bankers League '25-27; NHL Montreal Maroons, Ottawa, NY Americans, Boston, Canadiens, St. Louis, Detroit '27-38; 108g, 101a; only player to appear in NHL's 2 longest games; Ottawa District class A golf champion '49; secty-mgr. Ottawa Valley Curling Assn.'68-76, Ottawa District Golf Assn. '65-76; mem. Governor-General's Curling Club; mem. NB Sports Hall of Fame.

LAMB, Willie (golf); b. 15 Dec 1902, Montrose Angus, Scotland, d. 28 Jan 1969, St Petersburg, Fla.; asst. pro Toronto GC '24-28; pro Monterey GC Mexico (winter months) '25-30; head pro Toronto Uplands '29-33, Lambton Golf Club '34-64; 5 times CPGA champion, runnerup once; winner Ont. Open '32, 3 times runnerup; Que. Open '31-33; won Millar Trophy '30; capt. CPGA '29; pres. Ont. PGA '48-50; on '64 retirement made CPGA life mem., mem. Canadian Golf Hall of Fame.

LAMBERT, Claude (boxing): b. 16 Feb 1969, Repentigny, Que.; competes at 54 kg; '94 ntl champion; bronze '95 Pan-Am Games; competed '94 Commonwealth, '96 Olympic Games; res. Repentigny, Que.

LAMBERT, Laurie (field hockey); b. 18 Nov 1960, Lachine, Que.; given name: Laurie Jean; UNB, UBC, York; mem. Que. jr. team '73-79; mem. Que. Sr. team from '76; mem. '77 Canada Games, '78-82 CIAU championships; mem. national team from '80; mem. World Cup silver medal team '83, '84 Olympic team; fed. govt. excellence award '83; res. Downsview, Ont.

LAMBERT, Nathalie (speed skating): b. 12 Jan 1963, Montreal, Que.; Montreal BA, MA; communications; began skating age 12; mem. ntl team from '81; relay bronze '88, relay gold '92, silver '94 Olympics; world champion '91, '93, '94; world 1,000m record 1:32.70; CASSA female short track athlete of '91 (co-winner), '92, '93, athlete of '84-85, '86-87 (indoor), '85-86 (outdoor), '89-93; dream of competing in '98 Olympics shattered with broken ankle in '97 short-track meet; hon. capt./TV analyst '98 Olympics; mem. Cdn Amateur Sports Hall of Fame; res. Ville d'Anjou, Que.

LAMMENS, Hank (sailing/hockey): b. 21 Feb 1966, Brockville, Ont.; hockey player, sailor; coached by brother Mark made competitive sailing debut age 11; only Cdn sailor to win 3 ntl youth championships in 2 different events; Ont. male athlete of '90; switched from Laser to Finn class '88; world Finn Class titles '90, '91; NA, ntl Finn titles '93; disqualified for forgetting lifejacket '92 Olympics; competed '87 Pan-Am Games; CYA Rolex sailor of '90-91; defenceman St. Lawrence ECAC '84-88; drafted NY Islanders '85; AHL Springfield '88-90, Capital Dist AHL, Kansas City IHL '90-91; Team Canada '92-93; NHL Senators '93-95; AHL PEI '93-95; mem. Team Canada '93 worlds; 2 ECAC all-star 2nd teams, 1 NCAA East 2nd all-star team; mem. Cdn Amateur Sports Hall of Fame; res. Brockville, Ont.

LAMY, Gaetan (harness racing): b. 23 Feb 1947, Trois-Rivieres, Que.; c. Yannick; made pro debut at 18 driving father's pacing mare Miss Direct; Hippodrome Trois-Rivieres driving champion 22yrs; Cdn driver of '92; represented Canada '92 World Drivers championship in Moscow; home construction accident '93 almost cost him his life, but he rebounded to resume competitive career '94; through '97 4923 victories with purses topping $16M; res. St. Nicephore, Que.

LANCASTER, Mark (harness racing): b. 23 Sep 1948, Bishopton, Que.; introduced to sport by part-time trainer father he won driving titles at Hinsdale and was well-regarded at Foxboro before shifting base of operations to Yonkers and Meadowlands; competes primarily at Freehold; through '95 2607 victories and purses exceeding $14M; res. Columbus, N.J.

LANCASTER, Ron (football): b.14 Oct 1938, Fairchance, Pa.; m. Beverly Vaughan; c. Lana, Ronald David, Robert Lee; Wittenberg (Ohio) Coll., BEd; football coach; pro Ottawa '60-62; Saskatchewan '63-78; CFL record: 3384 pass completions, 6233 attempts, 50,535yds, 396 interceptions, 333tds; Sask. single season record 3869yds on 297 completions '76; TDs single season (28 '66); quarterbacked Sask. to 5 Grey Cup finals, 1 winner; mem. '60 Ottawa Grey Cup winner; 6 times WFC all-star, 4 times all-Canadian; 5 times Jeff Nicklin Memorial Trophy as WFC

MVP; Schenley outstanding player award '70, '76, runner-up '66; coach. Roughriders '79-80, Eskimos '91-97, Tiger-Cats from '98; Annis Stukus CFL coach of '96, '98 awards; CBC TV football color commentator; mem. Canada's, Sask. Sports, Cdn Football halls of fame; res. Hamilton, Ont.

LANDERS, Pete (softball): b. 3 Jan 1947, South Porcupine, Ont.; given name: Peter Michael; m. Patricia Morris; c. Michael, Julie, Paul; laborer; Jr. B hockey Oshawa '76, Sr. A Whitby; lefthanded pitcher; Int. A at 16 South Porcupine; Jr. A Oshawa '66-67; all-Ont. title '67; Sr. A Oshawa Tonys '68-70; mem. Ont. team '69 Canada Summer Games; won Cdn title with London '70; with Campbell River, B.C., '71, picked up by Victoria Bates for ntls; '72 ntl title with Weyburn, Sask, beating world champ Richmond Hill Dynes in final; Toronto Globals '73-74; enjoyed career year '74 with Ont. record 27 wins, 13 shutouts, 394 strikeouts, 4 perfect games; picked up by Oshawa Tonys to win ntl title '74; played with Oshawa '75 losing ntls to Victoria Bates who picked him up for worlds in which they wound up in 3-way title tie due to rain; arm problems restricted play in Oshawa '76-77; won Western Major Fastball League title with Red Deer '78; credited with all 21 putouts in '69 2-hitter as he fanned 19 and made 2 putouts on grounders; 2 ntl championships MVP awards; mem. Cdn Softball Hall of Fame; res. Orono, Ont.

LANDRY, Denis (t&f); b. 16 Apr 1948, Iroquois Falls, Ont.; m. Maureen Ann Commerford; c. Sean, Craig; Windsor, BPHE, UofOtt, MEd; teacher; mem. OFSAA X-C sr. boys title team '66-67; convenor '73, '78 OFSAA X-C championship North Bay; exec. co-ordinator CAHPERD ntl office, coached with Ottawa Kinsmen Harriers, UofOtt; mem. OTFA exec. from '74 serving as v-p '78, '98, pres. '79-83; dir. 1st Pan-Am jr. t&f championships '80; CdM Cdn team '82 jr. Pan-Am Games; coaching development mgr. CTFA '83-88; Ottawa elementary school athletic assn. pres. '95-96; coached such champions as Alain Boucher, Bob Rice, Richard Charette, OFSAA medalists; coached UofOtt X-C team '84-95 winning 3 OUAA, CIAU titles; also coached basketball, soccer; Ont. govt. special achievement award '82, 2 CIAU X-C coach of yr awards; OBE coaches award '97; res. Ottawa, Ont.

LANDRY, Robert (horse racing): b. 18 Sep 1962, Toronto, Ont.; persistence his strong suit as he struggled through more than a decade of disappointments, injuries and bad luck before putting together his 1st 100 victory season '92; claimed his niche in Cdn horse racing history winning consec. Sovereign top jockey awards '93-94; best season '94 winning 175 races; more than 1,300 career victories; res. Mississauga, Ont.

LANDS, Ben (basketball); b. 22 Feb 1921, Montreal, Que.; m. Rita Jodhan; c. Michael, Larry, Michelle; owner specialty printing co.; mem. 15 title teams, 5 ntl, '37-55; mem. '48 Olympic team, nominated to '52 team; 3 times mem. Maccabiah Games team; coached 2 Que. sr. B title teams '46-48; coached sr. basketball '56-67; played jr. football '38; 35 years recreational softball; commissioner Cote St. Luc Lob Ball League from '79; 6 YM-YWHA sr. MVP awards; YM-YWHA outstanding athlete of '56; mem. YM-YWHA Jewish Hall of Fame; res. Cote St. Luc, Que.

LANDY, Frank (football): b. 24 May 1950, Fort William, Ont.; given name: Francis; m. Jan; c. Alicia, Jorden; North Dakota; radio advertising sales; versatile athlete; standout in hockey, baseball, wrestling, basketball, football as a youth; received early football grounding with Ukes bantams, Selkirk Rams; attended Regina HS; rights held by Roughriders; received UND scholarship where he played def. tackle making all-conference; capt. Fighting Sioux '71-74; MVP in Camelia Bowl '72; pro in CFL with Sask. '72; mem. '76 western champs; dealt to BC '77; all-star def. tackle '77-78; returned to Sask. then dealt to Toronto '80; retd. '81; asst. coach Richmond (BC) Raiders '84; mem. NWO Sports Hall of Fame; res. Richmond, B.C.

LANE, Ken (canoeing): b. 16 Aug 1923, Toronto, Ont.; given name: Kenneth; m. Madge Wilson; c. Christine, Laurel, Robin, Lisa; UofT, hons. BA; retd. corporate GM Simpson-Sears; 19 Cdn C1, C2, C4, War Canoe titles '46-56; silver 10,000m C2 '52 Olympics; secty-treas. Balmy Beach Canoe Club '46-49; editor *The Canadian Paddler* '53-59; mem. CNE sports committee '55-81; Dominion Day Regatta Assn. exec. '55-81, pres. '61-65; Western Ont. Div. Canada Canoe Assn. secty. '50-54, exec.-flag officer '55-56, flag officer '57-60, treas. '62-81; CCA dir. '56-58, '61-76, v.-commodore '59, commodore '60, hon. commodore '80-81, mem. financial comm. '80-81, Olympic, International committees '69-72; mgr '67 Pan-Am, '72 Olympic canoe teams; mem. St. Catharines national canoe championships organizing comm. '68; NA Canoe Racing Assn.; key role in promoting development of sport throughout career; Ont. Sr. squash title '74, ntl doubles finalist '78; mem. Simpson-Sears curling league title rink '81; res. Scarborough, Ont.

LANE, Sharon (t&f): b. 24 Oct 1958, Hamilton, Ont.; given name: Sharon Marie; UWO., hons BA, MA; hurdles specialist; ntl sr. 100m title '78-79, '81; ntl 100m hurdles record 13.43 '79 FISU Games; silver '79 Pan-Am Games; mem. '78 Commonwealth, '80 Olympic Games teams; res. Ancaster, Ont.

LANG, Dale (ballooning): b. 18 Aug 1951, Calgary, Alta.; given name: Dale Frederick; m. Diane McMurry; c. Jeffrey, Mark; Anglican Church priest; professional balloonist; ntl champion '79; co-pilot 1st balloon over North Pole; ntl sales dir. Barnes Sport Balloon; pres. Balloon Adventures Calgary; youth minister St. James Anglican Church; res. Calgary, Alta.

LANG, Lorraine (curling): b. 8 Oct 1956, Port Arthur, Ont.; given name: Lorraine Edwards; m. Rick Lang; c. Adam, Sarah; X-ray technician; third for Heather Houston '88-89 Scott Tournament of Hearts title, '89 world title; also won Ont. women's titles '83, '88, '91; mem. '81 NO, ntl mixed title rinks; mem. Cdn Curling (team), NWO Sports halls of fame; res. Thunder Bay, Ont..

LANG, Rick (curling): b. 12 Dec 1953, Fort William Ont.; given name: Richard Porter; m. Lorraine Edwards; c. Adam, Sarah; Lakehead, hons BA social work; services mgr. Children's Aid Society; 3rd for Doug Smith '71 ntl jr. runnerup; 3rd or skip in 10 Brier appearances; with Bill Tetley '75 Brier, with Al Hackner '82, '85 Brier, World titles;

skipped '81 Seagram Mixed ntl champions; recipient '81 ntl mixed congeniality award, '82 Silver Broom Colin Campbell Award most sportsmanlike player. '91 Brier Ross Harstone award for sportsmanship/ability; mem. Cdn Curling (team), NWO Sports halls of fame; res. Thunder Bay, Ont.

LANGDON, Jeff (figure skating): b. 13 Aug 1975, Smiths Falls, Ont.; began skating age 5; mem. ntl team from '90; gold Nebelhorn, bronze International Grand Prix '93; competed jr. worlds '93; silver '97 ntl championships; competed '97 worlds; coached by Doug Leigh, Robert Tebby; competed '98 Olympics; res. Barrie, Ont.

LANGFORD, Sam (boxing): b. 12 Feb 1880, Weymouth, N.S., d. 12 Jan 1956, Cambridge, Mass.; nicknamed "Boston Tar Baby"; fought almost 300 bouts, many not recorded; among opponents were Jack McVey, Jack Johnson, Stanley Ketchel, Joe Jennette, Young Peter Jackson, Joe (the original) Walcott, Jack Blackburn; held Negro heavyweight title losing it 1919 to Harry Wills; won/lost Mexican heavyweight title '23; ranked by *Ring Magazine* among top 10 all-time heavyweights; stood 5'5" with 84" reach: 252 recorded bouts, 99 won by KO, 37 by decision, 1 on foul, 31 draws, 19 lost on decision, 4 by KO, 59 no decision, 2 no contest; mem. Canadian, US Boxing, NS, Canada's Sports halls of fame.

LANGLOIS, Al (curling): b. 4 Aug 1915, Winnipeg, Man. given name: Allan David; retired; skipped inter-HS champions '34; winner variety of events Manitoba Bonspiel; 3rd for Billy Walsh Sr. winning Man. Consols, Brier '52, '56; mem. Canadian Curling Hall of Fame; res. Winnipeg, Man.

LANGLOIS, Lloyd (skiing): b. 11 Nov 1962, Sherbrooke, Que.; freestyle aerials specialist; began skiing at 7, competing age 16; mem. ntl team Cdn "Air Force" from '85; 47 World Cup gold; '85, '93 World Cup champion; '86, '89 world champion; bronze '88, '94 Olympics; twice retd to recover from injuries, retd permanently '98; world champion awards '85, '86; Tribute to Champions sports excellence awards '87, '89; mem. Cdn Amateur Sports Hall of Fame; res. Magog, Que.

LAPALME, Denis (wheelchair basketball): 29 Apr 1959, Timmins, Ont.; given name: Denis Orval; m. Catherine Anne Mallette; c. Jennifer, Michelle; Waterloo, hons BA; media analyst Transport Canada; mem. ntl wheelchair basketball team '86-92; 5 times ntl championship all-star; MVP '87 ntls; mem. 4th place Barcelona Paralympics team; mem. Ottawa Shooters ntl champions '95; res. Nepean, Ont.

LAPERRIÈRE, Jacques (hockey): b. 22 Nov 1941, Rouyn-Noranda, Que.; m. Elaine; c. Martin, Daniel, Michele; hockey coach; defenceman Montreal Juniors; turned pro with Hull-Ottawa (EPHL) '59-63; Montreal '62-74; Calder Memorial Trophy '64; Norris Trophy '66; playing career ended due to knee injury; mem. 6 Stanley Cup winners plus 2 as asst. coach; 4 times all-star; NHL record: 691 scheduled games, 40g, 242a, 88 playoff games, 9g, 22a; coached junior hockey; asst. coach Canadiens '81-97, Bruins '97; mem. Hockey Hall of Fame; res. Montreal, Que.

LAPERRIÈRE, André (hockey); b. 12 Jun 1925, Montreal, Que.; given name: Henry André; m. Marthe Sabourin; c. Josée, Luc; Montreal, BA; retd. printer; forward/defence Verdun Maple Leaf jrs 2 yrs; UMtl 5yrs; mem. '48 Olympic gold medal Flyers; Que. league srs. with Sorel, Drummondville 3yrs; played in Montreal commercial league; 10yrs OT hockey; mem. as mem. of '48 Flyers Ottawa Sports Hall of Fame; res. Outremont, Que.

LAPOINTE, Francois (t&f); b. 23 Aug 1961, Montreal, Que.; m.; race walker; ntl jr. 10km, 20km, 50km, sr. 5km records; 3 Que., 2 Ont., 5 ntl titles; mem. '81 World Cup, '82 Commonwealth, '83 FISU, Pan-Am, '84 Olympic Games teams; res. Montreal, Que.

LAPOINTE, Guy (hockey); b. 18 Mar 1948, Montreal, Que.; given name: Guy Gerard; m. Louise; c. Guy Jr., Stephanie, Jordan; hockey scout; def. Montreal Jr. Canadiens; played in NHL with Montreal '68-82, St. Louis '82-83, Boston '83-84; mem 6 Stanley Cup winners; 4 all-star games; 1 1st, 3 2nd team all-star; NHL record: 884 scheduled games, 171g, 451a, 123 playoff games, 26g, 44a; asst. coach Quebec '84-85. '87-90; GM/head coach Longueuil (QMJHL) '85-87; 1 QMJHL title; scout Calgary '90-95, from '97; asst. coach Calgary '95-97; mem. Hockey Hall of Fame; res. Montreal, Que.

LAPORTE, Paul (shooting); b. 9 May 1928, Edmundston, N.B.; m. Irene Blais; c. Sonia, Richard; restaurateur; ntl high avg. titles all-around '69-70, 12 gauge '69, '73, 20 gauge '70, '72, 28 gauge '69-70; 34 high overall avg., 36 12ga, 17 20ga, 17 28ga, 13 410 bore titles '67-73; 12 world records; world tuna fishing record 1160lbs; mem. National Skeet Shooting Assn. Hall of Fame; res. Montreal, Que.

LAPPAGE, Ron (judo/wrestling): b. 27 Jun 1945, Dryden, Ont.; c. 3; Queen's, UAlta. PhD; educator, AD Lakehead; started judo age 12; capt. Queen's judo team, OUAA light-heavyweight title; capt. UAlta judo team, 5 WCIAA heavyweight titles; CIAU heavy, open champion '67; 5 Alta. light-heavy black belt titles; retired from judo with 3rd degree black belt '74; began wrestling age 22; 2 WCIAA 190lb titles; 4 Alta. titles; 1 ntl 198lb Greco-Roman title; mem. ntl team '70 worlds; retired from competition '74; in youth also active in football, road running, cross-country skiing; Queen's letterman '65; UAlta. male athlete of '67-68; UAlta Block A ring, numeral 4 awards; 2 Edmonton, 1 Thunder Bay awards; 1 Alta. achievement award; wrestling, judo coach Lakehead.; varied exec., comm. roles as associate PE prof. Lakehead; mem. Lakehead U Hall of Fame selection comm.; mem. NWO Sports Hall of Fame; res. Thunder Bay.

LAPRADE, Edgar (hockey); b. 10 Oct 1919, Mine Centre, Ont.; given name: Edgar Louis; m. Arline Whear (d); c. Diane (Bonnie), Judith, Marcia; retd. sporting goods store owner; nicknamed "Beaver"; fluid skater and expert stick handler; joined NHL NY Rangers '45-55; NHL record: 500 scheduled games, 108g, 172a, 18 playoff games, 4g, 9a; played in 4 NHL all-star games; Calder trophy winner '46; operated sporting goods store 30yrs; alderman Port Arthur/Thunder Bay 15yrs; retired from politics following unsuccessful bid for mayor's job; helped found NWO Sports

Hall of Fame; mem. NWO Sports, Hockey halls of fame; res. Thunder Bay, Ont.

LAPTHORNE, Whitey (baseball); b. 1 Apr 1942, London, Ont.; given name: David James; m. Mary Jane McDonald; c. Andrea, Heather, Joseph; UWO, BA, Wayne State, MEd; OCE; PS principal; infielder London Majors (Sr. Intercounty) 1960-78; .275 lifetime avg.; best season '63 with .346; twice 1st team all-star 3rd baseman; once 2nd team all-star 1st baseman; mem. Ont., ntl baseball championships, Pan-Am Games playdowns teams '70; res. London, Ont.

LAREAU, Sebastièn (tennis); b. 27 Apr 1973, Montreal, Que.; ntl -12, -16, -18, senior singles, doubles titles; career record (since '90) 11-9 in Davis Cup play; with Sebastien LeBlanc won '90 French Open, Wimbledon junior doubles titles, first Canadians to win a Grand Slam title; turned pro '91; scored victory over 6th ranked Michael Stich '94 European championships; twice ranked #1 in Canada; 2 ATP Tour doubles titles; with Sebastien Leblanc shared Viscount Alexander award '90; with Daniel Nestor won '98 Japan Open doubles; mem. '98 Davis Cup team; teamed with Alex O'Brien (US) to become 1st Cdn to claim grand slam victory with men's doubles US Open and ATP Tour world doubles title '99; res. Boucherville, Que.

LARGE, Bert (lacrosse); b. 12 May 1907, Brampton, Ont.; m. Alice Gibson; c. Alberta, Margi-Fay; retired plumber, apt. superintendant; mem. Brampton Amateur Lacrosse Assn. sr. champions '26; mem. Mann Cup winner '30; pro Toronto Maple Leafs '31, Toronto Tecumsehs '32; mem. Mimico-Brampton Combines Mann Cup winner '42, Mike Kelly Memorial Medal Mann Cup playoff MVP; mem. Ont. champion Mimico-Brampton Combines '43; mem. Cdn Lacrosse Hall of Fame; res. Brampton, Ont.

LARMER, Steve (hockey); b. 16 Jun 1961, Peterborough, Ont.; m. Rose; c. Bailey Rose; rw Peterborough (OHL) '77-78, Niagara Falls '79-81, New Brunswick (AHL) '81-82; drafted by Chicago '80; NHL with Chicago '80-93, NY Rangers '93-95; OHL, AHL all-star; NHL all-rookie team '83; Calder Memorial Trophy '83; 2 NHL all-star games; 1 Stanley Cup winner; ironman streak of 884 consecutive games ended '93; scored series clinching goal vs. US '91 Canada Cup; nicknamed "Grandpa"; NHL record: 1006 scheduled games, 441g, 571a, 140 playoff games, 56g, 75a; res. Peterborough, Ont.

LaROCHE, Alain (skiing); b. 20 Sep 1963, Quebec City, Que.; impressive record in alpine events from '77 led to competition as mem. national jr. freestyle team; competed at World Cup level from '82; 6 WC combined, 2 aerials titles; 2 ntl combined, 1 moguls, 1 ballet, 1 aerials titles; 1 NA combined, aerials titles; world title '84; fed. govt. excellence '83, world champion awards '84; mem. Cdn Amateur Sports Hall of Fame; res. Lac Beaufort, Que.

LaROCHE, Philippe (skiing); b. 12 Dec 1966, Quebec City, Que.; c. 1; freestyle aerials specialist; began skiing age 3, competing age 12; mem. ntl team "Cdn Air Force" from '87; 17 World Cup gold; 3 World Cup championships; 3 ntl titles; '92 Olympic gold, '94 silver; brothers Yves, Alain

Dominic, all freestylers, sister Lucie, alpine skier; Tribute to Champions sports excellence award '89; res. Lac Beauport, Que.

LaROCHE, Yves (skiing); b. 7 Jun 1959, Quebec City, Que.; aerials specialist; mem. ntl team '82-86; 4 1sts, 2 2nds 8 World Cup events '84; WC aerials titlist '84, '86; near fatal para-gliding accident '89 ended competitive career; ntl team aerials coach '94 Olympics; fed. govt. excellence award '84; mem. Cdn Skiing Hall of Fame; res. Lac Beauport, Que.

LAROCQUE, Bunny (hockey); b. 6 Apr 1952, Hull, Que.; d. 29 Jul 1992, Hull, Que.; given name: Michel Raymond; m. Helene Legris; c. Stephane, Philippe, Mathieu; pro hockey player; goaler Ottawa 67's jrs.; 2nd pick Montreal 6th overall '72 draft; Canadiens '73-81, Maple Leafs '81-83, Philadelphia '83, St. Louis '83-84; shared Vezina Trophy Ken Dryden '77-79, Denis Heron, Richard Sevigny '81; mem. 4 Stanley Cup winners; NHL record: 312 scheduled games, 17,615min, 160-89-45, 978ga, 17so, 3.33 ga avg, 14 playoff games, 6-6, 759min, 37ga, 1so, 2.92 ga avg.

LAROCQUE, Dominique (cycling/skating); b. 29 Dec 1962, Sturgeon Falls, Ont.; UofOtt, BA; athletic consultant; ntl mountain bike team mem. '91; represented Canada at world championships; '93-95 10km in-line skating record holder NY Central Park race; won 145km Athens to Atlanta in-line skating marathon '93; Cdn in-line skating title '96; gold 25km, silver 100km Kuopio, Finland, Ice Marathon speed skating competition '94; developed Creative Wheel Consulting; res. Ottawa, Ont.

La ROCQUE, Penny (curling); b. Yarmouth N.S.; given name: Penny Wilson; m. Guy La Rocque; Dalhousie, MSc; mem. NS rink women's championship '74, '78-79, '83, '86; skipped '83 ntl title rink; mem. NS rink ntl Mixed championships '79, '81-82. '84; 6th in Canada Gillette Fitness Challenge '79; Fitness & Amateur Sport athletic scholarship (curling) '79; mem. Canadian Curling Hall of Fame; res. Halifax, N.S.

LAROSE, Bob (football/basketball); b. 6 Mar 1946, Toronto Ont. given name: Robert Alexander; m. Marianne Jorgenson; c. Karen, Jennifer; UWO hons. BPhE, MPhE; asst. football coach UWO; football, basketball star UWO; grid team capt. '69; wide receiver Winnipeg '70-77; Bombers 1st draft choice; CFL record; 227 receptions, 4209yds, 18.5 avg., 29tds; coaching asst. UMan. '77, UWO '79, UofOtt '81, '83; Toronto Telegram HS athlete of '65; UWO athlete of '70; All-Cdn wide receiver CFL '72; Blue Bombers Cdn athlete of '75; color commentator CFL games CBC '78; tech. dir. CAFA '80-83, exec. dir. '83-84; mem. W-Club Sports Hall of Fame; res. London, Ont.

LAROSE, Gilbert (gymnastics); b. 13 Sep 1942, Montreal, Que.; m. Terri; c. Gil Jr., Glenn; Michigan, BSc; professor, businessman; ntl gymnastic champion '65, '68; mem. ntl team '62 World championships, European tour, '64, '68 Olympics; Big Ten all-around titlist; NCAA all-around, 4 events titlist '62-63; capt. Mich team; Mid-West, Flint Open titles; 7yrs pres. Que. Gymnastics Fed.; 7yrs gymnast, ntl judge, coach; res. Longueuil, Que.

LAROUCHE, Pierre (hockey); b. 16 Nov 1955, Taschereau, Que.; m. Cindy; product spokesman; centre, Quebec, Sorel Jr. Black Hawks '72-74; NHL Pittsburgh in '74 amateur draft; Pittsburgh '74-78, Montreal '78-'82, Hartford '82-83, NY Rangers '83-88; attained 50-goal plateau with 53 '76, 50 '80; NHL record: 812 scheduled games, 395g, 427a, 64 playoff games, 20g, 34a; mem 1 Stanley Cup winner; active in community charity work; res. Pittsburgh, Pa.

LARSEN, Christine (synchro swim); b. 15 Dec 1967, Coquitlam, B.C; began synchroswim career '74; mem. ntl team '76-92 and again from '95; with Kathy Glen won '90 Commonwealth Games, Swiss Open, '91 Petro-Canada Cup duet gold; team gold '96 French, '90 Swiss Opens, '88 Petro-Canada Cup; silver '91 worlds, '96 Olympics; sister Karen also ntl team mem.; retd from competition to coach Nanaimo Diamonds Club '93-94; returned to competition to qualify for '96 Olympics; res. Coquitlam, B.C.

LASHUK, Mike (football); b. 9 Dec 1938, Edmonton, Alta.; UAlta., BPhE Southern Illinois, MSc; assoc. prof.; Edmonton City jr. golf, prov. HS shot put titles; jr. A hockey Edmonton Oil Kings; pro Eskimos '57-63; Dr. Beattie Martin Trophy WFC rookie of '57; corner linebacker, twice selected by teammates top Cdn player; coached HS football 5yrs; head coach UCal Dinosaurs from '70 leading team to National College Bowl final '75, losing to UofOtt; res. Calgary, Alta.

LASKIN, Mark (equestrian); b. 19 Oct 1956, New York; N; UAlta; farm mgr.; dominated '79 Rothman's Grand Prix circuit winning 1st place ribbons in 9 of 11 events including Vancouver, Toronto World Cup competitions; Rothman's equestrian of '78-81; mem. ntl team; mem. gold medal Nations Cup, Olympic alternate team '80; res. Santa Fe, N.M.

LATULIPPE, Phil (t&f); b. 16 Mar 1919, Cabano, Que.; retd Cdn Forces; ultra runner; began running age 48 to lose weight, quit smoking; at 50 covered 100miles in Ottawa Miles for Millions charity walk; 3 Guinness Book of Records marks for world's longest non-stop runs; longest 300miles '72; completed documented across Canada run '81; also ran Alaska to Shawinigan, Que., ran 65-69 age group world 48hr 150miles, 1689yds record '89; 1st Cdn 70+ ultramarathoner; crossed Canada Vancouver to Halifax in 134 days '89; Foundation Phil Latulippe bears his name; mem. Order of Canada; res. Loretteville, Que.

LAUMANN, Silken (rowing); b. 14 Nov 1964, Mississauga, Ont.; m. John Wallace; c. William Laumann; operates Silken & Co.; gave up competitive running to concentrate on rowing '82; mem. ntl team '83-98, competing single, double and quadruple sculls; 5 Cdn Henley, 3 Amsterdam, 2 ntl, 1 San Diego gold; '87 Pan-Am Games single gold; competed '84, '88, '92, '96 Olympics winning silver '96, bronze '84 and '92, in amazing display of grit after serious training accident; overall women's World Cup single scull gold '91; won single scull gold '95 Pan-Am Games but stripped of quadruple gold when she inadvertently consumed banned substance in cough medicine; 2 fed. govt. meritorious service awards; Lou

Marsh, Velma Springstead trophies '91; 2 Bobbie Rosenfeld awards; BC female athlete of '91; CARA Centennial award; 2 ORA athlete of yr awards; Mississauga athlete of '84; Olympic champion award '85; Olympic Order '95; hon. Dr. of Laws degree UVic '94; subject of film feature '96; special Cdn citizen's gold medal '92; Grace Under Pressure award '96; mem. Cdn Amateur, Canada's Sports halls of fame; res. Victoria, B.C.

LAURIN, Lucien (horse racing); b. 1915, Montreal, Que.; c. Roger; horse trainer; moderately successful career as jockey '29-42; ruled off track at Narragansett '38 when battery was found in pocket; with aid of Alfred Vanderbilt reinstated '41; joined forced with Reg Webster and career as trainer blossomed; trained Quill juve. filly of '58, Amberoid Belmont Stakes winner '66; replaced son Roger at Meadow Stable '71; brought Riva Ridge to title honors at 2, double classic winner at 3, champion handicapper at 4; trained Triple Crown winner Secretariat; trained 34 major stakes winners; mem. Saratoga Springs, Canadian Horse Racing halls of fame; res. Florida.

LAURIN, Roger (horse racing); b. 11 Sep 1935, Montreal, Que.; m. Nina; c. Robert, Ricky; horse trainer; followed father Lucien's footsteps and established reputation as one of NA's top trainers; moved from Meadow Stable to Phipps family string; enjoyed best success with Numbered Account '71-72, Pearl Necklace '76-79, Miss Cavendish '64, Drumtop '70-71; res. Garden City, N.J.

LAVIOLETTE, Chantal (synchro swim); b. 12 Oct 1963, Montreal, Que.; m. Fernand Cholette; c. Mathieu; sports exec.; 1 Que., ntl figures, solo, duet titles; Rome solo, team titles; team titles Pan-Pacific, World, America Cup; team gold '83 Pan-Am Games; world championship tournament gold '82, '86; 3 fed. govt. world champion excellence awards; trustee Ottawa Sports Hall of Fame; res. Gatineau, Que.

LAVIOLETTE, Jack (hockey/lacrosse); b. 27 Aug 1879, Belleville, Ont., d. 10 Jan 1960, Montreal, Que.; amateur hockey 1899 Montreal Overland jrs.; CP Telegaphs 1900 then Nationals of Federal League in both hockey, lacrosse; with formation of IHL (1st pro league) '04 played 4 seasons Sault Ste. Marie, Mich., team, capt. '06; when league disbanded '07 played with Montreal Shamrocks, lacrosse with Nationals; with Newsy Lalonde mem. '10 team which lost Minto Cup to New Westminster; with formation '09 of NHA involved in recruiting, managing Montreal Canadiens, oldest pro hockey team still in existence in Canada; foward Canadiens 1st Stanley Cup win '16; became referee after injury '17; mem. Canada's Sports, Hockey halls of fame.

LAVOIE, Marc (fencing); b. 29 Apr 1954, Ottawa, Ont.; m. Camille Lafortune; c. Jérome, Adrien, Christopner; Carleton, BA, U of Paris, PhD; professor, UofOtt; won French team handball, baseball, class B team golf titles while attending HS in Paris; ntl jr. sabre champion '73-74; sr. sabre '75-79, '85-86; mem. '73-75, '78, '81-82 world championships, '76, '84 Olympic, '75, '79, '83 Pan-Am Games, '74, '78, '82 Commonwealth championships teams; team bronze '74, silver, sabre silver '78 Commonwealth championships, team bronze '83 Pan-Am Games; ntl team

capt. '78; retd. From competition '84; authored 2 hockey-related books; Carleton athlete of '74-75; Ottawa ACT fencer of '74; res. Hull, Que.

LAW, Kelley (Owen) (curling); b. 11 Jan 1966, Burnaby, B.C.; given name: Kelley Atkins; m. Bruce Law; c. Christopher; conveyancer law corp; began curling age 12; runnerup '87 BC Schoolgirl, jr. championships; skipped rink in 8 BC STOH competitions, 4 titles; bronze '92 ntl STOH; bronze '97 Olympic trials; Kamloops, Richmond, Saskatoon major bonspiel titles; res. Vancouver, B.C.

LAWES, Keith (curling); b. 15 Oct 1937, Montreal, Que.; given name: Leslie Keith; m. Judith Anne Northey; c. David Keith, Judith Andrea, Christopher Charles; Lower Canada Coll., McGill; retd. trust co. mgr.; twice Newfoundland, Ontario provincial finalist Brier playdowns; 3rd '69 Nfld. Brier entry; earned nickname "Super Broom" as substitute sweeper for Nfld 7 games '71 Brier, 4 games with NB '74 Brier; won '72 OCA Challenge Round; '73 OCA Silver Tankard with St. Thomas; sr. instructor Curl Canada; res. Winnipeg, Man..

LAWSON, Smirle (football); b. 1888, Guelph, Ont., d. 22 Dec 1963, Toronto, Ont.; given name: Alexander Smirle; m. Pearl Forsyth; c. Elizabeth, Amy, Isobel; UofT, MB, MD hons., MRCP (London), MRCS (Eng.); medical doctor; hard-charging halfback; led Varsity Blues to '09 Grey Cup; mem., capt. Argos '11-14; Canada's original "Big Train"; medical officer WWI; taught surgery UofT; mem. Toronto General Hospital staff; chief coroner of Ont. '37-62; gained international rep. as coroner; 1st white man admitted to Ojibway tribe at Moose Pt. Indian Reserve; mem. UofT, Ottawa, Cdn Football, Canada's Sports halls of fame.

LAY, Jeff (rowing): b. 6 Oct 1969, Ottawa, Ont.; UWO, BSc; varsity rowing coach; started rowing in HS; mem. ntl team from '93; gold lw coxed 8s '93 worlds, US championships, straight 4 '94 Amsterdam, '95 US championships; 2 silver '95 Pan-Am Games; silver lw 4's '96 Olympics; silver lw 8's Lucerne; involved in coaching at all levels; res. London, Ont.

LAY, Marion (swimming); b. 26 Nov 1948, Vancouver, B.C.; given name: Marion Beverly; CalState Poly., BA, CalState, MA; tech. chair. ntl sports centre Greater Vancouver; ntl 100m FS title '64-68, mem. '64, '68 Olympic, '66 Commonwealth, '67 Pan-Am Games teams; British Open 100m FS record '65 Blackpool, Eng.; team capt., won 2 gold, set world record 4x110yd FS relay '66 Commonwealth Games; team capt., 4 silver '67 Pan-Ams; bronze 100m FS US long course Nationals '67; South African open 100m FS record '68; capt. '68 Olympic swim team, 4th 100m FS, bronze 4x100m FS relay; coached UWO '71-72 swim team to 4th place '72 CWIAU championships; CBC swimming color commentator; asst. coach Ottawa Kingfish SC; dir. institute for study of sport in society '71-75; acting mgr. tech. programs Sport Canada; mem. Cdn Aquatic Hall of Fame; res. Vancouver, B.C.

LAYTON, Athol (wrestling): b. 20 Aug 1920, Sydney, Australia; d. 18 Jan 1984, Toronto, Ont.; given name: Athol Alfred; m. Leah Emma Kett; c. John Gordon, Christopher

Thomas; pro wrestler, TV sports commentator; Australian amateur heavyweight boxing champion '38-43; began pro wrestling career Singapore '49; began NA wrestling career Toronto '50; given nickname "Lord"; with Lord James Blears won NWA world tag team title '53; began career as TV wrestling commentator Buffalo '59; with Ilio Dipaulo won world tag team title '59; noted raconteur; promotions mgr FBM Distillery '78-84; noted for charitable work with Shriner's Hospitals, Variety Club of Ont., St. Alban's Boys & Girls Club, Easter Seals; Ont. citizenship medal '83.

LEA, Mary (shooting): b. 15 Sep, Alexandra, P.E.I.; given name: Mary MacLennan; m, Crilly Lea; retd teacher, creamery mgr.; 1st female to qualify for Cdn Bisley team; capt. Cdn Kalapore title team Bisley '51; mem. PEI Sports Hall of Fame; res. Crapaud, P.E.I.

LEACH, Al (all-around): b. 12 Jul 1917, Richmond, Ont.; given name: Alvin Douglas; m. Valerie Evelyn Bennett; c. Douglas John, Patricia Gail; retd chief mechanical inspector, plan examiner; HS swim champion '35-37; Kiwanis jr. Big 4 football champions '37; Oakwood Indians ORFU intermediate titlists '38-39; Toronto Sr. Commercial HL '38-40; Ottawa football (Combines, Trojans, Rough Riders) '41-47; Ottawa District Football (soccer) Assn. '43-48; ODFA title '48; Ottawa Mercantile Softball League '43-46, Eastern Ont. title '45; Ottawa Valley Curling Assn. dir., p-pres.; mem. Governor-General's Curling Club; mem. '81 Ont. Masters title rink; Curl Canada Level 1 instructor; res. Nepean, Ont.

LEACH, Reg (hockey): b. 23 Apr 1950, Riverton, Man.; given name: Reginald Joseph; jr. Flin Flon, set scoring record, league MVP; 1st pick Boston '70 draft; Bruins '70-72, California '72-74, Philadelphia '74-82, Detroit '82-83; topped 50-goal playeau 61 '76, 50 '80; Stanley Cup playoff record 19 goals '76; Team Canada '76; NHL record: 934 scheduled games, 381g, 285a, 94 playoff games, 47g, 22a; 2nd team all-star right wing '76; Conn Smythe trophy '76; mem. '75 Stanley Cup winner; nicknamed "Riverton Rifle"; mem. Man. Hockey Hall of Fame; res. Detroit, Mich.

LEADER, Al (builder/hockey/baseball): b. 4 Dec 1903, Barnsley, Man.; d. 8 May 1982, Rancho Mirage, Calif; given name: George Alfred; m. Alice Segerstrom; c. Albert, Ruth, Raymond, Dawn; organized, played for Sask. jr. title team '24; semipro baseball Northern Sask.; helped organize Seattle city HL '32; organized defence league Seattle, Portland '43-44; helped organize Pacific Coast HL '44; PCHL pres. '44-49 (name changed to Western HL '51); served in hockey as player, coach, mgr., referee, owner, pres.; v-p USAHA; naturalized US citizen '33; pres. Rainier G&CC Seattle; v-p Desert Island CC, Rancho Mirage, Calif., '79-81; Lester Patrick award '76; mem. Man., Cdn Hockey halls of fame.

LEADLAY, Pep (football): b. 7 Mar 1898, Hamilton, Ont.; d. 8 Sep 1984, Hamilton, Ont.; given name: Frank Robert; m. Vera Esther Rymal; Queen's, BSc; retd civil engineer; great exponent of drop kick; Hamilton Tigers intermediate ntl champions '15; Hamilton Tigers Interprovincial Union '19-20; Queen's '21-25 winning ntl coll. titles, Grey Cup '22-24, OQAA titles '22-25; Hamilton Tigers '26-30, league title '27; ORFU ntl title '30; capt. Queen's, Hamilton teams;

mem. Golden Gaels team which scored 26 consec. victories; mem. Queen's, Cdn Football, Canada's Sports halls of fame.

LEAH, Vince (builder): b. 29 Nov 1913, West Kildonan, Man.; d. 9 Aug 1993, Winnipeg, Man.; m. Mary; c. Donald; journalist; began sports writing *Winnipeg Tribune* '30; operated 1st soccer, hockey teams at age 13; authored 9 books on local history; hon. doctorate (LLD) UMan. '85; hon. chief Winnipeg Fire Dept. for work with Fire Fighters Historical Society and Fire Fighters Burn Fund; honored by Cdn Amateur Hockey Assn., Cdn Soccer Assn., Cdn Parks & Rec. Assn., Cdn Amateur Sports Federation; US ntl Rec. Assn.; mem. Order of Canada, Man. Sports, Hockey halls of fame.

LEAR, Les (football): b. 22 Aug 1918, Grafton, N.D.; d. 1979 Hollywood, Fla.; m. Betty Louise Neill; mem. Winnipeg Deer Lodge Jrs.; Blue Bombers '37-42; all-star lineman 3 times; helped Bombers win WIFU titles '37-39, Grey Cup '39, Cleveland Rams (NFL) '42-45, LA Rams '46-47; 2nd team US pro all-star '45; traded to Detroit '47 but retd to coach CFL Stampeders; guided Calgary to Grey Cup '48; following season won west but lost Grey Cup final to Montreal; mem. Cdn Football Hall of Fame.

LEARN, Ed (football): b. 30 Sep 1935, Welland, Ont.; given name: Harry Edward; div.; c. Billy, Paul, Janice; m. Bernadee; sc. Christopher, Kimberley; automobile dealer; def. halfback ORFU champion K-W Dutchman '56-57; 12yr def. halfback Montreal, Toronto; punt return specialist; CFL record: 508 punt returns, 3091yds, 6.1 avg., 578yds returning 51 pass interceptions; all-Eastern 3 times, All-Cdn once; Montreal nominee Cdn player of '61; EFC leading 7 interceptions '68; defensive back modern era Argo all-star team ('45-73); nicknamed "Spider"; res. St. Catharines, Ont.

LEARY, George (shooting): b. 19 Nov 1957, Newmarket, Ont.; toolmaker; trapshooting specialist; European jr. Grand Prix '77; team gold, individual bronze '78 Benito Juarez; silver '78, 2 silver '94 Commonwealth Games; team, individual gold '91, bronze '79, '99 Pan-Am Games; mem. '80, '88, '92, '96 Olympic, '78, '82, '86, '94 Commonwealth, '79, '83, '91 Pan-Am Games teams; 3 ntl, 8 Ont., 5 Que., 3 Benito Juarez, 1 European, 1 Welsh, 1 British trap titles; head ref. trap shooting '76 Olympics; Shooting Fed. of Canada Golden Anniversary award '82; res. Newmarket, Ont.

LEBEL, Bob (hockey): b. 21 Sep 1905, Quebec City, Que.; d. 20 Sep 1999, Longueuil, Que.; given name: Robert; m. Lucile Begin; c. Jean-Marc; Que. City Commercial Academy; retd Bennett Inc.; jr., sr., Que. City; coached int. teams Montreal; 11yrs amateur hockey referee; founder, pres. ISHL '44-47; pres. QAHL; trustee George T. Richardson Memorial Trophy (Eastern Jr. championship), W.G. Hardy Cup (ntl int.); 17yrs mem. governing board Cdn Hockey Hall of Fame; former Chambly, Que., mayor; Kent GC, Sherbrooke Opens, Bank of Montreal golf titles; Confederation medal; mem. Cdn Hockey, Que. Sports halls of fame.

LeBLANC, Eugene (baseball/hockey): b. 29 Jan 1929, College Bridge, N.B.; exec. dir. Memramcook Institute; coached Memramcook Rovers to '61, '65 Maritime Int. A,

NB sr. baseball titles; founder/dir. minor baseball league operations in Memramcook Valley '61-65; sub-commissioner NBABA '63-64; helped create baseball facilities Memramcook Valley '68-70; coached Moncton Beavers to Maritime juvenile '58-59, Maritime junior '59-60 hockey titles; founder/dir. Memramcook Valley minor hockey league '68-70; exec. NBAHA '75-76; U Moncton recognition award '88; mem. NB Sports Hall of Fame; res. College Bridge, N.B.

LeBLANC, Guillaume (t&f): b. 14 Apr 1962, Sept-Iles, Que.; Montreal; engineer; race walker; ntl 3km, 10km, 20km, 5000m titles; Swedish 20km title; Cdn records 10km 39:26.02 '90, 30km 2:04.56 '90; PB: 20km 1:21.12 '86, 50km 3:56.46 '92; 30km gold '90, silver '86, bronze '82 Commonwealth, gold '83, bronze '85 FISU, gold '89 Francophone Games; mem. '84, '88, '92 Olympic, '83 Pan-Am Games; fed. govt. excellence award '84; res. Rimouski, Que.

LeBLANC, Ken (bobsleigh): b. 13 Feb 1968, Ottawa, Ont.; crewman 4/2-man teams; ntl team '85-92, from '97; competed '88, '92, '98 Olympics; 3 WC 4-man, 1 2-man race titles; mem. 4-man crew which claimed '89-90 WC series championship; res. Beaverton, Ont.

LeBLANC, Louise-Marie (fencing): b. 8 Jan 1958, Ottawa, Ont.; UofOtt, BA; computer programmer analyst; ntl jr. foil champion '74-78, sr. '76-78, '81; Ottawa Shield '78-81; team silver '75, '79 Pan-Am Games; Governor-General's Cup '79; team silver '78 Commonwealth Games; silver foil '83 Commonwealth championships; brief '92 comeback winning ntl épée title; winner, at least once, every major competition in Canada; represented Canada World Youth, World University, Worlds, Ramon Fonst International, Michel Alaux, Debeaumont, NY Open tournaments; Cornell Open titles '77-79; D'Aoust trophy French Cdn amateur athlete of '75; res. Ottawa, Ont.

LECLERC, Andre (horseshoes): b. 13 Dec 1964, St. Hyacinthe, Que.; m. Sylvianne Moisan; administrator; Que. jr. singles title '79; 9 Que. men's singles titles; 7 Que. men's doubles titles; 8 ntl men's singles titles; 2 recognized perfect games; men's record for high ringer percentage complete tournament '87 Que. championship 81%, ntl 95.8% '85; 3 top 10 finishes in world tournament; Horseshoe Canada player of decade '80s; wrote "*Historique du lancer de fers au Quebec 1958-88*"; editor *Canadian Horseshoe Pitchers Yearbook* '91-96; men. Cdn Horseshoe Hall of Fame; res. Chertsey, Que.

LEDDY, Jack (golf): b. 27 Oct 1912, Saskatoon, Sask.; d. 27 Nov 1990, Saskatoon, Sask.; given name: John Edward; m. Rita Wilkinson; c. Mary, Joanne, Jennifer, Michael; UofSask., McGill, MD; surgeon; runnerup '30 Sask. jr., '68 sr. championships; pres. RCGA '62; non-playing capt. Cdn 2nd place team world amateur tournament '62; mem. Sask. Sports Hall of Fame.

LEDERHOUSE, Phil (golf): b. 23 Nov 1915, Prince Albert, Sask.; d. 15 Aug 1998, Prince Albert, Sask; m. Ruby; lost sight at age 19; at 34 took up golf and with no prior experience and 6 months coaching won Cdn title and placed 3rd in International Blind Golfers' championship; from '50

won 17 Sask, 16 Western Cdn, 5 ntl blind golfers titles; twice world runnerup; held world record '66-67 for round of 89; a threat in every tournament he entered due to natural technique; sponsored by Lions Club and had played with the likes of Jack Nicklaus, Walter Hagan, Bob Hope, Ed Sullivan; mem. Sask. Sports Hall of Fame.

LEDUC, Mark (boxing): b. 4 May 1962, Kingston, Ont.; construction worker; competed as light welterweight (63.5kg); 3 ntl titles; 2 gold, 1 silver, 1 bronze Canada Cup; President's Cup bronze '91; competed '91 Pan-Am Games, '92 Olympics, '92 Worlds; mem. Kingston Amateur BC; res. Kingston, Ont.

LEE, Knotty (baseball); b. 12 May 1877, Toronto, Ont.; d. 5 Sep 1962, Smiths Falls, Ont.; given name: George Joseph; m. Eva Hammer; c. Herbert, George, Louis, Raymond, William, Donald, Laurence; pro baseball player, hotel owner; in late 1890s he possessed awesome, then legal, spitball pitch and was regarded as best amateur pitcher in Toronto; 6 decade relationship with baseball; played for 11 minor league teams, managed 10 more; scout for legendary Connie Mack's Philadelphia Athletics 2 decades; worked for Joe McCarthy's Yankees; business mgr. Toronto Maple Leafs (IL) 7yrs; team owner/founder 6 leagues including 1st Cdn pro league '11, Mich.-Ont., Can-Am, Pony and Border leagues; during minor league centennial celebration at Cooperstown Baseball Hall of Fame '39 represented Abner Doubleday, alleged baseball game inventor, in special ceremonies; uniform he wore that day displayed at Cdn Baseball Hall of Fame in St. Mary's; mem. Cdn Baseball Hall of Fame.

LEE, Peter (hockey): b. 2 Jan 1956, Chester, Eng.; given name: Peter John; m. Judy Perry; c. Christopher, Jeremy, Joshua; coach; scored most OHA jr. A career goals (215), points (451) and in '75-76 most goals single season (81) as mem. Ottawa 67's; OHA MVP, Tilson Trophy, highest scoring right winger Mahon trophy '76; honored with Peter Lee Day Ottawa Civic Centre '76; twice Ottawa ACT hockey player of yr; pro Nova Scotia AHL '76-77; Pittsburgh NHL '77-83; played Dusseldorf, Germany, '83-93; NHL record: 431 scheduled games, 114g, 131a, 19 playoff games, 0g, 8a; jersey retd by 67's; asst. coach 67's '93, head coach '94-95; player-coach E.C. Wolfsburg, Germany, '95-96; CHL outstanding player '76; res. Orleans, Ont.

LEE, Scott (canoeing): b. 15 Mar 1949, Saskatoon, Sask.; given name: Thomas Garfield Scott; m. Mary Jane Lynch; c. Nicole, Christopher; McMaster, BA, Ont. Teachers Coll., BEd; teacher; age group ntl titles '63-68; with John Wood ntl, NA C2 '69-70; ntl C2 '72-73, C1 '73; trained in Budapest '70-71; mem. ntl team '68 Olympics, '70-72 world championships; retd from competition '73; coach Mississauga Canoe Club 3yrs; active distance runner; res. Acton, Ont.

LEE-GARTNER, Kerrin (skiing): b. 21 Sep 1966, Trail, B.C.; given name: Kerrin Lee; m. Max Gartner; c. Riana, Stephanie; started skiing age 3; mem. alpine development group '83-84, C team '84-86, B team '86-88, A team '88-94; 3 ntl downhill, 2 GS titles; WC record 0-3-4; 2 Fleishman Cup, 2 NA Cup, 4 FIS, 2 Nor-Am gold; competed '88, '92, '94 Olympics; '92 Olympic DH gold; CBC, TSN skiing analyst from '95; fed. govt meritorious service award '93; Velma Springstead award '92; Order of BC; mem. Cdn Amateur, Cdn Olympic, Cdn Skiing; Alta., BC, Canada's Sports halls of fame; res. Calgary, Alta.

LEEMAN, Gary (hockey): b. 19 Feb 1964, Toronto, Ont.; right wing; jr. WHL Regina '81-82; drafted by Toronto '82; NHL Toronto '83-91 with brief stints in AHL with St. Catharines '85-86, Fredericton '94, Gardena, Italy, '95, Worcester (AHL, Utah (IHL) '96-97; NHL Calgary '91-93, Montreal '93-94, Vancouver '95-96; NHL record: 667 scheduled games, 199g, 267a, 36 playoff games, 8g, 16a; attained 50-goal plateau with 51 '90; res. Vancouver, B.C.

LEEMING, Marjorie (tennis): b. 4 Jun 1903, Kamloops, B.C.; d. 10 Jun 1987, Victoria, B.C.; UBC, BA; teacher; BC -16 title '15-18; Victoria clay court ladies singles, doubles '22-24, '26, mixed doubles '22-23; BC singles '23, '25-26, ladies, mixed doubles '25; ntl singles '25-26, doubles '25, '30, '32, mixed doubles '25, '30; Oregon State singles '26; Eastern Cdn singles, doubles '32; competed Forest Hills '32; tennis, badminton, golf instructor UBC '47-59; 2nd seeded nationally badminton '29; 6 times outstanding BC tennis player; mem. BC, Greater Victoria Sports halls of fame.

LEFAIVE, Lou (administration): b. 13 Feb 1928, Windsor, Ont.; m. Winnifred; c. Louise, Michelle, Maria, Jacqueline; UofOtt, St. Patrick's Coll.; retd sports administrator; football, basketball, semipro softball Windsor; coached basketball UofOtt, St. Pat's; dir. Sport Canada '68-75, '78-80; pres. Ntl Sport Recreation Centre '75-78; pres. Hockey Canada '80-82; exec-dir. Cdn Figure Skating Assn. '83-85; exec-dir. Sport Marketing Canada '86-92; founding mem. Hockey Canada, Coaching Assn of Canada, Canada Games Council; dir. COA; res. Ottawa, Ont.

LEFRANCOIS, Charles (t&f): b. 19 Dec 1972, Montreal, Que.; Ahuntsic Coll.; high jumper; began competing age 14; Que. jr. indoor/outdoor, ntl indoor jr. titles '91; Canada Games HJ gold, TJ bronze '93; competed '94 Commonwealth, '95 Pan-Am, '96 Olympic Games, '95 world outdoor championships; ntl title '95; res. Montreal, Que.

LEGACE, Francois (weightlifting): b. 13 Oct 1971, St. Hyacinthe, Que.; began competing age 12; competed '91 Pan-Am Games, '93 Worlds; 54kg bronze snatch, overall total '94 Commonwealth Games; res. Ste-Rosalie, Que.

LEGGATT, Art (baseball): b. 29 May 1941, Chatham, N.B.; given name: Arthur Michael; m. Carol; millworker; pitcher; began career with Chatham Ironmen age 14; 2 NB, 2 Maritime titles; signed pro contract Cleveland Indians; minor pro stops with Dubuque A, Salinas AA making all-star with latter; returned to Ironmen '66-81; arm trouble brought shift to 1st base; 7 NB sr., 5 Atlantic championships; mem. NB Baseball, Chatham Wall, NB Sports halls of fame; res. Chatham, N.B.

LEHMAN, Hughie (hockey): b. 27 Oct 1885, Pembroke, Ont.; d. 8 Apr 1961, Toronto, Ont.; given name: Frederick Hugh; nickname "Old Eagle Eyes"; goaler Pembroke '05, Sault Ste. Marie (international pro league) '06, Pembroke

semipro '07, Berlin (Kitchener) Ont. pro league '08-10, New Westminster Royals '11-13, Vancouver Millionaires (PCL) '14-25, Chicago (NHL) '26-27; mem. 8 Stanley Cup challengers, won with Vancouver '14-15; with Percy LeSueur shares record for playing on 2 Stanley Cup challengers within 2 months (Galt vs. Ottawa, Berlin vs. Wanderers '09-10); mem. Hockey Hall of Fame.

LEHMANN, Ken (football): b. 13 Jan 1942, Louisville, Ky.; m. Bonnie Roos; c. Eric, Heidi, Bridget; Xavier, BSc; newspaper exec.; capt/MV lineman 2ys in coll.; Xavier legion of honor; linebacker Rough Riders '64-72; Schenley lineman of '68, runnerup '66; 6 times EFC all-star, 5 times all-Cdn; mem. 3 Grey Cup finalists, 2 winners; asst. coach UofOtt 1season; mem. Ottawa Sports Hall of Fame; res. Ottawa, Ont.

LEIBEL, Allan (sailing): b. 28 Feb 1945, Montreal, Que.; m. Barbara Nemoy; UofT, BComm, LLD; lawyer; won '72 Olympic Dragon Class trials, 8th in games; 8th Tempest Class world championships '75; won '76 Olympic Tempest class trials, 5th in Games; NA Star class title '79; CORK Star Class title '81; won '80 Olympic Star class trials, missed Games due to boycott; res. Toronto, Ont.

LEIGH, Doug (coaching/figure skating): b. 4 Apr 1950, Huntsville, Ont.; m. Michelle; c. Dustin; professional skating coach; silver medal ntl jr. men's championships '66 but lack of confidence in own skating ability cut short his competitive career and he began coaching Orillia '68; opened Mariposa School of Skating in Orillia at 24; coached Brian Orser to 8 ntl titles, 2 Olympic silver medals, 1 world title; has coached 26 ntl, 14 international titlists; coached at 16 worlds, 5 Olympics; coached Elvis Stojko to 4 ntl, 3 world titles, 2 Olympic silver medals; 3M coaching award; 7 Longines coaching awards; Paul Harris Fellowship award; Ont. coach of yr award; Ont, world achievement award; Air Canada award; mem. Cdn Figure Skating Hall of Fame; res. Barrie, Ont.

LEITCH, Kerry (figure skating/baseball): b.5 Mar 1941, Woodstock, Ont.; given name: Thomas Kerry; div.Barbara Still; m. Kathryn Stewart; c. Kristi Lee, Christine, James; Detroit; pro skating school owner, coach; catcher jr. IC age 15-18, sr. London Pontiacs, Guelph age 17-14; began skating age 10, teaching age 17; trained by Otto Gold, Marcus Nikkanen; passed 7th figures test, competed jr. nationals; level 3 certified coach; coached Cdns in worlds, Olympics, internationally in England, Australia, Finland, Holland, France, USA, Belgium; among his students Sheri Baier, Robert Cowan, Lloyd Eisler, Lyndon Johnston; NCCP master rated pro; dir. ntl Pairs Centre, Champions training centre, ntl ice skating centre; pres. Intl. Pro Skating Union from '91; dir. NA training camp Lake Placid; dir. Preston FSC 30yrs; ex-board mem. CFSA; FS coach of yr award; mem. Waterloo Region Hall of Fame; res. Ellenton, Fla.

LEITHAM, Bobby (boxing): b. 25 May 1906, Perth, Scotland; m. Ethel Gordon (d); c. Joyce, Doreen; m. Celine Pinet; retd Cdn Freight Assn inspector; juv. football Verdun, jr. Grand Trunk Railways; won several 5-mile road races; 2nd to Edouard Fabre in 1 major race; won several major distance swim events; ntl level diver; ntl amateur flyweight boxing title '25-27, Que., Montreal titles '26-27; 4

international titles; ranked 3rd pro bantamweight div.; lost 20-round decision to Johnny King in '33 BE title bid; Verdun city key '79; GT-CN Old Boys plaque; mem. Cdn Boxing Hall of Fame; res. Montreal, Que./St. Petersburg, Fla.

LEMAIRE, Jacques (hockey): b. 7 Sep 1945, LaSalle, Que.; given name: Jacques Gerard; m. Mychele; c. Patrice, Danyk, Magalie; hockey exec.; jr. Montreal Canadiens; NHL Canadiens '67-79; NHL playing record: 853 scheduled games, 366g, 469a, 145 playoff games, 61g, 78a; coaching record: 229 scheduled games, 117-80-32, 67 playoff games, 44-29; mem. 8 Stanley Cup winners as player; player/coach Europe '80-81; asst. coach SUNY College '81; coach Longueuil QMJHL '82-83; coach Canadiens '83-85; asst. GM Canadiens '86-92, '98-99; managing dir. Verdun Jr. Canadiens '88-89; coach New Jersey Devils '93-98; Stanley Cup '96, scout NJ '98; Adams trophy '94; 2 *Hockey News* coach of yr awards; mem. Hockey Hall of Fame; res. Vaudreuil sur la Lac, Que.

LEMAY, Lucille (archery): b. 20 Jul 1950, Montreal, Que.; given name: Lucille Goyette; m. Roger Lemay; c. Michele; secretary; competed in all ntl outdoor championships '76-84 winning titles '76-79; 5th '76 Olympic target competition; championship of the Americas field bronze '75-77; bronze US nationals '77; PB international showing 5th Double FITA Star tournament, replacement for boycotted '80 Olympics; bronze '82 Commonwealth Games; res. Boisbriand, Que.

LEMAY, Roger (archery): b. 9 Apr 1950, Montreal, Que.; m. Lucille Goyette; c. Michele; policeman; competed all ntl outdoor championships '74-84, winning target, field titles '79, runnerup '74; 1st 9yrs of competition shot lefthanded, switched to righthand shooting '78; mem. 5 Championship of the Americas, 4 world championships, 3 US nationals teams; 1st '80 Olympic trials; competed '80 Olympics alternative Double FITA tournament; silver '82 Commonwealth Games; res. Boisbriand, Que.

LE MAY-DOAN, Catriona (speed skating); b. 23 Dec 1970, Saskatoon, Sask.; given name: Catriona Le May; m. Bart Doan; UCal; soccer, ringette player who followed sister Ailsa into speed skating; competed in t&f as heptathlete for Sask. '93 Canada Games; skating long track specialist; World Cup 500m bronze '92; competed '94, '98 (gold, bronze) Olympics; 6 ntl sprint titles; 8 World Cup medals '96 including gold, silver World championships; spectacular '98 season earning Olympic, World Cup overall, world sprint, world single distance gold; 9 WC gold '98; mem. ntl team from '88; set 2 world records '97; silver '99 worlds; World Cup circuit overall 500m gold, 1000m bronze '99; 500m gold, 1000m bronze '99 world single distance championships; 2 ntl outstanding skater awards; Bobby Rosenfeld award '98; res. Calgary, Alta.

LEMIEUX, Claude (hockey): b. 16 Jul 1965, Buckingham, Que.; m. Deborah; c. Christopher, Michael, Brendan, Claudia; rw Trois-Rivieres, Verdun (QMJHL), Nova Scotia, Sherbrooke (AHL); drafted by Montreal '83; NHL with Montreal '83-90, New Jersey '90-95, Colorado '95-98; mem. 3 Stanley Cup winners (with 3 different teams); Conn Smythe trophy '95; competed in Rendez-Vous '87; Team Canada '96 World Cup; brother Jocelyn also in NHL;

attained 300 goal plateau '98; NHL record: (through '99) 918 scheduled games, 325g, 326a, 198 playoff games, 76g, 71a; QMJHL all-star, '85 Guy Lafleur QMJHL playoff MVP trophy; res. Parber, Colo.

LEMIEUX, Gerald (boxing): b. 1 Feb 1909, Levis, Que.; d. 26 May 1959, Edmundston, N.B.; nicknamed "Biff" or "Flying Frenchman"; career spanned '28-37; Maritime featherweight titles '30, '35; 226 pro bouts in bantam, featherweight classes; fought world champions Harry Jeffra, Joey Archibald; mem. NB Sports Hall of Fame.

LEMIEUX, Lawrence (sailing): b. 12 Nov 1955, Edmonton, Alta.; boat builder; began competing age 9; Finn Class specialist; mem. ntl team from '78; competed '84, '88 Olympics, 8 worlds; 1 US National, 5 Midwinter, 1 European, 2 CORK gold; NA Finn title '94; Pan-Am Games gold '91; best remembered for corageous and sportsmanlike act in '88 Olympics when he rescued another competitor whose boat had capsized; res. Edmonton, Alta.

LEMIEUX, Mario (hockey): b. 5 Oct 1965, Montreal, Que.; m. Nathalie Asselin; c. Lauren Rachel; hockey exec.; standout jr. centre Laval Titan '81-84; QMJHL MVP '84 with 133g, 149a; Cdn jr record: 247g, 315a, 562pts; Cdn major jr. player of '84; Pittsburgh's 1st pick, 1st overall '84 draft; Calder Memorial Trophy '85; mem. all-rookie team '85; 4 L.B. Pearson, 2 Conn Smythe, 1 Masterton, 6 Ross, 3 Hart, 2 Dodge performer of yr, 1 Dodge Ram Tough trophies, 1 Pro Set NHL player of yr award, 1 Alka Seltzer plus award; *Hockey News* player of '93; 5 1st team, 3 2nd team all-star; played in 8 NHL all-star games; mem. 2 Stanley Cup winners; mem. Team Canada '90 Canada Cup winner; 50 goals in 50 games '96; topped 50-goal plateau '87 (54), '88 (70), '89 (85), '93 (69), '96 (69), '97 (50); prolific scorer plagued by chronic back ailment; diagnosed with Hodgkin's disease '93; nicknamed "The Savior" by Pittsburgh fans; Lou Marsh Trophy '93; 2 Lionel Conacher awards; NHL record: 745 scheduled games, 613g, 881a; 89 playoff games, 70g, 85a; tied single-period goal scoring record with 4 in 3rd period vs. Montreal '97; reached 600g plateau '97; retd. following '96-97 season; named to CHL all-time team '99; key figure in purchase of Penguins '99; Pittsburgh street bears his name; mem. Hockey, Canada's Sports halls of fame; res. Sewickley, Pa.

LEMMERMAN, Bruce (football): b. 4 Oct 1945, Los Angeles, Calif.; m. Brigitte Jaeger; c. Lisa Nicole, Jennifer Leigh; San Fernando Valley State Coll., BA, Cal State Northridge; football exec.; 3yrs HS baseball, football, all-conference, all-city baseball sr. yr.; 3yrs baseball, football SFVS, all-conf. 2yrs each sport; athlete of sr. yr; all-American hon. mention; QB Atlanta (NFL)'69-71, Edmonton (CFL) '71-78; 6 Grey Cup finals, 3 winners; traded to Hamilton, retd '80; asst coach Edmonton '81-82, LA Express (USFL), Houston (NFL) '84-85, Winnipeg '87-88; dir. ops. Edmonton '90-93; dir. college scouting New Orleans Saints from '94; mem. Cal State Hall of Fame; res. Destrehan, La.

LENARD, Al (football): b. 6 Jan 1921, Windsor, Ont.; given name: Aldon Lewis; m. Jean Louise Bidwell; c. James Aldon; Queen's, BA, BPHE, Michigan, MA, Illinois, PhD; retd. prof. AD; Silverwood trophy, WOSSA t&f MVP '38;

ORFU football Hamilton Wildcats '40-42, '45, Imperial Oil trophy '41; Eastern Cdn scoring leader '41-42; QB Queen's '46-49; 1st Queen's capt. chosen twice '47-48; asst. coach '54-70; pres. ntl AD's Assn '72; v-p CIAU '73; chair. CIAU admin. comm. '73-74; chair. OUAA admin, council '74-76, pres. '82-88; coached intercollegiate champions in curling, golf; '57 Kingston golf champion; res.Kingston, Ont.

LENARDON, Norman (hockey): b. 20 Oct 1933, Trail, B.C.; m. Eugenia Kennedy; c. Therese, Jim, Elizabeth, Maria; bricklayer, restaurateur; HS baseball, basketball, volleyball; sr. softball, jr. baseball; minor, jr. hockey Trail, sr. Trail, Rossland; peewee hockey MVP award, 6g, 5a in 10 games for Seattle vs. New Westminster '58 playoffs; rejected pro offers '59; mem. '61 world champion Trail Smoke Eaters; scored title clinching goal vs. Soviets in final game; mem. '62 Trail Allan Cup champions; with entire Trail team mem. BC Sports Hall of Fame; res. Trail, B.C.

LENARDUZZI, Bob (soccer): b. 1 May 1955, Vancouver, B.C.; given name: Robert Italo; m. Deanne Veitch; soccer coach; at 15 mem. Vancouver Spartans in now-defunct Western Canada SL; 5ys Reading of English 3rd div.; loaned by Reading to Vancouver Whitecaps '74-75; contract purchased by Whitecaps '76; through '83 only original Whitecap still on team; became all-time Whitecap scoring leader '81; ntl team '73-86; represented Canada internationally more than 30 times; mem. '84 Olympic, '86 World Cup finals teams; 47 international caps; mem. '79 NASL Soccer Bowl champions; as midfielder scored 10g, 17a, named NA player of '78; NASL 2nd team all-star as defender '79; mem. Tacoma Stars MISL '84-85; playing coach Vancouver 86ers '86-92, 5 titles, GM from '98; ntl team coach '92-97; mem. CSA board '98; 1st Cdn named NA player of yr '78; only player to play all 11 positions on field; CSL coach of yr '88-89, CSL GM of '91; Lou Marsh trophy nominee '78; mem. BC Sports Hall of Fame; res. N. Vancouver, B.C.

LENARDUZZI, Sam (soccer): b. 19 Dec 1949, Udine, Italy; rejected Reading, Eng., pro offers; mem. ntl team '67-78; represented Canada internationally close to 50 times, including '67 Pan-Am Games; pro defence Vancouver Whitecaps '74-78; traded to Toronto Blizzard '79-81; polished raconteur, dir. PR Whitecaps '78; coached Blizzard reserves '82; res. Vancouver, B.C.

LENOVER, Max (t&f): b. 27 Aug 1918, Chatham, Ont.; given name: Roy Maxwell; m. Ruth Ione Maxwell; c. Ruth Ann, Robert Maxwell; Loyola, PHB; retd corporate industrial engineer; mem. Chatham Queen's AC int. OHA hockey team; Ont. int. schoolboy 440 recordholder; champion miler, capt. Loyola t&f team; in 4yrs at Loyola never lost a dual competition race; established numerous school, state, ntl records; Illinois cross-country titlist; nicknamed "Legs"; mem. '38 BEG team; mem. Loyola Sports Hall of Fame; recognized in US Colleges Who's Who; res. Jacksonville, Fla.

LEONARD, Stan (golf): b. 2 Feb 1915, Vancouver, B.C.; m. Chris Main; c. Linda; retd golf pro; won 1st tournament he entered, '32 BC Amateur, repeat '35; semifinalist Cdn Amateur '36-37; mem. 6 BC Willingdon Cup teams; touring

pro '55-63; included among 44 pro victories were '57 Greater Greensboro Open, '58 Tournament of Champions, '60 Western Open; twice low individual World Cup ('53-59), with Jules Huot '53 runnerup; 8 CPGA titles, 5 times runnerup; 9 Rivermead Cups as low Cdn in Cdn Open; 5 BC, 9 Alta., 2 Sask. Open, 1 Millar Trophy titles; mem. 9 Canada Cup, 6 Hopkins Cup teams; 3rd US Masters '58-59; ntl sr. pro title '75; golfer of '59; head pro Desert Island CC Rancho Mirage, Calif., '74-81; emeritus dir. of golf from '81; mem. RCGA, BC, Canada's Sports halls of Fame; res. Rancho Mirage, Calif./Vancouver, B.C.

LEPAGE, Carolyne (judo): b. 9 Jun 1975, Montreal, Que.; competes at 48 kg; 1st degree black belt; began competing age 15; bronze '94 Francophone Games 2 ntl titles; silver '95 Pan-Am Games; competed '96 Olympics; res. Verennes, Que.

LESLIE, Deardra (baton twirling): b. 17 Jun 1953, Kitchener, Ont.; given name: Deardra King; m. Trevor Leslie; NA twirling champion, Miss Majorette of Ont., Canada; 2 ntl titles; pro twirler; coach, judge; tech. advisor Ont. chapter IBTA; students have won prov, ntl, US titles; res. Kitchener, Ont.

LESPI, Kusti (hockey): b. 24 Feb 1915, Ft. William, Ont.; given name: Leo; nicknamed "Flying Finn"; developed hockey skills in Nipigon; played Jr. Port Arthur West Ends, Sudbury Cub Wolves; turned pro Boston organization 1 season Boston Cubs; loaned to AHA Minneapolis Millers where he played 10yrs; mem. 1 AHA title team; set record for right wingers with 35 goals; played in inaugural AHA all-star game '41; retired from pro ranks '47 returning to Nipigon to coach Flyers to '52 North Shore title; active many yrs with Nipigon Old Timers; day in his honor held in Nipigon '65; Celebration '88 award; mem. NWO Sports Hall of Fame; res. Nipigon, Ont.

LESSARD, Lucille (archery): b. 26 May 1957, Quebec City, Que.; m. Hutchinson; 5 ntl titles; '74 world field title; Pacific Coast field title '74; Champion of the Americas '75; mem. '80 Olympic team; Que. athlete of '74; Elaine Tanner award; mem. Canada's Sports Hall of Fame; res. Waterloo, Ont.

LeSUEUR, Percy (hockey): b. 18 Nov 1881, Quebec City, Que.; d. 27 Jan 1962, Hamilton, Ont.; m. Georgia Steele; c. Steve Douglas; hockey exec.; nicknamed "Peerless Percy"; jr. Que. Victorias, sr. Que.; Ottawa Silver Seven '06-13; mem. 2 Stanley Cup winners; 3yrs team capt.; mgr., coach '13-14; Toronto Arenas '14; career spanned 50yrs as player, coach, mgr., referee, equipment designer, arena mgr., broadcaster, columnist; designed gauntlet type goaler's gloves, net used by NHA, NHL '12-25; original mem. radio's Hot Stove League; retd '46; mem. Ottawa Sports, Hockey halls of Fame.

LETHEREN, Carol Anne (administration): b. 27 Jul 1942, Toronto, Ont.; UofT, BPhE, BA; York, MBA; CEO/Secty Gen. COA; assoc. prof Uof T '63-70; York '70-77; Cdn. Govt. consultant '77-79; sr. partner/co-owner marketing planning and consultant co. '79-94; active role in ntl, international affairs particularly concerning women/ athletes; IOC mem. in Canada '90; press commission IOC '92-94; served on variety of IOC, Ont., COA, educational committees from '81; coached archery, gymnastics, volleyball university varsity level; ntl women's gymnastics team '70 FISU Games; officiated international gymnastics '76, '84 Olympic, '78, '82 Commonwealth, '74, '79, '81, '83, '85 World, '73, '83 FISU Games, '77, '79 European championships, '78, '80 World Cup; won intercollegiate badminton titles in '50s, varsity volleyball player; masters marathon, 10km runner; varied admin roles ntl volleyball assn., Ont. Cdn, Itnl gymnastics fed.; pres. COA '90-94; CdM Cdn team '88 Olympics; Air Canada Official of '78; McCain's volunteer of '88; Cdn Gymnastics Fed. gold service pin '85; YMCA woman of distinction '92; York public contribution award '92; hon. LLD UofT '93; hon. life mem. Cdn, Intl Gymnastics Feds.; mem. UofT Sports Hall of Fame; res. Toronto, Ont.

LETTERI, Tony (soccer): b. 27 Sep 1957, Italy; goaler Minnesota Strikers (NASL) '80-81, '84, Vancouver Whitecaps '82-83; leading NASL goaler '83 with 0.86 goals against avg.; mem. '76, '84 Olympic teams; res. N. Vancouver, B.C.

LEUSZLER, Winnie Roach (swimming): b. 3 Feb 1926, Pt. Credit, Ont.; given name: Winnie Roach; m. Morris Leuszler; c. Frances, Sharon, Phyllis, Norman, Michael; took initial swimming plunge age 3; a natural swimmer; despite fact father Eddie was swim coach never had a formal lesson; began competing age 9 winning ist medal in Pt. Credit River swim age 9; frequent Trent Canal, Etobicoke distance swim victories; at 18 became 1st Cdn to win US AAU 2.5-mile swim; 1st Cdn woman to swim English Channel '51; competed in '54 Lake Ontario swim which brought fame to Marilyn Bell; competed in varied Toronto playground sports, t&f from age 6; softball, baseball; on single day '44 won 4 t&f races at distances from 50-440yds then won 5-mile St. Clair River swim; served in Cdn Armed Forces '44-45; 1st woman hired as YMCA swim coach in Kitchener; in each centre in which career soldier husband posted played active role in establishing recreational programs; established Calgary Stampeders swim club; set up athletic programs in Kingston, Calgary women's prisons; toured one season with Cypress Gardens water ski show; 1st official woman baseball/softball umpire; active in Canada-France student exchange programs; presented with keys to cities of Toronto, Kitchener, North York, Marshfield, WI; mayor's wife Cdn village Chensey Moselle, France; mayor for a day Vancouver; mem. Ont. Aquatic, Cdn Forces Sports halls of fame; res. Port Coquitlam, B.C.

LEVANTIS, Steve (football): b. 28 Jul 1916, Montreal, Que.; m. Lillian; Assumption Coll.; sales & Marketing; mem. 3 TDIAA champions; Ont. sr. baseball title team; Toronto Argos '36-41, '45-49; mem. 5 Grey Cup champions; EFC all-star '45; tackle all-Argos '21-41 team; res. Ancaster, Ont.

LEVER, Don (hockey); b. 14 Nov 1952, South Porcupine, Ont.; given name: Donald Richard; m. Karen; c. Michael, Sarah, Caitlin; centre/lw Niagara Falls OHA '70-72; drafted by Vancouver '72; NHL Vancouver '72-80, Atlanta '80, Calgary '80-81, Colorado '81-82, New Jersey '82-85, Buffalo '85-87; player/coach Rochester AHL '85-91; NHL record: 1020 scheduled games, 313g, 367a, 30 playoff

games, 7g, 10a; head coach Rochester '91-92; 2 Calder Cup finals, 1 winner; asst./assoc. coach Sabres '92-98; AHL coach of '91; res. Amherst, N.Y.

LEVESQUE, Jean-Louis (horse racing): b. 13 Apr 1911, Gaspe Peninsula, Que.; d. 29 Dec 1994, Montreal, Que.; m. Jeanne; c. Andree, Suzanne, Pierre; Gaspe Coll., St. Dunstan's., Laval., BA; hon. degrees Laval, Montreal, Moncton, St. Dunstan's; investment broker; with '56 purchase of 2 trotters became racing devotee; purchased Blue Bonnets Raceway '58; later owned Richelieu, Windsor Raceways; re-introduced thoroughbred racing to Montreal; further involved with purchase of racing stock, including 6 horse of year winners, '75 Queen's Plate winner L'Enjoleur; Moncton U PE complex bears his name; horse racing's man of '83; Eleanor Roosevelt award for world peace; trustee OJC; mem. Order of Canada, Cdn Business, Cdn Horse Racing, Canada's Sports halls of fame.

LEVY, Marv (football/coaching): b. 3 Aug 1928, Chicago, Ill; m. Mary Francis; Coe College, Harvard, MA; running back Coe Coll '48-50; 2yrs HS coach; coach Coe Coll. '53-55; asst. New Mexico '56-57, head coach '58-59, California '60-63, William & Mary '64-68; began pro coaching career as asst. with Philadelphia '69, LA '70, Washington '71-72, 1 Super Bowl; head coach Montreal '73-77 posting 50-34-4 record, 2 Grey Cup victories; head coach Kansas City '78-82; following 2yr hiatus from game became head coach Chicago Blitz (USFL) '84; Buffalo Bills '86-97; 6 AFC titles, coached 4 consecutive Super Bowl finalists; pro career coaching record 144-113; Phi Beta Kappa at Coe; res. Hamburg, N.Y.

LEWIS, Bill (curling): b. 8 Feb 1921, Angusville, Man.; given name: William Morris; div. Avis Slitch; c. Patricia, Dale, Guy; div. Carol Devereaux; m. Helen McDonald; retd CF, taxi co. owner; winner 2 Ont. Silver Tankards, 2 Burden Trophies; twice competed Ont. Consols, once runner-up; Ont. Mixed finalist; won Ont. Legion title; City of Ottawa grand aggregate champion, runnerup once; 3rd stone for Jake Edwards (delivering final rocks each end) 3 Ont. Srs. title rinks; res. Saskatoon, Sask.

LEWIS, Bryan (officiating/hockey); b. 10 Sep 1942, Alliston, Ont.; given name: Bryan Howard; m. Elaine Margaret Pallett; c. Janelle Lynn, Duane Howard, Alyson Megan; dir. officiating NHL; played Jr. C Georgetown, Jr. B Dixie, Burlington; worked OHA Jr. A, 2 Canada-Russia international exhibitions; joined NHL staff '67 working 3yrs WHL, CHL, AHL before appearing in initial NHL league game 6 Jan '70; NHL record: 1031 scheduled games over 19 seasons; worked '81 all-star, '84 Canada Cup; retd '86 to join supervisory staff; dir. officiating from '89; OHA referees' honor roll; res. Georgetown, Ont.

LEWIS, Dave (hockey): b. 3 Jul 1953, Kindersley, B.C.; given name: David Rodney; m. Brenda; c. Ryan, Meagan; coach; defence Saskatoon Blades Jr '71-73; drafted by N Y Islanders; NHL Islanders '73-80, Los Angeles '80-83, Minnesota '83, New Jersey '83-86, Detroit '86-87; NHL record: 1008 scheduled games; 36g, 187a, 91 playoff games, 1g, 20a; joined Detroit coaching staff '87 as asst.; assoc. coach '97-99; 2 Stanley Cup winner; actively involved in Make-A-Wish Foundation; res. Detroit, Mich.

LEWIS, Elinor (administration): b. 16 Nov 1918, Thurso, Que.; m. Ray Lewis (d); c. Terry, Shirley; mem. Tweedsmuir, Crystal Pebble title winners; pres. Ottawa Hunt Club curling section '68-69, v-p Dist. 2 LCA '69-70; charter mem. Ottawa Crystal Pebble comm.; publicity dir. CLCA sr. championships '73; pres. EOLCA, OLCA; Ont. delegate CLCA meetings Moncton, Winnipeg, Halifax; mem. CLCA exe.; charter mem. Ont. Curling Development Council; 1st woman dir. National Capital Region Amateur Sports Council; res. Nepean, Ont.

LEWIS, Herbie (hockey); b. 17 Apr 1907, Calgary, Alta; d. 20 Jan 1991, Indianapolis, Ind.; m. Ceverene Adams; c. Gerald, George; lw; with Calgary Jr. Canadians; nicknamed "Duke of Duluth" for 4yr stint with Duluth Hornets where he was undisputed chief drawing card in AHL; spent 11 seasons in NHL '28-39 with Detroit Cougars, Falcons, Red Wings; on line with Cooney Weiland, Larry Aurie; named Red Wings capt. '33; started in 1st-ever NHL all-star game '34; participated in longest game in NHL history; mem. 2 Stanley Cup winners; NHL record: 484 scheduled games, 148g, 161a, 38 playoff games, 13g, 10a; brought hockey to Indianapolis as player/coach AHL Indianapolis Capitols claiming Calder Cup '42; retd from hockey '43; mem. Hockey Hall of Fame.

LEWIS, Lennox (boxing): b. 2 Sep 1965, Stratford, Eng.; raised in Kitchener, Ont. from age 12; Canada Games 81kg heavyweight title '83; jr. world 91kg super heavyweight title '83; Stockholm Open, Canada vs. US, ntl 91kg titles '84; mem. '84, '88 Olympic teams; super heavyweight gold '86 Commonwealth Games, '88 Olympics; turned pro, returned to UK '89; won British, European heavyweight titles, Commonwealth title '92, WBC title '93 (lost '94, regained '97); fought Evander Holyfield in title unification match '99 and, although considered by most observers as winner, was deprived of titles when match ruled a draw sparking fix investigation; unanimous decision in '99 rematch gave him WBC, WBA, IBF titles; pro record: 34-1-1, 27 kos; Viscount Alexander Trophy '83; Norton Crowe award '88; fed. govt excellence award '84; mem. Order of Canada, Cdn Amateur Sports, Waterloo County halls of fame; res. London, Eng.

LEWIS, Leo (football): b. 4 Feb 1933, Des Moines, Iowa; given name: Leo Everett Jr.; m. Doris Marie; c. Leo III, Marc, Barry; Lincoln, BSc, Missouri, MEd; instructor, coach Lincoln.; all-city St. Paul, Minn., HS football, basketball; all-Midwest Athletic Assn. 1st team all-star running back '51-54; Pittsburgh Courier all-American 3 times; AP Little all-American twice; Philip Morris all-American '53; 4457yds rushing in 4 seasons, including 245yds single game, 1239yds single season, 623 carries for 7.15yd avg., 64 career TDs, 22 single season, 4 times scored 4 in one game, 132 scoring points 1 season, all Lincoln records; pro Blue Bombers '55-66; CFL record: 8856yds rushing, 1351 carries, 6.57 avg., 48tds; twice rushed over 1000yds single season; 234 passes caught for 4251yds, 26tds; CFL leader career kickoff returns 187 for 5444yds, 1td; 450 points on 75tds, 5 converts, 1 single; 6 times CFL all-star; mem. all-decade Blue Bombers team of '60s; 6 Grey Cup finals, 4 winners; head football coach Lincoln '73-75; dir. intramural sports, golf coach, women's basketball coach Lincoln; mem. Cdn Football Hall of Fame; res. Columbia, Mo.

LEWIS, Loyd (football): b. 23 Feb 1962, Dallas, Tex.; Texas A&I; defensive tackle; drafted by Houston Gamblers (USFL), by Minnesota Vikings (NFL) '84; played 1 season Houston; joined Ottawa (CFL) as free agent '85; played in CFL with Ottawa '85-91, '95-96, Edmonton '92, Winnipeg '93-94; CFL record: 180 games, 245 tackles, 83 QB sacks; 4 Eastern, 1 Western all-star; 7 playoff games, mem. '93 Grey Cup finalists; res. Ottawa, Ont.

LEWIS, Ray (t&f): b. 8 Oct 1910, Hamilton, Ont.; given name: Raymond Gray; m. Vivienne; c. Larry; retd. govt chauffer; HS 100yd, 220yd, 440yd, mile relay titles; twice ntl 440yd title; bronze 1500m relay '32 Olympics; silver '34 BEGmile relay; 5 ntl 600yd indoor titles; res. Hamilton, Ont.

LEWIS, Stanley (roller skating/canoeing): b. 29 Feb 1888, Ottawa, Ont.; d. 18 Aug 1970, Ottawa, Ont; m. Pearl Brooks; c. Elda; hon. LLD UofOtt; ntl roller skating titles '09-10; mem. Ottawa Harrier hockey club; mem. Britannia ntl champion war canoe team '15; active with Ottawa football club '12-14; mem. Ottawa branch exec. AAU of C; mayor of Ottawa '36-48; mem. OBE.

LEYSHON, Glynn (wrestling): b. 2 Aug 1929, Hamilton, Ont.; given name: Glynn Arthur; m. Judith; c. Sian, Gar, Rhysa, Tal; UWO, PhD; retd. asst dean, AD; twice intercollegiate wrestling champion; referee '67 Pan-Am Games; coach UWO '64-80; 8 league champions; coach ntl team 4 world championship tournaments, 2 FISU Games, 3 World Cup of Wrestling, '79 Pan-Am, '80 Olympic teams; CIAU coach of '76; Silver Star Award, Fédération Internationale de Lutte '76; co-author (with Frank Cosentino) *Olympic Gold*; author *Of Mats and Men*, *Judoka*; Ont. special achievement award; mem. Cdn Amateur Wrestling, W-Club Sports halls of fame; res. London, Ont.

L'HEUREUX, Bill (hockey/football): b. 28 Feb 1918, Port Arthur, Ont.; given name: Willard Joseph; m. Viola M. Suitor; c. Susan, Mary, Bill Jr.; Assumption Coll, BA, Michigan. MA, UNB, LLD; professor; college hockey Assumption '34-36, sr. Windsor '40, Cornwall Flyers Que. sr. '41-43; Arnprior, Hull, Renfrew, Cornwall, Alexandria ODHA '45-49; coach Maxville HS '39, Cornwall CIVS '40-43, Ottawa Tech '45-48, Ottawa St. Patrick's '49-50, UWO Mustangs '50-55, '63-65; coach women's intercollegiate hockey UWO ; football Assumption '34-37; coached Cornwall '40-43, Galt CIVS '43-45, Ottawa Tech '45-50. asst. UWO '50-56; chair. Ntl Advisory Council on Fitness, Amateur Sport '66-69; CAHPER Tait McKenzie honor award '67; Hockey Canada development comm. '75-76; wrote several books on hockey; mem. W-Club Sports Hall of Fame; res. London, Ont.

LICHTY, Kathy (rowing): b. 16 Oct 1957, North Bay, Ont.; m. David Boyes; sweep ntl team from '76; 2 Cdn Henley coxed 8s, 1 coxed 4s titles; 1 ntl, Holland Cup coxed 4s titles; mem. '77-79, '82-83 world championships, '84 Olympic teams; res. St. Catharines, Ont.

LIDSTONE, Dorothy (archery): b. 2 Nov 1938, Wetaskiwin, Alta.; given name; Dorothy Carole Wagar; div.; archery equipment manufacturer; 3 prov., 4 Pacific

Northwest titles; ntl, world championships '69; variety of records including 2361 points in world championships; retd from competition '70; mem. Cdn Amateur, Canada's, BC Sports halls of fame; res. Abbotsford, B.C.

LIEBERMAN, Moe (football); b. 16 Jun 1891, Toronto, Ont.; d. 2 May 1984, Edmonton, Alta.; given name: Moses Isaac; m. Emily Sereth (d); c. Ethel, Samuel; UAlta., BSc, MSc, UofT, LLB; lawyer, QC; quarterback UAlta. '15-18; mem. Eskimos '19-21; helped raise funds to finance 1st western challenge for Grey Cup '21; mgr. Eskimos '22; several yrs. offical in Western Canada; active in organizational aspect of game; p.-pres. Western Canada Rugby Football Union; mem. Eskimos directorate from late 30s to late 50s; v-p,pres. Eskimos; mem. Edmonton board of governors '58-84; active in formation Eskimos Alumni Club; mem. Alta. Sports, Canadian Football halls of fame.

LIEPA, Ingrid (speed skating); b. 24 Mar 1966, Ottawa, Ont.; UCal, LLB; lawyer; novice level figure skater; switched to speed skating as means of stress management when she moved to Calgary to pursue law studies '90; began competing age 24; long track specialist; ntl team from '92; ntl all-around title '95; 2 ntl records; competed '94, '98 Olympics, '96, '97 worlds; res. Calgary, Alta.

LIFFORD, Johnny (boxing); b. 19 Jan 1911, Fredericton, N.B.; d. 13 Aug 1972, South Boston, Mass.,; ring career spanned '24-44; Maritime lightweight, welterweight, middleweight titles; won 222 of 235 bouts; mem. NB Sports Hall of Fame.

LIMNIATIS, John (soccer): b. 24 Jun 1967, Athens, Greece; midfielder; mem. ntl team program from '83; made ntl team international debut '87; played in CSL with Ottawa Intrepid '87-88; Greek 1st div. Aris; Montreal Impact A League from '93; indoor with Kansas City Attack NPSL '95-96; res. Montreal, Que.

LIMPERT, Marianne (swimming): b. 10 Oct 1972, Matagami, Que.; UofT, UNB; father was ntl heavyweight boxing titlist '64-65; 10 ntl titles, 6 ntl records; mem. ntl team '92-98; world short course 4x200 FS gold '95; 2 gold, 1 silver '93 FISU Games; silver, 4 bronze '94, 1 gold, 1 bronze '98 Commonwealth Games; 5 silver, 1 bronze '95, 2 gold, 2 bronze '99 Pan-Am Games; 2 gold, 2 bronze '96 Canada Cup; 2 gold, 1 silver, 3 bronze '93 CIAU championships, 3 world cup gold '95; 200IM silver '96 Olympics; competed '92, '96 Olympic Games, '93 Pan-Pacific championships; Cdn flag-bearer '98 Commonwealth Games; res. Vancouver, B.C../Fredericton, N.B.

LINDEN, Trevor (hockey); b. 11 Apr 1970, Medicine Hat, Alta.; m. Cristina; centre/rw Medicine Hat (WHL) '86-88; 2 Memorial Cup winners; NHL Vancouver '88-98, NY Islanders (capt.) '98, Montreal '99; became youngest capt. in NHL at 20; youngest to play in NHL all-star game; 1st Canuck rookie to win Cyclone Taylor team MVP trophy; Hockey News rookie of yr award; mem. '88 world jr. gold medal team, Team Canada '91 worlds, '96 World Cup, '98 Olympics; NHL all-rookie team; competed 2 NHL all-star teams; NHL record: (through '99) 810 scheduled games, 275g, 358a, 79 playoff games, 30g, 50a; King Clancy Memorial trophy '97; Gillette world champion award; very

active in community, charitable work; hon. spokesperson Canuck Place; developed Captain's Crew program; active Youth Against Violence program, Ronald McDonald House, Cancer Society's Lottery for Hope; has done some BCTV commentary work; res. Vancouver, B.C.

LINDLEY, Earl (football); b. 13 Mar 1933, Wellsville, Utah; given name: Earl Leishman; m. Marilyn Jensen; c. Greg, Teresa, Lance, Corey, Wade; Utah State, BSc, MSc; teacher, football coach; 11 HS football, basketball, t&f, baseball letters; HS all-state 2yrs; led US scorers sr. year; linebacker, drafted by NFL Chicago, joined Edmonton '54-57; all-star '56; mem. 3 Grey Cup winners; head coach Idaho Falls HS 3yrs; asst. coach Brigham Young 7yrs; from '68 head coach Sky View HS, Logan, Utah; res. Smithfield, Utah.

LINDQUIST, Vic (hockey/officiating); b. 22 Mar 1908, Gold Rock, Ont., d. 30 Nov 1983, Winnipeg, Man.; given name: Carl Victor; m. Gertrude Anderson; c. Marlene, Vicki, Susan, Randall, Rodney; mem. Western finalist Kenora jrs.; Winnipeg Allan Cup team '31; mem. '32 Olympic, world champion gold medal teams; mem. '35 world champion Winnipeg Monarchs; coached Swedish ntl team '35-36; rheumatic fever terminated playing career '39; began officiating '41; refereed 35 years Pacific, Western pro leagues; CAHA referee-in-chief; officiated 9 Memorial, Allan Cup, 1 Alexander Cup final, 2 world championships; rejected offers to officiate in NHL; avid golfer, 2 holes-in-one, several club championships; mem. NWO Sports, Man. Hockey halls of fame.

LINDROS, Eric (hockey): b. 28 Feb 1973, London, Ont.; centre; played jr. Det. Compuware, Oshawa Generals '89-92; mem. 2 Team Canada world jr. gold medal teams; mem. Memorial Cup team Oshawa '90; OHL 1st team all-star '91; competed '91 Canada Cup, '93 worlds, '96 world cup, '92, (capt.) '98 Olympic teams; Cdn major jr. player of '90, '91; Memorial Cup all-star '90; 1st pick overall by Quebec '91 entry draft but refused to play for Nordiques as he had earlier with Sault Ste. Marie, which led to Lindros Rule in OHL; traded to Philadelphia; considered franchise player; mem. NHL Upper Deck rookie team '93; 1st team '95, 2nd team '96 all-star; played in 3 NHL all-star games; NHL record (through '99): 431 scheduled games, 263g, 337a, 48 playoff games, 23g, 33a; 3 Bobby Clarke, 1 L.B. Pearson, Hart trophies; Viscount Alexander award '91; res. Toronto, Ont.

LINDSAY, Ted (hockey); b. 29 Jul 1925, Renfrew, Ont.; given name: Robert Blake Theodore; m. Joanne; c. 3; auto equipment sales; jr. St. Mike's Majors, Oshawa's '44 Memorial Cup winner; Detroit '44-57, '64-65, Chicago '57-60, left wing on Wings' Production Line with Sid Abel, Gordie Howe; mem. 7 straight NHL league title, 4 Stanley Cup winners; frequent penalty leader; nicknamed 'Tempestuous Ted', 'Terrible Ted', 'Forever Furious'; 8 times 1st, once 2nd team all-star; NHL record: 1068 scheduled games, 379g, 472a, 1808pim, 133 playoff games, 47g, 49a; 5g, 5a in 11 all-star games; pres. NHL Players' Assn.; GM. Detroit '77-81; coach '79-80; *THN* exec. of '77; jersey #7 retd by Red Wings; 1 of 4 official ambassadors of hockey NHL 75th anniversary; mem. Hockey Hall of Fame; res. Rochester Hills, Mich.

LINSEMAN, Ken (hockey); b. 11 Aug 1958, Kingston, Ont.; m. Pam; c. Kyle, Holly Rae; real estate; OHA jr. centre Kingston '74-77; turned pro WHA Birmingham '77-78; joined Philadelphia (NHL) '78-82 with brief stint in Maine (AHL); dealt by Flyers to Hartford who traded him to Edmonton same day '82; with Edmonton '82-84, Boston '84-90, rejoined Flyers '90, Edmonton '90-91, Toronto '91-92; played in Italy briefly '91-92; centred line of Brian Propp and Paul Holmgren which was dubbed Rat Patrol and was nicknamed The Rat; OHA all-star '77; NHL record: 860 scheduled games, 256g, 551a, 113 playoff games, 43g, 77a; WHA record: 71 scheduled games, 38g, 38a, 5 playoff games, 2g, 2a; 1 Stanley Cup winner; landmark court case lowered NHL draft age to 18 from 20; res. Hampton Beach, N.H.

LINTON, Keith (harness racing); b. 5 Dec 1947, Regina, Sask.; nicknamed 'Mighty Mite from Moose Jaw'; UDR titles '73, '76; moved from Regina-Saskatoon fair circuit to Assiniboia Downs '67; later shifted to Cloverdale-Sandown circuit; more than 2000 victories, all in Canada; res. Moose Jaw, Sask.

LIPARI, Michel (weightlifting); b. 18 Dec 1933, Montreal, Que.; m. Antoinette Eusanio; c. Mickeal Angelo, Anne-Marie, Mark Anthony, Catherine; North Carolina State College; owner Lipari Moving & Cartage; Que. bodybuilding champion '51; Montreal lightweight wrestling champion '53; competed as light heavyweight weightlifter '58-63; flagbearer Cdn team '59, bronze '63 Pan-Am Games; mem. '58 BEG, '60 Olympic, '62 World championships teams; ntl press record 299lbs, clean & jerk 358lbs '60s; res. Baie d'Urfe, Que.

LISKE, Peter (football); b. 24 May 1941, Plainfield, N.J.; m. Debbie Hackwith; c. Kim, Tucker; Penn State, BSc, MBA; AD Toledo; Penn baseball star leading Nittany Lions to College World Series '63; led Penn to Gator Bowls '61-62, Hula Bowl (MVP) '63; quarterback, defensive back NY Jets AFL, Toronto (CFL) '65, Calgary '66-68, '73-74, Denver (NFL) '69-70, Philadelphia '71-72, BC Lions '74-75; capt. Broncos, Eagles, Stampeders; 3 times CFL passing leader; single season CFL TD pass record 40 '67; CFL record: 1449 completions, 2571 attempts for 21,266yds, 133int, 130tds; Schenley outstanding player award '67, Jeff Nicklin WFC MVP award '67; Western Athletic Conf. referee '77-83, NFL referee '82-89; assoc. AD UWash '85-92; AD UIdaho '93-96; noted for placing high emphasis on academics; res. Holland, Ohio

LISTER, Ralph (all-around); b. 30 Jul 1908, Harvey Station, N.B.; d. 31 Oct 1990, Moncton, N.B.; given name: Ralph William; Mount Allison; nicknamed 'Bull'; mem. NB sr. rugby/football title teams '26, '28; 6 intercollegiate, sr. basketball title teams, Eastern ntl finalists '28; NB sr. baseball titlists '28; AD Mount Allison '31-36, coached 26 NB, Maritime title teams; skipped Beaver Curling Club rink to Ganong Cup, berth in '56 Brier; mem. NB Sports Hall of Fame.

LITTLE, Laura (diving); b. 25 Jul, 1907, Toronto, Ont.; m. Miller; at 17 became 1st Cdn women's diving champion , both high and low boards '24; won 3 ntl titles; only Toronto girl to dive from 33-foot tower; officially opened Toronto Sunnyside pool '25 by diving off high tower with Cdn flag held aloft in each hand, res. Etobicoke, Ont.

LITZENBERGER, Eddie (hockey); b. 15 Jul 1932, Neudorf, Sask.; given name: Edward Charles John; m. Gayle Marie Goschen; c. Dean, Kelly Lynne, John; Regina Coll; retd.; rw Regina Pats 3yrs, 2yrs capt., 2 Memorial Cup finals; Montreal Royals, 2 championships; NHL Montreal '52-55, Chicago '55-61, Detroit '61-62, Toronto '62-64; AHL Rochester '65-66; Calder Memorial Trophy '55; team capt Chicago 4yrs; mem. 6 successive championship teams 4 Stanley Cups, 2 Calder Cups; res. Etobicoke, Ont.

LIUT, Mike (hockey); b. 7 Jan 1956, Weston, Ont.; m. Mary Ann Donnewald; c. Justin, Blake, Jenna; Bowling Green, BSc (business), Detroit Coll. of Law,Mich. State, JD; lawyer; became hockey devotee at 15 playing jr. B Markham, Dixie; played goal for Bowling Green; drafted by St. Louis (NHL) '76 but opted for 2 seasons in WHA with Cincinnati; joined NHL St. Louis '79-84, Hartford '84-89. Washington '89-92, mem. '81 Canada Cup; NHL record: 663 scheduled games, 294-271-74, 38,155 min, 2219ga, 25so, 67 playoff games, 29-32, 2so; NHL all-star game MVP '81; *Hockey News* player of '81; Lester B. Pearson trophy; Norris div. title '81, Adams div. title '87; 1st team all-star '81, 2nd team '87; did some hockey broadcasting; collective bargaining/other labor related issues with NHLPA; volunteer asst. coach Mich; res. Bloomfield Hills, Mich.

LLEWELLYN, Jaret (water skiing); b. 27 Jul 1970, Innisfail, Alta.; m. Britta Grebe; c. Dorien; pro water skier; began skiing age 6; ntl team from '86; won '94 Moomba Masters jumps, tricks, Pan-Am championships tricks, jumps, overall; gold team, individual tricks, jumps '95, tricks gold, jumps silver '99 Pan-Am Games; 1 US open jump, US masters overall titles; overall, jump gold '97 British masters; won jump titles '95, '96 Paddy Classic, '97 Portland pro tour; '96 Pan-Am championship overall, jump titles; '96, '98 World Cup jump titles; '97 world jump champion; set world jump record '92; PB: buoys 51 (slalom), tricks 10,820 points (ntl record), jump 67.5m (ntl record); mem. '91, '93 '95 (bronze), '97 (bronze) world championships teams, mem. Alta. Sports Hall of Fame; res. Innisfail, Alta./Florida.

LOARING, John (t&f/swimming); b. 3 Aug 1915, Winnipeg, Man., d. 20 Nov 1969, Windsor, Ont.; given name: John Wilfrid; m. Ellen Selina Ruston; c. Mary Ellen, David John (d), George Robert John, David Charles, Esther Ann; Huron College; pres. construction co.; sprint, hurdles specialist; high hurdles titlist, anchored winning mile relay team '34 Inter-Empire schoolboy games; silver low hurdles '36 Olympics; gold 440yd hurdles, 440yd relay, mile relay '38 BEG; .'35 sr. intercollegiate 100yd, 220yd low hurdles, 440yd titles; Ont. 440 hurdles '36; 4th 400m '37 Pan-Am Games; 4 ntl sr. intercollegiate swim titles; mem. '39 int. intercollegiate harrier title team; ntl 400m hurdles record; equalled British 440yd hurdles record '42; helped form Windsor Swim Club, pres. '47-52; officiated many Windsor track meets, Commonwealth Games '66; exec. mem. Commonwealth Games Assn., AAU of C, COA, Windsor recreation commission; coached Windsor Swim Club water polo team; athletic coordinator Windsor-Detroit Freedom

Festival '63; J.W. Davies track trophy '38; Windsor Boy Scout exec. award '58; Windsor SC award '69; trophies bearing his name awarded annually by UWindsor to HS swim champions, Kennedy relay 400m dash winners; numerous swimming pool design awards; mem. Cdn Amateur, Windsor-Essex, W-Club Sports halls of fame.

LOBEL, Art (curling); b. 13 May 1935, Virden, Man; m. Shirley Pollock; c. Rob, Steven; UMan, BSc; mechanical engineer; skipped Que. '66 ntl mixed title rink; lead on Que. Brier entry '70, 3rd '72, '75-77; won '77 Brier, runnerup Silver Broom; won '75 CBC curling classic; all-star 3rd '77 Brier; 3 Ont., 3 Cdn seniors titles; mem. Canadian Curling Hall of Fame; res. Thornhill, Ont.

LOCKETT, Donna (t&f); b. 26 Apr 1965, Montreal, Que.; given name: Donna-Marie; Carleton, PhD; researcher; duathlon specialist; 2 Ont. 5km, 1 10km road racing titles; cyclist Ont. triathlon team relay titlist '92; 3 Eastern Cdn, 1 Ont, 2 ntl duathlon titles; mem. ntl elite team '93-94; competed '93 world championships; won '91 Gloucester half-marathon, '90 Cdn international duathlon; '94 car accident threatened duathlon career but extensive therapy put her back on track as she turned attention to marathons; won '97 Marathon by the Sea in Saint John, N.B., in record time; res. Ottawa, Ont.

LOCKHART, Gene (swimming/football); b. 18 Jul 1891, London, Ont., d. 31 Mar 1957, Santa Monica, Calif.; m. Kathleen Arthur; c. June; St. Michael's Coll., De LaSalle Inst., Brompton Oratory School, London, Eng.; actor; capt St. Mike's hockey team; football for Toronto Argos; Canadian mile swimming title '09; appeared in about 300 movies, numerous stage plays.

LOCKING, Norm (hockey); b. 24 May 1911, Owen Sound, Ont.; d. 15 May 1995, Port Elgin, Ont.; m. Beth Daniel; c. Fred; retired salesman; Owen Sound Greys '28-31; pro Chicago (NHL) '31-32; Pittsburgh, Tulsa '32-34; brief service with Chicago '34-36; sold to Toronto organization, played in Syracuse through '38; Cleveland '39-44; led Syracuse, AHL scorers, earned MVP award.

LOGAN, Freddie (speed skating); b. 28 Feb 1884, Gondola Point, N.B., d. 12 Feb 1962, Ottawa, Ont.; given name: Frederick William; m. Hannah Elizabeth Murphy; c. Gertrude, Willie, Valentine, Bessie, Francis, Dorothy; store mgr.; NB, Maritime jr. champion '05-11; Maritime 440yd champion '05; international outdoor 220, 880, 3-mile titles, US, ntl outdoor 220, 880, mile titles '07; US outdoor 220, international mile, ntl 1-3 mile titles '08; world indoor 220, 440 records, 3 Maritime titles, records '10; mem. Canadian Speed Skating, NB Sports halls of fame.

LOGAN, Tip (football); b. 30 Nov 1927, St. Thomas, Ont.; given name: John Robert; m. Helen Marie Batt; c. Timothy John, Claudia Marie; Queen's, BA; retd.;amateur football St. Catharines jr. Rams, Queen's; pro Hamilton '50-55; twice CIAU all-star; led Big 4 scorers '51; placement specialist, CFL record (since surpassed) 85 consecutive conversions; Big 4 all-star 1yr.; mem. '53 Grey Cup champions; intercollegiate football official, 8 College Bowls; minor, intermediate baseball Fort Erie, pro Brooklyn Dodger chain in class D Flordia State, Pony Leagues; mem. Welland sr.

OBA champion '49; mem. COSSA basketball champions '48; officiated HS basketball 10yrs.; runnerup '73 Ont. Colts curling championship; skipped Hamilton City title rink '75-76; won CHCH-TV bonspiel 1st 3yrs of competition; founder, pres. Hamilton minor football assnn.; pres. Lakeshore Football Officials Assn.; pres. Ont. Amateur Football Assn; former exec.-dir. OAFA; former mem. amateur football rules comm.; dir. Hamilton football trust fund; mem. Queen's Sports Hall of Fame; res. Hamilton, Ont.

LOGAN, Willie (speed skating/rowing); b. 15 Mar 1907, Saint John, N.B., d. 6 Nov 1955, Sackville, N.B.; given name: William Frederick; m. Dorita Gould; c. Sylvia; plumbing store mgr.; competitive skater '20-36, oarsman '23-33; ntl skating titles '22-23, '25; Maritime titles '24-36; international champion '25; 2nd overall '26 worlds; mem. '28, '32 Olympic teams, capt., 2 bronze '32; mem. Canadian Speed Skating, NB Sports halls of fame.

LOHNES, Rita (golf); b. 4 Aug 1938, Riverport, N.S.; given name: Rita Leone; m. Gary Haines; c. Dorothy Ann, Sandra Leone; Bridgewater Commercial; competitive golfer '51-69, from '83; 4 NS, 2 Maritime jr. titles; 5 NS, Maritime women's titles; 12 club titles (Lunenburg Bluenose 4; Whitby 1; Daytona Volusia 1, Riviera 1; Thornhill Uplands 3; Burlington Indian Wells 2); Peterborough Invitational title '64; low net Ont. PGA pro-lady '64; ntl jr. runnerup '58; mem. 8 NS interprovincial teams; mem. ntl jr. team titlists '54; mem. NS Sports Hall of Fame; last known res. Oakville, Ont.

LOMBARDO, Guy (speedboat racing); b. 19 Jun 1902, London, Ont., d. 5 Nov 1977, Houston, Tex; m. Lilliebelle Glenn; band leader; won '46 International Gold Cup, ntl sweepstakes for unlimited hydroplanes with his Tempo boats; US ntl champion '46-49; secty. American Power Boating Assn.; began racing '38, winning every major trophy in Gold Cup unlimited class for 20-40' propellor driven boats; set then speed record 119.7mph '48; retd '52, returned '55-56 winning ntl titles; mem. US Speedboat Hall of Fame.

LONEY, Don (football); b. 16 Nov 1923, Ottawa, Ont.; given name: Donald John; North Carolina State.; retired school administrator; jr., service football Montreal, Halifax; pro Montreal, Toronto, Ottawa, Calgary; capt. Ottawa 3yrs.; mem. 3 Grey Cup finalists, 2 winners; retd '55; Jeff Russel Memorial trophy '50; frequent Eastern all-star, once all-Canadian; coached 3yrs Ottawa HS, 3yrs Navy, 17yrs college football; won 3 service league, 10 college conference titles, '66 ntl college crown; St.FX football '57-74 coaching record: 133 wins, 31 losses, 2 ties; 6 Atlantic Bowl finals, 4 winners; '74-76 with Devco; '77 National Defence consultant; '78 Fitness, Amateur Sport consultant; '78-82 alumni dir. St.FX; CAFA-CFL plaque, NS recognition award '73; Centennial Medal '67; CIAU trophy bearing his name presented annually to Atlantic Bowl MVP; former pres. Canadian Football Coaches Assn.; mem. NS, Ottawa, Canada's Sports, Canadian Football halls of fame; res. Sherbrooke, N.S.

LONG, Bill (hockey); b. 2 Jan 1918, Barrie, Ont.; given name: William Edwin; m. Dorothy Catharine Wiles; c. Terry;

retd. hockey exec.; Jr. B Barrie, sr. Port Colborne; pro Pittsburgh, Kansas City; Jr. B coach '50-51, Jr. A 'Sunday coach' before moving to Niagara Falls '60; coach Ottawa 67's '67-71; coach London Knights '72-80, GM '72-84; OHA jr. A coaching record: 15yrs, 439-383-100; coach jr. B champions '51, juve. champions '54, Memorial Cup finalists '63, Memorial Cup champions '65; res. London, Ont.

LONG, Warren (gymnastics); b. 16 Apr 1956, Victoria, B.C.; Calif.,UofSask; mem. ntl team '77-84; gold medals parallel bars '77 Pacific championships, ntl vault '77, '79, '82-84, floor exercises '79, parallel bars '82; vault Chunichi Cup '80; mem. '79, '83 FISU, '80, '84 Olympic, World Cup, '81, '83 World championships teams; 3 silver, 2 bronze '79 Pan-Am Games; silver vault '83 FISU Games; res. Saskatoon, Sask..

LONGBOAT, Tom (t&f); b. 4 Jul 1886, Brantford, Ont., d. 9 Jan 1949, Brantford, Ont.; given name: Thomas Charles; m. Lauretta Maracle (d); m. Martha Silversmith; c. Ted, Clifford, Tom Jr., Phyllis; outran horse over 12-mile course '06; 3 consecutive 15 mile Toronto marathons; set Boston marathon record '07; as pro beat Italian champion Dorando Pietri, Britain's Alf Shrubb several times; competed '08 Olympics; last major race '12; victim of exploitation by promoters; mem. Cdn Amateur, Canada's Sports, Ont. Sports Legends, Cdn Roadrunners halls of fame.

LONGDEN, Johnny (horse racing); b. 14 Feb 1910, Wakefield, Eng.; given name: Eric John; m. Hazel Tarn; c. Vance, Andrea, Eric; jockey, trainer; raised in Taber, Alta.; summer cowboy age 10; left school age 13 to work in mines; '25 worked for Spud Murphy ranch competing in country fairs; began thoroughbred racing Salt Lake City '27; unconventional riding style earned him nickname 'The Pumper'; until retirement to become trainer '66 rode then-record 6032 winners, 4914 seconds, 4273 thirds with $24,665,800 in earnings; 3 Sep '56 broke Sir Gordon Richards' existing record with 4871; scored 5000th victory '57; ntl champion jockey '38,'47-48; rode Count Fleet to Triple Crown (Kentucky Derby, Preakness, Belmont Stakes) '43; Frequent accident victim, 5 times told racing career was over but each time battled back to win more races; special Eclipse award '95; mem. Alta., Canada's Sports, Horse Racing, US National Jockey's halls of Fame; res. Banning, Calif.

LOOMER, Lorne (rowing); b. 1937, Penticton, B.C.; given name: Lorne Kenneth; m. Elisabeth Baess; c. Lise-Lotte, Anne-Lise; UBC, BA, BSc, PhC; pharmacist; gold '56 Olympics coxless 4; gold 8s '58 BEG; mem. '60 Olympic team; mem. Cdn Amateur, BC, Canada's Sports halls of fame; res. Victoria, B.C.

LORD, Hervé (t&f/wheelchair basketball): b. 3 Mar 1958, St. Pamphile, Que.; employment equity asst.; versatile wheelchair athlete competing in track, road racing, sledge hockey, basketball; world record 4x100m Berlin '94; gold '95 National Capital marathon; 4 ntl sledge hockey title teams; 2 World Cup title teams; bronze '94 Paralympics; competed '98 Paralympics sledge hockey team; 2 Ottawa Lions TC outstanding wheelchair athlete awards, OLTC

president's award; 2 Ottawa ACT awards; 3 sledge hockey MVP awards, World Cup, ntl all-star; OWSA athlete of '93; res. Ottawa, Ont.

LORD, Lovel (curling); b. 29 Sep 1942, Trenton, Ont.; m. Joan; c. Wendy, April; insurance broker; began curling Moose Jaw age 12; mem. Winnipeg Westwinn CC title rink '66; skipped Sault Ste. Marie 'spiel winner, NO playoff entry '70; mem. Bill Lewis Kingston rink '72-74, winner Ottawa Masters, *Whig-Standard* 'spiels; 2nd Earle Morris Ottawa Navy rink which lost provincial final in playoff vs. Joe Gurowka '76; 8 Ont. finals, 1 as skip; 3rd Morris Brier rink '85; mem. 2 OCA Silver Tankard title rinks; res. Ottawa, Ont.

LORD, Margaret (administration); b. 2 Oct, Hamilton, Ont.; d. Sep 1993, Burlington, Ont.; given name: Mary Margaret; Hamilton Teachers Coll.; teacher; active in amateur sports from '29; v-p British Commonwealth Games Assn. '54-76; from '76 hon. v-p; only woman in Commonwealth to serve as officer; only woman elected to AAU exec.; chair. AAU of C honors, awards comm. 15yrs.; only woman elected pres. AAU of C branch; dir. COA; mgr. '36, '52 Cdn. Olympic t&f teams; mgr. '54, '62 Cdn. Commonwealth Games teams; secty. '58 Cdn. Commonwealth Games team; 1 of 2 women mem. 1st Ntl Advisory Council for Fitness, Amateur Sport; Sports Federation of Canada award; Centennial Medal '67; life mem. Hamilton Olympic Club; mem. Cdn Amateur Sports Hall of Fame.

LORD, Tom (t&f); b. 26 Apr 1910, Hingham, Mass.; m. Helen Gzowski; c. Tom Jr., John; McGill, Sir George Williams; financial planner, Investors Syndicate Ltd.; ntl 880yd title '35; founding secty. QATFA '34-38; chair. ntl t&f comm. AAU of C '48-54; AGM., mgr. ntl t&f team, mem. jury of appeal '50, '54 BEG; chair. jury of appeal BE Commonwealth Games '66, '70, '74, '78; pres. QATFA, meet dir., Europe vs Americas Expo '67 Montreal; dir. CFTA '69-71; dir. Fed. d'Athletisme du Que. '70-75; CTFA ntl officials chair. '72-79; track ref. '75 Pan-Am Games; mgr. athletics officials '76 Olympics; chair. CTFA rules comm. '80-90; Air Canada sports official of '77; Queen's Jubilee Medal; MBE; mem. COA; mem. Canadian Amateur Athletic Hall of Fame; res. Kitchener, Ont.

LORI, Chris (bobsled): b. 24 Jul 1962, Windsor, Ont.; Royal Roads Military College, MBA; began competing age 22; driver ntl team '85-98; competed 10 world championships, '88, '92, '94, '98 Olympics; 1 CODA Cup 2 man, 3 ntl 2-man, 3 ntl 4-man, 2 World Cup 4-man gold; finished 1st '90 World Cup overall 4-man standings; bronze '91 World Cup 2,4, combined; 22 World Cup medals; res. W. Vancouver, B.C.

LORION, Guy (shooting); b. 23 Mar 1953, Montreal, Que.; m.; mem. smallbore rifle teams '79, '83 Pan-Am, '78, '81-82 world, '82 Commonwealth, '84 Olympic, 8 Benito Juarez Games; 1 gold, 1 silver, 3 bronze Pan-Am Games, silver, bronze Commonwealth Games; SFC golden anniversary award '82; res. Longueuil, Que.

LOVELL, Jocelyn (cycling); b. 19 Jul 1950, Eng.; given name: Jocelyn Bjorn; div. Sylvia Burka; cycling supplier;

36 ntl championships '63-81; mem. 3 Pan-Am; 3 Olympic; 9 world championships; 2 Commonwealth Games teams; gold, silver, bronze '70, 3 gold '78 Commonwealth Games; gold '71, '75 Pan-Am Games; 2nd world 1000m '78; silver '78 ntl speed skating championships; Norton Crowe award '75; paralyzed in truck-bike collision '83; mem. Cdn Amateur, Canada's Sports halls of fame; res. Mississauga, Ont.

LOVEROCK, Patty (t&f); b. 21 Feb 1953, Vancouver, B.C.; given name: Patricia Elaine; UBC, BRE, UWO, MA; journalist; ntl record holder 4x100 (43.63); bronze 4x100 Commonwealth Games '70; silver 100m, bronze 4x100 '75 Pan-Am Games; bronze 100m '75 FISU; semifinalist 100m, 200m '76 Olympics; silver 4x100 Commonwealth Games '78; retd from competition '78; mem. BC Sports Hall of Fame; res. Los Angeles, Calif.

LOVETT, Claire (all-around); b. 24 Oct, Regina, Sask.; given name: Clara Louise Ehman; m. Robert Frederick Lovett (d); retd secty.; ntl badminton singles titles '47-48, ladies' doubles '47-48, mixed open doubles '63, sr. ladies' doubles '73-76, 6 US state, 18 prov., 20 city championships; mem. '57 Uber Cup team; runnerup '82 Cdn., US Grand Masters ladies' doubles; '46-67 won 16 Vancouver Lawn Tennis & Badminton Club tennis titles, Western Canadian grass court mixed doubles '52, ntl singles '66; Vancouver srs singles '78, ladies' doubles '77, ntl ladies' doubles '81; mem. numerous basketball title teams in Regina, numerous scoring records; lone Canadian chosen to join all-star quintet; HS ice, field hockey, baseball, t&f; top rated bowler leading Regina Ramblers 5-pin team scoring; once engaged famed Mildred 'Babe' Zaharias in friendly afternoon of competitive matches in tennis, 5 & 10 pin bowling and upstaged US athletic great in each instance; active in badminton coaching, administration; '77 formed BC Tennis Assn. for Sr. Ladies; mem. Cdn Amateur, BC, Sask. Sports halls of fame; res. Vancouver, B.C.

LOWE, Kevin (hockey); b. 15 Apr 1959, Lachute, Que.; m. Karen Percy; c. Devyn Jean, Darby, Keegan; hockey coach; defence Quebec (QJHL) '77-79; only anglophone capt.; 1st Edmonton pick '79 draft; NHL with Edmonton '79-92, '96-98, NY Rangers '92-96; asst. coach Edmonton '98-99; head coach '99; mem. 6 Stanley Cup winners; 7 all-star games; 1st NHL player to claim both Bud man of yr, King Clancy Memorial awards in 1 season '90; scored 1st-ever Edmonton NHL goal; Edmonton capt. '90-91; holds Oilers' record regular and post-season games played; mem. Team Canada '82, '84; NHL record: 1254 scheduled games, 84g, 347a, 214 playoff games, 10g, 48a; res. Edmonton, Alta.

LOWERY, Ron (orienteering); b. 29 Nov 1955, Halifax, N.S.; given name: Ronald William; m. Denise DeMonte; McMaster, BA BPhE, UWO, MA; fitness consultant; 4 ntl jr., 1 NA championships; mem. ntl team from '74; competed 4 world championships; best international performance 30th '79 worlds, 8th team relay '78 worlds; ntl champion '75, runnerup 4 times; NA champion '77, runnerup once; US title '76, runnerup 3 times; New Eng. title '79, runnerup once; bronze Coureur de Bois Canadian Ski Marathon; Ont. Athletic Achievement award; res. Hamilton, Ont.

LUCAS, Joe (rodeo); b. 10 Jan 1959, Olds, Alta; m. Shoena; c. Rickey Joe, Kyle, Kaitlyn; Cross Fire Rope Co.; calf roping, steer wrestling specialist; joined CPRA ranks '80; NFR rookie of '83; 3 ntl CR titles; Calgary Stampede CR title '87; Bud pro tour, Sask., Alta, BC circuit CR titles '90; 2 ntl, Alta. circuit high point titles; Coors Chute Out, Brahma Boot CR titles, Skoal pro rodeo tour SW crown '96; cowboy of year award '96; res. Carstairs, Alta.

LUCE, Don (hockey); b. 2 Oct 1948, London, Ont.; given name: Donald Harold; m. Diane; c. Scott, Kim, Kelly, Kristin; hockey exec.; centre Kitchener Rangers jrs; pro Omaha (CHL) '68-70; NHL N Rangers '69-70, Detroit '70-71, Buffalo '71-80, Los Angeles '81, Toronto '82; NHL record: 894 scheduled games, 225g, 329a, 71 playoff games, 17g, 22a; record 8 short-handed goals single season, incredible +61 plus/minus ranking; Masterton trophy '75; standout penalty-killer; joined Buffalo front office '84 as scout, asst. coach '85-86, dir. player personnel from '87; key role in bringing Alexander Mogilny to America '89; mem. Buffalo Sabres, Greater Buffalo Sports halls of fame; res. Williamsville, N.Y.

LUCHT, Edward (basketball); b. 6 Nov 1931, Jeffrey, Alta.; m. Lyla May Ford; c. Gregory, Duane, Karen, Sandra; UAlta., BSc; CIL projects mgr.; center UAlta Golden Bears '50-54; Edmonton Townhallers '54-56; ntl finalists '56; mem. Montreal Snowdon Y ntl championship team '57; playing coach Lakeshore Flyers '58; retd from competitive basketball '60; mem. 2 WCIAU title teams, ntl CIAU finalists '52; ntl intercollegiate single game scoring record 88 points '53-54 season vs. UofSask.; ntl Sr. B title with Lakeshore Flyers '58; mem. '58 Pan-Am Games team; mem. team which defeated Soviets in international play '58; res. Etobicoke, Ont.

LUDTKE, Frank (cycling/speed skating); b. 12 Jan 1936, Cologne, Germany; given name: Frank Martin; m. Kay Robinson; c. Robert; graphics, communications art instructor; mem. 3 world championships speed skating teams; alternate '68 Olympics; ntl title '68; mem. '67, '71 Pan-Am Games, '70 Commonwealth Games, World championships, '72 Olympic cycling teams; specialized in individual, team pursuit; coach '78 ntl cycling track team; asst. ntl coach '79-80; res. Pt. Moody, B.C.

LUEDERS, Pierre (bobsleigh); b. 26 Sep 1970, Edmonton, Alta; given name: Pierre Fritz; UAlta; switched career aspirations from t&f to bobsleigh on suggestion from German cousin; mem. Alta Bobsleigh Assn; driver jr. ntl team '90; ntl men's team from '93; among premier drivers in world; became 1st driver to earn WC gold in debut race; 1st driver to win 2/4/combined titles in single season; 24 WC medals; 4 WC 2-man titles; 2 WC combined (2/4-man) titles; competed '94, '98 Olympics; with brakeman Dave MacEachern Olympic 2-man gold '98 (actually finishing in tie with Italian team); res. Calgary, Alta.

LUFTSPRING, Sammy (boxing); b. 14 May 1916, Toronto, Ont,; given name: Yisrael; m. Elsie Goodman; c. Brian, Orian; travel agent; lost just 5 of 105 amateur bouts '32-35 resulting in Gold Gloves titles from bantam to welterweight; protesting Germany's treatment of Jews, rejected '36 Olympic team trials; under guidance of Harry Sniderman began Spanish tour but was stopped by civil war; launched pro career '36; met Gordon Wallace for ntl welterweight title '37 losing split decision; under mgr. Al Weill won Cdn. welterweight title in 13th round TKO over Frank Genovese '38; world ranked '38 beating 3rd-ranked Salvy Saban; while prepping for title bout with Henry Armstrong lost left eye in bout vs. Steve Belloise, terminating career at 24; won 50 of 56 pro bouts; turned to refereeing, licensed by Ont. Athlete Commission; officiated more than 2,000 amateur, pro bouts including world heavyweight title match George Chuvalo-Ernie Terrell, 3 British Commonwealth, 20 ntl pro championship bouts; author "*Call Me Sammy*"; mem. Canada's Sports, Ont. Sports Legends, Cdn Boxing, Cdn Jewish halls of fame; res. Toronto, Ont.

LUKANOVICH, Karen (canoeing); b. 22 May 1960, Montreal, Que.; given name: Karen Leigh; UofOtt; competitive skier '72-76; raced on jr. circuit '73; mem. Viking Ski Club, ranked among best jr. cross-country skiers Que. '74-78; ntl juvenile K1, K2, K4, sr. K2, K4 paddling titles '77-78; sr. K4 '80-81; swept every kayak event in midget, juvenile, sr. classes '76 Que championships; at 16 youngest Cdn. Olympic competitor '76 Olympics; mem. '80 Olympic team, ntl team '77-79; res. Beaconsfield, Que.

LUKANOVICH, Louis (canoeing); b. 5 Dec 1930, Zagreb, Yugoslavia; m. Jean Alnes; c. Karen, Julianne; Concordia, BSc; MDCC Systems pres.; K4 Yugoslavian ntl team mem. '50 world championships; moved to Canada '51; mem. ntl canoe team '53-68; 21 ntl titles; 7 NA titles; mem. '60 Olympic team; coach Cartierville, Que., Lachine canoe clubs; ntl team coach; Olympic coach '72, '76; pro ski instructor '63-73; mem. Order of Canada; Jubilee Medal; res. Beaconsfield, Que.

LUKE, Michael (rugby); b. 10 Oct 1946, Penzance, Cornwall, Eng.; m. Arlene McCann; Bristol, BA, Bordeaux, SFU, MA; French prof.; mem. Stade Bordleais U Club French 1st division, Penzance, Newlyn teams; with Tony Evans, Mick, Tom, Noel Browne instrumental in formation of St. John's, Nfld., rugby club; standout hooker, later club pres.; Maritime title '72; mem. regional, ntl teams vs. international opponents from '73; capt. Canada's tour to Wales, Eng., France '79; invited to play with UK teams; coach, administrator; original mem., dir. CRC; capped 13 times for Canada; res. St. John's, Nfld.

LUKOWICH, Ed (curling); b. 1 Mar 1946, North Battleford, Sask.; given name: Edward Richard; m. Judy Marie Mayer; c. Pamela Ann; UofSask. BEd, BPhE; personal investor; 3rd on brother Mike's Sask. Cdn HS title rink '62; competed in 5 Briers; skip '78, '86 Alta. Brier winners, '83 runnerup; world champion '86; topped curling's Gold Trail money winners '89-90 ($175,000), '87-88 ($101,250); founder Canadian, World curling pro tours; founder Seagram's VO Cup championship; founder WCT Players Assn.; skipped Canadian rink in '88 Olympics (demonstration sport); innovator of rock testing method; founder *TSN* Skins Game; exec. dir. WCT; won 3 Western Intercollegiate titles, CBC Curling Classic '78. *TSN* Skins '87, Moncton 100 '90, 4 carspiels, authored six books on

curling; instructional videos; operated curling supply business; nicknamed 'Fast Eddie'; brother Morris pro hockey player; mem. Cdn Curling, UofSask Sports halls of fame; res. Calgary, Alta.

LUMLEY, Harry (hockey); b. 11 Nov 1926, Owen Sound, Ont.; d. 13 Sep 1998, London, Ont.; m. Frances Buckley; c. Kerri Ann, James, Frank, Harry Jr.; retd. livestock auction mgr.; goal Owen Sound intermediates, Barrie jrs.; pro Indianapolis (AHL) '43-44, Detroit (NHL) '45-50, Chicago '51, Toronto '52-56, Boston '57-61; Vezina Trophy (TML) with 1.85 avg.; J.P.Bickell Memorial Gold Cup as Leafs' MVP, 1st team all-star '54-55; NHL record: 803 scheduled games, 2210ga, 71so, 2.75 ga avg., 76 playoff games, 199ga, 7so, 2.62 ga avg., mem. 1 Stanley Cup winner; Owen Sound arena bears his name; mem. Owen Sound Sports, Hockey halls of fame.

LUMSDEN, Bill (curling/administration); b. 27 May 1907, Brandon, Man.; d. 5 Apr 1982, Winnipeg, Man.; m. Eve Wall; c. William (d), Jean, Patricia; insurance co. partner; mem. Winnipeg Parks Board 7yrs; held varied executive positions Elmwood CC 50yrs; hon. life mem. from '53; hon. secty MCA '46-47, pres. '47-48, hon. life mem. from '52; chair. '70 Brier comm.; secty MCA life members assn. 25yrs; life mem. Civic Caledonian, Charleswood, Deer Lodge, Maple Leaf, West Kildonan, Rossmere Curling Clubs, Winnipeg Clubs Secretaries Assn., Past Presidents of Manitoba Clubs Assn.; won Hudson Bay ('64), Ganong ('54) trophies MCA bonspiel; pres. DCA '66-67, hon. life mem. from '69; 4yrs chair. curling hall of fame selection comm.; 1st chair. DCA schoolboy championship comm.; negotiated Seagram sponsorship of sr. men's curling championships; v-p RCCC '67; life mem. Ont., Que., BC curling assocs.; dir. Winnipeg Silver Broom '78; 3yrs mem. Air Canada exec. of yr selection board; Air Canada exec. of '68; Man. govt. Buffalo award, Man. Sports Fed. merit certificate, Centennial Medal; hon. citizen St. Boniface; mem. Canadian Curling, Man. Sports halls of fame.

LUMSDEN, Neil (football); b. 19 Dec 1952, London, Ont.; given name: Neil James; m. Donna Warner; c. Jesse, Kristin; UofOtt, BA; football exec.; athlete of year at every school he attended; brilliant college career capped by '75 Yates Cup, Vanier Cup triumphs, produced CIAU record 410 career points, OUAA record 148 points single season, 36 career field goals, 41 single season converts, 15 single-season TDs (equalled record of Eric Walter of McGill, Toronto); league all-star 4 times, all-Cdn. 3 times, 3 times Omega Trophy (OUAA MVP); Ted Morris Trophy (MVP) '75 College Bowl; all-time UofOtt offensive records including 3111yds rushing; outstanding running back 4 times, MVP 3 times; athlete of '75; ACT (Ottawa) athlete of '75; pro Toronto '76-77, Hamilton '78-79, Edmonton '80-85; EFC, runnerup CFL rookie of '76; mem. 3 Grey Cup champions; following stint in real estate joined Ottawa Rough Riders front office '91-92, Hamilton Tiger-Cats '93-96 (GM); mem. UofOtt Football, OUAA, Ottawa Sports halls of fame; res. Burlington, Ont.

LUMSDON, Cliff (swimming); b. 13 Apr 1931, Toronto, Ont.; d. 31 Aug 1991, Toronto, Ont.; sep.; c. Kim; Humber College; parks & recreation supervisor; 5 world marathon swim championships; 1st to conquer Straits of Juan de Fuca '56; regarded as king of pro swimmers; coached by Gus Ryder; coached daughter Kim, Diane Nyad; manager Lakeshore Swim Club; Lou Marsh Trophy '49; mem. Order of Canada, Cdn, Ont. Aquatic, Etobicoke, Canada's Sports halls of fame.

LUMSDON, Kim (swimming); b. 3 Feb 1957, Toronto, Ont; m. Robert Ian Young; Branksome Hall; swimming teacher, coach; 6th AAU long distance (3-mile) nationals '73; 1st woman, 5th overall, Rio de la Plate Argentina 5-mile swim '74; 2nd woman, 5th overall, Lac St. Jean 5-mile swim '75; cold water, exhaustion ended '75 Lake Ontario bid; 3rd woman, 10th overall, Lac St. Jean 25-mile swim '76; conquered 32-mile Lake Ont. in 21hrs, 27 min., despite 4-6' waves '76; 3rd best women's marathon swimmer in world '76; won Gus Ryder, Borough of Etobicoke awards for Lake Ont. swim; res. Etobicoke, Ont.

LUND, Cathy (rowing); b. 23 Mar 1959, London, Ont.; UWO; sweep Cdn Henley jr. coxed 4s, 8s titlists '78, coxed 8s '81; OUAA coxed 8s titles '81-82; mem. '79, '81, '83 world championships, '84 Olympic teams; res. N.Vancouver, B.C.

LUND, Pentti (hockey): b. 6 Dec 1925, Karijoki, Finland; div.; c. Patricia, Judy, Joanne; retd. sports ed. *Times-News*; emigrated to Port Arthur age 6; learned hockey skills Port Arthur minor program; TBJHL jr. scoring titles '43-45; sr. EAHL Boston Olympics '45-47, 1 scoring title; ntl US amateur title '47; pro AHL Hershey Bears '47-48; NHL NY Rangers '48-51; Calder Memorial Trophy (rookie of yr); Boston '52-53; lost use of right eye 13 Nov 1951 hockey accident leading to voluntary retirement from pro game with Victoria WHL '53; played sr. amateur hockey with Sault Ste. Marie '54-55 before retiring from game; coached Ft. William sr. Beavers '58, Thunder Bay Oldtimers late '60s; NHL record: 259 scheduled games, 44g, 55a, 18 playoff games, 7g, 5a; scoring champ '50 Stanely Cup playoffs 6g, 5a; mem. NWO Sports Hall of Fame; res. Thunder Bay.

LUNSFORD, Earl (football); b. 19 Oct 1933, Stillwater, Okla.; m. Margot; c. Brenda, Lamar; Oklahoma State, BA, MA; retd. football exec.; all-American '55; drafted by Philadelpha (NFL) but turned pro with Calgary (CFL) '56 leading club in scoring 1st season; 1034yds, 10tds on 183 carries '59 seasons; single game WFC rushing record 211yds '60; 1st player to gain more than a mile rushing single season '61 with 296 carries for 1796yds; twice Eddie James Trophy winner as WFC leading rusher; CFL record: 1199 carries, 6994 yds., 56tds; 5tds vs Edmonton Sep '62; 5 times 1000-plus yds seasons, 3 times 200-plus carries in season,; GM Winnipeg '67-82, Calgary '85-87; mem. Cdn Football Hall of Fame; res. Ft. Worth, Tex.

LUSTER, Marv (football): b. 27 Nov 1939, Shreveport, La.; UCLA; defensive back; competed '61 East-West game, all-America Graduation Bowl (outstanding player award); drafted by LA Rams; CFL Montreal '61-64, '73-74, Toronto '64-72; 9 all-star berths in 13 seasons; 6 all-Canadian; began career at offensive end before moving to defence where he shone as linebacker and deep back; CFL record: 113 receptions for 1963yds, 11tds, 26 interceptions for 312yds;

2 Grey Cup finals, 1 winner; mem. Cdn Football Halll of Fame; res. Shreveport, La.

LUZZI, Don (football): b. 20 Aug 1935, North Branford, Conn.; Villanova; co-capt. '57 Villanova team; Catholic College all-American '56-57; played in '58 Senior Bowl, East-West Shrine Bowl; pro Calgary '58-69; off./def. tackle; Grey Cup finalist '68; 5 all-Western def. tackle, 2 all-Western off. tackle awards; 4 all-Canadian def. tackle awards; Schenley outstanding lineman award '58; Scott-Mamino Calgary athlete of yr '58; Becket-DeMarco outstanding WFC lineman award '58; mem. Cdn Football Hall of Fame; res. Florida.

LYLE, Dulcie (golf); b. 25 Mar 1918, Allan's Corners, Que.; given name: Dulcie Isabella Jessie Logan; m. Robert Lyle; Notre Dame Ladies Coll.; ntl HS javelin record; equalled ntl 100yd breaststroke mark during BEG trials; with Marian Macdonald won 3 MAAA, Montreal District badminton doubles titlest; MAAA squash titlist; began golf age 31, reduced handicap to 4 in 2 yrs; 14 Kaniwaki club titles, 10 Montreal & Dist., 14 provincial titles; '60 ntl Closed, '71 Srs., '73 US Srs. titles; mem. 14 Que. ladies', 5 srs. interprov. teams; non-playing capt. ntl World Cup team '68; semifinalist Doherty '62; 3rd US North-South '72; res. Montreal, Que./Delray Beach, Fla.

LYON, Don (skiing): b. 4 Oct 1944, Ottawa, Ont.; m. Jacqueline Rouvier; c. Pascal, Olivier; travel agent; mildly successful competitive career including 3 seasons on world pro tour; began coaching Mt. Tremblant late '60s; coached Ntl Capital Div.; joined ntl women's program '70-95; among skiers he coached were Judy Crawford, Betsy Clifford, Kathy Kreiner, Kerrin Lee-Gartner, Kate Pace, Karen Percy, Laurie Graham, Gerry Sorensen, Deedee Haight; mem. Ottawa Sports, Cdn Ski halls of fame; res. Ottawa, Ont.

LYON, George (golf); b. 27 Jul 1858, Richmond, Ont., d. 11 May 1938, Toronto Ont.; given name: George Seymour; m. Annette M. Martin; c. George S. Jr., Fred M.; ntl pole vault record 1876; with Toronto Rosedale vs. combined Peterborough-Toronto cricket team carried bat for ntl record 238; began golf at 38, 8 ntl amateurs, runnerup twice; at 46 only person in history to win Olympic gold in golf beating US champion Chandler Egan 3 & 2 St. Louis '04; mem. Goulbourn Wall, RCGA, Cdn Amateur, Canada's Sports halls of fame.

MABEY, Hap (curling); b. 25 Oct 1939, Saint John, N.B. given name: Harold Arthur; m. Lina Petrea Andersen; c. Joy, Kim, Nathalie, Tanya, Adonica, David, Peter; sporting goods agent; mem. '53 Maritime midget, '55 NB juve., '59 Maritime jr., '60 Maritime sr. A baseball title teams; Maritime Sr.A fastball title '60; NB Schoolboy curling title '57; 5 times NB Brier representative, mem. Oldtimers hockey team; mem. NB Sports Hall of Fame; res. Riverview, N.B.

MABEY, Harold (curling); b. 27 Mar 1904, Tryon, P.E.I.; m. Gladys Burden; c. Harold (Hap), Roger; Prince of Wales Coll.; retd; played coll. football, all-star hockey goalie; associated with minor baseball Moncton region several years, serving as assn. pres., dir.; 3 times teamed with son Hap, Harold Keith to win NB men's curling title, compete in Brier; 2 NB Srs. titles; 2 NB Diamond Srs.(over 60); pres., hon. mem. Moncton Curlers Assn.; pres. NBCA; coached 2 jr. men's, 1 jr. women's rink to NB title; mem. Canadian Curling Hall of Fame; res. Riverview, N.B.

MacASKILL, Klari (canoeing); b. 31 Dec 1964, Budapest Hungary. m. Neil MacAskill; former mem. Hungarian ntl team; moved to Canada 1988; ntl team from '89; competed '92. '96 Olympic Games; K-4 200 bronze '94 World championships; gold K-4 500, bronze K-2 500 '95 Pre-Olympic regatta; gold K-4 200 Szeged '96; 2 gold, 1 silver Milano '96; 4 ntl titles; Edmonton Grads team trophy '95; res. Renfrew, Ont.

MacBETH, Donald (horse racing); b. 29 Aug 1949, Red Deer, Alta.; d. 1 Mar 1987, Ocala, Fla.; m. Joanne; c. Tiffany, Heather, Don, Christina; won with 1st mount, Walking Box, '67; leading apprentice rider Ak-Sar-Ben Omaha; leading rider Atlantic City '73, Hialeah '79, Monmouth Park '78-80, Aqueduct '81; more than 2000 winners, $20 million in purses; 13 major stakes race victories; mem. Alta. Sports Hall of Fame.

MacBETH, Fred (t&f); b. 26 Dec 1909, Hamilton, Ont.; d. 20 Sep 1986, Nepean, Ont.; given name: Frederick William; m. Margaret Clark McLeod; c. William, Margaret; Notre Dame, BComm, UWO, Northwestern.; retd general marketing mgr. Bell Canada; t&f capt. Notre Dame; mem. '28 Olympic team.

MacDONALD, Byron (swimming); b. 23 Jul 1950, Chicago, Ill.; given name: Arthur Byron; div.. Paula Thomson; m. Lisha Van Leeuwen; c. Troy, Shane, Kenzie; Michigan, BComm, MA; university lecturer, coach; as polio therapy began swimming age 6; capt. HS, Mich. swim team; gold 100m butterfly, 4x100 medley relay, leading 1st ever Cdn 1-3 international sweep of medals '70 Commonwealth Games; bronze 100m fly, silver 4x100 medley relay '71 Pan-Am Games; silver 100m fly '73 FISU, '74 Commonwealth Games; mem. '72 Olympic team; ranked among top 15 butterflyers in world '70-75; 4 Commonwealth 100m fly records; ntl 100m fly record, 200m fly record; numerous prov. records; all-American 3yrs

Mich., NCAA finalist; all-Cdn, 3 gold CIAU championships '73; coach men's team FISU Games '79, '81, '93; coach '92 Olympic team; coach York, UofT, North York; 9 CIAU coach of yr awards; CBC-TV swimming color commentator; mem. Cdn Aquatic Hall of Fame; res. Toronto, Ont.

MacDONALD, Gary (swimming); b. 15 Dec 1953, Mission, B.C.; given name: Gary Wayne; SFU; mem. Dolphins Swim Club; mem. '73 FISU, '74 Commonwealth, '75 Pan-Am, '76 Olympic teams; gold, 2 bronze '74 Commonwealth, silver 400m FS '75 Pan-Am Games; silver 4x100m medley relay '76 Olympics; 4 gold '76 ntls; 1 CIAU male swimmer of yr award; PB: 100m FS 53.31, 200m FS 1:38.51; ntl records 400m FS relay 3:33.42, 400m medley relay 3:55.69; Governor-General's silver medal '76; res. Mission, B.C.

MacDONALD, Irene (diving); b. 22 Nov 1933, Hamilton, Ont. given name: Irene Margaret; retd. prov. diving development co-ordinator; coach to '88; 15 ntl titles '51-61, 6 US ntl '57-60, 2 Mexican titles '58-59; bronze 3m springboard '54, silver '58 Commonwealth Games; bronze '56, 6th '60 Olympics; Ont. 3m titles '51-55, BC '61, Que. '56; Velma Springstead Trophy '57; dir. BC Sports Fed.; chair. Diving for Canada '62-66; diving coach Commonwealth team '66, European tour team '71, world championships team '73-75; trustee BC Sports Hall of Fame; CADA tech. dir. '67-69; CBC analyst 2yrs; mem. BC Sports, Cdn Aquatic, Canada's Sports, Cdn Amateur Sports halls of fame; res. Vancouver, B.C.

MacDONALD, Jackie (t&f); b. 12 Oct 1932, Toronto, Ont.; m. Bill Gelling; c. Andrew, Steven; Carleton, BA; retd. teacher; Ont. jr. diving title '48; mem. Toronto Globetrotters jr. basketball champions '49-50; ntl shot put title '53; ntl shot put record, silver '54 BEG; 5th discus '55 Pan-Am Games; beat own record placing 10th shot put '56 Olympics; only Cdn rep. Moscow World Youth Games '57; bronze '58 Commonwealth Games; res. Gloucester, Ont.

MacDONALD, Kilby (hockey); b. 6 Sep 1913, Ottawa, Ont.; d. 14 May 1986, Florida; m. Mary Hayes (d); c. Kilby-Ann, Terry, Allan; retd. Labatts regional sales mgr.; mem. UofOtt, HS ntl title football team; hockey Lasalle jrs. '26-27, Montagnard jrs. '28-32, Kirkland Lake srs. '34-35, Noranda Copper Kings '35-36; pro NY Rangers organization '36, with Rovers, Philadelphia Ramblers; Rangers regular '39-40 winning Calder Memorial Trophy as rookie of year; except for '42-44 when he played with Montreal army during service stint WW2, remained with Rangers through '44-45 campaign; mem. Stanley Cup champions '39-40; 5 yrs Rangers Eastern Ont. scout; coach at West Point. Arvida, Baltimore, Quebec; Memorial Cup finalist vs. Barrie '51; helped with Ottawa Cradle League; coach St. Anthony srs.; mgr.-coach Babe Ruth baseball teams winning Ont., Cdn titles, competing in Washington, D.C., world championships; mem. Ottawa Sports Hall of Fame.

MacDONALD, Noel (basketball); b. 23 Jan 1915, Mortlach, Sask.; given name: Noel Marguerite; m. Harry Robertson; c. Donald, Dale Jean; business school; mem. Edmonton Grads '33-39, capt. '36-39; in 135 games scored 1874 points for 13.8 points-per-game avg., best in club's history; softball Gyro Pats, Muttart Pats; coached HS, UAlta. girls basketball; coached Libyan teams during 13 1/2yr stay in country; Bobbie Rosenfeld award '38; mem. Cdn Basketball, Alta., Canada's Sports halls of fame; res. Qualicum Beach, B.C./ Sun City W, Ariz.

MacDONALD, Ross (sailing); b. 27 Jan 1965, Vancouver, B.C.; m. Marcia Pellicano; production mgr.; began competing '82; Star class sailor; with Bruce MacDonald 3 ntl, 1 Pan-Am Games gold '87, with Pat Dion '95 NA title; with Eric Jespersen 2 ntl, 1 worlds titles; with Jespersen '92 Olympic bronze, '93 NA, '94 ntl, world, '95 European championship gold; competed '88, '92, '96 Olympics, '87, '95 Pan-Am Games; with Jespersen 1st all-Cdn crew to win world title in Star class; Tribute to Champions Sport Excellence award '89; CYA sailor of '87, '94; Rolex Cdn sailor of '90, '92; BC sailor of '89, '92, '93; res. Vancouver, B.C.

MACDONALD, Wen (curling); b. 20 Dec 1908, Charlottetown, P.E.I.; given name: Wendell Leigh; m. Elizabeth Matthew; c. Patricia Jane, Janet Leigh, Kenneth, Debra; Prince of Wales Coll., Dalhousie, Edinburgh, MD; radiologist; rep. PEI '46, '54-56 Brier; 13 prov. srs. titles; skip ntl srs. champions '72, '76-77; skip PEI entry '68 ntl mixed; pres. PEI curling assn.; CCA dir.; mem. Governor-Generals CC; mem. Canadian Curling (inducted as curler and builder), PEI Sports halls of fame; res. Charlottetown, P.E.I.

MacDONELL, Paul (harness racing); b. 29 Jan 1963, Oshawa, Ont.; launched career at 18 working with Doug Brown stable; since moving out on his own has emerged as one of top drivers on tough OJC circuit; scored major upset '90 by driving longshot Bay's Fella to victory over Topnotcher to record longest mutuel price in Breeders Crown history, $140,600, for a $2 wager; piloted Billyjojimbob to '91, Lifetime Dream to '93 and Village Jiffy to '94 Breeders Crown triumphs; leading driver Charlottetown Driving Park '87-88; piloted Village Jiffy to '94 top older pacer honors, Lifetime Dream to top aged trotting mare honors '93, Billyjojimbob '91 aged trotting horse; more than 2000 victories, including 40+ major stakes titles, and purses exceeding $20M; res. Orono, Ont.

MacDONNELL, Wayne (badminton); b. 28 June 1940, Vancouver, B.C.; given name: Wayne Barry; m. Gil Semadeni; c. Brian, Leanna; exec. officer Sears Ltd.; record 6 ntl men's singles titles '62-67; ntl doubles champion '63; 6 BC singles, 5 BC doubles, 7 Vancouver singles, 3 Oregon State, 14 Washington State singles; 4 NS singles, 2 NS men's doubles, 3 NS mixed doubles, '66 US mixed doubles, '71 Irish Open singles titles; record 6 times mem. Cdn Thomas Cup team; men's ntl record for international appearances; pres. CBA; res. Oakville, Ont.

MacDUFF, Alan (broomball); b. 25 Jun 1949, Hawkesbury, Ont.; m. Elaine Carol Arthurs; c. Erin Dawn, Emily Alanna;

dairy farmer; played competitive ball-hockey '83-93; began playing broomball '65; ntl gold '82 Pop Shoppe, '91-95 Embrun Plumbing, '96 Embrun Sport; ntl silver '86 Independent Radiator, '90 Embrun Plumbing; ntl bronze '79 Sun Life team; world gold '91 Embrun Plumbing; 6 MVP, 2 sportsmanship, 7 best defence awards; ntl championship 2nd team all-star '86; Canada Celebration award '88; res. St. Eugene, Ont.

MacEACHERN, Dave (bobsled); b. 4 Nov 1967, Charlottetown, P.E.I.; brakeman ntl team from '90; brakeman for Pierre Lueders winning Olympic 2-man gold '98 (actually tied with Italian team); also competed '92, '94 Olympics; 9 World Cup 2-man gold, 5 silver, 3 bronze; 1 WC 4-man gold, 1 silver, 4 bronze; 2 final WC standing 2-man gold, 1 silver, 1 combined silver; 1 world championship 2-man silver; res. Calgary, Alta.

MacEACHERN, Shanyn (gymnastics); b. 17 Feb 1980, Brampton, Ont.; all-around performer; mem. ntl team from '95; competed '95 worlds. Pan-Am, '96 Olympic Games; 1 ntl jr., 2 ntl elite titles; res. Brampton, Ont.

MacFARLANE, Gus (basketball); b. 19 Feb 1925, Montreal, Que.; d. 22 Feb 1991, Charlottetown, P.E.I.; given name: Angus McKechnie; McGill., BA, BEd; War Veterans Allowance Board mem.; playground supervisor, basketball statistician, referee, coach, football coach, Montreal region exec. '49-56; guided Verdun to Que. Boy's Brigade basketball title, jr. hockey title '49; coached Verdun Pats to Que. juve. football title '50; coached Verdun to Que. int. YMCA basketball title '52; coached Verdun HS sr. football titlists '54-55; athletic dir., coach Mount Allison '57-69, 2 NB football, 2 NB, PEI basketball titles; lifetime coaching record in basketball, football, hockey, softball, 326 wins, 122 losses, 3 ties; GM ntl basketball team '69-70; dean of men McMaster '71; resource asst. National Administrative Centre for Sport, Recreation Ottawa '70; MP (Lib) Hamilton Mountain '74-79; key role in creation of offices of Ministers of State for Fitness & Amateur Sport and Federal-Provincial relations; life mem. CAFC, hon. mem., pres. CAUAD, National Assn. of Basketball Coaches of Canada merit award.

MacGOWAN, Margaret (t&f); b. 21 Sep 1954, Waterford, Ont.; given name: Margaret Eleanor; div. Bryan Stride; c. Christopher; m. Ross Hendershot; c. Kyle; Brock, BPhE. BEd; teacher; mem. '74, '78 Commonwealth, '76 Olympic, '77 FISU, '75, Pan-Am Games, World Cup teams; team bronze 4x400 relay '74, '78 Commonwealth Games; team gold 4x400 relay '75 Pan-Am Games; finalist 4x400m relay '76 Olympics; PB: 100m (11.4), 200m (23.4), 400m (52.8); 2 ntl masters records; masters world gold, 2 bronze '91; Brock Hall of Fame; res. Mildmay, Ont.

MACH, Gerard (coaching); b. 16 Sep 1926, Poland; speed coach consultant; retd. CTFA ntl program dir., ntl team coach '73-92; sprinter '52 Polish Olympic team; Polish ntl sprints, hurdles coach '52-72; under his guidance Polish t&f team emerged as one of Europe's most powerful in '50s and '60s; Cdn team coach '76, '80, '84 Olympic, '78, '82 Commonwealth, '79 Pan-Am, '81 World Cup; res. Ottawa, Ont.

MacINNES, Bob (curling); b. 23 Sep 1932, Lochiel Twp., Ont.; m. Marie Cutbush; c. Brenda, Kent, Neil, Elizabeth; Fanshawe College; personnel officer; as third with Bob Knippelberg (Ottawa) twice runnerup Ont. Consols; with Bill Lewis (Trenton) won City of Ottawa bonspiel grand aggregate beating Kingston's Jake Edwards in playoff '66; with Lewis runnerup '67 Ont. Consols, won Ontario Tankard '67; skipped Trenton rink to '69 Ont. Tankard, competed in Ont. Consols; represented Canada in international matches in Scotland, Europe, res. Schumacher, Ont.

MacINNES, Kent (curling); b. 15 Feb 1938, Kirkland Lake, Ont.; given name: Errol Kent; m. June Quick; c. Deborah, David, Katherine; senior buyer mining operations; runnerup Ont. junior men's '56; with Jack Polyblank represented Northern Ont. 3 Briers; NO runnerup '62; Brier all-star 2nd '64; NO mixed title '67, twice runnerup; v.-chair. CCA mixed committee '78-80, chair. '81-82; CCA award of merit '84; res. Timmins, Ont.

MacINNIS, Al (hockey); b. 11 Jul 1963, Inverness, N.S.; given name: Allan; m. Jackie; c. Carson, Ryan; defence Kitchener (OHA) '80-83, Colorado (CHL) '84; 1st Calgary pick '81 draft; NHL with Calgary '81-94, St. Louis '94-99; 2 NHL 1st team, 3 2nd team all-star; Conn Smythe trophy '89; Norris trophy '99; played 8 all-star games; mem. 1 Stanley Cup winner; noted for booming slap-shot; competed '90 worlds, '91 Canada Cup; mem. '98 Olympic team; NHL record: (through '99) 1142 scheduled games, 290g, 776a, 142 playoff games, 36g, 102a; res. Town & Country, Mo.

MACKAY, Craig (speed skating); b. 1 Apr 1927, Banff, Atla.; given name: Craig Innis; m. Gwen Bibbey; c. Kim, Heather, Terri, Craig Jr. Cam, Tom; road building contractor; mem. Saskatoon Lions Speed Skating Club; 25yr competitive career; Saskatoon, Sask. titles '44-45; '47 Alta. sr. men's 220yd record, gold '47 ntl sr. men's 3-mile; *Star-Phoenix* road race 3-mile mark '48; Alta. champion '51; mem. '67 Canada Winter Games team; mem. '48, '52, alternate '56, '60 Olympic, '50 world championships teams; helped institute Olympic trials for skaters; key role '57 NA outdoor speed skating championships; mem. ISA; 2yrs pres. Saskatchewan branch CASA, 2yrs v-p CASA; chair '68 ntl outdoor, '73 indoor championships; chair Canada Winter Games Speed Skating comm. '70-71; chair CASA Hall of Fame comm. from '68; mem. Sask., Saskatoon Sports, Canadian Speed Skating Halls of fame; res. Saskatoon, Sask.

MacKAY, Elizabeth (diving); b. 9 May 1960, Chicoutimi, Que.; given name: Elizabeth Hugette; Laval; mem. '78 Commonwealth, World Games, '79 Pan-Am, '80 phantom Olympic team; silver 3m, bronze 10m Vienna International, silver 10m, bronze 3m, Bolzano Internations '80; silver 10m '78, bronze 10m '81 Canada Cup; gold 1m, 3m Norway Cup '80; 5 ntl championships '77-80; all-around ntl champion '79, '81; res. Cap Rouge, Que.

MACKAY, Gerry (baseball/builder); b. 19 Feb 1930, Kenton, Man.; with a passion for baseball inherited from famed father Curly Mackay joined ManDak League Brandon Greys at 19; 3 strong seasons earned contract with Chicago Cubs organization; with Northern League (Class C) Sioux Falls hit .349 '52, .337 '53; split '54 between

Visalia (California League) and Brandon Greys then moved to El Paso (B League) playing infield/outfield and batting .371 while earning all-star status; joined Yankee organization '56; returned to Brandon to stay '57 hitting .394; played/coached Brandon sr. Cloverleafs to consec. Man. sr. league titles; chosen mgr. 1st ntl team '67; competed in '67, '71 Pan-Am Games, '72 World championships; dir. Cdn Fed of Amateur Baseball '67-74; instrumental in establishing Old Timers baseball in Man.; talented curler reaching Man. sr. men's finals '87; mem. Man. Sports Hall of Fame; res. Brandon, Man.

MacKAY, Mickey (hockey); b. 21 May 1894, Chesley, Ont., d. 21 May 1940, Nelson, B.C.; given name: Duncan McMillan; nicknamed 'Wee Scot'; sr. hockey Edmonton, Grand Forks, B.C.; Vancouver Millionaires (PCL) '15, 33 goals rookie season missing scoring title by single point; remained with Vancouver through '25-26 season, three scoring titles, 202 goals, 242 games; Chicago team's leading scorer '27-28; played half of '28-29 season in Pittsburgh then joined Boston Bruins, mem. 2 Stanley Cup winners; Boston business mgr. '30; mem. Hockey Hall of Fame.

MACKELL, Fleming (hockey); b. 30 Apr 1929, Montreal, Que.; given name: Fleming David; div. Kathleen O'Brien; c. Rosemary, Kathy, Michael, Jo-Anne, Shaun, Maureen, Sheilagh, Fleming Jr.; St. Pat's Coll., St. Mike's Coll.; auto sales; quarterback football teams at St. Pat's, St. Mike's; at 15 played jr. Quebec; 2yrs jr. St. Mike's Coll.; Toronto (NHL) '47-52, Boston '52-60; at 18 youngest to that time ever to play in NHL all-star game; NHL record: 665 scheduled games, 149g, 220a, 80 playoff games, 22g, 41a; competed 4 all-star games; with father Jack, whose name was misspelled McKell on Stanley Cup while member of Ottawa Senators, one of few father-son combinations to play for two Stanley Cup winners each; coached Quebec (AHL) 1yr; 5 GM Grand Master salesman awards; res. Verdun, Que.

MACKEN, Brendan (tennis); b. 21 Jan 1923, Montreal, Que.; given name: Brendan Hubert; m. Elizabeth Gillam; c. Nancy, Ginny, Peggy, Helen, Bren Jr.; William and Mary, BSc; owner chemical co., lawn bowls distributor; mem. '46-52 Davis Cup teams, capt. '54; only Cdn to beat Australian in Davis Cup play (Billy Sidwell '49); one of two Cdns to beat US player in Davis Cup action (Bob Perry '52); Cdn men's singles title '50; with brother Jim ntl men's doubles '47, repeat '51 with Lorne Main; ntl mixed doubles (with sister Patricia) '47; Que., Ont. singles, doubles, mixed doubles titles '52; retired '54; 1st chairman CLTA junior development; '67 chairman Davis Cup selection comm.; 2yrs pres. QLTA; ntl veteran squash doubles title with late Paul Ouimet '68-69, US runnerup each year; A ranked squash singles player; ranked #1 over 55 category in tennis '82; active role in annual Gordon Trophy srs. matches; instrumental in arranging US scholarships for Cdn tennis players; pres. MAAA; life mem. Toronto Cricket & Skating Club; mem. Cdn Tennis Hall of Fame; res. Richmond Hill, Ont.

MACKEN, Jim (tennis); b. 29 July 1925, Montreal, Que.; m. Audrey Maureen; c. Gerald, Kathy, Chris, Patrick, Tony; William and Mary, BA; retd. distributor; capt. W&M tennis team '49; NCAA champions '47-48; playing mem. Davis Cup team '46, non-playing capt. '63, '65; with brother Bren ntl men's doubles champion '46; ranked in Canada's top 10 '46-58; NS, Que., Ont., BC titles; BC, Pacific Northwest, Pacific Coast squash titles; ranked #2 nationally over 55 bracket tennis '82; pres. BC Tennis Assn.; promoted first BC Umpires Assn. '81; TV color commentator regional, ntl jr. tennis championships; umpire Davis Cup, WCT matches; chair. '71 Davis Cup comm.; Centennial medal '67: avid golfer, scored hole-in-one '98; mem. NCAA Tennis Hall of Fame; res: Richmond, B.C.

MACKEN, Patricia (tennis); b. July 1928, Montreal, Que.; div. Eldon Smart; c. Jennifer, Sheila; William and Mary; jr. provincial titles Que., Ont. '43-45; Vermont State ladies' singles, doubles, mixed doubles (with Clark Taylor) '48; 5 Que. sr. ladies' singles, doubles; 7 Montreal City, District ladies' singles, doubles; ntl ladies' open singles, doubles, mixed doubles (with brother Brendan) '47; mem. Wightman Cup team vs Britian '48; Alberta, Manitoba ladies' doubles, mixed titles; '50 CP poll female tennis player of half century; res. W. Vancouver, B.C.

MacKENZIE, Ada (golf); b. 30 Oct 1891, Toronto, Ont., d. 25 Jan 1973, Richmond Hill, Ont.; Havergal College; 5 ntl ladies' open, closed, 8 seniors, 9 Ont. ladies, 2 seniors, 10 Toronto, district titles; 3 successive Havergal Cups; instrumental in formation Toronto Ladies' Golf Club '24; twice reached semifinals US women's amateur; 2 Bermuda titles; competed internationally for Scotland and Canada; last seniors title '69 at age 78; from '71 ntl seniors have competed for Ada MacKenzie Trophy; Bobbie Rosenfeld award '33; mem. RCGA, Cdn Amateur, Canada's Sports halls of fame.

MacKENZIE, Bill (baseball); b. 27 July 1946, Pictou, N.S.; given name: William Roy; m. Janet Eldridge; St. Clair Community College; dir. Canadian scouting for Expos;; catcher; pro Detroit organization '66; minor ball at Lakeland, Fla.; Erie, Pa.; Statesville, N.C.; Dubuque, Iowa; West Palm Beach, Fla.; broken shoulder ended playing career; minor league instructor Bristol, Tenn.; coached Bristol, Lakeland, Rocky Mount, N.C., West Palm Beach; 7yrs Expos administrative assistant, scout, player development assn.rdinator; signed David Palmer and recommended Tim Raines to Expos; tech. dir. Baseball Canada '79-89; managed '83 Pan-Am Games gold medal team; res. Gloucester, Ont.

MacKENZIE, Eric (baseball); b. 29 Aug 1932, Glendon, Atla.; given name: Eric Hugh; m. Gail McNaughton; c. Christine, Coleen, Lee; recreation dir.; pro baseball as catcher in Athletics' organization '51-58, brief major league service Kansas City A's '55; coach ntl amateur baseball team '78, '80 World Games, '79, '83 Pan-Am Games; '81,'83 Intercontinental Cup; son Lee mem. Kitchener Memorial Cup champions '81; res. Mooretown, Ont.

MacKENZIE, Shanty (football); b. 27 Aug 1920, Scotland; given name: Donald; m. Audrey Lock; c. Mary Louise, Catherine, Marion, William Hugh; building superintendent; Toronto Argos '40-41, '50-53; Toronto Balmy Beach (ORFU) '46-49, player-coach '49; capt. '50 Grey Cup champions; mem. 2 Grey Cup champions; line coach Parkdale Lions '57 jr. champions, North York Knights,

Scarborough Rams '55-63.; Jimmy Keith Memorial Trophy; res. Agincourt, Ont.

MACKIE, Baz (football); b. 8 Mar 1932, Weston, Ont.; given name: Clarence; m. Marilynn Ellins; c. Douglas, Jo-Anne, Stephen; UofT, BPHE, BA,BEd; secondary school principal; football, lacrosse, hockey, t&f Weston CI Ironmen; only player to make 1st and 2nd TDIAA all-star teams in history of league; '51 1st team tackle, 2nd team fullback; defensive guard UofT Varsity Blues '52-55; mem. '54 OUAA champions; pro Argos '55-57; mem. Big Four all-Cdn team '56; res. Rexdale, Ont.

MACKIE, Gordie (builder); b. 17 Jan 1922, Winnipeg, Man.; m. Marguerite; c. Heather, Holly, Bonnie, Craig; certified physiotherapist; boxing instructor Winnipeg YMCA '49; owned/operated St. Boniface-Madison Boxing/ Wrestling Club '55-60; Cdn Olympic team therapist '72, '76; chief therapist Blue Bombers '59-69; 5 times CFL all-stars therapist; therapist '70 Cdn Davis Cup, '74 Team Canada hockey Summit Series teams; UMan. therapist; founding mem. Cdn Athletic Therapists Assn. '66; mem. Man. Sports Hall of Fame; res. Winnipeg, Man.

MACKIE-MORELLI, Anne (t&f); b. 18 June 1955, Calgary, Alta.; given name: Anne Mackie; m. Claudio David Morelli; UBC, BPhE, SFU, MA; 2nd fastest 400m in Canada '74; while touring Europe with ntl team '75 sustained foot fracture which cost her berth on Pan-Am, Olympic teams; '76 ntl 400m title, '79 400m, 800m indoor, 800m outdoor titles, '80 800m ntl outdoor title; mem. Pacific Conference, World Cup, FISU, '78 Commonwealth, '79 Pan-Am, '80 Olympic teams; bronze '77 Berlin 800m, Melbourne 400m, silver 800m World Cup trials; bronze 4x400m relay '78 Commonwealth Games; silver 4x400m, bronze 4x100m relay '78 Pacific Conference Games; semifinalist 800m '77, '79, 400m '79 FISU Games; bronze 4x400m relay '79 Pan-Am Games; gold 800m '79, silver 800m '80 *Edmonton Journal* Games; fastest 800m in Canada '77, 3rd fastest ever with 2:01.6; UBC athlete of '76-77; mem. Alta. Sports Hall of Fame; last known res. Vanderhoof, B.C.

MacKINNON, Dan (harness racing/all-around); b. 12 Nov 1876, Highfield, P.E.I.; d. 24 Dec 1964, Charlottetown, P.E.I.; c. Morris; pharmacist, fox farmer, publisher; Maritime mile running titles 1897-99; DCRA, Governor-General's medals for shooting '20; during 12-day period '15 won 15 of 16 starts with pacer Helen R; his horse Volo Rico upset previously unbeaten US-owned Eula H. '31; world ice racing record Mt. Clemens, Mich., '23 with The Yank; Eastern harness racing promoter '30; USTA director, promoter '30-61; pres. Provincial Exhibition Assn.; DSO, Croix d'Guerre WW1; mem. Canadian Horse Racing, PEI, Canada's Sports halls of fame.

MacKINNON, Zoe (field hockey); b. 5 Oct 1959, Toronto, Ont.; given name: Zoe Elizabeth; UofT, BPHE; physical educator; mem. Ont. team from '75; ntl team '81-84; UofT team '78-83; goaltender World Cup silver medal team '83; mem. '84 Olympic team; fed. govt. excellence award '83; res. Bramalea, Ont.

MacLACHLAN, Alan (bobsleigh); b. 2 May 1957, Toronto, Ont.; given name: Alan William; m. Jill Henry; Upper

Canada College, UWO, BA; investment analyst; t&f competitor Toronto region as youth; mem. ntl bobsleigh team from '78; attained driver status '80; mem. 4-man crew which crashed in '80 Lake Placid Olympics; mem. '84 Olympic team; res. Bolton, Ont.

MacLAGGAN, James (administration); b. 10 Aug 1923, Blackville, N.B.; given name: James Coburn; v-p '68-71, pres. '71-75 NBAHA; mem. sr., int. CAHA councils; dir. NB Baseball Assn. '68-71; dir. NB Sports Fed. '72-74; chair. NB Sports Hall of Fame '79-80; CAHA service citations '65, '67; NB sports exec. of '82; mem. NB Sports Hall of Fame; res. Bathurst, N.B.

MacLEAN, Allan (jiu jitsu); b. 7 Feb 1953, Exeter, Ont.; given name: Allan John; Waterloo, BSc; pharmaceutical salesman; South Huron DHS most valuable male athlete '71; began jiu jitsu training Waterloo '71; 1st degree black belt '75, 2nd degree '78; organized Kitchener jiu jitsu club '77; mem. ntl team '78; instructor Kitchener club; res. Kitchener, Ont.

MacLEAN, John (hockey); b. 20 Nov 1964, Oshawa, Ont.; m. Adrienne; c. John Carter; rw Oshawa jrs. '81-84; Memorial Cup all-star '83; NHL with New Jersey '83-91, '92-97 (missed entire '91-92 season due to injury), San Jose '97-98, NYR '98-99; NHL record (through '99) 1067 scheduled games, 388g, 420a, 94 playoff games, 33g, 47a; 2 NHL all-star games; 1 Stanley Cup winner; mem. Team Canada '84 jr. worlds, '89 worlds; wife was former golf pro; res. Montclair, N.J.

MacLEAN, Lucella (baseball); b. 3 Jan 1921, Lloydminster, Sask; given name: Lucella Katherine; m. George Mervyn Ross; retd. TV factory inspector; active in hockey, basketball; catcher in AAGPBL with South Bend '43-44 playing 101 games .204ba, .953fa; following season of sr. ball in Edmonton returned to US National League finishing career with Chicago '46-52; in later years active in lawn bowling, curling; mem. Sask. Baseball Hall of Fame Battleford; honored by Cooperstown, Cdn Baseball halls of fame; res. Lloydminster, Alta.

MacLEISH, Rick (hockey); b. 3 Jan 1950, Lindsay, Ont.; given name: Richard George; m. Carolyn; c. Danielle; Jr. A Peterborough '68-70; Boston's 2nd pick, 4th overall '70; Oklahoma (CHL), Richmond (AHL); NHL Philadelphia '70-81, '83-84, Hartford '81, Pittsburgh '81-83, Detroit '84; reached 50-goal single season plateau '72-73 (50); NHL record: 846 scheduled games, 349g, 410a, 114 playoff games, 54g, 53a; mem. 2 Stanley Cup winners; res. Philadelphia, Pa.

MacLEOD, Tammy (diving); b. 3 Aug 1956, Vancouver, B.C.; given names Tammy Donna; m. John Percy; c. Matthew, Tia; sc. Gavin Logan; UBC, hons. Econ.; realtor;; gold 1m '71 ntls 13-14 age-group; bronze 3m '72 winter ntls; bronze 10m '74 summer ntls; silver 10m '71 world age-group finals; silver 3m, 10m '71 Bolzano competition; gold 1m, 3m '73 Australian jr. ntls, silver 10m, bronze 1m '73 Australian sr. ntls; bronze 3m '74 USSR; bronze 10m '75 NZ Games; mem. '76 Olympic team; retd. from competition '76; swimming, diving instructor,lifeguard; res. Vancouver, B.C.

MacMARTIN, Andrew (triathlon); b. 23 Jul 1972, Montreal, Que.; given name: Andrew Christopher; triathlete; bronze Cdn ski marathon '88; Que. triathlon title '89; jr. Commonwealth silver '90; 2 ntl men's titles; 5 world cup victories; mem. '92 gold medal team world championships; gold Tampa International '94; ranked #1 world ITU ratings '92; awarded Juan Antonio Samaranch trophy, *Triathlete Magazine* rookie of '92; res. Tucson, Ariz./Westmount, Que.

MacMILLAN, Billy (hockey); b. 7 Mar 1943, Charlottetown. P.E.I.; given name: William Stewart; m. Marjorie Linkletter; c. John, Anne, Susan; UMan, BPhE; hockey exec.; mem. ntl team '66-70; pro Toronto '70-72, Atlanta '72-73, NY Islanders '73-77; NHL playing record: 446 games, 74 goals, 77 assists, 53 playoff games, 6 goals, 6 assists; coached Fort Worth '77-79 winning '78 CHL title; asst. coach Islanders '79-80; coach Colorado '80-81, GM '81; New Jersey coach-GM '82-83; CHL coach of the year '77-78 season; coach UPEI; mem. PEI Sports Hall of Fame; res. Charlottetown, P.E.I.

MacMILLAN, Sandy (sailing); b. 1 Jul 1952, Lunenburg, N.S.; Dalhousie; sailmaker; teamed with Glen Dexter, Andreas Josenhans to win world Soling titles '77, '80; mem. '74-76 NS title crews, '76 Olympic team; NS achievement award '77, Moosehead Sports award '80; mem. NS, Canada's Sports halls of fame; res. Tantallon, N.S.

MacNEIL, Al (hockey); b. 27 Sep 1935, Sydney, N.S.; given name: Allister Wences; m. Norma; c. Allison, Alister; defence Toronto Marlboros jrs.; NHL '55-68 Toronto, Montreal, Chicago, NY Rangers, Pittsburgh; NHL record: 524 scheduled games, 17g, 75a, 37 playoff games, 0g, 4a; mem. 2 Stanley Cup winners; coach Houston Apollos; Canadiens, Stanley Cup rookie season '70; GM/coach NS Voyageurs (AHL) '71-77, 4 1st place finishes, 3 Calder Cups; asst. Team Canada Canada Cup teams '76, '81; head coach Calgary '79-92; NHL coaching record: 134-108-53; AGM Calgary '82-89; dir. hockey operations Calgary from '90; mem. Sydney, NS sports halls of fame; res. Calgary, Alta.

MacPHERSON, Kitch (basketball); b. 11 June 1916, Hamilton, Ont.; d. 17 Oct 1998, Hamilton, Ont.; given name: Herbert Horatio Kitchener; m. Jessie Park; c. Catharine, Edward; retd. stereotyper; officiated 27 years, 1st Canadian to hold international referee card; officiated Pan-Am Games '59, Russian ntl team tour of US '60, '62, Manila world games '62, Pan-Am Games '67, Philadelphia World Cup '68; supervisor Western Division OUAA referees; CIAU Coaches award, Ont. service to basketball award; mem. Canadian Basketball Hall of Fame.

MacPHERSON, Michelle (swimming); b. 11 May 1966, Toronto, Ont.; m. John Hojnacki; c. Zachary, Dylan; Cincinnati; began swimming at Pointe Claire, Que.; 5 ntl butterfly, 6 IM titles; 2 Canada Cup butterfly, 3 IM titles; 2 ntl, 1 Commonwealth Games records; gold 4x100 medley relay, bronze 100m butterfly, 400m IM '82 Commonwealth Games; silver 4x100 MR, 200m IM, 100m butterfly, bronze 400m IM '83 Pan-Am Games; mem. 4x100 bronze medley relay '84 Olympics; 4yrs all-American; asst. swim coach Cincinnati; Ont. achievement award '81, Metro Toronto recognition award '82, fed. govt. excellence award '83; mem. Ont. Aquatic Hall of Fame; res. Chandler, Ariz.

MacRITCHIE, Kay (basketball); b. 22 Jan 1922, Saskatoon, Sask.; m. Donald Ross MacBeth; c. Donald Malcolm, Kerry; mem. Edmonton, Vancouver softball title teams '34-51; HS high jump, long jump, swimming titles; basketball with variety of Edmonton, Vancouver teams '37-50; most notable was '39-40 tenure with famed Edmonton Grads, one of only 38 women to play on team during its 25yr history of unparalled success; as mem. of prov., Western Canadian title Vancouver Hedlunds '40-46, mem. BC Sports Hall of Fame; as Grad mem. Canadian Basketbal, Alta. Sports halls of fame; res. Comox, B.C.

MacTAVISH, Craig (hockey); b. 15 Aug 1958, London, Ont.; m. Debbie; c. Nathan, Sean; US college hockey Lowell, Mass.; coach; centre Binghamton, Springfield, Erie (AHL); drafted by Boston '79; NHL with Boston '79-84, Edmonton '85-94, NY Rangers '94, Philadelphia '94-96, St. Louis '96-97; mem. 4 Stanley Cup winners; 1 NHL all-star game; team capt. Edmonton '92-94; last player to play entire NHL career sans helmet; asst coach Rangers '97-99, Oilers '99; NHL record: 1093 scheduled games, 213g, 267a, 193 playoff games, 20g, 38a; res. Edmonton, Alta.

MACVICAR, Don (powerlifting); b. 10 Jun 1956, Glace Bay, N.S.; given name: Donald Frank; m. Carole; purchasing dept. Dofasco Steel; began lifting career '78; a diminutive 4-11, 114 pounds he lifted 10 times his body weight and in rookie year of lifting was described as the Wayne Gretzky of powerlifting; judged strongest man in Canada '82; 4 ntl, 5 Ont. titles; never defeated in Canada; 38 ntl records; 2 NA titles; 1 Eastern Cdn title; World Cup silver '80; World Games silver '81; competed throughout Canada and US and in England, India, Sweden; retd '83; organized church youth group, floor hockey league; basketball coach; plays flute in church band; NA weightlifting drug marshal; nicknamed 'Mighty Mite'; mem. Copps Coliseum Sports Wall of Fame; res. Stoney Creek, Ont.

MADDIN, Janet (t&f); b. 4 May 1949, Winnipeg, Man.; m. Allan Neale; c. Heather, David; SFU, BA, UMan, BEd; teacher; sprinter; set 6 ntl, 16 Man. records, won 4 ntl championship gold '64; 2 ntl age-group, 1 ntl open, 4 ntl championship gold '66; competed '66 BEG; silver '67 Pan-Am Games; set ntl age-group 400m record '68; mem. Cdn Commonwealth Games team '70; set world indoor 300m record '70; Olympic team alternate '64; Man. jr. athlete of '64; Daniel McIntyre CI outstanding athlete, Governor-General's medal '66; mem. Man. Sports Hall of Fame; res. Winnipeg, Man.

MADY, Levente (swimming); b. 2 Apr 1959, Arad, Romania; UCal; butterfly specialist; mem. '81 NZ, FISU Games, '82 Commonwealth, '83 Pan-Pacific Games, '79, '82 Canada Cup, '84 Olympic teams; 1 Canada Cup, NZ Games, Romanian championships, ntl championships golds; res. Scarborough, Ont.

MAGNUSON, Keith (hockey); b. 27 Apr 1947, Wadena, Sask.; given name: Keith Arlen; m. Cindy White; c. Kevin, Molly; Denver, BSc; sales exec. Coca-Cola; Denver '64-69, co-capt. Pioneers to 2 NCAA titles; defenceman Chicago

'69-79; NHL record: 589 scheduled games, 14g, 125a, 68 playoff games, 3g, 9a; mem. '69-70 league title team; chronic knee injury led to retirement '79; asst. coach Black Hawks '79-80, head coach '80-81; mem. Ill. AHA board; pres. Black Hawks alumni assn; res. Chicago, Ill.

MAGNUSSEN, Karen (figure skating); b. 4 Apr 1952, North Vancouver, B.C.; m. Tony Cella; c. 1 son; SFU.; skating teacher; ntl jr. singles '65, sr. '68, '70-73; mem. '68, '72 Olympic teams; NA title '71; silver '72 Olympics; world championship '73; pro Ice Capades to '73-77; BC junior athlete of '67; BC sports merit award '70; Bobbie Rosenfeld award '73; BC athlete of '72; 2 Velma Springstead awards; Officer Order of Canada '73; taught skating Boston area four years then retired to raise family; flag-bearer '72 winter Olympics; hon. head figure skating coach Special Olympics Assn.; mem. BC, Canada's Sports, Cdn Figure Skating halls of fame; res. N.Vancouver, B.C.

MAH, Sy (t&f); b. 2 Aug 1926, Bagshaw, Alta; d. 1988, Toledo, Ohio; given name: Thian; Toledo; physiology prof.; ran 1st marathon 6 May 1967 at Toronto; broke existing world marathon record with 198th '81; 200th marathon '81, 300th '83, 400th '86; at time of death had completed in world record 524 marathons; founder cardiac rehabilitation program Toledo; regarded by marathoners/ultramarathoners as outstanding competitor and inspiration to many distance runners.

MAHER, Peter (hockey); b. 11 Nov 1946, Campbellton, N.B.; m. Nancy; hockey broadcaster; played minor hockey from age 13; conceived/promoted idea of NB North-South All-Star hockey game to raise funds for children/adults with intellectual disability; became voice of Maple Leafs '78, Flames from '80; Campbellton Sportsman of yr awards '67, '88; mem. NB, Campbellton Sports halls of fame; res. Calgary, Alta.

MAHER, Peter (t&f); b. 30 Mar 1960, Ottawa,Ont.; m. Brenda; c. Kevin, Louise; radio station owner; investment consultant; marathon specialist; lived in Ireland '62-86 holding joint Cdn/Irish citizenship; Irish 800m, 1500m, 3000m titles; Irish road runner series title '86; 4 Around the Bay 30km titles, record 1:33.00; gold 2 Manitoba, 1 California, Montreal, National Capital, Barbados, Hamilton marathons; competed '88, '92 Olympics, '91, '93 Worlds, '95 Boston marathons; 3 Fred Begley Memorial trophies; marathon PB 2:11.46 '91; res. St. Petersburg, Fla.

MAHEY, Diane (field hockey); b. 20 Jan 1960, Victoria, B.C.; given name: Diane Lea; m. Shiaz Virjee; c. Arif; UVic; mem. UVic team '78-82, BC jr. team '78-80, BC sr. team '80-83; mem. ntl team '80-86 representing Canada in European competitions '80-82, World Cup competitions '80, '83; mem. '83 World Cup silver medal team; mem. '84 Olympic team; BC prov. team '80-92; UVic female athlete of '82; res. Vancouver, B.C.

MAHONY, Bill (swimming); b. 16 Sep 1949, New Westminster, B.C.; given name: William Victor; m. Fran Cruise; c. Cole, Laurel; UBC, BSc; investment research; bronze 200m breast stroke '66 Commonwealth Games; silver 4x100 medley relay '67 Pan -Am Games; semifinalist 100m breast stroke '68 Olympics; 3 gold in 100m, 200m breast stroke, 4x100 medley '70 Commonwealth Games; 4x100 medley relay silver '71 Pan-Am Games; bronze 4x100 medley, semifinalist 100 breast stroke '72 Olympics; gold 4x100 medley '74 Commonwealth Games; numerous ntl sr. records '66-74; 1st Cdn to break 2:40 and 2:30 breast stroke barriers; worked with handicapped children; helped establish BC Cerebral Palsey Sports Assn.; mem. BC Sports, Cdn Aquatic halls of fame; res. Surrey, B.C.

MAHORN, Atlee (t&f); b. 27 Oct 1965, Clarendon, Jamaica; California (Berkley); sprinter; moved to Canada '80; began competing age 16; competed '88, '92 Olympic, '86, '94 Commonwealth, '85 FISU Games; gold 200m, 4x100 relay '86 Commonwealth Games; gold 100m ntl outdoor jr., sr., BYU relays, 200m ntl outdoor jr, 3 sr., 2 Nice France, 1 Times-Colonist, Harry Jerome, 400m Arizona State, 300m Great Britain; 1 ntl jr, 5 ntl sr records; Phil Edwards Memorial Trophy '91; '87 sport excellence award; PB 10.16 100m, 20.17 200m; res. Montreal, Que.

MAHOVLICH, Frank (hockey); b. 10 Jan 1938, Timmins, Ont.; given name: Francis William; m. Marie; c. Michael, Nancy, Teddy; St. Michael's College, Assumption College; Senator, retd. travel agent; jr. St. Michael's College junior; OHA junior all-star, Red Tilson Memorial Trophy (MVP) '56-57; baseball talents attracted pro offer Boston Red Sox; strong competitive swimmer; pro Maple Leafs '57-68; Calder Memorial Trophy NHL rookie of year; Red Wings '68-71, Canadiens '71-74; Toronto (later Birmingham) WHA '74-78; 3 times NHL first team, 6 times 2nd team all-star left winger; tied Phil Esposito for Stanley Cup playoff points 1 yr with 27, including record 14 goals; NHL record: 1181 scheduled games, 533g, 570a, 137 playoff games, 51g, 67a; best single season '68-69 with Detroit scoring 49 goals; played with brother Pete while with Montreal; mem. Team Canada '72; appointed to Cdn Senate '98; mem. Order of Canada, Order of St. Michael's, Canada's Sports, Hockey halls of fame; res. Toronto, Ont.

MAHOVLICH, Pete (hockey); b. 10 Oct 1946, Timmins, Ont.; given name: Peter Joseph; div.; c. Peter Jr., Jeffrey, Margaret-Ann; m. Elise; broadcaster, hockey coach, scout; centre jr A Hamilton Red Wings; second overall '63 amateur draft; with brief stints at Pittsburgh (AHL), Fort Worth (CPHL) mem. Detroit '65-69; Montreal '69-78, Pittsburgh '78-79, Detroit '79-81, Adirondack (AHL) '80-83; NHL record: 884 scheduled games, 288g, 485a, 88 playoff games, 30g, 42a; mem. Team Canada '72, '76, 4 Stanley Cup winners; TV broadcaster New Jersey; area scout San Jose '92-94; GM/coach Ft. Worth (CHL); scout NY Rangers '86-87; coach Toledo (IHL); coach/GM Adirondack; coach Cape Breton (AHL) '94-95; scout Edmonton '95-97, Tampa Bay from '97; res. Bolton Landing, N.Y.

MAIN, Lorne (tennis); b. 9 Jul 1930, Vancouver, B.C.; given name: Lorne Garnet; m. Ivy Malloy (d); c. Kelly, Kevin, Kristine, Kasey; California (Berkeley); tennis pro; ntl jr. singles '46, '47, '48; US jr. hardcourt title '47; with Jim McGregor '46 jr. doubles; ntl men's doubles (with Brendan Macken) '51, (Luis Ayala) '54; ntl mixed doubles (Barbara Knapp) '50; playing mem. Davis Cup team '49-55, non-playing capt. 5 times; ranked #1 '51-54; with Bob Bedard defeated Chile, Australia and US team of Vic Seixas, Hugh Stewart to win '76 Stevens Cup; from '75-98 won 18 srs

singles titles in 45, 55, 60, 65 divs. mem. 20 Gordon Cup teams; competed 17 world srs. championships winning 5 singles titles; with Ken Sinclair 4 consec. Austria Cup over-55 team titles, Von Cramm Cup (60), Britannia Cup (65), 6 world doubles titles; mem. Cdn Tennis Hall of Fame; res. Aurora, Ont./Florida.

MAKOLOSKY, Randy (t&f); b. 26 Jul 1953, Calgary, Alta.; given name: Randall Samuel; m. Tina Maureen Groszko; UCal; Bay dept. mgr.; ntl jr. 800m record 1:48.9 ('70); with Bill Crothers shared sr. 800m indoor record 1:49.5 ('74); 3 times ntl sr. indoor 800m champion; mem. ntl team '73-75; last known res. Calgary, Alta.

MALAR, Joanne (swimming); b. 30 Oct 1975, Hamilton, Ont.; began swimming at 3; made intl debut '90 Commonwealth Games; 4 silver, 1 bronze '91, 2 gold, 3 silver, 1 bronze '95, 3 gold, 1 silver, 1 bronze '99 Pan-Am Games; competed '92, '96 Olympics, '93 Pan-Pacific, 3 world short course championships, bronze '94, 1 gold, 2 silver, 2 bronze '98 Commonwealth Games; 2 CIAU female swimmer of yr awards; 3 CIAU records; res. Hamilton, Ont.

MALCOLM, Andrew (all-around); b. 15 Sep 1901, Saint John N.B.; d. 23 Jan 1986, Saint John, N.B.; m. Jean Harding; c. Jean, Bruce; wholesale merchant; capt. Saint John HS rugby, basketball teams, co-captained t&f team; intermediate basketball through '21, sr. Trojans through '32, capt. 11yrs, 9 NB, 8 Maritime, 1 Eastern title; beat Windsor, Ont., for '32 Eastern title but lost international title to Winnipeg Toilers; led scorers in each series they played; coached Saint John HS basketball team '28-33; refereed basketball several yrs including Cdn Interscholastic championships '33. ntl sr. championships '30; Maritime shot put record '24, ntl title '24, '27; 3 gold, 1 silver, 2 bronze '25 ntl championships; led city league baseball batters '22; nicknamed 'Beef'; nominated '50 CP poll athletes of half century; Andrew Malcolm Trophy awarded annually by YMCA to Saint John male athlete of year; mem. NB Sports Hall of Fame.

MALONE, Joe (hockey); b. 28 Feb 1890, Quebec City, Que., d. 15 May 1969, Montreal, Que.; tool maker; began organized hockey '07 Crescent jrs; pro Waterloo '09, Quebec '10-17, '19-20, Montreal Canadiens '17-19, '22-24, Hamilton '20-22; NHL scoring record 7 goals in single game with Que. Bulldogs vs Toronto St. Pats '20; '17-18 season 44 goals in 22-game schedule; '19-20 scored 39 goals, 6 assists in 24-game schedule; pro career record 379 goals; capt.-coach 2 Que. Stanley Cup winners; nickname Phantom Joe; 9 goals vs. Sydney Millionaires '13 Stanley Cup playoff game, 8 goals one game vs. Wanderers '17; mem. Hockey Hall of Fame.

MALONEY, Don (hockey); b. 5 Sep 1958, Lindsay, Ont.; given name: Donald Michael; m. Toni; c. Donald Jr.,; hockey exec.; lw Kitchener jrs '75-77; minor pro New Haven (AHL); NHL with Rangers '79-89, Hartford '89-90, Islanders '90-91; NHL record: 765 scheduled games, 214g, 350a, 94 playoff games, 22g, 35a; played in 2 NHL all-star games, MVP '84 game; AGM Islanders '92-95; Eastern pro scout San Jose ;96-97; AGM Rangers '97-99 (simultaneously GM Hartford AHL); scored with initial shot in NHL vs. Boston '79; set record (since broken) for rookie point scoring (20) in Stanley Cup playoffs '79; Rangers Crumb Bum, Good Guy awards, 3 Rangers Players' Player awards; mem. silver medal Team Canada world championship team; res. Rye, N.Y.

MALOUF, Bob (boxing); b. 27 Jul 1931, Montreal, Que.; m. Pauline Salhany; c. Perri-Ann, Stephen; owner-pres. Perri-Ann Lingerie Ltd.; Quebec Golden Gloves champion '50-52; ntl amateur middleweight champion '52; mem. '52 Olympic team; 7 bouts as pro; last known res. Mount Royal, Que.

MANAHAN, Cliff (curling); b. 11 Oct 1888, Fort William, Ont., d. 20 Mar 1970, Edmonton, Alta.; given name: Clifford Ross; m. Elizabeth Ann Jones, (d), m. Mary Watson McAndrew Eckert; c. Ross (d), Robert, Donald, Doris, Kathleen, June, Marjorie, Dawn; civil servant; 8 Alberta, 9 Northern Alta. titles; mem. 5 Brier entries, '33, '37, winners; 7 Alta. CA and grand aggregate, 8 Edmonton grand challenge titles; winner 65 major championships; life mem. Alta. CA, Royal Glenora CC, Granite CC of Edmonton; mem. Edmonton, Alta. Sports, Canadian Curling halls of fame.

MANDARICH, Tony (football); b. 23 Sep 1966, Oakville, Ont.; Michigan State; NFL tackle Green Bay '89-92, Indianapolis '96-98; NFL record (through '97): 76 games, 53 as starter; 1st round draft Green Bay '89; res. Indianapolis, Ind.

MANLEY, Elizabeth (figure skating); b. 7 Aug 1965, Belleville, Ont.; given name: Elizabeth Ann; initial 1st place finish pre-novice ladies '74; 1st Eastern Ontario sectionals victory juve. B ladies '75; EO sectional novice ladies '77; EO sectionals, Eastern divisionals jr. ladies '79; 2nd ntl jr. ladies '80; 3rd Eastern Divisionals, ntl sr. ladies, jr. worlds '81; 2nd ntl sr. singles '84; mem. '84 Olympic, world championship teams; 1st woman in Canada to land a triple combination in competition; silver '88 Olympics; US Open pro title '97; Orleans Arena, park, pool named in her honor; authored *"Thumbs Up"*; co-owner skating tour; mem. Order of Canada, Cdn Amateur, Ottawa Sports halls of fame; res. Victoria, B.C.

MANN, Avard (curling); b. 18 Sep 1894, Elgin, N.B., d. 8 Apr 1984, Truro, N.S.; m. Mable; c. Lloyd (d), Bob (d), Phyllis; retired; class AA Maritime skeet title '38; 3 NS junior curling titles; 3 times NS Brier rep.; NS seniors title '65, Maritime Johnson senior championship; mem. NS Sports Hall of Fame.

MANN, Bob (curling); b. 5 Jan 1922, Truro, N.S.; d. 1995, Mississauga, Ont. m. Lena (d); c. Bob, Susan, Patricia, Sandy; retd. regional sales manager; mem. NS jr. hockey champions '39-40; 6yrs sr. hockey Truro Bearcats; refereed Big Six League '50-51; NS class A skeet title '48; 3 times NS Consols finalist, 5 times Ont. finalist; rep. NS '60 Brier, Ont. '63-64; OCA Silver Tankard '68., OCA intermediate '72, finalist OCA srs '75-76; 3rd Tournament of Champions Maple Leaf Gardens '64.

MANN, Dave (football); b. 6 Feb 1932, Berkeley, Calif; given name: David Carl; div. Gail; c. Angela, Melissa,

David; m. Susan; Oregon State; salesman, actor, restaurateur; Chicago Cardinals 3yrs; Argos '58, '60-70; offensive back, carried ball 107 times for 556 yds, caught 33 passes for 319 yds; appeared in 155 league, 13 playoff games; 2nd in Argos all-time scoring records with 435 points (33td, 73c, 22fg, 98s); punter '60-70 with 1261 punts for 55,745yds including 1 for 102 yds; twice scored TDs on punt returns; handled 139 kickoffs for 7862yds and as returner carried 36 for 755 yds; EFC all-star team '45-73; nicknamed 'Superman'; res. Mississauga, Ont.

MANN, David (archery); b. 1 Oct 1957, Vancouver, B.C.; given name: David Lorne; m. Wendy Killick; UBC, BPhE, UAlta, MSc; medical doctor; Vancouver target champion '72-73; mem. ntl team '75-78; mem. '75, '77 world target championship, '76 Olympic (7th), world field championship, '76, '78 Tournament of the Americas teams; 4 of 5 ntl records for single round international (FITA) competition; CAC coaching scholarship '79; level 4 coaching certificate; res. Calgary, Alta.

MANNING, Peter (t&f); b. 6 Apr 1931, Romford, Essex, Eng.; given name: Peter George; m. Myra Laycock; c. Helen Jane, Gillian Claire, Sarah Louise;London, UMan; retd. sports management co. owner; dir. Manitoba CTFA '67-70, CTFA coach of '74, runnerup Air Canada award '74; coached 1600m relays '76 Olympics; coached '76, '84, '88, '92 Olympic, '78, '90 Commonwealth, '79 Pan-Am Games teams; ntl assn.rdinator sr. sprints, relays '89-96; res. Guelph, Ont.

MANNING, Ron (curling); b. 1 Aug 1937, Orangeville, Ont.; m. Linda Dowds; c. Stacey, Jason; carpet salesman; nicknamed 'Moon'; began curling Haileybury '59; lead Alf Phillips Jr. rink '62-67; all-star lead '67 Brier champions; 11 times provincial championship competitor; res. Toronto, Ont.

MANTHA, Sylvio (hockey); b. 14 Apr 1903, Montreal, Que., d. Aug 1974, Montreal, Que.; Notre Dame de Grace jrs. '18-19; moved through intermediate, sr ranks to QSHL Nationals before turning pro; forward as amateur, defence as pro Montreal Canadiens '23-36, Boston '36-37; mem. 9 Prince of Wales Trophy, 3 Stanley Cup winners; player-coach with Habs '35-36; 2 seasons as NHL linesman, AHL referee; coach jr., sr. teams several years; twice 2nd team all-star; NHL record: scored 63g, 72a; mem. Hockey Hall of Fame.

MARA, George (hockey); b. 12 Dec 1921, Toronto, Ont.; given name: George Edward; m. Margaret Roddick; c. George Jr., Diane; Upper Canada College; chair. Jannock Ltd.; Jr. B at 15, Jr. A Toronto Marlboros '41; mem. Toronto Navy team '42; rejected pro offers from Toronto, NY Rangers, Detroit; mem. '48 RCAF Flyers Olympic champions; founded Olympic Trust '71; gov. Olympic Trust; Canada Medal, Cdn Olympic Order; mem. Order of Canada, Cdn Amateur, Ottawa Sports, Canada's Sports halls of fame; res. Don Mills, Ont.

MARCH, Bill (mountaineering); b. 14 Dec 1941, Chelmsford, Eng.; d. 8 Sep 1990, Inverness, B.C.; given name: William Joseph; m. Karen Louise Kreutzweiser; c.

Anthony James; King's Coll, London, Lougnborough Coll, Idaho State; prof.; began climbing UofLondon '59; deputy dir. Glenmore Lodge national outdoor training centre '67-74; dir. UK mountaineering centre '76-77; coordinator outdoor pursuit program UCal '77-83; 80 1st ascents Scotland, Canada, Ecuador, US; 4 Himalaya expeditions; leader '82 Mt. Everest expedition which placed 2 Cdns, 4 Sherpas on summit; author 3 mountaineering books; mem. International Assn. of Mountain Guides; Alta Sports Hall of Fame Special Award.

MARCHAND, Claude (parachuting); b. 20 Nov 1954, Quebec City, Que.; m. Louise Poitras; aviation mechanic; began skydiving '74; more than 1500 jumps; won ntl 8-way '78-80; 4-way '80; mem. Cdn 2nd place 8-way, alternate 1st place 4-way team France '79, 2nd place 4-way team China '80; res. Abbotsford, B.C.

MARCHILDON, Phil (baseball); b. 25 Oct 1913, Penetanguishene, Ont.; d. 10 Jan 1997, Toronto, Ont.; given name: Phillip Joseph; m. Irene Patience; c. Dawna, Carol; St. Michael's College; retd. hospital furnishing co. employee; pitched Penetang intermediates to Ont. finals '30's, Creighton Mines to Nickle Belt title and provincial finals '38; 2 seasons with Toronto Maple Leafs (IL), part of one with Cornwall (Can-Am) before joining Connie Mack's Athletics '40; 17-14 record with A's '42; honored by fans with Marchildon night Philadelphia '45; 19-9 record '47 with 1-hitter, 2 2-hitters; closed pro career Boston '50; Senior Intercounty Guelph, Waterloo; ML record: 185 games, 68-75, 481k, 6so, 3.93era; spent 9mos German POW camp WW2; co-authored *Ace, Phil Marchildon*; mem. Canadian Baseball, Etobicoke, Canada's, Ont. Legends Sports halls of fame.

MARECHEK, Bill (lacrosse); b. 12 Jun 1955, Kitchener, Ont.; department mgr.; began playing age 13; mem. McDonald's Bread Jr. A '74, Nepean Lumbermen Jr. '75-76, Victoria Payless '76-81, '92, Victoria Royal Waxmen '80-92, ntl team '81-96; 7 Cdn field lacrosse title teams; Victoria Shamrocks '79 Mann Cup winner; noted for strong stickhandling ability, deft scoring touch; named to '90 all-world team; res. Victoria, B.C.

MARECHEK, Tom (lacrosse); b. 25 Aug 1968, Kitchener, Ont.; Syracuse; coach; mem. Victoria Royal Waxmen '85-88, Esquimalt Jr. Legion '85-89, Syracuse Orangemen '89-92, Philadelphia Wings '94-98, ntl team '89-98; mem. 2 NCAA, 4 ntl field title teams; top scorer '88 Minto Cup winner; 4 all-American; 4th all-time NCAA goal scorer; 2 runnerup NCAA Attackman of year honors; mem. '90 Mann Cup winners; MILL rookie of '94; res. Baltimore, Md.

MAREK, Deb (ringette); b. 8 Mar 1962, Winnipeg, Man.; UManitoba B.Comm; coach; information/marketing officer Lethbridge leisure services; versatile athlete who played and coached both field and ice hockey as well as ringette at national level; as goaltender claimed ntl ringette gold '82, '83, '85-87 with Team Manitoba, '90, '92, '94 with Team Alberta; coached Team Alta. to gold '96-97; goaltender '90, '92, coach '96 Cdn world gold medal teams; coach ntl team '99; res. Lethbridge, Alta.

MARINKO, Max (table tennis); b. 30 Sep 1916, Ljubljana, Yugoslavia; d. 26 Aug 1975, Toronto, Ont.; teacher; only player to represent 3 countries, Yugoslavia (1), Czechoslovakia (2), Canada (1), world Swaythling Cup (men's team) championships; mem. 2 title winners Czechoslovakia; moved to Canada '54; 9 ntl men's closed singles, '58 men's open singles, doubles, '57 mixed open doubles; finalist '58 US men's open singles; mem. ITTF Swaythling Cup Club; mem. 30 Cdn international team competitions; Perc McLeod Memorial Award for contribution to table tennis.

MARION, Alain (shooting); b. 23 Dec 1946, Pointe Gatineau, Que.; div.; c. Karine; retd. police officer; 22 Que. smallbore prone rifle, 2 free rifle titles; mem. 4 ntl smallbore title teams; through '99 qualified Bisley teams record 31 times, competed 19 times; 14 Bisley Queen's finals; Queen's Prize Bisley '80, '83, '96 (Cdn record), silver medal '72, 3rd '87, '90; Bisley grand aggregate '90, silver cross '73-80; Cdn record 8 ntl (CTR Bisley Agg.) championships; 8 Macdonald Stewart grand aggregate titles; Governor-General's prize '85, '96, 5 times runnerup; gold, silver '86, silver '98 Commonwealth Games; mem. '74, '86, '98 Commonwealth Games team; mem. 8 Cdn Palma teams; team gold '72, '82, silver '92 Palma matches; mem. DCRA council, executive; mem. Order of Canada, Ottawa Sports Hall of Fame; res. Hull, Que.

MARKER, Gus (hockey); b. 1905, Wetaskewin, Alta.; d. 7 Oct 1997, Kingston, Ont.; given name: August Solberg; m. Lillian Malroney; owner building supply, concrete co.; didn't begin skating until he was 14 but proved a natural; began pro career Tulsa (AHA) '28; forward NHL 1932-42 with Detroit, Montreal Maroons, Toronto, Brooklyn; mem. 1 Stanley Cup winner; mgr./coach Tulsa 2yrs; NHL record: 322 scheduled games, 64g, 69a; 46 playoff games, 5g, 7a.

MARKLE, Jean (horseshoes); b. 22 Jul 1938, Clapham, London, Eng.; given name: Jean Palmer; m. Larry Markle; exec. secty; emigrated to Canada '61; asst. to ntl assn. pres. George Schummer '69-73; secty-treas. Horseshoe Canada '73-84; treas./tournament director Horseshoe Canada '79-91; asst. to regional dir. Jack Adams NHPA from '73; authored tournament manual; conducted numerous seminars; life mem. Horseshoe Canada; mem. '97 world championships org. comm.; charter mem. Horseshoe Canada, mem. Horseshoe Ont. halls of fame; res. Hamilton, Ont.

MARKLE, Larry (horseshoes); b. 8 Apr 1919, Napanee, Ont.; m. Jean Palmer; c. 1 daughter; carpenter; began pitching horseshoes age 14; military service interrupted play and he didn't return to game until '53; Hamilton champion '61; 6 Ont., Cdn senior men's titles; ntl intermediate men's title '82; mem. Horseshoe Ont. Hall of Fame; res. Hamilton, Ont.

MARQUETTE, Ulla (t&f); b. 28 Jun 1958, Edmonton, Alta.; m.; c. Maianna; teacher; long distance runner; 2 CIAU 1500m titles; '85 ntl 3000m title; CIAU 1500m record; competed world cup, cross-country, FISU Games; 3 CIAU X-C all-Cdn; ntl 10km titles '91-92, 3000m title '92; gold

10,000m Harry Jerome Classic '94; ntl 10,000m title '94; res. Sooke, B.C.

MARSH, Brad (hockey); b. 31 Mar 1958, London, Ont.; given name: Charles Bradley; m. Patty Quaile; c. Erik, Patrick, Victoria, Madeline; restaurateur, hockey exec.; defence London (OHA) '74-78; twice all-star; claimed by Atlanta '79 expansion draft; played in NHL with Atlanta '78-80, Calgary '80-81, Philadelphia '81-88, Toronto '88-91, Detroit '91-92, Ottawa '92-93; NHL record: 15 seasons, 1086 scheduled games, 23g, 175a, 97 playoff games, 6g, 18a; res. Kanata, Ont.

MARSH, Lou (builder); b. 1878 Campbellford, Ont., d. 4 Mar 1936, Toronto, Ont.; given name: Lewis Edwin; journalist; defeated Bobby Kerr in 100yd race; hockey, boxing referee; 43yrs *Toronto Star* sports dept., editor; trophy in his name awarded annually to Canada's outstanding athlete.

MARSHALL, Blake (football); b. 17 May 1965, Guelph, Ont.; UWO; fullback; pro Edmonton '87-93; CFL record: 88 scheduled games, 65tds, 523 carries for 2,449yds, 54tds, 143 receptions for 1,467yds, 11tds, 9 playoff games, 5tds; 3 all-Western, 3 all-CFL all-star; GMC outstanding Canadian '91; Dr. Beattie Martin trophy '91; tied CFL record 20tds single season '91; mem. 3 Grey Cup finalists, 2 winners; res. Edmonton, Alta.

MARSHALL, Don (hockey); b. 23 Mar 1932, Verdun, Que.; givenn name: Donald Robert; m. Betty; c. 4; lw Cincinnati Mohawks (IHL), Montreal Royals (QHL), Buffalo (AHL); NHL Montreal '51-52, '55-63, NY Rangers '63-70, Buffalo '70-71, Toronto '71-72; Red Garrett Memorial trophy (AHL) '54; mem. 5 Stanley Cup winners; NHL record: 1176 scheduled games, 265g, 324a, 94 playoff games, 8g, 15a; res. Stuart, Fla.

MARSHALL, Dru (field hockey/coaching); b. 2 Mar 1958, Winnipeg, Man.; given name: June Dru; U Man, BPhE, UAlta, MSc, PhD; assoc. prof/coach; a love of hockey stemmed from father Tom who played defence for Allen Cup champion Winnipeg Maroons, Cdn ntl team but translated itself into field variety; centre-half UMan '76-79, UA '80-81; twice shared scoring titles; coach UAlta Pandas '81-96; 2 CIAU ntl tournament bronze; 4 CWUAA, 2 CIAU, 1 3M Canada coach of yr awards; head coach ntl jr. women's team 9yrs; head coach ntl sr. women's team from '96; mem. UAlta Sports Wall of Fame; res. Edmonton, Alta.

MARSHALL, Greg (football); b. 9 Sep 1956, Beverley, Mass.; m. Cindy; c. Christine, Bryan, Caitlin, Kelsey; Oregon State; coach, teacher; PAC 10 all-star '77; drafted Philadelphia, played briefly NFL Baltimore '78; Ottawa '79-87; def. end; Schenley outstanding defensive player '83; CBC-TV Coaches all-star, Ottawa def. MVP, Bill Smyth Memorial Trophy, Rothman lineman of year '83; 4 Eastern, 2 CFL all-star; James McCaffrey Memorial Trophy '83; CFL all-time all-star team; coach Ottawa Bootleggers '90, Ottawa Sooners '91-93; Cdn. Junior coach of year; asst. Saskatchewan from '94; res. Regina, Sask.

MARSHALL, Jack (hockey); b. 14 Mar 1877, St. Vallier, Que., d. 7 Aug 1965, Montreal, Que.; mem 3 Caledonia Cup soccer winners 1890s; 1897 Britannia rugby title team; hockey forward, defenceman 17yrs 7 different teams, 5 Stanley Cup winners; Winnipeg Victorias '01, Montreal Victorias '02-03, Wanderers '04-05, '07, '10-12, '16-17, Montagnards '07, Shamrocks '08-09, Toronto Arenas '13-15, twice led league scorers; player-manager Arenas '13-14, guided club to '14 Stanley Cup; 99 career goals in 132 league games, 13 in 18 playoff games; scored 6 goals in 1 game, 5 goals in two others; mem. Hockey Hall of Fame.

MARSHALL, Neal (speed skating); b. 13 Jun 1969, Victoria, B.C.; following in steps of great grandfather Klaas Hanje, a Dutch champion, and uncle Joe Janje, former Cdn ntl team mem., Neal and brothers Steve, Mike and Kevin all became speed skaters; long track specialist; competed '94 Olympics; 1st Cdn to win a World Cup overall title '95; 2nd overall for '96 WC circuit; 3 ntl records; 4 ntl distance skating awards; 3 outstanding Cdn male skater awards; retd from competition '98; CTV commentator; res. Coquitlam, B.C.

MARTEL, Marty (bowling); b. 1887, Cape Breton, d. 1958, Halifax, N.S.; given name: Wilbert; world candlepin record for single string 213, total 496 for three strings; helped form NS Wolverines, Allan Cup winners; mem. NS, Canada's sports halls of fame.

MARTELL, Henry (golf); b. 1913, Edmonton, Alta., d. 12 Jun 1984, Edmonton, Alta.; policeman, golf pro; 14 Edmonton City Open, 12 Edmonton City amateur, 9 Alta. amateur, 4 Alta. Open, 4 Sask. Open, 1 Ont. Open, '49 Cdn Amateur, '53, '58 CPGA, '66, '71 CPGA Seniors titles; 1st Albertan to win major ntl title; mem. 3 ntl teams; pro Edmonton Highlands GC '48-79; Edmonton junior tennis champion, mem. basketball title team; mem. Alta. Sports, RCGA halls of fame.

MARTENS, Camille (rhythmic gymnastics); b. 1 Jun 1976, Vancouver, B.C.; began competing age 10; ntl jr '91, sr all-around title '94; competed '93 worlds, '94 Commonwealth, '96 Olympic Games; team gold, 4 individual silver '94 Commonwealth Games; BC novice title '86; Miss Elegance trophy '91 France international; res. Vancouver, B.C.

MARTIN, Carol (t&f); b. 19 Apr 1948, Toronto, Ont.; given name: Carol Lynne; SFU, York, BA; track coach; bronze discus '66 Commonwealth Games 159'3"; silver '67 Pan-Am Games 156'3"; silver '69 Pan-Pacific Games; bronze '70 Commonwealth Games 158'10"; won '72 Olympic trials; ntl record 55.45m '72; unexpectedly dropped from '72 Olympic team; gold '73 Pan-Pacific Games; bronze '74 Commonwealth Games, PB 56.60m; retd '76; discus, shot put coach UofT Track and Field Club; res. Palgrave, Ont.

MARTIN, Flora Greenwood (curling/softball); b. 21 Jun 1916, Treherne, Man.; given name: Flora Mae Greenwood; m. Geoff Martin; c. Bill; mem. Treherne softball team which won 8 of 9 Manitoba tournaments '38-39; won 9 Vancouver Island ladies' curling titles; 6 Vancouver Island Sr. ladies' titles; skipped BC ntl entries in both Macdonald Lassie, Srs

'74-75; ntl srs titles '74-75, '79-80, runnerup '81; mem. Vancouver Island O'Keefe mixed title rink '64; in lawn bowling Vancouver Island novice title '69; Vancouver Open singles '74, runnerup '75; runnerup BC pairs championships '74-75; master athlete of year finalist BC Sports Federation '74-75; hon. life mem. Victoria Curling Club; mem. Canadian Curling Hall of Fame; res. Victoria, B.C.

MARTIN, Frank (boxing); b. 25 Feb 1908, Montreal, Que.; m. Margot; c. Robert, Brian, Thelma; Strathcona Academy; retd. fur trader, mechanic, hotelman; Montreal junior flyweight (112 lbs) champion '27; senior provincial, ntl titles '28; mem. '28 Olympic team; Montreal city, provincial bantamweight (118 lb) titles '29; pro '29 winning ntl bantam title and ranking 3rd in world; when top 2 ranked bantams refused to fight he moved into featherweight (126 lb) ranks and won ntl title to hold 2 crowns simultaneously; fought professionally 10yrs; while living in NWT 20yrs did some competitive dogsled racing; res. Atikokan, Ont.

MARTIN, Fritz (golf); b. 15 Sep 1869, York, Ont.; d. 19 May 1934, Hamilton, Ont.; with brother-in-law George S. Lyon engaged in numerous legendary matches; Cdn amateur titles '02, '10, twice runnerup; 1st lefthander to win Cdn. Amateur; Cdn Srs. title '27; pres. Hamilton G&CC '10, 5 times club capt.; 9 HGCC titles, 5 times runnerup; 3 Hamilton Dist. titles; 3 times runnerup Niagara Invitation; Lambton Invitation title '06, twice runnerup; international cricketer, prominent curler, rugby football halfback; mem. RCGA Hall of Fame.

MARTIN, Jacques (hockey/coaching); b. 1 Oct 1952, St. Pascal, Ont.; m. Patricia; c. Angela, Nathalee; St. Lawrence Coll.; coach; began coaching career at St. Lawrence '76; coached at Algonquin Coll, Brockville, Hawkesbury in CJHL; asst./scout Peterborough; head coach Guelph (OHL) '86; won Memorial Cup; OHL coach of '86; head coach St. Louis (NHL) '86-88 winning 1 Norris div. title; asst. Chicago '88-90, Quebec '90-93; GM/head coach Cornwall (AHL) '93-94 winning Southern div. title; asst. Colorado '94-96; head coach Ottawa from '96; Adams Trophy nominee '97, winner '99; *SN* coach of '99; res. Kanata, Ont.

MARTIN, John (bowling); b. 30 Nov 1919, Toronto, Ont.; given name: John Martyn; sep.; c. Patricia, Wayne (d), Calvin, Michael, Ronald, Randall, John Jr., Kevin; bowling proprietor; 5-pin bowler, entered business with opening of O'Connor Bowl, Toronto, '51; major role in elimination of counter pin and adoption of new scoring system; through his efforts bowling became regular CBC-TV feature 9 yrs; annual O'Connor Open among country's top competitions from '57; staged attractions such as ntl Invitational Singles, Rotary '50' Marathon; founding mem. Bowling Proprietors Assn. of Ont, Canada, p.-pres. of each; Builders of Bowling Industry Award '74; mem. Ont. 5-pin Bowling Hall of Fame; res. Toronto, Ont.

MARTIN, Kevin (curling); b. 31 Jul 1966, Killam, Alta.; m. Shauna; c. Karrick, Kalycia; owner Kevin's Curling Supplies; skipped Alberta 5 Briers, winning twice; CCR 1st team all-star '96; silver '91 world championship; finalist '98 Olympic team qualifier bowing 6-5 to Ontario's Mike Harris; won '97 *TSN* Skins' Game, 2 WCT titles; res. Edmonton, Alta.

MARTIN, Peter (football); b. 20 Oct 1940, Toronto, Ont.; given name: Peter Thomas Ross; m. Wendy Warwick; c. Cindy, Kristi, Peter James, Jennifer; UWO,BPHE; retd. phys ed teacher, adult program leader Peel Board; co-capt., MVP UWO Mustangs '63; first college draft choice Ottawa '64; mem. East York Argos ntl sr. champions '64; CFL Argos linebacker '65-72; 103 league, 10 playoff games; radio commentator Argos games '77-94; SkyDome PA announcer for Argos games; res. Mississauga, Ont.

MARTIN, Pit (hockey); b. 9 Dec 1943, Noranda, Que.; given name: Hubert Jacques; m. Pat Gurniss; c. 4 daughters; McMaster; owns Windsor Pool Service; ex-restaurateur; mem. '58 NOHA title team; OHA Hamilton jrs.; 2 seasons Pittsburgh (AHL); centre Detroit '63-65, Boston '65-67, Chicago '67-77, Vancouver '78-79; NHL record: 1101 scheduled games, 324g, 485a, 100 playoff games, 27g, 31a; Bill Masterton Memorial Trophy '70; licensed pilot; res. Tecumseh, Ont.

MARTIN, Rick (hockey); b. 26 Jul 1951, Verdun, Que.; given name: Richard Lionel; m. Martha; c. 3 sons; computer consultant.; left winger; Montreal Canadiens jrs.; 1st Buffalo draft '71; mem. Sabres '71-81, Los Angeles '81-82; with Rene Robert, Gil Perreault formed Buffalo's French Connection line; twice 1st, 2nd team all-star; twice reached 50-goal plateau with 52 in both '74-75; Team Canada '76; retirement forced by injury; following lengthy court action was awarded $2.5M in medical malpractice suit '94; jersey #7 retd by Sabres; NHL record: 685 scheduled games, 384g, 317a, 63 playoff games, 24g, 29a; res. Buffalo, N.Y.

MARTIN, Robert (t&f); b. 23 Jul 1950, Paris, Ont.; given name: Robert John; m. Mary Kerr; c. Nicole Ann; St. Andrew's College,Oregon, BSc; pres. Marco Sales, Incentives Ltd.; mem. Hamilton Spartan TC; track scholarship Oregon '70-74; ntl jr. outdoor 100m, 200m titles '69, indoor 50m '70; NCAA all-American Oregon '71; ntl sr. 100m, 200m champion '72; Pan-Pacific finalist, ntl 200m titlist '73-74, '77; mem. '74 Commonwealth Games, '74-75 European tour, '75 Pan-Am, '76 Olympic, '77 FISU Games teams; bronze, Cdn record Pan-Am Games 4x100m relay, double silver medalist US Games, 4th NZ Games '75; national sr. indoor 50m title '76; ntl record 4x200m relay team '77; res. Brantford, Ont.

MARTIN, Seth (hockey); b. 4 May 1933, Rossland, B.C.; m. Beverley Linn; c. Lynne, Patti, Susan; fireman; Lethbridge jrs. '49-52; goaler Trail Smoke Eaters '52-63, '68-69, '70-72, Rossland Sr. Warriors '63-66, St. Louis NHL '67-68; Spokane Jets WIHL '69-70, '72-73; coach Spokane PCHL '78-79, Trail '82-84; best goaler '61 World Cup Smoke Eaters; ntl team '64, '68 Olympics, '63-66 world championships; most valuable goaler awards '61, '63, '64, '66; mem. 3 Allan Cup winners; PCHL coach of '79; BCAHA outstanding player of '65; BC Sports Hall of Fame; res. Trail, B.C.

MARTINEZ, Dennis (baseball); b. 14 May 1955, Granada, Nicaragua; given name: Jose Dennis; m. Luz Marina Garcia; c. Dennis, Erica, Gilberto, Ricardo; represented Nicaragua '72-73 amateur World Series; turned pro '74 playing in minors with Miami (A), Asheville (AA), Rochester, Indianapolis (AAA), in majors with Baltimore (AL) '76-

86, Montreal (NL) '86-93, Cleveland (AL) '94-96, Seattle (AL) '97, Atlanta (NL) '98; one of 7 pitchers to post 100 victories in both AL/NL; pitched perfect game for Montreal vs. Los Angeles '91; 4 all-star games; 2 World Series; nicknamed 'El Presidente'; res. Miami, Fla.

MARTINEZ, Pedro (baseball); b. 25 Oct 1971, Manoguayabo, D.R.; Ohio Dominican Coll.; rhp; signed by Dodgers as amateur free agent '88; played with Los Angeles '92-93, Montreal '94-97, Boston from '98; ML record: (through '98) 84-46; 218 games, 153 starts, 23cg, 10so, 3sv, 1146ip, 890h, 370r, 373bob, 1221k; recorded banner year with Montreal '97 pitching 1-hitter vs. Cincinnati, becoming 1st Latin pitcher to record 300k single season, 1st pitcher with 300k (305) and sub-2.00era (1.90) since Steve Carlton '72, 1st rhp since Walter Johnson '12; NL all-star; Montreal, *Sporting News* NL pitcher of yr, 3rd ML pitcher to win Cy Young awards both leagues NL '97, AL '99; res. Santo Domingo, D.R.

MARTINI, Paul (figure skating); b. 2 Nov 1960, Woodbridge, Ont.; given name: Paul Lloyd; m. Elizabeth Wallace; c. Kate Emily, Robert; York, BA; figure skating, hockey coach; with Barbara Underhill 5 ntl jr. & sr. titles; jr. world pairs title '78; St. Gervais Grand Prix France, Nebelhorn Trophy Germany '78; Ste. Ivel, England, NHK Trophy Japan '80; mem. world championships teams '79-84, Olympics '80, '84, Skate Moscow '79; bronze '83, gold '84 worlds; pro '84-98; 7 pro world pairs titles; CBC '92, '98 Olympic, 3 world, 1 European championships color commentator; mem. Canada's Sports, Cdn (Olympic) Amateur Sports, Cdn Figure Skating halls of fame; res. Bradford, Ont.

MARTITSCH, Karl (builder); b. 19 Nov 1917, Ratnitz, Austria; m. Beverly Ann Westman (d); c. Nicholas, Franchesca; Graz. MSc; consulting engineer; mem. Austrian ntl ski team 12yrs; participated in all four disciplines, downhill, slalom, cross-country, jumping; in 25 competitive yrs amassed 360 trophies/prizes; Austrian jr. slalom title '36; Austrian nordic, academic nordic combined, 3-way, 4-way combined titles '46; earned medals in competitions in Austria, Italy, Switzerland; competed '48 Olympics, '50 worlds; won NA 4-way title '50; academic rep. ski sports in Austria '46-49; moved to Canada '51Canadian rep. FIS from '63; FIS jumping judge; mem. FIS Council '79-92; played key role in construction of ski-jumping/recreational facilities Lake Placid, Calgary, Revelstoke, Thunder Bay, Banff, Mont Ste. Anne, Ironwood/Iron Mountain, Mich, Anchorage, Alaska; Austrian Olympic medal for contribution to '76 Innsbruck winter games; Cdn commerative medal; mem. Cdn Ski Hall of Fame; res. Toronto, Ont./Governor's Harbour, Eleutheva, Bahamas.

MARUK, Dennis (hockey); b. 17 Nov 1955, Toronto, Ont.; given name: Dennis John; m. Joni; c. Jonathan, 2 daughters; Creative Concepts marketing; 113 goals 2 seasons centre London Knights Jr. A; 2nd draft pick California '75; Cleveland '76-78, Minnesota '78, '83-89, Washington '78-83; twice reached 50-goal plateau with 50 '81, 60 '82; NHL record: 888 scheduled games, 356g, 522a, 34 playoff games, 14g, 22a; nicknamed 'Peewee'; HS hockey coach; res. Eden Prairie, Minn.

MASON, Janice (rowing); b. 23 Nov 1959, Edmonton, Alta.; West Coast Coll. of Massage Therapy; 7 ntl, Cdn Henley, 1 US title; gold double sculls '81 Royal Henley; mem. '79, '82, '83 world championships, '80, '84 Olympic teams; bronze double sculls '82 worlds; res. Vancouver, B.C.

MASON, Susan (swimming); b. 3 Jun 1960, Halifax, N.S.; given name: Susan Marguerite; m. Donald Allan MacLeod; Dalhousie, BSc; teacher, physiotherapist; mem. Halifax Trojan Aquatic Club under coach Nigel Kemp; ntl team mem. '77-84; 3 gold, 1 silver, 1 bronze '77 Canada Games; freestyle specialist at distances ranging from 100m to 1500m; 2 bronze Coca Cola Inter-nations '78, bronze 400m FS relay FISU Games '79; CIAU championships 200m FS '79, 400m, 800m FS '79-80; mem. '78 Commonwealth Games team; AUAA outstanding female swimmer awards '79-81, CIAU outstanding female swimmer award '79; Dalhousie outstanding female athlete award '79; mem. NS Sports Hall of Fame; res. Halifax, N.S.

MASOTTI, Paul (football); b. 10 Mar 1965, Hamilton, Ont.; m. Vivi; c. Andrin, Athena; Acadia; wide receiver, financial advisor; 2 AUAA, 1 CIAU all-star; drafted by Toronto '88; attended Washington NFL camp '88; with Argos '88-98; CFL record (through '98): 174 games, 36tds, 1cvt, 526 receptions for 8399yds, 44td, 1cvt, 266pts; 3 Grey Cup finals, 3 winner; 2 Eastern, 1 CFL all-star; Dick Suderman trophy '97; Stoney Creek community award; res. Stoney Creek, Ont.

MASTERS, Wally (football/baseball); b. 28 Mar 1907, Pen Argyl, Pa.; d. 12 Jul 1992, Ottawa, Ont.; given name: Walter Thomas; m. Ruth Anna Newman; c. Walter Thomas Jr.; Pennsylvania; public relations; all-American college baseball righthander '31 winning 15 in row, 28-3 record; Knute Rockne football all-American team '31; pro baseball 1yr each Washington, Philadephia (AL), Philadephia (NL), Ottawa Nationals Border League '47; pro quarterback Philadephia, Chicago-Pittsburgh combined teams; all-Cdn Ottawa '32; coached Riders '33-34 (simultaneously managed Ottawa Crains Can-Am baseball league), St. Patrick's College '35, Ottawa Trojans ORFU '47, Rough Riders '48-50; coached Wilmington Delaware Clippers in American Assn. '37-39; overall football coaching record 88 wins, 22 losses, 2 ties; ORFU title '47; guided Riders to '48 Grey Cup bowing to Calgary 12-7; mem. Ottawa Sports Hall of Fame.

MASTERTON, Bill (hockey); b. 13 Aug 1938, Winnipeg, Man.; d. 15 Jan 1968, Minneapolis, Minn.; given name: William; Denver, MB; centre St. Boniface Jrs., Man. champions '56; when NHL expanded '67-68 he joined Minnesota playing 38 games scoring 4g and adding 8a before disaster struck; on 13 Jan after being checked he struck his head on the ice and died 2 days later; NHL created Bill Masterton trophy in his memory; mem. Man. Hockey Hall of Fame.

MATHER, Eddie (archery/t&f); b. 4 Aug 1895, Hyde, Cheshire, Eng.; d. 16 Sep 1983, White Rock, B.C.; m. c. Marion; track star, archer, gunsmith and accomplished musician, machinist, violin-maker; emigrated to Saskatoon with parents '06; following WW1 service supervisor municipal swimming pool '28-39; competed in '24 Olympic trials but did not go to Olympics; master archer he played role in formation of Saskatoon, Bedford Road, RCAF Archery Clubs; helped found Western Development Museum, several bands in Saskatoon; lifetime and founding mem./asst. conductor Saskatoon Symphony Orchestra; at 88 swam 88 lengths of pool, about 1 1/4 miles.

MATHERS, Frank (builder/hockey); b. 29 Mar 1924, Winnipeg, Man.; given name: Frank Sydney; exceptional athlete who played both pro hockey and football; Ottawa srs; NHL with Toronto '48-52, 23 scheduled games, 1g, 3a; became AHL star defnceman with Hershey Bears, 5 consec. all-star teams; both player/coach with Hershey; retd as player '62; 3 Calder Cup titles; pres/GM Bears '73-91; 3 more Calder Cups; honored with Frank Mathers night by Bears; Lester Patrick Trophy '87; mem. Cdn, Man. Hockey halls of fame; res. Hershey, Pa.

MATHESON, Dan (wrestling/boxing); b. 11 Jul 1893, Emerald, P.E.I.; d. 20 Dec 1950, Regina, Sask.; given name: Donald John; m. Katie Belle McKenzie; c. James (d), Earl, Donald, Agnes; Regina police sergeant; gold '23-25, '31, silver '22, '32 AAU of C ntl heavyweight wrestling championships; Sask. boxing champion; mem. Regina boxing/wrestling commission; proficient in hammer throw, discus, shot put, pole vault events; trained numerous wrestling champions including Earl McCready; mem. PEI, Sask. Sports halls of fame.

MATHESON, Wayne (curling); b. 27 Sep 1944, Charlottetown, P.E.I.; psychologist; PEI schoolboy champion '62-63; skipped PEI entries '79, '84 Briers; Ross Harstone award '79; res. Crossroads, P.E.I.

MATOBA, Tom (baseball); b. 19 Sep 1898, Vancouver, B.C.; d. (circa 1990) Weston, Ont.; m. Hideko Yieno; c. Raye, Clara, Rumi, Eri; gardener; at 16 one of dominant players Japanese Cdn Archis team; united with Nippon Club '18; mem. Vancouver Sr. Terminal League pennant team '26; noted for home run power at Vancouver Athletic Park; never lost enthusiasm for game despite relocation ordeals inflicted on Japanese Canadians WW2; coach Niagara to Fruit Belt Softball League title; mem. Canadian Baseball Hall of Fame.

MATTHEWS, Don (coaching/football); b. 22 Jun 1939, Amesbury, Mass.; div. c. Mike, Mark, Pat; Idaho; football exec.; served in US Marine Corps; arrived at Idaho as walk-on; left 4yrs later as team capt.; began coaching as asst Idaho; successful HS coach Nevada, Washington, Oregon; 2 state titles; joined CFL as Edmonton asst. '77-82, '89; head coach BC '83-88, Toronto '90, '96-98, Edmonton '99, Orlando Thunder (WLAF) '91, Saskatchewan '91-93, Baltimore (CFL) '93-95; 4 Grey Cup finals, 2 titles; surpassed Frank Clair's 147 regular season victory total '97 to become CFL's winningest coach; 4 Annis Stukus coach of yr awards; res. Edmonton, Alta.

MATTHEWS, John (bowling); b. 2 May 1948, Winnipeg, Man.; given name: John Clifford; m. Phyllis Gail Jeske; c. Dorelle Dawn Lenore, Joel John Llewelyn; UMan, BA, BEd; teacher; 5-pin specialist; mem. Man. mixed title team '77, men's title team '78; coach Alta. mixed team titlists

'80; mem. Alta. Masters men's team titlists '80; representing Man. won '81 ntl Masters singles title; 4-handicap golfer; hole-in-one '70; Southwood Club match title '77; mem. Man. Colt (17-18) championship baseball team '77; Sr. B fastball league all-star '72; mem. Man. team handball champions '75; Winnipeg club singles, men's doubles tennis titles '77; coached several jr. HS basketball, volleyball, soccer teams; res. Winnipeg, Man.

MATTHEWS, Tam (sailing); b. 8 Oct 1955, Peterborough, Ont.; 470 sailor; 2 ntl, 1 CORK, 1 Hyeres, 2 NA titles; mem. '79 Pan-Am, '78-81 world championships, '80, '84 Olympic teams; res. Belleville, Ont.

MATTHIAS, Brendan (t&f); b. 12 Aug 1969, Toronto, Ont.; UofT; long distance runner; began competing age 10; Ont. HS champion '83-84; ntl jr. 1500m titlist; competed world jr. championships '88; ran 3:58.03 indoor mile; ntl indoor 1500m title '90; CIAU 10km title; won *Times-Colonist* 1500m '91; won Toronto 10km '92; ntl indoor, UofT Classic 3000m title '93; competed in world indoor meet '93; ntl 10,000 title '94; ntl indoor 3000m record 7:30.90 '93, 5000m record 13:41.73 '94; mem. UTTC; res. Thornhill, Ont.

MATTSON, Dale (shuffleboard); b. 24 Feb 1955, Victoria, B.C.; given name: Dale Christopher; m. Diane Weger; computer operator supervisor; mem. Man. champion, runnerup basketball, baseball, fastball, volleyball, football HS teams; capt. basketball, fastball title teams; highest winning percentage shuffleboard league play '78-84; won Man. singles, runnerup Cdn '78; mem. Man. title teams '78-84; Cdn men's doubles title '84-85; runnerup Cdn mixed doubles '84-85; Man. mixed champion '84-86; res. Winnipeg, Man.

MAUCH, Gene (baseball); b. 18 Nov 1925, Salina, Kan.; given name: Eugene William; m. Nina Lee Taylor; c. Leanne; retired baseball manager; pro Brooklyn Dodgers organization '43; minor clubs Durham, Montreal, St. Paul; Indianapolis, Milwaukee, Atlanta, Los Angeles, Minneapolis, ML Brooklyn, Pittsburgh, Chicago (NL), Boston (NL), St. Louis (NL), Boston (AL) through '59; 1st managerial assignment Atlanta (Southern) '53; managed Minneapolis (A.A.) '58-59; Philadelphia '60-68; 1st Montreal manager '69-75; Minnesota '76-80, California '81-82, '85; guided Angels to AL Western div. title '82; 3 times NL mgr. of yr.; *Sporting News* ML mgr. of yr.; Canada's baseball man of '73; once mgr, 3 times coach NL all-star team; res. Rancho Mirage, Calif.

MAUGHAN, George (boxing); b. 8 May 1910, Toronto, Ont.; given name: George Burwell; m. Joan Brais; c. Marilyn, G.B. Jr., Walter, David, Joanne, Carol; McGill, MD, MSc, FACS, FRCOG, FRCS(C); retd. professor emeritus McGill; intercollegiate football '28; intercollegiate shot put, swimming, water polo '30; began boxing '29, competed at college level '30-34; ntl title '32; semifinalist '32 Olympics; Canada Medal; res. Montreal, Que.

MAUNDER, Maria (rowing); b. 19 Mar 1972, St. John's, Nfld.; women's coxed 8s; learned to row at Ridley College; mem. ntl team from '92; gold 8s '93 FISU Games; silver 8's '96 Olympics; res. London, Ont./Victoria, B.C.

MAURICE, Pauline (softball); b. 17 Dec 1967, Welland, Ont.; Kent State, BSc; telephone customer service rep.; Kent State career batting avg. .397; competed '90, '94 world championships; '91 (bronze), '95 Pan-Am Games; '94 South Pacific Classic; '96 Olympics; Kent State female athlete of decade '92; 1st team all-region, 2nd team all-American NCAA Div. 1 '90; 2 ntl championship all-star awards; 2 Welland female athlete of yr awards; Kent State Sports Hall of Fame; res. Welland, Ont.

MAWHINNEY, Bill (golf); b. 7 May 1929, Vancouver, B.C.; d. 26 Jan 1995, Abbotsford, B.C.; given name: William Cecil; m. Jess; c. Chris, Jocelyn, Marilyn; golf pro; defeated Stan Leonard 1-up for 1st of 2 BC match titles '47; 2 BC jr., '52 Pacific Northwest Amateur titles; ntl jr. '48, ntl amateur title '50; mem. Willingdon Cup, Morse Cup, Hudson Cup, America's Cup teams; semifinalist '52 US Amateur; Seattle, Tacoma Open titles before turning pro; Millar Trophy CPGA match champion '57; BC Open title '57; mem. BC Sports Hall of Fame.

MAXWELL, Doug (builder/curling); b. 13 Jan 1928, Toronto, Ont.; given name: Douglas Dean; m. Shirley Ann Ward; c. Douglas Ward, Gordon Dean, Janet Louise, William James; UofT, BComm, MComm; retd. editor/publisher; earned school letters in variety of sports; part-time work at CBC during school days evolved into staff position on both radio/TV working in sports/children's program areas; utilized marketing skills with Ont, Centennial Commission; had role in establishment Ont. Sports Fed., and Ont. Sports Centre; business mgr. for Nancy Greene '68; special researcher fed, govt, task firce on sports '68-69; consultant COA '69-77; chef de communications COA 3 Olympic Games; began curling '49; 1 of 4 founding mem. Humber Highlands CC, served as secty/pres.; Toronto CA pres. '69; OCA mem.-at-large '67; exec. dir. Air Canada Silver Brooms '68-85; exec.dir. Hexagon world curling championships '86-88; consultant world curling championship comm. from '89; key role in obtaining Labatt's as Brier sponsor replacement for Macdonald Tobacco; exec.dir OCF '88-93; undistinguished playing career but did score an 8-ender; radio/TV curling commentator CBC/BBC many years; helped in developing *TSN* Skins Game; editor/publisher *Canadian Curling News* from late '70s; charter mem. secty-treas Canadian Curling Reporters; authored 2 curling books, Labatt draw book; inaugurated/organized Toronto, later ntl, mixed championships; organized/directed Tournament of Champions at Maple Leaf Gardens mid-60s; innovator who had hand in introduction of time clocks, baseball-style scoreboards and varied other game upgrading features; initiated international standardization of game rules; chief umpire Silver Brooms '68-72; organized Moncton 100, Las Vegas Desertspiel; Scotty Harper Memorial award; TCA curler of '74 award; hon. life mem Sask. CA; OCA media award; CCA achievement award; honored by Swedish, German, Italian, French, Swiss, Royal Caledonian CC; mem. Cdn Curling Hall of Fame; res. Markdale, Ont.

MAXWELL, Gavin (canoeing); b. 28 Aug 1970, Mississauga, Ont.; McMaster; ntl canoe team mem. from '90; 2 Pan-Am Games bronze '91; silver C-4 200 Szeged '96; gold C-4 200 Milano '96, C-1 1000 Hemespheric Olympic Qualifier '96; 3 ntl C-4 titles; competed '96 Olympics; res. Oakville, Ont.

MAXWELL, Steamer (hockey); b. 19 May 1890, Winnipeg, Man., d. 11 Sep 1975, Winnipeg, Man.; given name: Fred; skating prowess earned nickname 'Steamer'; began playing '10; received several pro offers during playing career but chose to remain amateur; rover Winnipeg Monarchs Allan Cup champions '14-15; retired as player '17, coach Monarchs 2 seasons; coached Winnipeg Falcons to '19 Allan Cup, '20 Olympics, world championships, Winnipeg Rangers to Manitoba title '25-26, Winnipeg Maroons (APHL) '26-28; guided Elmwood Millionaires to junior, senior Manitoba titles '29-30; Monarchs to world title '35; officiated many games, amateur and pro '10-40; mem. Man., Cdn Hockey halls of fame.

MAYER, Alfons (shooting); b. 1 Feb 1938, Weiler, Germany; div.; c. Anita, Linda; m. Irngard; mechanical foreman; several ntl, Ont. rifle championships; gold English Match '67 Pan-Am Games setting world record perfect 600; 4th world English Match competition; '68 NY State title; Ont. free rifle, sporting rifle, prone titles '82; team silver '79, '83, bronze '71, '79, '83 Pan-Am Games; mem. '68, '72, '80 Olympic, '66, '74, '78, '82 world teams, '77, '79, '81, '83 Benito Juarez teams; res. Kitchener, Ont.

MAYERS, Wallace (basketball); b. 5 Nov 1908, New Westminster, B.C., d. 3 Aug 1976, Vancouver, B.C.; UBC; university soccer star; '26 BC jr. claycourt tennis champion; 3rd '27 ntl swimming championships; mem. 4 ntl men's basketball title teams; led New Westminster Adanacs to BC's first ntl cage crown '29; mem. BC Sports Hall of Fame.

MAYES, Rueben (football); b. 6 Jun 1963, North Battleford, Sask.; Washington State; ret. pro football player; set NCAA, WSU running back records while leading Pac-10 rushers '84-85; twice Pac-10 player of year; all-American '85; 10th in Heisman voting '85; played in Senior, East-West Shrine, Blue-Gray Bowl games; twice Pac-10 all-conference; UPI, Football Writers of America 1st team, *AP, Football News* 2nd team all-star; pro New Orleans '86-90, Seattle Seahawks '91-93 UPI NFC rookie of '86; Football Writers NFL rookie of '86; Harry Jerome Award (Canada's outstanding black athlete) '84; Sask. male athlete of year '84-85; res. Pullman, Wash.

MAYNES, Billy (t&f); b. 1902, Saint John, N.B.; d. 4 Aug 1966, Saint John, N.B.; c. Douglas; Oxford, Rhodes Scholar '25; journalist; NB outdoor relay '21, 440yd '22 titlist; Maritime outdoor quarter-mile champion '22-23; described as "fastest quarter-miler Maritines have produced"; despite 3yd penalty lost '23 AAUC 440yd title by mere inches; mem. '24 Olympic team; mem. NB Sports Hall of Fame.

MAYOTTE, Roger (harness racing); b. 9 Aug 1956, Thunder Bay, Ont.; apprenticed with Gary Crowe, Keith Waples, Bill Troy, Percy Robillard before branching out on own '81; meteoric rise has ranked him among top reinsmen on OJC circuit; with Kingsbridge, That'll Be Me won Breeders Crown titles; Maple Leaf Trot with Earl '94; Take A Look one of his best horses; more than 3000 victories with purses exceeding $25M; res. Mississauga, Ont.

MAZINKE, Harvey (curling); b. 6 Apr 1937, Sewell, Man.; m. Marian Dickson; c. Scott, Dietta; UMan, BSc; engineer; 3rd for Bruce Hudson '64 Man. Brier entry; skipped 11 Sask.

finalist rinks, including mixed, '73, '75 Sask. men's titles, '73 Brier title, lost in Silver Broom final; all-star Brier skip '73; Ross Harstone award '75; Regina B'nai B'rith Sportsman of '73; coach '82 Sask. jr. title rink; pres. CCA; dir. Sask. Sports Admin. Centre, governorUofSask; mem. Cdn Curling, Sask. Sports halls of fame; res. Regina, Sask.

MAZUR, Eddie (hockey); b. 25 Jul 1929, Winnipeg, Man.; d. 3 Jul 1995, Winnipeg, Man.; given name: Edward Joseph; nickname 'Spider'; left wing with Winnipeg Monarchs winning prov. titles at all minor levels as well as juve. and jr.; a proven winner he also played with '51 PCHL champion Victoria, '53 Stanley Cup champion Montreal and '56 WHL titlist Winnipeg; NHL record: 6 seasons with Montreal, Chicago, 107 scheduled games, 8g, 20a, 25 playoff games, 4g, 5a; overall pro record 1086games, 391g, 461a; on retirement tireless hockey volunteer; mem. Man. Hockey Hall of Fame.

MAZURAK, Steve (football); b. 25 May 1951, Regina, Sask.; given name: Steven Lee; m. Heather Thomson; c. Lee, Jacklyn, Andrew; North Dakota; radio FB color commentator; mem. Regina Rams '71-72; Roughriders '73-81; TD '76 Grey Cup final; 2 all-star games; Schenley outstanding Cdn nominee; led wide receivers in catches '77; CFLPA exec. dir. '82-87; res. Regina, Sask.

McARTON, Cheryl (swimming); b. 25 Apr 1966, Ottawa, Ont.; given name: Cheryl Ann; m. Peter Ward; c. Rebecca Lynn, Rachel; Arkansas, BSc; ntl 800m FS relay record '81; 3 silver, 1 bronze '84 winter ntls; gold, 2 bronze '87 winter ntls; mem. '82 Commonwealth, '84 Olympic, '87 FISU, '87 Pan-Am Games teams; 2 silver, 1 bronze '87 Pan-Am Games; 4 NCAA all-American '85-88; 3 academic all-American; North York female athlete of '86; sister Jennifer ntl team diver; res. Indiana, Pa.

McARTON, Jennifer (diving); b. 2 Feb 1968, Ottawa, Ont.; m. Jeff Wright; c. Justin, Nicolas; UofT, BPHE, BA, BEd; HS teacher; 2 ntl 10m, 1 world age group 3m title; silver 10m '82 Commonwealth Games; mem. '82, '86 Commonwealth teams; finalist '82 World Aquatic Games, '83 World Cup; performed 20m high diving exhibitions Canada's Wonderland '89; avid skier, canoeist; sister Cheryl mem. ntl swim team; res. Orleans, Ont.

McBAIN, Barb (swimming); b. 9 Dec 1966, Vancouver, B.C.; backstroke specialist; 2 ntl, 1 Canada Cup, Hapoel Games titles; silver 4x100 MR, bronze 100m, 200m backstroke '83 Pan-Am Games; res. Vancouver, B.C.

McBEAN, Marnie (rowing); b. 28 Jan 1968, Vancouver, B.C.; UWO; public speaker/coach; launched career with Toronto Argonaut RC '85; mem. ntl jr. team '86, sr. team from '89; switched from sweep specialty to sculling '93; mem. '91 world, '92 Olympic straight pair (with Kathleen Heddle), 8s gold medal crews, '96 Olympic double sculls gold (Heddle), quad sculls bronze; 3 World Cup titles; Commonwealth single sculls gold '94; mem. '89, '93 FISU, '88 (spare), '92, '96 Olympic, '95, '99 Pan-Am Games teams; after winning double sculls gold, stripped of '95 Pan-Am Games quadruple sculls gold when teammate Silken Laumann tested positive for mistakenly taking illegal decongestant; 1st woman to reach Olympic/world podium

6 different boat classes; 11 medals '98 worlds; 7 international regatta gold, 8 US, 2 Cdn titles; single sculls gold '99 PAG; began mountain climbing '97; certified snowboard instructor; Dick Ellis Memorial trophy for sr. team of '91-92; ntl spokesperson Kids Help Phone; Cdn meritorious service award; UWO, ORA female athlete of '89; CARA centennial medal '91; mem. Canada's Sports Hall of Fame; res. Toronto, Ont.

McBLAIN, Liz (t&f); b. 30 Jan 1948, Bandung, Indonesia; given name: Elizabeth Vanderstam; m. Willian McBlain; Lethbridge, UAlta, BPhE; teacher; pentathlon specialist; PB: 3,951 pentathlon points, 400m hurdles 61.2, 400m 54.9, 53.88 in relay leg; outstanding Calgary athlete '67, outstandingLethbridge athlete '71; competitor masters circuit from '78; WR masters (35+) triple jump '84; ntl record masters javelin, 100m, 400m hurdles '84; res. Edmonton, Alta.

McBRIEN, Harry (football); b. 1910, Toronto, Ont., d. 31 Aug 1976, Toronto, Ont.; m. Kathleen; c. Derek, Scott; pres. Sterling Coffee Co., L.L. Garr Enterprises; football official '26-50; seriously injured officiating '50 national jr. final; organized Toronto District Board of Football officials; secty.-treas. Toronto Dist. Interscholastic AA; secty. CRU '51-66; mem. 3-man comm. which streamlined rules '67; governor, mem. Canadian Football Hall of Fame selection comm. '67-76; major role in developing Grey Cup into ntl festival; mem. Canada's Sports, Canadian Football halls of fame.

McBURNEY, Margaret (basketball); b. 10 Apr 1909, Fernie, B.C.; m. Victor Vasheresse (d); retd. secretary; 1st baseman Edmonton Toddies baseball team; mem. Monarch ladies hockey team, 3 championships; longest playing mem. legendary Edmonton Grads '26-36; played in 164 games amassing 2079 points for 12.6 avg.; world champion free throw artist 61 in succession '31; twice mem. team which claimed world title honors during exhibition tournaments staged in conjunction with Olympics; coached jr. girls basketball Edmonton, Vancouver; 5-pin bowling champion; mem. Canadian Basketball, Alta. Sports halls of fame; res. Edmonton, Alta.

McCAFFREY, Janice (t&f); b. 20 Oct 1959, Etobicoke, Ont.; given name: Janice Leslie Turner; m. Bill McCaffrey; c. Scott, Jamie; psychologist, workshop facilitator; pres. Success Coaching; began career as middle distance runner then switched to race walking to compete in '81 Canada Summer Games where she won bronze; 10 ntl titles; mem. '87, '95 Pan-Am, '90, '94, '98 Commonwealth, '92, '96 Olympic Games, 5 World championship teams; 10km RW bronze '94 Commonwealth Games, gold '94 Francophone Games; 3 Athletics Alta. female athlete of yr awards; '89 Alta. achievement award; ranked among top 10 marathoners in Canada; top Cdn woman, 20th overall '97 NY marathon; race walking coach; res. Calgary, Alta.

McCAFFREY, Jimmy (football); b. 1895, Alexandria, Ont., d. 29 Oct 1966, Alexandria, Ont.; m. Ella Krock (d); c. Patricia; government registrar of trademarks; managed St.Brigid's hockey club; pres. Ottawa Senators Que. Sr. League; mgr. Rough Riders '23-59, 7 Grey Cup finals, 4 titles; Big Four pres. '40, '56; helped form Eastern Football

Conference; Schenley award trustee '55; mem. Ottawa, Canadian Football halls of fame.

McCALL, Robert (figure skating); b. 14 Sep 1958, Halifax, N.S.; d. 15 Nov 1991, Toronto, Ont.; Dalhousie; ice dance specialist; teamed with Marie McNeil '75-81, Tracy Wilson '81-84; 5 ntl, 1 Skate Canada titles; jr. world bronze '77; mem. '84 Olympic, '80-84 world championships teams; mem. Order of Canada, Cdn Amateur Sports Hall of Fame.

McCANCE, Ches (football); b. 19 Feb 1915, Winnipeg, Man.; d. 8 May 1956, Winnipeg, Man.; given name: Chester William; m. Frances Elizabeth Carson; c. William Robert, Margaret Elizabeth; wine salesman; CFL with Winnipeg, Montreal; 8 Grey Cup finals, 3 winners; 2 field goals, 2 singles as Bombers edged Ottawa 18-16 '41 final; field goal, 3 converts, 1 single as Als beat Calgary '49 final; 3rd Ken Weldon's Que. entry '52, '53 Briers; lost title playoff '53; coached Isaac Newton jr. HS to Man. football title '40; asst. coach Blue Bombers '43; mem. Canadian Football Hall of Fame.

McCANN, Dave (football); b. 5 Feb 1889, Ottawa, Ont.; d. 27 Mar 1959, Ottawa, Ont.; m. 1. Florence Wilson (d), 2. May Stafford; c. Lenore, June; civil servant, insurance exec.; mem. Ottawa Senators (renamed Rough Riders) '07-20; credited with originating flying wing position '10; mem. '09 Interprovincial title team; intercollegiate football referee '21-24; coach Rough Riders (Senators) '26-27, 2 Grey Cups; pres. CRU '27; mem., chairman CRU rules comm. '27-58; prominent paddler New Edinburgh Canoe Club; Canadian Branch Governor-General's, Royal Victoria Jubilee curling trophies; mem. Ottawa CC '18-58; mem. Governor-General's CC; mem. '09 YMCA Eastern Cdn basketball, city baseball, ntl war canoe titlists; mem. Ottawa Sports, Canadian Football halls of fame.

McCANNELL, Don (speed skating); b. 11 Dec 1918, Minto, N.D.; d. 25 Apr 1985, Winnipeg, Man.; m. Florence Esler; c. Joan, Doreen, Donna; instrumental in Sargent Park skating track expansion to Olympic standards; liason Winnipeg Parks & Rec and Man. SSA '63-82; mem. Winnipeg SSC from '58, serving various exec. roles; exec. mem. MSSA; dir. CASSA, chair. Olympic development comm.; coached Man. team Canada Winter Games '67, '64 Olympic, '65, '67 ladies' world teams; tech. advisor, color commentator CTV '76 Winter Olympics; mem. Canadian Speed Skating Hall of Fame.

McCANNELL, Donna (speed skating); b. 20 Feb 1950, Winnipeg, Man.; m. Bob Keating; c. Kim, Andrea; UMan, BPhE; teacher; Man. mass start titles: midget '62, juve. '63-64; sr. indoor titles '69, '71; ntl mass start titles: juve. '63, jr. '66; intermediate indoor titles '67-68, sr. '71; mem. jr. Olympic team '66; mem. '72 Olympic team; res. Winnipeg, Man.

McCANNELL, Doreen (speed skating); b. 29 Jul 1947, Winnipeg, Man.; given name: Doreen Ann: m. Calvin Bruce Botterill; c. Jennifer, Jason; UMan, BPhE, Ed. Cert.; retd. teacher; 8 Man., ntl titles; NA, US Olympic style champion '66; mem. '64, '68 Olympic, '65, '67, '68 world championships teams; 5 gold Canada Winter Games '67; Man. jr. athlete of '61; Man. athlete of '65; Man. female athlete of '66; mem. Man. Sports, Cdn Speed Skating Hall of Fame; res. Winnipeg, Man.

McCASKILL, Kirk (baseball); b. 9 Apr 1961, Kapuskasing, Ont.; given name: Kirk Edward; m. Dana Metzger; c. Riley, Reese; Vermont; retd; rw drafted by Winnipeg Jets '82 but after part of minor league season opted for baseball; rhp; drafted by California '82; 10 seasons in California organization and at ML level '85-91; joined White Sox as free agent '92-96; ML record: 380 games, 242 started, 30 complete games, 1729ip, 1748h, 876r, 154hr, 665w,1003k, 72wp, 9bk, 106-108 w/l, 11so, 7sv, 4.12era; 0-2 in LCS; 1st pitcher in ML history to surrender back-to-back homers to a father/con combination (Ken Griffey Sr/Jr); played '97 season in Italy; res. Rancho Santa Fe, Calif.

McCAW, Doug (bowling); b. 26 Nov 1954, Regina, Sask.; given name:Douglas Ronald; m. Wendy Shewchuk; c. Ashley, Taylor; letter carrier; mem. 2 YBC Sask., 1 ntl title teams; '86 Sask. mixed, '93 men's title teams, '93 singles; made ntl history rolling perfect 450 game during '93 Cdn championships for which he received $50,000; twice ntl championship all-star; level 2 coach guiding numerous YBC teams at prov. level; mem. Regina 5-pin Assn. exec. 15yrs; chair. Coca-Cola Classic cash tournament; coached Sask. open all-stars '90, '93; sr. hockey referee to '91; level B basketball official; mem. 2 Sask. sr. men's B title fastball teams; res. Regina, Sask.

McCLEERY, Alan (canoeing); b. 13 Jun 1929, Montreal, Que.; m. Joan Louise Hart; c. Colin, Colleen, Gail, Shawn; Sir George Williams; retd. mgr. Bell Canada; 5yrs water polo Montreal Concordia; 8yrs football to sr. level; competed at 175lb class in Golden Glove boxing; competed nationally, internationally in canoeing; mem. 1000m kayak tandem team '60 Olympics; mem. Cdn Ski Instructors Alliance from '66; alpine skiing teacher Mont. Ste. Sauveur, Gray Rocks, Morin Heights, Vorlage; res. Ottawa, Ont.

McCLELLAN, Reg (wheelchair basketball); b. 2 Apr 1954, Pierceland, Sask.; m. Chantal Benoit; consultant; former exec.-dir. Cdn Wheelchair Basketball Assn.; significant role in development of wheelchair basketball throughout Canada; began career in Edmonton; founded Northern Lights organization; played with clubs in Vancouver, Calgary, Toronto, St. Hyacinthe, Halifax, Ottawa; player/coach various teams including ntl team '74-94; multiple all-star, MVP awards; mem. 11 ntl title teams; competed 4 Paralympic Games, 6 world championships; capt. '91 Stoke-Mandeville World Games gold medal team; CWBL gold '87 Calgary Grizzlies, '89, '95 Ottawa Royals; player/coach Gold Cup silver '86, bronze '90; silver '92, bronze '94 with Ottawa Royals NWBT final four; capt. Cdn team '92 Barcelona Paralympics; res. Orleans, Ont.

McCLINTOCK, Joel (water skiing); b. 9 Oct 1960, Mississauga, Ont.; given name: Joel Scott; m. Michelle; c. J.D., Justin; coach ntl team; mem. ntl team '77-85; 1st international competition '76; ntl jr. title '76; ntl boys title '77; skied in 1st world championship '77; won 1st international medal, gold, '78; ntl open overall titles '78-80; world overall title '79; California International Cup, Pan-American Group titles '80; ntl trick record 7300 points; ntl slalom record; author "*Complete Instructional Book of*

Waterskiing"; Viscount Alexander award '79; mem. Cdn Amateur, Mississauga Sports halls of fame; res. Florida.

McCLINTOCK, Judy (water skiing); b. 6 Sep 1963, Mississauga, Ont.; given name: Judith Louise; m. Perry Messer; c. Jamie, Jenna, Jay; fitness club co-owner; pro water skier; began skiing age 4; ntl jr. girls tricks title age 9, jr. girls overall titlist '74, '76-77; alternate '77 world championships team; 3rd slalom 1st international appearance '78 Group One championships; mem. '79, '83 world championships teams; '81 British Masters overall title; 3rd jumping, 4th overall '81 world championships; women's overall world title '95; jr. girls slalom, tricks, girls slalom, tricks, jump, open women's tricks, jumps records; with brothers Jim, Joel, Jeff, Lions Club citizens of '77; mem. Cdn Amateur Sports Hall of Fame; res. Northampton, Mass.

McCLOY, Paul (t&f): b. 6 Nov 1963, St. John's, Nfld.; Memorial; teacher; distance runner; ntl jr. 10,000m titlist; CIAU titlist; ntl cross country champion; Pan-Am, Canada Games bronze; ntl cross country title '90; silver 5000m ntls, Cdn Airlines; gold 10,000m Harry Jerome Classic; National Capital, Boston Milk Run 10km titles; competed '90, '94 Commonwealth Games, '94 world cross country; 3 CIAU X-C all-Cdn; 1 CIAU indoor t&f record; mem. Mount Pearl TC; brother Bill mem. ntl water polo team, sister Cora ntl rowing team; res. St. John's, Nfld.

McCOMB, Bill (hockey); b. 14 Dec 1920, Newmarket, Ont.; given name: William Eugene; m. Janet Allan; c. David, Bill Jr.; owner McComb Heating; Jr C, B Aurora '36-38; St. Catharines Jr B '39; Toronto Hockey League Major Sr. '40-42; army teams '42-44; pro Providence '45-46; St Louis '47-49; Indianapolis '50; mem. Owen Sound Mercurys '51-54, Meaford '55-57; coached several Western Ont. teams, Owen Sound Old Timers; res. Owen Sound, Ont.

McCONACHIE, John (football/hockey); b. 18 Jul 1941, Montreal, Que.; given name: John Alexander; m. Diane Gregory; c. Sean, Ryan; Sir George Williams, BA; retd. dir. marketing, communication CIAU; HS male athlete of '58-60; mem. Rosemount Bombers '60 ntl jr. football titlists, '61 ntl finalists; mem. '63-64 SGW ntl finalists hockey team; 3yrs head coach South Shore Colts juvenile football team; interscholastic gymnastics, badminton (singles, doubles titles), soccer (team capt. 2 seasons), volleyball (team capt.); pres. South Shore Colts football club 2 yrs; outstanding defenceman award South Shore intermediate HL '66-67; res. Stittsville, Ont.

McCONNELL, Russ (hockey/football); b. 7 Jan 1918, Montreal, Que.; d. 7 Sep 1942, Gulf of St. Lawrence; given name: Russell Henry; McGill.; while attending McGill mem. 3 Queen's Cup CIHU, 3 Alex Thompson Trophy IIHL title hockey teams, 2 football teams; 2 IIIHL scoring crowns; 12 McGill hockey records; capt. '39 squad; set career (94 games) records for goals (116), assists (95), points (211) which stood 4 decades; most points single game (10) in '39, accomplishing feat twice; rejected NY Rangers pro offers; died in WWII when ship torpedoed; Ken Stewart Cup as QSHL MVP '39; mem. McGill Sports Hall of Fame.

McCORMACK, Mildred (basketball); b. 21 Jun 1909, Buffalo, N.Y.; d. Mar 1991, New Westminster, B.C.; m. Walter Wilkie (d); c. Maurice, Jack; retd. secretary; catcher 3 Edmonton Toddies baseball title teams; forward famed Edmonton Grads '26-32, 94 games, 924 points, 9.8 avg.; husband mem. '28 Olympic lacrosse team; mem. Canadian Basketball, Alta. Sports halls of fame.

McCORMICK, Frank (shooting); b. 14 Sep 1924, Montreal, Que.; given name: Frank McLeod; m. Lillian Johnson; c. Brian, Theresa, Kathleen; Sir George Williams; dir. marketing, Information Science Industries Ltd.; sporting rifle, match rifle, handgun, trap, skeet shooting '48-74; ntl pro skeet champion '59, '61-62, '67, Que. '59-63, '67, Ont. '60; Can-Am '67; mem. ntl skeet team '59 Pan-Am Games, all-American team '62, all-Canadian trap team '65; mgr. ntl team '58, '62 world championships, '60, '64 Olympic, '59 Pan-Am Games; COA dir.; CASF dir., v-p; Cdn Pan-Am Games comm. secty; Cdn BEG Assn. dir.; Shooting Federation of Canada secty, treas, exec.-dir.; Cdn, Que. Skeet Shooting Assn. founding dir.; Que. Rifle Assn. dir.; Ont. Skeet Shooting Assn. secty; Cdn delegate International Shooting Union; conducted financial campaigns, arranged travel, participation for 12 Cdn internationazl shooting teams; tournament dir. NSSA world skeet championships '63-65; tournament dir. ntl skeet championships more than 20yrs; ISU Jubilee Medal '57; Confederation Medal '67; Que. Safety Award; res. Beaconsfield, Que.

McCOURT, Dan (officiating/hockey); b. 14 Aug 1954, Falconbridge, Ont.; m. Betty Behm; c. Lisa, Shari; oficiated at minor levels until joining NHL '79; appeared in initial NHL game as linesman 27 Dec '80; worked '90 all-star game; through '98 linesman 1215 NHL scheduled, 49 playoff games; active with Easter Seals Society; brother Dale played in NHL; res. Detroit, Mich./Garson, Ont.

McCRAE, Don (basketball/coaching); b. 14 Apr 1935, Guelph, Ont.; given name: Donald Glen; m. Judith Ann Moore; c. Susan, Kate; UWO, BA, McMaster, BPHE; coach Waterloo; jr. B hockey Guelph '53-55, sr.A Kingston '57; basketball Tillsonburg Livingstons '58-60; mem. '59 Pan-Am, '60 Olympic teams, intercollegiate titlists '61; coached 6 Kitchener HS basketball, 4 football title teams; coach Waterloo from '71; 8 consec. league titles; 3rd nationals 3 times; only undefeated team CIAU history '75; 1 CIAU coach of yr award; coach ntl women's team '77-84; bronze '79 worlds, Pan-Am, FISU Games; dispute with Basketball Canada exec. led to firing '83 but when players revolted was reinstated; mem. Cdn Basketball Hall of Fame; res. Elmira, Ont.

McCRAE, John (curling); b. 26 Apr 1940, Lindsay, Ont.; given name: John Duncan Sinclair; m. Eleanor; c. Carol, Scott, Steve; OCA general manager from '88; mem. Lindsay recreation commision '74-83, chair. '79-83; began curling '53; Ont. schoolboy finalist '57-59; 3 Governor-General's zone winner; Consols prov. finalist '71; Consols zone winner '73; Silver Tankard zone winner '75; pres. Lindsay CC '71, life mem. from '92; CCA award of merit '87; club rep., zone rep., chair. competitions comm. OCA in '70s; pres. OCA '82-83; promotions dir. OCA '84-88; res. Oshawa, Ont.

McCRAE, Judy (field hockey); b. 24 Apr 1947, Sarnia, Ont.; given name: Judith Ann Moore; m. Don McCrae; c. Susan, Kate; Western Michigan, BA, North Carolina, MSc; teacher, coach; Waterloo athletic dir., coach women's field hockey, badminton, curling; coordinator WO women's summer games Kitchener '74; 3yrs regional rep. OFHA; 4yrs publicity officer, exec. mem. OWIAA; mem. advisory council, 3yrs dir. Waterloo regional sports council; instructor ntl coaching development program; '76 pres. OWFHA; v-p CWFHA from '77; mem. steering comm. Ont. Sportplan '76; Ont. rep CWIAU; chairman Cdn team development comm. CWFHA; CBC-TV color commentator '84 Olympics; res. Elmira, Ont.

McCREADY, Earl (wrestling); b. 6 May 1905, Lansdowne, Ont., d. 6 Dec 1983, Seattle, Wash; m. Margaret; Oklahoma A&M, BPhE; masseur; launched wrestling career Regina CI, attending first tournament New Westminster, B.C., '26; lettered in A&M football, all-Oklahoma State guard; mem. varsity wrestling team '28-30 winning all matches in 30 major college meets over 3yr period; capt. '30 team; 4 Cdn heavyweight titles; 3 Dodder (top points) wrestling awards, 1 Curtis Cup (outstanding scholar-athlete), Roberts award (outstanding athlete), dean's honor roll 2 successive semesters; mem. '28 Olympic team; gold '30 BEG as Canadians swept all 7 wrestling categories; by '30 had won every amateur wrestling honor available in Canada, US, Commonwealth; wrestled as pro throughout world; BE pro title, defended it several times; ranked 2nd in world to Jim Londos, to whom he lost in world title bid '32; 1st wrestler to give demonstration on television; mem. US, Canadian Wrestling, Helm's, Cdn Amateur, Sask., Canada's Sports halls of fame.

McCREATH, Ralph (figure skating); b. 27 Apr 1919, Toronto, Ont., div.; c. Jim, Martin, Paul, Michelle; UofT, LLD; lawyer, QC; 19 ntl, NA singles, pairs, fours championships; nominated to '40 Olympic team but games not held due to WW2; from '56 International, Olympic judge, referee; chair./secty exec. comm/ gov. Olympic Trust; mem. Cdn Figure Skating Hall of Fame; res. Toronto, Ont.

McCREDIE, Nancy (t&f); b. 5 Feb 1945, Belleville, Ont.; animal groomer; shot put, discus specialist; ntl shot record placing 5th '64 Olympics; gold shot '63, '67, discus '63 Pan-Am; bronze shot '66 Commonwealth Games; ntl female track athlete of '63; PB: discus 169'31/2", shot 52'61/4"; mem. Cdn Amateur Sports Hall of Fame; res. Brampton, Ont.

McCRIMMON, Brad (hockey); b. 29 Mar 1959, Dodsland, Sask.; defence Brandon (WHL) '77-79; 2 WHL 1st team all-star; drafted by Boston '79; NHL with Boston '79-82, Philadelphia '82-87, Calgary '87-90, Detroit '90-93, Hartford '93-96, Phoenix '96-97; NHL plus/minus leader '88; NHL 2nd team all-star '88; asst coach NY Islanders '97; mem. 1 Stanely Cup winner; NHL record 1222 scheduled games, 81g, 322a, 116 playoff games, 11g, 18a; res. Dodsland, Sask.

McCULLOCH, Jack (speed skating); b. 15 Aug 1872, Perth, Ont., d. Jan 1918, Winnipeg, Man.; c. Marguerite; skate manufacturer; mem. Winnipeg Victorias who won 9 of 11 hockey games on Eastern tour and outscored rivals

76-36, 1890; Man. cycling champion 1892; Western roller skating titlist; ntl speed skating titles 1893, 1897; US nationals 1896, world title 1897; pro 1898 and barnstormed several yrs; made possibly 1st pair of tube skates in Canada; mem. Canadian Speed Skating, Canada's Sports halls of fame.

McCUSKER, Joan (curling); b. 8 Jun 1965, Yorkton, Sask.; m. Brian McCusker; c. Rory, Christina; teacher; began curling age 12; mem. '92 Sask. mixed title rink; 3 Sask. women's title rinks; 2nd Sandra Schmirler's 3-time STOH, world title rinks; gold '98 Olympics; res. Regina, Sask.

McDERMID, Heather (rowing); b. 17 Oct 1968, Calgary, Alta.; Rice; business owner; NCAA all-American track star '89-90; mem. ntl rowing team from '95; mem. women's coxed 8s silver medal crew '96 Olympics; Rice track MVP award '90; res. Calgary, Alta.

McDIARMID, Don (tennis); b. 21 Nov 1917, Ottawa, Ont.; given name: Donald Stuart; m. Janet Scanlon; c. Kimberley, Margo; ret. public servant; numerous Ottawa, Eastern Cdn, Que. doubles, singles titles; ntl open men's singles title '40; mem. '46 Davis Cup team vs. Mexico; with Jean Marois rep. Canada Pan-Am championships; twice played at Forest Hills; life mem. Rideau Tennis & Squash Club; mem. Ottawa Sports Hall of Fame; res. Ottawa, Ont.

McDONALD, Dennis (hockey); b. 10 Apr 1937, Flin Flon, Man.; given name: Dennis Francis; m. Valdeen Bremwell; c. Andrew, Marcia, Michelle; North Dakota, BSc, Michigan State, MSc; hockey administrator; football letterman UND '57; mem. St. Vital Bulldogs, Manitoba '58-60, ntl champions '60; coached football Winnipeg Kelvin HS, Man. title '62; hockey 20yrs from minor through college ranks; pres. Cdn Hockey Coaches Assn. '74; Winnipeg city sports, athletics supervisor 6yrs.; Scarborough Centennial College AD 7yrs.; Percy Genser HS sportsmanship award '64; UND football scholarship '64; St. Vital most valuable lineman '58; chair. IIHF coaches comm. '76; AGM/dir. hockey operations Winnipeg Jets, GM Moncton Hawks; res. River Heights, Man.

McDONALD, Doug (rowing); b. 11 May 1935, Thorsby, Alta.; given name: Douglas John; m. Diane Louise Wyma; c. Donald Andrew, Dustin Allan; UBC, BSF; corporation mgr.; 8-oared crew specialist; mem. '54 BEG, '55 Royal Henley, '56 Olympic teams; res. Garibaldi, B.C.

McDONALD, Joan (archery); b. 23 Feb 1943, Toronto, Ont.; given name: Joan Gallie; div.; c. David, Christopher; computer trainer; ntl FS target '62, '64-67, '92-93, FS field '64-66, '89, '91, '93-94; grand champion '64-66; mem. 6 world teams, '79 Pan-Am, Championships of the Americas teams; team silver, individual bronze '79 Pan-Ams; team gold '79 field Championships of the Americas; team leader '95 Olympic trials, world championships, '96 Olympics; head archery coach '99 Pan-Am Games; FCA coach of '92; figure skating judge; mem. Cdn Amateur Sports Hall of Fame; res. Toronto, Ont.

McDONALD, Lanny (hockey); b. 16 Feb 1953, Hanna, Alta.; given name: Lanny King; m. Ardelle Moyer; c. Andra, Leah, Barrett, Graham; hockey exec.; jr. Lethbridge,

Calgary, Medicine Hat; Toronto's 1st choice, 4th overall '73 amateur draft; Leafsrecord for right winger 93 points '75-76; mem. Team Canada '76; Colorado '79-81; Calgary '81-89; twice 2nd team NHL all-star; topped 50-goal plateau '83 with 66; NHL record: 1111 games, 500g, 506a, 117 playoff games, 44g, 40a; co-capt. '89 Stanley Cup winner; v-p/marketing dir., corporate development Flames from '90; Bill Masterton Memorial Trophy '83; King Clancy Memorial trophy '88; NHL Man of '89; 2 Ralph Scurfield Humanitarion awards; active in charitable work Special Olympics, Ronald McDonald House, Children's Miracle Network telethon; jersey 9 retd. by Flames; mem. Hockey, Alta. sports halls of fame; res. Calgary, Alta.

McDONALD, Vern (basketball); b. 5 Jul 1910, Winnipeg, Man.; d. 1999, Hamilton, Ont.; given name: Vern Henry; m. Ethel Fines; retd.; coached basketball teams to 5 city, 3 Ont. 1 ntl championship; secty-treas. Basketball Ont. 16 yrs.; treas. CABA '72-76; lacrosse coach; honored by Ont. government for contribution to sport, Cdn Coaches Assn. for contribution to basketball, International Assn. of Approved Basketball Officials for work on behalf of basketball in Canada; life mem. Basketball Ont.

McEACHERN, Archie (cycling); b. 1874, Woodville, Ont., d. 13 May 1902, Atlantic City, N.J.; ntl amateur welterweight boxing title 1898; fought briefly as pro; 25-mile Boston indoor cycling title 1900; world record 5-mile race, Chicago 6-day title '02;rapidly developing into one of most popular riders of his day, he died of injuries suffered in training accident.

McEACHERN, Ken (football); b. 14 Jan 1953, Regina, Sask.; m. Charlotte; Weber State Coll.; CFL Saskatchewan '74-82, '84, Toronto '83; CFL rookie of '74; 3 WFC, 1 EFC, 1 all-Cdn safety selections; CFL interception leader with 10 '80; all-time Saskatchewan interception leader; Schenley outstanding Canadian nominee '83; mem. '83 Grey Cup champions; Tom Pate award '81; res. Regina, Sask.

McELROY, Walter (golf); b. 11 Jul 1927, Vancouver, B.C.; given name: Walter Grassie; m. Jean Engbaum; c. Walter Jr., Bradley, Robert; pres. Grassie Jewelers Ltd.; ntl jr. runnerup '46; quarterfinalist '46 ntl men's match play championships; semifinalist '48; ranked top amateur in Canada '49; ntl amateur title '51; twice defeated Frank Stranahan to rank as top amateur in world '52; mem. America's Cup team '52, '54; 2nd '54 America's Cup; top amateur, 7th overall Canadian Open '54; 2nd '54 Commonwealth matches; quaterfinalist '54 British Amateur; mem. 7 BC Willingdon Cup teams, 3 winners; 2 Vancouver city jr. titles; '48 Vancouver city men's closed champion; 2 BC jr. titles; '51 BC men's closed champion; retired from competitive golf '54; mem. BC Sports Hall of Fame; res. Vancouver, B.C.

McEWEN, Don (t&f); b. 27 Aug 1928, Montreal, Que.; given name: Donald Scott; m. Amber Jean Clark; c. Scott Cameron, Anna Maria; Michigan, BBA, MA; sales rep, educator; Cdn jr/sr mile champion; set HS mile record 4:18.8; attended UMan on athletic scholarship; capt. UMan t&f team '52; Big 10 4-mile cross-country champion, record holder '49, 2 mile, indoor mile titles '50; NCAA 2 mile champion/record holder/all-American; Big 10 4-mile, 1 mile

titles/records; world indoor dirt track 2-mile record; anchored indoor/outdoor distance medley relay world records '51-52; anchored US record 4-mile relay team '51 Drake relays; Cdn/BE 2-mile indoor/outdoor records; ntl mile/2-mile records; anchored world distance medley relay record team '52; held Cdn scholastic mile/2-mile records several yrs; retd. from competition '52; coached UofT track team '53-54; coach UMan track '55-83; Big 10 medal for outstanding athletics/academics '52; Jack Davies trophy '51; mem. Michigan Hall of Honor; res. Ann Arbor, Mich.

McFARLAND, Packy (football/basketball); b. 25 Sep 1934, Bangor, Me.; given name: John; m. Irene; c. John Jr., Mike, Kathleen, Patricia, Joe, Debbi, David, Danny; St. Francis Xavier, BA, BEd, Springfield College, MPhE, DPhE; assoc. prof., phys ed chair. St.FX; mem. St.FX football, basketball teams '52-56, capt. both teams '56; head basketball coach '60-74; NSSFL offensive, defensive all-star teams '55; Halifax Herald outstanding lineman trophy '55; pres. Cdn Assn. Basketball Coaches '72-73; honor award CABC '76; pres. Antigonish Minor Basketball Assn. '75-77; mem. St.FX Sports Hall of Fame; res. Antigonish, N.S.

McFARLANE, Bob (t&f/football); b. 28 May 1927, London, Ont.; given name: Robert Malcolm: m. Patricia Jean Henderson; c. Janie, Wendy, Laurie; Ridley College,UWO,MD; retd. plastic surgeon, professor of surgery; backfielder UWO team which won CIAU titles '45-47, '49-50; mem. intercollegiate, Eastern Cdn all-star teams; ran 880yd relay 1:27.1, 440yd 47.5, mile relay 3:17.1 '47, ran 400m 47.3 '48; ran 500yd 48.00, 1000yd 2:18.1, mile relay 3:32.4, 300yd 30.00, 880yd 1:53.2 '50; flag-bearer '48 summer Olympics, mem. 4x100m relay team which placed fifth; harness race horse owner, breeder; Lou Marsh Trophy '50; John W. Davies trophy (AAU of C) '47, '50; mem. UWO W-Club Sports Hall of Fame; res. London, Ont.

McFARLANE, Brian (hockey); b. 10 Aug 1931, New Liskeard, Ont.; m. Joan; c. Michael, Lauren, Brenda; St. Lawrence; hockey historian, broadcaster; capt. Inkerman Rockets Jr. A hockey team; attended St. Lawrence on hockey scholarship; 3yrs class pres; 1st to score more than 100 career goals for school; as centre/capt. led team to 2 NCAA finals; all-American; 17yrs mem. NHL Oldtimers (only amateur); sports commentator CFRA Ottawa, WRGB-TV Schenectady, CFRB Toronto; 1st Cdn to work network hockey for CBS '60; sports dir. CFCF-TV Montreal, CFTO-TV Toronto; 26yrs Hockey Night in Canada; 3yrs NBC hockey; introduced animated Peter Puck character to hockey telecasts; author of more than 40 books on hockey; comes by writing skills honestly as his father Leslie (aka Franklin W. Dixon) authored first 23 books in famous Hardy Boys series; hon. pres. Society for International Hockey Research; editorial consultant Total Sports Raleigh, N.C.; operates hockey museum in Niagara Falls, Ont.; popular public speaker/MC; mem. Hockey (media section), St. Lawrence, Ottawa sports halls of fame; res. Willowdale, Ont.

McFARLANE, Don (football/t&f); b. 18 May 1926, London, Ont.; given name: Donald Cecil; m. Frances Smith; c. David, Donald, Karen, Joanne; Ridley College, UWO,MD; retd. ocular surgeon; with brother Bob mem. UWO Mustangs powerhouse backfield '44-50; ntl titles '45-47, '49-50; intercollegiate, Eastern Cdn all-star; George

McCullough MVP Trophy; mem. UWO track team '46-49 specializing 200m, 400m, 800m events; competed Eastern Canada vs Eastern US track meets '46-47; mem. 4x100m 5th place relay team '48 Olympics; qualified '50 BEG team but did not compete due to final year medical student obligations; mem. UWO W-Club Sports Hall of Fame; res. London, Ont.

McFATER, Allan (boxing); b. 6 Jan 1931, Mimico, Ont.; given name: Allan James; m. Joan Constance Allen; c. Bradley, Cheryl, Barbara, Grant, Jeffrey; Meisterschaft Coll.; retd. sales/marketing Molson Breweries; welterweight; began boxing age 10 Mimico Boys Clyb; fought 90 amateur bouts, winning 86, losing decisions to Norm Thompson, Ron Lacelle, Carl Zoba and drawing with Clayton Kenny; defeated each in rematches; fought 40 pro bouts, winning 34; held Cdn welterweight title '54-55; lost decision to world lightweight champion Jimmy Carter '52; mem. Cdn Boxing, Mississauga sports halls of fame; res. Mississauga, Ont.

McGEE, Doug (football/t&f); b. 6 Sep 1954, Ottawa, Ont.; m. Patricia McQuay; c. Raquel; Richmond, BA.; insurance exec. RBC Dominion Securities; 4 HS shot put titles; set records which stood for 17yrs; Ont. HS shot put title '73; mem. Ottawa Uplands Kinsmen Harriers TC '67-73; co-capt. Glebe HS jr. football titlists '69; O-lineman Ottawa Sooners '72; attended Richmond on football scholarship '73-77; Southern Conf. title '75; co-capt. sr. year; played all five O-line positions Rough Riders '77-81; coached O-Line Carleton '91, UofOtt '82, '85, ntl jr. champion Sooners '84; active in PR activities for Rough Riders and with MD Assn.; p.-pres. Mississauga chapter Cdn Life Underwriters; res. Scarborough, Ont.

McGEE, Frank (hockey); b. 1882, Ottawa, Ont.; d. 16 Sep 1916, Courcelette, France; given name: Francis; center, rover Ottawa Silver Seven '03-06; mem. 3 consecutive Stanley Cup winners; 71 goals, 23 regular season games; 22 playoff games, 63 goals, including 14 in single game vs. Dawson City '05 as Ottawa won 23-2, 8 consecutive goals in span of 8 minutes, 20 seconds; 7 times 5 goals single game; mem. Ottawa Sports, Hockey halls of fame.

McGILL, Frank (all-around); b. 20 Jun 1894, Montreal, Que., d. 2 Jul 1980, Montreal, Que.; given name: Frank Scholes; m. Margaret Williamson; c. Isabel, Nancy, John; McGill; retd. Air Vice-Marshall; quarterbacked Montreal Big Four '19 title team calling signals in French; ntl 100yd outdoor record '12; capt. MAAA water polo team, 3 ntl titles; mem. George Hamilton international sailing crew; pres. Interprovincial Football Union, MAAA Football Club; Sir Vincent Meredith Trophy as best all-around MAAA athlete; CFL Schenley awards trustee; Companion of Bath, Haakon VII Cross of Liberation, Order of Lafayette; mem. Canadian Football, Canada's Sports halls of fame.

McGILLIVRAY, David (figure skating); b. 30 Sep 1949, Sarnia, Ont.; given name: David Lachlan; UofT, MD, FRCPS, FAAP; pediatrician; '66 ntl jr. men's title; '70 sr. men's title; mem. worlds teams '68-70, '69 NA championships, '68 Olympics; turned to marathon running late '70's; competed Montreal marathon '79, Ottawa '80,

Boston '81; best time 2:45.41 Boston '81; last known res. Peterborough, Ont.

McGIMSIE, Billy (hockey); b. 7 Jun 1880, Woodsville, Ont., d. 28 Oct 1968, Calgary, Alta.; given name: William George; centre Kenora Thistles 10yrs; entire major league career with one club; mem. 4 Stanley Cup finalists, 1 winner; dislocated shoulder in Ottawa exhibition contest ended career; mem. Hockey, NWO Sports halls of fame.

McGRATH, Larry (curling); b. 14 Jun 1940, Dodsland, Sask.; given name: Larry Martin; m. Agnes Heit; c. Grant, Daryl, Scott; farmer; baseball, softball standout several years; 14 time competitor Northern Sask. Brier playdowns; 4 times prov. finals, twice runnerup; skip Sask entry to runnerup spot '74 Brier; skip '67-68, '71 Sask., Cdn mixed title rinks posting 28-2 record at nationals; 3 Edmonton carspiel titles; mem. Sask. Sports, Canadian Curling halls of fame; res. Dodsland, Sask.

McHALE, John (baseball); b. 21 Sep 1921, Detroit, Mich.; given name: John Joseph; m. Patricia Cameron; c. John Jr., Kevin, Brian, Cam, Anne, Mavie; Notre Dame.; retd. baseball exec.; city, state baseball, basketball, football all-star; center Fighting Irish early '40s; 1st baseman Detroit (AL) organization '41-48; with ML club '45 pennant drive, parts of '47-48 seasons; Detroit farm director, AGM, GM '48-58; v-p, GM Milwaukee Braves '59-60; pres. '61-66; incumbent when Braves moved franchise to Atlanta '66; administrator, asst. to commissioner '67; simultaneously advisor to city of Montreal in campaign for ML franchise; part-owner Expos; pres., CEO '68-91; GM '78-84; NL rep. exec. council of government of organized professional baseball; NL v-p '70-84; mem. baseball playing rules comm., joint drug comm.; dir. Baseball Hall of Fame; mem. Cdn Baseball Hall of Fame; res. Palm Beach, Fla.

McINNIS, Andy (t&f/coaching); b. 16 Mar 1954, London, Ont. given name: Aandrew Stuart; c. Emily Edith; UWO, BA, MA, Louisiana State.; coach; asst. t&f coach UWO '78-83; head coach London-Western TFC '80-84; asst. coach LSU '84-87; head coach Ottawa Lions TFC from '89; program dir. Ntl Capital t&f centre from '88; ntl sr. events coordinator Athletics Canada '92-96; head coach Athletics Canada speed/power events from '97; head coach Cdn Olympic team '96, world jr. team '92; has served in coaching capacity 4 Olympic, 2 Commonwealth, 5 world championships, 1 FISU Games; conducts frequent clinics for athletes/coaches; has coached 11 major international Games medallists, 48 Games representatives; coached Mark McKoy, Sheldon Blockburger to world records; coached 8 SEC, 2 NCAA title teams; LSU-coached teams 1st ever men's/women's NCAA title teams same year; 3 CIAU, 6 OWIAA title teams; coached 22 ntl sr. outdoor/indoor championships, 51 ntl medallists; 96 Ont. title athletes; 5 Ont. club championship teams; 3M coaching award '92, Wittnauer coaching excellence award '96; training consultant Bobsleigh Canada; res. Ottawa, Ont.

McINTOSH, Bob (harness racing); b. 11 Aug 1952, Windsor, Ont.; standardbred trainer; raised in the business with father Jack and brother Doug, he began working with brother's stable at 19; 5 yrs later developed his own stable and success followed rapidly; 6 Cdn trainer of yr awards; Cdn Horseman of '93 after leading Staying Together to Horse of '93 award; experienced similar result with Artsplace '92 and earned Glen Garnsey trainer of yr award from US Harness Writers Assn; res. Windsor, Ont.

McINTOSH, Pam (orienteering); b. 23 Mar 1949, Beaverlodge, Alta.; given name: Pamela Jean; Guelph BSc, UofT, BEd; phys ed teacher; Ont. elite ladies' title '72, 2nd ntl finals, '73 Ont., Ohio titles; '74 Ont. title; mem. ntl team, 35th (top Cdn) world championship; ntl elite title '75; Ont. Athletic Commission Award; last known res. Ridgeway, Ont.

McINTYRE, Jack (hockey); b. 8 Sep 1930, Brussels, Ont.; d. 16 Mar 1998, London, Ont.; given name: John Archibald; m. Donna; c. Randy, Rick, Robbie, Roger, Ronanye; auto salesman; def. St. Catharines jrs; pro Hershey, Buffalo (AHL), left wing Boston '49-53, Chicago '53-58, Detroit '58-60; NHL record: 499 scheduled games, 109g,102a, 29 playoff games, 7g, 6a; scored overtime goal which beat Detroit in '53 Stanley Cup semis; beat Toronto single-handedly scoring 4g, 2a in 6-2 Chicago victory; 1st head coach London Nationals; played London Oldtimers, Old Indians, London Huff 'N Puff; hon. chair. Great Lakes Cup tourney.

McKAY, Dave (baseball); b. 14 Mar 1950, Vancouver, B.C.; given name: David Lawrance; m. Lene Brondum Yjord; c. Cody Dean; Columbia Basin Junior College, Creighton; baseball coach; mem. '70 Pan-Am Games team; pro Wisconsin Rapids (Midwest) '70, Lynchburg (Carolina) '72-73, Orlando (Southern) '74, all-star 3rd baseman, Tacoma (PCL) '75, all-star shortstop; Minnesota (AL) '75; home run in first major league plate appearance; hit safely in first 5 games and 21 of 22; acquired by Toronto '76 expansion draft; Oakland '80-82; coach Oakland, St. Louis; res. Vancouver, B.C.

McKAY, Heather (squash/racquetball); b. 31 Jul 1941, Queanbeyan, New South Wales, Australia; given name: Heather Pamela Blundell; squash, racquetball instructor; Australian women's squash champion 14 consecutive years '60-73; British women's world champion '76, '79; mem. Australian women's ntl field hockey team '67, '71; US ntl amateur racquetball champion '79; women's pro racquetball assn. US ntl champion '80-81; Toronto, ntl racquetball titles '82; Australian Broadcasting Commission sportsman of '67; Squash Canada distinguished service award; MBE '69; Order of Australia '79; res. Australia.

McKAY, Roy (baseball); b. 1 Aug 1933, London, Ont.; d. 25 Dec 1995, London, Ont.; given name: Roy Alexander; m. Ruth McPherson; c. Alex, Rosemary (d), Jim (d); specifications writer; lefthanded pitcher; signed with Detroit organization following '52 trial with Dodgers; Douglas, Ga., Idaho Falls parts of '53, '55 seasons; Sr. IC, Great Lakes-Niagara Leagues with London, most valuable pitcher '57; best season '58 with 10-6 record, 2.79 ERA; led in complete games '58 with 13; topped circuit in hit batsmen '58 with 16; mgr. London '69-72, '74-76, '81-82; three-time IC all-star mgr.

McKAY, Willie (t&f/football); b. 30 Mar 1930, Toronto, Ont.; given name: William Earl; m. Barbara Ethel Askew; c. Robin, Paul; UofOtt, OCE; HS art teacher; football to semipro 15yrs; coached HS 14, officiated 7; pres. Oakville Black Knights '58-60; ran 100yds (10.2), 220yds (22.4) jr. Olympics; chair. Ont. t&f officials council '76; mem. OTFA exec. '76-77; comptroller ntl officials comm. CTFA '77-80, chair. '81; throws ref. '78 Commonwealth Games, '79 World Cup, '77, '81 Canada Games, '80 Pan-Am jr. championships; OFAS achievement award '64; Oakville award of merit '68; Alan Klarer Trophy for leadership in sports (Oakville Rec. Dept.); res. Nepean, Ont.

McKEAN, Jim (baseball/officiating); b. 26 May 1945, Montreal, Que.; given name: James Gilbert; m.; Sir George Williams., Concordia, BEd; pro baseball umpire; quarterback, punter NDG Maple Leafs; pro Alouettes '64; 3 seasons Als, 2 Saskatchewan; mem. '67 Grey Cup finalists; qualified OHA official working numerous junior games, 1 Memorial Cup championship series; baseball umpire from '70; AL from '74; worked AL playoff series '77; World Series '79; all-star games '80-82; off-season basketball coach; Fla. state doubles racquetball champion; Larry Smith Award '70; res. St. Petersburg, Fla.

McKEE, Jamie (badminton); b. 11 Aug 1951, Toronto, Ont.; given name: James Keating; m. Linda Mason; c. Tommy, Fiona; York, hons BSc; chemist; Ont. men's singles champion '73-78; twice Ont. men's doubles champion; ntl men's singles titles '77-78; Pan-Am men's singles titlist '78; 3 Pan-Am doubles titles; 2 Eastern, Western Opens singles titles; mem. silver medal team '78 Commonwealth Games; mem. '79 Thomas Cup team; twice Pepsi-Cola doubles champion; res. Markham, Ont.

McKEE, Joyce (curling); b. 29 Oct 1933, Asquith, Sask.; given name: Helen Joyce; stock control operator; mem. several Sask., Western Canada softball title teams early '50s; 8 Sask. ladies curling titles, 5 as skip, 3 as second; 6 ntl titles, 3 as skip, 3 as second, runnerup '62 ntl finals; Cdn sr. women's title '92; Saskatoon sportswoman of '69; Curl Canada Outstanding Contribution award '84; Governor-General's award; mem. Sask. Sports, Canadian Curling halls of fame; res. Saskatoon, Sask.

McKEE, Walt (football/soccer/coaching); b. 28 Jun 1949, Belfast, N. Ireland; given name: William, Walter Jeremiah; m. Terry Louise Schroeder; c. Darcie, Kathleen; UMan, BPhE, MEd; AD UMan.; mem. 2 CIAU Vanier Cup winners; pro football with Winnipeg '72-75, Edmonton '75; founding mem. Winnipeg Fury CPSL team; Level V soccer coach; mem. ntl soccer team '71; asst. coach ntl team '86; mem. ntl champion all-star soccer team '70; coached soccer at amateur/pro levels; pres. Great Plains Athletic Conference from '95; dir. CIAU from '95; dir. Manitoba Special Olympics '94-96, Sport Manitoba from '96; dir. soccer coaching '84-87; dir. player personnel Winnipeg Fury SC '86-90; dir. UMan high performance centre '93-96; co-chair. practice facilities '99 Pan-Am Games; res. Winnipeg, Man.

McKENZIE, Johnny (hockey); b. 12 Dec 1937, High River, Alta.; given name: John Albert; div.; c. Betty, Jacqueline, Lori, Amy, Megan; BMW salesman; at 15 mem. Calgary jrs followed by Medicine Hat, St. Catharines; pro Chicago (NHL) '58-59, '63-65, Detroit '59-61, NY Rangers '65-66, Boston '66-72; jumped to WHA Philadelphia, Vancouver,

Minnesota, Cincinnati, New England '72-80; saw minor league duty with Calgary, Hershey, Buffalo, St. Louis; set AHL playoff scoring record; NHL record: 691 scheduled games, 206g, 268a, 69 playoff games, 15g, 32a; spent off-seasons as calf roper in rodeos; mem. 2 Stanley Cup winners; on retirement in bid to help athletes operated full-service bank to '85; plays hockey, slo-pitch softball with Boston alumni; nicknamed 'Cowboy' or 'Pie'; res. Stoneham, Mass.

McKENZIE, Merv (all-around); b. 1 Dec 1920, Moose Jaw, Sask.; d. 23 Jan 1977, Mississauga, Ont.; given name: Lawrence Mervyn; m. Jean Elizabeth Trimbee; c. Marilyn, Kerry, Janis; Ontario Athletic Commissioner; raised in Orillia, Ont., he excelled in t&f, football, hockey, swimming, lacrosse; won 100yd backstroke CNE '39; capt. Orillia Minto Cup ntl jr. lacrosse title team '40; sr. lacrosse with Mimico, Hamilton, Peterborough; mem. Hamilton Mann Cup ntl sr title team '48, Peterborough Mann Cup title team '51; played lacrosse, hockey RCAF '41-46; set Trenton AFB 50yd backstroke record; played hockey Toronto Mercantile league; Ont. Athletic Commissioner '52-77; Ont. lacrosse Commissioner '54-77; coached Long Branch Ont. jr. lacrosse title team '55; pres. Cdn Boxing Assn. '59-61, World Boxing Assn. '64; Cdn Confederation medal; 2 trophies honoring his name awarded annually by Ont. Lacrosse Assn.; mem. Mississauga Sports, Cdn Lacrosse halls of fame.

McKENZIE, Tait (builder); b. 26 May 1867, Almonte, Ont., d. 28 Apr 1938, Philadelphia, Pa.; given name: Robert Tait; m. Ethel O'Neil; McGill, BA, MD, hon LLD, Springfield College, MPhE; developed own frail frame through exercise establishing foundation upon which he developed programs leading to recognization as father of NA phys ed programs; won Wickstead silver medal as 1887 intercollegiate jr. gymnastics champion, gold medal as sr. champion 1889; college high jump title; succeeded James Naismith as McGill gym instructor 1890; instrumental in forming McGill's 1st basketball team; 1st McGill medical dir., among forerunners in orthopedic surgery 1892; British army medical corps WWI; contributions to sport art through sculpting without peer; among best known works which exemplified perfection in physical development are The Onslaught, Brothers of the Wind; many of his works used in design of Olympic Medals; also noted for war memorials; wrote books on physical education, sports medicine; twice pres. American Physical Education Assn.; chair. Penn PE; mem. American Academy of Physical Education, Philadephia St. Andrews Society; instrumental in development Philadelphia playground system, Boy Scout movement; York athletic centre bears his name; mem. McGill Sports Hall of Fame.

McKENZIE, Tom (baseball); 11 Apr 1942, London, Ont.; m. Cheryl MacDonald; c. Kerry-Sue, Tommy-Jay; UWO, BA, Oregon, MA, teacher; all-Ont. honors as hockey goaler, in track, football; minor baseball London; London Majors Sr.IC team '60-65, Kitchener '66-80; 21yr IC batting average .314; twice batting champion; 438 IC games played, 570 career hits, 383 runs scored, 155 stolen bases; managed Kitchener '66-67, '80, '96; 16 times all-star shortstop or manager; IC MVP '70; men. 4 Kitchener IC title teams; mem. Ont. team '70, '76 national championships, '67, '71, '79 Pan-Am Games teams, '70, '71 world amateur

championships teams; coach Kitchener minor baseball, HS football, basketball; res. Kitchener, Ont.

McKEOWN, Bob (football); b. 10 Oct 1950, Ottawa, Ont.; given name: Robert Duff; div. Alice Ramo; c. Robert III; m. Sheilagh D'Arcy McGee; c. Alexander, D'Arcy, Liam; Yale, BA; TV journalist; CBC Fifth Estate; CBS news; NBC news correspondent; ntl age-group discus title '65; varsity football Yale; center Rough Riders '71-76; EFC all-star '74; mem. Grey Cup champions '73; 1 US Emmy, 2 Cdn Gemini awards; res. New York, N.Y.

McKERLICH, Bill (rowing); b. 2 Dec 1936, Vancouver, B.C.; given name: Willian Alister; m. Gail Turland; c. Ian, Ross, Leigh, Sarah; UBC, BEd, Oregon, MSc; asst. supertintendant of schools; pulling # 6 oar Cdn 8s crew won '56, '60 Olympic silver, '58 BEG gold; CRA referee, FISA international rowing official; last known res. Salmon Arm, B.C.

McKIBBON, John (basketball); b. 14 Sep 1940, Sudbury, Ont.; m. Patricia; c. Jeffrey, Tommy, Patti-Lyn, Susan; Laurentian, BA, UofT, MDiv; United Church minister; mem. ntl team '59 Pan-Am Games, '60, '64 Olympics, '72 China tour; head basketball coach Laurentian '67-69; Laurentian athlete of '70, '72; mem. Laurentian Sports Wall of Fame; res. Bobcaygeon, Ont.

McKILLOP, Bob (baseball/hockey); b. 1 Jun 1942, Toronto, Ont.; given name: Robert Commings; m. Margaret; c. Robert Jr., Barbara; Waterloo, BA, BPhE; phys ed teacher; catcher, pitcher Toronto People's Jewellers jr. team '59; pro White Sox organization '60-64; Kitchener Sr.IC '66-76; lifetime IC record: .342 BA, 31-11 w-l record, 2.37 ERA; managed Kitchener '68-69, '71, 56-24 record, '71 pennant; 3 IC home run, 5 RBI, 2 total bases leader titles; led IC hitters '69 with .381, pitchers '66 with 0.93 ERA; 7 times 1st team all-star catcher, once 1st team righthanded pitcher, manager; 4 times MVP; mem. Ont gold medal team '69 Canada Games, ntl team '67 Pan-Am Games; hockey, football coach Waterloo; pres. Kitchener Minor Baseball Assn.; mem. Waterloo County Hall of Fame; res. Kitchener, Ont.

McKINLEY, Harold (harness racing); b. 24 Dec 1921, Sault Ste. Marie, Ont.; d. 22 May 1998, Georgetown, Ont.; given name: Harold Andrew; m. Audrey (d); m. Myrna Noecker; c. (step) Janice, Lori, Tracy, Andrew Termano; horseman; raised in Peace River, Alta., he developed love of horses and built a life-long reputation as a harness driver and trainer; trained and drove horses for Armstrong Bros. stable '54-69 then with wife Audrey established Butterball Farm at Norval, Ont.; won numerous major races, including '72 Queen City Pace and '60 Maple Leaf Trot; winner of close to 1000 career races, several Greenwood dash titles; among his top horses were Lynden Bye Bye, Armbro Express, Vandella and Norbeth Hanover; mem. Cdn Horse Racing Hall of Fame.

McKINNON, Archie (all-around); b. 19 Aug 1896, Glasgow, Scotland, d. 25 Dec 1984, Victoria, B.C.; m. Dorothy Bell Aird; c. Dorothy Joan, Isabel Ann, Heather Anne; Washington, YMCA School Sealbeck, Wash.; phys ed dir.; competed and/or coached Commonwealth teams '28-

61; '28 Olympic competitor, '32 diving coach, '36 t&f coach, '48 diving, swimming coach, '52 swimming coach; various awards including naming of Victoria YM-YWCA pool, UVic athletic complex in his honor; Freeman City of Victoria '61; CAPHER Tait McKenzie award '81; mem. Cdn Amateur, BC Sports halls of fame.

McKINNON, Frank (all-around); b. 16 Jun 1934, Wellwood, Man.; m. Bonnie Lynn Cachran; c. Jeffrey, Kevin; Brandon College, BSc, BPaed, UMan, BEd; school principal; mem. divisional HS t&f title team '51; jr. hockey Brandon Wheat Kings; mem. 3 Man. sr. baseball title teams; 2 Western fastball title teams; '55 WIAU hockey scoring title; 10yrs MAHA exec., 5yrs pres; 5yrs dir. CAHA; chair. CAHA awards comm. '77-78; mem. CAHA restructing comm.; 2yrs v-pCAHA Senior, Intermediate hockey; 2yrs CAHA v-p in charge of development; mem. Man. Hockey Players Foundation; 4yrs v.-chair. Man. advisory council FAS; mem. ntl advisory council COTHA; mem. organizing comm. 1st world jr. hockey tournament; mem. Carman baseball comm. '67 Pan-Am Games; chair. '78 Pembina Valley winter games; 2yrs pres. Carman-Dufferin MHA; Centennial Cup trustee; coached provincial title basketball, baseball, hockey teams; also t&f, volleyball, soccer coach; dir., v-p SFC; v-p COA; mem. IIHF congress '79-81; chair. CAHA '79-81; CAHA award for contribution to minor hockey '77; mem. Man. Hockey, Sports halls of fame; res. Carman, Man.

McKNIGHT, Becky (table tennis); b. 25 Mar 1965, Brampton, Ont.; ntl mixed doubles '81, jr. singles '82; 2 US jr. singles titles; Elaine Tanner Trophy '80; last known res. Brampton, Ont.

McKOY, Mark (t&f); b. 10 Dec 1961, Georgetown, Guyana; York., Louisiana State; m. Yvette Grabner; c. 2; hurdle specialist; 4 ntl 110m hurdles, 2 50m hurdles, 1 4x200m relay titles; CIAU 50m, 50m hurdles, 4x200, 4x400 relay titles; gold 110m hurdles '82, '86, gold 4x100m relay '86, silver '82 Commonwealth Games; bronze 110m hurdles '83 FISU Games; world indoor 60m hurdles bronze '91; gold '92 Japan meet; Cdn 110m hurdles record 13.11 '92; mem. '83 Pan-Am, '84, '88, '92 Olympic Games teams; 7 ntl, 2 CIAU indoor t&f, 1 Commonwealth, Commonwealth Games, world records; outstanding male athlete '82 ntl outdoor championships; fed. govt. excellence award '83; 3rd international superstars competition '82; suspended 2yrs for leaving '88 Olympic team without notice; 1 CIAU indoor t&f male athlete of yr award; became Austrian citizen '94; mem. Cdn Amateur Sports Hall of Fame; res. Traun, Austria/ Toronto, Ont.

McLAREN, Grant (t&f); b. 19 Aug 1948, Paris, Ont.; m. Janet Manley; c. Christopher, Heather;Guelph, BSc, UWO, PhD; dairy farmer; CWOSSA 2-mile title '65, ntl jr. cross-country '67, OQAA 3-mile '68, Canada Games steeplechase, 5000m '69, OQAA 1500m, 5000m, steeplechase '70, Philadelphia 2-mile, Drake Relays 3-mile '72, Pan-Pacific Games 5000m '73, Montreal France-Canada dual meet 3000m '74; mem. Toronto Olympic Club;GuelphU athlete of '68-69; outstanding CIAU track athlete '70; UWO athlete of '72-73; ntl records indoor 2-mile, outdoor 3-mile, 3000m, 5000m, steeplechase, 2000m;

3:59 mile '72; mem. '71, '75 Pan-Am Games, '70, '74 Commonwealth Games, '72, '76 Olympic teams; mem. GuelphU, W-Club Sports halls of fame; res. Drumbo, Ont.

McLAREN, Robert (t&f); b. 19 Apr 1945, Victoria, B.C.; m. Nancy Oldfield; c. Lindsay, Brian; Oregon State, BSc; supervisor BC Telephone; equalled ntl HS 100yd record 9.8; 3-yr letterman Oregon State track team; '66 ntl indoor 300yd title; silver 1600m relay, ntl record 3:04.8, bronze 400m hurdles, ntl record 51.4, '67 Pan-Am Games; reduced 400m mark to 50.7 '68; mem. '68 Olympic team; res. N. Vancouver, B.C.

McLARNIN, Jimmy (boxing); b. 19 Dec 1907, Belfast, Ireland; m. Lillian Cupit; c. Grace Ellen, Jean, Nancy, Jim; retd. chromium plating business; began boxing age 12, pro at 16; unbeaten 19 straight bouts; protegee of Pop Foster who guided him through success and left him a fortune; lost world lightweight title bid in 15 to Sammy Mandell '28 NYC; KO'd Young Corbett III in 1st for world welterweight crown '33 LA; lost title in 15 to Barney Ross '34 NYC; regained title beating Ross in 15 same year; again lost title to Ross in 15 '35 NYC; retd. from ring '36; pro record 77 fights winning 20 by KO, 42 on decision, 1 on foul, 3 draws, 10 losses on decision, 1 on TKO (due to cut under eye); Canada's boxer of half century '50 CP poll; mem. US, Canadian Boxing, BC, Canada's Sports halls of fame; last known res. Glendale, Calif.

McLAUGHLIN, Dean (horseshoes); b. 7 Mar 1921, Oshawa, Ont.; m. Wilma; c. Steven Brant, Dale Mary; retd. store owner; 6 Ont. men's singles titles; 13 ntl men's singles titles; NA champion '60, runnerup '67; twice placed in top 16 world tournament; set world record 91.6% avg. 5 consec. games; 1st Cdn to qualify in championship division at World tournament; manufactured own brand of horseshoes; mem. NHPA. Horseshoe Canada, Oshawa Sports halls of fame; res. Oshawa, Ont.

McLAUGHLIN, Frank (sailing); b. 15 Apr 1960, Toronto, Ont.; UofT; lawyer; began sailing age 9; ntl jr. Fireball champion '77; mem. ntl team from '82; 3 ntl 420 titles; Ont. Laser titles '80-81; 470 bronze '83 Pan-Am Games; mem. '84, '88, '92 Olympic teams; '88 Olympic Flying Dutchman bronze with John Millen; CORK FD titles '89-90; worlds bronze '86; father Paul 2 time Olympian; brother FD skipper Terry McLaughlin; res. Toronto, Ont.

McLAUGHLIN, Jack (golf); b. 31 Dec 1933, Ottawa, Ont.; d. 23 Jan 1991,Palm Springs, Calif.; m. Marilyn; c. Jim, Mike, Kelly, Ed; St. Mike's Coll; jr. Scarborough G&CC; 2nd Ont. jr.; won Ont. jr. best ball; capt. St. Mike's golf team; turned pro '53; pro Cedar Brae '56-60, Bayview CC (Toronto) '61-73, Shaughnessy (Vancouver) '74-91; quarterfinalist Millar match; personal low 67 Brantford; served on numerous CPGA, Ont., BC committees; head coach CLGA ntl team '88-91; launched jr.-jr. golf programs for ages 4-11; helped start UBC golf program; 1st Cdn pro invited to teach US pros at their business school '73-74; ranked as one of Canada's top teaching pros.

McLAUGHLIN, Sam (horse racing); b. 8 Sep 1871, Enniskillen, Ont., d. 6 Jan 1972, Oshawa, Ont.; given name:

Robert Samuel; m. Adelaide Louise Mowbray (d); c. 5 daughters; York, LLD; chair. GMC; many cycling awards as youth; as sailor won '25 Richardson Cup and championship of Great Lakes; entered first horse show '26 with jumpers; won 1500 ribbons, 400 trophies on Canada, US circuit; concentrated on breeding, racing thoroughbreds with his Parkwood Stables; produced King's/Queen's Plate winners Horometer '34, Kingarvie '46, Moldy '47; v-p, dir. Jockey Club, Ltd.; mem. Canadian Horse Racing, Canada's, Oshawa Sports halls of fame.

McLAUGHLIN, Terry (sailing); b. 24 Jul 1956, Toronto, Ont.; stockbroker; national, NA, Can-Am, 2 CORK Flying Dutchman titles; skipper Clipper Xerox Challenge Cup series; skipper Canada 1 America's Cup series; gold FD '80, bronze '83 world championships; mem. '80, '84 Olympic team; with Ev Bastet FD silver '84 Olympics; mem. runnerup SFC team of '80; fed. govt. excellence award '83; res. Toronto, Ont.

McLEAN, Arnold (golf); b. 4 Jun 1928, Montreal, Que.; m. Lavina Jean Matheson; c. Arnold Jr., Brian, Donna; Sir George Williams.; golf dir., master pro; junior hockey, baseball; Que. jr. golf title '41; Que. PGA '54, Spring Open '61; runnerup Que. Open '54; pres. QPGA '59-60, CPGA '76-77; mem. Cdn Golf Superintendant's Assn., Professional Golf Club Repairman's Assn.; res. Lorraine, Que.

McLEAN, Kenny (rodeo); b. 17 May 1939, Penticton, B.C.; m. Penny Wise; c. Guy, Tracey, Steven, Jill; rancher; 5 ntl saddle bronc, 1 calf roping, steer wrestling, 3 all-around titles; US rodeo circuit rookie of '61; world saddle bronc title '62; 3 times winner of competition limited to participation by world's top 15 saddle bronc riders; twice winner Bill Linderman award (open only to winners of $1,000 in three events); has remodeled ancestral homestead to provide area in which he trains horses and conducts school for team roping; conducts team roping and saddle bronc clinics on request; mem. Order or Canada, Okanagan, BC Sports halls of fame; res. Okanagan Falls, B.C.

McLEISH, Robin (skiing); b. 3 Sep 1956, Ottawa, Ont.; given name: Robin Ramsay; m. Ann Holtshousen; downhill specialist; began skiing age 9; mem. national alpine team '77-84; Can-Am overall, dh titles '77; Pontiac Cup dh Mont. Ste. Anne '76-77, '80; '81 Shell Cup dh, combined, FIS dh; WC circuit 17th Crans Montana, Val Gardena dh '79; twice Ottawa ACT alpine award; Kanata civic award; last known res. Toronto, Ont.

McLELLAND, Ivan (hockey); b. 15 Mar 1931, Campbell's Bay, Que; m. Faye Amos; c. David, Bonnie, Rhonda; GM Okanagan Mfgrs. Ltd.; goaler South Porcupine jrs. '45-47; NO jr. title '47; mem. St. Catharines TeePees '47-48; South Porcupine Porkies '48-50; NO sr. title '49-50; Penticton Vees '50-56; Western Cdn sr. title '52-53, Allan Cup '53-54, World championship '55; from 14 Mar '55 to 15 Aug '81 was only goaler to shut out Russians in international competition; res. Pentiction, B.C.

McLEOD, Barbara (t&f); b. 20 Oct 1937, Timmins, Ont.; given name: Barbara Caswell; m. Bill McLeod; began running age 43 to "get in shape" and evolved into veritable running machine; ultramarathon specialist; women 50-54 world 6day 393miles, 48hours 177miles, indoor 24hours 113miles records; women 55-59 world 50mile, 50km road/ track records; 9 NA age 50-59 records; 27 Cdn Masters Women 40+ records; has run throughout world in such locales as Greece, China, Spain, USA and Canada; ran 4 ultras in '96 placing 1st woman, 4th overall in 3; 9 Gloucester Sports awards; 2 Gloucester outstanding achievement awards; Breakthrough award '90; Ottawa ACT award '89; 4 Ont. sports awards; mem. Cdn Road Running, Ottawa Sports halls of fame; res. Gloucester, Ont.

McLEOD, Jackie (hockey/baseball); b. 30 Apr 1930, Hazlet, Sask.; given name: Robert John; m. Beverly Evans; c. Don, Patti; Notre Dame College; hockey exec., chief pilot Concorde Group; jr. ND Coll. '45-47; jr. Moose Jaw Canucks '47-49; pro NY Rangers '49-55; Saskatoon, Vancouver, Calgary (WHL) '55-60; world champion Trail Smoke Eaters '61; sr. Saskatoon, Moose Jaw '62-65; coach/ GM ntl team '65-70; coach/GM/owner WHL Saskatoon Blades '70-80; scoring title, all-star right winger '61 World Cup; Centennial tournament champions '67; in youth star pitcher, 1st baseman; mem. Sask. jr. champ Gull Lake Lakers, North Battleford Beavers 4 titles; player/coach/mgr. Swift Current Indians 10yrs; developed Swift Current minor baseball system; retd from baseball '66; offered minor league contract by Chicago Cubs; mem. Sask. Baseball Hall of Fame; res. Saskatoon, Sask.

McLEOD, Lawrence (parachuting); b. 25 Feb 1957, Campbell River B.C.; UBC; commercial pilot, air traffic controller; began skydiving '76; A class instructor; 1st '80 Cdn 8-way; alternate 1st-place Cdn 4-way; last known res. Vancouver, B.C.

McLOUGHLIN, Mark (football); b. 26 Oct 1965, Liverpool, Eng.; South Dakota; kicker; CFL with Calgary '88-99; CFL record (through '98): 190gp, 469fg, 603cvts, 116s, 2126pts; 4 Western, 1 Northern, 1 CFL all-star; 3 CFL scoring titles; 3 Dave Dryburgh Memorial trophies; Tom Pate Memorial award '95; 3 Grey Cup finals, 1 winner; USD athlete/academic of yr award; implemented Calgary "Stay in School" program; involved in Calgary Educational Partnership Foundation; res. Calgary, Alta.

McMAHON, David (biathlon); b. 6 May 1964, Middleton, N.S.; div. Michelle; c. Katie, Christoph; RMC, B. Eng.; computer engineer; elite competitor in biathlon, cross-country skiing, mountain running; 2 Canada Cup biathlon series titles; 5 ntl biathlon championship medals; ntl title '93; once ranked 3rd in world summer biathlon; top North American '97 world Loppet ski racing circuit; 7th world masters '98; coach at Olympic level; conducts masters ski camps; res. Chelsea, Que.

McMAHON, Gary (shooting); b. 25 Feb 1932, Roland, Man.; given name: Garfield Walter; m. Ruby Bertha Fulton; Brandon, BSc, UBC, MSc; research scientist; 1st of 3 ntl open handgun titles '58; NS handgun title '59-66; mem. '60, '64 Olympic, '62 (5th free pistol), '66 world, '59, '63, '67, '71 Pan-Am Games, '66 Commonwealth Games teams; bronze individual centrefire, team free pistol '59 Pan-Am Games; 3 silver, 1 bronze indiviual centrefire '63 Pan-Am

Games; bronze free pistol '66 Commonwealth Games; silver centrefire team '72 Pan-Am Games; best international performer '62 worlds; res. Stewiacke, N.S.

McMAHON, John (soccer/administration); b. 9 Apr 1922, Glasgow, Scotland; m. Ivy; c. Bill, Marilyn; retd sports administrator; immigrated to Watrous, Sask., '23 but returned to Scotland during Depression where he honed soccer skills; played Glasgow jr. league; joined Scottish FA as referee '46; officiated Scottish pro league; returning to Canada officiated in Toronto '51-54; dir. Toronto Church SL; 1st pres. TDMSA '59; introduced minor soccer to Toronto boroughs; dir. OMSA; exec. Toronto City Eastern Canada pro team '61-82; had role in formation NASL; mgr. ntl team '71-73, GM '74-82; life mem. CSA; v-p CSA Alumni; mem. OSA Heritage comm.; res. Toronto, Ont.

McMANN, Chuck (football); b. 11 May 1951, Toronto, Ont., m. Margaret; c. Kristin, Jeffery, Jonathan; Wilfrid Laurier; teacher, football coach; 2 CIAU all-star teams, team MVP '75; running back 10 CFL seasons Montreal Alouette/ Concordes; asst. coach Waterloo '88-91; guest coach Calgary '90-91; asst. Calgary from '92; 3 Grey Cup winners; res. Calgary, Alta.

McMANUS, Danny (football); b. 17 Jun 1965, Dania, Fla.; m. Kim; c. Kelsey; Florida State; quarterback, distribution business owner; '88 Fiesta Bowl MVP; FSU player of yr '86-87; drafted by Kansas City (NFL) '88; joined CFL with Winnipeg '90-92, BC '93-95, Edmonton '96-97, Hamilton from '98; CFL record (through '98): 156gp, 2988passes, 1589comp., 23,998yds, 131int, 118td; 5 Grey Cup finals, 2 winners; res. Indianapolis, Indiana.

McMILLAN, Leigh (football); b. 8 Nov 1935, Edmonton Alta.; given name: Herbert Leigh; m. Aline Baril; c. Linda, Karen, John; Denver, BSc, UAlta, BEd, graduate dip. Vocational Guidance; HS teacher, counsellor; halfback, safety Edmonton '56-58; averaged 5.4yds per carry on 66 punt returns '56 Grey Cup champions; Edm. club record 93 punt returns '58; mem. Alta. champion Lacombe Rockets Intermediate A hockey team '60-61; UAlta Golden Bears CIAU hockey champions '63-64; coach minor hockey, soccer, fastball, sr. football Austin O'Brien HS; res. Edmonton, Alta.

McMILLAN, Roy (curling); b. 1 Apr 1893, Stratford, Ont. d. 28 Nov 1983, Ottawa, Ont.; m. Helen Belyea; c. Jean, Dorothy, Catherine, Donald; UofT; chemical engineer, teacher; won Royal Victoria Jubilee, Royal Caledonia; Branch Governor-General's 3 times, runnerup 4 times, srs. twice; twice reached Ont. srs. playdowns; mem. Governor-Generals CC; life mem. CBRCCC, OCA, Rideau CC.

McMURRAY, Mary (curling); b. 6 Mar 1896, Newcastle, N.B.; d, 1986, Bathurst, N.B.; m. Andrew M. McMurray (d); c. Betty; through 41 consecutive years played major role in spreading curling gospel through Maritimes; hon. mem. Bathurst CC, Que. City Cambrai CC; hon. life mem. NBLCA; mem. Canadian Curling Hall of Fame.

McNAB, Peter (hockey); b. 8 May 1952, Vancouver, B.C.; given name: Peter Maxwell; div. c. Shanon, Robyn; Denver;

hockey broadcaster; son of 47-yr hockey exec. Max McNab, brother Dave Anaheim AGM; centre Denver '71-73; pro AHL Cincinnati, NHL Buffalo '73-76, Boston '76-84, Vancouver '84-85, New Jersey '85-87; NHL record: 954 scheduled games, 363g, 450a, 107 playoff games, 40g, 42a; began broadcasting NJ Sports Channel '87-95; moved into similar role Colorado '95; highly involved in community affairs, charitable works; res. Littleton, Colo.

McNAMARA, Bob (football); b. 12 Aug 1931, Hastings, Minn.; m. Annette; c. Anne, Suzy, Bobby; Minnesota, BSc; all-American halfback Minn. '54; Winnipeg (CFL) '55-58; Denver (NFL) '60-61; all-Cdn '56 with 1101yds rushing on 178 carries for 17 TDs; CFL record 36 points single game at Vancouver tieing Lorne Benson for most TDs single game (6); US paddleball doubles title '58, singles '70; US International, Canadian masters racquetball champion '76; res. Minneapolis, Minn.

McNAMARA, George (hockey); b. 26 Aug 1886, Penetanguishene, Ont., d. 10 Mar 1952, Sault Ste. Marie, Ont.; major hockey debut with Michigan Sault; Montreal Shamrocks (ECL) '08-09, Halifax Cresents (MPL) 3 seasons, Toronto Tecumsehs '12-13, Toronto Ontarios '13-14 season; Cdn Army 228th Sportsman's Battalion team NHA; coached Sault Greyhounds to '24 Allan Cup; mem. Hockey Hall of Fame.

McNAMEE, Kathleen (swimming); b. 8 Jan 1931, Vancouver, B.C.; given name: Kathleen Mavis; div. Rich Ferguson; c. David, Jeanne, John; UBC,UofT, SFU; dir. volunteer personnel, Vancouver YWCA; competed 10yrs under coach Percy Norman at VASC; mem. '48, '52 Olympic, '50 BEG teams; ntl 200yd, 400yd FS records; organized, coached 1st competitive swim club Burlington, Ont. '69-75, guiding 5 swimmers to ntl team status, 1 to Olympic level; Beatrice Pines Trophy as Canada's outstanding female swimmer '52; last known res. N. Vancouver, B.C.

McNAUGHTON, Don (builder); b. 18 Jul 1926, Montreal, Que.; given name: Donald William; m. Barbara Ann Little; c. Tim, John, Susan, Ann; Sir George Williams, Loyola Coll, Concordia; retd. pres./CEO Schenley Canada; average athlete in youth earning swimming, mile running medals; coordinated CFL Schenley awards 1963-88; mem. Cdn Football Hall of Fame; res. Westmount, Que.

McNAUGHTON, Duncan (t&f); b. 7 Dec 1910, Cornwall, Ont.; d. 1998, Austin, Tex.; given name: Duncan Anderson; m. Eileen Frances Garrioch; c. Diane, Sheila, Ellen; SouthernCal, BA, PhD, CalTech, MSc; consulting geologist; capt., coach '29 provincial basketball champions; individual titles '29 Vancouver HS track meet, BC HS Olympiad; mem. USC track team; disqualified for illegal jumping techniques '30 BEG; change to conventional Western roll resulted in California state title, State high jump record; US intercollegiate high jump title '33; gold '32 Olympics clearing 6'6"; mem. Cdn Amateur, Cornwall, BC, Canada's Sports halls of fame.

McNICHOL, Doug (football); b. 29 Mar 1930, St. Catharines, Ont.; given name: Douglas Stewart; m. Clara

MacFarlane; c. Scott, Cameron, Clara;UWO, BA; retd. company pres.; basketball UWO '49-53, team capt. '51-52; football UWO '49-53, all-star status 3yrs; pro Montreal '53-60, 4yrs all-star defensive end; defensive end, tackle Toronto '61-63; twice *Weekend Magazine* all-star; asst. coach ntl sr. champion East York Argos '66, Bramalea Satellites '67; pres. Ont. Midget Football League '79-80; mem. UWO Sports Hall of Fame; res. Mississauga, Ont.

McNICOLL, Bruce (triathlon); b. 29 Aug 1958, Berne, Switzerland; m. LeeAnne; c. Mallory; Carleton, BA, UofOtt, BEd; teacher; victor in more than 50 triathlons '82-91; 5 Ntl Capital, 4 OAC-Gatineau triathlon titles; mem. Ntl Elite '86, Ont. Elite teams '89-90; ntl age group team '90; competed in Canada, US, Japan; 3 all-American status awards by *Triathlon Today* magazine; PB 1:51.59 for certified Olympic distance triathlon Boston; res. Gloucester, Ont.

McNIE, Murray (t&f); b. 17 Nov 1902, Glasgow, Scotland; d. 27 Nov 1982, London, Ont.; Glasgow Coll. of Electro-Therapy, Medical Massage; retired trainer, track coach; asst. t&f coach, trainer '36, '48 Olympic teams; coach, trainer UWO '34-68; CIAU, UWO citations for contribution to football over 35yrs.; mem. UWO Sports Hall of Fame.

McPHEE, Barry (curling); b. 24 Mar 1947, Kamloops, B.C.; m. Karen; c. Erin, Nicole, Spencer, Angela; golf professional; began curling age 12; skipped BC 4 Briers; lost extra-end semifinal to Russ Howard '86 Brier; res. Kamloops, B.C.

McPHEE, Peter (curling); b. 18 Oct 1946, Halifax, N.S.; given name: Peter Ross; m. Louise; promotions supervisor; 3rd NS entry '78-80, '82, '85 Brier; 2nd team all-star 3rd '78 Brier; res. Dartmouth, N.S.

McPHERSON, Don (builder); b. 1918, Regina, Sask.; d. 1973, Regina, Sask.; dir. Sask. Roughriders '49-73; pres. CFL '59, CRU '63, WFC '65; on invitation chaired comm. which reorganized BC Lions; life mem. BC Lions; mem. Cdn Football Hall of Fame.

McPHERSON, Donald (figure skating); b. 20 Feb 1945, Windsor, Ont.; given name: John Donald; figure skating teacher; Western Ont. novice title '57, sr. '58-59, ntl jr. '59; 1st Canadian to win ntl, NA, world amateur titles in single year ('63); world pro title '65; 10th '60 Olympics; 11yrs mem. Holiday on Ice show; mem. Canada's Sports Hall of Fame; res. Munich, Germany.

McQUARTERS, Ed (football); b. 16 Apr 1943, Tulsa, Okla.; given name: Eddie Lee; m. PaulElla; c. Ed Jr., Mike; Oklahoma; advertising supervisor; HS discus, shot put records; state wrestling title; 2nd Big 8 wrestling tournament '62; mem. '63 Gator Bowl team; St. Louis (NFL) '64-65, Saskatchewan (CFL) '66-74; Schenley lineman of '67; all-Cdn 3yrs; WFC outstanding lineman twice; mem. Cdn Football Hall of Fame; res. Regina, Sask.

McRAE, Ed (cycling); b. 13 Apr 1953, Kamloops, B.C.; given name: Edward Renner; SFU, BA; industrial sales rep.; NA jr. title '70; 5 times BC road racing champion; mem.

'71 Pan-Am, '72 Olympic, '73 world championships teams; only Canadian to win gold medal in international Grand Prix (US '73); res. Vancouver, B.C.

McREAVY, Pat (hockey); b. 16 Jan 1918, Owen Sound, Ont.; given name: Patrick Joseph; m. Evelyn Baker Burns; St. Michael's Coll.; auto service mgr.; jr. Owen Sound, St. Mike's Majors, Coppercliff Redmen, Sudbury Wolves; pro Boston '39-42; mem. '41 Stanley Cup winners; Detroit '42; closed pro career with St. Louis AHL; mem. Owen Sound Mercurys Allan Cup champions '51; coached Mercurys 2yrs; oldtimers hockey to retirement age 62; res. Owen Sound, Ont.

McROBERTS, Brit (t&f); b. 10 Feb 1957, Copenhagen, Denmark; given name: Brit Lind-Petersen; m. Dale McRoberts; SFU; 800m, 1500m specialist; mem. '79 Pan-Am, '84 Olympic Games, '79, '81 World Cup, '81 Pacific Conf. Games teams; ntl 1500m title '80-81; unbeaten outdoors '80; gold 1500m '81 Pacific Conf. Games; silver, bronze 1500m *Toronto Star, Ottawa Citizen*, gold 800m *Edmonton Journal* indoor Games '81; despite stress fracture in right foot, which sidelined her 7 weeks, claimed Dublin, WC trials gold; 2nd 5th Ave. mile New York with PB 4:28.3 '81, 2nd FA mile '83; *Toronto Star* 1500m, US ntl mile titles '84; 4 ntl records; PB 800m 2:01.6 (Zurich '81), 1500m 4:09.6 (Rome WC '81); ntl track athlete of '81 nominee; BC track athlete of '81; Vic Andrew Trophy (Lower Mainland amateur athlete of '81); last known res. Coquitlam, B.C.

McTAGUE, Mike (football); b. 31 May 1958, Toronto, Ont.; North Dakota State; all-conf. wide receiver, placement kicker '78-79; capt. NDS Bisons '79, MVP, hon. mention all-American; 7 school scoring, receiving records; 3 conf. records; all-time leading scorer; numerous HS triple, long jump records; territorial draft Toronto '78; CFL punter Calgary from '79-84; last known res. Calgary, Alta.

McTAVISH, Bill (curling); b. 13 Jul 1917, Winnipeg, Man.; given name: William Boyd; m. Ann; c. Jamie, John, Gordon, Billy; UMan, BSc, MD; retd. general practitioner; 22 consecutive victories '50 Winnipeg bonspiel, winning Brinks, Eatons, grand aggregate, British Consols trophies; runnerup '50 Brier, Man. srs. titles '73-74, ntl srs. '73; with sons John, Gordon, Billy competed in '76 Perth, Scotland, Invitational Master's; res. Winnipeg, Man.

McWHIRTER, Cliff (boxing); b. 19 Apr 1913, London, Ont.; given name: Clifford Gilbert; m. Mary Warbeck; c. Lloyd Gary, David Clifford; Wells Business Academy; retd. insurance co. supervisor; Western Ont. featherweight title age 14; several Golden Gloves titles before turning pro '32; campaigned under ring name of Babe La Varre; on 1st boxing card ever staged at Maple Leaf Gardens; career total: 157 bouts, won 136, lost 17, 4 draws; never KO'd; trainer, mgr., promoter; handled Bob Flannigan, Jackie 'Spider' Armstrong, Teddy Swain, Gil Geekie, all of Toronto; mem. Canadian Boxing Hall of Fame; res. London, Ont.

MEAD, Noel (speedboat racing); b. 10 Oct 1941, Ottawa, Ont.; given name: Noel Charles; m. Nartha Jose; c. Trisha, Wil, Scott; Ashbury Coll.; sales rep.; ntl record C service runabout '65; NA grand prix hydroplane champion '75 Gold Cup; originated Festival Canada hydroplane championships at Ottawa '72, title '74; originated, developed international GP hydroplane class competition; campaigned in 1st hydroplane GP circuit in history; retired from racing '76; last known res. Acapulco, Mexico.

MEAGHER, Aileen (t&f); b. 26 Nov 1910, Edmonton, Alta.; d. 2 Aug 1987, Halifax, N.S.; given name: Aileen Alethea; Dalhousie, BA; retired teacher; qualified '32 Olympics as sprinter but severe charley horse prevented participation; gold 660yds relay, silver 440yd relay, 220yd sprint '34 BEG; bronze 400m relay, 100m semifinalist '36 Olympics; silver 440yd, bronze 660yd relay, 4th 220yd finals '38 BEG; Bobbie Rosenfeld Trophy '35; mem. Cdn Amateur Sports Hall of Fame.

MEAGHER, Dan (basketball); b. 25 Oct 1962, Kingston, Ont.; Duke; travel agent; mem. national team '82-88; forward 2nd place Jones Cup team '82, gold medal FISU Games team '83; mem. '83 Pan-Am, '84 Olympic teams; fed. govt. excellence award '84; last known res. Miami, Fla.

MEAGHER, Robyn (t&f); b 17 Jun 1967, Antigonish, N.S.; UVic; research officer; middle distance specialist; started competing age 12; ntl jr. 1500 title '84; ntl indoors 1500m title '86; silver '88 CIAU championships; won '89NY Games mile; ntl 3000m title '91; CIAU, ntl indoor 1500m title '90; competed in '90, '94 Commonwealth, '91 Worlds, '92, '96 Olympic Games; silver 3000m '94 Commonwealth Games; President's Cup UVic '90, Athletics Canada athlete of '94; res. Victoria, B.C.

MEEKER, Howie (hockey); b. 4 Nov 1923, New Hamburg, Ont.; given name: Howard William; m. Grace Vera Hammer; c. Jane, Peggy, Kim, Howie Jr., Michael, Andy; corp. pres.; Maple Leafs '46-54; part of 2nd generation Kid Line with Vic Lynn, Teeder Kennedy; NHL Calder Trophy '47; mem. 4 Stanley Cup winners; coached Stratford '52, Pittsburgh (AHL) to '54 Calder Cup victory; at 32 youngest Maple Leafs coach '56-57; 5 months Leafs GM before being fired by Stafford Smythe; operates boys' hockey schools Parksville, B.C., Potsdam, N.Y., Vancouver; CBC Hockey Night in Canada color commentator, analyst; retd as TSN hockey analyst '98; author several hockey instruction books; autobiography "*Golly Gee - It's Me*"; MP (PC) Waterloo South '51-53; mem. Hockey, Waterloo County halls of fame; res. Parksville, B.C.

MEHLENBACHER, Jack (harness racing/officiating); b. 14 Mar 1922, Nelles Corners, Ont.; given name: Jack Leslie; m. Geraldine Austin; c. Jack Jr., Jerry, Jane, Joanne; seed merchant/farmer/standardbred horse breeder; catcher Ont. champion Hagersvile Int. B baseball team '39; referee OHA in '40s officiating in Memorial, Allan Cup finals; referee NHL '50s; driving Vanduzen won Toronto Maple Leaf trot at Thorncliffe Raceway '53; through '50s and '60s among leading drivers at Thorncliffe, Batavia Downs, Buffalo Raceway; res. Cayuga, Ont.

MEISSNER, Ernie (diving); b. 29 May 1937, Belgrade, Yugoslavia; Michigan; pres. travel bureau chain; all-American; 11 ntl titles '58-68; 3m bronze '62 Commonwealth Games; 5th 3m '60 Olympics; mem. Waterloo County Hall of Fame; res. Kitchener, Ont.

MEISZTER, Ernst (coaching); b. 18 Apr 1921, Cluj, Romania; accredited fencing master; 1st class water polo player; began fencing '39; mem. Romanian national team '46-58, capt. '52 Olympic team; coach Romanian team '49-62, Brazil national team '64-65; emigrated to Canada '66; coach Cdn team '75 Pan-Am, '76 Olympic Games; fencing instructor Humber Coll., Brock, Toronto Unicorn Club; operates Meister Fencing Academy Willowdale; res. Willowdale, Ont.

MELDRUM, Jenny (t&f); b. 12 Apr 1943, Northampton, Eng.; given name: Jennifer Anne Wingerson; div.; c. Samantha, Gregory; m. Stewart Madill; secretary; hurdles, pentathlon specialist; hurdles silver '63 Pan-Am, bronze '66BEG; pentathlon silver '67 Pan-Am, bronze '70 Commonwealth Games; mem. '63, '67, '71 Pan-Am, '66, '70 BE/Commonwealth, '64, '68 Olympic teams; qualified for '72 Olympics but opted for retirement; national pentathlon, hurdles, long jump records; asst. mgr. '75 Pan-Am t&f team; CBC t&f color commentator; res. Coquitlam, B.C.

MELESCHUK, Orest (curling); b. 11 Apr 1940, St. Boniface, Man.; m. Patricia Frances McSherry; c. Sean, Karin; United Coll.; engineering tech.; nicknamed 'Big O'; Man. University champion, Charleswood carspiel, CBC televised series; '74 Grey Cup 'spiel Toronto; competed 8 prov. championships winning Man. Consols, Brier, Silver Broom '72; Sudbury Superspiel '76; res. St. Boniface, Man.

MELOCHE, Gilles (hockey); b. 12 Jul 1950, Montreal, Que.; m. Sophie; c. Eric, Annie; coach/scout; goaltender Verdun jrs, Flint (IHL); NHL Chicago '70-71, California '71-76, Cleveland '76-78, Minnesota '78-85, Pittsburgh '85-88; NHL record: 988 scheduled games, 270-351-131, 45,401min, 2756ga, 20so, 45 playoff games, 21-19-0, 2464min, 143ga, 2so; turned to coaching '89-99; goalie coach/scout Pittsburgh; res. Rosemere, Que.

MELOCHE, Lise (biathlon); b. 19 Apr 1960, Ottawa, Ont.; Ottawa, B.Sc, B.Ed; teacher, exercise physiologist; 2 time Olympian, one of best technical skiers in country; mem. ntl biathlon, cross-country ski teams '84-94; 3rd overall ranking World Cup series '86; World Cup gold '91; pioneer in women's biathlon; won ntl, U.S., Swiss titles; competes as pro elite skier; coaches high performance athletes; res: Chelsea, Que.

MELVIN, Doug (administration/baseball); b. 8 Aug 1952, Chatham, Ont.; m. Ellen; c. Ashley, Cory; baseball exec.; standout HS athlete starring in football, basketball, hockey Chatham Kent SS; mem. CKSS athletic Hall of Fame; credits Ferguson Jenkins with helping him decide to pursue pro baseball career; pitched 6yrs Pittsburgh, Yankee organizations; worked in Yankee organization '79-85, scouting dir. '85; 9yrs Baltimore organization serving in such varied roles as dir. player personnel/asst. GM '86-94; became GM Texas '94, exec.v-p '96; *Sporting News* ML exec. of '96, Baseball America AL exec. of '96; mem. Texas Baseball Hall of Fame; res. Southlake, Tex.

MERAW, Ann (swimming); b. 23 Feb 1917, Powell River, B.C.; given name: Barbara Annabelle Mundigel; m. Joseph Meraw (d); c. William; Pittman Business College; retd. aquatic dir.; established reputation for swimming endurance by negotiating 10 miles across Howe Sound and back age 10; after claiming all available amateur honors turned pro at 17 and went on to establish 7 world speed and distance swimming records, including 42 miles in 25 hours 1 minute, 55 miles in 32 hours 12 minutes; became Canada's 1st registered female life guard; known as 'Queen of the Polar Bears', the hardy group of swimmers who brave icy English Bay on New Year's Day; organized 1st water babies program; conducted courses for military, civilian personnel in hazardous jobs and physically challenged; examiner/instructor Royal Life Saving Society `40-70; swim instructor Vancouver parks board `58-70; swim coach `58-82; with husband Joe trained field dogs; coached swimming, field hockey, skiing, basketball, tennis, synchronized swimming, diving, badminton, gymnastics, 1st Vancouver women's baseball team; tech. advisor *Beachcombers* TV series; Canada 125 commemorative medal; hon. life mem. Royal Life Saving Society; recognized in BC Who's Who; organized Ridge Meadows Hall of Fame; mem. BC Sports, Ridge Meadows halls of fame; res. Maple Ridge, B.C.

MERCIER, Michel (weightlifting); b. 2 Oct 1954, La Sarre, Que.; Laval, BPHE; phys ed teacher; Que. 60kg titles '73, '75; ntl 60kg '77-78, '80; Canada Games gold '75; Ottawa International silver 67.5kg '78; Commonwealth Games gold 60kg '78; gold 67.5kg silver, bronze 60kg Commonwealth championships; bronze 60kg Pan-Am championships; Que. weightlifter of year award; res. La Sarre, Que.

MERETSKY, Toots (basketball); b. 17 May 1912, Windsor, Ont.; given name: Irving; m. Eleanor; c. Warren, Lynn, Rodd (d); Assumption Coll.; retd. furniture store owner; began playing basketball in public school; established reputation as deadly shooter and strong court general; mem. '36 silver medal Olympic team; 2yrs playing coach Port Alberni; versatile athlete who quarterbacked HS football team, played shortstop with Windsor Olympics baseball team; mem. Cdn Basketball, Windsor-Essex Sports halls of fame; res. Windsor, Ont.

MERKLINGER, Anne (swimming/curling); b. 15 Nov 1958, London Ont. given name: Anne Lousie; m. Don Michie; c. Meagan, Connor; South Carolina, BSc; swim coach, sports administrator; mem. prominent curling family; curling: bronze '75 Canada Winter Games; silver ntl jr. ladies '76; silver Ont. jr. ladies '78; fifth mem. Alison Goring Ont. title rink '90; skip Ont. women's title rink `93-94, '98; semifinalist '93, finalist '98 Scott Tournament of Hearts; became involved in swimming for theraputic reasons following injury; East. Cdn. 100m, 200m breaststroke titles '76; silver 200m breaststroke '77 FISU Games; mem. ntl swim team '77-79; finalist Coca-Cola intl '79; capt. Uof SC swim team '81; all-American 8 events '79-81; dean's list Uof SC '78-81; Ottawa ACT swimming awards '77, '79; Breakthrough leadership award '97; Johnny F. Bassett award '98; exec. dir. Cdn Canoe Assn.; res. Ottawa, Ont.

MERKLINGER, Bill (curling); b. 30 May 1956, Montreal, Que.; given name: William Arthur; UofOtt, BPhE; federal government management consultant; competitive swimmer prior to turning attention to curling; Ont. jr men's curling champion '73; rep. PEI '75 Canada Winter Games; competed '75, '82 Maritime men's championships; 3rd for brother Dave '81 Ont. men's Tankard playdowns; skipped PEI to 3rd place with 8-5 record '82 Seagram Mixed; res. Ottawa, Ont.

MERKLINGER, Dave (curling); b. 14 Mar 1955, Montreal, Que.; given name: David Michael; m. Janet Davies; c. Michael, Jennifer; curling ice maker; Ont. jr. tankard '73; Ont. Silver Tankard '76-77, '79; 8 Ont. Tankard (Consols) appearances, 6 as skip; 1 Ont. mixed competition; lead for Earle Morris '85 Ont. Brier rink; skip McCain East Superspiel winner; icemaker ntl STOH '98; res. Nepean, Ont.

MERRICK, Wayne (hockey); b. 23 Apr 1952, Sarnia, Ont.; given name: Leonard Wayne; m. Carol Lee Moore; c. Courtney, Andrew; financial planner; Silver Stick midget tournament MVP '69; jr. Ottawa 67's '69-71; 1st pick St. Louis '72 draft; Denver (WHL) '72; 12 NHL seasons with St. Louis '72-75, California '75-76, Cleveland '76-78, NY Islanders '78-84; NHL record: 774 scheduled games, 191g, 265a, 102 playoff games, 19g, 30a; 4 Stanley Cup winners; scored final game winner vs. Minnesota '81 Stanley Cup; overtime winning goal vs. Quebec '82 Stanley Cup playoffs; res. Lindenhurst, NY/London, Ont.

MERRILL, Horace (canoeing/hockey); b. 30 Nov 1884, Toronto, Ont.; d. 24 Dec 1958, Ottawa, Ont.; given name: Horace Jefferson; m. Phyllis May Parker; c. Bill. Dorothy, Audrey, Lois; retd printing co. pres., school board trustee; standout paddler, hockey, football, soccer, basketball player; backbone of YMCA basketball, soccer, rugby teams `04-08; frequent MVP awards; 3 ntl sr. single blade canoe, 3 sr. war canoe, 1 sr. tandem canoe titles; defenceman Allan Cup champion Cliffsides `09; 7 seasons with Ottawa Senators; 3 Stanley Cup finals, 1 winner; mem. Glebe Curling Club Governor-General's Cup winner `24; secty-treas. Cdn Canoe Assn.; mem. Ottawa Sports Hall of Fame.

MERVYN, Glen (rowing); b. 17 Feb 1937, Vancouver, B.C.; given name: Glen Alexander; m. Christina Maclean; c. Tyler, Sasha; UBC, BSc, Harvard, MEd; pres.-GM ski lift importing, installation bus.; #6 seat '58 BEG gold medal crew, #6 seat '59 Pan-Am Games silver medal crew; stroke '60 Olympic Games silver medal crew; coached UBC crews '63-64; coached ntl crews '64 Olympics, including gold medal pairs Roger Jackson, George Hungerford; mem. 8s crew Cdn championships '58-60; unofficial 2501 full-twist situps record '58 while testing effect of vitamin E on athlete's diet; as mem. '60 Olympic 8s silver medalist inducted into BC Sports Hall of Fame; res. Kelowna, B.C.

MESSIER, Mark (hockey); b. 18 Jan 1961, Edmonton, Alta.; given name: Mark Douglas; c. Lyon; centre Portland (WHL) '77-78, Indianapolis, Cincinnati (WHA) '78-79, Houston (CHL) '79-80; Edmonton's 2nd choice '79 draft; NHL Edmonton '79-91, NY Rangers '91-97, Vancouver '97-99; mem. 3 Canada Cup teams, Team Canada '89 Worlds, '87 Rendez-Vous team; 4 1st team, 1 2nd team all-star; 2 Hart, 2 Pearson, 1 Conn Smythe trophies; mem. 6 Stanley

Cup winners; 14 all-star games; *Sporting, Hockey News* player of '90; NHL record: (through '99) 1413 scheduled games, 610g, 1050a, 236 playoff games, 109g, 186a; joined Wayne Gretzky, Gordie Howe, Marcel Dionne, Phil Esposito on 1500 point plateau '96; reached 600 goals, 1000 assist plateaus '98; proficient golfer; very active in children's charities; mem. Madison Square Gardens Walk of Fame; res. Hilton Head, S.C.

MESSNER, Joe (water skiing); b. 1 Mar 1924, Solbad Hall, Tirol, Austria; m. Linda Ohm-Meier; c. Peter, Bill (d), Patricia; Ferdinand Franzens U. Innsbruck, Handelsakademie, Austria; ntl exec-dir Friends of SOS, ex-exec-dir Children's Aid Society; 42 prov titles; 12 gold, 8 silver, 10 bronze in ntl competition; 4 golds Ont. Games, European srs. title '72, 43 other international medals; competitive record includes 102 1sts, 20 2nds, 9 3rds, variety of prov., ntl records; operator Mesle Sport; 14 special awards, 5 Ont. achievement, 8 Ont. sports achievement, 1 Command Sports award; mem. Cdn Hang Gliding Assn. holds special pilots license for paragliding; res. Ottawa, Ont.

MESSNER, Pat (water skiing); b. 17 Mar 1954, Hamilton, Ont.; given name: Patricia Marilyn; McGill, Carleton; Waterloo BA, UofOtt, BEd, Algonquin Coll.; musician, HS teacher; '64-81 dominated ntl water skiing scene; 15 ntl, 45 Ont. titles; '72 Carl Fisher Cup, '78 US Masters slalom (1st Cdn woman), '76 Western Hemisphere slalom, Aquaba international champion '79, world slalom champion '79 (1st Cdn woman), 44 other tournaments; bronze '69 Canada Summer Games; bronze '72 Olympics (only Cdn); silver '72 Western Hemisphere slalom; bronze '75 world championships (1st Cdn woman); silver '77 world championships (only Cdn); silver '80 World Cup; 10 Ont., 7 Ottawa ACT sports achievement awards, Ottawa ACT athlete of '79, SFC '79 international achievement award; Level 3 master coach; mem. athletes advisory comm. on ntl sports, ntl coaching '76-79; chief instructor Mesle Sport (recreational, competitive instruction for water skiing, windsurfing, kayaking, hang gliding) from '72; OCRAS academic excellence award '85; mem. ntl medical/science comm.; mem. Order of Canada, Ottawa Sports Hall of Fame; res. Carleton Place, Ont.

METRAS, John (coaching); b. 8 Apr 1909, Dowagiac, Mich., d. 13 Apr 1982, Naples, Fla.; given name: John Pius; m. Shirley Goodheart; c. John Jr., Robert, Mary Lynn; Detroit, hon. LLD UWO; coach, AD UWO; all-state HS halfback; all-American mention as center UDet; with St. Mike's Coll. starred in ORFU '33-34; all-Cdn center '34; joined Bill Stern as asst. coach UWO '35, head coach '39-69; football coaching record: 106 wins, 76 losses, 11 ties, 9 league titles; teams once had undefeated run of 29 games; basketball coach '45-64, teams won or shared 14 titles, 24 league-game winning streak; UWO athletic dir. '45-72; nicknamed 'The Bull'; various offical capacities in football, basketball rules-making bodies Canada, US; hon.-pres. Assn. of Cdn. Intercollegiate Football Coaches; trophy in his honor awarded to Cdn. coll. football lineman of year; mem. Cdn Football, UWO Sports halls of fame.

METZ, Nick (hockey); b. 16 Feb 1914, Wilcox, Sask.; d. 24 Aug 1990, Wilcox, Sask; Notre Dame Coll, St. Michael's Coll; began hockey career under Fr. Athol Murray; mem.

'34 Memorial Cup winner; signed with Maple Leafs; following stint with Syracuse farm team rejoined Toronto for playoffs; spent 12 seasons with Leafs scoring 131g, 119a while playing left wing/centre; 9 Stanley Cup finals, 4 winners; record 3 assists 1 period '41 Stanley Cup semifinals vs. Boston; while serving in army WW2 mem. Victoria team which lost to Ottawa in Allan Cup finals; also proficient curler, baseball, lacrosse player; mem. Sask. Sports Hall of Fame.

MEYER, Bill (water polo); b. 4 Nov 1958, Hamilton, Ont.; m. Cathy; c. Kayla; UofOtt; branch mgr. Canada Trust; gold '77 Canada Games; mem. jr. ntl team '76-77, ntl sr. team '77-85; bronze '79, '83 Pan-Am Games; mem. '82 world, '83 FISU, '84 Olympic teams; competed over 200 international games; res. Ottawa, Ont.

MICHEL, Yvette (swimming/t&f); b. 26 Aug 1965, Chilliwack, B.C.; blind swimmer, shot put, long jump specialist; 13 prov., 7 ntl, 23 world/Olympic Games for Disabled swimming records; res. Vancouver, B.C.

MICHIBATA, Glenn (tennis); b. 13 Jun 1962, Toronto, Ont.; m. Angie; Pepperdine; tennis club dir.; Cdn -12 singles '74, -18 singles, doubles '78, '80; ntl jr singles '80; ntl jr. indoor title '81; with Martin Wostenholme ntl under 18 doubles '78, '80; ntl sr singles titles '81-82, doubles '85, '89; 1st Cdn to win all-American ranking 3 straight years; NCAA '82 finalist; mem. 9 Davis Cup, '79-81 Galea Cup teams; won USTA Hawaiian Satellite singles, San Francisco, Springfield doubles '85; teamed with Grant Connell '88 to produce formidible doubles combination; semifinalist French Open; Wimbledon '91; 9 Tennis Canada excellence awards, twice player of year, 5 doubles team of year; retd. from competive circuit '94; res. Whistler, B.C.

MICHIENZI, Peter (wrestling); b. 22 Feb 1934, Curinga, Italy; m. Margaret Dixon; c. Peter (Piero), Marina, Mario; printer; 10 ntl FS titles, 5 Greco-Roman titles (15 titles a ntl record); Jewish Invitational Buffalo, Mich. State titles; silver '62 BEG; bronze '66 Commonwealth Games; mem. '62 world, '63, '67 Pan-Am, '68 Olympic Games teams; capt. ntl team '66-68; outstanding wrestler '66 ntl championships; Ont. Fitness, Sport Awards '66, '69; Ont. medallion of excellence in sport '67; Italo-Cdn. sports award '73; London Jaycees young man of '67; volunteer coach from '57 guiding London Y to 3 prov. titles, Ont. team to Canada Games gold '71; coach London Amateur Wrestling, Athletic Club, UWO to OQAA runnerup honors '70-71; A1 status as international amateur wrestling referee; dir. Olympic Club of Canada; silver medal '76 World Wrestling Assn.; mem. Canadian Amateur Wrestling Hall of Fame; res. London, Ont.

MICKOSKI, Nick (hockey); b. 7 Dec 1927, Winnipeg, Man.; left wing CUAC, St. James jrs., NY Rovers; minor pro New Haven, Cincinnati (AHL), NHL NY '47-60 season playing with NYR, Chicago, Detroit, Boston; NHL record: 703 scheduled games, 158g, 185a, 18 playoff games, 1g, 6a; played '63 season with San Francisco Seals winning WHL title; mem. Man. Hockey Hall of Fame; res. Winnipeg, Man.

MIDDAUGH, Wayne (curling); b. 20 Sep 1967, Brampton, Ont.; m. Pam; golf pro/icemaker; finalist '87 Pepsi jr.; 2nd for Russ Howard '91-94 Labatt Briers; '93 winner, '93 World champion; '91-94 TSN Skins; '93 VO Cup; skipped own rink from '95; won TSN Skins Game '95-96; skipped '98 Brier winner; top money winner WCT '98; WCT title '99; res. Brampton, Ont.

MIDDLETON, Rick (hockey); b. 4 Dec 1953, Toronto, Ont.; given name: Richard David; jr. Oshawa Generals; 1st draft NY Rangers '73; right wing Rangers '74-76; Boston '76-88; Garrett Memorial Trophy (AHL rookie of year) '73-74; Lady Byng '82; 2nd team all-star '82; 50-goal plateau '81-82 with 51; Team Canada '81, '84; NHL record: 1005 scheduled games, 448g, 540a, 114 playoff games, 45g, 55a; played in Europe; res. Boston, Mass.

MIDGLEY, Arnold (skiing); b. 28 Apr 1935, Ottawa, Ont.; given name: Philip Arnold Samuel; m. Caroline Morris; c. Eric, Adam; Carleton, Queen's, BSc; electrical engineer; mem. Ottawa Night Riders, Camp Fortune; OQAA Alpine title '57-57; won Robertson Kandahar, alpine races vs. ntl team '58; mem. ntl team '59-63; coach 251d Que. div. teams Camp Fortune '60-64; admin. FIS '63-79; tech delegate FIS; ntl alpine titles '60, '62; FIS Congress mem. '75-79; chair. Cdn Ski Museum; mem. Cdn Ski, Ottawa Sports halls of fame; res. Ottawa, Ont.

MIJOVIC, Danny (golf); b. 11 Dec 1960, Belgrade, Yugoslavia; Texas Wesleyan, BAdm; NAIA champion; 3 NAIA all-American; won '83 Cdn amateur, '84 Mid-Alantic, Porter Cup; mem. 3 Ont. Willingdon Cup, 2 world amateur teams; pro '84; won '84 Mexican Open, '85 Blue Light pro-am; competed on Asia, Australian/NZ, Europe, USTPA, US mini-tours; res. Toronto, Ont.

MIKAWOS, Stan (football); b. 11 May 1958, Gdansk, Poland; North Dakota; def. tackle; territorial exemption Blue Bombers; with Winnipeg '82-97; 5 Grey Cup finals, 3 winners; 1 Eastern all-star; res. Winnipeg, Man.

MIKI, Fuji (curling); b. 20 Sep 1941, Vancouver B.C.; given name: Fuji Roy; m. Mary Anne Uyele; c. Tracey Anne, Bryan; auto parts salesman; mem. '60 Pacific Coast hockey champions; mem. 3 Pacific Coast Zone 3 curling champions; mem. '79 BC Brier entry; prov. men's finalist '80-82; 2nd on '82 ntl Seagram Mixed title rink; mem. '77 Japanese Cdn. curling title team; res. Burnaby, B.C.

MIKITA, Stan (hockey); b. 20 May 1940, Sokolce, Czech.; given name: Stanislas Gvoth; m. Jill; c. Scott, Meg, Jane, Christopher; hon. LLD Brock; restaurateur; nicknamed 'Stash'; jr. St. Catharines TeePees; 3 times OHA all-star, MVP once, '58-59, scoring title; Black Hawks '59-80, NHL's 1st triple crown winner, (Ross, Hart, Lady Byng trophies) in single season '66-67, repeated '67-68; 4 Ross (scoring), 2 Hart (MVP), 2 Lady Byng (most gentlemanly); Lester Patrick Trophy '75-76; 6 times 1st, twice 2nd team all-star center; Team Canada '72; NHL season record: 1394 games, 541g, 926a, 155 playoff games, 59g, 91a; inventive player, developed suspension helmet, curved stick; with Ab McDonald, Ken Wharram formed Scooter Line; record 21 playoff points in 12 games, record 15 assists; jersey #21 retd by Hawks; mem. Hockey Hall of Fame; res. Oak Brook, Ill.

MIKOWETZ, Rudy (racquetball/tennis/golf); b. 30 May 1922, Rudig, Czechoslovakia; given name: Rudolf; sep., c. Lisa; businessman; '39 Czech jr. grenade throwing champion with 84m throw; mem. '51 Austrian Davis Cup team; NCTA singles titlist; national over 55 racquetball title '80; world finalist '79; Northeastern US title '79, Florida champion '77; ODGA seniors title '79, Que. Srs. golf title '80; Bedard Trophy '82, Rivermead GC Srs. title '83; Ottawa ACT racquetball awards '79-80; res. Ottawa, Ont.

MILES, Johnny (t&f); b. 30 Oct 1905, Halifax, Eng.; m. Elizabeth Connon; retd. mfgr. co. mgr.; ntl 5-mile, Halifax Herald 10-mile titles '25, Boston Marathon '26, '29; ntl 10,000m '28; bronze '30 BEG; mem. '28, '32 Olympic teams; mem. Order of Canada; Cnd Roadrunners, NS, Canada's Sports halls of fame; res. Hamilton, Ont.

MILES, Kay (swimming); b. 28 Jul 1931, London, Ont. m. Bob Easun; c. David, Jeff, Susan; UWO, hons BA; teacher; Central CI basketball, volleyball, t&f standout; mem. BEG swim team '50; excelled in coll. swimming, basketball, volleyball; Claude Brown Trophy for contribution to UWO sport '54; coached UWO women's swim teams to 2 intercollegiate titles '54-56; active Masters swimmer from '77, setting group ntl records; chairman Ont. Masters Swim Assn.; 1st woman elected to UWO W-Club Sports Hall of Fame; res. Thornhill, Ont.

MILES, Rollie (football); b. 16 Feb 1928, Washington, D.C.; d. 17 Aug 1995, Edmonton, Alta; m. Marianne; c. Rolanda, Tony, Monica, Mario, Michelle, Rollie Jr., Brett; St. Augustine Coll., BA, Arizona, MEd; phys ed supervisor; all-American '50; 10 athletic letters basketball, baseball, t&f; Class A baseball Boston's Regina farm team '51; Eskimos '51-62; CFL record: 278 punts returned 2085yds, 7.5 avg., 88 kickoff returns 2131yds, 24.2 avg., including 100yd TD, 38 interceptions returned 547yds; 8 times WFL all-star, 4 times all-Cdn; 3 times club MVP; variety of club records; most TDs 1 season, most yds gained single game, most interceptions 1 season; mem. Edmonton, Alta. Sports, Canadian Football halls of fame.

MILES, Wiff (officiating); b. 9 Nov 1931, Fredericton, N.B.; given name: William Boddington; c. Wendy, Susan, Allan; accounting officer; officiated every level hockey from schoolboy to sr. '47-89; formed NB referees assn.; pres./ chief official '68-80; at request of Soviet Sports Fed., officiated in Leningrad game '69; Charles Daigle top NB hockey exec.; Fredericton area MHA award; mem. NB Sports Hall of Fame; res. Fredericton, N.B.

MILFORD, Jake (hockey); b. 29 Jul 1914, Charlottetown, P.E.I.; d. 24 Dec 1984, Vancouver, B.C.; given name: John Calverley; standout junior Winnipeg Columbus, Kenora Thistles; rejected pro offers Detroit, NY to play 3yrs in England; minor pro Cleveland, Springfield, Buffalo (AHL); traded by Eddie Shore from Springfield to Buffalo for 2 sets used Art Ross nets; 14yrs Rangers system; Central League coach of year trophy bears his name; GM LA '73-77, Vancouver '77-84; mem. Man., Cdn Hockey halls of fame.

MILLAR, Ian (equestrian); b. 6 Jan 1947, Halifax, N.S.; m. Lynn Doran; c. Jonathon, Amy; horseman, businessman;

mem. ntl team from '71; mem. '72, '76, '80, '84, '88, '92, '96 Olympic, '71, '75, '79, '83, '87, '95, '99 Pan-Am Games, 5 World Show Jumping teams; 2 individual, 1 team gold, 3 team silver, 1 individual, 1 team bronze Pan-Am Games; team gold '80 alternative Olympics; world's most successful GP/derby riders, with Big Ben his most successful mount, unprecedented 130 victories; personal record 11 GP wins single season '92; 1st rider to lead World Cup League 9 times; 1st ever to successfully defend World Cup title '88-89; twice ranked #1 in world; competed in 84 Nations Cups; mem. 14 Nations Cup title teams; numerous ntl, NA, European titles; 8 ntl GP champion rider titles; Ottawa ACT equestrian of '75; retired Welcome Stakes Class Trophy NY International with 3rd straight win '80; riding Big Ben won 4 Fleischmann World Cup, 5 Smirnoff Cup, 2 du Maurier (world's richest GP) titles; with My Girl won Big Ben GP Challenge Toronto '96; ntl equestrian of '84; Ont. male athlete of '89; seriously injured in water jump spill '95; competed on European circuit '98-99; flag-bearer '99 PAG; co-authored *Riding High*; mem. Order of Canada, Cdn Amateur, Canada's, Ottawa Sports halls of fame; res. Perth, Ont.

MILLAR, Torchy (equestrian); b. 20 Aug 1945, Calgary, Alta.; given name: Terrance; m. Elizabeth Wiebe; c. Jessica Anne; Carleton, BA; farm manager; initial international competition '67; mem. '68, '72 Olympic, '71, '83 Pan-Am Games teams; individual bronze, team gold '71, team silver '83 Pan-Am Games; Rothman's NA GP '71, '73; NA, Eastern Cdn jumper titles '67; mem. '71 prix de nations title teams NY, Toronto horse shows; NY show jumping title '73; ntl show jumping title '73; ntl jumping derby '77; sole Cdn qualifier '79 WC finals; '80 jumper stakes title; res. Kettleby, Ont.

MILLER, Colin (soccer); b. 4 Oct 1964, Lanark, Scotland; given name: Colin Fyfe; honed skills in Vancouver; midfielder Hamilton Steelers CSL '88-90; Hearts, Dunfermline (Scottish League); mem. ntl team from '83; capt. team Canada in Gold Cup play '92-96; 13 WC qualifying matches; 53 International caps; res. Scotland.

MILLER, Colleen (rowing); b. 12 Dec 1967, Winnipeg, Man.; Comcheq services; former competitive swimmer who began rowing 1989; bow for Wendy Wiebe lightweight women's double scull; mem. ntl team '89-99; 4 world championship, 2 International regatta, 2 US championship golds; competed '96 Olympics; Man. female athlete of '95; Dick Ellis team award '90; mem. Man. Sports Hall of Fame; res. Winnipeg, Man.

MILLER, Dave (sailing); b. 18 Sep 1943, Vancouver, B.C.; given name: David Sidney; m. Susan Jean; UBC, BComm; sailmaker; with crew Colin Park, Kenneth Baxter '60 NA jr. sailing title, Sears Cup; at 19 skipper '64 Olympic Star Class; crew mem., tactician 4th place Dragon Class '68 Olympics; bronze medal skipper Soling Class '72 Olympics; res. Victoria, B.C.

MILLER, Doug Jr. (bowling); b. 25 Nov 1927, Peterborough, Ont.; given name: James Douglas; m. Colleen Smith; c. Douglas, Carol, Dan, Dave, Anne Marie; retd. tool designer, product mgr., exec., fund raiser; minor,

intermediate, sr. B lacrosse; jr., int., sr. football, hockey, boxing; 2 lacrosse seasons Toledo, Ohio, '48-49; coached Peterborough, Ont., juve. lacrosse titlist '52; built Allencourt Lanes Richmond Hill, mgr. '60-62; conceived, founded Youth Bowling Council (YBC) '62; launched world bantam tournament; key role in eliminating counter pin from 5-pin game; formed Bowling Proprietors Assn. of Canada; exec. dir. BPAO, BPAC '62-69; owned, operated Newmarket Redman hockey team '75-78; led Can-Am lacrosse league in penalties 2 seasons; model shipbuilder of note; pioneer in development of facial, eye protection for hockey players with CCM '75-78; Ont. achievement award, Builder of Bowling Industry award; grand marshall Variety bike-a-thon Toronto '81; mem. Ont. 5-pin Bowling Hall of Fame; res. Peterborough, Ont.

MILLER, Doug Sr. (lacrosse); b. 1904, Peterborough, Ont.; d. 8 Mar 1986, Seminole, Fla.; given name: Thomas Douglas; m. Alice Mary Ebbs; c. Douglas, Adele, Marilyn; retd. contractor; mem. champion Crescents Peterborough sr. city league; sr., jr., Oshawa '23, Wallaceburg '24; competitive career lasted 27yrs.; final game marked beginning of sr. play for son Doug as both appeared on field the same day; as contractor dominant force behind construction of 4000-seat Miller Bowl (named in his honor) by Peterborough Lacrosse Club; mem. Canadian Lacrosse, Peterborough Sports halls of fame.

MILLER, Esther (skiing); b. 10 Sep 1957, Edmonton, Alta.; given name: Esther Ruth; cross-country specialist; ntl jr. title '73; mem. ntl team '74-82; BC 5km champion '73; NA 3x5km '78-79; ntl 5km, 1st overall Dannon series '80; Ont. 5km, 10km, national 5km, 3x5km, NA 4x5km relay titles '81; mem. '76, '80 Olympic; '79, '81 Swedish Ski Games, '79, '81 Finland World Cup teams; res. Burns Lake, B.C.

MILLER, James (harness racing); b. 13 Sep 1945, Saint John, N.B.; after stints as commercial pilot and serious shot at professional hockey settled on career as horse trainer; from humble beginnings racing for $250 purses at Paterson Park, B.C. has made successful transition to Grand Circuit racing; first major acquisition was Invincible Shadow which earned Aged Pacer of '74; while training is his forte he does make the occasional catch drive which through '95 has produced 953 wins and purses exceeding $6M; among star horses he has trained are former world champion Brisco Hanover, million dollar winner J.D's Buck, Tijuana Taxi, Brace Yourself and Cheery Hello; winter-trains at Ben White Raceway; res. Clarcona, Fla.

MILLER, Leigh (t&f); b. 17 Aug 1905, Elmsdale, N.S.; d. 24 May 1998, Halifax, N.S.; m. Helen Oliver; c. James, Evan; Dalhousie, BComm; retd. production mgr.; Maritime sprint champion '25-31; Ont. sprint champion '28-31; ntl, NA indoor sprint titles '30; 3 world 100yd, 1 world 100m, 60m (indoor), ntl indoor 40yd record; mem. '30 BEG gold medal relay team; 25yrs t&f coach Toronto, Montreal, Halifax; head t&f coach '54 Empire Games; subject of S. M. Parker poem; Dalhousie gold medal, sports plaque; '30 BEG president's medal; mem. NS Sports Hall of Fame.

MILLER, Linda (shooting); b. 5 Jul 1952, Noranda, Que.; given name: Linda Karen; sep. Szulga; Ryerson, BA;

management consultant/entrepreneur; initial target shooting experience '85; moved to Olympic events '89; qualified for ntl smallbore rifle team '90; won World Cup medals '92-95; Commonwealth Games pairs (with Christina Ashcroft) bronze '94; switch to fullbore competition '96; 3 Que., 4 Ont., 3 ntl championships; nationally certified coach; founding mem. SFC ntl coaching comm; mgr/head coach Ont. rifle team '91-94; dir. ORA '97, Ont. smallbore fed. '89-91; conducts coaching seminars; founder/editor *CoachNet*; dir./mgr./administrator varied sports organizations; res. Toronto, Ont.

MILLER, Russ (curling/darts); b. 13 Sep 1918, London, Ont.; given name: Russell Edward; m. Frances Elizabeth Blakey (d); c. Bonnie Jean; retd. sheet metal worker; 26 London Curling Club championships,; Ont. Silver Tankard '48, '54, numerous City of London bonspiel titles; with wife Fran, won Auld London mixed, Tillsonburg Tobacco Belt; 3 8-enders; Ont. Points championship '58-59; 6 times competed Ont. Consols; 12 Royal Cdn Legion zone titles, provincal '59, 4th nationals; London Free Press sportsman of '59; mem. Ont. champion dart teams '55, '74, several city titles; numerous perfect 180 scores with either hand; flag-bearer '74 London Brier; life mem. LCC; ranked in London's top 10 5-pin bowlers '62; res. London, Ont.

MILLER, Shannon (hockey/coaching); b. 1964, Melfort, Sask.; UofSask, BPhE; coach; ex-police officer; played in 1st-ever women's ntl championship '82, also competed '83-85; ended competitive playing career '89; refereed university level women's hockey '82-85; moved from Sask. to Calgary to become police officer '88; started 1st-ever girl's minor hockey team in Calgary '89; began ntl coaching career '91 as asst. leading Alta women's team to Canada Games gold; asst. '92, '94 Cdn women's world gold medal team coached Canada to gold at 2 Pacific Rim championships; coached Calgary Classics to '95-96 Alta provincial gold;ntl bronze; chair. female hockey in Sask.; pres. Southern Alta Women's HL; mem. Cdn hockey's female council '85; hired by Olympic Oval '95 to lead 1st-ever international high performance female hockey program; coached ntl team to '97 women's world title; coach '98 Cdn women's silver medal Olympic team; head coach UMinn-Duluth women's hockey; Breakthrough award '98; res. Duluth, Minn.

MILLER, Zan (t&f); b. 26 Jan 1899, Sussex, N.B., d. 19 Mar 1957, Sussex, N.B.; given name: Andrew; Maritime high jump champion '20; ntl HJ, BJ titles '22-23; mem. '24 Olympic team; mem. NB Sports Hall of Fame.

MILLIKIN, Hugh (curling); b. 4 Jul 1957, N. Vancouver, B.C.; given name: Hugh Ronald Alexander; m. Sara Waller; c. Carlee; Algonquin Coll.; managing dir. JetForm; following mother Alma's lead honed curling skills in Ottawa area; all-star third '81, all-star second '88 Ontario Tankard; second for Dave Van Dine's Ottawa RCMP Canadian mixed title rink '86; skip Australia rink '92-99 Worlds, '92, '98 Winter Olympics, '92-96 Pacific titles; Colin Campbell award '93 Worlds; res. Sydney, Australia/Ottawa, Ont.

MILLS, Bob (rowing); b. 9 Dec 1958, Halifax, N.S.; sculling specialist; double sculls gold, quad 4s gold '83 Pan-Am Games; single sculls bronze '84 Olympics; mem. NS Sports Hall of Fame; res. Dartmouth, N.S.

MILLS, James (football); b. 24 Sep 1961, Vancouver, B.C.; Hawaii; offensive tackle; drafted by Baltimore NFL '83; dealt to Denver '86; joined CFL Lions '86-93, '95-98, Ottawa '94; 5 Western, 3 CFL all-star; 2 CFL outstandingoffensive lineman awards; 2 Becket-DeMarco Memorial awards; 7 playoff games; res. Vancouver, B.C.

MILNE, Howie (all-around); b. 1903, Park River, N.D.; d. (circa 1990) Weyburn, Sask.; given name: Howard; m. Violet Benallick Bartlett; retd.; hockey Regina jrs., Vic's 2 seasons, Pat's 2 seasons; 4 prov. jr. champions; mem. losing Pat's '22 Memorial Cup series; center, defence sr. Vic's '23-24; replaced Al Ritchie as coach Monarchs '27 winning Memorial Cup; reorganized sr. Vic's, coached 1 season; officiated '33 Western Canada jr. final series; jr. football YMCA Regina '18-20, 2 prov. titles; 4 seasons player/coach Roughriders; 1st Western offical to work Grey Cup final '31; Cdn football all-star '23; shortstop, 3rd base with Y Regina North Side Baseball League int., sr. divisions; mem. Champ's Hotel team '19-27; best season '23 leading Southern Baseball League batters with .423; pro offer from Minneapolis Millers of American Assn.; basketball Moose Jaw, Saskatoon, Regina, 2 prov. titles, lost ntl finals to Winnipeg Toilers '25; 1 of few to play, coach in Memorial Cup final, play, officiate in Grey Cup final; pres. Regina Juve. Baseball League '26; Regina outstanding athlete '23, '24; mem. Sask. Sports Hall of Fame, Roughriders Plaza of Honor.

MIMBS, Robert (football); b. 6 Aug 1964, Kansas City, Mo.; Kansas; running back; NFL with NY Jets, Dallas, Phoenix '86-89; CFL Winnipeg '90-92, BC '92-93, Sask. '95-97; CFL record: 81 games, 40tds, 1cvt, 1244 carries for 6162yds, 36tds, 178 receptions for 1726yds, 4tds; 2 Eastern, 1 Western, 3 CFL all-star; Jeff Russel Memorial Trophy '91, Jeff Nicklin Memorial Trophy '96; runnerup CFL outstanding player '91, '96; 3 playoff games, mem. '90 Grey Cup champion; res. Regina, Sask.

MINDORFF, Philip (swimming); b. 13 Jul 1963, Stratford, Ont.; m. Anne; c. Leah; Brock; computer programmer; class S8 swimmer; began swimming competitively age 13; competed Ont. Games '77; mem. Ont. team Games for Physically disabled; competed '78 ntls, '79 Stoke Mandeville Hames (100m backstroke bronze); '80, '84. '88 Paralympics; 2 silver '84, bronze '88; 3 Canada Games gold '83; 3 ntl records; Ont. Amputee Sport Assn. male athlete of '84; retd following '90 international disabled championships; also competed in triathlons/t&f/volleyball; mem. Ont. Aquatic Hall of Fame; res. North York, Ont.

MINER, Hazel (administration); b. 6 Apr 1935, Outlook, Sask.; given name: Hazel Jean Hopkins; m. William Manning Miner; c. Debbie, Max, Diana, Michael; secretary; formed Nepean Amateur Basketball Assn. '70, pres. '70-83; founded Ottawa Rookies League '73; Eastern Ont. pres. OABA '74; launched Ont. jr. development program '77; pres. National Capital BA '79; dir. Ont. player development OABA '83; operated annual summer basketball training camps '76-88; Ottawa ACT Sportswoman of '83; res. Nepean, Ont.

MINOR, Ron (t&f/wheelchair basketball); b. 13 Oct 1957, Magrath, Alta.; fed. govt claims officer; wheelchair athletics;

world records at 400m, 800m, 1000m, 1500m distances; gold 100m, 800m, 1500m '78, 2 silver, 2 bronze '82 Pan-Am Games for Disabled; 1 gold, 2 silver '79 Stoke Mandeville Games; gold 1500m Superchallenge '79; 2 gold, 2 silver, 1 bronze '83 ntl championships; mem. 5 Paralympic teams, 2 Gold Cup basketball teams; Alta. provincial award '79; CWSA athlete of '78; mem. Alta. Sports Hall of Fame; res. Edmonton, Alta.

MINSHALL, Barbara (horse racing); b. 6 Nov 1953, Montreal, Que.; given name: Barbara Stracey; m. Aubrey Minshall (d); s c. Shawn, Patrick; horse trainer; began riding as pony club mem.; dressage specialist; earned gold, silver in AHSA dressage events '73; gold, silver Cdn International dressage show '74; reserve Ont. advanced champion, silver with ntl dressage team '75 Pan-Am Games; GP silver Ont. dressage championships 4th with ntl team '76 Olympics; encouraged by husband developed into topnotch thoroughbred trainer; became licensed trainer '95 posting 23 race wins; 1st woman to saddle a Cdn triple crown race winner with Kiridashi in Prince of Wales Stakes; with 139 mounts claimed 40 wins, 25 seconds, 34 thirds '96; 15 stakes race winners, including 2nd Prince of Wales with Stephanotis, $2.1M in winnings brought Minshall Farms 15 Sovereign Award nominations; Mt. Sasafrass named horse of yr, champion older horse; Minshall Farms received outstanding breeder and owner Sovereign awards; 1st female to win Sovereign trainer of yr award; res. Hillsburgh, Ont.

MITCHELL, Bill (builder); b. 30 Oct 1914, Berlin, Ont.; given name: William; m. Eleanor Hales; c. William Jr.; Ont. Agricultural Coll.; retd. AD Guelph; HS all-around t&f champion all levels; rugby, basketball, boxing standout at college level; recipient football Wildman trophy; mem. Guelph Sports Hall of Fame; res. Guelph, Ont.

MITCHELL, Doug (administration); b. 19 Feb 1939, Calgary, Alta.; m. Lois; c. Shelley, Steven, Sue Ann, Scott; Colorado Coll, UBC, LLD; lawyer (QC); attended Colorado on hockey scholarship; football UBC, CFL BC, Hamilton '60-61; general counsel Calgary Flames, rep. Flames NHL governors; chair. advisory comm. ntl Olympic hockey team; credited with re-birth of hockey in Calgary; dir. Calgary Olympic Development Assn.; legal counsel '88 winter Olympics; color commentator Stampeder football broadcasts 9yrs; sponsored NBA exhibitions Calgary, Edmonton; established Willie deWit trust; CFL commissioner '84-89; res. Toronto, Ont.

MITCHELL, Doug (coaching); b. 14 Jul 1942, Windsor, Ont.; m. Irana Bellringer; c. Christina, Stacy, Todd; UWO, BA; football coach; HS, college football standout; pro Hamilton '67-74, Montreal '74; mem. 3 Grey Cup winners; OUAA heavyweight wrestling title '65, '67, Ont. amateur champion '65-67; coach NB wrestling team '83 Canada Winter Games; CIAU coach of '81; coached football 3yrs Burlington HS, 5yrs Mount Allison, UofT '83-85; UWO athlete of '67; mem. UWO W Club Hall of Fame; res. Toronto, Ont.

MITCHELL, Kurt (shooting); b. 19 Nov 1951, Lethbridge, Alta.; given name: Kurt Davison; Waterloo, BSc; electronic engineer; mem. bronze 300m team '73 Western Hemisphere championships; mem. '74, '79 World championships, '76, '80 Olympics, '75, '79 Pan-Am Games teams; individual 10m air rifle bronze '79 Pan-Am Games; unofficial world record 400/400 40 shots prone '80, 599/600 60 shots prone '81; ntl 3 position smallbore record 2308 '80 Olympic trials; ntl overall champion '76, prone champion '76-77, '80; res. Stratford, Ont.

MITCHELL, Ray (bowling); b. 22 Mar 1931, Peace River, Alta.; given name: Raymond Harold; m. Mari Dillon; c. Adrienne, Jocelyn; engineering mgr.; several UK regional swimming, boxing titles; '51 mem. Toronto Bell men's 5-pin league; started 10-pin bowling early '60's; '67-68 Southern Ont. singles, 3rd ntl singles; mem. Scarborough league champions who established ntl 3-game, 5-man record 3385; '72 SO, ntl singles titles, world 10-pin title Hamburg, Germany; mem. world team medal champions; 37 sanctioned tournament titles; tech. assn.rdinator Cdn 10-pin Federation, ntl coach; coached in Japan, Philippines, South America, Canada; bowling columnist *Globe & Mail*; pres. American Zone World Bowling Writers Assn. from '81; mem. Canada's Sports, Cdn 10-Pin Bowling halls of fame; res. Scarborough, Ont.

MITRUK, Steve (gymnastics); b. 17 Jan 1947, Hamilton, Ont.; given name: Stephen Frederick; m. Brigitte; c. Terry, Christopher; McMaster, BA, UofT, BEd; HS teacher; mem. '67 Winter Games, '68, '72 Olympic, '69 Cup of Americas, '71, '73 FISU, '71 Pan-Am, '70, '74 world teams; Werry Cup, OUAA gymnast of year award record 5 consec. yrs. '69-73; McMaster athlete of '72; mem. McMaster Sports Hall of Fame; res. Burlington, Ont.

MITTON, Randy (officiating/hockey); b. 22 Sep 1950, Fredericton, N.B. m. Maureen Loblaw; c. Michael, Jeffrey; working through minor ranks spent 2 seasons as linesman WHL, AHL; moved into NHL '72 appearing in initial game 26 Dec '73; gained international experience '87 Canada Cup; officiated '88 NHL all-star game; NHL record through '98: linesman 1701 scheduled, 142 playoff games; conducted officiating schools in off-season; res. Leduc, Alta.

MOBBERLEY, Herb (all-around); b. 18 Oct 1904, Dudley Staffordshire, Eng.; d. 26 Jun 1988, Winnipeg, Man.; m. Marcella; c. Terry, Dale (d), Patrick, Janet; retd. machinist CNR, superintendent TCA; nicknamed 'Mighty Atom'; mem. original Blue Bombers, 2 Grey Cup titles; baseball with Winnipeg Nifties; hockey with Winnipeg Maroons; credited with saving drowning swimmer; avid hunter, fisherman; inventor in both aeronautical, fishing fields; designed Flatfish Lures; noted gunsmith; mem. Man. Sports Hall of Fame.

MOBERG-PARKER, Tine (sailing); b. 4 Jun 1969, Honefoss, Norway; SFU; Europe class sailor; began sailing age 6; competed in first Optimist world championships age 12; mem. Norwegian ntl team 1985-93, Cdn ntl team from '93; World title '91; World Cup titles '90-92; since joining Cdn team has claimed gold in 8 regattas; mem. '96 Olympic team; brother Peer Moberg Laser sailor Norwegian Olympic team; coach Royal Vancouver Yacht Club; Norwegian YA female athlete of '91; Canadian YA female athlete of '94; BC Premier's athletic award '95; res. Vancouver, B.C.

MOBILIO, Domenic (soccer); b. 22 Apr 1973, North York, Ont.; mem. ntl -20 team '87 World Youth championships; striker, prolific scorer who in 6 CSL campaigns was all-time leading scorer with 81g in 121 scheduled games; 3 CSL all-star awards; '91 CSL scoring title with record 25g; CSL MVP '91; hamstring injury hampered play '95; comeback with Vancouver 86ers A-League '96; mem. ntl team from '86; 22 international caps; res. Vancouver, B.C.

MOFFATT, Rich (curling); b. 8 Mar 1959, Ottawa, Ont.; given name: Richard John; m. Denise Allan; Algonquin Coll.; rec. management; following in footsteps of grandfather Roy MacMillan and mother Kay, honed his skills as youngster; scored impressive victories in college championship ranks; competed in 9 Ont. men's championships, semifinalist '98, winner '99; skip runnerup rink '96 ntl mixed champioonship; skip runnerup McCain.TSN Skins game '89; skipped 3 OCA Silver Tankard title rinks, 2 Shorty Jenkins Classic, Toronto Royals, Welton Beauchamp, City of Ottawa 'spiel titles; res. Ottawa, Ont.

MOGILNY, Alexander (hockey); b. 18 Feb 1969, Khabarovsk, USSR; right wing; joined Central Red Army team at 17; mem. Soviet '88 Olympic gold medal team, youngest ever Soviet player; competed 3 world championships; top forward '88 jr. worlds; mem. Russia's World Cup team '96; selected by Buffalo '88 NHL entry draft; NHL Buffalo '89-95, Vancouver '95-99; scored 1st NHL goal 20 seconds into initial game; achieved 50-goal plateau with 76 '93, 55 '96; NHL record: (through '99) 646 scheduled games, 329g, 385a, 37 playoff games, 15g, 24a; recipient Buffalo's Frank Eddolls Memorial trophy, Vancouver's Cyrus McLean trophy; mem. 5 all-star teams; res. Vancouver, B.C.

MOHNS, Doug (hockey); b. 13 Dec 1933, Capreol, Ont.; given name: Douglas Allen; m. Tabor; def./lw Barrie Jr. Flyers; NHL Boston '53-64, Chicago '64-71, Minnesota '71-73, Atlanta '73-74, Washington '74-75; NHL record: 1390 scheduled games, 248g, 462a, 94 playoff games, 14g, 36a; founder, v-p Advantage Health Corp.; 19yrs; co-founder Dianne De Vanna Centre for abused children; res. Bedford, Mass.

MOIR, Darrell (football); b. 15 Aug 1958, Calgary, Alta.; m. Donna; c. Sean;UCal; fitness dir. Edgemont Racquet Club; 3 times HS athlete of year; sr. prov. 110m low hurdles record; QB UCal; CFL defensive back CFL Stampeders '79-85; res. Calgary, Alta.

MOISAN, Sylvianne (horseshoes); b. 21 Jul 1966, St. Raymond, Que.; m. Andre LeClerc; secretary; 5 Quebec women's doubles titles; twice runnerup Que. women's singles; 3 ntl women's singles titles; with Sue Snyder involved in best game ever thrown by women (130 shoes) '95 World tournament, with Myrna Kissick (126 shoes) '95 ntl championship; 5 world records, shares 2 others; 5 top 5 finishes in world tournament, runnerup '95; res. Chertsey, Que.

MOLITOR, Paul (baseball); b. 22 Aug 1956, St. Paul, Minn.; given name: Paul Lee; m. Linda; c. Blaire; Minn.; nicknamed 'Molly' or 'Ignitor'; all-state in baseball,

basketball, 2 all-conference awards; participated Montreal International Games '75; drafted by St. Louis (NL) '74; pro Milwaukee '77; played with Burlington in minors '77; in major leagues with Milwaukee '78-92, Toronto '93-95, Minnesota '96-98; mem. 2 World Series champions, winning World Series MVP award with Toronto '93; 5 AL all-star teams; career played with various injuries; Midwest League prospect of yr, MVP award, batting title '77; AL rookie of '78; 2 Harvey Kuenn hitting excellence awards; Milwaukee distinguished citizen award '90; 2 *Sporting News* Silver Slugger awards; Adults for Youth Good Guy award '86; Brewers' comeback player of '85 award; reached 2000 hit plateau '91, 3000 hit plateau '96; moved into 9th place on all-time ML hit list with 3309 27 Aug '98; Branch Rickey award '98; very active in community charitable projects; res. Mequon, Wisc.

MOLLE, Bob (wrestling); b. 23 Sep 1962, Saskatoon, Sask.; m. Karen; c. 3;SFU; wrestling coach; Saskatoon, provincial HS heavyweight titles; NAIA 100+kg FS title '83; 4 ntl FS titles; bronze '83 Pan-Am Games; bronze World Cup '84; back surgery three weeks before '84 Olympics threatened participation but came through to win silver medal; became 1st heavyweight to win 4 straight American Ntl Amateur Intercollegiate titles; coach UMan.; with Ned Brigante shared 2 CIAU coach of yr honors; mem. 4 Evan Hardy football teams, '80 provincial champions; 1 season Saskatoon Hilltops; all-American off. lineman honors at SFU '85; pro Blue Bombers '85-92; capt. '90 team; mem. '88, '90 Grey Cup title teams; mem. Saskatchewan Sports, Cdn Amateur Wrestling, NAIA halls of fame; res. Winnipeg, Man.

MOLNAR, Bill (shooting); b.21 Feb 1937, Brooks, Alta.; given name William Julius; m. Anne Bedford; c. Deborah, Leslie; Royal Roads MC; Lt. Col. Cdn Armed Forces; military rifle team '58-80, 4 Bisley teams; Queen's medal; ntl pistol team '75-78; silver free pistol '75 Pan-Am Games, free pistol team bronze Benito Juarez Games Mexico; mem. NB sporting rifle team Canada Winter Games '66; CISM competitions Chile, Nigeria, USA, Sweden, Italy; men. Cdn Forces Sports Hall of Fame; res. Kanata, Ont.

MOLSON, Hartland (hockey); b. 29 May 1907, Montreal, Que; given name: Hartland deMontarville; m. Maria Magdalene Posner; c. Zoe Anne; Royal Military Coll., LLd; senator from '55, dir. Molson Ltd., Bank of Montreal, CIL; mem. Kingston jr. OHA champion, Memorial Cup finalists '26; mem. RMC hockey teams '24-28; RMC Intermediate Intercollegiate football champions '27; coach Chamonix, France, hockey club '29; also active in t&f, soccer, cricket; pres./chairman Montreal Canadien's hockey club '57-68; v.-patron Que. Rifle Assn.; from '54 hon. pres. Cdn Commonwealth Games Assn.; governor Palestre Nationale; ex-pres. Cdn Arena Co.; hon. dir. Cdn Fed. of Silent Sports, Cdn Paraplegic Games; hon. mem. QMHA; life mem. AAU of C, Montreal Flying Club; hon. patron Olympic AC; patron Que. Rugger Union, Cdn Olympic Training Regatta (CORK); mem. advisory comm. COA; winter sports fair comm. Laurentian Ski Zone; hon.v-p Golden Glove tournament; hon. dir. QRCA; patron Little Grey Cup ntl jr. football championships; hon. pres. International Bantam hockey tournament; mem. advisory council Atlantic Salmon Assn., dir., mem. International advisory group IASF; OBE;

hon. degrees Montreal, Calgary, Bishop's, RMC; mem. Order of Canada, Hockey Hall of Fame; res. Westmount, Que.

MOLSON, Percy (all-around); b. 14 Aug 1880, Cacuona, Que.; d. 5 Jul 1917, Vimy Ridge, France; given name: Percival; McGill, BA; shone in t&f, hockey, tennis, badminton, golf, cricket, billiards, aquatics, football at McGill '98-01; at 16 mem. 1896 Stanley Cup champion Montreal Victorias; brilliant running back, exceptional kicker, capt. MAAA Winged Wheelers '02-06; set world long jump record 1900; epitomy of sportsmanship with unique distinction of never having been penalized for unfair play in any sport in which he participated; youngest mem. McGill bd of governors; served with distinction (Military Cross) as capt. in WWI until killed in action; left bequest to McGill which led to Molson Memorial Stadium; 3 McGill athlete of yr titles; mem. Cdn Football, McGill Sports halls of fame.

MONCKTON, Philip (rowing); b. 8 Apr 1952, St. Boniface, Man.; given name: John Philip; div. Deborah Holmes; m. Tracey Black; c. Geoffrey, Gillian; UWO, BA, MA; product mgr. Scepter Corp; mem. UWO Mustangs '71, '74 CIAU football title teams; all-Cdn defensive end '74; mem. straight 4s '76, single sculls '80 Olympic, '77, '79 World championships teams; silver '79 Pan-Am Games, mem. bronze coxless quad sculls crew '84 Olympics; 1st Cdn in 50yrs to advance to semifinals diamond sculls '80 Royal Henley Regatta; UWO male athlete of '76; coaching from '88; res. Toronto, Ont.

MONEY, Ken (t&f); b. 4 Jan 1935, Toronto, Ont.; given name: Kenneth Eric; m. Sheila Donelly; c. Laura; UofT, BA, MA, PhD; research scientist, astronaut; 5yrs ntl high jump champion; ntl record 6'7 3/4" set while placing 5th '56 Olympics; mem. '58 BEG team; candidate for possible space mission '85 but never got into orbit; teamed with Mark Grantham to win US international badminton +60 masters men's doubles title '98; mem. UofT, Cdn Forces Sports halls of fame; res. Willowdale, Ont.

MONNOT, Ray (basketball); b. 24 May 1932, Pittsburgh, Pa.; d. 6 Feb 1999, Ottawa, Ont.; div.; c. Christopher, Sandra, Susan; UWO, BA; PMO mgr. finance personnel/admin.; mem. Toronto Nortown Tri-Bells, ntl sr. champions '53-54; UWO intercollegiate titlists '54-55, '55-56, capt. UWO '55-57; UWO record 44pts 1 game '56-57; UWO single season 530, career 1278 scoring records; mem. Tillsonburg Livingstons ntl champions '59-60, '59 Pan-Am, '60 Olympic Games teams; UWO outstanding athlete '57; former bar owner; mem. Ottawa Dildo pickup football/basketball teams; accomplished singer; mem. UWO W-Club Hall of Fame.

MONOD, Peter (skiing); b. 7 Jan 1957, Banff, Alta.; part owner sporting goods store; mem. Alta. Ski Team '74-76; ntl team '77-81; slalom, GS specialist; Can-Am circuit '75-77; Europa, World Cup series '77-81; mem. '78 world title team; Alta. Cup champion '74-75, 1st FIS GS France '78; overall ntl Spring series titlist '78; 2nd Europa Cup GS France '79; US GS title '80; 6 ntl, 1 US titles; Alta. sports achievement awards '78-80; res. Banff, Alta.

MONROE, Jessica (rowing); b. 31 May 1966, Palo Alto, CA; moved to Canada '72; mem. ntl '88-92 and again from '95; gold 8s, straight 4s '92 Olympics, '91 Worlds, silver 8s '96 Olympics; 2 International regatta titles; 2 Dick Ellis team awards; res. Victoria, B.C.

MONSON, Walter (hockey); b. 29 Nov 1908, Winnipeg, Man.; d. 9 Jan 1988, Winnipeg, Man.; given name: Walter George; m. Mary Alderdice; c. Walter, Gail; retd. machinist; amateur hockey Elmwood Millionaires ('28 Man. jr. title), Jack King Srs., Selkirk Fishermen; 2. Man. sr. titles, 2 scoring crowns; pro Pittsburgh Yellow Jackets (AHL), Moncton (Maritime League), Harringay Racers (Eng.); coached Winnipeg Jr. Monarchs Memorial Cup winner '46; centre '32 Olympic gold medal team; mem. Man. Hockey, Sports halls of fame.

MONTABONE, Monty (t&f); b. 26 Aug 1903, Grand Rapids, Mich.; d. 27 Sep 1999, Nepean, Ont.; given name: Warren Joseph; m. Jean Margaret Collins (d); c. Sue-Ann, Carol Jane, Robert; Loyola Coll.; electrical engineer; retd. owner electrical supply bus.; US jr. ntl hurdles champion; mem. '24, '28 Canadian Olympic teams; ntl hurdles titles '24-28; competitive snowshoer, world record 120yds; dog sled racing gold medalist; hon. mem. Commonwealth Games Assn. of Canada; coached at YM-YWCA 2yrs; 38yrs mem. Kiwanis club; key role in creating Manotick Mini Run Heart Institute fund raiser; Kiwanian of '86 award for Eastern Canada, Caribbean; Illuminating Engineering Society of North America distinguished service award '86.

MONTGOMERY, Carol (triathlon); b. 24 Aug 1965, Sechelt, B.C.; 10,000m runner; represented Canada World cross-country championships, Commonwealth Games '94; silver 10,000m, bronze 5,000m '95 Pan-Am Games; silver '91 World Triathlon championships; bronze '99 PAG; won numerous triathlons throughout world; '93 Triathlete and Duathlete of year; res. N. Vancouver, B.C.

MONTGOMERY, Ken (football); b. 8 Jan 1907, Wetaskiwin, Alta., d. 17 May 1981, Edmonton, Alta.; m. Evelyn Wright; c. Douglas, Lawrence; McTavish Business Coll.; businessman; mem. '23 Central Alta. hockey champions; pres., exec. officer Edmonton Athletic Club '34-40; associated with 2 jr. hockey clubs, 2 Memorial Cup finals '34-39; co-founder, road secty. Eskimos football club '38-39; pres. '52-54, Grey Cup '54; pres. CRU '56, WIFU '57; co-founder CFL; mem. CRU Shrine Comm. initiating East-West Shrine charity games '54-56; v-p Eskimos football alumni '62; trustee Schenley Awards '58-63; v.-chairman Alta., Sask. Thoroughbred Racing Society '60-62; chairman Eskimos Football Club board of inquiry '63; mem. Canadian Football Hall of Fame.

MONTGOMERY, Willie (broomball/coaching); b. 25 May 1947, Cornwall, Ont.; given name: Wilson; m. Irene St. Louis; c. Deborah Anne, Darryl; float driver; coached Embrun Plumbing/Sports to 10 ntl, 1 world broomball titles; 2 Eastern, 3 I-Tech, 1 Russell Twp, 1 ntl coach of yr awards; 1 ntl all-star team coach award; 1 ntl, Ont. achievement awards; Federation of Broomball Assn. of Ont. Hall of Fame award; res. Embrun, Ont.

MONTMINY, Anne (diving); b. 28 Jan 1975, Montreal, Que.; John Abbott College; began competitive diving age 8; age-group competitor '85-89; ntl team from '90; silver 1m, 3m '90 Pan-Am invitational; gold 10m, team silver '93 FISU Games; 10m bronze '99 FISU Games; competed '92, '96 Olympics; gold 10m '94 Commonwealth, '95 Pan-Am Games; ntl 10m title '98, '99; Cdn flag-bearer '93 FISU Games; Elaine Tanner award '93; res. Pointe Claire, Que.

MOOG, Andy (hockey); b. 18 Feb 1960, Penticton, B.C.; given name: Donald Andrew; m. Karla Ziegler; c. Alyssa, Arielle, Abby; consultant; Tier 2 hockey Kamloops Braves, Penticton Vees; Tier 1 Billings Bighorns; drafted Edmonton '80; pro Wichita Winds '80; called up to NHL Oilers for Stanley Cup playoffs '81, turned in standout performance; mem. '83 Stanley Cup finalists; 2nd team all-star Billings (WHL) '80, Wichita (CHL) '82; Edmonton '81-87; Cdn Olympic team '88; Boston '88-92; Dallas '93-97, Montreal '97-98; shared Wm. Jennings trophy with Rejean Lemilin '90; 3 NHL all-star games; reached 300 victory milestone '94; NHL record: 713 scheduled games, 372-209-88, 40,151min, 28so, 132 playoff games, 7452min, 68-57, 4so; part owner Ft. Worth Broncos (WPHL); goaltending consultant NHL Atlanta Thrashers '99; financial interest in hockey equipment mfg. co.; res. Coppell, Tex.

MOOG, Don (hockey); b. 7 Oct 1932, Regina, Sask.; d. 16 Jun 1993, Penticton, B.C.; given name: Donald Ernest; m. Shirley Reading; c. Jan, Kelly, Mike, Andrew, Darrell; Greyhound bus driver; 4yrs backup goaler Penticton Vees; mem. '54 Allan Cup, '55 World title teams; mem. Kamloops Sr. Elks '55-56, Medicine Hat Intermediates '56-57; ntl intermediate finalist Penticton '60; mem. Penticton Old Timers.

MOON, Warren (football); b. 18 Nov 1956, Los Angeles, Calif.; m. Felicia; c. Joshua, Chelsea, Jeffrey; Washington; pro football player; HS MVP, all-American; Pac 8 player of '77; quarterback, MVP '78 Rose Bowl winner; pro Edmonton '78-83, Houston (NFL) '84-93, Minnesota '94-96, Seattle '97-98, Kansas City '99; CFL record: 2382 passes, 1369 completions for 21,228, 144tds, 77 interceptions; 5648yds '83 all-time single season record, topping own 5000yd mark set '82 which eclipsed all-pro standard 4802yds set by Dan Fouts, San Diego '81; effective ball carrier with 330 carries, 1700yds, 16tds; 5 Grey Cup victories; Schenley outstanding player '83; NFL record: (through '97) 195g, 3827 completions in 6528 attempts for 47,465yds, 279tds, 224int; 9 time Pro Bowl; NFL man of '89; formed foundation to assist disadvantaged youngsters and homeless in Houston; res. Seattle, Wash.

MOORE, Bob (t&f); b. 11 Nov 1940, Doveridge, Eng.; given name: Robert William; m. Barbara Jane McVicar; c. Fiona, Jennifer; Leeds, BSc, PhD,UofT, Dip. Clinical Chemistry; clinical biochemist; ntl 10-mile title '69-73; competed 4 Boston Marathons, 5th once, 7th 3 times; mem. '70 Commonwealth, '71 Pan-Am Games; PB: 3km 8:09, 5km 14:22, 10km 29:49, 10 miles 48:49, 1 mile 4:19, 3 miles 13:40, marathon 2:16.45; National Capital marathon '77; 40+ ntl marthon title '81; former pres., Toronto Olympic Club; co-founder, pres. Metro Toronto Road Running Assn.; res. Toronto, Ont.

MOORE, Buzz (rugby); b. 20 Apr 1921, Regina, Sask.; given name: Douglas Lorne; UBC athletic dept. bus. mgr.; mem. Meralomas '37-63; mem. almost every Vancouver, B.C., ntl representative team in that period; capt. BC team Japan tour '59, ntl team UK tour '62; invited to join famed Barbarian team; 1st Cdn made honorary Barbarian, rugby's most coveted honor; played/coached representitive teams against opponents from 9 countries; Jack Patterson Memorial Trophy, BCRU's premier individual trophy; pres. VRU '54-66; mem. BCRU 12 yrs; mem. BC Sports Hall of Fame; res. West Vancouver, B.C.

MOORE, Curt (baseball); b. 10 Oct 1920, Marysville, N.B.; given name: Curtis; m. Dorothy; retd.; won NB jr. title with Marysville Maroons '37, 4 NB sr. titles with Devon, Marysville; 4 league all-star; batting titles '53, '56; acknowledged as one of outstanding pitchers/clutch hitters starring in era of US imports; team leader and role model for younger players; retd. '58; mem. NB Baseball, Sports halls of fame; res. Fredericton, N.B.

MOORE, Dickie (hockey); b. 6 Jan 1931, Montreal, Que.; given name: Richard Winston; m. Joan; c. John, Lianne, Richard (d); property rentals; led Montreal Royals, Jr. Canadien's to Memorial Cup victories; mem. Royals (QSHL) '51-52; Canadiens '52-63, Toronto '64-65, St Louis '67-68; Art Ross Trophy '58, '59; twice 1st team all-star left winger, once 2nd team; NHL record: 719 scheduled games, 261g, 347a, 135 playoff games, 46g, 64a; mem. 6 Stanley Cup winners; mem. Hockey Hall of Fame; res. Ville Mount Royal, Que.

MOORE, Gail Harvey (golf); b. 13 Jun 1943, Toronto, Ont.; d. May 1993, Coquitlam, B.C.; given name: Gail Harvey; m. Dr. James B. Moore; c. Dana, Julie; UofT, BPHE; ntl jr. titles '58-60; ntl Closed '64-65; runnerup '63 Canadian Open, Closed; '70 ntl Open, BC titles; mem. 4 women's world teams, 2 Commonwealth teams; mem. Ont interprovincal team '58-66, BC team '68-72, '74-75, '83; mem. Cdn Golf Hall of Fame.

MOORE, Greg (motorsport); b. 22 Apr 1975, Maple Ridge, B.C.; d. 31 Oct 1999, Fontana, Calif.; began racing career with go-karts '86; NA Enduro go-kart title '90; Esso Protec Formula 1600 rookie of '91; USAC Formula 2000 West championship, rookie of yr '92; youngest at 18 to win IndyCar sanctioned event in Phoenix '94; mem. Player's Ltd. team winning 10 Indy Lights, 5 in succession, to run victory total through '95 to 13; PPG-Firestone IndyLights champion '95; youngest at 22yrs, 1 month, 10 days to win CART race with victory in '97 Miller 200; made it two in row Detroit; won '98 Rio De Janiero, US 500 CART races; Miami CART GP '99; killed in California Speedway crash; mem. Ridge Meadows Hall of Fame.

MOORE, Harry (baseball); b. 8 Dec 1914, Camlachie, Ont.; d. 1986, Sarnia, Ont.; m. Margaret Harriet Bayly; c. Sylvia Elaine; justice of the peace; at 15 mem. Detroit Triple A sandlot team but father's death brought him home never to return to Detroit play; pitched with above average control; competed 23yrs; 3 walks in 26 games 1 season; began coaching at 23; Detroit Tigers scout '58; dir. Sarnia baseball coaches '58-70; guided Sarnia teams to several OBA, 2 ntl sr. titles; coached Sarnia to Michigan Outstate title; had hand in development of such players as Ferguson Jenkins, Dick Drago, Jim Gosger, Jim Northrup; signed former Baseball Canada tech. dir. Bill MacKenzie to Det. pro contract '66; special asst. instructor ntl team from '77; hitting instructor Wes Rinker Fla. Baseball Schools; scout Expos from '72; operated baseball school from '80; author several hundred poems, some published, noted raconteur; nicknamed 'The Old Bear'; Ont. Centennial Achievement award '67; Canadian championship award '68; Sarnia-Lambton Sports Hall of Fame builders award.

MOORE, Linda (curling); b. 24 Feb 1954, Vancouver, B.C.; given name: Linda Tweedie;m. Allan Moore; UBC, BHE, MBA; exec-dir Curl BC, former teacher; began curling at 13; twice skipped BC entry Cdn Jr championships; from '80 in 6 BC women's championships; Scott Tournament of Hearts bronze '84, gold '85; team became first Team Canada with direct entry into '86 Cdn women's title tourney where they placed 2nd; '85 world champions; named BC team of year; all-star skip '85 Worlds, '86 STOH; skipped team to Olympic gold, *TSN* Skins title '88; Level II CCA certified coach; hon. life mem. North Shore Winter Club; mem. CCA marketing comm; *TSN* curling commentator; mem. BC Sports, Cdn Curling halls of fame; res. N. Vancouver, B.C.

MOORE, Marie (swimming); b. 1 May 1967, Sidney, N.S.; butterfly specialist; 2 ntl 100m, 1 200m titles; bronze 200m butterfly '83 Pan-Am Games; 2 ntl records; mem. '84 Olympic team; res. Dartmouth, N.S.

MOORE, Quip (baseball); b. 15 Sep 1904, Saint John, N.B.; d. 20 Oct 1994, Saint John, N.B.; given name: Clarence Francis; played amateur, semipro Saint John, Milltown, Salem, Reading, Mass., '21-41; set Maritime record 9 RBI 1 game '24; led league in triples, doubles, batting, stolen bases '24; offered St. Louis (NL)tryout '25; batted .300 or better throughout career; called greatest centrefielder to come out of NB; mem. NB Sports Hall of Fame.

MORAN, Paddy (hockey); b. 11 Mar 1877, Quebec City, Que., d. 14 Jan 1966, Que. City, Que.; given name: Patrick Joseph; 2yrs. Que. Dominion jrs.; Crescent intermediates 1895-1901, ntl intermediate title; standup goaler; Que. Bulldogs '01-02, except for '09-10 season with Haileybury, remained with Bulldogs 16 season posting 5.4 avg., 201 games; successive Stanley Cups '12-13; mem. Hockey Hall of Fame.

MORAND, Jim (harness racing); b. 30 Sep 1964, Windsor, Ont.; began career as groom for stepfather Gerry Bookmyer at 15; won Ohio Harness Horsemen's Assn. youth driving title '81; moved from Ohio fair circuit to Rosecroft where he established himself as a top driver; with Kiev Hanover won '90 Messenger, Bluegrass, Cleveland Classic, Tattersalls and Bret Hanover stakes; through '95 3426 victories with purses exceeding $13M; res. Upper Marlboro, Md.

MOREAU, Lucette (t&f); b. 17 Jan 1956, Pte. Cascades, Que; McGill, BPHE; national discus titles '76, '80-81, shotput '76; bronze shotput '75 Pan-Am Games; bronze discus '77 Adelaide International, shotput Pacific Conference Games; bronze discus '78 Commonwealth Games; silver discus '80 Colgate Games, Philadelphia Olympic alternative; mem. '75, '79 Pan-Am, '76, '80 Olympic, '78 Commonwealth Games teams; res. Pte. Cascades, Que.

MORENZ, Howie (hockey); b. 21 Sep 1902, Mitchell, Ont., d. 8 Mar 1937, Montreal, Que.; given name: Howarth; m. Mary McKay; c. Howie Jr., Donald (d), Marlene; nicknamed 'Stratford Streak', 'Mitchell Meteor'; Stratford OHA jrs.; Canadien's '23-34; briefly with Chicago, NY then returned to Habs '36; died of hockey injury; NHL record: 550 scheduled games, 270g, 197a, 47 playoff games, 21g, 11a; Art Ross Trophy '28, '31; Hart Trophy (MVP) 3 times; mem. 5 league championship teams, 3 Stanley Cup winners; Canada's hockey player of 1/2 century '50 CP poll; jersey #7 retd. by Canadiens; mem. Que. Sports, Hockey halls of fame.

MORGAN, Colin (judo); b. 12 Nov 1973, Calgary, Alta.; competes at 78 kg; Ntl title '93; bronze '95 Pan-Am Games; competed '96 Olympics; twin brother Keith also ntl team mem.; res. Calgary, Alta.

MORGAN, Keith (judo); b. 12 Nov 1973, Calgary, Alta.; competes at 92 kg; 2nd degree black belt; 3 ntl titles; gold '95, bronze '99 Pan-Am Games; competed '96 Olympics; 90kg FISU Games gold; twin brother Colin also ntl team mem.; res. Montreal, Que.

MORNEAU, Marie-Josee (judo); b. 4 Dec 1969, Longueuil, Que.; competes at 56 kg having moved up from 51 kg; 3 ntl sr titles; Canada Cup gold '91-92; competed '96 Olympics; res. Longueuil, Que.

MOROZ, Evelyn (baseball); b. 11 Nov 1924, Tyndall, Man.; given name: Evelyn Wawryshyn; m. 1. John Litwin (d), 2. Henry Moroz; c. Linda, Gregory, Dawn, Sheryl, Penny, Tammy; retd. teacher/Winnipeg Aquatics dept.; sprinter/jumper Man. t&f sr. champion '40; shortstop Man. women's softball title teams '41, '45; MVP Koman trophy; top scorer Winnipeg Sr. women's ntl champion hockey team '50; played 2B/OF in AAGPBL with Kenosha '46, Muskegon '46-47, Springfield '48, Ft. Wayne '49-51; hit .266 in 544 games; not noted for power but good clutch hitter driving in 193 runs; honored by Cooperstown, Cdn Baseball halls of fame; mem. Man. Baseball, Man. Sports halls of fame; res. Winnipeg, Man.

MORRIS, Alwyn (canoeing); b. 22 Nov 1957, Montreal, Que.; Capilano Coll.; public servant; mem. ntl team '77-87; '77 ntl jr. K1 500m, 1000m; '79 Continental Cup K1 1000m; '79-80 Zaandam regatta 4K 500m, '80 K1 1000m; '80 Olympic trials K1 1000m; ntl '80-83 K1 1000m, '81, '83 K1 500m; '82 Tata regatta K2 500m with Hugh Fisher; Moscow K1 10,000m '83; silver K2 1000m '82, bronze 500m '83 worlds; gold 1000m, bronze 500m K2 '84 Olympics; mem. 7 world championship, 3 Olympic teams; 6 ntl K1 titles; world K2 silver, bronze; commodore Onake Canoe Club; coach '87 FISU Games; '77, '85 Tom Longboat award (top NA Indian athlete); fed. govt. excellence awards '83-84; John F. Bassett Memorial award for community works '92; award bearing his name recognizes community service involvement, educational excellence, athletic prowess; youth ambassador for Canada during international youth year; mem. Order of Canada, Cdn Amateur, Que. Sports halls of fame; res. Wakefield, Que.

MORRIS, Earle (curling); b. 16 Aug 1945, Rosthern, Sask.; given name: Earle Harold Clifford; m. Maureen Phelan; c. Marie, Sarah, John; RMC, BSc; Canadian Forces sports consultant; skip '69-70 CFB title rinks; Ottawa Navy CC '76 Ont. Consols finalists; '78 Winnipeg Super League titlist; '79 Man. ACC points champion; '81 Montreal Super League titlist; lone curler to represent 3 provinces in Brier play, skip Man. '80 Brier entry; 3rd Que. '82 Brier entry; skip '85 Ont. Brier entry; finalist 3 City of Ottawa bonspiels; son John skipped ntl, world jr. men's title rinks '98-99; mem. Cdn Forces Sports Hall of Fame; res. Gloucester, Ont.

MORRIS, Frank (football); b. 14 May 1923, Toronto, Ont.; m. Dorothy Broad; c. Marsha, William, Frank Jr., Steven, Peter, David; football executive; lineman Toronto Navy '42, Halifax Navy '43-44, Argos '45-49, Eskimos '53-58; frequent all-star; coach UAlta '59-64; rejoined Eskimos organization '70; dir. player development; involved in 16 Grey Cup games, 12 winners; as player mem. 6 Grey Cup champions; key role in scouting of Canadian players for Edmonton dynasty of '70s and '80s; mem. Eskimos Wall of Honor, Alta., Canadian Football halls of fame; res. Edmonton, Alta.

MORRIS, Fred (ski jumping); b. 1 Aug 1917, Toronto, Ont.; d. 18 Feb 1994, Ottawa, Ont.; given name: Frederick George; m. Helen McSweeney; c. Patrick, Ted, Caroline, Gayle, Mary-Ann; retd. Canada Packers; began skiing, jumping recreationally mid-'20s; became involved in administrative end of sport Ottawa Ski Club '55; National Capital Division jumping chair. '63-76; v.-chair. CSA jumping comm. '64-68, chair. '69-70, '76-80; Olympic comm. jumping rep. '80-82; mgr. ntl jumping team '79, pre-Olympics, '80 Olympics, World Cup team '79-80; mgr., coach ntl jr. team '74, World jr. Nordics '79-80; v.-chair. CSA jumping; chair. NCD, OSC jumping comm. '82; ntl ski jumping judge, ntl coach numerous international competitions; Ottawa ACT Sportsman of '79; Ont. special achievement award '84; mem. Canadian Skiing, Ottawa Sports halls of fame.

MORRIS, Greg (baseball/hockey); b. 27 Oct 1943, Saint John N.B. given name: Clifford Gregory; m. Linda; St. Thomas U; HS principal; played hockey with NB Bantam champs '58 and baseball NB Midget '57, sr. '67-68; began coaching baseball teams to NB titles '61 winning in leagues from mosquito to sr.; several Maritime, Atlantic titles; coached sr. teams to 1 silver, 3 bronze at Cdn championships; coached gold '90, silver '88 medal teams ntl midget finals; coached ntl team at '78 worlds; coaches hockey teams to 10 prov. titles; St. Thomas athlete of '63; Moosehead coach of '78; 2 Baseball NB team of yr awards (Chatham Midget Ironmen); mem. Chatham Sports Wall, NB Sports Hall of Fame; res. Chatham, N.B.

MORRIS, Jim (all-around); b. 15 Dec 1911, Tacoma, Wash.; d. 27 Nov 1995, Trail, B.C.; given name: James Henry; m. Mary Isabel Wright; c. Gary Wayne, James

Thomas; retired personnel officer; excelled in t&f, baseball, lacrosse, hockey, basketball, swimming, softball, soccer, speed skating, curling, golf; mem. 27 BC championship teams, including 8 hockey titlists; mem. '38 Trail Allan Cup winners, '39 Smoke Eaters world championship team; began hockey career Trail Jrs., Smoke Eaters '32-46; mem. 3 Blaylock Bowl soccer title teams; pitched no-hitter, batted .400 1yr, struck out 18 batters 1 game; coached Smoke Eaters 3 seasons; coached/managed various other Trail teams in varity of sports; 8yrs hockey ref.; Jim Morris Award presented annually to Trail sportsman of year; mem. BC Sports Hall of Fame.

MORRIS, Price (weightlifting); b. 22 Oct 1941, Frankford, Ont.; given name: Ernest Price; m. Louise Mills; c. Jacqueline, Price Jr.; Guelph; farmer; competed 17yrs; 5 ntl titles; 4th '67 Pan-Am Games; 1st Cdn to lift 400lbs; bronze '70 Commonwealth Games; 4 bronze '71 Pan-Am Games; mem. '72 Olympic team; ntl records all categories; PB: clean & jerk 413lbs, press 382 1/2lbs, snatch 308lbs, total lift 1085lbs; 1st Cdn to unofficially total 1102lbs, to that time had lifted 400lbs more times than any other Cdn in history; res. Frankford, Ont.

MORRIS, Teddy (football); b. 1910, Toronto, Ont., d. 5 Sep 1965, Toronto, Ont.; career spanned 3 decades as football player, coach; at 16 softball Toronto Industrial League, halfback with brother Gord's jr. team; capt. Winnipeg Native Sons to Western jr. title, lost ntl title to jr. Argos; mem. Argos '31-41; backfield coach last 2 seasons; coach HMCS York WW2 winning '44 service title; coach Argos '45-49; 3 Grey Cups as player, 3 as coach; Jeff Russel Memorial Trophy '37; CIAU College Bowl MVP award bears his name; mem. Canadian Football Hall of Fame.

MORRISON, Bernie (football); b. 25 Mar 1955, Winnipeg, Man.; m. Debie; c. Annie, Carly, Marshall; UMan, BA; sales rep.; capt. Bisons '77; CIAU all-star linebacker '76-77; all-Cdn; mem. '78 Can-Am Bowl team; Winnipeg territorial draft '78; CFL linebacker Winnipeg '78, Calgary '78-88; noted for pass coverage ability; nicknamed 'Bunyud'; res. Calgary, Alta.

MORRISON, Lee (softball/curling); b. 14 Oct 1938, Regina, Sask.; given name: Lenore Pickrell; m. Larry Morrison; c. Lance, Layne; UofT, BPHE, UofSask, BEd, Oregon, MSc; assn. professor; softball '58, '60 Regina Lexiers, '64 Saskatoon Imperials prov. titlist; mem. UofT women's ice hockey team '60, UofSask. volleyball team '61-62; mem. winning rinks Saskatoon ladies' bonspiel '65-69; prov., ntl title rinks '69 (2nd Joyce McKee), '71-73 (lead Vera Pezer); coach UofSask. women's team '62-73, 6 conference titles; coached '72-73 ntl girls' champions; coach UofSask. women's field hockey team '67-70, 1 conference title; coached Sherry Sherick rink '96-98; Sask. srs title (3rd Sheila Rowan) '94; sr. T award UofT; mem. Sask., Saskatoon Sports, Cdn Curling halls of fame; res. Saskatoon, Sask.

MORRISON, Roland (fencing); b. 13 Mar 1951, Toronto, Ont.; UNB, BA, LLB; investigator; began fencing '69 CMR de St. Jean, Que.; mem. '71 NB Canada Winter Games fencing team; variety of NB foil, épée, sabre titles '72-81;

Lt. Governor's foil champion '76, sabre titlist '79-81; variety of executive positions with NB, Cdn Fencing Assn. '72-81; coach NB Winter Games fencing teams '75, '79; level II foil coach; res. Dartmouth, N.S.

MORRISON, Scotty (administration/officiating); b. 22 Apr 1930, Montreal, Que.; given name: Ian; m. Joan Perry; c. Ian, Perry (d), Donald, Cameron, Katharine, Karen, Joanne, Carolyn; retd. Hockey Hall of Fame administrator; jr. hockey Canadiens organization; turned to refereeing in QAHA, Que. Sr. League, WHL; at 24 youngest referee (to that time) to work NHL '54-56; entered sales field with Goodyear, Yardley '57-64; returned to NHL as referee-in-chief '65; NHL v-pres. officiating '81-86; appointed v-p, project development, pres. Hockey Hall of Fame '86-91; chair. Hockey Hall of Fame '91-98; served term as pres. Assn. of Sports Museums and halls of fame (ASMHF); mem. Hockey hall of fame; res. Etobicoke, Ont.

MORRISSEY, Janet (figure skating); b. 12 Oct 1959, Ottawa, Ont.; given name: Janet Katherine; Carleton, BA; broadcast journalist; Eastern Ont. juvenile ladies title '70; EO pre-novice '72; EO jr. '76-77, sr. '77-79; Eastern Canada jr. '77, sr. '79; ntl sr. champion '79; competed internationally St. Gervais GP (bronze), Nebelhorn Trophy (bronze), Skate Canada, Venna Worlds, Lake Placid pre-Olympics, Richmond Trophy; CFSA Bursary Award '79, Ont. achievement awards '75-80, Ottawa ACT figure skating award '79-80; mem. Nepean Wall, Ottawa Sports Hall of Fame; res. Ottawa, Ont.

MORROW, Al (rowing/coaching); b. 28 Dec 1949, Hamilton, Ont.; given name: Alan George; m. Julia Eutemia Santavicca; c. Claire, Gregory, Stefan, Marisa;UWO, BA; UBC, BPhE; rowing coach; through '97 rowed or coached with ntl team 26yrs; rowed or coached 5 Olympic, 5 Pan-Am, 1 Commonwealth, 2 FISU Games, 11 world championships; his crews earned 12 medals (9 gold) at world championships '92-96; head coach ntl women's team, UWO women's team; dir. ntl rowing centre; fed. govt meritorious service award; FISA coach of '99 award; mem. Cdn Olympic, UWO W Club halls of fame; res. London, Ont.

MORROW, Carol (diving); b. 6 Apr 1946, New Westminster, B.C.; given name: Carol Ann; m. Maurice Wright; c. Sean Cameron, Kerry Michael; UBC, BEd; retd. teacher; several BC jr. backstroke, synchronized swimming, diving titles; ntl jr. 100yd backstroke title; '63 ntl open tower diving title, '64 1m title; bronze '64 US ntl 3m championships; mem. '64 Olympic diving team; res. Surrey, B.C.

MORROW, Suzanne (figure skating); b. 14 Dec 1930, Toronto, Ont.; div.; c. Kristen Lyn Francis; Ont. Veterinary Coll.; veterinarian; only woman in Cdn figure skating history to hold sr. ntl titles in singles ('49-51), pairs ('47-48) and dance ('48); NA pairs champion with Wally Diestelmeyer '47; bronze Olympic pairs, world championships '48, '50-52; 5th singles '52 Olympics; international judge from '64, judging Olympic, world competitions; dir. CFSA; Doberman Pinscher breeder; res. Toronto, Ont.

MOSCA, Angelo (football/wrestling); b. 13 Feb 1937, Waltham, Mass.; m. Gwen (d); c. Jolene, Angelo Jr., Gino; Notre Dame; retd. wrestling promoter; lineman; played 15 CFL seasons with Hamilton, Ottawa, Montreal; 9 Grey Cup finals, 5 winners; 5 all-Eastern, 8 all-Cdn awards; runnerup Cdn defensive lineman of yr award '63-70; wrestled professionally 25yrs; occasional actor; goodwill ambassador for CFL; raconteur; mem. Cdn Football Hall of Fame; res. Hamilton, Ont.

MOSIENKO, Bill (hockey); b. 2 Nov 1921, Winnipeg, Man.; d. 9 Jul 1994, Winnipeg, Man.; m. Wanda; c. Billie, Brian, Wendy; bowling proprietor; Winnipeg Monarchs jrs.; pro Providence, Kansas City; Chicago '41-55; right wing on Pony Line with Max, Doug Bentley; Lady Byng Trophy '45; 2 2nd team all-star; record 21 seconds fastest 3 goals one game vs. NY Rangers Mar '52; NHL record: 711 scheduled games, 258g, 282a, 22 playoff games, 10g, 4a; in 1030 pro games over 20yrs accumulated only 129 penalty mins.; with Alf Pike launched pro hockey Winnipeg; their Warriors won Edinburgh Trophy inaugural season '56; mem. Warriors through '59, coach '60; mem. Man. Sports, Man., Cdn Hockey halls of fame.

MOSS, Joe (football/coaching); b. 9 Apr 1930, Elkins, W.Va.; div.; c. Joe Jr., Nancee Gay; m. Yvonne; c. 2 stepsons; Maryland, BSc; football coach, retired Lt.Col. USAF; offensive lineman Maryland, 2yrs univ. basketball; mem. '49 Gator Bowl, '51 Sugar Bowl, '52 College All-Star Game teams; tackle Washington Redskins '53; player-coach Bolling AFB service title team '53-54; all-service team; lineman Rough Riders '55; asst. coach Maryland '56, Texas Tech '57-59, West Texas State '60, USAF Academy '61-68, Philadelphia (NFL) '69-72, Argos '73-76, '83-84, '87-89, '93-96; Roughriders '77, Rough Riders '78-81, '96, Tiger-Cats '90-92, '97; head coach Argos (interim) '74, UofOtt (7-0 record) '82, Ottawa '85-86; res. Ancaster, Ont.

MOSS, Judy (diving); b. 7 Jun 1916, Winnipeg, Man.; m. Kennedy; UMan; '32 Man. springboard title; '34 ntl title; 4th '34 BEG trials, with backing of Winnipeg Winter club included on ntl team; 3m springboard gold '34 BEG; retired following '35 ntl championships; mem. Man. Sports, Cdn Aquatic halls of fame; res. W. Vancouver, B.C.

MOSS, Shona (sailing); b. 12 Apr 1969, Kitchener, Ont.; m. Steve Lorshin; UofOtt, BA, UAlta; considered pursuing career as world class cross-country skier but changed mind in late teens; began sailing age 8; won CORK Laser title '88; women's division Laser II gold '89 world championships; Radial women's world title '90; CORK Europe class bronze '90; Pan-Am Games Radial gold '91; mid-winter regatta radial gold '91; top Canadian '91 women's world championships; competed '92 Olympics; top IYRU world ranking 14; top IYRU women's world ranking 12; switched to 505 class '93; res. Edmonton, Alta.

MOST, Joe (bowling); b. 17 Nov 1926, Regina, Sask.; given name: Joseph Matthew; m. Betty Bellerby; c. Jack, Cathy; optician; with Red Glasser ntl 10-pin doubles title '64; mem. 4 Sask., numerous Sask., Regina singles, doubles title teams; co-founder Regina youth 10-pin program, coach, instructor; 4yrs dir. ntl 10-pin fed.; secty. Sask. 10-pin fed. 10yrs; secty. Regina 10-pin assn. more than 20yrs; mem. Sask. Sports Hall of Fame; res. Regina, Sask.

MOTZEK, Peter (field hockey); b. 1 Jun 1957, Vancouver, B.C.; CP Air commissary; mem. ntl team '72-81; represented Canada on tours of Great Britian, New Zealand, Malaysia, Australia, Holland, Germany; mem. '75, '79 Pan-Am Games, '76 Olympic; '77, '81 International Cup, '78 World Cup teams; res. Vancouver, B.C.

MOUAT, Michael (field hockey); b. 20 Mar 1954, Vancouver, B.C.; given name: Michael Malcolm; UBC, BSc; electrical engineer; foward ntl champion BC team '72; mem. ntl team '71-82; mem. '71 Pan-Am, '76 Olympic, '77 International Cup, '78 World Cup; mem. tour team in Great Britian, Argentina, Chile, Malaysia, Germany, Holland, Australia; res. Vancouver, B.C.

MOUNTIFIELD, Eleanor (basketball); b. 1902, Fort Yukon, Alaska; d. Feb 1985, Lewiston, Idaho; m. Charles D. Vogelsong; c. Charles M.; nicknamed 'Tattie'; mem. famed Edmonton Commercial Grads '20-24; mem. Canadian Basketball, Alta. Sports halls of fame.

MOYER, John (baseball/bowling); b. 4 Jan 1913, Waterloo, Ont.; d. 13 May 1987, Waterloo, Ont.; given name: Edward John; m. Isabelle Eadie; retd painter; pitched Waterloo Tigers to OBA Sr. B title hurling 13 successive playoff games, winning 10; mem. Waterloo '34-35 Intermediate B, '36 Intermediate A title teams; 24 strikeouts single games; pitched '39 OBA playoff no-hitter vs. Port Credit then ran no-hit string to 16 innings; in 7 '39 OBA games struck out 71, 217 for season; earlier in '39 campaign pitched no-hitter vs. Kitchener; as 5-pin bowler won '59 O'Connor Open, ntl men's singles title; 2 Eastern Cdn singles crowns '58-59; mem. 3 Ont. title teams; retired from competitive bowling '76; Elmira, Ont. srs. golf champion '80; mem. Ont. 5-Pin Bowling, Waterloo County halls of fame.

MOYNIHAN, Kerry (administration); b. 26 Jul 1956, New Westminster, B,C.; m. Helene St. Denis; c. Caroline, Dana; Laurentian, hons B Comm; pres. Alpine Canada; exec. dir. Ont, Cycling Assn. '79-80; tech. dir. Canadian Hostelling Assn. '79-80; exec. dir. Shooting Fed. of Canada ;81-85; asst. product mgr. American Express Canada '85-86; exec. dir. Ont. Gymnastics Fed. '86-89; exec. dir. Canadian Canoe Assn. '89-93; GM '95 Canada Games '93-95; GM '97 Canada Games '95-97; CEO CIAU '97-99; res. Markham, Ont.

MUCKLER, John (coaching/hockey); b. 3 Apr 1934, Midland, Ont.; m. Audrey; c. John, Cindy, Karen, Tracy, Jenny; hockey exec.; launched coaching career '59 serving in minors as coach and/or GM with NY Rovers, Long Island (EHL), Memphis, Dallas, Wichita (CHL), Cleveland, Jacksonville, Providence, Rhode Island (AHL) over a span of 14 seasons; EHL, AHL coach of yr awards; 1 CHL title; NHL head coach Minnesota '68-69, Edmonton '89-91, Buffalo '91-95, NY Rangers '97-99; pro scout 2yrs with Vancouver; has served in roles from scouting to asst., co-coach, head coach, GM with several organizations; had role in 5 Stanley Cup winners, 3 NHL all-star games; co-coach Team Canada '84, asst. coach '87 Canada Cup title teams; NHL coaching record (through '98) 488 scheduled games, 214-212-62, 67 playoff games 36-31; 2 *Hockey News* coach/ exec. of yr awards; mem. Brantford Wall of Distinction, Paris (Ont.) Sports Hall of Fame; res. New York.

MUIR, Debbie (synchro swim); b. 12 Jun 1953, Calgary, Alta.; given name: Debbie Humphrey; m. Neil Muir; UCal, BEd; synchronized swimming coach; mem. ntl team '71-73; silver team medal '71 Pan-Am Games, gold team '73 world aquatic championships; began coaching '73; ntl team coach from '76; coached 1st ntl duet (Helen Vanderburg, Michelle Calkins) to win international competition vs. top US swimmers '77 Pan-Pacific Games; coached gold medalists in duet, solo '78 World Aquatic championships, duet, solo '79 Pan-Am, FINA Cup; coached '79 Pan-Am silver medal team; '79 Pan-Pacific gold medalist solo; coached Kelly Kryczka to sweep of individual ntl sr. titles '80; Kryczka, Sharon Hambrook to titles in solo, duet British tri-meet; ntl all-stars Pan-Pacific Games '81; Canada's World champions '82; Air Canada coach of '86, runnerup '77; mem. Canada's, Alta. Sports, Cdn Aquatic halls of fame; res. Calgary, Alta.

MUIR, Lela (archery); b. 4 Nov 1934, Duncan, B.C.; given name: Lela Viola Yetman; div.; c. Ian William Muir; UVic; archery shop owner; local level championships in swimming, t&f, baseball, tennis, badminton '40-52; mem. BC jr. basketball champions '49-51, Sr. A champions '54, ntl runnerup '54; mem. ntl ladies archery team champions '70; ntl team '71 Ambassador Cup; '72 Olympic team; mem. BC team '70-71, '73-74, '77, '79; archery judge; res. Victoria, B.C.

MULLEN, Gary (skiing); b. 2 Oct 1969, Calgary, Alta.; champion gymnast in youth; allergy to cows, horses precluded pursuit of real love, rodeo; began skiing age 4, competing age 5; mem. ntl team from '90; 2 FIS slalom, GS gold; WC downhill gold, silver '94; WC record 1-2-0; competed '90 Pan-Am Winter Games, '92, '94, '98 Olympics; res. Banff, Alta.

MULLINS, Joe (t&f); b. 18 Oct 1937, Glace Bay, N.S.; m. Sally Kennedy; c. Patricia, Kathy; Nebraska, BSc, Maine, BEd; teacher; established numerous NS, Maritime 440, 880m standards mid-'50s; considered ntl king of the 880; frequent Big 8 Conf. titles '57-60; set world indoor record 1:11.4 for 600yds '56; mem. '58 BEG, '60 Olympic teams; Nebraska athlete of '60; Viscount Alexander trophy '55-56; mem. NS Sports Hall of Fame; res. Sydney, N.S.

MULLINS, Peter (basketball); b. 9 Jul 1926, Sydney, Australia; Washington State, EdD; assoc. professor; 6th decathlon '48 Olympics; mem. ntl basketball team '59 world tournament; coached ntl basketball team '69-71; coached UBC basketball, t&f; res. Vancouver, B.C.

MUMFORD, Peter (builder/figure skating); b. 1920, Ottawa, Ont.; d. 1986, Ottawa, Ont.; m. Mary; c. Ted, Blaize; retd. Brig. Gen.; regarded as one of the administrative giants of local, ntl figure skating; chair. '78 world championships; advisor jr. worlds '84; chair. '76 Skate Canada; pres. Nepean Figure Skating Club; v-chair, secty Eastern Ont. section '71-75; 4yrs exec/ dir. Sport Medicine Council of Canada; mem. Cdn Figure Skating Hall of Fame.

MUNDINGER, Karin (golf); b. 9 Nov 1959, Toronto, Ont.; c. Kasey; Ohio State; twice Cdn jr. runnerup; 2 Ont. titles; runnerup '81 Doherty Cup; 6 college titles, including Big

10 crown; shot round of 65 at 17; joined pro tour '85; res. Toronto, Ont.

MUNRO, Bruce (curling); b. 23 Mar 1947, Hanover, Ont.; m. Sandra Joan Ross; Ryerson Polytechnical; advertising sales mgr.; ranked among top shotmakers in prov.; competed Ont. Consols 7 times, runnerup 3 times; won Whitby Dunlop 'spiel '71; 3 times OCA Challenge round, winner '76, '82; '76 Royal Canadian Curling Classic; res. Kilworth, Ont.

MUNRO, Johnny (football); b. 27 Sep 1913, Toronto, Ont.; d. 26 Oct 1994, North York, Ont.; given name: John McCulloch; m. Bette Gilmour; c. Michael John, Elizabeth Anne, Brian Gilmour; Queen's, BA, UofT, Cambridge; retd sr. v-p life assurance co.; mem. numerous Toronto baseball teams; 3yrs HS all-star, 1yr all-Cdn with Queen's; mem. '33-38 Argos, 3 Grey Cup champions; hockey Marlboro jrs, 4yrs Queen's, leading coll. scorer; EFC referee 14yrs; past Schenley Award trustee; governor Canada's Sports Hall of Fame from '84; mem. Queen's Sports Hall of Fame.

MUNTON, Mabel (basketball); b. 30 Mar 1914, Edmonton, Alta.; d. 16 Jan 1994, Edmonton, Alta.; m. Jack McCloy; c. Patricia, Robert; retd. secretary; mem. famed Edmonton Grads '32-40, 148 games, 852 points, 5.7 avg.; mem. 2 Alta. ladies curling title teams; mem. Canadian Basketball, Alta. Sports halls of fame.

MURCHISON, Cliff (curling); b. 20 Oct 1896, Souris, Man.; d. 30 Dec 1987, Ottawa, Ont.; m. Grace Masterman; c. Kenneth, Grace Mary, Angus Clifford;UofT, BA, UMan, LLB; retd. Unemployment Ins. Commissioner; wounds sustained during overseas service WW1 curtailed some of his early athletic activities although he lost none of his enthusiasm; pres. Man. Baseball Assn. '21-22; co-founder, v-p Memorial Cup champion St. Boniface Seals '38; began curling in Man., brought interest in game to Ottawa '44; key role in formation Ottawa Valley Curling Assn., City of Ottawa Bonspiel, Granite Club of West Ottawa; pres. OVCA '59-60; chair. City of Ottawa bonspiel '61; King's Counsel '41; mem. Governor-General's Curling Club; mem. Ottawa Sports, Canadian Curling halls of fame.

MURPHY, Cal (coaching); b. 12 Mar 1932, Winnipeg, Man.; m. Joyce; c. Carol, Michael, Barbara, Erin, Shannon, Brian, Kelly; UBC, BA, Eastern Washington, MA; football executive; coached in HS by CFL Hall of Famer Greg Kabat; QB, linebacker UBC; brief stint def. back CFL Lions '56; HS/college coach '56-64, asst. EWU '65-67, Hawaii '68-72, San Jose State '73, Lions '74-75; head coach Lions '75-76, asst. Montreal '77, Edmonton Eskimos '78-82; head coach Winnipeg '83-86, '92-96; GM Winnipeg '87-96; asst. Sask. '97-98, head coach '99; Annis Stukus Trophy winner '83-84; involved in 11 Grey Cup finals, 9 winners; underwent heart transplant '92; res. Winnipeg, Man.

MURPHY, Larry (hockey); b. 8 Mar 1961, Scarborough, Ont.; m; c. 3; defence Peterborough (OHA) '78-80; 1st LA pick '80 draft; NHL with LA '80-83, Washington '83-89, Minnesota '89-90, Pittsburgh '90-95, Toronto '95-96, Detroit '97-99; OHA 1st team all-star, 3 NHL 2nd team all-star; mem. 1 Memorial Cup, 2 Canasa Cup, 4 Stanley Cup winners; 2 NHL all-star games; set NHL record for games

played by a defenceman (1447) '99; NHL record: (through '99) 1477 scheduled games, 275g, 981a, 200 playoff games, 35g, 111a; res. Peterborough, Ont.

MURPHY, Mike (football); b. 6 Jul 1955, Moncton N.B.; given name: Micheal Paul; m. Cathy Howard; c. Nathan; UofOtt, BComm; chartered accountant; mem. 2 Ottawa HS title teams, MVP Hillcrest Hawks '73; fullback UofOtt '75 College Bowl champions, '76 conf. champions; CIAU rushing record 1060yds '76; OQIFC scoring title 144pts; tied ex-teammate Neil Lumsden's single season TD record of 15; conf., Atlantic Bowl MVP; OQIFC all-star, all-Cdn '76; running back Rough Riders '77-80, Alouettes '81; EFC rookie of year nominee; conf. all-star '78; injury suffered in 1st exhibition game with Alouettes led to retirement; last known res. Thunder Bay, Ont.

MURPHY, Pat (cycling); b. 7 Nov 1933, South Norwich Twp., Ont.; given name: James Patrick; m. Marlene; sales exec.; ntl amateur track title '52, pursuit '53; mem. '54, '58 BEG, '56 Olympic teams; winner, record holder '56 Que.-Montreal road race; res. Schaumburg, Ill.

MURPHY, Ron (football); b. 13 Jun 1932, Hamilton, Ont.; m. Betty; c. Paula Jane, Douglas Paul, Gregory Ronald; McGill, BSc, MEd; educator; outstanding HS football career '46-52; MVP, most sportsmanlike player awards; Red Feather HS tournament title team, MVP '51; twice league all-star; mem. jr. Tiger-Cats '52, Grey Cup champion Ticats '53; McGill Redmen '54-58, MV lineman '54; 3 seasons sr. Redmen, all-star; joined McGill athletic staff '58-64; pro Alouettes; retd. following '61 campaign; asst. coach McGill '62, OUAA title; UofT phys ed staff, asst. coach Blues '64; head football coach Toronto Varsity '66-82; Old Crow Society CIAU coach of '74; res. Toronto, Ont.

MURPHY, Ron (hockey); b. 10 Apr 1933, Hamilton, Ont.; given name: Robert Ronald; m. Carole Audrea Gorrie; c. Ronald, Kimberley, Linda; hotel owner; jr. Guelph Biltmores '47-51; pro NY Rangers '52-56, Chicago '57-63, Detroit '63-65, Boston '66-70; retd. due to shoulder injury; mem. '61, '70 Stanley Cup winners; mem '65 league champions; NHL record: 889 scheduled games, 205g, 274a, 53 playoff games, 7g, 8a; coached Kitchener jr. Rangers '71-73; res. Hagersville, Ont.

MURRAY, Albert (golf); b. 3 Sep 1887, Nottingham, Eng.; d. 7 Jun 1974, Montreal, Que.; golf pro; migrated to Canada '02; asst. Toronto GC, Westmount GC; head pro Plains of Abraham Que. City, Outremont, Kanawaki, Montreal CC, Beaconsfield; at 20 youngest winner Canadian Open; twice Cdn Open titlist; launched Canada's 1st indoor golf school Montreal; CPGA title '24, 3 times runnerup; '30 Que. Open title; 3 times CPGA capt.; pres. CPGA '41; active in golf course design; mem. RCGA Hall of Fame.

MURRAY, Ben (football); b. 22 Jul 1916, St. Thomas, Ont., d. 1976, St. Thomas, Ont.; given name: Benjamin; m. Helen Foley; c. William, James, Margaret; railway police sergeant; nicknamed 'Brutus'; 4yrs. St. Thomas ORFU jrs.; intermediate basketball St. Thomas Y, Orioles; pitched softball intermediate, sr. OASA clubs; several years intercollegiate football official.

MURRAY, Bob (hockey); b. 26 Nov 1954, Kingston, Ont.; given name: Robert Frederick; m. Betsy; c. Kevin, Amanda, Andrew, Kathleen; hockey exec.; defence Cornwall Royals jrs. '72-74; pro Dallas (CHL) '74-75; Chicago (NHL) '75-90; NHL record: 1008 scheduled games, 132g, 382a, 112 playoff games, 19g, 37a; played in 3 all-star games; pro scout Chicago '90-95, dir. player personnel '91-95; asst. GM '95-97; GM '97-99; res. Chicago, Ill.

MURRAY, Bruce (golf); b. 29 Dec 1938, Ft. William, Ont.; given name: Robert Bruce; m. Nance Kirkland; c. Pam, Craig, Heather, Kirk; golf pro; Alta. jr. titles '56-57; club pro 2yrs Kitchener Rockaway, 13yrs St. Catharines GC, 6 yrs Royal Montreal; 2yrs CPGA educational chair.; CPGA capt., v-p, pres.; 3yrs dir. CPGA; founded Bill Burgoyne Memorial tournament for mentally retarded St. Catharines; chair. 1st CPGA Pan-Am Classic, Las Vegas; res. Hudson, Que

MURRAY, Bryan (coaching); b. 5 Dec 1942, Shawville, Que.; given name: Bryan Clarence; m. Geraldine Sutton; c. Heide, Brittany; McGill; hockey exec.; 4yrs AD/coach McGill; coached Pembroke CJHL; coached at college, minor pro level; guided Regina Pats to '80 WHL title; coached Hershey Bears AHL '80-81; Washington (NHL) '81-90; coach/GM Detroit '90-93; GM only '93-94; v.p./GM Forida Panthers from '94, coach '97; *Hockey News* minor league coach of '81; NHL coach of '84; div. titles '89, '92; GM Team Canada '99 worlds; NHL coaching record: 975 scheduled games, 484-368-123, 78 playoff games, 34-44; res. Ft. Lauderdae, Fla

MURRAY, Charlie (golf); b. 1880, Birmingham, Eng.; d. Jun 1939, Montreal, Que.; c. Ken; golf pro; teenage golf sensation; asst. Toronto GC; head pro Royal Montreal '06-39; twice Cdn Open titlist, once runnerup; 10 Que. Open titles; mem. RCGA Hall of Fame.

MURRAY, Dave (skiing); b. 5 Sep 1953, Montreal, Que.; d. 23 Oct 1990, Vancouver, B.C.; given name: William David; m. Stephanie Sloane; skier, instructor; mem. ntl World Cup team '73-82, '74, '78 world championships, '76, '80 Olympic teams; 2nd WC downhill Chamonix France '78, Schladming Austria '79, 3rd Lake Placid pre-Olympic '79; ranked 3rd world downhill '79; overall ntl champion '79; Europa Cup downhill Artesina, Limone '78; BC athlete of '79; mem. BC Sports, Cdn Skiing halls of fame.

MURRAY, Eddie (football); b. 29 Aug 1956, Halifax, N.S.; Tulane; place kicking specialist; 7th round NFL draft choice Detroit '80; played in NFL with Detroit '80-91, Kansas City/Tampa Bay '92, Dallas '93, Philadelphia '94, Washington '95, Minnesota '97; NFL record: 240g, 337FG, 521cvts, 1532pts; set NFL record 237 consec. cvts 12 Oct. '97; res. Minneapolis, Minn.

MURRAY, Ken (administration); b. 28 Nov 1911, Montreal, Que., d. 16 Oct 1979, Ottawa, Ont.; given name: Kenneth George; m. Evelyn Eileen Henderson; c. Glenn Andrew, Donna Lynn; Sir George Williams, McGill.; sport administrator; mem. 3 Allan Cup hockey champions, Montreal Big 4 football team; coached jr. B hockey 3yrs, jr. A 2yrs, McGill hockey 3yrs.; dir. MAAA; pres. Canadian Amateur Swimming Assn.; v-p British Commonwealth Games Assn. of Canada; mem. Institute of Assn. exec.; Cdn Diving Advisory Council; pres. Beaver Oil Co.; program assn.rdinator COA '71-79; mem. Canada's Sports Hall of Fame.

MURRAY, Pere (administration/coaching); b. 9 Jan 1892, Toronto, Ont.; d. 15 Dec 1975, Regina, Sask.; given name: Athol; Laval, BA, Osgoode Hall, UofOtt, hon. PhD, UAlta., hon LLD; ordained priest; following brief stint as newspaper reporter, law student entered seminary, ordained secular priest '18; brief stays in Orillia, Penetanguishene, Ont.; chancellor Regina diocese '23-27; organized predominantly Protestant group of boys into Regina Argos AC which in 8yrs gained reknown as hockey, football, baseball, lacrosse powers; with boys from his Argo club forming nucleus, established Notre Dame Coll. Wilcox, Sask. '27, degree-granting institution affiliated with UofOtt, now known as Athol Murray College of Notre Dame; man of vast energy, determination, he shepherded college through depression years; produced such noted alumni as Nick, Don Metz, Jackie McLeod, Garth Boesch, Gus Kyle of NHL fame, Gordon Currie of football repute; Hounds of Notre Dame rank among best-known names in Canadian sport; mem. Order of Canada; honored by Ottawa, Alta. educational institutions; testimonial dinner in his honor Regina '65; mem. Sask., Hockey, Canada's Sports halls of fame.

MURRAY, Scott (shooting); b. 1 Mar 1946, Guelph, Ont.; given name: David Scott; m. Eleanor Closs; Carleton, BA, UofOtt, LLB; lawyer; fullbore rifle specialist; with various victories in DCRA, Bisley competitions, including '94 DCRA Governor-General's trophy, '96 Macdonald Stewart Grand Aggregate, ranked among top marksmen in Canada; 16 consec. Bisley team qualification, competed each time; mem. Cdn winning teams in Kolapore, MacKinnon, Empire, Canada, Commonwealth matches; res. Arnprior, Ont.

MURRAY, Terry (hockey); b. 20 Jul 1950, Shawville, Que.; given name: Terry Rodney; m. Linda; c. Megan, Lindsey; hockey coach; defence Pembroke (CJHL) title team, Ottawa 67's (OHL); pro Providence, Baltimore, Boston, Richmond, Maine (AHL), Oklahoma City (CHL), Salt Lake (WHL), Cincinnati (IHL), NHL California, Philadelphia, Detroit, Washington '72-82; NHL playing record: 302 scheduled games, 4g, 76a, 18 playoff games, 2g, 2a; mem. 2 Calder Cup winners; turned to coaching Baltimore '88-90; asst. to brother Bryan at Washington 6yrs, head coach '90-94, Philadelphia '94-97, Florida '98-99; NHL coaching record: (through '98) 537 scheduled games, 281-198-58; scout Philadelphia '97; coach Team USA '99 worlds; res. Coral Springs, Fla.

MYDEN, Curtis (swimming); b. 31 Dec 1973, Calgary, Alta.; UCal; began swimming age 3, racing age 7; mother Barbara master level swim official; competed '92, '96 Olympics, '93 FISU, Pan-Pacific championships; gold 400m IM, bronze 200m IM '93 world short course championships; 2 silver '94 Commonwealth Games; 2 gold, 2 bronze '95, 1 gold '99 Pan-Am Games, 2 bronze '96 Olympics; ntl 200IM, 400IM records; 1 CIAU record; CIAU Howard. Mackie award; Cdn Aquatic Fed. male athlete '97; res. Calgary, Alta.

NADEAU, Daniel (shooting); b. 28 Feb 1954, Quebec City, Que.; Laval, BSc; Que. government biologist; mem. ntl team '74-78; running bore title '75 pre-Olympic match; rep. Canada world moving target matches '75, Puerto Rican championships '75, twice Benito Juarez matches, Championship of the Americas '76; ntl running bore champion '75-77; retd. from competition '78; res. Beaudry, Que.

NADIN, Robert (officiating/hockey); b. 15 Mar 1933, Toronto, Ont.; m. Nancy Wood; c. Kenneth, Janice; UofT, BPHE; mem. UofT hockey team; refereed OHA from '56; refereed more than 100 international hockey games in Canada, Europe, Asia including '72 Olympics, '74 Leningrad world jr.; supervisor of referees '76 Canada Cup series; referee-in-chief CAHA; mem. IIHF rules & referee comm.; conducted referee clinics China, Japan '77; runnerup '81 Air Canada referee award; res. Weston, Ont.

NAGURSKI, Bronco (football); b. 3 Nov 1908, Rainy River, Ont.; d. 7 Jan 1990, Chicago, Ill.; Minnesota; a symbol of power and ruggedness in pro football; a bulldozing runner and bone-crushing linebacker; rushed for 4031yds in 9 pro seasons with Chicago '30-37, '43; 3 times all-NFL; 2tds helped Bears win '33 title; after 6yr retirement returned to help Bears claim '43 crown; charter mem. NFL Hall of Fame.

NAGY, George (swimming); b. 9 Jul 1957, North York, Ont.; SouthernCal; butterfly specialist; ntl 200m fly champion from '75; mem. '75, '79 Pan-Am Games, '76, '80 Olympic, '78 Commonwealth Games, '75, '78 Worlds, '80 Japanese, US ntl championships teams; all-American '76-79; gold 200m fly Pan-Ams; bronze 200m fly '78 worlds; 6 Cdn sr., 2 Commonwealth records; last known res. Los Angeles, Calif.

NAGY, Imre (fencing); b. 7 May 1941, Kolozjvar, Hungary; sep.; c. Nataley, Gregory; administrator Dominion Textile; mem. ntl sabre team '70-79; silver team medal '74 Commonwealth Games; mem. '74 Worlds, Commonwealth Games, '75, '79 Pan-Am, '76 Olympic teams; 5 Que. prov. sabre titles, '75 Eastern Cdn champion; 3 times Governor-General's, Terre des Hommes tournament champion; Cupe du Que., Ottawa Shield tournament titles; res. Ville Lasalle, Que.

NAIMARK, Barry (curling); b. 1 Jul 1932, Regina, Sask.; m. Dell-Jean Miller; c. Benjamin, Carmella; lumberman; proficient trapshooter; mem. Cdn '65, '69 Maccabiah Games team; as lead, third, skip 4 BC Consols titles, 1 runnerup; lead '64 Brier, World title rinks; Brier runnerup '77; BC mixed title '69; BC seniors title '83, runnerup '84; res. Richmond, B.C.

NAIRN, Bill (football); b. 16 Nov 1912, Winnipeg, Man.; m. Stella Patricia King; c. Herbert Gordon; retd. regional mgr.; Deer Lake jrs. '31-33; guard, placement kicker Blue Bombers '34, '36-40; Winnipeg Victorias '35; officiated '41-70 including 20 Western finals, 18 Grey Cups; mem. Howie Wood curling rink 20yrs; res. Winnipeg, Man.

NAISMITH, James (basketball); b. 6 Nov 1861, Almonte, Ont.; d. 28 Nov 1939, Lawrence, Kan.; m. Maude Sherman; c. Margaret, Hellen, John, Maude, James Jr.; McGill, BA, DD, Presbyterian Theological Coll., Springfield Coll., Gross Medical School, MD, Kansas; 11 academic degrees; played football under Amos Alonzo Stagg at Springfield; top McGill gymnast; McGill's 1st phys ed dir.; inventor of basketball Springfield, Mass., 1891 using soccer ball, pair of peach baskets; also credited with designing 1st leather football helmet to protect players' ears; Naismith Memorial Basketball Hall of Fame, Springfield, Mass., completed '68; Cdn Basketball Hall of Fame in Almonte bears his name; ntl amateur sports centre in Gloucester, Ont., on street which bears his name; mem. US, Cdn, Ont. Basketball, Cdn Olympic, Canada's, Ont. Legends, Ottawa, Kansas, McGill Sports halls of fame.

NAKAMURA, Hiroshi (judo); b. 22 Jun 1942, Tokyo, Japan; m. Keiko Maruyama; c. Emi, Yumi, Karen; Chuo U, BEc, Kodokan Judo Institute (7th dan); judo coach; tech. dir. Que. Judo Assn. '76-84; mem. Japanese ntl team '62-67; silver all-Japan middleweight championships '66; coached Chuo U to all-Japan university title '66; among top 16 Japanese Open championships '64, '66; coach Montreal judo club '70-73, from '89; head coach QJA '68-70; ntl team coach '73-76, '84-89; coach Cdn '75, '87, '95 Pan-Am, '76, '88, '96 Olympic Games teams, 5 world championships teams, 2 FISU Games teams; level 3 ntl coaching certificate; international referee from '75; coaching excellence award '92; res. Pierrefonds, Que.

NANNE, Lou (hockey); b. 2 Jun 1941, Sault Ste. Marie, Ont.; given name: Louis Vincent; m. Francine Yvette Potvin; c. Michelle, Michael, Marc, Marty; Minn., BSB; exec. v-p/ ntl sales mgr. asset management co, hockey exec.; US citizen, capt./MVP/scoring champ/all-American Minn.; capt. '68 US Olympic, '75-77 world championships teams; def./rw North Stars '67-78; player rep./v-pres NHLPA '72-78; NHL record: 635 scheduled games, 68g, 157a, 32 playoff games 4g, 19a; coach North Stars '78; GM '78-88, pres. '88-90; NHL governor '74-91; GM Team USA '81, '84, '87 Canada Cup, '94 worlds; broadcaster Minn. State HS tournament from '64, active in hockey broadcasting for HNIC, NBC, CBS, ESPN, CFAN radio from '78; served on numerous NHL committees; wrote document for NHL-WHA merger; chair. CHL governors, NHL GMs comm.; liaison NHL-NCAA; mem. USA hockey international comm.; Cdn Hockey Hall of Fame board; North Stars most-popular player, most-valuable defenceman awards; Lester Patrick award '89; Hockey Hall of Fame Heritage award; 50yr WCHA team award; highly active in community affairs chairing many charitable events; mem. Minn. Sports Hall of Fame; res. Edina, Minn.

NAPPER, Jason (diving); b. 12 Feb 1972, Thunder Bay, Ont.; Lakehead; began diving age 10, competing age 11; 4yrs jr. ntl team; sr. ntl team from '90; bronze 1m '91 Cuba invitational; team bronze '91 FISU Games; gold 3m '93 Pan-Am invitational; silver 1m Rostock international '93; gold 1m, bronze 3m '94 Commonwealth Games; res. Thunder Bay, Ont.

NARCISSE, Donald (football); b. 26 Feb 1965, Port Arthur, Tex.; m. Cassandra; c. Donald Jr., 1 daughter; Texas Southern; wide receiver; pro Saskatchewan Roughriders '87-99; eclipsed Ray Elgaard's CFL career reception record of 830 by hitting 833 plateau '98; all pro record of 216 consecutive games with at least 1 reception; CFL record (through '98): 198gp, 872recp, 11,937yds, 74td, 4cvt, 452pts; 3 Western, 1 Northern, 3 CFL all-star teams; mem. '89 Grey Cup winner, '86 Freedom Bowl; res. Regina, Sask.

NASH, Jack (golf); b. 18 Dec 1911, London, Ont.; d. 4 Jan 1993, London, Ont.; m. Kelly; c. Becky, John, Rob, David; UofT, UWO; jeweller; runnerup Ont. jr. '29-30; 3 Ont. amateur titles; with father John A. Ont. father-son title '35; same crown 5 more times, twice each with sons Rob, David, once with John C; mem. 12 Ont. Willingdon Cup teams; l3 London Hunt & Country Club championships; 1 Ont., ntl Srs. title; quarterfinalist British Amateur '33; quarterfinalist US Amateur '35; mem. London Hunt George S. Lyon Trophy team '60; 3 Ont. men's doubles badminton titles, ntl finalist; 2 Ont. Silver Tankards with London Curling Club; competed 4 Ont. Consols playdowns.

NASH, John (diving); b. 1 Jul 1962, Ottawa, Ont.; given name: John Franklin; Carleton, UAlta; mem. ntl team '81-90; 3 ntl 1m, 10m, 1 3m titles; bronze 10m '82 Commonwealth Games; mem. '77, '79 world age group, '81 FISU, '82 world championships teams; 3 ntl records; mem. Nepean Sports Wall of Fame; res. Nepean, Ont.

NASH, Steve (basketball); b. 7 Feb 1974, Vancouver, B.C.; Santa Clara; West Coast conf. player of '95-96; Santa Clara all-time assists (510), free throw percentage (.861) leader; father John, brother Martin both played pro soccer in England; excelled at lacrosse, soccer, hockey; drafted by NBA Phoenix Suns '96-98, Dallas Mavericks '98; NBA record: 102 scheduled games, 4 playoff games; NBA game career high 20pts; subject of Jeff Rudd book *Long Shot: Steve Nash's Journey to the NBA*; participated '97 NBA rookie game; res. Phoenix, Ariz.

NATTRASS, Sue (shooting); b. 5 Nov 1950, Medicine Hat, Alta.; given name: Susan Marie; UAlta, BA, MA, PhD; medical research assn., ex-athletic dir., journalist; mem. ntl trapshooting team '69-82; 6 world titles; 4 world records; 1st woman trapshooter to compete in Olympics '76; mem. '92 Olympic team; silver '95 Pan-Am Games; 3 gold Benito Juarez International; gold '73, silver '81 Championship of the Americas; ntl women's title '68-83; capt. women's all-American trap team '73-78; 1st woman to win both high overall, all-around honors from 27yds; only woman to score perfect 200 three times; top woman all-around NA standing '73-77; won '77 European Grand Prix; coached skiing Cornell, McMaster, Blue Mountain; Order of Delta Gamma Rose Award '76; Canada's female athlete of '77, '81; Ont.

athlete of '77; Edmonton outstanding contribution to sport awards '68-76, '79, '81; Alta. achievement awards '69-77, '80; Ont. achievement awards '75-78; Shooting Fed. golden anniversary award '82; fed. govt. world champion award '82, excellence award '84; Edmonton Sports Reporters mem. Canada's Sports Hall of Fame selection comm.; amateur athlete of '81; Lou Marsh Trophy '81; 2 Velma Springstead awards; hon. Edm. Big Sister '79; mem. FAS ntl advisory council '81-83; SFC dir. '80; 2 WC doubles titles; AD St. Mary's.; Officer Order of Canada '81; mem. World Amateur Trapshooting, Cdn Amateur, Alta., Canada's Sports halls of fame; res. Seattle, Wash.

NEALE, Cynthia (equestrian); b. 19 Jun 1952, Edmonton, Alta.; m. Neil Ishoy; c. Kahla, Zachary; international debut as youngest mem. '71 Pan-Am Games gold medal dressage team; youngest mem. '72 Olympic team; Ont. medium dressage title '73; high point title Detroit Horse Show '74; reserve rider '76 Olympic dressage team, mem. '80, '88 Olympic teams; 11 ntl, international 1sts; 1st Cdn to compete world dressage championships '78, impressive 8th place finish; Martini & Rossi horseman of '78-79; mem. '88 Olympic bronze medal dressage team; res. Jerseyville, Ont.

NEALE, Doris (basketball); b. 26 Jun 1911, Ottawa, Ont.; d. 26 Feb 1992, Edmonton, Alta.; given name: Doris Edwina; m. Edward Chapman (d); c. Peter, Judith, Randall; retd. secretary; mem. famed Edmonton Grads '29-36, 116 games, 607 points, 5.2 avg.; mem. Canadian Basketball, Alta. Sports halls of fame.

NEALE, Harry (hockey); b. 9 Mar 1937, Sarnia, Ont.; given name: Harry Watson; UofT, McMaster, Ohio State; Hockey Night in Canada TV analyst; jr. Toronto Marlboros '55-58; mem. '55-56 Memorial Cup winners, all-star defenceman; sr. Galt Terriers '60 Allan Cup winners; Hamilton Hillpark SS, Westdale SS coach '60-66; Ohio State coach '66-70; Hamilton Red Wings coach '71, Hartford (WHA) '75-78, Vancouver (NHL) '78-82, '84, GM Canucks '82-85; coach Team USA '76 Canada Cup; CBC hockey analyst '98 Olympics; res. East Amherst, N.Y.

NEELY, Cam (hockey); b. 21 Jun 1965, Comox, B.C.; rw; jr with Portland (WHL); drafted '83 by Vancouver; played with Canucks '83-86, Boston '86-96; reached 50-goal plateau '90 55, '91 51, '94 50; NHL record: 726 scheduled games, 395g, 299a, 93 playoff games, 57g, 32a; Bill Masterton trophy '94; 4 2nd all-star team; frequent injuries curtailed even greater production and degenerative hip condition dictated retirement prior to '96-97 campaign; opened Martha's Vineyard restaurant '92; established Cam Neely Foundation, Neely House for families of hospitalized cancer patients; mem. Ridge Meadows Hall of Fame; res. Winchester, Mass.

NEILL, Cliff (softball); b. 8 Feb 1926, Ottawa, Ont.; given name: Clifton; m. McCaffrey (d); c. Bonnie, Bill; m. Coyne; c. Craig, Shelley; retd. Ont. Hydro; above average hockey player; outstanding softball pitcher; 7 Eastern Ont. sr. titles; numerous no-hitters including 2 perfect games '56; all-Ont. sr. title team '56; lifetime BA .290; 24k's single Eastern Ont. playoff game; mem. Ottawa Sports Hall of Fame; res. Nepean, Ont.

NEILL, Susan (administration); b. 17 May 1944, Toronto, Ont.; UofT, BPHE, UofOtt, PhD; educator, sport administrator; pres. Alta. WFHA '70-74; coach Alta. team '72-78; coach ntl women's field hockey team '74; pres. CWFHA; dir. Coaching Assn. of Canada from '79; assoc. professor of phys ed UAlta; dir. policy planning/evaluation Sport Canada; mem. UofT Sports Hall of Fame; res. Ottawa, Ont.

NEILSON, Roger (coaching); b. 16 Jun 1934, Toronto, Ont.; given name: Roger Paul; McMaster, BPHE; hockey coach; ex-HS teacher; former baseball coach; coach Peterborough jr. A 10yrs, 1 OHA title; Dallas (CHL) '76; Toronto '77-79; asst. Buffalo '79-80, head coach '80-81; Vancouver '81-83, Stanley Cup finalists '82; LA '83-84; asst. Chicago '84-87; scout/broadcaster Blackhawks '87-88; coach NY Rangers '89-93; coach Florida '93-95; coach Philadelphia '98-99; NHL coaching record: 381-326-132; dir. CJHL Pembroke '95; asst. coach St. Louis '97; 3 NHL div. Titles; 1st NHL coach to use video as training tool, hence name 'Captain Video'; hockey school operator; experimented with bunji jumping in NZ '93; res. Lakefield, Ont.

NEILSON, Scott (t&f); b. 31 Jan 1957, New Westminster, B.C.; given name: Robert Scott; Washington, BC, UBC; ntl records juvenile 12lb hammer throw 72.34m, jr. 16lb hammer 67.06, sr. hammer 72.74m; NA HS 12lb hammer throw; bronze '75, gold '79 Pan-Am Games; silver '78 Commonwealth Games; NCAA hammer titlist '76-79; mem. '80 Olympic team; Washington most valuable t&f performer '79; BCTFA male athlete of '80; last known res. New Westminster, B.C.

NEILSON, Terry (sailing); b. 2 Nov 1958, Toronto, Ont.; insurance agent; 3 ntl, 1 European laser class titles; CORK, mid-winter regatta, US Finn class titles; world laser title '82; Finn bronze '84 Olympics; Norton Crowe award '82; fed. govt. world champion award '82; Ont. excellence award '83; res. Islington, Ont.

NELFORD, Jim (golf); b. 28 Jun 1955, Vancouver, B.C.; given name: James Cameron; m. Linda; c. Blake; Brigham Young; pro golfer; outstanding jr, college career; '75-76 Canadian amateur, '77 Western amateur titles, French Nation's Cup; pro from '77; mem. 3 World Cup teams, with Dan Halldorson won '80 WC title; 1st PGA victory '84 Essex International; runnerup '83 Heritage Classic; lost '84 Crosby title to Hale Irwin in playoff; righthander who putts lefthanded; *Score* magazine Cdn pro of '83; boating accident threatened playing career but he bounced back; golf analyst *ESPN*; res. Phoenix, Ariz.

NELSON, Roger (football); b. 8 May 1932, Brady, Okla.; d. 29 Jul 1996, Houston, Tex.; given name: Roger Dean; m. Barbara Anne; c. Dianna, Mark, Carol, Michael; Oklahoma, KC Western Dental College; oil executive; guard/tackle/ centre; HS all-American; Big 7 Conf. all-American '51-53; co-capt. Oklahoma Sooners; drafted by Washington (NFL) '54 but opted for CFL with Edmonton; mem. Eskimos '54, '56-68; all-Western offensive tackle '57-60; offensive playing-line coach '62-63; Schenley outstanding lineman award '59; mem. Grey Cup winners '54, '56; became Cdn citizen '62; mem. Cdn Football Hall of Fame.

NEMESVARY, Mike (skiing/trampoline); b. 3 Mar 1961, Glasgow, Scotland; education assn. coordinator disability awareness and prevention program; mem. Ont. jr. lacrosse title team '71; freestyle ski specialist; Ont. Winter Games aerials title '76; 3 ntl jr, 5 int., 2 sr. titles; 1 NY State, Vermont titles; 4 Que., WC, 3 Europa Cup, 2 European, 5 British, 1 Scottish titles; European water ramp title; world record for skiers performing most black flips; ntl jr. trampoline title; injured in trampoline accident mid '80s and rendered a quadraplegic; recipient Perry medal for outstanding contribution to British skiing; 2 European TV documentary awards; 2 Ottawa ACT skiing awards; Celebrity Guild of Great Britain award; mem. Nepean Wall of Fame; res. Ottawa, Ont.

NESBITT, Keith (skiing); b. 14 Jan 1930, Montreal, Que.; m. Linda Miller; c. Karen, Brian, Christopher, Krista, Andrea; Sir George William; sport administrator, real estate agent; competitive skiing through '52; Laurentian ski zone official '53, pres. '56; pres. Que. Div. 2 terms; National Alpine chair. '63-65; 1st full-time mgr. CSA '67; helped create permanent ntl ski team '58; instrumental in bringing international ski racing to Canada through '66 du Maurier series; created coaching certification program, official suppliers program for ntl ski team, athletic grading or classification system, 1st officals courses; active SFC, COA; exec. dir. Canadian Ski Assn. '67-77, Canadian Weightlifting Assn. '78-85, Cdn Ski Museum from '96; mem. Cdn Skiing Hall of Fame; res. Ottawa, Ont.

NESTERENKO, Eric (hockey); b. 31 Oct 1933, Flin Flon, Man.; given name: Eric Paul; div. Barbara; c. Melanie, Donna, Paul; UofT, UWO; ski instructor; rw; jr scoring star with Toronto Marlboros; turned pro with Leafs at 18; played 21 NHL seasons with Toronto '51-56, Chicago '56-72; NHL record: 1219 scheduled games, 250g, 324a, 124 playoff games, 13g, 24a; mem. 1 Stanley Cup winner; on loan to Winnipeg Warriors '55-56 from Toronto won WHL title/ Edinburgh Cup; player/GM Trail Smoke Eaters at 43; learned to ski while coaching in Lausanne, Switzerland; dabbled in stockbroking, journalism; ran recreational hockey program Aspen; joined Aspen ski patrol '78; hockey consultant, actor in movie *Youngblood*; became ski instructor at Vail, Colo., from '81; guest lecturer Guelph; plays occasional oldtimers hockey games; mem. Man. Hockey Hall of Fame; res. Vail, Colo.

NESTOR, Daniel (tennis); b. 4 Sep 1972, Belgrade, Yugoslavia; lefthanded, two-handed backhand; moved to Canada '76; won ntl under-16, under-18 outdoor singles titles; -12, -14, -16, -18 doubles titles; Orange Bowl -16 doubles '88; 3 Cdn international doubles; 2 SunLife nationals doubles; attained #1 ntl doubles ranking in -12, -14, -16 categories; mem. world champion Sunshine Cup -18 team '89; turned pro '91; mem. ntl Davis Cup team '90-98, 5-5 in singles, 3-2 doubles; scored major victories over world #1 Stefan Edberg '92 Davis Cup, top-seed Thomas Muster '96 duMaurier Open; mem. '96 Olympic team; teamed with Mark Knowles of Bahamas '94 for doubles; won Bogota '94, New Zealand, Indianapolis titles, finalists Australian Open, Wimbledon semifinals '95, German Open doubles '96, Mason, Ohio ATP doubles '98; with Sebastien Lareau won '98 Japan Open; reached '99 Wimbledon 4th round before bowing to Pete Sampras; res. North York, Ont.

NESUKAITIS, Violetta (table tennis); b. 28 Mar 1951, Toronto, Ont. m. Josip Turcinovic; c. Carlo, Julio; bank data center clerk; among 28 jr. titles won Ont. midget girls, Ont. Open, Closed, girls under-15; won more than 100 ntl, US titles in singles, women's, mixed doubles including 10 ntl singles; finalist Commonwealth mixed doubles '75; trained in Europe, Japan; made promotional instruction film for Prudential Life; top-ranked Canada, 6th Commonwealth; retd '77; res. Toronto, Ont.

NETTLES, Ray (football); b. 1 Aug 1949, Jacksonville, Fla.; given name: Ernest Ray; div; Tennessee; trucker; coll. all-star; BC '72-76, Toronto '77-78; Ottawa '79; '73 WFC, CFL Schenley Award outstanding lineman; 4 times WFC all-star; HS coach Fla.; asst. coach UofOtt '82-84; res. Jacksonville, Fla.

NEUFELD, Chris (curling); b. 21 Apr 1957, Winnipeg, Man; m. Pearl; c. Denni, B.J., Michael; baker; began curling age 12; second for Vic Peters '92, '92, '97 Briers; winner '92; res. Gimli, Man.

NEUMANN, Peter (football); b. 10 Aug 1931, St. Catharines, Ont.; m. Edia Schellenberg; c. Peter, Kristine, Denise, Jimmy, Nancy; employee GM; def. end, linebacker Hamilton '51-63; 7 Grey Cup finals, 3 winners; mem. Canadian Football Hall of Fame; res. St. Catharines, Ont.

NEW, Maureen (swimming); b. 28 Dec 1963, Edmonton, Alta.; m. Mora; UAlta.; freestyle specialist; bronze 4x100 FS relay '83 FISU Games; ntl, Commonwealth record 4x100 medley relay '82; mem. '84 Olympic team; last known res. Pico Rivera, Calif.

NEWHOUSE, Ian (t&f); b. 25 Dec 1956, Calgary, Alta.; UBC; t&f coach Lakehead.; mem. Edm. Olympic Club; 3 ntl indoor 400m, 2 800m titles, 3 outdoor 400m hurdles titles; mem. '79, '83 Pan-Am, '80, '84 Olympic, '82 Commonwealth, '79, '81, '83 FISU Games teams; ntl record 400m hurdles (50.04), 500yds (57.7), 500m (1:03.6), 400m (47.63); fastest electronic time in world 600m (1:17.52) '81 CIAU championships; world record 300m hurdles (37.0) '81 Vandal International; male athlete of '81 CIAU championships; 2 CIAU indoor t&f male athlete of yr awards; res. Thunder Bay, Ont.

NEWMAN, Al (coaching); b. 2 Apr 1912, Detroit, Mich.; during 40-year career at Windsor Patterson CI won 30 titles in football and other sports; one of 20 student coaches invited by German Olympic Committee to attend '36 Berlin Olympics; most successful coach in Windsor AKO football team's history with 10 league, 4 Eastern Cdn and 2 ntl titles; OFSAA director; mem. Canadian Fitness Council 3yrs; mem. Windsor-Essex County Sports Hall of Fame; res. Windsor, Ont.

NEWMAN, Bernard (coaching); b. 4 Aug 1914, Windsor, Ont.; m. Lee Werbowecki; c. Bernard Jr., Leeann, Jane, Gary, Patricia; Assumption Coll.; teacher, politician; as Windsor teacher '34-58 gained reputation as gymnastics coach; among protegees ntl champions Ernestine Russell, Ed Gagnier; coached more than 170 individual titlists; only coach to guide ntl jr. male, sr. women's athlete of year same

year; ntl chair. of gymnastics AAU '55-56; coach ntl gymnastics team '56 Olympics, '58 world, '59 Pan-Am Games; Windsor alderman '55-60; MLA (Lib) Windsor; mem. Windsor-Essex County Sports Hall of Fame; res. Windsor, Ont.

NEWMAN, Pat (rowing); b. 7 Aug 1963, St. Catharines, Ont.; men's coxed 8s.; mem. ntl team from '87; competed '92, '96 Olympics; 2 Cdn, 3 US, 2 International regatta, 1 World championship gold; res. St. Catharines, Ont.

NEWSHAM, David (soccer); b. 21 Nov 1928, Saskatoon, Sask.; m. Pearl Hoogeveen; c. Stephanie, Noel, Andrea; UofSask, BA, LLB, QC; lawyer; 25yrs competitive soccer; mem. 3 prov. title teams; competed vs. 3 touring European teams; founder Saskatoon United Soccer Club; founding mem. Western Canada Soccer League; served at all levels of administration; 25yrs. Saskatoon Soccer Assn. exec., 20yrs prov. exec.; 5yrs CSA exec.; 5 terms pres., 10yrs secty. prov. SA; pres. Saskatoon SA; coach Arsenal Youth team; mem. Sask. Sports Council; res. Saskatoon, Sask.

NEWTON, Jack (football); b. 2 Jan 1887, Sarnia, Ont., d. 23 Dec 1967, Sarnia, Ont.; m. Eleanor Watson; c. John, Fred; UofT; educator; mem. '09 UofT Grey Cup winners, all-star; coached Varsity to 2 interprov. titles, '14 Grey Cup; head coach Sarnia CI, several Ont. championships; coached Sarnia intermediates 8yrs. numerous Ont., ntl championships; head coach Sarnia Imperials; mem. Cdn Football Hall of Fame.

NEZAN, Andy (golf); b. 10 Nov 1926, Ottawa, Ont.; d. 5 Feb 1997, Ottawa, Ont.; given name: Joseph Andre Rodolphe; m. Rose Sydor; c. Diane, Greg; engraver; 2 Que. amateur titles; 4 ODGA match, 2 ODGA medal, with Glen Seely 2 ODGA best ball titles; 2 Collie Cups; 8 Rivermead, 1 Chaudiere club titles; mem. '69 Que. Willingdon Cup team, '83 ntl triangular matches team; 2 O'Keefe Open, Renfrew, Buckingham Invitationals; 2 Ottawa ACT golf awards; ACT amateur athlete of '64; Charles Daoust French-speaking amateur athlete of '65; hon. life mem. Rivermead Golf Club; mem. Ottawa Sports Hall of Fame.

NG, Gideon Joe (table tennis); b. 15 Nov 1963, Toronto, Ont.; Seneca Coll., UofT; optician; mem. ntl team from '79; 1 US singles title; 1 CNE International mixed doubles title; overcame battle with cancer in '80s to win Pan-Am Games gold '87; mem. '88, '96 Olympic, '82, '94 Commonwealth championships, NA, world universities championships, '83, '87 Pan-Am Games teams; team silver '83 Pan-Am Games; won '90 Western Japan open; Canada Cup gold '91; NA singles titles '88-89, '91, men's doubles '93, '96; ntl men's singles '85, '89; ntl triple crown winner '89; with Johnny Huang doubles gold '94 Commonwealth championships; res. Toronto, Ont.

NICHOLAS, Cindy (swimming); b. 20 Aug 1957, Toronto, Ont.; given name: Cynthia Maria; m. Roy LeGrow; UofT, Windsor, LLB; lawyer; record 15h10m conquest of Lake Ont. 16 Aug '74; record 9h46m English Channel swim from France to England '75; record 1st 25km Syrian Jablak to Lattakia swim; women's division '76 Chibougama single-day 3-swim competition (10, 5, 1 1/2 miles), women's div.

25-mile Lake St. John swim; 1st woman to complete 2-way English Channel swim '77; 2-way record 19h12m '79; 1st person to complete 3, 2-way crossings 1yr '81; 1st woman to swim Chaleur Bay from Grand Anse, N.B., to Paspebiac, Que., '77; 2-way Chaleur Bay swim '78; women's div. International Cross Channel Race in record 10h10m '79; repeat '81; crowned 'Queen of the English Channel' with 19 crossings, including 5 2-way trips; World Federation of Swimming world's women's international swimming champion '76; Scarborough, Toronto, Ont. Cdn govt. awards; Capt. Webb Silver award; Sotiraki Trophy; Athletic Club of Columbus trophy; Ont., Bobbie Rosenfeld award '77; Vanier Award; recognized in *Guinness Book of World Records*; mem. Order of Canada; UK swimming, US International, Ont. Aquatic, Canada's Sports halls of fame; res. Scarborough, Ont.

NICHOLL, Jimmy (soccer); b. 28 Dec 1956, Hamilton, Ont.; m. Sue; c. Kate; midfielder N. Ireland Schoolboy Team; pro Manchester United '72; shifted to fullback, initial 2nd Div. English League game '75; club moved into 1st Div. '76; 1st Canadian-born player in FA Cup final; more than 200 games for Manchester United 1st team; on loan to 1st Div. Sunderland '82; sold to Toronto Blizzard '82; mem. N. Ireland World Cup team '82; res. Belfast, N.I./Toronto Ont.

NICHOLLS, Bernie (hockey); b. 24 Jun 1961, Haliburton, Ont.; given name: Bernie Irvine; m. Heather DeBrouwer; c. McKenna, Flynn, Jack (d); hockey exec.; ctr Kingston (OHA); drafted by LA '80; New Haven (AHL) '81-82; Kings '81-90, NY Rangers '90-91, Edmonton '91-93, New Jersey '93-94, Chicago '94-96, San Jose '96-98; 3 NHL all-star games; NHL record: 1117 scheduled games, 475g, 732a, 118 playoff games, 42g, 72a; topped 50-goal plateau with 70 '89; joined San Jose front office '98; proficient golfer, competes on celebrity tour; part-owner New Mexico Scorpions (WPHL); res. San Jose, Calif.

NICKS, Frank (t&f); b. 7 Feb 1914, Halifax, N.S.; given name: Frank Stanley; c. Barry William; retd. career soldier, exec. secretary; began competitive running age 10 and quickly emerged as standout sprint star setting records which stood for several decades; Maritime junior sprint champion; mem. '34 BEGteam; injury ended career '35; posted 80 1sts, 14 2nds, 7 3rds in races '24-35; also standout in rugby, soccer, badminton, tennis; 40yrs in Boy Scout movement; life mem. Kiwanis; NS athlete of '33; awarded OBE, Coronation medal; mem. NS Sports Hall of Fame; res. Halifax, N.S.

NICOL, Helen (baseball); b. 9 May 1920, Ardley, Alta.; given name: Helen Margaret; div. Gordon Fox; retd. Motorola Corp; right handed pitcher; began playing softball at 13; advanced to sr. women's league at 15; scouted by former hockey star Johnny Gotsleig and joined AAGPBL '43 remaining with Kenosha to '46 before shifting to Rockfoed; '46-52; during 10yr pro career appeared in 313 games with 163-118 w/l record, 2382ip, 1076k, 1.89era; also standout ice hockey player helping team to Western Cdn, Banff Winter Carnival titles; speed skater; competed in t&f, 7yrs club golf champion, has a hole-in-one to her record; honored by Cooperstown, Cdn Baseball halls of fame; mem. Alta. Sports Hall of Fame; res. Tempe, Ariz.

NICOL, Robert (curling); b. 10 Sep 1952, Ft. Frances, Ont.; m. Marion; plumbing assn.rdinator; mem. '79-80 Thunder Bay grand prix 'spiel title, '80 World Open, '81 Soo cashspiel; 2nd for Al Hackner rink 4 N O Brier reps; mem. '82 Brier, Silver Broom title rink; res. Thunder Bay, Ont.

NIELSEN, Ken (football); b. 10 May 1942, Hanna, Alta.; m. Marsha Murray; c. Alana, Jennifer, Grant, Keith; UAlta, DDS; dentist; halfback, end Blue Bombers '65-70; Western Conference all-star 3 times; '68 Schenley outstanding Canadian Award; caught CFL record-tieing 109yd TD pass from Kenny Ploen at Calgary '65; career total 280 passes for 4340yds (15.5 avg), 31tds; Man. male athlete of '67; completed Vancouver marathon '81; res. Winnipeg, Man.

NIEUWENDYK, Joe (hockey); b. 10 Sep 1966, Oshawa, Ont.; Cornell; centre Cornell (ECAC), ntl team '84-87; 2 NCAA East All-American, 2 ECAC 1st team all-star; ECAC rookie of '85; Cornell MVP '87; 2nd Calgary pick '85 draft; NHL with Calgary '86-95, Dallas '95-99; Calder Memorial trophy '88; NHL all-rookie team '88; Dodge Ram Tough award '88; King Clancy trophy '95; mem. 2 Stanley Cup winners; 4 NHL all-star games; competed worlds '90, world jr. '86; mem. '98 Olympic team; reached 50-goal plateau '88 51, '89 51; 400 career goals plateau '98; NHL record: (through '99) 835 scheduled games, 425g, 398a, 97 playoff games, 46g, 40a; hon. chair Capital Campaign for SPCA of Texas; res. Irving, Tex.

NIGHBOR, Frank (hockey); b. 26 Jan 1893, Pembroke, Ont., d. 13 Apr 1966, Pembroke, Ont; m. Dorothy Slattery (d); c. Frank Jr.; m. Ann Heney (d); c. Patrick, Pauline, Catharine; insurance exec.; Port Arthur '10-11 season; pro Toronto '13; Vancouver Millionaires Stanley Cup winners '14-15, Ottawa Senators '15-29, Toronto '29; with Senators 4 Stanley Cup winners; nicknamed 'Flying Dutchman', 'Pembroke Peach'; tied for '17 scoring lead 41 goals in 20 games; 233 goals in 281 regular season games, 16 in 33 playoffs; 1st recipient Lady Byng Trophy '25, repeat '26; 1st recipient Hart Trophy '24; noted for popularizing poke check; mem. Ottawa Sports, Hockey halls of fame.

NIGHTINGALE, Lynn (figure skating); b. 5 Aug 1956, Edmonton, Alta.; div. Bob Connor; c. Jessica; UWO; journalist, coach; EO sr. titles '70-72, ntl jr. '72, sr. '74-77, Skate Canada '73-74, Prague Skate '73, Moscow Skate '74; 9th '76 Olympics; mem. '73-77 worlds teams; pro Ice Capades '77-82; Cdn Ladies pro champion '81; skating double in movies *Youngblood* and *Skate*; City of Ottawa awards '72-74; Ottawa ACT athlete of '74; mem. Ottawa Sports Hall of Fame; res. Ottawa, Ont.

NILSSON, Kent (hockey); b. 31 Aug 1956, Nynashamn, Sweden; hockey scout; centre AIK Sweden '76-77; WHA Winnipeg Jets '77-79; WHA record: 158 scheduled games, 81g, 133a; NHL Atlanta Flames '79-80, Calgary Flames '80-85, Minnesota '85-86, Edmonton '86-87, '94-95; NHL record: 553 scheduled games, 264g, 422a, 59 games, 11g, 41a; mem. 1 Stanley Cup winner; became Edmonton scout '94 and, except for 6-game comeback bid '94-95, has remained as scout; brother Ulf also played in WHA/NHL; res. Edmonton, Alta./Sweden.

NOBLE, Reg (hockey); b. 23 Jun 1895, Collingwood, Ont.; d. 19 Jan 1962, Alliston, Ont.; given name: Edward Reginald; Collingwood jrs '15 OHA group titlist, prov. semifinalist; Toronto Riversides OHA sr. title team '16; pro Toronto '16-17, when team disbanded joined Montreal Canadiens; Toronto Arenas at inception of NHL '17-18, 28 goals in 22 games, Stanley Cup winner; St. Pat's '21-22 Stanley Cup winners; Montreal Maroons '24-26, '33, Stanley Cup winner '26; Detroit Cougars '27-32; 170 NHL goals; 1 season Cleveland (IHL); refereed 2yrs NHL; mem. Hockey Hall of Fame.

NOEL, Leo (boxing); b. 14 May 1940, Cocagne, N.B.; given name: Leo Joseph; Moncton city works supervisor; amateur record 19-0, with 16 KOs; Maritime Golden Gloves title '62; turned pro, won NB-PEI lightweight title '63; Maritime lightweight title, 5th ranked Canada '66; Eastern Cdn title '67; ranked #1 Cdn title contender '69-71; lost 8th round TKO to Al Ford in ntl title bout '71; retd. from ring '72; secty, chair. Moncton Boxing Commission; secty boxing/wrestling commission '81-84; Moncton city award '69, Moncton citizenship award '86; mem. Moncton Wall, Cdn Boxing, NB Sports halls of fame; res. Moncton, N.B.

NOGA, Arleene (baseball/softball/curling/bowling); b. 1 Jan 1924, Ogema, Sask; given name: Arleene Cecelia Johnson; m. Ronald Noga (d); c. Carol Lee, Robert Craig; retd admin. asst.; 3rd base All-American Girls Professional Baseball League '45-48; only player to play all league games over 2 seasons; set fielding record for 3rd base; played 1st organized softball '44 in Regina sr. league; played 9 provincial championships, 5 Western Cdn championships, '53 amateur softball world championship; 2 batting titles, 2 MVP awards, 1st team all-star; competitive curler '51-77; skipped Regina Ladies 'spiel grand aggregate winner '60; participated 5 Sask, 1 BC district playdowns; mem. Vics B mixed league 5-pin team '53; league organizer/administrator; held ladies high avg. several years; dir. AAGPBLPA from '87; mem. Sask. Baseball, Sask Sports halls of fame; honored by Cooperstown, St. Mary's Baseball halls of fame; res. Regina, Sask.

NOLAN, Frank Jr. (boxing); b. 24 Jan 1961, Sault Ste. Marie, Ont.; steelworker; Ont. 60kg title '78, ntl 60kg title '79; runnerup 60kg '78, US Golden Gloves, '79 NY State Golden Gloves; bronze 67kg '80 Acropolis Cup; quarterfinalist 60kg '78 Commonwealth Games; mem. '78 Commonwealth, '79 Pan-Am Games teams; res. Sault Ste. Marie.

NOLAN, Frank Sr. (boxing); b. 4 Oct 1932, Garden River, Ont.; m. Charlotte Gingras; c. Stephen, Frank Jr., Brien, Michael; steelworker; competitive boxer '42-58; began coaching '72; ntl team coach '78 Commonwealth, '79 Pan-Am Games, '78 Finnish International competition, '78 US Golden Gloves; res. Sault Ste. Marie, Ont.

NOLAN, Steve (boxing); b. 10 Feb 1960, Sault Ste. Marie, Ont.; given name: Stephen; m. Dory Lacasse; c. Deborah; steelworker; '74-75 jr. Olympics 57kg titles; ntl int. 57kg title '76-77, sr. '81-83; NA 57kg title '76; Tour de France 57kg title '79; Stockholm open 60kg title '84; bronze 57kg '80 New Zealand Games; mem. '80, Olympic, '82

Commonwealth, '83 Pan-Am Games teams; res. Sault Ste. Marie, Ont.

NOLET, Alan (gymnastics); b. 17 Dec 1967, Toronto, Ont.; McMaster; m. Tamara; began competing age 12; mem. ntl team from '86; all-around competitor; his high bar routine considered one of most difficult in world; competed '90, '94 Commonwealth, '94 University Cup, '91, '94 Worlds, '88, '92, '96 Olympic, '87, '95 Pan-Am, '93 FISU Games; 2 gold, 2 silver '90, 1 gold, 1 bronze '94 Commonwealth, 1 bronze '95 Pan-Am Games; 6 gold, 1 silver '94 University Cup; all-around gold '95, 2 gold '94 World Challenge; CIAU gold '94; 3 ntl sr titles, 8 ntl elite titles; res. Hamilton, Ont.

NOONEY, John (gymnastics); b. 21 Jun 1921, Bendon, Ireland; m. Patricia; Christian Brothers Coll., Ireland; retd. sr. civil servant Ont.; 14yrs PTI (all sports) RAF; emigrated to Canada '50; pioneer Ont. Gymnastics Assn.; wrote 1st gymnastics handbook for YMCA; coach Etobicoke; international judge Pan-Am Games; tech. dir. Ont. men's gymnastics; Ont. judging chairman; exec. mem. OGF; historian OGF, CGF; Cdn reporter Modern Gymnast mag.; mem. British Olympics Comm.; considered father of Ont. gymnastics; res. Mississagua, Ont.

NORD, Dennis (coaching); b. 8 Apr 1945, Winnipeg, Man.; m. Patricia; c. Christie, Lana, Danny; UWpg; teacher, coach; mem./coach numerous prov. volleyball, basketball title teams; coached Man. jr. men to 3 ntl volleyball titles; coached UWpg men to 3 ntl volleyball titles; coach ntl men's volleyball team '73 FISU games; asst. coach '67 men's Olympic team; head coach ntl team '77; CBC-TV ntl trivia champion '79-80; dir. Canadian Volleyball board from '82; res. Winnipeg, Man.

NORDHAGEN, Christine (wrestling); b. 26 Jun 1971, Valhalla Centre, Alta; UCal; teacher; competes in 68kg class; gold 4 world championships (3 in succession), 1 Pan-American, 1 German ntl, 1 Gilbert Schaub, 1 France International tournaments; 1 ntl 75kg, 5 ntl 68kg titles; Canada's female wrestler of yr '93-96; International female wrestler of '97; res. Calgary, Alta.

NORMAN, Clint (taekwon-do); b. 21 Jul 1955, Hamilton, Ont.; head instructor Norman's Taekwon-Do Centres; began taekwon-do training '73; pioneered ITF taekwon-do in Sask. '84; founding mem. Sask. Taekwon-Do Fed. International; level 3 coach; ITF Sask. tech. dir; head coach, trainer for Sask.; 2 ntl heavyweight titles; West Cdn sparring title; capt. ntl team '86-92; NA team gold '86; Intercontinental Cup, European championships team gold '86; individual patters silver, sparring bronze, '86 European championships; 2 gold, 2 silver, 1 bronze Pan-Am championships; 4 silver, 2 bronze world championships; active in conducting coaching/technical seminars; v-p ITF, chair. Pan-Am championships; v-p Western Cdn ITF; trainer/instructor more than 42 ntl champions; ITF outstanding instructor award; mem. Sask Sports Hall of Fame; res. Regina, Sask.

NORMAN, Larry (canoeing); b. 5 Apr 1966, Toronto, Ont.; UBC; kinesiologist; began paddling age 10; mem. ntl team '86-98; competed '92, '96 Olympic Games; 5 ntl C-1 titles; res. Chilliwack, B.C.

NORMAN, Moe (golf); b. 10 Jul 1929, Kitchener, Ont.; given name: Murray; pro golfer; ntl amateur title '55; pro '58; tied Stan Leonard low Cdn '57 Cdn Open; 3 Alta., 2 Sask., 3 Man. 1 Ont, Atlantic, Que. Open titles; Millar Trophy; 2 CPGA, 7 CPGA Sr. titles; record 9-hole 28 back 9 CPGA final Old Ashburn, Halifax; mem. numerous Ont. Willingdon Cup, ntl America's Cup teams; Rockway's George S. Lyon team matches, '71 World Cup team; 33 course records, twice recorded rounds of 59; considered by peers most proficient shotmaker despite impatient behavior; popular with fans due to running repartee throughout round; mem. RCGA, Waterloo County halls of fame; res. Gilford, Ont.

NORMAN, Percy (swimming/coaching); b. 14 Mar 1904, New Westminster, B.C.; d. May 1957, Vancouver, B.C.; began career as marathon swimmer but found greater satisfaction as coach; head coach Vancouver Amateur Swim Club '31-55; coached '36 Olympic, '54 BE-Commonwealth Games teams; among top students were: Helen & Mary Stewart, Jack Pomfret, Howard Firby, Lynda Adams, George Athans Sr.; Vancouver pool bears his name; mem. BC Sports Hall of Fame.

NORMANDIN, Pierre (table tennis); b. 11 Oct 1959, Montreal, Que.; given name: Pierre Gerard; McGill, BSc; with Marc Lesiege ntl jr. boys' boubles, with Mariann Domonkos jr. mixed doubles; twice Que. under-17 champion; final jr. year swept prov. singles, both doubles; silver singles, team gold Israel Hapoel Games; twice mem. English Open, once Italian Open teams; mem. bronze team '79 Pan-Am Games, bronze team World Student table tennis championships '81; 2nd ntl Top 12 tournament '80; mem. New Zealand Games, world championships teams '81; twice Ottawa Open titlist; res. Westmount, Que.

NORRIS, Edgar (rowing); b. 23 Dec 1902, Evesham, Eng.; d. (circa 1990), Toronto, Ont.; given name: Cyril Edgar; m. Renee Vielete; retd. Toronto city clerk; mem. Argonaut 8-oared bronze medal crew '28 Olympics; mem. ntl champion 140lb 8-oared Don Rowing Club crew, jr. 8-oared Argos crew, 8-oared open championship Argos crew; 8-oared Argos crew which finished in dead heat in English Henley then lost in row-over; Toronto Civic Award; pres. Ont. Municipal Assn., Scarborough Golf & Country Club.

NORTHCOTT, Ron (curling); b. 31 Dec 1935, Innisfail, Alta.; given name: Ronald Charles; m. Gerry McKay; c. Karen, Greg; steel production co. owner; launched curling career Vulcan jr. HS; skip Alta. entry '63-64, '66-69 Briers, won 3; 3 times world champion; nicknamed 'The Owl'; mem. Governor-General's CC; mem. Order of Canada, Alta., Canada's Sports, Curling halls of fame; res. Calgary, Alta.

NORTHUP, Helen (basketball); b. 16 Mar 1916, Arcadia, Fla.; m. Harry Arthur Alexander; c. James Barrie, Robert Keith; retd. secretary; softball Edmonton Gyro Pats; avid curler, golfer; mem. famed Edmonton Grads '34-40, 105 games, 1019 points, 9.7 avg.; mem. Canadian Basketball, Alta. Sports halls of fame; res. Edmonton, Alta.

NORTON, Wayne (baseball); b. 12 Nov 1942, Winnipeg, Man.; given name: Wayne Lester; m. Trudy Drake; c. Steve, Elizabeth; Whitworth Coll., Howard.; prov. baseball

development coordinator; pro '61-70 NY Yankees, Kansas City, Oakland organizations; rec. dir. Vancouver Jewish Community Center '66-74; BC Rec. & Fitness Branch assn.rdinator '75-80; BC Amateur Baseball assn.rdinator from '81; TV commentator; Montreal Expos Western Canada scout '75-80; part-time tech. dir. Cdn Fed. of Amateur Baseball 2yrs; CFAB ntl technical comm. '75-82; mem. BC mission staff '77 Canada Games; coached ntl team in international competition Italy, Nicaragua, US, Canada; '75 Pan-Am Games; conducted cross-Canada clinics for O'Keefe Sports Foundation; res. Port Moody, B.C.

NOSEWORTHY, Mark (curling); b. 3 Nov 1959, St. John's, Nfld.; m. Carol Power; c. Matthew, Nicole; Memorial, BA; exec. officer; silver '72 Canada Games; skipped Nfld. rink '82, '87, '94 Brier; total Brier record 21-12; 2 Ross Hartstone awards; 2nd team all-star skip '87; res. St. John's, Nfld.

NOWOSIELSKI, Dan (fencing); b. 16 Nov 1966, Montreal, Que.; McGill, BA; began fencing age 12; mem. ntl team from '84; épée specialist; competed '88, '92, '96 Olympic, 5 FISU, '87, '91, '95, '99 Pan-Am Games, 9 world championships; won ntl titles in both épée, foil; épée team gold '92 ntls; individual, team bronze '91 Pan-Am Games; equalled best-ever Cdn placing 7th men's épée Netherlands '95; bronze '96 World Cup; named top fencer '87 FISU Games; flag-bearer '91 FISU Games; brother Leszek also ntl team mem.; res. Ottawa, Ont./Montreal, Que.

NOWOSIELSKI, Leszek (fencing); b. 12 Sep 1968, Montreal, Que.; Notre Dame, MacDonald Coll.; began fencing age 11; 4 time all-American; mem. ntl team from '91; sabre specialist; Commonwealth championship gold '94; mem. '95 Pan-Am Games team; res. Ottawa, Ont./Ste. Anne de Bellevue, Que.

NUGENT, Andrea (swimming); b. 1 Nov 1968, Montreal, Que.; UCal; 8 ntl titles; ntl record 50m FS; bronze 4x100 MR '88 Olympic Games; silver, bronze '93 FISU Games; relay gold '86, FS bronze '90 Commonwealth Games; competed '94 Commonwealth, '92 Olympic Games; 2 CIAU records; '87 sports excellence award, '89 Olympic champions award; res. Calgary, Alta.

NUNNS, Brenda (tennis); b. 13 Sep 1945, Toronto, Ont.; m. John Michael Shoemaker; c. Adam, Alexandra, John, David, Victoria; Trinity Coll.,UofT, BA, UofOtt, MHA; father Gilbert 8 times Davis Cup team mem., mother Beatrice Eastern Cdn champion; with Faye Urban ntl girls -15 doubles '60, girls -18 doubles '61-63; with variety of partners Ont., Que., BC, Washington State -18 doubles; with Urban '64 Tennessee, Tri-State doubles; ntl women's open doubles '65; intercollegiate women's singles '63-66, Ont. -18 singles '62; with Cynthia Nowlan National Capital women's doubles '75; mem. Fed. Cup team '66; mem. Rockcliffe Lawn Tennis Club; teaching pro '78-81; mem. Intl. Lawn Tennis Club; res. North Saanich, B.C.

NUNNS, Gilbert (tennis); b. 30 Jun 1907, Leeds, Eng.; m. Beatrice Symons; c. Mary, Margot, Ruth, Brenda; Lower Canada Coll., UofT, BA; retired advertising agency v-p; at 15 Que. boys' champion; won both Ont., Que. jr., sr. titles; 7 times Davis Cup team mem., capt. '34; No. 1 Canada '30;

2 ntl jr. open titles; mem. UofT, Cdn Tennis halls of fame; res. Toronto, Ont.

NUTTER, Janet (diving); b. 2 Apr 1953, Montreal, Que.; m. Chris Rudge; c. Diane, Ryan; UMan, BA, Queen's, BEd; ED. OWIAA; CBC-TV sports commentator; bronze 1m, gold 3m '73 Canada Games; gold 3m CIAWU '73 championships; bronze 3m '73 summer nationals; silver 10m '75 USSR, Mexico; mem. '73 New Zealand, FISU Games, Canada Cup teams; gold 3m, bronze 10m '78 Commonwealth Games; 6th 3m '78 World Aquatic championships; silver 3m '79 FINA World Cup; bronze 3m '79 Pan-Am Games; mem. '80 Olympic team; '76-80 ntl 3m champion; mem. Cdn Aquatic Hall of Fame; res. Thornhill, Ont.

NYE, Barry (wrestling); b. 3 Jul 1936, Toronto, Ont.; given name: Barry William; m. Valerie Sampson; c. Stacey, Kimberley; comm. affairs mgr. Air Canada; Toronto 125.5lb titles '56-57; mem. Toronto Central YMCA Ont. Y title team '56; coach Scarborough Police Youth Club '57-60, Montreal Boys & Girls Club '61-67, Sir George Williams '68-69, Vanier Coll. '71-72, North Island WC '72-74, Pierrefonds WC '74-77, Riverdale WC '77-80; officiated '67 Pan-Am Games, '69 World jr., '70 World championships; coach, mgr. '70 jr. ntl team; mgr. '72 Olympic team; headed Cdn wrestling delegation '74 world championships, '78 Commonwealth, '79 Pan-Am Games; pres. Montreal pre-Olympic competitions '75; wrestling chair., host pres. Montreal Olympics; sec. QAWA '68-70, pres. Que. Olympic WA '70-72, v-p CAWA officials assn. '70-71, v-p CAWA '72-73, pres. '73-80; v-p Commonwealth Games Assn. Canada from '78, chair. '94; dir. COA from '73; mem. world wrestling body; hon. citizen Winnipeg '75; World Wrestling Fed. gold star, diploma '76; Air Canada merit award for contribution to wrestling '77; Queen's Medal '78; finalist '80 Air Canada sport exec. of year; mem. Cdn Amateur Wrestling Hall of Fame; res. Mississauga, Ont.

NYKOLUK, Danny (football); b. 16 Jun 1934, Scarborough, Ont.; m. Lois; offensive tackle Balmy Beach '54; Argos '55, '57-71; CFL record: 204 league, 16 playoff games; all-EFC '67, '69; mem. 1 Grey Cup finalist; brother Mike former NHL player, coach; named to All-Time Argos team '96; last known res. Toronto, Ont.

NYSTROM, Karen (hockey); b. 17 Jun 1969, Scarborough, Ont.; order mgr. Nike Canada; HS soccer/hockey MVP '84-89; mem. Scarborough United Ont. Cup soccer champs '83-88; Central Ont. WHL scoring title '92, twice runnerup; COWHL all-star '89-96; mem. OWHA Scarborough Firefighters '85-91; Ont. Winter Games gold '85-87; coached Scarborough Girls' Bantam A team 2yrs; forward 3 world title teams, '96 Pacific Rim, 3-Nation's Cup gold medal teams; res. Scarborough, Ont.

O

OAKLEY, Alex (t&f); b. 26 Apr 1926, St. John's, Nfld.; given name: Alexander Harold; auto worker; race walking specialist; mem. '60, '64, '72, '76 Olympic teams, 6th '60; gold 20km '63 Pan-Am Games, World Masters 5km, 25km titles '75; mem. 2 Commnwealth Games teams; Ont. athlete of '60; mem. Cdn Amateur, Oshawa Sports halls of fame; res. Hastings, Ont.

OATES, Adam (hockey/lacrosse); b. 27 Aug 1962, Weston, Ont.; Rensselaer Pokytechnic Institute; centre RPI '82-85; drafted by Detroit '85; Adirondack (AHL} '85; NHL Detroit '85-89, St. Louis '89-92, Boston '92-97, Washington '97-99; NHL record: (through '99) 967 scheduled games, 288g, 837a, 126 playoff games, 38g, 100a; reached 1000 point plateau '97; NHL record most assists 1 period (4); 4 time finalist for Lady Byng trophy; standout lacrosse player jr./sr./major Etobicoke, Port Elgin, Owen Sound, Brampton '79-84; lacrosse record: 120 scheduled games, 305g, 409a, 34 playoff games, 65g, 90a; record most assists (19), points (29) single jr. game '81; 3 Dennis McIntosh MVP awards; Advertiser top scorer trophy '81; res. Boston, Mass.

OBECK, Vic (football); b. 28 Mar 1921, Philadelphia, Pa., d. 21 Apr 1979, New York, N.Y.; Springfield Coll., BSc, Columbia, MA, NYU, PhD; owner public relations firm; coll. letters football, track, wrestling, swimming, lacrosse, boxing; pro football 3yrs Chicago Cardinals, Brooklyn Dodgers; coach, athletic dir. McGill '47-55; GM Alouettes 2yrs; athletic dir. NYU 12yrs. authored book on fitness, isometric exercises; public relations officer '76 Olympics.

OBERLANDER, Fred (wrestling/builder); b. 1913 Vienna, Austria; d. 1996, Montreal, Que.; c. Philip; considered one of the outstanding wrestlers to compete on world stage; 2 European, 6 French, 8 British championships; represented Britain '48 Olympics; moved to Canada '49; 2 ntl titles; with Joey Richman was driving force behind Cdn, NA Maccabi movement; high standards as wrestler, coach, leader were catalyst which produced many YMHA champion wrestlers; Maccabiah Games titles '50, '53; declared world's greatest Jewish athlete '53; dir. world Maccabiah Games comm. '65-75; pres. Cdn Amateur Wrestling Assn. '65-69; dir. Commonwealth Games '65-75; dir. Cdn Amateur Sports Fed. '65-69; dir. COA '65-73; FILA wrestling rep. '76 Olympics; hon. pres. Maccabi Can.; trustee Montreal YM-YWHA; recipient Olympic Order '84; mem. Cdn Olympic, Montreal YM-YWHA, CAWA halls of fame.

OBERLANDER, Phil (wrestling); b. 17 Aug 1939, London, Eng.; given name: Philip Mordechi; div.; c. Anthony, Joel, Karen; Cornell; sales rep; 5 ntl welterweight titles '60-65; gold Greco-Roman welterweight div. '61 Maccabiah Games; silver '62 Commonwealth Games; 5th welterweight FS '63 Toledo World Cup; 6th FS welterweight '64 Olympics; res. Ithaca, N.Y.

OBEY, Arthur (coaching/hockey/baseball); b. 25 Nov 1931, Piapot Reserve, Sask.; m. Yvonne Adams; c. 9; Notre Dame Coll.; school supervisor; coach Lebret Indians jr. B hockey champions '57-58; Lebret Indians juve. C, midget C champs '58-59; coach Lebret Indians HS basketball B champs; competitively he pitched baseball and recruited players for Notre Dame Hounds, Balcarres Braves, Fort Qu'Appellle Sioux; mem. Fort Qu'Appelle Sioux Indians Sask. Int. C hockey champs '56-57; 2 Tom Longboat awards; mem. Sask. Indian First Nations Sports Hall of Fame; res. Fort Qu'Appelle, Sask.

O'BILLOVICH, Bob (football/basketball/coaching); b. 30 Jun 1940, Butte, Montana; m. Judy Ristow; c. Tracey, Jodi, Coy; Montana, BA; football TV analyst; lettered in football, basketball, baseball Montana, all-Skyline Conference in each; twice Grizzly award for combining academic-athletic excellence; Dragstedt award, basketball MVP, '60-61; all-American football hon. mention; led US coll. pass interceptions '60; Earhart award best defensive basketballer Montana '61-62; Montana athlete of decade '60-70; St. Louis (NFL) draftee; late cut AFL Denver; all-star defensive back United League Indianapolis, led league in interceptions '62; Ottawa defensive back/back-up quarterback '63-67; twice EFC all-star; twice led EFC interceptions, CFL once; basketball coach Eastern Ont. Institute of Technology (later Algonquin) '65-69; football coach UofOtt '70 guiding team to Coll. Bowl; basketball coach, sports info. officer Carleton '71-73; basketball coach, asst-coordinator intercollegiate athletics UofOtt '73-77; asst. coach Rough Riders '76-81; head coach Argos '82-90, '93-94, '95, Lions '90-91; GM Argos '93-95; 3 Grey Cup finals, 1 winner; CFL coaching record: 113-112-3; CFL coach of '82 (Annis Stukus trophy); TV football analyst '96-97; dir. player personnel Sask. '98; mem. Montana Grizzlies Basketball, Butte Sports, UofOtt Football halls of fame; res. Mississauga, Ont.

OBODIAC, Stan (all-around); b. 7 Feb 1922, Yorkton, Sask.; d. 5 Nov 1984, Toronto, Ont.; m. Emma; c. Erin, Hadley; publicity dir., author; Sask. midget, juve. hockey; mem. Winston Churchill Cup winning team; leading scorer (12 goals) '51 world hockey Lethbridge Maple Leafs title team; coach Swiss ntl hockey team '52-53; mem. Sask. softball title team '39; mem. Regina Western Canada softball champions '42; Sask. sand greens golf titles '48-49; Eastern Sask. Open, Yorkton City Open, Melville City Open, Tisdale Open, Maple Leaf Gardens Open; author several sports books including *"No Substitute for Victory"*, *"Red Kelly"*, *"The Leafs, the 1st 50yrs"*; hon. dir. Timmy Tyke hockey tournament; publicity dir. Maple Leafs 25yrs; mem Sask., Yorkton Sports, British Ice Hockey, Canadian Hockey, Boxing halls of fame.

OBST, Herbert (fencing); b. 26 Jun 1936, Striegan, Germany; m. Elisabeth Hullay; c. Gregory; self employed sales agent; 10 Que., 3 ntl foil titles; mem. '66

Commonwealth, '67, '71, '75 Pan-Am, '72 Olympic teams; finalist men's foil '71 Pan-Am Games; last known res. Beaconsfield, Que.

O'BRIEN, J. Ambrose (hockey); b. 27 May 1885, Renfrew, Ont., d. 25 Apr 1968, Ottawa, Ont.; m. Mary Adele Gorman (d); c. Lawrence (d), Brian, Barry, Justin, Gerald; UofT; jr., intermediate, sr. hockey Renfrew, UofT; organized National Hockey Assn.; with father, Sen. M..J. O'Brien, financed 4 clubs including Renfrew Millionaires, Montreal Canadiens; mem. Ottawa Sports, Hockey halls of fame.

O'BRIEN, Joe (harness racing); b. 25 Jun 1917, Alberton, P.E.I.; d. 29 Sep 1984, Shafter, Calif.; m. Ilene Dyer; c. (stepsons) Stanley, Channing Bayless; driver, trainer; Maritimes circuit with father, 4 brothers to '35; operated own stable in Nova Scotia; '43-47 led all Maritime drivers in victories; US circuit '47; more than 4,500 winners, $20 million in purses; 3 Little Brown Jug, 2 Hambletonian winners; more than 500 sub 2:00 min. miles; in winning '55 Hambletonian drove Scott Frost to world's 1st 2 min. mile for a 2yr old; drove Steady Star to 1:52 mile for fastest clocking ever by a standardbred '71; drove world record 44 sub 2 min. miles, 32 2 min miles single season '75; drove Flower Child to 1:58.4 for 1st European sub 2 min trotting mile Sweden '75; instrumental in developing 2 Horse of Year winners, Scott Frost ('55-56), Fresh Yankee ('70); drove Scott Frost to '55 Hambletonian, Yonkers Futurity, Kentucky Futurity, 1st horse in history to claim harness racing's triple crown; with Clint Hodgins co-holder world record 11 wins single program (Truro, N S '42); USTA dir.; mem. PEI, Canada's Sports, Canadian Horse Racing, US Hall of Fame of the Trotter, Bob Elias, California Sports halls of fame.

O'BRIEN, John (baseball); b. 13 Jul 1866, West Saint John, N.B.; d. 13 May 1913, Lewiston, Me.; nicknamed 'Chewing Gum'; NL 1891-99, .254 lifetime avg., 229rbi, 501 games; played with Brooklyn, Chicago, Louisville, Washington, Baltimore, Pittsburgh; minor league umpire; mem. NB Sports Hall of Fame.

O'CONNOR, Buddy (hockey); b. 21 Jun 1916, Montreal, Que.; d. 24 Aug 1977, Montreal, Que.; given name: Herbert William; m. Jennie; ctr; standout minor career gaining reputation as a master playmaker, smoothly deceptive skater and brilliant stick handler; with Montreal Royals centred one of hockey's all-time great amateur forward lines, the Razzle Dazzle line of O'Connor, Pete Morin and Gerry Heffernan; NHL with Canadiens '41-47, NY Rangers '47-51; NHL record: 509 scheduled games, 140g, 257a, 53 playoff games, 15g, 21a; mem. 2 Stanley Cup winners; Hart, Lady Byng, Lionel Conacher trophies '48; mem. Hockey Hall of Fame.

O'CONNOR, Larry (t&f); b. 22 Sep 1916, Toronto, Ont.; d. 6 Sep 1995, Chatham, Ont.; given name: Lawrence Gerard; m. Helen Elizabeth Conway; c. Lawrence Jr., Thomas, Jane; UofT, Osgoode Hall, LLB; lawyer; ntl intercollegiate 120yd high hurdles '35-37; mem. '36 Olympic, 5th 110m hurdles, '38 BEG teams, silver 120yd high hurdles, gold 440yd relay; world record 60yd indoor

hurdles '37; Norton Crowe Memorial Trophy '39; mem. UofT, Cdn Amateur Sports halls of fame.

O'CONNOR, Zeke (football); b. 5 Feb 1926, New York, N.Y.; given name: William; m. Nancy Jean Seffing; c. Cathie, Karen, Christopher; Notre Dame, BSc, Columbia, MA; retd. business exec.; all-American '44; capt. Great Lakes Naval football team under Paul Brown, mem. Great Lakes basketball team under Weeb Ewbank '45; pro Buffalo Bills '48, Cleveland Browns '49, NY Yankees '50-51, Toronto Argos '52-53, Grey Cup champions '52; head coach Balmy Beach ORFU '54-56; active mountaineer, mem. Sir Edmund Hillary foundation; radio football commentator '58-81; pres. Sports Fed. of Canada '82-84; founder Nepal Special Olympics; governor Canada's Sports Hall of Fame from '84; res. Islington, Ont.

O'DONNELL, William (harness racing); b. 4 May 1948, Springhill, N.S.; m. Barbara McGregor; c. Faith, Christopher, Megan, Sean; entered business as second trainer for Jim Doherty in New England; became licensed driver at 24; moved to Saratoga to go head-to-head with J.P. Morel; set single season record 269 victories '79 (since broken) at Saratoga before moving to Meadowlands and Grand Circuit; broke old money winning standard by 50% with more than $9M '84 season in which he posted 422 victories then in '85 became sport's 1st $10M man with earnings of $10,207,372; drove Nihilator to '84 world record 1:49.2, later same day won Hambletonian with Prakas in record time; won 2 Little Brown Jug, 1 Hambletonian, 1 Cane Pace, 1 Yonkers Trot, 2 Cdn Pacing Derby, 12 Breeders Crown, 2 World Trotting Derby, 3 Kentucky Futurity, 2 Messenger Stakes among more than 200 major stakes titles; tabbed by NY racing fans as 'Magic Man'; drove '93 Horse of Year Staying Together; through '97 5359 victories and purses exceeding $90M; mem. Hall of Fame of the Trotter, Cdn Trotting, NS, Canada's Sports halls of fame; res. Franklin Lakes, N.J.

O'DOWDA, Ernie (builder); b. 1916, Elmwood, Man.; d. 25 Jun 1985, Winnipeg, Man.; following average athletic career was instrumental in revival of lacrosse in Winnipeg; coached/managed Elmwood Terriers, Elmwood Pats; pres. Man. Lacrosse Assn.; driving force behind establishment of Cdn Little League group during '50s; avid curler; hon. life mem. Elmwood CC; with Alex Irvin operated amateur boxing/wrestling cards; 1st Cdn recipient American National Recreation Assn. award '56; City of Winnipeg Community Service award '64, '72; Winnipeg park bears his name; mem. Man. Sports Hall of Fame.

ODUMS, Ray (football); b. 30 Oct 1951, Birmingham, Ala.; m. Jo-Ann; c. Alicia, Monique, Rozell, Tiffany; Alabama, BPHE; all-city, all-county HS football honors; never played college football; starred in college basketball; all-American, all-state, all-city track honors; numerous MVP awards; CFL cornerback Saskatchewan '75-76, Calgary '77-84; 3 WFC, 2 CFL, 2 coaches all-star teams; nicknamed 'Bama Blade'; last known res. Calgary, Alta.

O'GRADY, Diane (rowing); b. 23 Nov 1967, North Bay, Ont.; Queen's; former fencer she captained OWIAA team champions '87; began rowing age 21; captained Queen's team '91-92. 2nd seat women's quadruple sculls; mem. ntl team from '94; 3 Cdn, 2 US championships; FISU Games gold '93; Pan-Am Games gold '95; Olympic bronze '96; CARA, Ontario female sculler of year awards '94; last known res. Victoria, B.C.

OGDEN, Steve (curling); b. 21 Jun 1953, Moncton, N.B.; given name: Stephen Gerald; Dalhousie., BComm; mortgage officer; runnerup NB Schoolboy '71; runnerup NS Tankard '82; winner 3 NS mixed, 2 ntl mixed titles; NB 800m running championship '71; res. Halifax, N.S.

OGIBOWSKI, Diane (figure skating); b. 19 Jan 1965, Minnedosa, Man.; given name: Diane Mae; 1st competitive victory age 11; gold Central Canada novice div., Canada Games novice, Man. novice sectionals '79; novice nationals '80; 6th jr. worlds '80; gold '81 jr. divisionals, nationals; ntl bursary outstanding skater award '80; Winnipeg JayCees athlete of '81; runnerup Man. athlete of '81; last known res. Minnedosa, Man.

OGILVIE, Peter (t&f); b. 2 May 1972, Vancouver, B.C.; SFU; ntl jr.100, 200m titles; competed world jr. championships '88, '90, Pan-Am jr. '89, '91, Commonwealth Games '90, '94, Pan-Am Games, Worlds '91, Olympics '92, '96, FISU Games '93, Francophone Games '94; relay silver '91 Pan-Am Games; bronze 200m '94 Harry Jerome Classic; gold 60m, silver 300m Cargill Indoor Games, Winnipeg, '94; silver ntl 200m '94; PB: 10.29 100m, 20.46 200m; 3 Burnaby athlete of yr, 2 BC HS athlete of yr, BC t&f male athlete of '92; mem. Vancouver Olympic Club; res. Burnaby, B.C./Brisbane, Australia.

OGRODNICK, John (hockey); b. 20 Jun 1959, Ottawa, Ont.; given name: John Alexander; m. BettyAnne Leonelli; c. KelseyAnne, Breanne; investment consultant; left wing; jr. New Westminster WHL '77-79; drafted by Detroit '79; Adirondack AHL '79-80; Detroit NHL '79-86, '92-93, Quebec '87, NY Rangers '87-92; NHL record: 14 seasons, 928 scheduled games, 402g, 425a, 41 playoff games, 18g, 8a; shared WHL rookie of '78 award with Keith Brown; 1st NHL all-star '85; 5 all-star games; reached 50-goal plateau 55 '85; Fox TV hockey analyst; res. Farmington Hills, Mich.

O'HARA, Jane (tennis); b. 24 Jul 1951, Toronto, Ont.; given name: Jane Ellen; UofT, BA; journalist; ntl girls -12 closed singles '63; through '69 won girls -14, -16, -18 (twice) closed singles, Open girls -18 singles, doubles (with Karen Will); 4 times Wimbledon competitor reaching quarterfinals mixed doubles '70; 6 times mem. Fed. Cup team; 1st ntl women's rankings '75; retd. '76; ex-sports editor *Ottawa Sun;* employed *MacLean's;* res. Toronto, Ont.

OLAFSSON, Shirley (t&f); b. 10 Apr 1927, Vancouver, B.C.; given name: Shirley Gordon; m. Herbert Olafsson (d); c. Heather Sigrid, David Herbert; overcame club foot birth defect to excel in basketball, t&f, field hockey; mem. BC champion Int. A basketball team; '44-45 ntl sr. women's title basketball team; Sr. B, Cagett League, BC League, Vancouver City, Cdn Underwood trophies; '50 ntl high jump title; mem. '48 Olympic, '50 BEG teams; capt. '50 BEG t&f team; numerous ntl, international field hockey matches;

coached basketball, t&f several yrs; husband Herb mem. 2 Cdn basketball title teams, '55 world, '59 Pan-Am Games teams; level 3 curling coach; mem. BC Sports Hall of Fame as mem. '44-45 Hedlunds team; res. Richmond, B.C.

OLAND, Erick (cycling); b. 18 Mar 1924, Winnipeg, Man.; m. Rita; c. Janice, Lynda, Judy, Erick Jr.; Man. juve. champion '36-38; jr. title '38-40; 5 sr. titles; prairie overall jr. champ '40, sr. '43; 3 ntl titles; top ntl mile racer '47, '49; ntl 100km title '50; mem. '50 BEG team; set Cdn 100km, Man 5mile records; retd. from competition at 27; 2 terms pres. Man. Cycling Assn.; dir. Cdn Cycling Assn.; mem. Man. Sports Hall of Fame; res. Winnipeg, Man.

OLDERSHAW, Bert (canoeing); b. 10 Nov 1921, Toronto, Ont.; m. Marcelle; c. Dean, Reed, Scott, Lee, Lynn; retd. sales promotion; several ntl titles; only Cdn paddler to reach finals 3 successive Olympics; 5th 10,000m tandem canoe '48; 7th 1000m kayak '52; 5th 1000m tandem canoe '56; founded Mississauga Canoe Club '57; 12yrs dir. COA; dir. South Peel Red Cross Water Safety program; organized Mississauga Water Safety canoeing course; formed Canamtur Ltd., to assist in amateur sport funding; from '71 Canamtur has raised more than $1 million from private sector; dir. US International Swimming Hall of Fame; designed crests for CTFA, CASA; res. Burlington, Ont.

OLDERSHAW, Dean (canoeing); b. 7 Aug 1946, Toronto, Ont.; m. Diane Panet Raymond; c. Adri, Dana, Craig; Guelph, BSc-PE, UofT, BEd; teacher; 48 1st place finishes in all events (K1,K2,K4,C1,C2,C4) '62-78; 15 1st all events NA championships '66-77; 6 victories '69 Ottawa CCA championships; mem. 8 World Championships, '72, '76 Olympic teams; Ont. coaching certification asst.-coordinator '78-81; head coach Mississagua Canoe Club '70, Mohawk Canoe Club '73, Oakville CC '80-81, Ont. team '80-81, Canada Games team '81; res. Burlington, Ont.

OLDERSHAW, Scott (canoeing); b. 23 Feb 1954, Toronto, Ont.; m. Connie Lee Tipping; c. Adam; Sheridan Coll.; coach; claimed 23 national, 8 NA championships '67-83; mem. '84 Olympic, 8 world championships teams; semifinalist K1 500m, 1000m '81 worlds; gold 500m K4 '79-80 Zaandam international regatta; ntl kayak coach '95; res. Burlington, Ont.

O'LEARY, Kelly (canoeing); b. 31 Mar 1972, Halifax, N.S.; kayak specialist; 2 ntl jr. silver; K-2 500m silver '95 Pan-Am Games; competed '96 Olympics; res. Lower Sackville, N.S.

OLERUD, John (baseball); b. 5 Aug 1968, Seattle, Wash.; given name: John Garrett; m. Kelly; Washington State; 1b/lhp US ntl team Intercontinental Cup '88; lettered in 3 sports in HS; all-state baseball MVP; Baseball America's NCAA player of yr '87-88; set Washington State baseball records; drafted byYankees '86 but opted to continue education; never played in minors; 1b Toronto '89-96, Mets '97-99; made serious run at .400ba '93 finally winning AL batting title with .363; runnerup to Larry Walker '98 NL batting race with .354; Hutch Award '93; hit for elusive cycle vs. Montreal '97; mem. 2 World Series champions; res. Phoenix, Ariz.

OLESEN, Marc (t&f); b. 13 Oct 1964, Ottawa, Ont.; given name: Marc Christian; Stanford; 1500m, 3000m, 5000m, cross-country specialist; 9 Ont., 7 OFSAA, 2 Legion, 2 ntl, 1 Ont. Summer Games titles; Ont. midget outdoor 3000m record (8:53.1); ntl midget indoor 3,000m record (8:36.6); '81 *Ottawa Citizen* Indoor Games HS 1500m; ranked 2nd in world for age group '81 world championships; '82 Ont. 8000m cross-country title, Mitel 10k road race; 1st Cdn high schooler to break 4-min. mile barrier 3:58.08 Burnaby, B.C., 16 Jun '83; mem. '83 FISU Games team; mem. Ottawa Kinsmen Harriers; Ottawa ACT t&f award, Confederation HS Cardinal award; mem. Cdn HS Hall, Nepean Wall of Fame; last known res. California.

OLIN, Ralf (speed skating); b. 12 Apr 1925, Seattle, Wash.; given name: Ralf Emil; rep. Canada 5 Olympic Games, competitor '52, '56, '60, '64, flag-bearer '64; coach '68; mem. '56 world championships team; ntl metric champion '62-63, '66; variety ntl metric records; ntl mass start mile record; key role in promoting Olympic style competition which established Cdn strength in world outdoor events; mem. Alta. Sports, Canadian Speed Skating halls of fame; res. Ladysmith, B.C.

OLIVER, Al (baseball); b. 14 Oct 1946, Portsmouth, Ohio; given name: Albert Jr.; m. Donna; c. Aaron, Felisa; Kent State; baseball coach; outfielder-1st baseman; Pittsburgh '68-77, Texas '77-81, Montreal '82-83, San Francisco '84, Philadelphia '84; only player in history to combine 200 hits, 100 RBI single season both AL, NL; 8 consec. .300-plus seasons; 1st Expos NL batting champion with .331 '82; Expos player of '82, 2 Expos player of month awards; NL player of month, week awards; *Sporting News*, *UPI* all-star; mem. 5 NL, 2 AL all-star teams; AL record total bases doubleheader 21 '80; ML record: 18 seasons, .303 lifetime BA, 2743 hits, 1189 runs; 529 2Bs, 219 HRs, 1326 RBI; mem. '71 World Series finalists, 3 Silver Slugger awards; Canada's baseball man of '82; college baseball coach Portsmouth, Ohio; res. Portsmouth, Ohio.

OLIVER, Harry (hockey); b. 26 Oct 1898, Selkirk, Man.; d. 16 Jun 1985, Winnipeg, Man.; given name: Harold; Selkirk Fishermen, Man. jr. champions '17-18; Selkirk Srs. Western Cdn champions, Allan Cup finalists '18-19; pro Calgary '21-26; Western Canada champions, Stanley Cup finalists '23-34; Boston (NHL) '26-34; mem. '29 Stanley Cup winners;Rangers '34-37; with Calgary scored 91 goals, 49 assists; in 11 NHL campaigns scored 127 goals, 95 assists; pro record: 218g, 144a; mem. Cdn, Man. Hockey halls of fame.

OLIVER, Murray (hockey); b. 14 Nov 1937, Hamilton, Ont.; given name: Murray Clifford; m. Helen Marie Murray; c. Michael, Susan; hockey scout; baseball shortstop Hamilton, Galt (Sr. IC) pro tryout Cleveland Indians '57; Tilson Trophy as mem. Hamilton Tiger-Cubs Jr.A hockey team '58; pro Edmonton Flyers '58-59, 2nd in top rookie vote; Boston '61-66; Toronto '67-69; Minnesota '70-75; NHL record: 1127 games, 274 goals, 454 assists; asst. coach/scout Minnesota, '78-88, interim head coach '82-83 season; dir. pro scouting Vancouver '88-98; res. Edina, Minn.

OLIVER, Roy (t&f); b. 1909 Linden, N.S.; d. Jan 1991, New Glasgow, N.S.; m. Helen Rankin; CNR conductor; 1st race was 3-miler '27; won 9 *New Glasgow Evening News* 10-mile races; competed regularly in Canada, England and USA; won 4 *Halifax Herald* modified marathons; mem. Cdn Empire Games teams '34, '38; pushed Cy Bricker to Cdn record '32 Olympic trials; set ntl records for 5000m, 10,000m, 6miles; won 27 of 36 races '31-33, 6 2nds, 1 3rd; retd from competition '39; NS 10,000m record stood 39yrs; key role in inauguration of Johnny Miles marathon in New Glasgow; mem. NS Sports, Cdn Road Running halls of fame.

OLIVIER, Caroline (skiing); b. 22 Dec 1971, Quebec City, Que.; Laval; freestyle aerials specialist; began competing at 18; mem. ntl team '91-99; 2 ntl silver; competed '94, '98 Olympics, '95, '97 worlds; 3 World Cup race gold, 4 bronze; ranked 3rd WC finals standings '95, '97; res. Cap Rouge, Que.

OLMSTEAD, Bert (hockey); b. 4 Sep 1926, Sceptre, Sask.; given name: Murray Bert; m. Nora Jean Moffatt; c. Dennis, Bonnie; retd farmer; jr. Moose Jaw; pro Kansas City, Milwaukee (USHL); NHL Chicago '49-50, Montreal '50-58, Toronto '58-62; NHL record: 848 scheduled games, 181g, 421a, 115 playoff games, 16g, 43a; mem. 5 Stanley Cup winners; earned reputation as hardnosed player and team motivator; 2 2nd team all-star; twice led NHL in assists; scout for Rangers; coach 2yrs Vancouver (WHL); 1st coach Oakland expansion team '67; mem. Hockey, Sask. Sports halls of fame; res. Calgary, Alta.

OLMSTED, Barbara (canoeing); b. 17 Aug 1959, North Bay, Ont.; Queen's BA, BPhE, Bed, UWO, MA; teacher; kayak specialist; '77 Canada Games K2, K1, K4 500m titles; semifinalist '77 jr. worlds K2 500m; ntl sr. record 2:03.2 winning '79 K2 500m title; '81 Commonwealth Cup K2 500m, 1000m; '82 Vichy regatta K4 500m; '83 Pan-Am championships K4 500m; mem. 500m K4 bronze crew '84 Olympics; competed '88 Olympics, '81-83, '85-87 worlds; 2 ntl K2 500m, 1 K4 titles; retd. from competition '88; coach North Bay club '89-92, club exec. '93-96; sister Nancy ntl team mem.; res. North Bay, Ont.

OLMSTED, Nancy (canoeing); b. 25 Feb 1966, North Bay, Ont.; Queen's, BA, BPhE, Nipissing, BEd, McMaster, BSc; physiotherapist; kayak specialist; sister Barbara ntl team mem.; 5 ntl K1 500m, 4 K2 500m, 2 K4 500m titles; 1 K1, 2 K2, 2 K4 500m Pan-Am championships titles; mem. '84, '88 Olympic teams; retd. from competition '92; res. North Bay, Ont.

OLSEN, Phil (t&f); b. 31 Jan 1957, Nanaimo, B.C.; given name: Philip Einar; m. Anne Robinson; Tennessee; teaching asst, strength coach; ntl team '73-86; world javelin record for 16-19 yr-olds; holds oldest standing BC javelin record (71.46) from '74; 9 ntl sr. javelin titles; 4yr Tennessee letterman; 4 times all-American; NCAA javelin champion '76; gold '73 Canada Games, '78 Commonwealth Games; Commonwealth, ntl, junior world javelin record 87.72m '76 Olympic qualifying round; triple crown '77 Melbourne International, gold '77-79 Dogwood Relays, '80 France Olympic alternatives, '80 Tom Brown Classic, '81 Pacific Conf. Games; Viscount Alexander amateur athletic award '73; mem. '76, '80, '84 Olympic, '78, '82 Commonwealth, '75, '79, Pan-Am Games teams; 2 Tennesseeoutstanding athlete awards; named by *Athletics* magazine to Canada's all-time men's t&f team; res. Nanaimo, B.C.

OLSON, Betty (speed skating/t&f); b. 19 Sep 1928, Winnipeg, Man.; given name: Betty Mitchell; m. Robert Olson; c. Nancy, Karen, Barbara; business coll.; ssecty/real estate agent; 5 women's NA speed skating titles '46-50; represented Canada world championships '49; ntl 200-metre t&f champion '47; mem. Manitoba, Cdn Speed Skating halls of fame; res. Newport Beach, Calif.

OLSON, Billy (snooker); b. 14 Jan 1922, North Battleford, Sask.; d. 11 Feb 1995, Ottawa, Ont.; Dominion Wide photo processing co. owner; photographer; processed photographs for *Ottawa Journal, The Canadian Press, Globe & Mail, Toronto Telegram*, motion films Rough Riders, Alouettes, CBC; shift to video forced closure of film processing operation '86; became involved in snooker as hobby '64 after watching Joe and Fred Davis in UK; owned Karrys Bowling & Billiards, Century Club '64-85; mem. Ottawa team which competed 13 times in International Snooker Players amateur team championships, winning six titles; also claimed individual championship '84 in Bermuda; nicknamed 'Mr. Death' for intense approach to competition.

OLSON, Greg (golf); b. 21 Feb 1954, Bitburg, Germany; given name: Gregory Glenn; m. Tracy Miller; Florida Junior College, AA, Florida, BA, BSc; Apple USA advertising agency account exec.; mem. Que. jr. team '71-72, Que.-Ont. team '71-72, Que. Willingdon Cup team '74, '76, '80; mem. Fla. colleges all-state team '74-75; Fla. State colleges district champion '75; Cape Coral, Fla., Intercollegiate Invitational champion '78; mem.Florida golf team '77-78; '82 Que. Amateur title, runnerup '72, 3 Alexander of Tunis trophies; low amateur '77 Quebec Open; 4th Cdn amateur '79, won Cdn amateur '80; alternate Cdn world best-ball team '79; top-ranked Que. player '80; low individual '80 Que. Willingdon Cup champions; low Cdn, 13th overall '80 world amateur; CPGA tour card '83; '78 presidential recognition award Florida; Ottawa ACT athlete of '80; Que. golfer of '82, res. San Jose, Calif.

OLSON, Scott (boxing); b. 26 Feb 1968, Edmonton, Alta.; pro boxer; 48kg (flyweight) boxer; competed in '85 World Cup, '86 World championships, Commonwealth Games, '87 President's Cup, Pan-Am Games, '88 Olympics; gold Commonwealth Games, President's Cup; turned pro '88; nicknamed 'Bulldog'; twice broken right hand cost him world title bout shots; defeated Roger Espanola 10 Dec 1994 to claim International Boxing Organization world flyweight title; lost IBA world light-flyweight title on 10th round KO to Michael Carbajal '97; res. Edmonton, Alta.

O'MALLEY, Terry (hockey); b. 21 Oct 1940, Toronto, Ont.; m. Deborah Suzanne Hindle; c. Kathleen, Frank, Bridget; UBC, UMan; educator; St. Michael's College '61 Memorial Cup team; ntl team Olympic program '63-70; player-coach Japan '71-78; 1st Cdn to play on 3 Olympic hockey teams; at age 39, 124 days oldest Cdn to play on Olympic hockey team '80; coach Notre Dame Coll. Hounds ntl midget finalists '84; res. Wilcox, Sask.

OMHOLT-JENSEN, Jarl (skiing); b. 5 Jun 1947, Oslo, Norway; given name: Jarl Edvard; m. Tony Elaine Bishop; writer, broadcaster, photographer; mem. ntl cross-country ski team '69-73; ntl XC sr. 3x10km relay champion '71; 3rd 15km '71 NA championships; mem. '72 Olympic team; CTV color commentator '80, '84 Olympic XC, biathlon events; last known res. Mayerthorpe, Alta.

O'NEILL, Brian (administration); b. 25 Jan 1929, Montreal, Que.; m. Jean Yates; c. Sean, Darcy, Nancy, Patrick, Sandra; Loyola College, BA, McGill, BComm; consultant, former exec.-v-p National Hockey League; hockey, football Loyola College; varsity hockey McGill; junior B Montreal Winged Wheelers; mem. Montreal MAAA, Hockey halls of fame; res. Montreal, Que.

O'NEILL, John (rowing); b. 1877, Ketch Harbor, N.S., d. 1967, Halifax, N.S.; '04 Halifax harbor sculling title; Middle States regatta singles title '05, '07; US Assn. singles '08; US single sculls '09; mem. NS, Canada's Sports halls of fame.

O'NEILL, Kay (curling); b. 7 Dec 1926, Stratford, Ont.; given name: Catherine; m. Joe O'Neill; c. Michael, Kathy; launched curling career '67; competed 11 Eastern Ont. ladies championships, 10 as skip; skipped 3 EOLCA sr. finals; skipped 2 Lady Tweedsmuir titlists; won Southern Ont. silver tankard '72, runnerup '73; scored 8-ender '73; won EOLCA int. title '85; skipped in 5 Ont. ladies finals; rep. prov. '70 ntls; 3 mixed zone titles, 2 Ont. mixed finals; 3rd ntl mixed finals '76; 2 Kingston CC, 4 Cataraqui G&CC titles; Kingston Kiwanis outstanding achievement award '80; res. Kingston, Ont.

O'NEILL, Tip (baseball); b. 25 May 1858, Woodstock, Ont.; d. 31 Dec 1915, Montreal, Que.; given name: James Edward; restaurateur; early baseball Ont. leagues, pitched amateur ball Harriston, Woodstock, leading latter to ntl title 1880; semipro Detroit; major leagues N Metropolitans, St. Louis, Chicago, Cincinnati as pitcher-outfielder; with John Humphries formed 1st all-Cdn battery 1883; 10yr big league record of 16-16 as pitcher and .326ba through 1054 games; 38 World Series games; in 1887 compiled all-time record .492 single season avg. (walks were treated as hits that season), with walks removed avg. recalculated to .435; only batter to lead league in doubles, triples, homers same season; competed Players' League 1890; retd. to Montreal where he played key role in bringing pro baseball to that city; pres. Montreal (EL) team; served as umpire; mem. Windsor-Essex Sports, Cdn Baseball, Canada's Sports halls of fame.

ONESCHUK, Steve (football); b. 22 Nov 1930, St. Catharines, Ont.; d. 20 Apr 1996, Hamilton, Ont.; m. Marilyn McIntosh; c. Douglas, James; UofT, BPHE; HS principal; mem. St. Catharines jr. Athletics ('48 Minto Cup lacrosse finalist), sr. Athletics '49, '50; UofT football all-star 4yrs; Johnny Copp Memorial Trophy '54; George M. Biggs Trophy '53-54; Hamilton (CFL) '55-60, co-capt. 3yrs; 2 East-West Shrine games; EFC, *Globe and Mail* all-star 3 times; led Ticat scorers '57 as halfback, placement kicker; 3 Grey Cup finals, 1 winner; asst. coach Ticats '61; mem. UofT Sports Hall of Fame.

ONGARO, Alex (cycling); b. 5 Oct 1963, Edmonton, Alta.; bicycle builder; ntl jr. 1000m sprint title; Alta. 100m time trial, men's 1000m sprint titles; ntl men's 1000m sprint title

'83; mem. '82 Commonwealth, '83 FISU, '84 Olympic Games, '82-83 world championships teams; CCA jr. cyclist of '81; last known res. Edmonton, Alta.

OPSAL, Frank (shooting); b. 18 Nov 1928, Vancouver, B.C.; given name: Frank Edward; div.; c. Laura Louise, Frank Matthew, Cynthia Marie; financier; trap and skeet specialist; 6 BC skeet titles; 3 ntl, 10 BC trap titles; twice posted BC record perfect 200x200 trap singles in prov. competition; Western Zone singles trap champion '57; mem. 7 Pacific International Trapshooting Assn. all-star teams; mem. '62 Sports Afield all-American trap team, 4 *Sports Afield* all-Canada trap teams, *Hunting and Fishing in Canada* all-star team '60-64; *Rod and Gun in Canada* '66 all-star team; winner more than 300 tournaments; mem. BC combined trap and skeet all-star teams '54-67; 7 times capt.; capt. ntl team '62 world championships; mem. ntl trap team '56 Olympics; mem. BC Sports Hall of Fame; res. Vancouver, B.C.

O'QUINN, Red (football); b. 7 Sep 1925, Bluett Falls, N.C.; given name: John William; m. Dorothy Brown; c. Kathy, John III; Wake Forest, BSc, MA; retd. marketing manager; all-Southern receiver; pro Chicago (NFL) 2yrs; tight end Montreal (CFL) '52-59, combined with Sam Etcheverry for 377 receptions, 5679yds, 24tds (from '54 when EFC records were kept); frequent all-East, all-Canadian; honored by Montreal fans with 'day' '59; 3 Grey Cup finals; Grey Cup records '54 with 13 receptions, 316 yds, longest pass and run 90 yds.; best season '55 with 78 receptions; GM Ottawa '62-69, Montreal '70-71; with Etcheverry Montreal sportsman of year for '70 Grey Cup victory; mem. Wake Forest, North Carolina Sports, Canadian Football halls of fame; res. Manotick, Ont.

O'REE, Willie (hockey); b. 15 Oct 1935, Fredericton, N.B.; given name: William Eldon; NHL/USA dir. Diversity Task Force; pro debut Que. Aces '56; became 1st black man to play in NHL 18 Jan '58; played 45 NHL games with Boston '58-61; 13yrs WHL with Los Angeles, San Diego '61-74; New Haven (AHL) '73; San Diego (semipro) '74-76, PHL '79; led WHL scorers '64 with 38 goals; retd. '79; baseball Fredericton Tigers, Milwaukee Braves tryout '53; subject of TV documentary Echoes in the Rink '93; jersey #20 retd by San Diego Gulls; hon. doctorate Saint Thomas U '92; mem. San Diego, NB Sports halls of fame; res. La Mesa, Calif.

ORGAN, Gerry (football); b. 4 Dec 1944, Cheltenham, Eng.; m. Lore; c. Jamey, Leah; Guelph, BSc; pastor; all-Cdn Guelph Gryphons; place kicker Rough Riders '71-83; 4 EFC, 1 CFL scoring titles; 2nd only to Dave Cutler CFL all-time scoring; 6 FG single game '73, '80; shares CFL record 4 FG single quarter; PB 154 consec. converts '74-79; Schenley outstanding Canadian award '73, runnerup '72; CFL record: 2 tds, 391 converts, 318 field goals, 105 singles, 1462 points; 1st EFC player to pass 1000 point plateau; sweater #71 retired '84; mem. Athletes in Action; mem. Guelph, OUAA football, Ottawa Sports halls of fame; res. Orton, Ont.

O'ROURKE, Frank (baseball); b. 28 Nov 1894, Hamilton, Ont.; d. 14 May 1986, Chatham, N.J.; given name: James Francis; nicknamed 'Blackie'; spent 70yrs involved with baseball; began ML career at 17 as shortstop with Boston Braves; minor league stints with Bridgeport (Conn. League), Lawrence (New England League), Wilkes-Barre (NY State League) before joining Brooklyn Dodgers as 3rd baseman '17-18; back to minors with New London (EL), Birmingham (IL), Toronto (IL) before joining Washington (AL) as shortstop '20-21; dealt to Red Sox '22; back to Toronto '23-24 then claimed by Detroit to play 2nd base '24-26; dealt to St. Louis Browns he played 3rd base '27-31; player/mgr. Milwaukee (AA) '31-33, Montreal (IL) '34, Charlotte (Piedmont) '35, El Dorado (Cotton States) '36-39; minor league managerial record 536-534; scout Cincinnati '41-51, NY Yankees '52-83; ML record: 1131 games, 4069ab, 1032h, 196d, 42t, 15hr, 547r, 430rbi, 101sb, .254ba.

ORR, Bobby (hockey); b. 20 Mar 1948, Parry Sound, Ont.; given name: Robert Gordon; m. Peggy; c. Darren; North Eastern (Boston), hon. doctorate in humanities; hockey exec., player agent; shortstop MacTier Ont. provincial champion jr. baseball team '63; Oshawa Generals OHA Jr. A club at 14; led team to '66 OHA title; with help of Alan Eagleson signed reported $70,000 pro contract Boston Sep '66; deal considered cornerstone for NHL Players' Assn.; Calder Memorial Trophy NHL rookie of '67; 2 Art Ross scoring, 3 Hart MVP, 2 Conn Smythe, 8 James Norris Memorial Trophies; 8 times 1st team, once 2nd team all-star defenceman; NHL regular season assist record 102 '70-71; record point total for defenceman 139 same season; playoff assist record 19 '71-72; playoff point record for defenceman same season with 24; regular season goals record for defenceman 46 '74-75; 2 Stanley Cups; played out option, signed by Chicago '76; 6 knee operations led to retirement '78-79; asst. coach Chicago '76-77; MVP Canada Cup '76; NHL record: 657 scheduled games, 270g, 645a, 74 playoff games, 26g, 66a; asst. to NHL pres. '78-82; Lou Marsh, Lionel Conacher trophies '70; *Sport Magazine, Sports Illustrated* athlete of year awards; jersey #4 retd by Bruins; Jean Beliveau award '97; named to CHL all-time team '99; co-owner Lowell, Mass., AHL franchise '95; Officer Order of Canada '79; mem. Ont. Sports Legends, Oshawa, Canada's Sports, Hockey halls of fame, Canada's Walk of Fame; res. Weston, Mass.

ORSER, Brian (figure skating); b. 18 Dec 1961, Belleville, Ont.; given name: Brian Ernest; bottling co. rep.; began skating age 6; ntl novice singles title '77; jr. '79; Vienna Cup '79; Canada Games gold '75; '80 International Grand Prix title, 2nd Nebelhorn Trophy; ntl senior champion '81-84; '81 St. Ivel singles; gold Skate Canada '83; bronze '83, silver '84 worlds; silver '84 Olympics; fed. govt. excellence award '83, world champion award '84; flag-bearer '88 winter Olympics; CTV skating color commentator '93; Officer Order of Canada '88; mem. Cdn Amateur, Canada's Sports, Cdn Figure Skating halls of fame; res. Ottawa, Ont.

ORTON, George (t&f); b. 10 Jan 1873, Strathroy, Ont., d. 25 Jun 1958, Meredith, N.H.; m. Edith Wayne Martin; UofT, BC, Pennsylvania, MA, PhD; educator; middle, long distance runner; competing for Toronto Lacrosse Club won both Cdn, US mile titles 1892-93; captained Penn track team, mem. NYAC; regarded as most consistent runner and student of the sport; by 1900 had accumulated 121 victories, including 15 US titles; although Cdn by birth was invited to join US team for 1900 Olympics; as Canada did not compete he entered 2500m steeplechase for US; won gold medal and bronze in 400m hurdles to become 1st Cdn to strike Olympic gold; authored several articles and book on running; dir. Philadelphia Municipal Stadium '26; founded children's sports camp in New Hampshire; mem. UofT, Canada's Sports halls of fame.

ORYSZCYN, Eugene (gymnastics); b. 14 Oct 1914, Lwiw, Poland; d. 17 Aug 1997, Toronto, Ont.; Warsaw, LLD, BPhE; established solid reputation as gymnastics competitor, coach, judge in Europe before emigrating to Canada '60; chief trainer Polish Wlokniar Assn. training camp tech. dir. '49-54; trainer Gymnastic Centre of Technical Training Krakow '54-59; accepted as international judge '59; judged in 5 world championships, 2 Olympic, 1 Pan-Am, FISU Games; coached Etobicoke Jaycees; chair Ont. judges comm; mem. ntl judges comm.; chair. Ont. coaching comm.; co-author ntl men's technical manual; life mem. Cdn Gymnastics Fed.

OSBALDISTON, Paul (football); b. 27 Apr 1964, Oldham, Eng.; m, Leigh-Anne; Western Montana; punter/kicker; learned fundamentals at Kamloops, B.C., HS; mem. Richmond, B.C., jr. Raiders title teams; drafted by BC '86, dealt to Winnipeg '86, Hamilton '86-99; CFL record (through '98): 218gp, 477fg, 486cvt, 213s, 2130pts, 943kickoffs, 53,748yds, 14s, 1618punts, 66,527yds, 64s; 3 Eastern, 1 CFL all-star; set CFL single season points record with 233 '89 (later tied by Dave Ridgway); tied Ridgway with 8FG single game '96; Lew Hayman trophy '90; CFL outstanding Canadian runnerup '90; Dick Suderman trophy '86 Grey Cup; 3 Grey Cup finals, 1 winner; Tiger-Cats Charlotte Simmons humanitarian award '90; res. Beamsville, Ont.

OSBORNE, Bob (administration); b. 10 Apr 1913, Victoria, B.C.; given name: Robert Freer; m. Dorothy Beatrice McRae; c. Wayne McRae, Robert David; UBC, BA, BEd, SouthernCal, Oregon State, Washington; retd. professor; mem. '36, coach '48 Olympic basketball teams; mgr. '56 Olympic t&f team; 33yrs UBC professor, dir. school of Phys Ed and Rec.; mgr. '58 Commonwealth Games, '59, '63, '67 Pan-Am Games teams; liaison mem. '71, '75 Pan-Am Games comm., CdM '79 Pan-Am Games; pres AAU of C '50-51; chair. BC sports council '67-70; pres. Vancouver Field Sports Fed., dir. COA, exec. mem. Pan-Am sports organization, hon. v-p Cdn Commonwealth Games Assn., trustee BC Sports Hall of Fame; mem. National Advisory Council on fitness and amateur sport '61-62; CAHPER honor award, National Assn. of Cdn Basketball Coaches merit award, Confederation medal '67, Queen's Jubilee medal '77; mem. Order of Canada, Cdn Basketball, Cdn Amateur, BC Sports halls of fame; res. Vancouver, B.C.

O'SULLIVAN, Shawn (boxing); b. 9 May 1962, Toronto, Ont.; UofT; '78 ntl jr. light-middleweight (71kg) title; Ont. Golden Gloves '78-79, Ont. jr. 71kg '78, NY State Golden Gloves '79; Ont. Intermediate 71kg titles '80-81; ntl Intermediate 71kg '80; NZ Games 71kg '81; ntl sr. 71kg '81, '83; World Cup '81; silver '80 Finnish International meet; enroute to '81 Cordova Cardin tournament bronze defeated world, Olympic champion; NA light middleweight title '83; world championship challenge title '83; Commonwealth Games gold '82; silver '84 Olympics; outstanding boxer awards '81 NZ Games, '80 Finnish

International; CABA outstanding service award '80, SFC athlete of month (Nov '81) award, fed. govt. world champion award '82-83, Ont. excellence award '83, Viscount Alexander award '81; brief pro career '84-88; launched brief comeback bid 1991, again in 1996; retd. for good due to eye injury '97; res. Toronto, Ont.

OTTENBRITE, Anne (swimming); b. 12 May 1966, Whitby, Ont.; m. Marlin Muylaert; c. Cameron; Guelph, BComm; swim coach Burlington Olympian Swim Stars; breaststroke specialist; gold 100m, 200m '81 Canada Games, Canada Cup; 8 ntl sr., 5 Commonwealth, 3 Commonwealth Games records; 3 ntl 100m, 4 200m breaststroke titles; silver 100m, bronze 200m '82 world championships; gold 200m, 4x100 medley, silver 100m '82 Commonwealth Games; gold 100m breaststroke, silver 4x100m medley relay '83 Pan-Am; gold 200m, silver 100m breaststroke, bronze 4x100 medley relay '84 Olympic Games; CASA swimmer of '82, Cdn Aquatic Fed. female athlete of '83; hon. capt. '94 Commonwealth Games team; coached Guelph '93-97; OWIAA coach of '96; mem. Order of Canada, Cdn Amateur Sports, Aquatic, Canada's Sports halls of fame; res. Guelph Ont.

OTTEY, Milt (t&f); b. 29 Dec 1959, Jamaica; Texas; high jump specialist; coach Kent State.; mem. Scarborough Optimists TC; ntl team mem. from '78; 6 ntl, 1 US, 20 international titles; mem. '79 Pan-Am, '80, '84 Olympic, '82 Commonwealth, '83 FISU Games teams; bronze '79 Pan-Am, gold '82 Commonwealth Games; '82 NCAA title; ntl, Commonwealth records; Ont. athlete of '82; *Track and Field News* top high jumper in world '82; runnerup '82 Norton Crowe award; Jack Davies (top athlete), Cal Bricker (top jumper), Fred Rowell (top field athlete)awards '82; fed. govt. excellence award '83; res. Toronto, Ont.

OUELLETTE, Bert (tennis); 17 Aug 1916, Toronto, Ont.; given name: Herbert; retired postman, tennis teacher; began teaching tennis following WW2; pro, pres. La Boheme TC; teaching pro Brooklyn Park TC St. Lambert, club dir., shareholder 20yrs; tech. dir. jr. programming QLTF; 20yrs Montreal playgrounds teaching pro; master teacher; tech. advisor Quebec Games; pres. Que. chapter Cdn Assn. of Tennis Instructors and Counselors; taught game to more than 10,000 players; Centennial Medal '67; res. Montreal, Que.

OUELLETTE, Gerry (shooting); b. 14 Aug 1934, Windsor, Ont.; d. 25 Jun 1975, Windsor, Ont.; given name: Joseph Raymond Gerald; m. Judith; c. Mark; auto tool designer, teacher; ntl junior and cadet service rifle titles '51; Lt.-Governor's medal '52; small-bore prone gold '56 Olympics with perfect 600 score; ntl service pistol title '57; gold, 2 silver '59 Pan-Am Games, silver '67 Pan-Am Games; 6th '68 Olympics; mem. 13 ntl Bisley teams; 8 Queen's finals, finished in top 25 12 times; with wife Judy became 1st husband-wife team to represent Canada at Bisley '71; 3 CTR Bisley Agg. titles, 4 DCRA Macdonald Stewart grand aggregate titles; 7th world masters '58; Canada Post honored him with postage stamp '96; mem. Cdn Forces, Canada's, Cdn Amateur; Windsor-Essex County Sports halls of fame.

OUELLETTE, Luc (harness racing); b. 22 Jul 1965, St. Augustin, Que.; received grounding in sport with grandfather Gedeon and uncle Michel Lachance from age 11; as Michel's own driving career blossomed, Luc earned his A driving license and began campaigning his own 3-horse stable at Monticello Raceway; his stable grew as other owners grew to trust his training/driving skills; operated at Roosevelt '87, made Yonkers home base '88; became full-time catch driver '90 disposing of his own stable; drove free-for-all pacing sensation Riyadh on '95 five-race win string; HTA driver of '95 title; through '97 4102 victories with purses exceeding $29M; res. Fort Lee, N.J.

OUELLETTE, Red (hockey/baseball); b. 1 Nov 1938, Grand Falls, N.B.; given name: Gerald Adrian; retd. Campbellton sports dir.; Jr. B hockey OHA Waterloo Siskins '58-59; 12yrs pro hockey with EPHL Kingston Frontenacs '59-60, Boston NHL '60-61, Buffalo AHL '65-70, capt. Calder Cup champions '70, Omaha CHL '70-71, capt. Adams Cup titlists; prolific scorer; coached Campbellton Tigers to 3 Hardy Cups; amateur baseball Grand Falls Cataracts, NB title '62; mgr/player/coach Cabano Braves, 2 league titles; 6 batting titles '60-68; rookie of yr award '59; 3 Que.-NB sr. baseball league MVP/coach of yr awards; CHL MVP '71; mem. NB, Campbellton Sports halls of fame; res. Grand Falls, N.B.

OVEREND, Alan (speed skating); b. 22 Dec 1951, Abbotsford, B.C.; given name: Alan Howard; m. Shirley Inkster; c. Andrew, Christopher; UBC, BSc, UAlta., MSc; consulting engineer; 7 BC age-group titles; 9 Alta. sr. titles; ntl jr. '67, intermediate '68 short track titles; Alta master men's '89 short track title; exec. officer Calgary SSC '77-81; v-p AASSA '83-88; volunteer asst.-coordinator '88 Olympics; officials assn.rdinator '86 NA Short Track, '87 pre-Olympic World Cup, '88 Olympics; revised ntl officials certification program; developed officials manuals; Alta skater of '80, Calgary SSC master skater of '91-93; res. Calgary, Alta.

OVEREND, Bill (speed skating); b. 28 Oct 1959, Abbotsford, B.C.; given name: William Ernest; UofOtt, BA, King's College, BJ, UCal, MBA; print media specialist, Parks Canada; 4 BC age-class titles; mem. BC team '74-80, Ontario '80-82; BC team 2 Canada Winter Games; coached clubs in Ottawa, Abbotsford, Mission, Halifax/ Dartmouth; coorganizer/participant clinics in Hythe, St. Paul, Jasper, Anchorage, Whitehorse, Dawson Creek, Mission, Abbotsford; media liaison short track '88 Winter Olympics; res. Calgary, Alta.

OVEREND, Clara (speed skating); b. 13 Mar 1926, Kelowna, B.C.; given name: Clara Johanna Spall; m. William Howard Overall; c. Alan Howard, Thomas James, Laura Jean, William Ernest; UBC, UofT; occupational therapist; club coach Dawson Creek '65-72, Mission '72-77, Abbotsford '74-81, Whitehorse '81-85, Team BC '71, '75 Canada Winter Games; Yukon team coach '84 Arctic Winter Games; coordinator BC summer skating school; certified coach; founded skating clubs Mission, Abbotsford/ Matsqui, Sardis, Maple Ridge, Surrey in BC and Haines Junction, YT; formed Yukon Territorial Speed Skating Assn.; BCSSA exec. '68-80; v-p CASSA '71-76, '82-86; chaired various CASSA comms.'71-86; CASSA pres. '77-81; asst. team mgr. '76 Olympics; CASSA rep. '80 Olympics, World Short Track, '81 NA short track championships; runnerup

Air Canada sport administrator of '82; John Hurdis CASSA outstanding volunteer of '86 award; mem. Cdn Amateur Speed Skating Hall of Fame; res. Salmon Arm, B.C.

OVEREND, Howard (speed skating); b. 27 Feb 1917, Toronto, Ont.; given name: William Howard; m. Clara Johanna Spall; c. Alan Howard, Thomas James, Laura Jean, William Ernest; UofT, BA, BLS; retd. librarian; creator, 1st editor CASSA's *The Racer* '65; pres. Dawson Creek SSC '65-66, BC SSA '68-69; v-p CASSA '70-72; meet asst.-coordinator ntl outdoor championships '66; active in BC Seniors Games t&f; CASF award '68, John Hurdis award '73; mem. Cdn Amateur Speed Skating Hall of Fame; res. Salmon Arm, B.C.

OVEREND, Tom (speed skating); b. 30 Apr 1953, Abbotsford, B.C.; given name:Thomas James; m. Leslie Joy Post; UAlta, BPhE, UWO MA, 1000m gold '71 Canada Winter Games; mem. ntl team '71-78; mem. '76 Olympic, '755, '77 world championship teams; CASSA tech. dir. '78-82; dir. CASSA '86-87, '88-91; CTV color commentator '80 Lake Placid Olympics; mem. National Capital Runners Assn.; competed in National Capital Marathon; alumni gold medal as top graduating PE student '78; John Hurdis award '94; OSSA award of merit '93; res. London, Ont.

OVERLAND, Kevin (speed skating); b. 8 Jun 1974, Toronto, Ont.; long track specialist; mem. ntl team from '92; sister Cindy also ntl team mem.; 2 WC 1000m, 1 500m bronze; set Cdn 1500m record; competed 2 world sprint, 1 single distance championships; 500m bronze '98 Olympics; res. Kitchener, Ont./Calgary, Alta.

OWEN, Jon (baseball); b. 19 Jun 1958, Leatherhead, Eng.; m. Cathy Hesselman; c. Jesse, Travis; Southern Miss; Ont. ministry of transportation; pitcher London Majors, Sr. IC '76-97; through '97 994 ip in 166 games, 67 wins, 758k; 4 times league all-star; res. London, Ont.

OXENBURY, Noel (swimming); b. 25 Dec 1918, New Westminster, B.C.; given name: Noel Gertrude; m. James William Morrow; c. Carol Ann; ntl jr. girls 50yd FS record '33, 50yd FS, backstroke, 100yd FS '34, jr. world 50m FS, 150yd IM '34; 6 ntl 100yd backstroke titles; ntl jr. 100yd FS champion '35; mem. '34, '38BEG, '36 Olympic teams; gold 400yd FS relay '38 BEG; NZ 100yd backstroke record '38; ntl records 200yd, 100yd backstroke, world record 300yd medley relay; Pacific Coast international, Pacific Northwest 100yd backstroke champion; Crescent Beach SC coach '42-43, '49-54; coached BC synchronized swim champions Frances Lett, Carol Ann McPherson, ntl champion Allan Brew, jr. diving champion Margaret Mary Leeson; Vancouver Y swim club coach '44-46; founder, coach Kah-Mi Synchronized SC '54-60; UBC synchronized SC coach '57-58; chaperone '60 Olympic team; life mem. Crescent Beach SC, BCSSA; res. Surrey, B.C.

OYLER, Don (curling); b. 8 Mar 1907, Kentville, N.S.; d. 1990, Kentville, N.S.; given name: Herbert Donald; m. Dorothy Harris; c. Marilyn, John; retd. fuel merchant; established Brier record skipping '51 ntl men's title winner to 10-0 mark; performance made possible by addition of Newfoundland to Brier field; mem. NS Sports Hall of Fame.

P

PACE, Kate (skiing); b. 13 Feb 1969, North Bay, Ont.; m. Dr. Mark Lindsay; 3rd youngest 10 children; began skiing age 2, competing age 6; mem. ntl alpine development group '86-88, ntl team '88-98; won world championship '93; 3 ntl downhill, 1 combined, 1 FIS downhill, 2 slalom, 2 World Cup downhill gold; WC record 2-1-2; plagued by injuries throughout career but displayed true grit rebounding quickly to claim major victories; 5th downhill '94 Olympics; competed '98 Olympics; North Bay athlete of yr '87, '91; Cdn Sports Council athlete of '93; Ont. female athlete of '93; Bobbie Rosenfeld, Velma Springstead, John Semmelink trophies; res. White Lake, Ont.

PACHL, Carole (figure skating); b. 23 Nov 1938, Prague, Czechoslovakia; given name: Carole Jane; div.; c. Natalie, Kim Lerch; public relations; silver medal ntl jr. '51 only to have CFSA retract it and give her bronze instead; bronze '53 national championships; ntl title '55-57, only Que. skater to that time to reign as ntl champion; runnerup NA '57, 3rd '55; 4th worlds '57; 6th '56 Olympics despite suffering broken vertebrae in practice 2 days before competition; rep. Canada 4 times worlds, twice North Americans, once Olympics; retired '57; last known res. Montreal, Que.

PACHL, Vern (hockey); b. 4 Nov 1930, Yorkton, Sask; given name: Vernon Jack; m. Marilyn Kay Lowenberger; c. Kent, Kurt, Jane, Jill; UAlta, BA, BEd; teacher; Western Cdn jr. scoring champ '50-51; 3 UAlta scoring titles; mem. 3 Western Cdn college title teams; MVP Sask. Sr.HL '62; UAlta athlete of '60 award; played pro hockey Syracuse AHL; chair. Yorkton Sports Hall of Fame; res. Yorkton, Sask.

PAGAN, Dave (baseball); b. 15 Sep 1949, Nipawin, Sask.; given name: David Percy; m. Brigitta; c. Todd, Craig, Shari; Bellevue Community College (Seattle); carpenter; pitcher; pro '70 playing minor ball Johnson City, Oneonta, Ft. Lauderdale, Kingston, West Haven, Syracuse before promotion to NY Yankees '73-76; Baltimore '76; Seattle '77, Pittsburgh '77; farmed to Columbus; res. Nipawin, Sask.

PAGE, Fred (hockey); b. 29 Sep 1915, Port Arthur, Ont.; d. 22 Dec 1997, Vancouver, B.C.; given name: Frederick; m. Ethel Willianen; c. Elizabeth, Judith; retd manager; Port Arthur Jrs. '33-34, Srs. '34-35, Nipigon Intermediates '35-36; coached, managed teams in Fort William MHA '43-46; exec. mem. FWMHA '47-48, pres. '50-54; dir. Thunder Bay AHA '54-58, pres. '59-62; v.-pres. CAHA '63-65, pres. '66-68, p.-pres to '71; v-p IIHF '69-72; mem. hockey directorate '68, chair. '72 Olympics; pres. Pacific Junior A League '73-78; exec.-mgr. Central Div. BCJHL '81-90; life mem. CAHA, Fort William MHA; Centennial Medal; CAHA, AHAUS, IIHF, FWMHA citations; mem. Hockey Hall of Fame.

PAGE, Percy (coaching); b. 14 May 1887, Rochester, N.Y., d. 2 Mar 1973, Edmonton, Alta; m. Maude Roche; c. 1 daughter; Queen's; teacher, politician; coached Edmonton Grads '15-40, team played 522 games, won 502 for 96.2 percentage; attended Olympics Paris '24, Amsterdam '28, Los Angeles '32, Berlin '36, won 27 consecutive exhibition games constituting world championships; coached team to 23 of 24 prov. titles, 15 of 15 Western Canadian titles, 29 of 31 ntl championships games, 18 of 18 Underwood Trophy tournaments vs. US; during team's 25-year existence recorded victory streaks of 147 and 78 games; missed attendance at only 3 games in club's history, once while skipping Alta. rink to prov. title and twice while campaigning politically; MLA (PC) '52-59; Lt.-Gov. Alta. '59-66; mem. Alta., Canada's Sports, Cdn Basketball, Naismith Memorial Basketball halls of fame.

PAGÉ, Pierre (hockey); b. 30 Apr 1948, St. Hermas, Que.; m. Donna; c. Lauren; hockey coach; Dalhousie, MPHE; coach/lecturer Dalhousie '72; Maritime title '79; consultant Halifax Voyageurs 7yrs; guest coach Cdn Olympic team '80; asst. Team Canada '81, '95; served in several capacities with Calgary (NHL) organization '80-88; GM/coach Denver, Moncton; head coach Minnesota '88-90, Quebec '91-94, Calgary '95-97, Anaheim '97-98; pro scout Toronto '94-95; res. Tustin, Calif.

PAICE, Terry (wrestling); b. 22 Feb 1953, Whitewood, Sask.; given name: Terrence Ephraham; m. Lidia Pistillo; Lakehead, BPHE; contractor; initial major victory '71 Canada Winter Games; ntl jr. title '73; won '72, '74 CIAU titles; 2 ntl sr. FS, 4 sr. Greco-Roman titles; Commonwealth Games gold '74, Pan-Am Games bronze '75, 5th '76 Olympics; 2 World Cup bronze; USAAU championship bronze '76; 2 CAWA outstanding wrestler awards; Lakehead athlete of yr '72; Thunder Bay athlete of '74; accumulated 20 gold, 2 silver, 6 bronze in major competitions; 1st Sask. provincial wrestling coach; mem. Saskatchewan Sports, Cdn Amateur Wrestling halls of fame; res. Moose Jaw, Sask.

PAJACZKOWSKI, Tony (football); b. 31 May 1936, Verdun, Que.; regarded short on finesse and polish but long on desire, strength and brute ability as he shone in CFL with Calgary '55-65, Montreal '66-67; played defensive end/guard; 5 all-Western, 1 all-Eastern, 4 all-Canadian guard awards; 1 all-Western defensive end award; Schenley outstanding Canadian award '61, runnerup '60; mem. Cdn Football Hall of Fame; res. Mississauga, Ont.

PAL, Mohinder (field hockey); 1 Apr 1950, Sansarpur, India; m. Santysht Kayr; c. Manroop; Gyry Nanak U, BA; Holiday Inn asst. mgr.; mem. Punjab U team; all-India universities team; toured Australia with combined India universities team '71; moved to Canada '72; mem. Ontario team '73-88; ntl team Intercontinental Cup '77, '81, world tournament '78, '79; Pan-Am Games '79; last known res. Willowdale, Ont.

PALMASON, Diane (t&f); b. 15 Mar 1938, St. Catharines, Ont.; given name: Florence Diane; div. Hutton; c. Leanne, Craig, Eric, Tracy Hutton; m. Ben Johns; Queen's, BA; sports programmer; 220yds sprinter '54 BEG team; silver marathon World Veterans t&f championships '79; silver 10,000m World Veterans, ntl Masters record 39.10; bronze 5000m World Veterans '79; ntl Masters (40 plus) records, 1500m 4:53, 5000m 18:36.7, 10km 37:38:98; NA, ntl Masters records 800m 2:20.9, marathon 2:49.14; Ont. sports achievement award; asst. ed. *CMA Journal*; res. Engelwood, Colorado

PALMER, Alison (field hockey); b. 21 Aug 1960, Vancouver, B.C.; given name: Alison Gail; UBC; mem. UBC varsity team '80-83, BC -23 team '80, '82; ntl -23 team '82; mem. World Cup silver medal team '83; UBC female athlete of year co-winner '83; res. Vancouver, B.C.

PALMER, David (baseball); b. 19 Oct 1957, Glens Falls, N.Y.; given name: David William; m. Beverly Richey; c. John Brandon; righthanded pitcher; picked by Montreal '76 amateur draft; ML debut '78; Florida State League record 37 consec. innings without issuing a walk; in ML rookie season set club mark 8 consec. victories; elbow surgery appeared likely to shorten promising career and he saw limited action '81-83; returned to starting rotation '84 and hurled 5-inning perfect game (shortened by rain); res. Cordova, Tenn.

PALMER, Doug (curling); b. 9 Mar 1944, MacGregor, Man.; given name: Douglas Cyril; m. Margaret Phillips; c. Scott, Christine; insurance adjuster; jr. A, B hockey MacGregor, Winnipeg; sr.A fastball Portage La Prairie, Man., titlists '66; curled in '66 Man. Consols, 9 Ont. Consols (Tankards); winner every major 'spiel title Niagara Peninsula, record 6 Banana Belt titles; only skip to win every event in Whitby Sunlife; OCA Challenge Round winner; res. Welland, Ont.

PALMER, Lillian (t&f); b. 23 Jun 1913, Vancouver, B.C.; given name: Lillian Emily; m. Charles Collingwood Alderson (d); c. Donald, Blake; PS, HS 50, 100yd dash, high, broad jump records; as ineligible 15-year-old beat '28 Olympics seniors, set world record 50yd 5.4; mem. '32 Olympic silver medal relay team; with Hilda Strike, 2 British runners beat US gold medal team in post-Olympic match; '32, '34 BC women's 200m title; mem. gold medal relay team BEG; capt. ntl team, 4th 200m, flag bearer '34 Women's World Games; hole-in-one Point Grey Club '72; active in organizing junior women's golf McCleery GC; mem. Cdn Amateur, BC Sports halls of fame; res. Vancouver, B.C.

PALMER, Marilyn (golf); b. 17 Dec 1946, Vancouver, B.C.; m. Don O'Connor; c. Ryan, Sean; UBC, BEd; teacher; BC jr. titles '63-65, '66 ntl ladies' Closed, Open runnerup twice; ntl Open medalist '69, Pacific Northwest Golf Assn. title '73, medal '66, '72; with Joycelyne Bourassa NZ Foursomes title '71; with Dale Shaw national Foursomes '75, International Fourball '72; low amateur women's titleholder tournament '72; mem. 4 ladies' Commonwealth, World Cup teams, title '79; BC interprovincial team '64-75, Alta. interprovincial team '83; won '79 Sask., 6 Alta., 5 B.C. women's; low Canadian '81 ntl ladies; top Cdn ladies' amateur golfer '81; mem. Cdn Golf Hall of Fame; res. Calgary, Alta.

PALMER, Sue (cycling); b. 27 Jan 1967, Collingwood, Ont.; road racing specialist; following 3yrs on ntl team almost retired due to broken leg suffered in '91 criterium race; rehabilitation paid off with silver in individual road race, team time trial gold '92-93 Canadian championships; competed '94-95 Tour de France, '94 Commonwealth, '96 Olympic Games; ntl road racing title '96; res. Hamilton, Ont.

PANASIK, Bob (golf); b. 20 Oct 1941, Windsor, Ont; div. Dolores; c. Melissa; pro golfer; Ont. jr., best ball, ntl jr. '58, Ont. amateur '59, Ont. jr. '60; pro '60; 2 Brooks Bursary awards; pro from '59; Que. Open '74, Alta. Open '74-75, Sask. Open '74, Nfld. Open '73, Atlantic Open '75, NO PGA '66, CPGA '72-73, Cdn Tar Sands tournament of champions '76, Cdn TPC, Man. Open '86; '88-89 CPGA Winter Tour; top money winner CPGA Winter Tour '89; Peter Jackson Cup order of merit '75; limited success 1 yr US pro tour; 2 CPGA Seniors titles; mem. World Cup team '72-74; ntl golfer of '74; res. Tecumseh, Ont.

PANASIS, Rita (basketball/softball); b. 29 Mar 1921, Vancouver, B.C.; given name: Marietta; m. Samuel William Bell; c. Suzanne, Richard; Duffus Business School; mem. BC Intermediate A basketball title team '38-39, Senior B '39-40, Senior A '40-41; mem. ntl Senior A champion Hedlunds '42-46, Nut House '47, Eilers '53-54; 11 provincial, 8 ntl title teams; offer from Abe Saperstein to play with ladies' pro team; centre Percy Page personal all-Canadian all-star team; mem. several Vancouver city softball title teams; ntl team '44 World amateur softball championships; mem. '46 BC champion Ballards team; '49 Western Cdn champion Western Mutual team; rejected pro offers Chicago Bluebird team; mem. Eilers '55 Pan-Am Games team but didn't compete due to injury; mem. BC Sports Hall of Fame; res. Burnaby, B.C.

PANGMAN, Arthur (skiing); b. 1 Jul 1905, Montreal, Que.; d. 25 Jun 1996, Senneville, Que.; given name: Arthur Henry; m. Lois Martin; c. Peter, Jill; McGill, BSc; retd. engineer; mem. McGill ski team; Intercollegiate snowshoe title '28; mem. McGill rowing team Cdn Henley 140lb 4s, 8s titlists '29; mem. '32 Olympic team; mgr., coach, spare '36 Olympic ski team; mem. McGill '32 international intercollegiate relay title team; Que. Kandahar downhill title '32; chair. Laurentian Ski Zone '30-32; v-p CSA '36-37; founder, later pres., Red Birds SC '28; Mt. Tremblant peak bears his name; mem. Laurentian, Cdn Skiing halls of fame.

PANTING, Bill (speed skating); b. 6 Apr 1925, Winnipeg, Man.; given name: Arthur William; ntl jr. records '41; ntl outdoor champion '51; 1st commissioner CASA; mem. CASA rules comm.; asst. coach ntl team '73; ISU referee; exec. mem. Winnipeg Speed Skating Club; mem. Man. Centennial Commission; mem. Canadian Speed Skating Hall of Fame; res. Winnipeg, Man.

PAPASIDERIS, Peter (shooting); b. 19 Feb 1935, Greece; m. Lydia; c. Dimitrios, Diane; hair stylist; began shooting '67 winning 3 medals in first shoot; won numerous BC, Sask., Alta., provincial championships; City of Victoria medal; City of Ottawa gold watch (subsequently stolen); Hayhurst, Patron's DCRA matches; Sask. Lt.-Governor's, grand aggregate; 3 Alta. Lt.-Governor's, 2 ISU titles; tied for St. George's medal Bisley, losing shootoff; Bisley Queen's Silver medal '83, runnerup '84; qualified for 13 Cdn Bisley, 3 Cdn Palma teams; 2 Des Burke awards; Booster Club achievement award; Alta., Calgary achievement awards; res. Calgary, Alta.

PAPROSKI, Steve (football); b. 23 Sep 1928, Lwow, Poland; d. 8 Dec 1993, Smiths Falls, Ont.; given name: Steven Eugene; m. Mary Elizabeth Coburn; c. Patrick Steven, Peter John, Annamarie, Alexandra, Elizabeth; North Dakota, Arizona, Banff School of Advanced Management; sales mgr., politician; college football N.D., Arizona; pro Edmonton '49-54; Alta. HS heavyweight wrestling champion '43, runnerup ntl championship '43-44; MP (PC) '68-93; min. of state for multiculturism, fitness and amateur sport in Joe Clark government.

PAQUIN, Rollie (curling); b. 28 Feb 1951, Montreal, Que.; given name: Rolland; m. Helene; sales agent; '82 Que. Fed. A, Montreal Super League champion; '83 Royal Victoria Jubilee, Que. Labatt Tankard title; skipped Que. entry '84 Brier; Canadian Branch RCCC dist. councillor; res. St. Hyppolyte, Que.

PARADIS, Renéè (synchro swim); b. 27 Nov 1964, Charlesbourg, Que.; national jr. solo, duet, figures titles '80; with Nathalie Audet Spanish, Rome open duet titles '82; Spanish solo, team, Rome solo titles '82; team gold '83 America Cup, Pan-Am Games; fed. govt. excellence award '84; last known res. Charlesbourg, Que.

PARÉ, Mark (officiating/hockey); b. 26 Jul 1957, Windsor, Ont.; m. Debbie Glos; c. 2 daughters, 1 son; moved through Windsor minor hockey to OHA Major Jr. A (as referee) 2yrs; initial NHL game as linesman 11 Oct '79; made NHL all-star game debut '92; NHL record through '98: 1398 scheduled, 25 playoff games as linesman; res. Windsor, Ont.

PARENT, Bernie (hockey); b. 3 Apr 1945, Montreal, Que.; given name: Bernard Marcel; m. Carol Wilson; c. Chuck, Bernie, Kim; company v-p, ex-hockey coach; jr. Niagara Falls Flyers; goaler Boston '65-67, Philadelphia '67-71, '73-79, Toronto '71-72, Philadelphia (WHA) '72-73; NHL record: 608 scheduled games, 1493ga, 55so, 2.55ga avg., 71 playoff games, 174ga, 6so, 2.43ga avg.; WHA record: 63 games, 220ga, 2so, 3.61ga avg.; won/shared 2 Vezina Trophies; 2 Conn Smythe Trophies; twice 1st team all-star; mem. 2 Stanley Cup winners; playing career terminated 17 Feb '79 when Ranger defenceman Jimmy Watson's stick struck him in right eye; goaltending coach Philadelphia '82-96; jersey #1 retd. by Flyers; named to CHL all-time team '99; mem. Board of Advisors Schcio Eye Institute; mem. Flyers, Hockey halls of fame; res. Cherry Hill, N.J.

PARENTI, Eddie (swimming); b. 26 Jun 1971, Montreal, Que.; junior engineer; 200m, 400m freestyle, 100m, 200m butterfly specialist; mem. ntl team '90-97, 4yrs team capt.; 7 ntl titles; ntl record 4x200m FS relay 7:22.74 set in '91; silver 4x200 FS relay '89 Pan-Pacifics; silver 4x200 FS relay '90 Commonwealth Games; silver 4x50m FS relay '91 Worlds; bronze 4x200m FS relay '91 Pan-Pacifics; bronze 4x100m medley relay '95 Pan-Am Games; mem. '92, '96

Olympic teams, '94 Commonwealth Games; retd. from competition '97; mem. Nepean Sports Wall of Fame; res. West Vancouver, B.C.

PARFITT, Adam (rowing); b. 22 Apr 1974, Victoria, B.C.; UVic; began rowing in high school '89; mem. ntl team '94-98; 2 ntl HS, 1 US 2 ntl junior, 2 ntl senior, 1 International regatta golds; 2 silver '95 Pan-Am Games; competed '96 Olympics; Rowing Canada jr sculler of '91; res. Victoria B.C.

PARK, Brad (hockey); b. 6 Jul 1948, Toronto, Ont.; given name: Douglas Bradford; m. Gerry George; c. Jamie, Rob, Alexa, Kelly, Ben; consultant, partner Amesbury Sports Park; juvenile Scarborough Lions; jr. Toronto Marlboros; 1st choice NY Rangers '66 amateur draft; denceman Buffalo (AHL) '68, Rangers '68-75, Boston '75-83, Detroit '83-85; mem. Team Canada '72; 5 times 1st team, 2 2nd team all-star; NHL record: 1113 scheduled games, 213g, 683a, 158 playoff games, 35g, 90a; NHL career regular season assist record for defencemen; TV hockey broadcaster '85; coach Detroit '85-86; '83 Charlie Conacher Memorial Trophy, '84 Bill Masterton Trophy; mem. Hockey Hall of Fame; res. Lynnfield, Mass.

PARKER, Jackie (football); b. 1 Jan 1932, Knoxville, Tenn.; given name: John Dickerson; m. Peggy; c. Jere Jo, Peggy Mae, Jack Jr.; Mississippi State; retd. football coach; all-American, '52-53 Southeastern Conference MVP, scoring record 120 points '52; halfback, quarterback, wide receiver, place kicker, punter Eskimos '54-62; 3 Grey Cup titles; Argos '63-65; coach Toronto Rifles Continental League '66; Lions' asst. '68, head coach '69, GM '70-75; head coach Eskimos from '83; 7 Jeff Nicklin Memorial Trophies (WFC MVP), 3 times WFC, CFL all-star; CFL record: 88tds, 103c, 40fg, 19s, 750 points, 5210yds rushing, 135 receptions 2308yds, 2061 passes, 1089 completions, 16,476yds, 88tds; CFL player of quarter-century; mem. Alta., Canada's Sports, Football, Edmonton, Mississippi halls of fame; res. Edmonton, Alta.

PARKIN, Lorne (football); b. 3 Oct 1919, Toronto, Ont.; m. Ella Grace; c. John, Robert; retd. policeman; Toronto Indians '47, Toronto Indians Beaches ORFU '48; pro Argos '49-55; mem. '50, '52 Grey Cup winners; coached Toronto police tug-of-war team to NA titles '60-73; res. Toronto, Ont.

PARKS, Arnold (shooting); b. 14 Jun 1930, Saint John, N.B.; given name: Alfred Arnold; m. Zola Sypher; c. Victoria, Sonya Jane; certified general accountant; ntl cadet smallbore outdoor title '48; 4 NB Prince of Wales, Governor's Cups; NB, Atlantic Rifle championships; mem. 10 Bisley teams, adjutant '68 team, 3 Palma teams, 19 NB inter-Maritime, coach 3 times, titles twice; mem. 22 NB DCRA Ottawa shoot teams; won Governor-General's match twice; Bisley Century match '67, Clock Tower '69, St. George's Silver Cross '73, Queen's prize '68, in Queen's Hundred 5 times; mem. several Kolapore, MacKinnon match teams, several winners; NB indoor smallbore champion several times; DCRA smallbore title '70; life mem. DCRA, NBRA; pres. NBRA, Saint John Garrison Military Rifle Assn.; various exec. roles DCRA, NBRA;

coached juniors, cadets; mem. Cdn Forces, NB Sports halls of fame; res. Saint John, N.B.

PARNELL, Bill (t&f); b. 14 Feb 1928, Vancouver, B.C.; given name: Comer William; m. Joan Mary; c. John, Leslie, Keith, Jacquelyn; Washington State, BSc, BPhE, UBC, teacher's certificate; educator; all-American WSU miler; mem. '48, '52 Olympic, '50, '54 BEG; gold with 4:11 mile '50 games, capt. '52, '54 teams; several ntl titles, records; flag-bearer '52 summer Olympics; Norton Crowe Memorial Award, Canada's male athlete of '49; mem. Cdn Amateur, BC Sports halls of fame; res. N. Vancouver, B.C.

PARNELL, Paul (lacrosse); b. 28 Mar 1938, Peterborough, Ont.; given name: Paul Arthur; m. Joan Cundell; c. Randy, Penny; captain fire prevention office; int. football Peterborough '58-59, Victoria Drakes '60; Jr. B hockey Peterborough, int. Lakefield, Victoria, New Westminster; sr. lacrosse Peterborough '58-59, Victoria '60, New Westminster '61-75; mem. 9 Mann Cup, 2 World championship finals; record 441 league games, record 912 goals, 865 assists; league scoring title '65; twice Mann Cup MVP (Mike Kelly medal); 13 times all-star, 7 1st team; Commission Trophy '65 league MVP; Ellison Trophy '72 playoff MVP; playing-coach New Westminster Salmonbellies '71-72; jr. Salmonbellies '77; chair, treas. Canadian Lacrosse Hall of Fame '81-85; commissioner WLA '83-86; mem. Canadian Lacrosse, Peterborough Sports halls of fame; res. New Westminster, B.C.

PARRIS-WASHINGTON, Christine (softball); b. 23 Jan 1967, Truro, N.S.; given name: Christine Parris; m. Robert Washington; Crowder Jr. Coll,UNLV, BSc; asst. coach UNLV; played 3rd base/shortstop '90, '94 world championships, '91 (silver) Pan-Am Games, '94 South Pacific Classic; with Redding Rebels 4 Canada Cup championships, 2 titles, '96 Olympics; 3 NJCAA all-American awards; 3 NCAA all-American awards; 3 ASA ntl titles; 2 ASA all-American awards; Canada Cup batting title '93, MVP award '96; Big West Conf. player of '91; res. Las Vegas, Nev.

PARRISH, Larry (baseball); b. 10 Nov 1953, Winter Haven, Fla.; given name: Larry Alton; m. Jennifer Leigh Wetzel; c. Jessica, Joshua, Amanda; baseball exec.; Seminole Jr. Coll; all-conf. baseball/basketball Haines City HS '71; baseball coach; primarily 3B but also played other infield/outfield positions; uncanny knack for swinging with such force batting helmet fell off his head and he would catch it; Montreal '74-81, Texas '82-88, Boston '88; ML record: 1891g, 1789h, 360 2b, 33 3b, 256 hr, 851r, 992rbi, .263 BA; 2 seasons in Japan leading league in home runs with 42 '89; coached/managed Detroit farm system '92-96; bench-coach Detroit '97-98, mgr. '98-99; guided Niagara Falls to NY-Penn title '93, Jacksonville to AA title '96; 2 NL all-star teams; Expos player of '79; hit 3 grand slams in single week '82; 4 career 3-homer games; mem. Montreal Expos Hall of Fame; res. Haines City, Fla.

PARRY, Jack (all-around); b. 8 Jun 1922, Windsor, Ont.; d. 14 Dec 1990, Chatham, Ont.; given name: John Clayton; m. Anne Huffman; c. Jann, Jay, Jill, Jon;UWO., MD; anaesthesiologist; Windsor Forster CI, WOSSA, Ont. records in sprints, field events (long, triple jumps) several

years; 2yrs Windsor all-city football; '42 Grey Cup with Toronto Hurricanes; UWO Mustangs football MVP, t&f team '47-49; mem. Cdn record relay team '47; mem. '48 Olympic team but injury kept him from competing; ntl 100m, 200m champion '48; outfielder London Majors (Sr. IC), sr. baseball Windsor, signed by Cleveland (AL) but WW2 interferred; served as bomber pilot RCAF; awarded DFC; John Davies trophy Canada's top track athlete '48, Dr. Claude Brown Memorial trophy, George McCullogh trophy; mem. UWO W-Club, Windsor-Essex Sports halls of fame.

PART, John (darts); b. 29 Jun 1966, North York, Ont.; given name: John Eric; div. Holly Jean Boynton; pro darts player; 3 Ont, 2 ntl singles, 4 Hamilton Power Point Open, 2 Cleveland Extravaganza, 1 Chicago Windy City Open titles; Embassy world professional title '94; World Cup international open title '95; with Carl Mercer of Regina won '93 World Cup pairs, '94 Pacific Cup pairs; with Patricia Farrell '94 Pacific Cup mixed pairs; with Doug Scanlon 2, John Verwey 1 ntl pairs titles; ranked #1 in Canada from '93; res. Oshawa, Ont.

PASQUALE, Eli (basketball); b. 24 Aug 1960, Sudbury, Ont.; m. Karen Graham; c. Isiah, Emanuel; UVic, BA; auto sales mgr., sports camp operator; recruited by Ken Shields while starring for Lockerby HS; guard 5 UVic CIAU title teams; mem. ntl team '78-92, '97; competed 3 FISU, 2 Pan-Am, 4 world championships, 2 Olympic Games teams; gold '82 worlds fair tournament, '83 FISU Games; bronze '85 FISU Games; CIAU player of '82-83; NBA tryout Seattle (NBA) '84, Chicago '85; CIAU 2 MVP Jack Donohue trophies, 1 Mike Moser Memorial trophy; 2 CIAU all-Cdn; played pro ball in Argentina, Germany, Switzerland; BC athlete of '82; ntl sports excellence award '84; Victoria athlete of decade ('80-90); coaching, camps in 20 cities; res. Victoria, B.C.

PASSAGLIA, Lui (football); b. 7 Jun 1954, Vancouver, B.C.; m. Loa; c. Lea, Loren; SFU, BA; QB, receiver SFU, Dist. 1, all-Northwest all-star twice; top Lions draft '76; played with BC '76-99; CFL record (through '98): 372gp, 805fg, 956cvt, 291s, 3668pts, 1191kickoffs, 63,857yds, 20s;among most consistent placement kickers in CFL history; only 2 misses in 928 career convert tries, converting 511consecutively in one stretch; 6 WFC, 3 all-CFL; 3 CFL scoring titles; 12 CFL records; all-time CFL leader in 6 categories; 4 Grey Cup finals, 1 winner; kicked winning FG '94 Grey Cup game; 2 Dick Suderman trophies; res. Vancouver, B.C.

PATAKY, Bill (basketball); b. 12 May 1930, Windsor, Ont.; given name: William Andrew; m. Joan Monaghan; c. Maureen, Joanne, Monica, Margaret, Jane;Windsor, UWO, OCE; retd. educator; Windsor all-city football backfielder, basketball forward '48-49; shortstop Windsor jr. Ont. finalist '48-49; halfback Assumption College (Windsor) jr. ORFU all-Ont. finalist; varsity basketball Assumption Coll. '49-50; shortstop Frood Mine team Sudbury '51; UWO Mustangs basketball all-star '51-52; mem. Tillsonburg Livingstons '52 Olympic basketball team; football Sarnia Imperials ORFU '53; sr. basketball '53-65 Sarnia-Port Huron area; res. Sarnia, Ont.

PATERSON, Gord (football/curling); b. 7 Sep 1950, Winnipeg, Man.; m. Judy; c. Lyndsey; UMan; stockbroker; tight end Winnipeg '74-79, Hamilton '79-81; WFC Schenley top Canadian candidate '77; 2nd Man. entry '83 Brier; res. Winnipeg, Man.

PATON, Brian (softball); b. 17 Sep 1959, Woodstock, Ont.; given name: Brian Kenneth; m. Susanne Michelle; c. Lindsay, Bryan, Brittany, Jordan, Brendan; self-employed printer; played AHL hockey Detroit organization; mem. Team Canada fastball '87-99; mem. ISC world, ntl champion Toronto Gators '93, '95; Pan-Am gold '87, '91, '95, '99; mem. Green Bay All-Car '97, Tampa Bay (ISC Worlds) '98, Ballston Lake '99; res. Woodstock, Ont.

PATON, Jim (shooting); b. 24 May 1957, Newcastle, N.B.; given name: James Andrew MacMillan; m. Anna Huis; UVic, BA; liquor store mgr. BC govt.; ranked among nation's top fullbore marksmen; DCRA Governor-General's trophy triumphs '86, '95, '97, '99; Australian grand aggregate '88; mem. 3 Palma teams; mem. Cdn Bisley team 14 consec. yrs from '85; gold, silver '98 Commonwealth Games; once runnerup DCRA grand agg.; BC target rifle title '95; '97 Commonwealth championships individual gold; Bisley Aggregate (Cdn Match Rifle) title '99; 3 ISU match titles; 2 President's, Short Range Agg., G-G's qualifier match, 1 Letson match titles; Bisley George's Cross silver, Century, Wimbledon match titles; res. White Rock, B.C.

PATRICK, Frank (hockey); b. 23 Dec 1885, Ottawa, Ont., d. 29 Jun 1960, Vancouver, B.C.; m. Catherine Porter; c. Joseph, Gloria, Frances; McGill; hockey exec.; refereed MSL at 18, Stanley Cup playoffs at 20; defenceman Montreal Victorias (CAHL) '04, Westmount (CAHL) '05, Montreal Victorias (ECAHA) '08, Renfrew Millionaires (NHA) '10, Vancouver Millionaires (PCHA) '12-18, Vancouver Millionaires (WCHL) '25, coach Bruins '34-36; created Vancouver Millionaires, owner, coach, mgr.-capt. '15 Stanley Cup team; mgr. Canadiens; innovative genius put 22 pieces of legislation on NHL rule books, including origination of blue line; with brother Lester established Pacific Coast League, later sold entire league to eastern interests; managing-dir. NHL; mem. BC Sports, Hockey halls of fame.

PATRICK, Lester (hockey); b. 31 Dec 1883, Drummondville, Que., d. 1 Jun 1960, Victoria, B.C.; m. Grace Victoria Linn; c. Lynn, Murray; McGill; hockey exec.; defenceman Brandon, Man. '03, Westmount (CAHL) '05, Montreal Wanderers (ECAHA) '06-07, capt. 2 Stanley Cup winners; capt. Nelson, B.C., '08-09; Renfrew Millionaires '10; formed Victoria Aristocrats, helped establish Pacific Coast League, organized clubs and built artifical ice arenas in all league centres; played Victoria '12-16, '19-26, Spokane '17, Seattle '18; NY Rangers mgr.-coach, player '26-39, GM through '46; 7 times NHL all-star coach; with Aristocrats defeated Que. for '13 world title although Stanley Cup not at stake; won Stanley Cup '24 with Victoria Cougars ; 3 Stanley Cups Rangers; trophy in his memory for service to US hockey from '66; division of NHL given his name '74; nicknamed 'Silver Fox'; mem. BC, Greater Victoria Sports, Hockey halls of fame.

PATRICK, Lynn (hockey); b. 3 Feb 1912, Victoria B.C.; d. 26 Jan 1980, St. Louis, Mo.; given name: Joseph Lynn; div. Dorothy Davis, m. Bernice Pachal (d.); c. Lester Lee, Craig, Karen, Glenn, Dean; hockey exec.; mem. ntl champion Blue Ribbons basketball team, BC Reps rugby team, Winnipeg Blue Bombers; NY Rangers '35-43, '45-46; 1st team all-star '42; mem. '40 Stanley Cup winner; coached Rangers '50 Stanley Cup finals, Boston '50-53, coach-GM to '65; coach-GM St. Louis '66; exec. v.-pres '67-77; mem. BC Sports, Hockey halls of fame.

PATRICK, Muzz (hockey); b. 28 Jun 1915, Victoria, B.C.; d. 23 Jul 1998, Riverside, Conn; given name: Frederick Murray; m. Jessie Farr; c. Lynda, Richard, Paul, Lori; defenceman NY Rangers '37-41, '45-46; coach Rangers '54-55, GM '55-64, later v-p; retd from hockey scene '73; mem. Victoria Dominoes ntl basketball champions; ntl amateur heavyweight boxing title '36; with Art Coulter became one of Rangers' toughest defensive units; following WW2 US army duty, coached, managed in minors; competing for Victoria Y under coach Archie MacKinnon won city interscholastic mile, half-mile same day; mem. BC Sports Hall of Fame.

PATRICK, Steve (football); b. 24 Mar 1932, Glenella, Man.; given name: Stephen Clifford; m. Marjorie June mathieson ; c. Kim, Carolyn, Sandra, Stephen, James, Lisa, Tara; pres. Patrick Realty/Insurance; middle-guard Winnipeg '52-64; 290 CFL games; twice all-star, Bombers' top lineman '58, Schenley best Cdn nominee '59; twice CFL all-star game participant; most valuable Cdn '57; captained Bombers '61-64; mem. 6 Grey Cup , 4 winners; mem. Man. legislature (Lib.) '62-77; regarded as champion of all resolution makers; sons James, Steve Jr. both played in NHL; mem. Man. Sports Hall of Fame; res. Winnipeg, Man.

PATTERSON, Hal (football); b. 1933, Rozel, Kansas; given name: Harold; div.; c. 1 son; Kansas; road builder; nicknamed 'Prince Hal'; Kansas all-star baseball, basketball, football; Montreal '54-60, Hamilton '61-67; began pro career as defensive back, switched to receiver; CFL record: 460 pass receptions, 9473yds, 20.6 avg., 64tds, returned 105 kickoffs, 2871yds, 27.3 avg., 3tds, scored total 75tds, 432pts; best single season '56, 88 passes, CFL record 1914yds; best game 29 Sep '56 CFL record 338yds in receptions; longest single gain 109yds; longest kickoff return 105yds; Lord Calvert Trophy (Montreal MVP) 3 times; Jeff Russel Memorial Trophy '56; Schenley outstanding player award '56, runnerup '57; 8 times EFC all-star, twice all-Canadian; 9 Grey Cup finals, 3 winners; mem. Canadian Football Hall of Fame; last known res. Larned, Kansas.

PATTERSON, Joe (softball); b. 6 Feb 1936, Regina, Sask.; given name: Joseph James; m. Marylou Burton; c. Bradley, Angela; fire fighter; perennial all-star 1st baseman, outfielder Victoria '59-68; mem. 2 BC Sr. B title teams; Victoria Bate '69-74; 8 BC Sr. A titles; 3 ntl titles; coached Bate to co-world title '76; twice ntl softball coach of year; mem. Canadian Amateur Softball Hall of Fame; res. Victoria, B.C.

PATTON, Casey (boxing); b. 21 Nov 1974, London, Ont.; began competing with East London BC at 13; featherweight;

2 ntl titles; '94 Commonwealth Games gold 57kg; Pacific Ocean Games gold '95; competed '96 Olympics; Cdn boxer of '94 award; res. London, Ont.

PAUL, Donald (builder); b. 5 Mar 1933, Hamilton, Ont.; m. Joan; c. Margo, Gordon, Douglas; UofT; nicknamed 'Doc'; p-pres. Collingwood Shipbuilders HC; p-pres./charter mem. Collingwood Blue Mountain Golf & Country Club; played key exec. role in '91 Ontario Winter Games; exec./charter mem. Collingwood Sports Hall of Fame '74-90; mem. exec. comm. Collingwood YMCA '78; p-chair. Collingwood Recreation Board; player/coach/mgr. Christie's Men's Wear Slo-pitch all-Ont. finalists '78, '90, 3 Summerfest tournament titles, 3 league titles; chair Summerfest slo-pitch tourney '85-90; recipient Order of Collingwood '91; mem. Collingwood Sports Hall of Fame; res. Collingwood, Ont.

PAUL, Robert (figure skating); b. 2 Jun 1937, Toronto, Ont.; m. Sally Ann Welsh; skating choreographer, coach; 5 ntl, 2 NA, 4 world titles; '60 Olympic gold; Ice Capades '61-64; from '65 coached US world and Olympic competitors; choreographer '68 Olympic gold medalist Peggy Fleming; with Barbara Wagner shared '59 Lou Marsh Trophy; flagbearer '60 winter Olympics; mem. Cdn, US Figure Skating, Cdn Amateur, Canada's Sports halls of fame; res. Beverly Hills, Calif.

PAULETTO, Bruno (t&f); b. 21 Jan 1954, Portogruaro, Italy; Central Michigan, B.Sc, Tennessee, MEd; teacher; shot put specialist; mem. ntl jr. team '73-75, sr. team '76-84; 5th '77 World Cup; 4th '77 FISU Games; silver '77 Pacific Conference Games; gold '78 NCAA indoor, silver outdoor championships; 4 ntl titles; gold '79 Dogwood Relays, Florida Relays, '80 Tom Black Classic; silver '78 Commonwealth Games, '80 Copenhagen Games, Dogwood Relays; bronze '78 Helsinki Games, '79 Canada-Russia dual meet, *Edmonton Journal* Games, Pan-Am Games; 5 gold, 3 silver, 2 bronze '80 Olympic alternative meets; gold '82 Commonwealth Games; mem. '84 Olympic team; 3 times all-American; 3 times Mid-American Conference titlist and record holder; '78 university scholar-athlete of year; fed. govt. excellence award '83; last known res. Knoxville, Tenn.

PAULSON, Jamie (badminton); b. 26 Apr 1948, Calgary, Alta; m. Clair Wilson; c. Julie, Christopher, Daniel; UCal, BComm, UWO, MBA; investment broker; 4 ntl jr., sr. singles titles; with Yves Pare 5 ntl men's doubles; twice singles, doubles champion Jamaican, Mexican Opens; led Canada to 1st NA title over US '69; bronze Singapore world championships; gold singles, bronze doubles '70 Commonwealth Games; silver '74 Commonwealth Games; twice Thomas Cup team mem.; among top 5 singles players in world 5 consecutive years; mem. Alta. Sports Hall of Fame; res. Calgary, Alta.

PAVELICH, Matt (hockey/officiating); b. 12 Mar 1934, Park Hills Gold Mines, Ont.; began officiating minor hockey at 14; referee-in-chief Northern Michigan Int. League; personally worked Michigan Tech home games; following impressive performances in AHL games '55-56 he made NHL debut 11 Oct. '56; remained as linesman in NHL through '79 working 1727 scheduled games, 245 Stanley

Cup playoff games, 11 NHL all-star games; 1st linesman elected to Hockey Hall of Fame; res. Sault Ste. Marie, Mich.

PAYNE, Marita (t&f); b. 7 Oct 1960, Barbados; m. Mitchell Wiggins; c. Mitchell, Stephanie, Nicholas; Florida State; sprint specialist; mem. Scarborough Optimists TC; mem. bronze medal 4x400m relay team '79 Pan-Am Games; silver 4x100m relay '82 Commonwealth Games; 200m, 4x400m, 4x100m relay silvers '83 FISU, silvers 4x100, 4x400 relays '84 Olympics; ntl outdoor 4x100m relay title '80; silver 100m, 200m '80 Colgate Games; ntl outdoor 400m '81; '82 NCAA 400m title; 4 ntl sr. records; fed. govt. excellence award '82; res. Concord, Ont.

PEACOSH, Walter (hockey); b. 16 Sep 1935, The Pas, Man.; given name: Walter Nickolas; m. Alice Allen; c. Debra, Ricky, Carrie, Yvonne, Robert, David; millwright; jr. Flin Flon Bombers '53-55; mem. Penticton V's '56-58; MVP '58; Vancouver Canucks (WHL) '58-59, Western Cdn title '58; Spokane Comets '60; mem. Trail Smoke Eaters world title team '60-61; ntl int. finalist Summerland, B.C., '62; Trail Smoke Eaters '62-63, 4th in world championships; Kimberley Dynamiters '64-70; MVP, scoring champion '66-68; picked up by Allan Cup finalist Nelson Maple Leafs '66; coach Kimberley '70-72; mem. Trail Smoke Eaters Old Timers Sweden tour '73-74; East Kootney Old Timers from '75; ntl titles '77, '79; mem. BC Sports Hall of Fame with '61 Trail team; res. Kimberley, B.C.

PEAKER, Brian (rowing); b. 26 May 1959, London, Ont.; lightweight men's straight four stroke; began rowing age 16; mem. ntl team '85-86, '89, from '92; straight four bronze '86 Commonwealth Games, silver '96 Olympics; 3 US, 1 world championship; res. London, Ont.

PEARCE, Bobby (rowing); b. 30 Sep 1905, Sydney, Australia, d. 20 May 1976, Toronto, Ont.; m. Velma Hilda; c. Jon Robert, Jill Elizabeth, Robert Ernest; salesman; Australian army heavyweight boxing champion '26; world amateur sculling champion, gold '28, '32 Olympics; sculling gold '30 BEG; '31 diamond sculls Henley Eng.; competed for Australia '32 Olympics although Cdn resident; pro world title CNE '33; lost only 2 races in pro career; Lou Marsh Trophy '38; Australia's athlete of past 200 years '70; second only to Joe Wright Sr. as Canada's outstanding oarsman of half century '50 CP poll; mem. Cdn Amateur, Canada's Sports Hall of Fame.

PEARCE, Dave (softball); b. 10 Jul 1937, Montreal, Que.; given name: David Albert; div.; c. Karen, Kevin, Kyle; m. Jane Haigh; sc. Susan; retd. RCMP superintendent; softball ambassador; pitched at Sr. A level, 4 ntl, 1 world championships; playing career extended more than 30yrs; coached more than 20yrs at sr. level; 3 world tournaments, Italian men '78, Cdn women '82, Cdn men '84; mgr. Cdn men's ntl team '82-89; coached Italian women's European titlists '79, Canadian men's Pan-Am gold '83, Sask. Boys Canada Games gold team '93; authored 10 softball instruction books; organized Regina Gold program operating softball, baseball instruction camps for kids and sponsoring teams to ntl, intl events; in 10 intl events his teams won 4g 2s, 1b medals; conducts clinics throughout the world; competed judo 15yrs; 2nd degree black belt; coached community baseball, hockey in Ottawa, Regina; res. Regina, Sask.

PEARCE, John (equestrian); b. 3 May 1960, Toronto, Ont.; m. Cathy; Forestview Farm operator; spent many yrs in amateur/owner jumper class before launching Grand Prix career '90; mem. ntl team from '92; competed '92 World Cup final; winning Cdn Nations' Cup teams '92, '95; expert carpenter; 4 GP victories '96, 2 '97; res. Stouffville, Ont.

PEARSON, Mike (football/hockey/baseball); b. 23 Apr 1897, Toronto, Ont.; d. 27 Dec 1972, Ottawa, Ont.; given name: Lester Bowles; m. Maryon Moody; c. Geoffrey Arthur Holland, Patricia Lillian; Victoria College, BA, St. John's College, Oxford, BA, hon. degrees 48 universities; statesman; Prime Minister of Canada '63-68; interfaculty rugby, basketball, football, hockey, lacrosse at Oxford; coach sr. hockey '26-27, sr. football, lacrosse '26-27, sr. ORFU football '27-28; OBE '35, Nobel Peace Prize '57; trophy in his name presented annually by CIAU, NHL; mem. UofT Sports, Cdn Baseball halls of fame.

PEARSON, Paul (football); b. 15 Jun 1957, Campbell River, B.C.; m. Shan Williams; c. David, Michael; College of the Siskiyous, UBC, BA; deli operator; drafted by Calgary '78; slotback Toronto Argos '79-87; ranked among CFL's premier receivers; CFL record 424 receptions for 5867yds; 3 Grey Cup finals, 1 winner; Schenley outstanding Canadian nominee '81-83; co-chair. Metro Toronto Big Brothers Bowl for Millions; res. Kelowna, B.C.

PEDEN, Doug (all-around); b. 18 Apr 1916, Victoria, B.C.; given name: James Douglas; m. Trudy; retd. sports editor; competed professionally bicycle racing, basketball, baseball; rode 37 international 6-day races, won 7, 2nd 9 times; ntl pro sprint title '39; mem. House of David baseball team; player, manager minor league teams Pittsburgh organization; runnerup class B Interstate League batting .357 York, Pa., '46; guard 3 Victoria ntl basketball title teams; top Canadian scorer, silver medal '36 Olympic team; pro Buffalo Bisons, Vancouver Hornets; BC, regional jr. tennis titles; BC rugby fullback, punter, place kicker; all-around t&f performer; zone sr. golf champion '77; also competed in swimming, soccer, cricket, softball; mem. Cdn Basketball, BC, Canada's Sports halls of fame; res. Victoria, B.C.

PEDEN, Sandy (shooting); b. 3 May 1934, Edmonton, Alta.; m.; retired; cyclist '54 BEG; Man. fullbore title '63; BC titles '72, '74; ntl title '81; mem. '82 Commonwealth Games team; CTR Bisley aggregate gold cross '81; 5 individual DCRA aggregate titles; coach Malaysian ntl team 3yrs; coach Cdn Commonwealth Games team '98; res. Victoria, B.C.

PEDEN, Torchy (cycling); b. 16 Apr 1906, Victoria, B.C., d. 26 Jan 1980, Chicago, Ill.; given name: William John; m. Annamae; c. 4; retail sporting goods; competed '28 Olympics after winning ntl titles at 1, 5 miles, tieing for all-around ntl amateur title; 5 ntl amateur indoor titles, records in 4, '29; English 103-mile record 1h39:39; pro '29-48, 38 wins in 148 6-day races; US record for mile 73.5 mph '31; mem. Canada's, BC Sports halls of fame.

PEEL, Ann (t&f); b. 27 Feb 1961, Ottawa, Ont.; m. Robert Luba; c. Michael, Andrew; UofT, BA (hon), LLB; lawyer; race walking specialist; Pan-Am jr. gold '80; 5th '81 World Cup, 7th '83, 10th '85, 7th '87, 16th '89; Americas Cup gold '84, '88, silver '86; Pan-Am Games silver '87; Universiade 4th '85, bronze '87; world indoor championship bronze '85, '87, 6th '89; competed '90 Commonwealth Games; 18 ntl titles; ntl records 1500m, 3000m (indoor), 3km, 5km, 10km; 1st chair./founding mem. Athletes CAN (formerly Cdn Athletes Assn.) '93; mem. Canada's all-time women's t&f team '93; '99 Breakthrough award; mem. Ottawa Sports Hall of Fame; res. Toronto, Ont.

PELCHAT, Ann-Marie (skiing); b. 30 May 1974, Levis, Que.; freestyle moguls specialist; mem. ntl team '94-98; 4 ntl titles; competed '98 Olympics, '97 worlds; res. Levis, Que.

PELECH, Jack (builder); b. 21 Jun 1933, Hamilton, Ont.; given name: John; McMaster, BA; Osgoode Hall LLB; lawyer; played football, basketball, handball in youth; turned to coaching/administration; dir. Hamilton YMCA boards from '55, pres. '77; active as administrator in varied Hamilton sports/recreation/university organizations; chair. Pan-Am/Commonwealth Games bids committees; 8yr mem. National Advisory Council on Fitness & Amateur Sport; 7yrs governor ntl Youth Bowling Council; chair. ntl Canada Games council '71-99; 3yr chair. Fred Sgambati charity golf tournament; mem. Hamilton Copp's Coliseum Wall of Fame comm. '87-99; trustee Tiger-Cats trust fund for amateur sports '86-99; Ont. sport volunteer citation; '87 Hamilton citizen of yr; mem. McMaster Sports Hall of Fame; res. Hamilton, Ont.

PELKEY, Arthur (boxing); b. 27 Oct 1884, Chatham, Ont., d. 18 Feb 1921, Ford City, Ont.; given name: Andrew Arthur Peletier; fought Tommy Burns, Jess Willard, Jim Coffey to no decisions; KO victory '13 resulted in death of opponent Luther McCarty, Pelkey never again won a bout; KO'd by Gunboat Smith in lone title challenge '14; in 50-bout career won 12 by KO, 9 by decision, 4 draws, lost 1 decision, KO'd 13 times, 11 no decisions.

PELLETIER, Annie (diving); b. 22 Dec 1973, Montreal, Que.; College Andre-Grasset; company spokeswoman; competitive swimmer age 6-8; gymnast 8-13; began diving age 13; mem. Montreal CAMO Club; jr ntl 3m title '91; sr ntl 3m title '93; won 1m, 3m summer ntl sr. titles '94, 1m winter ntls '94, '95; 1m, 3m gold '94 Commonwealth, 3m gold, 1m silver '95 Pan-Am Games, 1m bronze '94 worlds, 3m bronze '96 Olympics; competed '91 Pan-Am, '93 FISU Games; 2 bronze '95 Dive Canada; Bev Boys outstanding diver awards '91, '93; 3 Que. female diver of year awards; retd. from competition '96; res. Montreal, Que.

PELLETIER, Leo-Charles (boxing); b. 26 Jan 1952, Eel River Crossing, N.B.; RCMP officer; mem. ntl team '72-78; Maritime Golden Gloves titles '68-78; Eastern Cdn GoldenGloves '72-76; Cdn amateur welterweight title '73-74; 39 international bouts, 34 wins; overall record 112 wins, 20 losses; 3 international gold medals; silver '73 NA championships; bronze '75 pre-Olympic tournament; NB boxer of '71-73; mem. NB Sports Hall of Fame; res. Balmoral, N.B.

PELLS, Leah (t&F); b. 9 Nov 1964, Vancouver, B.C.; SFU; child care counsellor; middle distance runner; ntl jr. 1500m titlist '83; NIAI 1500, 3000m titles '83, '88; ntl 3000m titles '90, '93, 1500m '95; competed '90, '94 Commonwealth, '92, '96 Olympic Games, '99 Pan-Am Games, '88, '90, '92, '94 world cross-country; won '94 *Times-Colonist* 1500m; silver 1500m '99 PAG; displayed essence of Olympics with amazing, albeit non-medal, performance '96; SFU female athlete, Burnaby outstanding athlete of '88; res, Coquitlam, B.C.

PELYK, Mike (hockey); b. 29 Sep 1947, Toronto, Ont.; given name: Michael Joseph; m. Sarah MacLean; c. Kimberley, Christopher, Leah, Stacy, Robert; UofT, BA, York, MBA; real estate development and acquisition; jr. defenceman Toronto Marlboros; Maple Leafs 3rd choice, 17th overall '63 amateur draft; NHL record: 441 scheduled games, 29g, 88a; 2 seasons Vancouver Blazers, Cincinnati Stingers WHA; capt. Stingers; mem. Toronto NHL Old Stars; res. Weston, Ont.

PERCIVAL, Lloyd (all-around); b. 3 Jun 1913, Toronto, Ont., d. 23 Jul 1974, Montreal, Que.; m. Dorothy Macdonell; c. Janet; physical educator; nicknamed 'Ace'; ntl jr. tennis finals at 16; ntl bantam Golden Gloves boxing title, qualified for Olympics but too young to participate; high scorer '36 Cdn cricket team touring England; coached '32 National Sea Flea midgets to undefeated hockey season; launched Sports College '41, at peak of program 800,00 students were registered; began Canadian Amateur Sports and Physical Fitness Development Service '56; founder Fitness Institute; t&f coach; formed Don Mills TC; Coronation medal from Queen Elizabeth.

PERCY, Karen (skiing); b. 10 Oct 1966, Edmonton, Alta.; given name: Karen Lynne; m. Kevin Lowe; c. Dervyn Jean, Darby, Keegan; alpine specialist; silver WC downhill Zinal, Switzerland, '88; bronze WC downhill Banff '86; WC record 0-2-3; 2 bronze '88 Olympics; mem. Order of Canada, Cdn Skiing, Cdn Olympic, Canada's Sports halls of fame; res. Edmonton, Alta.

PEREIRA, Ken (field hockey); b. 12 Jul 1973, Toronto, Ont.; given name: Kenneth; Centennial Coll.; quick, adept stick handler with accurate shot; represented Canada '95, '99 (gold) Pan-Am Games, '96 Olympic qualifier, '97 World Cup qualifier; mem. Cdn team which posted best ever sixth place finish '98 World Cup; res. Toronto, Ont.

PEROWNE, Ron (football); b. 5 Feb 1950, Montreal, Que.; given name: Ronald Grant; m. Gail Elizabeth Murphy; c. Charles; Bishop's., BA, McGill,BTheology; football, hockey coach; football, hockey Lower Canada College, 4yrs Bishop's, 1yr hockey McGill; pro football 2 1/2 seasons Alouettes; coach Bishop's football, hockey teams; mem. Bishop's Sports Wall of Fame; res. Lennoxville, Que.

PERREAULT, Annie (speed skating); b. 28 Jul 1971, Windsor, Que.; cashier; followed tradition set by family members such as sister Maryse who claimed world title honors and several world championship medals earlier; competed in age-class events from '84 earning gold at midget, junior, intermediate, senior levels; 3 Canada Winter Games gold '87; 2 Pacific Rim gold '91; 2 world short track team/relay gold; '92 Olympics relay gold; Bormio Cup 1500m, relay gold '95, 500m, 1000m, 1500m relay gold '94; world championships 500m silver '96; Cdn open overall bronze '96; Cdn International Challenge 500m gold '94; mem. '98 Olympic team; world team bronze, relay silver '98; res. Rock Forest, Que.

PERREAULT, Gil (hockey); b. 13 Nov 1950, Victoriaville, Que.; given name: Gilbert; Sabres PR ambassador from '97; Montreal Jr. Canadiens; twice OHA 1st team all-star centre; 1st Buffalo pick, 1st overall '70 amateur draft; Calder Memorial Trophy '71; Lady Byng Trophy '73; twice NHL 2nd team all-star; NHL record '70-87: 1191 scheduled games, 512g, 814a, 90 playoff games, 33g, 70a; mem. 5 Team Canada Canada Cup teams; jersey #11 retd by Sabres; mem. Hockey Hall of Fame; res. Buffalo, N.Y.

PERRIER, Ross (officiating/football); b. 26 Jun 1934, Toronto, Ont.; d. 29 Oct 1999, Scarborough, Ont.; m. Joan Halloran; c. Joanne, Karen, Michele, Michael; retd. fireman; officiated in CFL 18 seasons including 335 regular season and playoff games; worked 7 Grey Cup finals; retd after '90 season to become officiating supervisor; when league expanded into US he returned to active duty for '94 season; 1 of 2 CFL officiating supervisors to '95 when he was promoted to dir. of officiating.

PERROUD, Pat (curling); b. 31 Dec 1962, Thunder Bay; given name: Patrick Charles; m. Jane Hooper; c. Gabriel; software engineer; began curling as jr. in TB; competed 4 Briers, 2 winners; lead Al Hackner '85, Ed Werenich '90 Brier, world title rinks; with Werenich 1, Wayne Middaugh 2 TSN Skins Games titles; CCR 1st team all-star lead '90; mem. Ont. team of '85; ntl mixed finalist '95; mem. Cdn Curling Hall of Fame; res. Bradford, Ont.

PERRY, Gordon (football/curling); b. 18 Mar 1903, Moncton, N.B.; m. Jessie Keith (d), c. Gordon Jr., Marilyn, Patricia; m. Betty Bywater Thomas (d); m. Muriel Taggart; retd. Bank of Canada; Montreal city league baseball, hockey, Westward football intermediates '26-27; Montreal Winged Wheelers '28-34, capt. '31 unbeaten, untied (14 games) team to Grey Cup title; Jeff Russel Memorial Trophy '31; all-Eastern 4 times; Royal Victoria Jubilee in both irons ('53), granites ('56); Branch Governor-General's '61; hon. chair. '93 Ottawa Brier; mem. Governor-General's CC; bonspiel named in his honor by Ottawa CC; mem. Ottawa, NB, Que., Canada's Sports, Cdn Football halls of fame; res. Ottawa, Ont.

PERRY, Nellie (basketball); b. 4 Feb 1903, London, Eng.; d. Apr 1991, Victoria, B.C.; given name: Ellen; m. Gordon McIntosh; c. Tim, Bud, Alan, Ron, Barbara, Carol, Wendy; mem. famed Edmonton Grads '21-24, 40 games, 242 points, 6.5 avg.; mem. Canadian Basketball, Alta. Sports halls of fame.

PERRY, Norm (football); b. 1 Jun 1904, Sarnia, Ont., d. 17 Nov 1957, Sarnia, Ont.; m. Marie McPhail; c. Don, Dick; safety supervisor; running halfback 8 seasons jr., intermediate football; 8 seasons sr. ORFU Sarnia Imperials,

7 titles, 1 Grey Cup; capt. '34 Grey Cup champions, MVP that season; perennial all-star; ORFU exec. officer several years; CRU pres. '53; term as mayor of Sarnia; mem. Canadian Football Hall of Fame.

PESCHISOLIDO, Paul (soccer); b. 25 May 1971, Scarborough, Ont.; m.; c. 1 daughter; striker West Bromwich Albion; competed for Cdn -17 team '87 world championships; 1st pick CSL Toronto Blizzard '89; scored 32g during 4yr stint with Blizzard; twice CSL all-star; debuted for ntl sr. team '92 scoring 1st international goal in 3-1 win over Hong Kong; signed with Birmingham (English 1st Div) '92; transferred to Stoke City '94-95 scoring 22g before returning to Birmingham '96; sold to West Bromwich for '96-97, Fulham '97-98; represented Canada internationally from '92; Cdn player of '96 award; 22 international caps; res. Pickering, Ont./England.

PETERS, Vic (curling); b. 24 Mar 1955, Steinbach, Man.; m. Debora; c. Kasandra, Daley, Elisabeth; golf course superintendent; skipped Manitoba entry '92, '93, '97 Brier; won '92 Brier; bronze medal '92 world championships; CCR 1st team all-star '92; Ross Harstone award '97 Brier; res. Winnipeg, Man.

PETITCLERC, Chantal (t&f); b. 15 Dec 1969, Ste, Foy, Que.; wheelchair racer. 2 bronze '92, 2 gold, 3 silver '96 Paralympics; 2 gold '94 Francophone Games; 5 gold '95 Stoke Mandeville Games, Ian Hume Invitational; 2 gold '94 IPC World Athletic championships. 2 ntl 10km, marathon titles; ntl record in 100, 200, 400, 800, 1500, marathon; res. Montreal, Que.

PETTAPIECE, Jim (curling); b. 7 May 1943, Saskatoon, Sask.; given name: James Kenneth; Nevada; owner International Curling Promotions; Sask. jr., sr. baseball title teams; Nevada baseball scholarship; mem. Don Duguid Man. Consols, Brier, Silver Broom championships rinks '70-71; Brier all-star 2nd '70-71; mem. Dan Fink Man. Consols winner, Brier entry '73; instructor Silver Broom Curling Schools, Curl Canada Clinics '71-75; mem. Canadian Curling Hall of Fame; res. Langley, B.C.

PETTIGREW, Vern (wrestling); b. 30 Mar 1908, Durham, Ont.; given name: John Vernon; m. Jean Saunderson; c. Robert, Heather, Ronald; retd. stonecutter, firefighter; 6 ntl titles '33-40; 4th featherweight (134lbs) '36 Olympics; wrestling instructor Regina City Police '35-37; referee-in-chief ntl wrestling championships '55; Regina boxing/wrestling commission '56-86; mem. Cdn Amateur, Sask. Sports, Cdn Amateur Wrestling halls of fame; res. Regina, Sask.

PETTINGER, Glen (basketball); b. 27 Sep 1928, Toronto, Ont.; given name: Glen Murray; m. Nancy Louise Hayman; c. Wendy, Kim, Jill, Christopher; UofT, UWO, BA; retd. HS principal; mem. East York CI Ont. Golden Ball champions '46, York Belting ntl junior titlist '47; CIAU all-star UofT '49; UWO Mustangs CIAU winners '52, All-Canadian; mem. Tillsonburg Livingstons '52 Olympics; capt. Nortown Tri-Bells ntl sr. basketball titlist '53; mem. '55 Pan-Am Games team; Ottawa Fellers '59 ntl finalist; res. Gloucester, Ont.

PEZER, Vera (curling); b. 13 Jan 1939, Melfort, Sask.; given name: Vera Rose; UofSask, MA, PhD; asst. professor; won intercollegiate titles; 3rd Joyce McKee rink '69 ntl ladies' title; skipped ntl title rinks '71-73; coached ntl jr. champions '75; 3 Western intercollegiate champions; mem. Saskatoon Imperials '63-69 provincial women's softball champions, '69 ntl title; mem. Sask. interprovincial golf teams '70-77; Saskatoon sportswoman of '68; team psychologist '92 Olympics; mem. Sask. Sports, Canadian Curling halls of fame; res. Saskatoon, Sask.

PFEIFER, Alan (football); b. 27 Dec 1928, Newark, N.J.; m. Alva; c. Ross, Judy Ann, Linda, Mary; Fordham, BSc; equestrian equipment sales; HS all-state football 2 years, baseball 1 year; college all-Eastern, all-American '50; 6 years pro football NY Giants, Argos, Rough Riders; all-pro '51, '55; CFL scoring title '55; led EFC pass receivers 3 times; EFC record for most TD passes caught 1 season with 15; most receptions single game 13; with Hugh Campbell shares CFL record of catching 3 TD passes 1 game 3 times 1 season; Argos record holder most 100yd games 17; most 100yd games single season 8; res. Phoenix, Ariz.

PHIBBS, Bob (basketball); b. 26 May 1927, Windsor, Ont.; given name: Robert James; m. Mary; c. Lizabeth Jean, Christine Louise, Richard James; UWO, BA; company v-p; Ont. discus, javelin titles '46; 3 UWO intercollegiate football title teams, 4 basketball title teams; capt. '52 ntl sr. men's basketball champions, Olympic team; Claude Brown Memorial Trophy '49 as UWO outstanding athlete; res. Calgary, Alta.

PHILIP, Bob (hockey/coaching); b. 15 Apr 1944, Montreal, Que.; m. Linda Carey; c. Matthew; Sir George Williams, BA, McGill, BEd, Concordia, MA; AD UBC; starred with SGW hockey team '67-70, co-capt. '70; coached SGW hockey '72-75; QUAA coach of '73; asst. coach Concordia '75-84; AD Concordia '85-92; AD UBC from '92; res. Delta, B.C.

PHILLIPS, Alf Jr. (curling); b. 10 Sep 1938, Toronto, Ont.; given name: Alfred John; m. June Doreen Carnell; c. Cliff, Steve, Wayne; Ryerson business school; v-p Canadian Conklin Shows; Ont. -17 100yd FS swimming title; won Ont. jr. tankard '58; 3 Ont. Silver tankards; skipped Brier winner '67; City of Ottawa champion '75; mem. Governor-General's CC; publisher *Ontario Curling Report* from '74; res. Toronto, Ont.

PHILLIPS, Alf Sr. (diving/curling); b. 27 Jul 1908, Durham, Ont.; d. 28 Jul 1994, Toronto, Ont.; m. Margaret Dobson; c. Alf Jr., Dave; company pres.; Ont. springboard, platform fancy diving champion '26-34, ntl champion '26-34 retiring undefeated; 7th platform '28, 4th springboard '32 Olympics; 1st double winner '30 BEG; 4 Ont. Silver Tankard titles; 2 Canada Life, 5 Canada Life seniors titles; won Toronto International, ntl seniors '69; skip '56 Ont. champions, lost Brier extra-end playoff; mem. Governor-General's CC; mem. Canadian Curling, Amateur Sports, Cdn, Ont. Aquatic halls of fame.

PHILLIPS, Bill (baseball); b. 1857, Saint John, N.B.; d. 7 Oct 1900, Chicago, Ill; 1st baseman; 1st Cdn to play in major leagues with Cleveland Blues 1879-84; 1st Cdn to hit home run (1880); joined Brooklyn Bridegrooms (AA) 1885-87; finished ML career with Kansas City 1888; regarded as excellent fielder; ML record: 1038 games, 4255ab, 1130h, 562r, 214d, 98t, 17hr, .266ba.; mem. Cdn Baseball Hall of Fame.

PHILLIPS, Jerry (rodeo); b. Dec 1951, Claresholm, Alta.; given name: Patti Jerry Duce; m. Lee Phillips; c. Fallon; horse trainer, movie wrangler, stuntperson; began trick riding with sister Joy age 9; as Flying Duces they toured NA, Eng., Scotland, Bermuda, Japan; made barrel racing debut age 11; 9 ntl women's barrel racing titles; 1st Cdn rider to qualify for ntl rodeo finals; 3 ntl finals appearances; 1st Miss Rodeo Canada; rodeo queen judge Miss Worlds '81; won numerous Southern circuit titles and awards; mem. Cdn Rodeo Hall of Fame; res. Carseland, Alta.

PHILLIPS, Peter (curling); b. 9 May 1943, Toronto, Ont.; given name: Peter Edward; m. Beverley Johnstone; c. Monica, Ryan; Waterloo, Ryerson Polytechnical Inst.; partner printing co.; Ont. men's championship runner-up '72, '80; 2 Ont. Silver Tankard titles; 6 times provincial championship competitor; res. Willowdale, Ont.

PHILLIPS, Rudy (football); b. 25 Feb 1958, Dallas, Tex.; North Texas State; off. centre; pro Pittsburgh (NFL) '81, Ottawa (CFL) '81-84; off. guard, tackle; twice Schenley outstanding offensive lineman; twice Leo Dandurand Memorial Trophy (EFC); CBC-TV Coaches all-star team '83; twice CFL all-star; Bill Smyth Memorial Trophy '82; last known res. Dallas, Tex.

PHILLIPS, Tommy (hockey); b. 22 May 1883, Kenora, Ont., d. 30 Nov 1923, Toronto, Ont.; given name: Thomas Neil; m. Ella Gertrude Kilgour; c. Margery Merceline, Mary Margaret, James Kilgour; McGill, UofT; timber merchant; Toronto Marlboros '04, OHA sr. title; capt. Kenora Thistles 2 Stanley Cup challenges '06-07; 13 goals in 6 playoff games as Kenora won Stanley Cup '07; 26 goals in 10 games '07-08 Ottawa Senators; mem. 6 Stanley Cup challengers, 1 winner; closed career with Vancouver Millionaires '12; mem. Hockey Hall of Fame.

PHILP, Jerry (football); b. 6 Jun 1932, Windsor, Ont.; m. Joanne Lawrence; c. John, Mark, Ann; Florida State; all-city basketball Detroit '50; football Toronto '58-63, Montreal '64; coach Toronto De LaSalle, Windsor Assumption; 20-year record of 140 wins, 30 losses, 2 ties, coach Windsor AKO posting 30-21-2 record '74-78; last known res. Harrow, Ont.

PHINNEY, Gertrude (t&f); b. 18 Jan 1909, Lawrencetown, N.S.; m. Brannon Young (d); c. Bette, Fred, Harold, Carol, Richard; m. Thomas Beattie; Acadia, BSc, BEd; retd teacher; trained 2 weeks then entered '27 Maritime t&f championships "to win some points for her team;" by day's end had run 14 races (including heats) winning 5 titles, setting 2 sprint, 1 hurdles, 1 broad jump records; "some points" amounted to 28, sufficient to single-handedly win meet for her team; added 2 indoor sprint records '27; surpassed performance '28 Maritime meet with 6 titles, 4 records; ntl 220yd title '28; tied world 60yd record; 7

Maritime titles, 1 record '29; disuaded from competing in '28 Olympics by father on grounds t&f events too strenuous for female anatomy; mem. '26 ntl finalist Ex-Dalhousie basketball team; won numerous srs. tennis titles; 3 *Halifax Chronicle* trophies, Dalhousie Award; mem. NS, Kings County Sports halls of fame; res. Wolfville, N.S.

PHOENIX, Skip (diving); b. 19 Aug 1948, Addis Ababa, Ethiopia; m. Mary Turner; c. Kimberlee, Samantha; Guelph, BSc, BPhE., UWO, BEd, UofT, MEd; clubs supervisor UofT; bronze 3m springboard '73 winter, '74 summer nationals; silver '74 summer nationals, bronze 1m '75 winter nationals; mem. 2 Canada Cup, '76 Olympics; coach from '77-92; coached UofT to CIAU title '81; CIAU diving coach of year '80-82; Oly coach '88, '92; coached several divers to Commonwealth, World medals; mem. Guelph Sports Hall of Fame; res. Toronto, Ont.

PIASKOSKI, Jim (football); b. 10 Oct 1948, Levack, Ont.; given name: James Peter; m. Nancy Ross; c. Janna, Ross; Eastern Michigan College; PR Hugh Dolan Distribution; Sudbury Spartans juniors to offensive, defensive tackle Rough Riders '72-82; mem. '73, '76 Grey Cup champions; '76 City of Ottawa grand aggregate curling title rink; res. Manotick, Ont.

PICHE, Doris (badminton); b. 14 Oct 1965, La Sarre, Que.; m. Mike Bitten; c. William Michael; UofOtt; began competing age 15; mem. ntl team from '85; ntl women's doubles title with Si-An Deng '90, Denyse Julien '92; 2 French. 1 Spanish, 1 Irish Open singles gold; 1 Pan-Am championships singles, 2 women's doubles, 1 mixed doubles gold; Cdn Open women's, mixed doubles gold; 1 Welsh Open women's doubles title; team silver '90 Commonwealth Games; mem. 3 worlds, 2 Commonwealth, 1 Olympic Games teams; res. Ottawa, Ont.

PICKARD, Allan (builder/hockey); b. 2 Jan 1895, Exeter, Ont.; d. 7 Apr 1975, Exeter, Ont.; organizer/administrator Regina YMCA League mid-'20s from which grew Regina Parks League, one of largest and best organized in country; coach/pres/ Regina Aces sr. team; mem. SAHA exec, pres. '41, served 2 terms; pres. Sask. sr. league ' pres. Western Canada sr. league; governor Sask. jr., Western Canada jr. leagues' pres. CAHA '47-50; life mem. SAHA, CAHA; mem. Hockey Hall of Fame.

PICKARD, LeRoy (softball/basketball); b. 9 Sep 1919, St. Catharines, Ont.; given name: LeRoy Garnet; m. Lillian Louise Lohnes; c. Linda Christine, Laurel Marie; retd. general supervisor McKinnon Industries, GM Canada; accounting; in his youth won St. Catharines horseshoe, checker, softball titles; capt. 2b/3b '41 OABA Jr. A champions; player/secty-treas. Can-Am basketball assn. '47-50; player/secty. St. Catharines Softball Assn. mem. 2 OASA, 3 OABA title teams; 3 St. Catharines, 1 Ont. Mr. Softball awards; served in varied exec. capacities OASA '55-94; Royal Canadian Legion minor softball/hockey exec./ umpire '56-74; OCBA secty '49-51; OASA life mem. from '82; secty. Niagara Olde Tyme Sports Assn. '86-97; secty men's 10-pin league '86-97; active bowler from '90; mem. CASA, St. Catharines Sports halls of fame; res. St. Catharines, Ont.

PICKARD, Vic (t&f); b. 23 Oct 1903, Hamilton, Ont.; given name: Victor; m. Elizabeth Hershberger; c. Jane, Victor Jr., Carolyn Anne; Pittsburgh, BSc; retd. dept. store exec.; pole vault, javelin specialist; despite winning '20 Olympic trials was excluded from team; mem. '24, '28 Olympic teams; '24, '28 BE vs U S claiming polevault silvers each time; gold '24 Irish Olympics; 5 ntl pole vault titles; ntl record '28; silver US championships '29; '24 Scottish pole vault title, record; gold '27, silver '28-29 Penn Relays, gold '27, '29, silver '28 Ohio Relays; Pittsburgh vault mark of 13'10" which lasted until advent of fiberglass pole; twice 3rd NC4A championships; vault, javelin titles '24 NA Interscholastic championships; retd. from competition '31; mem. Pittsburgh, Western Pennsylvania, Canadian Amateur Sports halls of fame; res. Miami, Fla.

PICKELL, Bob (basketball); b. 2 Jul 1927, Kovna, Lithuania; d. 8 Aug 1987, Toronto, Ont.; given name: Bernard; m. Wendy; c. Al, Stephen; Portland;v-p TV Bureau of Canada; 4 times Portland all-star, mem. 3 NIT tournament teams; 5 ntl title teams; 5 MVP awards; mem. '59 Pan-Am, '52, '56 Olympic Games teams; football Edmonton '51-52, BC '54; AAU basketball '51 Hawaii; toured Far East with Universal Motors team '52-53; 2 Vancouver City handball singles, doubles titles; with Herb Capozzi ntl Masters racquetball doubles '73; drove in Shell 4,000 rally 4 times.

PICKELL, Stephen (swimming); b. 11 Aug 1957, Vancouver, B.C.; given name: Stephen John; m. Shelley Sanborn; c. Blake, Nicolas, Paul, Cooper; Capilano College,USC, insurance broker; asst. swim coach USC; 39 ntl championships '73-80; mem. ntl team '73-80; gold, silver '74 Commonwealth Games; silver '76 Olympics; silver, bronze '79 Pan-Am Games; 9 1sts '76 nationals, '75 World trials; 34 ntl sr. records; Viscount Alexander award '74; mem. '80 Olympic team; res. Tustin, Calif.

PICKERING, Bob (curling); b. 19 Sep 1932, Regina, Sask.; given name: Robert Hugh; m. Dorothy Somerville; c. Laurie, Pattie, Sheri; retd. politician; MLA Bengough '78-81, served as minister of Rural Development; Parks & Renewable Resources; nicknamed 'Peewee'; 6 times provincial champion, Brier rep., 2nd several times; '64 Massey-Ferguson ntl Farmers' title, Canadian Elks '75; twice winner Canadian Open Carspiel Edmonton; twice Calgary Masters champion; mem. Canadian Curling Hall of Fame; res. Phoenix, Ariz./Regina, Sask.

PIDSKALNY, Diane (t&f/wheelchair basketball); b. 3 May 1948, Ethelbert, Man.; m. Alex Hrychuk; c. A.J.; UMan; began competing in variety of sports '68; mem. ntl women's wheelchair basketball team '71-90; mem. Man. mixed wheelchair basketball team '68-92, Man. women's league '96-97; holds Class V women's discus, shot put, javelin records; with teammate Joanne MacDonald Pan-Am gold table tennis doubles '75, '78; ntl Class V table tennis singles champion; more than 100 medals, 20 in international competition; frequent all-star basketball honors; commissioner women's div. CWBA '98; res. Fork River, Man.

PIELAK, Casmer (baseball); b. 3 Feb 1939, Candiac, Sask.; m. Lavern Haider; c. Warren; businessman; played baseball,

hockey in both Candiac, Regina; coached juvenile Columbus boys baseball league; pres. Columbus Boys League '69-70; pres. Sask. Baseball Assn. '71-72; v-p Baseball Canada '73-75; pres. Baseball Canada '75-85; chair Sask. Sport '76; chair Sask. Lottery '77; v-p International Federation of Amateur Baseball '76-84; secty-general IBA '84-92; instrumental in baseball being '88 Olympic demonstration sport; founding mem. Sask. Sport; mem. Sask Sports Hall of Fame; res. Regina, Sask.

PIERCE, Glen (curling); b. 19 Sep 1941, Tisdale, Sask.; given name: Glen Arnold; m. Eleanor Vuksic; c. Brent, Shannon; mechanical contractor; 11 times Pacific Coast men's finalist; won 6 major cashspiels; skipped BC entry '79 Brier; provincial Tankard finalist '80-82; skipped BC entry to national Seagram Mixed title '82; res. New Westminster, B.C.

PIETRACUPA, Michel (weightlifting); b. 12 Jul 1959, Baie Comeau, Que.; ntl jr. record 232.5kg '78 jr. worlds; broke same record with 262.5kg '79 Canada vs England meet; ntl sr. snatch record 135.0kg '81 then broke own standard with 138.9kg '82; ntl sr., Commonwealth clean and jerk record 178.0kg '82; 60kg title Canada vs US '77, 67.5kg jr. America Cup '79, 75kg Que. championships '80, ntl titles '81-82; ntl sr. lift record 315.0kg '82; mem. '80 Olympic team; res. St-Thomas d'Aquin, Que.

PILCHER, Al (skiing); b. 18 Sep 1964, Toronto, Ont.; cross-country specialist; also active in duathlons/triathlons; '91 ntl cross-country champion; scored 2 1sts '91 Continental Cup series; NA 10km, 30km titles '90; competed '88 Olympics, '89 world championships; res. Orangeville, Ont.

PILON, Claude (wrestling); b. 13 Jun 1950, Ottawa, Ont.; m. Rosalie Sutherland; c. Jean-Marc, Jeffrey Thomas; UofOtt, hons. BPHE; financial advisor, fed. govt.; ntl jr. discus, hammer titles '69-70; def. end Ottawa Sooners ntl jr., sr. ORFU finalist '70-71; 1 ntl jr. 5 sr. FS wrestling titles; mem. '71, '75 Pan-Am, '73 FISU Games teams; bronze '70, gold '74 Commonwealth Games; silver World Cup '75; CIAU champion '71-74; alternate Greco-Roman team '76 Olympics; pro football Rough Riders '77; 3rd ntl judo black belt championships '82-83; judo black belt '83; consultant Sport Canada '76-80; res. Ottawa, Ont.

PILON, Jacques (t&f); b. 16 Aug 1957, Ottawa, Ont.; Dalhousie, UofOtt; launched competitive career B1 (0 vision to light perception) '75; 5 ntl 800m, 1500m, 2 5000m titles; gold 1500m, silver 10,000m '78 Pan-Ams for disabled; gold 1500m '80 Blind Olympics; 1st blind runner to crack 3 hour barrier 2h58:53 National Capital Marathon '83; world records for totally blind 800m, 1500m, ntl records 800m, 1500m, 5000m; silver 1500m Stoke-Mandeville Games for disabled; 1st blind competitor Ottawa Indoor Games; unbeaten at prov. level 800m, 1500m; pres. Ont. Blind Sports Assn. '77; mem. Ottawa Sports Hall of Fame; res. London, Ont.

PILOTE, Pierre (hockey); b. 11 Dec 1931, Kenogami, Que.; given name: Pierre Paul; m. Ann Greshchyshyn; c. Denise, Pierre, Renee, David; retd businessman, farmer; defenceman; began organized hockey career Fort Erie at

16; Jr. B Niagara Falls; Jr. A St. Catharines Tee Pees; pro Buffalo AHL '51-55, Chicago NHL '55-68, Toronto '68-69; effective defensively and offensively; 5 1st, 3 2nd team all-star; 3 Norris Trophy; capt. Black Hawks '63-68; 1 Stanley Cup; NHL record: 890 scheduled games, 80g, 418a, 86 playoff games, 8g, 53a; raised German Short Hair Pointers; mem. Hockey Hall of Fame; res. Elmvale, Ont.

PILOUS, Rudy (builder/hockey); b. 11 Aug 1914, Winnipeg, Man.; d. 5 Dec 1994, St. Catharines, Ont.; played jr. hockey Portage La Prairie, Winnipeg Monarchs; sr. Nelson, B.C., Eng., NY Rovers; established jr. club in St. Catharines; scout/promotions assistant Buffalo '46; helped Houston win USHL title ;47; sent by Buffalo to San Diego Skyhawks and helped them win PC title '49; reputation as trouble-shooter/promoter firmly established he went on to become mgr/coach St. Catharines Memorial Cup winners '54, '69; coached Black Hawks to '61 Stanley Cup; mgr./coach WHL champion Denver Invaders '64; mgr. WHA Avco Cup champion Winnipeg Jets '76, '78; scout Detroit, Los Angeles; GM Toronto's St. Catharines farm club; mem. Cdn, Man. Hockey halls of fame.

PINDER, Gerry (hockey); b. 15 Sep 1948, Saskatoon, Sask.; given name: Allan Gerald; m. Kaylene Cloward; c. Matt, Patrick, Brett; UofSask, BComm, UMan; real estate developer; mem. Nutana midgets; jr. Saskatoon Blades '65-67; MVP, scoring champion '67; mem. ntl bronze medal team '68 Olympics, '69 world championships; pro Chicago (NHL) '69-71, California (NHL) '72, Cleveland Crusaders (WHA) '72-76, San Diego Mariners (WHA) '76-77, Edmonton Oilers (WHA) '77-78; eye injury reduced efficiency; co-owner Regina Pats jr. team; scratch golfer; mem. 4 Sask. Willingdon Cup teams; mem. Sask, Saskatoon Sports halls of fame; res. Calgary, Alta.

PINDER, Herb (hockey); b. 29 Dec 1946, Boston, Mass.; given name: Herbert Charles; m. Madeleine Luiten; c. Scott, Danielle; UofSask, BA, UMan, LLB, Harvard Business School, MBA; businessman, player agent; from junior ranks to ntl team; mem. '68 bronze medal Olympic team; ankle fractured in skiing accident ended playing career; exec. asst. to pres. Calgary Broncs (WHA); became player rep. '73; clients have included Peter McNab, Kevin Maxwell, Mike Rogers, Ryan Walter, Dave Williams, Joe Nieuwendyk, Mike Richter, Trevor Kidd, Bill and Chris Hajt; co-owner Regina Pats jr. team; before injury enjoyed standout golfing career; competed in Sask. jr., Regina amateur; Sask. jr. champion; mem. Sask. Willingdon Cup team; has served on numerous corporate boards; governor Canada's Sports Hall of Fame; trustee Fraser Inst., Manning Awards; chair. PRIDE Canada; mem. Sask., Saskatoon Sports halls of fame; res. Saskatoon, Sask.

PINKNEY, David Sr. (harness racing); b. 16 Nov 1931, South Ohio, N.S.; c. Dave Jr., Greg; following father Kirk's footsteps he began driving '51 with most of his career spent campaigning in the Maritimes; despite more than 3200 victories has amassed purses totalling only $2.4M; with Team Hanover won '87 Haughton Memorial and Hanover Colt Stakes; res. Truro, N.S.

PINTEA, Horatio (table tennis); b. 11 Nov 1962, Oradea, Romania; m. Lijuan Geng; c. James Ross; UofOtt; operates pizza business; team, mixed doubles (Mariann Domonkos) silver '83 Pan-Am Games; men's doubles (Pradeenan Peter-Paul) bronze '99 PAG, '99 Butterfly Cup; 3 ntl, 1 Lousiana, CNE mixed doubles gold; 1 ntl, NA men's doubles gold; 1 ntl, NA, Louisiana men's singles gold; res. Ottawa, Ont.

PIOTROWSKI, Irene (t&f); b. 9 Jul 1941, Skaudvile, Lithuania; given name: Irena Macijauskas; div.; UBC; jewelry store owner/mgr.; BC cross-country title, ntl 100yd record '63; ntl, world record 11.4 for 100m '64; mem. '64 '68 Olympic teams; world indoor 300yd, 300m records; silver 100yd, bronze 220yd '66 Commonwealth Games; 5 first, ntl 220yd 23.5 mark BC vs Oregon meet; silver, bronze '67 Pan-Am Games; ntl record 11.3 100m '68 Olympics; Yukon Flour Packing title '74 backpacking 500lbs 100ft, 600lbs 50 ft; carried 342lbs 50 ft '75 Powell River Sea Festival; women's '74 European tour manager; PB: 100yd 10.4, 100m 11.3; mem. BC Sports Hall of Fame; res. Vancouver, B.C.

PIRNIE, Bruce (t&f); b. 20 Sep 1942, Boston, Mass.; div. Karen Hayton; c. Elizabeth, Catherine; m. Jane Edstrom; Yankton College, BA, South Dakota State; ex-teacher, CTFA ntl throwing coach, head coach high performance centre, t&f coach UMan.; college all-conference track, football; all-league defensive end St. Vital Bulldogs, ntl sr. champions '68; competed for U.S. '67 Pan-Am Games; co-capt. '72, '76 Olympic team; shot put silver '73 Pan-Pacific Games '73; bronze '74 Commonwealth Games; gold '75 Pan-Am Games; 5 ntl indoor, outdoor shot put titles; began coaching '66; 3 CIAU indoor t&f coach of yr awards; ntl Espoir team asst.-coordinator '87-98; coach 2 Commonwealth, 3 Pan-Am Games teams; v-p Manitoba Basketball Assn.; pres. Norwood Basketball Club; res. Winnipeg, Man.

PISCHKE, Garth (volleyball); b. 12 Aug 1955, Winnipeg, Man.; m. Cindy Lynn Shepherd; c. Dane, Taylor; UMan, BA; coach; played with UMan Bisons '77-79; 3 CIAU title teams; 3 ntl -20 titles; 5 CVA open, 3 USVBA open titles; mem. 29 ntl title teams including '91 Cdn beach doubles; mem. ntl team '76-90; competed '76, '84 Olympics; played pro IVA El Paso, Denver; IVA rookie of '78, MVP '79; 12 ntl championship all-star teams, 6 MVP awards; all-American at 7 USVBA championships, 1 MVP award; through '97 Bisons coach 20yrs, qualifying for ntls each year; 7 CIAU gold, 9 silver, 1 bronze; has amassed more than 1000 coaching triumphs; 5 CIAU coach of yr awards; coached varied developmental/experienced club teams to 3 -18, 4 -20, 4CVA open titles; mem. Manitoba Sports Hall of Fame; res. Winnipeg, Man.

PITCAIRN, Bob (shooting); b. 26 Jun 1938, Summerside, P.E.I.; given name: Robert Andrew; m. Kay Reade; c. Lee-Anne, Donald; Prince of Wales Coll.; retd. airline pilot; began smallbore shooting '52, target rifle shooting '60; 8 BC target rifle titles, BC sub machine gun title '83, 2 BC service rifle titles; 4 BC Lt.-Governor's prizes; qualified 28 Bisley teams; Bisley grand aggregate gold cross '65, silver cross '81; qualified 9 Cdn Palma Teams; DCRA ntl fullbore titles, Governor-General's '62, '64; CTR Agg. '90; Macdonald Stewart grand agg. gold cross '90, silver cross '82;. prov exec. pres. '74-78, '90-98; ntl exec., life-gov. BCRA, DCRA; nicknamed 'Mr. H'; mem. Cdn Forces, PEI Sports halls of fame; res. Chilliwack, B.C.

PITRE, Didier (hockey/lacrosse); b. 1884, Sault Ste. Marie, Ont., d. 29 Jul 1934, Sault Ste. Marie, Mich.; pro defenceman Nationals of Federal Amateur HL; teamed with Jack Laviolette Shamrocks international pro league '08; mem. Lester Patrick's Edmonton team '09; first player signed when Laviolette formed Montreal Canadiens '09-10 and remained with that club until '23 retirement except '13-14 season with Vancouver; moved to right wing '11, teamed with Laviolette, Newsy Lalonde to form top line which led Habs to '16 Stanley Cup, team became known as Flying Frenchmen; most productive season '15 with 30 goals; in 19 seasons, 282 games, 240 goals, 27 playoff games, 14 goals; lacrosse player with variety of teams; nicknamed 'Cannonball'; mem. Canadian Lacrosse, Hockey halls of fame.

PITTS, Allen (football); b. 28 Jun 1963, Tucson, Ariz; Cal State Fullerton; slotback; attended NFL LA Rams camps '86-87; made impressive CFL debut with Calgary '90 catching passes in 17 of 18 regular season games with 65 receptions; during 10yr CFL career set records for all-time receiving yardage (13,272), all-time receiving tds (106), most games catching a td pass (86), most 100yd plus receiving games (61), most td pass receptions single season (21); through '99 in 149 regular season games, 14 playoff games, 5 Grey Cup finals, 2 winners (through '98); 100yds or more receiving 61 times in regular season play; career receptions total 869 2nd in league behind Donald Narcisse of Sask.; 9 all-star awards; 4 Keith Spaith awards; President's ring award '94; res. Calgary, Alta.

PIZZEY, Blair (bowling); b. 5 Jan 1963, Saskatoon, Sask.; given name: Blair Kenneth; m.; c. Branden; UofSask.; auto sales mgr.; played hockey, baseball provincially, softball, provincially, nationally; five-pin bowler; silver '78 Saskatchewan Winter Games; bronze '83 Canada Winter Games; Saskatchewan, ntl singles titles '86; CBC singles title '87; Molson open singles titlist '88; res. Saskatoon, Sask.

PLAMONDON, Charles (biathlon); b. 4 May 1961, Charlesbourg, Que.; Laval; NA 4x7.5km relay title '84; ntl jr. 10km, 15km, 4x7.5km relay titles '81; ranked 16th in world '87; mem. '88 Olympic team; res. St. Augustine, Que.

PLANTE, Jacques (hockey); b. 17 Jan 1929, Mt. Carmel, Que.; d. 26 Feb 1986, Switzerland; m. Jacqueline; c. Michel (d.), Richard; hockey coach; jr. Quebec City; minor pro Montreal Royals (QHL), Buffalo (AHL); goaler Canadiens '52-63, Rangers '63-65, Blues '68-70, Maple Leafs '70-73, Bruins '73, Edmonton (WHA) '74-75; coach Quebec Nordiques (WHA) '73-74; goaler coach Flyers '79-82; Hart Trophy (MVP) '62, 7 times Vezina Trophy, including 5 in succession '56-60; 3 times 1st team, 4 times 2nd team NHL all-star; revolutionized netminding methods; pioneered modern-day goaler's masks; Montreal jr league commissioner; asst. coach California Seals '67-68; led Quebec minor pro baseball league hitters several seasons; jersey #1 retd by Canadiens; mem. Canada's Sports, Hockey halls of fame.

PLATTS, Robin (horse racing); b. 27 Apr 1947, Leicester, Eng.; father's letter to OJC president John Mooney led to opportunity to learn the jockey's art under famed trainer Lou Cavalaris Jr.; made riding debut '66; as apprentice '68 won 219 races including Cdn International championship aboard Frenetico; evolved into one of Woodbine's top money riders winning 4 Queen's Plates, 3 Prince of Wales Stakes, 4 Breeder's Stakes; Sovereign top jockey award '79; Avelino Gomez Memorial award '92; highly regarded by peers; more than 3,300 victories; mem. Cdn Horseracing Hall of Fame; res. Toronto, Ont.

PLATZ, Jim (shooting); b. 25 Jun 1931, Bruno, Sask.; given name: James Walter; m. Nadine Peters; c. Jerry, Tom, Randy, Jamie, Shelley, Debbie; St. Thomas Coll.; self-employed; trap specialist; mem. '72 Olympic team; gold '71, silver '75 worlds, Benito Juarez; 6 ntl titles; last known res. Sherwood Park, Alta.

PLAXTON, Hugh (hockey); b. 16 May 1904, Barrie, Ont.; d. 1 Dec 1982, Mississauga, Ont.; given name: Hugh John; m. Grace Livingstone Innes; c. Martha, Catherine, Charles Timothy, John Innes (d.); UofT, BA, Osgoode Hall, LLB; retired lawyer; mem. Varsity Grad hockey team; Allan Cup champions '27; Olympic gold '28; MP-Lib Toronto Trinity '35-39; mem. Mississauga Sports Hall of Fame.

PLESS, Willie (football); b. 21 Feb 1964, Anniston, Ala.; Kansas; linebacker; Lombardi, Butkus awards nominee; AP 2nd team all-American; MVP '85 Blue-Grey Game; participated Senior, East-West Shrine Bowls; pro CFL Toronto '86-89, BC '90, Edmonton '91-98, Sask '99; CFL record (through '98): 211gp, 77sacks; 2 Eastern, 9 CFL, 6 Western, 1 Northern all-star; Frank Gibson Eastern rookie trophy '86; 5 Norm Fieldgate trophies; 5 CFL outstanding defensive player awards, 1 runnerup; CFL career record most defensive tackles; 3 Grey Cup finals, 1 winner; res. Edmonton, Alta.

PLOEN, Ken (football); b. 3 Jun 1935, Lost Nation, Iowa; m. Janet Newcomer; c. Kendra, Douglas, Carol; Iowa, BSc; Blue Bombers sales/marketing chief; all-American, '57 Rose Bowl game; Winnipeg '57-67; as defensive back '59 established club interception record with 10; as quarterback completed 1084 of 1916 passes for 16,470yds, 119tds, 56.6 completion avg, 106 interceptions; shares CFL record for longest completed pass-109yds to Ken Nielsen '65; 3 times WFC all-star; 6 Grey Cup finals, 4 winners; Blue Bomber outstanding offensive player of half-century; mem. Canadian Football, Blue Bombers, Rose Bowl halls of fame; res. Winnipeg, Man.

PLOUDRE, Tony (fencing); b. 2 Feb 1966, Chibougamau, Que.; began fencing age 11; sabre specialist; mem. ntl team '85-98; competed '88, '92, '96 Olympics; NA Cup circuit gold '94, Continental Olympic qualifier team gold '95; 2 team silver Pan-Am Games; with triumph over former world champion Chris Etropolski of Bulgaria, helped Canada to best ever sabre team showing at worlds with 6th place '91, also 6th '93; ntl sabre title '96; 2 Petro-Canada fund scholarships; res. Montreal, Que.

PLUMMER, Reg (field hockey); b. 6 Aug 1953, Sudbury, Ont.; given name: Reginald Frederick; m. Gail Dawson; Carleton, UBC, BSc; economist; ntl team '73-92; gold '83, silver '75, '79 Pan-Am Games; mem. '76, '84 Olympic, '78 World Cup, '80 Intercontinental Cup teams; MVP Lahr,

Germany, international tournament '76; mem. BC gold medal team '80 ntl championships; asst coach ntl -21 team to '96; mem. ntl high performance team comm.; mem. Outaouais FHC; fed. govt. excellence award '84; res. Nepean, Ont.

POCE, Paul (t&f/coaching); b. 19 Sep 1929, Toronto, Ont; given name: Paul Francis; div. Ethel McKnight; m. Lorraine Watt; UofT; one of Canada's top milers in '40s and competitor over all distances up to 6 miles to '56; several prov., US distance race titles; ntl team coach from '60; coach team '66, '70, '78, '86, '90, '94 Commonwealth Games, '67, '75, '79, '83 Pan-Am Games, '72, '76, '80, '92 Olympic Games, '68 Scandinavia, '71 Italy, '74 European tour; res. Toronto, Ont.

POCKAR, Brian (figure skating); b. 27 Oct 1959, Calgary, Alta.; d. 28 Apr 1992, Calgary, Alta.; given name: Brian James; UCal; competed '71 Canada Games; at novice level nationally '72-73, ntl junior level '74-75, bronze world junior '76; silver '77 ntl sr. men's, St. Gervais Grand Prix; bronze '78 Skate Canada, '79 England Rotary; ntl sr. men's champion '78-80; world team mem. '77-81; silver '80 Skate Canada; gold '80 St. Ivel England; bronze worlds '82; mem. '80 Olympic team; retd. '83; artistic dir. '88 Olympic team; TV color commentator; Alberta achievement awards '76-81; Calgary Booster Club athlete of '80; pro skating lifetime achievement award; mem. Calgary Olympic advisory comm;mem. Alta Sports Hall of Fame.

POCKLINGTON, Peter (builder/hockey); b. 18 Nov 1941, Regina, Sask.; div. c. 4; chair. Pocklington Financial Corp.; at 23 Canada's youngest Ford dealer; in 3yrs built it into Canada's largest dealership; sport involvement began with Edmonton Oilers in WHA '77; played key role in moving team into NHL; 5 Stanley Cup winners; mem. Chairman's exec. comm. NHL board of governors; sport interest not confined to hockey; owner Edmonton Trappers (PCL) baseball club, Edmonton Drillers (ntl pro soccer league); involved in Can-Am auto racing with Paul Newman; among world's top jet boat racers; wide array of business interests; sold interest in Oilers '98; res. Edmonton, Alta.

PODBORSKI, Steve (skiing); b. 25 Jul 1957, Toronto, Ont.; given name: Stephen Gregory; div. Ann Rhomer; m. Cathy Rooney; c. Benjamin; ski instructor; mem. ntl team '73-84; ntl slalom champion '77, downhill runnerup '80; NA jr. downhill champion '75; 8 WC downhill victories moved him to forefront among 'Kamikaze Kids' as daredevil Canadian male downhillers were termed on World Cup circuit; '80-81 season runnerup for WC downhill title despite coming off knee surgery previous summer; WC downhill title '81-82; WC record 8-5-7; ranked by FIS as world's top downhiller '80-81 season; bronze '80 Olympics, mem. '84 Olympic team; ntl downhill title '84; Ont. athlete of '80, co-holder with Alex Baumann '81; 2 Norton Crowe awards; CSA John Semmelink Trophy '81; course record 1:55.48 in winning WC downhill Garmisch '81; Officer Order of Canada '82; mem. Cdn Amateur Sports, Cdn Skiing halls of fame; res. Don Mills, Ont.

PODIVINSKY, Edi (skiing); b. 8 Mar 1970, Edmonton, Alta.; UWO; began skiing age 3, competing age 6; mem. ntl alpine development group '87-89, ntl team '90-98; ntl juvenile downhill gold '85; 1 ntl, 1 jr. world, 4 FIS, 1 World Cup downhill gold; 1 FIS Super G, 2 FIS slalom gold; downhill bronze '94 Olympics; competed '98 Olympics; won US downhill title '98; WC record 1-0-1; res. Guelph, Ont.

POILE, Bud (builder/hockey); b. 10 Feb 1924, Fort William, Ont.; given name: Norman; retd. hockey exec.; began pro career Leafs '42; led team in playoff scoring '43; mem. Toronto Stanley Cup winner '47; played in NHL with Toronto, Chicago, Detroit, New York, Boston ;'42-50; NHL record: 311 scheduled games, 107g, 122a, 23 playoff games, 4g, 5a; turned talents to administration; coached minor league title winners in Edmonton, San Francisco; GM Philadelphia, Vancouver in NHL; played key role in building 2 Philadelphia Stanley Cup winners; exec/v-p WHA; commissioner CHL '76-84; during '83-84 season also commissioner IHL; forced to suspend CHL operations and stayed with IHL post through '89; Lester Patrick award '89; mem. Hockey Hall of Fame; res. Mesa, Ariz.

POIRIER, Joe (football); b. 30 Jul 1937, Montreal, Que.; given name: John Joseph; m. Geraldine Lavoie; c. Erin, J.J., Noemi, Sam; Loyola, BA; McGill, BSW; UofOtt, MSW; marketing/sales Cdn Tourism Commission; nicknamed 'The Fox'; following standout college career turned pro as defensive back with CFL Rough Riders '59-70; EFC rookie of year '59; annually *Globe & Mail* Eastern all-star from '59; CFL Eastern all-star '60-66; all-Canadian '66; 4 Grey Cups, 3 winners; Loyola sportsmanship award '57; McGill sportsmanship award '58; mem. Ottawa, Loyola Sports halls of fame; res. Aylmer, Que.

POITRAS, Tina (t&f); b. 5 Oct 1970, Thompson, Man.; McGill; race walk specialist; began competing '88; world jr. 5km walk gold '89; 5000m Pan-Am jr. championship gold; won 3000m Japan International; 2 ntl outdoor 10km walk gold; competed '92, '96 Olympics; '91, '93 FISU Games, '94 Francophone Games, 2 world championships; Shell scholarship best Quebec student athlete '91-92; Terry Fox award '92; res. Montreal, Que.

POLISOIS, Alex (table tennis); b. 19 Jan 1957, Cairo, Egypt; given name: Alexandre; Ecole Polytechnique de L'Universite de Montreal; men's A, D titles '72 Chateauguay Open; 3 years runnerup ntl title before winning '78; Que. jr., sr. champion '73; mem. ntl team '74-90; 2 gold (men's, mixed doubles), 2 bronze (singles, team matches) '79 Pan-Am Games; Sydney, Australia, Invitational title '81; mem. 4 English Open, 1 German Open, 3 Welsh Open, 2 Commonwealth championships, 3 world championships, 1 Pan-Ams, 1 Hungarian Open, 1 Yugoslavian Open teams; last knownn res. St. Laurent, Que.

POLLOCK, Lloyd (builder); b. 26 Jul 1909, Pine River, Ont.; given name: Lloyd Thompson; retd. railroader; secty-tres Windsor City HL; instrumental in bringing OHA Junior A hockey to Windsor with Spitfires '46; pres. OHA '61, CAHA '68; mem. Windsor-Essex Sports Hall of Fame; res. Windsor, Ont.

POLLOCK, Sam (hockey); b. 15 Dec 1925, Montreal, Que.; m. Mimi Kinsella; c. Rachel, Sam Jr., Mary; chair./CEO Toronto Blue Jays; former hockey exec.; coached

Junior Canadiens '47-53, 1 Memorial Cup winner; Hull-Ottawa Canadiens (EPHL) '59-62; GM Montreal Canadiens '64-78; 9 Stanley Cup winners; '76 *Sporting News* NHL exec. of year; managing dir. Team Canada '76; elected Great Montrealer in Sport past 2 decades '78; chair. John Labatt Ltd., '91-95; chair. Blue Jays '95-99; Officer Order of Canada '85; mem. Hockey, Canada's Sports halls of fame; res. Toronto, Ont.

POLSON, Lynn (basketball); b. 19 Apr 1962, St. Catharines, Ont.; m. Doug Hamilton; c. Frederick, Douglas; Bishop's, BA, Concordia, sports admin. diploma; guard ntl team '91-88; 2 CIAU title teams; gold Jones Cup '82; mem. '81, '83, '85 FISU, '83, '87 (bronze) Pan-Am, '84 Olympic teams; capt. '86 World championship bronze medal team; mem., all-star German semi-pro league '85-97; ntl tour all-star '88; MVP honors Hungary, Czechoslovakia, Canada-Russia series; 3 Bishop's athlete of yr awards; 3 CIAU all-Canadian awards; 2 ntl championship MVP awards; res. St. Catharines, Ont.

POMFRET, Jack (all-around); b. 22 Nov 1922, Vancouver, B.C.; given name: Jack Bradshaw; m. Marilyn; c. Lynne, Penny, Jay; Washington, BA, MSc; associate prof. UBC; national age group, sr. native, open swim records; '41 world record; mem. '40 Wash. world record medley relay team; Pacific Coast Conf. record holder; mem. Wash. conf. title team; NCAA all-American; swim coach White Rock SC, Vancouver SC, UAlta., UBC; '70-71 college coach of year; all-star 4yrs HS rugby title teams; mem. Meraloma Vancouver, BC title teams; capt. Washington Huskies basketball team; *AP* Pac. Conf. all-star; mem. 1 Meraloma, 3 Cloverleaf ntl title teams; mem. '48 Olympic team; *Daily Province* MVP Trophy; offered pro contract Northwest League; coached UBC juniors to 2 BC titles; coached UBC Thunderbirds 15yrs; asst. coach '56 ntl champion BC all-stars, Olympic team; coached RCAF Western Command service champions, Evergreen Conf. all-stars; football to college level, coached UBC 5yrs; mem. Vancouver, Edmonton sr. softball leagues; Edmonton league batting title; baseball Wash., Vancouver sr. league; pro offers Yankees; mem. Wash. boxing team winning all bouts on KO or TKO; jr. hockey Vancouver Lions; semipro Seattle McGregors; pro offers Vancouver Lions, NY Rangers; mem. Richmond Locarno juvenile, jr. lacrosse title teams; mem. 5 soccer title teams; active in swimming, basketball administration at ntl championship, BE, Pan-Am, Olympic Games levels from '62; meet manager, referee CASA swims more than 25 years; key role CIAU aquatic program development; founder BC basketball coaches assn.; pres. Wash. Big W Club; mem. Wash. Oval Club; considered one of greatest athletes in UW history; mem. BC Sports Hall of Fame selection comm.; mem. UBC, BC Sports halls of fame; res. Vancouver, B.C.

PONTING, Tom (swimming); b. 28 Jan 1965, Montreal, Que.; UCal; butterfly specialist; ntl sr 200m butterfly record; 2 200m, 1 100m CIAU, 16 ntl titles; silver 4x100 MR '83 Pan-Am, FISU, bronze 100m butterfly '83 FISU games; 1 world, 2 Cdn, Commonwealth, 3 CIAU records; 2 CIAU male swimmer of yr awards; 4x100 medley relay silver '84 Olympics; retd. from competition '94; mem. Alta. Sports Hall of Fame; res. Calgary, Alta.

POPLAWSKI, Joe (football); b. 2 Sep 1957, Edmonton, Alta.; m. Darlene Dick; UAlta, BSc, UMan; insurance agency partner; college standout receiver; wide receiver Blue Bombers '78-86; CFL record (through '85): 475 receptions, 7266yds, 40tds; Schenley rookie of '78; Jackie Parker Trophy, Dr. Beattie Martin Trophy '78; Schenley Outstanding Canadian '81; CFL all-Cdn. '81; radio football color commentator; mem. Cdn Football Hall of Fame; res. Winnipeg, Man.

PORTER, Bob (all-around); b. 3 Dec 1913, Toronto, Ont.; d. 14 Mar 1995, Toronto, Ont.; mem. 3 HS sr. football title teams, Balmy Beach '32-48; 6 amateur baseball title teams; pro East Texas League '36, Toronto (IL) '36-39, Springfield (IL), Washington (AL) '41; mem. '35 softball title team; '31 St. Simons juvenile lacrosse team; jr. hockey Marlboros, int. champion Toronto Royals; rejected pro offers Maple Leafs, Montreal Maroons; coach St. Andrew's College football title team '39; football referee 10yrs ORFU, CIAU; mem. Canada's Sports Hall of Fame.

PORTER, Derek (rowing); b. 2 Nov 1967, Belfast, Ireland; mem. ntl team '89-98; stroke for '92 Olympic gold medal 8s crew; switched to single sculls '93 winning gold World championships, '99 Pan-Am Games; silver '96 Olympics; 4 Cdn, 2 US, 3 International regatta golds; res. Victoria, B.C.

PORTER, John (hockey); b. 21 Jan 1904, Toronto, Ont.; given name: John Chester; m. Marjorie Reever; c. John Jr., Ruth; UofT, BA; retd v.-chair. Simpson's; defenceman '21 UTS jr. OHA team; group finalist UofT OHA jrs. '22; OHA finalist UofT '23; OHA semifinalist UofT seniors '25-26; mem. '27 Varsity Grads Allan Cup champions, '28 Olympic champions; flag-bearer '28 winter Olympics; coached '29-30 Varsity Srs to Intercollegiate, OHA titles; pres. Rosedale Golf Club '51, Toronto Hunt Club '69; res. Toronto, Ont.

PORTER, Ken (t&f); b. 27 Jul 1948, Montreal, Que.; given name: Thomas Kenneth; UAlta, BPhE; sport administrator, coach; mem. CTFA selection comm. '71-72, chair. '72-73; chair. Commonwealth Games Foundation Edmonton athletics '72-77, competition dir. '77-78, asst. sports coordinator '77-78; mem. COJO, Montreal Olympics organizing comm. '75-76; Commonwealth Games Foundation Brisbane '80-82; ntl, international t&f meet director '69-80; coach ntl sprint team from '73; head coach Edmonton Olympic Club '79-80; sr. sprints, hurdles coach Australia '80-81; coaching development assn. rdinator Alta. TFA '79-80; official observer '74 European championships, '75 Pan-Am, '77, '79 World Cup, '81 New Zealand games; res. Edmonton, Alta.

PORTER, Lewis (football); b. 3 Jul 1947, Clarksdale, Miss.; m. Christine Hendrix; c. Patricia, Connie; Southern, BA; real estate agent; 29th among US HS running backs; MVP Mississippi '65; all-conference 3 years, all-American twice; Denver (NFL) '69, Kansas City '70-71, Hamilton (CFL) '71-78; all-Canadian cornerback '73, all-Eastern '75; returned kickoff 98yds for TD '72; last known res. Hamilton, Ont.

PORTER, Muriel (curling); b. 1903, Toronto, Ont.; d. (circa 1980s) Vancouver, B.C.; given name: Muriel Kathleen

Steen; m. Dr. Alvin B. Porter (d.); c. Robert Thomas, Charles Beverly; UBC; retd. teacher; organized Vancouver Ladies Curling Club '48, pres. 2yrs; helped organize BC Ladies Curling Assn. '50; gold medal best HS female athlete; mem. Canadian Curling Hall of Fame.

POSCENTE, Vincent (skiing); b. 1 Oct 1962, Edmonton, Alta.; m. Michelle Lemmons; c. Max, Alexia; UAlta. BA; professional speaker; speed skiing specialist; luge racer; began skiing at 25; 2 ntl titles; 5 ntl records; ranked among world's top 10 '90-92; competed in speed skiing '92 Olympics; ntl speed record 135 m.p.h. (216.7 k.p.h.); an adventurer he dove among sharks off Australia's Great Barrier Reef, hang glided in Rockies, dove off world's largest permanent bungee jump (230'); overcame total malfunction while parachuting; pres. Olympians of Canada Calgary '94-95; chair. Olympic Academy of Can. Org. Comm. '95; chair./founder Alta. Youth Olympic symposium '87-95; dir. Olympic Hall of Fame '94-95; chair. Lillehammer Olympic team sendoff '93-94; selected to Intl. Cdn. Olympic Academy; host broadcaster media liason (luge) '88 Olympics; managing dir. Alta. Luge Assn. '85-88; real estate award winner; owner/operator video production co.; mem. ntl speakers assn.; res. Dallas, Tex.

POST, Sandra (golf); b. 4 Jun 1948, Oakville, Ont.; div.; m. John McDermid; teaching pro golfer; ntl jr. titles '64-66, 3 Ont. jr. 1 Ont. Open, South Atlantic titles; pro from '68; '68 LPGA title, beating Kathy Whitworth in playoff; LPGA rookie of year '68; hole-in-one '68 at Cypress Creek Club Boyton Fla.; 8 LPGA tournament victories through '84; nicknamed 'Post-O'; 1 Lou Marsh, 2 Bobbie Rosenfeld trophies; capt. inaugural Nation's Cup team; exec. *editor World of Women's Golf;* CTV, ABC golf color commentator; mem. Canada's Sports, RCGA halls of fame; res. Palgrave, Ont.

POTHIER, Hector (football); b. 13 Jun 1954, St. Catharines, Ont.; m. Louisa; St. Mary's, McGill; 4 conf. all-star, 1 all-Cdn awards; John Metras Trophy CIAU top lineman; originally drafted by Montreal; rights dealt to Edmonton; Eskimos regular '78-89; off. tackle; WFC all-star, all-Cdn '81; mem. Eskimos hockey team; res. Edmonton, Alta.

POTTER, Billy (hockey/baseball/football); b. 10 Oct 1951, Ottawa, Ont.; given name: William Lorne; m. Linda Walton; c. Bradley, David, Brendan, Jesse; Carleton, BComm; economic analyst; mem. peewee Silver Stick hockey title team; midget league scoring champion; mem. 2 CJHL title teams; capt. Carleton, 2 scoring titles; Doug Canton award for athletic excellence Carleton; Little League, Babe Ruth baseball; mem. Ont. Babe Ruth title team; twice represented Canada vs US; mem. 6 Interprovincial Sr. baseball league title teams; twice led league batters; mem. '80 OBA title team; 4 times league all-star; 3 times Ottawa Senior Touch Football League scoring champion; '80 top sportsman trophy OSTFL; mem. ntl Touch FB all-stars '79; mem. '79 Ont. Touch football title team; brother Dale former mem. Edmonton Eskimos; res. Nepean, Ont.

POTTER, Dale (football); b. 9 Nov 1949, Ottawa, Ont.; given name: Dale William; m. Janet Mary Stirton; c. Braydon, Kenzie; Lenoir Rhyne College, UofOtt, BPhE;

UAlta; teacher; HS football MVP '68; played baseball to age 20; excelled as linebacker 3 seasons UofOtt team capt. 2 years; MVP, top defensive player '71; missed '72 season due to injury after earning Roy Farran award as top training camp player; drafted Winnipeg '73; Edmonton '74-83, Toronto '84; 8 Grey Cup finals, 6 winners; Western all-star, all-Cdn '80; outstanding Cdn, most valuable defensive player '80 Grey Cup game; Joe Clarke award as Eskimo player doing most for team with least recognition '75-76; CFL Players' Assn. Western Conf. linebacker of '75; plays touch football; coached minor football 5yrs; mem. UofOtt Football Hall of Fame; res. Nepean, Ont.

POTVIN, Denis (hockey); b. 29 Oct 1953, Ottawa, Ont.; given name: Denis Charles; m. Valerie; c. Madeleine, Annabelle, Christian; hockey broadcaster; mem. Ottawa 67's jrs.; twice OHA junior A Max Kaminsky award as top defenceman; 1st pick NY Islanders, 1st overall '73 amateur draft; Calder Memorial Trophy NHL rookie of '74; 3 James Norris Memorial trophies; 5 times 1st team, once 2nd team all-star; mem. 4 Stanley Cup winners; mem. Team Canada '76, '81; Islander capt. '79-80, '86-87; NHL record 25 points by defenceman one playoff year; tied NHL records 3 power play goals 1 game, 2 in 1 period; NHL record: 15 seasons, 1060 games, 310g, 742a, 185 playoff games, 56g, 108a; hon. chairman Suffolk County United Cerebral Palsy Assn.; jerseys retd by 67's, Islanders; named to CHL all-time team '99; mem. Hockey, Ottawa Sports halls of fame; res. Lighthouse Point, Fla.

POTVIN, Jean (hockey); b. 25 Mar 1949, Hull, Que.; given name: Jean Rene; m. Lorraine Paluck; c. Kim, Leslie-Ann; UofOtt; broadcaster, stockbroker; Hull Hawks (CJHL) 2 seasons; mem. national team; 2 seasons Ottawa 67's; pro Springfield (AHL) '69-70; NHL with Los Angeles '70-71, Philadelphia '72-73, NY Islanders '73-78, '79-81, Cleveland '78, Minnesota '78-79; retired '81 after teaming with brother Denis on defence with Islanders and winning 2 Stanley Cups; NHL record: 613 games, 63g, 224a, 39 playoff games, 2g, 9a; res. Huntington Station, N.Y.

POUND, Richard (swimming/administration); b. 22 Mar 1942, St. Catharines, Ont.; given name: Richard William Duncan: div. Mary Sherrill Owen; c. William Trevor Whitley, Duncan Robert Fraser, Megan Christy; m. Julie Houghton Keith; McGill, B Comm, BCL., Sir George Williams, BA; lawyer, chartered accountant; 4 ntl FS, 1 butterfly, 3 relay titles; ntl records 40, 50, 100, 110, 200yd, 100m FS; 6 provincial FS titles, records 40, 50 100, 200, 220yd, 100, 200m; intercollegiate FS champion 5yrs, records 50, 100, 200, 220 yds; mem. '59 Pan-Am Games team; 6th 100m FS '60 Olympics, 4th 400m medley relay; gold 110yd FS record 55.8 '62 Commonwealth Games, silver 880yd, 440yd FS relays; pres. COA '77-82; mem. IOC from '78, v-p; gov. Olympic Trust; Officer Order of Canada '92; mem. Canadian Aquatic, Amateur, Que. Sports halls of fame; res. Montreal, Que.

POWELL, Bill (boxing/bowling); b. 14 Oct 1921, Moose Jaw, Sask., d. 28 Dec 1978, Thunder Bay, Ont.; given name: William Thomas; m. Treasure Corrigan; c. Bob, Faye, Lorrie, Donna Rae; mem. '38 BEG team; ntl bantam, feather, lightweight titles; '46 ntl welterweight title; organized Thunder Bay Legion 5-pin bowling programs; pres.

WCFPBA '72; 4yrs pres. TBFPBA; coach, pres. HS 5-pin tournaments; mem. Winnipeg, Thunder Bay, Boxing halls of fame; '80 sportsman's award Thunder Bay; George Crowe Memorial Award '48.

POWELL, Cliff (administration); b. 24 Jul 1899, Westmount, Que.; d. 18 Nov 1987, Montreal, Que.; given name: Clifford Baden; m. Doris Sharples; c. Brian, Tim, Ann; McGill.; company board chair.; capt. St. Lambert war canoe, competed tandem 4s '20-25; European baseball following WWI, also hockey, football, baseball Montreal region '20-25; dir. COA, patron Canadian Canoe Assn., pres. Canadian Bobsleigh, Luge Assn.; mem. Cdn Amateur Sports Hall of Fame.

POWELL, Lori-Jane (racquetball); b. 8 Nov 1971, Saskatoon, Sask.; UofSask, BA; numerous medals at ntl, world jr. level; mem. ntl team; women's singles gold tournament of Americas '94, ntl championship '95; singles silver '94 worlds; ntl singles gold '95, bronze '96; ntl mixed doubles gold '06; res. Saskatoon, Sask.

POWER, Dale (tennis/hockey); b. 2 Oct 1949, Toronto, Ont.; given name: Dale Thomas; m. Joan Kathryn Westman: Oklahoma City ; tennis pro; OHA jr. hockey St. Catharines, Peterborough Petes '67-68; 5th pick Montreal '69 draft; pro Fort Wayne Komets (IHL) 1 season; ntl -18 closed tennis title '67; OCU tennis scholarship '70; mem. '72, '76 Davis Cup teams; among Canada's top 10 singles players from '68; ntl men's doubles title '73; top men's singles player '75 Rothman's Summer Grand Prix tour '80; ntl indoor singles, doubles titles '78, outdoor '79; pro circuit '76-81; playing coach Canadian Alcan tennis team '83; Racquet Power touring pro; mgr. Pinecrest TC, Chateau Montebello; switched competitive attention to squash '95; res. Montebello, Que.

POWER, Jonathon (squash); b. 9 Aug 1974, Comox, B.C.; m. Sita; ntl jr. titles '85-92; ntl men's title '96; mem. ntl jr. men's team '90, '92; team placed 3rd, best ever by Canada, '92 worlds; his 2nd place finish best ever by Canadian; youngest-ever men's ntl team mem. '91; mem. ntl sr. men's team '93-98; individual silver, team gold '95 Pan-Am Games; silver '98 Commonwealth Games; won '95 MAAA invitational, '96 tournament of champions (1st NA player to win major world squash event), German masters, Val de Loire. Hungarian Open, '97 Qatar Open, finalist '97 worlds; top-ranked in Canada '97; 1st non-European to win Australian Open '98; won Cathay Pacific Open '98; won Flanders Open '99; 1st NA player to win world open title '98; 1st Canadian ranked No. 1 in world '99; res. Toronto, Ont.

POWLESS, Gaylord (lacrosse); b. 1 Dec 1946, Brantford, Ont.; given name: Gaylord Ross; m. Patty Broker; c. Gaylene, Chris; retd. construction; centre jr./sr./major/pro Oshawa, Detroit, Brantford, Six Nations, Coquitlam, Syracuse, Montreal, Brampton '64-77; cumulative record: 705 scheduled games, 588g, 914a, 118 playoff games, 207g, 317a; 4 Minto, 1 Mann Cup title teams; Jim McConaghy Minto Cup MVP awards '64, '67; 2 Ken Ross ability/ sportsmanship awards; 1 Bucko MacDonald, 2 *Advertiser* top scorer awards; 4 1st team, 1 2nd team all-star centre

awards; mem. Cdn Lacrosse Hall of Fame; res. Hagersville, Ont.

POWLESS, Ross (lacrosse); b. 29 Sep 1926, Six Nations of the Grand River, Ont.; given name: Alexander Ross; m. Margaret Wilma Bomberry; c. Gaylord, Gail, Gary, Audrey, Gregory, Harry, Arlene, Richard, Darryl, Karen, Anthony, Jeffrey, Jacqueline; retd construction supervisor/band council mem.; Sr. B Eastern Cdn Huntsville title team '50; mem. Peterborough Mann Cup titlists '51-54; player/coach Lewiston, NY/Tuscarora Indian Reserve Eastern Sr, B champs '55; '58-68 coach Brantford Warriors Ont. Int. A/ Sr. B titles, player/coach Hamilton Lincoln Burners Sr. A, coach Six Nations All-Indian sr. team; coach Cdn sr. men's team Expo '67; coach.mgr. Rochester NALA titlists '69; co-coach First Nations silver medal team '80 Nations Cup; 3 terms Six Nations rec. comm.; pres. Six Nations MHA '66; mem. building comm. Six Nations Sports/Cultural Memorial Centre; Mike Kelly Mann Cup MVP award '53; Ont. Municipal Rec. Assn. volunteer service award; mem. Cdn Lacrosse Hall of Fame; res. Hagersville, Ont.

PRATHER, Rollie (football); b. 17 Jul 1925, Eureka, Kan.; d. 28 May 1996, Calgary, Alta.; given name: Rollin Wayne; m. Gwyneth Mary Evans; c. Russell Rollin Wayne, Teresa Anne, Candice Louise, Shannon Maureen Kelly, Kathleen Moira Kelly; Kansas State, BSc; geologist; pres., chief ecec. officer gas dev. co.; all-American t&f '47-48; pro Edmonton '50-54; all-Cdn '51-52; CFL record most passes caught one game 15 '52; pro-am golf classic champion Willow Park G&CC '71; dir. Eskimos; mem. Kansas State Football Hall of Fame.

PRATT, Babe (hockey); b. 7 Jan 1916, Stoney Mountain, Man.; d. 16 Dec 1988, Vancouver, B.C.; given name: Walter; v-p, public relations asst. Vancouver Canucks; mem. 15 championship teams in 26-year playing career; Man. midget, juve. titles Elmwood Maple Leafs; Man. jr. title, scoring title Kenora; defenceman NY Rangers '35-36, Maple Leafs '42-46, Boston '46-47; NHL record: 517 scheduled games, 83g, 209a, 64 playoff games, 12g, 17a; on leaving NHL played with Hershey, New Westminster, Tacoma; Hart Trophy NHL MVP '44, mem. 1st, 2nd all-star teams once each; mem. '40 Stanley Cup, '42 Prince of Wales Trophy winners; mem. Cdn, Man. Hockey halls of fame.

PRATT, Ned (rowing); b. 15 Jul 1911, Boston, Mass.; given name: Charles Edward; m. Catherine Gordon Lang; m. Peter, Toni; UofT, BArch; architect; North Pacific junior singles '29, Sir Thomas Lipton Trophy '31; with Noel de Mille '32 North Pacific doubles, ntl championship, bronze doubles '32 Olympics, Pacific Coast title; mem. BC Sports Hall of Fame; res. West Vancouver, B.C.

PREDIGER, Pete (baseball); b. 1913, Odessa, Russia, d. 4 Feb 1974, Saskatoon, Sask.; given name: Peter John; raised in Macklin, Sask.; mem. Edmonton jrs. '32; mem. Neilberg Monarchs 38yrs, playing in remarkable 34 consec. Saskatoon Exhibition Baseball Tournaments; 5 title teams; semipro North Battleford Beavers '50-55, Lloydminster Meridians '57; retd. from play at 50; umpired to death from cancer; coached Legion baseball, softball, hockey 20yrs; toured Europe with Krefield Canadians hockey club '36; mem. Canadian Baseball, Sask. Sports halls of fame.

PRENTICE, Bob (baseball); b. 12 Aug 1928, Toronto, Ont.; d. 9 Feb 1995, Toronto, Ont.; given name: Robert Fergus; m. Nancy Sutherland; c. Jamie Susan, Richard Robert Scott; dir. Canadian scouting Blue Jays; all-star quarterback '44-46 Riverdale CI football team; mem. Ont. Jr. A Toronto Young Rangers hockey team '46-47; pro baseball Cleveland (AL) organization '48-57; Canadian chief scout Detroit '59-76; dir. Canadian scouting Blue Jays '76-95; freelance sports columnist *Toronto Telegram* '60-63; CBS TV broadcaster's asst. PGA golf tournaments '72-76.

PRENTICE, Bruce (administration); b. 31 Jul 1933, Toronto, Ont.; given name: Bruce Leslie; m. Audrey Grace Robertson; c. Brad, Laura, Graham, David; pres. Deamfield International Management Group; mem. OBA juve. baseball champions '50, sr. OBA titlists '53; Detroit Tiger prospect; coach/dir. playground baseball program '56-60, '59 Toronto city champions; founder/head coach 1st college/university baseball program in Canada Seneca Coll. '78-82; mem. NJCAA, NY-Penn conference; formed Metro College Baseball League '83; head coach Ryerson '83-84; Blue Jays scout '79-85; founder/pres. Cdn Baseball Hall of Fame '78-93; owner Proway baseball schools '81-84; skip bronze medal novice lawn bowling team '97; skip Balmy Beach Club curling league champions '96; brother Bob Blue Jay scouting dir.; operates Ont. Sport Legends, World Baseball, World Sport Legends, Royal Canadian Legion Sports halls of fame; res. Toronto, Ont.

PRENTICE, Dean (hockey); b. 5 Oct 1932, Schumacher, Ont.; given name: Dean Sutherland; m. June Collier; c. Kelly, Kerry; left winger; jr. Guelph Biltmores; played 22 seasons in NHL with NY Rangers '52-63, forming line with Andy Bathgate and Larry Popein, Boston '63-66, Detroit '66-69, Pittsburgh '69-71, Minnesota '71-74; NHL record: 1378 scheduled games, 391g, 469a, 54 playoff games, 13g, 17a; competed 4 NHL all-star games; coach New Haven (AHL) '75-77, Traverse City '77-78; with figure skating coach Kerry Leitch operated hockey school in Galt '64; assisted Glen Sather in Banff hockey school; setup Can-Am Hockey Schools; mgr./parks and rec. dir. Ayr 10yrs; active in Hockey Ministries International; plays old timers hockey; res. Cambridge, Ont.

PRESTON, Ken (football); b. 29 Oct 1917, Portland, Ont.; d. 2 Aug 1991, Regina, Sask.; m. Dorothy Barber (d); c. William, Douglas, Richard, Donna; Queen's, BComm; retired football exec.; football Queen's '36-39; pro Sask. '40, '46-48, Winnipeg '41 playing in Grey Cup victory, Ottawa '45; Saskatchewan GM '58-79; mem. Sask. Sports Hall of Fame.

PRICE, Harry (administration); b. 6 Apr 1896, Toronto, Ont.; d. 19 Feb 1985, Toronto, Ont.; given name: Harry Isaac; m. Ethel Hilker (d); c. Harry, Ethel Margaret; businessman; sports promoter; key role in establishment Canada's Sports Hall of Fame, chairman bd. of govs. '55-69; key role in establishment of govt. fitness, amateur sport administration; pres. CNE; MP York West; mem. Canada's Sports Hall of Fame.

PRICE, Noel (hockey); b. 9 Dec 1935, Brockville, Ont.; given name: Garry Noel; m. Joann Packota; c. Christine,

Joel; retd.; played minor hockey in Coniston; mem. Falconbridge Jr. A team at 15 where he was offered St. Michael's Coll. scholarship and played 4yrs in OHA Jr. A; turned pro '56; def. Rochester, Baltimore, Springfield, Quebec, Nova Scotia (AHL), Winnipeg (WHL); NHL with Toronto, NY Rangers, Detroit, Montreal, Pittsburgh, Los Angeles, Atlanta; NHL record: 499 scheduled games, 14g, 114a, 12 playoff games, 0g, 1a; retd. following '75-76 season; 4 Calder Cups, 1 Stanley Cup; 3 AHL 1st team, 1 2nd team all-star; only player to win 3 Eddie Shore best AHL defenceman awards; named top defenceman Springfield 50th anniversary team; mem. Springfield Hockey and with '72 Calder Cup title team Nova Scotia Sports halls of fame; res. Kanata, Ont.

PRICE, Pamela-Jean (baton twirling); b. 21 May 1958, Regina, Sask.; given name: Pamela-Jean Wilson; m. Marty Price; URegina, BA; systems analyst; mem. award winning Regina Optimist Buffalo Gals; ntl Miss Majorette title '76; ntl sr. women's title '80; certified Twirl Canada judge; last known res. Regina, Sask.

PRICE, Steve (softball); b. 24 Dec 1963, Toronto, Ont.; lhp/of; salesman; began as intermediate with Verona; played sr. with Kemptville Thunder, Toronto Gators, Middletown, NY, Heflin Builders Ballston Lake, NY, Decatur Pride, Vancouver Ravens, Green Bay; mem. ntl team; mem. ISC Toronto Gators world title team '93; Pan-Am gold '95, '99; res. Kingston, Ont.

PRIDHAM, Chris (tennis); b. 11 Apr 1965, Toronto, Ont.; ntl -16 singles, doubles titles; ntl -18 doubles; posted singles victories Hawaiian Satellite '87, Sun Life Classic '88, Troia Setubal '89, Bloomfield Hills Challenge '92; doubles victories Sun Life ntls '91, Munich Challenger '92; 3rd round singles Wimbledon '88, Australian Open '89, Player's International '92; Tennis Canada most improved award '87; pro '85; ranked 2nd Canada '92-93; mem. Cdn Davis Cup team from '88; mem. '88 Olympic team; active spokesperson, fundraiser CAVEAT (Canadians Against Violence Everywhere Advocating Its Termination); highest ATP ranking 75 in '88; res. Oakville, Ont.

PRIESTLEY, Gladys (swimming); b. 17 Jun 1938, Montreal, Que.; given name: Gladys Jean; m. Ross Watson; c. Ray Allan, Lori Anne; ntl FS relay titles, record times '50-58; mem. '52 (silver FS, medley relay), '56 Olympics; silver 400m FS '54, relay '58 BEG; FS finalist '55 Pan-Am Games; res. Arundel, Que.

PRIESTMAN, Keith (badminton); b. 21 Jan 1959, Scarborough, Ont.; given name: Keith Jack; m. Patti Bell; c. Ryan, Kelsey; Waterloo, BSc; mgr racquets div. Sportslines Intl.; 11 Ont. titles, including 2 jr. singles, '79 Open singles, 3 OUAA titles; 8 ntl titles; junior doubles with Jeff Goldsworthy; intermediate singles '79, '81; intermediate mixed doubles with Sandra Skillings '80; men's doubles with John Czich '82; mem. Pan-Am championships '80, Canadian Open, Devlin Cup, Am-Can, All-England teams; mem. ntl team '79-85; team silver '82 Commonwealth Games; turned to coaching '82-90; finalist Waterloo County amateur athlete of '78; mem. Waterloo Athletic Hall of Fame; res. Bowmanville, Ont.

PRIESTNER, Cathy (speed skating); b. 27 May 1956, Windsor, Ont.; given name: Catherine Ann; div. Merle Douglas Faminow; c. Leah Colette; m. Todd Allinger; c. Alicia, Colten; Mount Royal College; dir. ice events 2002 Salt Lake City winter Olympics; ex-asst. AD UCal; 6 ntl titles; gold 400m, silver 500m '71 Canada Games; silver 500m, 1000m '75 junior world; 5th overall world championships '75 with silver 500m, bronze 1000m, 14th 1500m, 3000m; third overall '75 world sprint championships with gold 500m, 4th 1000m, 6th 500m, 1000m; silver 500m, 6th 1000m '76 Olympics; ntl open records 500m, 1000m; fastest 500m award 3 times; '75 Calgary athlete of year; Governor-General's silver medal '76; coach ntl jr. team '76; coached Champaign, Ill., speed skating club; with Ken Read torch bearer '88 Olympics opening ceremonies; CBC '92, '98 Olympic speed skating analyst; mem. Alta. Sports, Cdn Speed Skating, Cdn Olympic halls of fame; res. Salt Lake City, Utah.

PRIMEAU, Joe (hockey); b. 29 Jan 1906, Lindsay, Ont.; d. 15 May 1989, Toronto, Ont.; m. Helen Marie Meagher; c. Joe Jr., Bill, Bob, Anne, Richard; St. Michael's College; hockey coach, businessman; ctr St. Michael's College jrs.; pro Toronto Ravinas '27, league scoring title; Maple Leafs '28-36; centred Kid Line with Charlie Conacher, Busher Jackson; twice runnerup NHL scoring race; Lady Byng Trophy '32; 2nd team all-star '34; coach 23 years, Memorial (2), Allan, Stanley Cup winners; mem. '32 Stanley Cup champions, coached '51 titlist; mem. Hockey, Canada's, Mississauga Sports halls of fame.

PRIMEAU, Keith (hockey); b. 24 Nov 1971, Toronto, Ont.; m. Lisa; c. Corey, Kylie, Chayse; ctr OHL Niagara Falls, AHL Adirondack, NHL Detroit '90-96, Hartford '96-97, Carolina '97-99; mem. Team Canada '96 World Cup, '97, '98 worlds, '98 Olympics; NHL record (through '99): 597 scheduled games, 179g, 227a, 70 playoff games, 6g, 17a; one of founders Hockey's Helping Hands; active with Drug Awareness Resistance Education program; res. Hartford, Conn.

PRIMROSE, John (shooting); b. 28 May 1942, Ottawa, Ont.; UofAlta, BPhE, MSc., self-employed investor, dir. Pinhead Components Inc.; mem. 13 world championships trapshooting teams, gold '75, '83, 4 silver; mem. '68, '72, '76, '84, '88, '92 Olympics; mem. '74, '78, '82, '86, '90 Commonwealth Games teams winning gold '74, '78; ntl doubles champion '69 Pan-Am championships; mem. '75, '79, '83, '87, '95 (team silver) Pan-Am Games teams; Benito Juarez title '77; 13 ntl titles; ntl record 386x400 '68, 296x300 '70; mem. Edmonton Gun Club, dir. '64-70; pres. Alberta International Style Trap Assn. '72-99; dir. Shooting Federation of Canada '73-75; chair. shooting tech. comm. '78 Commonwealth Games; flag bearer '82 Commonwealth Games; founding comm. mem. Alberta Federation of Shooting Sports; mem. COA athletes council '80-92; Golden Anniversary SFC award for contribution to sport '82; fed. govt. world champion award '84; mem. Order of Canada, Alta., UAlta, Edmonton; Cdn Amateur, Canada's Sports halls of fame; res. Edmonton, Alta.

PRINGLE, Mike (football); b. 1 Oct 1967, Los Angeles, Calif.; Washington State; Cal State (Fullerton); personal trainer; running back; led nation all-purpose yds with 2690

'89; NFL Atlanta '90-91, WLAF Sacramento Surge '92, CFL Edmonton '92, Sacramento '93, Baltimore '94-95, Montreal '96-98; CFL record (through '98): 99gp, 63tds, 1cvt, 380pts, 1481 carries for 8922yds, 56tds, 210 recep.,2102yds, 7tds; 1 Eastern, 1 Southern, 2 CFL all-star teams; set CFL single season rushing record 1972yds on 308 carries '94; 2 Terry Evanshen trophies; CFL outstanding player '97, MVP '95 Grey Cup; 3 playoff games, 2 Grey Cup finals, 1 winner; res. Los Angeles, Calif.

PRIOR, Russ (weightlifting); b. 11 Jul 1949, Hamilton, Ont.; m. Barbara Behan; c. Kyle, Scott, Heather; McMaster, Carleton, Queen's, UMan, North Dakota, BA, BEd, BSc; HS teacher; 28 Commonwealth, 74 ntl records, including all Commonwealth, ntl standards 110kg class; ntl, Commonwealth snatch record 172.5kg super heavyweight class; 9 ntl titles, 3 Commonwealth Games gold medals; 3 ntl teenage titles (2 at 82.5kg, 1 at 90kg); '68 American teenage champion 82.5kg; 2 NA 110kg titles; Pan-Am Games 110kg gold '75; silver Pan-Am championships twice; gold Western Canada Games 110kg '79; mem. '76, '80 Olympic Games, awarded (on paper) snatch bronze '76 Olympics when Bulgarian disqualified for steroid use; '73 world championships teams; 1st Cdn to win gold medals 3 successive Commonwealth Games; retd. from competition after winning silver '81 NA championships; regarded by many as Canada's strongest man of his time; res. Winnipeg, Man.

PROCHER, Theda (bowling); b. 24 Jun 1917, Chapleau, Ont.; given name: Theda Crowhurst; m. Bill Procher; c. Teddy, Ken; Ont. singles title '69; mem. 3 ntl ladies' title teams; PB: 420 single, 1029 triple; highest season avg. 272 in '69; top level coach, instructor Master Bowlers Assn. program; res. Toronto, Ont.

PRONGER, Chris (hockey); b. 10 Oct 1974, Dryden, Ont.; def. OHL Peterborough '91-93; NHL Hartford '93-95, St. Louis '95-99; team capt, '97; NHL record (through '99): 429 scheduled games, 50g, 135a, 42 playoff games, 4g, 19a; NHL all-rookie team; Hartford Most Valuable Defenceman award '94; CHL def. of '93; mem. Team Canada '98 Olympics; res. Dryden, Ont.

PRONOVOST, Marcel (hockey); b. 15 Jun 1930, Lac la Tortue, Que.; given name: Joseph Rene Marcel; m. Cindy Lapierre (d); c. Michel, Brigitte, Leo; m. Eva; hockey scout; def. jr. A Windsor Spitfires; pro Omaha (USHL) '49-50; Indianapolis (AHL) '50-51; Detroit '51-65, Toronto '65-70; player/coach Tulsa (CHL) '70-72, coach of year '71; coach Chicago Cougars (WHA) '72-73; Hull, Que. juniors '75-77, '79-80; Buffalo '78; asst. coach Detroit '79-81; Windsor Spitfires (OHL) '81-82; NHL Central Scouting Bureau 5yrs; scout New Jersey from '90; NHL record: 1206 scheduled games, 88g, 257a, 134 playoff games, 8g, 23a; mem. 8 Prince of Wales Trophy (league title), 5 Stanley Cup winners; twice 1st, 2nd team all-star; mem. Hockey Hall of Fame; res. Windsor, Ont.

PROPP, Brian (hockey); b.15 Feb 1959, Lanigan, Sask.; m. Kris Vollmer; c. Paige, Jackson; hockey TV color analyst; lw Melville (SJHL) '75-76, Brandon (WCJHL) '76-79; ntl jr. team '79; mem. Team Canada '79, '82, '83, '88, '93; Canada Cup, Spengler Cup winning teams; 1st draft choice

Philadelphia '79; with NHL Flyers '79-90, Boston '90, Minnesota '90-93, Hartford '93-94; Lugano (Switz) '93; twice all-star Brandon; 5 NHL all-star games; set several Flyers club records; NHL record: 1016 scheduled games, 425g, 579a, 160 playoff games, 64g, 84a; named to CHL all-time team '99; mem. Flyers Hall of Fame; res: Mount Laurel, N.J.

PROULX, Rita (curling); b. 16 Jun 1919, Quebec City, Que.; given name: Rita Louise Couture; m. Jean Noel Proulx; Montreal.; Cdn Red Cross volunteer; pres. Que. Winter Club '50-53; pres., organizer 1st International ladies' bonspiel '51; pres., organizer Que. Ladies' Curling Assn. '56; won 1st provincial curling title; organized Que. Ladies' Curling Council '68; pres. 1st ntl jr. girls curling championship '73; organized 1st curling school for jrs. in Canada, instructor '75; pres. CLCA '78-79; treasurer La Federation Québécoise de Curling Inc.; Cdn rep. ICF Ladies' Comm.; authored constitution, by-laws for women's curling in Que.; chair. Que. district golf course rating committee; pres. Ladies' Sr. golf championship '74; Cdn Red Cross Service Medal '45, Queen's jubilee medal '77; Quebec sports administrator of '78; mem. Canadian Curling Hall of Fame; last known res. Quebec City, Que.

PROVOST, Barry (curling); b. 15 Mar 1944, Ottawa, Ont.; given name: Barry Michael; m. Nancy Carol Jeffrey; c. James Warren, Tyler; Gould Business College; branch mgr. insurance group; North Eastern Alta. Schoolboy title '63; lead Eldon Coombe's Ottawa rink, 7 consecutive OCA Div. 1 titles; Ont. Consols title, Brier berth '72; 3 Cdn Branch Royal Caledonian Curling Club Royal Victoria Jubilee titles; 7 Red Anderson Memorial championships; CBC Curling Classic '72; Whitby Dunlop 'spiel '72; 3 Ottawa ACT curler of year awards, rated one of Canada's outstanding leads and sweepers; active in Stittsville minor softball program; res. Stittsville, Ont.

PRYSTAI, Metro (hockey); b. 7 Nov 1927, Yorkton, Sask.; m. 1. Evelyn Peppler (d), 2. Mavis Evans; c. David, Merrill (d), Karen, Michael, James; retd Prystai Insurance Agency owner; Moose Jaw jrs.; NHL centre for Chicago '47-50, '55-56, Detroit '50-54, '56-58; NHL record: 674 scheduled games, 151g, 179a, 43 playoff games, 12g, 14a; 3 NHL all-star games; 2 Stanley Cup winners; coached Omaha (CHL), Moose Jaw (SJHL) league titles '60-62, Melville (SJHL); salesman O'Keefe Brewery; operated International Hockey School, Nelson, B.C.; mem. Sask. Sports Hall of Fame; res. Yorkton, Sask.

PSUTKA, Harry (baseball/hockey); b. 19 Nov 1926, Kitchener, Ont.; m. Joan Rita Kipper; c. David, Thomas, Douglas, Andrew; St. Michael's Coll.; furniture salesman; catcher jr., sr. IC with Kitchener; 4yrs pro in Detroit chain with Jamestown (Pony), Durham (Carolina), Flint (Central), Williamsport (Eastern), Davenport (3I); defenceman Kitchener minor hockey system, St. Mike's Jr. A, Marlboroughs Sr. A; pro Pittsburgh Hornets (AHL), Maple Leafs (NHL), playoff backup '49; mem. Memorial Cup '46, Allan Cup '43, Stanley Cup '49 winners; res. Kitchener, Ont.

PUDDY, Bill (swimming); b. 19 Dec 1916, Toronto, Ont.; given name: William Albert; m. Eileen Anna Stoneburg (d.),

Marion Frances Forlong; c. Susan, John; retd company pres.; mem. Toronto Westend YMCA swim team age 10-12; competed international YMCA championships Ann Arbor, Mich., '31; ntl jr. titles ages 14-17; ntl open breaststroke titlist '34-36; gold, bronze '34 BEG; CNE breaststroke titlist '31-36; declined Michigan athletic scholarship; mem. '36 Olympic team; amassed 120 medals, trophies '30-36, establishing numerous records; Ont. open breaststroke jr., sr. titles '31-36; mem. Cdn, Ont. Aquatic halls of fame; res. Islington, Ont.

PUGH, Bob (football/hockey); b. 29 Oct 1928, Montreal, Que.; given name: Robert Wesley; m. Thora Doreen Sheppard; c. Paige, Stacey, Wesley, Corrie; Springfield Coll., BSc; retd. exec. v-p CIAU; quarterbacked Verdun Bulldogs, Westmount Warriors, '48 Dominion Int. champion HMCS Donnacona; sr. fastball Verdun Crawford Park; jr. B hockey Verdun Maple Leafs; dir. of athletics 14yrs Macdonald Coll., head coach football 14yrs, hockey coach 10yrs.; pres. Ottawa St. Lawrence Athletic Assn. 6yrs.; pres CIAU 2yrs.; dir. Hockey Canada, SFC; dir. school of sports admin. Laurentian; chef de mission '73 FISU Games; with John McConachie played major role in elevating several intercollegiate sports to ntl championship status; unsuccessful in initial foray into political wars; CIAU Austin-Matthews award; res. Pakenham, Ont.

PUGH, Lionel (t&f); b. 1 Apr 1922, Wales; given name: David Lionel; m. Irene Samuel; c. Jane; U of Wales, t&f coach UBC; Welsh HS javelin records; colors in rugby, soccer, squash, boxing; capt. boxing team; 1st class rugby for Headingley, Swansea; Great Britain ntl t&f coach '52-62; coach Oxford t&f '62-64; Canadian ntl t&f coach '69-73; coach Nigerian Commonwealth Games team '58, Canadian Commonwealth Games team '70, Pan-Am Games team '71, Olympic team '72; authored 3 t&f books; coach 45 top international athletes in Britain, Canada; Air Canada coach of '73; last known res. Vancouver, B.C.

PUGLIESE, Dan (administration); b. 7 May 1931, St. Catharines, Ont.; given name: Daniel Joseph; m. Carol Erb; c. 5; McMaster, BA, BPhE, Buffalo, MEd; businessman; coll. letters football, basketball; several yrs. exec. administrator National Sports, Recreation Center Ottawa; coach basketball, football, baseball, t&f at community, HS, university levels; designed numerous sports, recreation programs, facilities in Kitchener-Waterloo, Ottawa regions; with Jim Rose wrote *Basketball for the New Coach*; standardbred horse owner; res. St. Catharines, Ont.

PUGLIESE, Rick (water polo); b. 30 Oct 1952, Hamilton, Ont.; given name: Patrick; m. Carol MacCrimmon; c. David, Patrick, Matthew; McMaster, BA, Brock, BEd; HS teacher; mem. Hamilton Aquatic Water Polo Club winning 6 ntl titles; mem. ntl team '69-76; mem. silver medal team '69 Canada Games; mem. '71, '75 Pan-Am, '72, '76 Olympic, '75 World Aquatic Games; coach HS swimming, golf; mem. McMaster Sports Hall of Fame; res. Dundas, Ont.

PUHL, Terry (baseball); b. 8 Jul 1956, Melville, Sask.; given name: Terry Stephen; m. Jacqueline; stockbroker; MVP honors Barhead, Alta., tournament; rejected by Expos in tryout camp; pro Houston organization '73-90, Kansas City '91; hard-hitting outfielder who moved through farm chain with Covington, Dubuque, Columbus, Memphis, Charleston to Astros '77; in 60 rookie season games '77 batted .301; '78 NL all-star team; standout player '80 NL championship series; ML record: 1531 scheduled games, 4855ab, 1361h, 676r, 226d, 56t, 62hr, 435rbi, 217sb, .280ba; Canada's baseball man of '80; mem. Cdn Baseball, Sask Sports halls of fame; res. Missouri City, Tex.

PULFORD, Bob (hockey); b. 31 Mar 1936, Newton Robinson, Ont.; given name: Robert Jesse; m. Roslyn McIlroy; c. Rob, Lindsay, Jennifer; McMaster, BA; hockey exec.; mem. Toronto Marlboros, 2 successive Memorial Cups; Maple Leafs '56-70, LA '70-72; NHL record: 1079 scheduled games, 281g, 362a, 89 playoff games, 25g, 26a; mem. 4 Stanley Cup winners; 6 time all-star; NHL coach of '74-75; coach LA '72-77, coach/GM Chicago '77-90, GM to '97, sr.v-p '90-97; coach Team USA '76, co-GM Team USA '91 Canada Cup; NHL coaching record: 336-305-130; *Hockey News* coach of '78; 1st pres. NHL players union '67; mem. Brampton ntl jr. lacrosse champions, Weston CI football all-star; mem. Hockey Hall of Fame; res. Chicago, Ill.

PULFORD, Harvey (all-around); b. 22 Apr 1875, Toronto, Ont., d. 31 Oct 1940, Ottawa, Ont.; given name: Ernest Harvey; m. Jean Davison; c. Harvey P., Lawrence Moore; ins. salesman; HS hockey, football, paddling, lacrosse title teams; mem. Ottawa Silver Seven 1893-1909, 3 Stanley Cup winners; backfielder Rough Riders 1893-1909, 4 ntl title teams; lacrosse Captials 1896-1900, 4 ntl titles; Eastern Canadian light heavyweight, heavyweight boxing titles 1896-98; Eastern Canadian double-, single-blade paddling champion 1898; mem. 1900 war canoe title crew; ntl, US titles; mem. Hanlan Memorial, Canadian Henley, US International title crews '10; stroked Ottawa 8s to '11 Eng. Henley semifinals; Ottawa squash title '22-24; mem. Ottawa Sports, Hockey halls of fame.

PULLEN, Harry (football); b. 26 Dec 1907, Coventry, Eng.; m. Pansy Horel; c. Frances, Kathleen, Tom; UofSask, BA, UofT, BPaed, EdD, FCIS, FCCT, FOISE; professor, school superintendent; player-mgr. St. Thomas Tigers Junior ORFU champions '27-28; player-coach Saskatoon Quakers '29-33; Sask. sr. softball champions '35; Sask. Varsity Grads sr. basketball champions '35; coach Saskatoon Wesleys '35; res. White Rock, B.C.

PULLEN, Tom (football); b. 3 Jan 1945, Ottawa, Ont., given name: Thomas Robert; m. Judith Lynn O'Neil; c. Tracey-Lynn, Kevin Thomas; Michigan, BSc,UofOtt; pres. Kiptra Intl Marketing; jr. hockey Ottawa Montagnards; prov, city track meets in high jump, hurdles; Golden Ball basketball tournament with Glebe; Journal Trophy Ottawa HS lineman of '61; tight end Ottawa '68-70, '72-74, Montreal '70-71, Toronto '75; asst. coach Carleton '76; mem. 4 Grey Cup winners; mem. Ottawa Old Pros hockey club; res. Nepean, Ont.

PULLEN, Wayne (archery); b. 27 Feb 1945, St. Thomas, Ont.; m. Anne-Marie; c. Jason, Shannon; machinist; ntl men's titles '70-73, '80; mem. '72 Olympic, alternate '76, '80 Olympic, '71, '73, '75, '80, '81 world championships, '79, '80 Championship of Americas teams; bronze '71 world

championships; mem. '70 Ambassador Cup winning team; 2 golds field events Championships of America '73; ntl records in field, 1200 '72, broke both '74; FITA record '73; 10 ntl records; res. Dorchester, Ont.

PUNTOUS, Patricia (t&f); b. 28 Dec 1960, Montreal, Que.; Quebec (Montreal), BPHE; triathlete; with twin sister Sylviane tied 1st Orlando, Tampa, Panama City, Atlanta triathlons, won US triathlon series nl title; 2nd Hawaii Ironman triathlon '83-84; res. California.

PUNTOUS, Sylviane (t&f); b. 28 Dec 1960, Montreal, Que.; Quebec (Montreal), BPHE; triathlete; Que. 3000m record '79; hand in hand with twin sister Patricia shared 4 US triathlon titles, US triathlon series ntl championship; 1st Hawaii Ironman triathlon '83-84; res. California.

PURCELL, Jack (badminton); b. 24 Dec 1903, Guelph, Ont.; d. 10 Jun 1991, Toronto, Ont. given name: John Edward; m. Helen Colson (d); c. William, Nancy, Peter, Philip; m. June Copland; c. Robbie, Scott, Ian, Jack Fairclough; stockbroker; 5 consecutitve Ont. singles titles, numerous men's, mixed doubles titles '27-31; ntl singles champion '29, '30; pro '32, unbeaten world pro champion to '45 retirement; runnerup ntl jr. tennis title '22; outstanding athlete of 1/2 century miscellaneous sports division '50 CP poll; mem. Toronto Stock Exchange '49-60; life mem. RCYC; mem. Rosedale GC, RCYC, Tortuga Club, Fla.; mem. Cdn Amateur, Canada's Sports Hall of Fame.

PURDY, Margaret (tennis/badminton); b. 27 Nov 1907, Saint John, N.B., d. 4 Apr 1972, Saint John, N.B.; given name: Margaret Henderson; nicknamed 'Bunny', 'Henny'; active tennis player '22-59, 3 NB ladies' singles titles; 2 prov. mixed doubles; Turnbull Cup competition 2 singles, 6 ladies' doubles, 1 Maritime titles; ntl badminton title '31; mem. NB Sports Hall of Fame.

PYC, Jack (bobsleigh); b. 17 Jul 1972, Wroclaw, Poland; emigrated to Canada '81; parents both mem. Polish ntl track team; brakeman ntl team from '91; with Pierre Lueders 1 ntl 2-man, 2 4-man titles; teaming with drivers Lueders, Chris Lori won 55 gold, 3 silver, 1 bronze 2-man medals, 3 gold, 2 silver, 4 bronze 4-man World Cup circuit medals; world championship 2-man silver '95; competed '92, '94, '98 Olympics; res. Calgary, Alta.

PYLE, Dave (wrestling/coaching); b. 30 Jun 1917, Aberdeen, Scotland; emigrated to Moose Jaw, Sask. as a child; began wrestling as teenager; began coaching '50; over 3 decades guided provincial teams in ntl, international competitions; his charges amassed 25 ntl gold, 4 international gold, 2 silver, 2 bronze; among his charges were Olympians Ray Lougheed, Terry Paice; international coach of Canada-US combined wrestling vs, Japan '66; mem. Sask. Sports Hall of Fame; res. Moose Jaw, Sask.

PYZER, Doug (football); b. 8 Oct 1923, Toronto, Ont.; m. Noreen; c. Jeannie, Douglas, Ruth Linda; UofT; retd. mgr; Toronto Indians '42, RCAF Hurricanes '43-44, Toronto Indians '45-46, Argos '47, '49, '51-53, Toronto Beaches Indians '48, Edmonton Eskimos '50; mem. 2 Grey Cup champions; player-coach Toronto Beaches Sr. A fastball '49-

55, 2 titles; mem. Columbus Boy's Club Ont. bantam baseball champions '38, Webber Machinery Ont. jr. titlist '40; 1st in 100yd, 220yd dashes Ont. RCAF t&f championships '40-41, repeat RCAF Eastern Cdn championships '43; mem. Toronto, Ont. midget hockey champions '39; mem. Toronto, Ont. int. A basketball champions '50; res. Toronto, Ont.

Q

QUACKENBUSH, Bill (hockey); b. 2 Mar 1922, Toronto, Ont.; d. 11 Sep 1999, Pennsylvania; given name: Hubert George; m. Joan Kalloch; c. Bruce, Scott, Todd; Northeastern, ACE; athletic administrator, coach; mem. Toronto Native Sons Jr. A team '40-41, OHA champion Brantford Lions '41-42; pro Detroit '42-49, Boston '49-56; Red Wings MVP '44-45; Lady Byng Trophy '48-49 season; 3 times 1st team, twice 2nd team NHL all-star; NHL record: 774 games, 62 goals, 222 assists, 79 playoff games, 2 goals, 19 assists; through 13 seasons drew only 1 major penalty and career total 95 penalty minutes; among game's most effective defencemen, excellent checkers; coached hockey, golf Princeton U '67-85, 5 men's, 3 women's Ivy League golf titles; mem. Hockey Hall of Fame.

QUESSY, Marc (t&f); b. 20 Sep 1962, Cap-de-la-Madelaine, Que.; wheelchair racer; mem. ntl team from '86; 2 silver '92, 2 bronze '96 Paralympics; ntl 10km title '93; Athletics Canada 400m, 1500m titles '93; Francophone Games 100m gold '94. IPC 4x100 gold '94; Stoke-Mandeville Games 800m gold '95. 3 Black Top Invitational gold '96; 2 world, 4 ntl records; res. Sherbrooke, Que.

QUILTY, Silver (football); b. 8 Feb 1891, Renfrew, Ont., d. 2 Dec 1976, Toronto, Ont.; m. Irene Boyle; c. John (d), Helen (d), Bernadine, Ken, Bob; UofOtt, BA, McGill; insurance exec., civil servant; outside wing Uo ttO Sr. Intercollegiate champions '07; Rough Riders '13; coll. football McGill '14; refereed intercollegiate, interprov. football 5yrs; coach Ottawa; pres. CAHA '24-26; mem. Cdn Football, Ottawa, Canada's Sports halls of fame.

QUINN, Pat (hockey); b. 29 Jan 1943, Hamilton, Ont.; given name: John Brian Patrick; m. Sandra; c. Valerie, Kalli; San Diego, Widener, Delaware Law Schoo, LLBl; hockey coach; defenceman Knoxville Knights; pro Tulsa, Memphis, Houston, Seattle; claimed in draft by Montreal from Detroit then sold to St. Louis who dealt him to Toronto; NHL '68-77, Toronto, Vancouver, Atlanta; asst. coach Philadelphia '77; head coach Maine (AHL) '78, Philadelphia '78-80, Los Angeles '84-87, coach/GM Vancouver '90-94, coach Toronto '98, coach/GM '99; coached Team Canada world bronze '86; 2 Jack Adams NHL coach of year awards; *Sporting News, Hockey News* coach/exec. awards; pres./GM Vancouver '87-97; GM '98 Cdn world championships team; set NHL record 35-game undefeated streak '79-80; NHL playing record: 606 scheduled games, 18g, 113a, 11 playoff games, 0g, 1a; NHL coaching record (through '98): 744 scheduled games, 357-285-102, 97 playoff games, 51-46; Jake Milford award '95; Jack Diamond Sports Personality of '95 award; res. Toronto, Ont.

QUIRK, Wendy (swimming); b. 29 May 1959, Montreal, Que.; m. Dave Johnson; c. Michael, Rosemary; UAlta, BPHE; coach UCal SC; FS, butterfly specialist ranging from 100m-1500m; ranked among Canada's finest aquatic competitors; amassed 49 gold, 31 silver, 21 bronze medals; 25 ntl sr., 3 Commonwealth records; mem. '74, '78 Commonwealth, '75, '79 Pan-Am, '76, '80 Olympic, '75, '78 World championships, '79, '80 Canada Cup, '80 US, Japanese nationals teams; 3 ntl 100m, 2 200m butterfly, 4 400m FS, 1 200m FS, 4 4x100m FS relay, 2 4x50m FS relay, 1 4x100m medley relay, 1 4x200m FS relay titles; asst. mgr. '83 FISU Games swim team; Aquatic Fed. of Can. athlete of '80; res. Calgary, Alta.

RACINE, Moe (football); b. 14 Oct 1937, Cornwall, Ont.; given name: Maurice Joseph; m. Donna Donihee; c. Tom, Scott, Lee Ann, Bruce; retd. insurance exec.; tackle Ottawa (CFL) '60-74; as placement kicker recorded 176 converts, 62 field goals; 5 Grey Cup finals, 4 winners; 4 times EFC all-star, once all-Cdn; Gil O. Julien, Cornwall outstanding French Cdn athlete, Cornwall outstanding athlete awards; jersey # 62 retd.; mem. Rough Rider advisory board '82-92; mem. Cornwall, Ottawa Sports halls of fame; res. Metcalfe, Ont.

RADMORE, Joey (t&f); b. 18 Oct 1978, Ottawa, Ont.; to create active lifestyle this cerebral palsy athlete became involved with disabled sports age 12 focusing on competitive track/road racing; mem. ntl team from '96; competing in CP3/T33 class earned 100m silver, 400m PB '96 Paralympics; has established Cdn records in 100m, 400m, 800m, 1500m, 5000m as well as 10km, 15km road races; world records 200m, 800m; Ont. record 1500m; gold, silver '97 CP-ISRA world championships; world 100m, 200m records '99; mem. Panthers, Ottawa Lions TC; Ont. jr. CP athlete of '93; Ont. sr. CP athlete of '96; Cdn YTV Athletes div. award; 100m gold (record), 400m silver '98 worlds; 5 gold, 2 world records Southern Cross championships Sydney, Australia '99; res. Kemptville, Ont.

RAE, Al (basketball/officiating); b. 26 Dec 1932, Weyburn, Sask.; given name: Allen Gordon; m. Edna Beryl Bright; c. Allan Gordon William; Carleton, BA; importer/exporter; retd. Basketball Canada exec.-dir., retd. RCMP; officiated '64, '68, '72, '76 Olympics, '67, '71, '75, '79 Pan-Am, 3 FISU Games, 7 Asian, 7 Canadian, 4 CIAU, 1 Indian, 1 Japanese, 1 European championships, 1 A.W. Jones Taiwan tournament; mem. FIBA tech. comm. '76-94, v-p. '84-94; mem. tech. comm. '84, '88, '92 Olympics; mem. IAABO from '58; Air Canada sports official of year award; 1st Cdn official to receive FIBA Order of Merit; Sport Canada consultant '72-82; pres. SFC '90-92; mem. Man. Basketball Hall of Fame; res. Ottawa, Ont.

RAFFIN, Romel (basketball); b. 23 Apr 1954, Toronto, Ont.; m. Susan Kay Bergstrom; c Jessica, Kayley; Penn State, BSc, UCal; HS teacher; MVP, mem. all-Ont. title team; twice K-W all-star; Penn State on basketball scholarship; mem. ntl team '74-76, '79-84; mem. '76, '80, '84, '88 Olympic, '75, '79, '83, '87 Pan-Am Games teams; semipro Italy '76-78, Venezuela '80; mem. UCal Dinosaurs '79-80, hon. mention all-Cdn; brother Angelo mem. '70 Grey Cup champion Alouettes; mem. Cdn Basketball Hall of Fame; res. Calgary, Alta.

RAFTERY, John (boxing); b. 30 Dec 1956, Bristol, Eng.; m. Anna-Marie Tarrant; c. Julia; UofT, BA, Queen's, LLB; lawyer; 2 NY State Golden Gloves titles; 4 ntl, 5 Ont., 2 Eastern Cdn titles; gold '77 Tamner Turnaus tournament Finland; bronze '78 Commonwealth Games; gold Ireland '79; bronze World Cup '81; represented boxing in official

Commonwealth Games film *Going the Distance*; subject of NFB film on boxing; retired '83; res. Mississauga, Ont.

RAIKE, Stan (t&f); b. 20 Jan 1923, Hamilton, Ont.; m. Theona Gaudette; c. Denise, Maureen; retd. Ont. Police Commission; field specialist, hammer, discus, shot put; numerous athlete of meet awards annual Toronto police games '52-66; world record 56lb high throw 17'10"; mem. '54, '58 Commonwealth Games teams; ntl records discus, shot put, hammer; Fred Rowell Trophy '55, '60; res. Brampton, Ont.

RAINE, Al (coaching); b. 22 Oct 1941, Dauphin, Man.; m. Nancy Greene; c. Charles, William; ski development coordinator; co-owner Cahilty Lodge; coach ntl alpine ski team '68-70; CSA program dir. '70-73; exec.-dir. Whistler Resort Assn. to '82; mem. Canada's WC, Nor-Am comm.; TV color commentator international competitions; mem. Cdn Skiing Hall of Fame; res. Sun Peaks, B.C.

RAINES, Tim (baseball); b. 16 Sep 1959, Sanford, Fla.; given name: Timothy; m. Virginia Hilton; c. Tim Jr., Andre Darrel; standout HS tailback; drafted Expos '77; *Sporting News*, Topps, *Baseball Bulletin* minor league player of '80; Amer. Assn. batting champion, stolen base leader, rookie of year; Montreal regular '81-90, White Sox '91-95, Yankees '96-98, Oakland '99; ML rookie theft record 71 in 88 games as season shortened by strike; *TSN* rookie of year, *UPI* all-star; switch-hitting infielder, outfielder, ranked among game's premier base stealers; set AL record 37 consecutive steals '95; 3 Expos player of year awards; 7 NL all-star appearances; '86 Silver Slugger award; NL batting title with .334 '86; mem. '96, '98 World Series champion Yankees; nicknamed 'Rock'; diagnosed with Lupus disease '99; res. Palm Beach Gardens, Fla.

RAINVILLE, Marcel (tennis); b. 1903 Montreal, Que.; d. 1949 Montreal, Que.; McGill; lawyer; regarded as one of most colorful, tenacious and tragic characters in Cdn tennis; nicknamed 'Pee Wee'; mem. Cdn Davis Cup team '29-34; played on Florida's Orange Circuit in winter and returned to Canada for summer season; also spent time on French Riviera playing with famed Musketeers; one of 1st players to wear shorts and no socks, constantly changed shoes; while lacking most skill shots he compensated with steadiness and conditioning; won '34 Cdn Open singles; scored some amazing Davis Cup upsets beating Wimbledon champion Sydney Wood and George Lott of USA; adequate doubles player winning Cdn open with Jack Wright '31 and Lott '32; drinking problem led to suicide; mem. Cdn Tennis Hall of Fame.

RALEIGH, Don (hockey); b. 27 Jun 1926, Kenora, Ont.; given name: James Donald; m. Janice Pitblado; c. Susan, Jack; Brandon Coll.; retd. insurance broker; nicknamed 'Bones'; at 16 played jr. Winnipeg Monarchs; played 13 games with NY Rangers '43 before broken jaw sent him home; 2 more jr. seasons with Brandon winning MJHL scoring title `46; rejoined Rangers `47 later becoming team capt.; scored 2 overtime game winners `50 Stanley Cup final but Rangers lost series to Detroit in overtime in game 7; played 10 NHL seasons with NY appearing in 535 scheduled games, 101g, 219a, 18 playoff games, 6g, 5a; playing coach in WHL `57-58 before retiring; mem. Brandon U, Man. Hockey, Sports halls of fame; res. Winnipeg, Man.

RAMAGE, Pat (administration); b. 21 Jun 1922, Vancouver, B.C.; given name: Patricia Marie Doyle; m. Paul Ramage; St. Paul's Academy; involvement with Cdn Ski Assn. began '48 and covered variety of roles including director, comm. chair., hon. secty-treas., fund raiser; mgr. 8 Canadian ski teams in international competition; world ski congress rep. 8 times; mem. international jury of appeal 6 times; FIS technical delegate World Cup races 7 times; 1st Cdn named to an FIS comm. '61; 1st Cdn jury mem. Winter Olympics '64; COA mem. at large '53-64, '66-72; Pan-Am Games clothing coordinator '71, '75, same role '76 Olympics, '73, '77 Maccabiah Games, '78 Commonwealth Games; hon. treas. Cdn modern pentathlon '78-80, co-organizer '79 ntl championships; CSA dir. to COA '72-82; chair. biathlon comm., team mgr. biathlon world championships '81; co-chair. Laurentian Ski Zone; CSA merit award '65; Centennial Medal '67; Ont. Athletic merit award '68; finalist Air Canada Amateur Sport exec. award '70; Queen's jubilee medal '78; mem. Order of Canada; Cdn Skiing, Cdn Amateur, Canada's Sports halls of fame; res. Nuns' Island, Montreal, Que.

RANDALL, Sam (horse racing); b. 25 Sep 1881, Bruce County, Ont., d. 2 Nov 1961, Vancouver, B.C.; c. William, John, Robert; stove business operator, horseman; entered horse racing '19; key role in developing thoroughbred racing Western Canada; dir. Vancouver Ascot Jockey Club, Vancouver Thoroughbred Assn., Hastings (now Exhibition) Park; constructed Lansdowne Park, Williams Track, Victoria; operated Brighouse Park, Colwood, Vancouver Island; 1st to install photo-finish cameras; backed construction of 1st closed-in electric starting gate '39; instrumental in developing breed in BC; developed Ascot Stock, Dairy Farm; mem. Canadian Horse Racing Hall of Fame.

RANGER, Melissa (lawn bowling); b. 16 May 1981, Espanola, Ont.; began lawn bowling age 10; won Ont. -16 junior singles titles '93, '97; won Ont. Summer Games -16 junior singles '94, '96; at 17 became youngest ever to win sr. ladies' provincial singles title '98; standout 5-pin bowler winning Ont. bantam title, ntl bronze '92; Ont. jr. title '96; res. London, Ont.

RANKIN, Callie (harness racing); b. 22 May 1950, North Sydney, N.S.; given name: William; standardbred racing is a way of life for the Rankin family; tested talents one season at Foxboro Raceway before establishing strong presence at Exhibition Park in Saint John; after a decade had 5yr stint at Tartan Downs Sydney before shifting to Flamboro Downs; more than 2800 victories with purses exceeding $5M; Flamboro horseman of year `88-89; Flamboro driving title `90; res. Dundas, Ont.

RANKIN, Frank (hockey); b. 1 Apr 1889, Stratford, Ont., d. 23 Jul 1932, Toronto, Ont.; rover in 7-man hockey era; led Statford jrs. to 3 consecutive OHA titles; capt. Eaton Athletic Assn. to Ont. titles '10-11, '11-12, lost Allan Cup to Winnipeg Victorias each time; with Toronto St. Mike's in OHA finals '12-13, '13-14, lost to Toronto R&AA each time; coached Toronto Granites to '24 Olympic title; mem. Hockey Hall of Fame.

RANKIN, Heather (curling); b. 30 Apr 1965, Halifax, N.S.; given name: Heather Velma; m. Brian Murray Fowlie; Acadia, BSc; computer consultant, co. pres.; began curling age 9 coached by parents; sister Beth played 3rd for her for 20yrs; NS jr title '84; attended Acadia on scholarship; AUAA title '85; all-star ntl STOH skip '90; 3rd for Colleen Jones '93 STOH; mem. NS volleyball title team '82; starting setter Acadia volleyball '84-85; goaler undefeated girls HS field hockey team; res. Calgary, Alta.

RANKINE, Scotty (t&f); b. 6 Jan 1909, Hamilton, Scotland; d. 10 Jan 1995, Wasaga Beach, Ont.; given name: Robert Scade; m. Edna May Hodgkiss; c. Ian, Lynne, Craig; retd. deputy sheriff; 2 ntl marathon titles; competed 3 Boston Marathons, placing 4th, 5th, 7th; 2 US 15km, 1 20km titles; ntl 5000m title to qualify for '32 Olympics, 5000m finalist; mem. '36 Olympic team but leg cramps at 7500m mark of 10,000m race forced him out; silver 6-mile, 4th 3-mile '34, silver 6-mile, bronze 3-mile '38 BEG; Lionel Cconacher Trophy '35; mem. Cdn Road Racing Hall of Fame.

RANNELLI, William Jr. (boxing); b. 15 May 1958, Sudbury, Ont.; given name: William Raymond; m. Sue Davlut; contractor; Ont. titles '76-81; ntl titles '76-79, '81; US Golden Gloves silver '77; Tampere Finland silver '78; bronze Commonwealth Games '78; mem. '79 Pan-Am Games team; silver Canada vs Ireland '79; bronze East Germany Chemical Cup tournament '81; bronze Greece Acropolis Cup tournament '81; nominee Kinsmen male athlete of '78-80; CABA Hall of Fame; res. Val Caron, Ont.

RANSOM, James (fencing); b. 2 Apr 1971, Toronto, Ont.; UofOtt; accomplished t&f athlete before switching to fencing; mem. Algonquin First Nation; aspiring film director; jr. ntl épée title '92 sr. '97; ntl men's épée team gold '96; won Can-Am Open epee title '93; mem. OUAA epee title team '93; mem. ntl team from '94; competed 5 sr. World Cup events; mem. '94 Commonwealth, '95 world, '96 Olympic teams; Cdn flag bearer '97 FISU Games; res. Nepean, Ont.

RASHOVICH, Dan (football); b. 30 Nov 1960, Toronto, Ont.; SFU; linebacker; drafted by Ottawa '84, Toronto '85-86, Montreal property but went to Sask. '87 dispersal draft; mem. '89 Grey Cup champions; res. Regina, Sask.

RATANASEANGSUANG, Channarong (badminton); b. 26 Apr 1939, Bangkok, Thailand; m. Joyce Rati; c. Paul, David; San Diego City College; badminton pro, coach; Thailand ntl champion '61-62; ranked 2nd in world with 2nd place finish All-England tournament '62; pro teacher Calgary Glencoe Club '67-98; ntl team coach '84-96; under his guidance, players like Jamie Paulson, Wendy Clarkson emerged as world status performers; team mgr. 4 world, 3 Commonwealth Games, '96 Olympic teams; 3 ntl doubles, 4 Mexican ntl titles, US, Scottish, Denmark, Asian Commonwealth Games titles; Alberta achievement awards '75-76; International Badminton Federation Meritorious Service Award '88; mem. US., Sweden, Thailand, Alta. Sports halls of fame; res. Calgary, Alta.

RATCLIFFE, Frank (administration); b. 11 Sep 1944, Montreal, Que.; d. 3 Apr 1995, Toronto, Ont.; given name: Frank Ronald; m. Kathy MacDonald; c. Tracey, Christopher; communication dir. COA '82-95; info dir. NSRC '78-82; PR coordinator Coaching Assn. of Canada '77-78; founding editor *Coaching Review* magazine; head Cdn team communication unit '84, '88, '92 summer, winter Olympics, '83, '87, '91, '95 Pan-Am Games; press attache '82 Commonwealth Games.

RATELLE, Jean (hockey); b. 3 Oct 1940, Lac St. Jean, Que.; given name: Joseph Gilbert Yvon Jean; m. Nancy; c. 3 daughters; hockey scout; Guelph Jr. Royals; minor pro Trois-Rivieres, Kitchener-Waterloo (EPHL), Baltimore (AHL); NHL NY Rangers '64-75, Boston '75-81; baseball Guelph Sr. IC, attracted ML offers from Milwaukee, Los Angeles organizations; 2nd team NHL all-star centre; Bill Masterton Memorial, Lester B. Pearson, 2 Lady Byng trophies; Team Canada '72; NHL record: 1281 scheduled games, 491g, 776a, 123 playoff games, 32g, 66a; asst. coach '81-85, scout Boston '81-99; mem. Hockey Hall of Fame; res. Lynnfield, Mass.

RATHGEB, Chuck (all-around); b. 2 Dec 1921, Trois-Rivieres, Que.; m. Rosemary; Upper Canada College, UofT; board chair.; mem. '35 Canadian Commonwealth cricket team; mem. '50-51 team which climbed Mount Edith Cavell, Mount Robson; founding mem. Cdn Bobsleigh, Luge Assn.; competed '59-61 world bobsled championships; organized, coached '64 Olympic gold medal sledders; mgr.-driver Comstock auto racing team; with late Peter Ryan driving won 1st Canadian Grand Prix; twice won Shell Trans-Canada rally, 3 times ntl winter rally; 1st Cdn to campaign cars at Daytona, Sebring, LeMans in world class races, at 52 finished 10th '73 Targa Florio road race Sicily; drove '75 Trans-Sahara World Cup rally; founding mem., pres. Balloon Club of Canada; entry Trans-Canada balloon race Calgary to Winnipeg; flew over Alps by balloon from Zurich to Milan '67; entry London-to-Monte Carlo powerboat race '72; won Cdn Handicap Gulfstream Park, Fl., Canada Day '72; 1 of 3 Cdns to have taken the Big Six animals (lion, leopard, elephant, buffalo, rhino, tiger) in big game hunting; Cdn entry international tuna championships; gov. Olympic Trust; mem. Cdn Motorsport Hall of Fame; res. Toronto, Ont.

RATHWELL, Bob (administration); b. 23 Jun 1929, Lachine, Que.; m. Ruth Rawn; c. David, Douglas, Leslie; UWO, hons BA; retd. computer systems analyst/programmer/consultant; involved in amateur sport from age 19 as Little League coach; not a particularly gifted athlete; mgr. HS soccer team; 2 terms Ottawa RA exec. mem.; instrumental in creating Riverside Dr. playing fields; coached house-league/inter-club competitive hockey Nepean MHA 10yrs;coached sofftball and began soccer

involvement '70; pres. Lynwood Minor soccer club 10yrs before becoming involved in game at league/district levels; served as chair./secty/statistician Ottawa Carleton SL as well as pres/secty EODSA from '75; 8yrs dir. Ontario SA; developed computerized sports record keeping system; chair United Way campaign; certified Level 1 hockey/soccer coach; Ottawa ACT sportsman of '88; res. Nepean,Ont.

RATUSHNY, Ed (builder); b. 18 May 1942, Kamsack, Sask.; given name: Edward Joseph; m. Lynn Diane Allen; c. Kimberly Anne, Daniel Paul John, Gregory Allen (d); UofSask. BA, LLB, London LLM, Michigan LLM, SJD; law professor, player agent, arbitrator; registered player agent NHLPA; independent adjudicator Cdn Centre for Drug-Free Sport; arbitrator international court of arbitration for sport Lausanne, Switzerland; arbitrator/mediator, ADR program for amateur sport, centre for sport and law; mem. bd of regents Ont. women's HA; mem. bd of regents Sport Medicine and Science Council of Canada; QC; mem. Order of Canada; res. Ottawa, Ont.

RAU, Richard (t&f); b. 17 Jun 1939, Windsor, Ont.; given name: Richard Frederick; m. Dianne Verrege; c. Robyn; Michigan, Assumption College; salesman; all-Windsor basketball '57-58, leading scorer; ntl HS record 120yd low hurdles (13.2), triple jump (46'4"); nen, 2 WOSSA soccer, volleyball champions; WOSSA high jump, long jump, high hurdle records; Ont. long jump, triple jump records; basketball Assumption Lancers '60-61; Mic-Mac baseball batting champion .395 '57; mem. BEG team '58; ankle injury playing football at Mich. '59 ended track career; fastball Hamilton Big Four league '65-67; Royal Arcanum Trophy HS athlete of year '58, Viscount Alexander Trophy Canada's outstanding HS athlete '58; res. London, Ont.

RAUHANEN, Eric (biathlon); b. 3 May 1959, Winnipeg, Man.; sep. Shauna White; retd. Canadian Forces, big game outfitter; mem. ntl team '82-88; ntl 10km title '83, 20km, 4x7.5km relay '84, NA 4x7.5km relay title '84; ntl 20km aggregate titles '85-86; mem. Que. 4x7.5km relay ntl title team '89; mem. Cdn Forces Sports Hall of Fame; res. Edson, Alta.

RAUTINS, Leo (basketball); b. 20 Mar 1960, Toronto, Ont.; m. Maria; c. Michael, Andy, Jay; Minnesota, Syracuse; basketball announcer; 4yrs. St. Michael's College; rated best player in Canada sr. year; at 16 youngest ever to qualify for Olympic basketball team; toured Europe with junior Olympic team because he was too young to play in FISU Games; 150 US college scholarship offers, chose Minnesota; transferred to Syracuse after rookie year in which he received Big 10 honorable mention; all-star '80 Olympic qualifying tournament as team became first Canadian squad to qualify for Olympics through tournament play; with Syracuse '80-81 Big East tournament MVP, all-tournament NIT finalist; as 16-year-old led Cdn scorers vs Yugoslavia, Russia; MVP '78 Commonwealth basketball tournament; 2nd top scorer world championships, 2nd team all-world; 2nd team all-star '79 Pan-Am Games; FISU Games all-star '79; Viscount Alexander Trophy '78; 1st Canadian 1st round pick (17th overall Philadelphia '76ers) '83 NBA draft; subsequently traded to Indiana Pacers, Atlanta Hawks before injuries forced him to broadcast booth; Syracuse basketball broadcaster; comeback with teams in Europe 5yrs; ntl team '92; color commentator Toronto Raptors (NBA) from '95; mem. Canadian Basketball Hall of Fame; res. DeWitt, N.Y.

RAYMOND, Claude (baseball); b. 7 May 1937, St. Jean, Que.; given name: Jean Claude Marc; m. Rita Duval; c. Natalie, Claude-Marc; Académie Commerciale Catholique, St. Jean; sportcaster; strong right arm led to 17 year pro baseball career, 12 in major leagues; particularly effective as relief pitcher; with Chicago White Sox, Milwaukee Braves, Houston Astros, Atlanta Braves, Montreal Expos; Milwaukee rookie of '62; mem. NL all-star team '66; career 46-53, 3.66era, 83sv in 449 games; 23 saves with Expos '70; honored as Canada's baseball man of '70; 3 times St. Jean athlete of year; St. Jean man of '70; French radio network baseball broadcaster with Expos; mem. Cdn Baseball, Montreal Expos, Que. Sports halls of fame; res. St. Luc and Mt. Orford, Que.

RAYNER, Chuck (hockey); b. 11 Aug 1920, Sutherland, Sask.; given name: Claude Earl; m. Ina Lackey; c. Roberta; retd. rental business; Saskatoon Jr. Wesleys, Western Cdn jr. finalists '35-36; goaler Kenora Thistles 3 seasons; capt. Memorial Cup finalist '38-39; pro Springfield Indians '39-40; NY (Brooklyn) Americans '40-42; following navy stint WW2 NHL Rangers '45-53; NHL record: 424 scheduled games, 25so, 3.06ga avg., 18 playoff games, 1so, 2.43 avg.; Hart Trophy '50; 3 times NHL 2nd team all-star; coached in Edmonton, Nelson, Kenora; NHL milestone award; mem. Cdn, Man. Hockey, Saskatoon Sports halls of fame; res. Langley, B.C.

REA, Harold (administration); b. 26 Sep 1907, Kincardine, Ont.; d. 19 Jul 1985, Toronto, Ont; m. Marion Josephine Currie; c. Marilyn, Barbara; Inst. Chartered Accountants, CA, FCA; retd. business exec.; ntl pres. YMCA '63-65; chair. fed. govt. task force on sport '69; 1st chair. Cdn Coaching Assn.; chair. bd. of governors Canada's Sports Hall of Fame '69-75; mem. Order of Canada, Canada's Sports Hall of Fame.

READ, Cari (synchro swim); b. 4 Sep 1970, Edmonton, Alta.; began synchro age 9; mem. ntl team from '88; solo, duet gold '92 Loano Cup; '94 German Open; duet gold '93 ntl championship, Optrex World Challenge; team gold '90 Swiss Open, '93 Nationals, '94 Titrex Cup, '96 French Open; figures gold '92 Loano Cup; '95 Pan-Am, '96 Olympic Games team silver; res. Calgary, Alta.

READ, Frank (coaching); b. 1 Mar 1911, Vancouver, B.C.; d. Jan 1994, Mexico; given name: Frank Harold; m. Beatrice Emma Davis; c. Hugh David, Charles Anthony; retd. hotelman; football Vancouver AC '30-34; rower Vancouver RC '31-34, '39; coached UBC rowing crews to BEG 8s gold '54, Henley Royal Regatta Grand Challenge Cup 8s silver '55, Olympic 4s gold, 8s silver '56, 8s silver '60; Cdn Amateur Assn. of Rowing award of merit; mem. Cdn Amateur, BC Sports halls of fame.

READ, Ken (skiing); b. 6 Nov 1955, Ann Arbor, Mich.; given name: Kenneth John; m. Lynda Robbins; c. Erik, Kevyn, Jeffrey; UCal, UWO; consulting firm IOC athletes commission; mem. World Cup teams '73-83; WC record 5-

3-6, Val D'Isere, France, '75-76, Cortina, Italy, '76, Schladming, Austria, '78, Kitzbuhel, Austria, Wegen, Switzerland, '80, twice runner-up, twice 3rd; leader of 'Crazy Canucks'; mem. Olympic team '76 (5th downhill), '80; 5 ntl downhill titles, 1 combined title; Lou Marsh Trophy (with Graham Smith) '78; Norton Crowe award '79; Calgary athlete of '80; Premiers' outstanding achievement award '80; CBC, CBS Olympic skiing analyst; freelance journalist; '80 winter Olympic flag-bearer; mem. IOC athletes commission from '85; CdM '92 Olympics; ISF Olympic downhill design expert; mem. ISF exec. board from '88; operates Cystic Fibrosis fundraisers; author "*White Circus*"; mem. Order of Canada, Canada's, Cdn Skiing, Cdn Amateur, Alta. Sports halls of fame; res. Calgary, Alta.

REARDON, Ken (hockey); b. 1 Apr 1921, Winnipeg, Man.; given name: Kenneth Joseph; m. Suzanne Raymond; c. Catherine Anne, Donat Raymond, Kenneth Anthony, Anthony Kelly; retd. hockey exec.; Winnipeg -12 champions, Edmonton jr.; mem. Ottawa Commandos '43 Allan Cup winner; Canadiens '40-42, '45-50, all-star defenceman; mem. 1 Stanley Cup winner; NHL record: 341 scheduled games, 26g, 96a; 3 all-star games; exec. Montreal organization; Field Marshall Montgomery award of merit WW2; mem. Cdn, Man. Hockey halls of fame; res. Montreal, Que.

REAY, Billy (hockey); b. 21 Aug 1918, Winnipeg, Man.; m. Clare; c. Adele, Billy Jr.; retired hockey exec.; unique among NHL coaches because he coached before he played; player-coach Que. Aces '43-44, Allan Cup winner; coached 1 Memorial Cup winner; centre Detroit 4 games over 2 seasons, Montreal '45-53; NHL record: 479 scheduled games, 105 goals, 162 assists, 63 playoff games, 13 goals, 16 assists; coached Victoria Cougars (WHL) 2 seasons, Seattle (WHL) 1, Rochester (AHL), Maple Leafs '57-58; replaced by Punch Imalch early following season, joined Chicago organization and coached Sault Ste. Marie (EPHL) 1 season, Buffalo (AHL) 2 seasons; coach Black Hawks '63-77, Prince of Wales Trophy '67, Clarence Campbell Bowl '71-73; NHL coaching record: 532 wins, 366 losses, 170 ties, .578 percentage regular season play, 57 wins, 60 losses, .487 playoff percentage; mem. Man. Hockey Hall of Fame; res. Chicago, Ill.

REBAGLIATI, Ross (snowboarding); b. 14 Jul 1971, Vancouver, B.C.; Langers.; pro snowboarder; giant slalom specialist; WC circuit overall gold, silver, 3 bronze; ntl team from '96; burst into world prominence winning '98 Olympic gold at Nagano, Japan, as snowboarding made Olympic debut; marginal traces of marijuana in urine sample led to IOC bid to strip him of medal but subsequent COA appeal overturned IOC ruling and he retained medal; resulting publicity led to US talk show circuit appearances (Jay Leno Tonight Show); res. Whistler, B.C.

REBHOLZ, Russ (football); b. 11 Sep 1908, Portage, Wisc.; m. June Simonson; c. Ted, James, Tim, Bonnie; Wisconsin, BSc, MSc; retd. teacher, coach; nicknamed 'Doss'; HS standout baseball, t&f, basketball, football; all-conf. basketball 4 years, football 3 years; all-tournament basketball honors as a centre despite standing only 5'7"; all-state centre '26; played both offence, defence in football at Wisconsin; 3 letters each in football, basketball; played '32 East-West Shrine football game; joined Winnipeg in club's initial season '33 and quickly earned reputation as prolific passer, outstanding blocker and kicker and an elusive, shifty runner; threw what is believed longest pass in CFL history (68yds in air) to Lynn Patrick who galloped additional 10yds for TD; 5 times all-Cdn; helped Winnipeg win first Grey Cup '35 by tossing 2 TD passes and kicking both converts; player-coach '32 Winnipeg St. John's rugby team; mem., second leading scorer '33 Toiler basketball team; following 5yr Cdn grid career coached HS, college athletics in US guiding teams to several regional, state honors; mem. Canadian Football Hall of Fame; res. Portage, Wisc.

RECCHI, Mark (hockey); b. 1 Feb 1968, Kamloops, B.C.; m. Alexa; right wing; jr New Westminster WHL '85-86, Kamloops '86-88; drafted by Pittsburgh '88; NHL Pittsburgh '88-92, Philadelphia '92-95, '99, Montreal '95-99; brief Muskeogon IHL stints '89, '90; reached 50-goal plateau with 53 '93; 5 NHL all-star games; '97 MVP; 1 Stanley Cup; 2 Molson Cup player-of-yr awards; mem. 2 Team Canada gold medal teams; NHL record (through '99): 781 scheduled games, 333g, 510a, 51 playoff games, 21g, 38a; WHL, IHL, NHL 2nd team all-star; mem. '98 Olympic team; res. Kamloops, B.C./ Pittsburgh, Pa.

REDDON, Lesley (hockey); b. 15 Nov 1970, Mississauga, Ont.; UofT; all-star goaltender 4 OWIAA champion Lady Blues teams '89-93; mem. 2 ntl sr. women's, 4 Ont. Sr. AA title teams; mem. Maritime Sports Blades (NB) in 3 ntl women's championship tournaments, silver '95, bronze '96; competitive softball player '90, '94 nationals; goalie '92 world champion roller hockey team, '94 silver medallist; ntl women's hockey team mem. from '94; 2 world, 1 Pacific Rim, 1 3-Nations Cup titles; attends Olympic Oval high performance female hockey program; res. Calgary, Alta.

REDMOND, Mickey (hockey); b. 27 Dec 1947, Kirkland Lake, Ont.; given name: Michael Edward; div; c. Kelley, Shannon; automotive steel sales rep.; tour business operator; 4yrs OHA Jr. A Peterborough Petes; pro Montreal '67-70, Detroit '70-76; back injury led to retirement; NHL record: 538 scheduled games, 233g, 195a; twice achieved 50-goals plateau in single season with 52 in '73, 51 in '74; twice NHL all-star; Hockey Night in Canada TV analyst; mem. Peterborough Sports Hall of Fame; res. Franklin, Mich.

REED, George (football); b. 2 Oct 1939, Vicksburg, Miss.; given name: George Robert; m. Angelina; c. Keith, Vicky, Georgette; Washington State, BEd; sales promotion mgr.; 44 CFL records; 3245 carries for all-pro record 16,115yds, all-pro 137tds; 11 1000yd seasons for career avg. 4.97 yds-per-carry; caught 300 passes for 2772yds, 3tds; mem. 1 Grey Cup winner; CFL all-star 11 times; Jeff Nicklin Memorial Trophy (WFC MVP) '66; Schenley outstanding player award '65, runnerup '68, '69; Tom Pate Memorial Trophy '76; City of Regina, Province of Saskatchewan 'day' in his honor '74; pres. CFL Players' Assn. '72-81; mem. Order of Canada; mem. Sask., Canada's Sports, Canadian Football halls of fame; res. Calgary, Alta.

REED, Georgette (t&f); b. 26 Jan 1967, Regina, Sask.; Washington State; daughter of CFL Hall of Famer George

Reed; throw specialist; Canada Games record '89; shot put gold Oregon International, bronze Pac-10 championships '91; ntl indoor shot title '93; 5 ntl outdoor shot titles; mem. '89, '94 Francophone, '91, '95 Pan Am, '92 Olympic, '94 Commonwealth Games teams; gold shot '94 Harry Jerome Classic; Athletic Alta. sr. female athlete of '90, Alta. achievement award '91; outstanding sr. female athlete '90-91; NCAA all-American '90-91; res. Calgary, Alta.

REES, David (skiing); b. 25 Feb 1943, Barnard Castle, Eng.; m. Gail Fortey; c. Stephanie, Andrew; Carleton, BSc, MA, UofOtt, PhD; professor; cross-country specialist; mem. ntl team '62-72; 5 gold, 6 silver, 6 bronze at ntl championship level; winner numerous Ont., NA titles; 2 gold, 1 bronze '71 Canada Games; won every university cross-country ski race entered '61-64; coached at club level Ottawa, North Bay; ntl cross-country team coach '74-78; chair. NO Div. 2yrs; v.-chair. CSA 5yrs; 1st pres. Cdn Assn. of Nordic Ski Instructors; v-p. Cdn Masters cross-country Ski Assn.; authored cross-country skiing book, numerous magazine articles, coaching manuals; key speaker Ottawa Ski Symposium '75; Carleton athlete of '62, Ottawa ACT skiing award '62; pres. Cross-Country Canada; coach '92 Olympic team; ski coach Nipissing U; mem. North Bay Sports Hall of Fame; res. North Bay, Ont.

REES, Gareth (rugby); b. 30 Jun 1967, Duncan, B.C.; Oxford; teacher/pro rugby player; Oxford Blue '93-94; made international debut vs. US '86; mem. London Wasps in John Player Cup as teenager '86; fly-half, capt. Team Canada '95 World Cup, '97 Pacific Rim title teams; at 19 youngest player in inaugural World Cup game '87; played in all 11 World Cup games for Canada; Canada's top all-time scorer (through '98) 45 tests, 388 points of 7 tries, 7 d-gs, 89pens, 34cvt; scored all the points in tests vs. US, France, Wales '94; English Courage League scoring title '96-97; Pacific Rim scoring title '97; mem. BC Castaway Wanderers, London Wasps (pro) teams; res. London, Eng.

REEVE, Ted (lacrosse/football); b. 6 Jan 1902, Toronto, Ont., d. 27 Aug 1983, Toronto, Ont.; given name: Edward Henry; m. Alvern Florence Donaldson; c. Joseph, Susan; sportswriter; nicknamed 'The Moaner'; early football Toronto St. Aidan jrs, Argonauts; coach, player Toronto Beaches FC '24-30; ORFU title '27; Grey Cup victories '27, '30; 4yrs lacrosse Brampton Excelsiors; Mann Cup Brampton '26, '30, Oshawa '28; coached Queen's to 3 intercollegiate football titles '33-38; Ont., federal government acheivement awards; Fred Sgambati award '82; mem. Canada's Sports, Lacrosse, Football, News halls of fame.

REGAN, Larry (hockey/administration); b. 7 Aug 1930, North Bay, Ont.; given name: Lawrence Emmett; m. Pauline LeBlanc; c. Natalie; UCLA; retd. Sports administrator; played jr. Toronto Marlboros '48-50; sr. Ottawa Senators (OSHL) at 17; Allan Cup finalists '47; MVP Shawinigan Falls '51-52; Quebec Aces '52-55, MVP '54; NHL Boston '56-59, Toronto '59-61; NHL record: 280 scheduled games, 41g, 95a, 42 playoff games, 7g, 14a; Calder Memorial trophy '57; 2yrs Stanley Cup finals; player/coach Pittsburgh Hornets (AHL) '62, Innbruck, Austria '62-65; coach Baltimore (AHL) '65-66; head scout LA Kings '65-66; GM LA Kings '66-74; coach Montreal srs '74-75; pres. Cdn

Oldtimers Hockey Assn. '75-95; organized Relive the Dream hockey series; mem. Ottawa Sports Hall of Fame; res. Ottawa, Ont.

REGNIER, Claude (skateboarding); b. 30 Dec 1958, Cornwall, Ont.; given name: Claude Emery; m. Ginette Larivierre; c. Richard, Lindsay, Jason; SK8 City consultant; ntl slalom champion '81-98; made pro debut '86; Expo '86, PSL '90 pro titles; coach/instructor from '77; coached minor hockey '91-98; coached minor football '94; coached/played broomball '81-91; '82-83 coach of yr award; in-line skating instructor/coach '92-96; BMX biking coach; 16yrs competitive 5-pin bowler excelling at YBC competitions; deesigned/built slateboard facilities in various communities; dir. Cdn Amateur Skateboard Assn; res. Ottawa, Ont.

REID, Bobby (soccer/hockey/boxing); b. 13 Sep 1890, Hamilton, Scotland, d. Dec 1982, Saskatoon, Sask.; given name: Robert John; soccer as player, coach, mgr., administrator, trainer '14-51; 8 title teams; key role in developing schoolboy soccer in Sask.; 96th Highlanders boxing title '16; boxing trainer, coach administrator '16-39; coached-managed Ozzie Herlen to '37 Sask. lightweight, '38 welterweight titles; while employed in NY Rangers organization designed team jacket; trainer Western Canadian girls' fastball titlist, '54 Little World Series rep.; trainer Saskatoon Commodores baseball team '58-74; mem. Sask. Sports Hall of Fame.

REID, Brigitte (t&f); b. 22 Aug 1955, Weddinghofen, West Germany; given name: Brigitte Bittner; div. Pat Reid; UofOtt; real estate agent; high jump specialist; ntl jr. titles '72-74; Can. Games gold '73, Games record 1.80m; bronze '74 Commonwealth Games; silver '81 Pan-Pacific Games; ntl indoor record 1.87m, 5th ranked world indoor '76; 5 ntl sr. indoor titles; 3 ntl outdoor titles; mem. 3 FISU Games, World Cup trials teams; alternate '76, mem. '80, '84 Olympic, '82 Commonwealth Games team; PB: 1.90m; exec. dir. Lawn Bowls Canada; last known res. London, Ont.

REID, Bruce (water skiing); b. 23 May 1956, Selkirk, Man.; given name: Alexander Bruce; m. Elizabeth Christine Allan; c. James Brody; UMan, BPE, MD, FRCSC; orthopaedic surgeon; mem. ntl team '70-83; 21 ntl titles, 17 ntl records; 4 Man. barefoot titles; competed 6 Worlds; silver overall, team '82 World Cup, bronze jump '79 world championships, '80 World Cup; mem. Man., Cdn WSA, Man. Underwater Council , Cdn Fencing Assn., CAHPER; Alta., Sask water ski coach '82-83; man. WS pres., tech comm. chair. '76-77; Man. sports excellence award, Queen's Jubilee medal, Winnipeg outstanding sport achievement award; hockey referee, girls basketball coach; mem. Man. Sports Hall of Fame; res. Alton, Ill.

REID, Cam (swimming); b. 14 Nov 1960, Minneapolis, Minn.; Arizona State; freestyle, individual medley specialist; 2 national 400m IM, 1 4x200m FS relay titles; mem. '79, '83 FISU, '82 Commonwealth, '83 Pan-Am Games teams; ntl record FS relay; res. Vancouver, B.C.

REID, Ian (water skiing); b. 7 Apr 1931, Selkirk, Man.; given name: Ian Livingstone; m. Ruth; c. Kim, Patricia, Bruce; MD; with father William became founding members Selkirk Seals Water Ski Club, Masn. Water Ski Assn.; a pioneer and daredevil once reaching speed of 80mph skiing behind an airplane; 8 Man. Open titles; never competed nationally although all three children were ntl team members/champions; mem. prov., ntl, intl water ski associations; instrumental in making helmets/life jackets mandatory jumping equipment; noted historian of sport; established country's only water skiing museum in Selkirk; judge of prov., ntl, intl competitions; mem. Order of Canada, Man. Sports Hall of Fame; res. Selkirk, Man.

REID, Lefty (softball/bowling); b. 25 Sep 1927, Mersea Twp, Ont.; given name: Maurice Hugh; m. Evelyn Dorothy Wickens (d); c. Dale, Janet, Gary, Scott, Terry; Geo. Brown College; retd. hockey administrator; southpaw fastball pitcher with wide array of Ont. teams; Leamington, Ont., HS mile record; mem. Portage La Prairie, Man., RCAF softball title team '46, Ont. jr. finalist '47, Peterborough city champs '49; active pitcher through '78, Toronto Press League MVP, all-star honors; one of 65 world masters 5-pin finalists '60; numerous city, regional singles, match play, team titles, all-star bowling honors; twice Ont. Legion titlist, singles '58, doubles '60; sports journalist Trenton, Belleville, Chatham, Galt, Peterborough, *Toronto Telegram*; awards for school sport coverage; charter mem. Cdn Bowling Writers Assn.; v.p. Ont. Bowlers Assn; managed 20-lane bowling house 3 1/2 years; Jr. B hockey league convenor '53-54; sr. OHA statistician '53; asst. to Bobby Hewitson, then curator Canada's Sports, Hockey halls of fame '67; curator both halls '68-74; Hockey only '75-90; mem. Hot Stove Club, Ont. Museum Assn., Cdn Assn. for Sport Heritage, co-founder, v.p. American Society of Museums and halls of fame; volunteer curator Peterborough Sports Hall of Fame; res. Peterborough, Ont.

REID, Leslie (equestrian); b. 2 Jul 1956, Vancouver, B.C.; began riding age 2; mem. ntl team '91-98; dressage specialist and coach; dressage team gold '95 Pan-Am Games; competed '96 Olympics; BC Horse Council coach of year '89; res. Langley, B.C.

REID, Pat (coaching/administration); b. 17 Mar 1949, Edmonton, Alta.; div. Brigitte Bittner; m. Beverly McDonald; c. Taylor, Brett; Waterloo, hons. BSc, UWO, MA, Pacific Western, PhD; former dir. sponsorship & promotions Corel Corp.; former dir. gen. Sport Medicine & Science Council of Canada, dir. Swimming Canada, CAHA v-p. intl. operations, Sport Canada consultant '74-88; mgr. Best Ever '88 program '83-88; IAABO official '69-79; ntl high jump coach; European tour jumps coach '79-81; competed '72 Boston, Cdn marathons; head field event coach Ont. t&f title team '77 Canada Games; coached 16 ntl HJ title winners; founder, meet dir. Ottawa Indoor Games '78-82; high jump coach Americas team '81 World Cup; head t&f coach '84 Olympics, hj coach '86 Commonwealth, '87 Pan-Am, '88 world jr. championships; mem. NA Meet Directors Assn. from '78; chair. Ont. T&F Coaches Assn. '78-82; 1st person to direct 3 CAHA consec. world championship ice hockey teams, jr. men '90-91, sr. women '91; coach/tech. consultant/administrator '72, '76, '84, '88, '92 summer Olympics, '80, '84, '88 '78 Commonwealth, '79 Moscow Spartakaide, '81 pre-Commonwealth Games; tech. consultant '80 Winter Olympic team; intl. IAAF hj lecturer from '78 ; responsible for name change of Palladium to Corel Centre in Kanata '96; responsible for pitch that led to $1M Alexi Yashin contribution to NAC '98; res. Ottawa, Ont.

REID, Robert (golf); b. 10 Mar 1917, Swift Current, Sask.; d. 29 Dec 1994, Prince Albert, Sask.; given name: Robert Douglas; m. Eleanor Young; c. Bob, Gordon; UofT, DDS; dentist; back-to-back individual Cdn Intercollegiate titles '37-38; 5 Sask. amateur titles; mem. 7 Willingdon Cup teams; '34 Sask. junior title, twice Sask. senior champion; pres. Sask. Golf Assn. '55; pres. Sask. Seniors Golf Assn. '76-77; mem. Sask. Sports Hall of Fame.

REILLY, Keith (curling); b. 2 Sep 1938, Ochre River, Man.; m. Rosemary Lanzarotta; c. Lisa, Chris; Waterloo Lutheran, BA; retd. teacher, Wheels in Action Co. owner; began curling '48; all-star lead Alf Phillips Jr. rink '67 Brier winner; competed 7 Ont. Consols; twice OCA intermediate champion; mem. 2 Canada Life, 2 Toronto Metro Major League, 1 Whitby Dunlop, 3 Avonlea Beef-O-Rama, 1 Kirkland Lake cash, 2 OCA Challenge Round, 1 Molson Carspiel title rinks; coach 2 Toronto Curling Assn. Jr. girls, 3 Ont. Jr. women's, 1 Cdn Jr. women's title rinks '81-85; coach Canada Games gold medallists '83, TCA Sun Life winner '83; hon. life mem. OCA; TCA curler of year '84; mem. Phillips rink which forced OCA to rethink code of ethics and paved way for cashspiels in Ont. '68; active in coaching, officiating, supervisory, organizational capacity with Curl Canada from '73; conducted clinics, Japanese curlers in Japan and Canada '97-98; res. Rexdale, Ont.

REISER, Glenda (t&f); b. 16 Jun 1955, Ottawa, Ont.; UofOtt, MD; physician; Cdn native, open record 4:06.7 for 1500m '72 Olympics; 3 ntl 1500m titles; gold '74 Commonwealth Games; Elaine Tanner award '73; mem. Ottawa Sports Hall of Fame; res. Ottawa, Ont.

REMMEN, Ray (harness racing); b. 28 May 1947, Saskatoon, Sask. m. Shirley; c. Kati, Tammy; drove 1st race at 16 at Ladner, B.C.; campaigned with moderate success on Sask., Alta. circuits (won 3 Western Canada pacing derbys) and Windsor Raceway before moving to Meadowlands, N.J., where he ranks among top drivers; posted 1st- ever Western Canada sub-2 min. mile with Stormin Stephen '75; with Shiaway Pat won 1st Hambletonian raced at Meadowlands '81; with Dance Spell won '82 World Trotting Derby; with Grade One Woodrow Wilson Stakes '85; drove Beach Towel to Little Brown Jug, Horse of Year titles '90; 2 Breeders Crown titles; only driver to win Woodrow Wilson, Peter Haughton Memorial, Hambletonian; mem. Cdn Horse Racing Hall of Fame; res. Westwood, N.J.

RENAUD, Ab (hockey); b. 2 Oct 1920, Ottawa, Ont.; given name: Albert Romeo; retired public servant; mem. Woodroffe juveniles '36; Lasalle jrs. '37-39; Hull Volants Sr. A '40-41; various armed forces teams '41-46; mem. Cdn Forces title team in Eng. '45; mem. Ottawa Senators '46, Ottawa Montagnards '47; mem. gold medal Olympic, World champion RCAF Flyers '48; mem. Flyers in Eastern Canada HL '49-50; mem. Ottawa army team ECHL '51; player-coach Brockville Magedomas NY-Ont. League '52-57; mem. Ottawa Old Pros; with '48 Olympic title team mem. Ottawa Sports Hall of Fame; res. Ottawa, Ont.

RENAUD, Chris (swimming); b. 29 Aug 1976, Fredericton. N.B.; 100m, 200m backstroke specialist; 5 ntl titles; mem. ntl team from '95; silver 100m, 200m back '93 Eight nations youth meet; silver 4x100m medley relay '94 Commonwealth Games; bronze 4x100m medley relay '95 Pan-Am Games; silver 200m back '95 World short course championships; gold 200m back, silver 100m back '96 Olympic trials; gold 200m back, 4x100m medley relay, silver 100m back, bronze 200m IM '96 Canada Cup; silver 200m back, bronze 50m back, 100m back '96 World Cup; competed '96 Olympics; 4 CIAU records; res. Calgary, Alta

RENAUD, Don (golf); b. 17 May 1937, Ottawa, Ont.; m. Teri Bertrand; c. Debbie; golf pro; mem. CPGA/PGA 45yrs; winner 58 pro/pro-am tournaments; low pro Pebble Beach, Scotland world pro-ams; won '57 Rochester Open; 3 OV asst. titles, runnerup OV pro championship; 2 OV seniors titles; ntl asst. title; low pro Bermuda Goodwill; teaching pro averaging 1500 lessons per yr; assoc. pro Ottawa Hunt, Cleveland Oakwood, Rochester Oakhill; served as head pro Ottawa Rideau View, Cedarhill, Peterborough Kawartha; dir. of golf Blockbuster, Ft. Lauderdale, Fla., Eagle Creek, Dunrobin, Ont.; res. Kanata, Ont./Tamarac, Fla.

RENKEN, Brian (wrestling); b. 21 Jun 1955, Ft. William, Ont.; UWO, BA, UofOtt; ntl jr. FS, GR champion 74kg '74-75; mem. '75 ntl jr. world team; gold Canada Games '75; gold CIAU '75-78, '80; CIAU outstanding wrestler '80; mem. '76 Olympic team both categories; mem. '80 Olympic team; UWO most valuable wrestler '75-76, '77-78; mem. '77 FISU, '78 world championships teams; bronze '79 Pan-Am Games, '80 World Cup; ntl sr. GR. 2 FS titles; brother Lloyd ntl team wrestler; mem. UWO-W Club, NWO Sports halls of fame; res. Meaford, Ont.

RENKEN, Lloyd (wrestling); b. 27 Jun 1957, Dryden, Ont.; UWO, hons. BA, Lakehead, BEd; phys ed. teacher; freestyle specialist; Pan-Am jr. 62kg title '76; CIAU 68kg titles '79-80; ntl 68kg FS title, outstanding wrestler award '82; bronze 68kg '82 Commonwealth Games, '84 World Cup; competed '81 FISU, '82 world championships; UWO MVP award '80; brother ntl team wrestler Brian Renken; res. Thunder Bay, Ont.

RENNEY, Tom (coaching); b. 1 Mar 1955, Cranbrook, B.C.; m. Glenda; c. Jessica, Jamie; North Dakota, BPhE; began coaching career with Kamloops Blazers WHL '90; 2 league titles, 1 Memorial Cup; asst. Team Canada '92 world jrs.; head coach ntl -18 Phoenix Cup winners '92; joined ntl team sr. program '92, head coach '93-96, silver '94 Olympics, bronze '95, silver '96 Worlds; head coach Vancouver (NHL) '96; replaced by Mike Keenan '97; CHA v-p. '97-98; head coach ntl jr. team '98-99; 3M Coaches Canada, WHL coach of '91 awards; Sport BC. coach of '92 award; res. Calgary, Alta.

RESTIVO, John (coaching); b. 30 Jul 1946, Winnipeg, Man.; given name: John Phillip; m. Vivian Brown; c. Kevin, Kimberly, Heather; UWpg, BA,UMan, BPhE; sports marketing/promotion; mgr. ntl basketball team '72-73; asst. athletic dir. UMan '71-72; pres. Bison Booster Club '70-72; PR dir. Man. Central Soccer League '71; mgr. Bisons basketball team '70-72; exec. dir. Cdn Amateur Basketball Assn. '73-76; mgr. special programming, exec. asst. to pres.

NSRC '76-96; head basketball coach UofOtt '79-88; OUAA coach of '83; res. Kanata, Ont.

RETI, Harvey; (boxing); b. 1 Sep 1937, Paddock Wood, Sask.; given name: Harvey Neil; m. Mabel Martin; c. Douglas, Lawrence, Tyler, Debra Leigh; retd. soldier, correctional service employee; ntl amateurwelterweight title '61; light welterweight title '62-64; bronze '62 Commonwealth Games; mem. '64 Olympic team; mem. Alta. Sports, Canadian Forces Sports halls of fame; res. Whitehorse, Y.T.

REVILLE, Ralph (golf); b. 1867, Witney, Eng.; d. 1957, Brantford, Ont.; publisher; emigrated to Canada 1882; launched golfing career Brantford 1884; sold interests in *Brantford Courier* 1913; founder, publisher, managing editor Canada's 1st golf magazine *Canadian Golfer* 1915-33; publication recognized internationally as "best golf journal in world;" secty RCGA rules comm. '16-21; helped found Canadian Seniors' Golf Assn. '18; secty CSGA '18-26; governor CSGA to death; mem. RCGA Hall of Fame.

REYNOLDS, Kirk (shooting); b. 20 Nov 1974, Outlook, Sask.; trapshooting specialist; mem. ntl team from '91; 2 '95 Pan-Am Games silver; competed '96 Olympic Games; res. Outlook, Sask.

REYNOLDS, Shelley (ringette); b. 3 Apr 1975, Edmonton, Alta.; NATE; competed in 8 ntl championships winning gold '90, silver '94, bronze '95; mem. 2 gold, 1 bronze world championships; forward 4 ntl all-star teams; played 8 months in Finland; versatile athlete who excels in volleyball, soccer, hockey; res. Fort Saskatchewan, Alta.

REYNOLDS, Warren (basketball); b. 26 May 1936, Winnipeg, Man.; given name: Warren Alfred; div.; c. Jeffrey, Jodie; Windsor (Assumption); TDIAA sr. football titlists, all-star '55; 2 TDIAA scholastic basketball title teams with Etobicoke, all-star '55; 2 ntl Jr. A title teams; intercollegiate intermediate title team '59; mem. Tillsonburg Livingstons ntl Sr. A title team '60; competed '59 Pan-Am, '60, '64 Olympic teams; champion Ont. Sr. B Toronto Dow Kings '63, ntl Sr. A '64; ntl 46+ squash title '82; ntl platform tennis sr. title '87; res. Etobicoke, Ont.

RHEAUME, Manon (hockey); b. 2 Feb 1972, Trois-Rivieres, Que.; m. Gerry St-Cyr; c. Dylan; pro hockey goaltender, coach; began playing hockey at 6; 1st girl to play in annual Que. peewee tournament; made hockey history as 1st female to play in regular season Quebec Major Junior Hockey League game; made NHL history when signed by Phil Esposito to play with Tampa Bay Lightning; appeared in one exhibition game before being sent to Knoxville (ECHL); traded to Nashville Knights, Las Vegas Thunder, Tallahasse Stars; loaned to Austrian team and beat Swiss elite team; mem. NJ Rockin Rollers '95, Ottawa Loggers '96, Sacramento River Rats '97; mem. '92 Team Canada world champions, '98 Olympic team; world all-star; asst. coach U Minn-Duluth women's team; published book "*Manon, alone in front of the net*"; res. Trois-Rivieres, Que./ Duluth, Minn.

RIBBINS, Peter (football); b. 31 Aug 1948, Belfast, Northern Ireland; m. Siobhan Flanigan; c. Emily, Taylor;

East Carolina., UofOtt, BSc; pres/COO Cayman Water Co.; football East Carolina, UofOtt; 3 years all-conf. defensive halfback, flanker UofOtt; 1yr all-Cdn; mem. '70 College Bowl finalist; pro Winnipeg '71-76; all-Cdn defensive back '72; Hamilton '73, Edmonton '77; mem. UofOtt Football Hall of Fame; res. Grand Cayman, B.W.I.

RICHARD, Henri (hockey); b. 29 Feb 1936, Montreal, Que.; given name: Joseph Henri; m. Lise Villiard; c. Michèle, Gilles, Denis, France; sports columnist, club owner; 50 goals in single season as jr. before joining Canadiens '55 at 19; centred line with brother Maurice on right, Dickie Moore on left; mem. Habs '55-75, retd. holding club record for most seasons (20), most games (1256); NHL record: 1256 scheduled games, 358g, 688a, 180 playoff games, 49g, 80a; mem. 11 Stanley Cup winners; once 1st team, 3 times 2nd team all-star centre; tied playoff record 3 assists one period vs. Maple Leafs '60; nicknamed 'Pocket Rocket'; jersey #16 retd. by Canadiens; Canadiens special ambassador; mem. Canada's Sports, Hockey halls of fame; res. Montreal, Que.

RICHARD, Jacques (hockey); b. 7 Oct 1952, Quebec City, Que.; Que. jr. Remparts; QMJHL 1st team all-star left wing '72; 1st Atlanta pick, 2nd overall '72 draft; Atlanta '72-75, Buffalo '75-79, Quebec '79-83; topped 50-goal single season plateau with 52 '80-81; NHL record: 556 scheduled games, 160g, 187a, 35 playoff games, 5g, 5a; res. Quebec City, Que.

RICHARD, Maurice (hockey); b. 4 Aug 1921, Montreal, Que.; m. Lucille; c. Hugettte, Maurice Jr. Norman, André, Suzannne, Paul, Jean; retd. fishing supply company owner; Verdun jrs., Canadiens srs.; NHL Canadiens '42-60; NHL record: 978 scheduled games, 544g, 421a, 133 playoff games, 82g, 44a; record 83 game-winning, 28 game-tieing goals; 1st to score 50 goals in 50 games '44-45; record 5 goals, 3 assists Dec '44; 8 times 1st, 6 times 2nd team all-star; nicknamed 'Rocket'; Hart Trophy (MVP) '47; never won league scoring title; capt. Habs several seasons; 8 Stanley Cup winners; suspension from playoffs for striking official triggered Montreal Forum riot; coached Quebec Nordiques WHA; 3 Lionel Conacher awards; Lou Marsh Trophy '57; special ambassador Canadiens from '80; jersey #9 retd by Canadiens; museum honoring his life in Montreal; NHL top goal scorer award bears his name; Officer Order of Canada '67, upgraded to Companion '98; mem. Que., Canada's Sports, Hockey halls of fame; res. Montreal, Que.

RICHARDSON, Arnold (curling); b. 2 Oct 1928, Estevan, Sask.; given name: Arnold Wellington; m. Edna Shirley Fleming; c. Shelley Joanne, Kimbal Brian, Laurie Susan, Nancy Anne; retd. carpenter; 3rd on Richardson family rink with cousins Ernie, Garnet and Wes; best-known foursome in Canadian curling history winning unprecedented 4 Briers, 4 world championships (Scotch Cup) '59-63; mem. Sask. Sports, Canadian Curling, Canada's Sports halls of fame; res. Silton, Sask.

RICHARDSON, Bert (rowing); b. 25 Nov 1903, Toronto, Ont., d. 17 Jan 1982, Toronto; given name: Herbert Trenchard; m. Betty McPherson (d); sc. John; carpenter, salesman; minor baseball '22-24; Argos jr. football '25; rowing with Argonaut Club from '25; US jr. championship

'26; bronze with Argos crew '28 Olympics; mem. '30 BEG team.

RICHARDSON, Blair (boxing); b. 1940, South Bar, N.S., d. 5 Mar 1971, Boston, Mass.; m. Beverly MacDowell; c. Lisa; Canadian, BE middleweight titles, twice vs Gomeo Brennan of the Bahamas for the latter '65, lost 1st, won 2nd; death from brain tumor; mem. NS Sports, Canadian Boxing halls of fame.

RICHARDSON, Ernie (curling); b. 4 Aug 1931, Stoughton, Sask.; div. Marcia Carle; c. Don, Judy, Jim; m. Edith Jordan Ricki Eventon; retd. owner electrical wholesale-retail business; skipped 5 Saskatchewan title rinks, record 4 Briers, world championships; CBC Cross Canada, Calgary Masters, numerous car, cash 'spiels; authored several books on curling; mem. Order of Canada; Governor-General's CC; Canadian Curling, Sask., Canada's Sports halls of fame; res. Regina, Sask.

RICHARDSON, Garnet (curling); b. 6 Nov 1933, Stoughton, Sask.; given name: Garnet Sam; m. Kay Meronuk; c. Brenda, Robert; retd. contractor; teamed with brother Ernie, cousins Arnold, Wes, later Mel Perry, to win 5 Saskatchewan men's championships, 4 Macdonald Briers, 4 Scotch Cups; CBC Cross-Canada title, numerous western carspiels; rep. Regina 10 prov. championships, 3 as skip, 7 as 2nd; skipped Sask. mixed title rink '73; catcher with Sask. -18 baseball champions; freelance sportscaster for curling competitions at prov., national levels; mem. Curling Reporters of Canada; mem. Canadian Curling, Canada's Sports halls of fame; res. Regina, Sask.

RICHARDSON, George (hockey); b. 1880s, Kingston, Ont., d. 9 Feb 1916, France; mem. Queen's '09 Allan Cup winner; OHA sr. finals with 14th Regiment team '06-07; killed in WW1 action in France; George Richardson Memorial Stadium is home of Queen's Golden Gaels Kingston; mem. Hockey Hall of Fame.

RICHARDSON, Jillian (t&f); b. 10 Mar 1965, Trinidad; m. William Briscoe; c. Sterling, Paris, Trey; UCal, BA; sprint specialist; gold 4x400m relay '82, '86, silver 400m '86 Commonwealth Games; silver 4x400m relay '83 FISU, Pan-Am; bronze 4x100m relay '83 Pan-Am Games; silver 400m '91 world indoor championships; 3 ntl 400m, 2 200m titles; Colgate Games 200m, 400m titles; silver 4x400 relay '84 Olympics; competed '88, '92 Olympics; gold 400m '91 IAAF Grand Prix; '93 indoor GP title; 4 ntl jr, 1 sr. records; ranked in top 2 400m, top 3 200 m '86-92; flag bearer '93 world championships; fed. govt. excellence award '83; 1 CIAU indoor t&f female athlete of yr award; 3 Calgary Booster Club, 4 Alta. achievement awards; UCal. female athlete of '87, 2 UCal merit awardsl ATFA athlete of '97 award; Cdn HS Hall of Fame award; active in community activities; parade marshal '85 Calgary Stampede; subject of CBC documentary; hon. chair. Terry Fox Foundation, '93 run; hon. starter '94 Mayor's Day Stampede runoff marathon; Olympic rep. 3 Stampede parades; seriously injured in '93 auto accident; rebounded to become active coach; res. Calgary, Alta.

RICHARDSON, John (water polo/administration); b. 6 Mar 1937, Toronto, Ont.; d. 5 Jul 1981, Puerto Rico; m.

June; c. Cynthia, Suzanne; UofT, BSc, UAlta, MSc, Mich. PhD; professor UWO; competitive swimmer Etobicoke SC; Cdn backstroke record; began playing water polo UofT; founded Alta. , Ont. Water Polo Assns; secty '61-67, pres. '67-75 Cdn Water Polo Assn.; 2yrs secty FINA; mem. COA '68-80; instrumental in expanding water polo competition in CIAU; helped develop coaching assn. certification program for water polo; helped create ntl women's team, '81 Canada Games participants; dir., exec. comm. mem. Sport Ontario '70-80; team mgr. '72 Olympics, water polo referee '76 Olympics, '71 Pan-Am Games, '81 world juvenile championships; life hon. pres. CWPA; Royal Life award; mem. London Aquatic Wall, Cdn, Ont. Aquatic halls of fame.

RICHARDSON, Kathy (swimming); b. 17 Oct 1963, Toronto, Ont.; Brock; bronze 200m breaststroke '82 Commonwealth Games; mem. '80 Olympic, '83 FISU Games teams; 3 CIAU 400m IM, 2 200m breaststroke, 800m FS, 1 400m FS titles; Pan-Pacific, Speedo 400m IM, 4-Nations 400m FS titles; res. Toronto, Ont.

RICHARDSON, Stephanie (swimming); b. 11 Feb 1977, Toronto, Ont.; 200m, 400m, 800m freestyle specialist. mem. ntl team from '95; gold 4x100m, 4x200m FS relay '91 Eight Nations youth meet; bronze 4x200m FS relay '94 Commonwealth Games; gold 800m, silver 200m FS '96 Olympic trials; silver 400m FS '96 Canada Cup; competed '96 Olympics; res. Toronto, Ont.

RICHER, Stéphane (hockey); b. 7 Jun 1966, Ripon, Que.; m. Sabrina; right wing; jr. Granby, Chicoutimi QMJHL '83-85; drafted by Montreal '84; Sherbrooke AHL '87; Montreal NHL '85-91, '96-97, New Jersey '91-96, Tampa Bay '98-99; reached 50-goal plateau 50 '88, 51 '90; QMJHL rookie of '84; QMJHL all-star '85; mem. '86, '95 Stanley Cup winners, 1 NHL all-star game; NHL record (through '99): 930 scheduled games, 392g, 362a, 128 playoff games, 52g, 45a; res. Montpellier, Que.

RICHMAN, Joey (all-around); b. 25 Apr 1915, Montreal, Que.; m. Roz Shizgai; c. Steve, Mark; retd. owner sales agency; played, coached basketball '32-57; mem. 4 ntl finalists, 7 Que. titlists as player, 3 ntl champions as coach; frequent league, tournament MVP, all-star, scoring champion; instrumental in making YMHA respected force in Montreal, ntl cage circles; coached YMHA to unblemished 29-0 record, ntl title '56-57 season; end Montreal Cubs '39-41, halfback RCAF Hurricanes '41-42, Grey Cup winner '42; played with Lachine, Hamilton, Ottawa Trojans, Alouettes (CFL) through '47; pres. Alouette Alumni Assn. '77-80; without formal training coached RCAF t&f team '42; began competing as sprinter at 27; PB: 100yds 9.7, 220yds 21.9; with Fred Oberlander organized 1st Canadian entry Maccabiah Games; coached '50 basketball team, '53, '57 t&f teams; chair. athletic co-ordinating comm. Maccabiah Games from '57; coach ntl women's t&f team '52 Olympics; mem. HS soccer title team '31; novice 126lb Golden Gloves boxing title '37; semipro baseball Hamilton '44; Que. sr. singles tennis titles '56, '66, 5 Martini masters titles, 5 ntl srs. titles; Montreal outstanding athlete '46; mem. Montreal YM-YWHA Sports Hall of Fame; res. Montreal, Que.

RICHMAN, Ruby (basketball); b. 22 Sep 1934, Toronto, Ont.; given name: Reuben; m. Eileen Young; c. Alana, Jacqueline, Steven; UofT, BComm, LLB, Osgoode Hall; sports administrator; capt. TDHS champions '52; 7 years mem. Varsity Blues basketball team, capt. '56-59, champion '58; player-coach Maccabiah Games teams '61, '65, '69, '73 (bronze), Sao Paulo, Brazil, '66, Olympics '64, '68, '72, Pan-Am Games '67; player-coach ntl sr. men's champions '63-64; mem. 3 Ont. jr. softball titlists, 2 Toronto sr. titlists, 1 Ont. jr. baseball titlist, 2 Toronto jr. champions, capt. Ont. midget, juvenile, Jr. B. hockey champions; pres. Basketball Ont., Basketball Canada, Sports Federation of Canada, Sport Ont.; outstanding all-around athlete UofT; W.A. Potter Trophy UofT Blues MVP '58; chair. ntl selection comm. Cdn Maccabiah Games Assn.; mem. Cdn Basketball Hall of Fame; res. Willowdale, Ont.

RICKER, Maelle (snowboarding); b. 2 Dec 1978, N. Vancouver, B.C.; halfpipe specialist; began snowboarding '94; ntl team mem. from '96; ISF world jr. gold; '97 ntl champion; mem. '98 Olympic team; 1 FIS WC silver, 3 bronze; res. W.Vancouver, B.C.

RIDD, Carl (basketball); b. 17 Aug 1929, Winnipeg, Man.; m. Beverley Tozer; c. Laurel, Brian, Karen; UMan, BA, MA, United College, BD., Drew., PhD; retd. university prof., United Church minister; mem. 8 consecutive Man. champion basketball teams '48-55, all-star '50-55; mem. 3 Western Canada title teams (UMan Bisons '50, Varsity Grads '52, Winnipeg Paulins '54); latter team won ntl title; mem. '52 Olympic team; 2nd all-star world tournament team '54; '49-50 4th highest college basketball scorer NA; nicknamed 'King Carl'; mem. Cdn Basketball, Man. Sports halls of fame; res. Winnipeg, Man.

RIDGWAY, Dave (football); b. 24 Apr 1959, Stockport, Eng.; m. Nancy; c. Christopher Dallas, Drew Bradley; Toledo; retd. kicker; drafted/released by Montreal '81, Saskatchewan '82-95; 7 all-Western, 6 all-CFL all-star; set/tied 8 CFL records; most consec. FG 28 '93; most FG 1 game 8 '88 (tied by Paul Osbaldiston '96); longest FG 60yds; Dick Suderman outstanding Cdn Grey Cup '89; mem. 1 Grey Cup winner; res. Regina, Sask.

RIGNEY, Frank (football); b. 4 Sep 1936, East St. Louis, Ill.; given name: Frank Joseph; div; c. Mitchell Frank, Lisa Karen, Kathy Dawn; Iowa, BA; investment broker, golf club distributor, TV commentator; played in North-South, Senior Bowl games, Rose Bowl '57; 3rd draft Philadelphia (NFL); offensive tackle Blue Bombers '58-67; 5 Grey Cup finals, 4 winners; 7 times all-pro; Beckett-DeMarco Trophy twice; Schenley defensive player of '61; CBC-TV football commentator 20yrs; mem. Canadian Football Hall of Fame; res. North Vancouver, B.C.

RILEY, Con (rowing); b. 25 Aug 1875, Atlantic Ocean, d. 20 Nov 1960, Winnipeg, Man.; given name: Conrad Stephenson; m. Jean Isabel Culver; c. 6 sons, 2 daughters; dir. Hudson's Bay Co.; Winnipeg Rowing Club 1892-1929 as rower, coach, official; WRC pres. '11, hon. pres. '29; Steward's Challenge Cup in 4s as stroke Winnipeg crew '10 Royal Henley regatta; led 14 WRC rowers to 7 NA titles (8s, 4s, sr., int. doubles, singles) '12; last race at age 70; mem. Canada's, Manitoba's Sports halls of fame.

RILEY, Culver (rowing); b. 21 Jun 1907, Winnipeg, Man., d. 1970, Winnipeg, Man.; given name: William Culver; m. Elizabeth Hamilton; c. William Culver Jr., Evelyn Hamilton, Christopher Hamilton; St. John's College, McGill, LLD; bd. chair. Cdn Indemnity Co.; dir. Royal Bank, Great-West Life, Dominion Bronze, Union Oil, Southam Press; mem. ntl title crew '27-28; exec. mem. Winnipeg Football Club, pres. '50-51; key role in construction Winnipeg football, baseball, hockey complex; pres. Winnipeg '67 Pan-Am Games comm.; dir., mem. OBE, National Hockey Foundation, Canada's, Man. Sports halls of fame.

RILEY, Martin (basketball); b. 8 May 1955, Winnipeg, Man.; given name: Martin James; m. June Fick; UMan, BPhE; basketball coach; mem. undefeated Manitoba HS title team; provincial title, MVP, all-star honors; 4 times 1st team, once 2nd team GPAC all-star; all-time points, assists leader; mem. CIAU titlist '76, championship series MVP; 3 times all-Cdn; Mike Moser award '77; 3 CIAU all-Cdn; 1st HS player to qualify for men's ntl team; ntl team mem. '75-82, capt. '78-82; mem. 2 Intercontinental tournament, '76, '80 Olympic, '75, '79 Pan-Am Games, 2 FISU Games, 2 world championships teams; semipro Argentina 1yr; Man. male athlete of '76; coach UMan men's varsity team '83-84; mem. Cdn Basketball, Man. Sports halls of fame; res. Winnipeg, Man.

RINKE, Chris (wrestling); b. 26 Oct 1960, Port Coquitlam, B.C.; SFU; freestyle specialist; gold 82kg '82 Commonwealth Games; bronze 82kg '82-83 World Cup, '83 Pan-Am, '84 Olympic Games; 7 ntl FS titles; 1st Cdn gold medalist Freiburg International tournament '84; fed. govt. excellence award '83; res. Port Coquitlam, B.C.

RISEBROUGH, Doug (hockey); b. 29 Jan 1954, Guelph, Ont.; m. Marilyn; c. Allison, Lindsay; hockey exec.; jr. Guelph, Kitchener; Nova Scotia (AHL), NHL Montreal '74-82, Calgary '82-87 (capt. 4 yrs); NHL playing record: 740 scheduled games, 185g, 286a, 124 playoff games, 21g, 37a; mem. 4 Stanley Cup winners; asst. Calgary '87-89; head coach '90-92; 2 President's Cups, 1 Stanley Cup; AGM Calgary; GM '91-95; held various positions with ntl team '95-96; v-p. hockey operations Edmonton Oilers '96-99; GM Minnesota Wild '99; res. Edmonton, Alta.

RITCHIE, Alvin (coaching); b. 12 Dec 1890, Cobden, Ont.; d. Apr 1966, Regina, Sask.; given name: Alvin Horace; customs officer; among Canada's coaching greats; nicknamed 'Silver Fox'; often called "The Knute Rockne of Canada"; best known for football coaching exploits, also gained prominence in hockey; only coach in Cdn history to guide teams to Little Grey Cup, Memorial Cup titles; asst. coach Regina sr. football club '21; major role in organizing Regina Pats hockey team, coached them to Memorial Cup triumphs '25, '28, '30; instrumental in organizing Sask. Jr. Hockey League; coached Regina Pats jr. football club to Western Cdn titles '25-28, ntl title (Little Grey Cup) '28; head coach Regina Roughriders (he gave them their name), consecutive Grey Cup finals '29-32 but never a winner; football teams he coached recorded 56 consecutive league victories, 9 western titles, 1 ntl crown; retd. from coaching '36; scouted for NY Rangers hockey club more than 30yrs; strong crusader for Cdn football rule changes trimming from 14 to 12 players, encouraging forward pass 2yrs before East approved it, importing of US players; mem. Canadian Football, Sask., Canada's Sports halls of fame.

RITCHIE, Andy (swimming); b. 6 Dec 1958, Thunder Bay, Ont.; given name: Andrew James Allan; Florida, Lakehead, BPHE; ntl team '74-81; mem. '76 Olympic, '77 FISU, '78 Commonwealth Games teams; world 400IM, 200m breaststroke ranking; 2 silvers Florida conf. championships; bronze 400IM '77 FISU Games; 3rd 200m breaststroke '78 Commonwealth Games trials; 2nd 400IM European tour meet Paris '79; gold 200m breaststroke, silver 200IM, 100m breaststroke '80 CIAU championships; silver 200m breaststroke '81 CIAU championships; res. Thunder Bay, Ont.

RITCHIE, Bill (basketball); b. 6 Apr 1923, Saint John, N.B.; given name: William Struan; St. Francis Xavier; active official '50-72; formed NB Assn Approved Basketball Officials '57; authored basketball coaches manual '63; chair. officials selection comm. for ntl, intl championships '79-85; mem. ntl comm. Cdn Assn. Basketball Officials '74-85; pres. Cdn Assn. Basketball Officials '79-85; pres. Atlantic provinces CAHPER '68-69; dir. Cdn School Sports Fed. '70-82; chair. NB Sports Hall of Fame selection comm. '70-73; chair./governor NB Sports Hall of Fame '77-78; APAHPER honor award; IAABO merit award; CSSF award; NBOA honor award; Basketball NB special award; life mem. IAABO; mem. St. FX,NB Sports, Canadian Basketball halls of fame; res. Fredericton, N.B.

RITCHIE, Dale (ballooning); b. 19 Oct 1952, London, Ont.; m. Cynthia Egbert; c. Michael Dale, Christopher Paul; UCal, UAlta, BSc; operations mgr. Balloon Adventures; competed '81 world hot air balloon championships; 3rd ntl hot air balloon championships; won '81 Foothills Balloon race; res. Calgary, Alta.

RITCHIE, Dave (football); b. 3 Sep 1938, New Bedford, Mass.; m. Sharon; c. Phyllis, Susan, Dave; Cincinnati; fullback, linebacker at Cincinnati; football coach; coached Fairmount State Coll '78-82, 1 ntl title; coached Marshall, Brown, Cincinnati; asst. coach Montreal '83-86; Winnipeg '90 Grey Cup; Ottawa; headcoach BC 3yrs, '94 Grey Cup; head coach Montreal '97-98, coach/GM Winnipeg '99; res. Winnipeg, Man.

RITCHIE, Jo-Anne (triathlon); b. 9 Mar 1960, Vancouver, B.C.; given name: Jo-Anne Lynne; m. Blake William Dean; c. William, Jillian, Spencer; SFU, BBA; homemaker, part-time fitness trainer; 9 Cdn Grand Prix titles; gold '91 ITU short course worl' championship; silver '92 ITU worlds; bronze '93 ITU worlds; ntl women's titles '91-93; res. Kelowna, B.C.

RITCHIE, John (skiing); b. 4 Jul 1948, Thunder Bay, Ont.; given name: John Francis Stewart; m. Eileen Grimsgaard; c. Damien, Max; Lakehead, MA; financial officer; mem. ntl team '67-71, Lakehead team '71-73; head coach Kootenay Zone '73-75; head coach women's ntl ski team '75-76; men's ntl team '76-83; Level IV Cdn Ski Coaches Federation; Level III Cdn Ski Instructors Alliance; master coach, Coaching Assn. of Canada; co-authored "*Ski the Canadian Way*"; v.-chair Rough Riders 2yrs; res. Invermere, B.C.

RITCHIE, Trevor (harness racing); b. 14 Jun 1956, London, Ont.; displayed interest in racing at age 10; began driving London's Western Fair Raceway then shifted to Flamboro and Windsor; 3 dash, 2 UDR titles Windsor; moved on to OJC circuit; with Quite A Sensation won '86 and Frugal Gourmet '87 NA Cup; piloted Ready To Rumble to Cdn Pacing Derby title '94; through '97 2356 victories with purses exceeding $24M; res. Acton, Ont.

RIZAK, Gene (basketball); b. 27 Aug 1938, Windsor, Ont.; div. Claire Anna Best; c. John, Anna, Joe, Susan, Samantha, Joshua; Assumption College, BA, McMaster, BPhE, UBC, MPhE; retd. educator, basketball coach; all-star Windsor HS champions '57; Assumption '57-60, Ont. intercollegiate title '59, co-champions '58; led league scorers, set record 44 points 1 game vs UofT, NA record 26 of 28 free throws; averaged 25 points per game, led McMaster scorers '60-61; mem. Tillsonburg Lvingstons, London Fredericksons, Eastern Cdn title '61-62; Montreal Yvon Coutu Huskies '62-64, '62 Eastern Cdn title; UBC '64-65; 3 ntl titles IGA '65-67; Art Willoughby Trophy, Vancouver men's rookie of '65; mem. ntl team '67 Pan-Am Games; Vancouver White Spots '68 ntl finalist; coached HS '60-67, SFU '68-70, Regina '70-79; varied administrative roles SABA; wrote "*Basketball for the Beginning Coach and Teacher*"; pitched 2 seasons London Senior IC Baseball League; Sask. 55+, Alta. 60+ tennis titles, runnerup ntl 60+ championships; res. Calgary, Alta.

ROBERT, Magli (orienteering); b. 18 Sep 1964, Sherbrooke, Que.; m. Farshad Sepadj; c. Jasmine, Darya; UofOtt, MD; gynecologist; won OFSAA cross-country ski titles while attending Gloucester HS; represented Canada in 3 world orienteering championships; 6 ntl, 2 NA elite women's titles; retd '91; res. Calgary, Alta.

ROBERTS, Gary (hockey); b. 23 May 1966, North York, Ont.; m. Tamra; c. Jordan; standout lacrosse player, mem. Minto Cup jr. title team; left wing, capt. Ottawa 67's '82-85, Guelph '86; 2 Memorial Cup winners; 2 OHL 2nd team all-star; 1st round draft Calgary '84; Moncton (AHL); NHL Calgary '86-96, missed '96-97 season with injury, Carolina '97-99 topped 50-goal plateau 53 '92; 2 NHL all-star games; NHL record (through '99): 723 scheduled games, 291g, 305a, 64 playoff games, 14g, 31a; mem. Stanley Cup winner '89; Bill Masterton trophy '96; spokesman Alberta Lung Assn.; res. Calgary, Alta.

ROBERTS, Gordon (hockey); b. 5 Sep 1891, Ottawa, Ont., d. 2 Sep 1966, Ottawa, Ont; McGill, MD; physician; Ottawa Senators (NHA) '10, Montreal Wanderers (NHA) '11-16; Vancouver Millionaires '17 setting PCHA record 43 goals 23 games; Seattle Metropolitans (PCHA) '18, Vancouver '20; 203 goals in 166 regular season games but never played on title team; twice scored 6 goals in single games; once scored five; mem. Ottawa Sports, Hockey halls of fame.

ROBERTS, Jay (football); b. 20 Oct 1942, Des Moines, Iowa; c. Jed, Kimberly, Kelley; Kansas, BA; public servant; earned all-state recognition in football, basketball; ntl merit scholarship finalist; 7 varsity letters in football, basketball, t&f at Kansas '61-63; tight end Ottawa '64-70; 3 Grey Cup finals, 2 winners; son Jed with Edmonton '91-98; res. Ottawa, Ont..

ROBERTS, Jim (hockey/coaching); b. 9 Apr 1940, Toronto, Ont.; given name: James Wilfred; m. Judy; c. Vicki, Corey; coach; def./rw Peterborough Petes jr.; NHL with Montreal '63-67, '71-77, St. Louis '67-'71, '77-78; NHL record: 1006 scheduled games, 126g, 194a, 153 playoff games, 20g, 16a; 5 Stanley Cup winners; began coaching career as asst. Buffalo '79-84; asst. Pittsburgh '84-88; head coach Springfield '88-90 winning 2 Calder Cups; brief stints as NHL head coach Buffalo '81-82, Hartford '91-92, St. Louis '96-97; GM/head coach Worcester Ice Cats (AHL) '94-96; asst. coach St. Louis '96-99; res. St. Louis, Mo.

ROBERTSON, Bruce (swimming); b. 27 Apr 1953, Vancouver, B.C.; given name: Bruce Richard; m. Sheila Jocelyn Hurtig Bresalier; c. Andrew Alexander; sc. Michael, Julie; UBC; SFU, BA, CA; management consultant; silver 100m butterfly (55.56), bronze 4x100 medley relay '72 Olympics; gold 100m butterfly (55.67), bronze 4x100 medley relay '73 world championships; gold 4x100 medley relay, 4x100 FS relay, silver 100m FS (53.67), 200m FS (1:57.22), bronze 100m butterfly (56.8) '74 Commonwealth Games; bronze 4x200 FS relay, 4th 100m butterfly (56.31), 4x100 medley relay '75 world championships; silver 4x100 FS relay, 4x100 butterfly (56.8), 100m FS (53.44) '75 Pan-Am Games; Canada's male athlete of '73; mem. '76 Olympic team; 5 1sts, 1 2nd '77 NAIA championships; 1 world, 5 ntl masters records while claiming 7 gold, 2 silver ntl masters championships '99; shared '73 Norton Crowe award with George Athans Jr.; mem. Order of Canada; mem. BC, Cdn Aquatic, Amateur, Canada's Sports halls of fame; res. Manotick, Ont.

ROBERTSON, Doug (weightlifting); b. 27 Mar 1949, Vancouver, B.C.; given name: Douglas Stewart; m. Peggy Phillips; c. Stewart, Ashton; foreman BC Rail; 2nd 123lb class '69-70 ntl championships; 132lb title '71 Canada Winter Games; 2nd 132lb class '71-72 ntl championships; mem. '73 world championships, '74 Commonwealth, '75 Pan-Am Games teams; ntl 132lb titles '73, '75-76; BC champion '68-76, '78; res. Backendale, B.C.

ROBERTSON, Lisa (rowing); b. 13 Oct 1961, Victoria, B.C.; UVic; sweep ntl coxed 4s titlists '82; 2 CIAU coxed 8s, 1 coxed 4s titles; Cdn Henley coxed 8s, 4s titles; mem. '84 Olympic team; res. Sidney, B.C.

ROBERTSON, Nancy (diving); b. 25 Dec 1949, Saskatoon, Sask.; given name: Nancy Jean; m. Larry Brawley; c. Kristen, Tara; UMan, exec.-dir. Kitchener business development org.; 4th '67 Pan-Am Games 3m; 8th 10m, 13th 3m '68 Olympics; silver 10m '70 Commonwealth Games; gold 10m '71 Pan-Am Games; 7th 10m '72 Olympics; ntl team mgr. '86-87; FINA intl judge; mem. Cdn., Ont. Aquatic halls of fame; res. Waterloo, Ont.

ROBERTSON, Sandy (all-around); b. 26 Feb 1923, Vancouver, B.C.; given name: Edward Alastair Sandy; m. Mary Patricia; c. Barbara Joyce, Bruce Richard, Carolyn Patricia; UBC, BSc; retd. consulting engineer, baseball Vancouver srs. '39-46, Louisville Colonels, Durham Bulls '46-47, Vancouver Capilanos '47-53; basketball UBC Thunderbirds '42-46, ntl champion Vancouver Meralomas '47, Vancouver Clover Leafs '48-53, 4 ntl titles; soccer UBC

'46, Vancouver City, Pacific Coast League '52; squash '63-64 Vancouver City, BC, Pacific Northwest titles; semifinalist ntl sr. doubles '75-76; coach UBC, Pony, Babe Ruth, Jr. Pacific Coast baseball teams, Clover Leaf jr. basketball; George Pringle Trophy, rookie of year UBC basketball '43; MVP UBC basketball '46; basketball MVP '47-48; baseball MVP, all-star '50; mem. Vancouver Baseball, BC Sports halls of fame; res. Vancouver, B.C.

ROBILLARD, Gene (football/tennis); b. 15 Jan 1929, Ottawa, Ont.; given name: Eugene Thomas; div.; c. Matthew Thomas, Timothy John; McGill, BSc; retd. HS teacher; mayor's trophy Ottawa Tech top athlete; Gerry Boucher Memorial Trophy OHSAA best football player, Kinsmen Shield OHSAA best hockey player 1st player to win both city awards; McGill quarterback int., sr. football; 3yrs varsity hockey; int. shot put champion '50; intercollegiate all-star defensive back '51; quarterbacked Ottawa Seconds ORFU '52; pro BC '54; 2 Ottawa int. men's doubles tennis title, with Rick Marshall, Jacques Tamaro; int. men's singles title; Ottawa men's sr. doubles with Murray Wiggins; Ottawa and Rideau Tennis club int., sr. singles, men's doubles, mixed doubles titles; mem. '78 Ottawa team sr. hockey Olympics; chair. '80 ntl tennis championships; mem. Ottawa, Ont.

ROBINSON, Bill (basketball); b. 2 Feb 1949, Chemainus, B.C.; m. Susan Ford; c. Ella, Leah; SFU, U of Americas, Mexico, Waterloo; self employed; HS all-star; NAIA all-American (1st Cdn) at SFU; 3yrs. conf. all-star; sparkplug for Jack Donohue's ntl team '69-76 excluding 2 seasons; frequent all-star guard, tournament MVP; 2 Intercontinental Cup, '74 World, '75 Pan-Am, '76 Olympic Games teams; all-Cdn status SFU, Waterloo; NBA trial with Buffalo, ABA Virginia Squires; semipro Belgium, Mexico; res. Chemainus, B.C.

ROBINSON, Bill (football); b. 23 Apr 1951, Toronto, Ont.; given name: William Robert; m. Barbara-Jo MacNeil; c. Kristi-Jo, Billy Jr.; St. Mary's U, BComm;UWO; exec.-dir. Sport Heritage Nova Scotia; quarterbacked undefeated HS team '68-69; Maritime CIAU college MVP '71-73; conf. title winners '71-73; College Bowl title over McGill '73; all-star 4 consec. years; helped UWO win Western Bowl, College Bowl '74; all-Cdn quarterback; George McCullah UWO MVP award; pro Ottawa '75; mem. '76 Grey Cup champions; mem. Ont. basketball B champions '78, '80; Ont. touch football champions '79; Ont. sr. baseball champions '80; pres. Senior Interprovincial Baseball League '81; exec.-dir. CAFA '77-83; chair. CIAU final eight basketball tournament; res. Halifax, N.S.

ROBINSON, Bill (harness racing); b. 5 Sep 1946, Hamilton, Ont.; left tire factory to pursue career in standardbred racing; has established himself as one of the finest trainers in business with the likes of Precious Bunny, Cam's Card Shary, Riyadh, Presidential Ball, Pacific Rocket, Panifesto, Rule The Wind, Abbatom, All I Ask, Dream Maker, Lime Time, Topnotcher, Western Dreamer and Silent Spring; USHWA Glen Garnsey Trainer of '93 award; CTA Trainer of '91, '94; Breeders Crown trainer of '95; frequent OJC non-driving Trainer of Year awards; several of his charges have claimed horse of year honors as well as victories in the Little Brown Jug, Messenger Stakes, Cane

Pace, Cdn Pacing Derby and varied world records; his Western Dreamer set Little Brown Jug record 1:51 1/5 '97; res: Hagersville, Ont.

ROBINSON, Blondie (bowling); b. 3 Jan 1928, Kirkland Lake, Ont.; given name: Graydon Ormiston; m. Phyllis Jones; sheet metal mechanic; led Intercounty 5-pin League '49-50 with 245; 3rd Cdn Bowling Assn. singles tournament '46; with Ken Drury of Sarnia 2nd '52 CBA doubles; averaged 265, rolled high triple of 1066 (418) Regina '53-54; '62 10-pin rookie season avg. 189; 2 perfect 300 games (1 sanctioned); 3 299 sanctioned games, 3 unsanctioned, 796 sanctioned triple, 802 unsanctioned; nore than 75 700s; ntl all-events 9 game record 1941 '66; with Ray Mitchell mem. of team which set record 3385 games; twice winner, 3 times runnerup provincial 700 tournament; 3 times winner Toronto 700 tournament; with Ray Mitchell Toronto scratch doubles; 3 times Toronto scratch all-events, twice city singles; Jim Brace ntl all-stars tournament, runnerup twice; CPBA singles champion '66, '78; averaged career high 212 for '80 season; Ont. scratch singles title '80; topped field of 25 to win '69 world 10-pin title; won Osaka Challenge tourney '69; failed in world title defence '70; Toronto bowler of year; mem. Canada's Sports, Greater Toronto 10-pin BA halls of fame; res. Weston, Ont.

ROBINSON, Bob (wrestling); b. 10 Sep 1958, Montreal, Que.; UWO; freestyle specialist; 62kg gold '82 Commonwealth, bronze '83 Pan-Am Games; 3 ntl 62kg FS, 1 52kg GR titles; mem. '81 FISU, '83 World Cup, world championships, '84 Olympic teams; silver Freiburg tournament '84; fed. govt. excellence award '83; res. Pierrefonds, Que.

ROBINSON, Bobby (builder); b. 8 Apr 1888, Peterborough, Ont.; d. 6 Jun 1974, Burlington, Ont.; given name: Melville Marks; m. Maribel Fair Hawkins; c. Edna Margaret; editor; organized first Empire (later Commonwealth) Games in Hamilton '30; ntl team mgr. '34, '38; Olympic team mgr. '28, '32; mem. Canadian Amateur Sports Hall of Fame.

ROBINSON, Claude (builder/hockey); b. 17 Dec 1881, Harriston, Ont.; d. 27 Jun 1976, Vancouver, B.C.; mem. Winnipeg Victorias as player/exec. Victorias brought Allan, Stanley Cups to Winnipeg during his tenure; recognizing need he suggested formation of ntl assn. to compete for amateur hockey championships; result was CAHA formed '14 with him as 1st secty.; mgr. Cdn Olympic squad '32; life member CAHA; mem. Man., Cdn Hockey halls of fame.

ROBINSON, Emma (rowing); b. 26 Nov 1971, Montreal, Que.; UofT; started rowing at university; mem. ntl team from '93; gold World University 8s '93; 2 US titles; women's coxed 8s silver '96 Olympics; with Alison Korn pairs gold '97, '98 worlds; with Theresa Luke '99 Pan-Am Games coxless pairs gold; with Luke set WR in heat then won gold Lucerne WC regatta; diagnosed with thyroid cancer '99; res. Victoria, B.C.

ROBINSON, Jackie (baseball); b. 31 Jan 1919, Cairo, Gga.; d. 24 Oct 1972, Stamford, Conn.; given name: Jack Roosevelt; m. Rachel Isum; c. Jackie Jr. (d), Sharon, David; UCLA; standout college football/baseball player; played in Negro Baseball League; broke baseball's color barrier when signed by Branch Rickey to become 1st modern era negro to compete in major leagues with Brooklyn Dodgers; made pro ball debut with Montreal Royals 1946; played initial ML game with Dodgers 15 Apr 1947; overcame major racist pressure of time to establish himself as standout ML player; with Dodgers played 1b, 2b, ss, 3b, of '47-56 amassing 1382 games and .311BA; subject of numerous movies, TV specials, books; wife established Jackie Robinson Foundation to assist minority students; UCLA stadium bears his name; special tribute paid on 50th anniversary of his ML debut; mem. Baseball Hall of Fame; hon. mem. Cdn Baseball Hall of Fame.

ROBINSON, Larry (football); b. 18 Apr 1942, Calgary, Alta.; m. Donna; c. Kirk, Tyler, Wesley; Mt. Royal College; OPI sales rep.; quarterback Calgary Western Canada HS champions '59; guided Mt. Royal Cougars to '60 Western Cdn jr. finals; Stampeders '61-75, WFC rookie of year; twice Dave Dryburgh WFC scoring title; 3 times WFC all-star; twice runnerup Schenley nominee; at retirement CFL all-time scoring leader; CFL record: 9tds, 362 converts, 171 field goals, 101 singles, 1030 points (record since surpassed); 50 pass interceptions for 717yds, 3tds; returned fumble recoveries for 219yds; mem. 3 Grey Cup finalists, 1 winner; mem. Cdn Football Hall of Fame; res. Calgary, Alta.

ROBINSON, Larry (hockey); b. 2 Jun 1951, Winchester, Ont.; given name: Larry Clark; m. Jeannette; c. Jeffrey, Rachelle; jr. Brockville, Kitchener '69-71; 4th pick Montreal, 20th overall '71 draft; Nova Scotia (AHL) '71-72; defenceman Canadiens '72-89, LA Kings '89-92; James Norris Memorial Trophy '77, '80, Conn Smythe Trophy '78; 3 times 1st team, 3 2nd team all-star; mem. 5 Stanley Cup winners; NHL playing record: 1384 scheduled games, 208g, 750a, 227 playoff games, 28g, 116a; mem. Team Canada '76, '81, '84; asst. coach New Jerse '93-95, Stanley Cup '95; head coach Kings '95-99; active polo player; growing interest in thoroughbred racehorse ownership; mem. Hockey Hall of Fame; res. Peterborough, Ont./Florida.

ROBITAILLE, Daniel (weightlifting); b. 11 Nov 1953, Val d'Or, Que.; m. Claudette Leblanc; UofOtt; ntl jr. featherweight title '70; numerous Ont. jr., sr. records; 3 bronze '75 Pan-Am Games; ntl 75kg title '77 with 282.5 overall lift; asst. coach jr. world championship team '80; res. Elliot Lake, Ont.

ROBITAILLE, Luc (hockey); b. 17 Feb 1966, Montreal, Que. m. Stacia Rae; c. Steven, Jesse; left wing Hull Olympiques '83-86; QMJHL, Cdn major junior player of '86; 9th round draft choice LA Kings '86; NHL with Kings '86-94, '97-99, Pittsburgh '94-95, NY Rangers '95-97; Calder Memorial Trophy '87; NHL all-rookie team; 5 1st, 2 2nd all-star; 6 NHL all-star games; topped 50-goal plateau 53 '88, 52 '90, 63 '93; reached 1000pt plateau '98; NHL record: (through '99) 971 scheduled games, 517g, 559a, 111 playoff games, 46g, 57a; mem. Team Canada World title team '94; nicknamed 'Lucky'; res. Los Angeles, Calif.

ROBSON, Fred (speed skating); b. 1879, Toronto, Ont.; d. 1944, Toronto, Ont; piano repairman; Toronto jr. champion 1897; Ont. champion 1897-1902; at 19 3 world records; at

22 world records 220yd, 440yd hurdles, 60yd, 75yd sprints; at peak of career 1899-1916 held 9 world records, shared mile mark of 2:41.2 with Philadephia's Morris Wood; ntl barrel jumping record with 11, running high jump record 4'2"; mem. Cdn Speed Skating, Canada's Sports halls of fame.

ROBSON, Lex (golf); b. 7 Feb 1898, Scotland; d. 27 Jan 1976, Peterborough, Ont.; given name: Alexander Laurie; Cdn match play champion; 6 Millar trophies, 1 runnerup; CPGA title '33, runnerup '34; won Ont. Open '35, 3 times runnerup; 2nd Que. Open '33; head pro Kawartha G&CC '40-64; mem. Peterborough Sports Hall of Fame.

ROCHON, Henri (tennis); b. 12 Mar 1924, Montreal, Que.; given name: Henri Denis; m. Yolande Belisle; c. Danielle, France; insurance salesman; various Que. age-group titles, at 17 Que. jr. crown; ntl men's open singles '49; mem. Davis Cup team '46-53, '55-56, capt. '56; with Dr. Breen Marian ntl sr. men's doubles '72; ntl 60+ outdoor '89, 65+ indoor title '91; 3yrs teaching pro including year as resident pro Ville St. Laurent Indoor Tennis Club; res. Montreal, Que.

ROCHON, John (shooting); b. 11 Dec 1941, Cadillac, Que.; given name: Jean Louis Arthur Joseph; m. Donna Francis Green; c. Christine, Judy, John Jr., Tony; retd mechanic, firearms instructor; mem. ntl team '85-98; handgun specialist; 42 ntl titles (all disciplines); gold '91, bronze '95 Pan-Am Games; competed '90, won silver, bronze '94, silver, 3 bronze '98 Commonwealth Games; competed 5 Crossman air gun championships winning 1 gold, silver, bronze; mem. Elliot Lake Sharpshooters Handgun Club, Algoma Rod & Gun Club; res. Elliot Lake, Ont.

ROCHON, Stéphane (skiing); b. 15 Mar 1974, Laval, Que.; freestyle moguls specialist; mem. ntl team from '93; ntl gold '96, bronze '97; 3 World Cup race gold, 4 silver, 3 bronze; world championship silver '97; ranked 2nd '96 WC final standings; competed '98 Olympics; res. St. Saveur, Que.

ROCK, Richard (t&f); b. 6 Nov 1957, Reading, Eng.; given name: Richard Oliver; Southern Illinois; ntl jr. long jump champion '75; mem. '76, '80 Olympic, '77 FISU, '78 Commonwealth, '79 Pan-Am Games teams; Missouri Valley Conf. indoor long jump record 24'5" '76; bronze NCAA indoor championships '77; Southern Ill. indoor, outdoor long jump record holder at 25'3", 26'8" respectively; PB: 26'8"; ntl long jump champion '78-80; res. Agincourt, Ont.

RODDEN, Mike (hockey/football); b. 24 Apr 1891, Mattawa, Ont., d. 11 Jan 1978, Kingston, Ont.; given name: Michael James; m. Mildred Alice Wormith; c. William Bernard, Richard John; Queen's, McGill; retd. sports editor; football, hockey, soccer, lacrosse as player, coach, official, chronicler; 4 football seasons Queen's, 1 McGill, all-star 4 times, each at a different position; 15 Tricolor letters, record never equalled; hockey Queen's, Haileybury, Toronto St. Pat's; coached Queen's football '16; middle wing Toronto Argos '19; coached Argos to '20 Grey Cup final, lost to UofT; Parkdale Canoe Club ORFU titles '21-22; guided Balmy Beach to '24 Grey Cup final, lost to Queen's; won Grey Cup '28-29 as Hamilton coach; coached 42 football teams, 27 league titles, 2 of 5 Grey Cup appearances; coached Toronto de LaSalle, St. Mary's, St. Pat's, UotT

hockey; refereed 2864 hockey games, 1187 in NHL; mem. Canadian Football, Hockey halls of fame.

RODGERS, Johnny (football); b. 5 Jul 1951, Omaha, Neb.; div, Daryl; c. Terry, Latonya, Johnni; m. Jawana; c. Jewel; Nebraska, BA; mgr. Jetware/Mannatech spokesman; all-time leading Nebraska pass receiver with 143 catches for 2479yds ('70-72); awarded Heisman trophy '72; played in CFL with Montreal '73-76; earned nickname 'Ordinary Superstar'; CFL rookie of yr; all-CFL 3yrs; runnerup CFL MVP '76; joined NFL with San Diego '76; remained for 3 injury-plagued seasons; founded 1st weekly cable TV magazine *Tuned In*; key figure in '97 Pro Flag tour; res. Lincoln, Neb.

ROE, Lot (speed skating); b. 2 Sep 1881, Kincardine, Ont., d. 28 Oct 1964, Toronto, Ont.; m. Fannie May; c. John Murray, Arthur Edward, Anna May, Clarice Isabel; compositor; international 220yd sprint titles '10-12, '15-16; ntl all-around indoor titles '10, '13, outdoor '13; competitive skater 1897-1924; world 1 1/2 mile record 4:10; New England 1/2 mile title '10; developed point system to determine all-around international champions; 2 CNE 100yd dash (t&f) titles; mem. Canadian Speed Skating Hall of Fame.

ROGERS, Bruce (swimming); b. 4 Jun 1957, Toronto, Ont.; given name: Bruce Hibbert; Miami, UofT, Indiana, BA, UWO, MBA; ntl butterfly champion '74-75, records each time; 2 silver, 1 bronze '63 Canada Games; mem. '74 Commonwealth, '75 Pan-Am, worlds, '76 Olympic, '77 FISU Games teams; bronze 200m butterfly '77 FISU Games; res. Oakville, Ont.

ROGERS, Chris (horse racing); b. 1924, Hamilton, Ont.; d. 29 Oct 1976, Hamilton, Ont.; jockey; began riding '41; quickly developed into what Eddie Arcaro described as "the complete rider"; 3 Queen's Plate winners, Epic '49, McGill '50, Collisteo '54; 2nd aboard Lincoln Road '58 Kentucky Derby; lifetime totals: 2043 wins, 2127 seconds, 2207 thirds from 21,424 mounts; successfully overcame alcholism which threatened career; while enjoying good '76 season, sustained broken leg in Woodbine spill 30 Sep; died of lung cancer; mem. Canadian Horse Racing Hall of Fame.

ROGERS, Danny (swimming); b. 19 Sep 1958, Toronto, Ont.; given name: Daniel Clive; Indiana, BA; 3 silver, 1 bronze (backstroke, IM races) '77 winter nationals; silver (100m backstroke), bronze (200m backstroke) '78 summer nationals; 3 gold, 2 silver '77 Canada Games; mem. '79 FISU Games team; res. Mississauga, Ont.

ROGERS, Doug (judo); b. 26 Jan 1941, Truro, N.S.; given name: Alfred Harold Douglas; University in Japan; airline pilot; ntl judo titles '64-72; gold Canada Winter Games '71; silver '64 Olympics; bronze '65 Worlds; gold, silver '67 Pan-Am Games; flag-bearer '72 summer Olympics; capt. all-Japan university judo team tiltists, 1st Caucasian so named; coached judo UBC, guiding team to Western Canada university titles '75-77; mem. Cdn Amateur, BC, Canada's Sports halls of fame; res. Vancouver, B.C.

ROGERS, Melville (figure skating/builder); b. 5 Jan 1899, Ottawa, Ont.; d. 26 Sep 1973, Ottawa, Ont.; m. Isobel (Tish)

Blyth (d); c. David, Pamela; UofT, BA, Osgoode Hall, LLB; active in hockey, rugby, tennis; 18 sr. ntl figure skating titles in singles, pairs, fours; 5 Cdn, 2NA singles titles; with sister Gladys won '27 ntl pairs and with Margaret Davis '38 ntl dance title; mem. Cdn and 4 NA fours title teams; 1st male to represent Canada in Olympic figure skating '24; mem. '32 Olympic team; International Skating Union gold medal; 4 Royal Ottawa, 2 Rivermead golf club titles; RCGA governor; key role in formation and served 14yrs pres. Cdn Sports Advisory Council (later Sports Federation of Canada); drafted that body's constitution; associated with Minto Skating Club 60yrs; founded Minto Follies; life mem., hon. pres. Minto Club; 2 terms pres. CFSA; chaired international judges comm. 15yrs; Minto FS Club scholarship fund bears his name; COA dir.; nicknamed 'Mev'; mem. Cdn Amateur, Cdn Figure Skating, Ottawa Sports halls of fame.

ROGERS, Shotty (rowing); b. 1887, St. John's Nfld.; d. 1963, St. John's, Nfld.; given name: Levi; coxed more than 300 crews to victory; last victory '62 at age 75; mem. Newfoundland, Canada's Sports halls of fame.

ROGERS, Steve (baseball); b. 26 Oct 1949, Jefferson City, Mo.; given name: Stephen Douglas; m. Barbara Bodnarchuk; c. Colleen, Stephen Jason, Geoffrey Douglas; Tulsa, BSc; 4yr college record 31-5, outstanding amateur athlete US Southwest '71, college world series all-star; pro Montreal organization '71; ML roster '73-85; *Sporting News* rookie pitcher of '73, Topps ML rookie all-star team; 100th ML victory 9 Sep '80, 150th 7 Sep '83; 4 1-hitters; 6 NL player of month awards, Apr '82 NL player of month; 5 all-star games; runnerup Cy Young balloting '82; nicknamed 'Cy'; Expos player rep.; res. Springfield, Okla.

ROGIN, Bill (basketball); b. 9 Jun 1915, Windsor, Ont.; d. 7 Mar 1987, Windsor, Ont.; m. Florence Fisher; c. Ann, Steven, Howard; Assumption Coll., BA, UofT, BPHE; retd. HS principal; nicknamed 'Moose'; Windsor HS shot put record '31-50; mem. Assumption Coll. '5 Fighting Freshmen' '33-37; 4yrs top scorer; Eastern Cdn finalists '34, ntl champions '35; NCAA single game scoring record, world record 16 successive foul shots; mem. Victoria Dominoes '37-38; football, basketball UofT '38-39; semipro basketball Detroit '40-44; named to '36 Olympic team at own expense but did not attend; tryout as catcher with Philadelphia Athletics; coached Sarnia CI '39-44, Toronto YMHA '45-48; refereed basketball '32-65, ORFU football '39-48, EFC, Grey Cup final '47; life mem. Windsor Dist. Football, Basketball Refs., Umpires Assns.; son Steve QB Matt Anthony's unbeaten UofOtt Gee-Gees team, wife Florence mem. Windsor Alumni ntl finalist basketball team vs. Edmonton Grads '35; founding mem./dir. Windsor Essex County Sports Hall of Fame; mem. Windsor Essex County Sports, U Windsor, Cdn Basketball halls of fame.

ROKOSH, Greg (rowing); b. 24 Jan 1942, Flin Flon, Man.; given name: Gregory Joseph; m. Gillian Green; c. Amanda, Jennifer; UofSask, BA, BComm; sport administrator; 5yrs varsity football guard, linebacker Sask.; 2yrs capt.; founder Sask. Letterman's club; school's top athletic award; capt. wrestling team competing at 191lbs, heavyweight levels; Toronto Open FS title; began rowing as theraphy '68; mem.

Toronto Argonaut RC '68-74; 5 ntl titles in pairs, 4s, 8s; several Ont. titles; semifinalist Royal Henley England '70, '72; with Ian Gordon, Karl Jonker, Don Curphey 9th (best by Cdns) '72 Olympics; won '72 Martini-Achter coxless 4s; turned to marathon running '74; PB 2h52min; coached rowing York, UofT, Ottawa; coaching coordinator CARA; created *Catch* magazine for CARA; designed ntl team program used by CARA; CBC-TV color commentator '84 Olympics; res. Russell, Ont.

ROLLICK, Bruce (badminton); b. 11 Apr 1943, Vancouver, B.C.; given name: Bruce Irwin Alexander; m. Judith Ellen Humber; c. Lisa Jane, Elayne Alexandra; UBC,BSc; consulting actuary; won all age-group prov. jr. titles; ntl men's open singles '68; with wife Judi closed mixed doubles '69, 5 times ntl men's closed singles; with Rolf Patterson '72 men's doubles; with Mimi Nilsson '77 mixed doubles; mem. 4 Thomas Cup, '70 Commonwealth Games, '72 China tour teams; active as coach for jrs., srs.; mem. silver medal team '98 Nike World games; res. Vancouver, B.C.

ROLLICK, Judi (badminton); b. 17 Aug 1944, Seattle, Wash.; given name: Judith Ellen Humber; m. Bruce Rollick; c. Lisa Jane, Elayne Alexandra; teacher; ntl jr. champion, ladies' closed singles, mixed doubles once each, with Mimi Nilsson ladies' closed doubles twice; mem. 2 Uber Cup, China tour '72, 3 Commonwealth Games teams; twice ntl veteran ladies singles, doubles champion; proficient golfer; mem. Greater Victoria Sports Hall of Fame; res. Vancouver, B.C.

ROLLO, Kathy (diving); b. 30 Oct 1951, Warroad, Minn.; given name: Kathleen Mary; m. Donald Seaman; c. Erin Rae, Rebecca Rollo; Saskatoon, BSc, Central Mich., MA; registered nurse, nursing teacher; Saskatchewan diving champion '65-72; 4th tower '67 Pan-Am, '70 Commonwealth Games; mem. '72 Olympic team; FINA International judge from '82; res. Regina, Sask.

ROMANO, Rocco (football); b. 1 Jan 1963, Hamilton, Ont.; Concordia; offensive guard; drafted Calgary '87, from '92, Toronto '88, Ottawa '89, BC '90-91; CFL record (through '95): 144 games; 3 Western, 1 Northern, 3 CFL all-star; Becket-DeMarcoMemorial Trophy '94; runnerup CFL outstanding offensive lineman '94; 3 Grey Cup finals, 1 winner; res. Calgary, Alta.

RONEY, Jean (lawn bowling); b. 11 Sep 1945, Nokomis, Sask; given name: Jean Marie Berkan; m. Keith Norman; UofSask, BA; forensic scientist RCMP; skipped Sask women's pairs '87, '90-92 Cdn championships; mem. ntl team from '90; ntl women's singles titles '89, '93; skip 1st Cdn women's gold medal fours in international competition '93 Pacific Bowls; skip women's fours silver '94, gold '95 ntl championships; competed '94 Commonwealth Games women's singles; skip '95 women's fours bronze Pacific Bowls; competed world bowls '96, world women's indoor singles '93; res. Regina, Sask.

RONEY, Keith (lawn bowling); b. 7 Feb 1948, Regina, Sask; given name: Keith Norman; m. Jean Marie Berkan; Regina, BA; curator Royal Sask. Museum; 16 provincial titles; 3 ntl pairs, 2 ntl fours gold; 1 ntl singles, 1 pair silver;

2 ntl singles, pairs bronze; mem. ntl team '85, from '88; represented Canada 2 Hong Kong, 2 Pacific Rim, 1 world indoor singles, 1 world bowls championships; WOBA singles gold '96; 2 Sun City Fla. triples, 1 LA pairs gold; '93 LA bowler of tournament award; res. Regina, Sask.

ROOST, Ain (t&f); b. 5 Dec 1947, Upsala, Sweden; m. Dianne; c. Lindsey Melissa; Minnesota, PhD; psychologist; 5th javelin '66 Commonwealth Games; 4th discus '74 Commonwealth Games; bronze discus '71 Pan-Am Games; 5th discus '75 Pan-Am Games; silver discus '73 Pan-Pacific Games; mem. '72 Olympic team; ntl discus title '71-74; res. San Diego, Calif.

RORVIG, Ed (football); b. 24 May 1913, Binford, N.D.; given name: Edward Carlyl; m. Frances McQueen; c. Suzanne Caldarello, Paul Edward, Peter Gordon; North Dakota, BSc; sales manager; pro Calgary '36; '37 WFL all-star fullback, all-Cdn; res. Boonville, Mo.

ROSE, Bob (golf); b. 19 Apr 1939, Toronto, Ont.; m. Kathy; c. Steven, Ruth Ann; golf pro; qualified in 1st tour school in US '66; played on PGA tour '66; 3 CPGA seniors titles; shot 57 on par 71, 6500yd Beverly Golf Club course '81; 1 CPGA title; res. Waterdown, Ont.

ROSEN, David (squash); b. 14 Mar 1970, Ottawa, Ont.; given name: David Jonathan; Franklin & Marshall College; squash pro; nicknamed 'Duddy'; ranked top 5 in Cdn jr. hardball/softball squash '82-88; gold Pan-Am Maccabiah Youth Games '86; mem. F&M varsity squash team '88-92, team capt., MVP, all-American '91-92; ranked 12 US softball singles, 6 US men's doubles '93-94; ranked 5 US men's doubles '94-95, mixed doubles '96-97, 21 softball men's singles '85-96; mem. US Maccabiah Games squash team '97; coached Agnes Irwin School girls team to 3 undefeated championship seasons '92-95; coached 9 US nationally ranked jr. players; head squash pro Philadelphia Country Club, Gladwyn, Pa., '95-97; res. Superior, Colo.

ROSEN, Goody (baseball); b. 28 Aug 1912, Toronto, Ont.; d. 6 Apr 1994, Toronto, Ont.; given name: Goodwin George; m. Mildred Rothberg; c. John Michael, Cecil Brendan; retd sales mgr; outfielder; Toronto amateur baseball product; pro Louisville (AAA); Brooklyn Dodgers '37-39, '44-46, NY Giants '46; runnerup NL batting race '45 with .325 avg.; ML record: 551 games, 1916ab, 557h, 71d, 34t, 22hr, 197rbi, .291ba; mem. NL all-star team '45; 1st game with NY went 7 for 9 vs. Dodgers in doubleheader, winning RBI each game; ended career Toronto (IL); mem. Canada's Baseball Hall of Fame.

ROSENFELD, Bobbie (t&f); b. 28 Dec 1903, Russia, d. 14 Nov 1969, Toronto, Ont.; given name: Fanny; sportswriter; Canada's female athlete of half century '50 *CP* poll; silver 100m, gold 4x100 women's relay '28 Olympics, record 48.2; co-holder 11.00 100yd world record; '25 world 220yd record 26.00 disallowed when track found to be foot short; during '25 Ont. ladies' t&f championships scored 1st in shot put, discus, running broad jump, 200yd dash, 100yd low hurdles, 2nd 100yd dash, javelin (all in one afternoon); '24 Toronto grass courts tennis title; Cdn. Female Athlete of yr award named for her; mem. Barrie,

Cdn Amateur, Cdn Jewish, Canada's,Ont. Legends Sports halls of fame.

ROSS, Art (hockey); b. 13 Jan 1886, Naughton, Ont., d. 5 Aug 1964, Boston, Mass.; given name: Arthur Howie; developed nets, pucks still in use in NHL; defenceman 14 years with Westmount (CAHL), Brandon (MHL), Kenora (MHL), Montreal Wanderers (ECAHA), Haileybury (NHA), Wanderers (NHA), Ottawa Senators (NHA); 85 goals in 167 games; best single season '12 with 16 goals in 18 games; mem. Kenora '07, Wanderers '08 Stanley Cup winners; retired '18 to referee; mgr. Hamilton Tigers, coach-mgr. Boston Bruins when they joined NHL '24, won 3 Stanley Cups; Lester Patrick award; Art Ross Trophy awarded to NHL scoring champion; mem. Hockey, Canada's Sports halls of fame.

ROSS, Betty (basketball); b. Apr 1915, Edmonton, Alta.; m. Ray Bellamy; c. Penny, Betty-Raye, Douglas; retd. secretary; mem. legendary Edmonton Grads '37-39; mem. Canadian Basketball, Alta. Sports halls of fame; res. Summerland, B.C.

ROSS, Chucker (curling); b. 4 Dec 1934, Montreal, Que.; m. Sheila Peever Seltzer; c. Becki, Brenda, Larry, Karey, Julie; Institute of Chartered Accountants of Ont.; chartered accountant; skipped NO rink '74 Brier; skipped NO entry '82 ntl Seagram Mixed; skipped '81 Bowling Green Ohio International mixed title winner; NO jr. men's golf champion '53; mem. NOSAA sr. basketball title team '53, national Sr. B title team '56; avid windsurfer; with wife Sheila has achieved official instructor status and has windsurfed as far south as Caribbean; res. Sudbury, Ont.

ROSS, Earl (motorsport); b. 4 Sep 1941, Charlottetown, P.E.I.; given name: Earl Seymour; m. Yvonne; c. 3 daughters; auto mechanic, racing driver; raced stock cars as hobby Delaware, Nilestown tracks; '72 Export A grand championship; competed in 21 NASCAR races '74, 1st Canadian to win Grand National race, Old Dominion 500 at Martinsville Va.; 2nd Michigan International Speedway Motor State 400, NASCAR Grand National rookie of '74; Canadian Motorsport's man of '74; res. Ailsa Craig, Ont.

ROSS, George (boxing); b. 22 Mar 1922, Sydney, N.S.; dockworker; ring career spanned '46-53, '57-58; 22 amateur, 52 pro bouts; pro record: 42 wins, 1 draw, 9 losses; ntl middleweight title '48-50; mem. NS Sports Hall of Fame; res. Halifax, N.S.

ROSS, John (trampoline); b. 19 Feb 1961, Arnprior, Ont.; given name: John David; Carleton, Algonquin Coll.; runnerup Ont. jr. '78; ntl sr. title '80-84; 3rd '82 world championships; US ntl, Ennia Cup titles '82, 2 world cup title events '82, 3rd Hermesetas championships '83; turned attention to freestyle skiing '90s; mem. Nepean Sports Wall of Fame; res. Nepean, Ont.

ROSS, Marie Claire (swimming); b. 21 Nov 1975, Kingston, Ont.; UWO; B3 blind athlete; standout in all swimming disciplines; mem. London Aquatic Club; 1 silver, 1 bronze '92 Paralympics; 1 gold, 1 silver, 4 bronze IPC World championships '94; 3 gold, 3 silver IPC swim trials

'95; 2 gold, 1 silver, 3 bronze Paralympics '96; 3 gold, 3 silver World blind championships '98; world records 50, 100, 200m breaststroke; res. London, Ont.

ROSS, P.D. (rowing); b. 1 Jan 1858, Montreal, Que., d. 5 Jul 1949, Ottawa, Ont.; given name: Philip Dansken; m. Mary Littlejohn; McGill; publisher; Que. single sculls title, twice stroked 4-oared crews to ntl championships; capt. McGill football team 1876; standout hockey, lacrosse player; founder several golf clubs; hockey, lacrosse referee; Minto Cup, Stanley Cup trustee; mem. Hockey Hall of Fame.

ROSS-GIFFEN, Jill (t&f); b. 23 Feb 1958, London, Ont.; given name: Jillian Margaret Ross; div. Frank Giffen; UofT; heptathlon specialist; ntl jr. pentathlon title '76; gold pentathlon '77 Canada Games; mem. '78, '82 Commonwealth, '79, '83 Pan-Am Games, '80, '83 FISU, '84 Olympic Games teams; pentathlon bronze '79 Pan-Am Games; long jump gold Tom Black Classic '79; CIAU long jump titles '80-81; heptathlon bronze '82 Commonwealth Games; ntl heptathlon record 6110 points '82; ntl pentathlon, long jump, heptathlon titles; 1st Cdn woman to win 8 events in 7-event heptathlon '83 winning 200m twice; res. Toronto, Ont.

ROTHWELL, Nigel (gymnastics); b. 29 Apr 1957, Romford, Essex, Eng.; given name: Nigel Mark; Michigan, BSc, MSc; coach, athlete; mem. ntl team from '75; mem. '75, '79 Pan-Am, '77, '81 FISU, '78 Commonwealth Games teams, numerous major international meets; team silver '79 Pan-Am Games; gold floor exercises, silver horizontal bar, all around, bronze parallel bars, rings, vault '81 ntl championships; twice runnerup all-around Big 10 Conf.; res. Switzerland.

ROUGHTON, William (speed skating); b. 14 Jan 1883, London, Eng., d. 19 Nov 1963, Montreal, Que.; playing pres. Montreal Soccer Club; founder Montreal Hockey League; pres. Amateur Skating Assn. of Canada '31-58; starter '32 Winter Olympics; life mem. MAAA; mem. Canadian Speed Skating Hall of Fame.

ROUNTREE, Jim (football); b. 21 Apr 1936, Miami, Fla.; m. Nan; c. James Jr., Taren; Florida; construction industry; HS all-state, all-American; all-Southeastern Conf., Gators' MVP '57; halfback Toronto '58-67; combined with Tobin Rote 10 Sep '61 for 108yd TD pass-run play; all-time Argos interception record 41; all-Cdn '62; 7 all-Eastern Conf. selections; asst. coach Argos '68-72, '77-78, Memphis Southmen '74-75; mem. Florida Sports Hall of Fame; res. Pompano Beach, Fla.

ROUSSEAU, Bobby (hockey); b. 26 Jul 1940, Montreal, Que.; given name: Joseph Jean-Paul Robert; golf pro; St. Jean jrs. at 15, jr., sr. Hull-Ottawa; mem. '60 Olympic silver medal team; pro Rochester (AHL), Hull-Ottawa (EPHL); right wing Montreal '61-70; Calder Memorial Trophy; Minnesota '70-71, Rangers '71-75; one of first to use helmet; mem. 4 Stanley Cup winners; 2nd team all-star '66; twice scored 30 goals 1 season; NHL record: 942 scheduled games, 245 goals, 458 assists, 128 playoff games, 27 goals, 57 assists; 5 goals 1 game vs. Detroit '64; pitched no-hit game for St. Hyacinthe baseball jrs.; Joliette Country Club competitive golf course record 66; res. Sorel, Que.

ROUSSEAU, Yves (biathlon); b. 5 Apr 1960, Blind River, Ont.; Canadian Forces; NA 4x7.5km relay title, bronze NA 10km '84; national 10km, 20km, 4x7.5km relay, overall titles; res. Blind River, Ont.

ROWAN, Sheila (softball/curling); b. 22 Apr 1940, Young, Sask.; given name: Sheila Anne; stenographer; all-star Saskatoon Imperials '68 ntl women's softball championships, ntl titles '69-70; mem. ntl team '70 world tournament, Sask. team '69 Canada Summer Games; coach Saskatoon Baldwinettes 2 seasons, 1 ntl title; 3rd with Vera Pezer ntl women's title rink '71-73; defeated '72 ntl men's champion Orest Meleschuk in televised match; ntl sr. women's title rink '92; mem. Sask Sports, Canadian Curling halls of fame; res. Saskatoon, Sask.

ROWE, Earl (harness racing); b. 13 May 1894, Hull, Iowa, d. 10 Feb 1984, Toronto, Ont.; given name: William Earl; m. Treva Lennox; c. Bill, Jean, Lennox; UofOtt, DSS, UWO, LLD; horseman, business exec., politician; drove harness horses '13-'70; operated Rowelands Farm; 7 Standardbred Horse Society Trotting Futurity titles; '52 Maple Leaf Trotting Classic; with son Bill instrumental in founding Windsor, Barrie Raceways; MLA Ont. '23-25; federal MP '25-35, '37-62; cabinet minister Bennett govt.; Ont. PC leader '36; Ont. Lt.-Gov. '63-68; pres. CSHS '27-28, '58-61; prominent as breeder/trainer; hon. dir. Ont. Harness Horsemen's Assoc.; mem. Canadian Horse Racing Hall of Fame.

ROWE, Paul (football); b. 25 Jan 1917, Victoria, B.C.; d. 26 Aug 1990, Calgary, Alta.; div.; c. Barry, Robert, Virginia; Oregon; retd.; all-Canadian as mem. Victoria, BC English rugby teams; t&f with Victoria YMCA; footballOregon, Calgary Bronks '38-40; Canadian Army '44, Stampeders '45-50; named greatest plunging fullback in Canadian Football '48; led Calgary to '48 Grey Cup; Western all-star 4 times; Dave Dryburgh scoring champion trophy '39, '48; retired due to injuries and served as coach, advisor in minor football; mem. Alta., BC, Cdn Football, Canada's Sports halls of fame.

ROWELL, Fred (builder); b. 20 May 1916, Toronto, Ont.; given name: Frederick Newton Alexander; active t&f athlete from youth to masters level; founded Vancouver Olympic Club; initiated Vancouver relays '49; asst. track coach UBC '48-53; ED/head coach VOC '49-57, pres. '57-63, dir. to '65, hon. dir from '65; established selection standards for CTFA teams; dir, COA '46-50, '53-56; mgr t&f team '48 Olympics; AAU of C exec. '47-56, pres. BC branch '55-57; mem. Vancouver mayor's special BEG comm. '50-51; comm. chair. '54 BEG; established Canada's 1st accredited coaching school at UBC '53; CdM '55 Pan-Am Games; editor *T&F Digest* and *Around the Track*; dir. BC Amateur Sports Council from '64; mem. BC Sports Hall of Fame; res. Vancouver, B.C.

ROWLAND, Gordie (football); b. 1 Sep 1930, Montreal, Que.; m. Joan Lloyd; c. Jill, Janet, Gary; retd. Gladden Paint mgr; football Montreal Orfuns intermediates, soccer Stelco srs., ntl champions '54; Blue Bombers '54-63; 5 Grey Cup finals, 4 winners; 5 times WFC all-star defensive halfback; leading Canadian WFC '58, Schenley runnerup; returned career total 324 punts for 2395yds, 7.8 avg.; returned 215 kickoffs for 9546yds; intercepted 31 passes, 4 for TDs; 4yrs UMan. asst. coach, Vanier Cup '70; coached minor football several yrs; res. Winnipeg, Man.

ROXBURGH, Doug (golf); b. 28 Dec 1951, Santo Domingo, Dominion Republic; given name: Douglas Ian; m. Lorna McPherson; c. James, Geordie; Oregon,SFU, BComm; retd. accountant; dir. RCGA player development '99; golf range operator; BC junior title '69-70; ntl junior '70; 3 Vancouver city jr. titles; 13 BC amateur, 4 runnerup, 5 Vancouver City sr. titles; 4 ntl amateur titles, twice runnerup; semifinalist British Amateur '79; mem. 19 BC Willingdon Cup, 4 BC jr. teams; 7 Eisenhower World team matches, 2 Commonwealth Trophy matches, '77 Nations Cup Paris, '81 Simon Bolivar Cup Maracaibo; mem. RCGA, BC Sports halls of fame; res. Vancouver, B.C.

ROY, Aldo (weightlifting); b. 22 Mar 1942, Sudbury, Ont.; given name: Aldo Robert Joseph; Laurentian, BA, UofOtt, MA; HS history dept. head; at 17 ntl sr. titlist, 3 ntl sr., open records; mem. '62 Commonwealth Games, '63, '67 Pan-Am, '65 world championships, '68 Olympics teams; coach from '72; asst. and/or head coach '78 jr. world team, '79 Pan-Am Games, America's team '80 Pan-Am championships, '80 Olympics, '81 Commonwealth championships; TV colorcaster Olympic, Commonwealth, Pan-Am Games; res. Ottawa, Ont.

ROY, Andy (sailing); b. 3 Jan 1958, Halifax, N.S.; ntl Laser champion '81; silver Laser '82 worlds, '83 Pan-Am Games; crewman Canada II '87 America's Cup competition; fed. govt. excellence award '82; res. Toronto, Ottawa, Ont.

ROY, Kevin (weightlifting); b. 21 Apr 1963, Sudbury, Ont.; Laurentian; jr. America Cup 90kg title '79; 3 ntl 100kg, 1 Ont. 100kg titles; 9 ntl, Commonwealth jr., 3 ntl, Commonwealth sr. records; bronze 100kg '82 Commonwealth, 3 silver 110kg '83 Pan-Am Games; mem. '84 Olympic team; res. Coniston, Ont.

ROY, Patrick (hockey); b. 5 Oct 1965, Quebec City, Que.; m. Michele; c. Jonathan, Frederick. Jana; goalie Granby Bisons; 4th round pick Montreal '84 draft; Sherbrooke (AHL), Granby '84-85, Montreal '85-95, Colorado '95-99; 2 Conn Smythe trophies; 4 William Jenning awards; NHL all-rookie team; 3 Vezina trophies; *Hockey News* playoff MVP award '93; 2 Trico goaltending awards; 3 1st, 2 2nd team all-star; played 7 NHL all-star games; mem. 3 Stanley Cup winners, '98 Olympic team; reached 400 career victory plateau '99; NHL record: (through '99) 778 scheduled games, 412-243-95, 45,404min, 39so, 140 playoff games, 8567min, 355ga, 6so, 84-54; part-owner QMJHL Quebec Remparts; res. Denver, Colo./Ste-Foy, Que.

ROY, Simon (racquetball); b. 4 Mar 1969, Quebec City, Que.; Southwest Missouri State; marketing; ntl juve., jr. titles; singles silver tournament of Americas '94; men's doubles gold '96, silver '92 world championships; 5 ntl men's doubles titles; 5 ntl singles silver; res. Ste-Foy, Que.

RUBENSTEIN, Louis (figure skating); b. 23 Sep 1861, Montreal, Que.; d. 3 Jan 1931, Montreal, Que.; partner, silverplaters and manufacturers; learned skating skills Jackson Haines school; Montreal skating title at 17; ntl title

1882-89; US titles 1888-89, 1891; world title 1890; key role in founding Canadian Amateur Skating Assn. 1878; pres. International Skating Union of America 1907-09; monument to his memory Montreal '39; 18yrs pres. Cdn Wheelman's Assn.; ranked by some father of bowling in Canada; mem. US Figure Skating, Cdn Amateur, Cdn Speed Skating, Canada's, Montreal YM-YWHA Sports halls of fame.

RUBES, Jan (tennis); b. 6 Jun 1920, Volyne, Czechoslovakia; m. Susan Douglas Burstein; c. Jonathan, Anthony; Prague Academy of Music; actor/singer; claimed several Czech junior club tennis titles, Czech jr. cross-country ski champion; claimed several Ont. seniors age-group singles/doubles titles; ntl seniors singles title '82; has represented Canada in Crawford Cup play in Australia, France; mem. Cdn team Venice, Fla., tennis league; 3 Ont. athletic excellence awards; opera singer, active TV/Movies actor; res. Collingwood, Ont.

RUBY, Martin (football); b. 1922 Waco, Tex; m. Delmar; c. Marsha. Deanna; Texas A&M; competed 3 Bowl Games; SW Intercollegiate Conf. MVP '41; following WW2 service played several seasons with Brooklyn Dodgers, NY Yankees (football); two-way tackle Roughriders '51-57; 4 all-West off. tackle, 3 all-West def. tackle awards; 3 times two-way all-star; mem. Cdn Football Hall of Fame; res. Salmon Arm, B.C.

RUEGGER, Silvia (t&f); b. 23 Feb 1961, Ottawa, Ont.; UGuelph; mem. Etobicoke Huskies-Striders; National Capital Marathon (1st ever marathon) course record 2:03.37 '84; mem. '84 Olympic team; 1 CIAU X-C all-Cdn; seriously injured '85 car accident; mem. Guelph Sports Hall of Fame; res. Guelph, Ont.

RUEL, Claude (hockey/coaching); b. 12 Sep 1938, Sherbrooke, Que.; given name: Claude Robert; hockey exec.; loss of sight in left eye when struck with a stick playing jr. hockey ended his playing career; began working in Montreal organization at 15; coached Jr. Canadiens 5yrs; chief scout Montreal 2yrs; dir. player development '66-68, '81-98; became youngest NHL coach '68; guided Canadiens to Stanley Cup in initial season; replaced as coach '71 by Al MacNeil; asst coach '73, '76-79 Stanley Cup winners; replaced Bernie Geoffrion as head coach '80-81; NHL coaching record: 305 games, 172-82-51; res. Montreal, Que.

RUITER, Garth (curling/baseball/basketball); b. 26 Jun 1920, St. Jerome, Que.; given name: Garth George Ward; m. Dorothy Jean Stephen; c. Allan Van, Stephen; UofT; manufacturers' agent; jr. baseball Guelph '35-36; Toronto Viaduct, Beach Leagues '37-39; Navy '43; mem. Snowdon softball league Montreal '56-57; coached Dorval to ntl Little League finals '67; mem. Interscholastic baseball title team Guelph '36-37; West End Y Toronto Sr. League '38-39; mem. Service League titlist Victoria Navy team '41-42; mem. Maritime champion New Waterford Strands Cape Breton, N.S., '43; mem. Halifax Stadacona service, prov. titlist '44-45; mem. East York Grads Ont. Sr. League '46-48; YMHA Toronto Sr. League '49-51; player-coach Orillia Int. Ont. champions '53; mem. Montreal YMHA Que. sr. champions '56; began curling Orillia '53; 2nd Que. rink '62 Brier; skipped City of Ottawa grand aggregate winner

'65; skipped Que. rinks to 1 Governor-General's Trophy, 4 Royal Canadian Legion ntl finals, title '66; 4 Que. srs titles; 3rd Jim Wilson's Que. ntl srs champions '81; res. Dorval, Que.

RUMBOLD, Dave (shooting); b. 30 Dec 1934, Guilford, Surrey, Eng.; given name: David William; m. Audrey Florence Solly; c. Yvonne Susan, Joanne Elisabeth, Ian David; aeronautical engineer, retd. major Cdn Forces; mem. 12 Ont. target rifle teams from '62, capt. '78; Ont. champion '79; mem. 4 RCAF, 12 ntl Bisley teams, adjutant '74, v.-capt. '83, commandant '86; mem. 4 Cdn Palma teams, adjutant '72, coach '85; competed twice US nationals, '80 world championships; 30 individual medals at prov., ntl, international levels; shooter, capt. or coach ntl teams which won 1 Palma, 1 Empire, 3 Kolapore, 5 Overseas, 3 Commonwealth, 6 Canada matches; coached team to WR short-range 1182x1200 vs. Britain '84; mem. council, exec. comm. ORA from '74, DCRA from '69; dir. DCRA support operations '76-78, chair. several committees; organized DCRA ntl matches '76-82; editor *Canadian Marksman* '75-76; DCRA life governor; res. Ottawa, Ont.

RUNGE, Paul (baseball/officiating); b. 20 Oct 1941, St. Catharines, Ont.; given name: Paul Edward; m. Anastasia Mouzas; c. Brian, Renee; Arizona State; umpire, real estate broker; minor ball Houston, California chains; umpired California, Eastern, Pacific Coast Leagues; 1st ML game '73; mem. NL umpiring staff from '74; '78 all-star, '77, '81-82 championship series, '79 World Series games; res. El Cajon, Calif.

RUOFF, Bernie (football); b. 12 Oct 1951, Hiedenheim-Wurtemberg, W. Germany; given name: Bernd; m. Colette; Syracuse, BA; sr. yr. MVP; raised in Kitchener; kicking specialist; pro NE Patriots; CFL Winnipeg '75-79, Hamilton '80-87; 4 EFC, 2 WFC scoring titles; 4 div. punting titles; 4 times EFC all-star; 1 Grey Cup winner; kicked 58yd FG '75; Ticats career FG, single season points, all-time scoring records; dog breeder; last known res. Fisherville, Ont.

RUPERTUS, Glenn (biathlon); b. 26 Jul 1964, Wetaskwin, Alta.; given name: Glenn Richard; m. Dorothy Joan Denroche; c. Stephanie Kathryn May; Augustana BA; Cdn Forces; nicknamed Rockit; began as cross-country skier '77; competitive skier, runner to '80; mem. ntl biathlon team from '83; co0mpeted '88, '92, '94 Winter Olympics; 6 world championships; 4 world military championships; competed World Cup circuit from '86; 2 NA 10km, 1 20km, 1 relay titles; 6 ntl 20km gold, 2 silver, 2 bronze, 2 10km gold, 2 silver, 3 bronze, 6 ntl relay gold; won 20km, 10km gold '96 Australian championships; Level IV coaching certificate; 4 Biathlon Canada athlete of yr, 9 Alta. Achievement awards, '94 award of excellence; Rudy Setz Memorial award '98; res. Courtenay, B.C.

RUSEDSKI, Greg (tennis); b. 6 Sep 1973, Montreal, Que.; lefthander; turned pro '91; won 1st major tournament at Newport, R.I., '93; ranked 1 in Canada '93; mem. Cdn Davis Cup team; TC player of '93, most improved player award '93; opted to compete for England '95; reached final '97 US Open before bowing to Patrick Rafter; ranked 10 ATP rankings '97; defeated #1 Pete Sampras to win '98 French

Open; European Community title '98; BBC British sports personality of '97; res. London, Eng.

RUSSEL, Blair (hockey); b. 17 Sep 1880, Montreal, Que., d. 7 Dec 1961, Montreal, Que.; all-star Montreal Victorias 1899-1908; scoring 110 goals in 67 games; once 7 goals in single game, also 6 and 5 goal games; mem. Hockey Hall of Fame.

RUSSEL, Jeff (football); b. 27 Oct 1900, Ouray, Colo.; d. 3 May 1926, Montreal, Que.; given name: Jeffrey Cameron; Lower Canada Coll., RMC, McGill; power co. lineman; starred as halfback RMC '17-20, McGill '20-22, Montreal Winged Wheelers '22-25; killed while repairing power lines during a storm; trophy in his honor awarded annually to EFC outstanding player; mem. Cdn Football Hall of Fame.

RUSSELL, Ernest (hockey); b. 21 Oct 1883, Montreal, Que., d. 23 Feb 1963, Montreal, Que.; capt. Sterling hockey jrs., MAAA football jrs. ntl titles same year; sr. hockey Winged Wheelers '05; Montreal Wanderers '06-14; 180 goals in 98 games, 3-goal hat-tricks 5 successive games, 42 goals in 9 games '07; mem. 4 Stanley Cup winners; 2 league scoring titles, once scored in 10 consecutive games; mem. Hockey Hall of Fame.

RUSSELL, Ernestine (gymnastics); b. 10 Jun 1938, Windsor, Ont.; div, John Carter; m. Jim Weaver; c. Kelly; Michigan State, BSc; coach, PE prof.Florida; ntl women's gymnastic champion '55-60; 4 times NA champion; mem. '56, '60 Olympic teams; 5 golds '58 Pan-Am Games; competed '59 world championships; Velma Springstead Trophy '55-57; authored several gymnastics books; coach US women's gym team '77 FISU, '80 Olympics; mem. Cdn Amateur, Windsor-Essex County Sports Hall of Fame; res. Gainesville, Fla.

RUTHERFORD, Jim (hockey/administration); b. 17 Feb 1949, Beeton, Ont.; div.; c. Andrea; goal tender Hamilton jrs; pro Fort Worth (CHL) '69-71, Hershey '71-72; NHL Detroit '70-71, '74-81, '82-83, Pittsburgh '71-74, Toronto '81, Los Angeles '81-82; NHL record: 457 scheduled games, 25,895min, 1576ga, 14so, 8 playoff games, 440min, 28ga; 5yrs Detroit player rep. mem. Team Canada '77, '79 worlds; on retirement from play joined Compuware serving as dir. hockey operations; key role in Compuware purchase Windsor Spitfires '84; GM Spitfires '84-89; reached Memorial Cup finals '88; led Compuware efforts to bring Detroit 1st OHL franchise '89; pres./GM Hartford '94; 1st GM Carolina; OHL exec. of '87-88; CHL exec. of '87; res. Cary, N.C.

RUTTAN, Jack (hockey); b. 5 Apr 1889, Winnipeg, Man., d. 7 Jan 1973, Winnipeg, Man.; Winnipeg juvenile title '05-06; St. John's College '07-08 Man. University HL title; Man. Varsity '09-10 Winnipeg Sr. HL title; Winnipeg Hockey Club '12-13, won league title, Allan Cup; coach Winnipeg srs. '19-20, UMan '23; officiated Winnipeg Senior League '20-22; mem. Cdn, Man. Hockey halls of fame.

RUYS, Henk (soccer); b. 27 Jan 1934, Veghel, Holland; m. Riek; c. Ingrid, Robert, Steve, Christene; fire fighter; Dutch 3rd div. before emigrating to Canada '57; mem. several

Saskatoon, prov. all-star teams; several scoring titles; coached Saskatoon Hollandia '58; Hollandia rep. Saskatchewan Soccer Assn.; club secty. '59; mem. Saskatoon SA council '59; various administrative roles from local through ntl levels; founding pres. Saskatoon Minor SA '66-74; active referee and referees administrator; Queen's anniversary medal '77; Saskatchewan sport recognition award; Saskatoon and Dist. SA appreciation award; Cdn Youth Soccer Assn. outstanding achievement award; mem. Sask Sports Hall of Fame; res. Coquitlam, B.C.

RYAN, Doc (basketball); b. 30 Jun 1950, Orangestad, Dutch Antilles; given name: Peter; Florida A&M; Quebec (Trois-Rivieres), St. Francis Xavier, Dalhousie; women's basketball coach; mem. CYO titlist '58-59, gold medal team '70 Canada Winter Games; Rutger League all-star '72; mem. Knoxville Coll. SIAC champions '72-73; Florida A&M '75-76; CIAU leading scorer UQTR '76-77; all-Cdn, all-conf. '76-77, AUAA all-conf. '77-79; mem. Olympic teams '76, '80; coach Dalhousie, St.FX; mem. ntl sr. champions '80-81, ntl tournament MVP; '79-80 "Do it with the Doc" international 3 on 3 champion; outstanding NS adult male athlete '81; res. Antigonish, N.S.

RYAN, Doreen (all-around); b. 27 Sep 1931, Edmonton, Alta.; given name: Doreen Delores McLeod; div; c. Ken, Debby, Dave; UAlta, BEd; PE consultant; 39 major speed skating titles include 17 Alta. (indoor, outdoor), 7 Sask., 2 Man. and 10 ntl championships; tied for NA title '52, runnerup '62; ntl jr. '47, intermediate '49, sr. '51, '53-54, '57-59, '62-63; mem. '60, '64 Olympic, '64 Worlds teams; won '59 Olympic time trials, '64 Swiss International time trials; jr. long jump, high jump, 60m Edmonton Highland Games; scholastic 60m, 100m, 60m hurdles, high jump; ntl discus, 60m hurdles, 100m, softball throw '47; Myrtle Cook Trophy for highest aggregate points; sr. 100m, long jump '48 Highland Games, discus, 60m, 100m scholastic meet; sr. 220yds, discus '49 Highland Games; mem. Edmonton HS, prov. title basketball teams; city softball teams; HS badminton singles titles; swam backstroke competitively 1 year; mgr. ntl t&f team '74 Commonwealth, '76, '80 Olympic, '79 Pan-Am Games; administrative duties '78, '82 Commonwealth Games, Alta. Sportswoman of '64; 1st women inducted into Edmonton Sports Hall of Fame; mem. Cdn Speed Skating, Alta. Sports halls of fame; res. Edmonton, Alta.

RYAN, Joe (football); b. 1900, Starbuck, Man., d. 2 Jun 1979, Victoria, B.C.; given name: Joseph Bernard; m. Helen Katherine Killeen; c. Mary Jo, Kathleen, James Timothy, Cynthia Ann; securities officer, football administrator; promoted rugby football Winnipeg '31-35, amalgamated Winnipeg Rugby, St. John's Club '32; imported Carl Cronin from Notre Dame as player-coach and won '33 title, Grey Cup (first for West) '35; developed intercity league '36-40; managed Winnipeg club 7 of first 11 years of operation winning 6 league titles, 3 Grey Cups; 14yrs mem. CRU rules comm.; with Lew Hayman, Eric Cradock, Leo Dandurand helped establish Montreal Alouettes; scouted talent like Frank Filchock, Joey Pal, Pete Thodos, Rod Pantages to help Als win '49 Grey Cup; GM Edmonton 5 years; launched night football Winnipeg; hon. life mem.

Winnipeg Football Club, Winnipeg FC Alumni Assoc.; CRU plaque for service to football in Canada; mem. Canadian Football, Canada's Sports halls of fame.

RYAN, Pat (curling); b. 28 Sep 1955, Winnipeg, Man.; given name: Pat John Charles; m. Penny; c. Lynsay; management accountant; Man. jr. men's title '73; 2nd for Paul Devlin '79 Brier; all-star skip, lost title in extra end playoff to Al Hackner '85 Brier; finalist '86 ntl mixed; skip '88-89 Brier winners, 3rd for Rick Folk '93-94 Brier, '94 winner; skip '89, 3rd '94 world title rinks; Dick Ellis team award '89; mem. Cdn Curling Hall of Fame; res. Kelowna, B.C.

RYAN, Peter (motorsport/skiing); b. 10 Jun 1940, Philadelphia, Pa., d. 2 Jul 1962, Paris, France; as teenager won major Que. ski titles Taschereau, Ryan Cup, Que. Kandahar; 2nd to Buddy Werner US Nationals; mem. ntl water-ski team, among top 5 2 years; won auto racing Vanderbilt Cup, Canadian Grand Prix; injured while competing for Lotus factory team at Reims, France, and died in hospital; mem. Cdn Motorsport Hall of Fame.

RYAN, Tommy (bowling/builder); b. 1882, Guelph, Ont., d. 19 Nov 1961, Toronto, Ont.; m. Ruth Robins; auctioneer, art gallery owner; credited with inventing 5-pin bowling; opened Toronto's 1st bowling house '05; founded Miss Toronto beauty contest; mem. Ont. 5-pin Bowling, Canada's Sports halls of fame.

RYAN, Vinnie (boxing); b. 1 Jul 1939, Dublin, Ireland; m. Valerie; c. Sean, Jackie; master plumber, mechanical contractor; Irish jr./intermediate boxing titles; schoolboy champion for GB; Irish sr. welterweight champion; dir. coaching, pres. Boxing Ontario; exec mem. Cdn Amateur Boxing Assn.; res. Ancaster, Ont.

RYDER, Gus (swimming); b. 11 Jan 1899, Toronto, Ont.; d. 23 May 1991, Toronto, Ont.; given name: Augustus Joseph; m. Phyllis Hamilton; customs broker; jr. hockey Auralee; football Excelsiors, Argos intermediates; rowed 4yrs Argos; represented Canada 4 times internationally in handball; swam in several across-the-bay races Toronto; formed 700-mem. New Toronto (later Lakeshore) swim club; taught thousands of crippled children to swim; personally credited with 47 rescues from drowning; coached Marilyn Bell, Cliff Lumsdon; Canada's man of year twice; US Presidental sports award '75; hon. chief Six-Nations Indian tribe; handball award 70-80 age-group sr. Olympics '76; Argo Rowing Club medal; wide array of honors from service clubs for work on behalf of crippled children; Toronto, Victoria awards of merit; Ont. government medal; mem. Order of Canada; mem. Etobicoke, Mississauga, Toronto Playground, US, Ont. Aquatic, Canada's Sports halls of fame.

RYPIEN, Mark (football); b. 2 Oct 1962, Calgary, Alta.; m. Annette; c. Andrew (d), 2 daughters; Washington State; quarterback ; NFL Washington '87-93, Cleveland '94, St. Louis '95, '97, Philadelphia '96, Atlanta '98; NFL record 100g completed 1461 of 2604 attempts for 18,416yds, 115tds, 88int; 1 Super Bowl victory; res. Post Falls, Idaho.

S

SABOURIN, Jamie (karate); b. 30 Sep 1967, Toronto, Ont.; given name: Jamie Michael; m. Joanne Leclerc; c. Nickolas, Brittany; Algonquin Coll.; investigator/martial arts instructor; became involved in sport age 12; winner of more than 150 tournament titles; competing in 64kg class; WKA world sparring, European FS Forms gold, FS Weapons silver '93; WKA world sparring, FS Weapons gold '95; WKC world FS Forms gold '96; mem. Team Canada '98; 4 Gloucester outstanding achievement awards; res. Nepean, Ont.

SAGEMAN, Randy (diving); b. 9 Apr 1960, London, Ont.; UofT; 4 ntl, 2 CIAU, 1 Ont 1 m titles; 1 CIAU, 1 Ont. 3m titles; mem. '83 FISU, '84 Olympic Games teams; outstanding male diver '81 CIAU championships; res. Toronto, Ont.

SAKIC, Joe (hockey): b. 7 Jul 1969, Burnaby, B.C.; given name: Joseph Steve; m. Debbie; c. Mitchell; part-owner restaurant; centre Swift Current (WHL) '86-88; drafted by Quebec '87; pro Quebec '88-95, Colorado '95-99; WHL rookie '87, twice player of year; Cdn major jr. player of '88; NHL record: (through '99) 792 scheduled games, 375g, 604a, 76 playoff games, 41g, 53a; reached 50-goal plateau with 51 '96; 6 NHL all-star games; team capt. from '92; mem. Team Canada '88 world jr., '90, '93, '94 worlds, '96 World Cup, '98 Olympic teams; Conn Smythe Trophy; '96 Stanley Cup champs; res. Aurora, Co.

SALLY, Kevin (archery); b. 12 May 1972, Richmond Hill, Ont.; mem. ntl team '92-98; ntl outdoor title '95; gold '93 Canada Summer Games; competed '95 Pan-Am Games, World championships, '96 Olympics, Championship of Americas; res. Pickering, Ont.

SALMING, Borje (hockey); b. 17 Apr 1951, Kiruna, Sweden; given name: Anders Borje; m. Margitta; c. Anders; underwear mfgr.; Swedish ntl jr. team, champion Brynas club Swedish Division 1, Swedish ntl team; all-star '73 world amateur championships; pro Toronto '73-89, Detroit '89-90; ended playing days in Sweden '90-94; NHL record: 1148 scheduled games, 150g, 637a, 81 playoff games, 12g, 37a; 1 1st, 5 2nd all-star teams; with clubmate Inge Hammarstrom became first of European stars to attain NHL stardom; rated one of game's finest defensive defencemen; mem. Hockey Hall of Fame; res. Stockholm, Sweden.

SALMOND, Gary (t&f); b. 28 Apr 1947, Vancouver, B.C.; given name: Garfield Donald; Vancouver, district HS hammer champion; ntl record 67.30m (220'9 1/2") since broken by Murray Keating with 67.46; mem. '67 Pan-Am, '70 Commonwealth Games, '69 Pacific Conf. teams; 5 ntl hammer titles; last known res. New Westminster, B.C.

SALTER, Allen (weightlifting); b. 11 Oct 1936, Almonte, Ont.; m. Waveney Morphy; CGA; fed. govt. auditor; ntl bantamweight (123lb) champion '60-63; 280 3/4lb clean and jerk record for that class which stood '63-76; ntl featherweight (132lb) champion '64-66; lightweight champion (148lb) '68; silver bantamweight '62, bronze featherweight '66 Commonwealth Games; mem. 2 World, 1 Olympic Games teams; City of Ottawa crest, Ottawa ACT outstanding amateur athlete award '62; res. Carp, Ont.

SAMIS, John (badminton); b. 15 Nov 1918, Swift Current, Sask.; m. Grace Peggy; c. Page, Julie; retd. investment dealer; 7 Vancouver City, provincial titles; 3 ntl singles titles; ranked 4th in world '41; mem. Canada's 1st international Thomas Cup team; at 15 youngest ntl sr. singles titlist; while serving in Cdn navy competed in British War Relief exhibition matches; mem. BC Sports Hall of Fame; res. W. Vancouver, B.C.

SAMPLE, Bonnie (canoeing); b. 9 Apr 1948, Port Credit, Ont.; given name: Bonnie Jane Buchanan; m. Tim Sample; c: Kirsten, Tomas, Lindsay; McMaster, BA, BPhE, Oregon, MSc; real estate agent; competitive paddler '62-75; coach Mississauga Canoe Club '70-75, Rideau Canoe Club '75-77; ntl canoeing jr. development/sr. team coach '77-83; ntl canoe team program mgr. '84-87; coached Canadian teams '75 NA, '77, '79, '81 jr. worlds, 3 Continental Cups; coached Ont. team Canada Games; CBC-Radio analyst '84 Olympics; Rideau Canoe Club executive of year award; co-chair fencing Ontario winter games; taught program for disabled UofOtt; author *It's Got to be Fun*; res. Barrie, Ont.

SAMPLE, Tim (builder): b. 6 Jul 1947, Barrie, Ont.; m. Bonnie Buchanan; c. Kirsten, Tomas, Lindsay; sports marketing; coached basketball, hockey, soccer to intermediate level '68-97; founder, exec. St. Lambert hockey school; mem. Cdn paddling comm. '78-80; vice-commodore Rideau Canoe Club '78-81; chair. '81 canoe ntls; co-ordinator '93 Ottawa Twining Games; mem. mayor's council '86 Ottawa Commonwealth Games bid; ntl canoe team mgr, 4 world, 2 Olympic Games, 3 Continental Cup, 2 Canada/America Cups, varied international regattas; founder/chair Canada Day international regatta '85-89; fencing chair. '91 Ont. Winter Games; event/volunteer operations chair. '93 world indoor championships; chair. volunteer operations Hockey Canada Cdn Olympic team Ont. tour '93-94; chair. volunteer operations '94 world basketball championships; dir. volunteer operations '97 Special Olympics world winter games; dir. operations review 2001 Peterborough Canada Games feasibility study; dir. Barrie Sports Hall of Fame; event mgr. '96 Fr. Bauer Cup hockey tournament; res. Barrie, Ont.

SAMPLONIUS, Anne (cycling); b. 11 Feb 1968, Grand Rapids, Mich.; UAlta, York; moved to Canada '72; began road racing competitively '92; played competitive women's hockey at UAlta and York; mem. Timex Racing Team; claimed yellow jersey for 2 days at '94 women's Tour de France; silver '94 worlds; competed '94, '98 Commonwealth, '95 Pan-Am Games, '93-94 worlds; res. Brampton, Ont.

SAMPSON, Darryl (football); b. 21 Sep 1963, Scarborough, Ont.; York; def. back; CFL Winnipeg '86-98' 1 Eastern, CFL all-star; 4 Grey Cup finals, 2 winners; res. Winnipeg, Man.

SAMS, Judy (golf): b. 7 Oct 1957, Toronto, Ont.; m. William Ralph Sams; c. Jennifer; Ohio State; as jr. at Ohio State won '79 Midwest region title; '80 Ontario amateur title; turned pro '82; career low round 67; Cdn amateur golfer of '80; res. Sarasota, Fla.

SAMUEL, Randy (soccer): b. 23 Dec 1963, Trinidad & Tobago; given name: Randolph Fitzgerald; centre back; began play age 12 Southam Warriors, Richmond, B.C.; defender Edmonton Eagles '83, Vancouver Whitecaps '83-84, PSV Eindhoven '86-88, Volendam '88-90, Fortuna Sittard '90-96, Port Vale, Harstad, Norway, '96-97, Vancouver 86ers '98; mem. BC -16, -18 Selects, ntl -18; competed in World Cup '86; mem. PSV Eindhoven Dutch title team; made intl debut '83 with Team Canada vs. Hondouras; Canada's all-time leading intl match performer with 82 caps; res. Richmond, B.C.

SANDERLIN, Don (shooting): b. 26 Feb 1933, Viking, Alta.; given name: Donald Edward; m. Rita Zima; c. Roxanna; electrical construction firm owner; skeet shooting specialist; ntl champion '67-69, '71-72; US champion '68, '73; won Olympic trials '68, '72, Pan-Am trials '75; mem. 3 Pan-Am, 2 Olympic, 9 world championships teams; 4 times all-American; res. Edmonton, Alta.

SANDERSON, Derek (hockey): b. 16 Jun 1946, Niagara Falls, Ont.; youth counsellor, hockey broadcaster; Jr. A Niagara Falls; centre Boston '65-74, Philadelphia (WHA) '72, Rangers '74-75, St. Louis '75-77, Vancouver '77, Pittsburgh '78; NHL record: 598 scheduled games, 202g, 250a, 56 playoff games, 18g, 12a; Calder rookie of year trophy '68; mem. 2 Stanley Cup winners; highest paid athlete '73 when he jumped to WHA briefly; earned reputation as bon vivant and addiction to high living, alcohol and drugs led to dissipation of wealth and health; at 38 hired by Boston mayor to work on alcohol and drug abuse commission; res. Boston, Mass.

SANDERSON, Gus (shooting): b. 3 Jan 1929, Ottawa, Ont.; m. Betty Benedict; c. Janet, Jeffrey; retd. engineer; skeet shooting specialist; Ottawa Valley Club, Ont. titles '55; ntl titles '63-64, '66, '74, '79, '83; world title '79; sub-seniors world title '80; 6 Capital of Canada shoot titles; 6 times all-American skeet team; 3 Ottawa ACT skeet shooting awards; mem. Ottawa Sports Hall of Fame; res. Ottawa, Ont.

SANDERSON, Lyle (coaching): b. 8 Nov 1938, Maple Creek, Sask.; given name: Lyle Kingman; m. Carol Wood; c. Michael, Krista; UofSask, BA, MSc; assoc. prof. of PE, UofSask.; middle distance runner; head t&f coach UofSask from '65; 13 conf. team titles; ntl teams coach '76, '80 Olympics, '78 Commonwealth Games; Air Canada amateur coach of yr nominee '77, '79; 1 CIAU X-C coach of yr award; chairman CTFA tech. comm. 3 years; CTFA multiple event coordinator; t&f coach UofSask.; mem. Saskatoon Sports Hall of Fame; res. Saskatoon, Sask.

SANDS, Johnny (speed skating): b. 17 Apr 1933, Saskatoon, Sask.; given name: John Valance; halfback Saskatoon Hilltops '51-53; ntl jr title '53; ntl outdoor titles '55, '57-58, shared '53 title with Frank Stack; mem. '56, '60 Olympic teams; ntl 220yds record '56-64, 500m record '56-68; coach Que. '60s; mem. Cdn Speed Skating, Saskatoon Sports halls of fame; res. Mississauga, Ont.

SANDULO, Joey (boxing): b. 5 May 1931, Ottawa, Ont.; given name: Joseph Oleg; m. Mary Theresa Lewis; c. Patrick, Mary Jane, Kelly; retd. cartographer; Ottawa Golden Gloves novice title '46; Que. Golden Gloves 106lb novice, Jack Dempsey Trophy '47; Ont., Eastern Canadian, ntl flyweight titles '48; youngest boxer to represent Canada in Olympics '48; Cdn Forces, BC bantam titles '49; with Gord Montagano operated boxing classes Ottawa '50-53; started Ottawa RA fitness program '59; launched Beaver Boxing Club '74, pres. '75; ring record shows 5 losses in 75 bouts; refereed pro, amateur boxing bouts from '53; Ottawa ACT sportsman of '80; mem. Canadian Boxing, Ottawa Sports halls of fame; res. Nepean, Ont.

SANDUSKY, Jim (football): b. 9 Sep 1961, Othello, Wash.; m.; c. 2; Nevada, San Diego State; football coach; 1st team all-Western; played in Japan Bowl; MVP Hula Bowl; coach, wide receiver; drafted USFL Philadelphia Stars, NFL Detroit '84; joined CFL BC '84-87, Edmonton '88, '91-96; NFL Seattle '89-90 but sat out with injuries; CFL record: 170 scheduled games, 70tds, 1 2-point convert, 586 receptions for 9737yds, 69tds, 147 punt returns for 1399yds, 1td; 3 Western, 2 CFL all-star; 3 Grey Cup finals, 2 winners; asst. coach BC '97; active in Athletes in Action; res. Vancouver, B.C.

SANFORD, Aubrey (soccer): b. 4 Sep 1905, Nanaimo, B.C.; d. 5 Jan 1985, Vancouver, B.C.; m. Muriel Audrey; c. Judith Ann, Anthony Albert; UBC; retd. chartered accountant; 45yr involvement with soccer; mem. 3 ntl champions with Westminster Royals '28, '30-31; managed same club to ntl titles '53, '55; CSA pres. '69-72; runnerup Air Canada Amateur Sport Award '72; mem. BC Sports Hall of Fame.

SANKEY, Derek (basketball): b. 17 Dec 1948, Vancouver, B.C.; given name: Derek William; m. Irene Sigismund; c. Jordan, Adrienne; UBC, BA, MEd; teacher, ex-mgr. education BC Central Credit Union; HS basketball '60-66, 2 city titles; mem. ntl jr. men's title team '67; UBC Thunderbirds '67-71, ntl champions '70; Vancouver sr. men's Dogwood League '72-79; MVP, all-star '75; ntl team '70-76; mem. '71, '75 Pan-Am, '76 Olympics, '70 World championships, '73 FISU Games teams; coached UBC jr. varsity '71-72, '75-77, HS teams '72-75, '77-98; mem. UBC Block Club, pres. '71; mem. Cdn Basketball Hall of Fame; res. Richmond, B.C.

SAPUNJIS, Dave (football): b. 7 Sep 1967, Toronto, Ont.; UWO, BA; oil co. sales rep.; slotback; mem. '90 Vanier Cup winner; CFL Calgary '90-96; CFL record: 120 scheduled games, 47tds, 2 2-point converts, 460 receptions for 6586yds, 46tds, 10 punt returns for 124yds, 1td, 9 playoff games, 3tds; 1 Western, 1 Northern, 2 CFL all-star; Dr. Beattie Martin trophy '93; Jeff Nicklin Memorial trophy '95; Lew Hayman trophy '95; CFL outstanding Cdn '93, '95; most valuable Cdn '91-92, '95 Grey Cup; 9 playoff games, 3tds; 3 Grey Cup finals, 1 winner; res. Calgary, Alta.

SASKAMOOSE, Fred (hockey): b. 25 Dec 1933, Sandy Lake Indian Reserve, Sask.; given name: Frederick George; m. Loretta Isbester; c. Algin, Phyllis (d), Garth, Beverley, Kevin, Karen, Derrick, Neil, Ryan; farmer/hunter; learned to skate on bobskates as child; attended St. Michael residential school in Duck Lake age 8; mem. St. Michael provincial midget title team '49; 4yrs with Moose Jaw (WHL); MVP '53; jumped from jr. to Chicago (NHL) at 19 playing in 11 games; 1st Treaty Indian to play in NHL; played in minors with New Westminster, Calgary, Chicoutimi, Kamloops; refusal of Chicago to give him release to regain amateur status cost him opportunity to join Penticton Vees for Allan Cup and World championships; Kamloops paid $10,000 for his release and he remained with that sr. club 7yrs; hon. chief Kamloops Indian reserve; became involved in Indian leadership serving as band councilor several years, 7yrs chief; developed Indian hockey schools for youth; established Sask. Indian bantams travelling team; builder Indian Sports/Recreation programs.facilities; nicknamed 'Chief Thunder Stick'; mem. Sask. First Nations Sports Hall, Meadow Lake Sask Wall of Fame; res. Shell Lake, Sask.

SATHER, Glen (hockey): b. 2 Sep 1943, High River, Alta.; given name: Glen Cameron; m. Ann; c. Justin, Shannon; hockey exec.; left wing Edmonton jrs., Memphis, Oklahoma City; NHL '66-76 with Boston, Pittsburgh,Rangers, St. Louis, Montreal, Minnesota; Oilers (WHA) '76; NHL record: 658 scheduled games, 80g, 113a, 72 playoff games, 1g, 5a; turned to coaching '77; coach Team Canada '84 Canada Cup; GM Team Canada '94, '96 Worlds; mem. management comm. '87 Rendez-Vous; coach/GM Edmonton Oilers '78-89, pres./GM '89-99; architect of 5 Edmonton Stanley Cup winners; Jack Adams coach of '86 award; Fr. David Bauer award '97; 1 of only 6 coaches in NHL history to coach 5 all-star games; mem. Alta. Sports, Cdn Hockey halls of fame; res. Edmonton/Banff, Alta.

SAUNDERS, Alex (football): b. 20 Apr 1929, Stratford, Ont.; given name: Robert Alexander; m. Beverley Joynt; c. Alex, Julia, Tim, Sheila; CF Staff College; retd. military officer, public servant; as teenager earned Ottawa all-star guard award, Rough Riders outstanding lineman award; Ottawa, Ontario all-star centre '48; played guard, centre, linebacker with Rough Riders '48, rookie lineman of year nominee; moved into coaching ranks in Ottawa-Carleton MFA '72-81; Football Ont. Northeastern coach of '80; held varied exec. roles with North Eastern Region Amateur Football organization '81-88; mem. '84-85 Camp Olympia coaching staff; offensive line coach, interim GM Ottawa Bootleggers NAMLFA runnerup '89; coach 2 Sir Robert Borden HS jr. National Capital champions; ntl Level III coaching certificate; player/coach Cdn Forces Western Canada basketball title team '56; mem. Rivers, Man., Air Training centre lacrosse team; shot put, relay specialist in t&f; forces rugby '57-62; forces volleyball '65-73; exec. Rough Riders Alumni Assn.; res. Nepean, Ont.

SAUNDERS, Billy (baseball): b. 26 May 1946, Fredericton, N.B.; m. Mary; civil technician; one of NB's most successful coaches in ntl competition (43-30) winning 2 gold, 1 silver, 3 bronze medals; coach/manager/owner Marysville Royals for 3 prov, 3 Atlantic championships; ntl championship silver, bronze medals; coached 1st ever NB Cdn title team '81; instrumental in forming NB jr. baseball league; founding mem. NB baseball coaches assn.; 9ys part-time NY Yankees scout; 2 Baseball NB coach of yr awards; mem. NB, Fredericton, Saint John, NB Baseball halls of fame; res. Fredericton, N.B.

SAUNDERS, Bryan (t&f); b. 9 Jul 1952, Trinidad; div. Andrea Lynch; c. Shannon; m. Metta Gordon; c. Dorice, Blaine; North Platt (Neb), Bishop State (Mobile), Long Beach State Coll.; bakery business; began racing at 21; mem. Scarborough Optimist TC; 400m specialist; ntl sr. record '77; mem. '75, '79, '83 Pan-Am, '76, '80, '84 Olympic, '78 Commonwealth, '75, '77 FISU Games. '77, '79 World Cup teams; bronze '75 FISU Games; 5 ntl 400m titles; retd. '84; coached HS girls 3yrs Compton, Calif.; res. Willowdale, Ont.

SAUNDERS, Dyce (cricket): b. 22 Mar 1862, Guelph, Ont., d. 12 Jun 1930, London, Ont.; c. Thomas (d); Trinity College; finest wicket keeper in Canadian history; capt. Trinity Coll.; at 19 mem. ntl team vs. US; mem. 12 international match teams; final international match at 43; starred 1887 UK tour; considered 'Grand Old Man' of Canadian cricket.

SAUNDERS, Jim (boxing): b. 4 Jan 1932, Winnipeg, Man.; given name: James Allan; m. Marion; c. James, Cole, June; retd. truck driver; Man. amateur champion, ntl champion '49, '52-53; mem. '52 Olympic team; retd. from ring '61; honored by COA '76; nicknamed 'Babyface'; res. Winnipeg, Man.

SAUNDERS, Sandy (rowing): b. 25 Jan 1912, Hamilton, Ont.; given name: Thomas Vassar Claude; m. Florence Papps; c. Claude, Lois, Janice; retd. Stelco; 17yr competitive career; stroked Leander Boat Club jr. 8s to '34 ntl title, Ned Hanlan Trophy; identical honors heavy 8s '35, '39; stroked heavy 8s to Dominion Day, CNE regatta victories '37-38; mem. '36, '48 (alternate) Olympics; won Olympic trials '39 but '40 games cancelled due to WW2; Henley, ntl junior double sculls '40; Henley single sculls '44; ORFU football Hamilton Tiger-Cubs '37; mgr. '60 Olympic crews; mgr. Leander BC '33-38; Leander rowing chair. '39-46, v-p. '48; charter mem. Central Ont. Rowing Assn.; hon. pres. '54-58, secty. '58-66; mem. exec. Cdn Secondary School RA '53-61, pres. '61-62; Leander rep. to CAAO '49-52, v-p. '52-56, pres. '57-58, p-pres. '58-60, hon. pres. from '92; Cdn Henley regatta chair. '52-98; starter, referee '49-98; 1st Cdn international referee '60 Olympics; life mem. Leander BC; Argonaut RC club award; Ottawa RC award; St. Catharines RC award; B'nai B'rith, Shamrock Boystown, CAAO president's awards; 3 Ont. achievement awards; CAAO award of merit; Centennial Medal; life mem., alumni award St. Catharines RC; mem. Order of Canada, Canada's Sports Hall of Fame; res. Hamilton, Ont.

SAUNDERS, William (horse racing): b. 13 Apr 1915, Calgary, Alta; m. Marguerite Chisholm; horseman; nicknamed 'Smoky'; began riding career '32 in Calgary area; gained prominence riding Omaha to throughbred racing's triple crown (Kentucky Derby, Preakness, Belmont Stakes) '35; recorded victories in Louisiana Derby, Detroit

Derby, Chicago Derby, San Juan Capistrano Handicap, Fashion Stakes, Saratoga Handicap; retired from saddle '50 to serve as race steward, placing judge, patrol judge; New York Turf Writers' Man of Year; mem. Canadian Horse Racing Hall of Fame; res. Hallandale, Fla.

SAUVÉ, Gordon (boxing); b. 16 Mar 1906, St. Zotique, Que.; m. Blanche Brisset; c. Laurent; retd.; gained 1st boxing training through Mike Gibbons correspondence course; 1st novice title MAAA; mem. Palestre Nationale training under Joe Flanagan, Gene Brosseau; 1st rate amateur in '30s; national amateur bantamweight (118lbs) title; never knocked down or out in his career; retiring from competition he became highly regarded referee; when Que. boxing commission overruled one of his decisions he quit officiating for QABA; officiated national title bouts for CBF; coach national boxing team '48 Olympics; AAU of C boxing official; citations from AAU of C, Olympic Club; 15yrs chief QABA referee, 10yrs chief judge, 10yrs professional referee; res. Verdun, Que.

SAVAGE, Marilyn (coaching); b. 3 Jun 1934, Toronto, Ont.; given name: Marilyn Florence Charters; m. Frederick James Savage; c. Frederick James; UofT, BPHE; teaching master Seneca College; coach ntl women's gymnastics teams '66-70 world championships, '67 Pan-Am, '68, '72 Olympic, '67-75 Canada Games teams; coach Scarborough Winstonettes gymnastics club '64-78; coached 11 competitors to Olympic status; coached ntl champions Jennifer Diachun, Nancy McDonnell; mem. National Advisory Council on Fitness, Amateur Sport '68-77; founding mem., dir. Coaching Assn. of Canada '70-78; founder Seneca College coaching program, Canada's 1st sports school; runnerup Air Canada coach of '73 award; mem. COA '68-81; Ont. achievement awards '69, '71; Centennial Medal '67; Jubilee Medal '77; res. Hillsborough, Ont.

SAVAGE, Paul (curling); b. 25 Jun 1947, Toronto, Ont; given name: Allin Paul; m. Barbara Lee; c. Bradley, Lisa; Seneca College; partner Sporteck Software, '65 Ont. Schoolboy title; Ont. jr. title '66; 7 times Ont. Brier rep.; skipped winning provincial Consols rinks '70, '73, '74, '77, '87; 3rd with Ed Werenich's '83-84 Ont. Tankard, '83 Brier, Silver Broom champions; won '78 CBC Classic; author *"Canadian Curling Hack to House"* ('74); mem. Hamilton World Curling comm.; Dick Ellis team award '83; mem. Cdn Curling Hall of Fame; res. Markham, Ont.

SAVARD, Denis (hockey); b. 4 Feb 1961, Pointe Gatineau, Que.; m. Mona; c. Tanya Lee; hockey coach; ctr Verdun Jr; 1st pick Chicago '80 draft; pro Chicago '80-90, '95-97, Montreal '90-93, Tampa Bay '93-95; QMJHL all-star, MVP '80; 1 2nd team NHL all-star; mem. 1 Stanley Cup winner; NHL record: 1196 scheduled games, 473g, 865a, 169 playoff games, 66g, 109a; jersey #18 retd. by Chicago; Chicago development coach/community relations ambassador; mem. Hockey Hall of Fame; res. Chicago, Ill.

SAVARD, Serge (hockey); b. 22 Jan 1946, Montreal, Que.; hockey exec. realtor; jr. Montreal Canadiens; defenceman NHL Canadiens '66-81, Winnipeg '81-83; Team Canada '72, '76; NHL record: 1040 scheduled games, 106g, 333a, 130 playoff games, 19g, 49a; mem. 7 Stanley Cup winners;

Conn Smythe Trophy '69, Bill Masterton Trophy '79; once 2nd team all-star; v-p./managing dir./GM Canadiens '83-95; consultant Expos, Alouettes; Officer Order of Canada '94; mem. Hockey Hall of Fame; res. Montreal, Que.

SAWCHUK, Bill (swimming); b. 8 Jan 1959, Roblin, Man.; Florida.; swim coach; began competitive swimming career with Thunder Bay Thunderbolts '73; mem. ntl team '75-82; close to 40 top 3 finishes in ntl, interntl competitions; several ntl records; Pan-Am Games 200 IM bronze '75, 3 silver 2 bronze '79; 7 medals '78 Commonwealth Games, including 2 medley gold; competed '76 Olympics, qualified for '80 boycotted Olympics; Southeastern Conf. swimmer of '80; turned to coaching following '82 retirement; mem. Cdn, Ont. Aquatic, NWO Sports halls of fame; res. Vancouver, B.C.

SAWCHUK, Terry (hockey); b. 28 Dec 1929, Winnipeg, Man, d. 31 May 1970, New York, N.Y.; given name: Terrance Gordon; div.; c. 7; goaler Winnipeg Rangers jrs., Windsor Spitfires jrs; USHL, AHL, NHL rookie of year awards; NHL Detroit '49-55, '57-64, '68-69, Boston '55-56, Toronto '64-67, Los Angeles '67-68, Rangers '69-70; NHL record: 971 scheduled games, 953 complete games, 2401 goals-against, 2.52 avg., 103so, 106 playoff games, 267 goals-against, 2.64 avg., 12 so; mem. 4 Stanley Cup winners; 3 times 1st, 4 times 2nd team all-star; Vezina Trophy 4 times (1 shared with Johnny Bower); died following altercation with teammate Ron Stewart (cleared of guilt); jersey #1 retd. by Red Wings; Winnipeg arena named in his honor; mem. Cdn, Man. Hockey halls of fame.

SAWICKI, Ted (lacrosse); b. 31 Jan 1962, St. Catharines, Ont.; teacher; ntl team goalie from '81; mem. Niagara Warriors '81, St. Catharines Jr. A '82-84, Victoria Payless '84-87, Brooklin Redmen '88-89, Oshawa Blue Knights '88-90, Detroit Turbos from '89; mem. Niagara Founders Cup winner '81, Brooklin Mann Cup winner '88; defensive MVP award '83 Lacrosse International tournament, Oshawa '90; mem. 3 ntl title teams; 3 ntl championship all-star goalie; mem. MILL '91 title team; 3 MILL 1st team all-star awards; res. St. Catharines, Ont.

SAWULA, Lorne (volleyball); b. 19 Feb 1947, Edmonton, Alta.; given name: Lorne William; UAlta, BPhE, MA, PhD; hi-performance dir. Australian VBA; mem. '67 Alta. Canada Winter Games volleyball team; mem. UAlta men's volleyball team '64-69; WCIAA all-star '64-69; mem. Alta. champion Edmonton Phoenix, Dalhousie Volleyball Clubs '69-74; coach UAlta men's team '71-73, Dalhousie women's Montreal, Atlantic champions '73-75, UBC Thunderbirds CIAU men's titlists '75-77, UofOtt '78-81; asst. coach women's ntl team '74-75; coach ntl jr. women's team '76; tech. dir. CVA '77-84; ntl women's coach '81-85; hi-perf. dir. VB Canada '86-90; head coach Swiss women's team '91-93; sole Cdn mem. International Volleyball Assn., Coaches Commission; appointed master coach '79; authored most of CVA coaching manuals from levels 1-4; has given coaching clinics in more than 40 countries; res. Sydney, Australia.

SAX, Joe (t&f); b. 5 Nov 1952, Toronto, Ont.; given name: Joseph Anton; UofT, BPHE, UWO, BEd; teacher; ntl record 3000m steeplechase '74 with 8:36.8; mem. '78

Commonwealth Games team; ntl 3,000m title '78; Tor. Star Invitational 1500m '79; 3rd Tor. Marathon '80; res. Toronto, Ont.

SAZIO, Ralph (football); b. 22 Jul 1922, South Orange, N.J.; given name: Ralph Joseph; m. Rose Louise Matthews; c. Mark, Peggy; College of William and Mary, BSc, Columbia, MA; retd. football exec.; capt. William and Mary football team; pro Brooklyn Dodgers; tackle, asst. coach Hamilton '50, head coach '63-67; CFL coaching record: 59-25-1, 4 Grey Cup finals, 3 winners; GM, dir. Tiger-Cats '68-72; club pres. '73-81; CFL pres. '75; pres. Argos '81-89; mem. Cdn Football Hall of Fame; res. Burlington, Ont.

SCAPINELLO, Ray (officiating/hockey); b. 5 Nov 1946, Guelph, Ont.; m. Maureen Flaherty; c. Ryan; joined NHL as linesman '71; worked 3 NHL all-star games, 17 consec. Stanley Cup finals, Canada Cup, Challenge Cup, Rendez-Vous '87, Olympics '98; NHL record: (through '98) 2090 scheduled, 347 playoff games; low handicap golfer; active in Make A Wish Foundation activities; res. Guelph, Ont.

SCHALM, Sherraine (fencing): b. 21 Jun 1975, Brooks, Alta.; UofOtt; began fencing at 14; excelled at all age categories; won ntl cadet, 2 junior épée titles; U of O MVP awards '94-95; ranked #1 sr. nationally; competed '95 (team bronze), '99 (team silver) Pan-Am Games; mem. ntl women's épée team from '94; Ottawa Shield women's épée title '98; Elite Circuit, French Circuit gold, 2 World Cup bronze '99; NA Cup silver '98; 6th world sr. championships '99, best ever by Cdn fencer; res. Ottawa, Ont./Brooks, Alta.

SCHERER, Sue (hockey/softball): b. 27 Aug 1956, Kitchener, Ont.; given name: Susan; Guelph, BA; consultant; mem. Cdn women's softball teams '83 (gold), '87 (bronze) Pan-Am Games; competed in '82, '86 world softball championships; capt. '90, mem. '92 Team Canada world ice hockey champions; coach Guelph varsity women's hockey team '93-96; Fair Play Canada ambassador '91-98; Ont. mission staff '93, '97 Canada summer games; CIAU planning comm. ntl coaching school for women '93-98; Met. Life foundation for athletic scholarships comm. '94-98; CAAWS board mem. '94-98; Johnny F. Bassett Memorial award '96; program coordinator F.A.M.E. '91-95, program consultant '95-96; Women onn Move award '98; consultant Scherer Energy Unlimited from '96; res. London, Ont.

SCHLEGEL, Elfi (gymnastics); b. 17 May 1964, Toronto, Ont.; Florida State; coach, broadcaster; 3 all-American, 11 NCAA Southeast regional, 4 Southeast Conf. titles; 4 Ont. titles; '78 national, Commonwealth champion; team gold, silver uneven bars, vault, bronze all-around '79 Pan-Am Games; mem. '80 Olympic, 4 world championships teams; bronze vault '80 World Cup; gold vault, bronze all-around, uneven bars '81 New Zealand Games; 4 gold '81 Canada vs Great Britain; 5 gold Canada vs Norway '81; silver beam '81 Ennia Gold Cup; Cdn FISU Games teams '83, '85; asst. coach Florida; Olympic games TV commentator; Ont. Gymnastics Fed. special achievement award '85; last known res. Florida.

SCHLEIMER, Joseph (wrestling): b. 31 May 1909, Austria; d. 23 Nov 1988, Mississauga, Ont.; m. Margaret;

c. Ewin; retd. architectural draftsman, manufacturer wood products and construction; ntl 164lb title '34-36; gold '34 BEG; bronze '36 Olympics; coach ntl wrestling team '59, '63 Pan-Am Games, '62 Commonwealth Games, world championships, '64 Olympic; chair. AAU of C wrestling comm. '60-64; pres. OAWF '55-60; wrestling coach Broadview YMCA Toronto '50-71; Ont. achievement awards '70-72, '75 for service to sport; dir. CAWA many years; mem. Cdn Amateur Sports, Cdn Amateur Wrestling halls of fame.

SCHMALZ, Tubby (administration); b. 19 Dec 1916, Breslau, Ont., d. 7 Dec 1981, Walkerton, Ont.; given name: Clarence; m. Dorothy Wolfe; c. Marilyn, Susan, Ann, Jacqueline; innkeeper; jr. hockey Kitchener, Brantford; coached, managed Walkerton OHA int. champions '54-55; mem. OHA exec. 25yrs, 3 terms pres.; commissioner OMJHL '74-79; board mem. Hockey Canada; board chairman CAHA; instituted coaching, refereeing clinics in OHA, a program adopted throughout CAHA; OHA Gold Stick award, CAHA meritorious service award; life mem. OHA; 17yrs. mem. Walkerton town council, reeve at time of death.

SCHMIDT, Milt (hockey); b. 5 Mar 1918, Kitchener, Ont.; given name: Milton Conrad; m. Marie Peterson; c. Milton Jr., Nancy; retd. hockey exec., Boston Madison Square Garden Club mgr.; ctr Bruins '36-55, excluding 3 WW2 seasons RCAF, mem. Allan Cup champion Ottawa Hurricanes; centered famed Boston Kraut Line of Woody Dumart, Bobby Bauer; NHL record: 776 scheduled games, 229g, 336a, 80 playoff games, 24g, 25a; NHL scoring title '40; Hart Trophy (MVP) '52; mem. 2 Stanley Cup winners; 3 times 1st team, once 2nd team all-star; coached Bruins '55-61, '62-66, also GM; coach-GM Washington in NHL expansion program '73-78; served as corporate season ticket sales chief Bruins; mem. Hockey, Canada's Sports halls of fame; res. Dover, Mass.

SCHMIDT-FOSTER, Angela (skiing); b. 6 Jan 1960, Woodstock, Ont. m. Don Foster; c. Joey, Stephen, Suzanne; self-employed; top Cdn jr. cross-country skier '77-79; ntl cross-country ski team mem. '76-92; competed 4 Olympic, world championships; 1st Cdn to crack top 3 world cup competition '87; top Canadian in most international competitions; 12yrs on WC circuit; runs Jackrabbit program; Kerri Lotion award of excellence '91; Midland highway junction bears her name; res. Midland, Ont.

SCHMIRLER, Sandra (curling): b. 11 Jun 1963, Biggar, Sask.; given name: Sandra Marie Peterson; m. Shannon England Schmirler; c. Sara, Jenna; leisure centre supervisor; began curling age 13; won '92 Sask. mixed title; 3 Sask. women's championships; skipped Saskatchewan to Scott Tournament of Hearts titles '93-94, '97; 1st to skip 3 world curling title rinks; skipped rink to '98 Olympic gold; skipped *TSN* women's skins game winner '98; res. Regina, Sask.

SCHNEIDER, Angela (rowing): b. 28 Oct 1959, St. Thomas, Ont.; UofT; asst. dean ethics/equity UWO; sweep 2 Cdn Henley coxed 4s, 8s crews; 1 ntl coxed 4s, 8s; 2 Dominion Day, Head of Charles regatta coxed 8s titlists; mem. silver coxed 4s '84 Olympics; res. London, Ont.

SCHNEIDER, Bert (boxing); b. 1 Jul 1897, Cleveland, Ohio; d. 20 Feb 1986, Stanwood, Wash.; given name: Albert; m. Mary Ellen Henderson (d.); US immigration service; with Montreal Swimming Club water polo team, skier, diver, swimmer and boxer; joined Montreal Casquette Club training under Eugene Brosseau; MAAA welterweight title, 1 city title 2 ntl titles; gold '20 Olympics scoring 4 wins in 3 days; 90 pro bouts; mem. Canadian Boxing, Canada's Sports, Amateur Sports halls of fame.

SCHNURR, Paula (t&f): b. 15 Jan 1964, Kirkland Lake, Ont.; McMaster; teacher; middle distance runner; represented Canada '92, '96 Olympic, '94 Commonwealth Games; double gold '88 CIAU championships; 2 ntl 3000m, 2 1500m, 1 800m titles; silver 1500m '94 Commonwealth Games; McMaster female athlete of 1985; res. Burlington, Ont.

SCHOENFELD, Jim (hockey/coaching); b. 4 Sep 1952, Galt, Ont,; given name: James Grant; m. Theresa; c. Justin, Katie, Adam, Nathan; hockey coach; def. Niagara Falls Flyers jr; pro AHL Cincinnati, NHL Buffalo '72-81, '84-85, Detroit '81-83, Boston '83-84; NHL playing record: 719 scheduled games, 51g, 204a, 75 playoff games, 3g, 13a; youngest team capt. to that time '74; 2nd team all-star '80; NHL's top rookie defenceman '72; played in 2 all-star games; launched coaching career Rochester (AHL) '84; NHL with Buffalo '85-86, New Jersey '87-90, Washington '93-97, Phoenix '97-99; NHL record (through '98) 498 scheduled games, 217-215-66, 50 playoff games, 23-27; *ESPN* hockey analyst; mem. Sabres Hall of Fame; res. Phoenix, Ariz.

SCHOENHALS, Dorenda (curling); b. 14 Jun 1947, Moose Jaw, Sask.; given name: Dorenda Alene Stirton; div. Paul Schoenhals; c. Susan, Ryan, Karyn; m. Bill Bailey; UofSask, BSc; nurse, heart patient educator; skipped HS rink to prov. title at 15; 5 consecutive WCIAA titles '64-69; ntl Intercollegiate title '67; with sister Cheryl playing 3rd skipped ntl Lassies title rink '70; 3rd on Rick Folk mixed provincial title rinks '75, '81-83; ntl title '83, twice runnerup; mem. UofSask Sports Wall, Sask Sports Hall of Fame; res. Calgary, Alta.

SCHOENHALS, Paul (football); b. 5 Nov 1941, Clinton, Ont.; given name: Paul John; div. Dorenda Stirton; c. Susan, Ryan, Karyn; div. Pat Bugera; U of UofSask, BEd, MEd; pres. Petroleum Industry Training Service; jr. football Saskatoon; asst. coach Saskatoon Hilltops 7yrs, head coach 6yrs; assisted Al Ledingham in guiding Hilltops to ntl junior title '68; head coach '78 ntl jr. champions; mem. Sask. legislature '82-86 holding various ministerial portfolios; mem. Cdn Srs Golf Assn.; res. Calgary, Alta.

SCHOLES, Louis (rowing); b. 1880, Toronto, Ont., d. 1942, Toronto, Ont; US intermediate singles '01; 2 major sr. sculls events defeating US champion C.S. Titus at '02 Harlem Regatta; with partner Frank Smith won both Canadian, US double sculls titles '03; Dominion Day Regatta, Cdn Henley, USNRA singles titles '03; 1st Canadian to win English Henley diamond sculls in record 8:23.2 '04; brother Jack held ntl featherweight, lightweight boxing titles, 1900-01 US amateur featherweight title; mem. Cdn Amateur, Canada's Sports Hall of Fame.

SCHOOLEY, Dennis (baseball): b. 10 Mar 1953, Stratford, Ont.; div.; Wilfrid Laurier, BComm; chartered accountant; played varsity hockey at WLU; 3b Stratford Jr. Optimists; saw 1st Sr. Intercounty action while still jr. age; 1st full sr. season with Stratford Hillers at 1B '72; all-star 2B '75; played half of '83 season in Waterloo; made managerial debut with Hillers '79; managed Hillers to 7 Sr. IC titles, 3 times runnerup; as player competed in 566 games, 444 hits; as mgr. (through '97) 815 career games, 484 wins, both league records; operates top-rated baseball school; brother Pat 12 seasons infielder with Hillers; David Hastings exec. of '89 trophy; res. Stratford, Ont.

SCHOOTMAN, Teddy (administration); b. 28 Aug 1918, Ridgewood, N.J.; m. Mies de Chavonnes Vrugt; c. Anneke, Roel, Joke; Rotterdam Technical College; sr. engineer BC Hydro and Power Authority; moved to Canada '53; mem. Dolphin SC '61-80; chief of officials BC Centennial meet '64; organized officials clinics '65-67; v-p. Dolphin SC '66, pres. '68-73; v-p. BC section CASA '68-73, pres. '74; dir. CASA '75; ntl swim team chair. '70-73; mem., chair. ntl team selection comm.; chair. '67 BC championships, short course nationals '69, summer nationals '76, winter nationals '78; BC team mgr. '68 nationals; organized, managed Dolphin European tour '69; Olympic aquatic team mgr. '72; deck official '73, '75 worlds; organized West Van. Dolphin SC as Dolphin affiliate, also club at Tsawwassen and Master SC; res. West Vancouver, B.C.

SCHREIDER, Gary (football); b. 21 Apr 1934, Belleville, Ont.; m. Patricia; c. Gary Jr., Ronald, Thomas, Michael, Suzanne; Queen's, BA, UofOtt, LLB; lawyer, QC; mem. 3 Toronto St. Michael's Ont. Catholic Conf. champions; intercollegiate champion Queen's Golden Gaels '55; 9 CFL seasons '56-64 with Ottawa, BC, Hamilton; halfback, place kicker; 3 times all-star; ntl jr. 60yd dash record 6.3 in HS training under Lloyd Percival; 1st pres. CFL Players' Assn. '63; appointed sole arbitrator player salaries, disputes by NHL and NHLPA '76-93; mem. Ottawa, Belleville Sports halls of fame; res. Ottawa, Ont.

SCHREINER, Andrea (rowing); b. 27 Apr 1959, St. Catharines, Ont.; sculler; 5 Canadian Henley, 4 ntl, 1 Rotsee regatta single sculls titles; mem. '77-79, '81-83 world championships, '80, '84 Olympic Games teams; res. North Beath, WA, Australia.

SCHRIEWER, Tex (football); b. 30 Sep 1934, New Braunfels, Texas; given name: Menan; m. Sandra Jefferies; c. 6; Texas (Austin), BBA; insurance, real estate exec.; all-South, Western Conf. honors '54-55, hon. mention all-American '55; pro Toronto '56; led Argos in receptions with 43 for 691yds, 1td '57; dealt to Saskatchewan for Cookie Gilchrist '59; rejoined Argos '60-62; all-Eastern with Argos '57; res. San Antonio, Tex.

SCHRINER, Sweeney (hockey); b. 30 Nov 1911, Calgary, Alta.; d. 4 Jul 1990, Calgary, Alta.; given name: David; m. Mary; c. Joanne, Norman; retired Fina Petroleum; jr., sr. Calgary; pro Syracuse '33-34; NY Americans '34-39, Maple Leafs '39-46; Calder Memorial Trophy '35; NHL scoring titles '35-36; mem. 2 Stanley Cup winners; once each 1st, 2nd all-star teams; NHL record: 201g, 204a; mem. Alta. Sports, Hockey Hall of Fame.

SCHROETER, Reg (hockey); b. 11 Sep 1921, Ottawa, Ont.; m. Norma Elizabeth Thomas (d); c. Thomas, Carol Ann; m. Shirley Luce Howe; retd. Air Transport Board, retd. dept Indian & Northern Affairs; mem. '48 RCAF Flyers Olympic (12g, 5a), world amateur hockey champions; refereed for 17yrs; as '48 Olympic team mem. Ottawa Sports Hall of Fame; res. Ottawa, Ont.

SCHUETTE, Tom (football); b. 10 Jan 1945, East St. Louis, Ill.; given name: Thomas Paul; Indiana, BSc; realtor associate, restaurateur; all-American coaches 1st team, *Sport Magazine* 2nd team, hon. mention AP, UPI as offensive guard Indiana; all-Big 10; all-academic Big 10 '66; played in East-West Shrine all-star game '66; Balfour Award Indiana for athletic, academic excellence; pro Ottawa '67-77; mem. 4 Grey Cup champions, 2 all-star games; twice topped East in CFL all-pro countdown series, 2nd, 3rd nationally; res. St. Agustine, Fla.

SCHULER, Laura (hockey): b. 3 Dec 1970, Scarborough, Ont.; Northeastern,UofT; attended 3 ntl soccer championships with Scarborough United; hockey forward with Toronto Aeros '81-84, Scarborough Firefighters '84-89; Northeastern Huskies '89-94, Toronto Red Wings in COWHL, UofT Lady Blues from '94; 3 world, 2 Pacific Rim, 1 3-Nations Cup titles; mem. '98 Olympic team; res. Scarborough, Ont.

SCHULZE, Rudy (shooting); b. 31 Oct 1928, Berlin, Germany; m. Eva; c. Karin, Christina; merchant; began competitive shooting with sporting rifles Woodstock '55; 1st major competition '56 Ont. outdoor championships; organized Norwich Rifle Club; instrumental in formation Ont. Sporting Rifle Assn.; founding pres.; chair. sporting rifle section CCAM '62; mem. '66 world championships, '67 Pan-Am, '68 Olympic, '61, '65 Pershing Trophy teams; ntl sporting rifle champion '65; mem. silver medal teams '67 Canada Winter Games, Pan-Ams; mem. Germany's Wiesbadener Schutzengellschaft organization '69-75; German Landesmeister (provincial) champion; v-p., coach Ont. ISU rifle team; res. Waterloo, Ont.

SCHWENDE, Carl (fencing); b. 20 Feb 1920, Basel, Switzerland; m. Claire; c. Heidi, Maria; estimator-designer; competed in Switzerland, France '33-47; competed for Montreal Palestre Nationale from '49; coach Immaculate Conception '56, Notre Dame Centre '59; mem. '54, '58, '62 BE, '59 Pan-Am, '60 Olympic Games teams; gold team sabre, silver team épée, individual épée, bronze team foil '54, silver team épée '58, silver team sabre, bronze team foil, épée '62 BEG; bronze team foil, sabre '59 Pan-Am Games; flag-bearer '60 summer Olympics; supervisor PQFA '52-56; mem. National Fencing Comm. '53-61; pres. PQFA '56; coach McGill fencing team '59, '66-67; pres. Que. Branch AAU of C '62-67; pres. CFA; pres./dir. Que. Sports Hall of Fame; mem. Cdn Amateur, Que. Sports halls of fame; res. Laval, Que.

SCHWENGERS, Bernie (tennis): b. 26 May 1880, Surrey, Eng.; d. 6 Dec 1946, Victoria, B.C.; given name: Bernhard Peter; gifted all-around athlete excelling in tennis, baseball, soccer, rugby, t&f, polo, basketball, field hockey, cricket, golf, lacrosse; 3 Vancouver LTC titles; 7 Victoria LTC titles;

6 BC Open, 7 BC Mainland titles; 6 Pacific Northwest titles; Oregon, Quebec singles titles; 2 ntl open singles titles; Middlesex, Eng., all-England singles titles; mem. '13-14 Davis Cup teams; mem. Cdn Amateur, Cdn Tennis, BC, Canada's Sports halls of fame.

SCOCCIA, Sam (football): b. 27 Jul 1928, Hamilton; d. 12 May 1996, Hamilton, Ont.; givan name: Samuel Patrick; m. Mary Elizabeth; c. Susan, Debra, Jacqueline; refrigeration mechanic; middle guard CFL Hamilton '51, Saskatchewan '52-54, Ottawa '55-65; *Globe & Mail* IRFU Cdn all-star '57; all-Cdn '63; mem. '60 Grey Cup champions; line coach Hamilton Hurricanes '69-70; line coach McMaster early '70s; mem. Ticats alumni assn.; mem. McMaster Lettermen's/friends of distinction Hall of Fame.

SCODELLARO, Duke (hockey); b. 23 May 1914, Maple Leaf, Alta.; given name: Dulio Joseph; m. Jeanne Marie Lepage; c. Janice, Darrel; retd. office equipment technician; goaler Bellevue Intermediates '31-35, Coleman Srs. '35-37; mem. Trail Smoke Eaters '37-41, '45-52; Allan Cup, World championship teams '38-39; 7 shutouts in 12 playoff games, acclaimed Western Cdn Amateur Hockey's outstanding goaler; pro tryouts NY Rangers, Vancouver Lions; mem. Toronto RCAF all-Ont. champions '43-45; BCAHA outstanding player award; res. Trail, B.C.

SCORRAR, Doug (t&f); b. 9 Sep 1948, Auckland, N.Z.; given name: Douglas Alfred; m. Janis Grace Anderson; c. Brendan Alfred Anderson, Grace Margaret Anderson; Ohio State, BSc, MA; financial analyst Agriculture Canada; Sport Canada consultant '80-94; ntl midget mile record 4:24.9 '64; ntl HS 2-mile record 9:16.6 '65, 9:12.3 '67; OFSSA 2-mile title '65-67, jr. international 3-mile title '67; Big 10 Conf. cross-country '68, 3-mile runnerup '70; Ohio State records 2-mile indoor, 1, 2, 3, 6-mile outdoor, 2, 4-mile outdoor relay; mem. ntl team winning 3-mile vs Norway, Sweden; Ont. team 10,000m, marathon '74-76; mem. ntl team '75-76; 10,000m champion '76; Bermuda international marathon '77; res. Ottawa, Ont.

SCOTT, Abbie (basketball); b. 6 Oct 1902, Cheyenne, Wyo.; d. 24 Feb 1991, Edmonton, Alta.; given name: Abigail Esther; m. Robert Kennedy (d); c. Lois Anne; Edmonton Business Coll.; retd. secretary; mem. famed Edmonton Grads '22-24, 30 games 184 points, 6.1 avg.; mem. Canadian Basketball, Alta. Sports halls of fame.

SCOTT, Alex (curling); b. 7 Mar 1940, Willowdale, Ont.; given name: Alex Victor Ferguson; m. Janet Isabel Ritchie; c. Sandy, Kathy, Jamie; Queen's, MD; physician; Ont. Intercollegiate curling title; Ont. Governor-General's double rink title '69, Whitby Dunlop 'spiel; 1st Ont. rep. Edmonton carspiel; Toronto Royal Canadians carspiel (Ontario's 1st) '71; skipped Kingston rink of Ted Brown, Tom Miller, Mike Boyd to '75 Ont. Consols title, Brier berth; res. Kingston, Ont.

SCOTT, Barbara Ann (figure skating); b. 9 May 1928, Ottawa, Ont.; m. Thomas V. King; began skating career Minto Skating club at 6; at 10 youngest to pass gold figures test; ntl jr. title '40; sr. champion '44-48; NA titlist '45-48; world champion '47-48; Olympic gold '48; 1st NA to win

European, Olympic titles same year; pro '49-54 with Skating Sensation, Hollywood Ice Review; trains, shows horses as hobby; with Tipper, who died at 34, won more than 400 trophies during 30-year span; Lou Marsh Trophy '45, '47, '48; 3 Bobbie Rosenfeld awards; Officer Order of Canada; mem. US Figure Skating, Cdn Amateur, Ottawa, Canada's Sports Halls, Canada's Walk of Fame; res. Chicago, Ill.

SCOTT, Debbie (t&f); b. 16 Dec 1958, Victoria, B.C.; m. Ron Bowker; UVic, BEd; teacher; mem. UVRC; BC jr. 3000m, ntl jr. 1500m, 3000m '76; ntl 1500m '77; mem. '77 Pacific Conf., World Cup, FISU Games, '78, '82, '86, '90, '94 Commonwealth, '87 Pan Am, '84, '88, '92 Olympic Games; '79, '81 World Cup cross-country, '81-82 European tour teams; CIAU 1500m, 3000m titles '81-82, Sweden International 800m, Oslo Games, ntl 1500m, WC trials 3000m '81; ntl outdoor 1500m, 3000m, 5th Avenue mile '82; ntl sr. 5000m record (15:48.99) '82 Prefontaine Classic; ntl outdoor 1500 title '91; sr. ntl, Commonwealth record (4:29.67) '82 Oslo mile, (4:23.96) '82 5th Ave. mile; ntl record (8:48.85) 3000m Koblenz, Germany '82; 1500, 3000 silver '86 Commonwealth, 1500 silver '87 Pan Am Games; res. Victoria, B.C.

SCOTT, Mike (canoeing); b. 1 Dec 1930, Ottawa, Ont.; given name: Patrick; m. Lola Lewis; c. Jennifer, David, Judy; Carleton; retd. asst. product planner; competitive paddler '49-61; cross-country ski racer '52-60; mem. RCAF Rockcliffe, YMCA boxing clubs '53-58; coached boxing YMCA, Ottawa Boys Club, Beaver Boxing Club; coach, administrator and, from '61, commodore Rideau Canoe Club; organizing chair. 7 ntl championship regattas; coached minor hockey '74-75; competitor several Canadian Ski Marathons; competed annually in National Capital Marathon from inception, '78 Skylon Marathon, '79 NY Marathon; Ottawa ACT Sportsman of '71; National Health & Welfare Operation Lifestyle award '79; mem. Ottawa Sports Hall of Fame; res. Nepean, Ont.

SCOTT, Tom (football); b. 19 Nov 1951, California; m. Susan; c. Carey, Elizabeth; San Mateo Jr. Coll., Washington; Wash. receiving record; all-Pac. 8, 2nd team all-American; drafted Detroit NFL; opted for CFL Winnipeg '74-77, Edmonton '78-83, Calgary '84; CFL rookie of '74; established all-time CFL reception yardage record with 10,837 on 649 catches '84; 6 times 1000yds plus season; CFL record 88 TD passes; mem. 5 consec. Grey Cup winners; mem. Cdn Football Hall of Fame; res. Sherwood Park, Alta.

SCOTT, Vince (football); b. 10 Jul 1925, Leroy, N.Y.; d. 13 Jul 1992, Hamilton, Ont.; div.; c. Joseph, Robert, Vincent Jr., Gail; Notre Dame, BSc; radio sports commentator; 9 athletic letters HS football, track, baseball; twice Western NY State football all-star; mem. '43 Western NY State championship football team; NY State sectional shot put champion '43; mem. '46 ntl football champions; Pitts all-opponents team '45; pro Buffalo (NFL '47-48, title game vs Cleveland '48; Hamilton (CFL) '49-62, Eastern all-star 10 times; Stuke's '54 dream team; twice Ted Reeves' all-Canada team; '55 coaches dream team; Jack Matheson's '67 all-pro team chosen for *US All-Pro Magazine*; Hamilton's Fabulous Fifty's all-star team; Eastern team of century; in 4 all-star games; twice honored by 'day' ('48

Buffalo, Hamilton quarterback club); Batavia, N.Y., Notre Dame Booster Club outstanding athlete of decade; coached Oakville Black Knights (ORFU) 3yrs, Hillfield College Hamilton 3yrs; mem. 6 Grey Cup finalists, 2 winners; mem. Canadian Football Hall of Fame.

SEAGRAM, Joseph (horse racing); b. 15 Apr 1841, Fisher's Mill, Ont., d. 18 Aug 1919, Waterloo, Ont.; m. Stephanie Urbs; c. Edward, Thomas, Norman, Joseph, Alice; Brant Stratton's Business Coll.; distiller; parlayed business success into horse racing dynasty; his horses claimed 15 Queen's Plate winners; obtaining English broodmares he established a string of Ont.-bred champions on his Waterloo farm; pres. OJC; only Cdn hon. mem. English Jockey Club; mem. Canadian Horse Racing Hall of Fame.

SEARS, John (golf): b. 17 Jan 1936, Fredericton, N.B.; given name: John Patrick; mem. FHS Class L NB basketball title team '53, NB interscholastic rugby title team '53, Fredericton Capitals Maritime Intermediate A '60 title team; Fredericton GC jr. title '51-53, sr. '68; NB-PEI amateur titles '60, '65, Nfld. '72; 4 NB-PEI district titles, 2 Madawaska Invitationals, 2 PEI Opens, runnerup once; low scorer 4 NB-PEI Willingdon Cup trials; mem. 8 NB-PEI Willingdon Cup teams; 4 Frank Robertson trophies; mem. NB Sports Hall of Fame; res. Fredericton, N.B.

SECORD, Al (hockey): b. 3 Mar 1958, Sudbury, Ont.; given name: Alan Edward William; m. Tracy Shaw; pilot American Airlines; lw; jr. St. Catharines, Hamilton OHA '76-78; drafted by Boston '78; minor pro Rochester, Springfield AHL; NHL Boston '78-81, Chicago '81-87, '89-90, Toronto '87-89, Philadelphia '89; NHL record: 12 seasons, 766 scheduled games, 273g, 222a, 102 playoff games, 21g, 34a; reached 50-goal plateau with 54 '83; res. Dallas, TX/Elmhurst, Ill.

SEELY, Glen (golf/baseball); b. 4 Sep 1928, Saint John, N.B.; m. Pauline Rouleau; c. Kim, Jamie, Cindy; merchant; pitcher Ottawa Nationals baseball team '48, '50, Sudbury '48-49, Ogdensburg, N.Y., part of '50 season; lefthander 40-5 record over 2 seasons; mem. Rivermead GC from '63; 3 Alexander of Tunis titles; Que. Willingdon Cup team mem.; res. Nepean, Ont.

SEIBERT, Earl (hockey); b. 7 Dec 1911, Kitchener, Ont.; d. 16 May 1990, Agawam, Mass.; given name: Earl Walter; def. Springfield (AHL) '29-31, NY Rangers '31-35, Chicago '35-45, Detroit '45-46; all-star 10 consecutive seasons, 4 times first team; NHL record: 89g, 187a, plus 11g, 8a in playoffs; following serious concussion became 1st player to wear helmet in AHL; with father Oliver, 1st father-son combination Hockey Hall of Fame.

SEIBERT, Oliver (hockey); b. 18 Mar 1881, Berlin, Ont., d. 15 May 1944, Kitchener, Ont.; goaler, later forward, on team comprised solely of family members; 6 seasons mem. champion Berlin Rangers (WOHA); pro Houghton, Mich., '07; London, Guelph in Ont. pro, Northwestern Mich. leagues; wearing old rocker skates once beat a trotter in one-mile match race on Grand River ice despite fact trotter set mile record 2:13; with son Earl first father-son combination Hockey Hall of Fame.

SEILING, Rod (hockey/administration); b. 14 Nov 1944, Elmira, Ont.; given name: Rodney Albert; m. Sharon Bland; c. Michael, Bradley; Wilfrid Laurier, BA; pres. Greater Toronto Hotel Assn., Ontario Hotel & Motel Assn.; former exec.v-p. Racetracks of Canada; def. Rangers '64-75, Toronto '75-76, St.Louis '77-79, Atlanta '79; Team Canada '72; NHL record: 979 scheduled games, 62 goals, 269 assists, 77 playoff games, 4 goals, 8 assists; licensed standardbred owner, trainer; GM Elmira Raceway '79-82; exec. v-p. Racetracks of Canada '82; helped found NHLPA, mem. player-owner council which negotiated 1st collective agreement in NHL; turned Elmira track from losing to profitable operation; former mem. ORC advisory board; dir. Racetracks of Canada, Racing Hall of Fame, Harness Tracks of Ont.; former mem. CTA, USTA, Cdn Standardbred Horse Society, Ont. Standardbred Breeders Improvement Assn.; pres. NHL Oldtimers charity hockey team; ex-co-ordinator ntl Race Against MS harness div.; chair. Team Canada '72 Representation Inc.; v-p. corp. dev. OJC 3yrs; res. Toronto, Ont.

SELANNE, Teemu (hockey): b. 3 Jul 1970, Helsinki, Finland; m. Sirpa; c. Eemil, Eetu; played with Jokerit, Finland, '87-92, league leading scorer, mem. Finnish ntl. title team; mem. Finnish team '91 Canada Cup, '92, '98 Olympics; drafted by Winnipeg '88 but didn't join Jets until '92-93; to Anaheim '96-99; impressive rookie season with 76 goals; attained 50 goal plateau '93 76, '97 51, '98 52; Calder Memorial trophy '93; HN Rookie of '93; NHL/Upper Deck rookie team; 2 1st team all-star; 4 NHL all-star games; nicknamed 'Finnish Flash', 'Salami', 'Flying Finn'; active interest in auto racing; NHL record (through '99): 464 scheduled games, 313g, 330a, 21 playoff games, 13g, 7a; reached 300g plateau '99; initial recipient Rocket Richard trophy '99; active in children's charities; res. Helsinki, Finland/Anaheim, Calif.

SELKE, Frank Sr. (hockey/builder); b. 7 May 1893, Berlin, Ont.; d. 3 Jul 1985, Rigaud, Que.; given name: Frank Joseph Aloysius; m. Mary Agnes Schmidt; c. Blanche, Chilton, Evelyn, Audrey, Delphine, Frank, Geraldine; electrician, retd. hockey exec.; managed first hockey team (bantam) at 13; also managed team to minor city, provincial softball, baseball, hockey titles; managed 3 Memorial Cup winners; associated with Conn Smythe in early days of Maple Leafs; managed Toronto to 3 Stanley Cups; GM Canadiens '46-64, 6 Stanley Cup champions; also managed 1 Allan Cup champion; founding dir. Hockey Hall of Fame; prominent in construction Maple Leaf Gardens, Cincinnati Gardens, Rochester War Memorial, numerous other arenas; Frank J. Selke Trophy awarded annually to best defensive forward in NHL; mem. Canada's Sports, Hockey halls of fame.

SELKIRK, George (baseball); b. 4 Jan 1899, Huntsville, Ont.; d. 19 Jan 1987, Ft. Lauderdale, Fla.; given name: George Alexander; nicknamed 'Twinkletoes'; led Toronto (IL) in HRs '32; mem. Yankees '34-42; became regular replacing Babe Ruth in outfield; ML record: 846 games, 810h, 503r, 576rbi, 49sb, .290ba; GM Washington Senators '64-69; 6 World Series, batting .265 in 21 games; twice drove in 100 or more runs; mem. Canadian Baseball Hall of Fame.

SELLER, Peggy (all-around); b. 23 Jan 1905, Edinburgh, Scotland; d. 31 Mar 1996, Newmarket, Ont.; given name:

Margaret Cameron Shearer; m. Dr. Reg Seller; c. Marna, Donald; competing in 1st competition in world sanctioned by a swimming governing body won Que. synchronized swim title '24; all Royal Life Saving Awards '24; 5 Que., ntl 3m diving titles; capt. 3 ntl water polo title teams; helped write rules for Gale Trophy, emblematic of ntl synchro. swim championship; won Gale Trophy 1st 4 times; standout in hockey, basketball, volleyball, baseball, tennis, figure skating, t&f; provincial titles javelin, 100yd dash, broad jump, relays; first woman secty. FINA, CASA Que. section; secty.-treas. CASA '48-50, Cdn Royal Life Saving Society 10yrs; wrote FINA synchro. swim rules '52; wrote descriptive rule book on sport, co-authored with US champion Beulah Gundling book on Aquatic Art; v-p. International Academy of Aquatic Art '54; hon. mem. IAAA, CSSA; mem. Pointe Claire SC advisory board; mem. Canadian, US Aquatic, Intl. Swimming, Canada's Sports halls of fame.

SELTZER, Sheila (curling); b. 29 Oct 1938, Iroquois Falls, Ont.; given name: Sheila Evelyn Peever; m. J.R. Chucker Ross; Stratford Teachers' College; retd. school teacher; from '70-84 curled in 15 Ont. title playdowns in business girls, ladies, srs., mixed; runnerup '75 Ont. Business Girls; skipped '78, '81 Ont. Lassie title rinks; 3rd on NO Seagram Mixed title winner '82; skip 2 ntl sr. women's title rinks; 3rd on Toronto Royals Molson's champions '77; skipped Ottawa Crystal Pebble winner '79, '97, Ottawa Molson's Masters champion '80; 3rd on '81 Bowling Green, Ohio, International mixed title rink; all-star skip NO sr. women's title rink '94; mem. Sudbury Northland AC; Burlington 12-mile relay road race champion, Brantford 6-mile masters road race, 10-mile Hamilton masters road race titles '78; avid windsurfer; with husband has achieved official instructor status andhas windsurfed as far south as Caribbean; Sudbury female athlete of '81; res. Subury, Ont.

SENECAL, Jean-François (shooting); b. 29 Jun 1961, Laval, Que.; engineer; mem. '79-83 Benito Juarez, '82, '86, '90, '94 Commonwealth, '83, '87, '95 Pan-Am, '84, '88, '92. '96 Olympic, '82-83 world championship teams; 2 gold, 2 silver, 1 bronze Commonwealth Games; 2 gold, 7 silver, 1 bronze Pan-Am Games; Shooting Fed. golden anniversary award '82; fed. govt. excellence award '83; res. Chomedy, Que.

SENKLER, Harry (rowing); b. 24 Jul 1866, Brockville, Ont.; d. 1926, Vancouver, B.C.; given name: John Henry; m. Margaret Richards; Upper Canada College, Osgoode Hall; lawyer (KC); capt. Argonaut ntl title crews 1891-92; rugby star UofT; international cricketer; standout sprinter UofT; standout baseball player; capt. Vancouver Boating Club 1895-98, Vancouver Rowing Club 1899-1900, 1923; mem. Cdn. Olympic Comm.

SENOS, Eddie (boxing); b. 25 Mar 1928, Ottawa, Ont.; given name: Edward; m. Lorraine Lecusson; c. Stephen, Thomas, James Scott; exec. salesman; Ont. golden gloves title '45, Que. '46; bronze '48 Olympic trials; Ont. middleweight titles '50, '52; bronze '54 BEG trials; mem. Canadian Boxing Hall of Fame; res. Nepean, Ont.

SERVOLD, Clarence (skiing); b. 1927, Camrose, Alta.; retd.; as mem. Camrose jr ski club developed interest in

Nordic skiing; won ntl 15km, 30km X-C titles '55; mem. '56 Olympic team where 19th in 15km, 22 in 50km was highest finish to that time by any NA X-C skier; ntl seniors 15km X-C title '64; enjoyed considerable success at masters level; involved in coaching Alta. jr., ntl X-C teams; played active role in establishing Nordic Combined skiing popularity across Canada; chair. jumping/Nordic combined '90 Alta. winter games; mem. Alta. Sports Hall of Fame; res. Canmore, Alta.

SERVOLD, Irvin (skiing); b. 14 Nov 1932, Camrose, Alta.; given name: Irvin Benjamen; m. Eleanor Bernice Vekved; c. Mark, Helen-Marie, Jon, Niel, Ingrid, Daniel; Seattle, UAlta, BEd, PPhE; teacher; learned to ski using barrel staves as skis, poplar trees for poles; Alta. cross-country, jumping titles; ntl jr. jumping title '50; 11 ntl sr. mordic combined titles '53-68; mem. '56, '60 Olympic teams; ntl team coach; conducted officials' clinics for Canada Winter Games '72, '75; UAlta nordic coach '57-62; coach FISU Games '72; cross-country coach Miasama ski games Japan '73; co-founder Devon Nordic Ski Club; ntl cross-country ski chairman '68-69, '71, '73; mem. ntl cross-country program comm. '68-75; Alta. div. tech. chair. '76-98; UAlta male athlete of '62; International Intercollegiate cross-country champion '58-61; Alta. sports service award '80; mem. Cdn Skiing; Alta. Sports halls of fame; res. Devon, Alta.

SEVIGNY, Chantal (speed skating): b. 13 Jul 1975, Sherbrooke, Que.; Ahuntsic Coll.; began speed skating age 8; although deaf she relies on coaches and shadows cast by fellow competitors to help her during competition; 2 gold, 3 silver '95 Canada Games; qualified as substitute on Cdn world team '95; mem. '98 Olympic team; res. Montreal, Que.

SEWELL, Don (shooting): b. 22 Jun 1927, Winnipeg, Man.; given name: Donald Ferrand; m. Doran Westhead; c. Dena, Lori, Gren, Michael, Kip; UMan; retd Air Canada; began target shooting age 8; 1st major win Man. Air Cadet League sporting rifle high aggregate '43; joined St. James Rifle Club '47; Man. title '48; won every division indoor, outdoor match '49-60; mem. 4 Cdn Dewar teams; perfect 400 '58; won Red River Valley titles '53-57; final .22 competition '62; switched to fullbore '60; mem. 18 Bisley teams, 3 McKinnon match, 1 Africa, Empire match, St. Georges Cross, *Daily Telegraph* match titles; Cdn Target Rifle title '65, '89, '94; competed '73 Canada Summer Games; 5 Man. Lt.-Gov. gold medals, 9 Man. target rifle titles; mem. 4 Palma teams, 2 silver medals; Man. Intl Honors Supreme '75; twice missed opportunity to compete in Commonwealth Games due to work/injury; mem. Man. Sports Hall of Fame; res. Winnipeg, Man.

SEWELL, Doran (shooting): b. 26 Dec 1932, Manchester, Eng.; given name: Doran Westhead; m. Don Sewell; c. Dena, Lori, Gren, Michael, Kip; retd Revenue Canada appeals officer; developed interest in fullbore shooting while serving with Northern Rhodesia police force '53; 1st woman in Africa to win NRA Donegall medal '56; numerous Rhodesian titles '54-60; served on exec. Northern Rhodesia RA, Chingola RC; moved to Canada '60 after making initial Bisley appearance; represented Alta. provincially, internationally '61-67; wed and moved to Man. '67; 1st

woman in world mem. Palma team '67, won gold; mem. 3 Cdn Palma teams, '73 silver; ntl smallbore postal title '71; ntl women's title '90; numerous provincial titles from '68; MPRA team adjutant '73, commandant '76; competed '73 Canada Summer Games; capt. Cdn Commonwealth team '84, adjutant '87, commandant '95 Cdn Bisley team; competed 4 Bisley teams; Man. target rifle title '94; Man. Lt.-Gov gold medal '93, Intl Honors Supreme award '75; exec. MPRA from '68; DCRA exec.; Man. Sports Fed. dir. 2yrs; res. Winnipeg, Man.

SGRO, Joe (hockey); b. 21 Jan 1939, South Porcupine, Ont.; div.; c. Tony-Joe, Rebecca; salesman Victoriaville Hockey Inc.; mem. South Porcupine NO bantam champions; spare goaler Guelph Biltmore Jr. A '59; int., sr. hockey South Porcupine; trainer Nashville Dixie Flyers (EHL) '62-66, Tulsa (CHL) '66-68, Toronto (NHL) '68-77; Team Canada '72, '79, '81, '82; res. Toronto, Ont.

SHACK, Eddie (hockey); b. 11 Feb 1937, Sudbury, Ont.; given name: Edward Steven Phillip; m. Norma Given; c. Cathy, Timmy; businessman; jr. Guelph Biltmores; NY Rangers '58-61, Toronto '61-67, Boston '67-69, Los Angeles '69-71, Buffalo '71-72, Pittsburgh '72-75; NHL record: 1047 scheduled games, 239g, 226a, 74 playoff games, 6g, 7a; mem. 4 Stanley Cup winners; res. Toronto, Ont.

SHAKESPEARE, Shannon (swimming): b. 6 May 1977, Mission, B.C.; began swimming age 4; freestyle, breaststroke specialist; mem. ntl team from '93; 7 ntl titles, 88 ntl records; gold, silver '95 world short course championships; ntl, Commonwealth 50m FS (sc) record, ntl 100m FS (sc) record; competed '92 eight-nations youth meet, '93 Pan-Pacific, world short course championships; 2 bronze '94 Commonwealth Games; 4 silver '95 Pan-Am Games; 4 Canada Cup gold '96; mem. '96 Olympic team; res. Winnipeg, Man.

SHANAHAN, Brendan (hockey): b. 23 Jan 1969, Mimico, Ont.; left wing; jr. London OHL '85-87; drafted by New Jersey '87; NHL New Jersey '87-91, St. Louis '91-95, Hartford '95-96, Detroit '96-99; NHL record (through '99): 869 scheduled games, 394g, 407a, 101 playoff games, 37g, 44a; reached 50-goal plateau with 51 '93, 52 '94; reached 400g plateau '99; 2 Stanley Cup winners; 1 NHL 1st team all-star; 3 NHL all-star games; mem. Team Canada '87 Jr. Worlds, Team Canada '91 Canada Cup, '94 worlds, '96 World Cup, '98 Olympics; hon. chair. Michigan Alzheimer's Disease Research Centre charity softball game; res. Simsbury, CT.

SHANKS, Vicki (racquetball); b. 14 Feb 1965, N. Vancouver, B.C.;UBC, BPhE; 4 ntl women's doubles titles; 4 Tournament of the Americas silver; 4 world women's doubles silver; women's doubles (with partner Debbie Ward) silver '95 Pan-Am Games; res. N. Vancouver, B.C.

SHANNON, Carver (football); b. 28 Apr 1938, Corinth, Miss.; given name: Carver Beauregard; m. Loraine; c. Michael; Southern Illinois, B.S., UCLA, MA; aircraft co. mgr; numerous Southern Illinois football records including scoring for one game, season and career, best rushing avg.

game, season, career; track record 9.4 for 100yds; led US major college scorers '56; twice all-American; voted school's greatest athlete '75; pro Winnipeg '59-61, Hamilton '61; 2 Grey Cup finals, 1 winner; Los Angeles (NFL) '62; led Rams in yardage, best avg. single game on punt returns, most pass interceptions '62; second in NFL kickoff returns, 3rd punt returns '63; all pro defensive halfback '64; pro tennis umpire; Pac-10 football official; last known res. Los Angeles, Calif.

SHARPE, Tony (t&f); b. 28 Jun 1961, Jamaica; m. Colleen Taffe; employee Xerox; sprint specialist; York; mem. Scarborough Optimists TC; mem. '79, '83 Pan-Am, '80, '84 Olympic, '82 Commonwealth, '83 FISU Games teams; ntl 100m, 400m, 4x200m relay titles; silver 4x100m relay '82 Commonwealth Games; bronze 4x100m relay '84 Olympics; ntl sr. record 200m (20.22), 4x100 relay (38.43); ntl sr. record, world best 4x200m (1:23.97) '83; Dr. Fred Tees Memorial Trophy (top CIAU athlete) '82; last known res. Pickering, Ont.

SHARPLES, Jim (curling): b. 16 Mar 1936, Oshawa, Ont.; given name: James Douglas; m. Sandra; c. Donna, Grant; UofT, BComm; Cornell, MA; Osgoode Hall, LLB; lawyer; competed 9 Ont. Consols/Tankard; won 3 Labatt Challenge Rounds; 3 Silver Tankard titles; 3 Ont. seniors titles, twice runnerup; Canadian seniors champion skip '89, '92; chair. organization, constitution, rules comm. OCA '87-93; v-p. OCA '92-94, pres. '95-96; res. Markham, Ont.

SHASKE, Ed Jr. (shooting); b. 19 Jan 1957, Edmonton, Alta., d. 31 Mar 1982, Edmonton, Alta.; given name: Edward Mark; UAlta; real estate appraiser; above avg. jr. hockey player; offered several US college hockey scholarships; coach midget B team; Industrial HL dir. '79-81; trap shooting specialist; ntl trapshooting team mem. '77-82; 5 international world trapshooting title competitions; officiated '76 Olympics, trapshooting chairman '78 Commonwealth Games; US Pacific Coast champion '77; mem. gold medal team '78 Benito Juarez matches; mem. '80 Olympic team; tied for 1st '80 British Grand Prix; tied 2nd '80 Brazilian Grand Prix; runnerup '81 Cdn International trapshoot; '81 Western Cdn title; organized, coached Edmonton jr. shooting program '79-80; mem. organizing comm. '83 World Moving Target championships; Edmonton achievement awards '77-78, '81; Alta. achievement awards '78, '80; mem. Alta. Sports Hall of Fame.

SHATTO, Cindy (diving); b. 16 May 1957, Toronto, Ont.; div; c. Richard Darland; m. Richard Weingartner; exec.-scty Xerox; daughter of Football Hall of Fame mem. Dick Shatto; mem. ntl team '71-79; 4 ntl 1m, 2 3m titles; gold 3m '74 Commonwealth Games; mem. '73 worlds, '76 Olympic, 3 Canada Cup teams; coached by Don Webb; last known res. Ft. Lauderdale, Fla.

SHATTO, Dick (football); b. 23 Jun 1933, Springfield, Ohio; given name: Richard Darrell; m. Lynne Garlough; c. Randy, Becky, Cindy, Jay, Kathy; Kentucky; resort exec.; football, track star Kentucky; pro Toronto '54-65; fullback, halfback, slotback, flanker; 15 Argos offensive records; most points (career) 542, most TDs (career) 91, (game) 4, most

carries (career) 1322, most yds gained rushing (career) 6958, most 100yd games (career) 16, most receptions (career) 466, most yds gained receiving (career) 6584, most TDs rushing (career) 39, (game) 3, most TDs receiving (career) 52, most kickoff returns (career) 83, (season) 25, most yds kickoff returns (career) 1991, (season) 636; twice Jeff Russel Memorial Trophy winner; twice runnerup Schenley outstanding player award; 6 times EFC all-star, once all-Cdn; rejoined Argos '74 as marketing mgr., media and public relations; managing dir. '76-79; named to All-Time Argos team '96; jersey #22 retd by Argos; mem. Canadian Football Hall of Fame; last known res. Dunedin, Fla.

SHAUGHNESSY, Frank Jr. (hockey/football/golf); b. 21 Jun 1911, Roanoke, Va., d. 12 Jun 1982, Montreal, Que.; Loyola, BA, McGill; Bell Canada; son of Shag Shaughnessy; football all-star McGill '34; mem. McGill intercollegiate hockey champions '34-35, Canadian Olympic hockey team '36; coach freshman football, hockey McGill; v-p. Laurentian Ski Zone '52-55; tech. chair. Que. div. CSA '54-55; ntl ski team chair. '54-55; CdM winter Olympic teams '56, '60, '64, '68, '72; COA v-p. '57-82; dir. QGA '58-64, pres. '64; governor RCGA '65-69, chair. '67; pres. Montreal Sportsmen's Assn. '68-72; chair. Air Canada amateur sport exec. of year award comm. '68-72; mem. Loyola, Cdn Amateur, Canada's Sports halls of fame.

SHAUGHNESSY, Shag (baseball); b. 8 Apr 1884, Amboy, Ill., d. 15 May 1969, Montreal, Que.; given name: Francis Joseph; m. Katherine Quinn; c. 8 sons, 1 daughter; Notre Dame; capt. Notre Dame football, baseball teams '03-04; pro baseball Washington '05, Philadelphia '08, mgr. Roanoke, Va., Fort Wayne, Ind.; coached football 1yr Clemson; introduced option play to US football while coaching at Yale, Cornell; 1st pro McGill football coach '12-28, won 2 Yates Cups, overall record 32-52-4; introduced forward pass to Cdn university football; coached McGill men's, women's hockey teams; managed Ottawa baseball team to 3 straight pennants; formed Cdn Pro Baseball League with teams from Ottawa, Brantford, Guelph, Kitchener and Peterborough; GM Ottawa hockey club; mgr. Hamilton baseball club '19; coach, scout Detroit Tigers; rebuilt Montreal Royals and won 1st Montreal pennant of century '35; instituted playoff system (adopted from hockey) initiating Little World Series; International League pres. '36-60; broke pro baseball's color bar by signing Jackie Robinson to Montreal Royals '46; appointed by baseball commissioner Happy Chandler to recodify baseball rules '49; mem. McGill. Cdn Baseball, Football halls of fame.

SHAVER, Ron (figure skating); b. 16 Jun 1951, Galt, Ont.; Detroit; gold Skate Canada '74, '76, silver '73, '75; silver Skate Moscow '73; ntl men's singles title '77; competed 4 world championships, best placement fifth '74; pro Ice Capades '77; mem. Waterloo County Hall of Fame; res. Cambridge, Ont.

SHAW, Colin (canoeing); b. 17 Mar 1954, Powell River, B.C.; carpenter; ntl jr. K2, K4, sr. K4 1000m '75; sr. K1, K2 500m, 1000m, jr. 500m (ntl jr. record 1:53.24) '79; Olympic trials, Zaandan regatta K4 1000m, ntl K2 500m, 1000m '80; semifinalist K4 500m '81 world championships;

Commonwealth Cup K1 500m, 10,000m, K2 500m, ntl K2 500m, 1000m, K4 1000m '81-83; mem. '84 Olympic team; res. Coquitlam, B.C.

SHAW, Dan (football); b. 18 Dec 1933, Toronto, Ont.; d. 5 Mar 1992, Toronto, Ont.; given name: Dan Ross; m. Beverley Ford; c. Stephen, Susan, Dani; sporting goods salesman; Toronto HS all-star two-way guard, tackle '48-51; Toronto Balmy Beach sr. ORFU '52-53 winning league title latter year, losing to Winnipeg Grey Cup semifinal; Toronto '54-57; secty.-treas. Argo Old Boys; convenor Ont. Junior Football Conf. '65-72, exec. dir. '72-77; mem. founding comm. Argo Playback Club '67, dir. '67-74; v.-chair. Argo Double Blue Club; chair. founding comm. Cdn Football Hall of Fame Club '76; Ont. achievement award '72; CAFA-CFL award '80.

SHAW, Gerry (football); b. 6 Dec 1942, Hamilton, Ont.; given name: Robert Gerald; m. Norma Inkster; c. Bradley, Keri; Washington State, BA; v-p.,dir., investment dealer; college football '62-64; pro Calgary '65-74; twice mem. Western Conf. champions; mem. '71 Grey Cup champions; twice in CFL all-star games; led CFL receivers in TD receptions '72 with 12; caught 65 passes for 1002yds '72 season; CFL record: 310 receptions for 4732yds, 34tds; res. Calgary, Alta.

SHAW, Paul (shooting); b. 20 Jun 1949, Collingwood, Ont.; given name: Ian Paul; lawyer; trapshooting specialist; 3 ntl titles; mem. ntl team from '86; ntl double trap titles '91-93; Pan-Am Games silver, bronze '87; competed '96 Olympics; res. Collingwood, Ont

SHAW, Wayne (football); b. 24 Feb 1939, Bladworth, Sask. m. Joan; c. Kimberly; Notre Dame College, UofSask; businessman; football '56-58 Notre Dame College; jr. Saskatoon Hilltops '59-60, all-star middle linebacker '59, offensive tackle '60, Man.-Sask. Jr. League MVP '60; ntl jr. championship '60; outside linebacker Roughriders '61-72; 5 times WFC all-star, once all-Cdn; club's nominee for Schenley award once; mem. 4 Grey Cup finalists, 1 winner; last known res. Winnipeg, Man.

SHEA, Stu (shooting); b. 5 Jul 1926, Dartford, Ont.; given name Stuart Wallace; skeet shooting specialist; Ont. open overall title '61; NO title, 1 of 3 tied for world crown '62; Cdn open 28-guage title '64; Ont title, father/son 12-guage champion '68; Ont. 410 guage title '75; Cdn high overall, 28-guage titlist, Ont. all-star '76; top all-around shooter over 50, open 20-guage inter-American champion, Ont. all-star '77; NO high overall '78; Cdn Open 2-man, 5-man, sub-senior overall winner '79; 400-target marathon 410-guage title '81; mem. Peterborough Sports Hall of Fame; res. Peterborough, Ont.

SHEAHAN, Pat (football/coaching); b. 10 Oct 1956, Pembroke, Ont.; given name: Patrick; m. Lee McClure; c. Ryan, Erin, Devan; Concordia, BSc, DSA, MA, McGill, BEd; football coach; QB Brockville HS team '72-75; TE, OT, OG, C Concordia '75-79; 2 tryouts with Edmonton (CFL); O-line coach Montreal Jr. Concordes '82-83; Eastern Cdn title '82; asst. coach McGill '84-88, Vanier Cup '87; head coach Concordia '89-98; outstanding lineman award '77; OQIFC coach of '90; res. Kirkland, Que.

SHEDD, Marjory (badminton); b. 17 Mar 1926, Toronto, Ont.; given name: Marjory Jean; retd. lab technician, sport instructor; guard '45 ntl jr. basketball champion Carltonettes; led Toronto Montgomery Maids to '50 ntl sr. title; volleyball '59 ntl champion Broadview Y, '60-62 University Settlement Blacks, '65 University Settlement Rebels; coached UofT Ladies volleyball tean '64-74; mem. '67 Pan-Am volleyball, '70 Commonwealth Games badminton teams; finalist ntl badminton singles '51-52; 6 ntl singles, 5 mixed, 14 ladies' doubles titles; mem. 6 Uber Cup teams; mem. Cdn Amateur, Canada's Sports halls of fame; res. Toronto, Ont.

SHEEHAN, Jeff (swimming); b. 18 Nov 1964, Connecticut; UCal; gold 200m IM, 400m IM, 100m FS '83 CIAU championships, 200m IM '82 Canada Cup, 100m FS, 200m IM '81 Canada Games; bronze 200m IM '82 Commonwealth Games, 4x100m FS relay '83 FISU Games; last known res. Calgary, Alta.

SHEFFIELD, Cathy (judo); b. 6 Aug 1959, Toronto, Ont.; m. Phil Takahashi; c. Christy, Jenny, Emily; York, BA, UofOtt, BEd; mem. ntl team '76-83; 52kg gold '80 Pan-Am championships; ntl 52kg titles '78-79; res. Kanata, Ont.

SHEPHERD, George (t&f); b. 23 Apr 1938, Port Colborne, Ont.; m. Sylvia Mary; c. Craig Andrew; UWO BPHE; HS teacher; ntl 400m hurdles champion '58-63, ntl record '58-65; mem. East York track club 1-mile relay team '60-68, ntl titles, 3:08.6 record; mem. '60 Olympic team; p.-pres. Olympic Club of Canada; res. Toronto, Ont.

SHEPPARD, Ray (hockey); b. 27 May, 1966, Pembroke, Ont.; m. Lucie; c. Lyndsay, Douglas; right wing Cornwall (OHL), Rochester (AHL); Buffalo '87-90, NY Rangers '90-91, Detroit '91-95, San Jose '95-96, Florida '96-97, '99, Carolina '97-99; reached 50-goal plateau with 52 '94; NHL record (through '99): 771 scheduled games, 347g, 290a, 81 playoff games, 30g, 20a; OHL 1st team all-star; NHL all-rookie team; res. Boca Raton, Fla.

SHERIDAN, Juan (football); b. 2 Feb 1925, Havana, Cuba, d. 7 Oct 1969, Ormstown, Que.; m. Elizabeth Hedrick; c. Martha, Gordon, Bob, Bruce, John; UofT; sales rep.; sports dir. HMCS Donnacona, mem. '44 Grey Cup champions; played with Toronto Balmy Beach, Toronto Indians; Montreal Alouettes '48-59, mem. '49 Grey Cup winner; frequent all-star, all-Cdn centre; nicknamed 'The Pear'; asst. coach Queen's.

SHERK, Cathy (golf); b. 17 Jun 1970, Fonthill, Ont.; div.; c. 1 son; golf administrator; Ont. amateur titles '76, '78; ntl amateur titles '77-78; US amateur champ '78; North-South Women's amateur title '78; low individual world amateur '78; CPGA championship '88, '90-91; Ont athlete of '78; *Golf Digest* women's amateur golfer of '78; co-winner (with Diane Konihowski) Velma Springstead award '78; CLGA advisor/coach '94-95; player dir. du Maurier series; pro co-ordinator Ont. jr. girls camp; mem. RCGA Hall of Fame; res. Toronto, Ont.

SHERO, Fred (hockey/coaching); b. 23 Oct 1925, Winnipeg, Man.; d. 24 Nov 1990, Camden, N.J.; given name: Fred Alexander; c. Ray; jr. St. James, Winnipeg Rangers; 3 seasons NY Rangers; 2 Calder Cups with

Cleveland (AHL); mem. '56 WHL champion Winnipeg Warriors; turned to coaching piloting Buffalo Bisons to '70 AHL title; named coach of yr; coached Philadelphia '71-78; Stanley Cup victories '74-75; concluded coaching career with Rangers '78-81; NHL coaching record: 734 scheduled games, 390-225-119; mem. Man. Hockey Hall of Fame.

SHERRING, William (t&f); b. 1877, Hamilton, Ont., d. 1964, Hamilton, Ont.; railway brakeman; at 16 won races at Ont. fairs; at 20 3rd Hamilton's around-the-bay race (about 19 miles); won same race 1899, 1903; 2nd 1900 Boston Marthon; gold 1906 special Athens Olympics; took race lead after 2 1/2 hours, finished in record 2:51:23.6; accompanied over line by Prince George of Greece; finished race weighing 98lbs, a loss of 14lbs during race; mem. Cdn Amateur, Canada's Sports Hall of Fame.

SHERWOOD, Liv (sailing); b.27 Nov 1923, Ottawa, Ont.; given name: Livius Anglin; m. Anne Galligan (d.); c. Christopher, Mary; UofT, BA, Osgoode Hall; retd provincial court judge; international 14' dinghy champion BYC '54-57; Dragon Class '58-60, Shark Class '64-67; Shark Class ntl '64, NA '65 champion; 3 Severn Trophy dinghy titles; p.-pres. St. Lawrence Valley Yachting Assn.; founded BYC jr. program '56; dir. CYA '57-67, '70-83, councillor from '83; CYA rules committee '70-98, chair. '78-81; mem. CYA appeals comm. '70-98, chair. '70-75; International Yachting Racing Union racing rules comm. '74-98; certified international yachting judge '80-98; jury mem./chair. 7 America's Cup, 1 Canada's Cup, 27 world championships; dir. sailing '76 Olympics; Ottawa citizen of '71; mem. Governor-General's Curling Club; res. Ottawa, Ont.

SHIBICKY, Alex (hockey); b. 19 May 1914, Winnipeg, Man.; given name: Alexis Dimitri; m. Gloria May Aspinall; c. Alex, Kathy, Lori, Nancy, Bill; retd; rw jr. Selkirk Fishermen; pro NY Rangers '36-42, '45-46; mem. Allan Cup champion Ottawa Commandos '42-43; New Haven Ramblers '46-47; coached WHL New Westminster Royals '47-49, '53-54, Flin Flon Bombers SJHL '49-53, Kelowna Packers '54-55, IHL Indianapolis Chiefs '60-61; mem. '40 Stanley Cup champions; NHL record: 322 scheduled games, 110g, 91a, 40 playoff games, 12g, 12a; mem. Man. Hockey Hall of Fame; res. Burnaby, B.C.

SHIELDS, Kathy (basketball/coaching); b. 18 Jan 1951, W.Vancouver, B.C.; m. Ken Shields; Laurentian, BComm, UBC, BPhE; coach UVic; competed as ntl team mem. '70-74; coach jr. varsity '76-77; varsity asst. coach '77-78; head basketball coach '78-99; coached 12 CWUAA, 8 ntl CIAU title teams; BC team of '92; groomed 13 UVic athletes for ntl women's team; ntl jr team coach '83; development team coach '86; asst. sr. ntl team '82-84, '88-92; head coach sr. ntl team '92-95; coached '93 America's Zone world qualification bronze medal team '93, '94 world championships team; 2 CIAU, 7 Canada West coach of yr awards; 2 Basketball BC, 1 Sport BC coaching awards' Coaching Assn of Canada 3M award '92; master coach ntl coaching institute '86-98; level 4 coaching cert.; dir. Commonwealth Games board '93-94; former UVic AD; res. Victoria, B.C./Tokyo, Japan.

SHIELDS, Ken (basketball/coaching); b. 7 Dec 1945, Beaverlodge, Alta.; m. Kathy; UCal, BA, UBC, BPhE,

MPhE; coach; ex-pres. Commonwealth Centre for Sport Development; AD/basketball coach UVic '78-89; 7 consec CIAU ntl titles; coached BC ream, ntl jr, ntl B teams; ntl men's team head coach 5yrs; directed establishment of National Coaching Institute '86; led in creation of high-performance training centres for rowing, soccer, middle-distance running; CCA certified master coach for basketball; 4 CIAU coach of year awards; '81 BC coach of year; George Pearkes Memorial award for leadership in university sports; dir. CCA, NCI; mem. '94 Commonwealth Games bids comm., governor Victoria Commonwealth Games Society; pres. CPCA '93-98; mem. Cdn Basketball Hall of Fame; res. Tokyo, Japan.

SHOCKEY-MILANESE, Barbara (swimming); b. 16 May 1962, Saskatoon, Sask.; given name: Barbara Shockey; m. Thomas Jay Milanese; c. Anthony, Jamie, Thomas;Miami, Dowling Coll., BA; art teacher; began swimming age 6; coached by Harry Bailey attained ntl level; at 14 set 2 provincial records; forte 800m FS; coached by Ken Olsen competed '78 Commonwealth Games, World championships; 800m FS bronze '79 Pan-Am Games; 3 masters gold Empire State Games '93; silver, bronze '95 US ntl masters; mem. Sask, Saskatoon Sports halls of fame; res. Boca Raton, Fla.

SHONG, Laurie (modern pentathlon/fencing); b. 2 Jan 1971, Vancouver, B.C.; Vancouver Community College; actor/model; successful age-group swimmer; only Cdn to win world fencing title jr. épée '88 world cadet championships; silver '91 junior worlds; 5th '91 jr. worlds Modern Pentathlon best-ever result by Cdn male; 1st Cdn to qualify for two sports in same summer Olympics '92; Pan-Pacific MP bronze '91; team épée gold, individual bronze '90 Commonwealth championships; rebounded from near fatal auto accident '93 to win fencing titles NA Cup circuit, Tournoi des Grands Vins, Commonwealth championships '94; Pro Fencing League gold '98; épée bronze '99 Pan-Am Games; Harry Jerome, Fair Play awards, BC jr.athlete of '88; res. Vancouver, B.C.

SHORE, Eddie (hockey); b. 25 Nov 1902, Ft. Qu'Apelle, Sask.; d. 16 Mar 1985, Agawam, Mass.; given name: Edward William; m. Katie McRae (d.); c. Ted; Manitoba Agricultural College; retd. hockey exec.; wife mem. famed Edmonton Grads basketball team '24-29; Melville Millionaires '23-24; def. Regina Caps, Edmonton (WCL); Boston (NHL) '26-39, NY Americans '39-40; season; NHL record: 105 goals, 179 assists; 4 Hart Trophy (MVP awards); 7 1st, 1 2nd team all-star; mem. 2 Stanley Cup winners; owned, operated Springfield (AHL) '40-78, excluding WW2 yrs as GM, coach Buffalo Bisons; briefly operated New Haven franchise, owned Fort Worth (USHL), Oakland (PCHL) until sold to California Seals; past v-p. AHL; '70 Lester Patrick Trophy for contribution to US hockey; hon. governor AHL; jersey #2 retd. by Bruins; mem. Hockey, Canada's Sports halls of fame.

SHORT, George (football/t&f); b. 5 May 1941, Saskatoon, Sask.; given name: George Douglas; m. Margaret Jean Parr; c. Stacey Lynn, Lesley Anne;UAlta, BPhE, UCal, BEd, Windsor, MPhE; retd. asst. athletic dir.; defensive halfback '58 Sask. HS champs, '59 ntl jr. champion Saskatoon Hilltops; mem. WCIAA champion Alta. Bears '62-64,

Calgary Dinosaurs '67, CCIFC champion, Prairie Bowl finalist Windsor Lancers '69; ntl jr. sprint champion '59, setting 100yd dash record 9.8 sec.; mem. '59 Pan-Am, '60 Olympic teams; WCIAA all-star, hon. mention all-Cdn '64, CIAU all-Cdn. '69; pres. Cdn Assn. University Athletic Directors '75; Hong Kong delegation Olympic attache '76; pres. Olympic Club of Canada '77; retd. asst. AD, lecturer Concordia.; mem. Sask. Sports (as '59 Hilltops member), Saskatoon Sports halls of fame; res. Beaconsfield, Que.

SHOULDICE, Hap (football/officiating); b. 12 Mar 1907, Ottawa, Ont., d. 21 May 1981, Ottawa, Ont.; given name: Hans; m. Lois McCulloch; c. Don, Doug, Drew (d); retd. chief administrator customer accounting, CFL dir. of officiating; organized, managed, coached, Gowlings to '27 ntl juvenile basketball title; coach Rideau Aquatic sr. ladies' canoe team; juvenile lacrosse Strathconas '22-25; catcher Ottawa Hydro Mercantile softball league, Masonic League early '30s; paddled Rideau club '25-35, 5yrs war canoe capt., ladies' war canoe capt.; paddler '30 BEG; coach Shamrock Jr. hockey team '27-29; coach-mgr. Rideau Jr. '30 Memorial Cup semifinalists; began hockey, football officiating '27; worked 9 ntl hockey finals, Memorial, Allan, Alexander Cup; CFL official '35-58, 8 Grey Cup finals; EFC supervisor of officials '58, same role for CFL '72; organized first hockey, football officials assn. in Canada; mem. Ottawa Sports, Canadian Football halls of fame.

SHRUBB, Alf (t&f); b. 1878, Slinfield, Sussex, Eng., d. 23 Apr 1964, Bowmanville, Ont.; tobacconist; dominated world distance running scene 2-20 miles around turn of century; mem. Horsham Blue Star Harriers 1898, 1, 3, 4 mile titles; South London Harriers 1900; Eng. sr. cross-country titles 1901-04, international cross-country titles '03-04, 10 AAA track titles in 4 years; 6 world, 6 GB records; missed Olympic opportunity when Britain failed to send team to '04 Games; pro '05, moving to Boston '05, Toronto '09; competed with and defeated Dorando Pietri, Johnny Hayes, Bill Sherring, Tom Longboat in all races less than 20 miles; lost to Longboat '09 NY marathon; engaged in profitable (reported $3,000 per win, $2,000 per loss) 10-race series with Longboat winning 7 at 10-16 miles, losing 3 at 20 or more miles; fan pleaser with varying running styles; trainer, cross-country coach Harvard '15; 1st pro coach Oxford '15-26.

SHUTT, Steve (hockey); b. 1 Jul 1952, Toronto, Ont.; given name: Stephen John; ice making equipment dealer; hockey coach; jr. Toronto Marlboros; 1st Montreal pick, 4th overall '72 draft; lw Canadiens '72-84, Los Angeles '84-85; attained 60 goal plateau '76-77 season; once 1st, twice 2nd team all-star; Team Canada '76; NHL record: 935 scheduled games, 424g, 393a, 99 playoff games, 50g, 48a; mem. 5 Stanley Cup winners; color commentator on radio 3yrs; asst. coach Canadiens '93-97; mem. Hockey Hall of Fame; res. Montreal, Que.

SIDDERS, George (boxing); 2 Jun 1907, London, Eng.; d. (circa) 1990, Galiano Island, B.C.; given name: George William; m. 3 times; Sir George Williams, College of Divine Metaphysics, Indianapolis; Que. military dist. lightweight title '25; Montreal, Que. lightweight crowns '26; claimed ntl amateur lightweight, welterweight titles during span of

1 hour on a single night '26; ntl pro welterweight crown '28; British army PT instructor Aldershot, Eng., '40; chief instructor remedial, physical exercise training for Cdn army in England '40-45; active in soccer, baseball, swimming, golf, tennis.

SIEBERT, Babe (hockey); b. 14 Jan 1904, Plattsville, Ont.; d. 25 Aug 1939, St. Joseph, Ont.; given name: Albert Charles; Kitchener OHA jrs. '22-23; Niagara Falls srs. '24-25, NHL Montreal Maroons '25-32, Rangers '32-34, Boston '34-36, Canadiens '36-39; with Maroons lw 5yrs on Big S line with Nels Stewart, Hooley Smith; 1st team all-star def. 3 successive years; Hart Trophy '37; captain '39 team, signed to coach Canadiens following season but drowned during summer; mem. Hockey Hall of Fame.

SIGFUSSON, Svein (t&f); b. 15 Jul 1912, Lundar, Man.; d. 1993, Winnipeg, Man.; m. Thelma Goodman; c. Skuli Norman, Darlene Sigridur, Linda Gudran, Lois Olive Iris, Charles Svein; owner Sigfusson Transportation Co.; ntl discus record '38 in initial competitive performance; hammer throw gold, discus, shot, triple jump, javelin silvers '38 ntl championships; won hammer '47-48, silver discus '48 nationals; bronze discus '50 BEG; mem. '54 BEG team; lost records make totals incomplete but it is known he won at least 8 Man., 9 ntl titles '38-54; all-Canada t&f team '54, councilman Cdn Commonwealth Games Assn.; Manitoba Centennial Medal, Order of Canada; mem. Manitoba Sports Hall of Fame.

SILCOTT, Liz (basketball); b. 14 Dec 1950, Montreal, Que.; given name: Helen Elizabeth; UBC, Concordia; mem. women's ntl basketball team '72-78; leading scorer UBC ntl women's champions, all-conf. guard '72-74, all-Cdn '74; led Concordia scorers '75, all-conf. guard, ntl record points in 2-game championship series with 77; mem. '75 Pan-Am, '76 Olympic teams; Que. athlete of '74, '75; MVP '74 Genoa, Italy, tournament; MVP '75 Szombathely, Hungary; pro basketball St. Louis Streak, San Francisco Pioneers, New Mexico Energee '79-80; last known res. Cornwall, Ont.

SILVERBERG, Doug (golf); b. 16 Jan 1933, Red Deer, Alta.; given name: Douglas Howard; m. Carole Barber; c. Douglas Kirk, Kyle Robert, Scott William; Colorado Coll.; London Life insurance exec.; jr. hockey Port Arthur; all-American, all-Cdn; 2 Alta. juvenile, 2 Alta HS, 3 Alta. jr. golf titles; Cdn jr. '50, runnerup '51; 6 Alta. amateur, 3 runnerup, 1 Alta. Open, lost 2nd in playoff, twice runnerup, 8 times low amateur; 2 Alta match play pro-am; 8 Central Alta amateur, 3 Central Alta Open titles; Sask. Amateur '55, Open '58; mem. 23 Willingdon Cup (3 winners); 5 Commonwealth teams, '71 winner; 4 Americas Cup, 2 World Amateur teams; 3yrs pres. Calgary GA; mem. RCGA, Alta. Sports halls of fame; res. Calgary, Alta.

SILVERHEELS, Jay (lacrosse/boxing); b. 26 May 1912, Six Nations of the Grand River, Ont.; d. 5 Mar 1980, Canoga Park, Calif; given name: Harry Smith; m. 1. Laura Bailey; c. Sharon; m. 2. Mary; c. Jay Jr., Karen, Pamela, Marilyn; actor; a superb athlete, he played professional lacrosse with Buffalo, Toronto Tecumsehs and semi-pro hockey; won NY State Golden Gloves middleweight boxing title '37; while competing in lacrosse and hockey in California '33 was encouraged by Joe E. Brown and Richard Dix to try acting as film extra; career took off when he earned role of Tonto on Lone Ranger TV series; appeared in numerous movies, three times playing Geronimo in major movies; among movie credits were*: Broken Arrow, Saskatchewan, Captain from Castile*; in later years raised and drove standardbred horses; mem. Brantford Wall of Recognition, Cdn Lacrosse, Western NY Entertainment halls of fame.

SIMARD, Martine (synchro swim); b. 29 Mar 1961, Quebec City; Laval.; competitive diver, swimmer before focusing attention on synchronized swimming '69; mem. Que. 15 and under team '74; 2nd duet, team '76 ntl championships; ntl title team '78-80; mem. '78 world championships, '80 FINA Cup, American Challenge Cup teams; mem. Pan-Pacific Games gold medal team '79; res. Sillery, Que.

SIMBOLI, Chris (skiing): b. 18 Sep 1962, Ottawa, Ont.; m. Melanie Palenik;Windsor LLB, Detroit JD; lawyer; freestyle specialist; moved from Ont. to ntl team '84; ntl men's aerials title '86; 1st skier to achieve freestyle grand slam winning world title, World Cup, Grand Prix '89; 3 Ont., 7 ntl titles; won 46 WP, GP medals '84-89; retd. from competition '89; CSA John Semmelink trophy, 1st FS skier so honored; finalist Cdn male athlete of '89; Ottawa ACT athlete of '89; mem. Nepean Wall, Cdn Skiing, Ottawa Sports halls of fame; res. Nepean, Ont.

SIMMER, Charlie (hockey); b. 20 Mar 1954, Terrace Bay, Ont.; given name: Charles Robert; div.; c. Brittany Ann; m. Jody,; c. Jake, Austin; sales recruiter, TV hockey analyst; jr. Sault Ste. Marie Greyhounds; 4th California pick, 39th overall '74 draft; lw California '74-76, Cleveland '76-77, Los Angeles '77-84, Boston '84-87, Pittsburgh '87-88; Team Canada '83; 1 season Frankfurt, Germany; asst. coach San Diego Gulls (IHL) '89-90; successive 56 goal seasons Kings '79-81; 2 2nd team all-star; with Marcel Dionne, Dave Taylor formed LA's Triple Crown Line; played 3 NHL all-star games; NHL record: 712 scheduled games, 342g, 369a, 24 playoff games, 9g, 9a; Bill Masterton trophy '86;radio analyst Anaheim Mighty Ducks, TV analyst Phoenix ; active in varied charitable organizations; mem. NWO Sports Hall of Fame; res. Scottsdale, Ariz.

SIMMS, Tony (basketball); b. 16 Feb 1959, Jamaica; guard ntl team '81-92; mem. '83 FISU Games gold team; '83 Pan-Am, '84 Olympic teams; fed. govt. excellence award '84; res. Toronto, Ont.

SIMONS, Pop (softball); b. 15 Jan 1894, Penzance, Eng.; d. (circa) 1990, Vancouver, B.C.; given name: Richard Percy; retd storekeeper; mediocre playing career as shortstop failed to dull enthusiasm for game; sponsored 1st team '37; with Cece White arranged for installation of lights Vancouver South Memorial Park, instrumental in formation of BCASA, CASA; treasurer BCASA '48-77; CASA's 1st secty '65, later v-p., dir. to '71; secty BC Amateur Basketball Assn. 5yrs; 1st life mem. CSA '72; mem. Softball Canada Hall of Fame.

SIMPSON, Ben (football); b. 1878, Peterborough, Ont., d. 20 Oct 1964, Guelph, Ont.; Queen's, MA, Normal School; educator; int. football Queen's; Hamilton Tigers '04-10, 2

Ont., 1 ntl titles; captain '10 team; referee 3yrs intercollegiate ranks, 7 interprovincial league; mem. Tiger team which, with Ottawa, demonstrated Cdn game to US fans; mem. Canada's Sports, Canadian Football halls of fame.

SIMPSON, Bill (soccer); b. 13 Sep 1894, Paisley, Scotland, d. 1974, Toronto, Ont.; foreman; mem. Fraserburg team Toronto, Toronto City in National Soccer League, Davenport Albion, Toronto Scottish, '19 league title; 15yrs secty.-treas. Ont. Soccer Assn., 14yrs pres. Toronto District Soccer Assn.; 4yrs pres. CSFA; credited with many innovations in Cdn soccer; mgr. 1st Cdn team to play USSR; launched Canada's soccer coaching schools; mem. Canada's Sports Hall of Fame.

SIMPSON, Bob (football); b. 20 Apr 1930, Windsor, Ont.; div. Cecile; c. Robert John, Gary Lee, Lynn Patricia, Mark Stanley; m. Mary Francis; c. Mary Leigh; Assumption College; retd. LCBO clerk; forward 2 Ont. HS basketball title teams; 4ys Tillsonburg Livingstons; mem. '52 Olympic team; 1yr Windor Rockets (ORFU); Rough Riders '50-62; CFL record: caught 65 TD passes, record surpassed '75 by Terry Evanshan; 386 lifetime points, 12 other defensive TDs, 274 receptions 9 recorded seasons, 6034yds (22.0yds-per-catch avg. 2nd only to Whit Tucker 22.4); best single season 47 receptions '56; 6 times EFC all-star, 4 times all-Cdn; outstanding player (Gordon Sturtridge Memorial Trophy) '57 East-West Game; runnerup Schenley outstanding Cdn '56; mem. 2 Grey Cup winners; jersey #70 retired by Riders; coach Ashbury College football several years; PR director Ottawa; several years Ottawa sr. basketball league; exec.-dir. National Capital Regional Sports Council; mem. Cdn Football, Ottawa, Windsor-Essex Sports halls of fame; res. Nepean, Ont.

SIMPSON, Bruce (t&f); b. 6 Mar 1950, Toronto, Ont.; div. Joanne; m. Senga Nicholson; c. Colin, Katie; UCLA, UofT BSc, UofOtt, LLB; lawyer; ntl pole vault title '65, ntl record 12'6 1/2" (3.81m); ranked among top 6 indoor vaulters in world '68; mem. '70, '78, '82 Commonwealth, '72, '76 Olympic, '71, '75, '79 Pan-Am, '75 FISU Games, '77, '79 World Cup teams; bronze '71, gold '79 Pan-Am Games; gold '78 Commonwealth Games; silver '75 FISU Games; ntl indoor record 17'4 3/4" (5.30m); '77 Adelaide Interntl, Pacific Conf titles; gold Melbourne Interntl, *Etobicoke Guardian*, ntl championships '80; ntl indoor, outdoor titles '81; does some coaching in Toronto area; res. Toronto, Ont.

SIMPSON, Bullet Joe (hockey); b. 13 Aug 1893, Selkirk, Man., d. 26 Dec 1973, Florida; given name: Harold Joseph; compensated for lightweight stature with speed to become great defenceman and earn nickname "Bullet Joe"; amateur hockey Winnipeg Victorias '14-15; mem. Winnipeg 61st Battalion Allan Cup winner; Selkirk Fishermen '19-20; Edmonton Eskimos '21-25, 2 WCHL titles; NY Americans (NHL) '25-31; managed Americans '32-35; New Haven, Minneapolis before retiring; awarded Military Medal; mem. Canada's Sports, Man., Cdn Hockey halls of fame.

SIMPSON, Craig (hockey); b. 15 Feb 1967, London, Ont.; m. Christine Kirkland; c. Dillon; Michigan State; TV hockey color commentator; lw; Mich. State CCHA '83-85; CCHA all-star; NCAA all-American; drafted by Pittsburgh '85-88, Edmonton '87-93, Buffalo '93-95; NHL record: 634 scheduled games, 247g, 250a, 67 playoff games, 36g, 32a; res. Edmonton, Alta./Los Angeles, Calif

SIMPSON, Jimmy (football/builder): b. 1 Nov 1906, Hamilton, Ont.; d. 16 Nov 1975, Hamilton, Ont.; c. Jim Jr.; began football career with Hamilton Tigers '28 and remained affiliated with game as player/official/trainer almost 50yrs; outside wing with 6 Grey Cup finalists, 4 winners; scored 4 Grey Cup Tds; turned to officiating '45-56; joined Tiger-Cats as asst. trainer '57; head trainer '60-75; nicknamed "The Rooster"; affiliated with 19 Grey Cup games, 6 as player, 3 as official and 10 as trainer; mem. Cdn Football Hall of Fame.

SIMPSON, John (equestrian): b. 3 Jul 1949, Calgary, Alta.; m. Tracy Bowman; c. Christy, Luke; rancher; ntl team '73-80; US President's Cup '78; Rotterdam GP title '77; jumping team silver '79 Pan-Am Games; mem. '76 Olympic, '79 Pan-Am Games teams; res. Cochrane, Alta.

SIMPSON, Rene (tennis): b. 14 Jan 1966, Sarnia, Ont.; given name: Norine Karen; div. Barry Alter; Texas Christian, BA (business/accounting); Tennis Canada player services mgr. from '98; Ont. Open singles titles '87-90; mem. Cdn Federation Cup team '88-98, coach '99; mem. '88, '92 Olympic team; all-American singles, doubles TCU '88, all-American Southwest Conf. MVP '88, Southwest region sr. player of '88, all-Southwest Conf. academic team; mem. TCU all-decade team; ntl singles title '92; ntl women's, mixed doubles titles '93-94; with Helen Kelesi Tennis Canada doubles team of '92; TC most improved player '88; highest WTA ranking 70 in '89; 3 intl doubles titles; res. Toronto, Ont.

SINCLAIR, Ken (tennis): b. 4 Jan 1930, Toronto, Ont.; given name: Kenneth Donald; m. Elizabeth Stella Aston; c Bill, Bob, Pat, Kelly; insurance broker; 3 world championships for journalists; won over-45 and over-55 indoor, outdoor ntl singles titles; with Lorne Main 6 world srs. doubles titles, 4 consec. Austria Cups, Von Cramm Cup '92, Britannia Cup '98; European indoor singles, doubles '91; chair. Cdn open championships in '70s and '80s. mem. Cdn Tennis Hall of Fame; res. Aurora, Ont.

SINCLAIR, Marjorie (curling): b. 25 Jan 1911, England; given name: Marjorie Helen; m. Duncan S. Sinclair; c. Jaclyn, John; secty. Western Canada Ladies' Curling Assn. '49-50; delegate for Northern Alta. LCA on WCLCA '50-52; WCLCA secty. '54; pres. Eaton NALCA '55-56; pres. NALCA '57-58; pres. Edmonton LCC '59-60; Western Canada delegate CLCA '61-63; Sinclair Trophy presented annually to NALCA champions; pres. CLCA '63-64; secty. NALCA '61-68, also ALCA twice during that period; mem. 1st women's baseball team Calgary; mem. Canadian Curling Hall of Fame; res. Edmonton, Alta./Sun City, Ariz.

SINDEN, Harry (hockey): b. 14 Sep 1932, Collins Bay, Ont.; given name: Harry James; m. Eleanor; c. Nancy, Carol, Donna, Julie; hockey exec.; 5yrs def sr. OHA guiding Whitby Dunlops to '57 Allan Cup, '58 world amateur championship; player-coach Kingston (EPHL),

Minneapolis, Oklahoma City (CPHL) 6yrs; CPHL championship '66; never played in NHL; coach Boston '67-70, '79-80, GM from '72, pres. from '89; coached '60 Team Canada Olympic silver medal team, '72 Team Canada victory over USSR; NHL coaching record: 142 wins, 106 losses, 55 ties regular season, 22 wins, 16 losses in playoffs; 1 Stanley Cup; 1st NHL GM to reach 1000 victories during his tenure with same club; Lester Patrick award '99; dir. Hockey Hall of Fame; mem. IIHF, Hockey halls of fame; res. Winchester, Mass.

SINGLETON, Gordon (cycling): b. 9 Aug 1956, Niagara Falls, Ont.; m. Louann Godak; c. Christopher, James; auto store mgr.; began competitive cycling '74 winning Ont. jr title; ntl sr. sprint titles '75-77; mem. '75-77 World championships, '75, '79 Pan-Ams, '76 Olympic, '78 Commonwealth Games teams; gold, bronze '78 Commonwealth Games; 2 gold '79 Pan-Am Games, silver worlds; within 24-hour span set world 200m, 500m, 1000m sprint records '80, 1st cyclist to accomplish feat in so short a time; NA records 200m, 1000m; mem. ntl team '75-80; pro with AMF Wheel Goods '81; silver world sprints '81; 2 world pro records; world title '82; 1st Cdn cyclist to win coveted rainbow jersey; career ended following '82 track crash; Ont. athlete of '79; twice runnerup Cdn athlete of yr; CBC-TV color commentator '84 Olympics, '94 Commonwealth Games; also TV analyst for CTV, TSN; does some coaching; mem. selection comm. NF Sports Wall of Fame; mem. Order of Canada, Niagara Falls Sports Wall of Fame; res. St. Catharines, Ont.

SINGLETON, Harvey (football/basketball/t&f): b. 22 Dec 1932, Chicago, Ill.; m. Sonja Matwichuk; c. Patti-Jo, Todd; Kentucky State, BSc, Eastern Michigan, MSc; teacher; 12 athletic letters Kentucky State; 4yrs all-conf. receiver, little all-American status; mem. Argos '52; ORFU champion Toronto Balmy Beach; 2yrs all-conf. basketball KSU; mem. Dow Kings Ont. Sr. A champions, YMHA Sr. A champions; played briefly Harlem Globetrotters; vertical jumps referee '76 Montreal Olympics; co-operator, co-director VYTIS basketball camp 5yrs; coach HS basketball several years; res. Oakville, Ont.

SIPPEL, Lori (softball): b. 16 May 1965, Stratford, Ont.; given name: Lori Anne; Nebraska, BScEd.; coach; righthanded pitcher; competed '81 World Youth Games; mem. '84 ntl title team; 3 US ntl gold, 1 silver; Pan Am Games gold '83, silver '91, bronze '87; college world series silver; competed 4 world championships; mem. ntl team 15yrs; mem. '96, 2000 Olympic team; retd but came back to help Team Canada qualify for 2000 Olympics; most inspirational player award '98 Canada Cup; jersey #16 retd by Nebraska; asst. softball coach Nebraska; Academic All-American '88; TV softball analyst '99 Pan-Am Games; mem. Cdn Softball Hall of Fame; res. Lincoln, Neb.

SISSAOURI, Guivi (wrestling): b. 15 Apr 1971, Russia; immigrated to Canada '92; 3 ntl sr 57kg, 1 62kg titles; gold '94 Francophone Games, silver '95, bronze '97 world championships; gold '95, silver '97 Canada Cup; gold '96 Pan-American championships; silver '96 Olympic Games; gold Austrian, Poland GP, NY, Romanian Open; res. Montreal, Que.

SITTLER, Darryl (hockey); b. 18 Sep 1950, St. Jacob's, Ont.; given name: Darryl Glen; m. Wendy; c. Ryan, Megan, Ashley; hockey exec.; OHA junior A London Knights; 1st pick Maple Leafs, 8th overall '70 amateur draft; Toronto '70-82, Philadelphia '82-84, Detroit '84-85; once 2nd team all-star ctr; NHL record 10 point game Feb '76 vs Boston with 6 goals, 4 assists; 6 goals tied modern NHL mark shared by Syd Howe, Red Berenson; in playoffs vs Philadelphia same season scored 5 goals in single game; 1 league, 5 Toronto club records; mem. Team Canada '76; scored overtime winner vs Czechoslovakia which gave Canada title; Leafs captain '75-'81; NHL record: 1096 scheduled games, 484g, 637a, 76 playoff games, 29g, 45a; hon. chair. McDonald House, prominent numerous charities; special consultant to Toronto pres. Cliff Fletcher '91-96; dir. marketing/community relations '97; fan choice as Leafs all-time team centre; mem. Waterloo County, Hockey halls of fame; res. East Amherst, N.Y.

SKILLINGS-HARNEY, Sandra (badminton); b. 29 Aug 1959, Vancouver, B.C.; m. Greg Harney; c. Stewart. Kathleem; Langara Coll; racquets pro; ntl intermediate doubles, mixed doubles, singles titles '80; Pepsi-Cola mixed doubles '80; silver singles, mixed doubles (with Ken Priestman) '80 Pan-Am championships; ntl doubles (with Wendy Carter) '82; quarterfinalist Scotland '83; mem. '84 Uber Cup team; team silver '82, '86 Commonwealth Games; retd. '86 and turned to squash, coaching; #1 ranked BC squash 1yr; competitive squash '86-93; coached squash/badminton '89-98; mgr. BC Canada Winter Games badminton team '99; dir. CG Sports Dev. board; res. Victoria, B.C.

SKINNER, Archie (golf); b. 21 Aug 1913, St. Andrews, Scotland; d. 19 May 1989, Fredericton, N.B.; NB, PEI, Maritime Open champion '33-60; course record St. Andrews '41, Digby Pines '36; mem. NB Sports Hall of Fame.

SKINNER, Grant (softball); b. 5 Jun 1952, Vancouver, B.C.; given name: Grant Thomas; m. Cheryl Murphy; c. Bryan; Molson Breweries rep.; second baseman; mem. ntl team '80-93; ntl championship MVP '80; gold '83 Pan-Am Games, silver '84 worlds; 4 time all-Canadian at ntl championships; mem. '93 Toronto Gators ISC world, ntl title teams; head coach CJHL Ottawa Jr. Senators '98; mem. Nepean Wall of Fame; res. Kanata, Ont.

SKINNER, Jim (hockey); b. 12 Jan 1917, Selkirk, Man.; given name: James Donald; m. Vivian Reynolds; c. Holly, Karen, Teresa, Jim Jr.; hockey consultant; defenceman with Flin Flon Bombers; pro Indianapolis (AHL); player-capt.-asst. coach Omaha (USHL); retd. as player '47; 6yrs coach Windsor Spitfires, 1yr Hamilton Red Wings; coach Detroit (NHL) '54-58, 2 league titles, 1 Stanley Cup; served many roles with Detroit including head scout, dir. farm club operations, asst. GM, dir. hockey operations, GM; mem. Man. Hockey Hall of Fame; res. Windsor, Ont.

SKINNER, Larry Jr. (hockey/softball); b. 21 Apr 1956, Vancouver, B.C.; given name: Larry Foster; m. Laurie McRae; c. Jordan, Angela; newspaper circulation mgr.; Jr. A hockey with Ottawa 67's '75-76; Colorado Rockies (NHL) '76-80; 2yrs Austria, 5yrs France; won French Cup B div. title '82; scored 1st goal in Colorado Rockies franchise history; NHL record: 47 scheduled games, 10g, 12a, 2 playoff games, 0g, 0a; all-star 3rd baseman ntl fastball championships '80, '81, '86, '90; batting champion ntl championships PEI; mem. ntl '84 world silver medal team; asst. coach CJHL Ottawa Jr. Senators '98; mem. Nepean Wall of Fame; res. Kanata, Ont.

SKINNER, Larry Sr. (hockey/softball); b. 25 Jul 1930, Keyes, Man.; m. Marjorie Blair; c. Grant, David, Ruth, Larry, Shannon; Oregon; retd. dir. marketing, communication CAHA; softball player, coach, manager 30yrs; participated in 3 world softball championships, 6 ntl finals; 5yrs Pacific Coast Soccer League; 1 ntl soccer championship; exec.-dir. CASA 3yrs; dir. marketing CAHA '73-95; res. Manotick, Ont.

SKRESLET, Laurie (mountaineering); b. 25 Oct 1949, Calgary, Alta.; m. Monique Viau; c. Natasha; mountain guide/motivational speaker; began mountaineering age 20; graduate of Colorado Outward Bound school; 7yrs instructor Cdn Outward Bound School; 1st Cdn to summit Mount Everest; certified mem. Assn. of Cdn Mountain Guides; as mem. '82 Mt. Everest expedition mem. Alta. Sports Hall of Fame; res. Calgary, Alta.

SKRIEN, Dave (football/coaching); b. 1929, Brooten, Minn.; m. Dee; c. Scott, Bruce, Christopher; Minnesota, BSc, MA; retd. parks and recreation supervisor; fullback Sask., Winnipeg '53, Grey Cup finalist; HS coach Minnesota; backfield coach Ball State College, Minn.; asst. coach BC (CFL) '59-60, head coach '61-67; WFC titles '63-64, Grey Cup victory '64; asst. Boise State College '67, Eskimos '68; head coach Roughriders '69-72 losing Grey Cup final to Hamilton '72; asst. WFL Memphis Southmen '73-75; part-time coach '79-81 nationally-ranked Golden Valley Lutheran Jr. College; full time parks and recreation dir. Richfield, Minn., '76-94; Annis Stukus Trophy as CFL coach of '63; res. Eden Prairie, Minn.

SLACK, Bill (harness racing/baseball); b. 24 Oct 1929, Toronto, Ont.; given name: William Michael Blakeley; sep.; c. Steven, Michael, Brian; St. Michael's College; retd. racing secty. Blue Bonnets Raceway; mem. Toronto Marlboros midget hockey champions '46; Ont. jr. baseball championship team '50; pro tryout Brooklyn Dodgers; played briefly Boston Braves farm system; Que. area scout Detroit '72-77, Toronto '77-98; asst. program dir. Thorncliffe Raceway '50; program dir. Dufferin Park Raceway '51; program dir. Richelieu Park, Blue Bonnets Raceways '52-67; racing secty. Blue Bonnets '67-94; feature columnist Harness World from '65; TV commentator Que. Derby '60s; developed harness racing charts, past performance program for Que.; res. Anjou, Que.

SLACK, Bill (baseball); b. 3 May 1933, Petrolia, Ont.; given name: William Henry; m. Patricia; c. Victor, Cindy, Karen, Timmy; baseball coach; mem. Sarnia Jr. B hockey champs '50-51; pitcher, Sr. Intercounty with London; drafted by Chicago (NHL) but opted for baseball signing with Boston (AL)organization; spent 33yrs in Boston organization as player, manager, pitching coach; 10yrs Atlanta organization as minor league pitching coach Danville Braves; mem. Sarnia/Lambton Sports Hall of Fame; res. Winston Salem, N.C.

SLACK, Stan (baseball): b. 2 Jun 1930, Petrolia, Ont.; given name: Stanley Frederick; m. Marnie Marie; c. Linda, William, Lori, Julie, Brian (d); retd. steamfitter; signed with St. Louis (NL) organization as pitcher age 14; won 1st pro game in Appalachian League before turning 15; 8 seasons with Cardinals, Braves winning 69 games; mem. OBA champion Lou Ball Jrs., London Majors Srs.; coached minor, senior teams in Sarnia area several yrs; mgr. London Majors Sr, IC '91; mem, Sarnia/Lambton Sports Hall of Fame; res. Sarnia, Ont.

SLATER, Bill (swimming); b. 18 Apr 1940, Vancouver, B.C.; m. Carol Picard; c. David, Jamie, Scott, Bradley; Pennsylvania, Bsc (Econ); investment counsellor; ntl jr., sr. records 440, 880, 1650, mile FS, 220, 440 IM; mem. '56 Olympic, '58 BEG teams; bronze men's 4x220yd FS relay '58 BEG; res. West Vancouver, B.C.

SLEEMAN, George (baseball); b. 1841, St. David's, Ont., d. 1926, Guelph, Ont.; businessman, politician; mgr. Silver Creek Brewery team 1872; pres. Guelph Maple Leafs 1874; imported US players to bolster team; world semipro tournament title 1874, ntl championships 1874-75; pres. co-founder Canadian Assn. of Ballplayers; rated a petty despot and pioneer of Canadian baseball; key role in formation International Assn. 1877; mem. Cdn Baseball Hall of Fame.

SLOAN, Susan (swimming); b. 5 Apr 1958, Stettler, Alta.; given name: Susan Estelle; m. Kelsey; Arizona State; butterfly specialist; Stettler Centennial, Vancouver Dolphins, Etobicoke Olympian swim clubs; medalist nationals '74-80; mem. several ntl record setting relay teams; won 100m butterfly, Olympic trials with Commonwealth record 1:02.41 '76; bronze 4x100m medley relay '76 Montreal Olympics; ntl record 100m butterfly 1:02.0 '77; 4 times all-American; gold 4x100m FS relay, '78 Commonwealth Games; bronze 4x100m relay '78 Berlin World Games; mem. '79 Pan-Am Games team; last known res. res. Comox, B.C.

SLOAN, Tod (hockey); b. 30 Nov 1927, Vinton, Que.; given name: Aloysius Martin; m. Jean Aird; c. Marilyn, Joanne, Donald; St. Michael's College; salesman; Jr. A St. Mike's Majors; ctr Toronto '47-58, Chicago '58-61; once 2nd team all-star; mem. 4 Stanley Cup winners; NHL record: 745 scheduled games, 220g, 262a, 47 playoff games, 9g, 12a; played in 3 all-star games; coached minor hockey several years; mem. Toronto Oldtimers hockey team; res. Jackson's Point, Ont.

SLYTHE, Christine (t&f); b. 10 Aug 1961, Montreal, Que.; Sherbrooke; silver 4x400m relay '83 Pan-Am Games; 2 CIAU 1000m, 1 1500m titles; Canada Games, ntl 800m titles; mem. '84 Olympic team; res. Rock Forest, Que.

SMALE, Ted (football); b. 23 Jun 1932, Toronto, Ont.; given name: Fred; m. Dorothea Mary Hoffman; c. Frederick Douglas, Elizabeth Dawne, Karen Lorraine, Randall Scott; UofT, BASc., PEng; retd. mgr. Nordion International; o/d end Humberside CI Toronto HS champions; all-star end engineering faculty title team '51; all-star o-end Balmy Beach ORFU '52; 3yrs o-end UofT Blues; '54 intercollegiate champions; co-capt sr. yr; 3yrs all-star; drafted by Toronto CFL but job with AEC in Ottawa led to

sale to Ottawa '56-62; 3yrs d-end, 4 o-end; mem. '60 Grey Cup champions but knee injury kept him from game; *Globe & Mail* all-Canadian '56-59; mem. Kanata B League badminton title team '79; Kanata golf club champion '68-69; OVGA 2-ball title (with Fred Drummie) '86; res. Kanata, Ont.

SMEATON, Cooper (hockey/officiating); b. 22 Jul 1890, Carleton Place, Ont.; d. 3 Oct 1978, Montreal. Que.; a proficient hockey. baseball, football and basketball player with Westmount AAA, he rejected pro hockey offers choosing instead to devote his attention to officiating, first in amateur then from '13 in pro ranks, for more than 25yrs he handled numerous Stanley, Allan Cup games; mgr. Philadelphia Quakers '30-31; head NHL referee '31-37; served overseas WW1 earning Military Medal; Stanley Cup trustee '46-78; mem. Hockey Hall of Fame.

SMITH, Adam (softball): b. 29 Dec 1964, Hagersville, Ont.; given name: Adam Jeffery; m. Lauren English; c. Rachel Marie Bennett, Jon (sc); dairy farmer; mem. Owen Sound Tiremen '89-92, Toronto Gators '93-96, Green Bay All-Car '97, Decatur '98, Oshawa Gators '99; mem. ntl team '89-98; 2 ISC World silver, 1 gold, 1 ISF World gold; 2 ntl title teams; '91, '95, '99 Pan-Am gold; ISC all-world 1st team '94-95; res. Hagersville, Ont.

SMITH, Alfred E. (hockey); b. 3 Jun 1873, Ottawa, Ont., d. 21 Aug 1953, Ottawa, Ont.; mem. 1st Ottawa team (Electrics) to compete in organized hockey 1890 OHA; played 3yrs then retd.; returned to hockey age 30 helping Ottawa win 2 Stanley Cups; Kenora '07, Ottawa '07-08, Pittsburgh in city pro league; retd. to coach Renfrew, Ottawa, NY Americans, Moncton, N.B., North Bay; player-coach Ottawa Cliffsides '09 Allan Cup winners; Bully's Acres lacrosse team 1889; coach Ottawa lacrosse club, 1922 Eastern Ont. title; quarterback Rough Riders, '03 Que. titlist; with brother Tommy mem. Ottawa Sports, Hockey halls of fame.

SMITH, Becky (swimming); b. 3 Jun 1959, Edmonton, Alta.; given name: Rebecca Gwendolyn; m. Bruce Wiber; c. Davis; UAlta BEd; teacher; ntl team '73-78; gold, 2 silvers '74, silver, bronze '78 Commonwealth Games; bronze 400IM, 400FS relay '76 Olympics; 2 bronze world aquatic games '78; 2 golds '73 youth team Sweden; 6 gold Coca-Cola meets; 5 gold, 1 silver Canada Summer Games; gold, silver, 2 bronze '75 NZ Games; 3 Commonwealth records; numerous ntl titles; mem. sr. women's water polo team '79-81; asst. coach Olympian Club '79-81; City of Edmonton awards '73-78; Alta. awards '73-78, Edmonton Sport Reporters Assn. award '74, Governor-General's medal '76; CWIAU outstanding female swimmer '78; mem. UAlta Wall, Edmonton, Alta. Sports halls of fame; res. Edmonton, Alta.

SMITH, Bev (basketball); b. 4 Apr 1960, Armstrong, B.C.; coach/consultant; forward ntl team '79-96; gold Jones Cup '82; bronze '79 Pan-Am, '79, '86 world championships, '79 FISU Games, '82 Federation Cup; mem. '79, '81 FISU, '84, '96 (capt) Olympic Games teams; all-star '79 world championships; 12yrs Vivo Vicenza, Italy, team, all-star each yr; head coach sr. women's div. 1 league Italy; level 4 coaching cert.; coach Cdn ntl women's team from '97; res. Salmon Arm, B.C.

SMITH, Billy (hockey): b. 12 Dec 1950, Perth, Ont.; m. Debbie; c. Chad, Corey; hockey coach; goaltender Cornwall jr. Royals; drafted by L.A. (NHL) '70; 2 seasons Springfield (AHL); picked in '72 expansion draft by NY Islanders; NHL record '71-89, 680 scheduled games, 305w, 233l, 105t, 22so, 2031g, 3.17 goal/game avg., 132 playoff games, 88w, 36l, 348g, 5so, 2.73ga; mem. 4 Stanley Cup winners; jersey 31 retd. by Islanders; 1 Vezina, shared William Jennings trophy with Roland Melanson; Conn Smythe trophy '83; became 1st NHL goalie credited with goal (vs Colorado) 28 Nov '79, (shot actually made by Colorado player from behind Islanders net and travelling length of ice into empty net); 4yrs NYI goaltending coach; Florida goaltending coach 5yrs; asst. Coach from '98; mem. Hockey, Ottawa Sports halls of fame; res. West Palm Beach, Fla.

SMITH, Bobby (hockey); b. 12 Feb 1958, North Sydney, N.S.; given name: Robert David; m. Elizabeth Robertson; c. Ryan, Megan, Daniel; UofOtt, Minn. Curt Carlson School of Management, BSc, MBA; hockey executive; Jr. A Ottawa 67's '75-78; OHA record 192 points, including 123 assists, '77-78; Ottawa, OHA (Red Tilson Trophy) MVP '78; twice OHA all-star; Eddie Powers Memorial Trophy '78; Ontario MVP Labatt Cup international tournament '77; Cdn junior player of '78; mem. Team Canada jr. World Cup '78; 1st pick Minnesota (NHL), 1st overall '78 amateur draft; North Stars '78-83, '90-93, Montreal '83-90; Calder Memorial Trophy; mem. Stanley Cup finalist '81, winner '86; NHL record: 1077 scheduled games, 357g, 679a, 184 playoff games, 64g, 96a; played 4 NHL all-star games; shares NHL single season playoff record of 5 game-winning goals '91; v-p. NHLPA '81-90; v-p. dir. hockey operations Phoenix '96, GM '96-98; 67's retd. jersey #15; mem. Ottawa Sports Hall of Fame; res. Scottsdale, Ariz.

SMITH, Brian (hockey); b. 6 Sep 1941, Ottawa, Ont.; d. 2 Aug 1995, Ottawa, Ont.; given name: Brian Desmond; m. Alana Kainz; TV sportscaster; jr. Ottawa Montagnards '57-58, jr. Canadiens '59-61; pro Hull-Ottawa (EPHL) '61-63; Innsbruck, Austria, '63-64; Springfield Indians (AHL) '64-67; Los Angeles (NHL) '67-68; Minnesota '68-69; Denver Spurs (WHL) '69-70; Berne, Switzerland, '70-72; Houston Aeros (WHA) '72-73; victim of random shooting at Ottawa TV station; charitable foundation founded in his honor; mem. Ottawa Sports Hall of Fame.

SMITH, Clint (hockey): b. 12 Dec 1913, Assiniboia, Sask.; given name: Clinton James; m. Ella Keys (d); c. Judith Ella, Virginia Jane; retd. businessman; mem. Saskatoon Wesley Jrs.; pro at 18 Rangers organization; 6 seasons NY, 4 Chicago '37-47; NHL record: 483 scheduled games, 161g, 236a, 44 playoff games, 10g, 14a, mere 24pim; mem. 1 Stanley Cup winner; 2 Lady Byng trophies, 3 runnerup; 1st player to win Lady Byng with 2 different teams; set NHL record 49a in 50 game schedule '43-44; played 4 penalty-free seasons in NHL; centred line of Bill Mosienko and Doug Bentley which set single line single season record 219 points; playing-coach Tulsa Oilers (USHL), league MVP '47-48; coached St. Paul to USHL title '48-49; founder/6ys pres. BC Benevolent HA; mem. Hockey Hall of Fame; res. W. Vancouver, B.C.

SMITH, Connie (basketball); b. 1903, Walsall, Staffordshire, Eng.; d. 9 Jan 1990, Viking, Alta.; m. Lloyd Clark McIntyre; c. Alan Lloyd; retd. civil servant; mem. famed Edmonton Grads '20-26, 78 games, 637 points, 8.3 avg.; mem. Canadian Basketball, Alta. Sports halls of fame.

SMITH, Dallas (hockey); b. 10 Oct 1941, Hamiota, Man.; given name: Dallas Earl; def Estevan jrs; turned pro Boston '60; to minors following '61 season mem. CPHL champion Oklahoma City Blazers '66-67; rejoined Boston '68 and remained in NHL with Boston, NY Rangers through '78; NHL record: 890 scheduled games, 55g, 252a, 86 playoff games, 3g, 29a, 2 Stanley Cup winners; mem. Man. Hockey Hall of Fame; res. Hamiota, Man.

SMITH, Darrell K. (football): b. 5 Nov 1961, Youngstown, Ohio; Central State (Ohio); coach Tuskegee; slotback; brief NFL stints Dallas '84, Cincinnati '85; CFL Toronto '86-92, Edmonton '93, Shreveport '94; CFL record: 120 scheduled games, 489 pass receptions for 8,427yds, 52tds, 22 carries, 101yds, 1td; 8 playoff games, 34 catches, 640yds, 5tds; 5 all-Eastern, 2 all-CFL all-star; set/tied 2 CFL records; most tds on passes single season 20 '90; mem. 2 Grey Cup finalists, 1 winner; res. Youngstown, Ohio.

SMITH, David (curling): b. 1 Oct 1919 Saint John, N.B.; d. 5 Jan 1984, Saint John, N.B.; given name: David Charles; m. Beryl; mgr. Saint John Harbor Bridge Authority; pres. Lancaster Little League baseball '62-68; pres. NB MHA '62-63; mem. NB Sports Hall of Fame founding comm. '70; secty '77, '85 Canada Summer Games comms.; NB Curling Assn. secty-treas. '61-83, v-p. '72-76; CCA pres. '76-77, v-p. Royal Caledonian CC '76; competed for Canada '79 Lord Strathcona matches in Scotland; hon. life mem. CCA, Carleton CC; mem. Cdn Curling, NB Sports halls of fame.

SMITH, Don (coaching/administration): b. 30 May 1921, Port Colborne, Ont.; d. 1 Sep 1976, Edmonton, Alta.; given name: William Donald; m. Gwen Lewis; c. George, Graham, Scott, Lewis, Sandra, Sue, Rebecca, Allison; UofT, BPHE, Columbia MA, Buffalo, DPHE; educator; UofT outstanding athlete award '46; asst. football coach UofT; associated with Red Cross Society 29yrs; chair. ntl Water Safety '71-76; fb, basketball, hockey coach UAlta 10yrs; administrator, coach UAlta swimming '70-76; chair. '78 Commonwealth Games swim comm.; key role in building Kinsmen Aquatic Centre, competitive pool named in his memory; avid outdoorsman; exec. Alta. Camping Assn. '63-67; ntl pres. Cdn Camping Assn.; CAHPER pres. '67-69; pres. Sport Alta. '74-76; CAHPER honor award; Cdn Red Cross badge of service; Cdn Council in cooperation with Aquatics award; mem. UAlta Sports Wall of Fame, Alta., Edmonton Sports halls of fame.

SMITH, Donn (football); b. 3 Sep 1949, Rochester, Minn.; given name: Laton Donn Frederick; m. Pauline Leger; c. Simon, Natasha; Purdue, BSc; football coach; ex-property mgr. Public Works Can.; mem. Nepean HS (Ottawa) city title team '66; mem. Windsor Vincent Massey HS city titlist team '67-68; all-city Windsor '67-68; pro Ottawa '73-80; offensive lineman, mostly centre; 3 times EFC all-star centre; Schenley nominee top rookie '73; Schenley nominee best offensive lineman '76; mem. '73, '76 Grey Cup champions; CFL all-time all-star centre; asst. coach UofOtt

'86-90, Ottawa Sooners '91-92, 1 ntl jr. final; coach Carleton Ravens from '93; guest coach Sask. (CFL) '98; res. Chelsea, Que.

SMITH, Doug (football); b. 16 Jun 1952, Galt, Ont.; m. Kim; c. Veronica, Cameron; Wilfrid Laurier; salesman Imperial Tobacco; ctr Montreal '74-81, '83-84, Toronto '81-82; EFC all-star '79; mem. 4 Grey Cup finalists, 1 winner; last known res. Rockton, Ont.

SMITH, Ethel (t&f); b. 1907, Toronto, Ont.; d. 31 Dec 1979, Toronto, Ont.; m. Stewart; natural athlete who excelled in basketball, softball; mem. hydro commission-sponsored t&f team at 16; mem. Cdn Ladies' AC, teamed with Bobbie Rosenfeld, Jane Bell to win major meets, including New York's Millrose Games; ntl 220yd champion '28, bronze 100m '28 Olympics, ran 2nd leg with Rosenfeld, Bell and Myrtle Cook of gold medal 400m relay; 1 of 3 Cdn women to win 2 Olympic track medals (Rosenfeld, Hilda Strike); retd from competition '29; mem. Cdn Amateur; Canada's Sports Hall of Fame.

SMITH, Frank (builder/hockey); b. 1 Jun 1894, Chatham, Ont.; d. 11 Jun 1964, Toronto, Ont.; at 17 helped organize Beaches HL which evolved into Metropolitan Toronto HL, probably biggest minor league in world today; became 1st secty '11 and held position until he resigned '62; MTHL life mem.; OHA Gold Stick award; top CAHA award; Toronto award of merit; mem. Hockey Hall of Fame.

SMITH, Gary (hockey): b. 4 Feb 1944, Ottawa, Ont.; given name: Gary Edward; div.; c. Marshall, Sunny, Chelsea; race track official; goalie; mem. '64 Toronto Marlies Memorial Cup winner; pro Toronto Maple Leafs '64; earned nickname "Suitcase" as he saw pro service with Rochester, Hershey AHL, Tulsa CPHL, Victoria WHL, Fort Worth CHL, Indianapolis, Winnipeg WHA, Toronto, Oakland, California, Chicago, Vancouver, Minnesota, Washington, Winnipeg NHL in '64-80 pro career; NHL record: 14 seasons, 532 scheduled games, 152w, 237l, 67t, 29,619min, 1675ga, 26so, 3.39 GA avg., 20 playoff games, 5w, 13l, 0t, 1153min, 62ga, 1so, 3.23 GA avg.; shared Vezina trophy with Tony Esposito '71; father Des, brother Brian both played in NHL; Brian became 1st brother to score goal against his brother in NHL; mem. Ottawa Sports Hall of Fame; res. Vancouver, B.C.

SMITH, George (swimming); b. 20 Nov 1949, Edmonton, Alta.; given name: George Warren; m. Lorraine Powell; c. Warren, Lindsey, Trent, Fraser; Indiana, UBC, BSc, Athabaska U, MBA; international new franchise owner; 9 ntl age group records; mem. '67, '71 Pan-Ams, '70 Commonwealth, '68 Olympic teams; 3 gold New Zealand, England '68; Cdn, Commonwealth records 200m, 400IM '68 Olympics; 2 gold, 2 silver '70 Commonwealth Games; 2 3rds NCAA championships '69; suffered near fatal motorcycle accident '71; attended UBC and swam for remedial reasons; 1st swimmer to win Bobby Gaul Trophy since '30 inception '75; CIAU 200, 400IM titles, CIAU outstanding swimmer award '77; coached swimming '72-74; City of Edmonton awards '60, '67-71; Alta. awards '69-71; CASA outstanding male swimmer '69; CIAU outstanding male swimmer '74; 6 times CASA Alta. section outstanding male swimmer; presented gold medal to brother Graham for 200IM victory '78 Commonwealth Games;

ardent sailor; mem. UAlta Wall, Edmonton, Alta. Sports, Canadian Aquatic halls of fame; res. Nanaimo, B.C.

SMITH, Gina (equestrian): b. 11 Nov 1957, Saskatoon, Sask.; began riding age 12; turning attention to dressage; mem. ntl team from '84; reserve rider '84 Olympics; team bronze '88 Olympics; team gold '91 Pan-Am Games; competed '96 Olympics; ntl dressage title '97, '99; Saskatchewan Horse Federation President's award '85; German Bereiter award '86. Saskatchewan athlete of year '89; suffered serious injury in riding accident '98; mem. Saskatoon Sports Hall of Fame; res. Brockville, Ont.

SMITH, Glen (rowing); b. 5 Aug 1931, Grand Forks, B.C.; given name: Glen William; m. Jean McKerrow; c. JoAnne, Maureen, Gregory; UBC; physician; mem. '54 BEG gold medal coxed 8-oared crew; runnerup Grand Challenge Cup '55 Royal Henley Regatta; '56 Olympic team; silver medal crew '58 BEG; mem. Cdn Amateur, BC Sports Hall of Fame; res. New Westminster, B.C.

SMITH, Graham (swimming); b. 9 May 1958, Edmonton, Alta.; given name: Donald Graham; m. Linanne Cameron; c. Cameron; UCal, Cal. (Berkley), B Comm, MBA; exec. Pitney Bowes; mem. ntl team '73-82; 56 golds, 23 silvers, 8 bronze medals in competition ranging from ntl championships to Commonwealth and Olympic Games; in process set 17 Cdn, 5 Commonwealth Games, 3 Commonwealth, 2 world, 2 US Open records; achieved pinnacle of stardom in home town '78 Commonwealth Games with 6 gold (100m, 200m, breaststroke, 200m, 400m IM, 4x100 FS, 4x100 medley relays), set 5 Commonwealth Games, 3 Commonwealth records; 1st Cdn to win NCAA triple crown (3 individual golds, one relay) '79 NCAA championships; 6 CIAU, NCAA titles; 8 city of Edmonton, 7 Alta. awards, CIAU swimmer of yr award, Lou Marsh Trophy, Lionel Conacher award, Canada Sporting Goods Assn. award, Edmonton Sports Reporters Assn. award, Premier's award for performance, Norton Crowe award '78; hon. citizen of Winnipeg '79; fed. govt. excellence award '82; Governor-General's medal '76; mem. Order of Canada; mem. Berkley, UAlta Walls, Canada's, Alta., Edmonton Sports, Cdn Aquatic halls of fame; res. Albany, Calif.

SMITH, Gwen (administration); b. 31 Aug 1925, Toronto, Ont.; given name: Lorna Gwendolyn Lewis; m. William Donald Smith (d); c. George, Graham, Scott, Lewis, Allison, Sandra, Sue, Rebecca; UofT, BPHE; 1st women's PE dir. McMaster; dir. PHE Edmonton YWCA; has coached, officiated and supported swimming at all levels; coached competitive swimmers '62-74; officiated '67 Pan-Am, '73 FISU, '78 Commonwealth Games; served in nearly all exec. capacities CASA Alta. section '62-85; 1st master official in Alta.; chair. Alta. swim officials '62-85; dir. Alta Sports Council '84-92; pres. Sports Alta. '81-84; dir. SFC; mem. Ntl Advisory Council on Fitness and AmateurSport; served on exec. Cdn Council of Provincial and Territorial Sport Federations; chair. Edmonton Salute to Excellence comm. '90-97; mem. Alta., Edmonton Sports Halls of Fame; res. Edmonton, Alta.

SMITH, Helen (shooting); b. 26 Jul 1950, Kirkland Lake, Ont.; given name: Helen Mae Mann; m. Welland "Smokey" Smith; London Teachers' Coll.; retd. accounting clerk;

handgun specialist; began shooting as a form of recreation '84; entered 1st competition same yr; mem. ntl team '86-97; 5 ntl women's sport pistol, 2 ntl women's air pistol titles; team silver '91 Pan-Am Games; air pistol gold, sport pistol pairs silver (with Sharon Cozzarin) '94 Commonwealth Games; lost to Cozzarin in '92 Olympic qualifying shootorff; res. London, Ont.

SMITH, Hooley (hockey); b. 7 Jan 1903, Toronto, Ont., d. 24 Aug 1963, Montreal, Que.; given name: Reginald Joseph; mem. Granites '24 Olympic gold medal team; pro Ottawa '24-27, Montreal Maroons '27-36, Boston '36-37, NY Americans '37-41; 3 Stanley Cup finals, 2 winners; with Nels Stewart, Babe Siebert formed famed Maroons' Big S line; once 1st, 2nd team all-star; NHL record: 200g, 215a; mem. Hockey Hall of Fame.

SMITH, Larry (football): b. 28 Apr 1951, Montreal, Que.; given name: Lawrence William; m. Leesa Clark MacLean; c. Wesley, Ashley, Bradley; Bishop's, BA, McGill, BCL; football exec.; 1st overall '72 CFL draft by Montreal; running back, slotback Alouettes '72-80 playing 140 consecutive regular season, 13 playoff games; competed in 5 Grey Cups, 2 winners; 9th CFL commissioner '92-96; instrumental in league expansion into the US.; pres./CEO Alouettes from '97; p.-pres. Bishop's Alumni Assn.; governor Bishop's; res. Montreal, Que.

SMITH, Mark (softball): b. 27 Jun 1959, Halifax, NS; given name: Robert Mark; m. Ann Dodge; c. Jasmine; NS dept. of justice; left handed pitcher/strong hitter; competed 18 ntl championships; co-founder Halifax-Windsor Keiths; Pan-Am Games gold '79, '83, '91; ISC world titles with Camarillo Kings '81-82; 1 ISF world title with Team Canada; playing coach Halifax Jaguars; pitching coach Team Canada from '98; res. Coldbrook, N.S.

SMITH, Michael (t&f): b. 16 Sep 1967, Kenora, Ont.; UofT; under coach Andy Higgins turned full attention to decathlon '85; became 1st NA to win gruelling Gotzis decathlon '91 with 8,427 points; same year world championship silver with Cdn record 8,549 points; gold '90, '94 Commonwealth, '89 Francophone Games; bronze '95 worlds, '98 Commonwealth Games; competed '86, '90, '94, '98 Commonwealth, '88, '92, '96 (flag-bearer '92) Olympic Games, 4 world championships; 1 Cdn jr., 3 Cdn sr., 1 Commonwealth record; 1 Arizona State, Florida Relays decathlon gold; 3 ntl outdoor decathlon titles, 1 indoor heptathlon title, 1 pentathlon title; 2 Jack Davies outstanding t&f athlete awards; Athletic Canada athlete of '94; 3 Fred Rowell field athlete of yr awards; res. Calgary, Alta.

SMITH, Murray (hockey); b. 23 Oct 1945, Thunder Bay, Ont.; given name: Murray Edward; m. Sharon Wilson; c. Shannon Leigh; Lakehead, BA; personnel mgr.; sr. baseball Thunder Bay; coach Little League baseball; all-time Lakehead hockey records in 4-year college career; most career points 226, single game points 8, career assists 134, single game assists 5, season assists 39 shared with Rick Alexander, 6 career hat-tricks shared with Dwight Stirrett, 3 season hat-tricks shared with Dave Vaillant; led team scoring 3 seasons, team goals 3 seasons, team assists twice; twice league MVP; 4yrs NAIA all-American; res. Sudbury, Ont.

SMITH, Neil (hockey/administration); b. 9 Jan 1954, Toronto, Ont.; m. Katia; c. Viktor; Western Mich.; pres./ GM NY Rangers; def. Brockville Jr. (CJHL), team capt./ all-American WMU; drafted by NY Islanders and spent 2 seasons in IHS; became Islanders scout '80-81; joined Detroit as dir. pro scouting, later dir. entire farm system; dir. scouting/GM/ governor Adirondack (AHL), 2 Calder Cups; became GM Rangers '89, pres. from '92; 3 div., 2 President's, 1 Stanley Cup titles; *Hockey News* exec. of '94, *Sporting News* hockey exec. of '92, New Jersey Sports Writers Assn. exec. of '94 awards; mem. WMU Sports Hall of Fame; res. New York, N.Y.

SMITH, Pop (baseball); b. 12 Oct 1856, Digby, N.S.; d. 18 Apr 1927, Boston, Mass.; given name: Charles Marvin; his initial exposure to baseball was probably to rounders, referred to as the Massachusetts game; arrived on ML scene as "elderly" 23-year-old and was tagged "Pop"; referred to as an agile fielder, with sure hands and an accurate arm; never a great hitter but showed flashes of power and was a good base stealer; normally a 2nd baseman he was regarded as a good utility player; joined Cincinnati (NL) 1880; played with Cleveland, Worcester, Buffalo 1881, Baltimore, Louisville 1882, Columbus 1883-84, Pittsburgh 1885-89, Boston 1890, Washington 1891; ML record: 1093 games, 4176ab, 935h, 633r, 141d, 87t, 24hr, .224ba.

SMITH, Rosaire (weightlifting); b. 9 Jan 1914, St. Rosaire, Que.; m. Auree Cardin; c. Armand, Gaston, Denis, Claire, Marcel, Jacqueline, Line; retired; competed at 123lb (56kg) level; ntl title '41; 3rd worlds '47; mem. '48, '52 Olympics; silver '50 BEG; '48 Commonwealth title; St. Jean Bosco trophy best lifter in class Montreal '48; Que. old timers title '59; taught dumbbell manipulation for high schoolers several years; res. Drummondville N., Que.

SMITH, Sandra (swimming); b. 29 Feb 1952, Edmonton, Alta.; given name: Sandra Irene; div. Gordon Osborne; c. Michael Bradley; m. Wayne Harris; c. Christa Lee, Shana Lynn; Montpellier (France), UAlta, BPhE; swim coach; mem. ntl team '67-71; mem. '67, '71 Pan-Am, '70 Commonwealth, FISU Games; ntl 50, 100, 200, 400 FS records; only Cdn medalist (bronze 400FS) '70 FISU Games; tied with sister Sue high point female as mem. UAlta swim team; asst. coach women's team '73-74; head coach '74-77; asst. coach Edmonton Olympic SC '77-81; coach Alta. team Western Canada Games '79; Edmonton awards '69-70; CWIAU outstanding female swimmer '72; Alta. section CASA outstanding female swimmer awards '66-67; mem. UAlta Wall, Edmonton, Alta. Sports halls of fame; res. Swift Current, Sask.

SMITH, Shannon (swimming); b. 28 Sep 1961, Vancouver, B.C.; m. Mark Jones; c. Celestina, Wesani; Hawaii, SFU, Guelph, UBC; ex-kayak guide; mem. Hyack Swim Club coached by Ron Jacks; mem. ntl swim team '74-78; mem. '75 world, '76 Olympic teams; bronze 400m FS with PB 4:14.60 '76 Olympics; 4 gold, 4 silver '77 Canada Cup; ntl record 800m FS 8:41.17 '77; BC jr. athlete of '76; Governor-General's silver medal; Elaine Tanner award '76; conducted kayak tours in varied areas throughout world from Caribbean to Queen Charlotte Islands, Fiji and Hawaii; mem. BC Sports Hall of Fame; res. Whistler, B.C.

SMITH, Sheldon (motorsport); b. 10 Sep 1928, Peterborough, Ont.; given name: Sheldon Louis; began motorcycling age 16; 3 ntl 500-mile, 500 cc endurance titles; ntl motocross scrambles champion 500 cc expert class '58; ntl 500 cc jr. dirt bike title '57; Ont. 500 cc expert class road race title '58; held numerous exec. positions at prov., ntl levels of CMA; ntl CMA pres. '59-60; primarily responsible for development of motocross in Ont.; mem. Peterborough Sports Hall of Fame; res. Peterborough, Ont.

SMITH, Sid (hockey); b. 11 Jul 1925, Toronto, Ont.; given name: Sidney James; m. June Millen; c. Scott, Blaine, Megan; retd. salesman, court officer; Jr. A Oshawa Generals, Stafford srs., Que. Aces; pro Toronto '46-58; mem. 3 Stanley Cup winners; 2 Lady Byng awards; once 1st, twice 2nd team all-star lw; playing coach Whitby Dunlops, '58 World, '59 Allan Cup champions; NHL record: 601 scheduled games, 186 goals, 183 assists, 44 playoff games, 17 goals, 10 assists; 7 NHL all-star gmes; coached midget, Jr. C hockey briefly; mem. Toronto Oldtimers team; mem. Hockey Hall of Fame; res. Newmarket, Ont.

SMITH, Stanley (administration); b. 18 Jun 1897, Vancouver, B.C., d. 20 Mar 1975, Vancouver; tireless worker in field of amateur sport administration in BC 50yrs; general chair. '54 BEG; freeman city of Vancouver; mem. BC Sports Hall of Fame.

SMITH, Sue (swimming); b. 7 Dec 1950, Edmonton, Alta.; given name: Susan Evelyn; m. Terry Halak; c. Michael, Leslie; Montpellier (France), UAlta, BEd; teacher; mem. ntl team '67-72; alternate '68 Olympic team; mem. '70 Commonwealth, '71 Pan-Am, '72 Olympic teams; 6 ntl titles 100m, 200m butterfly, 200IM, 400IM; 2 ntl records; 2 silver, 1 bronze '70 Commonwealth Games; bronze 200 butterfly '71 Pan-Ams; 100yd FS, 200yd butterfly titles '69 NZ; CWIAU high point female mem. UAlta team '72-73; head coach Royal Glenora SC '72-73; Olympian SC '74-75; asst. to husband Terry Halak Olympian SC '76-78; coached sister Becky, brother Graham and Cheryl Gibson to their first Games teams; Alta. team coach Western Canada Games '75; 1st female Cdn coaching staff '75 World Aquatic championships; Edmonton awards '65, '68-71; Alta. awards '68-72; CWIAU outstanding female swimmer awards '72-73; CASA Alta. Section outstanding female swimmer 7 times; mem. UAlta Wall, Edmonton, Alta. Sports Hall of Fame; res. Edmonton, Alta.

SMITH, Tommy (hockey); b. 27 Sep 1885, Ottawa, Ont., d. 1 Aug 1966, Ottawa, Ont.; St. Patrick's Lyceum jrs., Ottawa Victorias srs. '06, led scorers; Pittsburgh (IL) '07, led team with 23 goals in 22 games; rover, OPHL scoring champion with 33 goals 13 games Brantford '09; top scorer, league title Galt '11, lost Stanley Cup bid to Ottawa; Moncton Maritime pro league '12, league crown, lost SC bid to Que. Bulldogs (NHA); Que. Bulldogs '13-16, formed line with Joe Malone, Jack Marks; trailed Malone by 4 goals 39-43 in scoring race, won only Stanley Cup; nicknamed 'Little Bulldog' (5'4" 150lbs); mem. Canadiens '17, when NHA dissolved '18 left hockey; returned for 10 games with Que. '19; in 171 recorded games, 239 goals, 15 in 15 playoff games; 5 times led league scorers, during '13 campaign scored in 14 consecutive games; twice scored 9 goals in

single game, one 8-goal game, 4 5-goal games, 10 4-goal games, 15 3-goal games; no records for International or Maritime League play; mem. Ottawa Sports, Hockey halls of fame.

SMITH, Tricia (rowing); b. 14 Apr 1957, Vancouver, B.C.; given name: Tricia Catherine; UBC, BA; mem. athletically oriented family, father Marshal UBC rugby star, mother Patricia Pan-Am Games basketball player, sister Shannon Olympic swimmer, brothers Jeff, Dean, sister Lori active in various sports; ntl coxed 4 titles '74, '80; coxed 8 '75, '80; with Betty Craig '76, '80 straight pair titles; gold straight pairs '76 West German, Swiss regattas; silver women's pairs '84 Olympics; mem. '76, '80, '84 Olympic, '77-79, '81-82 worlds teams; bronze coxed 8s Worlds '77, '78; gold straight pairs '80 Holland, '83 Moscow regattas; bronze coxless pairs '82-83 worlds; BC athletic achievement award '81; fed. govt. athletic achievement awards '82-84; mem. UBC Sports Hall of Fame; res. Vancouver, B.C.

SMITH, Wayne (weightlifting); b. 13 Jul 1955, Halifax, N.S.; self-employed welder; NS jr. 67kg title at 13; Maritime sr. 75kg title at 14; 2 Maritime records; ntl jr., sr. clean & jerk record 162.5kg 110kg class '73; 3rd NA '74; ntl 100kg title '77; 3 ntl jr., 1 Commonwealth jr. records '75; ntl sr. snatch record 140kg in 90kg class '76, sr. C&J record 100kg class '77; mem. '78 Commonwealth, '79 Pan-Am Games, '81 Commonwealth championships; res. Truro, N.S.

SMITH-JOHANNSEN, Herman (skiing); b. 15 Jun 1875, Olso, Norway; d. 5 Jan 1987, Tonsberg, Norway; m. Alice Robinson (d); c. Alice Elizabeth, Robert, Ella Margaret; Norwegian Military Academy, U of Berlin; retired engineer; instrumental in introducing skiing as form of travel to NA; nicknamed 'Jackrabbit' by Cree and Ojibway Indians; opened Maple Leaf Trail Labelle to Shawbridge 30s; from '54 (age 75) confined skiing to cross-country; instrumental in setting trail for Lachute-Ottawa National Ski Marathon; at 99 honored by King Olav V of Norway with Medal of St. Olav, first time to non-resident; subject of CBC films *"Jackrabbit"* and *"The Long Ski Trail"* and book *"Jackrabbit-his first 100 years"*; Dubonnet skier of '75; mem. Order of Canada, Cdn Skiing, Canada's Sports halls of fame.

SMREK, Mike (basketball): b. 31 Aug 1962, Port Robinson, Ont.; given name: Michael Frank; m. Sanja; Canisius Coll.; pro basketball player; set single season/career field goal percentage record at Canisius; *AP* all-American hon. mention; ECAC North Atlantic 1st team all-star; drafted by Portland (NBA), traded to Chicago '85-86, Los Angeles '86-88, San Antonio '88-89, Golden State '89-92, L.A. Clippers; backup centre to Kareen Abdul-Jabbar '86-88 winning 2 NBA titles; NBA record: 194 scheduled games, 554pts; 21 playoff games, 11pts; mem. ntl team '92; played in Greece '93, Croatia '96; YMCA fitness instructor Port Robinson; res. Split, Croatia.

SMYL, Stan (hockey); b. 28 Jan 1958, Glendon, Alta.; given name: Stanley Philip; m. Jennifer; c. Jilian, Natalie, Spencer; hockey coach; rw New Westminster jrs '75-78; pro Dallas (CHL) '78, Vancouver (NHL) '78-91; NHL record: 896 scheduled games, 262g, 411a, 41 playoff games, 16g, 17a;

Canucks team capt. '82-90; 3 Canucks MVP awards; described as "heart & soul" of Canucks during playing days; 1st NHL player to lead a team in goals, assists, points, penalty minutes in single season '79-80; asst. coach Vancouver '91-99; jersey #12 retd. by Canucks; res. W. Vancouver, B.C.

SMYLIE, Doug (football); b. 3 Jun 1922, Toronto, Ont., d. 19 Mar 1983, Toronto, Ont.; given name: Douglas John; div.; c. Randy, Cheryl, Craig; Cornell.; insurance agent; junior OHA; rejected pro hockey offers to join RCAF; won RCAF heavyweight boxing title; 5 gold medals RCAF t&f championships; football Cornell, Ottawa Trojan ORFU title team '47; pro Toronto '45, '49-53, Montreal '46, Ottawa '48; mem. 4 Grey Cup champions; CFL kickoff runback record 95yds '51 (broken '81); 4-handicap golfer, frequent club tourney winner; nicknamed "Big Ci".

SMYLIE, Rod Jr. (football); b. 25 Dec 1924, Toronto, Ont.; d. 8 Nov 1991, Toronto, Ont.; given name: Roderick; m. Helen Quebec; c. Catharine, Diane, Kristin, Rod; retd. commercial traveller; nicknamed "Little Citation" while playing 11yrs in CFL with Argos '45-45, '48-55, Ottawa Trojans ORFU champions '47; captain Argos '51; mem. 4 Grey Cup champions; modern era ('45-73) Argo all-star team as slotback.

SMYLIE, Rod Sr. (hockey/t&f); b. 28 Sep 1895, Toronto, Ont.; d. 3 Mar 1985, Toronto, Ont.; given name: Roderick Thomas; m. Mary Black (d); c. Anne, Douglas, Rod; UofT, MD; retd. physician; capt. UofT track team; ntl 440yd champion '17; mem. Toronto Dentals hockey team '16-20; left wing, capt. '20 world amateur champions; pro Toronto St. Pat's '21-22; rw '22 Stanley Cup winners.

SMYTH, Harry (speed skating); b. 21 Feb 1910, Moncton, N.B.; d. 20 Sep 1992, Moncton, N.B.; given name: Charles Henry; m. Marion Sharpe (d); c. Robert, Richard, Ron, Tom; retd. CNR shop foreman; trained by his father, a former Maritime speed skating champion; world jr. outdoor title '26; all possible NA titles '26; Maritime cycling champion several times over 20yr span; mem. NB, inter-Maritime rifle team several times; mem. '32 Olympic skating team; managed provincial midget hockey title team; received personally autographed silver skates from actress Norma Talmadge for '26 world title win; Moncton city award for contribution to skating; mem. NB Sports Hall of Fame.

SMYTH, Jack (t&f); b. 24 Mar 1936, Winnipeg, Man.; m. Val; c. John, Kathleen; Houston, BSc, UMan, MEd; retd. school superintendent; ntl jr., juve. triple jump records; mem. '54 BEG, '55 Pan-Am Games teams; 4 ntl sr. TJ records; Mo. Valley Conf. hurdles record; Drake relays TJ, sprint relay records; outstanding t&f athlete Houston '58-59; exec. mem. Man. TFA; mem. Man. Sports Hall of Fame; res. Winnipeg, Man.

SMYTHE, Conn (hockey); b. 1 Feb 1895, Toronto, Ont., d. 18 Nov 1980, Toronto, Ont.; m. Irene; c. Hugh, Mariam, Stafford (d), Patricia; UofT; pres. sand and gravel co., hockey exec.; capt. Toronto Varsity '15 Ont. champions; coached Varsity to '27 Allan Cup, Varsity Grads to '28 Olympic title; coach NY Rangers, released after assembling team that went on to win '28 Stanley Cup; purchased Toronto

Pats, changed name to Maple Leafs; involved in Maple Leaf Gardens construction '31; managing dir., later pres. of Gardens, retired '61 after his team had won 7 Stanley Cups; supervisd construction Toronto CNE's Hockey Hall of Fame; his racing stable produced 3 Queen's Plate winners; long involved with Ont. Society for Crippled Children; awarded Military Cross WW1; mem. UofT, Hockey, Canada's Sports halls of fame.

SMYTHE, Don (badminton); b. 27 Apr 1924, Toronto, Ont.; given name: Donald Keith; m. Betty Rennie; c. Rennie, Jackie, Heather, Kelly, Nancy; UWO; retd. pres. Donsco Adhesives; 5 Ont. singles, 4 doubles titles; 4 ntl singles, 3 men's doubles titles; semifinalist all-England (World) badminton championships '53, finalist '54; ranked 2nd in world '54; mem. 3 Thomas Cup teams; non-playing capt. '73; mem. 3 Commonwealth teams; mem. Cdn Amateur Sports Hall of Fame; res. Islington, Ont.

SNELGROVE, Karen (softball); b. 12 Mar 1969, London, Ont.; Missouri; sporting goods sales; righthanded pitcher; NCAA all-American '91-92; academic all-American '91; pitched back-to-back no-hitters Missouri '91; mem. ntl youth team '87, sr. team '90-96; competed Pan-Ams '91 (silver), '95; '96 Olympics, NCAA College World Series '91; played for 3 time ntl jr. champion K-W Civitans, '94 ntl sr. champion Dorchester Jesters; posted 0.18era to lead NCAA '91; res. Kitchener, Ont.

SNELLING, Charles (figure skating); b. 17 Sep 1937, Toronto, Ont; m. Velma Green; c. Bradley, Lisa, Scott; UofT, MD; plastic surgeon; ntl jr. men's title '52; sr. titles '54-58, '64; NA silver '57; bronze '57 worlds; mem. '56, '64 Olympic teams; res. Vancouver, B.C.

SNELLING, Deryk (swimming); b. 22 Jul 1933, Darwen, Lancashire, Eng.; pro swim coach; British ntl champion; coach Southhampton SC '62; head coach Vancouver Dolphins '67-76, ntl team titles each year; protegees won gold, silver, bronze medals in Commonwealth, Pan-Am, Olympic, World Aquatic Games; coached Cdn ntl team '71 Pan-Am, '72, '76, '80, Olympic, '73 world aquatic, '74 Commonwealth Games teams; coach Etobicoke '77-79, UCal from '80; 7 CIAU coach of yr awards; author *All about Individual Medley*, co-authored *Swimming Coaching at Club Level*; mem. Order of Canada, Cdn Aquatic Hall of Fame; res. Calgary, Alta.

SNIPES, Angelo (football): b. 1 Nov 1963, Atlanta, Ga.; given name: Angelo Bernard; West Georgia Coll. '81-84; linebacker; mem. ntl Div. III title team '82; drafted USFL Oakland Invaders '85, dealt to Memphis Showboats '86; NFL Washington '86, San Diego '87, Kansas City '88-90; CFL Ottawa '91-93, BC '94, Birmingham '95, Winnipeg '96-97; 3 Eastern, 2 CFL all-star; Jeff Russell Memorial Trophy '92; James McCaffrey trophy '92; runnerup CFL most outstanding player, outstanding defensive player '92; mem. 1 Grey Cup winner; res. Winnipeg, Man.

SNYDER, Brad (t&f): b. 8 Jan 1976, Windsor, Ont.; South Carolina; Ont HS shot put champion '94-95; ntl jr champion '94-95; set ntl jr record 17.34-metres '95; gold '95 Canada-US jr dual meet, '96 Gatorade Classic, Gamecock Invitational, LSU Alumni, Midland Walwyn Freedom

Festival; javelin gold SEC championships '96; competed for South Carolina in NCAA championships '96-98; mem. '96 Olympic team; bronze '99 Pan-Am Games; res. Windsor, Ont./South Carolina.

SOBRIAN, Jules (shooting); b. 22 Jan 1935, San Fernando, Trinidad; m. Frances; c. Camille, Glenn; St. Mary's College, Trinidad, UofT, MD; physician; pistol shooting specialist; '63-84 frequent ntl titles; silver free pistol, bronze rapid fire '66 Commonwealth Games; bronze centre fire, silver team '67, '71 Pan-Am Games; silver rapid fire, gold free pistol '74 Commonwealth Games; gold free pistol '73 Western Hemisphere championships; bronze free pistol, silver rapid fire '75 Pan-Am Games; gold free pistol, rapid fire '75 pre-Olympic intl; gold rapid fire '78 Commonwealth games; mem. '68, '72, '76, '80, '84 Olympic teams; Ont. handgun champion '69-73; SFC golden anniversary award '82; life mem. SFC; res. Omemee, Ont.

SOLES, Michael (football): b. 8 Nov 1966, Pointe Claire, Que.; m. Catherine; c. Justine (Montreal's 1st baby of '97); McGill; financial broker Nesbitt Burns; Vanier Cup MVP; CIAU rookie of '86; 2 McGill athlete of yr awards; Que. male student-athlete of '88; running back CFL Edmonton '89-95, Montreal '96-98; CFL record (through '98): 177gp, 42tds, 1cvt, 254pts, 568carries, 2961yds, 20tds, 288recpt, 3112yds, 22tds; 1 Northern, 1 Eastern all-star; Lew Hayman trophy '96; runnerup outstanding Cdn '96; 2 Grey Cup finals, 1 winner; res. Montreal, Que.

SOMERVILLE, Sandy (golf/cricket); b. 4 May 1903, London, Ont.; d. 17 May 1991, London, Ont.; given name: Charles Ross; m. Eleanor Elizabeth Lyle; c. Philip, Kenneth; Ridley College, UofT; retd. life insurance exec.; played in last international cricket match between Canada, US '21; holds highest score for school cricket in Canada, 212 not out; mem. 12th Battery Ont. int. hockey champions '26; 6 Cdn amateur golf titles between '26-39, runnerup 4 times; Man. amateur, 1st of 4 Ont. amateurs '26; 1st Cdn to win US amateur beating Johnny Goodman in Baltimore '32, Lionel Conacher award '32; '38 semifinalist British amateur; CP poll golfer of half century '50; 2 Canadian Seniors Golf Assn. titles, shared title twice; pres. RCGA '57, CSGA '69-70; mem. UofT, RCGA, Cdn Amateur, Canada's Sports halls of fame.

SONMOR, Glen (hockey); b. 22 Apr 1929, Moose Jaw, Sask.; given name: Glen Robert; m. Marcia Stowe; c. Kathleen; Minnesota, BSc, Ohio State, MPhE; retd. hockey exec.; Cleveland (AHL), New York (NHL); loss of eye as a result of hockey injury terminated playing career; Minnesota coach '56; subsequently coach Jr. A St. Catharines; pro Springfield (AHL), Minnesota, Birmingham (WHA); chief scout Minnesota (NHL); GM Minnesota (WHA); coach Minnesota (NHL) '78-83, '84-85; scout Philadelphia '92-96, Phoenix '98-99; res. Hopkins, Minn.

SONNENBERG, Debbie (softball): b. 4 Jan 1971, Edmonton, Alta.; Delta State, MSc, MEd; asst. softball coach Delta State.; lefthanded pitcher; competed '93 Canada Cup; ntl jr. championship gold '94; NAIA ntl bronze '94; ntl sr. gold '95; competed '94 sr. women's worlds, '95 Pan-Ams, '96 Olympics; MAIA all-American '91-94; ntl jr.

championships MVP '93-94; top pitcher '94 Pan-Am qualifier; res. Cleveland, Ohio/Winnipeg, Man.

SOPER, Alice (golf); b. 6 Mar 1894, Montreal, Que.; d. 8 Oct 1994, Montreal, Que.; given name: Alice Ross; m. Harold Warren Soper; c. Warren, Anne; Bryn Mawr College; active golfer '12-74; 16 club championships; 1 Montreal Dist. title; mem. 3 Interprovincial teams, 2 Que. Srs. titles; ntl Srs. title '51; women's course records Murray Bay, Delray Beach; 3 Kennebunk, Me., titles; 4 Royal Montreal Charles Murray Memorial Trophy titles; competed '37 US women's amateur; CLGU v-p. '38-40, pres. '41-46.

SOPER, Barry (figure skating); b. 2 Jul 1948, Vancouver, B.C.; given name: Robert Barrett; m. Louise Ann Lind; c. Amy, Tiffany, Sean;UBC, BEd; real estate dev. mgr., coach; hockey, jr. tennis to age 15; teamed competitively with future wife '66; ntl ice dance gold medalist '68; US ice dance gold '69; ntl novice dance '67, jr. dance '69; sr. dance '71-74; 4th NA ice dance '71; mem. world championships '71-74; silver Skate Canada '73; silver dance BC '67, gold dance BC '68-69, BC sr. dance '68; taught elementary school phys ed. '70-72; Hartshorne Memorial Trophy Squaw Valley '69; BC special achievement award (with Louise) '73; with Louise mem. BC Sports Hall of Fame; res. N. Vancouver, B.C.

SOPER, Louise (figure skating); b. 11 Apr 1948, Vancouver, B.C.; given name: Louise Ann Lind; m. Robert Barrett Soper; c. Amy, Tiffany, Sean;UBC; dental hygienist; gold medalist figures, free skating; 1st teamed with future husband '66; (see Barry Soper for competitive record); Hartshorne Memorial Trophy for highest avg. gold dance test Sun Valley '68; mem. BC Sports Hall of Fame; res. N. Vancouver, B.C.

SOPINKA, John (football); b. 19 Mar 1933, Broderick, Sask.; d. 24 Nov 1997, Ottawa, Ont.; m. Marie Ethel Wilson; c. Randy, Melanie; Queen's, UofT, BA, LLB; lawyer, QC Supreme Court judge; halfback Queen's Golden Gaels '52-53; halfback UofT Blues '53-54; mem. Intercollegiate champions '54; pro halfback, defensive capt. Argos '55-56; Alouettes '57; frequent legal lecturer; authored 1 book, several articles on law; accomplished violinist.

SORENSEN, Arne (shooting); b. 21 Jan 1934, Denmark; m. Rosemarie Monkman; c. Anna-Marie, Wayne, Stephen; drywall finisher; ntl team '71-84; mem. '71, '75, '79 Pan-Am, '76, '84 Olympic, '78 Commonwealth Games teams; team silver '79, bronze '71, '75 Pan-Am Games; Benito Juarez small bore air rifle title '77, Championship of Americas air rifle individual, team titles '77; ntl English match (small bore 3-position) titles '71-75; SFC golden anniversary award '82; res. Calgary, Alta.

SORENSEN, Gerry (skiing); b. 15 Oct 1958, Kimberley, B.C.; given name: Geraldine Ann; m. Brendan Lenihan; cashier; mem. ntl team '80-84; Pontiac Cup downhill title '80; 3rd ntl downhill '80; initial world cup victory Haus downhill Feb '81; ntl, FIS downhill champion '81, '83; successive WC victories Grindelwald, Switzerland, 13-14 Jan '82; WC downhill France '84; WC record 5-0-1; BC athlete of '81-82; Bobbie Rosenfeld award '82; mem. '84

Olympic team; mem. Cdn Skiing, Cdn Amateur, Canada's, BC Sports halls of fame; res. Kimberley, B.C.

SORENSEN, Ole (wrestling); b. 23 Apr 1948, Randers, Denmark; given name: Ole Toft; m. Claude Tellier, c. Cody, Catherine; UWO, BA,UAlta., BPhE; sr. consultant Sport Canada; Ont. HS titles gymnastics, wrestling; bronze W (most valuable wrestler), Claude Brown Memorial Cup (most valuable male athlete) UWO; block A most valuable wrestler UAlta; Alta, Ont. provincial sports achievement awards, several aquatic awards; high jump, pole vault, wrestling titles in college; Alta., Ont., Western Canada Open, college, YMCA, 2 ntl FS wrestling titles; mem. '70 world, Commonwealth (bronze), '72 Olympics, '73 FISU Games teams; coached wrestling, gymnastics, aquatics; mem. CAWA ntl coaching staff; CAWA tech. dir. '75-77; lecturer Windsor '74-75; Sport Canada consultant from '77; CBC-TV color commentator '84 Olympics; res. Ottawa, Ont.

SORENSEN, Wayne (shooting); b. 8 Jul 1963, Calgary, Alta.; financial planner; following father Arne's lead began shooting at 13; rifle specialist; set ntl record in kneeling stage of 3-position event '82; competed 3 Benito Juarez, World Cup competitions, '92, '96 Olympic, '94, '98 Commonwealth Games, '95, '99 Pan-Am Games; with Michel Dion 3-position smallbore pairs gold, individual 3-position silver '94, '98 Commonwealth Games; air rifle team silver '95, individual air rifle bronze '99 Pan-Am Games; 50m prone free rifle silver '99 PAG; Gil Boa Memorial award '88; Alta. achievement award '79; res. Calgary, Alta.

SOUCHEREAU, Kelsey (squash); b. 28 Jul 1969, Calgary, Alta.; Alberta College of Art; graphic designer; began playing squash age 12; ntl jr. titles '83-85; mem. ntl jr. women's team '85-87; mem. ntl sr. team from '94, team gold '96 ntl championships; 1 individual, 2 team silver '94 Pan-Am championships; 2 team gold, '95 Pan-Am Games; competed inaugural World Cup '96; res. Calgary, Alta.

SOVRAN, Gino (basketball/t&f); b. 17 Dec 1924, Windsor, Ont.; m. Inger Kathryn Seim; c. Daniel Louis, Victoria Gene, Ralph Edward, Andrew Lars; Assumption Coll,. BA, Detroit, BME, Northwestern, MSc, Minnesota, PhD; retd. General Motors research engineer; 4yrs jr., 1yr sr basketball Kennedy CI, 1 WOSSA title, all-star, scoring title; capt. Assumption Coll 2yrs, 1st to score 1000 points in 3 seasons; leading scorer Det. '45-46; competed '46 Eastern Cdn championships; pro Toronto Huskies '46-47; mem. Ont. champion Windsor Alumni '48; high jump specialist; winning city, WOSSA, Ont. jr., int., sr. titles; set hj, hop, step & jump (triple jump) records; also claimed broad jump, pole vault, relay titles; competed in some t&f meets with Det. but WW2 curtailed normal activity; mem. Windsor Sports Hall of Fame; res. Troy, Mich.

SOWIETA, Rick (football); b. 16 Jan 1954, Huesden, Belgium; m. Joanne Elizabeth; c. Katie, Sara; Richmond, BA; restaurateur; mem. Glebe HS jr. football champions '69, coaches def. MVP award; Glebe sr. def. MVP '71; Glebe sr. basketball MVP '71; Glebe Don Lewicki, Dick Stewart awards; def. lineman Ottawa Sooners Eastern jr. football finalists, outstanding DL award; attended Richmond on football scholarship, 2 conf. titles; Toronto CFL '77-78,

Ottawa '79-86; 4 all-Eastern all-star awards; Ottawa specialty team award, Schenley top Canadian nominee; '81 Grey Cup finalist; played in '83 CFL all-star game; received Ottawa 100th regular season game award '85; hon. chair. CF 65 Roses Club '86-87; co-chair. '88 Grey Cup breakfast comm.; asst. coach Ottawa Bootleggers '90-91; asst. coach Ottawa Sooners '92-94; res. Gloucester, Ont.

SPACK, Mike (basketball); b. 5 Mar 1922, Winnipeg, Man.; m. Kathleen Saint; c. Suzanne, Jamie, Catherine; UMan, MEd; retd educator; played college, prov. sr. basketball simultaneously (no longer allowed); mem. Winnipeg Paulins prov. title teams; 2 Western Intercollegiate title teams; mem. '54 ntl sr. championship team; '54 World Cup team; retd. from active play after 47 years; coached several teams including YMHA ntl jr. finalists; Man. HS basketball commissioner; bantam league organizer; officiated several years, Man. officials commissioner; racquetball competitor, instructor; mem. Brandon U faculty '66-87; several basketball awards in his name competed for annually in Man.; res. Brandon, Man.

SPARKES, Bernie (curling); b. 15 Oct 1940, Claresholm, Alta.; given name: Bernard Leslie; div. Lindsay Davie; c. Christopher, Karen, Lisda, Selena; salesman; mem. ntl Pony League baseball champions '55, Babe Ruth League champions '56; mem. '58 Alta. HS curling champions; Edmonton world open carspiel title '65; mem. record 11 Brier rinks, 3 winners, 3 world championship rinks; all-star 2nd Ron Northcott's Brier title rinks '66, '68-69; skip 7 BC Brier reps.; Evergreen, Dogwood, Kamloops, Prince George cashspiels '76; Saskatoon cashspiel '77; finalist Edmonton cashspiel '79, Vernon car spiel '80; noted artist; mem. Canadian Curling, Southern Alta., BC Sports halls of fame; res. N. Vancouver, B.C.

SPARKES, Lindsay (curling); b. 8 Jun 1950, N. Vancouver, B.C.; given name: Lindsay Davie; div. Bernie Sparkes; teacher/librarian; skipped ntl women's title rinks '76, '79; 3rd for Linda Moore '85 STOH, world title, '88 Olympic (demonstration) gold medal rink; ntl women's team leader (coach) from '92 at world, Olympic levels; with Linda Moore competed in first women's skins game; level 4 coach; proficient golfer, skier; res. N. Vancouver, B.C.

SPARLING, Jean (t&f); b. 26 Feb 1955, Vancouver, B.C.; given name: Jean Donalda; m. Bill Gairdner; c. Christine, Emilie, Ruthann, Billy, Franklin; U of British UBC, UofT, BSc; ntl juvenile 200m hurdles record '72; gold 100m, 100m hurdles, 200m hurdles, silver 4x100 relay '73 Canada Games; 4th '76 Olympic trials 200m; mem. '77 FISU Games team; ntl 60yd hurdles record 6.63 '78; mem. '74 ntl title BC jr. field hockey team; BC high school athlete of year; res. King City, Ont.

SPEERS, Jim (horse racing); b. 1882, Elmbank, Ont., d. 19 Jul 1955, Winnipeg, Man.; given name: Robert James; "Mr. Racing" in Western Canada; key role fostering Man., Sask., Alta., BC thoroughbred racing; built, operated Whittier, Polo, Chinook Parks; also operated summer race meetings for exhibition associations in Regina, Saskatoon, Edmonton, Calgary; 1st Canadian breeder to raise winners of more than $1 million on NA tracks; 6 consec. Cdn breeder of yr awards; founder Prairie, Canadian Thoroughbred Breeders Assns.; founded Canadian Derby for 3-year-old foals; introduced pari-mutuel betting to Canada; pioneered daily double in NA; installed 1st closed automatic starting gate in NA Whittier Park '39; launched Red Book of Canadian Racing '30; mem. Canadian Horse Racing, Man., Canada's Sports halls of fame.

SPEIER, Chris (baseball); b. 28 Jun 1950, Alameda, Calif.; given name: Chris Edward; m. Aleta; c. Justin, Erika, Luke, Travis; California (Santa Barbara); baseball mgr.; semipro Stratford Sr. IC '70; SF Giants '71-77, Montreal '77-84, St. Louis '84, Minnesota '84; helped Giants reach '71 Western Div. title, batted .375 in losing playoff cause; NL all-star shortstop *Sporting News* poll '72; AP ML all-star '73; mem. 3 NL all-star teams; 1 of 2 Expos (other Tim Foli) to hit for cycle in game '78; Expos single game RBI record 8 '82; batted .400 in Expos' div. series playoff vs. Phillies '81; minor league mgr. Arizona Diamondbacks org. '98; mem. Athletes for Life; res. Phoenix, Ariz.

SPENCER, Jim (soccer); b. 13 Feb 1915, N. Vancouver, B.C.; d. 14 Apr 1990, Vancouver, B.C.; given name: James Haggarty; m. Sheina Kathleen Murray; c. Jesslen Helen; retd. fire chief; capt. N. Van. HS bantam title team; coach, mgr. 4 consecutive Van. all-star teams vs visiting Europeans; Sr. A basketball with Lauries; rejected '38 offers to play in Eng. League 1st Div., with West Brom, Derby County; refereed juve. soccer; dir. chair. BC Juve. Soccer Assn. '62-76; 2 ntl titles; mem. every BC all-star team during 1st div. career; 7 goals, 3 games for BC all-stars California World's Fair; secty. Pacific Coast Soccer League; mem. soccer discipline board and referee assessor; life mem. BC Youth Soccer Assn.; mem. North Shore, BC Sports halls of fame.

SPENCER, Victor (rowing); b. 6 Oct 1882, Victoria, B.C., d. 21 Feb 1969, Vancouver, B.C.; Columbia Coll.; Boer War, WW1 vet.; mem. VRC 60yrs; club pres. '24-25, '28, hon. pres. '29-69.

SPIR, Peter (t&f); b. 6 Nov 1955, Manchester, Eng.; given name: Peter Charles Francis; m. Kimberley Conner; Oregon, BSc; BC, ntl jr. mile record 4:02.9 '74, jr. 1500m record 3:41.4 '75; ntl sr. 1500m title '75; ntl jr. 800m title, ntl, BC jr. 3000m steeplechase record 8:53.4, BC sr. 2000m 5:11.4, BC jr. 3000m 8:18 '75; Pac-8 Conf. 1500m record 3:46; mem. '75 FISU, '76 Olympic, '79 Pan-Am Games teams; res. Eugene, Ore.

SPOONER, Hugh (t&f); b. 25 Nov 1957, Toronto, Ont.; given name: Hugh Gordon;Texas, BSc; sprint specialist; Ont. HS champion '73-77; jr. Olympics finalist '74; 4x100 relay team finalist '76 Olympics; 4x100 relay team finalist '78 Pan-AM Games; 4x100 relay team finalist NCAA championships '79; last known res. Willowdale, Ont.

SPOWAGE, Cheryl (t&f/rowing); b. 30 Jan 1953, Comox, B.C.; given name: Cheryl Lynne; div. Tom Howard; c. Francine Louise; UBC, BPhE; teacher; competed at 800m, 1500m, 1 mile distances, '67-72; midget all-around athlete Richmond championships, BC midget 800m champion '67; BC juve. mile title '68; bronze open 1500m '69; ntl juve. 800m title '69; BC HS 1500m titles '70-71; Stanley Park

15 mile road race title '72; ran '81 Vancouver International marathon in 2:58.19; rowing '74-78; with Pam Gilmore BC double sculls title '75; singles, doubles titles '76; with Bev Cameron 6th Olympic double sculls finals '76; with Cameron BC doubles title '77, singles, doubles, quad titles '78; ntl, Royal Henley titles '78; 4 Richmond Outstanding Athletic Achievement awards; top jr., sr. HS track athlete awards; res. Surrey, B.C.

SPRAGUE, Dave (football): b. 11 Aug 1910, Dunkirk, N.Y., d. 20 Feb 1968, Ottawa, Ont.; given name: David Shafer; m. Catherine Anderson; c. David Jr., John, Judy, Peter, James; company v-p.; teamed with Huck Welch to lead Delta CI to ntl HS title; capt. HS t&f team specializing in 1/4 mile; football Hamilton Tigers '30-32; 2 interprovincial, 1 Grey Cup winner; Ottawa '33-41; twice capt. Riders, 3 Big Four titles, 1 Grey Cup; all-Eastern, all-Cdn almost every year of 10yr career; mem. Ottawa, Cdn Football, Canada's Sports halls of fame.

SPRATLEY, Jim (shooting); b. 9 Nov 1962, York Twp., Ont.; Centennial Coll.; only sponsored shooter in NA; youngest mem. ntl team; 2nd jr. smallbore prone '84 Benito Juarez; 3rd '84 ntl championships; PB: unofficial world record tie 600x600 sr. men's English match prone; last known res. Pickering, Ont.

SPRAY, Robert (rugby); b. 22 May 1913, Surrey, Eng.; d. 10 Apr 1991, Vancouver, B.C.; m. Joan; c. Rosemary, Andrew; insurance agent; knee injury cut playing career short, turned to administration; emigrated to Vancouver '47, became referee; chair. Cdn rugby tours committee '60-65; pres. CRU '65-72; Jack Patterson Memorial Trophy; Air Canada Amateur Sport Exec. of year award candidate; mem. BC Sports Hall of Fame.

SPRING, Doughy (lacrosse); b. 24 Jan 1888, Draper, Ont., d. 1974, New Westminster, B.C.; given name: Clifford; baker, mechanic; mem. New Westminster Salmonbellies '05-36, 5 Minto Cup winners; prolific scorer judged by peers as outstanding player of his day; at 49 scored 9 goals single box lacrosse game; mem. Lacrosse, BC Sports halls of fame.

SPRING, Harry (administration); b. 27 Sep 1912, Moose Jaw, Sask.; given name: Harry Charles Frederick; m. Constance Hicks; c. Robert, Elaine;UBC, BA, LLB; lawyer; jr. soccer Moose Jaw; quarterback 2 Meraloma BC sr. football title teams; pres. Meraloma Club '37, hon. life mem. from '81; chair. BC Lions organizing group; exec. mem. Lions '53-60, life mem. from '60; CFL commissioner's Vancouver rep. '61-80; mem. Lions bd. of governors from '61; mem. Roughriders board; CFL contribution to game award '67, Centennial Medal '67; mem. Canadian Football Hall of Fame; res. W.Vancouver, B.C.

SPRINGSTEAD, Velma (t&f); b. 22 Aug 1906, Hamilton, Ont., d. 27 Mar 1926, Hamilton, Ont.; given name: Velma Agnes; bronze high jump, Lord Decies Trophy (meet's best all-around competitor) '25 UK Canada-UK-Czechoslovakia tri-meet; pneumonia victim at 20; trophy in her honor presented to Women's Amateur Athletic Fed. of Canada (later absorbed by SFC) by Alexandrine Gibb '32 to be awarded to nation's outstanding female athlete annually.

SQUIRES, Bert (weightlifting); b. 17 Aug 1954, St. John's, Nfld.; PE teacher; ntl 100kg title '79, 90kg title '82, 110kg title '84; ntl sr. records snatch 156kg, C&J 186kg, total 337.5kg; silver 100kg '80-81, team bronze '80 Commonwealth championships; bronze 100kg Pan-Am championships, Shanghai invitational '80; silver 100kg '81 Pan-Am championships, Cuban invitational; bronze snatch '83 Pan-Am Games; mem. '79, '83 Pan-Am, '80, '84 Olympic, '82 Commonwealth Games teams; res. Pangnirtung, NWT.

ST. GODARD, Emile (dogsledding); b. 15 Aug 1905, Winnipeg, Man., d. 26 Mar 1948, The Pas, Man.; dog breeder, trainer; gained fame in series of races vs Leonard Seppala; 200-mile The Pas race winner '25, '26; beat Seppala Que. City '27; pair met annually at Que. City over next 6 years with St. Godard winning 4 times, Seppala twice; pair also competed The Pas, Alaska, Minnesota, Laconia, North Conway with St. Godard winning majority of encounters; last meeting '32 Lake Placid as Olympic demonstration sport following which Seppala, 54, conceded St. Godard's superiority; at peak, '25-35, St. Godard and team raced 1500 miles per season; noted for kindness and concern for his dogs; when lead dog was no longer up to rigors of racing St. Godard retired from competition; mem. Man., Canada's Sports halls of fame.

ST. LOUIS, France (hockey); b. 17 Oct 1958, St. Hubert, Que.; PE teacher, sports dir.; competed in sr. women's ntl championships '83-94; forward 6 ntl sr. women's title teams; 3 Sr. A league MVP awards; 2 Sr. A league scoring titles; 3 ntl championship MVP awards; mem. 5 Team Canada world championship teams; Pacific Rim, 3-Nations Cup gold; mem. '98 Olympic silver medal team; retd. '99; mem. ntl women's lacrosse teams '85-89, 2 world championships; Que. athlete of '86, athlete of decade '80-90; asst. coach Team Quebec '91 Canada Winter Games; res. St. Hubert, Que.

ST. MARTIN, Pierre (handball); b. 4 Sep 1957, St. Jean sur Richelieu, Que.; teacher; ntl team '75-80; mem. 5 ntl title teams; mem. '76 Olympic team; 2nd '80 Pan-Am handball championships; Que. handball player of '80; res. St. Jean sur Richelieu.

ST. PIERRE, Martin (t&f); b. 4 Mar 1972, Ripon, Que.; racewalker; represented Canada '91, '93, '95 World Cup of racewalking, '94 Commonwealth, '95 Pan-Am, '96 Olympic Games; gold 10km '93 Canada Games; ntl 20km title '95; Cdn male athletic prospect of year '94. Quebec University male athlete of '90; res. Montreal, Que.

STACEY, Nelles (rowing); b. 9 May 1888, Vancouver, B.C.; d. 31 Jan 1968, Vancouver, B.C.; given name: George Nelles; mem. Vancouver Rowing Club from '06; 'Mr. Rowing" Vancouver region; mem. '10-11 Miller Cup rugby titlists; rowed in 2 slot '09 NPAAO 4s title Seattle in record 7:49.5 for 1 1/2 miles; varied exec. roles Vancouver Rugby Assn., Vancouver Rowing Club; chief fund raiser VRC/UBC mid-'50s BE, Commonwealth Games winners; mgr. '55 Henley 8s, '57-59 Pan-Am teams; trophy in his name awarded annually by VRC to jr. coxless 4s; mem. Cdn Amateur, BC Sports halls of fame.

STACK, Frank (speed skating); b. 1 Jan 1906, Winnipeg, Man.; d. 25 Jan 1987, Winnipeg, Man.; m. Edith Nixon; c. Bonnie, Diane; retd. salesman; competed regularly '19-54 winning varied honors; Western Canada jr. titles '19-23, sr. '24-29; Western Open indoor title '31-33, world 5-mile record 15:42.2; bronze 10,000m, 4th 500m, 1500m '32 Olympics; 6 ntl titles; US outdoor title '31; world indoor 500m record 47.0; rep. Canada 6 Olympics, 3 as competitor, others as official; only Cdn to win 10,000 Lakes championships also Silver Skate competition Minneapolis, set points record; following 12-year retirement, competed ntl indoor championships at age 60, taking 3 2nds, 2 3rds; life mem. St. James Speed Skating Club Winnipeg; Man. Centennial Comm. '70 speedskater of century; mem. Canadian Speed Skating, Man., Canada's Sports halls of fame.

STAIRS, Matt (baseball) b. 27 Feb 1969, Fredericton, N.B.; given name: Matthew Wade; m. Lisa; c. Nicole, Alicia, Chandler; outfielder; signed as free agent with Expos '89; spent several seasons in minors with Rockford, West Palm Beach, Jacksonville, Harrisburg, Ottawa, New Britain; Pawtuckett, Edmonton; brief stints in ML with Montreal; played with Chunichi Dragons of Japanese Central League '93 before returning to Expos; traded to Boston '94; joined Oakland as free agent '95; shunted between majors and minors until '97 when he blossomed as a power hitting outfielder smashing 27 homers, followed with 26 '98; ; 1st Cdn to hit 25 or more HRs in successive seasons; won batting titles Mexican Winter League and Eastern League; EL MVP with Harrisburg and EL all-star game MVP '94; tied Triple-A record with 6rbi single inning; res. Cardigan, N.B.

STANLEY, Allen (hockey); b. 1 Mar 1926, Timmins, Ont.; given name: Allan Herbert; m. Barbara Bowie; owner, operator resort, golf course; Boston Olympics srs.; pro Providence Reds (AHL); def NY Rangers '48-54, Chicago '54-56, Boston '56-57, Toronto '58-69; rejected coaching offer Quebec Aces (AHL); operates successful hockey school; NHL record: 1244 scheduled games, 100g, 333a, 110 playoff games, 7g, 36a; 4 Stanely Cups; asst. coach Buffalo '77; mem. Hockey Hall of Fame; res. Bobcaygeon, Ont.

STANLEY, Barney (hockey); b. 1 Jun 1893, Paisley, Ont., d. 16 May 1971, Edmonton, Alta.; given name: Russell; jr. Paisley; amateur Edmonton Maritimes, Dominions, Albertas '09-15; mem. Vancouver Millionaires '15-19, 1 Stanley Cup; player-coach amateur Edmonton Eskimos '19-20; player-coach pro Calgary Tigers '20-22, Regina Capitals '23-24, Edmonton Eskimos '24-26, Winnipeg Maroons '26-27; coach-mgr. Chicago Black Hawks '27-28; Minneapolis Millers '28-29; coach Edmonton Pooler jrs. 3 years; as pro played every position on ice except goaler; in 216 games, 144 goals; twice 5 goals single game; mem. Hockey Hall of Fame.

STANOWSKI, Wally (hockey); b. 28 Apr 1919, Winnipeg, Man.; given name: Walter Peter; m. Joyce DuBrule; c. Wally Jr., Adair, Adrian, Craig; salesman; jr. football MVP '37; mem. St. Boniface Seals '38 Memorial Cup champions; pro AHL Syracuse Stars '38-39; excluding '42-44 when he served in RCAF, mem. Maple Leafs '39-48; Rangers '48-51; Cincinnati '51-52; all-star NHL def '41; NHL record: 428 scheduled games, 23g, 88a, 60 playoff games, 3g, 13a; mem. 4 Stanley Cup winners; mem. Toronto NHL Oldtimers to '81; mem. Man. Hockey Hall of Fame; res. Etobicoke, Ont.

STAPLETON, Pat (hockey); b. 4 Jul 1940, Sarnia, Ont.; given name: Patrick James; m. Jacqueline Prudence; c.Mary, Maureen, Tommy, Susan, Michael, Christopher; nicknamed 'Whitey'; retd. farmer; Jr. B Sarnia, Jr. A St. Catharines, all-star OHA defenceman, mem. Memorial Cup winner; minor pro Sault Ste. Marie, Kingston (EPHL), Portland (WHL) '60-65; Boston, Toronto property, Chicago '65-73; player-coach WHA Chicago Cougars; with Ralph Backstrom, Dave Dryden, bought team to become 1st person in major league histroy to own team, manage, coach and play simultaneously; when Cougars collapsed joined Indianapolis Racers as player; mem. Team Canada '72, WHA Team Canada '74; tied NHL playoff assists record with 13 '71, set new standard of 15 '73 playoffs; NHL, WHA record 6 assists single game; Dennis Murphy Award top WHA defenceman '74; 3 times NHL 2nd team, once WHA 1st team all-star; NHL record: 635 scheduled games, 43g, 294a; mem. Oldtimers hockey, ntl advisory council '83; mem. Sarnia/Lambton Sports Hall of Fame; res. Strathroy, Ont.

STASIUK, Vic (hockey); b. 23 May 1929, Lethbridge, Alta.; given name: Victor John; m. Mary Ragnfrid Lenning; c. Vanessa, Elsa, Victor Guy, Jae Jae; retd farmer/golf course owner; minor hockey Lethbridge Native Sons, jr. Edmonton-Wetaskwin Canadians; pro Kansas City '48-49; NHL Chicago '49-50, '55-60. Boston '50-55, '60-63; left wing Bruins' famed Uke Line with Bronco Horvath, Johnny Bucyk; NHL record: 745 scheduled games, 183g, 254a, 69 playoff games, 16g, 18a; 1 all-star game, 2 Stanley Cup winners; turned to coaching '63-75 with minor league stints in Pittsburgh, Memphis, NJ, Quebec, California, Denver and NHL stops in Philadelphia, Vancouver, St. Louis; developed Paradise Canyon Golf & Country Club; recipient Elizabeth Dufresne trophy (Boston); res. Lethbridge, Alta.

STASTNY, Peter (hockey); b.18 Sep 1956, Bratislava, Czechoslovakia; m. Darina; c. Katarina, Kristina, Paul-Peter, Yan-Pavol; special assignments St. Louis; played with HC Slovan Bratislava '73-80, winning ntl title '79; Czech player of '80; defected to Canada '80; NHL Quebec '80-90, New Jersey '90-93, St. Louis '94-95; Calder Memorial Trophy '81; set 1st yr player record 70a, 109pts; capt.Nordiques '85-90; 6 NHL all-star games; NHL record: 977 scheduled games, 450g, 789a, 93 playoff games, 33g, 72a; at '95 retirement was highest scoring European-born and trained player in NHL history; mem. Czech ntl team '75-76 jr. worlds, '76-77 sr worlds, '76 Canada Cup, '80, '94 Olympics, '95 worlds; became Canadian citizen '84; mem. Team Canada '84 Canada Cup; mem. Hockey Hall of Fame; res. St. Louis, Mo.

STAUB, Rusty (baseball); b. 1 Apr 1944, New Orleans, La.; given name: Daniel Joseph; retd. restaurateur/chef; Louisiana Scholastic athlete of '61; $100,000 signing bonus Houston organization; limited minor league seasoning at Durham, Oklahoma City; Astros '63-68, Montreal '69-71,

'79, NY Mets '72-75, '81-84, Detroit '76-79, Texas '80; 1st genuine Expos superstar; nicknamed "Le Grande Orange" for his red hair; 6 all-star game appearances; '73 World Series; uniform #10 retired by Expos; mem. Montreal Expos Wall of Fame; res. New York City, N.Y.

STAUDER, Zlatica (rhythmic gymnastics/builder): b. 10 Sep 1946, Bratislava, Czechoslovakia; given name: Zlatica Takacova; m. Milan Stauder; c. Zuzanna; U J.A. Komenski, UMan. BPhE; emigrated to Canada '68; joined Man. Gymnastics Assn. exec and introduced rhythmics discipline to province; developed, taught 1st courses for coaches, teachers, judges in Western Canada; created 1st independent rhythmic gymnastics club in Manitoba; founder, head coach Manitoba High Performance Centre for Rhythmic Gymnastics; instrumental in establishing comm. for alternate education of elite athletes in province; Cdn RGF, international judges comm. high performance coach, official of '89; mem. Man. Sports Hall of Fame; res. Winnipeg, Man.

STEAD, Ron (baseball); b. 24 Sep 1936, London, Ont.; m. Betty; c. Ron, David, Heather, Jeff; training supervisor; batboy Toronto (IL) '45-54; minor baseball Toronto; London Sr. IC '55; minor pro Toronto organization '56-57; Sr. IC Brantford '58-66, Guelph '67-72; 16-year IC record: 104 wins, 44 losses, 1365 innings pitched, 1231 strike outs, 262 walks, 119 complete games, 2.08 lifetime ERA; IC record lowest ERA 1 season, 0.35 in 77 innings Guelph '67 (since surpassed); 4 times 1st team, twice 2nd team all-star; IC MVP '60, '63, '65, '67; single season shutout record (7) '67; mem. Ont. gold medal team '69 Canada Summer Games; mem. '67 Pan-Am Games team; res. Chatham, Ont.

STECKLE, Bob (wrestling): b. 21 Aug 1930, Waterloo Twp; given name: Robert John; m. Kay Allison Francis; c. David, Jane, James, Susan; Ont. Agricultural Coll. BSA; farmer; OQAA heavyweight champion '50-52; 9 ntl open FS titles; US open Greco-Roman champion '55-57; mem. 3 Cdn Olympic teams; silver '54, bronze '58 Commonwealth Games; silver '63 Pan-Am Games; flag-bearer, 4th Greco-Roman '56 Olympics; mem. U Guelph Sports Hall of Fame; res. New Hamburg, Ont.

STEELE, David (soccer/hockey/baseball); b. 31 Dec 1914, Muskeg Lake Reserve, Sask.; d. 22 Jul 1996, Regina, Sask.; given name: David Greyeyes; retd. Dept. Indian Affairs; he excelled in soccer and was 3 times Sask. all-star team mem.; represented Sask. vs. Newcastle United '49 following WW2 service; mem. Cdn Machine Gun Reinforcement Unit soccer team which won Overseas army title '42; also played in inter-Allied games; player/coach following WW2; mem. Sask. Sports, Sask. Indian First Nations Sports halls of fame.

STEELE, Don (administration); b. 11 Mar 1948, Toronto, Ont.; div.; c. Lisa, Rebecca; UofT, BA; exec. dir. Tennis Canada '82-88; nationally ranked jr.; coached 8 ntl champions; assisted with ntl certification program; former exec. dir. Ont. Tennis Assn.; former tech. dir. Tennis Canada; res. Toronto, Ont.

STEEN, Dave (t&f); b. 2 Jan 1942, Vancouver, B.C.; m. Cassie Gairdner; c. Laura, Heather, Stefan; Oregon, BSc; writer-author; shot put specialist; ntl shot record 53'10" '60, held (with improvements to 63' 1/4") to '72; bronze '62, gold, Games record '66 Commonwealth Games; mem. ntl track team more than decade; retd. from shot put competition '71; competed '80 Ottawa marathon; res. Terra Cotta, Ont.

STEEN, Dave (t&f); b. 14 Nov 1959, New Westminster, B.C.; m. Andrea Page;UofT; fireman; decathlon specialist; father Dan '56 Cdn decathlon champion; uncle Dave Commonwealth Games shot put gold medalist; '77 Canada Games decathlon, long jump, ntl outdoor long jump; mem. '79, '83 Pan-Am Games, '80, '84, '88 Olympic, '81, '83 FISU, '82 Commonwealth Games teams; '80 ntl indoor pentathlon, '81-82 decathlon, '84 heptathlon titles; '82 CIAU long jump; '83-84 UofT track classic pentathlon; decathlon gold '83 FISU, Pan-Am Games, silver '82, '86 Commonwealth Games, bronze '88 Olympics; 1st Cdn to score more than 8000 points in decathlon with record 8019 '82 LSU Invitational; 7 Cdn decathlon records; world pentathlon record 4,104 points '83; 4 Fred Rowell trophies; PB: 8205 decathlon points, 4108 pentathlon points; fed. govt. excellence award '84; Canada Games spokesperson; mem. Canada's Fair Play commission; mem. Order of Canada; Cdn Amateur, Canada's, BC Sports halls of fame; res. Tecumseh, Ont.

STEEVES, Ed (curling); b. 17 Oct 1936, Moncton, N.B.; m. Helen; chiropractor; 3rd for Hap Mabey '69-70 Briers; all-star skip '74 ntl mixed; coached 3 NB jr. title rinks; NB curling exec. '76-80; NB pres. '78-79, NB delegate to CCA '78; CCA dir. '85-91; CCA pres. '89-91; Intl Curling Fed. pres. '88; v-p. World Fed. '90-94; key role in amalgamation of ntl. assn into CCA; worked hard to secure Olympic status for curling; CCA exec. of '92; Ross Harstone award '70; mem. Moncton Sports Wall, Cdn Curling, NB Sports halls of fame; res. Gibsons, B.C.

STEMMLE, Brian (skiing); b. 12 Oct 1966, Toronto, Ont.; began skiing age 3, competing age 4; mem. ntl team '85-99; competed '88, '92, '94, '98 Olympics; downhill specialist; sister Karen former ntl team mem.; WC Super G bronze '85, downhill bronze '87; career dogged by injuries; res. Aurora, Ont.

STEPHENS, Richard (figure skating); b. 8 Dec 1947, Port Perry, Ont.; given name: Richard Warren; m. Barbara Lasalle; c. Brett Aaron; pro skating instructor; ntl jr. title '66; ntl, NA srs. '69; mem. '68 Olympic team; pro ice shows, teaching '70; last known res. Port Perry, Ont.

STEPHENSON, Linda (golf); b. 3 Aug 1944, Domville, Ont.; given name: Linda Mae; Algonquin Coll.; Stats Canada programmer analyst; played competitive softball; began golfing '68; left hander; mem. Prescott GC '68-83, '98, Carleton Golf & Yacht Club '84-97; winner of 26 consec. and 27 in 28yrs club championships; Que. sr. title; Ottawa City & District titles '85, '86, '88; 4 tournament of champions titles; 6 ladies' course records; 2 holes-in-one; 4 consec. Brockville sr. titles, 21 (20 consec) Prescott, 5 Mississippi, 4 Cornwall field day titles; with Jim MacKay teamed to win 19 Prescott, 2 Tecumseh, 11 Smiths Falls, 3 Cornwall (2 more with Jean Lachance), 3 Ottawa Hunt, 1 Buckingham mixed 2-ball titles; res. Nepean, Ont.

STERNBERG, Gerry (football); b. 18 Mar 1943, Orsk, Russia; given name: Gerald; m. Tania; c. Arlen, Samantha, Zachary, Ryne; UofT, BA, Osgoode Hall, LLB; barrister, solicitor, player agent; pro Edmonton '65, Montreal '66-67, Toronto '69-71, '73, Hamilton '71-72; 2nd to Jim Copeland in Argos records for punt returns with 151 for 861yds; res. Toronto, Ont.

STEVENS, Rick (cricket); b. 18 Mar 1945, London, Eng.; given name: Richard John; m. Jane; emigrated to Canada at 14; mem. Ont. interprov. team '62; ntl Colts cap '63; 5 sr. ntl caps; considered all-arounder who utilizes natural skills to fullest degree; mem. Rest of World team vs. Bermuda '73; mem. Eastern ntl XI in victory over Australian WC team; res. Ajax, Ont.

STEVENS, Scott (hockey); b. 1 Apr 1964, Kitchener, Ont.; m. Donna; c. Kaitlin, Ryan, Kara; defence Kitchener (OHL) '80-82; Memorial Cup '82; 1st Washington pick '82 draft; NHL with Washington '82-90, St. Louis '90-91, New Jersey '91-99; NHL all-rookie team '83; 2 NHL 1st team, 2 2nd team all-star; Alka Seltzer Plus award '94; acquired by New Jersey as compensation for St. Louis signing of free agent Brendan Shanahan; played 8 all-star games; mem. Team Canada '83, '85, '87, '89 worlds, '91 Canada Cup, '96 world cup, '98 Olympics; mem. 1 Stanley Cup winner; NHL record: (through '99) 1275 scheduled games, 171g, 628a, 155 playoff games, 19g, 71a; res. Essex Falls, N.J.

STEVENS, Warren (football); b. 1905, Syracue, N.Y., d. 25 Oct 1978, Melbourne, Aust.; m. Charlotte "Chubby" Tickner; c. Jacqueline; Syracuse, BSc; retd UofT athletic dir.; reputation as passing quarterback while leading Syracuse HS to city football title; all-American mention in university sr. year; rejected pro baseball offers Philadelpia Athletics; mem. MAAA Winged Wheelers, McGill backfield coach; made Cdn rugby football history '31 tossing 1st legal forward pass to end Frank Robinson; Wheelers won Grey Cup that year and Stevens completed 1st Grey Cup 40yd TD pass to Ken Grant; 1st to score convert on fake placement and run in Grey Cup; 1st AD UofT '32-70; as head coach (roles he yielded '41) 3 Intercollegiate football and basketball championships; mem. UofT Sports Hall of Fame.

STEVENSON, Art (football); b. 30 May 1916, Gothenburg, Neb.; given name: Arthur Clement; m. Dorothy Bowden; c. Sally, Curtis, Gary; Hastings College MD; retd. obstetrician, gynecologist; Little all-American, hon. mention in basketball; Little all-American football '36, conf. discus championship; pro Winnipeg '37-41; after WW2 coached Bomber backfield; best all-time all-around athlete Hastings College; mem. Canadian Football Hall of Fame; last known res. Phoenix, Ariz.

STEVENSON, Bill (football); b. 20 Aug 1950, Edmonton, Alta.; given name: William George; m. Carol; c. Stephanie, Tanner; Drake; territorial draft Eskimos; NFL draft Miami; opted for WFL Memphis Southmen '74-75; CFL offensive, defensive lineman Edmonton '75-88; mem. 6 Grey Cup winners; 3 WFC, 2 CFL all-star selections; res. Edmonton, Alta.

STEVENSON, Douglas Roy (football); b. 21 Oct 1930, Drumbo, Ont.; m. Barbara Jean St. Pierre; c. Chrystal Ann, Roderick Michael (d), Tevy Joan, Reme Marie, Wendy May; UofT, UAlta, MSc; hydrogeologist, company pres.; mem. UofT boxing team '51-52; football Kitchener-Waterloo Dutchmen '53-54, ORFU title '54 losing Little Grey Cup game to Edmonton Eskimos; mem. Eskimos '55-62, Grey Cup champions '55, '56; line coach UAlta Golden Bears '64-70, CIAU title '67; res. Langley, B.C.

STEVENSON, Forbis (curling/golf): b. 17 Nov 1913, Saint John, N.B.; d. 14 June 1995, Cold Lake, Alta.; given name: Forbis Beatrice McGeouch; m. Otty Stevenson; c. Norman, Nancy; mem. Mable Deware Dominion Diamond D title rink; noted for sportsmanship she served as pres. Paragon Ladies Golf Club, Kingston, NS mem. Grand Centre, Paragon, Westfield, Moncton, Amberdale golf clubs, Middleton, Thistle St. Andrews, Moncton Beaver, Mayflower curling clubs; mem. NB, Moncton Sports halls of fame.

STEVENSON, Greg (rowing): b. 27 Feb 1969, Sherbrooke, Que.; entrepreneur; began rowing age 20; men's coxed 8s; mem. ntl team from '91; bronze coxless 4s '91 Pan-Am Games; 2 silver '95 Pan-Am Games; 1 ntl 8s title; competed '92. '96 Olympics; Quebec Rowing Assn. athlete of year '91; res. Victoria, B.C.

STEVENSON, Lori (bowling): b. 28 Oct 1965, Neepawa, Man,; given name: Lori Lynne Greider; m. Peter Stevenson; c. Amy, Sarah; Man. research asst.; began bowling age 9; YBC Man. singles title '83, ntl bronze; Man. record 4 provincial singles titles; ntl gold '93, '95, silver '84-85; ntl all-star '84, '93, '95; repeat ntl title tied record; ntl women's Hiram Walker Special Old Pins Game title '94; pres. Minnedosa bowlers assn.; received early training from father Wilf and brother Bob, both prominent bowlers; holds Level 2 ntl coaching certificate; res. Minnedosa, Man.

STEVENSON, Ross (horseshoes): b. 11 Jun 1948, Kitchener, Ont.; c. William; owns Horseshoe Express courier; 5 ntl jr. boys titles; 1 Manitoba, 8 Alta. men's singles titles; ntl men's singles title '88; world B class crown '72; 1st Cdn to win world title claiming jr. boys title '65; HS chess, scrabble champion; res. Calgary, Alta.

STEVENSON, Victor (football): b. 22 Sep 1960, New Westminster, B.C.; UCal; tackle; CFL Sask. '82-92, BC '93-95, Toronto '96, Winnipeg '97; 2 Western, 1 Northern, 1 CFL all-star; Becket-DeMarco Memorial trophy '92; runnerup CFL outstanding offensive lineman '92; 2 Grey Cup winners; res. Vancouver, B.C.

STEWART, Black Jack (hockey): b. 6 May 1917, Pilot Mound, Man., d. 25 May 1983, Detroit, Mich.; given name: John Sherratt; race track judge; jr. Portage La Prairie; pro '38 Detroit but spent all but 33 games with Pittsburgh (AHL); Detroit regular '39-50, Chicago '50-52; mem. 2 Stanley Cup winners; 3 times 1st, twice 2nd team all-star defenceman; Detroit MVP '42-43; coached Chatham Maroons, sr. OHA teams Windsor, Kitchener, Pittsburgh (AHL); retd. from hockey '63; NHL record: 503 scheduled games, 30g, 79a; Florida State harness racing commissioner; mem. Cdn, Man. Hockey halls of fame.

STEWART, Brian (motorsport); b. 27 May 1942, Port Glasgow, Scotland; m. Sharon; c. Kimberley; aggressive racer who began motorsports career '65; Cdn Formula Vee title '69; Cdn Formula Ford title '72; 12th Formula Ford world championships '72; turned attention to team ownership fielding cars in FF1600, FF2000, Super Vee, Atlantic; Brian Stewart Racing drivers earned 10 titles before he entered full-time Indy Lights competition '89 as team mgr Landford Racing; BSR team, including Bryan Herta, P.J. Jones, Gualter Salles, Paul Tracy claimed 7 poles, 9 wins '90; most successful owner in Indy Lights history boasting back-to-back titles, 30 victories, '90-91; 6 victories, 2 poles, 2 rookie titles, 3rd place finishes '95-97; res. Pefferlaw, Ont.

STEWART, Gordon (t&f); b. 6 Sep 1948, Toronto, Ont.; given name: Gordon William; m. Sandra Maynard; SFU, BA, MSc; fitness consultant, freelance writer, editor; city all-star basketball '67; North Toronto CI athlete of '66-67; Toronto jr. pole vault, triple jump records '62-67; ntl midget triple jump title '64; ntl jr. decathlon title record 6150 points '68; Canada Games decathlon '69; mem. '70 Commonwealth, '71 Pan-Am, '73 FISU Games teams; 4 ntl decathlon titles; record 7438 points '72; ntl team '70-76; authored *Every Body's Fitness Book*; res. Victoria, B.C.

STEWART, Mary (swimming); b. 8 Dec 1945, Vancouver, B.C.; m. R.H. McIlwaine;UBC, BE; teacher; coached by Howard Firby; silver 4x100 FS relay '59 Pan-Am Games team at 13; finalist 100m FS '60, 100m butterfly '64 Olympic teams; gold 110yd butterfly, silver 4x110 medley, FS relays, bronze 110yd FS '62 Commonwealth Games; silver 100m butterfly, FS, 4x100 medley, FS relays '63 Pan-Am Games; world records 100m, 110yd butterfly '61-62; UK, US, Cdn ntl butterfly, Cdn ntl FS, backstroke titles; 2 Velma Springstead awards; 2 Beatrice Pines Cdn outstanding female swimmer awards; mem. '75 Pan-Am Games headquarters comm.; BC Lions football team mascot '56-63; mem. Cdn Aquatic, Amateur, BC Sports Hall of Fame; res. Vancouver, B.C.

STEWART, Nels (hockey); b. 29 Dec 1900, Montreal, Que., d. 21 Aug 1957, Wasaga Beach, Ont.; given name: Nelson Robert; brewery rep.; Montreal Maroons '25-32, 34 goals rookie season; nicknamed "Old Poison"; with Babe Siebert, Hooley Smith formed S Line; 134 goals, 56 assists 5 years on S Line; 1st NHL player to score more than 300 goals (324 goals, 191 assists, 653 league games); Boston '32-35, NY Americans '35-40; twice Hart Trophy; mem. 1 Stanley Cup winner; coach Port Colborne Srs.; mem. Canada's Sports, Hockey halls of fame.

STEWART, Ray (golf); b. 13 Dec 1953, Matsqui, B.C.; m. Maureen; c. Brett, Tyler; UBC; turned pro '80; Cdn tour victories '99 Telus Edmonton Open, Cdn Masters; with Dave Barr/Rick Gibson won '94 Dunhill Cup; on PGA tour '83, '87-95; runnerup '89 Chattanooga Classic, '87 Bank of Boston Classic; also played Asian, European tours; twice Dunhill Cup team mem.; ranked 2nd '99 Cdn tour McDonald's Order of Merit; mem. Cdn World Cup of Golf team '99; res. Abbotsford, B.C.

STEWART, Ron (football); b. 25 Sep 1934, Toronto, Ont.; m. Wendy Thomas; c. Melissa, Christian; Queen's, BA,

BPHE, UofOtt, LLB.; lawyer, ombudsman, Solicitor General's dept.; mem. Queen's '55-56 Yates Cup winners, league MVP '57, Webster scholarship '58; pro Ottawa '58-70, 4 Grey Cup finals, 3 winners; Jeff Russel Memorial Trophy '60, '67; Schenley top Canadian '60; Lionel Conacher award '60; Walker Trophy (Ottawa club MVP) '60, '67; Eastern Conference all-star '60, '64; Ottawa Jaycees young man of year, Ont. Achievement Award '70; sweater #11 retd. by Rough Riders; CFL record most yds gained single game (287 Montreal Oct '60); 13-season CFL record: 983 carries, 5690yds, 5.8yds-per-carry avg., 41tds; dir. Ottawa Football Club; mem. Canadian Football, Canada's, Queen's, Ottawa Sports, OUAA Football Legends halls of fame; res. Ottawa, Ont.

STEWART, Ron (hockey); b. 11 Jul 1932, Calgary, Alta.; given name: Ronald George; m. Barbara Christie; hockey exec.; jr. Toronto Marlboros, Windsor Spitfires, Barrie Flyers, Guelph Biltmores all in one season helping latter win Memorial Cup '52; pro Toronto '52-65, Boston '65-67, St. Louis '67-68, NY Rangers '68-71, '72, Vancouver '71, NY Islanders '72-73; NHL record: 1353 games, 276 goals, 253 assists, 119 playoff games, 14 goals, 21 assists; coached '74-74 Portland (WHL) team from last place to playoff final, '74-57 Springfield Kings to AHL championship; Ranger coach '75-76; player personnel dir. '77; mem. 3 Stanley Cup winners; res. Kelowna, B.C./ Surprise, Ariz.

STEWART, Susan (basketball); b. 14 Nov 1969, Toronto, Ont.; Laurentian, BA (law & justice); civilian employee RCMP; mem. 5 OWIAA, 2 CIAU title teams; 5yrs OWIAA all-star; mem. '87 jr., '90-97 sr. ntl teams; 1st team all-Canadian; competed '91 Pan-Am, 2 FISU Games; mem. Athletes in Action tournament team; attended WNBA draft camp; Laurentian athlete of '94 award; Nan Copp award '94; res. Mississauga, Ont.

STICKLE, Leon (officiating/hockey); b. 20 Apr 1948, Toronto, Ont.; given name: Leon Evan; m. Nancy Smith; c. Jayne, Christine, David; played minor hockey Milton, Jr. B. Sarnia, Jr. A St. Catharines; 12yrs minor league officiating; joined NHL '69 as linesman working initial game '70; worked 8 Stanley Cup finals, 4 NHL all-star games, '81, '84 Canada Cup tournaments; worked 1967 NHL scheduled games; active with Ont., Cdn Special Olympics; coach minor baseball; res. Mt. Forest, Ont.

STIEB, Dave (baseball); 22 Jul 1957, Santa Ana, Calif.; given name: David Andrew; m. Patti Faso; c. Andrew David; Southern Illinois; baseball player; *Sporting News* college all-American outfielder; semipro Alaska; drafted Toronto '78; among premier AL righthanded pitchers; Blue Jays regular '79-92, '98; 439 games, 407 starts, 2871.2ip, 175-134, 103cg, 1658k, 1017bob; youngest pitcher '80 all-star game; twice AL pitcher of month; Labatt's, Toronto BBWAA MVP '80, 3 Labatt's pitcher of month awards; mem. 7 all-star games; pitched no-hitter vs. Cleveland '90; mem. '92 World Series winner; co-author *Tomorrow I'll be Perfect*; retd. from baseball '93; made brief comeback in Blue Jays organization '98; mem. Blue Jays Level of Excellence; res. Incline Village, Nev.

STIEDA, Alex (cycling); b. 13 Apr 1961, Belleville, Ont.; given name: Alexander Nicholas Ernst; SFU; mem. jr. world pursuit team '79; ntl jr. track champion '79-80, sr. '81; BC, jr. track, road champion '80; won Tour L'Abitibi '80; mem. world pursuit team '81; mem. '82 Commonwealth, '84 Olympic Games teams; criticism of FISU Games cycling competition '83 led to CCA rescinding Sport Canada B card; reinstated A Card; 3 gold, 2 bronze '82 Trinidad Tesoro Games; bronze 4000m individual pursuit '83 FISU Games; last known res. Coquitlam, B.C.

STILLWAGON, Jim (football); b. 11 Feb 1949, Mt. Vernon, Ohio; m. Effie; c. Nicole, Angela, Electra; Ohio State; utilities co. employee; interior lineman; mem. Rose Bowl title team; recipient Knute Rockne, Outland trophies; drafted by Green Bay Packers but opted for CFL with Toronto '71-75; 1 Grey Cup final; 3 all-Canadian awards; res. Columbus, Ohio.

STIMPSON, Bob (golf): b. 10 Jun 1930, St. Vital, Man.; m. Carol; c. Kerry; sales; won 3 Alexander of Tunis, 1 Duke of Kent titles; mem. 1 Man., 3 Que. Willingdon Cup teams; Ottawa and district medal, match champion; Ottawa ACT athlete of '63; res. Stittsville, Ont.

STIMPSON, Earl (golf); b. 22 May 1914, Ottawa, Ont.; d. 15 Dec 1995, Ottawa, Ont.; m. Cecile O'Hara; c. Beverley Anne, Colleen; golf pro; life mem. CPGA; owned, operated Ottawa region's largest driving range 17 years; '66 taught game to UN troops in Egypt; 28 years operated winter golf school for YM-YWCA in Ottawa; operated Kiwanis golf school 22 years; 1st pres., only lifetime mem. Manderley Golf Club; trophy bearing name awarded annually to top pro Ottawa Valley; putter league established bearing his name.

STINSON, Wally (administration); b. 2 Jun 1918, Austin, Man.; given name: Edgar Wallace; div.; c. Donna, Allan, Ronald; UMan., BA, UofSask. retd. educator; branch AAU of C '51-58, pres. '59; pres. AAU of C '63; mem. National Council on Physical Fitness '48-53, National Advisory Council '61; '65-82 v-p. Commonwealth Games Assn. of Canada; dir. SFC, CTFA; chair. tech. advisory board Canada Winter Games '71; asst. mgr. '70 Commonwealth Games team; GM '74 Commonwealth Games team; track referee '67 Pan-Am Games, Canada Summer Games Halifax; CAPHER award of honor '72; pres. BC Commonwealth Games Comm.; mem. Sask. Sports Hall of Fame; res. Saskatoon, Sask./Gabriola, B.C./Mexico.

STIRLING, Bummer (football); b. 23 Oct 1907, London, Ont.; d. 28 May 1994, Calgary, Alta.; given name: Hugh; m. Jean; c. Heather, Susan; retd. dir. employee relations; mem. '28 Dominion jr. football champions, Sarnia Imperials (ORFU) '29; starred with Imperials through '37, all-star '32-37, all-Eastern '34-36, ORFU MVP '36; mem. 2 Grey Cup winners; Lionel Conacher award '38; mem. Cdn Football, Sarnia/Lambton, Canada's Sports halls of fame.

STIRTON, Erike-Leigh (rhythmic gymnastics); b. 8 Aug 1980, Oakville, Ont.; studied ballet as youngster but on suggestion of rhythmics judge Tamara Bompa switched to rhythmics; mem. Etobicoke Olympium Club; mem. ntl team '95-99; competed '97 worlds; 5 gold, 1 silver '98 Commonwealth Games; qualified for 2000 Olympics; group bronze '99 Pan-Am Games; res. Oakville, Ont.

STOCK, Ed (lawn bowling); b. 25 Nov 1924, Toronto, Ont.; given name: Edward Hodgins; m. Mary Margaret Meikle; c. Margaret Eileen, Gordon Edward;UWO., BSc, Syracuse, MPA; financial administrator; won several trophies while sailing GP-14s Malaysia '69-71; mem. Brockville Yacht Club; mem. numerous club trophy winning rinks with Ottawa RCN Curling Club; regional convenor Ont. PLBA '77-78; past sec.-treas. OPLBA District 16 '72-77; p.-pres. Elmdale LBC Ottawa '76-77; Disict 16 4s champion '75, singles '73; sec.-treas. '76 ntl championship; Level 2 Ont. Coaching program; res. Brampton, Ont.

STOCKTON, Donald (wrestling); b. 22 Feb 1904, Montreal, Que., d. 16 Jun 1978, Montreal, Que.; given name: Donald Parker; m. Margaret Connolly; c. Alan, Barbara, Patricia, Eric; retd. foreman; at 19 Que. 160lb wrestling title; mem. '24, '28, '32 Olympic teams, silver 174lbs class '28; 11 Que., 6 ntl titles at varying weights 160-191lbs; aside from Olympics, lost only 1 major match in career, '25 ntl 174lb title to Arthur Coleman; defeated Coleman following night in 191lb title match; '30 BE 174lb title; mem. Verdun jr. football team '24; CNR Int. ORFU title '25; Montreal Winged Wheelers '27-29; mem. Verdun AC lacrosse team mid-'20s; coached Montreal juvenile, int. city and district title teams; chief ref., chief judge, supervisor of referees and judges for Que.; mem. Canadian Amateur Sports, Wrestling halls of fame.

STOJKO, Elvis (figure skating): b. 22 Mar 1972, Newmarket, Ont.; York; began skating age 5, competing age 9; ntl jr. champ '88; mem. ntl team from '90; 5 Skate Canada gold; 6 ntl sr. titles, 4 runnerup; NHK Trophy gold '95, silver '92; competed 6 worlds winning gold '94, '95, '97; competed 3 Olympics winning silver '94, '98 (despite serious injury; Lalique trophy bronze '90; 1st skater to complete quadruple toe loop in combination with another jump (double axel) '91 worlds; coached by Doug and Michelle Leigh; Ont. male athlete of '93; Norton Crowe, Lionel Conacher awards '94; Cdn meritorious service award; res. Richmond Hill, Ont.

STONE, Edith (basketball); b. 9 Apr 1912, Edmonton, Alta.; m. Elmer Sutton (d); c. Philip, Margaret; retd. secretary; mem. famed Edmonton Grads '30-34; Alta. mixed doubles badminton playdowns '50; twin sister Helen also mem. Grads; mem. Alta. Sports, Canadian Basketball halls of fame; res. Edmonton, Alta.

STONE, Helen (basketball); b. 9 Apr 1912, Edmonton, Alta.; given name: Helen Cecilia; m. William James Stewart; Langaro Coll.; retd. secretary; mem. famed Edmonton Grads team '31-34; with sister Edith only twins ever on team; played 61 games, 412 points, 6.7 avg.; mem. Alta. Sports, Canadian Basketball halls of fame; res. Vancouver, B.C.

STONE, Reg (curling); b. 9 Apr 1914, Vancouver, B.C.; given name: Reginald Elliot; m. Ruby Elizabeth Morton; retd. Trail Parks & Rec. superintendent; with brother Roy

at 2nd, later 3rd 7 BC championships; '45 BC crown but there was no Brier that year due to WW2; competed in 6 Briers; won Saskatoon carspiel '56; with Roy skipping, Reg at 3rd, '73 BC Seniors title, lost ntl title playoff; mem. BC Senior-Seniors (over 60) title rinks '77-81; 9yrs golf pro, greenskeeper Rossland-Trail Country Club; dir. BC Golf Assn.; major role in construction of numerous regional golf clubs; hon. life mem. Trail, Kelowna Curling Clubs, BC Curling Assn., BC Golf Assn., Rossland-Trail Country Club; mem. Canadian Curling, BC Sports halls of fame; res. Victoria B.C.

STONE, Rocky (football): b. 16 Apr 1923, Moncton, N.B.; d. 19 Jan 1977, Moncton, N.B.; given name: Charles Frederick; c. Richard; founder NB Amateur Football Union, 1st FA in province '66; organized 1st celebrity dinner to raise funds for Moncton MFL '70; CAFA service award; CFL/CAFA award; life mem. Moncton FA; scholarship in his name awarded annually from '77; Moncton park football field bears his name; mem. NB Sports Hall of Fame.

STONE, Roy (curling); b. 21 Jun 1915, Lena, Man.; given name: Roy Hannah; m. Olive Mary Howlett; c. Larry Roy, Ronald Alfred; retd. golf pro; mem. 7 provincial title rinks; competed in 6 Briers; won Saskatoon carspiel '56; skipped BC sr. title rink '73, lost ntl title playoff; skipped BC Senior-Seniors (over 60) title winners '77-81; like brother, a baker by trade but for 30yrs golf pro, club mgr. Rossland-Trail Country Club; BC Senior PGA title; involved in construction of numerous golf clubs in Trail area; mgr. Trail Curling Club several years; hon. life mem. Trail, Kelowna Curling Clubs, BC Curling Assn., Rossland-Trail Country Club; mem. Canadian Curling, BC Sports halls of fame; res. Trail, B.C.

STONEBURGH, Norm (football); b. 31 Mar 1935, Toronto, Ont.; given name: Norman Joseph; m. Dolores Joyce Gore; c. Brad, Blake, Charyl-Ann, Terri-Lynn, Dan, James; De LaSalle Coll.; builder, land developer; 2yrs East York, 1 Balmy Beach, 1 Parkdale Lions; centre Argonauts '55-58, '60-67; missed entire '59 after suffering broken leg in exhibition game against NFL St. Louis Cardinals; appeared in 155 league, 8 playoff games over 12 seasons; 6 times EFC all-star centre; res. Etobicoke, Ont.

STONEMAN, Bill (baseball); b. 7 Apr 1944, Oak Park, Ill.; given name: William Hambly; m. Diane Falardeau; c. Jill, Jeff; Idaho, BSc, Oklahoma, MA; all-Big Sky conf. '65-66, all-NCAA '66; baseball exec.; righthanded pitcher; ML service Chicago Cubs '67-68, Montreal '69-73, California '74; w-l record 54-85; pitched no-hitters vs. Philadelphia 17 Apr 1969, New York 2 Oct 1972; pitched 1 1-hitter, 2 2-hitters; asst. to Expos pres. John McHale '83, v-p. baseball operations '84-99; GM Anaheim Angels 2000; mem. Expos Hall of Fame; res. Hudson, Que.

STOQUA, Pat (basketball/football): b. 29 Apr 1956, Ottawa, Ont.; given name: Patrick Charles Joseph; m. Elizabeth Gilmour; c. Jennifer, Sean, Brendan; Carleton, BA; account exec. Dollco Printing; v-p. sales Cepac Technologies; standout basketball/football player Lisgar CI; mem. '74 all-Ont. basketball title team; Lisgar athlete of yr; 4yrs basketball Carleton, 3 all-star, MVP awards; 3yrs football Carleton; OUAA rookie of yr; 2 conf. defensive back, 1 slotback all-star; all-Cdn slotback '79; Carleton football MVP '79; 2 Carleton athlete of yr awards; Jack Vogan graduating athlete award; Rough Riders CFL territorial exemption '79; played with Ottawa as slotback (occasional def. back) '79-85; mem. Carleton Sports Wall of Fame; res. Stittsville, Ont.

STOREY, Bob (bobsleigh/builder); b. 3 Dec 1942, London, Ont.; given name: Robert Hargan; m. Catherine Sullivan; c. Max, Sarah, Ben; investment co. owner; communications co. exec.; mem. ntl bobsleigh team '66-73; mem. Olympic bobsleigh teams '68 (brakeman), '72 (driver, capt.), '76 (coach); v-p. Cdn Amateur Bobsleigh and Toboggan Assn. '77, '80; pres. '81-82; Cdn rep. to Federation International de Bobsleigh and Toboggan '76-77, '80-82, v-p. '84-94, pres. '94-2002; FIBT International juror from '76; mem. Cdn Olympic Hall of Fame; res. Ottawa, Ont.

STOREY, Fred (curling); b. 3 Mar 1932, Empress, Alta.; given name: Frederick Lewis; m. Vivian Fullerton; c. Debbie, Wayne, Sandie, Cheryl, Ron, James; Mount Royal College; retd. administrative supervisor; 2nd Alta. rink '51 ntl schoolboy championships; lead 7 Alta. title rinks, 7 Briers appearances, 3 titles, world championship as lead for Ron Northcott; mem. '61 Edmonton Tournament of Champions titlist; with Northcott *CBC* Cross Canada curling title Winnipeg '64, Cdn Open Carspiel Edmonton '65, Vancouver Evergreen Tournament of Champions '71, repeat as lead for George Fink '73; Calgary Masters title '72; Brier all-star lead; from '69 hon. life mem. Calgary Curling Club, pres. '74-75; mem. Canadian Curling, Alta. Sports halls of fame; res. Calgary, Alta.

STOREY, Irene (t&f); b. 10 May 1915, Allendale, Ont.; d. 19 Mar 1986, Toronto, Ont.; m. Pat Weber; c. Lee, Lorrie, Gordon, Pamela; overshadowed in Barrie region by brother Red and Bobbie Rosenfeld; encouraged by mother began running competitively age 10; also standout softball, basketball player; gained attention outside Barrie region defeating Grace Morrison, Mary Frizell in 100yd dash at age 13; Ont. -14 girls 100yds title '28; Ont./Cdn 60m jr. titles '30; CNE -18 100yd title '30; impressed observers beating sr. champion Rosa Grosse O'Neill in 60m run '30; ntl intermediate 60m title '32; recruited by Toronto Lakeside Ladies Club to compete for team; competed but insisted on wearing Allendale jacket which became her trademark; teamed with Frizell, Peggy Matheson, Dot Brookshaw to win 32 consecutive relay titles; mem. ntl relay team '34 World Games; in only 2nd 220yd race of career set ntl record 25.5 beating '28 Olympic 100m titlist Elizabeth Robinson; although placing 3rd in trials was bypassed in favor of Aileen Meagher for '34 games, but, with help of Barrie backers trip to games was underwritten; on retirement, late '30s had amassed 8 cups, 75 medals; mem. Barrie Sports Hall of Fame.

STOREY, Red (football/hockey); b. 5 Mar 1918, Barrie, Ont.; given name: Roy Alvin; m. Helen Saint Pierre (d); c. Bob, Doug; m Bunnie Lyons; public relations; football Argos '36-41 leading team to Grey Cup victories '37-38; record 3 TDs in final quarter '38 Grey Cup; offers from NY Giants, Chicago Bears in NFL; officiated 14yrs Que. Football League, 12yrs Intercollegiate, 12yrs CFL; hockey Barrie

jrs., RCAF Camp Borden, Atlantic City (EHL), Sault Ste. Marie (Michigan League), Montreal Royals (Que. sr.); refereed 7yrs Que. jr., provincial, sr. leagues, 9yrs AHL, 9yrs NHL; 8yrs lacrosse Orillia, Hamilton Tigers, Lachine, Montreal Canadiens; scored 12 goals single game; refereed 10yrs Que. sr. league; with son Bob (Hamilton '67, Montreal '70) only father-son combination Grey Cup history to play on 2 title winners each; autobiography "*Red's Story*"; mem. Order of Canada, Barrie Sports, Hockey halls of fame; res. Montreal, Que.

STORM, Tim (rowing); b. 18 Jul 1956, Rotterdam, Holland; Ridley Coll.; accountant; sculling specialist; mem. 6 ntl jr., sr. coxed 8s, 4s, coxless 4s, pairs, 4-sculls titles; 5 Canadian Henley titles, 2 US titles; gold coxless pairs '79 Pan-Am Games; mem. '77-78, '82-83 world championships, '84 Olympic Games teams; res. St. Catharines, Ont.

STOTT, Arthur (diving); b. 21 Nov 1909, Victoria, B.C.; given name: Arthur Harling; m. Patricia Clare Copeland; c. Gael, Sheridan, Jon; Victoria College; retired mewspaper editor; jr. boys Pacific Northwest 3-metre title in 1st competition '23; Vancouver Island sr. men's titles, BC sr. championships late '20s; 2 golds, 2 silvers, 1 bronze in 5 ntl championships; bronze '30 BEG; mem. '32 Olympic team; mem. founding board of trustees BC Sports Hall of Fame; last known res. Victoria, B.C.

STOUGHTON, Blaine (hockey); b. 13 Mar 1953, Gilbert Plains, Man.; hockey exec.; right/left wing; jr. Flin Flon Bombers '69-73; drafted by Pittsburgh '73; minor pro stints Hershey, New Haven AHL, Oklahoma City CHL; WHA with Cincinnati, Indianapolis, New England '76-79; NHL Pittsburgh '73-74, Toronto '74-76, Hartford '79-83, NY Rangers '83-84; 1 WHL, NHL all-star; reached 50-goal plateau WHA with 52 '77, NHL with 56 '80, 52 '82; NHL/WHA record: 11 seasons, 745 scheduled games, 347g, 281a; coach Austin Ice Bats '96-97; v-p./GM from '97; mem. Man. Hockey Hall of Fame; res. Austin, Tex.

STOUGHTON, Jeff (curling); b. 26 Jul 1963, Winnipeg, Man.; given name: Jeffrey Roy; m. Susan Leone McElrea; c. Riley John, Cole Jeffrey; Air Canada finance system specialist; 4 Man., 2 ntl mixed titles; represented Man. 3 Briers, winning '96 and adding world title; competed '98 Olympic trials; competing on WCT recorded wins in MT&T, Inn of Woods, Labatt's Valour Road, West Kildonan, McDonalds Curling Classic, SGI Charity Classic, Steeltown Classic, CIBC Shorty Jenkins 'spiel, playoff qualifier in several others; mem. Man. Curling Hall of Fame; res. Winnipeg, Man.

STOYKA, Darlene (field hockey); b. 30 Nov 1956, Toronto, Ont.; given name: Darlene Anne; St. Mary's, BA; Canada Post; mem. Toronto Gopher's FH club, 4 prov. titles, 4 Bermuda tournament titles; mem. Ont. team '73-83; ntl titles '81-82; ntl team '76-85; mem. '83 World Cup silver, '84 Olympic teams; accomplished squash player; res. Ottawa, Ont.

STRACHAN, Bill (shooting); b. 10 Oct 1912, Ottawa, Ont.; given name: William James; m. Ethelena Burgess (d); c. Bill Jr.; m. Frances Holomon; retd Lt. Col.; mem. 12 Bisley,

4 Palma (capt.'71), 6 Kalapore, 11 MacKinnon teams; 3 times capt. Cdn army Bisley team; Macdonald Stewart grand aggregate title '62, runnerup '61; Bisley aggregate Canadian target rifle titles '61-62; Bisley team commandant '66; only Cdn Commonwealth sniping champion; pres. NDHQRA '47-49; v-p. GBNRA from '60; v-p. Commonwealth RA; past exec. v-p. DCRA; sr. life gov. DCRA; res. Ottawa, Ont./ Holiday, Fla.

STRANGE, Michael (boxing): b. 6 Aug 1970, Niagara Falls, Ont.; bar owner; lightweight; competed '90, '94, '98 Commonwealth, '92, '96 Olympic, '95 Pan-Am Games, '93 Worlds; gold 60kg '94, 63.5kg '98 Commonwealth Games; bronze '95 Pan-Am Games; gold 2 Canada vs. USA competitions '93; gold Stockholm Open '93, Tammer Finland '95; best boxer award '90 ntls, '91 Ont. championships; 5 ntl titles; res. Niagara Falls, Ont.

STRATTEN, Gaye (swimming/coaching): b. 25 Apr 1943, Toronto, Ont.; m. Lynn Sellors; c. Todd, Taryn; UofT BPHE, North Carolina; swim coach McMaster; Level III NCCP theory/practical/swimming technical, Level II course conductor; ntl 100/200m backstroke titlist '62-65; attended UNC on swim scholarship 64-66; CIAU swimmer of yr '67-69; UofT swimmer of yr (Bickle award), athlete of yr (Biggs award) '69; 9 OUAA, 2 CIAU, 1 Cdn, 3 Ont. swim coach of yr awards; aquatics innovator/developer; PE dir. University Settlement House Toronto '66; GM/coach Etobicoke Aquatic Club '69-76; asst. coach Olympium SC '76-77; GM/coach Hamilton Wentworth Aquatic Club from '77; aquatic sports co-ordinator/coach McMaster from '78; mem. Cdn/Ont. swimming coaches assn. from '69; mem.Coaching Assn of Canada from '75; dir. Ont. Amateur Swimming Coaches Assn '69-74, Ont. Amateur Swimming Assn. '69-70; pres. CIAU swim coaches assn '79-86; tech. dir. swimming OUAA from '86; FINA tech sub-comm. for swimming '91 FISU Games; developed financial assistance plan for A/B carded athletes; started 1st masters swim program; trainer of coaches; coached numerous international level swimmers; ntl team coach at varied worlds, Olympic, Pan-Am, FISU Games from '72; mem. UofT Sports Hall of Fame; res. Burlington, Ont.

STREETER, Val (golf); b. 1895 Duxbury, Mass., d. 7 Jul 1981, Saint John, N.B.; given name: Percival; 3 NB, PEI, 2 Maritime amateur titles; mem. 3 ntl teams; national srs. (over 70) champion '67; mem. NB Sports Hall of Fame.

STREIT, Marlene Stewart (golf); b. 9 Mar 1934, Cereal Alta.; m. J. Douglas Streit; c. Darlene, Lynn; Rollins College; 9 ntl Closed, 11 Open titles; '53 British women's amateur, 1st of 4 US ntl mixed foursomes; '56 US women's amateur; US North-South '56, '74, US Intercollegiate '56, won 34 consecutive matches, a feat unequalled; 9 Ont. ladies', 3 Helen Lee Doherty titles; only woman to win Canadian, British, Australian, US ntl amateur titles; '56 Shell Wonderful World of Golf title beating pro Marilyn Smith Oslo, Norway, '57 runnerup to Mickey Wright; '61 low amateur US Open; non-playing capt. 3 women's world amateur teams; 2 US sr. women's titles; mem. Ont. interprov. team '83, Cdn. international title team '83; ranked #5 Canada '83; 5 Bobbie Rosenfeld awards; Lou Marsh Trophy '51, '56; Officer Order of Canada '67; mem. RCGA, Canada's

Sports, Ont. Sports Legends halls of fame; res. Streetsville, Ont.

STRIDE, Bryan (t&f); b. 9 Feb 1951, Guelph, Ont.; given name: Bryan Alexander; div. Margaret MacGowan; c. Christopher; Brock, BPhE; teacher; middle distance, cross-sountry specialist; ntl team '74-78; 4th 3000m steeplechase '75 Pan-Am Games, 2nd 3000m steeplechase '75 ntl championships; OUAA cross-country title '75; 2nd Cdn indoor 3000m '76; PB: 800m (1:52), 1500m (3:48), 3000m steeplechase (8:45); res. St. Catharines, Ont.

STRIKE, Hilda (t&f); b. 1 Sep 1910, Montreal, Que.; d. 9 Mar 1989, Ottawa, Ont.; m. Fred Sisson; c. Barbara; Canadian Commercial college; stenographer; spotted '29 by Olympic gold medalist Myrtle Cook while playing softball, joined Cdn Ladies AC Montreal; by '32 Que., ntl sprint champion; finalist '30 BEG; silver 100m sprint losing narrowly to Stella Walsh, who, when murdered '80, was discovered to be a male, anchored silver medal relay team '32 Olympics; shortstop Murray's AC Montreal Ladies' Softball title team; with Myrtle Cook formed Murray's AC, Mercury Track Club and became coach; silver 100yd, 4x110 relay '34 BEG; Cdn female athlete of '32; life mem. COA; mem. Canadian Amateur, Canada's Sports halls of fame.

STRONACH, Frank (horse racing); b. 6 Sep 1932, Austria; m. Frieda; c. Andy, Belinda; owns Magna International Inc.; moved to Canada '54; K-W hospital dishwasher before entering tool & die business; formed Multi Matic Investments '57, merged with Magna Electronics '69; Magna International produces automobile components; became involved in horse racing early '60s; operates breeding farms, stallion stations Ont., Kentucky, Fla.; has campaigned more than 80 stakes winners including Touch Gold '97 Belmont Stakes; Glorious Song '80 Eclipse award winner and Canada's horse of yr; 8 ntl champions; Sovereign awards leading breeder '84, leading owner '93; purchased Santa Anita track '98; pres. Austrian major soccer league '99; res. Switzerland/Canada/Fla./ Colo/Ky.

STRONG, Karen (cycling); b. 23 Sep 1953, Toronto, Ont.; given name: Karen Ann Strong; div. Colin Hearth; Brock; coach; 5 ntl road, 3 1000m time trial, 5 1000m sprint, 7 3000m individual pursuit, 4 10km, 5 mile titles; won '81 25 mile Can. time trial title; represented Canada 5 world 3000m pursuit, 2nd '80, 3rd '77; 5 world road race championships, best finish 4th '77; mem. '84 Olympic team; ranked among world's top 10 cyclist 5th time '83; St. Catharines athlete of '75; ntl women's road coach from '89; last known res. Calgary, Alta.

STRONG, Lawrence (tennis); b. 17 May 1940, London, Eng.; given name: Lawrence Franklin; m. Vivienne Russel Cox; c. Nicole, Danielle, Suzette; London, BSc; general management; UK schoolboy title, English international honors; with wife ntl mixed doubles title '68, mixed doubles gold '69 Canada games; capt. Davis Cup team '70-71; pres. CLTA '76; Air Canada Sports Exec. of '77; res. Willowdale, Ont.

STRONGE, Stan (soccer/coaching); b. 29 Dec 1910, Montreal, Que.; d. Aug 1991, Vancouver, B.C.; given name:

Stanley Noble; rehabilitation consultant, Cdn Paraplegic Assn.; soccer goaler '23-40 when accident left him paralyzed from waist down; 9 times all-star goaler; mem. New Westminster Royals '35 ntl titlists; ntl rules chair. for Cdn Wheelchair Sports from '75; BC, ntl swim coach for disabled '67-79; coached Canada's paraplegic swimmers and attended all ntl and international games for disabled; swimmimg pool named in his honor '80; mem. Order of Canada; double inductee into BC Sports Hall of Fame for disabled sports builder and soccer.

STROULGER, Ken (canoeing); b. 9 Feb 1913, Ottawa, Ont.; d. 15 Feb 1990, Ottawa, Ont.; given name: Charles Kenneth; m. Barbara Taylor; Carleton.; retd. public servant; stroke C4 Rideau Aquatic Club '36 ntl champions; commodore CCA '50; commodore Rideau Canoe Club '50-60; mgr. ntl team '56 Olympics; hon. commodore Rideau Canoe Club '80-81; mem. Ottawa Sports Hall of Fame; Olympic Club Canada.

STRUMM, Gil (all-around); b. 29 Oct 1920, Saskatoon, Sask.; given name: Gilbert Roger; m. Jean Kemp (d); c. Beverly, Bob; m. Marnie Garbe; retd. mgr. Sask. Tel.; softball centre fielder 27yrs; Sr. A coach '43-83; 14 Sask., 6 Western Canadian, 1 ntl title; coached 2 world championship entries; 12yrs mem. Sask. Grads, Navy, Regina Legion basketball teams; 20yrs basketball coach, 8 prov. titles, 1 university crown; refereed basketball 20yrs; 5yrs semipro baseball; 39yrs dir. Saskatoon Hilltops football club; pres. Saskatoon Sr. Men's Softball League '57; Saskatoon sportsman of '69; ntl championships all-star softball coach '70; sr. prov. curling champion '73; skipped srs rink Sweden '79, Swizerland '81, Scotland '83; scout Vancouver Canucks 9yrs; Queen's Medal '77; avid golfer from '81; mem. Sask., Saskatoon Sports halls of fame; res. Saskatoon, Sask.

STUART, Bruce (hockey); b. 30 Nov 1881, Ottawa, Ont., d. 28 Oct 1961, Ottawa, Ont.; m. Irene; shoe store owner; rover, left wing Ottawa Senators 1898-99, 12 goals in 6 games; Que. Bulldogs 1900; rejoined Ottawa '01-02 then moved to International pro league with Pittsburgh, Houghton Mich., Portage Lakes; helped Montreal Wanderers win '08 Stanley Cup; returned to Ottawa following season, capt. '11 Stanley Cup winner; in 3 Cup victories scored 17 goals in 7 games; in 45 career scheduled games posted 63 goals including 6 in single game vs Que.; 2 5-goal games; mem. Ottawa Sports, Hockey halls of fame.

STUART, Hod (hockey); b. 1879, Ottawa, Ont., d. 23 Jun 1907, Belleville, Ont.; given name: William Hodgson; mem. Ironsides, Ottawa Senators, Que., Pittsburgh Victorias teams; mgr. Calumet Mich. 2 seasons before joining Pittsburgh, captain '06; Montreal Wanderers '07 Stanley Cup; 16 goals in 33-game career; flying wing 8yrs Rough Riders; mem. Ottawa Sports, Hockey halls of fame.

STUBBS, Lorraine (equestrian); b. 9 Jun 1950, Toronto, Ont.; given name: Constance Lorraine; York, BA, MA; dressage specialist; mem. ntl equestrian team from '71; mem. '71, '75 Pan-Am, '72, '76 Olympic teams; silver '75 Pan-Am Games; 3rd Aachen, W.Germany, international horse show '74; 2nd Norten-Hardenburg, Germany, '75; won Grand Prix, Special, Ont. dressage championships '76; London dressage title '81; res. Rockwood, Ont.

STUEBBING, Jeff (wrestling); b. 27 Mar 1959, Hamilton, Ont.; weight training centre mgr.; 74kg Greco Roman gold '83 Pan-Am Games; mem. '84 Olympic team; fed. govt. excellence award '84; res. Paso Robles, Calif.

STUKUS, Annis (football/hockey); b. 25 Oct 1914, Toronto, Ont.; given name: Annis Paul; m. Doris Louise Shannon; c. Suzanne, Sally, Mary Louise; sportcaster; Argos '35-41; Oakwood Indians '42, Balmy Beach '43, Toronto Navy '44, Toronto Indians '45-46; organized Eskimos '49, coach 3 seasons; organized, coached BC Lions '53-55; GM Vancouver Canucks (WHL) '67, Winnipeg Jets '71-74; helped sign Bobby Hull to WHA contract and instigated sorties into Sweden to sign hockey talent; trophy in his honor awarded CFL coach of year annually; promotions dir. Vancouver Whitecaps '74; mem. Cdn Football, Football Reporters of Canada, Canada's Sports halls of fame; res. West Vancouver, B.C.

STUKUS, Bill (football); b. 18 May 1916, Toronto, Ont.; given name: William Joseph; St. Michael's College; bookkeeper, camp athletic director; quarterback/safety Argos '36-41, '47, RCAF Hurricanes '42-44, Toronto Indians '45-46, Edmonton '49-51; mem. 4 Grey Cup winners; coached minor hockey; AD brother Frank's Fenlon Falls summer camp; res. Toronto, Ont.

STUKUS, Frank (football); b. 7 Aug 1918, Toronto, Ont.; m. Anna Havery (d.); c. Frank Jr. (d), Maureen Elizabeth; m. Pauline Audrey Woolings; retd resort, camp operator; fullback Argos '38-41, Toronto Indians '42, Toronto Indians '45; became Indians owner; established 1st-ever summer hockey camp Fenlon Falls, Ont., '61; coached 1 season int. football Oshawa; owner Byrnell Manor '61-75; 13yrs Etobicoke parks & rec. dept.; back room power in federal Conservative party from '50's through mid-'80s when actions of PM Brian Mulroney soured him on politics; res. Mississauga, Ont.

STULAC, George (all-around); b. 28 Jun 1933, Toronto, Ont.; given name: George William; UofT; teacher; HS gymnastics, diving titles; Intercollegiate swimming titles, mem. football, basketball title teams; mem. ntl water polo title team; Ont. Y diving titlist; 9 1st T awards UofT; Hec Phillips t&f trophy; mem. Toronto West End Y, Tillsonburg Livingstons basketball teams; 1st Cdn to qualify for Olympics in 2 sports same year '60; swimming alternate '52 Olympics; mem. '56 Olympic basketball, '60 Olympic basketball, t&f, '64 basketball teams; decathlon bronze '59 Pan-Am Games; res. Toronto, Ont.

STUMON, Gregg (football): b. 26 May 1963, Plain Dealing, La.; Southern Arkansas; defensive end; joined CFL BC '86-88, Edmonton '89, Ottawa '90-93, Shreveport '94-95; CFL record: 145 games, 1td, 87 QB sacks, 381 tackles; Norm Fieldgate trophy '87; Schenley outstanding def. player '87; 2 all-Western, 2 all-Eastern, 3 all-CFL all-star; mem. 1 Grey Cup finalist; last known res. Shreveport, La.

STUPP, Heather (racquetball): b. 28 Feb 1964, Montreal, Que.; McGill, BComm, Cdn Inst of Chartered Accountants CA, Harvard, MBA; management consultant; Canada Games singles title '79; 6 ntl singles, 4 ntl doubles titles; 2 world singles, 2 world team titles; Pan-Am Games team silver, singles bronze '87; Torneo de las Americas singles gold '87, silver '91; Pacific Rim silver '91; Japan open singles gold '89; last known res. Montreal, Que.

STUPP, Howard (wrestling); b. 3 May 1955, Montreal, Que.; McGill, BSc, LLD; lawyer; ntl open jr. FS, GR titles '75; sr. open GR champion '76, '78-79, '81; won '81, 2nd '79-80 Cdn Open FS championships; gold 68kg FS, GR '77 Maccabiah Games; '78, '81 CIAU FS titles; most outstanding wrestler award '78 CIAU championships; mem. '77-79 world championships, '76, '80 Olympic teams; mem. Montreal YM-YWHA Sports Hall of Fame; res. Lausanne, Switzerland.

STYNER, Dale (squash); b. 9 Nov 1961, Lethbridge, Alta.; m. Lori; c. 2; 4 ntl titles; mem. 5 ntl world championships teams; won Sask., Alta., Calgary, Husky, Pacific Coast Open, Calgary Closed titles; Squash Canada distinguished service award; res. Calgary, Alta.

STYNER, Lori (squash); b. 6 Jan 1963, Burlington, Ont.; m. Dale; c. 2; UCal, BN; medical research; began play age 16 in Sarnia; won Alta., Glencoe Open, Calgary Closed, Triumph Tubular titles; mem. '94 ntl women's team; res. Calgary, Alta.

SUGARMAN, Ken (football); b. 16 Jun 1942, Portland, Ore.; given name: Kenneth Lee; m. Carolyn; c. Kenny, Trevor; Whitworth College, BA, SFU; apple rancher, warehouse operator; Little All-American Whitworth '63; 7th draft Baltimore (NFL), last cut '64; BC '64-72; 3 all-star games; capt., Lions' most popular player '69; Laurie Neimi award as outstanding BC lineman '72; res. Tieton, Wash.

SUKUNDA, Eli (fencing); b. 10 Apr 1949, Windsor, Ont.; m. Marie Vielleux; c. Adrienne, Zachary; Wayne State., BA, UofT, MA; teacher Carleton; mem. '75, '79, '83 (sabre team bronze) Pan-Am, '76, '84, '88 (capt.) Olympic Games teams; twice mem. 4th place Pan-Am team; 1st '84, 2nd '75, '78, '82 ntl championships; gold '75 Canada Games, Governor-General's Cup '79-80, 5 Ottawa Shield, 4 London Heroes gold, Fred Wach Memorial '82; team gold, silver, sabre bronze Commonwealth championships; coach '93 FISU Games team; Windsor Kiwanis Club athlete of '76; fencing coach RA Centre; mem. Windsor-Essex Sports Hall of Fame; res. Manotick, Ont.

SULLIVAN, Frank (hockey/football); b. 26 Jul 1898, Toronto, Ont.; d. 8 Jan 1989, Toronto, Ont.; given name: Francis Gerald; m. Ursula Colleran; c. Catharine, John, Frank Jr., Lee, Edward, Michael, Mary, Patsy, Peter; UofT; retd.; mem. Harbord CI jr. HS football champions '15; UofT Schools Jr. ORFU champions '17; Central YMCA Jr. ORFU champions '18; UofT '19-20 Intercollegiate champions, '20 Grey Cup champions; Argos Big Four, Grey Cup champions '21; mem. Harbord CI sr. HS hockey champions '16; Aura Lee OHA Jr. champs '17; UofT Intercollegiate champs '20-21; Granite Hockey Club OHA Sr. champions '22; 3 Allan Cup winners; Varsity Grads '27 OHA Sr. champs, '28 Olympic gold medalists; mem. 9 ntl title teams in 10yr span; coached UofT jr. hockey '29-30, srs. '31-33, Intercollegiate title '31-32.

SULLIVAN, Joe (hockey); b. 8 Jan 1901, Toronto, Ont.; d. 3 Sep 1988, Scarborough, Ont.; given name: Joseph Albert; UofT, MD; surgeon, senator; mem. UTS '18-19 Memorial Cup champions; goaler Varsity Grads '28 Olympic gold medalists; mem. '50 CP poll team of half century; Intercollegiate golf title, Ont. amateur, runnerup '24 ntl amateur; CIAU goalie of year trophy bears his name; hon. Surgeon to Her Majesty; gov. UofT; hon. Fellow Royal Society of Medicine; chief otolaryngology Cdn. Forces; recipient Canada Medal; mem. UofT Sports Hall of Fame.

SULLIVAN, Kevin (t&f); b. 20 Mar 1974, Brantford, Ont.; Michigan; middle distance specialist; began competing age 12; brilliant HS career led to Michigan scholarship; Ont.800m, 1500m titles '89, ntl 800 title '89; ntl jr. 800m, 1500m titles '92-93; bronze 1500m world jr. championships; won jr. ntl cross-country, ntl indoor 1500m, gold 800m, 1500m Tokyo Invitational, gold 800m, bronze 4x100 relay Pan-Am jr. championships '93; competed '93 world championships, '94 Commonwealth, '96 Olympic Games; ntl sr. 1500m title '94; silver 1500m '94 Commonwealth Games; 1500m gold Gugl IAAF grand prix Austria '99; set Cdn mile record 3:52.25 '95 Zurich GP; NCAA 1500m, indoor mile titles '95; PB: 3:39.07 1500m; Viscount Alexander Trophy runnerup '93; res. Brantford, Ont.

SULLIVAN, Red (hockey): b. 24 Dec 1929, Peterborough, Ont.; given name: George James; m. Marion Redmond; c. Danny, Jane, Suzanne, Kate; retd. hockey exec.; relative lightweight at 152 pounds; sensational jr. career with St. Catharines; pro stints Boston, Chicago, NY Rangers '49-61; starred in AHL with Hershey; set scoring record 30g, 89a '53-54 season; NHL record: 557 scheduled games, 107g, 239a, 18 playoff games, 1g, 2a; voted by NHL coaches "hardest worker, hustler" in league; coached Rangers, Pittsburgh, Washington; scout for Boston, Philadelphia, NHL Central Scouting; power-hitting fastball infielder; mem. Peterborough Sports Hall of Fame; res. Indian River, Ont.

SULLIVAN, Tommy (boxing); b. 29 Dec 1904, Dublin, Ireland; d. 10 May 1990, Chapeau, Que.; m. Claire Carroll; c. Sharon, Deirdre; retd.; amateur boxer '21-31; Que. 147lb title '31; Lions Newsboy title Toronto '31; finalist US jr. nationals Boston '31; refereed Montreal Athletic Commission '36-56; coach RCAF St. Thomas, Trenton, Moncton '39-45, Grenadier Guards Montreal '48-56; '52 Olympic boxing coach; ntl coach CABA '71-72.

SUNDIN, Mats (hockey); b. 13 Feb 1971, Bromma, Sweden; began playing hockey age 5; played with Nacka, Djurgarden, Sweden, '88-90; 1st European drafted 1st overall in NHL entry draft; NHL Quebec '90-94, Toronto '94-99; Leafs capt. from '97; NHL record: (through '99) 693 scheduled hames, 296g, 419a, 36 playoff games, 19g, 14a; 4 NHL all-star games; mem. Team Sweden 4 world championships, '98 title team; competed for Sweden '98 Olympics; hon. capt. Street Buds, Leafs youth ball hockey pgm.; active in Swedish charity pgms. for players with debilitating injuries; res. Toronto, Ont./Sweden.

SUNOHARA, Vicky (hockey): b. 18 May 1970, Scarborough, Ont.; UofT, Northeastern; quality control technician; honed skills in Scarborough boys/girls hockey '75-88; all-American forward Northeastern '88-90; NCAA championship rookie of '88; UofT rookie of '90; Scarborough Firefighters/UofT '91-94; Toronto Red Wings '95-96; 3 world championship, 1 3-Nations Cup gold; mem. '98 Olympic silver medal team; res. Scarborough, Ont.

SUNTER, Ian (football); b. 21 Dec 1952, Dundee, Scotland; m. Karen; c. Kelly, David; owner CWS Sports; emigrated to Canada age 15; jr. football Burlington '70-71; moved into CFL from HS ranks as placement specialist; among 1st soccer-style kickers; with Hamilton '72-75; NFL trials Detroit, Buffalo, LA Rams; returned to CFL with Toronto '78-79; mem. '72 Grey Cup winner; res. Burlington, Ont.

SURETTE, Ron (shooting): b. 26 Aug 1943, Shediac, N.B.; given name: Ronald Alfred; m. Juliette; c. Michelle, Travis; retd. Cdn Forces; 6 Queen's medals; 3 Cdn Service Rifle titles; 6 ntl combined rifle titles; 15 CF Bisley teams; 3 DCRA Bisley teams; mem. Bicentennial rifle championship/ Palma teams '88; Atlantic Milita Small Arms team '89-98; Cdn Palma team '92; CFCISM team '92, '94; mem. Cdn Forces Sports Hall of Fame; res. Scoudouc, N.B.

SURIN, Bruny (t&f): b. 12 Jul 1967, Au Cap Haitien, Haiti; m. Birinall; c. Kimberley; Quebec; sprinter; came to Canada '75; began competing in long and triple jump '84; switched to sprints '89; competed '88 (lj),'92, '96 Olympic, '87 Pan-Am, '90, '94 Commonwealth, '87 FISU, '89, '94 Francophone Games, 4 world championships; 1 ntl outdoor TJ, 3 100m titles; 2 ntl 60m indoor titles; Francophone 100m gold '94; 10 ntl, 1 Commonwealth sr. records; PB 9.92 (100m), 20.48 (200m); 100m bronze '90, 4x100 gold '94 Commonwealth Games; gold 100m '94 Francophone Games; silver world 100m '95; world 60m indoor sprint title '95; mem. '96 Olympic, world gold 4x100m relay team; Jack Davies, Phil Edwards awards '93; Que. t&f athlete of '90; Cy Bricker jump events award '88; 2 Dick Ellis team awards; res. Pierrefonds, Que.

SUTHERIN, Don (football); b. 29 Feb 1936, Empire, Ohio; given name: Don Paul; m. Nancy Carolyn Jones; c. Julie, Gail, Becky, Jill; Ohio State, Malone College, BA, BScPhE; football coach; HS all-American, all-state; 4 seasons Ohio State under coach Woody Hayes; hon. mention all-American; all-Big Ten defence; kicked winning field goal '58 Rose Bowl game; drafted NFL New York Giants ; 1 year Giants, 1 Pittsburgh; Tiger-Cats '58, '60-66, Rough Riders '67-69, Argos '70; all-star, all-pro honors, 8 Grey Cup finals, 5 winners; 13 CFL records; CFL record: 4tds, 270c, 114fg, 78ss, 714pts; EFC scoring leader '61, '64-65, '68; as defensive back intercepted 58 passes for 599yds; shared CFL record 4 interceptions single game; scout Pittsburgh; asst. coach Ottawa '81-84, Edmonton '85-90, Montreal Machine (WFL) '91, Calgary '91-93; head coach Hamilton '94-97, asst. '98; 7 Grey Cups as coach, 2 winners; mem. Cdn Football Hall of Fame; res. Hamilton, Ont.

SUTHERLAND, Hugh (hockey); b. 2 Feb 1907, Winnipeg, Man.; d. 9 Sep 1990, Winnipeg, Man.; given name: Hugh Robert; m. Cecilia Anderson; retired sales mgr. Sask. Wheat Pool; defence Elmwood Millionaires Man. midget, jr. champions; mem. league champion Grain Exchange '29;

Winnipeg '31 Allan Cup, '32 Olympic title teams; Selkirk HC '33-36; midget, juvenile, jr. baseball Elmwood Giants, sr. Norwood '29-38.

SUTHERLAND, James (builder/hockey); b. 19 Oct 1870, Kingston, Ont.; d. 30 Sep 1955, Kingston, Ont.; often referred to as "father of hockey", Capt. Sutherland coached Kingston Frontenacs Jrs. to several championships and played key role in popularizing sport in Eastern Ont.; became connected with OHA as district rep.; moved through exec. ranks to pres. '15-17; following WW1 service became pres. CAHA '19; life mem. OHA, CAHA; mem. Hockey Hall of Fame.

SUTTER, Brent (hockey); b. 10 Jun 1962, Viking, Alta; m. Connie; c. Merrick, Brandon, Brooke; centre Red Deer, Lethbridge (WHL); 1st pick NY Islanders '80 draft; one of six brothers who played in NHL; played in NHL with Islanders '80-91, Chicago '91-97; Team Canada '84; NHL record: (through '98) 1111 scheduled games, 363g, 466a, 144 playoff games, 30g, 44a; mem. 2 Stanley Cup winners; res. Chicago, Ill./Sylvan Lake, Alta.

SUTTER, Brian (hockey); b. 7 Oct 1956, Viking, Alta.; m. Judy; c. Shaun, Abigail; hockey coach; one of 6 brothers who played in NHL; left wing jr. Lethbridge Broncos (WHL); Kansas City (CHL) '76-77; NHL with St. Louis '76-88; NHL record: 779 scheduled games, 303g, 333a, 65 playoff games, 21g, 21a; 9yrs Blues capt.; coach St. Louis '88-92, Boston '92-95, Calgary since '97; Jack Adams trophy '91; NHL coaching record (through '98): 618 scheduled games, 299-238-81, 63 playoff games, 27-36; res. Sylvan Lake, Alta.

SUTTER, Darryl (hockey); b. 19 Aug 1958, Viking, Alta.; given name: Darryl John; m. Wanda; c. Jessie, Brett, Christopher; hockey coach; 1 of 6 brothers who played in NHL; jr. Lethbridge '76-78; pro AHL New Brunswick '78-80, Japan '78-79, Chicago (NHL) '80-87; NHL playing record: 406 scheduled games, 161g, 118a, 51 playoff games, 24g, 19a; launched coaching career Saginaw (IHL) '88-89, Indianapolis (IHL) '89-90 (won Turner Cup), Chicago (NHL) '92-95 (1 div. title); consultant Chicago '95-97, head coach San Jose '97-99; 5ys team capt. Chicago; asst.coach Chicago '87-88, assoc. coach '90-92; AHL rookie of yr '80; IHL coach of yr '90; helped launch Sutter Foundation charitable organization; res. Viking, Alta.

SUTTER, Duane (hockey); b. 16 Mar 1960, Viking, Alta.; m. Cindy; c. Darby, Kassie, Brady; hockey exec.; 1 of 6 brothers who played in NHL; nicknamed 'Dog'; rw Lethbridge (WHL) jrs '76-80; NHL Islanders '79-87, Chicago '87-90; NHL record: 731 scheduled games, 139g, 203a, 161 playoff games, 26g, 32a; 4 Stanley Cup winners; scout Chicago 2yrs, head coach Indianapolis (IHL) 3yrs; asst. coach Florida '95-98; scout Panthers '98-99; res. Coral Springs, Fla.

SUTTER, Ron (hockey); b. 2 Dec 1963, Viking, Alta.; m. Margo; c. Madison, Reigan; centre Lethbridge jrs. '80-83; NHL Philadelphia '82-91, St. Louis '91-94, Quebec '94, Islanders '94-95, Phoenix '95-96, Boston '96, San Jose '96-99; NHL record: (through '99) 994 scheduled games, 199g,

320a, 92 playoff games, 8g, 30a; active role in Sutter Foundation and other charitable works; res. Whitefish, Mont.

SUTTON, Warren (basketball/coaching); b. 12 Mar 1939, Chester, Pa.; given name: Warren Leroy; Acadia, Sir George Williams; teacher, coach; Little All-American hon. mention Div. 3 schools; mem. SGW ntl champions, MVP title tournament; 1st NBA draftee from Cdn coll. ranks; mem. Montreal, Ottawa, Kitchener club teams, frequent MVP; began coaching '63; coached Ottawa Ont. jr. girls title team '71, Kitchener sr. women's Ont. title team '81; asst.Waterloo '84-85; res. Waterloo, Ont.

SUZUKI, Arthur (basketball); b. 29 Jul 1937, New Westminster, B.C.; m. Marlene Dubrick; c. Robert, William, Karen; UWO; supervisor production, inventory control; mem. 2 London Ont. city title football, 1 basketball teams; mem. Tillsonburg Livingstons, ntl finalists '58, Ont. title '59; Sr. A London Five B's '65; Ont. Int. A champion 3M '66; Ont. Sr. A champion Sarnia Drawbridge Inn '67 Canada Winter Games gold medal team; Ont. Sr. A champion London Celtics '73; basketball official '61-66; Ont. Masters (over 40) champions '80-81; res. London, Ont.

SWARTMAN, Mel (boxing); b. 3 Nov 1896, Arnprior, Ont.; d. 2 Jan 1985, Ottawa, Ont.; m. Irene Riffon; retd. armed forces, dog breeder; boxed briefly as welterweight in Hamilton; 25yrs military sports sergeant; organized Ottawa Beaver Boxing Club '30s; BEG boxing team coach '50; coached Olympians Joey Sandulo, Harvey Lacelle, Clayton Kenny; boxing instructor Ottawa Boys' Club; breeder minature long-haired dachshund champions; mem. Ottawa Sports Hall of Fame.

SWEENEY, Sylvia (basketball); b. 3 Oct 1956, Montreal, Que.; McGill, St. Mary's, Concordia, Sherbrooke, Laurentian, BA, also attended schools in France, Italy, Australia; owner Portal Entertainment Services; ntl team '74-84; mem. '76, '84 Olympic, '75, '79, '83 Pan-Am, '77, '79 FISU Games teams; centre '79 CIAU title team; bronze '79 Pan-Am, FISU Games, '82 Federation Cup; gold '82 Jones Cup; MVP '79 world, CIAU championships; flag-bearer '79 Pan-Am Games; 3 times all-Cdn; Que. athlete of '79; asst. CdM '96 Olympics; worked with group which brought NBA Raptors to Toronto; CIAU-TSN award bears her name; mem. Cdn Basketball Hall of Fame; res. Forest Hill, Ont.

SWEENY, Bimbo (rowing); b. 1888, Vancouver, B.C., d. 12 Feb 1966, Vancouver, B.C.; given name: Campbell; m. Violet Pooley; capt., fullback Vancouver Rowing Club rugby team '12, Miller Cup champions '10-11; mem. VRC from 1906; stroked NPAAO jr. 4s, sr. champions '08; strokes '09 4s which won Seattle North Pacific title in record time; VRC pres. '33-35, '46-49.

SWEENY, Violet (golf); b. Dec 1886, Victoria, B.C., d. Mar 1965, Victoria, B.C.; given name: Violet Pooley; m. Bimbo Sweeny; unprecedented 7 Pacific Northwest Golf Assn., 9 BC ladies championships; pres. CLGU '33-42; hon. life mem. BC exec.; 2 trophies bearing her name awarded annually for BC junior golf; mem. BC, Greater Victoria Sports, Cdn Golf halls of fame.

SWEET, Don (football); b. 13 Jul 1948, Vancouver, B.C.; m. Marilyn; c. 2; WSU; pro football player, teacher; placement kicker, punter; attended WSU on soccer scholarship; standout baseball player, golfer; signed by BC but traded to Montreal '72; CFL record 21 consecutive field goals '76; CFL record through '84: 325c, 312fg, 72s, 1333pts; 3 EFC scoring titles; 3 times EFC all-star; 2 Grey Cup winners; res. Dollard des Ormeaux, Que.

SWEETNAM, Nancy (swimming): b. 14 Aug 1973, Lindsay, Ont.; Laurentian; began swimming age 4, competing age 5; mother Marian female swimming coach of '90; breaststroke, IM specialist; mem. ntl team '88-97; 13 ntl titles; ntl short course 200m, 400m FS, 200m breaststroke records; ntl 400 IM record; gold 200IM, bronze 4x100 medley relay '90, silver 400IM, bronze 200IM '94 Commonwealth Games; 3 gold, 1 silver '93 FISU Games; competed '91, '94 world aquatic championships, '95 world short course, '92, '96 Olympics, 4 World Cup gold '96; 1 CIAAU female swimmer of yr award; Swimming Canada female athlete of '90; mem. Ont. Aquatic Hall of Fame; res. Sudbury, Ont.

SWIFT, Bob (football); b. 29 Nov 1943, Shawinigan, Que.; m. Sandy; c. Joelle, Jonathan, Bobby; Clemson, Millersville State Coll.; football coach; CFL running back BC '64-65, offensive guard Toronto '66-70, centre Winnipeg '70-78; rushed for 1054yds rookie season; scored BC's 1st TD '64 Grey Cup game; nicknamed 'Boss Hogg'; 4 all-WFC, CFL centre selections; 2 Schenley outstanding Cdn, 3 outstanding lineman nominations; launched coaching career Millersville State; asst. coach Saskatchewan '83-84, Ottawa '85-86, '88, '95, Montreal '87, Upsala Coll '87, Edmonton '89, Calgary '90-91; dir. CAFA relations for Sask. '84; res. Mastersonville, Pa.

SYDIE, Iain (badminton): b.12 Nov 1969, Richmond Hill, Ont.; began playing at 13 following footsteps of '65 Scottish singles champion father; '95 Pan-Am Games singles silver, doubles gold; competed '96 Olympics; '99 PAG men's (Brent Olynyk), mixed (Denyse Julien) doubles gold; res. Calgary, Alta.

SYDOR, Alison (cycling): b. 9 Sept 1966, Edmonton, Alta.; pro athlete; began competing as triathlete age 10; Alta. jr. champion; played ice hockey, volleyball, basketball in high school; burst onto ntl cycling scene at age 21 winning 3 gold '87 Western Canada Summer Games; mem. ntl road team '88-98; 1st Cdn to win world title medal with individual road race bronze '91; intl breakthrough came '90 Tour de L'Aude in France as mem. Cdn team time trial champs; wore leader's yellow jersey 6 days '91 Tour de L'Aude; competed 1st mountain bike cross country '91; 1st Cdn woman to win world cup gold '94; 5 ntl road race, 1 ntl mountain bike, 1 ntl criterium, 1 ntl team time trial gold; silver team time trial, bronze road race '94 Commonwealth Games; competed '92, '96 Olympic, '90, '94 Commonwealth, '95, '99 Pan-Am Games; Pan-Am Games mountain bike cross country gold '95, silver '99; women's mountain bike silver '96 Olympics; 3 world mountain bike overall titles; '98 world team gold, cross country bronze; '98 Sea Otter, Cactus Cup gold; 2 Velma Springstead, 1 Bobbie Rosenfeld awards; res. N. Vancouver, B.C.

SYLVAIN, Jules (weightlifting): b. 20 Dec 1925, Quebec City, Que.; m. Martha; c. Danielle, Ginette; butcher; competitive lifter 13 years; 10 ntl 60kg titles; mem. '52, '56 Olympic, '50, '54, '58 Commonwealth Games teams; coached 15 years; international referee; res. Charlesbourg, Que.

SYMONS, Bill (football); b. 14 Jun 1943, Nucla, Colo.; m. Connie Willden (d); c. Kellie, Stalor, Curt, Myles; m. Trish Peacock; Colorado, BEd; salesman/farmer; Green Bay (NFL) '64-65, BC '66, Toronto '67-73; 2 EFC rushing titles; 11 games 100-plus yards rushing, 6 in 1 season; CFL record: 4280yds, 807 rushes, 44tds, 264 points, 72 kickoff returns for 1878yds; 3 times led Argos KO retruns, 4 times leading rusher; best single game 7 Sep '70 vs Ottawa scoring 4tds, 3 rushing, 1 on pass reception; Argos single-season rushing record 1107yds; CFL all-star '68-70; Jeff Russel Memorial Trophy '70; Schenley Outstanding Player award '68; names to All-Time Argos team '96; 1 NFL Title; mem. Cdn Football Hall of Fame; res. Hockley Valley, Ont.

SZMIDT, Peter (swimming); b. 12 Aug 1961, Montreal, Que.; m. Donna Ross; UAlta, Cal. (Berkeley); Imperial Oil; freestyle specialist; NCAA team silver '80; AAU FS gold '81; mem. ntl team '77-84; 15 ntl, 1 Commonwealth, 1 world records; ntl titles: 7 400m, 5 1500m, 4 200m, 2 100m, 4x200m FS relay; Commonwealth Games gold 4x100m FS relay '78, silver 4x200m FSR '78, 200m, 400m FS '82, bronze 4x100m FSR '82; Pan-Am Games silver 4x100 FSR, bronze 400 FS, 4x200 FSR '79; FISU Games bronze 4x200 FSR '83; mem. '78, '82 Commonwealth, '80, '84 Olympic, '79, '83 Pan-Am, '83 FISU Games teams; 3 silver '83 CIAU championships; Cdn. Aquatic Fed. athlete of '80; dir. Swim Canada; mem. Quebec Swimming, Cdn Aquatic halls of fame; res. Toronto, Ont.

SZNAJDER, Andrew (tennis): b. 25 May 1967, Preston, Eng.; m. Kathya Ponce; c. Krystof Ernesto; Pepperdine; PageNet Canada sales exec.; NCAA rookie of year; 2 all-American awards; NCAA indoor singles title '88; mem. 2 Sunshine Cup -18 teams; won Bacardi indoor, Sporting Life singles '86; 3 Tennis Canada player of year awards; Tennis Canada most improved player '85; mem. Cdn Davis Cup team '89-93; pro circuit '88-94; wins over Mats Vilander, Bjorn Borg; 6 ntl singles titles; 46 in ATP rankings '89, highest by Cdn male in open era; plays charity fund raiser exhibitions Royal Bank tour; conducts nation-wide adult clinics; tennis rep COA athletes council; dir. ntl sports centre Toronto; res. Mississauga, Ont.

SZTEHLO, Zoltan (equestrian); b. 27 Nov 1921, Budapest, Hungary; d. 16 Jun 1990, Guatemala City; m. Rhonda; Royal Hungarian Military Academy, Debrecen, LLD; retd. lawyer; accredited dressage judge International Equestrian Federation; Hungarian jr. sabre champion; dressage team gold '71 Pan-Am Games; mem. '68 Olympic team; 3 Western Canadian dressage titles; Western Canada Games dressage gold '75; trainer-coach Alta. modern pentathlon gold team '75 WCG; mem. '67 Pan-Am Games equestrian jury; award winning course designer; coach jr. riding teams '80-90; organized 1st NA young riders championship in Maple Ridge, B.C., '82; authored book *The Art of Riding* in Hungarian.

T

TAKACS, Ed (t&f); b. 12 Feb 1954, Brantford, Ont.; given name: Edward Donald; Villanova, BSc; asst. hospital administrator; OFSSA 800m title '73; Ont. sr. 800m, Jr. Olympics, Ont. Games titles '74; Toronto Invitational 1500m, Metropolitan Games mile, IC4A 800m '75; res. Fredericton, N.B.

TAKAHASHI, Allyn (judo); b. 20 May 1956, Montreal, Que.; given name: Masao Allyn; div. Kiyomi Tomita; Waterloo, BA, MA; GM Isuzu Japan; 3 Ont. 120lb, 1 127lb title; winner 30, runnerup 9 of 40 competitions entered 120-139lb categories '69-76; bronze USJA nationals '72; 3 Eastern Cdn, Ont. HS, CNE invitational, 2 Kingston Y Asahi, jr. Olympic, 1 world junior Shiai title; Ottawa ACT award '72-74, Merivale HS phys ed award '72-73; Shodan black belt '72; res. Tokyo, Japan.

TAKAHASHI, June (judo); b. 17 Jun 1933, Vancouver, B.C.; given name: June Hayami; m. Masao; c. Allyn, Philip, Ray, Tina; sport administrator; 1st degree (Shodan) black belt '68, 2nd degree (Nidan) black belt '75; 5th degree black belt '97; assists husband Mas in operation of Japanese Martial Arts Centre; North East Region Cdn Judo Assn. secty-treas., dir. of judo for women '75-76; ntl councillor Judo Canada '76-78; regional rep. Judo Ont.; NA referee; ED Judo Canada; Ont. Achievement Award; res. Nepean, Ont.

TAKAHASHI, Masao (judo); b. 24 Jun 1929, Vancouver, B.C.; m. June Hayami; c. Allyn, Philip, Ray, Tina; judo instructor, operator Japanese Martial Arts Centre; 5th degree black belt; 3 ntl unlimited weight titles; mem. '61 Paris world championships team; pitched Alta. Japanese evacuees (relocated from BC) to baseball league championship '47; RCAF swimming, diving medalist '50; ntl councillor Judo Canada, v-p./councillor/regional dir. Judo Ont., mem. grading committee; past referee-in-chief Judo Ont.; referee Pan-American Judo Federation; Centennial medal '67; tech. official for judo '76 Olympics; chair. Judo Ont. grading board; mem. Cdn Forces Sports, Cdn Judo halls of fame; res. Nepean, Ont.

TAKAHASHI, Philip (judo); b. 12 Jun 1957, Toronto, Ont.; given name: Philip Masato; m. Cathy Sheffield; c. Christy, Jenny, Emily; Algonquin College, UofOtt; HS teacher; Eastern Ont. Open 80lb title '69; gold 58kg Sonthofen, Bavaria, Stuttgart, Germany, Ont. Winter Games '74, Canada Games '75, Ont. jr. Olympics (twice), Cdn Youth Games, Ont. HS; 6th degree judo black belt; 4 ntl 60kg, 2 Ont., Que., 1 Dutch, international teams, Canada Cup titles; bronze '79 Pan-Am Games; gold Pan-Am championships '80; bronze '81 worlds, '82 World University Games; silver 60kg Pacific Rim '83; gold '84 Canada Cup; mem. '80, '84 Olympic team; Detroit Mayor's Trophy for outstanding performance '71-72; ACT (Ottawa) sports award for judo '71, '74, '75; Ont. Sports Achievement Award '70-75; fed. govt. sport excellence award '82; mem. Nepean Wall, Judo Canada Hall of Fame; res. Kanata, Ont.

TAKAHASHI, Ray (judo, wrestling); b. 7 Aug 1958, Downsview, Ont.; given name: Raymond Hugh; m. Janet Dick; c. Mariko, Steven; UWO; UWO wrestling coach; gold '72 US jr. nationals; 10 ntl, 1 Pan-Am jr. titles; ntl team from '75; mem. '76, '80, '84 Olympic, '79, '83 Pan-Am, '78, '82 Commonwealth, '81, '83 FISU, '81-82 CIAU, '80, '82 World Cup teams; gold 52kg '78 Commonwealth, 57kg '80-81 CIAU, 52kg '83 Pan-Am Games; ACT (Ottawa) amateur sports award for wrestling, Ont. Sports Achievement Award '75, ntl outstanding wrestler award '80; 1 CIAU coach of yr award; fed. govt. excellence award '84; mem. Cdn Amateur Wrestling, UWO, Ottawa Sports Halls, Nepean Wall of Fame; res. London Ont.

TAKAHASHI, Tina (judo); b. 13 Jan 1960, North York, Ont.; given name: Alice Christina; m. Sean MacFadyen; c. Torn Sean, Adam Takahashi; UofOtt, BPhE, BEd; teacher, judo instructor; dominated jr. Ont. ranks; 7 ntl, 6 Ont., 3 Que. 2 Pacific Rim, 1 Desert Open, Canada Cup titles; ntl team '78-87; bronze 48kg '83 Pan-Am Games; silver '84 Canada Cup; 1st Cdn world champion '84; coach ntl team '88 Olympics; 5th degree black belt; mem. Nepean Wall, Judo Canada Hall of Fame; res. Ottawa, Ont.

TALBOT, Jean Guy (hockey); b. 11 Jul 1932, Cap de la Madelaine, Que.; m. Pierette Cormier; c. Carole, Danny, Michel; jr. Trois Rivieres Reds; defenceman Que. Aces '53-54, Shawingan '54-55, Montreal (NHL) '55-67; mem. 7 Stanley Cup winners; Minnesota, Detroit '67, St. Louis '68-70, Buffalo '70; NHL record: 1056 scheduled games, 43g, 242a, 150 playoff games, 4g, 26a; asst. coach NY Rangers '76-77, head coach '77-78; res. Montreal, Que.

TALLON, Dale (hockey/golf); b. 19 Oct 1950, Noranda, Que.; given name: Michael Dale Lee; m. Meg; c. Lauren, Kirsten; Ryerson Polytechnical Inst.; hockey exec., ex-broadcaster, pro golfer; ntl jr. golf championship '69; missed Ont. title same year by single stroke; defence jr. OHA Oshawa Generals, Toronto Marlboros; 1st Vancouver choice, 2nd overall '70 amateur draft; Chicago '73-78, Pittsburgh '78-80; played in 2 all-star games NHL record: 642 scheduled games, 98g, 238a, 33 playoff games, 2g, 10a; radio broadcaster, color commentator Leafs hockey '80-82, Hawks '82-98; dir. player personnel Chicago '98; res. Chicago, Ill.

TALLON, Wayne (curling): b. 22 May 1956, Ottawa, Ont. given name: Wayne William; m. Susan Fleck; c. Anne-Marie, Mireille; Algonquin Coll., CGA; town manager; competed 5 Ont. men's Tankards, runnerup '86; skip 2 City of Ottawa grand aggregate title rinks; 4 Ont. Silver Tankard titles; 3rd for Russ Howard '99 Brier; 2 hdcp golfer; St. Stephen club champion; res. St. Stephen, N.B.

TAM, Selwyn (wrestling): b. 8 Dec 1968, Vancouver, B.C.; SFU; began wrestling at 15; competed '90, '92 Canada Cup. '92 Sunkist Intl Open, Clansman Intl, '94 Cerro Pelado; 52km gold '93 Slovak Grand Prix, 2 ntl championships,

'94 Commonwealth Games; bronze '95 Pan-Am Games; res. Vancouver, B.C.

TAN, Taro (judo): b. 13 Aug 1967, Montreal, Que.; began competing age 14; mem. ntl team '86-98; 4th degree black belt; 4 ntl 65kg titles; bronze '95 Pan-Am Games; US Open title '94; competed '96 Olympics; res. Montreal, Que.

TANNER, Elaine (swimming); b. 22 Feb 1951, Vancouver, B.C.; div.; c. Scott, Shannon Nahrgang; UAlta.; butterfly, backstroke specialist; 17 ntl titles '65-68; PB: FS 61.5 (100m), 2:14.8 (200m), 4:43.8 (400m), backstroke 66.7 (100m), 2:24.5 (200m), butterfly 65.4 (100m), 2:29.9 (200m), medley 2:31.8 (200m), 5:26.3 (400m); most successful woman swimmer '66 Commonwealth Games at 15 with 4 gold, 3 silver, 2 world records; backstroke golds world record times '67 Pan-Am Games; Cdn, US, UK butterfly sprint titles '65; final competitive appearance '68 Olympics, 1 silver, 1 bronze; Lou Marsh, Bobbie Rosenfeld awards '66; trophy awarded annually to Canada's top jr. female athlete bears her name; Officer Order of Canada '70; nicknamed 'Mighty Mouse'; mem. Cdn, International Aquatic, Cdn Amateur, BC, Canada's Sports halls of fame; res. Toronto, Ont.

TAPP, Jay (swimming); b. 12 Dec 1959, Toronto, Ont.; given name: John Grenville; div.; c. Jake, Charlie; UCal, BComm; owns Tapp Technologies; mem. '77 Canada Games, '78 Worlds, '79 Pan-Am Games teams; gold 4x100 medley relay, bronze 100m backstroke '78 Commonwealth Games; CIAU backstroke gold; mem. Cdn Aquatic Hall of Fame; res. Langley, B.C.

TAPP, Larry (administration/swimming); b. 6 Oct 1937, Fort William, Ont.; given name: Lawrence; m. Joanne Fuller; c. John (Jay), Jill; McMaster, BA, Kansas, Bus. Dip; dean Richard Ivey school of business UWO; became involved in competitive swimming as dir. Etobicoke Aquatic Club '67-69; chair. finance Ont. section CASA; Ont. dir/pres. '71-74; CASA pres. '74-76; key role in fund-raising programs for '76 Olympics; master official '76 Olympics, '78 Commonwealth, Worlds, '79 Pan-Am Games; chair. Aquatic Federation of Canada, Amateur Swimming Union of the Americas tech. swim comm., FINA age group swim comm., Aquatic Trust of Canada; Ont. achievement award; mem. Ont., Cdn Aquatic halls of fame; res. London, Ont.

TASHLIN, Lesley (t&f): b. 27 May 1969, Toronto. Ont.; m. Craig Taylor; c. Emma; hurdler; represented Canada '94 Commonwealth, '95, '99 Pan-Am, '96 Olympic Games; ntl 100mH title '95; 5 intl meet titles; res. Ottawa, Ont./Calgary, Alta.

TATARCHUK, Hank (basketball); b. 2 Aug 1930, Vegreville; given name: Waldmar Eli; m. Arlene Hauberg; c. Erik; UAlta, BPhE, UofOtt, MPhE; pres. Triple T Diversified Associates; retd RCAF, asst. dean PE&R; PE specialist training, fitness, research, sports programming; coach RMC basketball '63-67; asst. coach, UAlta. basketball '67-68, '79-81, UMan. '68-71, Carleton '71-73, UofOtt '73-78; offfical, Pan-Am games '67; dir. basketball competition, '76 Olympics; v-p. sports div. FISU Games comm. '81-83; National Assn. of Basketball Coaches merit award '77; v-p. LA Olympic organizing comm. '83-84;

consultant/evaluator Seoul Olympic organizing comm. '84-88; FISU Games consultant "85, '97, '95; v-p. World jr. basketball championships '91; dir. sports/venues FISU Games '92-93; v.-chair FISU tech. comm. '87-91; consultant du Maurier LPGA Classic '94-96; commissioner/convenor basketball CWUAA '93-99; mem. Cdn Forces Sports Hall of Fame; res. Edmonton, Alta.

TAVARES, John (lacrosse): b. 4 Sep 1968, Toronto, Ont.; resource worker; began playing age 7; mem. Mississauga Tomahawks '85-90, Vancouver Bandits '91, Brampton Excelsiors, Buffalo Bandits '92-98, Team Canada '93-98; 2 Mann Cup champions; 2 Mike Kelly MVP awards; 2 Major Indoor Lacrosse League titles, 2 playoff MVP awards; MILL MVP '94, league scoring title, 1st team all-star; Mississauga pro athlete of '93; Governor-General's award '93; res. Mississauga, Ont.

TAYLOR, Betty (t&f); b. 22 Feb 1916, Ingersoll, Ont., d. 2 Feb 1977, Ottawa, Ont.; m. William Campbell; c. Margaret, David; McMaster; ntl int. hurdles title '30 in record time; mem. '32, '36 Olympic, '34 BEG, women's world games teams; London, Eng.; final competitive event Berlin Olympics '36 winning bronze when first 4 runners were given same time; Bobbie Rosenfeld award '36; mem. Cdn Amateur, McMaster Sports halls of fame.

TAYLOR, Bobby (football/hockey); b. 5 Mar 1939, Barrow-in-Furness, Lancashire, Eng.; div.; c. Janet Lee, Bobby Jr.; hotel/bar owner; football Mount Royal College Cougars; wide receiver Calgary '61-65, Toronto '66-70, '74, Hamilton '71, Edmonton '71-73; CFL record: 521 passes caught for 8223yds, 15.8 avg., 50td; WFC record 74 receptions Calgary '63; twice led EFC receivers; all-Eastern '69; 10 years pro hockey in Toronto, Philadelphia chains with Que. City (AHL), Victoria, Seattle (WHL), Long Island, Tulsa, Rochester, Cherry Hill, N.J., Johnstown, Pa. (EHL), South Peace HL; Toronto Oldtimers hockey; operates Black Bull Tavern in Toronto and Banff lodge; res. Toronto, Ont.

TAYLOR, Bryce (administration); b. 14 Nov 1933, Delisle, Sask.; d. 16 Feb 1989, Toronto, Ont.; given name: Bryce Malcolm; div Patricia; c. Deborah, Barbara, Nancy; m. Cheryl; c. Bryche; Springfield College, DPhE, BSc,UBC, MPhE; York professor; pres. Cdn Gymnastics Fed. '74, '78; pres. Coaching Assn. of Canada '76-77, v-p. '75; dir. National Sport and Recreation Centre '76, COA '75; secty-treas. Mission Dome Inc., '71-73; field rep. Ont. Jr. Olympics '73-74; chair. organizing comm. international gymnastics competition Montreal '75; chair. comm. for unification of sport in Canada '75; mem. Task Force on sport, Ont. reasearch council on leisure; CAC scholarship selection comm. '75; chair. Cdn gymnastic seminar '67-89; mem. American College of Sports Medicine '64; dir. intl sport coaches exchange '65; CdM FISU Games '67; involved in study of sports movement, ntl gymnastics development; CAHPER R. Tait McKenzie award of honor '76, Air Canada amateur sports exec. of '76 year; author gymnastic coaching manuals, several books, articles on gymnastics, tennis, sport studies.

TAYLOR, Cyclone (hockey); b. 23 Jun 1883, Tara, Ont., d. 9 Jun 1979, Vancouver, B.C.; given name: Fredrick

Wellington; m. Thirza Cook; c. Fred Jr., John, Mary, Edward, Joan; civil servant; amateur Listowel, Thessalon, Ont., Portage La Prairie, Man.; pro defenceman Houghton, Mich., '06; 2yrs with both Ottawa, Renfrew; Vancouver '12-21; as rover, centre scored 194 goals in 186 league games, 15 more in 19 playoff games; 5 scoring titles; 32 goals in 18-game '17-18 season, 6 in single game vs Victoria '16-17; nickname Cyclone given him at Ottawa CY Arena '07 by Governor-General Earl Grey; mem. 2 Stanley Cup winners; Ottawa Capitals lacrosse team '08-10, Mann Cup '08; OBE; mem. Hockey, Lacrosse, Ottawa, BC Sports halls of fame.

TAYLOR, Dave (hockey); b. 4 Dec 1955, Levack, Ont.; given name: David Andrew; m. Beth; c. Jamie, Katie; Clarkson College; hockey exec.; 14th LA pick, 210th overall '75 draft; with Marcel Dionne, Charlie Simmer formed Triple Crown Line; nicknamed 'Stitch'; 2nd team all-star right wing '81; played entire NHL career with LA '75-94; 4 yrs captain; NHL record: 1111 scheduled games, 431g, 638a, 70 playoff games, 23g, 28a; 1st player to win Masterton, King Clancy awards same year '91; active mem, Kings' charity golf, softball tournaments; twice Kings' unsung hero award; jersey 18 retd. by LA; AGM Kings 3yrs, GM/v-p. '97-98; mem. Hockey Hall of Fame; res. Tarzana, Calif.

TAYLOR, E.P. (horse racing); b. 29 Jan 1901, Ottawa, Ont.; d. 14 May 1989, Lyford Cay, BWI; given name: Edward Plunkett; m. Winnifred Thorton Duguid; c. Judith Winifred, Mary Louise, Charles; Ashbury College, McGill, BSc; retired investment broker, brewer; owner Winfield Farms; owner Northern Dancer '64 Kentucky Derby, Preakness, Nijinsky II '70 Epson Derby, English triple crown; pres. Ont. Jockey Club '53-73; did much to revitalize and raise standard of racing in Ont.; 9 Taylor horses won Cdn horse of year, 15 Queen's Plate winners; world's leading breeder '70; 10 NA breeder of yr awards; Thoroughbred Racing Assoc. man of '73; instrumental in forming Jockey Club of Canada; Woodbine turf course named in his honor; mem. Canadian Horse Racing, Canada's , Ont. Legends Sports halls of fame.

TAYLOR, Graham (parachuting); b. 26 Apr 1949, New Zealand; given name: Graham Michael; M. Melody Hydman; c. Warren, Jason; New Zealand, Capilano College; contractor; rugby '53-73; MVP Trojan Rugby Club Vancouver '73; HS athletic champion award '67; began skydiving '73; 4-way, 8-way ntl titles '77, '79-80; world champion '77, '79; Australian 4-way title '77; French 4-way title, runnerup 8-way '79; 2nd 4-way China '80; more than 2,500 jumps; res. Claresholm, Alta.

TAYLOR, John (skiing); b. 12 Jan 1908, Toronto, Ont.; d. 4 Nov 1989, Ottawa, Ont.; given name: John Pringle; m. Nattalie Skinner; c. Alex, Robert; retd.; mem. '32 Olympic team; 2nd ntl cross-country championships '34; ntl, Ont., cross-country titles '35; dir. Ottawa Ski Club; chair. Gatineau Ski Zone; pres. Heron Park Community Assn.; secty-treas. Ottawa Tennis Club; dir. Canadian Ski Museum.

TAYLOR, Piffles (football): b. 1894, Collingwood, Ont.; d. 24 May 1946, Regina, Sask.; given name: Neil Joseph; UofT; played football at UofT, Regina Roughriders '14-16, '19-20, Regina Boat Club '20-21; coached Regina Boat Club '22-23; pres. Roughriders '34-36, WIFU '37, '41-42, CRU

'46; considered largely responsbile for development of football in Western Canada; Regina stadium bears his name and CFL Western champions annually receive trophy bearing his name; mem. Cdn Football, Sask Sports halls of fame.

TAYLOR, Ron (baseball); b. 13 Dec 1937, Toronto, Ont.; given name: Ronald Wesley; m. Rona Douglas; UotT, BA, PPSc., MD; medical doctor, operates sports medicine clinic; right hand relief specialist Cleveland '62, St. Louis '63-65, Houston '65-66, New York Mets '67-71, San Diego '72; ML record 491 scheduled games, 800ip, 45-43, 72sv, 3.93era; mem. '64 St. Louis, '69 Mets World Series champions; perfect WS record of 7 innings pitched allowing no hits, no runs and recording a save in each series; 1 win, 1 save '69 playoff vs Atlanta; runnerup NL rookie pitcher of year; mgr. Alta. amateur team while awaiting medical school entrance marks; team doctor Blue Jays; mem. Canada's Sports, Cdn Baseball halls of fame; res. Toronto, Ont.

TAYLOR, Russ (curling); b. 27 Oct 1943, Ottawa, Ont.; given name: Gordon Russell; m. Nicole Boily; c. Candy, Russell Jr., James; private investigator; nicknamed 'The Hawk'; competed in 4 Ont. men's championships; skipped Governor-General'stitle rink `81; 3 OCA Intermediate, Quebec International titles; won City of Ottawa Grand Aggregate, Eastern Ont. Major League `85; in 2yr span `85-86 reached 2 intermediate (won both), 2 men's, 1 mixed provincial championships; unique distinction of having curled in competitive bonspiels every month for 2yr period; res. Cumberland, Ont.

TENNANT, Mark (coaching); b. 22 Jun 1944, Miniota, Man.; given name: James Mark; m. Gail Marie Olver; c. John Darcy, James Derek, Jodie Breanne; UMan., BPhE, UBC, MPhE; assoc. professor UofSask. Where coach of women's intercollegiate volleyball team '71-98; 3 CIAU ntl titles; 4 CIAU coach of year; coach of '79; pres. CIAU volleyball coaches assoc. '80; mem. master coaches review board CVA '77-98; IVBF instructor world class coaching courses '80-98; author *"Volleyball Team Play"* '75; chef adjoint secretariat Volleyball organizing Comm. '76 Olympics; mem. tech. comm. for volleyball FISU Games `84-98; mem. FIVB rules of game, sports organizing comms.; CIAU women's volleyball rookie of yr award bears his name; AMTEC award `78; life mem. Sask VBA; mem. UofSask Sports Wall, Saskatoon, Sask. Sports halls of fame; res. Saskatoon, Sask.

TERPENNING, Barbara (figure skating); b. 7 Sep 1956, Burnaby, B.C.; given name: Barbara Anne; m. Paul Wolfe; Capilano Coll., UBC; teacher; BC sr. titles '72-73; runnerup ntl jr. '72, Skate Canada '73, ntl sr. '74; pro Ice Follies '76-78; res. North Vancouver, B.C.

TERRY, Jackie (shooting); b. 29 May 1954, Owen Sound, Ont.; chemical technologist; mem. '81-83 world championships, '83 Pan-Am, '84 Olympic Games teams; silver ladies air rifle, 3-position teams '83 Pan-Am Games; Ont. air, standard rifle titles, Benito Juarez, Championship of Americas, Cuban small bore prone titles; SFC golden anniversary award '82; res. Burlington, Ont.

TESSIER, Orv (hockey); b. 30 Jun 1933, Cornwall, Ont.; given name: Orval Ray; m. Charlotte Chouinard; c. Adele, Andre, Michael, Julie; hockey exec.; leading scorer '53 Barrie Memorial Cup winner; pro '53-63 Montreal Royals (QHL), Canadiens, Bruins (NHL), Hershey Bears, Springfield Indians (AHL), Kingston Frontenacs (EPHL), Portland Buckaroos (WHL); reinstated amateur Clinton (EHL), Jersey Devils; pro scoring record '59-60 Kingston 59g, 67a; league scoring title '61-62 as player-coach Frontenacs scoring 54g, 60a; league MVP, good conduct awards; coached Cornwall Royals to Memorial Cup '72; Que. Remparts '73 Memorial Cup finalists; Kitchener '81 Memorial Cup finalists; Jr. A coaching record: 12yrs 446-304-74; coached NB Hawks to AHL title '81-82; coach Chicago '82-85; scout Colorado '97-98; NHL, Hockey News coach of '83; res. Fraser's Point, Ont.

TETLEY, Bill (curling); b. 11 Jul 1933, Lionshead, Ont.; given name: William Ross; m. Elaine Lord; c. Russ, Allan, Ian, Tanis; RIA cost accountant; executive; lead '51, skip '71, '75 Brier, '75 winner; semifinalist '75 Silver Broom; skip NO rinks 2 ntl mixed, 1 ntl srs; Thunder Bay sportsman of '68; mem. NWO Sports Hall of Fame; res. Thunder Bay, Ont.

TETLEY, Ian (curling); b. 14 Aug 1962, Port Arthur, Ont.; given name: Ian James; m. Sherry; c. Nicklaus; Lakehead, hons BComm; golf sales specialist; leftfielder '75 Cdn Major Little League baseball title team; competed Cdn juve. ski championships '78; 2nd stone Al Hackner's Cdn, World championship rink '85; 2nd Ed Werenich's Cdn, World title rink '90; 2nd Wayne Middaugh's Cdn, World title rink '98; '93 VO Cup winner; with Wayne Middaugh '95-96 TSN Skins Game titles; father Bill skipped '75 Brier winner; res. Mississauga, Ont.

TEWKSBURY, Mark (swimming): b. 7 Feb 1968, Calgary, Alta.; UCal, BA, New South Wales; motivational speaker, consultant; backstroke specialist; began competing age 8; mem. ntl team '84-92; competed '86, '91 worlds, '88, '92 Olympic, '86, '90 Commonwealth Games teams; 4 Commonwealth Games gold, 1 Olympic silver, 1 bronze; 35 World Cup gold, 12 winter ntls, 13 summer ntls gold; 3 overall World Cup backstroke titles; 11 Cdn sr., 4 world, 4 Commonwealth records; COA jr. athlete of '85; Calgary athlete of '90; Aquatics Canada athlete of '87, '90; 3 Swimming Canada jr. male athlete, 2 sr. male athlete awards; '87 fed. govt. Sports Excellence award; '89 Olympic champion award; Lionel Conacher, Norton Crowe awards '92; Johnny F. Bassett award '95; Sydney Morning Herald academic prize; resigned from COA/Toronto Olympic bid comm. due to ongoing bidding scandal; mem. Cdn Amateur, Canada's, Alta. Sports halls of fame; res. Toronto, Ont.

THACKER, Mary Rose (figure skating); b. 9 Apr 1922, Winnipeg, Man., d. Jul 1983, Victoria, B.C.; m. Roy Temple; c. 1 daughter; began skating age 3; Winnipeg Winter Club champion at 13; Cdn jr. champion at 14; Cdn sr. titles '39, '41-42, NA titles '40-41; Bobbie Rosenfeld Trophy '39, '41; named to '40 Olympic team but WW2 negated participation; turned pro and performed in numerous ice shows; operated skating rink Bremerton, Wash., summer skating school Nelson, B.C.; pro Victoria Figure Skating Club; among

protegees was Karen Magnussen; mem. Cdn Figure Skating, Man. Sports halls of fame.

THAIN, Ken (curling); b. 1 Jun 1913, Burks Falls, Ont.; d. 24 Oct 1986, Ottawa, Ont.; given name: Kenneth Bassett; m. Adrienne Belanger; c. Gary Clare; UofT; retd. surveyor, chief of construction claims Public Works Can.; charter mem. Granite Club of West Ottawa; won 3 trophy events City of Ottawa bonspiel; OVCA drawmaster '70-75, secty-mgr. '76-82; mem. Governor-General's Curling Club.

THEISMANN, Joe (football); b. 9 Sep 1949, New Brunswick, N.J.; m. Cheryl Lynn Brown; c. Joey, Amy, Patrick; Notre Dame; retd. pro athlete; restaurateur, disc jockey, actor, author; quarterbacked Notre Dame to consec. Cotton Bowls; runnerup Heismann Trophy; academic/athletic all-American; rejected pro baseball offers; Virginia State racquetball champion; drafted Miami (NFL) '71 but opted for Toronto (CFL) '71-73; competed '71 Grey Cup final; twice led EFC in passing yardage; Washington (NFL); 2 Super Bowls, 1 winner; frequent team MVP awards, NFL MVP '83; numerous club records; active in Washington, D.C., charity work, Fellowship of Christian Athletes; finalist TV Superstars competition; Redskins NFL man-of-year; Lions International humanitarian award; ESPN football commentator; res. Vienna, Va.

THELEN, Dave (football); b. 2 Sep 1936, Canton, Ohio; m. Bonnie; c. David Jr., Dayna, Lana, John; Miami of Ohio, BA; partner electric fixtures stores; semipro baseball; 17th round draft choice Cleveland Browns; pro Ottawa '58-64, '65-66 Toronto; CFL record: 8463yds in 1530 carries for 5.5 avg., 47tds; best single game Sep '60 Toronto at Ottawa with 209yds in 33 carries; lead CFL with 1407yds on 245 carries '60; 4tds single game '59; rushed ball 87 consecutive games; mem. Ottawa Sports, Canadian Football halls of fame; res. Nepean, Ont.

THÉRIAULT, Jean-Yves (kick boxing); b. 15 Jan 1955, Caraquette, N.B.; div. Suzanne Anderson; c. Chantal, Brigitte; fitness consultant; world middleweight champion '80-94, world light heavyweight title '94-95; 23 times world champion; over 15yr span 51 consecutive victories; pro record: 69-6-1, 60kos; lost title Jun '92 to Rob Kaman, regained it Dec. '92 and lost it again to Australian Tesis Petridis '93; retd. from ring as Cdn lightheavy champion '95; competed '83 Canadian Superstars; 4 times Gil O. Julien Trophy nominee; authored kick boxing book, series of instructional cassette tapes; conducts frequent intl seminars; mem. Black Belt Hall of Fame; res. Orleans, Ont.

THIBAULT, Jacques (speed skating); b. 13 Feb 1958, Quebec City, Que.; Laval; GM Calgary Olympic speed skating oval; ntl indoor all-around title '78, outdoor 1500m '79; mem. '80, '84 Olympic Games, '78, '80-84 world sprint championships teams; ntl team coach; fed. govt. excellence award '84; res. Calgary, Alta.

THIBODEAU, Nick (curling/shooting); b. 28 Apr 1885, Bathurst, N.B., d. 16 May 1959, Janeville, N.B.; given name: Nicholas Joseph; mem. '14 Bisley rifle team; 5 provincial curling titles, skipped NB entry 5 Briers; '31 skipped Bathurst CC rink to victory over champion Man. dealing

Winnipeg rink lone loss; vs Montreal in same competition was victim of first end 'seven'; 3rd place tie '40; mem. Canadian Curling, NB Sports halls of fame.

THIERRY, Nick (swimming/builder); b. 2 Dec 1938, Budapest, Hungary; UofT, B Arch; editor/publisher; swimming coach '61-82; ntl team coach European tour '65, Commonwealth Games '70; founded International Swimming Statisticians Assn. '86; secty ISSA from '86; FINA world statisticians from '92; edits world swimming annual; editor/publisher *Swim News* from '74; Ont. Merit award; Doug Gilbert media award '80; Swim Canada service award; mem. Ont. Aquatic Hall of Fame; res. Toronto, Ont.

THIVIÈRGE, Jojo (synchro swim); b. 10 Oct 1955, Quebec City, Que.; given name: Jocelyne Carrier; div; Laval, BA; coach; ntl jr. solo title '66; Que. all-events champion '67-73; bronze solo Copenhagen international, bronze duet, team Osaka international '70; ntl sr. solo champion '71-73, figures, duet '69-73; silver solo, duet '71 Pan-Am, '73 world aquatic Games; silver solo, duet '73 World Aquatic championships; began coaching '74; assisted Cuban coach '75 Pan-Am Games; choreographer, asst. coach Que. YWCA '74-78, head coach '79; guided Que. to team title '79 Canada Games, sr. nationals; coached ntl team FINA World Cup, Coventry Intl '80, Swiss Open '81; head coach Que. Synchro Elite '76-99; Suzanne Eon most promising coach trophy '77; res. Quebec City, Que.

THOM, Linda (shooting); b. 30 Dec 1943, Hamilton, Ont; given name: Linda Mary Alice Malcolm; m. Donald Cullen Thom; c. Samantha, Murray; Carleton, B.J., Cordon Bleu School of Cooking, Paris; operator L'Academie de Cuisine, caterer, real estate agent; pistol specialist; Ntl Handgun postal matches title '69; ntl titles '70-75, '82-83, record '70; mem. ntl handgun team '70-76, from '82; mem. French SA; 2 gold Federation of the Americas championships '73, unofficial world record; 4th overall US International air pistol, match pistol '82-83; mem. 70, '74, '82 world championship teams; gold Zurich International Matchweek '83; silver match, bronze air '83 Pan-Am Games, 2 silver Cuban International '83; bronze air '83 Benito Juarez; 7th world ranked '84; gold in shootoff, ntl record Zurich, bronze Munich '84; 1st woman to win gold sport pistol '84 Olympics; 2 ntl air pistol records '85; grand marshall '84 Central Canada Exhibition; Velma Springstead Trophy '84; Ottawa ACT athlete of '84; chaired govt. sports medicine, safety comm. from '85; RA President's trophy '84; unsuccessful bid for PC MPP '95; mem. Order of Canada, Canada's, Ottawa, Cdn Amateur, Ottawa CSRA Sports halls of fame; res. Ottawa, Ont.

THOMAS, Bronwen (skiing); b. 17 Mar 1969, Richmond, B.C.; freestyle moguls specialist; began skiing age 3, competing age 17; mem. ntl team '89-94; ntl title '90; competed '92, '94 Olympics; res. Delta, B.C.

THOMAS, Fred (all-around); b. 26 Dec 1923, Windsor, Ont., d. 20 May 1981, Toronto, Ont.; m. Arminta; c. Gregory, Tony, Dennis; Assumption College; educator; 2059 Assumption career points at time 3rd all-time NA college basketball scoring list; mem. Harlem Globetrotters; ntl champion Toronto Tri-Bells; 2nd in balloting Canada's basketball player of half century '50; baseball Cleveland

Indians chain, Waterloo, Kitchener Sr. IC; MVP; intl calibre softball player; pro football Toronto '49; Windsor park named in his honor; mem. Windsor-Essex Sports, Cdn Basketball halls of fame.

THOMAS, Howard (wrestling); b. 18 Jan 1905, London, Eng.; d. Mar 1995, Montreal, Que.; given name: Howard Vincent MacKenzie; m. Catherine Ellen Mary Nichol; c. Murray, Sylvia; retd.; as teenager played soccer, hockey, basketball, tennis; in his 20's turned to boxing and wrestling; '28-34 ntl lightweight (145lbs) wrestling champion; '30 BE lightweight titlist; mem. '32, '36 Olympic, '34 BEG teams.

THOMAS, Jeff (curling); b. 2 Jul 1958, St. John's, Nfld.; given name: Jeffrey Reynold; m. Candy; c. Colin, Mitchell; nicknamed 'Stache'; GM Thomas Glass; skipped Nfld. '75 ntl schoolboy, '77-78 ntl jr. men's, '83 Seagram ntl mixed; skip Nfld. entry '79, '84-85, '97 Briers, lead for Glenn Goss '90 Brier; res. St. John's, Nfld.

THOMAS, Jim (football); b. 1940, Columbus, Miss.; m. Lillian; c. Sheila, Darryl; Mississippi Industrial; teacher; nicknamed 'Long Gone'; pro Dallas (NFL) '62, led Louisville US League farm club scorers; running back Edmonton '63-71; as running back; frequent WFC, all-Cdn all-star; twice Canada Packers Trophy outstanding Eskimo player on fan's vote; 1006yds rushing 172 carries '67; CFL record: 1111 carries, 6060yds, 5.5 avg., 37tds; longest run 104yds from scrimmage; res. Columbus, Miss.

THOMAS, Jo (squash): b. 23 Feb 1975, Ottawa, Ont.; given name: Johanna; Queen's; began playing age 10; '91 ntl jr. title; mem. ntl jr. women's team '91-93; Ont. team gold '91 Canada Winter Games; 2 OWIAA championships; playing-coach Queen's; res. Kingston/Ottawa, Ont.

THOMAS, Misty (basketball): b. 1 Jul 1964, Santa Monica, Calif.; given name. Misty Paige; UNLV, BSc (sports medicine), Arizona State, BSc (fitness programming); dir. Vancouver Night Hoops program for high risk teenagers; 5 Windsor all-city HS awards; 3 WSSA/SWOSSA title teams; OFSAA silver, bronze medals; leading scorer 4 HS years; also excelled in volleyball, t&f, tennis, badminton; 2 Windsor outstanding female athlete awards; mem. '80 Windsor juveniles all-Ont. basketball champs; Rhodes Scholar nominee at UNLV; career scoring/assists/free throw/ field goal leader UNLV; 2 all-American, 4 Big-West conf. awards; 3 academic all-American awards; UNLV athlete of year award; jersey #4 retd. (1st female athlete so honored); mem. ntl team '82-89 competing in FISU, Olympic, World, Jones Cup, America's Cup; leading scorer, all-star, bronze medal '86 worlds; 9 knee operations aborted her playing career; asst. coach ntl team '90-93; asst. Arizona State '88-89; head coach UBC '89-95; guided UBC to CWUAA title '94; CWUAA coach of '95; mem. Cdn Basketball, UNLV, Windsor-Essex Sports halls of fame; res. Vancouver, B.C.

THOMAS, Paul (basketball); b. 14 Apr 1926, Saint John, N.B.; given name: Paul Ernest; div. Barbara Diane Baker; c. Scott Paul, Misty Paige, Brett Arthur; m. Kerri Lynn Towers; UWO, BA, UofT, teacher's certificate, Michigan, MSc, U of SouthernCal, PhD; retd. university prof., basketball coach; pro baseball Chicago Cubs system 1 1/2yrs; MVP Greater Niagara Falls Basketball Assn.; all-Cdn guard UWO 4yrs; mem. 4 CIAU title teams; mem. '52 ntl champion Tillsonburg Livingstons; at 24 youngest ever coach '52 Olympic team, not permitted to play because of pro baseball background; mem. 2 Toronto Tri-Bells ntl title teams; coached college level basketball, baseball, tennis; ntl men's basketball team coach '72-74; pres. National Assn. of Basketball Coaches '74-77; coach of year awards; mem. Niagara Falls Sports Wall, Cdn Basketball, UWO W Club, Windsor, Windsor-Essex Sports halls of fame; res. Windsor, Ont.

THOMAS, Shirley (equestrian); b. 12 Jul 1936, Ottawa, Ont.; given name: Shirley Laura; m. Donald Prosser; c. Christopher, Laura, Ruth; Elmwood Ladies College; 1st female rider to claim international class honors at Madison Square Garden '53; 1st woman named to Canada's 3-mem. intl equestrian team '53; shared Royal Winter Fair puissance title '53; toured UK and Europe winning Ostende intl ladies' jumping, Rotterdam ladies championship; Government of Ireland Trophy; Ottawa ACT athlete of year; Internationl Equestrian Assn. Cup; Montreal Press Assn. woman of '54; thoroughbred horse breeder; mem. Ottawa Sports Hall of Fame; res. Alexander Bay, N.Y./Portland, Ont.

THOMAS, Ted (coaching); b. 29 Sep 1919, Taber, Alta.; given name: Edward; m. Hilda Thomas; c. Hilda Ann, Glynis; retd. regional manager Alta. Govt. Telephones; mgr. YWCA Sharkettes '59-60, coach '61-64; head coach Killarney SC Calgary '64-68; coach Jasper Place SC '68; coached Alta. team to ntls '66-68; coach women's team '68 Olympics, ntl team China tour '74; pres. Alta. Coaches Council 4 years; v-p. National Swim Coaches '71, pres. '72; Calgary sportsman of year nominee '68; Edmonton recreation citation '74; res. Calgary, Alta.

THOMAS, Wayne (hockey); b. 9 Oct 1947, Ottawa, Ont.; given name: Robert Wayne; m. Barbara; c. Gretchen, Abby; Wisconsin, BPhE; goaltender 3yrs Wisc.; pro AHL Montreal Voyageurs '70-71, Nova Scotia '71-72, New Haven '80, NHL Canadiens '72-74, Maple Leafs '75-77, Rangers '77-80; NHL record: 243 scheduled games, 193-93-34, 13,768min, 766ga, 10so, 15 playoff games, 6-8-0, 849min, 50ga, 1so; asst. coach Rangers '82-85, Black Hawks '87-88, Blues '90-93, Sharks '93-96; head coach Peoria (IHL) '88-90, Salt Lake City '85-87 winning '86 IHL Turner Cup title; San Jose AGM '96-99; GM Kentucky Thoroughblades; res. San Jose, Calif.

THOMAS, Willie (football); b. 14 Aug 1955, Calgary, Alta.; m. Joanne; c. Sarah, Landa; UCal; investment co. owner; Calgary Dinosaurs rookie of year; CFL linebacker, centre Calgary '77-79, '83-84, Winnipeg '79-82; nicknamed "Bluto"; res. Calgary, Alta.

THOMPSON, Clif (curling); b. 8 Aug 1913, Brandon, Man.; given name: George Clifton; m. Helen Elizabeth; c. Nancy, Ross, Rick; UofSask, BSc; retd. engineer; mem. prov. baseball title, curling finalist teams; NO jr. development chair. 6yrs; 1st ever T&NO pres, CCA; chaired CCA Brier sponsorship comm.; ICF pres.; Claude H. Allard award '84; mem. Governor-General's CC; mem. Cdn Curling Hall of Fame; res. Stroud, Ont.

THOMPSON, Dan (swimming); b. 15 Jun 1956, Toronto, Ont.; given name: Daniel David; UofT, BPHE; butterfly, relay specialist; silver 100 fly, 400MR '77 FISU Games; gold 100 fly, 400MR '78 Commonwealth Games; 2nd world 100 fly '78; 13 ntl, 3 intl, 5 CIAU titles; mem. '78, '82 world championships, '80 Olympic teams; silver 100 fly, 400MR '79 Pan-Am Games; tied world record 100m fly 53.17 winter ntls short course; 8 ntl, 3 Commonwealth, 2Commonwealth Games records; gold 100m butterfly '82 Commonwealth Games; capt. ntl team '78-81, UofT swim team '78-80; 2 CIAU male swimmer of yr awards; UofT male athlete of '80; dir. CASA '78-81; mem. '80 Olympic swim trials organizing comm.; mem. Cdn Athletes Assn. board '93; mem. Cdn, Ont. Aquatic, UofT Sports halls of fame; res. Don Mills, Ont.

THOMPSON, George (lacrosse); b. 3 May 1910, Bowmanville, Ont.; given name: Walter George; m. Margaret McLaren; c. James, Gordon, Wayne, Barbara Jane; machine operator; mem. Brampton OLA jr. champions '30, Brampton Excelsiors Mann Cup winners '30-31, Mimico-Brampton Combines Mann Cup winners '42; coached Brampton Ont. title peewees '47, Brampton Minto Cup finalists '56, Brampton Excelsiors jrs to successive Minto Cups '57-59; pres. Lacrosse Old Timers '69-70; from '75 governor Canadian Lacrosse Hall of Fame; life mem. Brampton Excelsior Lacrosse Club; mem. Canadian Lacrosse Hall of Fame; res. Brampton, Ont.

THOMPSON, Jim (speedboat racing); b. 18 Dec 1926, London, Ont.; given name: James Gordon; m. Beverly Smith; c. Adair, Leslie, Ann, Robin, Gordon; Ridley Coll., Royal Roads, UofT, BSc, UWO, MBA; co. pres.; designed, built Miss Supertest series unlimited hydroplanes; developed propellor driven boat that set world record 184.24 mph; with Bob Hayward driving Miss Supertest III won Harmsworth Trophy '59-61; crafts set ntl, BE speed records; retd. from racing when Hayward was killed in Detroit River Silver Cup race '61; mem. Canada's Sports Hall of Fame; res. London, Ont.

THOMPSON, Jim (shooting): 4 Jan 1941, Horseforth, York, Eng.; given name: James Charlton; m. Marion; c. Claire, Eva; UofT, BA, PhD; UofT chemistry professor; qualified for 4 DCRA Bisley teams, competed 2, coached 2, commandant 1, adjutant 1; capt. 2 of 5 Palma teams; mem. 3 Ont. Bisley teams; represented Canada in New Zealand, West Indies, Australia competitions; won '76 Ont. Lt.-Gov. match; Ont. govt. special award '85; exec. v-p. DCRA '85-96; outstanding DCRA '98 F-Class competition winning 5g, 7s, 7b medals; res. Whitevale, Ont.

THOMPSON, Lesley (rowing); b. 20 Sep 1959, Toronto, Ont.; UWO; teacher; former gymnast who began rowing at UWO; sweep ntl coxed 4s, 8s title crews '80-83; Canadian Henley coxed 4s, 8s title crews '81-82; coxswain for ntl teams '84-98; mem. '80, '84, '88, '92, '96 Olympic teams; 1 Olympic gold, 2 silver, 1 Commonwealth Games gold, 1 World gold, 3 bronze, 10 ntl, 4 US, 4 international regatta titles; coached Ont. team '85 Canada Games; 2 Dick Ellis team awards; mem. Cdn Olympic Sports Hall of Fame; res. London, Ont.

THOMPSON, Stanley (golf); b. 17 Sep 1893, Toronto, Ont.; d. 4 Jan 1953, Toronto, Ont.; m. 1. Ruth McAinch (d), 2. Helen Duffy; golf course designer; mem. prominent Cdn golfing families; brother Frank twice Cdn Amateur titlist, brother Bill twice Ont., once Cdn amateur titlist, brothers Matt, Nicol long-time golf pros; ranked on par with Robert Trent Jones, Dr. Alister MacKenzie among world's finest course designers; designed more than 200 courses mostly in Canada, but also at such sites as Brazil, Colombia, British West Indies and US; among his designs were Toronto St. George's, Vancouver Capilano, Montebello's Seigniory Club, Nova Scotia's Digby Pines and Jasper, Alta., GC; mem. RCGA Hall of Fame.

THOMPSON, Tiny (hockey); b. 31 May 1905, Sandon, B.C., d. 9 Feb 1981, Calgary, Alta.; given name: Cecil; hockey scout; Calgary Monarchs jrs., Pacific Grain srs., Bellvue Bulldogs, Duluth, Minneapolis; pro Minneapolis; Boston (NHL) '28-39, Detroit '39-40; lifetime NHL goals-against avg. 2.27 regular season, 2.00 playoffs; 4 times Vezina Trophy; twice both 1st, 2nd all-star teams; vs Toronto '33 worked 104 minutes, 45 seconds of shutout hockey before being beaten 1-0; chief Western scout Chicago; mem. Hockey Hall of Fame.

THOMPSON, Tommy (baseball): b. 16 Jun 1918, Fredericton, N.B.; d. 21 Jul 1987, Fredericton, N.B.; given name: Thomas George; m. Lawanda; men's wear mgr.; involved 48yrs as player, coach, mgr., owner of teams in Fredericton; coached 5 NB, 1 Maritime jr. title teams; coached 2 jr. Vikings ntl title teams; asst. coach '74 ntl jr. titlist Fredericton Condors; coached 6 NB teams in ntl sr. finals, 2 winners; '72 Maritime sr. title; 3 times to sr. ntls; '76 coach of yr award; hon. citizen Republic of Madawaska '81; NB recognition certificate '81; baseball field, HS trophy, NB jr. baseball title trophy named in his honor; mem. NB Baseball, Fredericton Sports Wall and NB Sports halls of fame.

THOMPSON, William (skiing); b. 18 May 1905, Westmount, Que.; d. 3 Apr 1994, Ottawa, Ont.; given name: William Brown; m. Margaret Stuart Fraser; McGill, BSc; retd. chemical consultant; cross-country specialist; mem. title winning Westmount HS team '23 Montreal and district HS cross-country championships; 3 consecutive Mount Royal cross-country race titles; CIAU cross-country champion '25, 3rd in ski jumping; Lake Placid college 7-mile titles '26-27; 2nd '27, 3rd '25 Dartmouth Winter Carnival 7-mile race; 2nd (1st Cdn) '27 ntl 10-mile championships; mem. 1st Canadian Olympic ski team '28; cross country; capt. McGill ski team '26-27; secty. Intl Intercollegiate Winter Sports Union '26-27; co-founder, with A.H. Pangman, H.S. Maxwell, McGill Red Birds Ski Club, pres. '28-31; pres. CASA '33-36; chair. Olympic Ski Team comm. '36; mem. Cdn Skiing Hall of Fame.

THOMSON, Earl (t&f); b. 15 Feb 1895, Birch Hills, Sask., d. 19 May 1971, Oceanside, Calif.; South Carolina, Dartmouth Coll., BSc; as SC freshman set world record 14.8 for 110yd high hurdles; as mem. Royal Flying Corps 5 firsts, 1 2nd, 6 cups, gold medal service track meet Toronto; '19 world 110yd high hurdles mark of 14.4; IC4A high hurdles '19-21, low hurdles title '21; gold high hurdles '20 setting 14.8 Olympic mark; track coach West Virginia 1 year, asst. coach Yale to '27; coach US Naval Academy track teams more than 25 years; mem. Cdn Amateur, Canada's, Sask. Sports halls of fame.

THOMSON, Kay (figure skating); b. 18 Feb 1964, Toronto, Ont.; coached by Louis Stong; '79 ntl jr. title; 2nd '80 jr. worlds; '81 Moscow Skate title; '82-84 ntl sr. titles; silver Skate Canada '83; pro Ice Capades '84; res. Toronto, Ont.

THOMSON, Mabel (golf); b. 28 Sep 1874, Saint John, N.B., d. 13 Aug 1950, Saint John N.B.; given name: Mabel Gordon; Canada's top woman golfer turn of century; ntl Open, amateur titles '02, '05-08; numerous regional, provincial competition honors; mem. RCGA, NB Sports halls of fame.

THORBURN, Cliff (snooker); b. 16 Jan 1948, Victoria, B.C.; given name: Clifford Charles Devlin; m. Barbara Lynn Jalbert; c. James Edouard, Andrew Clifford; pro snooker player; pitched 2 no-hitters leading team to BC Little League baseball title; 9yrs minor soccer, 6yrs minor lacrosse; '70 Toronto snooker title; '71 NA title with 2 perfect 147 games; 3 perfect games in 8 days '73; ntl title '74-76; brought perfect game total to 9 with 3 '75; world quarterfinalist '75; 1st Cdn ever seeded in world play; world tournament record 13 straight black balls, tied record 2 consecutive century breaks reaching world finals '77; World champion '80, runnerup '83; recorded first 147 (perfect) break in world pro title play '83; world masters titles '83, '85; mem. Order of Canada, BC Sports Hall of Fame; res. Markham, Ont.

THORNTON, Bernie (football); b. 18 Jul 1912, Hamilton, Ont.; given name: Bernard David; m. June; c. Carr Alison, Bernard Joseph; Queen's; retired salesman; mem. Queen's Intercollegiate title team '37; mem. '32 Tiger-Cats Grey Cup champions; end Argos '38-40; all-Cdn '38-39, mem. '38 Grey Cup winner; Big Four all-star outside '38-40; mem. '41 Winnipeg Grey Cup winner; end all-Argo ('21-41) team; res. Toronto, Ont.

THURLOW, Jim (shooting); b. 20 May 1948, Bridgewater, N.S.; given name: James Maxwell; m. Deborah Anne Egan; c. Christopher, Karen; Ashbury College, Queen's; garage operator; pistol specialist; NRA ntl title '74; holds several provincial records; specializes in standard pistol, centrefire competitions; mem. Bentio Juarez Games, Federation of Americas shoot teams '72-73; standard pistol silver, team gold standard pistol, team silver centerfire world '74; Ottawa RA Gun Club shooting award, NDHQ club championship award, Ottawa Valley League top gun award; res. Edwards, Ont.

TIHANYI, Jeno (coaching/swimming); b. 13 Jul 1936, Nagybaracska, Hungary; m. Catherine Elizabeth Ennis; c. Miklos, Sacha, Andrey; Normal School of PE, Hungary; UBC, BPhE, MPhE; UAlta, PhD; child physiology professor; swim coach 38yrs; prov team coach Alta 1yr, Ont. 6yrs; ntl team coach '78-87, '93; dir./chair. Ont. Swim Coaches Assn. '74-81; v-p. (research) CSA '80; dir/pres. Cdn Swim Coaches Assn. '82-87; coached 54 ntl, 24 CIAU titlists, 13 world record holders, 2 Olympic gold medallists, 11 ntl team members; 4 Swim Ont., Swim Canada coach of yr awards; OUAA '90, CIAU '93, CWIAA '94 coach of yr awards; 2 fed. govt achievement awards; Air Canada award '94; Ont. govt. special achievement award '94; Sudbury Sportsman of '80; 44 academic/professional/scientific conferences presentations; authored numerous articles, 1 book; life mem. Sudbury Science North Life; mem. Sudbury Kinsmen Sports, Ont. Aquatic, Laurentian Sports halls of fame; res. Sudbury, Ont.

TILLEMAN, Karl (basketball); b. 11 Jan 1960, Ogden, Utah; UCal, BSc, Brigham Young; lawyer; CIAU all-star guard, smooth ball handler with deft shooting touch; mem. ntl team '81-88; mem. '83 FISU Games gold medal, '83 Pan-Am, '84, '88 Olympic teams; 2 CIAU scoring titles; UCal all-time scoring leader with 2090pts in 79 games; 3 CWUAA all-star, scoring titles; 3 CIAU all-Canadian awards; jersey 30 retd. by UCal; 2 Mike Moser Memorial CIAU player yr awards; Calgary athlete of '82; tryout Denver (NBA) '84; fed. govt. excellence award '84; mem. UCal Sports Hall of Fame; res. Phoenix, Ariz.

TILLEY, Ray (softball): b. 27 Aug 1953, Toronto, Ont.; given name: Raymond Warren; m. Tracey Hopkins; c. Reagan, David, Evan; correctional officer; with Petrolia Squires won Allan Cup hockey title; smooth fielder and steady hitter; ntl men's fastball team; 4 Pan-Am Games gold; 2 ntl sr. titles; 1 ISC World gold medal with Toronto Gators; res. Bright's Grove, Ont.

TIMMERMAN, Jim (shooting); b. 23 Sep 1950, Amsterdam, Holland; Mount Royal Coll., UCal; accountant, tax consultant; pistol specialist; mem. ntl team '73-74, '77, '79-83; nationally ranked 1st rapid fire '81-82; silver individual rapid fire pistol, bronze team air pistol '82 Commonwealth Games; secty.-treas '78-79, v-p. Alta. Fed. of Shooting Sports; secty. Alta. Handgun Assn. '78-80; pres. Calgary Rifle and Pistol Club '81-85; intl Level IV coaches certificate; ntl Level III officials certificate; res. Calgary, Alta.

TIMMIS, Brian (football); b. 5 Dec 1899, Winnipeg, Man., d. 22 Aug 1971, Hamilton, Ont.; m. Ada Clements; c. Brian Jr.; distillers rep.; halfback, fullback Ottawa '24, Hamilton '25-35, '37; Grey Cup champions '28, '29, '32; noted for powerful, grinding, battering ram style rushes; played without helmet and suffered many injuries; coached Hamilton to '43 Grey Cup triumph over Winnipeg; mem. Canadian Football, Ottawa, Canada's Sports halls of fame.

TINDALE, Bill (skiing): b. 10 Jul 1925, Toronto, Ont.; d. 24 Aug 1996, Ottawa, Ont.; m. Barbara; c. Chrystie, Katharine; McGill; retd Fisher Scientific; began skiing mid-30s; Ottawa SC Night Rider '42-43; mem. Dawson Coll. CIAU champs '48; mgr. McGill ski team '50; co-chair. McGill Winter Carnival '51; average racer; Osler Bluff SC champion '56; chair. Laurentian Ski Zone competitions '56; conceived 1st race rating system in Canada; chair. CSA intl competitions comm. '57-59; founded ntl team '57; rewrote constitution/by-laws CASA; pres. CASA '65-67; CASA FIS comm. chair '68; dir. COA '67-76; helped establish Olympic Trust; established Young Olympians of Canada, jr. Olympics program; played role in bringing Olympics to Montreal '76, Calgary '88; chair. Cdn Ski Museum from '87; Montreal Sportsman's Assn. award of merit '66; Gala des Skiers award

'66; Air Canada ntl sports exec of '67; fed. govt. Centennial medal '67; Queen's Jubilee medal '70; hon. life mem. COA; mem. Cdn Skiing Hall of Fame.

TINDALL, Frank (football); b. 16 Oct 1908, Syracuse, N.Y.; d. 5 Oct 1993, Kingston, Ont.; m. Mary; c. Frank Jr., Charles; Syracuse, BA, BPHE; retd. professor phys ed, football, basketball coach; '32 all-Eastern guard, hon. mention all-American, Syracuse MVP; '33 all-star lineman Argos, Grey Cup champions; all-time all-star Argos tackle '21-41 era; football coach Queen's Golden Gaels '39-75, basketball '48-75; 8 Intercollegiate football titles, 1 ntl championship '68, OUAA co-champions basketball '56-57; college football coaching record: 112 wins, 84 losses, 2 ties; CAFA-CFL plaque for outstanding services to football in Canada; trophy in his honor awarded annually by CIAU via Carleton Old Crows to CIAU Football coach of year; mem. Canadian Football, Queen's Sports halls of fame.

TINDLE, Janice (tennis); b. 3 Jul 1950, Vancouver, B.C.; given name: Janice Lee; UBC, Arizona BA; avalanche predictor; ex-tennis pro; ntl -16 singles '66, -18 '67, with Michelle Carey -18 doubles '68, Jr. Federation Cup singles '68, ntl women's Closed '72; mem. 3 Federation Cup teams; Pepsi-Cola Sportsmanship Trophy '66; competed briefly as pro; coached Delta Airport Inn and with Tony Bardsley conducted numerous teaching clinics; avid skier, mem. ski patrol; Yukon mining field worker; res. Alta Lake, B.C.

TINLINE, Dorothy (badminton); b. 25 Dec 1921, Scott, Sask.; given name: Dorothy Carol; Brandon College, UofT; retd. HS phys ed teacher; 4 ntl open, closed ladies doubles, '62 open mixed, 8 Ont. doubles, '64 Ont. singles, 2 ntl sr. mixed, ladies' doubles, 7 Masters singles, 5 ladies doubles, ntl grand masters singles '81; mem. 3 Uber Cup teams; twice umpire world games, once Uber Cup; Cdn rep. IBF '81; ntl senior ladies's tennis doubles title '65; pres. Toronto Dist. BA '64-65, '73-76; chair. Cdn Badminton Officials Assn. '67-81; 1st Cdn to umpire All-England '73; head badminton staff York seminars '75-81; Ont. coach '73-81; 3 terms pres. OBA; chair. Uber Cup program '69; chair. Devlin Cup championships '68-75; CBA dir. '60-81, pres. '81; Sr. examiner IBA; intl badminton fed. exec. 6yrs; Centennial medal; Canada Winter Games silver team medal; H.I. Evans Memorial award; Ont. awards '71-81; special fitness and amateur sports achievement award; Donald Smythe award; Queen's Jubilee medal; mem. Canadian Amateur Sports Hall of Fame; res. Toronto, Ont.

TINSLEY, Buddy (football); b. 16 Aug 1924, Damon Tex.; given name: Robert Porter Jr.; m. Hazel George Stevens; c. Cynthia Diane, Jack Steven; Baylor, BPhE; retd. sales mgr.; tackle Los Angeles Dons '49; Winnipeg '50-60, 7 times WFC all-star, 4 all-Cdn 4; capt. Bombers 10 years; mem. 4 East-West Shrine all-star game teams; coached St. James Rams to 2 Western Cdn sr., 1 ntl championship; wife Hazel founded Winnipeg Bomberettes '52; mem. Canadian, Winnipeg Football, Man. Sports halls of fame; last known res. Winnipeg, Man.

TIPPETT, Karen (canoeing); b. 7 Apr 1955, Winnipeg, Man.; given name: Karen Mary; m. Gerry Irving; Carleton; BSc, UWO; accountant; mem. Rideau Canoe Club; ntl team '73-77; ntl sr. K2, K4 titles '73-76; with Sue Holloway NA

K2 title '74; mem. '73-75 worlds, '76 Olympic teams; treas. City of Gloucester; res. Nepean, Ont.

TIPPING, Cam (speed skating); b. 24 May 1955, Winnipeg, Man.; given name: Cameron John; UAlta; ntl team '73-80; ntl champion '77-80; 10,000m ntl record holder; mem. 2 jr. world teams; competed in sailing at ntl level; avid cross-country ski racer, cyclist; last known res. Nelson, B.C.

TKACZUK, Walt (hockey); b. 29 Sep 1947, Emsdetten, Germany; given name: Walter Robert; m. Valerie Kelford; c. Michael, David, Sarah; co-owner River Valley Golf & Country Club; centre Kitchener Rangers OHA jrs; minor pro Omaha, Buffalo; NY Rangers '68-81; NHL record: 945 scheduled games, 227g, 451a, 93 playoff games, 19g, 32a; asst. coach Rangers '81-83; res. St. Mary's, Ont.

TOBACCO, Terry (t&f); b. 2 Mar 1936, Cumberland, B.C.; given name: Charles Terrence; m. Norine Irving; c. David, Tom, Judy, Michael; Washington, BA, MSc; teacher; bronze 440, anchor silver 4x400 relay team '54 BEG; semifinalist 400m, anchored 5th place 4x400 Olympic relay team '56; bronze 440, anchored bronze 4x400 relay team '58 BEG; semifinalist '60 Olympics; 3rd 440 NCAA championships '59; NCAA all-American track team; 3rd ranked in world for 440 '58-59; ntl 440 champion '54-60; Pacific Coast 440 titlist '56-58; capt. Wash. track team '59; res. Victoria, B.C.

TOBIN, Lee (curling); b. 2 Feb 1922, Huntingdon, Que.; given name: Eileen Herdman; m. Bill Tobin; c. Sharon, Bill Jr., Bob; pitcher Montreal Royals softball team; skipped Ont. tankard runnerup '63, 4 Que. ladies' title rinks '70-75; ntl ladies' title rink '75 beating late Marj Mitchell in playoff; 3rd Que. mixed title rink '76; key role in boosting calibre of jr. curling in Que., NB, NS through clinics; mem. Canadian Curling Hall of Fame; res. Montreal, Que.

TOCCHET, Rick (hockey); b. 9 Apr 1964, Scarborough, Ont.; m. Lynne; power forward Sault Ste. Marie jrs. '81-84; NHL Philadelphia '84-92 (capt. '91-92), Pittsburgh '92-94, Los Angeles '94-96, Boston '96-97, Washington '97, Phoenix '97-99; NHL record: (through '99) 990 scheduled games, 411g, 466a, 121 playoff games, 47g, 53a; played in 4 NHL all-star games; 1 Stanley Cup winner; mem. Team Canada '87, '91 World Cup, '91 World championships; res. Phoenix, Ariz.

TODD, Margaret (golf); b. 31 May 1918, Montreal, Que.; given name: Margaret Sutcliffe; m. John Todd; c. John, Rick, David; 11 Victoria, 3 BC Ladies, 2 BC Srs., 2 ntl Srs., 6 Jasper Totem Pole, 1 Victoria srs. titles; mem. 9 BC amateur, 8 srs., 4 intl teams; 2yrs club capt., 3 yrs pres. Van. branch BCCLGA, 8yrs. BCCLGA exec.; 3yrs ntl rating dir.; devised rating system for Canada's female golfers '61; ntl teams dir. 3yrs.; CLGA board ntl rules, handicap dir. '83-85; life mem. Victoria Golf Club; with husband conducted weekly swim class for blind; mem. BC, Greater Victoria Sports halls of fame; res. Victoria, B.C.

TOLCHINSKY, Sol (basketball); b. 2 Jan 1929, Montreal, Que.; m. Margot Blatt; c. Ivy, Neil, Leslie; McGill, BA; exposition service contractor; mem. Eastern Cdn champion, ntl finalist Montreal YMHA juve. basketball team '44-45;

Eastern Cdn champion, ntl finalist Montreal YMHA jr. team '45-46; Horace Baitle Award jr. team MVP '46; mem. Que. jr. title team '46-47; ntl finalist sr. team '47-48; mem. '48 Olympic, '50 Maccabiah Games teams; Eastern Cdn finalist sr. team '48-49, ntl champions '49-50; mem. Golden Ball champion McGill team '50-51; mem. Montreal YM-YWHA Sports Hall of Fame; res. Westmount, Que.

TOMBS, Tina (golf); b. 4 Apr 1962, Montreal, Que.; given name: Tina Tombs; div. Tom Purtzer; c. Sarah, Heidi; Arizona State; 2 titles, twice all-American; won '79 NH jr., '81 NH state title, New England amateur '82, Eastern amateur '84; joined pro tour '87, career low round 64; won LPGA Jamie Farr Toledo Classic '90; res. Minneapolis, Minn.

TOMLINSON, Lesley (cycling); b. 26 Dec 1959, Vancouver, B.C; full-time athlete; former marketing mgr.; long competitive career in cross-country, marathon running before turning energy to mountain-biking and road racing; Commonwealth Games team time trial silver '94; competed '96 Olympics; res. Vancouver, B.C.

TOMLINSON, William (administration); b. 31 Jan 1912, Cedar Rapids, Iowa; d. 4 Aug 1991, Thunder Bay, Ont.; given name: William Sherwood; m. Marion Elizabeth McKay (d), m. Hazel Jean Campbell; c. William Sherwood, Laren Campbell, Colin Campbell; St. John's Coll., UMan., Queen's, BSc; construction co. pres.; played football UMan,; avid golfer, duck hunter; owner Port Arthur Arena; pres. Port Arthur Bruins '48 Memorial Cup team; life mem. Port Arthur Golf & Country Club; mem. NWO Sports Hall of Fame.

TOMMY, Andy Jr. (skiing); b. 1 Nov 1932, Ottawa, Ont.; given name: Andrew Bailie; m. Marion Dunning; c. Sarah Jane, Randy, Lisa, Michael; ski resort owner; prominent alpine skier 40s, 50s; mem. ntl team '50 world championship, '56 Olympic teams; ntl alpine champion '50; head coach, mgr. '60 Olympic ski team; mem. Canadian Skiing; Ottawa Sports Hall of Fame; res. Edelweiss Valley, Que.

TOMMY, Andy Sr. (football); b. 24 Dec 1911, Hartland, N.B., d. 23 Apr 1972, Wakefield, Que.; m. Helen Bailie; c. Andrew B, Arthur, Frederick; agronomist, statistician; backfielder Ottawa Rangers '31-32, Rough Riders '33-45 excluding 2 seasons with Argos WW2; 5 Grey Cup finals, 2 winners; Jeff Russel Memorial Trophy Big Four MVP '40; mem. Ottawa CSRA, NB, Ottawa, Canada's Sports halls of fame.

TOMMY, Art (skiing); b. 15 Dec 1933, Ottawa, Ont.; d. 25 Nov 1994, Ottawa, Ont.; given name: Arthur Roland Bailie; m. Marilyn Thorpe; c. Natalie, Jedson, Lizbeth; merchant, enterpreneur; dominated ntl alpine skiing '52-60; ntl alpine, Arlberg Kandahar, Ottawa Ski Club, Gatineau Zone, NY State, Que. Taschereau, Que., titles, 11th in world as mem. FIS team '54 world championships; mem. ntl team '54-60; broke ankle world's 1st pro ski race; coach Ottawa Ski Club, Gatineau Zone, ntl team; mem. Intl Competitions Comm.; coach Gatineau Zone, Que. teams through '74; mem. Canadian Skiing, Ottawa Sports halls of fame.

TOMMY, Fred (skiing); b. 24 Sep 1941, Ottawa, Ont.; sep.; c. Alexander Frederic; UofOtt, BComm; chartered acountant, dir., v-p. of finance, realty firm; mem. Canada FIS team '58 world championships, '60 Olympic team; res. Ottawa, Ont.

TOMSETT, Arthur (shooting); b. 19 Feb 1928, Vancouver, B.C.; m. Shirley; c. Terry, Danny, Kevin, Richard, Susan; Vancouver Institute of Engineering; retd. engineer; mem. gold medal team Canada Games '57; BC indoor, outdoor titles '73, Vancouver Island titles '73-74; mem. ntl handgun team, free pistol, centerfire, standard pistol '73-95; mem. Benito Juarez Games, '74 world championships, '75, '79 Pan-Am Games teams; mem. bronze medal centrefire team '75 Benito Juarez Games; team gold '79 Pan-Am Games; '82 SFC golden anniversary award for outstanding contribution to shooting; res. Saanichton, B.C.

TONELLO, Jerry (wheelchair basketball): b. 29 Dec 1956, Toronto, Ont.; York, BA, UofT, BEd; financial planner, Revenue Canada; 1st able-bodied player to compete in Canadian Wheelchair Basketball ntl championships; mem. Toronto Spitfires WBA team; coached basketball from '80; ntl team asst. from '91; res. Toronto, Ont.

TONER, Vance (administration): b. 10 Apr 1926, Edmunston, N.B.; m. Pauline; St.Thomas; retd. prof., dir. Moncton PhE&R dept.; coached intercollegiate hockey, football; founder, 1st dir. '65-76 school of PhE&R and Institut de Leadership, Moncton; NB rep. Ntl Advisory Council on Fitness/Amateur Sport; chair. task force on hockey in NB; mem. NBSHF, Canada's SHF selection comms; mem. Canada's Olympic Hockey comm.; chair NBSHF '70-71; consultant on fed. gvt. Ntl Sports Admin, Centre development, 7yrs dir.; co-author *Master Plan for Sport in NB*"; Queen's Jubilee medal; Moncton man of yr; St. Thomas Alumni, CIAU Austin-Matthews, CAHPER Tait McKenzie awards; mem. Order of Canada, Moncton Sports Wall, NB Sports halls of fame; res. Moncton, N.B.

TOOGOOD, Ted (football); b. 27 Aug 1924, Toronto, Ont.; given name: Alex Edgar; m. Joan Davidson; c. Sharon, Sandra, Sylvia, Shirley, Sonya, Glen; UofT, BA, BPHE, West Virginia, MSc; retd. teacher, Etobicoke HS, RIT AD; pro Toronto (CFL) '50-54, capt. '52, mem. 2 Grey Cup winners; Argos, CFL record for TDs scored on punt returns single game with 2 vs Hamilton '50; single-game punt return yardage mark with 155 on dashes of 90 and 65 yds for majors; Eastern all-star '53; res. Islington, Ont.

TOOHY, Ralph (football); b. 9 Oct 1926, Montreal, Que.; d. 20 Jul 1998, Oakville, Ont.; given name: Ralph Joseph Edward; m. Teresa Lyon; c. Gary, Gail (d), Sharon, Bruce, Colleen, Ralph Jr., Kevin; Loyola, Colorado Coll.; retd. salesman; offensive, defensive end 5yrs Montreal, 7yrs Hamilton; earned reputation as hard rock; mem. 3 Grey Cup winners; 3 time CFL all-star; shortstop, outfielder Snowden Fastball League, MVP, batting titles; Memorial Cup hockey semifinalist; mem. Loyola Sports Hall of Fame.

TORREY, Bill (builder/hockey); b. 23 Jun 1934, Montreal, Que.; given name: William; div. c. William, Richard, Peter, Arthur; St. Lawrence, BA; began NHL career '67 as exec.

v-p. expansion California Seals; GM expansion NY Islanders '72-92; built Islanders into dynasty which claimed 4 consec. Stanley Cups; club pres. '80-89, board chair. '89-92; stepped down remaining with club as consultant to '93; pres. Florida Panthers from '93; Panthers reached Stanley Cup finals in their third season, fastest ever for expansion team; Lester Patrick trophy '83; mem. Hockey Hall of Fame; res. West Palm Beach, Fla.

TOSH, Wayne (football); b. 7 Aug 1947, Kitchener, Ont.; given name: Wayne Kenneth; m. Marlene Grubbs; c. Tim, Amy, Casey; Richmond, BSc, BA; civil servant; Sarnia Northern HS athlete of '67; lettered 4 yrs football Richmond; pro Rough Riders '71-77; led EFC in interceptions '75 with 9; EFC all-star '75; mem. Grey Cup winners '73, '76; mem. Athletes in Action; mem. Sarnia/Lambton Sports Hall of Fame; res. Orleans, Ont.

TOTZKE, Bob (bowling); b. 6 Nov 1917, Kitchner, Ont., d. 13 Dec 1980, Kitchener, Ont.; m. Martha; c. Marilyn, John, Steve; bowling proprieter; helped organize K-W 5-pin bowling assn.; hosted ntl 5-pin finals, BPAO convention; 15yrs Zone C pres. BPAO; coach 3 ntl tournament title teams; chairman, treas. 32-team Golden Horseshoe Intercity League 24 years; averaged 255 in '70; mem. 2 Ont. title teams, rolled 21 400-plus singles; Builders of Bowling Industry Award '76; mem. Waterloo sr. baseball exec. '48-54; jr., int., sr. ORFU football; 2 holes-in-one.

TOTZKE, Carl (football/basketball); b. 25 May 1926, Waterloo, Ont.; given name: Carl Andrew; m. Lois Joan Pfeiffer; c. Sarah, Paul, Susan; Waterloo College, BA, McGill; retd. AD; football, basketball, hockey, t&f Waterloo College '44-49, football at McGill '49-50; K-W Dutchman ORFU titlists '53-55; mem. YMCA ntl int. basketball champions '51-52; coach Waterloo football '54-67; delegate FISU Games '73, '75; CIAU pres. '71-72, '84-85; CAUAD pres. '69-70; CIAU Austin-Matthews award; res. Waterloo, Ont.

TOUSEK, Yvonne (gymnastics): b. 23 Feb 1980, Kitchener, Ont.; strong on uneven bars, beam, floor exercises; competed '95-96 Worlds, '96 America Cup, Olympics; team, indiv. Floor exercises, uneven bars gold '99 Pan-Am Games; Cdn female gymnast of '95 award; res. Cambridge, Ont.

TOWN, Bob (basketball); b. 4 Oct 1949, Winnipeg, Man.; given name: Robert Frederick; m. Barbara Diane Bock; c. Sean Cameron, Andrew Curtis; UMan, BPhE, BEd, MEd; HS principal; second team all-Cdn UMan '72; mem. ntl team '72-73, '75-76; '76 Olympics; mem. St. Andrews Super Saints ntl sr. men's title team '75-76; 4 times ntl championships all-star; mem. Gillette All-Star touring team '72; plays at Masters level; coach regionally. provincially; res. Winnipeg, Man.

TOWN, Tom (t&f); b. 7 Aug 1893, London, Eng.; d. 29 Mar 1957, White Rock, B.C.; m. Roseta Chapman; c. Jean, Lillian, June, Tom; decorator; began competitive road running career age 10; English all-schoolboy champion, English jr champion at 16; emigrated to Brandon, Man., '10 making presence felt at provincial,, local levels before moving into ntl ranks '19; ntl 5-mile champion '19-22;

5000m title '20; 3-mile title '21; 800yd, 1-mile titles '24; competed '20 Olympics; named to '24 Olympic team but lack of funding forced him to decline; offered Chicago U coaching job; defeated only once in a Cdn championship meet when he lost a shoe in '14 race; awarded permanent possession of Coldwell Cup for winning Manitoba 5-mile Labor Day race so often; mem. Manitoba Sports Hall of Fame.

TOWNS, Tom (football); b. 17 Mar 1953, Edmonton, Alta.; given name: Thomas Leslie; UAlta; mem. varsity wrestling team; impressive running back Golden Bears before switching to linebacker; twice Western Intercollegiate all-star; CIAU all-Cdn lienbacker '74; on Eskimos protected list '75; mem. Eskimos '75-84; twice WFC all-star; mem. 7 Grey Cup finalists, 6 winners; res. Edmonton, Alta.

TOWNSEND, Billy (boxing); b. 6 May 1909, Durham, Eng.; d. 12 May 1985, Nanaimo, B.C.; came to Canada age 2; began boxing age 14; nicknamed 'Blond Tiger'; Cdn lightweight, welterweight titles before turning pro at 16; 300 career bouts, only 22 losses; fought 11 main events (including 4 world champions) at Madison Square Gardens against such big names as Billy Petrolle, Bat Battalino, Tony Canzoneri, Benny Leonard, Joe Glick; retd. from ring '34 but made comeback '36; had comeback run of 12 straight wins before being beaten on KO in 13th round of 13th bout; regarded by *Ring Magazine* as "greatest lightweight ever produced in Canada"; mem. BC Sports Hall of Fame.

TOWNSEND, Cathy (bowling); b. 8 Jun 1937, Campbellton, N.B.; given name: Catherine Champoux; m. Douglas Townsend; bank employee; lefthander; 6th world championships '69; with Joanne Walker of Montreal gold women's doubles FIQ American Zone championships, record 2285 pins, also silver, bronze medals; 3rd Cdn, first woman World Cup title winner '75; all-events title 23-nation Tournament of Americas '76 with 67,333 for 36 games; with Glen Watson, Diane Langlois, Jean Benard mixed foursome title; bronze women's singles; Montreal's Bowler of Year as chosen by Montreal Sports Writers; mem. Cdn 10-Pin Bowling, Canada's Sports halls of fame; res. St. Thérèse, Que.

TOWNSEND, Stephanie (skiing); b. 21 Mar 1948, Calgary, Alta.; given name: Stephanie Margaret; div. Dexter Williams; m. Gary Bucher; Notre Dame, BA; Alberta juvenile champion '60-61, jr. '62-64; ntl team '65-69; slalom, combined titles Lowell Thomas Classic '68; instructor Aspen, Colo., ski club '69-70; Rotary Sportsman's Award '63, Alta. Sportswoman's Assn. Award '67; res. Houston, Texas.

TRACY, Paul (motorsport); b. 17 Dec 1968, Toronto, Ont.; given name: Paul Anthony; div. Tara; c. Alysha Rachelle, Conrad; m. Liisa Hunter; race car driver; began racing karts age 8; ntl Formula Ford title age 16, youngest FF champion ever; competed in FF2000 '86 becoming youngest ever Can-Am winner at 17; raced in SCCA Escort endurance series, Mosport 24-hour, British Grandstand series '87; entered Indy Lights series '88 winning initial race at Phoenix; won 9 of 14 Indy Lights races '90 setting 4 race records, 6 qualifying records, 7 poles single season record, Bruce McLaren most promising driver award; mem. Dale Coyne,

Penske, Newman/Haas, Kool Green racing teams; 10 Indy Lights victories, 8 seconds, 7 thirds, 10 poles in 77 starts; competed on CART circuit from '96; regarded as one of quickest drivers in sport; most improved driver award '93; 14 CART PPG victories; joined Reynard-Honda team '98; res. Scarborough, Ont./Paradise Valley, Ariz.

TRAGER, John (bowling); b. 12 May 1927, Winnipeg, Man.; given name: John Emil Joseph; m. Elsie Hrenchuk; c. Mary Anne, Kathryn, Barbara; retd.; began 5-pin bowling '44; shifted to 10-pins '48; St. Joseph's league secty from '48; turned talents to administrative end of game '52 as director Winnipeg 10-pin Assn., pres. '61; founding mem. Man. 10-pin BA '94, secty-treas to '95; instrumental in formation Man. 10-pin Fed., pres. 17yrs; founding mem. Cdn 10-pin Fed, 5yrs sect-treas, 5yrs pres.; exec. mem. FIQ, auditor '87-91; dir. COA; life mem. Cdn, Man 10-Pin Feds; life mem. Winnipeg Bowling Assn.; Man. Sports Federation Outstanding Volunteer award '81; mem. Manitoba Bowling, Sports, Cdn 10-Pin halls of fame; res. Winnipeg, Man.

TRAWICK, Herb (football); b. Pittsburgh, Pa.; d. 16 Sep 1986, Hawkesbury, Ont.; off. lineman; one of 1st imports selected by Lew Hayman and Leo Dandurand for new Alouettes team '46; played 12 CFL seasons; noted for quickness he was 1st player 7 times all-Eastern, 5 as tackle, 2 as guard; one of few linemen to score a touchdown in Grey Cup competition; mem. '49 Grey Cup title team; retd '57; noted for outstanding charitable work in community; mem. Cdn Football Hall of Fame.

TREGUNNO, Jane (rowing); b. 9 Jul 1962, St. Catharines, Ont.; Cdn. Henley jr. pairs '78; sweep coxed 8s ntl championships '78, jr. worlds '79; silver coxed 4s '81 Royal Henley; won coxed 4s '83 Head of the Charles; silver coxed 4s '84 Olympics; mem. '80, '84 Olympic teams; res. St. Catharines, Ont.

TRELLE, Herman (t&f/wrestling); b. 8 Dec 1894, Kendrick, Idaho, d. 4 Sep 1947, Fontana, Calif.; m. Bernice Irene Burdick; c. 1 son, 1 daughter; Blairmore, Alberta College, UAlta; grain grower; 2 ntl field records; Alta. heavyweight wrestling title.

TREMBLAY, Thalie (fencing); b. 6 Jun 1967, Montreal, Que.; m. Denis Lauriault; c. Mathieu, Camille; UofOtt, BA; ex-SRC, self-employed; followed footsteps of grandparents, both world champions for France, by winning 3 ntl jr., sr. women's foil titles; achieved Canada's best-ever performance by placing 7th women's world foils '91; best-ever Cdn Olympic women's foil standing with 14th '92 Olympics; competed '88, '92 Olympic, '90 Commonwealth Games; fencing coach UofOtt; res. Hull, Que.

TRIANO, Jay (basketball); b. 21 Sep 1958, Tillsonburg, Ont.; SFU; coach; former Vancouver Grizzlies (NBA) dir. community relations, TV-radio color analyst; ex-SFU basketball coach; son of former Tillsonburg Livingston's star Howie Triano; guard ntl team '78-90; mem. Commonwealth Cup champions '78, FISU gold medal team '83; silver medal pre-Olympic '80, Jones Cup '82; mem. '79, '83 Pan-Am, '80, '84 Olympic, '79, '81, '83 FISU, '82 Brazil tournament teams; BC university athlete of '78; 6th round draft CFL Stampeders, 8th round draft NBA Lakers

'81, tryout Jazz '84; coach ntl team '99; mem. Cdn Basketball, Olympic halls of fame; res. Burnaby, B.C.

TRIFUNOV, Jim (wrestling); b. 18 Jul 1908, Yugoslavia; d. 27 Jun 1993, Winnipeg, Man.; m. Mary; c. Donald; retd. promotion mgr.; 10 ntl titles (9 bantam, 1 featherweight) '23-32; mem. '24, '28, '32 Olympic teams, bronze '28; gold '30 BEG; coached YMCA jrs., UWpg, Olympic teams '52-60; mgr. ntl teams '54, '70 BE, Commonwealth Games, '66, '70 worlds; pres. MWA 25yrs; v-p. CAWA; sec.-founding dir. Man. Sports Federation; chairman Man. Sports Hall of Fame; pres. Winnipeg Bowling Assn. '51-52; FILA medal '67 Pan-Am Games organizational work; gold star medal, dip. of honor IAWF for outstanding service to wrestling '76; Man. merit award; Centennial, Jubilee medals; Winnipeg Community Service award; street in Regina named in his honor; life mem. Winnipeg Central YMCA; hon. dir. Man. Sports Fed.; mem. Order of Canada, Cdn Amateur, Sask., Man., Canada's Sports, Cdn Amateur Wrestling halls of fame.

TRIHEY, Harry (hockey); b. 25 Dec 1877, Montreal, Que., d. 9 Dec 1942, Montreal, Que.; given name: Henry Judah; McGill; 1st man to utilize 3-man line leaving rover ro roam free and encourage defencemen to carry puck; starred in hockey with McGill, Montreal Shamrocks; rover, capt. Shamrocks Stanley Cup winners 1899, 1900; retired '01 with record of 46 goals in 30 games and 16 in 8 playoff games; secty-treas., later pres. CAHL leading league through disputes with Federal League '04-05; advisor to Wanderers; refereed many league, Stanley Cup playoff games; pre-NHL record of 10 goals in single game during regular season; mem. Hockey Hall of Fame.

TRIPUCKA, Frank (football); b. 8 Dec 1927, Bloomfield, N.J.; given name: Francis Joseph; m. Randy; c. Heather, Tracy, Mark, Todd, T.K., Kelly, Chris; Notre Dame, BA; pres. distributing co.; pro Detroit Lions, Chicago Cardinals, Dallas Texans '49-53; Saskatchewan '53-58, '63, Ottawa '59; all-conf. quarterback '54; record 216 completions '56 (since topped by Ron Lancaster), 3274yds passing; completed 158 of 257 passes for .615 percentage '55; had 29 intercepted '57; CFL record: 15,506yds on 1090 completions in 1930 attempts, .565 avg., 136 intercepted, 83tds; res. Essex Fells, N.J.

TRITES, Ev (curling/golf); b. 18 Sep 1912, New Glasgow, N.S.; d. 6 May 1984, Saint John, N.B.; given name: Evan Allison; m. Jean; ntl sales dir.; chair. CCA ntl mixed curling comm. '71-76; ntl sr. comm. '77-81; exec. NBCA '73-75, NBMCA '74-76; secty-treas. NBGA '75-83; exec.-dir. CPGA Atlantic Zone '77-83; chair. Saint John Canada Summer Games comm. '77, '85; nicknamed 'Mr. Organization'; Moosehead Sports exec. of '78; CCA award of merit '83; mem. Cdn Curling, NB, Saint John Sports halls of fame.

TROTTIER, Bryan (hockey); b. 17 Jul 1956, Redvers, Sask.; given name: Bryan John; div.; c. Bryan Jr., Lindsay Ann, Taylor Noelle; treaty Indian status; hockey coach; jr. Lethbridge Broncos; 2nd choice NY Islanders '74 draft; minor pro Swift Current, Lethbridge (WHL) '72-75; WHL MVP, 1st team all-star centre '75; Islanders '75-90, Pittsburgh '90-96; Calder Memorial Trophy '76; Ross, Hart

trophies '79; Conn Smythe Trophy '80, KingClancy Trophy '89; led Stanley Cup playoff scorers '80 with 29 points; twice NHL 1st team, 2nd team all-star; mem. 6 Stanley Cup winners; competed 8 all-star games; shares NHL record fastest goal from start of game (5sec.), record 27 playoff points consecutive yrs '80-82; holds/shared 6 NHL scoring records; topped 50-goal plateau with 50 '82; asst. Coach Pittsburgh '94-97; head coach Portland Pirates (AHL) '97; asst. Coach Colorado '98; NHL man of year '88; US citizen '84; mem. Team Canada '81, Team USA '84 Canada Cup series; NHL record: 1279 scheduled games, 524g, 901a, 221 playoff games, 71g, 113a; mem. Cdn Hockey, AHL halls of fame; res. McMurray, Pa.

TSANG, Tosha (rowing): b. 17 Oct 1970, Saskatoon, Sask.; McGill; mem. ntl team from '95; gold straight pairs, double sculls '93, quad '94 ntl championships; silver 8s '96 Olympics; McGill University Rowing Club most valuable female player '91-92; Association Quebecois d'Aviron volunteer of year award '91; res. Victoria, B.C.

TUBMAN, Joe (football); b. 18 Aug 1897, Ottawa, Ont., d. 29 Nov 1975, Ottawa, Ont.; given name: Robert Elmer; m. Madge Whyte (d.); c. Mary; railway employee; kicking halfback Rough Riders '19-29; capt. '25-26 Grey Cup winners; refereed, umpired interprovincial, ORFU 15 years; retd. end of '44 season; as canoeist Eastern tandem and ntl war canoe tiltes for New Edinburgh club; played city league lacrosse, cricket, golf, lawn bowling; mem. Canadian Football, Ottawa, Canada's Sports halls of fame.

TUCKER, Murray (golf); b. 2 Nov 1922, Mitchell, Ont.; given name: Murray Carlyle; m. Fleurette Prevost; c. Terry; retd. golf professional; Ont. Open champion '50, runnerup twice; Ont. PGA champion '58, runnerup twice; mem. Cdn intl teams; mem. Ont. team; CPGA match play champion; 3 OPGA srs. titles; CPGA srs champion '78; tied 1st Que. Open; twice runnerup CPGA; pres. OPGA, CPGA; Ont., Cdn club pro of year; Canada's 1st Master Golf Professional; mem. Cdn Golf Hall of Fame; res. Willowdale, Ont.

TUCKER, Whit (football); b. 15 Nov 1940, Windsor, Ont.; given name: Whitman; m. Heather McCuaig; c. Ken, Kelly, Diane, Wendy; UWO, BA; resident dir., investment consultant firm; all-city football, basketball Windsor '58-59; Ont. scholastic long jump record '58; Royal Arcanum Trophy Windsor's outstanding HS athlete '59; Intercollegiate all-star football '61; pro Ottawa '62-70; Gruen Award Big Four Cdn rookie of year; all-star twice; 3 Grey Cup finals, 2 winners; CFL record: 272 pass receptions for 6092yds, 52tds; avg. gain 22.5 per-catch, best in CFL; runnerup outstanding Cdn award '68; dir. Ottawa Football Club; trustee Ottawa Sports Hall of Fame; mem. Ottawa Sports, Cdn Football, UWO W-Club, Windsor-Essex halls of fame; res. Ottawa, Ont.

TUDIN, Conny (hockey); b. 21 Sep 1917, Ottawa, Ont.; d. 24 Oct 1988, Ottawa, Ont.; given name: Cornell; m. Lois Darlene Sinnett; c. Terry, Rick; St. Patrick's College; supervisor HS tech. training; mem. Rideau Jrs., 1st team to employ red line, '35-37, Eastern Cdn title '37; Harringay Greyhounds English League champions '38-39, first UK team to have games televised in Eng.; pro Montreal organization '39-40; defence, all forward positions Lachine

Rapides, Washington Lyons, New Haven Eagles, Canadiens; mem. RCAF Flyers '42-46, Eastern Cdn Allan Cup finalists; mem. Ottawa Allan Cup finalists '48, champions '49; Smith Falls Rideaus '50-52 Eastern Cdn finalists; '52-53 Brockville St. Lawrence League titlists; organized Ottaw Riverside Park minor hockey league '61 coaching mosquito, peewee, midget teams; coach Glebe midgets Ottawa Cradle League, St. Jean's jr. city league, St. James UC midgets; scoring titles Rideau Jrs, Lachine Rapides, RCAF Flyers; mem. Ottawa Old Timers Hockey comm. '71-88; mem. Hockey Hall of Fame as mem. Flyers and Senators.

TULLY, George (fencing); b. 29 Aug 1914, Montreal, Que.; d. (circa 1990), Montreal, Que.; given name: George Victor; m. Rita Lumsden Seale; m. Barbara, Ann, Dianne Olivia, George Cornelius; retd. salesman; NBYMCA 3-weapon champion '29-35, '37-39; Que. sabre champion '33, '36-39; Que. foil champion '38-39; ntl sabre champion '33, '37-39; ntl foil champion '37-39; ntl épée champion '37-39; Que. duelling sword champion '34; ntl duelling sworld champion '35; Open City (Montreal) 3-weapon champion '39; mem. '36 Olympic team; coached McGill '40-70, BEG team '58; taught fencing 12 years NBYMCA, West Montreal YMCA.

TUPPER, Stephen (sailing); b. 6 Feb 1941, Vancouver, B.C.; given name: Stephen McGirr; m. Anne; c. Peter, Paul; UBC, BEd; exec. dir. BC Sailing Assn.; ntl team coach '73-80; 3 national Dragon Class titles; twice 3rd NA Dragon championships; 4th '68 Olympics Dragon Class; mem. Cdn One Ton crew New Zealand '71; mem. Cdn Onion Patch crew Bermuda '74, 2nd place; mem. Cdn Admiral's crew '75; coach Pan-Am Games team '75; res. Vancouver, B.C.

TURCOTTE, Bob (curling): b. 5 Mar 1944, Pembroke, Ont.; m. Kristin Holman; c. Jared, Sean, David, Alison; supervisor Ont. Hydro; competed 11 Ont. Tankards; 3rd for Bob Fedosa '79 Brier; skipped 2 ntl srs. title rinks; rep. Ont. 2 ntl mixed; wife Kristin 3rd Alison Goring '83 ntl jr., '90 ntl women's title rinks; res. Ajax, Ont.

TURCOTTE, Mel (harness racing): b. 30 Nov 1938, Mattawa, Ont.; 7th of 10 brothers educated in sport by father Theo; received P license at Batavia '58 but upgraded to A license after winning seven of 1st 10 races; criss-crossed US-Canada border for 12yrs before settling on Northfield Park as base of operations; enjoyed racing success with Essence Bear and Royal Cold; more than 2900 victories with purses exceeding $8M; res. Coconut Creek, Fla.

TURCOTTE, Ron (horse racing); b. 22 Jul 1941, Drummond, N.B.; given name: Ronald Morel; m. Gaetane; c. 4 daughters; Academie Notre Dame; ntl jockey of '62-63; 1st Cdn jockey to win successive Kentucky Derbys with Riva Ridge, Secretariat; twice winner Kentucky Derby, Preakness, Belmont; 1 of 3 Cdn jockeys to win thoroughbred racing's Triple Crown with Secretariat '73; Man. Centennial Derby '70; twice winner Cdn International Stakes; other major stakes wins include Wood Memorial, Coaching Club American Oaks; career record: 3032 victories, 2897 seconds, 2559 thirds with purses totalling $28,606,490; career ended with crippling injury sustained in race mishap '78; Cdn horse racing man of yr '78; French Cdn athlete of '73 award; mem.

Order of Canada, Canadian Horse Racing, Ntl Museum of Racing (US), Long Island, Canada's, NB Sports halls of fame; res. Grand Falls, N.B.

TURGEON, Melanie (skiing); b. 21 Oct 1976, Alma, Que.; began skiing age 3; ntl team mem. from '92; combined bronze '93 world jr. championships; ntl GS title '93; EC Super G silver '93; competed '94, '98 Olympics; res. Quebec City, Que.

TURGEON, Pierre (hockey); b. 28 Aug 1969, Rouyn, Que.; m. Elizabeth; c. Elizabeth, Alexandra, Dominic; pitched in Little League World Series; centre Granby '85-87; Cdn ntl team '86; 1st overall draft pick Buffalo '87-91, NY Islanders '91-95, Montreal '95-96, St. Louis '97-99; QMJHL Michel Beregeron rookie, Mike Bossy top pro prospect awards '87; Lady Byng trophy '93; 4 NHL all-star games; topped 50-goal plateau 58 '93; reached 1000 point plateau '99; NHL record: (through '99) 877 scheduled games, 397g, 600a, 72 playoff games, 29g, 39a; res. Rosemere, Que.

TURNBULL, Alex (lacrosse); b. 6 Dec 1883, Paris, Ont., d. 27 Aug 1956, Vancouver, B.C.; top scorer '08 Olympic team; mem. New Westminster Salmonbellies 1897-1909; 6 championship teams including 1900 world title team; mem. Canadian Lacrosse, BC Sports halls of fame.

TURNBULL, Barbara (golf); b. 6 Apr 1933, Saskatoon, Sask; given name: Barbara Lois Stone; m. William Turnbull (d); m. Danahar; 18 Saskatoon Riverside Club titles; from '58 mem. 24 provincial amateur teams; 9 Sask. titles, 6 times runnerup; runnerup ntl women's amateur '69; mem. Sask. team which tied BC for '67 interprovincial title; capt. Women's World Games team '70; mem. '73 international matches team; 13 Saskatoon city titles; low amateur Winnipeg Glendale pro-amateur; Saskatoon sportswoman of '67; mem. Sask., Saskatoon Sports halls of fame; last known res. Saskatoon, Sask.

TURNBULL, Ian (hockey); b. 22 Dec 1953, Montreal, Que.; given name: Ian Wayne; m. Inge Plug; c. Thea, William; UofOtt; financial advisor; Jr. A Ottawa 67's; 3rd Toronto choice, 15th overall '73 amateur draft; pro Maple Leafs '73-81, Los Angeles '81-82, Pittsburgh '82; Toronto club record for defenceman with 22 goals '76-77; club, NHL record most goals 1 game by defenceman with 5 vs Detroit 2 Feb '77; NHL record: 626 scheduled games, 123 goals, 317 assists, 55 playoff games, 13 goals, 32 assists; with partners opened Toronto's first wine bar 'Grapes' '77; res. Redondo Beach, Calif.

TURNBULL, Ray (curling); b. 19 Jul 1939, Huntsville, Ont.; given name: Charles William; m. Valerie Marcia Kaplan; c. Scott Douglas, Lori Dawn, Leanne Elizabeth; insurance agent, TSN curling color commentator; all-star jr. linebacker; mem. Man, jr. title rink '58; all-star lead '65 Man., Brier title rink, world championships; trained 11 world champions; 1 of 4 ICF umpires; chief umpire 6 world jr., 4 Silver Brooms; mem. Cdn Curling Hall of Fame; res. Winnipeg, Man.

TURNER, Dave (soccer); b. 11 Oct 1903, Edinburgh, Scotland; d. 6 Apr 1989, Victoria, B.C.; given name: David

Binnie; m. Margaret; c. Sandra Jean, David Robert; UBC, BSA, BA, MA, hon. PhD, Cornwall '46; retd. deputy minister; standout St. Andrews, Cumberland United; vs ntl champion Nanaimo kicked 5 goals in 2-games series; BC title, Connaught Cup semifinals with Cumberland; 1yr pro in US then joined Toronto Ulster United; rejected '24 offer to join ntl all-stars on Australian tour but accepted '27 invitation for New Zealand tour; 9 seasons New Westminster Royals, 4 ntl titles; mem. BC, Canada's Sports halls of fame.

TURNER, John (t&f); b. 7 Jun 1929, Richmond, Surrey, Eng; given name: John Napier; m. Geills McCrae Kilgour; c. Elizabeth, Michael, David, Andrew; St. Patrick's College, UBC, BA, Oxford, BA, BCL., MA, Paris; lawyer (QC), retd. politician; ntl jr. 100, 220yd sprint champion '47; mem. English t&f team '50-51; Lib MP '62-76; cabinet minister various portfolios '65-76; Cdn. Prime Minister '84; leader of opposition '84-86; res. Toronto, Ont.

TURNER, Lloyd (builder/hockey); b. 1884 Elmvale, Ont.; d. 7 Apr 1976, Calgary, Alta.; played with Sault Ste. Marie Ont. McNamaras; player/coach/mgr. Ft. William; moving to Calgary had ice installed in old roller rink and organized team and league from which Calgary Tigers emerged to unsuccessfully challenge for '24 Stanley Cup; moved to Minneapolis and Seattle before returning to Calgary and organizing Western Canada League '31; instrumental in resurgence of Allan Cup early '30s; organized Alta. Indian tribes into tournament competition; mem. Hockey Hall of Fame.

TURVILLE, Frank (football); b. 23 Sep 1907, Port Arthur, Ont., d. 8 Jan 1984, Toronto, Ont.; given name: Franklin David; m. Reta Lowry; c. Mary Ann, Nancy, William David; UWO, BA, Osgoode Hall, LLD; lawyer, QC; outstanding scholar-athlete Windsor HS '25; punter, receiver, running back Argos '28-31, capt., Jeff Russel award '30; Hamilton Tigers '32-36; mem. '32 Grey Cup winner; mem. 1st CP all-star team '32, repeat through '35; powerful punter; 116 CFL career singles, 27 in '32 season; Hamilton alderman '35; mem. W-Club Sports Hall of Fame.

TWA, Don (curling); b. 2 Nov 1935, Coronation, Alta.; given name: Donald Ross; m. Kathleen Ellen McGinnis; c. Sherry Leigh, Kelly Ross, Ronald Terrence, Donald Wade, Mark Jeffery; hotelman, journeyman plumber, pipefitter; 4 Northern Alta. zone men's titles, 1 mixed; 8 Yukon zone men's, 3 mixed titles; 1st skip NWT-Yukon entry '75 Brier posting 8-3 record, all-star skip; '77 Brier was 5-6; last known res. Whitehorse, Yukon.

TWADDLE, Tim (harness racing): b. 21 Aug 1962, St. Catharines, Ont.; Niagara College; broke into sport with John Burns stable in '80s; plagued by injuries throughout career, he has even undergone heart surgery but managed to forge impressive record; through '97 1385 victories with purses exceeding $10M; 27 major stakes race victories; drove Hardie Hanover to '94 Breeders Crown; res. Meadow Lands, Pa.

TYTLER, Donald (sailing); b. 8 Mar 1924, Toronto, Ont.; given name: Donald Milne; m. Elizabeth Osbourne; c. John, Ian, Margaret; UofT, BASc.; retd. mechanical engineer; crew mem. 6-metre team '52 Olympics, '56 Olympics Dragon team; mem. *Globe and Mail* 6-metre NA title team '54; mem. '46-48 Bartnel Trophy 8-metre title crew for Great Lakes; res. Don Mills, Ont.

U

UDVARI, Frank (hockey/officiating); b. 2 Jan 1924, Miltec, Yugoslavia; m. Colette Reinhardt; c. Martin, Jane; supervisor NHL officials; officiated OMHA 2yrs, OHA 4yrs; pro '51 refereeing 718 regular season, 70 NHL playoff games, 229 AHL, 7 WHL, 15 EHL, 7 CHL games; AHL referee-in-chief; conducted hockey schools across Canada and US, 2 in Germany for Cdn army; introduced 3-man officiating system to Finland '74; mem. Waterloo County, Hockey halls of fame; res. Waterloo, Ont.

ULLMAN, Norm (hockey); b. 26 Dec 1935, Provost, Alta.; given name: Norman Victor Alexander; m. Bibiane Goueffic; c. Gordon, Linda, Lori; business exec.; mem. 2 provincial bantam title teams, leading scorer bantam, peewee, midget, juvenile, junior; mem. provincial midget, juvenile title teams; Memorial Cup finals Edmonton Jr. Oil Kings; jr. league scoring record 55 goals, 46 assists in 36-game schedule; pro Edmonton Flyers (WHL), Detroit (NHL) '55-68, Toronto '68-75, WHA Edmonton Oilers '75-77; p.-pres. NHL Players Assn.; 7th in NHL history to score 400 goals; NHL-WHA record: 537g, 822a, 106 playoff games, 30g, 53a; mem. Toronto Old Stars HC; mem. Hockey, Alta. Sports halls of fame; res. Toronto, Ont.

UMEH, Stella (gymnastics): b. 27 May 1975, Toronto, Ont.; all-around competitor; began competing age 6; called in as last minute replacement '90 Commonwealth Games and led Cdn team to gold medal; subsequently competed in '92 Olympics, worlds, '93 world gymnastics challenge; 2 gold, 1 silver '94 Commonwealth Games; retd. from competition '94; res. Mississauga, Ont.

UNDERHILL, Barbara (figure skating); b. 24 Jun 1963, Pembroke, Ont.; given name: Barbara Ann; m. Rick Gaetz; c. Stephanie (d), Samantha, Matthew; with Paul Martini ntl, world jr. pairs titles '78; International GP; '79 St. Gervais, Oberstdoff; ntl srs. '79-84; St. Ivel, NHK Challenge Cup, Ennia Challenge, Skate America; mem. '79-84 Worlds, '80, '84 Olympic, '79 Moscow Skate teams; bronze '83, gold '84 Worlds; pro '84-98; TV skating analyst; mem. Cdn Amateur Sports, Cdn Figure Skating halls of fame; res. Mississauga, Ont.

UNDERHILL, Beth (equestrian): b. 5 Sep 1962, Guelph, Ont.; began riding age 7 at Georgetown Y; despite winning singing awards from Royal Conservatory her riding interests took precedence; following successful junior/amateur career moved into jumper competition at 21 with Sagan, winning Ont. Open jr. titles '84, '86; with Monopoly won 6 World Cup qualifying events; mem. ntl team from '90; mem. 3 Bank of Montreal Nations Cup title teams; team, individual silver '91, team bronze '99 Pan-Am Games; 2 ntl show jumping titles; Cdn World Cup League champion '93; competed '92 Olympics; coached by Torchy Millar; res. Schomberg, Ont.

UNDERHILL, Eileen (badminton); b. 1 Apr 1899, Moosomin, Sask.; d. 31 Jul 1988, Vancouver, B.C.; given name: Margaret Eileen Stuart George; m. John Edward Underhill (d); c. John Gerald, Charles Stuart; 12 BC singles titles, shared 11 BC ladies' doubles, 5 BC mixed doubles; ntl singles title '27, shared 4 doubles and with husband John 4 mixed doubles; 1st husband-wife team BC Sports Hall of Fame.

UNDERHILL, John (badminton); b. 3 Sep 1902, Vancouver, B.C., d. 3 Sep 1972, Vancouver, B.C.; given name: John Edward; m. Margaret Eileen Stuart George; c. John Gerald, Charles Stuart; 5 BC, 2 ntl singles titles; 5 BC men's doubles, each time with different partner; with wife Eileen 4 ntl mixed doubles titles; first husband-wife team elected to BC Sports Hall of Fame.

UNDERHILL, Pat (speed skating); b. 24 Jul 1928, Edmonton, Alta.; given name: Patricia Gunn; m. John C. Underhill; ntl outdoor titles '55-56, '60-61, indoor '58; NA indoor '56, Alta. outdoor '56, '61, indoor '56-59, '61, Illinois State indoor '56, Montana State indoor '56-58, BC outdoor '59-61, indoor '59, '61, Northwest Intl indoor '60; 4 ntl, 9 Montana records; mem. 2 world championship teams; alternate '60 Olympics; directly responsible for starting, developing clubs in Edmonton, Red Deer, Dawson Creek, Fort St. John, Regina, Calgary; conducted coaching clinics across Canada reactivating clubs in Montreal, Quebec City, Kitchener, Ottawa; mem. ntl exec., pres. CASSA '66; mem. Cdn Speed Skating, Alta Sports halls of fame; res. Toronto, Ont.

UNDERWOOD, Brad (softball): b. 27 May 1959, Owen Sound, Ont.; regarded as one of the outstanding left handed pitchers of his era; toiled with variety of top-notch teams including Owen Sound Tiremen, Toronto Gators, Green Bay All-Car; while noted for his brilliant pitching performances he also was a standout hitter; pitched 4 no-hitters in ISC world championship play, including perfect game '91; mem. Gators' '95, Green Bay '94 ISC gold medal teams; mem. 5 ntl title teams; wide array of ISC, ASA MVP awards; mem. ntl team '96, Owen Sound Tiremen '97; won total of 29 ISC tournament games '95; res. Owen Sound, Ont.

UNDERWOOD, Reg (softball): b. 7 May 1951, Sidney, B.C.; given name: Reginald Wayne; m. Julie May Wilson; Camouson College; carpenter; mem. Victoria Howard Russell rugby champions '70-71; Brentwood basketball tournament all-star centre '67, bantam sportsmanship award '66, Cordova Bay tournament all-star centre '68, Saanicton tournament all-star centre '68; Victoria all-star '71, Songhees Totem tour all-star '73; mem. 5-10 pin title teams '68-75; mem. Victoria Bate fastball team '74-77; Victoria Budget team '78-81; 7 BC, 4 ntl title teams; mem. '76 world, '78 Pan-Am title teams; 2 tournament MVP awards; 11 times tournament all-star; 5 team of year awards; '75 City of Victoria plaque; Brentwood League MVP '71; Stuffy McGinnis Invitational top batter, MVP '73; Senior C batting champion '72; major men's, Campbell River batting titles '73; Victoria all-native tournament all-star; Tom Longboat top native athlete award; mem. Greater Victoria Sports Hall of Fame; res. Victoria, B.C.

UNGER, Garry (hockey); b. 7 Dec 1947, Edmonton, Alta.; given name: Garry Douglas; hockey coach; jr. Calgary, London Nationals; pro '66-67 Tulsa (CPHL), Rochester (AHL); Toronto '67-68, Detroit '68-71, St. Louis '71-79, Atlanta '79-80, Los Angeles '80-81, Edmonton '81-83; NHL consec. games played record 914 from 24 Feb '68-21 Dec '79; NHL record: 1105 scheduled games, 413g, 391a, 52 playoff games, 12g, 18a; coach Tulsa Oilers, '93 CHL champions, CHL coach of '93; coach New Mexico Scorpions (WPHL); res. New Mexico.

UNGERMAN, Irv (boxing); b. 1 Feb 1923, Toronto, Ont.; given name: Irving; m. Sylvia Rothstein; c. Shelley, Howard, Temmi; retd. poultry processor, real estate agent, boxing promoter; active soccer, hockey player, boxer at YMCA; fought for Toronto 105lb title '39; during 3 years RCAF service fought at 135lbs, also served as phys ed officer; managed, promoted careers of numerous fighters in ntl heavyweight champion George Chuvalo, Cdn, Commonwealth welterweight champion Clyde Gray; agent for Trevor Berbick; *All-Canada Sports and City TV* Trophy '73; Jack Allen Trophy for contribution to world boxing '65-66; active fund raiser Cdn Maccabiah Games Assn.; mem. Canadian Boxing Hall of Fame; res. Toronto, Ont.

UPPER, Wray (baseball); b. 18 May 1931, Port Colborne, Ont.; m. Helen Bartok; c. Cindy, Shawn, Lisa; retd. supervisor; NY Giants organization '51-52; Sr. IC Galt '53-55, '57-72, Kitchener '56, Brantford '73-74; Sr. IC record: .289 lifetime BA; led league hitters '58 with .413; twice led league in hits, triples, once runs scored; managed Galt '62-67, '70-72, 113-157 record; 1st team all-star third base 6 times, mgr once, 2nd team third base 5 times; mem. Ont. team '69 Canada Games; res. Cambridge, Ont.

UPTON, Eric (football); b. 29 Apr 1953, Ottawa, Ont.; given name: Eric Thomas; m. Nancy; Colorado, UofOtt; son of former Rough Rider star Joe Upton; jr. Ottawa Sooners; twice OQIFC all-star offensive guard; UofOtt outstanding lineman award '74; pro Edmonton '76-85; WFC all-star guard; mem. 5 Grey Cup winners; mem. Nepean Sports Wall of Fame; res. Ottawa, Ont.

URBAN, Faye (tennis); b. 28 Oct 1945, Windsor, Ont.; m. William Mlacak; Windsor Teachers' College; bank employee; ntl -13 singles '58; with Brenda Nunns -15 doubles '60, -18 doubles, singles '61-62; with Nunns women's doubles, with David Body mixed doubles '65; with Vicki Berner women's doubles '66-69; closed singles '68-69, open singles '69; mem. '66-70 Federation Cup team, capt. '68; mem. Windsor-Essex County Sports Hall of Fame; res. Toronto, Ont.

URNESS, Ted (football); b. 23 Jun 1937, Regina, Sask; given name: Harold; m. Jacquelyn Joy; c. Mark, Dee Anne, Daniel; Arizona, BSc; pres. auto equipment sales co.; Governor's Trophy UAlta MVP '60;. Roughriders '61-70; all-Cdn centre '65-70; runnerup Schenley CFL lineman of '68; 3 Grey Cup finals, 1 winner; res. Saskatoon, Sask.

URSEL, Jim (curling); b. 22 Jan 1937, Glenella, Man.; given name: James William; m. Carol; c. Robert, Michael, Jill; retd. personnel mgr. Air Canada; Man. schoolboy title, ntl final playoff loser '54; all-star third '62 Brier; skipped Que. to 6 Briers, '77 title; finalist '77 Silver Broom; '77-78 Kronenbourg Trophy, Switzerland; twice Brier all-star skip; CBC championship '75; Ross Harstone Trophy '77 Brier; overall Brier record 48-27; 2 ntl sr. men's titles; coached sons to '84 Pepsi Jr. title rink; coached 3 other ntl jr title, 2 men's world rinks; mem. Man., Canadian Curling Hall of Fame; res. Kelowna, B.C.

URSULIAK, Wally (curling); b. 30 Jun 1929, Edmonton, Alta.; m. Kathleen VanKleek; c. Ken, Robin, Kelly; pro curling instructor, freelance broadcaster; Pittsburgh Pirates baseball training camp '51; lead for Hec Gervais '61-62 Briers, Brier, world titles '61; ntl Open, Edmonton Masters, Tournament of Champions titles '65; coached European curlers including world champions Otto Danieli of Switzerland, Kjell Oscarius of Sweden; coached '75 ntl Lassies champion Lee Tobin of Que.; res. Edmonton, Alta.

UTECK, Larry (football/coaching): b. 9 Oct 1952, Thornhill, Ont.; m. Sue; c. Luke, Cain; Colorado, Wilfrid Laurier; athletic dir., football coach, politician; guard/db in CFL with Toronto (74-76), BC ('77), Montreal ('78-80); Eastern all-star '75-76; competed in Gator Bowl, Atlantic Bowl; asst. coach Saint Mary's '82, head coach '83-98; AD from '96; 2 Frank Tindall CIAU coach of year awards; ex-Halifax alderman; diagnosed with ALS '98; res. Halifax, N.S.

VACHON, Brian (bobsleigh); b. 10 Aug 1951, Moncton, N.B.; m. Marla Marino; c. Margo;Carleton, BSc; marketing consultant; offensive tackle Carleton football team '71-76; mem. natl. team 2- & 4-man crews, generally as brakeman, '72, '77-78 World championships; '76, '80 Olympics; driver '80; TV Olympic sports commentator'88, '92; res. Gloucester, Ont..

VACHON, Rogie (hockey); b. 8 Sep 1945, Palmarolle, Que.; given name: Rogatien Rosaire; m. Nicole Blanchard; c. Nicholas, Jade, Mary Joie; hockey exec.; jr. Thetford Mines; pro Quebec (AHL) '65-66, Houston (CPHL) '66-67; Montreal for Stanley Cup playoffs '67; remained until '71, Los Angeles '71-78, Detroit '78-80, Boston '80-82; shared '67-68 Vezina Trophy with Gump Worsley; twice 2nd team all-star; MVP Team Canada '76; Kings' most inspirational player '73; *Hockey News* player of '75; Red Rose award by Hospital Charities Assn., Brian Piccolo award nominee '75; NHL record: 795 scheduled games, 355-291-127, 51so, 2.99 avg.; 48 playoff games, 2so, 2.77 avg,; mem. 2 Stanley Cup winners; asst. coach LA '82-84, '95, GM '84-92; asst. to chair Bruce McNall '92-95; LA pres. '95-97; v-p. special projects '97-99; jersey #30 retired by Kings; res. Los Angeles, Calif.

VADNAIS, Carol (hockey); b. 25 Sep 1945, Montreal, Que.; given name: Carol Marcel; hockey scout; jr. Montreal OHA; defenceman Montreal '66-68, Oakland '68-70, California '70-72, Boston '72-75, NY Rangers '75-82, New Jersey '82-83; NHL playing record: 1087 scheduled games, 169g, 418a, 106 playoff games, 10g, 40a; mem. 2 Stanley Cup winners; asst. coach Rangers '83-84; scout/asst coach Canadiens '93-95; res. New York, N.Y.

VAIL, Red (football); b. 10 Dec 1908, St. Thomas, Ont.; given name: Howard; m. Vivien Beardall (d); c. Barry; retd credit mgr.; 5-mile cross-country HS titlist; middle wing St. Thomas Jr. ORFU '27-29, Eastern Cdn title '28; Ont., Eastern, ntl titles '29; Argos '30-38, 3yrs middle wing under coach Buck McKenna; coach Lew Hayman switched him to snapback (centre) 5yrs; mem. 3 Grey Cup title teams; res. Weston, Ont.

VAILLANCOURT, Michel (equestrian); b. 26 Jul 1954, St. Felix de Valois, Que.; m. Carolyn; Ottawa Winter Fair puissance title '72; only Cdn to place (3rd) in Lake Placid Grand Prix '75; rode Branch County, a converted race horse, placed high in variety of Rothman's Grand Prix competitions; silver '76 Olympics; mem. bronze jumping team '75 Pan-Am Games; Royal Winter Fair Nation's Cup '79; Spruce Meadows jumping title '80; team gold Rotterdam Nations Cup '80; World Cup preliminary title Spruce Meadows '80; ntl, World Cup jumping titles '82; res. Mt. Albert, Ont.

VAIVE, Rick (hockey); b. 14 May 1959, Ottawa, Ont.; given name: Rick Claude; m. Joyce; c. Jeffrey, Justin; hockey coach; jr. Sherbrooke '76-78, Birmingham (WHA) '78-79;

1st Vancouver pick, 5th overall '79 amateur draft; Vancouver '79-80, '92, Toronto '80-87, Chicago '87-89; Buffalo '89-92; reached 50-goal plateau 54 '82, 51 '83, 52 '84; asst. coach Hamilton Canucks '92; coach/GM South Carolina Stingrays (ECHL) '93-98; head coach Saint John Flames (AHL) '98-99; NHL record: 877 scheduled games, 441g, 347a, 54 playoff games, 27g, 16a; WHA record: 75 scheduled games, 26g, 33a; res. Saint John, N.B.

VALENTAN, Walter (bowling); b. 23 Jun 1929, Graz, Austria; given name: Walter Johm; m. Connie West; c. Monica, Anita; tool engineer, bowling administrator; pres. Kitchener Bowlers' Assn. '68; dir. Ont. Bowlers' Congress '70; dir. public relations OBC '72; administrator Bowling Proprietors Assn. of Ont.; mem. Ont. 5-pin Bowling Hall of Fame; res. West Hill, Ont.

VAMPLEW, Des (shooting); b. 20 Aug 1955, Toronto, Ont.; given name: Desmond George Paul; m. Mary Gemorija; c. Timothy, Jonathon; York, BA; sales manager Dansk International Designs; hockey league MVP bantam, midget; '72 Strathcona award Canada's top cadet shooter, ntl prone indoor jr. smallbore titlist '72, '74; ntl jr. highpower champion '73-74; mem. '74 Royal Cdn Army Cadet Bisley team, top cadet honors (Bell Trophy) at Bisley; Lt.-Governor's gold medal '75-76 Que. HP championships; Que. HP title '77-78; Ont. HP '76, '79; Ont. SB '76, '78; Alta. HP '78; Atlantic HP '79; mem. ntl fullbore team '77-84; silver '77 ntl HP, 4th Governor-General's match; gold fullbore '78 Commonwealth Games; ntl HP title '79; bronze '79 Governor-General's match; Queen's Prize finalist Bisley '79, '81; mem. world fullbore championships team '80; gold Lord Tedder aggregate Bisley, finalist St. George's Prize Bisley '74, '81; mem. 9 Bisley teams, 3 as coach; mem. ntl smallbore team '82-84; gold English Match '84 Benito Juarez; 7 Ont. achievement awards; 4 Ont. championship certificates; hon. life mem. DCRA, ORA; life gov. ORA; res. Scarborough, Ont.

VAMPLEW, Edith (shooting): b. 15 Jun 1924, Toronto, Ont.; m. Thomas Vamplew (d); c. Patrick, Desmond; UofT; retd.; fullbore rifle specialist; mem. Ont. team '73 Canada Games; DCRA Tess Spencer award '78; commandant Cdn Bisley team '94; capt. Canada, Commonwealth, Unde-25 match teams; gov. Ont. Army Cadet League; mem. ntl Army Cadet League; life mem. ORA, DCRA; res. Whitby, Ont.

VAMPLEW, Pat (shooting); b. 24 Nov 1952, Toronto, Ont.; given name: Patrick Blakely; m. Donna Maria Marchand; c. Thomas Gil, Katherine Edith; UofT, BPHE, UWO, BEd; teacher; mem. '69 Bisley cadet team; ntl jr. fullbore rifle champion '73; mem. ntl smallbore team from '75; Florida State champion '76; Ont. indoor SB title '76; ntl 3-position title, pre-Olympic gold SB prone '76; team bronze Benito Juarez Games '77, '79-80; ntl open fullbore rifle title, Governor-General's gold '77; Ont. air rifle, standard rifletitles, Commonwealth Games fullbore bronze '78, smallbore prone team bronze '82; 3 team silver, 300m prone free rifle bronze '83, smallbore rifle gold '87 Pan-Am Games; tied 3rd world fullbore Bisley '80; 4 ntl prone championships; mem. '84, '88 Olympic teams; holder/co-holder 4 ntl records; 23 provincial titles; qualified for 13 Bisley teams; coach '90 cadet Bisley team; 9 provincial achievement awards; 2 Ont. championship certificates; SFC golden anniversary award '82; mem. bantam, midget hockey title teams; MVP awards;cross-country runner, winning '71 York League 300m, 3,000m, steeplechase titles, HS most valuable runner award '71; mem. Cdn Forces Sports Hall of Fame; res. Whitby, Ont.

van der KAMP, Anna (rowing): b. 19 Jun 1972, Abbotsford, B.C.; UVic; lifeguard, swimming instructor, recycling education co-ordinator; mem. ntl team from '94; 2 ntl titles; mem. women's 8s silver medal crew '96 Olympics; CARA female crew of year award with UVic '93; res. Port Hardy, B.C.

van der MERWE, Marina (coaching/field hockey); b. 7 Feb 1937, Cape Town, S.A.; Cape Town, Fredensborg, Denmark, Loughborough, Eng., teaching cert., Syracuse, BSc, Iowa, MA, Ohio State, PhD; asst. prof. York; mem. ntl team '65, '71; coached ntl team '76-95; guided ntl team from 16th ranking '76 to silver medal '83 world championships; coach '84 Olympic team; coach York.; fed. govt. excellence award '83; Air Canada coach of '83; CIAU FH coach of '95; res. Downsview, Ont.

VAN DINE, David (curling); b. 25 Jun 1948, Ottawa, Ont.; Carleton, BA, UofOtt, LLB; personnel mgr.; 3rd for Harry Adams 3 Ont. men's finals, skip for 2 others; competed 6 Ont. mixed finals, 5 as skip, Ont. champion '82, '86; ntl mixed champion '86; all-star skip '82 ntl mixed championships; res. Ottawa, Ont.

VAN HEES, Christie (racquetball); b. 5 Jul 1977, Kelowna, B.C.; Douglas Coll.; 7 ntl jr. titles; doubles gold '95 jr. worlds; 2 gold, 1 silver sr. ntls; bronze '96 sr. worlds; gold US women's open '96; 2 monitoring event gold; US Intercollegiate gold '98; world gold '98; competed '96 Tournament of Americas; '99 Pan-Am Games silver; res. Kelowna, B.C.

VAN HELLEMOND, Andy (officiating/hockey); b. 16 Feb 1948, Winnipeg, Man.; m. Cheryl MacDonald; c. Susan, Vanessa, Cynthia; retd hockey referee/hockey exec.; joined NHL ranks '71 making on-ice debut 22 Nov '72; went on to become one of top senior officials; worked 2 NHL all-star games, Rendez-Vous '87 series; worked 19 Stanley Cup finals; NHL record: 1475 scheduled games, 221 playoff games; as a '96 sendoff gesture on retirement after 25 yrs was fined $250 for incident year previous; v-p. hockey operations East Coast HL; mem. Cdn, Man. Hockey halls of fame; res. Princeton, N.J.

VAN KIEKEBELT, Debbie (t&f); b. 1 Mar 1954, Kitchener, Ont.; m.; c. 3; York, Ryerson PTI; broadcaster; mem. Scarborough Lions Track Club; ntl records midget hj (5'10"), lj (19'5 1/2") '70; 5th hj '70 Commonwealth Games, native, NA women's pentathlon record 5052 points '71; gold '71 Pan-Am Games penthathlon; mem. '72 Olympic team; shared Bobbie Rosenfeld '71 award with Debbie Brill; res. Toronto, Ont.

VAN RUYVEN, Andy (rowing); b. 9 Sep 1952, St. Catharines, Ont.; UWO, hons BA; salesman Xerox Canada; mem. Ont. gold medal 4s, 8s, 500m 8s dash '69 Canada Games; mem. ntl team '70-77, '80; mem. '72, '76, '80 Olympic, '71, '75 Pan-Am, 6 world championships teams; gold '72 English Henley, '75 Pan-Am, '76 Lucerne Intl Regatta, Yugoslavian Intl Regatta coxed 4s, '80 Nottingham Intl Regatta coxless 4s; ntl champion '70-77, '80; Cdn Henley champion '72-75, '78; UWO athlete of '75-76; St. Catharines achievement awards '75-76, '80; res. N. Vancouver, B.C.

VAN VLIET, Maury (administration); b. 3 Aug 1913, Bellingham, Wash.; m. Virginia Gaddis; c. Vicki, Maury Jr., Katharine Pieter; Oregon, BSc, MSc, UCLA, EdD; hon. LLD UWO, Windsor, UAlta., Dalhousie, Queen's; educator; coached basketball (2 ntl champions, 3 runnersup) t&f, football (6 Western Intercollegiate champions), rugby, gymnastics; responsible for 1st PhD program in PhE in Canada; 1st dean field of PhE in Commonwealth; dir PhE UBC '36-45; UAlta '45-75; pres. Commonwealth Games Foundation '75-78; exec. roles BC, Alta., ntl athletic, academic organizations; hon. pres. CAHPER, Edmonton Paralympic Sports Assn; mem. Cdn Assn. for Sports Sciences, National College PhE Assn. for men; fellow, American College of Sports Medicine; mem. Alta. Sports Council, chair. Advisory Comm.; Centennial Medal, Alta. Premier's Achievement award, Edmonton builder of the community award, Edmonton meritorious service certificate, Edmonton parks & recreation honor award, Citrus College, Calif. alumnus of year award, ntl, Edmonton CAHPER honor awards, CPSA pre-eminent service recognition; Churchill Bowl MVP award bears his name; mem. Order of Canada, Edmonton Sportsmen's, Alta., BC, Canada's Sports halls of fame; res. Edmonton, Alta.

VANDERBURG, Helen (synchro swim); b. 12 Jan 1959, Calgary, Alta.; given name: Helen Lena; m. Les Shaw; UCal, BPHE; operator Heaven's Fitness Club; mem. ntl team '71-79; jr. team titles '71-73, sr. team titles '75-77; 11 ntl solo, duet, figures titles; silver team '75, '79 Pan-Am, '76 Pan-Pacific, '79 FINA World Cup; gold duet, solo, figures '78 Worlds; gold solo, duet '79 Pan-Ams; gold solo, duet, figures '79 FINA world Cup; gold solo '79 Pan-Pacific; all events sweep '78 worlds, '79 Pan-Ams, Pan-Pacific, FINA Cup constituted unprecedented grand slam; Olympic team coach '96; 2 Elaine Tanner, 1 Velma Springstead award; Calgary athlete of '78; 3 times Booster Club of Canada athlete of year; Aquatic Federation of Canada female athlete of '79; mem. Cdn, World Aquatic, Alta., Cdn Amateur, Canada's Sports halls of fame; res. Calgary, Alta.

VANDERVLIET, Mary (t&f); b. 23 Jul 1912, Montreal, Que.; given name: Mary Catherine; m. Harold Graydon (d); c. James, Peter, William, Colleen; retd. telephone operator; 100m, 200m records Ont. championships '28; mem. '30 BEG, '32 Olympic teams; New Liskeard Hall of Fame bowling award; res. New Liskeard, Ont.

VARALEAU, Jack (weightlifting); b. 22 May 1922, Eastview (Vanier), Ont.; given name: James Patrick; rec. dir., retired RCAF; mem. '48, '52 Olympic, '50 BEG teams; placed 6th, broke Olympic press record '48; BE championship '48-50; gold '50 BEG; asst. mgr-coach '60

Olympic weightlifting team; Gil O. Julien trophy French Cdn athlete of '50; Ont. Sports Achievement Award; mem. Ottawa, Canadian Forces Sports halls of fame; res. Vancouver, B.C.

VARALJAY, George (fencing); b. 9 Mar 1941, Budapest, Hungary; m. Ilona Teglas; c. Shary, Nora; self employed; mem. Hungarian jr. fencing team; 1st class foil, épée ranking Hungary '58-61; competitive sailor '57-61; moved to Canada '69, Cdn citizen '75; Governor-General's tournament titles '70, '72; ntl champion '72-73; Eastern, Western Cdn titles '70-71, '75-76; mem. '75 Pan-Am, '76 Olympic Games teams; began coaching '77; last known res. N. Vancouver, B.C.

VARGO, Ken (football); b. 10 Jul 1934, Martins Ferry, OH; given name: Kenneth William; c. Laura, Bill; Ohio State, BSc; owner Capital Office Interiors; captained Martin's Ferry HS teams in football/basketball/t&f; Wigwam Wisemen ntl HS football all-American; centre Ohio State '53-55, co-capt, all-Big 10 '55; mem. '54 ntl title team; Hula Bowl, East-West Shrine game participant, Rose Bowl title team '55; centre Rough Riders (CFL) '56-58, all-star '56; participated East-West game '56; res. Nepean, Ont.

VAUGHAN, Eileen (parachuting); b. 1 Oct 1958, Halifax, N.S.; North Texas State, Dalhousie, BRec; versatile athlete competing in gymnastics, t&f, curling, basketball, volleyball, field hockey, ice hockey, soccer, box lacrosse, parachuting; competed nationally, internationally in box lacrosse; mem. '75 Cdn title team; 1st team accuracy parachuting Ont. Summer Games; 2nd junior style event '80; ranked 8th in world style '82; certified scuba diver; senior parachuting instructor; ntl Level III lacrosse referee; 3 times Canada Fitness award of excellence recipient; accomplished musician 5 instruments; made Dean's list North Texas State; technical asst. CSPA '81-82; mem. Cdn Forces Sports Hall of Fame; res. Halifax, N.S.

VAUGHAN, Kaye (football); b. 30 Jun 1931, Concordia, Kansas; given name: Charles Kaye; m. Lucile Wheeler; c. Myrle, Jake; Tulsa, BA, Kansas, MSc, McGill; school adminisrtator; lineman Tulsa '50-53; pro tackle Ottawa '53-64; team capt.; Schenley lineman of '56-57, runnerup '60; 10 times EFC all-star; mem. '60 Grey Cup winner, recovering fumble for game winning TD; above avg. skier, skilled diver; mem. Ottawa Sports, Canadian Football halls of fame; res. Knowlton, Que.

VAVRA, Greg (football); b. 19 Feb 1961, Red Deer, Alta.; given name: Gregory; m. Jody Jensen; c. Mitchell, Tyler, Jade; UCal, BComm, LLB; self-employed oil/gas consultant; quarterback HS MVP '79; WIFL leading passer 4yrs, twice player of year; quarterbacked Calgary Dinosaurs to Vanier Cup '83; Hec Crighton Trophy '83; North American single game passing record 627yds; QB Stampeders '84-85, BC '86-87, Edmonton '88; CFL record: 161 completions in 324 attempts, 1901yds, 10tds, 16 interceptions; jersey #17 retd. by UCal; UCal Sports Hall of Fame; res. Calgary, Alta.

VENTURA, Dawn (curling/softball); b. 23 Apr 1940, Ottawa, Ont.; statistician; catcher sr. softball teams '53-63; mem. 4 Eastern Ont. Sr. title teams, 2 Ottawa

Interdepartmental League titles; 3rd 6 OCA Divisional mixed title rinks, Ont., ntl titlists '86; '71 OVCA mixed champions, '72 Lady Gilmour Lem Cushing trophy winners, runnerup '73; skipped Ottawa Crystal Pebble grand aggregate title rink '71, 8 Eastern Ont. ladies' championships, 2 Ont. titles; mem. Ottawa RA Curling Club, Rideau CC; 3 times RA curler of year; twice RA female athlete of year; twice Ottawa ACT curling award winner; Ont. achievement award '74; mem. Ottawa CSRA Sports Hall of Fame; res. Ottawa, Ont.

VERBEEK, Pat (hockey): b. 24 May 1964, Sarnia, Ont.; m. Dianne; c. Kyle, Stephanie, Kendall, Haley; r/l wing Sudbury (OHL); league MVP '81; chosen by OHL coaches as hardest working player; drafted by New Jersey '82; played NHL with New Jersey '82-89, Hartford '89-95, NY Rangers '95-96, Dallas '96-99, Detroit '99; 1 Stanley Cup winner; played 2 NHL all-star games; NHL record: (through '99) 1225 scheduled games, 478g, 487a, 103 playoff games, 23g, 35a; active in Special Olympics, Leukemia Society; res. Avon, CT.

VERCHEVAL, Pierre (football); b. 22 Nov 1964, Quebec City, Que.; c. Samuel; UWO; 2 CIAU all-star; CIAU outstanding lineman '88; Eastern Cdn rep. '88 Shrine Bowl; pro CFL centre/guard Edmonton '88-92, Toronto '93-96; NFL tryouts New England, Detroit; CFL East, West, Northern all-star; 2 Grey Cup finals, 1 winner; res. Quebec City, Que.

VERNON, Mike (hockey); b. 24 Feb 1963, Calgary, Alta.; m. Jane; c. Amelia, Matthew, Dean; goalie (WHL), Oklahoma City, Colorado (CHL), Moncton (AHL), Salt Lake (IHL); drafted by Calgary '81; NHL with Calgary '80-94, Detroit '94-97, San Jose '97-99; 2 WHL 1st team all-star; Hap Emms Memorial Cup top goalie award '83; 4 NHL all-star games; mem. Stanley Cup winners '89, '97; NHL record: (through '99) 673 scheduled games, 347-223-83, 38,587min, 22so, 134 playoff games, 77-52, 7977min, 6so; shared William Jennings trophy '96 with Chris Osgoode; Conn Smythe trophy '97; 2 Calgary booster club athlete of yr awards; mem. '91 Team Canada World silver medal team; res. Calgary, Alta.

VERRECCHIA, Wendy (basketball); b. 27 Nov 1959, Montreal, Que.; Bishop's; centre Bishop's CIAU title team '83; MVP CEGEP nationals '78; 2nd team Que. all-star '81; mem. '81, '83 FISU, '83 Pan-Am Games teams; res. Montreal, Que.

VERSFELD, Mark (swimming); 13 Jun 1976, Edmonton, Alta; UBC; began swimming age 8; mem. Pacific Dolphins; coach Tom Johnson; backstroke specialist; mem. ntl team '94-99; competed '94, '98 Commonwealth Games; 100, 200m gold, 4x100 medley relay bronze '98 CG; set Commonwealth 200m backstroke record 1:59.39; bronze '95, silver, 2 bronze '97 Pan-Pacifics; silver, bronze '98 worlds; gold 100m backstroke '98 summer ntls; relay bronze '99 Pan-Am Games; res. Vancouver, B.C./Fort McMurray, Alta.

VESSELS, Billy (football); b. 22 Mar 1931, Cleveland, Okla; m. Susanne Wilson; c. Jane, Lance, Chase: Oklahoma, BSc; retd. Mackler Real Estate Dev. Co. exec.; 3 seasons under coach Bud Wilkinson Oklahoma Sooners; all-American '50, '52; Heisman Trophy winner '52; college record: 35tds, 2085yds rushing, 21 pass receptions for 391 yds; Sooners record (since broken) 1072yds rushing '52; rushed 100 or more yds single game 7 times, 5 in succession; 1st draft Baltimore Colts '53; opted for Edmonton CFL; initial recipient Schenley outstanding player award '53; joined Colts '56 after sitting out 2 seasons; 1 season with Baltimore, 215yds, 44 carries, 2tds, 11 pass receptions, 16yd avg., 1td; shelved by leg injury; TV football color commentator; avid fisherman; mem. Oklahoma, Sooners Sports halls of fame; res. Miami, Fla.

VÉZINA, Gèorges (hockey); b. 7 Jan 1888, Chicoutimi, Que., d. 26 Mar 1926, Chicoutimi, Que.; nicknamed "Chicoutimi Cucumber"; never missed league or playoff game in 15 NHL seasons; pro Montreal 1910-25; 328 consec. league, 39 playoff games allowing 1267 goals; mem. 5 title teams, 2 Stanley Cup winners; played most of career in era when goalers weren't permitted to drop to knees to muffle shots; trophy in his memory awarded annually to NHL goaler with best goals-against avg.; Chicoutimi arena bears his name; mem. Hockey, Que. Sports halls of fame.

VIDRUK, Kas (builder): b. 6 Oct 1925, Lithuania; d. 21 Oct 1986, Winnipeg, Man.; m. Phyllis; c. Michael, Shirley, Robin, Cheryl; educator; played football in CFL with Winnipeg '42-43, '52-56, Montreal '48-51; officiated CFL '57-74; mem. Man. Amateur Football Officials Assn. '56-76; founding mem. Man. HS Athletic Assn; mem. Pan-Am Games society facilities board '66-69; chair. Man. Sports Fed '78-81; board mem. SFC '82-85; v.-chair. Man. Sports Hall of Fame '79-85; mem. Man. Sports Hall of Fame.

VIELE, Vincent (jiu jitsu); b. 26 Nov 1938, Niagara Falls, N.Y.; m. Jean Jack; c. Wendy, Cindy, Billy; ironworker; judo brown belt '66-70; 1 year Tae Kwon Do; 4th degree black belt jiu jitsu; 3rd all-Cdn Randori competition '80; chief instructor Niagara College; Ont. distinguished service award '79; res. Niagara Falls, Ont.

VIGARS, Robert (coaching); b. 20 Feb 1944, St. Thomas, Ont.; given name: Robert Joseph; m. Julie Crouch; c. Jessica, Michele; Southern Illinois, BSc, CalState, MA; professor UWO; lettered in HS swimming, gymnastics, basketball, football, t&f; coach UWO men's cross country, t&f team from '68, women's teams from '72; head coach UWO men's, women's gymnastic teams '69-72; head coach London-Western t&f Club from '70; coached 3 CIAU cross country title teams, 3 OUAA cross country title teams, 5 OUAA t&f title teams, 7 ntl individual events t&f champions from '74, 29 OUAA individual events t&f champions from '68; Ont. coach men's decathlon from '74; co-coach ntl team intl decathlon/pentathlon '76; men's, women's Ont. t&f team '76 Olympic trials; Ont. coach women's pentathlon from '77; coach '79, '81 FISU Games; head coach t&f '81 Maccabiah Games; 5 CIAU X-C coach of yr awards; outstanding young Londoner award; top level coaching certification; meet dir. 10 gymnastics, 37 cross country, 128 t&f meets '68-80; noted for innovations in t&f programming at Intercollegiate level, particularly indoor meets; res. London, Ont.

VIGER, Andre (t&f); b. 27 Sep 1952, Windsor, Ont.; wheelchair equipment supplier; wheelchair athletics, specialist in long distances; gold 200m, 400m, 800m, 1500m '82 Pan-Am Games for Disabled; 5 gold ntl championships '83; gold, 2 silver '92 Paralympics; 3 world, 1 Pan-Am Games records; placed 10th '95 Boston Marathon; Officer Order of Canada '89; mem. Quebec, Terry Fox Sports halls of fame; res. Sherbrooke, Que.

VILAGOS, Penny (synchro swim); b. 17 Apr 1963, Brampton, Ont.; McGill; systems analyst; with twin sister Vicky 5 ntl sr., 1 Canada Games, 2 Swiss, 2 Rome, 1 Petro Canada Cup, 1 German, 1 Czechoslovakian duet titles; duet silver, team gold '83 Pan-Am Games; world team gold '82; FINA World Cup team gold '85; 1st duet in world to score perfect 10 '80 Swiss Open; fed. govt. world champion award '83, excellence award '84; retd. '85 then made comeback '90; res. Vaudreuil, Que.

VILAGOS, Vicky (synchro swim); b. 17 Apr 1963, Brampton, Ont.; McGillU; account exec.; see twin sister Penny for competitive, awards records; res. Pte. Claire, Que.

VILLENEUVE, Gilles (motorsport); b. 18 Jan 1952, St. Jean, Que.; d. 8 May 1982, Zolder, Belgium; m. Joanne; c. Melanie, Jacques; racing driver; ntl snowmobile titles '73, '75, world championship '74; Que. Formula Ford title '73; ntl driving title '76-77; US Formula Atlantic title '77; Molson Grand Prix Trois-Rivieres beating world class drivers James Hunt, Allan Jones; mem. Marlboro McLaren Formula 1 auto racing team '77; 1st GP victory for Ferrari Montreal '78; other GP victories Kyalami, Long Beach, Watkins Glen '79, Monaco, Spanish '81; in 67 GP starts won 6; runnerup to teammate Jody Scheckter '79 world driving title; fatally injured during qualifying run for Belgian GP when car crashed; shared Que. athlete of year honors with Guy Lafleur '75; Julien Trophy, Lionel Conacher trophy '79; spawned concert, became first patron Cdn Motor Sport Foundation; mem. Cdn Motorsport, Que., Canada's Sports halls of fame.

VILLENEUVE, Jacques (motorsport); b. 9 Apr 1971, St-Jean-sur-Richelieu, Que.; son of late racing great Gilles; Jim Russell racing school Mont-Tremblant Formula Ford 1600 title '86; Spenard-David racing school Shannonville F-2000 title '87; competed Italian Formula 3 circuit '88-91; Japanese Formula 3 circuit '92, 3 victories, 2nd overall; 3rd in first NA event Trois-Rivieres GP; mem. Player's Ltd. IndyCar team '93; won '94 Elkhart Lake 200, '95 Miami IndyCar; won '95 Indianapolis 500, 2nd '94; IndyCar rookie of '94; 1st Cdn winner Indy 500 '95; 3rd Toronto Molson '95; shifted to Formula One circuit with Williams-Renault team '96 placing 2nd initial race then scoring 4 GP race victories in rookie season to place 2nd in top driver race; added Brazilian, Argentinan, Spanish, British, Hungarian, Austrian, Luxembourg GP victories '97 to eclipse father's career GP victory total with 11; 1st Cdn to earn F1 driving championship '97; only driver to win on oval (Indy), permanent road course (Road America), street circuits (Miami, Cleveland); talented skier; 2 Lou Marsh, 2 Lionel Conacher trophies; mem. Canada's Walk of Fame; res. Monte Carlo, Monaco.

VILLENEUVE, Jacques (motorsport); b. 4 Nov 1955, Chambly, Que.; m. Celine; younger brother of Gilles; Que. snowmobile champion; moved into Formula Ford racing and established strong credentials; rookie of '79 NA Formula Atlantic circuit; NA Formula Atlantic title '81-82; Can-Am series title '83; qualified '84 Indianapolis 500 but accident in practice run kept him from race; world record qualifying for pole position '84 Phoenix IndyCar race; res. St. Cuthbert, Que.

VINCE, Anthony (t&f); b. 30 Jul 1902, Baltimore, Md.; d. circa 1990, Toronto, Ont.; given name: Anthony Joseph; m. Dorothy Margaret Cowan; c. Robert John, Dennis Jordon; UofT, DDS; dentist; sprint specialist; Riverdale HS champion; Broadview YMCA '22 gold medal 100yd dash champion; won '23 ntl YMCA title; gold 100yd dash, silver 200m '23 ntl championships; mem. '24 Olympic team; 3 Ont. 100yd dash gold medals.

VINCENT, Mark (parachuting); b. 12 Aug 1957, Winnipeg, Man.; given name: Mark Kenneth; contractor; m. Carol Whiteman; c. 1 son; 10yrs organized hockey, 3yrs competitive diver, 2yrs baseball; 10yrs competitive water skier, 3yrs snow skier, active gymnast; skydiving from '77; more than 1000 jumps; ntl 8-way, 3rd 4-way '79; ntl 4-way, 8-way '80; 2nd 8-way France '79, 4-way China '80; res. Victoria, B.C.

VINE, Bill (coaching); b. 27 Nov 1910, St. Catharines, Ont., d. 16 Jun 1983, Ottawa, Ont.; m. Winnifred Timmins; c. James, Joseph, William, Douglas; CIMA (Ind. Eng. & Management), IMMS (intl material man. & handling); Atomic Energy Canada; jumping coach Ottawa Uplands Harriers TC from '62; Ont. sr. jumping coach, advisor to Ont. tech. dir. t&f; Ont. official, Grade 5 referee; ntl instructor of officials; referee long, triple jumps '76 Olympics; officiated 2 Canada Games, provincial, ntl championships, Olympics, AAU meets; mem. jury of appeal Special Olympics '81.

VITARELLI, Dootch (lacrosse/hockey); b. 4 Aug 1921, Peterborough, Ont.; given name: Donato Anthony; natural athlete starring at rw in hockey, forward in lacrosse and standout golfer; mem. '49 Legion Ont. Sr. B title hockey team; mem. 3 Ont. Sr. B lacrosse title teams; 3 Mann Cup Sr. A title winners; retd. as player '53; mem. Peterborough Sports Hall of Fame; res. Peterborough, Ont.

VOGT, Kathy (speed skating); b. 7 Mar 1959, Elkhart, Ind.; m. Gregg;UMan, BPHE, UAlta.; 1 gold, 2 silver, 1 bronze '75 Canada Winter Games; ntl indoor, outdoor jr. champion '75; NA outdoor jr. champion, 3rd NA indoor '75; gold 500m, bronze 1000m, jr. world 500m record '76 world championships; 2nd world indoor championships '76-77; 6th overall, silver 1000m '79 jr. worlds; mem. '76, '80 Olympic, '76-81 world championships teams; Man. jr. athlete of '75; coach '81; res. Edmonton, Alta.

VOLPE, Jon (football); b. 17 Apr 1968, Kincheloe, Mich.; Stanford; running back; joined CFL BC '91-93, Las Vegas '94; CFL record 40 scheduled games, 42tds, 1 2-pt cvt, 511 carries for 2,654yds, 37tds, 100 receptions for 896yds, 6tds; 1 playoff game, 3tds; Jackie Parker, GMC rookie awards; 2 all-Western, 2 all-CFL all-star; set 2 CFL rookie records; res. Nevada.

VOLPE, Nick (football/administration); b. 23 Feb 1926, Toronto, Ont.; given name: Nicholas Peter; m. Rose Marie Masiello; c. Helen, Donna, Frank, Peter, Steven; UofT, BEd, MEd, BPHE; football administrator; retd. school supertindent, special education; mem. '48 Yates Cup winner; quarterback, defensive half Toronto '49-52; led Argos punt returners '49; 53 of 58 convert attempts '50; mem. 2 Grey Cup champions; HS football coach Port Credit 15yrs, 8 TCIAA, 2 all-Toronto titles; coached Lakeshore Bears '55-63, 1 Ont. jr. title; backfield coach Toronto Balmy Beach, '53 ORFU title; backfield coach. scout Argos '53-56; recruited Dick Shatto for Argos; scout Ottawa '56-58; author football text for CAHPER; CFRB radio football broadcasts spotter '65-68; isolation dir. CTV football '72-87; Argos player personnel dir. '90-93; Argos dir. college scouting from '94; East York CI athlete of '42, Wm. Burgess gold medal for leadership '44; T award football, basketball; awarded game ball by mates for '50 Grey Cup 13-0 victory in which he kicked 2 field goals and made key tackle of Winnipeg's Lee McPhail on 5yd line to preserve Mud Bowl shutout; res. Mississauga, Ont.

VOSS, Carl (all-around); b. 1 Jan 1907, Chelsea, Mass.; d. 13 Sep 1993, Lake Park, Fla.; given name: Carl Potter; m. Pearl; Queen's; retd. hockey official; born of Cdn parents, raised, educated Toronto; mem. '23-24 Queen's Intercollegiate, Grey Cup title team; jr. hockey Kingston, OHA, Eastern Cdn titles, Memorial Cup finalists; 1st player signed to Maple Leafs contract when they purchased St. Pat's club of NHL '27; mem. '32 Buffalo Bisons (IHL) title team; league scoring leader, all-star; Detroit '33, rookie of year, first such NHL award (preceded Calder Trophy); mem. '38 Chicago, Stanley Cup; leading playoff scorer; pres. USHL '49; NHL referee-in-chief '50-65; NHL playing service also took him to NY Rangers, Ottawa, St. Louis, NY Americans, Montreal Maroons; mem. Hockey Hall of Fame.

VOYLES, Carl (football/coaching); b. 11 Aug 1898, McLowd, Okla., d. 11 Jan 1982, Ft. Meyers, Fla.; m. Gertrude M. Hall (d); c. Carl Jr., Robert; m. Dorothy Belknap; Oklahoma State, BSc; coach, realtor; capt. college football team sr. year, basketball team 3yrs; coached HS conf. football, basketball title teams, tied for state wrestling title; coach Southwestern State College 3yrs, guided football team to 22-5-3 record, basketball team to ntl tournament twice; freshman football coach Illinois '25-31, head scout for coach Bob Zuppke; 8yrs asst. athletic dir., asst. football coach Duke; head coach, athletic dir. William and Mary, Southern Conf. title; athletic dir., head coach Auburn '44-47; coach, GM Brooklyn Dodgers (all-American Conf.) '48-49; coach/GM newly combined Tiger-Cats '50; Grey Cup '53; scout Hamilton '54-80.

WADE, Harry (basketball); b. 12 Mar 1928, Windsor, Ont.; m. Helen Lucas; c. Paul, William; UWO; business exec.; mem. all-Ont. HS basketball champions '47-48; 3 CIAU title teams '49-51; 2yrs football UWO, '49 league champions; mem. ntl sr. basketball champion Tillsonburg Livingstons '51, '52; Olympic team '52; res. Tillsonburg, Ont.

WADSWORTH, Mike (football): b. 4 Jun 1943, Toronto, Ont.; m. Bernadette; c. Carolan, Mary, Jane; Notre Dame, BA, Osgoode Hall, LLB, Harvard Business School; AD Notre Dame; son of '36-43 CFL all-star Bunny Wadsworth; attended ND on football scholarship '63-65; def. tackle; CFL Argos '66-70; 1st pres. CFL Players Assn.; practiced law '71-81; *Toronto Star* columnist '72-72; CFL broadcaster '71-81; v-p. Tyco Laboratories '81-84; v-p. Crownx Inc. '84-89; v-p. Crown Life '87-89; Cdn ambassador to Ireland '89-94; ND Advisory Council for International Activities; lecturer; ND athletic dir. from '95; res. South Bend, Ind.

WAGHORNE, Fred (builder/hockey); b. 1866, Tunbridge Wells, Eng.; d. 1956, Toronto, Ont.; over 50yr span officiated more than 2000 hockey, 1500 lacrosse games; earned reputation as innovator; credited with system of dropping puck on faceoffs (previously placed on ice between players sticks), use of whistle to stop play (ringing cow bell previous methiod); noted for unusual no-goal ruling in game in which puck (then two glued together pieces) split on hitting goal post with only half entering net, his argument was a legal size puck did not enter goal; pioneer '11 in what is now Metro Toronto HL; mem. Hockey Hall of Fame.

WAGNER, Barbara (figure skating); b. 5 May 1938, Toronto, Ont.; given name: Barbara Aileen; div. Grogan; c. James David Grogan; m. Michael Hofmann; Ryerson PTI; figure skating coach; with Robert Paul 5 ntl, 4 world, 2 NA, '60 Olympic pairs championships; Lou Marsh Trophy '57; Torch Award Canada's outstanding winter athlete of half-century '76; mem. Cdn, US Figure Skating, Cdn Amateur, Canada's Sports halls of fame; res. Valley Home, Calif.

WAGNER, Bill (curling); b. 19 Dec 1919, Wimborne, Alta.; m. Elaine Flynn; c. Darce, Kirk, Wendy, Heather, Douglas; UBC, BSA; civil servant; hockey Nanaimo Clippers '40 Western Canada Int. finalists, '44 Northwest Air Command RCAF champions, Alberta, UBC champions; softball BC sr. titlists '41; skip Ont. Seniors champion '75, '77, Masters champion '81, '83; ACT trophy Ottawa's outstanding curler '65, ACT curling team trophy '78; res. Ottawa, Ont.

WAGNER, Lauren (squash): b. 6 Jul 1968, Johannesburg, S.A.; accountant/office mgr/coach; South African -19 champion 3yrs; played on provincial A team 7yrs; won provincial -21 title; mem. BC team '96 Cdn championships; mem. '96 Cdn ntl women's team; 1 BC open, closed, Pacific Coast open titles; bronze '96 ntl championships; res. N. Vancouver, B.C.

WAGNER, Victor (squash); b. 19 Dec 1958, Ottawa, Ont.; Yale.; men's Que. Criterium title '76; Ont. jr. open champion '76-77; ntl jr. softball title '76-77; mem. first ntl squash racquets men's team; competed Drysdale Cup jr. open tournament London, Eng.,'77; mem. world championships team '77; Man. Open, Ottawa amateur titles '78; NCAA all-American '80; Boodles Open NYC, Yale Invitation titles '80; Intercollegiate all-American, all-Ivy League team '81; mem. Ont. Games jr. gold medal, ntl silver medal field hockey teams '74; mem. Ottawa Ont. Games gold, ntl jr. Olympics bronze teams '75; played field hockey internationally vs Holland '77; twice Little League baseball all-star team mem.; mem. Ont. jr. tennis team; 2 HS tennis trophies; 2 Ottawa ACT squash awards; last known res. Ottawa, Ont.

WAGNER, Virgil (football); b. 27 Feb 1922, Belleville, Ill.; d. Aug 1997, Belleville, Ill.; given name: Virgil Edwin; m. Mary Jeanette Rothgangel; c. Michael, Martha, Rebecca, Sara; Millikin, BSc US govt. inventory mgr.; all-conf., all-state HS football '38; lettered in football, basketball, baseball at Millikin; all-conf. '40-42, Little all-American '41-42; listed Who's Who in American Colleges and Universities '43; football Iowa Seahawks Naval Aircorps service team '43; pro Montreal '46-54; led Big Four scorers '46-49; 4 times all-Big Four, all-Eastern all-star; all-Cdn '46-49; Jeff Russel Memorial Trophy '47; CFL career, Alouettes team record 55tds; mem. Belleville Area, Millikin, Canadian Football halls of fame.

WAINMAN, Tracey (figure skating); b. 27 May 1967, Kirkland Lake, Ont.; ntl novice title '79, at 14 youngest ntl sr. titlist '81; Skate Canada, St. Ivel titles '81; coached by Doug Leigh; Bobbie Rosenfeld Trophy '81; res. Willowdale, Ont.

WAITE, Gary (squash); b. 9 Sep 1966, Quebec City; pro athlete; British jr. open finalist '84; world jr. hardball champion '85; NA open champion '93; NA open doubles titlist '94; ranked 12 in world, highest ranking ever by Pan-American '93; capt. men's ntl team to highest ever finish world championships '95; 3 gold '95 Pan-Am Games; Squash Canada delegate for COA from '95; dir. PSA from '95; Viscount Alexander Trophy '86; res. New York, N.Y.

WAITE, Jim (curling/golf); b. 17 Feb 1941, St. Thomas, Ont.; given name: James Frederick; m. Sue Richardson; c. Chris, David; McMaster, UWO, BA, MEd; retd. PS principal; 1st of 14 Ont. title bids as lead '66; won '68 Ont. title; 3 OCA Challenge Round titles; with Stan Curtis skipping other rink won '70 Governor-General's double rink title; with Don Gilbert other skip Ont. Silver Tankard '73, '75; Curl Canada ntl course conductor; gen. chair. '79 Consols; head umpire '81 Air Canada Silver Broom; Worlds head official '89, '91, '92; ntl coach Canada's Worlds teams '93-97; Olympic coach '98; 5 St. Thomas G&CC golf titles; 2 St. Thomas Early Bird golf titles; '73 father and 3 sons championship; golf coach UWO; res. St. Thomas, Ont.

WALBY, Chris (football): b. 23 Oct 1956, Winnipeg, Man.; Dickinson State; TV football analyst; tackle; drafted by Montreal '81, Winnipeg from '81-96; CFL record: 254 scheduled games, 1td, 15 tackles, 21 playoff games; 4 Western, 7 Eastern, 9 CFL all-star; 4 Leo Dandurand trophies; 2 CFL outstanding offensive lineman awards, 2 runnerup; 4 Grey Cup finals, 3 winners; retd '97 to become CBC-TV football analyst; res. Winnipeg, Man.

WALCHUK, Don (curling): b. 3 Jun 1963, Melville, Sask; stockbroker; m. Shelley; c. Michelle, Chad; began curling age 10; skipped '80 Sask. HS bronze medal rink, '81 Sask. jr men's title rink; competed 6 Briers, 3 winners; all-star lead for Pat Ryan '85 Brier runnerup; all-star 2nd with Ryan '87-89 Briers; 3rd Kevin Martin '96, '97 Briers; all-star 3rd '96; runnerup '87 Olympic Curling trials; 2 Alta Achievement awards; all-star 2nd '89 world title rink; Dick Ellis team award '89; mem. Cdn Curling Hall of Fame; res. Sherwood Park, Alta.

WALDO, Carolyn (synchro swim); b. 11 Dec 1964, Montreal, Que.; given name: Carolyn Jane; m. Tom Baltzer; c. Brittany, Corey; UCal; TV sports reporter; team gold, figures silver '83 Pan-Am Games; team gold, figures bronze '83 America Cup; team gold, figures bronze '82 world championships; team gold '81 Pan-Pacific Games; solo silver '84 Olympics; fed. govt. world champion award '83, excellence award '84; flag-bearer, single, duet gold '88 Olympics; Lou Marsh Trophy '88; 2 Bobbie Rosenfeld, 4 Velma Springstead, 2 Dick Ellis team awards; Officer Order of Canada '88; mem. Cdn Amateur, Alta, Que, Intl Swimming, Cdn Aquatic, Canada's Sports halls of fame; res. Kanata, Ont.

WALKER, Bill (football); b. 11 May 1933, Pittsburgh, Pa.; m. Nancy Jean Antrim; c. William, Richard, John; Maryland, BA; auto dealer; Maryland all-American jr. year; receiver, punter Edmonton '56-58; mem. '56 Grey Cup champions; last known res. Doylestown, Pa.

WALKER, Dennis (swimming); b. 10 Nov 1913, Victoria, B.C.; given name: Dennis Gerald; m. Ruby Elizabeth Davidson; c. Ruby, Linda, Ken; retired; mem. '32 Olympic team; Wrigley 1-mile ntl title, 2 *Victoria Times* 3-mile titles; mem. Navy swim, water polo teams; Y swim coach; res. Victoria, B.C.

WALKER, Elisabeth (swimming): b. 5 Feb 1977, Saskatoon, Sask.; as part of physiotherapy began swimming age 1, competing age 13; world 50m butterfly, 100m backstroke record holder; competed '92, '96 Paralympics; gold 100 FS '93 Cdn Foresters ntl championships; mem. '94 Commonwealth Games team; res. Toronto, Ont.

WALKER, Gord (administration); b. 17 Jul 1915, Kincardine, Ont.; d. 9 Jul 1988, Toronto, Ont.; given name: Gordon Sinclair; m. Victoria Burgess; c. Gordon Jr., Barry, Terry, Shirley; retd.; sports writer *Globe* '35-42, *Toronto Star* '42-47, excluding WW2 navy stint, *Globe & Mail* '47-49, '50-73; business mgr. Toronto Maple Leafs baseball club '49; CFL information dir. '73-82; instrumental in organizing Ont. Sportswriters, Sportscasters Assn. '48, initial v-p., later pres., secty-treas.; pres. Intl Baseball League Writers' Assn.

'56; prime organizer, 1st pres. Football Reporters of Canada '57; 10yrs FRC secty-treas.; authored 1st Big Four statistical, record manual '55; instrumental in establishing practice of including goal number following scorer's name in NHL summaries; brother Hal sports editor *Toronto Telegram, Calgary Herald*; mem. Canadian Football Reporters Hall of Fame.

WALKER, Jack (hockey); b. 28 Nov 1888, Silver Mountain, Ont., d. 16 Feb 1950, Seattle, Wash.; given name: John Phillip; from '06 mem. 4 consecutive Port Arthur city title teams; mem. Toronto Arenas, Seattle, Victoria Cougars Stanley Cup winners; mem. Moncton, Toronto Arenas, Seattle, Victoria, Detroit, Edmonton teams '12-30; player-mgr. Hollywood Stars '31-32; retired to manage, coach, referee in PCL; originator of hook check; noted for ability to teach young players; 2 PCL, NHL MVP awards; mem. Hockey Hall of Fame.

WALKER, Larry (baseball): b. 1 Dec 1966, Maple Ridge, B.C.; given name: Larry Kenneth Robert; div. Christa Vandenbrink; c. Brittany Marie; m. Angela; outfielder; played , goal in minor hockey; mem. ntl jr. baseball team; pro Montreal organization '84; minor league stops Utica, Burlington, West Palm Beach, Jacksonville, Indianapolis, Salem, Colorado Springs; promoted to Expos '87-94, Colorado '95-98; Expos player of '92; 5 Gold Glove awards; Silver Bat '92; 1st all-star selection '92, '97, '99; *AP, Sporting News* post-season all-star '92; runnerup *CP* male athlete of '92, '97; Lou Marsh, Conacher trophies '98; Tip O'Neill award '87, '97; runnerup '97 NL batting race with .366, .720 slugging avg, 49hrs, 130rbi; 1st Cdn named NL MVP '97; became 1st Cdn in modern baseball annals to win NL batting title with .363 '98, repeat '99 with .379; best Cdn position player in history; combines power with solid defence to rank among game's best right fielders; signed 6yr $75M contract extension with Rockies '99; youth baseball fields in Maple Ridge, Denver, Ft. Collins named in his honor; mem. Ridge Meadows Hall of Fame; res. Aurora, Colo.

WALKER, Larry (harness racing): b. 5 Apr 1947, Owen Sound, Ont.; regarded by peers as one of the most proficient handlers of trotters in the standardbred business; earned that reputation starting with Erin's Jet in '82 Roosevelt International trot; other square gaiters who have enhanced that reputation are Ambro Ermine, Shipps Dream, Armbro Flori, Ashley Jane, Mark's Marathon, Going Smartly and Veras Image; no slouch training pacers either, he guided Witsend Gypsy to Canadian Pacing Derby title '86; through '97 2165 victories with purses seeking $18M; winner of 23 major stakes races; res. Puslinch, Ont.

WALKER, Louise (t&f); b. 21 Mar 1951, Toronto, Ont.; given name: Marilyn Louise Hanna; m. James Douglas Walker; c. Kathryn, Bradley; UofT, BSc, MD; specializing in sports medicine; high jump specialist; ntl jr. title '70; ntl sr. titles '73, '75; silver '74 Commonwealth, '75 Pan-Am Games; ntl record 1:87m '75; mem. '72, '76 Olympic teams; finalist '76; switched to rowing '84 won 3 Head of Rideau Masters events; 1st female pres. Cdn Academy of Sport Medicine; mem. UofT Sports Hall of Fame; res. Nepean, Ont.

WALKER, Peahead (football/coaching); b. 1899, Birmingham, Ala., d. 16 Jul 1970, Charlotte, N.C.; given name: Douglas Clyde; m. Flonnie; c. Gwen; football exec.; head coach '37-50 Wake Forest compiling 79-47 w-l record; asst. to Herman Hickman Yale 2 seasons; head coach Montreal '52-59, 3 consecutive Grey Cup finals losing each time to Pop Ivy's Eskimos; NY Giants (NFL) scout.

WALKER, Skip (football); b. 11 Sep 1954, Houston, Tex.; given name: Alvin; m. Lisa; Texas A&M; pro running back Montreal '80-81, Ottawa '82-84; twice led CFL ground gainers; Ottawa single season rushing record 1431yds '83; twice CFL all-star, Carlsberg player of year; Ottawa team MVP '83, CBC-TV Coaches all-star team '83; brother Cornelius mem. '78 Ottawa club; CFL record '84: 648 carries, 3574yds, 114 receptions, 1625yds, 49 kickoff returns, 1118yds, 41tds; res. Austin, Tex.

WALL, Dave (harness racing); b. 9 Nov 1946, Kincardine, Ont.; in hockey he might be considered a "grinder", a player whose work ethic translates into success; through '97 had amassed 5462 victories with purses exceeding $38M; string of 25 consecutive years winning 100 or more races and 16 straight years topping $1M purses mark; pacer Odds Against and trotters Armbro Luxury and Goodtimes among his best horses; 1 NA Cup, 1 Canadian Pacing Derby, 2 Robert Stewart classic titles; res. Komoka, Ont.

WALL, Gwen (t&f); b. 16 Jan 1963, Saskatoon, Sask.; m. Brian Ridout; c. Paige, Jay; UofSask, BEd; HS teacher; hurdles specialist; 2 ntl 400m hurdles titles; silver 4x400m relay, bronze 400m hurdles '83 Pan-Am Games; bronze 400m hurdles '83 FISU Games; mem. '82, '86 Commonwealth Games teams; broke ntl 400m record 13 times '83; 2 ntl jr., sr. records; mem. Saskatoon Sports Hall of Fame; res. Calgary, Alta.

WALL, Nick (horse racing); b. 18 Dec 1906, Lower Gully, Kelligrews, Conception Bay, Ireland; d. 17 Mar 1983, Bellerose, N.Y.; emigrated to Cape Breton age 9; raised Glace Bay, Montreal; apprentice jockey Montreal; '26-57 rode 11,164 mounts, 1419 1sts, 1305 2nds, 1352 3rds; leading US jockey '38 with purses exceeding $3.5 million; rode in all major US races including Kentucky Derby, Preakness, Belmont Stakes; riding Stagehand '38 Santa Anita Handicap defeated famed Seabiscuit in photo-finish; double winner world's richest stakes race by riding Bay View through sea of mud to defeat Mouland '40; mem. Nfld, Canada's Sports halls of fame.

WALLACE, Heather (squash); b. 4 Dec 1962, Kitwe, Zambia; Bedford (Eng.) Coll., BSc; squash pro Goodlife Fitness Club; began playing squash age 16; Rhodesian, South African titles; 12 ntl titles, tieing Cdn record for consec. ntl title wins in any sport with 12 '97 (knee injury kept her from '98 title play); undefeated by any Cdn woman '87-98; 6 Western Cdn, 5 Pacific Coast Open, 5 Que. Open, 4 Ont. Open, 4 Pacific Rim Open, 1 BC Open titles; '93 Japan, San Francisco Open titles; '95 US Rolex Open, 3 gold '95 Pan-Am Games; mem. '98 Commonwealth Games team; frequently competed vs. men in tournament play and beat them; mem. ntl team 3 world championships; with Jamie Crombie world doubles bronze '97; retd. from

intertnational stage '98; coach jr. women's ntl team '91-93; level 4 NCCP coach; res. Ottawa, Ont.

WALLENIUS, Rob (swimming); b. 21 Apr 1962, Sudbury, Ont.; Laurentian; backstroke specialist; 2 ntl 200m backstroke titles; CIAU 100m, 200m backstroke titles '84; mem. '79 Pan-Am, '81 FISU Games teams; ntl sr. record; last known res. Sudbury, Ont.

WALLIN, Terry (softball); b. 19 Feb 1961, Moose Jaw, Sask.; m. Patsy Leah; c. Harrison David Micheal; Air Canada station services; mem. Legion 141 Winnipeg ntl jr. baseball champions '81; played fastball Portage Diamonds, Remple Bros, Toronto Gators, Decatur Pride; mem. ntl developmental team '92, ntl team from '94; capt. Rempel Bros '94 ntl title team; Pan-Am gold '95; all-Canadian 2nd baseman '91-92; res. Saskatoon, Sask.

WALLING, Brian (football); b. 16 Sep 1963, Toronto, Ont.; Acadia; running back; CFL Toronto '87, Edmonton '88-95, Saskatchewan '89, Hamilton '96; CFL record: 122 games, 213 carries for 1059yds, 2tds, 32 pass receptions for 219yds, 4tds; 13 playoff games, 3tds, 3 Grey Cup finals, 2 winners; res. Toronto, Ont.

WALLINGFORD, Ron (t&f); b. 13 Sep 1933, Ottawa, Ont.; given name: Ronald Roy; m. Heather Jane Magwood; c. Randy Roy, Anthony Alexander, Roxanne Rae, Cassandra Carmen, Darcy Dale; Michigan, BSc, McMaster, BPhE, Buffalo, MEd, EdD; retd. dir. PE Laurentian; distance runner, steeplechase specialist; ntl jr. 3-mile record '52, indoor mile, 3000m, steeplechase, 5000m, marathon records; mem. ntl record medley relay; 3rd '64 Boston marathon, 9th '71; mem. '66 Commonwealth, '71 Pan-Am Games teams; 2nd world masters marathon '74; chairman Ont. Coaches Assn. '71-73; marathon race mgr. '76 Olympics; dir. OTFA '71-73; former tech. co-ordinator CTFA; ntl t&f coach '65, '77, '79 FISU Games; res. Sudbury, Ont.

WALLIS, Kevin (harness racing); b. 18 Oct 1956, London, Ont.; enjoyed relative success in Canada before shifting to Hazel Park in Detroit and Pompano Beach in Florida where he is ranked among best catch drivers since '81; leading Hazel Park driver '94-95; career high season '96 posting 651 victories; also conditions solid stable; through '97 amassed 4341 victories with purses exceeding $15M; res. Deerfield Beach, Fla.

WALLS, Ken (builder); b. 21 Apr 1907, Elmvale, Ont.; d. 4 Nov 1984, Barrie, Ont.; given name: William Kenneth; Barrie Business Coll., UofT (Victoria Coll.), BA; newspaper publisher; versatile athlete; mem. varied baseball teams, Ont. finalists '35; batted .429 with North Simcoe title team; played intermediate lacrosse '31-33; mem. Barrie Colts hockey team '26-27; played hockey with Victoria Coll., Barrie intermediates; accomplished golfer; with Fred Anderton won '39 Georgian Bay district men's badminton doubles; established *Barrie Examiner* sports desk and played key role in boosting sport profile in region; mem. N. Simcoe baseball league exec. '30-36; publicity chair. Grey-Simcoe baseball league '47; mem. Barrie intermediate hockey club finance comm.; v-p. Barrie Town HL; pres. Barrie Garrison badminton club '47; pres. Georgian Bay District badminton assn.; club capt. Barrie Country Club; mem. Barrie Arena Commission; mem. Barrie Sports Hall of Fame.

WALLS, Mickey (horse racing): b. 1 Jun 1974, Vancouver, B.C.; began race-riding at 16 in Vancouver; after dominating jockey standings at Exhibition (now Hastings) Park moved East '90; although OJC rules prohibit licensing before age 18, his BC license was honored and he went on to win Sovereign apprentice jockey award '90; repeated award victory '91 posting 230 wins and claiming NA Eclipse apprentice jockey award; broken leg cost him much of '92 season; moved to Chicago/Oaklawn Park '94-95 before returning to OJC circuit '96; won two-thirds of Cdn thoroughbred racing's Triple Crown (Prince of Wales, Breeder's Stakes) '96; Sovereign top jockey award '91; outstanding performance Breeders' Cup X111 at Woodbine '96; res. Toronto, Ont.

WALSH, Billy Jr. (curling): b. 8 Oct 1948, Winnipeg, Man.; given name: William Joseph; div. Tannys Aspevig; c. Casey, Kiley, Steven; UMan; chartered accountant; skipped Fort Rouge CC Man. bonspiel grand aggregate winner '74; skipped Red Anderson Memorial Trophy winning Ottawa Navy rink '83; finalist '83 Ont. Tankard; skipped Ottawa Rideau rink to third place '93 *TSN* Skins Game; Shorty Jenkins Sportsmanship award '97; ex-wife Tanys 3 time Man. ladies golf champion; baseball scout for LA Dodgers; active on executive Ottawa Nationals minor baseball; Camelot Golf Club championship; res. Ottawa, Ont.

WALSH, Billy Sr. (curling): b. 20 Jan 1917, Haileybury, Ont., d. 7 Oct 1971, Winnipeg, Man.; given name: William James; m. Madeline Mary Metcalfe; c. William Joseph; provincial auditor; skipped Fort Rouge CC to '52 Man. Consols, Brier titles, 10-0 record; unprecedented 17 consecutive Brier playdown victories; won '56 Brier beating Ont. skipped by Alf Phillips Sr. in extra end playoff; mem. Canadian Curling Hall of Fame.

WALSH, Brenda (t&f): b. 31 Dec 1952, Edmonton, Alta.; given name: Brenda Constance; UAlta, BPhE; teacher; ntl jr. 400m title '70; ntl indoor jr. 400m record 54.9 '72; world indoor 300m 38.8 '73; ntl open indoor 400m 54.1 '73; mem. '71 Pan-Am, '73 FISU, '74 Commonwealth Games (bronze 4x400m relay) teams; Alta. open record 400m hurdles 59.9 '79; Bakewell Memorial Trophy (UAlta outstanding female athlete), Edmonton athlete of '73; res. Edmonton, Alta.

WALSH, Marty (hockey): b. 1883, Kingston, Ont., d. 1915, Gravenhurst, Ont.; given name: Martin; Queen's, BA; mem. Queen's OHA team which unsuccessfully challenged Ottawa Silver Seven for '06 Stanley Cup; Ottawa sought his services as replacement for centre Frank McGee but he elected to go to intl pro league where he broke his leg; with Ottawa '08-12, scored 135 goals 59 games, 26 goals 8 playoff games; mem. 2 Stanley Cup winners; 3 NHA scoring titles; 10 goals 1 game vs Port Arthur '11, 7 vs Montreal '08, 6 vs Galt '10, Renfrew '11, 5 vs Wanderers '08, Shamrocks '10; mem. Hockey Hall of Fame.

WALSH, Tarp (football): b. 21 Sep 1921, Sydney, N.S.; given name: Gerald; m. Bernadette Layden; c. Michael,

Patricia, Karen, Maureen; St. Francis Xavier, BSc, McGill, BEng; electrical engineer, retd. production supervisor Stelco; Jr. hockey Sydney; mem. St. FX Maritime English rugby champions; Maritime heavyweight boxing titlist; end, fullback Hamilton Tigers '46-48; St. FX Larkin Trophy; mem. St. FX, NS Sports halls of fame; res. Hamilton, Ont.

WALTERS, Angus (sailing): b. 1882, Lunenburg, N.S., d. 12 Aug 1968, Lunenburg, N.S.; sailor, dairy farmer; from '21-42 managing owner schooner Bluenose in which he won 5 international races; took Bluenose to Chicago '33 to represent Canada at Century of Progress exhibition; sailed to Eng. '37 to compete in Silver Jubilee of King George V and Queen Mary; mem. NS, Canada's Sports halls of fame.

WALTERS, Dale (boxing): b. 27 Sep 1963, Port Alice, B.C.; actor; bantamweight; BC Emerald, Silver Gloves titles '73-79; BC jr. Golden Gloves titles '77-79; BC sr. Golden Gloves titles '80-82; ntl bantamweight titles 81-84; mem. '82 Worlds, Commonwealth, '83 Pan-Am Games teams; bantamweight bronze '84 Olympics; played role of Robert Ritter in 26 episode CBC-TV series Ritter's Cove; appeared in 6 segments Huckleberry Finn TV series; father Len mem. '50 Commonwealth, '52 Olympic Games, Cdn athlete of '51; res. Burnaby, B.C.

WALTERS, Lisa (golf): b. 9 Jan 1960, Prince Rupert, B.C.; given name: Lisa Evelyn Young; m. Mike Walters; UVic, Florida State, BSc; mem. BC jr. team '76-77; ntl jr. team '77-78; BC jr. title '77; BC Ladies titles '79-81; mem. Cdn Ladies' team British Amateur '81; mem. FSU golf team '78-82; Lady Gator tournament title '80; 1st ranked US college golf '80-81 season; 3rd overall '81 AIAW ntl tournament; led FSU team to '81 AIAW title; all-American, regional SE US team '81; FSU team MVP '80-81; joined pro circuit '83; 2 career holes-in-one; career low 65; LPGA Itoki Hawaiian Open '92-93; LPGA Oldsmobile Classic '98 with record 23-under par; res. Tampa, Fla.

WALTON, Brian (cycling): b. 18 Dec 1965, Ottawa, Ont.; roadracing specialist; 10 ntl championships; rode for 7-11 amateur team before turning pro '89. 2 gold, 1 bronze '95, gold '99 Pan-Am, bronze '94 Commonwealth, silver '96 Olympic Games; Cdn Individual Pursuit record '94. 2 Canadian Tire overall titles and turned in strong performances on European circuit; competed '87, '95, '99 Pan-Am, '88, '96 Olympic, '94 Commonwealth Games; res. North Delta, B.C.

WALTON, Dorothy (badminton): b. 7 Aug 1909, Swift Current, Sask., d. 16 Oct 1981, Toronto, Ont.; given name: Dorothy Louise McKenzie; m. W.R.Walton Jr.; c. 1 son; UofSask, BA, MA; Sask., Western Canada tennis titles; ntl badminton singles titles '36, '38, '40, ladies' doubles '40; world badminton titles '39-47; Bobbie Rosenfeld award '40; 1 of 6 outstanding female athletes of half century '50 CP poll; mem. Order of Canada, Sask., Cdn Amateur, Canada's Sports halls of fame.

WALTON, Mike (hockey): b. 3 Jan 1945, Kirkland Lake, Ont.; given name: Michael Robert; m. Candy Hoult; nicknamed 'Shaky'; real estate broker, bar owner; mem. Toronto Marlboro Memorial Cup winners; pro rookie of year Tulsa (CPHL) '65, Rochester (AHL) '66; Maple Leafs '66-71, Bruins '70-73, Minnesota Fighting Saints (WHA) '73-75, Canucks '75-78, St. Louis, Boston, Chicago '78-79; 1 Stanely Cup; WHA scoring title '74; 2nd team centre WHA all-stars' mem. '74 WHA Team Canada; pro record (NHL, WHA): 799 scheduled games, 337g, 392a, 70 playoff games, 34g, 25a; res. Toronto, Ont.

WAPLES, Keith (harness racing); b. 8 Dec 1923, Victoria Harbour, Ont.; m. Eileen Devitt; c. Barbara, Donna, Karen, Gordon; drove Mighty Dudley to Canada's 1st sub 2:00 mile clocking 1:59.3 on 1/2 mile Richelieu Park track '59; won '62 Roosevelt International trot with Tie Silk; record 246 wins on Canadian tracks '67; drove Strike Out at Blue Bonnets '72 for 1st $100,000 race win in Canada (standardbred or thoroughbred); with Strike Out won '72 Little Brown Jug, Adios Pace, Prix d'Été, Tattersalls Pace; top Canadian dash winner '67-68; career win record exceeds 3000, purses exceed $5 million; more than 30 sub 2:00 minute miles; active in operation Orangeville (Ont.), Cloverdale (B.C.) harness tracks; mem. Canada's Sports, Canadian Horse Racing halls of fame; res. Durham, Ont.

WAPLES, Ron (harness racing); b. 21 Jul 1944, Toronto, Ont.; m. Josephine; c. Ronnie, Randy; cousin of Keith; 5 Canadian horseman of year awards; NA dash champion '79; through '97 6399 victories, purses exceeding $66M; 1st to surpass $1 million in purses racing almost exclusively on Canadian tracks '78; drove Ralph Hanover, pacing triple crown winner, to fastest mile Messenger Stakes history 1:57 Jun '83; 9 Breeders Crown triumphs; drove No Sex Please to 2 world records; among other noteworthy horses Dream Maker, Armbro Dallas, Super Flora, Presidential Ball, Park Avenue Joe; 191 major stakes victories, including Hambletonian, 2 Little Brown Jugs, 1 Cane Pace, 1 NA Cup, 1 Cdn Pacing Derby, 4 Maple Leaf Trots; mem. Cdn Horse Racing, Harness Racing's Living halls of fame; res. Puslinch, Ont.

WARD, Clint (water skiing); b. 11 Jun 1932, Saskatoon, Sask.; div.; c. Rande, Kim, Clint Jr.; UofSask; retd. capt. Air Canada; ntl age-group titles '61-74; coach-mgr. ntl team '65-71; organizing chair. 10th world championships '67; pres. CWSA '68-70; pres. Group 1 World Water-Ski Union '71-75; Group 1 secty-gen. '76-80; exec. v-p. Sports Fed. of Canada '73-74; mem. board of dir. National Sports Administration Centre '74-76; COA administration staff mem. '76 Winter Olympics team; CBC water-ski commentator; with George Athans Jr. authored "*Water Skiing*"; pres. OWSA '77-79; Air Canada sport merit award '74, finalist '79; Ont. special achievement award '79; mem. Sask. Sports Hall of Fame; res. Toronto, Ont.

WARD, Pete (baseball); b. 26 Jul 1939, Montreal, Que.; given name: Peter Thomas; Portland, BSc; travel agency operator; infielder; son of Jimmy Ward, former NHL standout with Montreal Maroons; a power hitter, he played in minors with Vancouver (PCL), Stockton (Class C), Fox Cities (3-I), Little Rock, Ardmore, Rochester (IL), led IL in runs (114), doubles (34) while batting .328 with 22hr; made ML debut with Baltimore '62 as outfielder; dealt to Chicago White Sox '63; *Sporting News* AL rookie of yr '63; injuries suffered in car accident plagued balance of career; dealt to

NY Yankees '69-70; retd.as player '70 but remained with Yankees organization as coach Rochester, mgr. Fort Lauderdale, West Haven, winning pennants '75-76; coach Atlanta '78; ML record: 973 scheduled games over 9 seasons, 3060ab, 345r, 776h, 136d, 17t, 98hr, 427rbi, .254ba; mem. Cdn Baseball Hall of Fame; res. Portland, Ore.

WARD, Peter (swimming); b. 18 Jul 1963, North York, Ont.; given name: Peter Francis; m. Cheryl McArton; c. Rebecca; Arkansas, BA; coach; butterfly specialist; 3 ntl 200 fly titles; Cdn record 2:00.78 for 200m fly '81; competed '84 Olympic, '87 FISU Games; silver 400m medley relay '87 Pan-Am Games; silver '81, bronze '83 Pan-Pacific championships; head swim coach Indiana University of Pa; Southeast/Southwest Conf. titles; produced 10 all-Americans at NCAA Div II '95; res. Indiana, Pa.

WARDEN, Donald (archery); b. 27 Dec 1931, Arthur, Ont.; given name: Donald Elgin; m. Jean Marie Brown; c. Donna, David, Dianne, Joan; Guelph Bus. College; real estate; early hockey interests terminated when injured pursuing duties as fireman '74; class III paraplegic; ntl archery records; ntl silver, bronze air rifle, air pistol; 5th Holland archery competition '80; mem. Stayner Rod and Gun Club; proficient in .22 rifle; mem. Base Borden Archery Club; Ont. good citizenship award '81; active in community life, activities for physically handicapped; last known res: Stayner, Ont.

WARNER, Edson (shooting); b. 6 Mar 1930, Sawyerville, Que.; given name: Edson Lyman; m. Edith; c. Patrick, Robert, Terry , Susan; McGill, BComm, Bishop's, BA; retd. accountant; mem. '52, '60 Olympic, '52, '58, '66 world championships teams; mem. 7 Bisley teams; 13 ntl .22 rifle titles; mem. '74 Commonwealth Games team; 3 Macdonald Stewart silver badge titles, 5 Queen's medals; '56 runnerup Queen's Prize Bisley, Duke of Gloucester award '56; 3 Bisley Argentina medals; p-pres, PQRA; 22yrs service Cdn army militia Sherbrooke Hussars; res. Lennoxville, Que.

WARREN, Harry (field hockey/t&f/cricket); b. 27 Aug 1904, Anacortes, Wash.; d. 14 Mar 1998, Vancouver, B.C.; given name: Harry Verney; m. Margaret Bessie Tisdall; c. Charlotte Louisa Verney, Victor Henry Verney; UBC, BA, BASc.; hon. DSc, Rhodes Scholar, Oxford, MSc, PhD; joined UBC faculty '32; retd. geology prof., consulting geological engineer; t&f alternate '28 Olympic team; 100m (on grass) Irish record Tailteann Games, 2 intervarsity relay records Oxford-Cambridge meet '29; capt. Queen's Coll. AC '28-29; introduced badminton, cricket, rugby, men's field hockey to Cal Tech '29-32; hon. life mem., founder Calif. Wanderers FHC; father of Canadian field hockey; organized UBC club '23; hon. pres. CWFHA; 1st pres., co-founder CFHA '62; instrumental in sending Canada's 1st field hockey entry to Olympics '64; twice UBC Big Block for rugby, track; Oxford track honors; University Hill's Men's Forum award for contribution to amateur sport '65; Warren pitch Thunderbird Park named in his honor '70; BC cricket cap '23; IHF award of merit '77; fellow Royal Society of Canada, Geological Society of America, Geochemical Society; served on UBC senate '39-60, '63-72; mem. Order of Canada, BC Sports Hall of Fame.

WARREN, Rod (rodeo); b. 24 Feb 1968, Valleyview, Alta.; rancher; rose through amateur to pro ranks '88 following path of brother Rick; began with bull riding but soon switched to saddle bronc riding, steer wrestling; Calgary Stampede bronze; Alta. circuit AA titles '93-96; Aalta. HP/SB title '94; Skoal, Bud pro circuit SB titles '94; 2 ntl AA titles; Dodge pro tour SB title '95; 2 BC circuit AA titles; Wrangler circuit AA title '96; 2 ntl all-around, 1 ntl high point titles, 9 ntl finals; res. Valleyview, Alta.

WARREN, Victor (field hockey); b. 19 Aug 1937, Vancouver, B.C.; given name: Victor Henry Verney; m. Cindy Secord; c. Devon, Davey, Steven;UBC, BA; civil servant; mem. 11 test match ntl teams; '64 Olympic team; mgr. ntl team '74-79; 98 test matches including '74, '79 Pan-Ams, '76 Olympics, '78 World Cup; pres. CFHA; res. West Vancouver, B.C.

WARWICK, Bert (football): b. 1902, Fort Chipewyan, NWT; d. 1963, Winnipeg, Man.; as player/coach/exec. at all levels served Cdn football for more than 50yrs; played with St. John's College of Wpg.; coach Western champion Blue Bombers '45; pres. jr. Bombers, chair. CRU/CFL rules comm. 8yrs; life mem. Blue Bombers; CFL commissioner's Western rep at time of death; mem. Cdn Football Hall of Fame.

WARWICK, Billy (hockey); b. 17 Nov 1924, Regina, Sask.; given name: William Harvey; m. Beatrice Powell (d); c. Jane Anne, Linda Caroline; m. Jackie Schoeneich; c. William Christopher, Richard Rudolph (d); publisher *Billy's Guide*; mem. Regina Sask jr. title team; attended Oshawa jr. camp but turned pro NY Rangers organization '42; played in minors with NY Rovers, Hershey, Providence, Philadelphia, Fort Worth, Cleveland, Memphia, Denver, Ottawa, Halifax; NHL with Rangers 14 games, 3g, 3a; retd from pro ranks '52; with brothers Dick and Grant formed famed Warwick line which led Penticton Vees to Allan Cup '54 and world title over Russia '55; mem. Intl, BC Hockey, BC, Sask. Sports halls of fame; res. Edmonton, Alta.

WARWICK, Claude (boxing); b. 28 Oct 1922, Regina, Sask.; d. 1 Mar 1945, Montreal, Que.; given name: Claude Carl; Cdn Forces; defensive back Regina Roughriders and Navy football teams; southpaw boxer who reigned as Cdn Navy featherweight champion; won ntl amateur featherweight title '41 with 29th straight victory; died as result of vehicular accident; ring record 51 bouts, 50 wins, 1 draw; mem. Sask. Sports Hall of Fame.

WARWICK, Grant (hockey); b. 11 Oct 1921, Regina, Sask; given name: Grant David; div.; c. Grant, William, Gayle; restaurateur; pro Rangers '41-47, Boston '47-49, Montreal '49-50; NHL record: 399 scheduled games, 147g, 142a, 16 playoff games, 2g, 4a; Calder, Jacobson rookie trophy '41; scored 1st goal in inaugural NHL all-star game '47; made history as 1st playing coach to win Allan Cup ('54), World championship ('55) with Penticton Vees; with brothers Billy, Claude, Dick and sister Millie inducted into Sask. Sports Hall of Fame same cermony; mem. International, BC Hockey, BC Sports halls of fame; res. Edmonton, Alta.

WARWICK, Millie (all-around); b. 28 Oct 1922, Regina, Sask.; given name: Mildred Marion; m. Kenneth McAuley (d); c. Ken Jr., Todd; retd. public servant; versatile athlete who excelled in basketball, t&f, softball, speed skating, 5-pin bowling, curling, baseball; set Sask. HS softball throw record; mem. '51 ntl champion Edmonton Mortons softball team; '38 Sask. speed skating champion; 3rd base Rockford Peaches in AAGPBL '43-44; with brothers Billy, Claude, Dick, Grant inducted into Sask. Sports Hall of Fame in same ceremony; honored Cooperstown, Cdn Baseball halls of fame; mem. North Battleford Baseball Hall of Fame; res. Edmonton, Alta.

WARWICK, Richard (hockey); b. 28 Apr 1927, Regina, Sask.; given name: Richard McAllister; m. Pam Gates; c. Claude, Sheryl; retd. Canada Dry sales/restaurateur; fine playmaker/prolific scorer; played jr. Humboldt, Medicine Hat, sr. Nanaimo, Penticton; played key role in formation of Penticton Vees and got brothers Billy and Grant to join him forming famed Warwick line which led Vees to '54 Allan Cup, '55 world championship over Russia; mem. Sask., BC Sports, International, BC Hockey halls of fame; res. Saanichton, B.C.

WASHBURN, LeRoy (t&f): b. 16 Jun 1934, Blackville, N.B.; AD St. Thomas U; overall NB t&f title '74; t&f official '67 Pan-Am, '76, '96 Olympic, '78, '86 Commonwealth Games; mem. IAAF tech. officials comm '85; CTFA officials comm., NBTFA dir., pres. '84-87; CdM '87 FISU Games; v-p. NB Special Olympics Assn.; consultant NB Indian Summer Games; Myer Budovitch Memorial trophy Fredericton athlete of '58; Lt. Gov. trophy '61; mem. NB Assembly '74; mem. NB Sports Hall of Fame; res. Oromocto, N.B.

WASZCZUK, Henry (fishing/football); b. 26 Aug 1950, Peterborough, Ont.; m. Mary Louise Duncanson; c. Michael, Jessica; Kent, BSc, MA; TV personality, producer, publisher; centre Tiger-Cats '75-84; 7 all-Eastern awards; Tom Pate Memorial award recipient; 3 Schenley outstanding lineman nominations; co-host *TSN Canadian Sportfishing* series; writer/partner *Canadian Sportfishing* magazine; authored more than 10 books on fishing; res. Campbellville, Ont.

WATKINS, Bill (baseball); b. 5 May 1858, Brantford, Ont.; d. 9 Jun 1937, Port Huron, Mich.; given name: William Henry; played briefly as infielder with Indianapolis (AA) 1884; same yr became team mgr.; became mgr. Detroit (NL) 1885-88, Kansas City (AA) 1888-89, St. Louis (NL) 1893, Pittsburgh (NL) 1898-99; ML managerial record: 914 games, 452-444; mgr. 1887 pennant, World Series winner.

WATLING, Wallace (all-around): b. 16 Mar 1888, Chatham, N.B.; d. 19 Sep 1929, Chatham, N.B.; mayor Chatham, N.B.; competed in hockey, t&f, baseball, basketball, rugby, boxing; excelled in 100, 200yd dashes, 400 relay, broad jump, shot put; many NB, Maritime titles; capt. Chatham's basketball, football teams; mem. NB Sports Hall of Fame.

WATSON, Bev (parachuting); b. 4 Dec 1953, Montreal, Que.; given name: Beverly Dale; Queen's, BA, York, MBA, CA; chartered accountant; mem. OUAA title ski team '74; provincially ranked squash player; 1st style Alta. parachuting championships '79; 4th style, accuracy, overall '80 ntl championships; mem. ntl team '80 world championships; para skier; res. Calgary, Alta.

WATSON, Harry (hockey); b. 6 May 1923, Saskatoon, Sask.; given name: Harry Percival; m. Lillian Thomson; c. Barry, Ron, Dale; retd. sales agency operator; Saskatoon jr. Quakers; pro Brooklyn Americans '41, Detroit '42-43, '45-46, Toronto '46-55, Chicago '55-57; mem. 5 Stanley Cup winners; left wing on Leafs' line of Syl Apps Sr., Bill Ezinicki; NHL record: 809 scheduled games, 236g, 207a, 62 playoff games, 16g, 9a; 7 NHL all-star games; 12yrs mgr. Tam O'Shanter hockey school; coach '63 Windsor Bulldogs Allan Cup champions; co-chair. Timmy Tyke hockey tournament; mem. Toronto Oldtimers hockey team 20yrs; mem. Sask., Saskatoon Sports, Hockey halls of fame; res. Markham, Ont.

WATSON, Ken (curling); b. 12 Aug 1904, Minnedosa, Man.; d. 26 Jul 1986, St. Boniface, Man.; m. Marcella Dowdall; UMan, BA; retd. insurance exec., teacher; lead 1st Man. bonspiel '23; 1st of 32 major trophies Man. 'spiel '26; 7 MCA grand aggregate titles including unprecedented 6 in succession '42-47; 4 Man. Consols titles; Brier championships '36, '42, '49; promoted, helped organize Scotch Cup '59; founder 1st Man. HS 'spiel '40; authored 4 curling books; hon. life mem. Strathcona CC, MCA, CCA; Elmer Freytag Memorial award; mem. Order of Canada, Man., Canada's Sports, Canadian Curling halls of fame.

WATSON, Mark (soccer): b. 7 Sep 1970, Vancouver, B.C.; made pro debut as defender Ottawa Intrepid CSL '90; mem. Hamilton Steelers '91, Montreal Supra '92, Watford English 1st div. '93-95, Vancouver 86ers A-League, Columbus Crew MSL, New England Revolution '96; international debut age 21; mem. ntl team from '91; 37 international caps; res. Vancouver, B.C.

WATSON, Moose (hockey); b. 14 Jul 1898, St. John's, Nfld., d. 11 Sep 1957, Toronto, Ont.; given name: Harry; St. Andrew's Coll.; St. Andrew's, Aura Lee jrs; Toronto Dentals '19; Toronto Granites, 2 Allan Cups, '24 Olympic title; scored 13 of 30 Canadian goals vs. Czechoslovakia in Olympics; player-coach Toronto National Sea Fleas Allan Cup winner '31; mem. Hockey Hall of Fame.

WATSON, Sandy (hockey/builder); b. 28 Mar 1918, Scotland; given name: Alexander Gardner; m. Patricia Brown; c. John Alexander; St. Andrews, Harvard, Cambridge, Columbia Presbyterian; eye surgeon; prof. of opthalmology; architect/mgr. RCAF Flyers '48 Eastern Canada League, world, Olympic title teams; mgr. IHF team; mem. COA, former governor Hockey Canada; with '48 Olympic team mem. Ottawa Sports Hall of Fame; res. Ottawa, Ont.

WATSON, Whipper Billy (wrestling); b. 25 Jun 1917, Toronto, Ont.; d. 4 Feb 1990, Orlando, Fla.; given name: William Potts; m. Eileen; c. John, Georgina, Phillip; pitched, played 2nd base Legion softball team; defence in hockey; football Eastside, Balmy Beach jrs; marathon swimmer CNE, across Hamilton Bay, down Humber River swims; European light heavyweight champion; twice held world title, beat Bill Longson '47, lost to Lou Thesz '48, reclaimed

from Thesz '56, lost in rematch; in 31yrs of wrestling more than 7400 bouts Europe, NA; forced into retirement following '70 auto mishap; prominent fund raiser Ont. Society for Crippled Children, Easter Seals telethon, other charities; B'Nai Brith citizen of '55 award; Ont. good citizenship medal '78; hon. life mem. Easter Seals Society; hon. LLD York; hon. citizen awards from myriad of Cdn cities; mem. Ont. Sports Legends Hall of Fame.

WATT, David (t&f); b. 24 Feb 1952, Barrie, Ont.; UofT, BA, MA; economist; ntl juve. tj title '70-71; ntl jr. title '72; mem. ntl '74-78; ntl sr. tj title '75-77, record 16.05; mem. '75 Pan-Am, FISU, '77 Pacific Conf., '78 Commonwealth Games teams; varsity basketball UofT '71-73, OUAA all-star '73; UofT outstanding athlete '74; res. Scarborough, Ont.

WATT, Laird (tennis); b. 21 May 1913, Montreal, Que.; given name: Malcolm Laird; m. Anne Fraser; c. Nancy, Linda, Sherrill; McGill, BComm; retd chartered accountant; playing mem. Davis Cup team '34, '38, '46; number 1 nationally '38-39; with father 3 US father-son titles; 2 Cdn Intercollegiate singles, doubles titles; 2 ntl indoor men's doubles titles; 1 Maryland state men's doubles title; 3 Que. singles titles, 5 men's doubles; 1 Ont. singles, doubles title; pres. CLTA '62-63, QLTA '51-52, ILTC of Canada '65-69; hon. treas. Commonwealth Games Assn. of Canada '53-59, v-p. '59-63; Centennial medal '67; mem. Cdn Amateur Sports, Cdn Tennis halls of fame; res. Montreal, Que.

WATT, R.N. (tennis); b. 11 Oct 1885, Tara, Ont., d. 4 Jul 1971, Montreal, Que.; given name: Robert; m. Marguerita Vittie; c. Laird, Robert Jr. (d); business exec.; with son Laird US ntl father-son doubles titles '33, '34, '37; CLTA pres. '37-45; only Cdn pres. Intl Lawn Tennis Federation '57; mem. Cdn Amateur Sports, Cdn Tennis halls of fame.

WATT, Sandra (baton twirling); b. 26 Feb 1948, Hamilton, Ont.; given name: Sandra Kelter; div.; c. Christopher; McMaster, BA; leader award winning Hamilton Tiger-Cat Majorettes; coach 20yrs; Ont. chapter chair.; created coaching program adopted by Twirl Canada; coaches' chair. Twirl Canada; Eastern v-p. TCF; res. Burlington, Ont.

WATT, Tom (coaching); b. 17 Jun 1935, Toronto, Ont.; m. Mabs MacPherson; c. Kelly, Ruth Anne, Robert; UofT, BPHE, MEd; hockey coach; coached Toronto Jarvis CI '59-64, Monarch Park HS '64-65; asst. football coach UofT '65-73; asst. coach Vancouver '80, head coach '85-87, Winnipeg '81-83, Toronto '90-92; asst coach Calgary '87-89; head hockey coach UofT '65-80, '84-85, 11 OUAA, 9 CIAU championships; coach Saint John AHL '94; wrote "*How to Play Hockey*"; CIAU coach of '71; TV color commentator '77 world, '84, '94 Olympic hockey tournaments; coach '80 Olympic team; NHL coach of '81-82; scout Toronto '97; mem. UofT Sports Hall of Fame; res. Toronto, Ont.

WATTERS, Lynn (sailing); b. 20 Nov 1916, Montreal, Que.; given name: Lynn Alexander; m. Gretchen; c. Penny, Sally, Alex, Nancy; Lower Canada College, McHill, BEng; chair. Plow & Watters Printing Canada Ltd.; mem. '60, '64, Olympic Dragon, '63 Pan-Am gold Dragon crew; coach '68 Olympic Dragon crew; commodore Royal St. Lawrence

Yacht Club; hon. dir. CYA; chair. CYA racing rules comm., NA Yacht Racing Union racing rules comm.; chairman Intl YRU racing rules comm.; dir. for yachting COA; IYRU rep. organizing comm. for yachting Kingston '76; pres. intl jury '67, '75 Pan-Am Games, F.D. World championships '67, Finn Gold Cup '69, '71; pres. jury Canada Games '69; pres. jury Laser World championships '74; mem. intl jury '71 Pan-Am Games, '72, '76, '80 Olympics, Finn Gold Cup '74, Canada Games '77, '81, finalist Air Canada official of year award '78; last known res. Cornwall, Ont.

WATTS, J.C. (football); b. 18 Nov 1957, Eufala, Okla.; given name: Julius Caesar; Oklahoma; US congressman, chair. house Republican conf.; high-profile US college quarterback; twice led Oklahoma to Orange Bowl victories, twice MVP; joined CFL Ottawa '81, '83-85, Toronto '86; CFL record: 63 scheduled games, completed 785 of 1487 passes for 11,550yds, 59tds, 315 carries for 2106yds, 12tds; 1 Grey Cup final; retiring from football became Baptist youth minister then entered politics becoming 2nd black Republican congressman elected in 60yrs '94; res. Washington, D.C.

WAWRYN, Alexandra (fencing): b. 1 Sep 1978, Warsaw, Poland; following in brother Borys' (former ntl jr. team mem.) footsteps, began as foil fencer then switched to épée. 2 Ont, titles, 2 cadet ntl titles; earned ntl team berth at 15; ntl sr. title '96; set Cdn best-ever performance '95 Cadet worlds in Paris with 2nd; undefeated double medalist '95 Canada Games leading Ont. to team title; Elaine Tanner award '95; res. Ottawa, Ont.

WAY, Kelly Ann (cycling): b. 18 Sep 1964, Windsor, Ont.; chiropractic asst/therapist; road race, pursuit specialist; began racing '75; 1st North Americanto win Tour de France stage '84, 8th stage; only Cdn woman to have worn leaders yellow jersey '89 Tour de France; competed '88, '92 Olympic, '90 Commonwealth, '83 FISU Games, 8 world championships, 6 Tour de L'Aube, 4 Tour de France; gold '87 Tour de L'Aube individual time trial; mem. Windsor/Essex Sports Hall of Fame; res. Windsor, Ont.

WEARRING, George (basketball); b. 2 Jun 1928, London, Ont.; given name: George Arthur; m. Marilyn Krueger; c. Matthew, Olin, Andrew, Joel; UWO, BA, SouthernCal, Michigan, MA, UofSask, PhD; retd. educator; 4yrs basketball, football standout UWO; mem. Ont. all-star basketball, football teams; mem. '52 Olympic team; mem. ntl champion Nortown Tri-Bells '53; res. London, Ont.

WEATHERALL, Jim (football); b. 26 Oct 1929, Texas; m. Ruth Williams; c. Tracy, Clay, Jamie; Oklahoma, BBA; retd. insurance, securities broker; Sooners all-American '50-51, Outland award '51, East-West Shrine Game '51, Senior Bowl, College all-star games '52; pro Edmonton '54, Grey Cup; Philadelphia (NFL) '55-57, Pro Bowl '57, Washington '58-59, Detroit '60-62; mem. Panhandle of Texas, US College Football, Big Eight Football Conf. halls of fame; res. Moore, Oklahoma.

WEBB, Don (coaching); b. 7 Apr 1933, Toronto, Ont.; div.; c. Michaele (d), Kelly; diving coach; pro diver at 15 competing in major water shows throughout world; pro high diving title '63; gymnastics coach '57-59; diving coach from

'60; diving coach at 7 Olympic, 7 Pan-Am, 7 Commonwealth Games, 10 FINA World Cup, 7 World championships, 2 FISU Games; personal coach David Bedard; mem. Cdn Amateur Sports halls of fame; res. Pointe Claire, Que.

WEBER, Richard (skiing/mountaineering); b. 9 Jun 1959, Edmonton, Alta.; m. Josée Auclair; c. Tessum, Nansen; Vermont, BEng; expedition organizer, lecturer; began skiing age 2, competing age 6; 3 ntl jr. boys, 4 ntl sr. cross-country ski titles; ntl biathlon title '81; mem. Cdn team '77, '79 world jr., '82, '85 world men's championships; with teammate Brent Boddy became 1st Cdns to reach North Pole on foot '86; Cdn team leader '88 Soviet-Canadian transpolar ski 1800km expedition from Northern Siberia to Ellesmere Island ntl park via North Pole; guided '89 environmental group that launched 1st hot air balloon from North Pole; with Russian Misha Malakhov set record 102 day two-way polar journey without benifit of dogs, airplanes, resupplies '92; 1st to reach North Pole four times; with Malakhov lead 1st commercial North Pole expedition '93 when two groups totalling 19 persons from 8 countries skied final 100km to Pole; UNESCO International Fairplay award '89; medal of Friendship of Nations from Soviet govt. '89, '96; Russian medal for personal courage '93; Cdn govt. Confederation Medal '93; meritorious service medal '94; wrote *Polar Attack; Polar Bridge, an Arctic Odyssey*; noted lecturer, photographer, writer; mem. Cdn Skiing Hall of Fame; res. Aylmer, Que.

WEDGE, Cathy (equestrian); b. 29 Dec 1950, Saskatoon, Sask.; given name: Katherine; UofSask, hons. BA, LLB; lawyer; working hunter title Seattle '69; mem. ntl team '70-78; mem. '71 Pan-Am 3-day event gold team; ntl 3-day title with City Fella '74; mem. '76 Olympic team; injuries prevented participation '72 Olympic, '75 Pan-Am Games; team gold '78 world championships; US reserve combined title '78; CEF award of merit '78; mem. Saskatoon, Sask. Sports halls of fame; last known res. Vancouver, B.C.

WEDLEY, Jack (football); b. 19 Sep 1917, England; m. Becky MacDonald; c. Joanne, Jacqueline; retd. Seagram's sales mgr; mem. 2 Toronto city HS football title teams; pro football, both offensive, defensive end, Argos, Navy, Regina '37-51; 7 Grey Cup finals, 6 winners; 5 times all-star; mem. 6 Metro Toronto jr., sr. baseball title teams, 2 Maritime titles, 2 Que. titles; scouted by NL teams; 6yrs basketball, 3 Toronto city title teams; mem. ntl champion Navy softball team '42, competed world championships; WW2 Navy phys ed instructor; helped organize Scarborough Kiwanis Little-4 FBL; mem. Scarborough P&R Commission; charter mem. Scarborough Rams FB exec.; league pres., coach Stouffville Whitchurch baseball title team '73; groom for horses daughter Jacqueline shows on Ont. jumping circuit; res. Stouffville, Ont.

WEDMANN, Wilf (t&f); b. 17 Apr 1948, Wagenetz, Germany; SFU, hons BA, Rhodes Scholar, Oxford, MA; pres/CEO Gymnastics Canada; high jump specialist; ntl midget HJ champion '63, ntl jr. '67, 4 ntl sr. titles; mem. '68 Olympic, '67, '71 Pan-Am, '69 Pacific Conference Games teams; silver '71 Pan-Am Games, gold Canada Games '69; ntl jr., sr. record holder; with partner Harry Jerome developed BC premier's sports award program;

varied exec. roles '79-88; dir./coach Kajaks TFC '78-85; pres. BC Athletics '81-85; GM/pres./CEO Athletics Canada '85-88; dir. Athletics Canada '83-85; pres./CEO Cdn Sport & Fitness Admin. Centre '88-96; COA dir. '83-93; pres./CEO Gymnastics Canada from '97; res. Vanier, Ont.

WEILAND, Cooney (hockey); b. 5 Nov 1904, Seaforth, Ont.; d. 7 Jul 1985, Boston, Mass.; given name: Ralph; m. Gertrude; Minnesota; retd.; mem. Owen Sound Memorial Cup winner '24; pro Minneapolis '25-28, NHL Boston '28-32, '35-39, Ottawa '32-33, Detroit '34-35; formed Boston's Dynamite Line with Dit Clapper, Dutch Gainor; Stanley Cup winners '29, '39; NHL record: 509 scheduled games, 173 goals; best season '29-30, 43 goals in 44-game schedule; 2nd team all-star '34-35; coach Bruins, '41 Stanley Cup winners; coach Harvard to '71 retirement; mem. Hockey Hall of Fame.

WEILER, Willie (gymnastics); b. 1 Mar 1936, Rastatt, Germany; given name: Wilhelm Friedrich; m. Fay Joy Prosser; c. Rick, Kimberley; retd. soldier, tool and die maker; '56 jr. all-around German gymnastics title; Cdn gymnastics titles '57-58, '60, '62, '66 working without coach; 1st in NA to perform Yamashita vault in competition; '60 US vaulting title; 1st in NA to perform piked back somersault dismount off horizontal bar; 3 gold, 4 silver, 1 bronze '63 Pan-Am Games; mem. '64, '68 Olympic, '66 worlds teams; mgr '71 Pan-Am Games gym team; mem. Cdn Amateur, Cdn Forces Sports halls of fame; mem. Order of Canada; res. London, Ont.

WEINMEISTER, Arnie (football); b. 23 Mar 1923, Rhein, Sask; Washington; defensive tackle who began pro career with NY Yankees (AAFC) '48; mem. Brooklyn-NY Yankees (AAFC) '49; became mem. NY Giants in NFL merger '50-53; all-AAFC '49; all-NFL '50-53; mem. 4 Pro Bowl teams; dominant defensive tackle of his time; mem. NFL Hall of Fame; res. New York, N.Y.

WEIR, Glen (football); b. 23 Jul 1951, London, Ont.; m. Elizabeth; c. Rachel, Jeannette, Jacqueline; pro football player, employee Imperial Tobacco; nicknamed "Fuzzy"; HS wrestling champion; mem. London Lords Sr. ORFU; launched CFL career as defensive lineman Hamilton '72; dealt to Montreal same season; '72-84 defensive mainstay with Alouettes/Concordes; runnerup '77 Schenley defensive award; James McCaffrey EFC defensive award '77; O'Keefe Cup Alouette player of '77; 5 EFC, 2 CFL all-star awards; politically active; last known res. Dorchester, Ont.

WEIR, Mike (golf); b. 12 May 1970, Bright's Grove, Ont.; m. Bricia; c. Elle Marisa; Brigham Young; Cdn juvenile title '86; Ont. Jr. title '88; Ont. Amateur title '90, '92; twice runnerup Cdn amateur; 2nd team all-American, WAC player of '92; turned pro '93; Cdn tour rookie of '93 award; PGA tour mem. from '98; 3 Cdn tour victories through '99; PGA Air Canada '99; Qualifying tournament '98; Cdn tour Order of Merit and Stroke Average award '97; won '96 Desert tour event; mem. '97 World Cup team; won '99 Cdn Skins Game title; res. Draper, Utah.

WELBOURN, Graham (swimming); b. 11 Jan 1961, Calgary, Alta.; UBC; freestyle sprint specialist; ntl team from '77; 6 ntl titles, 2 ntl, 2 commonwealth records; 2 silver, 1

bronze '79 Pan-Am, 2 bronze '83 FISU, 1 bronze '82 Commonwealth Games; mem. '80 Olympic, '82 world championships teams; res. Claresholm, Alta.

WELCH, Barbara (badminton); b. 28 Feb 1948, Toronto, Ont.; given name: Barbara Hood; m. Garry Welch; sports clothing sales; 5 ntl ladies' doubles titles; ntl mixed doubles '73; mem. 3 Uber Cup, '74 Commonwealth Games, '72 People's Republic of China tour teams; '72; ntl jr. ladies' doubles, finalist Danish Open mixed doubles '71; ntl Open ladies', mixed doubles '74; res. Toronto, Ont.

WELCH, Huck (football); b. 12 Dec 1907, Toronto, Ont., d. 15 May 1979, Ancaster, Ont.; given name: Hawley; m. Helen (d); c. Sandra, Patricia, Douglas, Robert; sales mgr. florist shop; twice topped scorers while helping Delta to 3 national interscholastic titles; Hamilton Tigers '28 helping club to interprovincial titles, Grey Cup '28-29; Montreal Winged Wheelers Grey Cup winners '31; Jeff Russel Memorial Trophy '33; frequent Big Four, all-Cdn all-star; rejoined Hamilton '35-37; twice interprovincial scoring champion, twice runnerup; coach Delta CI srs, Eastwood CI jrs; 1st post-war pres. Tigers '46; coach Kelvin CI, Winnipeg '48-50, Regina jrs '53; Hamilton rep. CFL commissioner '59; mem. Collingwood, Canadian Football, Canada's Sports halls of fame.

WELDON, Craig (judo); b. 5 Jul 1960, Scarborough, Ont.; given name: Craig Steven; m. Elizabeth; Concordia, BA; Ministry of Transportation examiner; black belt age 16; gold ntl jr. championships '77; silver Arizona Desert Open '78, Dutch Open, ntl championships '79; bronze Canada Cup international '79, 3 ntl sr. championships; gold '80 national jr. championships; silver '80 Canada Cup international; '86 Pan-Am silver; competed '88 Olympics; Que., British open titles; 4th degree black belt; Michigan governor's award; Ont. sports achievement awards; res. Whitby, Ont.

WELLS, Jay (hockey): b. 18 May 1959, Paris, Ont.; hockey coach; played defence Kingston (OHA), Binghamton (AHL) '77-80; OHA 1st team all-star; 1st LA choice '79 draft; NHL with Los Angeles '79-88, Philadelphia '88-90, Buffalo '90-92, NY Rangers '92-95, St. Louis '96, Tampa Bay '96-97; NHL record: 1098 scheduled games, 47g, 216a, 114 playoff games, 3g, 14a; asst. coach Portland Pirates (AHL); res. Portland, Maine.

WELLWOOD, William (harness racing); b. 22 Jul 1940, Chatham, Ont.; given name: William Edwin; m. Jean Bailey; c. Paula; began honing skills at 16 in stable of uncle Harold Wellwood; following 11yr apprenticeship launched own stable; 4 times horseman of year Ont. Jockey Club circuit; 2 CTA horseman of year awards; 2 Cdn O'Brien trainer of yr awards; campaigns throughout NA but enjoys greatest success on Greenwood, Mohawk tracks; through '97 2887 victories, $15 million in purses; with Surge Hanover won '73 Batavia Colt & Filly, Hanover Stake, '74 Dexter Cup, Reynolds Memorial Trot; with Village Jiffy won '92. '94 Breeders Crowns; operates training centre Acton, Ont.; res. Cambridge, Ont.

WELSH, Alex (curling); b. 12 Oct 1907, Edinburgh, Scotland, d. 4 Jan 1971, Winnipeg, Man.; m. Edna Howard; c. Judy, Heather, Alexander Jr.; insurance co. mgr.; 3 Man.

Consols titles, 3rd for John Douglas '33 Brier, 3rd for brother Jim '47 (title), '54 Brier entries; twice MCA grand aggregate champion.

WELSH, Jim (curling); b. 18 Feb 1910, Leith, Scotland; m. Kathleen Lloyd; c. Kathleen, Patricia; retd.; 4 Man. Consols titles; 2nd for John Douglas '33 Brier, skipped '37 Brier runnerup, '47 Brier champion (9-0 record), '54 Brier entry; pres. MCA '64-65; 3 MCA bonspiel grand aggregate titles; mem. Canadian Curling Hall of Fame; res. Winnipeg, Man.

WELTON, John (football); b. 9 Dec 1929, Ottawa, Ont.; m. Joan King; c. John Jr., Dan, Caroline; Wake Forest, BBA, Stanford, MBA; retd. pres. development co.; Ottawa '52-54, top rookie '52; Toronto '55-58, Eastern all-star '57; Ottawa sr. city basketball '52-54; res. Mississauga, Ont.

WENDEL, Fred (curling); b. 11 May 1909, Neudorf, Sask.; given name: Louis Fred; m. Betty McLuckie; retd. smelterman; mem. Trail's BC Consols finalists '39-40, '42; Brier runnerup '47. winner '48; Edmonton carspiel winner '49, runnerup '50; 2nd Cdn Legion title team '70; res. Trail, B.C.

WENDLING, Wendy (t&f/football); b. 4 Jun 1901, Brockville, Ont.; d. 26 Nov 1985, Woodstock, Ont.; m. Margaret McKay (d); c. Mary Joan, Peter, Paul; Loyola College, BA, UofT, BPHE; retd. teacher, business exec.; Que. jr. track champion '16-18; mem. Loyola sr. track champions '19-22; coached Jean Thompson ('The Penetang Pansy') to 880 berth '28 Olympics; coached Woodstock CI to 1st WOSSA championship '29 moulding team which scored 408 points while yielding only 6, and no touchdowns all season; repeated title triumphs '30-31; helped organize, coached Oxford Rifles, later called Grads, to ORFU jr. title and defeated Moose Jaw for ntl title '31; coached last provincial title team, the Grads, '36.

WENNINGTON, Bill (basketball); b. 26 Apr 1963, Montreal, Que.; given name: William Percy; St. John's Coll; 7ft centre ntl team '82-94; mem. '83 FISU Games gold team, '84, '92 Olympic teams; 2nd place Jones Cup team '82; 1st round (16th overall) NBA draft pick Dallas '85; dealt to Sacramento '90; played in Knorr, Bologna, Italy, '91-93; signed as free agent by Chicago '93; with Bulls through '98, 3 NBA title teams; joined Sacramento '99; fed. govt. excellence award '84; res. Chicage, Ill.

WENZEL, Joan (t&f); b. 24 Dec 1953, Hamilton, Ont.; given name: Joan Evelyn Eddy; div.; Waterloo, BA, UCal, BEd; teacher, coach; ntl jr. 400m record; mem. '71, '75 Pan-Am, '76 Olympic, '74 Commonwealth Games teams; bronze 800m '75 Pan-Am Games, lost it because she took a cold remedy containing prohibited drug; res. Vancouver, B.C.

WERENICH, Ed (curling); b. 23 Jun 1947, Benito, Man.; given name: Edrick; m. Linda Louise Goulsbra; c. Darren, Ryan; Ryerson PTI; fireman; competed in 11 Ont. Consols/ Tankard/Nokia Cup championships; 3rd Paul Savage rink 4 Consols, 1 Tankard titles; skipped '83-84, '90, '97 Ont. Tankard (Nokia Cup) winners; 10 Briers, '83, '90 winners;

skipped '83, '90 World title winners; twice winner Royal Canadian Classic, Thunder Bay Grand Prix; '82 Molson cashspiel title; skipped 4 *TSN* Skins Game winners; skipped 8 Ont., 4 ntl Firefighters title rinks; fed. govt. champions award '83; Ont. team of '83; Dick Ellis team award '83; mem. Cdn Curling Hall of Fame; res. Holland Landing, Ont.

WERTHNER, Penny (t&f); b. 5 Jul 1951, Ottawa, Ont.; given name: Penny Christine; m. John Bales; c. Neill, Elena; McMaster, BA, Carleton, Waterloo, UofOtt, MSc, PhD; sport psychologist; ntl midget 440yds, juvenile, junior 880yds, juvenile 1500m records; mem. '70, '78 Commonwealth, '71, '79 Pan-Am. '76 Olympic, '77 FISU Games teams; bronze 800m '71 Pan-Am Games, 1500m '78 Commonwealth, '79 Pan-Am Games; world 1000m record '72; Bryce Taylor Momorial award '98; mem. Ottawa Sports Hall of Fame; res. Ottawa, Ont.

WESLOCK, Nick (golf); b. 13 Dec 1917, Winnipeg, Man.; given name: Nick Wisnock; m. Elsie; c. Sheri-lee; retd. company owner, pres., sales rep.; US citizen; using borrowed clubs scored 1st tournament victory '39 Southern Ont. amateur; 405 tournament victories including 4 ntl, 8 Ont. amateurs, 7 Ont. opens, 4 ntl, 11 Ont. srs titles; 16 times leading amateur Canadian Open; mem. 25 Ont. Willingdon Cup, 7 America's Cup teams; 40yrs carried RCGA, OGA certified scratch handicap; 4 times invited to US Masters; special players rep., dir., OGA; mem. RCGA, Canada's Sports halls of fame; res. Burlington, Ont.

WEST, Art (football); b. 29 Jul 1918, Newport, Wales; given name: Arthur Philip; m. Veronica Ferriman; c. Arthur Jr.; Michigan State; retd. distilling industry; centerfielder Maher Shoes Toronto Sr. Baseball League, batting, home run leader '36-38; guard Broadview Rascals, Simpson Grads Toronto Sr. Basketball League; halfback Toronto '36-40, '45-46, 4 Grey Cup champions; '42 Grey Cup champion RCAF Hurricanes; end Montreal '47; captain '40 Argos; league TD leader '37-38; CFL single game interception record with 6 vs Ottawa '36; 1st Argo to return interception for TD 6 Oct '36; all-star Lionel Conacher's all-Cdn team '38; halfback all-Argo dream team '21-41 era; nicknamed "Whippet"; coach Jr. Argos '48-49, Parkdale Lions Intermediates '50, Balmy Beach ORFU '51, Cobourg Galloping Ghosts Srs. '52; v-p. in charge of coaches, playing personnel Kitchener-Waterloo Dutchmen ORFU '64; res. Thornhill, Ont.

WEST, James (football); b. 19 Dec 1956, Fort Worth, Tex.; Texas Southern; linebacker; signed/released NFL Oakland '80; Houston Gamblers USFL '85; CFL Calgary '82-84, Winnipeg '85-92, BC '93; CFL record: 164 scheduled games, 3tds, 21 interceptions, 51.5 QB sacks, 481 tackles, 14 playoff games, 7 QB sacks, 48 tackles; 1 all-Western, 3 all-Eastern, 2 all-CFL all-star; James McCaffrey trophy '87; runnerup Schenley outstanding defensive player '87; mem. 3 Grey Ckp finalists, 2 winners; res. Texas.

WEST, Mike (swimming); b. 31 Aug 1964, Kitchener, Ont.; Waterloo; backstroke specialist; 8 ntl, 1 US titles; 8 ntl sr., 1 Commonwealth Games records; world's best time 200m backstroke 1:57.90 Jan '84; gold 100m backstroke, bronze 200m '82 Commonwealth, silver, 2 bronze '83 Pan-Am, gold 100m, silver, bronze '83 FISU Games; silver 4x100 medley relay, bronze 100m backstroke '84 Olympics; fed. govt. excellence awards '83-84; res. Hamilton, Ont.

WEST-MAHONEY, Stacey (golf); b. 8 Sep 1958, Toronto, Ont.; given name: Stacey Louise West; m. Robert Mahoney; Florida, BA; 3 Ont., ntl jr. titles; ntl Ladies amateur '79; twice low amateur Peter Jackson Golf Classic; mem. 2nd place team world amateur championships '78, Commonwealth championship team '80; mem. 5th ranked UFla. team; res. Thornhill, Ont.

WESTLING, Gunnar (shooting); b. 25 Dec 1907, Trandstrand, Sweden; d. 25 Oct 1997, Vancouver, B.C.; m. Gertrude Norman; c. Kenneth; retd. welder; from '48 mem. DCRA ntl team specializing in fullbore, smallbore rifles and pistols; qualified 8 times for Cdn Bisley team competing on 7 occasions; Duke of Gloucester prize '60, Clocktower award '72; Bisley aggregate winner '66, with son Ken Bisley Families match '78; silver cross ntl champion '66; rep. Canada 6 times NRA prize meetings; helped team win overseas match '70, '72, Kalapore team match '72; 1 of 7 Canadians to win Bisley Queen's prize; only marksman to win BC title in grand-slam style; 5 BC, 1 Cdn target rifle titles; 4 BC Lt.-Governor'smatch titles; won every match, aggregate and team event at least once at BCRA annual prize meet; provincial handgun champion '56, centrefire titlist twice, smallbore titlist '47; mem. BC Sports Hall of Fame.

WESTLING, Ken (shooting); b. 18 Oct 1942, Vancouver, B.C.; m. Marilyn Orchard; c. Wesley, Warren, Wade; banker; grand aggregate champion DCRA '91 shoot; gold '91, '97, silver '94-95 Cdn target rifle; mem. 3 Cdn Palma teams, 6 Cdn Bisley teams; 2 BC championships; with father Gunnar Bisley Families match '78; res, Vancouver, B.C.

WESTPHAL, Don (curling): 26 Aug 1963, Buckingham, Que.; m. Joanne; c. Mathieu; asst. golf pro; began curling age 13; represented Quebec 4 Briers, 2nd for Pierre Charette '89, '93, skip '96 (semifinalist) '97 Briers; res. Buckingham, Que.

WESTWICK, Harry (hockey); b. 23 Apr 1876, Ottawa, Ont., d. 3 Apr 1957, Ottawa, Ont.; m. Ruby Duval; c. Bill, Thomas, Barberry, Elaine, Ula, Beatrice; civil servant; at 17 mem. Ottawa's 1892-93 title winners; Capitals (Silver Seven) 1895-97, 1900-08, Waterloo 1899; mem. 3 successive Ottawa Stanley Cup winners; best season '04-05, 24 goals 13 games; '06 named to 1st sr. all-star team in Cdn hockey; nicknamed "Rat"; refereed in NHA; mem. 1896-1904 Ottawa Capitals lacrosse team, 3 world titles; '02 National Lacrosse Union all-star; football Rough Riders; mem. Ottawa, Hockey halls of fame.

WHALLEY, Joan (administration); b. 17 Dec 1918, Wolverhampton, Eng.; given name: Joan White; m. Evan Whalley; c. Ellen, Leslie, Geraldine, Doree; pres. Deer Lodge (Winnipeg) CC '59-60, hon. life mem., instrumental in development business girls, jr. girls programs; varied exec, roles MLCA, pres. '66-67; chair. '67 ntl championships; pres. CLCA '75; instrumental in development Curl Canada uniform coaching program; CLCA service award; mem.

Canadian Curling, Man. Sports halls of fame; res. Winnipeg, Man.

WHATLEY, Chris (shooting): b. 29 Nov 1970, North York, Ont.; given name: Christopher Russell; Carleton; industrial designer; started shooting age 6; began competing at 14; mem. Queen's York Rangers Army Cadet Corps; mem. RCAC, Ont., Cdn, under-25 (2) Bisley teams; qualified for 5 ntl Bisley, 1 Palma team; DCRA Patron's, Gatineau match gold, Letson silver; ntl under-25 champion '94; competed '93 Bisley Queen's final, '87, '94 St. George's final; twice top 50 Bisley grand aggregate; mem. under-25 title team Bisley '87, Canada '89, '91; capt. Ont. team '92 ntls; capt./ head coach ntl under-25 Bisley team '94; res. Kettleby, Ont.

WHEATON, Robert (swimming); b. 28 Dec 1941, Victoria, B.C.; m. Julie Banfield; c. Fraser, Spencer, Ashley; UVic, UBC, SFU; construction co. pres.; backstroke specialist; silver, bronze '58 BEG, relay silver '59 Pan-Am, 4th relay '60 Olympic Games teams; res. Victoria, B.C.

WHEELER, Lucile (skiing); b. 14 Jan 1935, Montreal, Que.; m. Kaye Vaughan; c. Myrle, Jake; ski coach; ntl jr. downhill title age 12; mem. ntl team at 14; 1st Canadian to claim Olympic skiing medal with '56 downhill bronze; downhill, combined Hakenkammen, Kitzbuhel, Austria, titles '57; 1st NA world title winner downhill, GS, silver combined '58; Bobbie Rosenfeld, Lou Marsh trophies '58, Perry medal Ski Club of Great Britain '58; mem. Order of Canada, Que., Cdn Amateur, Canada's Sports, US National, Cdn Skiing halls of fame; res. Knowlton, Que.

WHITAKER, Denis (builder): b. 27 Feb 1915, Calgary, Alta.; m. Juanita Bergey; c. Gail, Clarke, Michael; RMC; retd. Brig. Gen.; successful college football career played for Hamilton Tigers until war intervened; overseas mem. Cdn team which competed vs. US squad in football; turned attention to horses following WW2 and played key role in developing strong Cdn equestrian program; founded Hamilton Hunt Club; twice horseman of year; chair. Cdn Equestrian team board '60-80; under his guidance Cdn jumping, 3-day event, dressage teams achieved impressive medal collection, Olympic gold, silver, 2 world gold, 1 bronze, 6 Pan-Am gold, 5 silver, 5 bronze; dir, COA; chef de mission '80 Olympic team; governor Olympic Trust; mem. Royal Winter Fair exec. comm.; mem. Canada's Sports Hall of Fame; res. Oakville, Ont./Mexico.

WHITCROFT, Frederick (hockey); b. 1883, Port Perry, Ont., d. 1931, Vancouver, B.C.; mem. Peterborough Colts '01 OHA jr. champions; rover in 7-man hockey days; capt. Peterborough '06 OHA Int. title team; Kenora Thistles '07 Stanley Cup; capt. Edmonton sr. team which challenged Ottawa for '08 Stanley Cup (losing 2 straight); 49 goals that season; Renfrew Millionaires '09-10 season; mem. Hockey Hall of Fame.

WHITE, Al (t&f); b. 28 Mar 1904, Catlin, Ill.; d. circa 1990, Peterborough, Ont.; given name: Albert; m. Louise (d); c. Don, Scott; Wayne, BA, Michigan Tech, BSc; retd. engineer; osteomyelitis of right leg at age 8 threatened athletic career almost from outset; turned to racing horses; HS tennis champion '22; Mich. Tech 100, 220, 440 dash, long jump awards; QB football squad; mem. world champion rifle team '34; semipro football Detroit '34-40; moved to Canada '56; at son Scott's urging competed in Ont. Masters t&f meet Oshawa '74; gold shot put, discus, javelin, hammer, 4x100 relay; from '74 competed regularly in Masters meets at local, provincial, ntl levels, also New Zealand; among top 10 4 world championships; world pentathlon record for men 76 '80, men 77 '81, surpassing '80 performance by 47 points; Grade V ranking as judge for intnl throws, Grade III field referee; officiated Canada, US, Mexico, Sweden, NZ; Governor-General's plaque for youth work; founder, exec. mem. Peterborough TC; officiated '76 Olympics; mem. Ont. t&f, Cdn Masters committees; res. Peterborough, Ont.

WHITE, Ben (harness racing); b. 5 Feb 1873, Whitevale, Ont., d. 1958, Orlando, Fla.; given name: Benjamin Franklin; horseman; drove 1st race at 15; groom for Hamlin Village Farm, East Aurora, N.Y.; assisted trainer Edward 'Pops' Geers; head trainer '03-05; drove 4 Hambletonian, 7 Kentucky Futurity winners plus impressive list of other major stakes and futurity winners; noted as developer, trainer of trotting colts; nicknamed "Dean of Colt Trainers"; among his trainees 3-year-old world champion trotter The Abbe; active driver more than 50 years; Ben White Raceway Orlando, Fla., dedicated in his honor; mem. Harness Racing's, Canadian Horse Racing halls of fame.

WHITE, Betty (t&f); b. 14 May 1915, Niagara Falls, Ont.; given name: Elizabeth McCallum; m. Frank Lewington; c. Nancy, Bill; retd. sales clerk; won 100yd dash Canada vs US meet CNE '32; 2nd 100m, 200m '33 ntl championships, ntl 200m record, outstanding female athlete; mem. gold medal 660yd relay team '34 BEG; res. Hamilton, Ont.

WHITE, Bill (hockey); b. 26 Aug 1939, Toronto, Ont.; given name: William Earl; div. Gail Rice; c. Kimberly, Karrie, Kristen, Kortnee, Kameron; plumbing wholesaler; jr. Toronto Marlboros; defenceman Rochester (AHL) '59-60, '61-62, Sudbury (EPHL) '60-61, Springfield (AHL) '62-63, Los Angeles (NHL) '67-68, Chicago '69-77; 3 times 2nd team all-star; mem. Team Canada '72; coach Chicago '76-77, Toronto Marlboros '80-81; NHL record: 604 scheduled games, 50g, 215a, 91 playoff games, 7g, 32a; played 5yrs Labatt's touring team, 7yrs Canadiens touring team; res. Toronto, Ont.

WHITE, Dalt (coaching); b. 6 Jul 1917, Toronto, Ont.; given name: Alexander Dalton; m. Margaret; c. Peter, Edward, Laurie-Ann, Jeffrey, Brian, Douglas, Janet; UofT, BA, BEd, MEd, OCE; retd. AD; mem. Orillia ntl jr. lacrosse champions '37; lacrosse Toronto Marlboros, Hamilton Tigers, Brampton Excelsiors, UofT; sr. basketball Toronto West End Y; coached Port Colborne to Central Ont. HS football title '40; Toronto Western Tech city, provincial basketball title teams; asst. dir. P&HE branch Ont. govt. '47-57; asst. football coach UofT '51-55, head coach '56-65; Yates Cup '58, '65; AD UofT, '70-76; Thomas R. Loudon Award for contribution to OUAA; mem. UofT Sports Hall of Fame; res. Toronto, Ont.

WHITE, Dennis (boxing); b. 4 Dec 1898, Waterloo, Que; d. circa 1980, St. Laurent, Que; ret'd railway employee; AAU of C boxing supervisor '28, ntl chair. '37-63; mgr. ntl boxing team '30 BEG; coach '32 Olympic team; mgr.

Olympic boxing teams '48, '52, '60; AIBA exec. comm. '71-74; mem. Cdn Amateur Sports, Cdn Boxing halls of fame.

WHITE, Devon (baseball); b. 29 Dec 1962, Kingston, Jamaica; m. Colleen; c. Thaddeus, Davellyn Rae, Anaya Jade; outfielder; drafted by California '81; began pro career Idaho Falls (Pioneer); moved through minors with stops at Danville (A), Peoria (A), Nashua (AA), Redford (A), Midland (AA), Edmonton (AAA); made ML debut with Angels '85, became regular '87 earning berth on Topps all-rookie team; traded to Toronto '91; signed as free agent by Florida '96; traded to Arizona '98, Los Angeles '99; mem. 3 World Series champions; 2 all-star games; 4 Rawlings Gold Glove awards; noted for dramatic catches in centrefield; res. Mesa, Ariz.

WHITE, Donald (shooting): b. 7 Mar 1908, Grand Falls, N.B.; d. 28 Sep 1988, Victoria, B.C.; given name: Donald Odell; c. Charles; attended 1st DCRA matches at 15; qualified 4 Bisley teams, competed in 3; Governor-General's gold medal '32; 5th King's Prize event '33; won MacDonald Challenge Trophy '53; retd from competition '55; grand aggregate silver medal '32, '53; mem. NB Sports Hall of Fame.

WHITE, Julie (t&f); b. 1 Jun 1960, Bancroft, Ont.; given name: Julie Margaret; Boston.; high jump specialist; world age-class record 1.85m '75; ntl jr. record 1.88m '79; US indoor title '76; AIWA pentathlon gold '82; mem. '76 Olympic, '79 Pan-Am, '82 Commonwealth Games teams; ntl jr. pentathlon record 3998 points '78; res. Brampton, Ont.

WHITE, Nancy (golf): b. 26 May 1959, Montague, P.E.I.; m. John Brophy; won '82 Ont. amateur; speedskater turned golfer; just missed qualifying for '80 Olympic speed skating team; joined LPGA tour '84; career low round 66; mem. PEI Sports Hall of Fame; res. Virginia Beach, Va.

WHITE, Tommy (baseball); b. 19 Apr 1922, Regina, Sask., d. 27 Feb 1982, St. Thomas, Ont.; given name: Thomas Towersey; m. Sally Anne Jones; c. Thomas Barry, James Joseph; Assumption College; sporting goods store manager, HS phys ed teacher; pitched Windsor sr. OBA '39, Welland OBA '40; Cleveland farm system Appleton, Wausau, Wis.,. '41-42, London, Ont., army team '43, London Majors Sr.IC '44-53, St. Thomas Elgins Sr. IC player-mgr. '53-60; twice led league won-lost percentage; Sr. IC record: 18 seasons 108 wins, 57 losses; 25-1 record '47; 3 victories 7-game World Sandlot series triumph by London Majors over Fort Wayne '48; frequent IC all-star, MVP '49; mem. Assumption College Eastern Cdn Sr. champion basketball team '45-46.

WHITE, Vance (bobsleigh); b. 26 Oct 1944, Toronto, Ont.; given name: Harvey Vance; m. Margaret Louise Law; Upper Canada College, UofT, BPHE; natural resource exec., pres. Dickenson Mines Ltd.; teenager provincial level diver, swimmer; mem. ntl bobsled team '69-73; mgr. ntl team '74-76; res. Toronto, Ont.

WHITEHOUSE, Reg (football); b. 8 Oct 1933, Montreal, Que.; given name: Reginald Alfred; m. Joanne Lee; c. Timber, Lee; self employed, electrical co.; mem. Notre

Dame de Grace '51 Que. Jr. champions; Saskatchean (CFL) '52-64, 1st string offensive guard, defensive tackle, linebacker, placement kicker 15 seasons; CFL record: 167 converts, 59 field goals; 5 converts '56 all-star game; Tibbits trophy Saskatchewan MVP; WFC record for field goal completion percentage 76.4; organized Saskatchewan players' assn. '64; '66 Grey Cup winner; coached Verdun Invictus to Que. jr. football title '71; res. Cranbrook, B.C.

WHITLEY, Gerry (lawn bowling); b. 22 Apr 1921, Ottawa, Ont.; div.; c. Scott, Steven; Carleton Coll; real estate agent; skipped rinks entry '68 Ont., ntl championships; skipped pairs team to '76 Ont. title, runnerup in ntl championship; res. Ottawa, Ont.

WHITTALL, Beth (swimming); b. 26 May 1936, Montreal, Que.; div.; c. Lyne, Helen, Marc Couvrette; Purdue, BSc; pres. Leader Sports Products LSP Inc.; silver 400m FS relay, finalist 400m FS '54 BEG; gold 100m butterfly, 400m FS, silver 400m medley relay, 400m FS relay '55 Pan-Am Games; 7th 100m butterfly '56 Olympics; Lou Marsh Trophy '55; mem. Cdn Aquatic, Cdn Amateur Sports halls of fame; res. Meaford, Ont.

WHITTIER, Heather (archery); b. 13 Dec 1950, Edmundston, N.B.; given name: Heather Margaret Horricks; m. Carl James Whittier; c. Crystal Louise; UWO hon. BA, UofT, MEd; French immersion teacher; began shooting on husband's team in La Tuque, Que., and, in a span of four yrs blossomed into a ntl and world champion; a natural who works hard perfecting her skills, she has garnered gold at every level, club, regional, provincial, national and world and set 3 ntl records; competes in both target and field events and holds records in both; broke all records in FCA FITA field, bowhunter unlimited class championships '98 to qualify for Canada's gold team; 3 ntl CFAA, 1 IFA, 1 NAFA titles; silver '98 US nationals; world field championship '98; Peel Bd of Ed award of excellence '97; res. Caledon East, Ont.

WHITTINGHAM, Dianne (field hockey); b. 27 Apr 1953, Vernon, B.C.; given name: Dianne Louise; UVic, BEd, UBC, MPhE; UAlta;teacher; mem. BC sr. women's field hockey team '70-80, ntl team '72-80; nen, FIH World Cup team '78; mem. BC jr. softball team '73 Canada Games; finalist '74 Victoria female athlete of year; '79 Vancouver Island women's FHA MVP; '80-81 Vancouver women's FHA MVP; res. Victoria, B.C.

WHITTLE, Doug (gymnastics); b. 25 Mar 1917, Calgary, Alta.; d. 3 Apr 1998, Vancouver, B.C. c. 3; UofT BPHE; Oregon MSc, PhD; retd. professor UBC; received early gymnastics training Calgary YMCA '35-38; physical dir. Winnipeg Y '38-42; coached gymnastics/swimming/diving/ basketball UBC '45-65; organizer/pres. BC Gymnastic Assn '48-62; mgr. ntl team '59 Pan-Am Games, '62 worlds; ntl gymnastics chair '62; organized 1st international gymnastics clinics in Canada '65; gymnastic men's judge '65-77; aquatic dir. Cranbrook pool '38; rec. dir. Geraldton, Ont., '42; hon. mem. Cdn, BC gymnastic bodies; ntl physical fitness scholarship '49; Cdn Red Cross 25yr service cross; Royal Life Saving Society 25yr service cross; Varsity T for gymnastics '43-45.

WHITTON, John (soccer); b. 8 May 1942, Norwich, Eng.; given name: John Michael; m. Noreen Ella Turnham; c. Carie Anne, Amanda Jayne, Michael John; London School of Economics, MSc, Aberystwyth, hons. BA; civil servant; 20yrs competitive soccer in Britain; coached girls soccer taking teams age 11 through sr. to tournament action throughout NA; organized National Capital Invitational girls tournament '83 starting with 2 divisions and 24 teams and growing to 9 divisions and 180 teams and international in scope; Cdn. Assn. for Advancement of Women in Sport award '94; Ottawa ACT Gord Trivett Memorial trophy '98; res. Nepean, Ont.

WICKENHEISER, Hayley (hockey); b. 12 Aug 1978, Calgary, Alta.; UCal; competed for Calgary Northwest Bruins boys bantam AA team; bronze with Edmonton Chimos '95 sr. women's nationals; MVP in title winning '91 Canada Winter Games match; 3 world, 2 Pacific Rim, 3-Nations Cup gold; mem. '98 Olympic silver medal team; competed '95 world jr. softball championships; referred to as the "Wayne Gretzky of women's hockey"; mem. Olympic Oval high performance female hockey program; invited to Philadelphia Flyers prospect camp '98; res. Calgary, Alta.

WIEBE, Wendy (rowing); b. 6 Jun 1965, St. Catharines, Ont.; m.; began rowing '81; mem. '83 ntl jr team; mem. ntl team from '84; with Colleen Miller 3 consec. worlds double sculls gold; single scull silver '95 Pan-Am Games; straight 4s bronze '86 Commonwealth Games; single scull gold '93 FISU Games; 1 Cdn, 7 US titles; competed '86 Commonwealth, '90 Goodwill, '95 Pan-Am, '96 Olympic Games; res. St. Catharines, Ont.

WIEBUSCH, Harry (boxing); b. 16 Jan 1916, Montreal, Que.; m. Heidi, Karen;UWO; retd. fuel co. pres.; '33 Que. junior 160lb title; '34-36 Que. 175lb title; boxing coach '36 Olympics; mem. Olympic Club Canada; res. Mount Royal, Que.

WIEDEL, Gerry (fencing); b. 1 May 1933, Germany; m. Pacita Dumenieux; contractor; ntl épée champion '65, foil '65, '69, '70; mem. '67 Pan-Am, '70 Commonwealth (bronze team foil), '68, '72 Olympic teams; res. Toronto, Ont.

WIEDEL, Pacita (fencing); b. 31 Mar 1933, Spain; given name; Pacitia Dumenieux; m. Gerry Wiedel; ntl women's foil title '59-64, '66, runnerup '67-68, '71; topped rankings '70-71; 9 Ont. titles; 5th US championships '65, 2nd US team championships '64; mem. '64 Olympic, '63, '67 Pan-Am, bronze individual, team foil '67, '70 Commonwealth Games teams, bronze team '70; res. Toronto, Ont.

WIETZES, Eppie (motorsport); b. 28 May 1938, Groningen, Holland; sep.; c. Michael, Douglas, Marlain; Ont. Trade School; class A mechanic, owner auto dealership; drove Comstock Mustang, GT40 '65-67; mem. Ford team Winter Rally, Shell 4000; drove Formula 1 Lotus '67 ntl GP rand; ntl Road Racing title with Lola T142 '69; sponsored by Formula Racing, drove McLaren M10B in Canadian, US Formula A competition repeating Cdn triumph; never placed lower than 6th ntl driving title series '70-75; returned to racing with Swiss Chalet team after 6 year retirement '81 and won 1st round CRC Chemical Trans-Am series; mem. Cdn Motorsport Hall of Fame; res. Thornhill, Ont.

WIGSTON, Fran (volleyball); b. 28 May 1935, North Bay, Ont.; given name: Frances Anne; m. John Eberhard; UWO, BA, MA; university prof.; mem. ntl volleyball title teams '66-68, ntl basketball team '67-68; coach-player London Grads basketball team '69-74; basketball silver '67, gold '71 Canada Winter Games; coached UWO 6 Ont., 3 ntl women's volleyball titles, UWO women's t&f team '69-71, team mem. '64-74; coached London Junos volleyball team '71-75, Ont. sr. women's title '73-74, ntl finalists '74; coached sr. men's London Kineldiego volleyball team '73-75; ntl women's volleyball team '73 FISU Games; coached London Lions Olympic t&f Club '64-68; mem. National Advisory Council on Fitness and Amateur Sport; res. Komoka, Ont.

WILEY, Alison (t&f): b. 11 Oct 1963, Toronto, Ont.; Stanford; middle distance specialist; 2 ntl 3000m, 1 1500m, 5000m, cross-country titles; Canada Games gold 1500m, 3000m; 4 Ont. HS titles; silver world cross-country championships; res. Toronto, Ont.

WILHELMSEN, Franz (builder): b. 7 Oct 1918, Trondheim, Norway; m. Annette Seagram; c. Annette Gina, Franz Philip; Norway Business Coll., UBC; businessman, ski resort developer; extensive speed skating/skiing as youngster in Norway; served in Norweigan military; Cdn citizen '47; real estate developer; earned nickname 'Whistler's Father' serving as pres. Garibaldi Lifts '60-84, developer of Whistler Mountain; Greater Vancouver man of '66; fed. govt Queen's Medal '77, tourism medallion '84, certificate of merit '88; Canada West Ski Areas Marshall Award; freeman of resort municipality of Whistler; mem. Canadian Skiing Hall of Fame; res. Vancouver, B.C.

WILKES, Debbi (figure skating); b. 16 Dec 1946, Toronto, Ont.; m. John Darroch; c. Christopher, Jillian; YorkU., hons. BA, Mich. State, MA; *CTV Sportsnet* broadcaster; with late Guy Revell won Canadian, NA pairs titles '63-64; Olympic silver '64; CTV color commentator for international, ntl skating events; Ont. Achievement Award; res. Scarborough, Ont.

WILKES, Jimmy (baseball); b. 1 Oct 1925, Philadelphia, Pa.; given name: James Eugene; div. Hattie; c. James, Janice, Patricia, Eugene; m. Donna Newton; retd municipal employee; mem. Negro American League '45 teaming with Larry Doby, Monte Irvin, Don Newcombe, same league as Jackie Robinson, Josh Gibson, Willie Mays, Satchel Paige, Bob Thurman; Dodgers organization '50, 2 seasons Eastern League at Elmira, N.Y., Trois-Rivieres, Lancaster, Pa., Interstate League; '52 season Hank Aaron teammate Indianapolis Clowns; Brantford (Sr. IC) '53-62; all-star centrefielder; 10yr IC career BA .294; best season '56 batted .344, led league in hits, doubles, times at bat, walks, only player to appear in all league, playoff games; mgr. Brantford '58; mem. 3 pennant winners, 5 playoff champions; umpire Brantford city league '64, Senior Intercounty '65-86; mem. Brantford & Area Wall of Recognition; res. Brantford, Ont.

WILKINS, Bruce (shooting); b. 29 May 1933, Hamilton, Ont.; given name: Bruce Gray; m. Bertha Stewart; c. Sandie, Janet; Mohawk College; retd. electronics draftsman; ntl open sporting rifle champion '66; ntl indoor standard rifle champion '70; 7 Ont. titles '67-74; mem. ntl champion Inter-Cities teams '63-75; mem. ntl rifle team '69-72; mem. '70 world, '71 Pan-Am Games teams; Ont. rifle coaching chair. '73-76, ntl chair. '73-97; ntl rifle team mgr.-coach from '76; rifle shooting chair. '76 Olympiad for physically disabled; coach '77 Ont. gold medal Canada Games rifle team; coach 2 Commonwealth Games, 9 world championships, 6 Olympic Games, 8 Benito Juarez, 1 Pan-Am Games, 5 World Cup, 1 World Air Gun, 1NA championship rifle teams; res. Ancaster, Ont.

WILKINSON, Tom (football); b. 4 Jan 1943, Greybull, Wyo.; given name: Thomas Edward; m. Anna Louise Michelena; c. Sherry, Tom Jr., Jodi; Wyoming; football coach; pro Toronto Rifles Continental League '66, Toronto '67-70, BC '71, Edmonton '72-82; led CFL pass completions avg. '72; quarterbacked Edmonton 9 Grey Cup finals, 6 winners; CFL record: completed 1613 of 2662 pass attempts for 22,579 yds, 154tds, .606 percentage, 126 intercepted; league record holder best single game .905 (19-21) vs. Ottawa '74, single season .6604 (177-268) '72; Edmonton athlete of '74; Jackie Parker Trophy, Canada Packers Award '72, '74; Schenley outstanding player award '74, runnerup '78; top QB '79 all-pro voting; head coach UAlta Golden Bears; mem. Edmonton Eskimo Wall of Honor, UAlta., Cdn Football, Alta. Sports halls of fame; res. Sherwood Park, Alta.

WILLIAMS, David (football): b. 1 Jun 1964, Los Angeles, CA; Illinois; wide receiver; NFL Chicago, Tampa Bay, LA Raiders '86-87, CFL BC '88-89, Ottawa '90, Edmonton '91, Toronto '91-92, Winnipeg '93-95; CFL record: 101 scheduled games, 79tds, 439 receptions for 7197yds, 78tds, 5 playoff games, 2tds; 2 Western, 2 Eastern, 2 CFL all-star; Schenley outstanding player award '91; Jeff Nicklin Memorial trophy '88; tied 1 CFL record; 3 Grey Cup finals, 1 winner; res. Los Angeles, CA.

WILLIAMS, Dawn (canoeing): b. 13 Nov 1959, Sao Paulo, Brazil; given name: Dawn Elizabeth; m. Maks Zupar; Guelph, BA, MSc, UofT, BEd; teacher; represented Canada 5 world cup marathon canoeing championships; US C2 women's open sprint title '92; amassed 8 gold, 6 silver, 6 bronze in international competition '87-92; also cross-country ski competitor; res. Paisley, Ont.

WILLIAMS, Desai (t&f); b. 12 Jun 1959, Basseterre, St. Kitts; m. Hazel; York; sprint specialist; ntl 200m outdoor title '77, '82, 100m, 200m titles '79-81; mem. '77, '81 Pacific Conf., '78, '82 Commonwealth, '79, '83 Pan-Am, '80, '84 Olympic, '83 FISU Games teams; '83 CIAU 300m, 60m titles; silver 4x100m relay '82 Commonwealth Games, 100m, 4x100m relay silvers '83 FISU Games; bronze 4x100 relay '84 Olympics; ntl sr. record, world best 1:23.97 4x200m relay '83 ntl indoor championships; ntl sr. record 33.53 300m, 6.66 60m '83 CIAU championships; male athlete of meet '82 8-nation invitational; 2 CIAU indoor t&f male athlete of yr awards; 2 CIAU indoor t&f records; res. Baltimore, Md.

WILLIAMS, Dick (baseball); b. 7 May 1929, St. Louis, Mo.; given name: Richard Hirshfeld; m. Norma Marie Mussato; c. Kathi, Ricky, Marc; Pasadena City College; baseball mgr.; minor pro Dodgers organization '47-50; 14 ML seasons outfielder, utility infielder Brooklyn, Baltimore, Cleveland, Kansas City, Boston; 1023 games, .260 career BA; '53 World Series; mgr. Toronto Maple Leafs (IL), consecutive Governor's Cup titles '65-66; Red Sox '67-69, AL pennant '67; coach Expos '70; mgr. Oakland A's '71-73, consecutive AL pennants, World Series victories '72-73; mgr. California Angels '74-76, Expos '76-81, Padres from '82, NL pennant '84; reached 1000 victory plateau 5 Aug '80 vs Mets in Montreal; ML mgr. of year (*Sporting News*) '67; AL mgr. of year (*AP*) '71; NL mgr. of year (*AP*) '79; res. Tampa, Fla.

WILLIAMS, Freddie (t&f); b. 24 Feb 1962, Cape Town, S.A.; m.; c. Lesley-Ann, Megan; teacher; emigrated to Canada '89; 800m specialist; began competing age 15; ntl sr. 800m record 1:45.13 '93 worlds; 6 NCAA, 11 International Invitational, 4 ntl outdoor, 1 Ont. gold; competed '92 Olympic Games, '93 world indoor, outdoor meets; mem. Toronto Olympic Club; 1st Cdn man to achieve berth in 800m final 8 at either Olympic or outdoor world championships '93 Worlds; TOC athlete of '91; res. Mississauga, Ont.

WILLIAMS, Gizmo (football): b. 31 May 1963, Memphis, Tenn.; given name: Henry; specialty teams/wide receiver; 2yrs Northwest Miss jr. coll, 2yrs East Carolina; Memphis Showboats USFL '85; CFL Edmonton '86-88, '90-99, Philadelphia NFL '89; CFL record (through '98): 183gp. 51tds, 306pts, 199recept, 3644yds, 21tds, 8844 punt ret., 10,099yds, 26tds, 317koret., 6917yds, 1td; all-time CFL leader punt return tds; 7 Western, 5 CFL all-star; most punt return yardage single game (221); most punt return tds single season (4); set/tied 13 CFL punt return records, 1 Grey Cup record; 4 Grey Cup finals, 2 winners; res. Edmonton, Alta.

WILLIAMS, Jerry (football); b. 1 Nov 1923, Spokane, Wash.; m. Marian Munroe; c. Jerry Bill, Rebecca Sue, Todd David, Julie Ann, Tyler Laurie; Washington State, BSc, Temple; rancher, retd. charter flying service owner; football coach; competed East-West Shrine Game, Chicago college all-star game; pro Los Angeles '49-52, world champions '51, Philadelphia '53-54; head coachMontana '55-57; defensive coach Philadelphia '58-63; asst. coach Calgary (CFL) '64, head coach '65-68, Grey Cup final '68, WFC pennant '65; head coach Philadelphia '69-71, Hamilton '72-75; asst. coach Calgary '81-82; guided '72 Ticats to single season team won-lost record 11-3, Grey Cup victory; CFL coach of '67; Dan Reeves' all-time Rams team; res. Prescott, Ariz.

WILLIAMS, John (motorsport); b. 26 Mar 1939, Toronto; m. Marilyn Lake; c. Greg, Wade, Terry; pro rider, STP team mgr.; 5 world hill climbing titles; 5 US grand ntl titles; once recognized in *Guinness Book of World Records* as only Cdn world champion in any motor sport in Cdn history; 25 consec. 1-2 finishes '80-81 season; 9 ntl hill climbing titles; with sons Greg, Wade only Cdn pro hill climbers; mem. Cdn Motorsport Hall of Fame; res. Markham, Ont.

WILLIAMS, Lynn (t&f); b. 11 Jul 1960, Regina, Sask.; given name: Lynn Kanuka; m. Paul Williams; UofSask, San Diego State; TV commentator; 3000m specialist; ntl 3000m title '83; gold 2000m West German Intl meet, 1500m Sweden International meet '83; bronze 3000m '83 FISU, '84 Olympics; 11 Cdn running records; won 5th Ave. mile '85; gold 3000, bronze 1500 '86 Commonwealth Games; bronze '89 World Cross-Country; competed '84, '88 Olympics; 6 BC athlete of yr, BC Premier's awards; Sport BC athlete of '85; Dr. Phil Edwards awards '88-89, Vanier award '90; spokesperson for anti-drug, stay in school programs; mem. Cdn Olympic, Sask Sports halls of fame; res. Vancouver, B.C.

WILLIAMS, Paul (t&f); b. 8 Jul 1956, Ottawa, Ont.; given name: Paul Gregory; m. Lynn Kanuka; Guelph, UofT, UBC; mem. OFSAA cross-country title team '73; ntl juve. cross-country title '74; CIAU cross-country '77-78, '80; ntl sr. indoor 3000m, outdoor 5000m '79; indoor record 3000m 7:54.1; 3000m steeplechase record 8:35.8 FISU Games '79; mem. '80, '84 Olympic, world cross-country teams '80, World Cup team '81; won Toronto Inter-Regionals 10,000m '81, Americas' trials 5000m '81, Nice France 5000m '81, MTRAA Toronto 10 miles '81; grandfather Jack Tait mem. '08, '12 Olympic t&f teams; res. Vancouver, B.C.

WILLIAMS, Percy (t&f); b. 19 May 1908, Vancouver, B.C.; d. 29 Nov 1982, Vancouver, B.C.; insurance consultant; gold 100m, 200m '28 Olympics; tied world record 100m (10.6) on grass track '25, tied world mark 100yds (9.6); won 21 of 22 races during 21-day span on US indoor circuit '29; world record 100m (10.3) '30; gold 100yds '30 BEG; mem. '32 Olympic team; retd. from racing at 22; Canada's t&f athlete of half century; mem. Officer Order of Canada '79; BC, Cdn Amateur, Canada's Sports halls of fame.

WILLIAMS, Roy (basketball); b. 8 Jul 1927, Winnipeg, Man.; given name: Roy Edward; m. Lenore Johannesson; c. Christopher, Cynthia, Andrea, Alison;UMan, BComm, CLU; retd. branch mgr. Great West Life; mem. city, provincial HS title teams, team capt. '44-45; mem. Lazy L jr. city league title teams '43-45; UMan Bisons jr. varsity city, provincial title teams '45-46; 4yrs mem. UMan sr. varsity team; Winnipeg sr. league champions '50, Western Cdn titlists, ntl finalist '50; mem. Winnipeg Paulins, twice Winnipeg sr. champs, Western Cdn finalist; mem. league champion Kings Best '55-56, UMan Grads '50-53, 3 consec. league titles, '52 Western Cdn champions, ntl finalists; mem. '52 Olympic team; Winnipeg sr. league MVP '51; all-star team mem. '49-53; Birks Trophy winner '64 Man. bonspiel; Winnipeg Granite Club champion '64; res. W.Vancouver, B.C.

WILLIAMS, Tiger (hockey); b. 3 Feb 1954, Weyburn, Sask.; given name: David James; owner Tigermen Developments; 4yrs jr. Swift Current (WHL); prolific scorer noted for pugilistic efforts as enforcer, hence nickname "Tiger"; NHL Toronto `74-80, Vancouver `80-84, Detroit `84-85, Los Angeles `85-87, Hartford `87-88; NHL record: 962 scheduled games, 2441g, 272a, 3966pim, 83 playoff games, 12g, 23a, 455pim; authored *Tiger-A Hockey Story*; dir. 5 public companies; partner snowboard mfgr. One Track;

owner Merrick, B.C., jr. hockey team; involved with roller hockey as player, team owner; plays regularly in adult sr. league; competed `98 Heroes of Hockey game; res. Vancouver, B.C.

WILLIAMSON, Jean (basketball): b. 4 Feb 1919, Edmonton, Alta.; m. Thomas Quilley (d); c. Wendy, Ronald; McDougall Commercial; retd.; competitive swimmer winning numerous medals as youngster; also active in t&f, tennis; member of famed Edmonton Grads basketball team; brother Gordon was "voice" of Grads on radio; standout 5-pin bowler earning several Alta trophies; won Cdn Legion singles title '75; mem. Alta., Cdn Basketball halls of fame; res. Edmonton, Alta.

WILLIAMSON, Peter (speed skating): b. 1 Aug 1946, Winnipeg, Man.; d. 7 Jul 1991, Winnipeg, Man.; m. Lori Toshack; c. Chris, Tyler, Reece, Elizabeth; ski centre mgr.; Calif. jr. cross-country running title '62; ntl indoor mass start gold '66-67; mem. Man. team '67 Canada Winter Games; mem. ntl pursuit cycle team '67 Pan-Am Games; ntl Olympic style speed skating gold '68; mem. Cdn Speed skating team '68 Winter Olympics, cycling team Summer Olympics; Man. Olympic style speed skating gold '68; Man. coach/tech. dir. MSSA '83-88; Man. cycling coach '83-87; helped launch Roller Sport Man.; helped found Man. Coaching Assn, 1st pres.; helped launch Snowman Triathlon, Cobblestone Classic; torch bearer '88 Olympic relay; tech. dir CASSA '89-91; CAM coach of yr award bears his name; ntl women's short track relay team dedicated '92 Olympic gold to his memory; color commentator CBC, TSN world championships; Man. order of sports excellence; mem. Cdn Speed Skating, Man. Sports halls of fame.

WILLS, Stan (shooting): b. 31 Dec 1950, Lethbridge, Alta.; ex-carpenter, family pre-cast concrete co. mgr.; handgun specialist; mem. ntl team from '82; competed 1 world championship, 30 World Cup, 3 Benito Juarez, 2 Pan-Am, 2 Commonwealth Games; with Mark Howkins pairs rapid fire silver '90, with John Rochon bronze '94 Commonwealth Games; team air pistol bronze '95 Pan-Am Games; 3 ntl free pistol, 1 men's air pistol, 2 rapid fire, 3 standard, 2 centrefire pistol, 1 Cdn 1800, 2700 centrefire titles; 3 Crossman air pistol titles, 11 grand aggregate titles; Alta. achievement award; mem. Lethbridge Sports Hall of Fame; res. Lethbridge, Alta.

WILLSEY, Ray (football): b. 30 Sep 1929, Griffin, Sask.; m. Barbara Bigelow; c. Lee Ann, Janet, Louise; California, BSc; retd. football coach; pro Edmonton '53-55, all-Western defensive back rookie season; mem. coaching staff NFL St. Louis Cardinals, Los Angeles Raiders, WLAF London Monarchs; res. Los Angeles, Calif.

WILLSIE, Harry (shooting): b. 20 Dec 1928, Jacksonville, Mo.; div.; c. Billie, Alan, Carol Dean, Debora; Missouri, BA; retd. real estate agent; p-pres. Cdn Skeet Shooting Assn.; dir. Shooting Federation of Canada; dir. QSSF, COJO Tir Mission '76, QTSA '59-67, Amateur Trap Shooting Assn. of America '59-68; pres. CTSA '63-67; gold, record '74 Commonwealth Games; mem. '64, '68 Olympic, '67, '71, '74 Pan-Am Games teams; mgr. '78 Commonwealth Games team; 6 ntl trap/skeet titles; only Cdn to score perfect 100x100 in American trap doubles; res. Ville d'Esterel, Que.

WILMSMEYER, Klaus (football): b. 4 Dec 1967, Mississauga, Ont.; m. Deborah Lynn; c. Kasey Nicole; Louisville; punter; lettered in football/soccer at Lorne Park HS; punter/place kicker at Louisville; *AP* 1st team all-South Independent '90; career longrest punt 84yds '90; tied school record 52yd field goal vs. Virginia '89; drafted in NFL by Tampa Bay '92; signed as free agent by San Francisco '92 earning all-rookie status *Football News, Pro Football Weekly, College & Pro Football Newsweekly*; joined New Orleans Saints '95; sat out '97 season then joined Miami '98; best season punting avg 41.4yds '94; best NFL punt 63yds '96; through '97 only 1 of 305 career punts blocked; mem. Super Bowl XXIX title team; res. Louisville, Ky.

WILSON, Al (football): b. 6 Apr 1950, Duncan, B.C.; given name: Alan Douglas; m. Robin Knowles; c. Chelsea, Alana, Colby; Montana State, BA; entrepreneur; all-Big Sky Conf. centre; mem. BC '72-86; all-WFC, all-Cdn centre '75-81; 3 times Schenley lineman award finalist, winner '77; knee injury suffered '82 season ended remarkable record of never having missed a practice, pre-season or regular season game in his career, 167 consecutive regular season games with Lions; jersey 52 retd. by Lions; mem. Cdn Football Hall of Fame; res. N. Vancouver, B.C.

WILSON, Alex (rowing): b. 2 Feb 1931, Toronto, Ont.; m. Sheila Sherman; c. Doug, Bruce, Sandra; Brock; policeman; competed at Cdn, US championship level; coached Olympic rowing team '60; coached HS rowers to Cdn, US schoolboy victories; FISA licensed rowing official; officiated at world, Olympic, Pan-Am Games level; mem. Cdn Amateur Sports Hall of Fame; res. St. Catharines, Ont.

WILSON, Ben (football): b. 12 Jul 1926, London, Ont.; d. 11 Jan 1995, Toronto, Ont.; given name: Benson Andrus; m. Charlotte Henry Harrington; c. Benson Andrus 2nd, Meredith Jane; UWO, BSc, Oxford, BSc; asst. deputy minister, Ministry of Colleges and Universities; outstanding lineman UWO Mustangs '44-47; '48-50; Oxford basketball team capt. '49-50; University College (Oxford) rugger team, Inter-College Cup semifinalists '49-50; coach football, basketball Ridley College, St. Catharines '50-51.

WILSON, Bruce (soccer): b. 20 Jun 1951, Vancouver, B.C.; sep. Donna Beltley; c. Derek, Colin; soccer coach UVic; minor soccer BC; rejected pro overtures Everton English League; mem. ntl team '74-86; capt. '76-79; pro Vancouver Whitecaps '74-78, Chicago Sting '78-80, NY Cosmos '80, Toronto Blizzard '81-85; mem. NY Soccer Bowl champions '80; capt. Chicago, Toronto, Vancouver teams; NASL "iron man" record playing 161 consec. games '75-80; played every minute of every league and playoff game over 6.5-year span; mem. '86 World Cup team; 1st Cdn to receive NASL all-star ranking; 1st team 3, 2nd team 3, hon. mention 1; coach '93 FISU Games team; coach UVic; 2 CIAU coach of yr awards; named to Pele's '88 world all-star team; mem. BC Sports Hall of Fame; res. Victoria, B.C.

WILSON, Chris (wrestling): b. 30 Dec 1967, Winnipeg, Man.; SFU; began competing age 13; mem. ntl team '87-94; World Cup 68kg silver '91, bronze '89-90; gold US, Polish Grand Prix '93, Czech GP '92; 5 ntl FS titles; Canada Cup silver '92; competed '90 Goodwill, '92 Olympic, '94 Commonwealth Games; Viscount Alexander award '87; BC male athlete of '87; CAWA wrestler of '90-91; Danny Gallivan Fair Play award '92; BC sr. and overall athlete of '91; Intl Fair Play award '93; Johnny F. Bassett award '93; res. Coquitlam, B.C.

WILSON, Don (football): b. 21 Jul 1961, Washington, D.C.; North Carolina State; def. back; Buffalo Bills (NFL) '84-86, signed by Montreal (CFL) '87 but picked in dispersal draft by Winnipeg '87, moved to Edmonton same month; played in CFL with Edmonton '87-89, '93-94, '98, Toronto '90-92, '95-96. BC '97; CFL record: 188 games, 640 tackles, 59int for 990yds, 5tds, 12 fumble returns for 197yds, 3tds; 13 playoff games, 1td; 4 Grey Cup finals, 4 winners; 3 Western, 4 CFL, 3 Eastern all-star; last known res. Edmonton, Alta.

WILSON, Doug Jr. (hockey): b. 5 Jul 1957, Ottawa, Ont.; given name: Douglas Frederick; m. Kathy Kovisto; c. Lacey, Douglas III, Chelsea, Charles; AGM/dir. player development San Jose '97-99; former coordinator player relations/ business development NHLPA; minor hockey Ottawa; jr. Ottawa 67's '74-75; OHA all-star defenceman; Memorial Cup finalist '77; Memorial Cup tournament all-star defenceman '77; pro Chicago '77-91, 1st draft choice, 6th overall, traded to expansion San Jose '91-93, team capt.; mem. Team Canada '84 Canada Cup, '87 Rendez-Vous series; Norris trophy '82; pres. NHLPA '91-93; mem. pension dispute bargaining comm.; NHL record: 1024 scheduled games, 237g, 590a, 95 playoff games, 19g, 61a; Cedarhill Golf Club champion '76; Toronto Thunderbird Invitational '76; co-owner San Jose Rhinos roller hockey team; board mem. CHA, Black Hawks Alumni, San Jose Children's Shelter; oversees Doug Wilson Foundation; Ottawa 67's retd. his jersey #7; mem. Ottawa Sports Hall of Fame; res. Los Altos, California.

WILSON, Doug Sr. (t&f/hockey): b. 25 Oct 1929, Toronto, Ont.; d. 29 Aug 1983, Ottawa, Ont.; given name: Douglas Frederick; m. Verna Myers; c. Murray, Victoria, Patricia, Douglas Jr.; UWO, BA; staff relations officer Carleton Board of Education; mem. UWO track team; involved with Ottawa 67's hockey organization from inception working with minor league development program; v-p. Man. t&f Assoc.; mem. ntl selection comm.; chief scout Ottawa 67's hockey club '74-78.

WILSON, Harold (speedboat racing): b. 12 Oct 1911, St. Catharines, Ont.; d. 11 Dec 1995, Montserrat, W.I.; given name: Harold Albert; m. Lorna Margaret Reid; c. Ernest, Launi, Marion, Harold, Patricia; Ridley College, UofT, BSc; manufacturer, pres. Ingersoll Machine and Tool Co., pres. Morrow Screw and Nut Co.; world 225 cubic inch class title Toronto '33-34 with 1st in series of inboard hydroplanes, Little Miss Canada series boats III, IV, V, VI, before moving up to 12 litre Gold Cup class and competing for this trophy at Lake George and Detroit; won Silver Cup at Detroit, President's Cup Washington with Gold Cup class hydroplane Miss Canada III; NA speed record for this class, world 12 litre title; challenged for Harmsworth Trophy '47 with unlimited hydroplane Miss Canada IV; world speed record at Picton; also made unofficial 173 mph run; retired from competitive races although he drove Miss Canada IV in Gar Wood Memorial race at Detroit and Gravenhurst Antique Boat Show; turned to auto racing; 2 terms pres. Cdn

Automobile Sports Clubs; dir., pres. Mosport race track in formative years; avid sail boater; mem. Gulf 100 mph club; life mem. Picton Yacht Club; author *Boats Unlimited*; mem. Gulf Marine, Canada's Sports halls of fame.

WILSON, Jean (speed skating): b. 1910, Glasgow, Scotland, d. 1933, Toronto, Ont.; Toronto indoor, NA champion '31; rep. Canada '32 Olympic demonstration event, 500m in record 58:00, world record for 1500m (2:54.2); died from progressive muscular disease; *Toronto Telegram* donated Jean Wilson Trophy in her memory to fastest indoor woman skater '34; mem. Cdn Speed Skating, Amateur, Canada's Sports halls of fame.

WILSON, Lefty (hockey): b. 15 Oct 1919, Toronto, Ont.; given name: Ross Ingram; m. Lillian Bhowe; c. Ross Martin; retd. athletic trainer; mem. Toronto Shirley St. School softball title team, Ont. title Brock Grads lacrosse team, K of C juve. baseball title team; goal Toronto Lions OHA jr. team; baseball St. Catharines, Niagara district teams '38-43; service softball batting title; minor pro 1st baseman Roanoke Piedmont League, Savannah Sally League; Brantford (Sr.IC); goaler Calder Cup champion Indianapolis (AHL); 3 partial games in NHL as fillin for Boston, Toronto, Detroit; head trainer Red Wings; 3 terms pres. NHL Trainers' Assn.; res. West Bloomfield, Mich..

WILSON, Montgomery (figure skating): b. 20 Aug 1909, Toronto, Ont.; d. 15 Nov 1964, Lincoln, Mass.; m. Mary Ann Winston; c. Marsha, Stewart Kimbrough, Winston; nicknamed 'Bud'; Toronto Skating Club jr. champion `22; 9 sr. men's ntl singles titles; with Constance Wilson Samuel 5 ntl pairs titles; 4 ntl fours titles; 6 NA sr. men's singles titles; 3 NA pairs, 1 NA fours titles; competed 4 world championships earning 1st world medal by Cdn male with singles silver `32; competed `28, `32, `36 Olympics winning 1st Cdn figure skating Olympic medal with bronze `32; turned pro St. Paul, Minn. `39; 18yrs coaching Boston SC; mem. US, Cdn Figure Skating halls of fame.

WILSON, Murray (hockey): b. 7 Nov 1951, Toronto, Ont.; given name: Murray Charles; div. Cathy Lewis; c. Emily, Matthew; Carleton; marketing consultant; jr. A Ottawa 67's; 3rd Montreal choice, 11th overall '71 amateur draft; 1 season Nova Scotia Voyageurs (AHL); left wing Montreal '72-78, Los Angeles '78-79; mem. 4 Stanley Cup winners; NHL record: 386 scheduled games, 94g, 95a, 53 playoff games, 5g, 14a; ntl juve. discus record; Ottawa HS discus record 51.86m '70; Ottawa Lynx community relations '93-96; mem. Ottawa Sports Hall of Fame; res. Nepean, Ont.

WILSON, Peter (ski jumping): b. 22 Oct 1952, Ottawa, Ont.; derrickman; mem. ntl ski team '70-76; '72, '76 Olympic teams; 2nd NA jumping championships '72; mem. Ottawa Rowing Club, ntl jr, sr. cox 4s; res. Burnaby, B.C.

WILSON, Phat (hockey): b. 29 Dec 1895, Port Arthur, Ont.; d. 26 Jul 1970, Thunder Bay, Ont.; given name: Gordon Allan; amateur throughout career as player, coach; defence Port Arthur War Veterans srs '18-20; Iroquois Falls NOHA, league title; Port Arthur Bearcats, Allan Cup '26, '27, '29, Western Cdn title '30; coach Bearcats '38, '40; mem. Northwestern Ont. Sports, Hockey halls of fame.

WILSON, Robert (rowing); b. 14 Oct 1935, Kamloops, B.C.; given name: Robert Andrew; m. Barbara Evon Andrews; c. Sharon Marie, Douglas James;UBC, BSc; mem. gold medal 8-oared crew '54, '58 BE, Commonwealth Games; silver '56 Olympics; mem. BC Sports Hall of Fame; res. Calgary, Alta.

WILSON, Robin (curling); b. 22 Apr 1951, Vancouver, B.C.; given name: Robin Leigh Knowles; m. Alan Douglas Wilson; c. Chelsea, Alana, Colby;UBC, BComm; marketing consultant; 2nd stone Cdn women's title rinks '76, '79; rink skipped by Lindsay Sparkes placed 3rd in 1st women's world championship; coordinated Scott Tournament of Hearts ntl women's championships from '82 when Scott Paper assumed sponsorship; res. N. Vancouver, B.C.

WILSON, Rod (baseball): b. 8 Sep 1938, Fredericton, N.B.; given name: Harold Rodney; m. Judith Marilyn; P.S. v-principal; nicknamed "Silver Fox"; coachd St. Stephen HS girls to 8 NB softball titles; St. Stephen Sabres to NB, Atlantic titles (midget) '78, (juvenile) '79, ntl bronze '79, NB jr. titles '80-81, Marysville Royals to '97 NB sr title; St. Stephen basketball team to NB bantam A crown, Eastern Cdn silver '85; mem. ntl youth baseball coaching staff '87; scout Blue Jays; Intl yr of Child award '79; Moosehead Sports coach of '80; Canada Summer Games merit award '81; Baseball NB coach of '87; NB coach of '89; mem. NB Sports Hall of Fame; res. St. Stephen, N.B.

WILSON, Ruth (tennis/golf/basketball); b. 27 Apr 1919, Calgary, Alta.; given name: Ruth Plant; UBC, BA, Western Washington State College, MEd; teacher, counsellor; mem. 5 ntl basketball title teams; coached 3 ntl sr. A titlists (Eilers '50-51, Buzz Bombs '75), bronze '67 Pan-Am Games; mgr. '59 Pan-Am Games team; mem. 2 women's softball world series, coached a third; mem. 8 BC interprovincial golf teams, 4 ntl titles; mem. 1 international team; runnerup ntl Closed championship '61; BC jr. tennis doubles, mixed doubles; Whistle Award for basketball contributions by BC referees; dir. CABA '52-61, BCABA '76-81; mem. BC Sports Hall of Fame; res. Vancouver, B.C.

WILSON, Seymour (football/officiating); b. 1911, Hamilton, Ont., d. 23 Sep 1974, India; c. Kerry, Simone; chief clerk treasury dept.; backfielder Victoria Park juvenile, jr. teams; made ORFU Hamilton Tigers '29 but persuaded by family to forego game because of size; made Tigers as end '30-37; mem. 2 Grey Cup finalists, 1 winner; began officiating '30; IRFU '38-57, CFL '58-70; umpire, head linesman, referee more than 10 Grey Cup finals; mem. Canadian Football Hall of Fame.

WILSON, Stacy (hockey): b. 12 May 1965, Salisbury, N.B.; P.E. teacher, coach; forward Team NB sr. women's ntl championships '87-96, Maritime Sports Blades '94 finals; ntl tournament MVP '95; top scorer '86 ntls, '88 all-star, '90, '96 most sportsmanlike player; MVP, top scorer NB sr. league '90; mem. 4 Team Canada world, 2 Pacific Rim title teams; mem. '98 Olympic team; asst. coach NB '95 Canada Winter Games team; rep. hockey at Cdn Athletes Assn. forum; volunteer with NB women's hockey council; attended Olympic Oval high performance program; asst. coach UMinn.-Duluth; res. Duluth, Minn.

WILSON, Tom (curling); b. 2 Jul 1948, Saskatoon, Sask.; given name: Thomas Robert; UofSaskatoon, BA; sales mgr. Q.S.P. (Reader's Digest/McLean-Hunter); 2nd Rick Folk's ntl mixed title rinks '74, '83, runnerup '81-82; all-star status; mem. Folk's '78-79 ntl men's championship runnerup, '80 Brier, Silver Broom champions; '76 Calgary Grey Cup 'spiel, '77 Edmonton Christmas car 'spiel, '78 Vernon car 'spiel, '80 Lausanne, Switzerland, Classic, Victoria invitational, '81 Scotland international; Dick Ellis team award '80; mem. Saskatchewan Sports Hall of Fame; res. Toronto, Ont.

WILSON, Tracy (figure skating); b. 25 Sep 1961, Lachine, Que.; m. Brad Kinsella; c. 2; TV broadcaster; with Mark Stokes ntl jr. dance title '80; with Robert McCall '82-84 ntl dance titles, Skate Canada '83; mem. '84 Olympic, '82-84 world championships teams; *TSN Women in Sport* show host; mem. Order of Canada, Cdn Amateur Sports Hall of Fame; res. Port Moody, B.C.

WILTJER, Greg (basketball); b. 26 Nov 1960, Whitehorse, Y.T.; m. Carol; Oregon State, UVic; all-American Idaho Junior College; centre ntl team '81-86, '91, '94; gold Worlds Fair tournament '82, FISU Games '83; mem. '83 Pan-Am, '84 Olympic teams; 1 CIAU MVP Jack Donohue trophy; 1 CIAU all-Cdn; mem. Canada's '82, '86, '94 World Championships teams; 2nd round draft Chicago NBA '84 but opted to play in Europe with Brescia (Italy), Barcelona (Spain), Madrid (Spain), Thessalioniki (Greece); CBA Omaha Racers '89-90; fed. govt. excellence award '84; res. Victoria, B.C.

WINDEYER, Walter (sailing); b. 1900, Toronto, Ont., d. 1964, Toronto, Ont.; mem. Royal Cdn Yacht Club; 4 Townsend Cups for International 14ft dinghies; Canada's 1st International Dragon Class world championship '59; at 19 Douglas Cup; 3 consecutive Wilton Morse Trophies; mem. Cdn entry which won Currie Cup International 14ft class '36; skipper Invader II '32 Canada's Cup challenge; '58 with Corte on Great Lakes; '59 Dragon Gold Cup, O'Keefe Trophy, Telegram Trophy, Olympic trials; Duke of Edinburgh Trophy Lake Ont. '61; permanent possession O'Keefe Trophy with 3rd victory; mem. Canada's Sports Hall of Fame.

WINFIELD, Dave (baseball); b. 3 Oct 1951, St. Paul, Minn; given name: David Mark; m. Tonya Turner; c. Shanel; Minnesota, hon. degree Syracuse;capt. Minn baseball team as pitcher/outfielder; also standout in football, basketball; 1st team all-American, college world series MVP; drafted in baseball by San Diego, football Minnesota, basketball Utah (ABA), Atlanta (NBA); founded David M. Winfield Foundation '77; ML player San Diego '73-80, NY Yankees '81-90, California '90-91, Toronto '92, Minnesota '93-94; reached 3000 hit plateau '93; ML record: 2850 scheduled games, 10,594ab, 1623r, 3014h, 520d, 85t, 453hr, 1786rbi, 1173w, 1609so, 220sb, .285ba; 2 world series, 1 winner; 5 Dick Siebert Upper Midwest player of yr awards; 7 Rawlings Gold Glove awards; 2 Silver Slugger awards; outstanding DH award; AL comeback player of yr award '90; 12 consec all-star games; played key role in Toronto '92 World Series victory; YMCA Brian Piccolo humanitarian award '79; Branch Rickey Community Service award; Arete award '92; Joe Cronin award '93; res. Minnesota.

WINFIELD, Earl (football): b. 6 Aug 1961, Petersburg, Va.; North Carolina; wide receiver; NFL Seattle tryout '86, San Francisco '89; CFL Hamilton '87-96; 3 Eastern, 1 Northern, 1 CFL all-star; Jeff Russell Memorial trophy '88; runnerup Schenley outstanding player award '88; tied CFL record 2td punt returns single game '93; 8 playoff games, 1 Grey Cup final; res. Hamilton, Ont.

WINNING, Craig (parachuting); b. 7 Jan 1950, Windsor, Eng.; given name: Craig Stuart; m. Susan Fry; Waterloo Lutheran, BA; salesman; ntl overall champion '79-80; mem. ntl team world championships '74, '76, '78, '80; silver accuracy '80 Worlds; ntl record 10 consecutive dead-centre landings on electronic accuracy pad '80 world meet; diamond wings (2000-plus jumps); coached ntl team '78 world meet; res. Hamilton, Ont.

WINTERS, Shelley (field hockey); b. 24 Jun 1953, Victoria, B.C.; given name: Shelley Ann; m. Rod Andrews; c. Robin, Brendan, Charlotte; UBC, BPhE; teacher; UBC varsity team '71-76; defence ntl team '75-86; mem. silver medal World Cup team '83; mem. '84 Olympic team; mem. BC ntl title team '80; mem. 4 World Cup, 2 world championships teams; Oak Bay sportsmanship award '71; UBC female athlete of '76; UBC Joan Livesey sportsmanship award '73; VFHA MVP '72, VIFHA MVP '80, '82; fed. govt. excellence award '83; res. Victoria, B.C.

WIRKOWSKI, Nobby (football); b. 20 Aug 1926, Chicago, Ill.; given name: Norbert; m. Therea Ann Lombardo; c. Linda Mary, Norbie J., Carol Julie, Ricky Patrick; Miami of Ohio, BSc; retd. AD; mem. '48 Sun Bowl, '51 Salad Bowl champions; pro Toronto '51-54, Hamilton '55-56, Calgary '57-59; quarterbacked '52 Argos Grey Cup winners; asst. coach Argos '60-61, head coach '62-64, dir. player personnel '66-68; football coach York '68-74; athletic dir. York.; res. Mississauga, Ont.

WISEMAN, Eddie (hockey); b. 28 Dec 1909, Newcastle, N.B., d. 4 May 1977, Red Deer, Alta.; given name: Edward Randall; mem. Regina Pats '30 Memorial Cup winner; pro Chicago Shamrocks (AHL); NHL Detroit '32-35, NY Americans '35-39, Boston '40-42; NHL record: 115 goals, 165 assists; led Bruins playoff goal scorers with 6 en route to '41 Stanley Cup victory; mem. NB Sports Hall of Fame.

WISHART, Carol (fencing); b. 20 Dec 1953, Jonquiere, Que.; given name: Carol Anne; m. Winston Esnard; c. Victoria, Elizabeth; UofOtt, hons BSc;v-p. Tree Canada Foundation from '92; mem. intercollegiate team '72-75; mem. ntl team '78-80; Ont. women's foil champion '79-80; mem. Ont. women's gold medal team '79-80; team gold ntl foil championships '77-78, individual silver; mem. Ont. women's intercollegiate gold foil team '73-74, individual silvers; fencing instructor UofOtt '75-76; secty-treas. Region IV OFA '79-86; holder levels I, II coaching certificates; UofOtt female athlete of '75; nominee RA female athlete of '78; ED freestyle Ski Canada '82-86; ED Cdn Fencing Fed. '86-89; v-p. marketing United Way Canada '89-92; res. Carleton Place, Ont.

WISHART, Wyatt (wrestling); b. 10 Jun 1958, Fort William, Ont.; Concordia, BA; weights mfgr.; Pan-Am jr.

100kg FS, GR titles '76, '78; ntl jr. 100kg FS, GR champion '78; 3 ntl 100kg FS, 1 GR titles; gold 100kg FS '78 Commonwealth Games; bronze '79 Pan-Am Games 100kg FS; bronze 100kg FS '78-79 Cerro Pelado, silver '80; 4th US Nationals '79; bronze 100kg FS '80 World Cup; gold super heavyweight '82 Commonwealth Games; outstanding wrestler (Greco Roman) '78 Pan-Am championships; Que. judo titles '80-81; middle guard Concordia football '80; drafted 6th round Edmonton Eskimos '81; competed for Lakehead U Weightlifting Club; mem. NWO Sports Hall of Fame; res. Suzhou, China.

WITTMEIER, Bonnie (gymnastics); b. 15 Sep 1966, Winnipeg, Man.; div. John Withington; 2 ntl all-around, beam, vault, 1 floor, uneven bars titles; 4 Canada Games gold medals; '82 Commonwealth championships floor exercise, team titles; sister Robin ntl diving team mem.; mem. Man. Sports Hall of Fame; res. N. Vancouver, B.C.

WOHLBERG, Eric (cycling); b. 8 Jan 1965, Sudbury, Ont.; roadracing specialist; mem. ntl team '91-98; won '93 Victoria Grand Prix; established Cdn record while placing 5th in team time trial '94 Commonwealth Games; represented Canada '95-96 World championships; 1 gold, 1 bronze '98 Commonwealth Games; gold '99 Pan-Am Games; Cdn Cycling Online male, road cyclist of '98 awards; res. Oakville, Ont.

WOLF, Walter (motorsport); b. 5 Oct 1939, Graz, Austria; m. Elizabeth; c. Wendy Heather, Alexandra Justin, Walter Maximillian, Fiona Elizabeth; purchased Williams Formula 1 racing team '75; ran '76 F1 world championship under Williams name with varied drivers including Jacky Ickx but scored no points; entered '77 F1 world championships as Walter Wolf Racing with Jody Scheckter as premier driver; won Argentina, Monaco, Mosport races; Scheckter runnerup to Niki Lauda in driver race and Wolf 4th in constructors' championship; entered a Wolf-Dallara in '77 Can-Am Challenge series with Gilles Villeneuve placing 3rd at Road America; Wolf team 5th in '78 constructors' championship; ran '79 F1 earning no points; ran a team in '85-86 Can-Am Motorcycle series; mem. Cdn Motorsport Hall of Fame; res. Austria/Canada.

WOLFF, Doreen (t&f); b. 23 Jul 1931, Kelvington, Sask.; given name: Doreen Mae Dredge; m. Bernard Wolff; c. Diane, Larry, Barbara; teacher's certif.; high/long jumper, sprinter; displayed versatility with participation in softball, volleyball, curling, snowmobiling, skiing; set Sask., Cdn HJ records; mem. '48 Cdn Olympic team; mem. Sask. Sports Hall of Fame; res. Arizona/Liberty, Sask.

WONG, Charlene (figure skating); b. 4 Mar 1966, Montreal, Que.; Que. juve. champion '75-76; Que. Ladies Novice title '78; Eastern Canada novice '78; 2 Eastern div. titles; runnerup ntl sr. singles '83, '88-90; GP intl title '81; won '88 Skate Electric invitational; guest skater Tour of World Champions Montreal Forum '79, '81; Que. athlete of '78; res. Pierrefonds, Que.

WONG, Chi Chong (table tennis); b. 2 May 1965, Hong Kong; mem. Ont. team ntl championships '78-81, title '81; mem. international jr. title team '81; 14 ntl, Eastern Cdn age group singles, doubles titles; ntl jr. champion '81; Scarborough PS chess champion '77, '79; mem. title winning PS soccer team '74; res. Scarborough, Ont.

WONG, Lester (fencing); b. 28 Aug 1944, China; m. Donna; UAlta, BSc; production mgr.; individual silver épée, team bronze '70 Commonwealth Games; ntl épée title '71, foil '75; mem. '71, '75 Pan-Am, '72, '76 Olympic teams; res. Caledon, Ont.

WONG SHUI, Mike (shooting); b. 24 Aug 1952, Montego Bay, Jamaica; given name: Herbert Michael; m. Dianne Ngo; Carleton, BEng; optician; mem. 10 Cdn Bisley teams, 2 others as coach; finalist St. George match, 3rd Queen's Prize '81 Bisley matches; competed ORA 100th matches '81; 3rd Lt.-Governor's final; 4 Palma teams; Ottawa ACT shooting award '82; res. Mississauga, Ont.

WOO, Wes (weightlifting); b. 11 Sep 1939, Vancouver, B.C.; given name: Westley; m. Joyce; UBC, BSP; fitness centre dir.; ntl teenage middleweight lifting title '56; BC jr. champion, record holder '60; UBC record holder; pres. BC Weightlifting Assn. '66-70; mem. ntl Senior Coaches Assn., chair. '74-78; coach ntl teams '68, '76, '80 Olympic, '71, '75 Pan-Am, '74, '77 world championships, '78 Commonwealth Games, '79 IWF world superheavyweight championships, '81 Commonwealth championships; '71 Canada Winter Games; coach BC teams 13 ntl championships; formed Spartak Weightlifting Club '68; runnerup Air Canada coach of '75; res. Vancouver, B.C.

WOOD, Bryan (curling); b. 10 Mar 1944, Brandon, Man.; given name: Bryan David; m. Thelma Davis; c. Kevin, Robbie; real estate, farming; played for skips Don Duguid, Barry Fry, Rod Hunter as well as 2 seasons skipping own rink; mem. CBC televised series winners '70, '71, runnerup '76; Heather carspiel title '70; runnerup with Bob Pickering Toronto Grey Cup 'spiel '74; mem. Duguid's '70, '71 Man. Consols, Brier, Silver Broom champions; mem. '79 Fry Man. Consols, Brier winners; mem. Canadian Curling Hall of Fame; res. Winnipeg, Man.

WOOD, Howie (curling); b. 8 Jul 1918, Winnipeg, Man.; given name: Howard Francis Jr.; m. Christine Romano; c. Larry, Victor, Betty, Bob, Howie, Bruce, Ken, Dave; retd. division mgr. Investors' Syndicate; semifinalist Man. 21-and-under championships age 11; with father beat Gordon Hudson for Winnipeg city title age 16; with father 1st carspiel Nipawin '47; 2nd for father '40 Brier winner with 9-0 record; skipped '57 Man. Brier entry comprising Bill Sharpe, Don and Lorne Duguid; skipped '54 Man. Bonspiel winner; Man. seniors title '70; pres. Man. Jr. (21-and-under) CA at 16; res. Winnipeg, Man.

WOOD, John (canoeing); b. 7 Jun 1950, Toronto, Ont.; given name: John Joseph; UofT, BA; stockbroker; mem. '68, '72, '76 Olympics, silver 500m solo canoe '76; '70, '73, '74, '75, '77 world championships teams, silver C2 (with Gregg Smith) '77; NA CI, C2 100m titles '74; ntl 500m, 1000m CI, C2 titles '72-77; bronze soling class sailing '79 Pan-Am Games; *CBC-TV* color commentator '84 Olympics; res. Oakville, Ont.

WOOD, Lionel (curling); b. 5 Dec 1924, Winnipeg, Man.; given name: Lionel Lawrence; m. Colleen Margaret Warner; c. Craig Wynn, Paul Daniel, Jayanne; UMan, LLB; retd. owner-mgr., office equipment; mem. '38 Man. PS softball champions; '39 soccer champions; Man. schoolboy curling title '41; Man. Consols '45; mem. Man.-Lakehead lacrosse champions '47; mem. Man. provincial HS football champions '42; mem. '46-47 Grey Cup finalist Blue Bombers; frequent Man. bonspiel trophy winner including grand aggregate; res. Edmonton, Alta.

WOOD, Nora (curling); b. 19 Jan 1903, Arnprior, Ont.; d. 12 Feb 1988, Arnprior, Ont.; given name: Nora Ward; m. Roy Wood; active curler '20-75; runnerup '52 Tweedsmuir Trophy double rink competition using irons, winner '54 Tweedsmuir using granites; pres. EOLCA '61, '70-72, OLCA '70-71; mem. Canadian Curling Hall of Fame.

WOOD, Pappy (curling); b. 29 Aug 1888, Winnipeg, Man., d. 28 Dec 1978, Winnipeg, Man.; given name: Howard; m. Elizabeth Gillespie; c. Howard Jr., Lionel; business college; pres. contracting firm; mem. Dominion Beavers soccer club '15, 1 of 2 Cdns on all-Scottish team; recognized in *Guinness Book of World Records* for curling longevity by competing in 65 consec. Man. bonspiels '08-72; 8 MCA 'spiel grand aggregate titles; won original Macdonald Brier '25 in conjuction with MCA 'spiel; skipped Brier winners '30, '40, 3rd Jim Congalton's '32 title winner; with son Howie 1st Nipawin carspiel '47; mem. Canadian Curling, Man., Canada's Sports halls of fame.

WOOD, Sharon (mountaineering); b. 10 May 1957, Halifax, N.S.; given name: Sharon Adele; m. Christopher Jon Stethem; c. Robin, Daniel Layne; UCal, hon. LLD; co. pres./mountain guide/motivational speaker; began climbing '68; achieved international recognition as 1st Cdn woman to reach summit Mount Everest '86; in addition to Everest has climbed numerous 20,000-foot-plus summits around the world; 1st woman to achieve full climbing guide status within Assn. of Cdn Mountain Guides; Tenzing Norgay award as pro mountaineer of yr.; Alta. achievement award; Breakthrough Award; *MacLeans* honor roll for outstanding achievement award; *Outside Magazine* 10 who made the difference award; co-founded Mountain Gate Community School; pres. Canmore Society for Community Education; Bill March Summit of Excellence award; Alta. Sports Hall of Fame special award; res. Canmore, Alta.

WOODCROFT, Greg (wrestling): b. 27 Aug 1970, Hamilton, Ont.; McMaster; teacher; 2 CIAU 52kg titles; mem. ntl team from '89; 9 ntl sr titles; silver '94 Francophone Games; bronze '93 World Cup; competed '93 World Cup, '96 Olympics, '90, '96 Pan-Am championships; res. Hamilton, Ont.

WOODHOUSE, Hedley (horse racing); b. 23 Jan 1920, Vancouver, B.C., d. 29 Dec 1984, New York, N.Y.; given name: Hedley John; m. Elsie Martens; c. Marten, Robert, Deborah; retired jockey; apprentice jockey Vancouver at 17; rode initial winner at 20; riding career spanned 31 years and involved every major race track in US, Canada; noted for ability to handle highly tempermental fillies, mares; 2642 victories including phenomenal 103 stakes races; won all major NY races, except Belmont Stakes, at least once; top year '55 with 148 winners; twice NY riding champion, once runnerup; retired age 51; Woodbine Park security guard '72-83; mem. Canadian Horse Racing, BC Sports, BC Thoroughbred Breeders Society halls of fame.

WOODLEY, Erin (synchro swim): b. 6 Jun 1972, Mississauga, Ont.; began competing '81; team silver '91 Pan-Am Games; competed 2 Petro Canada Cups, 1 Loano, Fina, America Cups; duet gold (Lisa Alexander) '94 Commonwealth Games; 2 silver '95 Pan-Am Games; team silver '96 Olympics; Unysis quest for excellence award '91 Canada Games; res. Etobicoke, Ont.

WOODS, Bob (curling): b. 2 Sep 1933, Carman, Man.; div.; c. Rolf, Keith; pres. importing firm; skipped Sweden to 2nd '67 Scotch Cup; skipped Toronto Royal Canadians rink to Ont. title '77; res. Toronto, Ont.

WOODS, Larry (sailing): b. 2 Aug 1939, Hamilton, Ont.; given name: Larry Earl; m. Elizabeth Helen Pleli; c. Larry David, Todd Michael; McMaster, BA, UofT, MEd; educator; ntl champion Tornado catamaran '74, '78; CORK title '78, in top 3 '76-80; NA champion '73, '80; 7th '76 Olympics; mem. '80 Olympic team; mem. 5 world championships teams; res. Winona, Ont.

WOODS, Maggie (t&f): b. 9 Jan 1960, Weston, Ont.; given name: Margaret Ann; Purdue., BA; midget OFSAA '75 hj title (1.70m), lj (5.25m); '76 senior OFSAA HJ (1.76), LJ (5.60); best for 100m hurdles 14.8; LJ gold '77 Canada Games; ntl HJ title '77; ntl indoor HJ title '79, competed HAPOEL Games, 2nd ntl outdoor pentathlon '79; retired following '82 NAIA championships; res. Weston, Ont.

WOODWARD, Reggie (rowing/rugby): b. Feb 1869, Constantinople, Turkey, d. 6 Jul 1957, Vancouver, B.C.; given name: Reginald Purves; c. Tommy (d), Marjorie (d), Buster (d); emigrated to Vancouver 1887; joined Burrard Inlet Rowing Club 1890, it later merged with Boating Club to form Vancouver RC 1899; mem. VRC 67 years; rugby at local, ntl, intl levels; coached several years; nicknamed "Mr. Rugby"; guided team to Miller Cup '10; cricket, rowing standout; VRC club capt. '16; VRC pres. '19-21, dir. '22-28, v-p. '29-33, hon. v-p. to death; hon. life mem. VRC; mem. BC Sports Hall of Fame.

WOODWARD, Rod (football): b. 22 Sep 1944, Vancouver, B.C.; given name: Rodney William; m. Kay Whitacre; c. Tod William Brian, Carilena Mae; Idaho, BSc; teacher, football coach; all-conf. def. halfback, hon. mention off. half Everett Junior College '63-64; pro Montreal '67-69, Ottawa '70-76, Calgary '77, Hamilton '78; CFL record: 39 interceptions; CFL record interceptions 7 consecutive games; twice intercepted 3 passes single game; all-Eastern Conf. 3 times, all-Cdn once; '75 Ottawa Schenley nominee def. back of year; mem. Athletes in Action; res. Burnaby, B.C.

WOOLF, George (horse racing): b. 1910, Cardston, Alta., d. 3 Jan 1946, Santa Anita, Calif; nicknamed 'The Iceman'; won '36 Preakness on Bolt Venture, '38 Pimlico Special on Seabiscuit; American Derby, Harve de Grace Handicap, Belmont Futurity, Hollywood Gold Cup 3 consecutive years; '45 Santa Anita Derby on Bymeabond; killed while riding Please Me at Santa Anita '46; in 19yr racing career 721 wins, 589 2nds, 468 3rds; George Woolf Memorial award for most sportsmanlike jockey in his honor; mem. Canada's Sports, American Jockey, Canadian Horse Racing halls of fame.

WOOLLEY, Emily (curling): b. 24 Jan 1899, Sarnia, Ont.; d. 1967, Toronto, Ont.; given name: Emily Clark; m. LeRoy Woolley; c. Jane; lefthanded standout in tennis, golf, badminton, curling; Royal Life Saving Society gold medal swimmer; began curling '32; mem. 14 Ont. Ladies' Tankard winners; with sisters Dadie, Janie, Redd formed famed Clark sisters rink; mem. 13 Toronto Granite Club Robertson Trophies, 7 Seigniory Club 'spiel titles, 5 Ont. title rinks; rep. Ont. '61, '63 ntl Diamond D competitions; SOLCA seniors trophy bears her name; recipient Ont. govt. achievement award; charter mem. Sarnia CC; life mem. Toronto Granite CC; mem. Canadian Curling Hall of Fame.

WOOTTON, Moon (lacrosse): b. 17 Sep 1926, Owen Sound, Ont.; d. 8 Feb 1989, Port Hope, Ont.; given name: William Lloyd; goaltender; played jr. Owen Sound; mem. 5 consec. Mann Cup winners, 1 Owen Sound, 4 Peterborough; ranked top goalie in Canada several seasons; 3 times Mann Cup MVP; played 10 seasons with Peterborough; mem. Cdn Lacrosse, Peterborough Sports halls of fame.

WORRALL, Jim (t&f/administration): b. 23 Jun 1914, Bury, Lancashire, Eng., m. Aileen McGuire (d); c. Anna Jane, Brian, Brenda; div. Lisbet Svensen; c. Ingrid; McGill, BSc, Osgoode Hall, LLB; retd. lawyer; Rector's Trophy all-around athlete Montreal HS; silver 120yds hurdles '34 BEG; flag-bearer '36 summer Olympics; 2yrs pres. Ont. t&f comm. AAU of C; 8yrs v-p. COA; 1st pres. Cdn Sports Advisory Council; mem. National Advisory Council on Fitness, Amateur Sport '61-66, chair. 2yrs; 1st Cdn IOC exec. board; Officer Order of Canada '76; mem. Cdn Olympic Order, Canadian Amateur, McGillU Sports halls of fame; res. Don Mills, Ont.

WORSLEY, Gump (hockey): b. 14 May 1929, Montreal, Que.; given name: Lorne John; m. Doreen; c. Lorne Jr., Dean, Drew, Lianne; retd.; from NY Sr. Rovers (EHL) to New Haven (AHL), St. Paul (USHL), Saskatoon (PCHL, WHL), Vancouver (WHL); NY Rangers '52-63, Calder Trophy rookie of year, Montreal '63-70, Minnesota '70-74; scout Minnesota; coach Belleville (OHL) '82; NHL record: 860 games, playing 50,201 minutes, 2432g, 43so, 2.91avg., 70 playoff games, 4080 minutes, 192g, 5so, 2.82avg.; 1st, 2nd team all-stars once each; mem. 4 Stanley Cup winners; USHL rookie of year Charles Gardiner Memorial Trophy; WHL MVP; WHL leading goaler; 2 Vezina Trophies ('66 with Charlie Hodge, '68 with Rogie Vachon); mem. Hockey Hall of Fame; res. Beloeil, Que.

WORTERS, Roy (hockey): b. 19 Oct 1900, Toronto, Ont., d. 7 Nov 1957, Toronto, Ont.; nicknamed "The Shrimp"; Pittsburgh Yellowjackets (USAHA); Pittsburgh Pirates '26-28, NY Americans '28-29, '30-37, Canadiens '30; averaged

2.36 goals-against in 488 league games, Vezina Trophy '31 with 1.68 avg.; twice 2nd team all-star; 1st goaler to win Hart Trophy (MVP) '28-29 season; 1st goaler to use back of gloves to direct pucks to corners; mem. Hockey Hall of Fame.

WOSTENHOLME, Martin (tennis); b. 11 Oct 1962, Toronto, Ont.; given name: Martin Clark; Yale, BA, NYU (Stern School Business) MBA; pres./CEO ME2 Corp; ; div. 1 Eastern conf. singles '84; ntl under 12 doubles '75, under 14 singles, doubles '76, under 18 doubles (with Glenn Michibata) '78, '80; mem. Galea Cup team '79-81, Davis Cup team '81-93; reached 3rd round '82 Players International; best ATP ranking #84 in '84; Tennis Canada player of '84; pro circuit '84-94; TSN color commentator; res. New York, N.Y.

WOTHERSPOON, Jeremy (speed skating); b. 26 Oct 1976, Humboldt, Sask.; long track specialist; mem. ntl team from '96; silver 500m '96 world jr;; 8 gold, 2 silver world cup; ntl overall gold '96, 500 bronze '97; Cdn, world 500m, 1000m records; 500m silver '98 Olympics; bettered own world 1000m 1:08.66, 500m 34.76 records '99; won '99 world title; won 8 consec. 500m WC races, overall WC gold '99; res. Calgary, Alta.

WOYCENKO, Karen (baton twirling); b. 8 Nov 1954, Calgary, Alta.; UCal, BPHE; teacher; competitive twirler '63-76; ntl jr. Miss Majorette title '69; U S TA 2-baton champion '76; certified USTA coach from '72; NBTA, Twirl Canada judge from '73; Western v-p., mem. rules, regulations comm. from '82-84; wrote judges' freestyle manual; res. Calgary, Alta.

WRIGHT, Doug (wheelchair basketball); b. 4 Feb 1938, Hamilton, Ont.; m. Dannielle; c. Douglas,Michael; CPO1 Cdn navy; played numerous sports for service teams '55-70; football MVP Bluenose conf. '66; Maritime Command athlete of '68; asst. football coach St. Mary's '70-82, 7 AAU titles, Vanier Cup '73; coached SMU Huskies varsity basketball '73-78, 2 ntl titles; head coach NS Flying Wheels, ntl wheelchair basketball silver medal team '81 Pan-Am Games, bronze medal team '90 Stoke-Mandiville Games; asst coach ntl women's team '76 Olympics; mem. NS, Cdn Forces Sports halls of fame; res. Dartmouth, N.S.

WRIGHT, Harold (t&f/administration); b. 10 Dec 1908, Winnipeg, Man.; d. 11 Dec 1997, Vancouver, B.C.; m. Edna May Robinson; c. Linda Catherine, Lee Madison, James Kirkland; UAlta, Utah, BSc, MSc; UBC, MA, LLD; retd engineer; sprinter '32 Olympic team; dir., pres., life mem. Vancouver Olympic Club; pres. CFHA '65-69; pres., dir., COA; governor Olympic Trust '70-97; dir. Montreal Olympics organizing comm.; dir. BC Amateur Sports Council; trustee BC Sports Hall of Fame; gov. Canada's Sports Hall of Fame; dir. Calgary Olympic Development Assn.; mem. Olympic Club Canada; special achievement award BC Sports Fed., Olmpic comm. order of merit, Queen's Jubilee medal, IOC order of merit, silver medal; mem. Order of Canada; mem. BC, Canada's Sports halls of fame.

WRIGHT, Jack (tennis); b. 11 Nov 1901, Nelson, B.C.; d. Sep 1949, Montreal, Que.; given name: John; MD; won Washington, Oregon, Idaho, BC, Northwest, Inland Empire jr. titles; 3 ntl singles titles; with Willard Crocker 3 and Marcel Rainville 1 ntl indoor doubles titles; mem. Cdn Davis Cup team '23-33, Cdn record 40 Cup matches; defeated world #3 ranked Tacheichi Harada of Japan in 3 straight sets; Que. titlist '31; voted Canada's outstanding tennis player of half century by CP '50; mem. Cdn Tennis, Canada's, BC Sports halls of fame.

WRIGHT, Joseph Jr. (rowing); b. 28 Mar 1906, Toronto, Ont., d. 7 Jun 1981, Toronto, Ont.; m. Dorothy; c. Dianne; pres. coal co.; centre, guard Argos '24-36; Grey Cup '33; stroked jr., sr. Argos 8s to Cdn Henley titles; mem. Penn AC crew '25 Middle States regatta title; 3 US ntl sculling titles, record times; 9 ntl titles; diamond sculls Royal Henley, England '28, runnerup '29; flag-bearer, silver, bronze medals '28 Olympics; 2 bronze '32 Olympics; pres. Eastern Football Conf.; mem. Canadian Amateur, Canada's Sports halls of fame.

WRIGHT, Joseph Sr. (all-around); b. 14 Jan 1864, Villanova, Ont., d. 18 Oct 1950, Toronto, Ont; m. Alethea Ainley Spink; c. George, Jessie, Nancy, Margaret, Joseph Jr.; UofT; rowing coach; Canadian amateur heavyweight boxing title at 35; among 1st Canadians to run 100yds in 10:00, ntl shot put, hammer throw records; 18yrs mem. Argos, '11 Grey Cup match with son George; ntl amateur wrestling titlist; ntl billiards champion; stroked 1st Cdn 8-oared crew to win US ntl title '01; 1st Cdn to win heat British Henley diamond sculls; Bedford Cup, English amateur singles title 1895 (1st ever by Cdn); US jr. singles 1891, int. singles 1892; honored by King of Sweden '12 Olympics; coached sr. 8s '05, '07, '11, int. 8s '05-06, '09-11 Cdn Henley, US ntl titles; coachPenn. '16-26; Cdn oarsman of half century '50 CP poll; mem. Cdn Amateur, Canada's Sports halls of fame.

WRIGHT, Ken (builder/all-around); b. 24 Jun 1913, Chaplin, Sask.; d. 8 Apr 1996, New Westminster, B.C.; given name: Kenneth William Thomas; UBC; nicknamed "Hooker" for famed hook shot in basketball; mem. New Westminster Adanacs, UBC Thunderbirds before turning to coaching and administration; founder BC HS boys basketball tournament '45, active comm. mem. 36yrs; co-founder/pres./hon. life mem. BCHSBBA; co-authored written/pictoral history of BCHSBBA tournament; coach BC women's relay team to '52 ntl t&f championship; coached New Westminster t&f club athletes to 5 gold, 3 silver, 2 ntl records '52 Cdn age class championships; chair. '54 BEG t&f officials; founding mem./governor Cdn Lacrosse Hall of Fame; pres./hon. life mem. New Westminster Tennis Club; mem. BC Sports Hall of Fame.

WRIGHT, Lee (field hockey); b. 28 Aug 1944, Vancouver, B.C.; given name: Lee Madison; m. Thelma Fynn; c. Lindsay, Aanthony, Philip, Gillian;UBC, BPhE, SouthernCal, MA; phys ed co-ordinator/coach; mem. '64, '76 Olympic, '67, '71, '75 Pan-Am Games teams; more than 60 intl matches; bronze '71, silver '75 Pan-Ams; both he and wife Thelma, a 1500m runner, won silver medals '75 Pan-Am Games; retd '76; coached BC team '78-79, '82; coached ntl team Colorado Springs tourney '82; dir. Olympic Club Canada; res. Vancouver, B.C.

WRIGHT, Thelma (t&f); b. 9 Oct 1951, Eastbourne, Eng.; given name: Thelma Sonia Fynn; m. Lee Madison Wright; c. Lindsay, Aanthony, Philip, Gillian; UBC, BPhE; teacher; ntl team '69-77; 800-3000m specialist; silver '75 FISU (3000m 8:54.9), '75 Pan-Am (1500m 4:22.3), bronze '70 Commonwealth (1500m 4:18), '74 Commonwealth (1500m 4:12.3), '75 NZ Games (1500m 4:19); 4 ntl 1500m titles; 3 ntl 2 1/2-miles cross-country titles; bronze '70 US cross-sountry; '74 Springbank 4 miles, Puerto Rico 6 1/4 miles road race titles; PB: 800m 2:05.1 '74, 1500m 4:10.5 '74, 3000m 8:54.9 '75; ntl open 3000m record '73-75; mem. '72, '76 Olympic, '70, '74, Commonwealth, '75 Pan-Am Games teams; mem.'77 world cross-country then retired; coach Vancouver Olympic TC, asst. coach UBC track team; mgr. BC t&f team '78-82; mgr. ntl cross-country team '80-81; won 3 ntl masters cross-country titles; dir. Olympic Club Canada; res. Vancouver, B.C.

WRUCK, Larry (football); b. 29 Oct 1962, Saskatoon, Sask.; linebacker Saskatoon Jr. Hilltops; CFL Edmonton '85-96; CFL record: 213 scheduled games, 673 tackles, 40 QB sacks, 15 fumble recoveries, 13 interceptions, 19 playoff games, 60 tackles; 1 Western all-star; 2 Dr. Beattie Martin trophies; twice CFL most outstanding Canadian runnerup; 4 Grey Cup finals, 2 winners; res. Edmonton, Alta.

WU, Walter (swimming); b. 14 Aug 1972, Vancouver, B.C.; travel agent; B3 blind athlete; strong swimmer in FS, butterfly, backstroke and IM; mem. Pacific Dolphin Swimming Assn.; 5 gold '94 Kinsmen/Kinette Cup; 5 gold IPC World championships '94; 5 gold Superior Propane Cup '95; 5 gold IPC Swim trials '95; 5 gold, 1 bronze '96 Paralympics; 7 gold World Blind championships '98; world records 200, 400m FS; mem. Terry Fox Hall of Fame; res. Richmond, B.C.

WURR, Alfred (wrestling); b. 28 Jun 1934, Germany; m. Beverly Bamendine; c. Alfred, Elke; iron worker; competitive at provincial, ntl, international levels '57-72; 11 FS, 8 GR ntl titles; silver '70 Commonwealth Games 163lb GR; mem. '70 world championships, '71 Pan-Am, '72 Olympic Games teams; AAU male athlete of '64; YMCA athlete of '64-65; Man. athlete of '68; mem. Canadian Amateur Wrestling, Man. Sports halls of fame; res. Winnipeg, Man.

WURTELE, Rhoda (skiing); b. 21 Jan 1922, Montreal, Que.; given name: Rhoda Isabella; m. Arnold Eaves; c. David Wurtele, John Ironside, Bruce Arnold; Trafalgar School for Girls, Notre Dame Secretarial School; ski club dir.; mem. '48, '52 Olympic teams; US ntl downhill, combined '47; ntl downhill, slalom, combined '51, Norwegian National Holmenkollen Vos slalom, giant slalom, combined '52, Que. Kandahar, Far West Kandahar, Harriman Cup Sun Valley, Roch Cup Aspen '57, NA combined '57; 3rd Arleberg Kandahar downhill Chamonix, France, '48; with twin sister Rhona female athlete of '44, runnerup to Joe Krol Cdn athlete of '45; dir. Ski Jay (1st children's club NA); mem. Que. Srs Golf team '72-78; pro-celebrity ski ballet competition with son John '77; mem. US National Ski, Cdn Amateur Sports, Skiing halls of fame; res. Etobicoke, Ont.

WURTELE, Rhona (skiing/swimming); b. 21 Jan 1922, Montreal, Que.; div. Gene Alan Gillis; c. Christopher Wurtele, Margaret Rose, Nancy Joanne, Jere Alan; Trafalgar School for Girls, Mother House secretarial school, Sir George Williams, Oregon; ski club dir.; Que., ntl 50, 100yd FS swim titles, provincial records in both; Idaho State 1m diving title; with twin sister Rhoda female athlete of '44, runnerup to Joe Krol Cdn athlete of '45, Cdn, US ntl titles slalom, downhill, GS; mem. US FIS team '50; mem. '48 Olympic team; mem. '73 Que. ladies' interprovincial golf team; Summerlea club champion; competed '80 Montreal marathon; mem. US National Ski, Cdn Amateur Sports, Skiing halls of fame; res. Actonvale, Que.

WYATT, Dave (coaching); b. 25 Jan 1940, Sherbrooke, Que.; m. Judith Stone; c. Chris; Queen's, hons BSc; retd. teacher; Little League baseball coach more than 25yrs; 17 District, 3 provincial, 1 ntl title teams; coach '71 Little League World Series team; Brockville sportsman of '75; mem. Brockville Sports Hall of Fame; res. Brockville, Ont.

WYATT, Jennifer (golf); b. 10 Dec 1965, Vancouver, B.C.; Lamar; graphic artist, retd. pro golfer; competitive hockey player before concentrating on golf; '84 BC jr. title; ranked top jr. in Canada '85-87; won NZ amateur '87; mem. Cdn Commonwealth team '87; 2 university tournament titles; played on LPGA tour '88-98; career low round 66; won Crestar Farm Fresh Classic '92; mem. LPGA softball team; res. Vancouver, B.C.

WYDARENY, John (football); b. 15 Feb 1941, Hearst, Ont.; m. Janet Elizabeth Gowans; c. John Christopher, Erin Jean; UWO, BA, UofT, BEd; teacher; Ont. 440yd titles '55-57; OQAA all-star backfielder Western Mustangs; pro Argos '63-65, *Globe and Mail* all-star def. back each year; Eskimos '66-72; 3 times WFC all-star, twice all-Cdn; Jackie Parker Eskimo's MVP trophy '69; CFL record: 52 interceptions for 747yds; gained 208yds on interceptions '67, 127yds Edmonton at Calgary game '67; 11 interceptions lead WFC, CFL '69-70; res. St. Albert, Alta.

WYKEHAM-MARTIN, Simon (parachuting); b. 23 Dec 1937, Ryde, Isle of Wight, Eng.; d. 1992; given name: Simon Fairfax; div.; c. Cathy Lynn, Douglas Fairfax; retired Cdn Forces, safety dir.; mem. Cdn Sports Parachuting Assoc. team '62, '64, '66, '68, '70; world championships '62, '64, '66; 1st Cdn parachute medalist world competition with 2 silver, 1 bronze '66; silver, bronze '70 Worlds; 2 silver, 1 bronze military team European intl meets; former mem., pres., p.-pres. CSPA; ntl overall Sport Parachuting, accuracy champion; qualified CSPA instructor/examiner, rigger; responsible for establishing Cdn Forces Military Freefall Training program and CF parachute team Skyhawks; 5yrs Skyhawks team leader; mem. CF Airborne Trials and Evaluation Section; 2600 freefall descents; qualified for airborne wings of Belgium, France, U.S.A., Canada; mem. Canadian Forces Sports Hall of Fame.

WYLIE, Bob (golf); b. 25 Sep 1929, Lamont, Alta.; given name: Robert Lenwood Duncan; m. Joan Cuthbert; c. Robert Scott, Michael, Jock; Mt. Royal Coll., Fullerton Jr. Coll.; retd. steel co. mgr.; 4 Alta. Amateur titles, 3 times runnerup; 2 Alta. Open titles, lost 3rd in playoff, 3 times runnerup;

Mexican Amateur title '61, Sask. Open '62; quarterfinalist British Amateur '70; rep. Canada 7 times internationally; mem. 14 Willingdon Cup teams; mem. Alta Sports, RCGA halls of fame; res. Calgary, Alta.

WYLIE, Harvey (football); b. Apr 1933, Lamont, Alta.; m. Pat Muir; c. Barbara, Wesley; Montana State; retd. engineer; baseball tryout Chicago White Sox; jr. A hockey Calgary; pro football Calgary '56-64; WFC all-star safety 5 seccessive years; twice all-Cdn; CFL record 5 tds on kickoff returns; 35 career interceptions; 20 fumble recoveries; career record 151 kickoff returns for 4293yds; mem. Alta. Sports, Canadian Football halls of fame; res. Rocky Mountain House, Alta.

WYNNE, Ivor (coaching); b. 2 Nov 1918, Wales, d. 1 Nov 1970, Hamilton, Ont.; m. Frances; c. Bob, John; McMaster, BA, Syracuse, MA, OCE; educator; nicknamed 'The Driver'; 2 seasons ntl champion Cloverleafs basketball team; athletic dir. McMaster from '48; pres. CIAU, governor OQAA; 16yrs color commentator for pro, intercollegiate football games on radio, TV with sportscaster Norm Marshall; Hamilton Civic Stadium renamed in his honor; McMaster athletic complex bears his name; mem. McMaster Sports Hall of Fame.

YAKUBOWICH, Joyce (t&f); b. 29 May 1953, Toronto, Ont.; given name: Joyce Louise Sadowick; m. Bradley Yakubowich; c. Jennifer, Lee; SFU, UVic; computer support; ntl HS record 54.7 for 400m '70; mem. bronze 4x100m relay team '70 Commonwealth Games; mem. '71, '75 Pan-Am, '72, '76 Olympic, '73 FISU Games, '77 European tour teams; gold 400m, 4x400m relay, bronze 4x100m relay '75 Pan-Am Games; Pan-Am, ntl records (51.60) in 400m, (23.2) 200m, ntl relay records; ntl 400m titles '71-78, 200m '72, '75; retd '78 due to blood disorder; coaches fitness training; res. Victoria, B.C.

YALLOP, Frank (soccer); b. 4 Apr 1964, Watford, Eng.; honed talents Port Coquitlam; 12 seasons as defender Ipswich Town, Blackpool; moved to MLS with Tampa Bay Mutiny '96; mem. ntl team from '90; competed '91, '93 Gold Cup, '92-93 World Cup qualifiers; 43 international caps; res. Tampa, Fla./Vancouver, B.C.

YASHIN, Alexei (hockey); b. 5 Nov 1973, Sverdlovsk, Russia; centre; represented Russia '92, '93 world jr, gold '92; gold Russia '93 worlds; competed for Russia '96 World Cup, '98 Olympics; Ottawa 1st choice '92 NHL entry draft; made NHL debut '93; NHL record (through '99): 431 scheduled games, 178g, 225a, 22 playoff games, 6g, 8a; only rookie '93-94 all-star game scoring 2g, including winner; donated $1M to National Arts Centre '98, withdrew donation '99 after first $200,000 payment made; Senators team capt. '98-99; *SN* all-star team '99; suspended by Senators for entire '99-2000 season for refusal to honor $3.6M contract; res. Ottawa, Ont./Kloten, Switzerland.

YEATS, Doug (wrestling); b. 1 Nov 1957, Montreal, Que.; Concordia; engineer; Greco-Roman specialist; 2 ntl 68kg GR, 1 62kg GR titles; 3 US 68kg GR titles; gold 62kg '79 Pan-Am Games; mem. '79, '83 Pan-Am, '76, '80, '84, '88, '92 Olympic, '77-79, '81-83, '86-87, '91 world championships teams; silver '92 Pan-Am championships; res. Montreal, Que.

YETMAN, Wayne (t&f); b. 8 Oct 1946, Toronto, Ont.; given name: Wayne Douglas; UWO, BA, UofT; mgr. creative services; '68 Detroit, '75 Toronto Police Games, '76 National Capital marathon titles; 19th '69, 10th '70 Boston marathons; mem. '76 Olympic team; 2nd '75 Skylon (Buffalo to Niagara Falls) marathon; res. Toronto, Ont.

YORK, Patrick (t&f/wrestling); b. 12 Jul 1951, Winnipeg, Man.; blind all-around athlete; brother of ntl team diver Teri; 23 gold BC Games for Disabled '77-81; 5 gold BC indoor games '79; 3 wrestling, 2 t&f, 1 canoeing gold Canada summer games; 3 silver, 1 bronze '78 Pan-Am, relay bronze, 400m gold '80 disabled Olympics; world record 400m; res. Vancouver, B.C.

YORK, Teri (diving); b. 11 Nov 1955, Winnipeg, Man.; given name: Theresa Kathleen; SFU, BA; teacher; ntl jr. 3m, 1m diving champion '69-72; mem. '72, '76 Olympic

teams, 6th 10m '76 Olympics; bronze '74 Swedish Cup, silver 10m Finnish championships, Czech 3m, U S ntl 10m titles '74; ntl 3m, tower titles '73-75; bronze '74 Commonwealth Games; 6th 10m, 7th 3m '75 world championships; Australian 3m title '77; res. White Rock, B.C.

YOST, Ken (coaching); b. 2 Sep 1905, Winnipeg, Man.; d. 12 Jul 1990, Winnipeg, Man.; given name: Elmer Kenneth; m. Leona Pearl Tetrault (d); c. Raymond, Carolyn, Greg; business college; retd. railroad employee; coach '48 Olympic t&f team; records chair. '52 BEG; p.-pres. Winnipeg AA, Greater Winnipeg Girls' Sr. Softball League, MSA, WCSA, CSA; treas., later secty. AAU of C; convenor Winnipeg Sr. HL; mem. Canadian Amateur Sports Hall of Fame.

YOSURACK, Joe (baseball); b. 1926, Juneau, Pa.; d. 1983, Waterloo, Ont.; m. Dorothy; c. Becky, Michael; rhp for several amateur teams in Pennsylvania and Kentucky before moving to Canada '47; played for St. Catharines Stags in Niagara District Sr. League posting 15-3 record before signing with Waterloo Tigers of SrIC; led SrIC pitchers with 11-6, 13-6 records '50-51; fine hitter and outfielder he shared '57 RBI title with Listowel's Jim Dickey with 26; mgr. Waterloo Junior Expos; umpired in SrIC; mem. Indiana, Pa. Sports Hall of Fame.

YOUNG, Dolores (rowing); b. 2 May 1957, Picton, Ont.; given name: Dolores Robina Mary; m. Robert Bailey; c. Graham, Emma; York, hons. BPhE, Queen's, BEd; ED Manitoba Rowing Assn.; US HS cox 4s, ntl cox 8s titles '75; mem. '76, '84 Olympic teams; West German cox 4s, 8s titles, bronze cox 8s '77 world championships; cox 4s title Cdn Henley, cox 8s Australia International regatta, bronze '78 Worlds; won cox 8s Amsterdam '79; quad title '80 nationals, '80-82 Cdn Henley, US nationals '83; competed '83 worlds; Ont., ntl jr. single sculls '82; Ont. achievement awards; co-chair rowing '99 PAG; res. Winnipeg, Man.

YOUNG, Don (all-around); b. 15 Feb 1906, Blakney, Ont.; d. 2 Mar 1988, Ottawa, Ont.; m. Frances Boomer (d), Alice Taylor McArton; c. Kenneth (d), Debbie, Jack McArton, Ron McArton; McGill, MD; general practitioner; starred in basketball, football with McGill; mem. Rideau Aquatic Club sr Cdn basketball titlists '24-25; mem. Rough Riders '25-27. 2 Grey Cup winners; centre (capt. '30) McGill basketball squad undefeated over 4yrs; Intercollegiate champs '28; captained 3 McGill football squads where he was a backfielder '28-34; 1st Ottawa native named *CP* university football all-star; played outside wing and rated superb tackler; mem. Rideau jr. football club; cousin of basketball inventor James Naismith; also shone in lacrosse, baseball where he caught for Renfrew, Smiths Falls, Ottawa Gunners city champs '31; scored hole-in-one at Ottawa Hunt; served overseas as medic WW2; McGill athlete of yr; OBE; mem. Ottawa, McGill Sports halls of fame.

YOUNG, Frank (rowing/basketball/racquetball); b. 5 Aug 1929, Toronto, Ont.; given name: Frank David; m. Jean Lockhart; c. John, James, Bob, Elizabeth; retd. insurance agent; mem. heavyweight 8s crew '52 Olympics; Sr. A basketball Toronto West End Y '50-54, Sr. B Andy's AC '55-56; mem. Kitchener-Waterloo Ont. Sr. B basketball champions '57-58; Eastern Cdn men's masters racquetball champion '76; Ont. men's masters racquetball titles '77, '80, 3rd '79, '81; co-capt. Central Tech sr. football, basketball teams; res. Hamilton, Ont.

YOUNG, George (swimming); b. 1910, Scotland, d. 6 Aug 1972, Niagara Falls, Ont.; m. 1. Margaret Ravior, 2. Gay Booth, 3. Georgina Stokoe; c. George, Margaret, Thomas; parks commission employee; emigrated to Canada age 2; learned to swim in Toronto's Don River; coached by Johnny Walker at Toronto West End YMCA; as amateur won 5 ntl titles; 4 Toronto across-the-bay, 3 Montreal bridge-to-bridge swim titles; Catalina channel in 15:45 '27; nicknamed "Catalina Kid"; staged own Lake Ont. marathon '28 but pulled from water after only 5 miles; failed to finish 3 more CNE swims, won '31; named Canada's outstanding swimmer of half century '50; mem. Canada's Sports, International Marathon Swimmers, Ont. Aquatic halls of fame.

YOUNG, Jim (football); b. 6 Jun 1943, Hamilton, Ont.; given name: James Norman; div.; c.Jamie, Sean, Cory; Queen's, BA; freelance broadcaster, Barter Business Exchange exec.; Omega Trophy OUAA MVP '64; 2yrs Minnesota (NFL); BC Lions '67-79; CFL record: 522 pass receptions for 9248yds, 17.7 avg., 65tds; club records receptions, yds receiving, TDs on passes; 5th all-time CFL receivers, all-Cdn '72, twice WFC all-star; Schenley outstanding Cdn award '70, '72, runnerup '69; asst. coach BC '89-90; v-p. community relations '90-92; rep. BC in Countdown, Superstars competitions; subject of book *Dirty 30* by Jim Taylor; mem. Cdn, OUAA Football, BC Sports halls of fame; res. Vancouver, B.C.

YOUNG, Joe (t&f); b. 4 May 1920, Hamilton, Ont.; given name: Joseph Riley; m. Mary (Molly) O'Neil; c. Joseph, Jennifer, Martha; McMaster, BA, BPhE, OCE; retd. supervisor phys ed Hamilton Board of Education; Ont. int. 440yd championship '36, ntl jr. 440yd '38, mem. ntl sr. mile relay champions '38; coached HS teams t&f, basketball, football '46-66 Woodstock, Ottawa, Hamilton; from '60 registered CTFA official; chief starter '76 Olympics, '78 Commonwealth, '79 World Cup, '81 Caribbean Games, World Cup Americas II trials; res. Ancaster, Ont.

YOUNG, Neil (curling); b. 27 Sep 1958, St. John's, Nfld.; given name: Jeffrey Neil; chemist; mem. Nfld. rink '78 ntl jr. men's; lead Nfld. Brier entries '81, '84-85; res. St. John's. Nfld.

YOUNG, Preston (football); b. 15 Jul 1954, Regina, Sask.; m. Nadine; c. Daniel; SFU; partner fitness club; mem. undefeated jr. Regina Rams 2yrs; def. back Sask. '78, Toronto '79-80, '85, Hamilton '81, Montreal '82-84; ranked among premier deep backs in CFL; record 134 punt returns 1477yds, 23 interceptions 317yds, 7 fumble returns 100yds, 1td; res. Regina, Sask.

YOUNG, Walter (t&f); b. 14 Mar 1913, Lime Ridge, Que.; m. Muriel Smith; c. Stanley; retd. fireman; 2 undistinguished Boston Marathon appearances preceeded '37 victory; 2nd N.Melford, Mass., 20-mile race '37; Salisbury Beach marathon title '31; mem. '38 BEG team; mem. Montreal Castor AC; welter, middleweight boxer, 3 pro bouts, won 1, lost 2 by KO; 10 consecutive snowshoe race victories including 10-mile record Hull race; expert marksman; ntl .22 100yd accuracy title '64; res. Longueuil, Que.

YOUNG-BLACK, Stuart (equestrian); b. 21 Jul 1959, Macclesfield, Eng.; began riding age 3; short-listed for British jr team; moved to Canada at 17; Ontario jr team '77-80; mem. ntl three-day event team from '87; 1st Canadian to win international advanced 3-day event in foreign country; competed '92, '96 Olympics; team gold '91, silver '87 Pan-Am Games; res. Millwood, VA.

YOUNGBERG, Jane (badminton); b. 25 Dec 1948, Alysbury, Eng.; given name: Jane Marie Dubord; m. Edward Youngberg; c. Marion, Brett; UBC, BEd; teacher; with Sue Latournier '65 jr. doubles age 15; with Barbara Nash ntl ladies' jr. doubles '67-68; ntl ladies' Open, Closed singles titles, with Barb Welch Open, Closed doubles '74-75, '77; mem. Uber Cup team '72, '75 beating former world champion Etsuko Takenaka of Japan '75; competed '74 Christchurch Commonwealth Games, Devlin Cup Matches vs US; with Sherry Boyce ntl women's doubles '76, quarterfinals all-Eng. singles; '77 Cdn women's singles; World Cup semifinals with Wendy Clarkson; mem. '78 Commonwealth Games silver medal team; res. Surrey, B.C.

YOUNGSON, Les (curling); b. 1900 Neury, County Down, Ireland, d. 28 May 1979, Regina, Sask.; given name: Lesley; m. Muriel Armstrong; c. Dorothy; car salesman; skip '36 Sask. Brier entry; South Sask. champion '43, '48; 43 consec. yrs Regina bonspiel competitor; 3yrs secty. SCA, pres. '43-44; life mem. SCA from ;51; pres. Regina CC '49-50; hon. life mem. Regina CC; mem. Sask. Sports Hall of Fame.

YOUNGSON, Muriel (curling); b. 15 Aug 1906, Pearson, Man.; d. 17 Feb 1986, Regina, Sask; given name: Muriel Armstrong; m. Les Youngson (d); c. Dorothy; retired nurse; competitive curler '31-62; Regina Ladies' Bonspiel grand aggregate '43, '45; pres. Caledonian Ladies' CC '45-47; active role formation Sask. LCA; mem. exec. council SLCA, pres. '59; exec. mem. WCLCA, pres. '60; key role in formation of CLCA, v-p. '61, pres. '62; with Addie Bright formed Sask. Sr. LCA, pres. '67-71; life mem.Caledonian LCC; with husband Les mem. Sask. Sports Hall of Fame.

YUNG, Darryl (badminton); b. 5 Aug 1972, Victoria, B.C.; mem. ntl team from '94; competed '94 Commonwealth, '96 Olympic Games; mixed doubles gold, men's doubles bronze '95 Pan-Am Games; res. Calgary, Alta.

YZERMAN, Steve (hockey); b. 9 May 1965, Cranbrook, B.C.; m. Lisa Brennan; c. Isabella, Maria, Sophia; came up through Nepean, Ont., minor program to Nepean Raiders (CJHL) then Peterborough Petes (OHL) '81-83; 1st pick Detroit '83 draft; pro Detroit from '83; youngest Red Wing capt. '86-87; NHL rookie team; set several rookie records; L.B. Pearson award '89; mem. Team Canada '83 world jr,

'85, '89, '90 worlds, '96 World Cup, '98 Olympics; topped 50-goal plateau with 50 '88, 65 '89, 62 '90, 51 '91, 58 '93; Central Junior league div. bears his name; 8 NHL all-star games; NHL record: (through '99) 1178 scheduled games, 592g, 891a, 145 playoff games, 61g, 87a; reached 600g plateau '99; capt. '97, '98 Stanley Cup champions; Conn Smythe trophy '98; '99-2000 became the 8th player to reach 600g and the 5th to reach 1500 points; Nepean arena bears his name; mem. Nepean Wall of Fame; res. Bloomington Hills, Mich.

Z

ZACK, Darren (softball); b. 9 Aug 1960, Sault Ste. Marie, Ont.; m. Charlotte Syrette; c. Darren, Molli Ann; natural resources; right handed pitcher; mem. NIAA (native) softball champions '84-85, '87, '89, '94; 1st world class exposure in Labatt's Challenge Cup '90; gold '91, '95, '99 Pan-Am Games; mem. 2 ntl title teams; ISF World title '92; with Toronto Gators ISC world title team '93, repeat '95; set world record with '92 Magicians hurling all but 1 inning of team's 9 games winning 7 ISC record 136 km in 76 innings, 0.38 ERA; 3rd pitcher in ISC world championship history to win back-to-back outstanding pitcher awards with 15-3 record and 108 strikeouts in 61 innings, hiked record to 150 SO '95; ranked number 1 pitcher in world '92-94; pitched with Tampa Bay Smokers '97-98, Oshawa Gators '99; res. Garden River, Ont.

ZAHAR, Michael (parachuting); b. 30 Oct 1954, Port Alberni, B.C.; m. Marlene Marsin; commercial jet pilot; former master rigger for parachute manufacturer; ntl 10-way title '75, 4-way, 8-way titles '77-80; Australian 4-way '77, French 4-way '79; 2nd French 8-way '79, China 4-way '80; world titles '77, '79; dir. CSPA; more than 2000 jumps; res. Paris, France.

ZAIPEC, Chuck (football); b. 1 Jul 1949, Philadelphia, Pa; given name: Charles; m. Mary Roberts; c. Emily, Sydney; Penn State, BA; financial advisor; def. capt., 1st team all-American Penn State '71; 8yrs pro with Dallas, Miami, Kansas City (NFL), Montreal (CFL); radio/TV analyst for NFL/CFL games; res. New Hope, Pa.

ZAMUNER, Rob (hockey); b. 17 Sep 1969, Oakville, Ont.; lw OHL Guelph '86-89, IHL Flint '89-90, AHL Binghamton '90-92, NHL NY Rangers '91, Tampa Bay '92-99, Ottawa '99; mem. Team Canada '97 worlds, '98 Olympics; NHL record (through '99): 484 scheduled games, 85g, 118a, 6 playoff games, 2g, 3a; res. Oakville, Ont.

ZEBCHUCK, Peter (golf); b. 20 May 1927, Ottawa, Ont.; d. 10 Aug 1995, Ottawa, Ont.; m. Marilyn Kearney; c. Colleen, Patti; businessman; began playing golf as teenager; noted for prodigious drives, expertise with wedge, putter; 4 Ottawa City & District medal, 1 match titles; set course records Chaudiere 65, Glenlea 65, Ottaw Hunt 67; only scratch golfer Ottawa area '54; won Chaudiere, Glenlea Opens; twice capt. Que. Seniors teams; won Alexander of Tunis title '65; 3 Chaudiere, 9 Hunt club titles; mem. several Que. Willingdon Cup teams; competed Cdn. Amateur.

ZEMAN, Joe (builder); b. 6 Feb 1914, Outlook, Sask.; m. Mary Schewan; c. Gary, Dale, Brenda, Blair; UofSask, BEd, BSc; agricultural economist; mgr. ntl baseball team '67 Pan-Am Games; founding mem. 3 hockey, several baseball organizations; mem. Saskatoon Parks & Rec. board, Sask. P&R Assn. council; board, comm. mem. 18 sports organizations; qualified baseball, hockey coach; dir. Sask.

Sport, Sask. Sports Hall of Fame; co-author *"Hockey Heritage: 88 Years of Puck Chasing in Saskatchewan"*; mem. Sask. Sports Hall of Fame; res. Saskatoon, Sask.

ZERON, Rick (harness racing); b. 8 Sep 1956, Ottawa, Ont.; honed skills in Ottawa area before switching to Blue Bonnets '82 where he rapidly rose to top billing; from '86-94 leading Blue Bonnets dash winner 7 times; led Blue Bonnets drivers in earnings 7 straight years; won 5 UDR titles; shifted operations to OJC circuit '95; career best season 437 wins '89; also highly regarded trainer; through '97 4165 victories with purses exceeding $23M; res. Oakville, Ont.

ZILBERMAN, Victor (wrestling); b. 28 Mar 1947, Kishinev, USSR; m. Christine Siciliano; c. Victoria, David; educator, coach; USSR jr champion '64-65; gold Israel ntls '74, Finland, Berlin internationals, USSR sr ntls '72, European team championships '73, Cdn sr FS titles '75, '78; silver World Cup Toledo, Spain (Sambo), '78 Commonwealth Games; impressive coaching record with USSR '65-66, Israel '74, Thunder Bay '75-76, Que. provincial '76-80, McGill '77-81, Snowdon YMHA Montreal '80-84, Concordia '96-98; CIAU coach of '84. '86, Que. wrestling coach of '85; pres. Cdn Amateur Wrestling Coaches Assn; Ont., Soviet achievement awards; USSR master of sport award; res. Montreal, Que.

ZIMMERMAN, Jeff (baseball); b. 9 Aug 1972, Kelowna, B.C.; given name: Jeffrey Ross; Texas Christian BS, SFU MBA; rhp; pitched in France '94; extensive experience with ntl sr men's team '95-97; 2 seasons at TCU '92-93; made pro debut Winnipeg '97; Northern League rookie of '97; named to '97 Independent Leagues all-star team by *Baseball America;* pitched for Peoria (Arizona Fall League); joined Texas Rangers organization '98 playing with Charlotte, Tulsa; Nolan Ryan Texas Rangers Minor League pitcher of '98 award; made major league debut '99 quickly establishing himself as premier relief pitcher and earning berth on AL all-star game team as rookie; res. Vancouver, B.C.

ZMICH, Rick (football); b. 18 Sep 1958, Ottawa, Ont.; UofOtt, hons Bsc; football coach; quarterbacked UofOtt Gee-Gees '78-82; noted for strong, accurate passing arm; competed '80 Vanier Cup; all-Cdn '82; Hec Crighton award winner '82; head coach Wilfrid Laurier; CIAU coach of '95; mem. UofOtt football Hall of Fame; res. Waterloo, Ont.

ZOCK, Bill (football); b. 26 Jan 1918, Toronto, Ont.; d. 29 Apr 1988, Toronto, Ont.; m. Mildred Eason (d); c. William Jr., Gordon, Arlene; steamfitter; hard-nosed guard/tackle who played 18yrs in CFL with Toronto, Edmonton; mem. 7 Grey Cup finals, 6 winners; all-Cdn guard '46-47; coached Balmy Beach, Argos; respected as a tough competitor on the field but true gentleman off field; accomplished singer who was musical dir. Invictones male chorus 20yrs; mem. Cdn Football Hall of Fame.

ZOKOL, Richard (golf); b. 21 Aug 1958, Kitimat, B.C.; Brigham Young; Cdn. amateur champion '81; mem. BYU NCAA title team, 2nd team all-American '81; International amateur champion of Morocco '80; joined PGA tour '81; won '92 Milwaukee Open, Deposit Guaranty Classic; nicknamed "Disco Dick"; golf columnist *Vancouver Sun*; res. Vancouver, B.C.

ZUGER, Joe (football); b. 25 Feb 1940, Homestead, Pa.; given name: Joseph Mark; m. Eleanor Townsend; c. Beth, Joe Jr., Amy; Arizona State; retd. football exec.; led all US colleges in punting, passing; Arizona State MVP '61; pro Hamilton '62 as defensive back until injury to Bernie Faloney provided opportunity to quarterback team; QB'd team to 2 Grey Cup wins; CFL record '62-71: 1618 passes, 814 completions for 12,676yds, 95 interceptions, 76tds, 1075 punts for 48,930yds, 68 singles, record 45.5 avg.; outstanding player award '67 Grey Cup; mgr. Hamilton Wentworth Curling Club; coached Mount Hamilton peewee hockey teams to 2 league titles; closed playing career Detroit (NFL) '72; asst. coach Hamilton '79, player coordinator '80, GM '81-92; 3 div. titles, 4 Grey Cup finals, 1 winner; v.-chair CFL governors '86-92; mem. Ariz. State Sports Hall of Fame; res. Hamilton, Ont.

GLOSSARY OF TERMS

a– assist
AAFC - All-America Football Conference
AAGPBL - All America Girls Professional Baseball League
AAGPBLPA - All America Girls Professional Baseball League Players Association
AAHA - American Amateur Hockey Association
AASSA - American Amateur Speed Skating Association
AAU - Amateur Athletic Union
AAU of C - Amateur Athletic Union of Canada
ab - at bats
ABA - American Basketball Association
ABC - American Bowling Congress
AC - athletic club
ACT - Associated Canadian Travellers
AD - athletic director
ADM - Assistant Deputy Minister
AEC - Atomic Energy Commission
AFB - Air Force Base
AFL - American Football League
AFL - Arena Football League
AGM - assistant general manager
AHA - Atlantic Hockey Association
AHL - American Hockey League
AIAW - Association of Intercollegiate Athletics for Women
AIS - Australian Institute of Sport
AIWA - Association of International Women's Athletics
AL - American League
ALCA - Alberta Curling Association
ALCS - American League Championship Series
Alta. - Alberta
AKO - Alpha Kai Omega fraternity
AMA - Automobile Manufacturer's Association
Amer. - American
ANAF - Army, Navy, Air Force
AP - Associated Press
APAHPER - Atlantic Provinces Association for Health, Physical Education & Recreation
APSL - American Professional Soccer League
APRC - Association of Professional Rodeo Cowboys
ASA - American Softball Association
ASMHF - Association of Sport Museums and Halls of Fame
assn - association
assoc. - associate
asst. - assistant
ATP - Association of Tennis Professionals

AUAA - Atlantic Universities Athletic Association
avg. - average

b. - born
BA - batting average
BA - bachelor of arts
BBA - bachelor of business administration
bob - base on balls
BB - bare back (rodeo riding)
BBHOF - Baseball Hall of Fame
BBWAA - Baseball Writers Association of America
B.C. (BC) - British Columbia
BCABA - British Columbia Amateur Basketball Association
BCABA - British Columbia Amateur Boxing Association
BCAHA - British Columbia Amateur Hockey Association
BCASA - British Columbia Amateur Softball Association
BCJHL - British Columbia Junior Hockey League
BCLA - British Columbia Lacrosse Assn.
BCPGA - British Columbia Professional Golf Association
BCU - Boston College University
BComm - Bachelor of Commerce
BD - Bachelor of Divinity
BE - British Empire
BE& C - British Empire & Commonwealth
BEc - Bachelor of Economics
BEd - Bachelor of Education
BEG - British Empire Games
BM - Boston Marathon
BMX – Bicycle Motor Cross
BPA - Bowling Proprietor's Association
BPAC - Bowling Proprietor's Association of Canada
BPAO - Bowling Proprietor's Association of Ontario
BPhE - Bachelor of Physical Education
BPharm - Bachelor of Pharmocology
BPHE - Bachelor of Physical, Health Education
BSc - Bachelor of Science
BSA - Bachelor of Science Agriculture
BScPhE - Bachelor of Science Physical Education
BYU - Brigham Young University

c. - children
C - centre
C1 - canoe singles
C2 - canoe doubles
C4 - canoe fours

CA - Curling Association
CA - chartered accountant
CAAO - Canadian Association of Amateur Oarsmen
CAAWS - Canadian Association for the Advancement of Women and Sport and Physical Activity
CABA - Canadian Amateur Basketball Association
CABA - Canadian Amateur Boxing Association
CABC - Canadian Association of Basketball Coaches
CABO - Canadian Association of Basketball Officials
CAC - Canadian Association of Coaches
CADA - Canadian Amateur Diving Association
CADORA - Canadian Dressage Owners & Riders Association
CAFA - Canadian Amateur Football Association
CAFC - Canadian Association of Football Coaches
CAHA - Canadian Amateur Hockey Association
CAHL - Canadian Amateur Hockey League
CAHPER - Canadian Association for Health, Physical Education and Recreation
Calif.(CAL) - California
CAM - Club and membership
CANZ - Canada New Zealand
capt. - captain
CARA - Canadian Amateur Rowing Association
CART – Championship Auto Racing Teams
CASA - Canadian Amateur Swimming Association; Canadian Amateur Skiing Association
CASH – Canadian Association for Sport Heritage
CASSA - Canadian Amateur Speed Skating Association; Canadian Amateur Synchronized Swimming Association
CAUAD - Canadian Association of University Athletic Directors
CAWA - Canadian Amateur Wrestling Association
CBA - Canadian Badminton Association
CBC - Canadian Bowling Congress
CBF - Canadian Boating Federation
CBRCCC - Canadian Branch Royal Caledonian Curling Club
CC - curling club
cc - cubic centimetres
CCA - Canadian Canoe Association

CCA - Canadian Cricket Association
CCA - Canadian Curling Association
CCA - Canadian Cycling Association
CCAM - Canadian Civilian Association of Marksmen
CCF - Co-operative Commonwealth Federation
CCGA - Canadian Commonwealth Games Association
CCHA - Central Conference Hockey Association
CCIFC - Central Canada Intercollegiate Football Conference
CCR - Canadian Curling Reporters
CD - Canada decoration
CdM - chef de mission
Cdn - Canadian
CEF - Canadian Equestrian Federation
CEO - Chief executive officer
CF - Canadian Forces
CFA - Canadian Fencing Association; Canadian Football Association
CFAB - Canadian Federation of Amateur Baseball
CFB - Canadian Forces Base
CFHA - Canadian Field Hockey Association
CFL - Canadian Football League
CFLPA - Canadian Football League Players Association
CFO - chief financial officer
CFSA - Canadian Figure Skating Association
CFSAC - Canadian Forces Small Arms Competition
CGA - Certified general accountant
CGF - Canadian Golf Foundation; Canadian Gymnastics Federation
CHL - Canadian Hockey League; Central Hockey League
CIAU - Canadian Interuniversity Athletic Union
CI - Collegiate Institute
CIBC - Canadian Imperial Bank of Commerce
CIHU - Canadian Intercollegiate Hockey Union
CIL - Canadian Industries Limited
CIRU - Canadian Intercollegiate Rugby Union
CISM - Conseil Internationale du Sport Militaire
c&j - clean & jerk
CJA - Canadian Jiu-jitsu Association
CJHL - Central Junior Hockey League
CKSS - Chatham Kent Secondary School
CLA - Canadian Lacrosse Association
CLBC - Canadian Lawn Bowling Council
CLCA - Canadian Ladies' Curling Association
CLGA - Canadian Ladies' Golf Association
CLGU - Canadian Ladies' Golf Union

CLLBC - Canadian Ladies' Lawn Bowling Council
CLTA - Canadian Lawn Tennis Association
CMA - Canadian Medical Association; Canadian Motorcycle Association
CMHA - Canadian Minor Hockey Association
CMJHL - Canadian Major Junior Hockey League
CNE - Canadian National Exhibition
CNR - Canadian National Railways
co. - company
CO - Commanding Officer
COA - Canadian Olympic Association
CODA - Calgary Olympics Development Association
COF - Canadian Orienteering Federation
CofO - City of Ottawa
COJO - Montreal Olympics organizing committee
coll. - college
Colo. - Colorado
comm. - committee
conf. - conference
consec. - consecutive
COPABA - Confederacion Pan-Americana de Baloncesto
CORK - Canadian Olympic Regatta, Kingston
COTHA - Canadian Old-Timers Hockey Association
COWHL - Central Ontario Women's Hockey League
CP - The Canadian Press
CPCA - Canadian Professional Coaches Association
CPGA - Canadian Professional Golfers Association
CPHL - Central Professional Hockey League
CPRA - Canadian Professional Rodeo Association
CRCA - Canadian Race Car Association
CRDA - Canadian Race Drivers Association
CRU - Canadian Rugby Union
CSA - Canadian Ski Association; Canadian Soccer Association; Canadian Softball Association
CSC – Canadian Silver Cross
CSCC – Canadian Snooker Control Council
CSCF – Canadian Ski Coaches Federation
CSFA - Canadian Soccer Football Association
CSGA - Canadian Seniors Golf Association
CSIA - Canadian Ski Instructors Alliance
CSL - Canadian Soccer League
CSPA - Canadian Sport Parachuting Association
CSRA - Civil Service Recreation Association

CSSA - Canadian Synchronized Swimming Association
CSSF - Canadian School Sports Federation
CSSIA - Canadian Ski School & Instructors Alliance
CT. - Connecticut
CTA - Canadian Trotting Association
CTF - Canadian Teachers Federation
CTFA - Canadian Track and Field Association
CTR - Canadian Target Rifle
CTTA - Canadian Table Tennis Association
CVA - Canadian Volleyball Association
CVHL - Central Valley Hockey League
CWA - Canadian Weightlifting Association
CWFHA - Canadian Women's Field Hockey Association
CWIAA - Canadian Women's Intercollegiate Athletic Association
CWIAU - Canadian Women's Intercollegiate Athletic Union
CWSA - Canadian Water Skiing Association
CWSA - Canadian Wheelchair Sports Association
CWUAA - Canadian Women's University Athletic Association
CYA - Canadian Yachting Association

d. - death
(d) - deceased
D or d - doubles
D.C. - District of Columbia
DCRA - Dominion of Canada Rifle Association
DD - Doctor of Divinity
DDS - Doctor of Dental Surgery
de. - defensive end
DEd - Doctor of Education
def. - defence
dept. - department
d-gs -drop goals (rugby)
dh - downhill
DL - dart league
DMD - (Gregoire - dentistry degree)
DND - Department of National Defence
dir. - director
div. - divorced
DPhE - Doctor of Physical Education
DPHE - Doctor of Physical and Health Education
DQ or dq - disqualified
D.R. - Dominican Republic
DSA - (Pat Sheahan degree)
DSc - Doctor of Science
DSO - Distinguished Service Order

EAHL - Eastern Amateur Hockey League
ECAC - Eastern Colleges Athletic Conference
ECAHA - Eastern Canadian Amateur Hockey Association

ED - Executive Director
EdD - Doctorate of Education
EFC - Eastern Football Conference
EFC - Equestrian Federation of Canada
EHL - Eastern Hockey League
EL - Eastern League
EO - Eastern Ontario
EOLCA - Eastern Ontario Ladies' Curling Association
EOSSA - Eastern Ontario Secondary School Athletics
EOSSA - Eastern Ontario Speed Skating Association
EPBL - Eastern Professional Basketball League
EPHL - Eastern Pro Hockey League
era - earned run average
EWU - East Washington University
exec. - executive
EYTC - East York Track Club

FA - Football Association
F.A.M.E. - Female Athletes Motivating Excellence
FAQ - Federation of Quebec Athletics
FAS - Fitness and Amateur Sport
FBI - Federal Bureau of Investigation
FCA - Federation of Canadian Archers
FCA - Football Coaches Association
FD - Flying Dutchman
fed. - federation or federal
FG (fg) - field goal
FH - field hockey
FHA - Field Hockey Association
FIA - Federation Internationale de l'Automobile
FIBL - Federation Internationale Bobsleigh & Luge
FIE - Federation Internationale de Escrime
FIFA - Federation Internationale de Football Associations
FIH - Federation Internationale de Hockey
FILA - Federation Internationale de Lute Amateur
FINA - Federation Internationale de Natation Amateur
FIQ - Federation Internationale de Quilles
FIS - Federation Internationale de Ski
FISU - World University Games
FIVB - Federation internationale de Volleyball
Fla. - Florida
Fr. - Father
FS - Figure Skating; freestyle
FSL - Florida State League
FSR - freestyle record
FSU - Florida State University
Ft. - Fort

g. - goal
GB - Great Britain
GBNRA - Great Britain National Rifle Association
G&CC - golf and curling club

GF - Gymnastics Federation
GM - general manager
Gov.-Gen. - Governor-General
govt - government
GP - grand prix
GPAC - Great Plains Athletic Conference
GR - Greco-Roman
GS - giant slalom
GT-CN - Grand Trunk-Canadian National

H&D - Halifax & District
HJ or hj - high jump
HL - Hockey League
HMCS - Her (His) Majesty's Canadian Ship
HN - Hockey News
HNIC - Hockey Night in Canada
hon. - honorary or honorable
hons. - honors
HP - high powered
HPA - Horseshoe Pitching Association
HR - home run
HS - high school

IAAA - International Amateur Aquatic Association
IAABO - International Association of Amateur Basketball Officials
IAAF - International Amateur Athletic Federation
IC - Inter County
ICF - International Curling Federation
IC4A - Intercollegiate Amateur Athletic Association of America
IEF - International Equestrian Federation
IESS - International Equestrian Sport Services
IHF - International Hockey Federation
IHL - International Hockey League
IIHF - International Ice Hockey Federation
IIHFM - International Ice Hockey Hall of Fame & Museum
IL - International League
Ill. - Illinois
ILTC - International Lawn Tennis Championship
ILTF - International Lawn Tennis Federation
IM - individual medley
IMSA - International Motor Sport Association
Inc. - Incorporated
Ind. - Indiana; Industries
inst. - institute
INS - International News Service
int. - intermediate
intl. - international
IOC - International Olympic Committee
IP - individual pursuit
IPRU - Interprovincial Rugby Union
IRFU - Interprovincial Rugby Football Union
IRL - Indy Racing League

ISC - International Softball Congress
ISF - International Softball Federation
ISSA - International Swimming Statisticians Association
ISU - International Shooting Union
ITF - International Tennis Federation
ITTF - International Table Tennis Federation
ITU - International Triathletes Union
IVBF - International Volleyball Federation
IWF - International Weightlifting Federation; International Wrestling Federation
IYRU - International Yacht Racing Union
jr. - junior
juve. - juvenile
K1 - kayak singles
K2 - kayak doubles
K4 - kayak fours
K of C - Knights of Columbus
kg - kilograms
km - kilometres
KO - knockout or kickoff
KOCR - King's Own Calgary Regiment
KSU - Kentucky State University
K-W - Kitchener-Waterloo

LA - Los Angeles
lb - pound
LBR - Ladies Barrel Racing
LCA - Ladies' Curling Association
LCBO - Liquor Control Board of Ontario
LCC - Ladies Curling Club
lhp - left-handed pitcher
Lib - Liberal
LJ (lj) - long jump
LLB - Bachelor of Laws
LLD - Doctor of Laws
LLM - Master of Laws
LPGA - Ladies' Professional Golf Association
LSU - Louisiana State University
LTC - Lawn and Tennis Club
Lt.-Gov. - Lieutenant-Governor

m. - married
m - metres
MA - Master of Arts
MAAA - Montreal Amateur Athletic Association
MAC - Mid-Atlantic Conference

MAHA - Manitoba Amateur Hockey Association
Man. - Manitoba
ManDak - Manitoba-Dakota
Mass. - Massachusetts
MB - Master Bowler
MBA - Master Bowlers' Association; master of business administration
MBE - Member of the British Empire
MCA - Manitoba Curling Association
MD - Doctor of medicine
mech. - mechanical

MEd - Master of Education
mem. - member
MFA - Manitoba Football Association
mfgr. - manufacturer
MFL - Minor Football League
mgr. - manager
MHA - Minor Hockey Association
Mich. - Michigan
MILL - Major Indoor Lacrosse League
MIT - Massachusetts Institute of Technology
ML - major league
MLA - member legislative assembly
MM - Military Medal
mos. - months
MP - modern pentathlon
MPhE - Master of Physical Education
MPP - Member Provincial Parliament
MPRA - Manitoba Provincial Rifle Association
MR - medley relay
MRA - Military Rifle Association
MSA - Manitoba Softball Association
MSA - Manitoba Soccer Association
MSc - Master of Science
MSL - Metro Soccer League
MSSA - Manitoba Speed Skating Association
MSU - Michigan State University
Mt. - Mount
MTHL - Metro Toronto Hockey League
MVD - most valuable defence
MVP - most valuable player

N. - North
NA - North American
NAIA - National Association of Intercollegiate Athletics
NAHL - North American Hockey League
NALA - North American Lacrosse Association
NALCA - Northern Alberta Ladies' Curling Association
NAMLFA - North American Minor League Footabll Alliance
NASCAR - National Association for Stock Car Auto Racing
NASKA - North American Sport Karate Association
NASL - North American Soccer League
NASO – National Association of Sports Officials
N.B.(NB) - New Brunswick
NBA - National Basketball Association
NBABA - New Brunswick Amateur Basketball Association
NBFHA - New Brunswick Field Hockey Association
NBGA - New Brunswick Golf Association
NBLCA - New Brunswick Ladies' Curling Association
NBOA - New Brunswick Officials Association
NBRA - New Brunswick Rifle Association

NBSA - New Brunswick Softball Association
NBSBL - New Brunswick Senior Baseball League
NBTFA - New Brunswick Track & Field Association
N.C.(NC) - North Carolina
NCAA- National Colleagiate Athletic Association
NCCP - National Coaching Certification Program
NCD - National Capital Division
NCI - National Coaching Institute
NCRRA - National Capital Region Rifle Association
NCTA - National Capital Tennis Association
N.D.(ND) - North Dakota
ND - Notre Dame
NDG - Notre Dame de Grace
NDHQ - National Defence Headquarters
NDHQRA - National Defence Headquarters Rifle Association
NDS - North Dakota State
N.E.(NE) - New England
NEA - News Enterprises of America
NF - Niagara Falls
NFL - National Football League
Nfld. - Newfoundland
NHA - National Hockey Association
NHL - National Hockey League
NHLPA - National Hockey League Players' Association
NIT – National Invitation Tournament
N.J.(NJ) - New Jersey
NL - National League
NLL - National Lacrosse League
NO - Northern Ontario
NOHA - Northern Ontario Hockey Association
NORCECA - North Central America and Caribbean zone
NMMI - New Mexico Military Institute
NPAAO - North Pacific Association of Amateur Oarsmen
NPSL - National Professional Soccer League
NRA - National Rifle Association; National Rodeo Association
NRC - National Research Council
N.S.(NS) - Nova Scotia
NSB - National Speakers Bureau
NSFAS - Nova Scotia Fitness & Amateur Sport
NSR - North Saskatchewan Regiment
NSRC - National Sport & Recreation Centre
NSSA - National Skeet Shooting Association
NSSFL - Nova Scotia Senior Football League
ntl -national
NTS - North Texas State
NWA - National Wrestling Association

NWBT - National Wheelchair Basketball Tournament
NWO - North Western Ontario
NWT - Northwest Territories
NWTCA - Northwest Territories Curling Association
NYC - New York City
NYP - New York-Pennsylvania
NYU - New York University
N.Z.(NZ) - New Zealand

OAC - Ottawa Athletic Club
OALA - Ontario Amateur Lacrosse Association
OASA - Ontario Amateur Softball Association
OAWF - Ontario Amateur Wrestling Federation
OBA - Ontario Baseball Association
OBE - Order of the British Empire
OCA - Ontario Curling Association
OCE - Ontario College of Education
OCWSA - Ottawa-Carleton Wheelchair Sports Association
O&D - Ottawa and District
ODFA - Ottawa District Football Association
ODHA - Ottawa District Hockey Association
ODGA - Ottawa District Golf Association
OFA - Ontario Fencing Association
OFC - Ontario Football Conference
off - offensive
OFSAA - Ontario Federation of School Athletic Associations
og - offensive guard
OGA - Ontario Golf Association
OGF - Ontario Gymnastics Federation
OHA - Ontario Hockey Association
OHL - Ontario Hockey League
OIAA - Ontario Intercollegiate Athletic Association
OJC - Ontario Jockey Club
OLA - Ontario Lacrosse Association
OLBA - Ontario Ladies' Basketball Association
OLCA - Ontario Ladies' Curling Association
OLGA - Ontario Ladies' Golf Association
OLTA - Ontario Lawn Tennis Association
OMJHL - Ontario Major Junior Hockey League
OMSA - Ontario Minor Soccer Association
Ont. - Ontario
OPGA - Ontario Professional Golfers' Association
OPHL - Ontario Professional Hockey League
OPLBA - Ontario Provincial Lawn Bowling Association
OQAA - Ontario-Quebec Athletic Association

OQIFC - Ontario-Quebec Interuniversity
Football Conference
ORA - Ontario Rifle Association
Ore. - Oregon
ORFU - Ontario Rugby Football Union
OSC - Ottawa Ski Club
OSL - Ontario Soccer League
OSSA - Ontario Speed Skating
Association
OSTFL - Ottawa Senior Touch Football
League
ot - offensive tackle
OTA - Ontario Tennis Association
OTFA - Ontario Track & Field Association
OUAA - Ontario Universities Athletic
Association
OVCA - Ottawa Valley Curling
Association
OVGA - Ottawa Valley Golf Association
OWA - Ontario Weightlifting Association
OWFHA - Ontario Women's Field Hockey
Association
OWHA - Ontario Women's Hockey
Association
OWIAA - Ontario Women's
Interuniversity Athletic Association
OWPA - Ontario Water Polo Association
OWSA - Ontario Water Skiing Association

p. - place
Pa. - Pennsylvania
Pac. - Pacific
Pan-Am - Pan American
PB - personal best
PC - Progressive Conservative
PCCA - Pacific Coast Curling Association
PCCHL - Peterborough Community
Centre Hockey League
PCHL - Pacific Coast Hockey League
PCL - Pacific Coast League
PE - physical education
P.E.I.(PEI) - Prince Edward Island
PEIJHL - Prince Edward Island Junior
Hockey League
PEng - Professional Engineer
PGA - Professional Golfers Association
PhD - Doctor of Philosophy
phys ed - physical education
PITA – Pacific International Trapshooting
Association
PLBA - Provincial Lawn Bowling
Association
POM - Piscine Olympique Montreal
POW - Prisoner of War
PQ - Province of Quebec
PQFA - Province of Quebec Fencing
Association
PQLTA - Province of Quebec Lawn Tennis
Association
PR - Puerto Rico
PR - public relations
P&R - parks and recreation
pres. - president

p.-pres - past president
prof. - professor
prov. - province or provincial
PS - public school
PT - physical training

QABA - Quebec Amateur Boxing
Association
QAHA - Quebec Amateur Hockey
Association
QAHL - Quebec Amateur Hockey League
QATFA - Quebec Amateur Track & Field
Association
QAWA - Quebec Amateur Wrestling
Association
QB - quarterback
QBA - Quebec Badminton Association
QC - Queen's Council
QCA - Quebec Curling Association
QFSAA - Quebec Federation of School
Athletic Associations
QGA - Quebec Golf Association
QHL - Quebec Hockey League
QJA - Quebec Judo Association
QJAHL - Quebec Junior Amateur Hockey
League
QJHL - Quebec Junior Hockey League
QLTA - Quebec Lawn Tennis Association
QLTF - Quebec Lawn Tennis Federation
QMJHL - Quebec Major Junior Hockey
League
QSF - Quebec Sailing Federation
QSHL - Quebec Senior Hockey League
QSM - Quartermaster Sergeant Major
QTF - Quebec Tennis Federation
QTFF - Quebec Track & Field Federation
Que. - Quebec

RA - recreation association
RAF - Royal Air Force
RB - running back
rbi - runs batted in
RC - rowing club; Royal Canadian
RCAF - Royal Canadian Air Force
RCCC - Royal Caledonian Curling Club
RCGA - Royal Canadian Golf Association
RCMP - Royal Canadian Mounted Police
RCN(R) - Royal Canadian Navy (reserve)
RCSSB - Roman Catholic Separate School
Board
RDA - Race Drivers Association
recept. - reception
rep. - representative
res. - residence
retd. - retired
RGF - Rhythmic Gymnastic Federation
RHIL - Roller Hockey International
League
RHYC - Royal Hamilton Yacht Club
RIT - Ryerson Institute of Technology
RMC - Royal Military College
RPI - Rensselaer Polytechnic Institute
RVC - Royal Victoria College

s - singles; show; silver
SA - Shooting Association
SABR - Society for American Baseball
Research
SAIT - Southern Alberta Institute of
Technology
SAL - South Atlantic League
Sask. - Saskatchewan
SB - smallbore
SB - saddle bronc
sb - stolen base
SC - swimming club; South Carolina
SCA - Saskatchewan Curling Association
SCCA - Sports Car Club of America
SD - South Dakota
SDSU - San Diego State University
SEC - South East Conference
secty - secretary
sep. - separated
SFC - Shooting Federation of Canada
SFC - Sports Federation of Canada
SFU - Simon Fraser University
St.FX - St. Francis Xavier University
SGW - Sir George Williams University
SJD - Doctor of Juridical Science
SJHL - Saskatchewan Junior Hockey
League
SLCA - Saskatchewan Ladies' Curling
Association
SLTA - Saskatchewan Lawn Tennis
Association
SO - Southern Ontario
so - strikeouts; shutouts
SOU - Southern League
S.P.O.R.T. - St. Petersburg Olympic
Regatta for Training
SPRA - Saskatchewan Provincial Rifle
Association
sr. - senior
S&R - sport & recreation
Sr. IC - Senior Intercounty
SSA - Speed Skating Association
SSC - Speed Skating Club
SSM - Sault Ste. Marie
St. - Saint
STOH - Scott Tournament of Hearts
SUNY - State University of New York
SWC - South West Conference

t - triples
TB - Thunder Bay
TBFPBA - Thunder Bay Five Pin Bowlers
Association
TC - track club; tennis club
TCA - Toronto Curling Association
TCIAA - Toronto Collegiate Institute
Athletic Association
TCU - Texas Christian University
td - touchdown
TDIAA - Toronto District Interscholastic
Athletic Association
TDMSA - Toronto & District Minor
Soccer Association

t&f - track and field
TFA - track & field association
TFC - track & field club
tj - triple jump
TKO - Technical Knock Out
TL - Texas League
treas. - treasurer
Tor. - Toronto
TPC - Tour Players' Championship
TSN - The Sports Network
TSSAA - Toronto Secondary School
Athletic Association
TT - time trials

UAlta - University of Alberta
UBC - University of British Columbia
UBCSC - University of British Columbia
Swim Club
-(age)- -(age)
UCal - University of Calgary
UCLA - University of California Los
Angeles
UDR - Universal Driver Rating
UDRS - Universal Driver Rating System
UFL - United Football League
UK - United Kingdom
UKOA - British Olympic Association
UMan - University of Manitoba
UMich - University of Michigan
UNB - University of New Brunswick
UNC - University of North Carolina
UND - University of North Dakota
UNLV - University of Nevada Las Vegas
UofOtt - University of Ottawa
UPI - United Press International
UQTR - University of Quebec Trois-
Rivieres
US - United States
USAC - United States Auto Club
USAHA - United States Amateur Hockey
Asociation
UofSask - University of Saskatchewan
USC (SouthernCal) - University of
Southern California
USFL - United States Football League
USGF - United States Gymnastics
Federation
USHL - United States Hockey League
USHWA - United States Harness Writers
Association
USNRA - United States National Rifle
Association
USNRA - United States National Rowing
Association
USRRC - United States Road Racing Club
USSR - Union of Soviet Socialist
Republics
USTA - United States Trotting Association
USTPA - United States Tour Players
Association
UofT - University of Toronto
UTEP - University Texas El Paso
UTS - University of Toronto Schools

UVic - University of Victoria
UVRC - University of Victoria Rowing
Club
UWash - University of Washington
UWO - University of Western Ontario

Va. - Virginia
VASC - Vancouver Amateur Swim Club
VB - volleyball
VBA - Volleyball Association
v.capt - vice captain
v-p - vice president
V&D - Vancouver & District
VFHA - Vancouver Field Hockey
Association
VIFHA - Vancouver Island Field Hockey
Association
VRC - Vancouver Rowing Club
vs. - versus
Vt. - Vermont

w – win(s)
WAKO - World Amateur Kickboxing
Organization
WBL - World Basketball League
WBTF - World Baton Twirling Federation
WC - World Cup; wrestling club
WCC - Winnipeg Canoe Club
WCFPBA - Western Canada Five-Pin
Bowling Association
WCG - Western Canada Games
WCIAA - Western Canada Intercollegiate
Athletic Association
WCL - Western Canada League
WCLCA - Western Canada Ladies'
Curling Association
WCSA - Western Canada Softball
Association
WCT - World Curling Tour
WFC - Western Football Conference
WFL - World Football League
WHA - World Hockey Association
WHL - Western Hockey League
WIAU - Western Intercollegiate Athletic
Union
WIFU - Western Interprovincial Football
Union
WKA - World Karate Association
WKC - World Karate Commission
w-l - wins-losses
WLA - Western Lacrosse Association
WLAF - World League of American
Football
WLCA - Western Ladies' Curling
Association
W&M - William & Mary
WO - Western Ontario
WOHA - Western Ontario Hockey
Association
WOSSA - Western Ontario Secondary
School Athletics
WP - Water Polo
Wpg - Winnipeg

WR - world record
WSU - Washington State University
WTA - World Tennis Association
WW1 - World War 1
WW2 - World War 2
Wyo. - Wyoming

XC - cross country

YBC - Youth Bowling Council
yds - yards
YMCA - Young Men's Christian
Association
YMHA - Young Men's Hebrew
Association
yr(s) - year(s)
YM-YWCA - Young Men's-Young
Women's Christian Association
YTV - Youth Television

CROSS-INDEX

ADMINISTRATION

Abramowitz, Moe
Ackles, Bob
Adams, Bob
Adams, Jack
Albrecht, J.I.
Allan, Maurice
Andersen, Roxy
Anderson, Dave
Anderson, George
Andru, John
Armitage, Rolly
Ash, Gord
Back, Len
Baird, Vaughan
Baker, Bill
Baker, Charles
Bales, John
Ballard, Harold
Barrow, John
Bauer, David
Bayer, Jim
Beach, Pete
Bedecki, Tom
Beeston, Paul
Bell, Bobby
Bigras, Sylvie
Binns, Hilda
Bishop, Jim
Bitz, Ed
Blair, Wren
Bouchard, Butch
Box, Charlie
Branch, David
Britton, Bill
Brochu, Claude
Brock, Henry
Buddo, Don
Bulloch, Jim
Burelle, Jacques
Burns, Leo
Campbell, Clarence
Campbell, Colin
Capozzi, Herb
Chipman, A.U.
Chynoweth, Ed
Clair, Frank
Clancy, King
Clifford, John
Condon, Eddie
Cook, Murray
Corey, Ron
Costello, Murray
Crowe, Norton
Davies, Jack
Dawson, Earl
DeBlonde, Garry
Delvecchio, Alex
Deschamps, Claude
Devine, Jack
Dilio, Frank
Dojack, Paul
Donaghey, Sam
Donohue, Jack

Dorsch, Henry
Dowell, Hanson
Duncan, Cecil
Dunlap, Jake
Duthie, George
Eagleson, Alan
Elliott, Allen
Elliott, Bob
Elliott, Geoff
Enos, Ed
Etcheverry, Sam
Fanning, Jim
Farmer, Jim
Farmer, Ken
Farrell, Neil
Fauquier, Harry
Fedoruk, Sylvia
Ferguson, John
Ferguson, Merv
Fitch, Ed
Fitzpatrick, Allan
Fletcher, Cliff
Fletcher, Doug
Fleury, Lionel
Fontana, Don
Foster, Red
Fournier, Lionel
Fox, Fred
Francis, Emile
Fraser, Bud
Frost, Stan
Fryatt, Dave
Fulton, Greg
Gainey, Bob
Garside, Bert
Gaudaur, Jake Jr.
Gauthier, Pierre
Giardino, Wayne
Gillick, Pat
Gloag, Norm
Glynn, Hugh
Godbout, Francois
Goplen, Henrietta
Goulding, Bev
Gowan, Geoff
Grant, Duncan
Gribbin, Chris
Griffith, Cal
Grinnell, Rae
Gurowka, Joe
Halder, Wally
Halter, G. Sydney
Hamilton, Jack
Hammond, Gord
Hansen, Warren
Hart, David
Hart, Nelson
Hauch, Paul
Hayman, Lew
Hayter, Ron
Heikkila, Bill
Helliwell, David
Hendrie, George Jr.
Hendrie, George Sr.

Hershfield, Leible
Hewitson, Bobby
Hewitt, W.A.
Hill, Harvey
Hilton, Geordie
Histed, Jack
Hoffman, Abby
Holmes, Derek
Hudson, John
Hume, Ian
Imlach, Punch
Irvin, Dick Sr.
Jackson, Roger
Johnson, Don
Juckes, Gordon
Kihn, Richard
Kilrea, Brian
Kimball, Norm
King, Peter
Kingsmith, Ray
Kirkconnell, Herb
Kryczka, Joe
Lamb, Joe
Larose, Bob
LeBel, Bob
Lefaive, Lou
Lenard, Al
Letheren, Carol Anne
Lewis, Elinor
L'Heureux, Bill
Lindsay, Ted
Lister, Ralph
Loaring, John
Logan, Tip
Long, Bill
Lord, Margaret
Lord, Tom
Lumsden, Bill
Lumsden, Neil
Lunsford, Earl
MacFarlane, Gus
MacInnes, Kent
Macken, Jim
MacKenzie, Bill
MacLaggan, James
MacMillan, Billy
Mara, George
Martin, John
Mazurak, Steve
McBrien, Harry
McCaffrey, Jimmy
McCann, Dave
McCannell, Don
McConachie, John
McCormick, Frank
McCrae, John
McCrae, Judy
McDonald, Dennis
McDonald, Vern
McGill, Frank
McHale, John
McKinnon, Frank
McMahon, John
Melvin, Doug

Merklinger, Anne
Miller, Doug Jr.
Miner, Hazel
Mitchell, Doug
Molnar, Bill
Molson, Hartland
Montgomery, Ken
Morris, Fred
Morrison, Scotty
Moynihan, Kerry
Murray, Ken
Murray, Pere
Nanne, Lou
Neill, Susan
Nesbitt, Keith
Newsham, David
Nooney, John
Nye, Barry
Obeck, Vic
Obodiac, Stan
O'Connor. Zeke
O'Neill, Brian
O'Quinn, Red
Osborne, Bob
Ouellette, Bert
Overend, Tom
Page, Fred
Page, Percy
Panting, Bill
Parker, Jackie
Patrick, Frank
Patrick, Lester
Patrick, Muzz
Perry, Norm
Phillips, Alf Sr.
Pielak, Casmer
Pinder, Gerry
Pinder, Herb
Poce, Paul
Pollock, Sam
Pomfret, Jack
Porter, Ken
Pound, Richard
Powell, Cliff
Prentice, Bob
Prentice, Bruce
Preston, Ken
Price, Harry
Primrose, John
Proulx, Rita
Pugh, Bob
Pugliese, Dan
Pulford, Bob
Quilty, Silver
Rae, Al
Ramage, Pat
Ratcliffe, Frank
Rathwell, Bob
Rea, Harold
Reed, George
Regan, Larry
Reid, Lefty
Reid, Pat
Restivo, John

Richardson, John
Richman, Ruby
Robillard, Gene
Robinson, Bill
Robinson, Bobby
Rokosh, Greg
Rumbold, Dave
Rutherford, Jim
Ruys, Henk
Ryan, Doreen
Ryan, Joe
Saunders, Sandy
Savage, Marilyn
Sawula, Lorne
Sazio, Ralph
Schmalz, Tubby
Schmidt, Milt
Schootman, Teddy
Schreider, Gary
Schwende, Carl
Scorrar, Doug
Scott, Mike
Seiling, Rod
Seller, Peggy
Servold, Irvin
Shatto, Dick
Shaughnessy, Fraank Jr.
Shaughnessy, Shag
Shaw, Dan
Sherwood, Liv
Shore, Eddie
Short, George
Simons, Pop
Sinclair, Marjorie
Sinden, Harry
Skinner, Jim
Skinner, Larry Sr.
Slack, Bill
Smith, Bobby
Smith, Don
Smith, Gwen
Smith, Neil
Smith, Stanley
Smyth, Jack
Smythe, Conn
Spack, Mike
Spencer, Jim
Spencer, Victor
Spray, Robert
Spring, Harry
Stacey, Nelles
Steele, Don
Stevens, Warren
Stinson, Wally
Stock, Ed
Stockton, Don
Storey, Bob
Strong, Lawrence
Strumm, Gil
Tapp, Larry
Tatarchuk, Hank
Taylor, Bryce
Tennant, Mark
Thompson, Clif
Thompson, George
Thompson, William
Tinline, Dorothy
Tomlinson, William

Toner, Vance
Totzke, Carl
Trifunov, Jim
Trihey, Harry
Udvari, Frank
Ungerman, Irv
Van Vliet, Maury
Volpe, Nick
Voss, Carl
Walker, Gord
Wallingford, Ron
Watt, Laird
Watt, R.N.
Watt, Tom
Watters, Lynn
Whalley, Joan
Willsie, Harry
Wishart, Carol
Wood, Nora
Worrall, Jim
Wright, Harold
Yost, Ed
Zuger, Joe

ALL-AROUND
Abelson, Jess
Akervall, Henry
Anderson, Dave
Bain, Dan
Bath, Doc
Bauld, Donald
Beaton, Bob
Beck, Ross
Beckman, Jim
Benson, Lorne
Box, Charlie
Brockway, Dot
Bronson, Pat
Browne, Cec
Buddo, Don
Cameron, Jack
Chiarelli, John
Clarkson, Reg
Conacher, Lionel Sr.
Connell, Charlie
Cook, Myrtle
Cooke, Stan
Deacon, Tom
Desjardins, Larry
Devenney, Sandra
Dibben, Hugh
Dunsmore, Fred
Ellefson, Steve
Elliott, Bob
Evon, Russ
Fedoruk, Sylvia
Fletcher, Douglas
Halpenny, Rachelle
Hansen, Rick
Harpell, Winnifred
Hershfield, Leible
Hill, Jim
Huband, Deb
Hughes, Billy
Hunt, Ted
Johnstone, Charlie
Junor, Daisy
Laing, George

Leach, Al
Lister, Ralph
Lovett, Claire
MacKinnon, Dan
Malcolm, Andrew
McGill, Frank
McKenzie, Merv
McKinnon, Archie
McKinnon, Frank
Milne, Howie
Mobberley, Herb
Molson, Percy
Morris, Jim
Obodiac, Stan
Parry, Jack
Patrick, Lynn
Patrick, Muzz
Peden, Doug
Percival, Lloyd
Pomfret, Jack
Porter, Bob
Pulford, Harvey
Rathgeb, Chuck
Richman, Joey
Robertson, Sandy
Ryan, Doreen
Seller, Peggy
Strumm, Gil
Stulac, George
Thomas, Fred
Voss, Carl
Warwick, Millie
Watling, Wallace
Wright, Joseph Sr.
Wright, Ken
Young, Don

ARCHERY
Albert, Herb
Allan, Wanda
Anderson, Les
Buscombe, Lisa
Ewert, Elmer
Genge, Ronald
Jackson, Don
Jackson, Rose Ann
Kazienko, Linda
Lemay, Lucille
Lemay, Roger
Lessard, Lucille
Lidstone, Dorothy
Mann, David
Mather, Eddie
McDonald, Joan
Muir, Lela
Pullen, Wayne
Sally, Kevin
Warden, Donald
Whittier, Heather

BADMINTON
Backhouse-Sharpe, Claire
Bauld, Don
Bitten, Mike
Blanshard, Bryan
Cameron, Jack
Carnwath, Jim
Carter, Wendy

Cornish, Ray
Czich, John
Dawson, Jamie
Deng, Si-An
Fabris, Lucio
Falardeau, Johanne
Fergus, Bert
Fitzpatrick, Allan
Harris, Lesley
Julien, Denyse
Kanchanaraphi, Raphi
Kaul, Anil
Kirkconnell, Herb
Lovett, Claire
MacDonnell, Wayne
McKee, Jamie
Money, Ken
Nash, Jack
Paulson, Jamie
Piche, Doris
Priestman, Keith
Purcell, Jack
Purdy, Margaret
Ratanaseangsuang,
+ Channarong
Rollick, Bruce
Rollick, Judi
Ryan, Doreen
Samis, John
Shedd, Marjory
Skillings-Harney, Sandra
Smythe, Don
Sydie, Iain
Tinline, Dorothy
Underhill, Eileen
Underhill, John
Walton, Dorothy
Welch, Barbara
Youngberg, Jane
Yung, Darryl

BALLOONING
Lang, Dale
Rathgeb, Chuck
Ritchie, Dale

BARREL JUMPING
Jolin, Yvon Jr.

BASEBALL
Allbon, Ackie
Alomar, Robbie
Alou, Felipe
Ambrose, John
Anderson, Gabby
Ash, Gord
Atkinson, Bill
Baker, Mary
Barr, Doris
Bawn, Bev
Bedecki, Tom
Bell, George
Bend, Olive
Benson, Lorne
Bertoia, Reno
Biasatti, Hank
Boniface, George
Boss, Leonard

Bowsfield, Ted
Bronfman, Charles
Brown, Robert
Browne, Cec
Burgess, Tim
Callaghan, Helen
Callaghan, Margaret
Carter, Gary
Carter, Joe
Casanova, Bruno
Casanova, Willie
Cass, Eddie
Clarke, Nig
Clarkson, Reg
Clemens, Roger
Cleveland, Reggie
Clifford, Shanty
Colman, Frank
Conacher, Lionel Sr.
Condy, Buddy
Congalton, William
Connell, Alex
Cooke, Jack Kent
Corkey, Joe
Cosentino, Frank
Cox, Bobby
Creighton, Dale
Cripps, Ken
Curran, Randy
Dalton, Chuck
Dawson, Andre
Delgado, Carlos
Ducey, John
Eddie, Arden
Edwards, Jake
Elliott, Bob
Elliott, Chaucer
Emslie, Bob
Evon, Russ
Fairs, Jack
Fanning, Jim
Ferguson, Dorothy
Ferguson, Skit
Ferguson, Vince
Fergusson, Layton
Fernandez, Tony
Finnamore, Arthur
Ford, Russ
Fowler, Dick
Fox, Fred
Frobel, Doug
Gaston, Cito
Gibson, George
Gillick, Pat
Gillis, Eddie
Gorbus, Glen
Gorman, Charles
Gorman, T.P.
Graney, Jack
Greaves, Joe
Green, Shawn
Griffith, Cal
Grimsley, Ross
Guerrero, Vladimir
Guzzo, Patrick
Haine, Audrey
Harvey, Scott Jr.
Harvey, Scott Sr.

Hayter, Ron
Heath, Jeff
Hentgen, Pat
Hiller, John
Hodgson, Paul
Irwin, Arthur
Jackson, Russ
Jenkins, Ferguson
Johnson, Donnie
Judd, Oscar
Kane, Frank
Karpuk, Pete
Keating, Jack
Lapthorne, Whitey
Leader, Al
Leblanc, Eugene
Lee, Knotty
Leggatt, Art
Leitch, Kerry
Lister, Ralph
Mabey, Hap
MacKay, Gerry
MacKenzie, Bill
MacKenzie, Eric
MacLean, Lucella
Malcolm, Andrew
Marchildon, Phil
Martinez, Dennis
Martinez, Pedro
Masters, Wally
Matoba, Tom
Matthews, John
Mauch, Gene
McCaskill, Kirk
McHale, John
McKay, Dave
McKay, Roy
McKean, Jim
McKenzie, Tom
McKillop, Bob
McKinnon, Frank
McLeod, Jackie
Melvin, Doug
Miles, Rollie
Milne, Howie
Molitor, Paul
Moore, Curt
Moore, Harry
Moore, Quip
Moroz, Evelyn
Morris, Greg
Morris, Jim
Moyer, John
Nicol, Helen
Noga, Arleene
Norton, Wayne
O'Brien, John
O'Neill, Tip
O'Rourke, Frank
Obey, Arthur
Olerud, John
Oliver, Al
Oliver, Murray
Ouellette, Red
Owen, Jon
Pagan, Dave
Palmer, David
Parrish, Larry

Parry, Jack
Pataky, Bill
Pearson, Mike
Peden, Doug
Phillips, Bill
Pielak, Casmer
Plante, Jacques
Pomfret, Jack
Porter, Bob
Potter, Billy
Prediger, Pete
Prentice, Bob
Psutka, Harry
Puhl, Terry
Raines, Tim
Rau, Richard
Raymond, Claude
Richman, Joey
Richman, Ruby
Rizak, Gene
Robertson, Sandy
Robinson, Jackie
Rogers, Steve
Rosen, Goody
Rousseau, Bobby
Ruiter, Garth
Runge, Paul
Saunders, Billy
Schooley, Dennis
Seely, Glen
Selkirk, George
Shaughnessy, Shag
Sinclair, Marjorie
Slack, Bill
Slack, Bill
Slack, Stan
Sleeman, George
Smith, Pop
Speier, Chris
Stairs, Matt
Staub, Rusty
Stead, Ron
Steele, David
Stieb, Dave
Stoneman, Bill
Strumm, Gil
Sutherland, Hugh
Takahashi, Masao
Taylor, Ron
Thomas, Fred
Thomas, Paul
Thompson, Tommy
Thorburn, Cliff
Upper, Wray
Walker, Gord
Walker, Larry
Ward, Pete
Watkins, Bill
Wedley, Jack
West, Art
White, Devon
White, Tommy
Wilkes, Jimmy
Williams, Dick
Wilson, Lefty
Wilson, Rod
Winfield, Dave
Yosurack, Joe

Zeaman, Joe
Zimmerman, Jeff

BASKETBALL
Abramowitz, Moe
Ager, Barry
Aitchison, Gordon
Allison, Ian
Andrews, Porky
Bailey, Marguerite
Baker, Norm
Baldwin, Frank
Bardsley, Jim
Barnes, Bev
Baryluk, Mitch
Bauld, Don
Bawden, Betty
Beck, Ross
Belanger, Babe
Bennie, Elsie
Biasatti, Hank
Blackwell, Andrea
Boland, Pat
Boucher, Kelly
Box, Charlie
Brockway, Dot
Brown, Bob
Brown, Mae
Brown, Sophie
Bruno, Al
Bulloch, Jim
Burnham, Faye
Campbell, David
Campbell, R.D.
Campbell, Woody
Casanova, Willie
Chapman, Art
Chapman, Chuck
Clarkson, Candy
Clarkson, Reg
Cline, Paddy
Colistro, Peter
Connell, Charlie
Cooke, Jack Kent
Coulson, Evelyn
Coulthard, Bill
Critelli, Chris
Czaja, Mitch
Dalton, Chuck
Daniel, Babe
Dann, Etta
Dawson, Eddie
Devlin, Alex
Donohue, Jack
Douthwright, Joyce
Dufresne, Coleen
Dukeshire, Kelly
Dunn, Mary
Edwards, Ted
Elliott, Bob
Elrick, Elizabeth
Ennis, Peter
Evans, Jodi
Farmer, Jim
Fedoruk, Sylvia
Ferraro, John
Fox, Rick
Foxcroft, Ron

Fraser, Bud
Fry, Gladys
Gallen, Winnie
Garrow, Alex
Gloag, Norm
Gordon, Frances
Gurunlian, Varouj
Hallas, Kory
Hansen, Lars
Harris, Merelynn
Hatch, John
Heaney, Brian
Herbert, Gord
Hevenor, George
Horgan, Fred
Horwood, Don
Howson, Barry
Huband, Deb
Hutchison, Patti
Innis, Jessie
Jerant, Martina
Johnson, Daisy
Johnson, Dorothy
Johnston, Cynthia
Karch, Karla
Kazanowski, Gerald
Kelsey, Howard
Kinney, Margaret
Konchalski, Steve
Kootnekoff, John
Kristmanson, Alan
Lands, Ben
Larose, Bob
Lister, Ralph
Lovett, Claire
Lucht, Edward
MacDonald, Jackie
MacDonald, Noel
MacFarlane, Gus
MacPherson, Kitch
MacRitchie, Kay
Mayers, Wallace
McBurney, Margaret
McCormack, Mildred
McCrae, Don
McDonald, Vern
McFarland, Packy
McKibbon, John
McNaughton, Duncan
Meagher, Dan
Meretsky, Toots
Metras, John
Monnot, Ray
Milne, Howie
Miner, Hazel
Mountifield, Eleanor
Mullins, Peter
Munton, Mabel
Naismith, James
Nash, Steve
Neale, Doris
Nord, Dennis
Northup, Helen
O'Billovich, Bob
O'Connor, Zeke
Olafsson, Shirley
Osborne, Bob
Page, Percy

Panasis, Rita
Pasquale, Eli
Pataky, Bill
Patrick, Lynn
Patrick, Muzz
Peden, Doug
Perry, Nellie
Pettinger, Glen
Phibbs, Bob
Philp, Jerry
Phinney, Gertrude
Pickard, Leroy
Pickell, Bob
Polson, Lynn
Pomfret, Jack
Pullen, Harry
Pullen, Tom
Rae, Al
Raffin, Romel
Rau, Richard
Rautins, Leo
Restivo, John
Reynolds, Warren
Richman, Joey
Richman, Ruby
Ridd, Carl
Riley, Martin
Ritchie, Bill
Rizak, Gene
Robertson, Sandy
Robinson, Bill
Rogin, Bill
Ross, Betty
Ross, Chucker
Ruiter, Garth
Ryan, Doc
Sankey, Derek
Scott, Abbie
Shields, Kathy
Shields, Ken
Silcott, Liz
Simms, Tony
Simpson, Bob
Singleton, Harvey
Smith, Bev
Smith, Connie
Smrek, Mike
Sovran, Gino
Spack, Mike
Spencer, Jim
Stewart, Susan
Stone, Edith
Stone, Helen
Stoqua, Pat
Strumm, Gil
Stulac, George
Sutton, Warren
Suzuki, Arthur
Sweeney, Sylvia
Tatarchuk, Hank
Thomas, Fred
Thomas, Misty
Thomas, Paul
Tilleman, Karl
Tindall, Frank
Tolchinsky, Sol
Totzke, Carl
Town, Bob

Triano, Jay
Underwood, Reg
Verrecchia, Wendy
Wade, Harry
Wearring, George
Wedley, Jack
Wennington, Bill
West, Art
White, Dalt
White, Tommy
Wigston, Fran
Williams, Roy
Williamson, Jean
Wilson, Ruth
Wiltjer, Greg
Wynne, Ivor
Young, Frank

BATON TWIRLING
Fisher, Darlene
Garland, Lynda
Harmen, Wendy
Johnson, Maureen
King, Tim
Kopas, Ron
Leslie, Deardra
Price, Pamela_Jean
Watt, Sandra
Woycenko, Karen

BIATHLON
Bedard, Myriam
Plamondon, Charles
McMahon, David
Meloche, Lise
Rauhanen, Eric
Rousseau, Yves
Rupertus, Glenn

BILLIARDS
/POOL
/SNOOKER
Budge, Ervin
Chenier, Georges
Emerson, Eddie
Miller, Doug Jr.
Olson, Billy
Thorburn, Cliff
Wright, Joe. Sr.

BOARDSAILING
/WINDSURFING
Alie, Caroll-Ann
Bolduc, Alain

BOBSLEDDING
Anakin, Doug
Baptiste, Sheridon
Currier, Doug
Emery, John
Emery, Victor
Flynn, Clarke
Frank, Chris
Gilbert, Glenroy
Graham, John
Greenidge, Ricardo
Haydenluck, Greg
Kilburn, Joey

Kirby, Peter
Leblanc, Ken
Lori, Chris
Lueders, Pierre
MacEachern, Dave
MacLachlan, Alan
Pyc, Jack
Rathgeb, Chuck
Storey, Bob
Vachon, Brian
White, Vance

BOWLING
Bagguley, Howard
Bala, Ray Sr.
Ballantine, Bonny
Bigras, Orv
Blake, Terry
Boehm, Frank
Carey, Jim
Chibi, Tony
Coghill, Sandi
Connerty, Doug
Crane, Cec
Cripps, Ken
Cutting, Flo
Edge, Ken
Evon, Russ
Fine, Jack
Garside, Bert
Glasser, Red
Hambly, Fraser
Hershfield, Leible
Hohl, Elmer
Hong, Al
Hoult, Billy
Hynduik, Ollie
Lovett, Claire
Martel, Marty
Martin, John
Matthews, John
McCaw, Doug
Miller, Doug Jr.
Miller, Russ
Mitchell, Ray
Most, Joe
Moyer, John
Noga, Arleene
Pizzey, Blair
Powell, Bill
Procher, Theda
Reid, Lefty
Robinson, Blondie
Ryan, Tommy
Stevenson, Lori
Totzke, Bob
Townsend, Cathy
Trager, John
Underwood, Reg
Valentan, Walter

BOXING
Alleyne, Jeff
Andersen, Dale
Anderson, Dave
Anderson, Ricky
Bath, Doc
Battaglia, Frankie

Beaton, Bob
Belanger, Frenchy
Benson, Lorne
Bergeron, Jean François
Box, Charlie
Brosseau, Eugene
Brouillard, Lou
Brown, Dale
Burke, Jack
Burns, Leo
Burns, Tommy
Callura, Jackie
Chuvalo, George
Clyde, Ian
Conacher, Lionel Sr.
Connell, Charlie
Connolly, Edward
Cotton, Harry
Coulon, Johnny
Czich, John
Daigle, Nora
Darwin, Howard
Décarie, Al
Defiagbon, David
Delaney, Jack
de Wit, Willie
Dixon, George
Donaldson, Ron
Donison, Lee
Doucet, Paul
Downey, Raymond
Dugan, Jackie
Durelle, Yvon
Dwyer, John
Faul, Adam
Fennell, Pat
Ferguson, Merv
Filane, Domenic
Findlay, Dick
Foley, Joe
Gallinger, Stephen
Gardiner, Tyrone
Gibson, Bryan
Glesby, Tom
Goff, Ken
Gordon, Taylor
Gordon, Wayne
Graham, Charles
Gray, Clyde
Gwynne, Lefty
Hafey, Art
Hart, Gaètan
Hayter, Ron
Herlen, Ossie
Hewitt, Foster
Hilton, Alex
Hilton, Dave Jr.
Hilton, Dave Sr.
Hilton, Matthew
Howard, Kid
Huard, Camille
Hunt, Ted
Ius, Chris
Johnson, Chris
Johnson, Greg
Keenan, Roy
Kenny, Clayton
Kerwin, Gale

Kyvelos, Hercules
Lablanche, George
Lacelle, Ron
Lambert, Claude
Langford, Sam
Leduc, Mark
Leitham, Bobby
Lemieux, Gerald
Lewis, Lennox
Lifford, Johnny
Luftspring, Sammy
Malouf, Bob
Martin, Frank
Matheson, Dan
Maughan, George
McEachern, Archie
McFater, Allan
McLarnin, Jimmy
McWhirter, Cliff
Noel, Leo
Nolan, Frank Jr.
Nolan, Frank Sr.
Nolan, Steve
O'Sullivan, Shawn
Olson, Scott
Patrick, Muzz
Patton, Casey
Pearce, Bobby
Pelkey, Arthur
Pelletier, Leo_Charles
Percival, Lloyd
Pomfret, Jack
Powell, Bill
Pulford, Harvey
Raftery, John
Rannelli, William Jr.
Reid, Bobby
Reti, Harvey;
Richardson, Blair
Richman, Joey
Ross, George
Ryan, Vinnie
Sandulo, Joey
Saunders, Jim
Sauve, Gordon
Schneider, Bert
Scott, Mike
Senos, Eddie
Sidders, George
Silverheels, Jay
Smylie, Doug
Strange, Michael
Sullivan, Tommy
Swartman, Mel
Townsend, Billy
Ungerman, Irv
Walsh, Tarp
Walters, Dale
Warwick, Claude
White, Dennis
Wiebusch, Harry
Wright, Joe Sr.
Young, Walter

BROOMBALL
Breton, Skip
MacDuff, Alan
Montgomery, Willie

BUILDER
Adams, Jack
Adkin, Dennis
Ahearn, Frank
Allen, Keith
Andersen, Roxy
Anderson, Nint
Armstrong, Lesley
Ballard, Harold
Baird, Vaughan
Bauer, David
Bean, Gladys
Beers, William George
Bickell, J.P.
Bonnycastle, Charles
Bronfman, Charles
Brook, Tom
Brown, D. Wes
Brown, Robert
Butterfield, Jack
Caithness, Charlie
Callaghan, Pius
Campbell, Angus
Campbell, Clarence
Cartwright, Ethel Mary
Cattarinich, Joseph
Chick, John
Chynoweth, Ed
Class, Harry
Clifford, John
Combe, Harvey
Condon, Eddie
Cooper, Ralph
Daniels, Danny
Desjardins, Larry
Dudley, George
Dunn, James
Eagleson, Al
Fabro, Sam
Fink, Hardy
Fireman, Jack
Gage, Bob
Gibson, Jack
Gorman, T.P.
Griffiths, Frank
Hanley, Bill
Hannibal, Frank
Hatskin, Ben
Hay, Charles
Hayman, Lew
Hill, Harvey
Hind, Terry
Hume, Ian
Hurdis, John
Kelly, Henry
Kinsella, J.J.
Kinsella, Ray
Krupp, Charlie
Leader, Al
Leah, Vince
MacKay, Gerry
Mackie, Gordie
Marsh, Lou
Martitsch, Karl
Mathers, Frank
Maxwell, Doug
McKenzie, Tait
McNaughton, Don

McPherson, Don
Miller, Doug Jr.
Miller, Doug Sr.
Mitchell, Bill
Molson, Gartland
Mumford, Peter
Murchison, Cliff
Murray, Pere
Naismith, James
Nesbitt, Keith
O'Brien, J. Ambrose
O'Dowda, Ernie
Oberlander, Fred
Oldershaw, Bert
Patrick, Frank
Patrick, Lester
Paul, Donald
Pelech, Jack
Percival, Lloyd
Pickard, Allan
Pilous, Rudy
Pocklington, Peter
Poile, Bud
Pollock, Lloyd
Porter, Muriel
Randall, Sam
Ratushny, Ed
Reville, Ralph
Richman, Joey
Ritchie, Alvin
Robinson, Bobby
Robinson, Claude
Roe, Lot
Rogers, Melville
Ross, Art
Ross, P.D.
Rowell, Fred
Ryan, Joe
Ryan, Tommy
Sample, Tim
Selke, Frank Sr.
Shaughnessy, Shag
Simons, Pop
Simpson, Bill
Simpson, Jimmy
Smith, Frank
Smith-Johannsen, Herman
Smythe, Conn
Speers, Jim
Spencer, Jim
Stauder, Zlatica
Stevens, Warren
Storey, Bob
Stronge, Stan
Stukus, Annis
Sutherland, James
Thierry, Nick
Thompson, Jim
Thompson, Stanley
Torrey, Bill
Totzke, Bob
Trifunov, Jim
Turner, Lloyd
Underhill, Pat
Vidruk, Kas
Waghorne, Fred
Walker, Gord
Walls, Ken

Warren, Harold
Watson, Sandy
Wendling, Wendy
Whitaker, Denis
Wilhelmsen, Franz
Wright, Ken
Wykeham-Martin, Simon
Zeman, Joe

**CANOEING
/KAYAKING**
Amyot, Frank
Arnold, Elisabeth
Bales, John
Barre, Alexandra
Barre, Denis
Barre, Jean
Beedell, John
Behrens, Norman
Bennett, Douglas
Botting, Steve
Boyle, Sheryl
Brien, Alvin
Brien, Don
Brigden, William
Brunet, Caroline
Buday, Attila
Buday, Tamas Jr.
Cain, Larry
Charters, Harvey
Cleevely, Bill
Crichlow, Renn
Dodge, Ann
Edwards, John
Faloon, Joanna
Findlay, Dave
Fisher, Hugh
Ford, David
Fraser, Martin
Gibeau, Marie-Josée
Giles, Peter
Giles, Steve
Groff, Doug
Guay, Lucie
Herst, Alison
Hevenor, George
Hickox, Mac
Holloway, Sue
Homer-Dixon, Marjorie
Howe, Dan
Hunt, Claudia
Kennedy, Corrina
Kerckhoff, Hermann
Lalonde, Bernie
Lane, Ken
Lee, Scott
Lewis, Stanley
Lukanovich, Karen
Lukanovich, Louis
MacAskill, Klari
Maxwell, Gavin
McCleery, Alan
Merrill, Horace
Morris, Alwyn
Norman, Larry
O'Leary, Kelly
Oldershaw, Bert
Oldershaw, Dean

Oldershaw, Scott
Olmsted, Barbara
Olmsted, Nancy
Pulford, Harvey
Sample, Bonnie
Scott, Mike
Shaw, Colin
Stroulger, Ken
Tippett, Karen
Williams, Dawn
Wood, John

COACHING
Abbruzzi, Pat
Abel, Sid
Abramowicz, Moe
Adams, Dick
Adams, Jack
Adams, Robert
Allan, Robert
Alleyne, Jeff
Alou, Felipe
Anderson, Dave
Anderson, Vberne
Andrews, Porky
Anthony, Matt
ApSimon, John
Arbour, Al
Armstrong, Charles
Armstrong, George
Arseneault, Lise
Arsenault, Paul
Arusoo, Toomas
Backstrom, Ralph
Baert, Jean-Paul
Baillie, Charlie
Bajin, Boris
Baldwin, Frank
Bales, John
Barry, Cliff
Bauer, David
Beaton, Bob
Bedecki, Tom
Bell, Bobby
Bennett, Doug
Berenson, Red
Berry, Bob
Blair, Wren
Blake, Toe
Boadway, Bob
Boland, Pat
Botting, Steve
Bottoms, Lynn
Boucher, Bob
Boucher, Frank
Bowman, Scotty
Brabenec, Hana
Brabenec, Josef Sr.
Brancato, George
Breck, Ian
Breen, Joe
Broda, Turk
Brown, Hal
Brown, Wally
Browne, Cec
Bruno, Al
Buckna, Mike
Bulloch, Jim

Burka, Ellen
Burns, Pat
Bush, Eddie
Cahill, Leo
Campbell, Hugh
Campbell, R.D.
Casanova, Willie
Chambers, Dave
Cheevers, Gerry
Clair, Frank
Clark, Jim
Connellan, Peter
Cosentino, Frank
Coulter, Bruce
Cox, Bobby
Crawford, Marc
Cullen, Ronald
Currie, Gordon
Custis, Bernie
Daigneault, Doug
Daley, Jim
Danyluk, Terry
David, Tracy
Davis, Pat
Day, Hap
Delahey, Wally
Demers, Jacques
Desclouds, Rick
Dimitroff, Tom
Donohue, Jack
Drake, Clare
Duff, Alexander
Dussault, Jacques
Edwards, Ted
Eisler, Laurie
Elliott, Bob
Elliott, Geoff
Elmer, Wally
Ennis, Peter
Eon, Suzanne
Etcheverry, Sam
Eynon, Bob
Faulkner, John
Fedoruk, Sylvia
Filchock, Frank
Findlay, Dave
Firby, Howard
Fletcher, Doug
Foot, Fred
Forder, Anna
Fowlie, Jim
Fracas, Gino
Francis, Emile
Fraser, Bud
Frederickson, Frank
Galbraith, Sheldon
Garvie, Clarence
Gaston, Cito
Gate, George
Gilbert, Don
Gillis, Eddie
Goermann, Elfriede
Goermann, Monica
Gold, Otto
Gordon, Jack
Gordon, Taylor
Gordon, Wayne
Gowan, Geoff

Graham, Charles
Grant, Bud
Grant, Martha
Grassick, Greg
Green, Gary
Griffing, Dean
Griffith, Harry
Griffiths, Joe
Gurney, Helen
Hall, Chris
Hamilton, Jack
Hargreaves, Doug
Hayes, Bob
Hayes, John
Hayman, Lew
Heaney, Brian
Heikkila, Bill
Henley, Garney
Hildebrand, Ike
Hill, Harvey
Hindmarch, Bob
Hitchcock, Ken
Horwood, Don
Huband, Deb
Hughes, George
Hume, Ian
Hunt, Lynda Adams
Hyland, Bruce
Hyland, Margaret
Imlach, Punch
Innes, Cam
Irvin, Dick Sr.
Irwin, Arthur
Ivan, Tommy
Jackson, Russ
Jacobs, Dave
Jacobs, Jack
Janzen, Henry
Johnson, Dave
Johnson, Tom
Kadatz, Dennis
Keenan, Mike
Kemp, Nigel
Kemp, Sally
Kerwin, Gale
Keys, Eagle
Kilrea, Brian
Knight, Tuffy
Konchalski, Steve
Krause, Willi
Kromm, Bobby
Lalonde, Lally
L'Heureux, Bill
Leigh, Doug
Leitch, Kerry
Lemaire, Jacques
Lenard, Al
Levy, Marv
Lindquist, Vic
Loaring, John
Long, Bill
MacDonald, Irene
MacDonald, Noel
MacFarlane, Gus
Mach, Gerard
MacKenzie, Bill
MacKenzie, Eric
MacKenzie, Shanty

MacMillan, Billy
Main, Lorne
Manning, Peter
Mantha, Sylvio
Marek, Deb
Marshall, Dru
Martin, Jacques
Masters, Wally
Matthews, Don
Mauch, Gene
McCannell, Don
McCrae, Don
McCrae, Judy
McDonald, Dennis
McFarland, Packy
McInnis, Andy
McKay, Willie
McKee, Walt
McKenzie, Tom
McKillop, Bob
McKinnon, Archie
McLeod, Jackie
McNie, Murray
McWhirter, Cliff
Meeker, Howie
Meiszter, Ernst
Mervyn, Glen
Metras, John
Michienzi, Pete
Miller, Doug Jr.
Miller, Leigh
Miller, Shannon
Milne, Howie
Mitchell, Doug
Mitchell, Ray
Montgomery, Willie
Moore, Harry
Morris, Fred
Morris, Jim
Morris, Teddy
Morrison, Roland
Morrow, Al
Moss, Joe
Most, Joe
Muckler, John
Muir, Debbie
Mullins, Peter
Murphy, Cal
Murphy, Ron
Murray, Bryan
Murray, Pere
Murray, Terry
Nakamura, Hiroshi
Neilson, Roger
Nettles, Ray
Newman, Al
Newman, Bernard
Nolan, Frank Sr.
Nooney, John
Nord, Dennis
Norman, Percy
Norton, Wayne
Nye, Barry
O'Billovich, Bob
Obeck, Vic
Obey, Arthur
Oldershaw, Dean
O'Malley, Terry

Osborne, Bob
Ouellette, Bert
Oxenbury, Noel
Page, Percy
Parker, Jackie
Patrick, Lester
Patterson, Joe
Peden, Sandy
Percival, Lloyd
Philip, Bob
Philp, Jerry
Phoenix, Skip
Pischke, Garth
Plante, Jacques
Poce, Paul
Pomfret, Jack
Porter, John
Porter, Ken
Primeau, Joe
Pronovost, Marcel
Pugh, Bob
Pugh, Lionel
Pyle, Dave
Quilty, Silver
Quinn, Pat
Raine, Al
Rankin, Frank
Ratanaseangsuang,
    Channarong
Rathgeb, Chuck
Read, Frank
Reay, Billy
Rebholz, Russ
Reid, Pat
Renney, Tom
Restivo, John
Richman, Joey
Riley, Martin
Ritchie, Alvin
Ritchie, John
Roberts, Jim
Robinson, Larry
Rodden, Mike
Rogers, Doug
Rogin, Bill
Rokosh, Greg
Rollick, Bruce
Ross, Art
Rowan, Sheila
Roy, Aldo
Ruel, Claude
Ruiter, Garth
Rumbold, Dave
Russell, Ernestine
Ryan, Doc
Ryder, Gus
Sanderson, Lyle
Sandulo, Joey
Sauve, Gordon
Savage, Marilyn
Sawula, Lorne
Sazio, Ralph
Schleimer, Joe
Schmidt, Milt
Schoenfeld, Jim
Schoenhals, Paul
Schulze, Rudy
Servold, Irvin

Shaughnessy, Shag
Sheahan, Pat
Shero, Fred
Shields, Kathy
Shields, Ken
Shore, Eddie
Sinden, Harry
Skrien, Dave
Smith, Alf
Smith, Don
Smith, Gwen
Smith, Sandra
Snelling, Deryk
Sonmor, Glen
Spencer, Jim
Stanley, Barney
Stevens, Warren
Stewart, Ron
Stratten, Gaye
Stronge, Stan
Stukus, Annis
Sullivan, Tommy
Sutton, Warren
Sztehlo, Zoltan
Takahashi, June
Takahashi, Masao
Takahashi, Ray
Takahashi, Tina
Tennant, Mark
Tessier, Orv
Thomas, Paul
Thomas, Ted
Thomson, Earl
Tihanyi, Jeno
Timmis, Brian
Tindall, Frank
Tommy, Andy Jr.
Trifunov, Jim
Upper, Wray
Ursuliak, Wally
Uteck, Larry
van der Merwe, Marina
Van Vliet, Maury
Vigars, Robert
Vine, Bill
Volpe, Nick
Voyles, Carl
Walker, Peahead
Watson, Moose
Watt, Tom
Webb, Don
Weiland, Cooney
Wendling, Wendy
West, Art
White, Dalt
White, Dennis
Wigston, Fran
Wilkins, Bruce
Williams, Dick
Willsey, Ray
Wilson, Alex
Wirkowski, Nobby
Woo, Wes
Wright, Joe Sr.
Wright, Lee
Wyatt, Dave
Wynne, Ivor
Yost, Ken

Young, Joe

CRICKET
Brewster, Ken
Cameron, Jack
Fletcher, Doug
King, Donald
Laing, John
Lyon, George
Martin, Fritz
Percival, Lloyd
Rathgeb, Chuck
Saunders, Dyce
Somerville, Sandy
Stevens, Rick
Warren, Harry

CURLING
Adams, Diane
Adams, Harry
Aitken, Don
Anderson, Nint
Anton, Ron
Armstrong, Jim
Arnott, Jan
Avery, Frank
Baldwin, Matt
Bartlett, Don
Bartlett, Sue Anne
Base, John
Bauld, Don
Begin, Terry
Belcourt, Tim
Benson, Lorne
Betker, Jan
Biron, Louis
Black, Elmer
Bodogh, Marilyn
Bodogh-Jurgenson, Christine
Borst, Cathy
Boyd, Mike
Braunstein, Terry
Bray, Shirley
Brown, Gord
Brown, Ted
Bubbs, John
Buchan, Ken
Burtnyk, Kerry
Buxton, Noel
Calles, Ada
Cameron, Doug
Campbell, Clarence
Campbell, Colin
Campbell, Garnet
Carney, Laurie
Carruthers, Bob
Carstairs, Kent
Charette, Agnés
Charette, France
Charette, Pierre
Chernoff, Mike
Chiarelli, John
Coben, Muriel
Cole, Betty
Congalton, Jim
Coombe, Eldon
Corkey, Joe
Corner, Peter

Creber, Bill
Cunningham, Cathy
Cunningham, Jake
Czaja, Mitch
D'Amour, Frenchy
DeBlonde, Clare
DeBlonde, Garry
Delmage, Al
Devlin, Paul
Deware, Mabel
Dewitte, Marcel
Dolan, Kim
Dugre, Lou
Duguid, Don
Dunbar, William
Edwards, Jake
Elliott, Bob
Fedoruk, Sylvia
Fedosa, Bob
Ferbey, Randy
Ferguson, Reid
Ferguson, Skit
Fletcher, Bill
Folk, Rick
Forgues, Keith
Fraser, Sherry
Fry, Barry
Gallant, Peter
Gee, Gordon
Geiger, Marla
Gellard, Kim
Gervais, Hec
Gilbert, Don
Goring, Alison
Gowanlock, Ab
Gowsell, Paul
Greaves, Joe
Green, Ron
Gretsinger, Bert
Gudereit, Marcia
Gunnlaugson, Lloyd
Gurowka, Joe
Hackner, Al
Hansen, Ina
Hansen, Warren
Harris, Mike
Harrison, Neil
Herlinveaux, Louise
Hermann, Tiny
Houck, Norm
Houston, Heather
Houston, Neil
Howard, Glenn
Howard, Russ
Hritzuk, Eugene
Hudson, Bruce
Hudson, Gordon
Hunter, Rod
Hushagen, Earle
Hushagen, Sandra
Jackson, Virginia
Jenkins, Bill
Jenkins, Peter
Jenkins, Shorty
Jones, Colleen
Jones, Debbie
Kawaja, John
Keith, Harold

Kempster, Ray
Kennedy, Bruce
Kennedy, Tracy
Kingsmith, Ray
Laliberte, Connie
Lang, Lorraine
Lang, Rick
Langlois, Al
LaRocque, Penny
Law, Kelley (Owen)
Lawes, Keith
Lewis, Bill
Lobel, Art
Lord, Lovel
Lukowich, Ed
Lumsden, Bill
Mabey, Hap
Mabey, Harold
MacDonald, Wen
MacInnes, Bob
MacInnes, Kent
Manahan, Cliff
Mann, Avard
Mann, Bob
Manning, Ron
Martin, Flora Greenwood
Martin, Kevin
Matheson, Wayne
Maxwell, Doug
Mazinke, Harvey
McCrae, John
McCusker, Joan
McGrath, Larry
McKee, Joyce
McMillan, Roy
McMurray, Mary
McPhee, Barry
McPhee, Peter
McTavish, Bill
Meleschuk, Orest
Merklinger, Anne
Merklinger, Bill
Merklinger, Dave
Middaugh, Wayne
Miki, Fuji
Miller, Russ
Millikin, Hugh
Moffatt, Rich
Moore, Linda
Morris, Earle
Morrison, Lee
Munro, Bruce
Murchison, Cliff
Naimark, Barry
Nairn, Bill
Nash, Jack
Neufeld, Chris
Nicol, Robert
Noga, Arleene
Northcott, Ron
Noseworthy, Mark
O'Neill, Kay
Ogden, Steve
Oyler, Don
Palmer, Doug
Paquin, Rollie
Paterson, Gord
Perroud, Pat

Perry, Gordon
Peters, Vic
Pettapiece, Jim
Pezer, Vera
Phillips, Alf Jr.
Phillips, Alf Sr.
Phillips, Peter
Piaskoski, Jim
Pickering, Bob
Pierce, Glen
Porter, Muriel
Proulx, Rita
Provost, Barry
Rankin, Heather
Reilly, Keith
Richardson, Arnold
Richardson, Ernie
Richardson, Garnet
Ross, Chucker
Rowan, Sheila
Ruiter, Garth
Ryan, Pat
Savage, Paul
Schmirler, Sandra
Schoenhals, Dorenda
Scott, Alex
Seltzer, Sheila
Sharples, Jim
Sinclair, Marjorie
Smith, David
Sparkes, Bernie
Sparkes, Lindsay
Steeves, Ed
Stevenson, Forbis
Stone, Reg
Stone, Roy
Storey, Fred
Stoughton, Jeff
Tallon, Wayne
Taylor, Russ
Tetley, Bill
Tetley, Ian
Thain, Ken
Thibodeau, Nick
Thomas, Jeff
Thompson, Clif
Tobin, Lee
Trites, Ev
Turcotte, Bob
Turnbull, Ray
Twa, Don
Ursel, Jim
Ursuliak, Wally
Van Dine, David
Ventura, Dawn
Wagner, Bill
Waite, Jim
Walchuk, Don
Walsh, Billy Jr.
Walsh, Billy Sr.
Watson, Ken
Welsh, Alex
Welsh, Jim
Wendel, Fred
Werenich, Ed
Westphal, Don
Wilson, Robin
Wilson, Tom

Wood, Bryan
Wood, Howie
Wood, Lionel
Wood, Nora
Wood, Pappy
Woods, Bob
Woolley, Emily
Young, Neil
Youngson, Les
Youngson, Muriel

CYCLING
Atkinson, Lorne
Bauer, Steve
Blouin, Marc
Boucher, Gaetan
Burka, Sylvia
Carter-Erdman, Kelly Ann
Davies, Jim
Dietiker, Judy
Dubnicoff, Tanya
Fraser, Gord
Gagne, Maurice
Garneau, Louis
Harnett, Curt
Harper, Ted
Harvey, Pierre
Hayman, Ron
Hughes, Clara
Jackson, Linda
Keast, Brian
Larocque, Dominique
Lovell, Jocelyn
Ludtke, Frank
McCulloch, Jack
McEachern, Archie
McRae, Ed
Murphy, Pat
Oland, Erick
Ongaro, Alex
Palmer, Sue
Peden, Doug
Peden, Torchy
Samplonius, Anne
Singleton, Gordon
Stieda, Alex
Strong, Karen
Sydor, Alison
Tomlinson, Lesley
Walton, Brian
Way, Kelly Ann
Wohlberg, Eric

DARTS
Astra, Duke
Cripps, Ken
Miller, Russ
Part, John

DIVING
Armstrong, Ken
Athans, George Sr.
Bedard, David
Bernier, Sylvie
Boileau, Myriam
Boys, Bev
Bulmer, Eryn
Carruthers, Liz

Class, Harry
Cranham, Scott
Crighton, Hec
Cuthbert, Linda
Dacyshyn, Anna
Depiero, Mary
Despatie, Alexandre
Dinsley, Tom
Flewwelling, Larry
Friesen, Ron
Fuller, Debbie
Fuller, Wendy
Gordon, Megan
Gordon, Paige
Grout, Glen
Hunt, Lynda Adams
Kelemen, Kathy
Kiefer, Eniko
Little, Laura
MacDonald, Irene
MacKay, Elizabeth
MacLeod, Tammy
McArton, Jennifer
McKinnon, Archie
Meissner, Ernie
Montminy, Anne
Morrow, Carol
Moss, Judy
Napper, Jason
Nash, John
Nutter, Janet
Pelletier, Annie
Phillips, Alf Sr.
Phoenix, Skip
Robertson, Nancy
Rollo, Kathy
Sageman, Randy
Shatto, Cindy
Stott, Arthur
Stulac, George
Webb, Don
York, Teri

DOG-SLEDDING
Martin, Frank
Montabone, Monty
St. Godard, Emile

ENTREPRENEUR
Ballard, Harold
Bassett, John Jr.
Berger, Sam
Cooke, Jack Kent
Darwin, Howard
Gorman, T.P. Tommy

EQUESTRIAN
Ashton, Elizabeth
Baker, Charles
Bonnello, Bonny
Boylen, Christilot
Cone, Mac
Day, James
Deslauriers, Mario
Dunlap, Moffatt
Dvorak, Tom
Ehrlick, Allan
Elder, Jim

Gayford, Tom
Graham, Hugh
Grant, Martha
Greenough, Gail
Hahn, Robin
Hayes, Jay
Henselwood, Jill
Herbert, Michael
Irving, Wendy
Ishoy, Mark
Jacobsen, George
Kerr, Barbara
Kozak, Chelan
Lamaze, Eric
Laskin, Mark
Millar, Ian
Millar, Torchy
Neale, Cynthia
Pearce, John
Reid, Leslie
Scott, Barbara Ann
Simpson, John
Smith, Gina
Stubbs, Lorraine
Sztehlo, Zoltan
Thomas, Shirley
Underhill, Beth
Vaillancourt, Michel
Wedge, Cathy
Young-Black, Stuart

FENCING
Andru, John
ApSimon, John
Archibald, Joan
Archibald, Nancy
Bakonyi, Peter
Banos, Jean-Marie
Banos, Jean-Paul
Beaudry, Paul
Chatel, Sigrid
Chouinard, Jean-Marc
Conyd, Magdy
Desjarlais, Robert
Dessureault, Michel
Fekete, Tim
Foxcroft, Bob
Hennyey, Donna
Hennyey, Imre
Horn, Alf
Lavoie, Marc
Leblanc, Louise-Marie
Meiszter, Ernst
Morrison, Roland
Nagy, Imre
Nowosielski, Dan
Nowosielski, Leszek
Obst, Herbert
Ploudre, Tony
Ransom, James
Schalm, Sherraine
Schwende, Carl
Shong, Laurie
Sukunda, Eli
Tremblay, Thalie
Tully, George
Varaljay, George
Wawryn, Alexandra

Wiedel, Gerry
Wiedel, Pacita
Wishart, Carol
Wong, Lester

FIELD HOCKEY
Beecroft, Lynne
Benson, Heather
Bissett, David
Blaxland, Jody
Borowy, Janet
Brafield, Leslie
Brewster, Ken
Broderick, Kathleen
Burrows, Pat
Charlton, Nancy
Conn, Michelle
Creelman, Sharon
Crook, Jan
Douthwright, Joyce
Dube, Ajay
Ellis, Phyllis
Forrest, Robin
Forshaw, Sheila
Gourlay, Jean
Haig, Cathy
Hartley, Errol
Hewlett, Karen
Hobkirk, Alan
Kanjee, Hashmuk
Kant, Hari
Lambert, Laurie
MacKinnon, Zoe
Mahey, Diane
Marshall, Dru
McCrae, Judy
Motzek, Peter
Mouat, Michael
Neill, Susan
Olafsson, Shirley
Pal, Mohinder
Palmer, Alison
Pereira, Ken
Plummer, Reg
Sparling, Jean
Stoyka, Darlene
van der Merwe, Marina
Warren, Harry
Warren, Victor
Whittingham, Dianne
Winters, Shelley
Wright, Lee

FIGURE SKATING
Albright, Debbie
Alletson, Kim
Bain, Dan
Baptie, Norval
Beacom, Gary
Beland, Daniel
Belyea, Arthur
Berezowski, Barbara
Bezic, Sandra
Bezic, Val
Bourne, Shae-Lynn
Bowden, Norris
Brasseur, Isabelle
Browning, Kurt

Burka, Ellen
Burka, Petra
Carscallen, Susan
Chouinard, Josée
Colman, Ann
Cranston, Toller
Dafoe, Frances
Dowding, John
Duchesnay, Isabelle
Duchesnay, Paul
Eisler, Lloyd Jr.
Forder, Anna
Galbraith, Sheldon
Gold, Otto
Griner, Wendy
Humphry, Jay
Hyland, Bruce
Hyland, Margaret
Irwin, Cathy Lee
Jackson, Donald
Jelinek, Maria
Jelinek, Otto
Jones, Candy
Kemkaren, Heather
Kraatz, Victor
Langdon, Jeff
Leigh, Doug
Leitch, Kerry
Magnussen, Karen
Manley, Elizabeth
Martini, Paul
McCall, Robert
McCreath, Ralph
McGillivray, David
McPherson, Donald
Morrissey, Janet
Morrow, Suzanne
Mumford, Peter
Nightingale, Lynn
Ogibowski, Diane
Orser, Brian
Pachl, Carole
Paul, Robert
Pockar, Brian
Rogers, Melville
Rubenstein, Louis
Scott, Barbara Ann
Shaver, Ron
Snelling, Charles
Soper, Barry
Soper, Louise
Stephens, Richard
Stojko, Elvis
Terpenning, Barbara
Thacker, Mary Rose
Thomson, Kay
Underhill, Barbara
Wagner, Barbara
Wainman, Tracey
Wilkes, Debbi
Wilson, Montgomery
Wilson, Tracy
Wong, Charlene

FISHING
Deval, Gordon
Labignan, Italo
Rathgeb, Chuck

Waszczuk, Henry

FOOTBALL
Abbruzzi, Pat
Abendschan, Jack
Ackles, Bob
Adams, Dick
Adelman, Louis
Ah You, Junior
Aird, Stu
Albrecht, J.I.
Aldag, Roger
Aldridge, Dick
Alexander, Ray
Allen, Damon
Anderson, Dave
Andreotti, Jim
Andrusyshyn, Zenon
Anthony, Matt
Arakgi, Nick
Atchison, Ron
Avery, Jeff
Back, Len
Bailey, By
Baillie, Charlie
Baker, Bill
Baker, Terry
Ballard, Harold
Barrett, Danny
Barrow, John
Barwell, Gord
Bass, Danny
Bastaja, Nick
Batstone, Harry
Battle, Greg
Bauer, Lyle
Beach, Ormand
Beckstead, Ian
Belcher, Val
Belec, Jacques
Belsher, Don
Bennett, Bruce
Bennett, Paul
Benson, Lorne
Berger, Sam
Berryman, Tim
Bevan, Eddie
Bevan, Marv
Beynon, Tom
Bitkowski, Bruno
Black, Fred
Blair, Don
Blanchard, Leo
Bonk, John
Bottoms, Lynn
Box, Ab
Bragagnolo, Mark
Brancato, George
Brazley, Carl
Breck, Ian
Breen, Joe
Bright, Johnny
Britton, Bill
Brock, Dieter
Brown, Clayton
Brown, D. Wes
Brown, Dick
Brown, Tom

Browne, Cec
Browne, Less
Bruce, Lou
Bruno, Al
Buddo, Don
Buono, Wally
Burgess, Tom
Burkholder, Dave
Cahill, Leo
Cain, Jim
Cameron, Bob
Campbell, Hugh
Campbell, Jerry
Campbell, R.D.
Capozzi, Herb
Carpenter, Ken
Casanova, Bruno
Casanova, Willie
Casey, Tom
Chalupka, Ed
Champion, Tony
Charlton, Ken
Chipper, Eric
Chomyc, Lance
Christie, Steve
Clair, Frank
Clare, Lou
Claridge, Pat
Clark, Jim
Clark, Ken
Clarke, Bill
Clarkson, Reg
Clements, Tom
Clemons, Mike
Climie, Jock
Coffey, Tommy-Joe
Coleman, Lovell
Collins, Merv
Conacher, Lionel Jr.
Conacher, Lionel Sr.
Connell, Charlie
Conroy, Jim
Cooke, Jack Kent
Cooper, Ralph
Copeland, Royal
Corrigall, Jim
Cosentino, Frank
Cotton, Harry
Coulter, Bruce
Coulter, Tex
Cox, Ernie
Creighton, Dale
Crighton, Hec
Cronin, Carl
Cummings, Bruce
Currie, Andy
Curtis, Ulysses
Custis, Bernie
Cutler, Dave
Cutler, Wes
Cyncar, Marco
Daigneault, Doug
Dalla Riva, Peter
Danychuk, Bill
Darch, Art
Dattilio, Gerry
Davies, Bill
Dawson, Bob

Daymond, Irv
Deacon, Tom
Dean, Bob
Degruchy, John
Dekdebrun, Al
Delahey, Wally
Desjardins, Paul
Dimitroff, Tom
DiPietro, Rocky
Dixon, George
Dojack, Paul
Dorsch, Henry
Dorsey, Dean
Doty, Frederick
Doucette, Gerry
Drake, Clare
Dublinski, Tom
Dumelie, Larry
Dumoulin, Seppi
Dunigan, Matt
Dunlap, Frank
Dunlap, Jake
Dussault, Jacques
Eben, Mike
Ecuyer, Al
Edwards, Ted
Elford, Gear
Elgaard, Ray
Eliowitz, Abe
Ellingson, James
Elliott, Chaucer
Ellis, Craig
Elsby, Ted
Emerson, Eddie
Enos, Ed
Etcheverry, Sam
Evans, Art
Evanshen, Terry
Exelby, Clare
Fairbanks, Lloyd
Fairholm, Jeff
Fairs, Jack
Faloney, Bernie
Farmer, Jim
Fear, Cap
Fennell, Dave
Ferraro, John
Ferrone, Dan
Fieldgate, Norm
Filchock, Frank
Fisher, Frank
Flanagan, Flin
Fleming, Willie
Flutie, Darren
Flutie, Doug
Flynn, Chris
Foley, Jim
Ford, Alan
Foster, Red
Foulds, William C
Fracas, Gino
Frank, Bill
Fraser, Cam
Fraser, Frank
Fraser, George
Fritz, Bob
Fry, Jay
Fryer, Brian

Furlong, Jim
Gabler, Wally
Gabriel, Tony
Gain, Bob
Gaines, Gene
Garvie, Clarence
Gaudaur, Jake Jr.
Gerela, Ted
Getty, Don
Giardino, Wayne
Gilbert, Don
Glasser, Sully
Golab, Tony
Gorrell, Miles
Gotta, Jack
Graham, Milt
Grant, Bud
Grant, Tommy
Grassick, Greg
Gray, Herb
Griffing, Dean
Gurney, Jack
Halter, G. Sydney
Ham, Tracy
Hanson, Fritzie
Harding, Rodney
Harper, Glenn
Harrington, Ed
Harris, Wayne
Harrison, Herm
Hatanaka, Bill
Hayes, Bob
Hayman, Lew
Hedges, Brian
Hees, George
Hegan, Larry
Hendrickson, Lefty
Henley, Garney
Hermann, Tiny
Hershfeld, Leible
Hevenor, George
Heydenfeldt, Bob
Highbaugh, Larry
Hill, Stewart
Hilzinger, Karl
Hinds, Sterling
Hinton, Tom
Hirst, Elgin
Hollimon, Joe
Holloway, Condredge
Howell, Ron
Howes, Bob
Hufnagel, John
Hughes, George
Hunt, Ted
Hutton, Bouse
Ilesic, Hank
Innes, Cam
Irwin, Al
Isbister, Robert Jr.
Isbister, Robert Sr.
Jackson, Glen
Jackson, Russ
Jacobs, Jack
James, Eddie
James, Gerry
Janzen, Henry
Jauch, Ray

Johnson, William
Johnstone, Chris
Jonas, Don
Jones, Tyrone
Jurasin, Bobby
Kabat, Greg
Kadatz, Dennis
Kapp, Joe
Karcz, Zeno
Karpuk, Pete
Karrys, Steve
Keeling, Jerry
Kelly, Brian
Kelly, Con
Kelly, Ellison
Kennerd, Trevor
Kepley, Dan
Kerns, John
Kerrigan, Mike
Keys, Eagle
Kimball, Norm
King, Don
King, Mike
Kiniski, Gene
Kirzinger, Dave
Knight, Lee
Knight, Tuffy
Konihowski, John
Kosmos, Mark
Kraemer, Bob
Krol, Joe
Krouse, Bob
Kruger, Harry
Kulka, Glenn
Kwong, Normie
L'Heureux, Bill
Laird, Stu
Lalonde, Lally
Lancaster, Ron
Landy, Frank
Larose, Bob
Lashuk, Mike
Lawson, Smirle
Leach, Al
Leadlay, Pep
Lear, Les
Learn, Ed
Lehmann, Ken
Lemmerman, Bruce
Lenard, Al
Levantis, Steve
Levy, Marv
Lewis, Leo
Lewis, Loyd
Lieberman, Moe
Lindley, Earl
Liske, Peter
Lister, Ralph
Lockhart, Gene
Logan, Tip
Loney, Don
Lumsden, Neil
Lunsford, Earl
Luster, Marv
Luzzi, Don
MacKenzie, Shanty
Mackie, Baz
Mandarich, Tony

Mann, Dave
Marshall, Blake
Marshall, Greg
Martin, Peter
Masotti, Paul
Masters, Wally
Matthews, Don
Maughan, George
Mayes, Rueben
Mazurak, Steve
McBrien, Harry
McCaffrey, Jimmy
McCance, Ches
McCann, Dave
McConachie, John
McConnell, Russ
McEachern, Ken
McFarland, Packy
McFarlane, Bob
McFarlane, Don
McGee, Doug
McGill, Frank
McKay, Willie
McKee, Walt
McKeown, Bob
McLoughlin, Mark
McMann, Chuck
McManus, Danny
McMillan, Leigh
McNamara, Bob
McNichol, Doug
McQuarters, Ed
McTague, Mike
Mikawos, Stan
Miles, Rollie
Mills, James
Milne, Howie
Mimbs, Robert
Mitchell, Doug
Mitchell, Doug
Moir, Darrell
Montgomery, Ken
Moon, Warren
Morris, Frank
Morris, Teddy
Morrison, Bernie
Mosca, Angelo
Moss, Joe
Munro, Johnny
Murphy, Cal
Murphy, Mike
Murphy, Ron
Murray, Ben
Murray, Eddie
Murray, Ken
Nagurski, Bronco
Nairn, Bill
Narcisse, Donald
Nelson, Roger
Nettles, Ray
Neumann, Peter
Newton, Jack
Nielsen, Ken
Nykoluk, Danny
O'Billovich, Bob
O'Connor, Zeke
O'Quinn, Red
Obeck, Vic

Odums, Ray
Oneschuk, Steve
Organ, Gerry
Osbaldiston, Paul
Pajaczkowski, Tony
Paproski, Steve
Parker, Jackie
Parkin, Lorne
Parry, Jack
Passaglia, Lui
Pataky, Bill
Paterson, Gord
Patrick, Lynn
Patrick, Steve
Patterson, Hal
Pearson, Mike
Pearson, Paul
Perowne, Ron
Perrier, Ross
Perry, Gordon
Perry, Norm
Pfeifer, Alan
Phibbs, Bob
Phillips, Rudy
Philp, Jerry
Piaskoski, Jim
Pickell, Bob
Pilon, Claude
Pitts, Allen
Pless, Willie
Ploen, Ken
Poirier, Joe
Pomfret, Jack
Poplawski, Joe
Porter, Lewis
Pothier, Hector
Potter, Billy
Potter, Dale
Prather, Rollie
Preston, Ken
Pringle, Mike
Pugh, Bob
Pulford, Harvey
Pullen, Harry
Pullen, Tom
Pyzer, Doug
Quilty, Silver
Racine, Moe
Rashovich, Dan
Rebholz, Russ
Reed, George
Reeve, Ted
Ribbins, Peter
Richman, Joey
Ridgway, Dave
Rigney, Frank
Ritchie, Alvin
Ritchie, Dave
Roberts, Jay
Robillard, Gene
Robinson, Bill
Robinson, Larry
Rodden, Mike
Rodgers, Johnny
Rogin, Bill
Romano, Rocco
Rokosh, Greg
Rorvig, Ed

Rountree, Jim
Rowe, Paul
Rowland, Gordie
Ruby, Martin
Ruoff, Bernie
Russel, Jeff
Ryan, Joe
Rypien, Mark
Sampson, Darryl
Sandusky, Jim
Sapunjis, Dave
Saunders, Alex
Sazio, Ralph
Schoenhals, Paul
Schreider, Gary
Schriewer, Tex
Schuette, Tom
Scoccia, Sam
Scott, Tom
Scott, Vince
Shannon, Carver
Shatto, Dick
Shaughnessy, Frank Jr.
Shaughnessy, Shag
Shaw, Dan
Shaw, Gerry
Shaw, Wayne
Sheahan, Pat
Sheridan, Juan
Short, George
Shouldice, Hap
Simpson, Ben
Simpson, Bob
Simpson, Jimmy
Singleton, Harvey
Skrien, Dave
Smale, Ted
Smith, Alf
Smith, Darrell K.
Smith, Donn
Smith, Doug
Smith, Larry
Smylie, Doug
Smylie, Rod Jr.
Snipes, Angelo
Soles, Michael
Sopinka, John
Sowieta, Rick
Sprague, Dave
Sternberg, Gerry
Stevens, Warren
Stevenson, Art
Stevenson, Bill
Stevenson, Douglas Roy
Stevenson, Victor
Stewart, Ron
Stillwagon, Jim
Stirling, Bummer
Stone, Rocky
Stoneburgh, Norm
Stoqua, Pat
Storey, Red
Strumm, Gil
Stukus, Annis
Stukus, Bill
Stukus, Frank
Stumon, Gregg
Sugarman, Ken

Sullivan, Frank
Sunter, Ian
Sutherin, Don
Sweet, Don
Swift, Bob
Symons, Bill
Taylor, Bobby
Taylor, Piffles
Theismann, Joe
Thelen, Dave
Thomas, Fred
Thomas, Jim
Thomas, Willie
Thornton, Bernie
Timmis, Brian
Tindall, Frank
Tinsley, Buddy
Tommy, Andy Sr.
Toogood, Ted
Toohy, Ralph
Tosh, Wayne
Totzke, Carl
Towns, Tom
Trawick, Herb
Tripucka, Frank
Tubman, Joe
Tucker, Whit
Turville, Frank
Upton, Eric
Urness, Ted
Uteck, Larry
Vail, Red
Van Vliet, Maury
Vargo, Ken
Vaughan, Kaye
Vavra, Greg
Vercheval, Pierre
Vessels, Billy
Volpe, Jon
Volpe, Nick
Voyles, Carl
Wadsworth, Mike
Wagner, Virgil
Walby, Chris
Walker, Bill
Walker, Gord
Walker, Peahead
Walker, Skip
Walling, Brian
Walsh, Tarp
Warwick, Bert
Waszczuk, Henry
Watson, Whipper Billy
Watts, J.C.
Weatherall, Jim
Wedley, Jack
Weinmeister, Arnie
Weir, Glen
Welch, Huck
Welton, John
Wendling, Wendy
West, Art
West, James
White, Al
Whitehouse, Reg
Wilkinson, Tom
Williams, David
Williams, Gizmo

Williams, Jerry
Willsey, Ray
Wilmsmeyer, Klaus
Wilson, Al
Wilson, Ben
Wilson, Don
Wilson, Seymour
Winfield, Earl
Wirkowski, Nobby
Wood, Lionel
Woodward, Rod
Wright, Joe Jr.
Wright, Joe Sr.
Wruck, Larry
Wydareny, John
Wylie, Harvey
Young, Jim
Young, Preston
Zaipec, Chuck
Zmich, Rick
Zock, Bill
Zuger, Joe

GOAL BALL
Hope, Gord

GOLF
Alexander, Keith
Anderson, Jerry
Balding, Al
Barr, Dave
Bathgate, Andy
Belec, Jacques
Beatty, Lou
Bigras, Adrien
Black, David
Black, Ken
Boes, Allan
Borthwick, Gayle
Bouchard, Rèmi
Bourassa, Jocelyne
Bowlan, David
Brockway, Dot
Brydson, Gordie
Buder, Jeff
Bulina, Bruce
Bunkowsky, Barbara
Burelle, Jacques
Cameron, Jack
Campbell, Dorothy
Charette, Agnes
Charette, Pierre
Charlebois, Vera
Coe-Jones, Dawn
Cole, Betty
Combe, Harvey
Cooke, Graham
Cordukes, Don
Cornish, Geoffrey
Costello, Ralph
Cowan, Gary
Crowell, Eddie
Cumming, George
Darling, Dora
Darling, Judy
Dickeson, Jean
Doyle, Jimmy
Driscoll, Mary Ellen

Eathorne, A.J.
Edey, Marjorie
Ervasti, Ed
Ezinicki, Bill
Farley, Phil
Fedoruk, Sylvia
Fletcher, Doug
Fletcher, Pat
Folk, Rick
Fraser, Alexa Stirling
Fulton, Ken
Gay, Mary
Getliffe, Ray
Girard, Ken
Goulet, Joanne
Graham, Gail
Grant, Benny
Guilbault, Michele
Halldorson, Dan
Harris, Mike
Harvey, Nancy
Hevenor, George
Hewson, Joanne
Hilton, Geordie
Hilzinger, Karl
Holzscheiter, Herb
Homenuik, Wilf
Horne, Stan
Howard, Russ
Huot, Jules
Jensen, Al
Johnston, John
Kane, Lorie
Kaufmanis, Eric
Kay, Jack Jr
Kern, Ben
Kerr, Bill
Knudson, George
Kolar, Stan
Kuzmich, Heather
Lamb, Willie
Leddy, Jack
Lederhouse, Phil
Leonard, Stan
Lewis, Elinor
Lohnes, Rita
Lyle, Dulcie
Lyon, George
MacKenzie, Ada
Martell, Henry
Martin, Fritz
Mawhinney, Bill
McElroy, Walter
McLaughlin, Jack
McLean, Arnold
Middaugh, Wayne
Mijovic, Danny
Mikowetz, Rudy
Moore, Gail Harvey
Mundinger, Karin
Murray, Albert
Murray, Bruce
Murray, Charlie
Nash, Jack
Nelford, Jim
Nezan, Andy
Norman, Moe
Obodiac, Stan

Olson, Greg
Palmer, Marilyn
Panasik, Bob
Post, Sandra
Proulx, Rita
Reid, Robert
Renaud, Don
Reville, Ralph
Robson, Lex
Rose, Bob
Ross, Chucker
Rousseau, Bobby
Roxburgh, Doug
Sams, Judy
Sears, John
Seely, Glen
Shaughnessy, Frank Jr.
Sherk, Cathy
Silverberg, Doug
Skinner, Archie
Somerville, Sandy
Soper, Alice
Stephenson, Linda
Stevenson, Forbis
Stewart, Ray
Stimpson, Bob
Stimpson, Earl
Stone, Reg
Stone, Roy
Streeter, Val
Streit, Marlene Stewart
Sweeny, Violet
Tallon, Dale
Thompson, Stanley
Thomson, Mabel
Todd, Margaret
Tombs, Tina
Trites, Ev
Tucker, Murray
Turnbull, Barbara
Waite, Jim
Walters, Lisa
Weir, Mike
Weslock, Nick
West-Mahoney, Stacey
White, Nancy
Wilson, Ruth
Wyatt, Jennifer
Wylie, Bob
Zebchuck, Peter
Zokol, Richard

GYMNASTICS
Arsenault, Lise
Bajin, Boris
Burley, Kris
Chartrand, Philippe
Choquette, Jean
Daley, Gail
Delasalle, Philip
Diachun, Jennifer
Eagle, Don
Gagnier, Ed
Goermann, Elfriede
Goermann, Monica
Hawco, Sherry
Hibbert, Curtis
Ikeda, Richard

Kelsall, Karen
Kihn, Richard
Lacy, Irene
Larose, Gilbert
Long, Warren
MacEachern, Shanyn
Mitruk, Steve
Newman, Bernard
Nolet, Alan
Nooney, John
Oryszcyn, Eugene
Rothwell, Nigel
Russell, Ernestine
Savage, Marilyn
Schlegel, Elfi
Taylor, Bryce
Tousek, Yvonne
Umeh, Stella
Weiler, Willie
Whittle, Doug
Wittmeier, Bonnie

HANDBALL
de Roussan, Hugues
Deckert, Merv
Fry, Harry
Pickell, Bob
St. Martin, Pierre

HARNESS RACING
Armitage, Rolly
Aubin, Marc
Avery, Earle
Baldwin, Ralph
Belanger, Bertrand
Brown, Doug
Burgess, Blair
Campbell, John
Chapman, John
Condren, Stephen
Cote, Benoit
Daigneault, Réjean
Doherty, James
Feagan, Ron
Filion, Henri
Filion, Hervé,
Filion, Yves
Findley, John
Firlotte, Stewart
Fleming, Vic
Fontaine, Lucien
Fritz, Bud
Galbraith, Clint
Gale, Bill
Gassien, Reg
Gendron, Gilles
Gilmour, Buddy
Gorman, T.P.
Grant, Fred
Hamilton, Douglas
Hebert, Jacques
Hennessey, Walter
Hodgins, Clint
Hudon, Joe Jr.
James, Jeff
Johnson, Danny
Kerr, Randy
Kerr, Terry

Kerwood, Tony
Kopas, Jack
Lachance, Michel
Lamy, Gaetan
Lancaster, Mark
Linton, Keith
MacDonell, Paul
MacKinnon, Dan
Mayotte, Roger
McIntosh, Bob
McKinley, Harold
Mehlenbacher, Jack
Miller, James
Morand, Jim
O'Brien, Joe
O'Donnell, William
Ouellette, Luc
Pinkney, David Sr.
Rankin, Callie
Remmen, Ray
Ritchie, Trevor
Robinson, Bill
Rowe, Earl
Seiling, Rod
Slack, Bill
Turcotte, Mel
Twaddle, Tim
Walker, Larry
Wall, Dave
Wallis, Kevin
Waples, Keith
Waples, Ron
Wellwood, William
White, Ben
Zeron, Rick

HIGHLAND GAMES
Harrington, Dave

HOCKEY
Abel, Sid
Acton, Keith
Adams, Jack
Ahearn, Frank
Alfredsson, Daniel
Allen, Keith
Anderson, Glenn
Andreychuk, Dave
Apps, Syl Sr.
Arbour, Al
Armstrong, George
Armstrong, Neil
Ashley, John
Awrey, Don
Babych, Dave
Babych, Wayne
Backstrom, Ralph
Bailey, Ace
Ballard, Harold
Balon, Dave
Barber, Bill
Barrie, Rachel
Barry, Martin
Bath, Doc
Bathgate, Andy
Bauer, Bobby
Bauer, David
Baun, Bobby

Bawn, Bev
Beaupre, Don
Bedard, Bob
Bedecki, Tom
Belfour, Ed
Beliveau, Jean
Bellows, Brian
Belsher, Don
Benedict, Clint
Bentley, Doug
Bentley, Max
Berenson, Red
Bergman, Gary
Berry, Bob
Beveridge, Bill
Bickell, J.P.
Bionda, Jack
Bishop, Jim
Blair, Wren
Blake, Rob
Blake, Toe
Boivin, Leo
Boldirev, Ivan
Boll, Buzz
Bonney, Wayne
Boon, Dickie
Boschman, Laurie
Bossy, Mike
Bouchard, Butch
Bouchard, Dan
Boucher, Bill
Boucher, Bob
Boucher, Frank
Boucher, Frank
Boucher, George
Bourque, Ray
Bower, Johnny
Bowie, Russell
Bowman, Scotty
Bowman, Scotty
Bowness, Rick
Branch, David
Branchaud, Mike
Brewer, Carl
Brind'Amour, Rod
Brisson, Thérèse
Broadbent, Punch
Broda, Turk
Brodeur, Martin
Browne, Cec
Bruneteau, Mud
Brydson, Gordie
Buckna, Mike
Bucyk, John
Bullard, Mike
Burch, Billy
Bure, Pavel
Burns, Pat
Bush, Eddie
Butterfield, Jack
Cameron, Harry
Cameron, Jack
Campbell, Angus
Campbell, Cassie
Campbell, Clarence
Carbonneau, Guy
Carlyle, Randy
Cashman, Wayne

Cattarinich, Joseph
Chabot, Lorne
Charlebois, Bob
Charron, Guy
Cheevers, Gerry
Cherry, Don
Chiarelli, John
Chouinard, Guy
Chynoweth, Ed
Ciccarelli, Dino
Clancy, King
Clapper, Dit
Clark, Wendel
Clarke, Bobby
Cleghorn, Odie
Cleghorn, Sprague
Coffey, Paul
Colville, Neil
Conacher, Brian
Conacher, Charlie
Conacher, Lionel Sr.
Conacher, Pete
Conacher, Roy
Connell, Alex
Cook, Bill
Cook, Bun
Cook, Tommy
Copp, Bobby
Corson, Shayne
Costello, Murray
Coulter, Art
Cournoyer, Yvan
Cowley, Bill
Craven, Murray
Crawford, Marc
Crawford, Rusty
Cristofoli, Ed
Cronie, Ab
Cunneyworth, Randy
Curry, Floyd
D'Amico, John
Daigle, Alexandre
Damphousse, Vincent
Darragh, Jack
Darwin, Howard
Davidson, Bob
Davidson, Scotty
Dawson, Earl
Day, Hap
Deacon, Tom
Delvecchio, Alex
Demers, Jacques
Denneny, Cy
Desjardins, Eric
Desjardins, Gerry
Devine, Jack
Dickie, Bill
Diduck, Judy
Dilio, Frank
Dineen, Bill
Dineen, Kevin
Dionne, Marcel
Doraty, Ken
Dowell, Hanson
Drillon, Gord
Drinkwater, Graham
Drolet, Nancy
Dryden, Dave

Dryden, Ken	Gibson, Jack	Howe, Gordie	Leblanc, Eugene
Dube, Danielle	Gilbert, Rod	Howe, Syd	Lee, Peter
Duchesne, Gaétan	Gilmour, Billy	Howell, Harry	Leeman, Gary
Dudley, George	Gilmour, Doug	Howell, Ron	Lehman, Hughie
Duff, Dick	Girard, Ken	Hrudey, Kelly	Lemaire, Jacques
Dugan, Arnie	Goldham, Bob	Huddy, Charlie	Lemieux, Claude
Dumart, Woody	Goodfellow, Ebbie	Hull, Bobby	Lemieux, Mario
Duncanson, Albert	Gordon, Jackie	Hull, Brett	Lenardon, Norman
Dunderdale, Tommy	Goring, Butch	Hull, Dennis	Lespi, Kusti
Dunlap, Frank	Gorman, T. P.	Hume, Fred	LeSueur, Percy
Dunn, James	Goulet, Michel	Hunter, Dale	Lever, Don
Durnan, Bill	Goyette, Danielle	Hutton, Bouse	Lewis, Bryan
Dutton, Mervyn Red	Grant, Benny	Hyland, Harry	Lewis, Dave
Dye, Babe	Grant, Danny	Imlach, Punch	Lewis, Herbie
Eagleson, Alan	Grant, Mike	Ingarfield, Earl	Linden, Trevor
Ellett, Dave	Gravelle, Red	Ion, Mickey	Lindquist, Vic
Elliott, Chaucer	Graves, Adam	Irvin, Dick Sr.	Lindros, Eric
Ellis, Ron	Green, Gary	Ivan, Tommy	Lindsay, Ted
Elmer, Wally	Green, Shorty	Jackson, Busher	Linseman, Ken
Emms, Hap	Green, Ted	James, Angela	Liut, Mike
Esposito, Phil	Grenda, Ed	James, Gerry	Litzenberger, Eddie
Esposito, Tony	Gretzky, Wayne	Jarvis, Doug	Locking, Norm
Evon, Russ	Griffis, Si	Johnson, Ching	Long, Bill
Ezinicki, Bill	Griffiths, Frank	Johnson, Don	Lowe, Kevin
Farmer, Ken	Guzzo, Patrick	Johnson, Moose	Luce, Don
Faulkner, Alex	Hadfield, Vic	Johnson, Tom	Lumley, Harry
Federko, Bernie	Haight, Jim	Johnston, Ed	Lund, Pentti
Ferguson, John	Hainsworth, George	Joliat, Aurel	MacDonald, Kilby
Ferguson, Lorne	Halder, Wally	Joseph, Curtis	MacInnis, Al
Ferguson, Skit	Hall, Glenn	Juckes, Gordon	MacKay, Mickey
Ferguson, Vince	Hall, Joe	Kane, Frank	MacKell, Fleming
Finn, Ron	Halliday, Milton	Kariya, Paul	MacLean, John
Fisher, Frank	Hammond, Alvin	Keating, Jack	MacLeish, Rick
Flaman, Fern	Hanley, Bill	Keats, Duke	MacMillan, Billy
Fletcher, Cliff	Harper, Terry	Keeling, Butch	MacNeil, Al
Fletcher, Doug	Hartsburg, Craig	Keenan, Mike	MacTavish, Craig
Fleury, Lionel	Harvey, Buster	Kehoe, Rick	Magnuson, Keith
Fleury, Theoren	Harvey, Doug	Kelly, Pete	Maher, Peter
Foligno, Mike	Harvey, Scott Jr.	Kelly, Red	Mahovlich, Frank
Fontinato, Lou	Hawerchuk, Dale	Kennedy, Sheldon	Mahovlich, Pete
Foote, Adam	Hay, Bill	Kennedy, Ted	Malone, Joe
Forhan, Bob	Hay, Charles	Keon, Dave	Maloney, Don
Foster, Red	Hay, George	Kerr, Tim	Mann, Bob
Fox, Fred	Hayes, George	Kilrea, Brian	Mantha, Sylvio
Foyston, Frank	Heaney, Geraldine	Kilrea, Hec	Mara, George
Francis, Emile	Hebenton, Andy	King, Dave	Marker, Gus
Francis, Ron	Hedberg, Anders	Knox, Swede	Marsh, Brad
Fraser, Kerry	Henderson, Paul	Koharski, Don	Marshall, Don
Fredrickson, Frank	Henry, Camille	Kromm, Bobby	Marshall, Jack
Fuhr, Grant	Hern, Riley	Kurri, Jari	Martin, Jacques
Gadsby, Bill	Hewitson, Bobby	L'Heureux, Bill	Martin, Pit
Gainey, Bob	Hewitt, Foster	Lach, Elmer	Martin, Rick
Galley, Garry	Hewitt, W.A.	Lafleur, Guy	Martin, Seth
Gamble, Dick	Hextall, Bryan Sr.	Lalonde, Lally	Maruk, Dennis
Gardiner, Charlie	Hextall, Ron	Lalonde, Newsy	Masterton, Bill
Gardiner, Herb	Hibberd, Ted	Lamb, Joe	Mathers, Frank
Gardner, Cal	Hildebrand, Ike	Lammens, Hank	Maxwell, Steamer
Gare, Danny	Hillman, Larry	Laperrière, André	Mazur, Eddie
Gartner, Mike	Hindmarch, Robert	Laperrière, Jacques	McCaffrey, Jimmy
Gaudet, Oscar	Hitchcock, Ken	Lapointe, Guy	McComb, Bill
Gauthier, Gèrard	Hodge, Ken	Laprade, Edgar	McConachie, John
Gauthier, Pierre	Holmes, Derek	Larmer, Steve	McConnell, Russ
Gelineau, Jack	Holmes, Hap	Larocque, Bunny	McCourt, Dan
Geoffrion, Bernie	Hooper, Tom	Larouche, Pierre	McCrimmon, Brad
Gerard, Eddie	Horner, Red	Laviolette, Jack	McCulloch, Jack
Getliffe, Ray	Horton, Tim	Leach, Reg	McDonald, Dennis
Giacomin, Ed	Horvath, Bronco	Leader, Al	McDonald, Lanny
Gibson, Doug	Houle, Réjean	LeBel, Bob	McFarlane, Brian

McGee, Frank
McGimsie, Billy
McIntyre, Jack
McKenzie, Johnny
McKillop, Bob
McKinnon, Frank
McLelland, Ivan
McLeod, Jackie
McNab, Peter
McNamara, George
McReavy, Pat
Meeker, Howie
Meloche, Gilles
Merrick, Wayne
Merrill, Horace
Messier, Mark
Metz, Nick
Mickoski, Nick
Middleton, Rick
Mikita, Stan
Milford, Jake
Miller, Shannon
Milne, Howie
Mitton, Randy
Mogilny, Alexander
Mohns, Doug
Molson, Hartland
Montgomery, Ken
Monson, Walter
Moog, Andy
Moog, Don
Moore, Dickie
Moran, Paddy
Morenz, Howie
Morris, Greg
Mosienko, Bill
Muckler, John
Murphy, Larry
Murphy, Ron
Murray, Bob
Murray, Bryan
Murray Ken
Murray, Pere
Murray, Terry
Nadin, Robert
Nanne, Lou
Neale, Harry
Neely, Cam
Neilson, Roger
Nesterenko, Eric
Nicholls, Bernie
Nieuwendyk, Joe
Nighbor, Frank
Nilsson, Kent
Noble, Reg
Nystrom, Karen
O'Brien, J. Ambrose
O'Connor, Buddy
O'Malley, Terry
O'Neill, Brian
O'Ree, Willie
Oates, Adam
Obey, Arthur
Obodiac, Stan
Ogrodnick, John
Oliver, Harry
Oliver, Murray
Olmstead, Bert

Orr, Bobby
Ouellette, Red
Pachl, Vern
Page, Fred
Page, Pierre
Pare, Mark
Parent, Bernie
Park, Brad
Patrick, Frank
Patrick, Lester
Patrick, Lynn
Patrick, Muzz
Pavelich, Matt
Peacosh, Walter
Pearson, Mike
Pelyk, Mike
Perreault, Gil
Philip, Bob
Phillips, Tommy
Pickard, Allan
Pilote, Pierre
Pilous, Rudy
Pinder, Gerry
Pinder, Herb
Pitre, Didier
Plante, Jacques
Plaxton, Hugh
Pocklington, Peter
Poile, Bud
Pollock, Sam
Pomfret, Jack
Porter, Bob
Porter, John
Potter, Billy
Potvin, Denis
Potvin, Jean
Power, Dale
Pratt, Babe
Prentice, Dean
Price, Noel
Primeau, Joe
Primeau, Keith
Pronger, Chris
Pronovost, Marcel
Propp, Brian
Prystai, Metro
Psutka, Harry
Pugh, Bob
Pulford, Bob
Pulford, Harvey
Quackenbush, Bill
Quinn, Pat
Raleigh, Don
Rankin, Frank
Ratelle, Jean
Rayner, Chuck
Reardon, Ken
Reay, Billy
Recchi, Mark
Reddon, Lesley
Redmond, Mickey
Regan, Larry
Reid, Bobby
Reid, Lefty
Renaud, Ab
Rheaume, Manon
Richard, Henri
Richard, Jacques

Richard, Maurice
Richardson, George
Richer, Stephane
Richman, Ruby
Risebrough, Doug
Ritchie, Alvin
Roberts, Gary
Roberts, Gordon
Roberts, Jim
Robinson, Claude
Robinson, Larry
Robitaille, Luc
Rodden, Mike
Ross, Art
Rousseau, Bobby
Roy, Patrick
Ruel, Claude
Russel, Blair
Russell, Ernest
Rutherford, Jim
Ruttan, Jack
Sakic, Joe
Salming, Borje
Sanderson, Derek
Saskamoose, Fred
Sather, Glen
Savard, Denis
Savard, Serge
Sawchuk, Terry
Scapinello, Ray
Scherer, Sue
Schmalz, Tubby
Schmidt, Milt
Schoenfeld, Jim
Schriner, Sweeney
Schroeter, Reg
Schuler, Laura
Scodellaro, Duke
Secord, Al
Seibert, Earl
Seibert, Oliver
Seiling, Rod
Selanne, Teemu
Selke, Frank Sr.
Sgro, Joe
Shack, Eddie
Shanahan, Brendan
Shaske, Ed Jr.
Shaughnessy, Frank Jr.
Sheppard, Ray
Shero, Fred
Shibicky, Alex
Shore, Eddie
Shutt, Steve
Siebert, Babe
Simmer, Charlie
Simpson, Bullet Joe
Simpson, Craig
Sinden, Harry
Sittler, Darryl
Skinner, Jim
Skinner, Larry Jr.
Skinner, Larry Sr.
Sloan, Tod
Smeaton, Cooper
Smith, Alfred E.
Smith, Billy
Smith, Bobby

Smith, Brian
Smith, Clint
Smith, Dallas
Smith, Frank
Smith, Gary
Smith, Hooley
Smith, Murray
Smith, Neil
Smith, Sid
Smith, Tommy
Smyl, Stan
Smylie, Doug
Smylie, Rod Sr.
Smythe, Conn
Somerville, Sandy
Sonmor, Glen
St. Louis, France
Stanley, Allen
Stanley, Barney
Stanowski, Wally
Stapleton, Pat
Stasiuk, Vic
Stastny, Peter
Steele, David
Stevens, Scott
Stewart, Black Jack
Stewart, Nels
Stewart, Ron
Stickle, Leon
Storey, Red
Stoughton, Blaine
Stuart, Bruce
Stuart, Hod
Stukus, Annis
Sullivan, Frank
Sullivan, Joe
Sullivan, Red
Sundin, Mats
Sunohara, Vicky
Sutherland, Hugh
Sutherland, James
Sutter, Brent
Sutter, Brian
Sutter, Darryl
Sutter, Duane
Sutter, Ron
Talbot, Jean Guy
Tallon, Dale
Taylor, Bobby
Taylor, Cyclone
Taylor, Dave
Tessier, Orv
Thomas, Wayne
Thompson, Tiny
Tkaczuk, Walt
Tocchet, Rick
Torrey, Bill
Trihey, Harry
Trottier, Bryan
Tudin, Conny
Turgeon, Pierre
Turnbull, Ian
Turner, Lloyd
Udvari, Frank
Ullman, Norm
Unger, Garry
Vachon, Rogie
Vadnais, Carol

447

Vaive, Rick
Van Hellemond, Andy
Verbeek, Pat
Vernon, Mike
Vezina, Georges
Vitarelli, Dootch
Voss, Carl
Waghorne, Fred
Walker, Jack
Walsh, Marty
Walton, Mike
Warwick, Billy
Warwick, Grant
Warwick, Richard
Watson, Harry
Watson, Moose
Watson, Sandy
Weiland, Cooney
Wells, Jay
Westwick, Harry
Whitcroft, Frederick
White, Bill
Wickenheiser, Hayley
Williams, Tiger
Wilson, Doug Jr.
Wilson, Doug Sr.
Wilson, Lefty
Wilson, Murray
Wilson, Phat
Wilson, Stacy
Wiseman, Eddie
Worsley, Gump
Worters, Roy
Yashin, Alexei
Yzerman, Steve
Zamuner, Rob
Zeman, Joe

HORSE RACING
Atkinson, Ted
Attfield, Roger
Bell, Max
Cheevers, Gerry
Fell, Jeffrey
Ferguson, John
Frostad, Mark
Gomez, Avelino
Gorman, T.P.
Hawley, Sandy
Hendrie, George Jr.
Hendrie, George Sr.
Hewitt, W.A.
Huntley, Gordon
Kabel, Todd
Landry, Robert
Laurin, Lucien
Laurin, Roger
Levesque, Jean-Louis
Longden, Johnny
MacBeth, Donald
McLaughlin, Sam
Minshall, Barbara
Platts, Robin
Randall, Sam
Rathgeb, Chuck
Rogers, Chris
Saunders, William
Seagram, Joseph

Smythe, Conn
Speers, Jim
Stronach, Frank
Taylor, E.P.
Turcotte, Ron
Wall, Nick
Walls, Mickey
Woodhouse, Hedley
Woolf, George

HORSESHOES
Bigras, Orv
Cantin, Diane
Curtis, Crystal
Hohl, Elmer
Hohl, Steve
Janssens, Sandy
Kissick, Myrna
LeClerc, Andre
Markle, Jean
Markle, Larry
McLaughlin, Dean
Moisan, Sylvianne
Stevenson, Ross

JIU JITSU
Forrester, Ron
MacLean, Allan
Viele, Vincent

JUDO
Beaton, Ewan
Berger, Mark
Blaney, Fred
Bolger, Pat
Buckingham, Michelle
Cyr, Alain
Doherty, Kevin
Erdman, Wayne
Farnsworth, Terry
Farrow, Brad
Filteau, Nancy
Gill, Nicolas
Gosselin, Nathalie
Greenway, Tom
Hirose, Tim
Jani, Louis
Kawasaki, Mitch
Lappage, Ron
Lepage, Carolyne
Morgan, Colin
Morgan, Keith
Morneau, Marie-Josee
Nakamura, Hiroshi
Pilon, Claude
Rogers, Doug
Sheffield, Cathy
Takahashi, Allyn
Takahashi, June
Takahashi, Masao
Takahashi, Philip
Takahashi, Ray
Takahashi, Tina
Tan, Taro
Weldon, Craig

KARATE
Anderson, Steve

Hayes, Cheryl
Sabourin, Jamie

KICK-BOXING
Thériault, Jean-Yves

LACROSSE
Aird, Stu
Alexander, Kevin
Allan, Robert
Batley, Jamie
Beers, William George
Benson, Lorne
Bionda, Jack
Bishop, Jim
Box, Charlie
Buddo, Don
Campbell, David
Cavallin, Roy
Conacher, Lionel Sr.
Connell, Alex
Connell, Charlie
Coombes, Cy
Crookall, Dot
Dean, Geordie
Dickinson, William
Douglas, Jim
Dugan, Arnie
Ferguson, Arnold
Ferguson, John
Ferguson, Larry
Ferguson, Merv
Fitzgerald, Billy
Fletcher, Doug
Foster, Red
Fulton, Jack
Gait, Gary
Gait, Paul
Gaudaur, Jake Jr.
Gisiger, Michelle
Goldham, Bob
Gorman, T.P.
Hall, Chris
Hammond, Gord
Hieltjes, Ben
Hildebrand, Ike
Hume, Fred
Hunt, Ted
Hutton, Bouse
Ion, Mickey
Kells, Morley
Lally, Joe
Lalonde, Lally
Lalonde, Newsy
Large, Bert
Laviolette, Jack
Marechek, Bill
Marechek, Tom
Miller, Doug Jr.
Miller, Doug Sr.
Oates, Adam
Oneschuk, Steve
Parnell, Paul
Pitre, Didier
Pomfret, Jack
Porter, Bob
Powless, Gaylord
Powless, Ross

Reeve, Ted
Sawicki, Ted
Silverheels, Jay
Smith, Alf
Spring, Doughy
Stockton, Don
Tavares, John
Thompson, George
Thorburn, Cliff
Turnbull, Alex
Vaughan, Eileen
Vitarelli, Dootch
White, Dalt
Wilson, Lefty
Wootton, Moon

LAWN BOWLING
Au, On-Kow
Bennett, Dot
Boettger, Bill
Clayton, Harold
Creaney, Doreen
Elliff, Jim
Forrest, Robin
Hart, Nelson
Kempster, Ray
Martin, Flora Greenwood
Ranger, Melissa
Roney, Jean
Roney, Keith
Stock, Ed
Whitley, Gerry

LUGE
Bowie, Mary Jane
Crutchfield, Linda
Keyes, Carole

MODERN PENTATHLON
Alexander, John
Chornobrywy, Lynn
Keyte, Lawrence
Shong, Laurie

MOTORSPORT
Bentham, Lee
Boyce, Walter
Brack, Bill
Carpentier, Patrick
Carter, Mo
Duff, Mike
Duhamel, Miguel
Duhamel, Yvon
Empringham, David
Emerson, Eddie
Fellows, Ron
Gee, Gordon
Goodyear, Scott
Headland, Martin
Heimrath, Ludwig Sr.
Hill, Craig
Jones, John
Jones, Tom
Kelly, Jim
Kroll, Horst
Moore, Greg
Pickell, Bob
Rathgeb, Chuck

Ross, Earl
Ryan, Peter
Smith, Sheldon
Stewart, Brian
Tracy, Paul
Villeneuve, Gilles
Villeneuve, Jacques
Villeneuve, Jacques
Wietzes, Eppie
Williams, John
Wilson, Harold
Wolf, Walter

MOUNTAINEERING
Amatt, John
Gmoser, Hans
March, Bill
O'Connor, Zeke
Rathgeb, Chuck
Skreslet, Laurie
Weber, Richard
Wood, Sharon

OFFICIATING
Adams, Robert
Armstrong, Neil
Ashley, John
Beaton, Bob
Bonney, Wayne
Cameron, Jack
Campbell, Clarence
D'Amico, John
Denoncourt, Sonia
Dojack, Paul
Elliott, Chaucer
Emslie, Bob
Evon, Russ
Farmer, Jim
Ferguson, Arnold
Findlay, Dick
Finn, Ron
Fletcher, Doug
Foxcroft, Ron
Fraser, Kerry
Frost, Barclay
Gauthier, Gèrard
Gravelle, Red
Gurney, Jack
Hammond, Gord
Hayes, George
Hewitson, Bobby
Hill, Harvey
Ion, Mickey
Isbister, Bob Sr.
King, Don
Knox, Swede
Koharski, Don
Lewis, Bryan
Lindquist, Vic
Loaring, John
Logan, Tip
Lowery, Ron
Luftspring, Sammy
Macken, Jim
Malcolm, Andrew
Mantha, Sylvio
Maxwell, Steamer
McBrien, Harry

McCourt, Dan
McKay, Willie
McKean, Jim
McKerlich, Bill
Mehlenbacher, Jack
Michienzi, Pete
Miles, Wiff
Milne, Howie
Mitton, Randy
Morris, Jim
Morrison, Scotty
Morrow, Suzanne
Murray, Ben
Nadin, Robert
Nairn, Bill
Pare, Mark
Pavelich, Matt
Perrier, Ross
Porter, Bob
Quilty, Silver
Rae, Al
Rodden, Mike
Rogin, Bill
Runge, Paul
Ruttan, Jack
Sauve, Gordon
Scapinello, Ray
Shannon, Carver
Shouldice, Hap
Simpson, Ben
Smeaton, Cooper
Smith, Gwen
Spencer, Jim
Spray, Robert
Stack, Frank
Stickle, Leon
Storey, Red
Strumm, Gil
Sylvain, Jules
Tinline, Dorothy
Trihey, Harry
Turnbull, Ray
Udvari, Frank
Van Hellemond, Andy
Vaughan, Eileen
Voss, Carl
Waite, Jim
White, Al
Wilkes, Jimmy
Wilson, Alex
Wilson, Seymour
Young, Joe

ORIENTEERING
Budge, Susan
Demonte, Denise
de St. Croix, Ted
Hunter, Gord
Kaill, Bob
Lowery, Ron
McIntosh, Pam
Robert, Magli

PARACHUTING
Bradley, Eric
Cox, Kathy
Grant, Duncan
Henry, Daryl

Kangas, Katherine
Laidlaw, Robert
Marchand, Claude
McLeod, Lawrence
Taylor, Graham
Vaughan, Eileen
Vincent, Mark
Watson, Bev
Winning, Craig
Wykeham-Martin, Simon
Zahar, Michael

POWER LIFTING
Macvicar, Don

RACQUETBALL
Capozzi, Herb
Ceresia, Mike
Grand'Maitre, Josée
Greenfeld, Sherman
King, Tim
McKay, Heather
McNamara, Bob
Mikowetz, Rudy
Pickell, Bob
Powell, Lori_Jane
Roy, Simon
Shanks, Vicki
Stupp, Heather
Theismann, Joe
Van Hees, Christie
Young, Frank

RHYTHMIC GYMNASTICS
Fung, Lori
Fuzesi, Mary
Martens, Camille
Stauder, Zlatica
Stirton, Erike-Leigh

RINGETTE
Anderson, Tamara
Brisson, Thérèse
Brown, Cara
Brown, Lisa
Coggles, Susan
Diduck, Judy
Jacks, Sam
Marek, Deb
Reynolds, Shelley

RODEO
Bews, Tom
Bruce, Winston
Butterfield, Joe
Coleman, Mel
Daines, Duane
Dunham, Steve
Eirikson, Tom
Girletz, Wilf
Gladstone, Jim
Guelly, Debbie
Hay, Denny
Kesler, Reg
Knight, Pete
Lucas, Joe
McLean, Kenny
Phillips, Jerry

Warren, Rod

ROLLER SKATING
Bain, Dan
Domik, Bernard
Lewis, Stanley
McCulloch, Jack

ROWING
Arnold, Don
Barber, Darren
Barnes, Kirsten
Battersby, Robert
Belyea, Arthur
Biesenthal, Laryssa
Bonnycastle, Charles
Boyes, Dave
Brain, Marilyn
Brodie, Scott
Brown, Clayton
Brown, George
Cameron, Bev
Cameron, Trice
Catherall, Robin
Clarke, Christine
Clarke, Heather
Cline, Paddy
Cort, Gail
Craig-Eaton, Betty
Crosby, Andy
Davidson, Chris
Delahanty, Megan
Doey, Jennifer
Dubois, Theo
Evans, Mark
Evans, Michael
Ford, Bruce
Forgeron, Mike
Fry, Harry
Gatley, Lyle
Gaudaur, Jake Jr.
Gaudaur, Jake Sr.
Gotfredsen, Leif
Graham, Phil
Green, Peter
Griffis, Sy
Guest, Jack
Hallett, Todd
Hamilton, Doug
Hanlan, Ned
Hassett, Gavin
Hattin, Heather
Heddle, Kathleen
Hegan, Larry
Helliwell, David
Hungerford, George
Jackson, Roger
Jespersen, Julie
Johnston, Bob
Jonker, Karel
Kaysmith, Henry
King, Peter
Korn, Alison
Kovits, Herman
Kueber, Philip
Laumann, Silken
Lay, Jeff
Lichty, Kathy

Logan, Willie
Loomer, Lorne
Lund, Cathy
Mason, Janice
Maunder, Maria
McBean, Marnie
McDermid, Heather
McDonald, Doug
McKerlich, Bill
Mervyn, Glen
Miller, Colleen
Mills, Bob
Monckton, Philip
Monroe, Jessica
Morrow, Al
Newman, Pat
Norris, Edgar
O'Grady, Diane
O'Neill, John
Parfitt, Adam
Peaker, Brian
Pearce, Bobby
Porter, Derek
Pratt, Ned
Pulford, Harvey
Read, Frank
Richardson, Bert
Riley, Con
Riley, Culver
Robertson, Lisa
Robinson, Emma
Rogers, Shotty
Rokosh, Greg
Ross, P.D.
Ryder, Gus
Saunders, Sandy
Schneider, Angela
Scholes, Louis
Schreiner, Andrea
Senkler, Harry
Smith, Glen
Smith, Tricia
Spencer, Victor
Spowage, Cheryl
Stacey, Nelles
Stevenson, Greg
Storm, Tim
Sweeny, Bimbo
Thompson, Lesley
Tregunno, Jane
Tsang, Tosha
van der Kamp, Anna
Van Ruyven, Andy
Wiebe, Wendy
Wilson, Alex
Wilson, Robert
Woodward, Reggie
Wright, Joseph Jr.
Wright, Joseph Sr.
Young, Dolores
Young, Frank

RUGBY
Bauld, Donald
Bedecki, Tom
Browne, Cec
Burnham, Barrie
Charron, Al

Conacher, Lionel Sr.
Elliott, Geoff
Evans, Eddie
Gray, Steve
Harper, George
Howe, Bruce
Hunt, Ted
Jackart, Dan
King, Donald
Lister, Ralph
Luke, Michael
Moore, Buzz
Patrick, Lynn
Peden, Doug
Pomfret, Jack
Rees, Gareth
Spray, Robert
Sweeny, Bimbo
Taylor, Graham
Van Vliet, Maury
Wilson, Ben
Woodward, Reggie

SAILING
Abbott, Bill Jr.
Abbott, Joanne
Bastet, Evert
Bjorn, Tyler
Bruce, Ian
Clarke, Richard
Cochrane, Nigel
Cross, Jay
Davies, Rod
Davis, Penny
Dexter, Glen
Duggan, Herrick
Eckard, Jeff
Emery, Vic
Fogh, Hans
Green, Donald
Hall, Peter
Henderson, Paul
Innes, Marjorie
Janse, Roy
Jespersen, Eric
Josenhans, Andreas
Kerr, John
Kidd, James
Kirby, Bruce
Konantz, Gordon
Lammens, Hank
Leibel, Allan
Lemieux, Lawrence
MacDonald, Ross
MacMillan, Sandy
Matthews, Tam
McGill, Frank
McLaughlin, Frank
McLaughlin, Sam
McLaughlin, Terry
Miller, Dave
Moberg_Parker, Tine
Moss, Shona
Neilson, Terry
Roy, Andy
Sherwood, Liv
Stock, Ed
Tupper, Stephen

Tytler, Donald
Walters, Angus
Watters, Lynn
Windeyer, Walter
Woods, Larry

SHOOTING
Adlhoch, Hans
Alexander, Jeremy
Altmann, Fred
Arnold, Sherman
Ashcroft, Christina
Ashcroft, Michael
Bain, Dan
Baldwin, Bill
Barwise, Bob
Beckett, Norman
Best, Bob
Bissonnette, Serge
Boa, Andrew
Boa, Gil
Boa, James Sr.
Boa, Sandy
Boa, Stuart
Boa, Vicki
Boll, Rod
Bowes, Sharon
Bowman, Gary
Brown, Colin
Bullock, Bruce
Bullock, Jim
Burke, Des
Caldwell, Earl
Carty, Hank
Carver, Julie
Chase, George
Clifford, William
Colville, Nelson
Cozzarin, Sharon
Cunningham, Keith
D'Amour, Léo
Dahlstrom, Clint
Dahlstrom, Patricia
Decsi, Laszlo
Dion, Michel
Dombroski, Ben
Ewing, Walter
Ferguson, Bruce
Ferguson, Ken
Fitch, Ed
Frazer, Gerry
Frost, Stan
Gabriel, Brian
Genereux, George
George, Ed
George, Ron
Graham, Sally
Grundy, Art
Guinn, Tom
Gunter, Andy
Gutnick, Paul
Hampton, Richard
Hare, William
Harper, George
Hartl, Gus
Hartman, Barney
Hayhurst, Tom
Henderson, Gil

Houlden, Jim
Howkins, Mark
Huot, Jean-Pierre
Igorov, Metodi
Jans, Edward
Jasiak, Andrew
Jmaeff, Peter
Kelly, Steven
Kwasnycia, Don
Laporte, Paul
Lea, Mary
Leary, George
Lorion, Guy
Mann, Avard
Mann, Bob
Marion, Alain
Mayer, Alfons
McCormick, Frank
McMahon, Gary
Miller, Linda
Mitchell, Kurt
Molnar, Bill
Murray, Scott
Nadeau, Daniel
Nattrass, Sue
Opsal, Frank
Ouellette, Gerry
Papasideris, Peter
Parks, Arnold
Paton, Jim
Peden, Sandy
Pitcairn, Bob
Platz, Jim
Primrose, John
Reynolds, Kirk
Rochon, John
Rumbold, Dave
Sanderlin, Don
Sanderson, Gus
Schulze, Rudy
Senecal, Jean-Francois
Sewell, Don
Sewell, Doran
Shaske, Ed Jr.
Shaw, Paul
Shea, Stu
Smith, Helen
Sobrian, Jules
Sorensen, Arne
Sorensen, Wayne
Spratley, Jim
Strachan, Bill
Surette, Ron
Terry, Jackie
Thibodeau, Nick
Thom, Linda
Thompson, Jim
Thurlow, Jim
Timmerman, Jim
Tomsett, Arthur
Vamplew, Des
Vamplew, Edith
Vamplew, Pat
Warner, Edson
Westling, Gunnar
Westling, Ken
Whatley, Chris
White, Al

White, Donald
Wilkins, Bruce
Wills, Stan
Willsie, Harry
Wong Shui, Mike
Young, Walter

SHUFFLEBOARD
Mattson, Dale

SKATEBOARD
Regnier, Claude

SKIING
Anderson, Verne
Asselin, Marie-Claude
Athans, Gary
Athans, George Jr.
Athans, Greg
Bagguley, Howard
Bott, Punch
Boyd, Rob
Brassard, Jean-Luc
Brenner, Veronica
Brooker, Todd
Champagne, Ed
Chapman, Currie
Clark, Bud
Clifford, Betsy
Clifford, Harvey
Clifford, John
Clow, Craig
Cochand, Louis
Condon, Eddie
Cousineau, Alain
Crawford, Judy
Crutchfield, Linda
Culver, Diane
Downs, Darcy
Dubois, Luc
Eaves, John
Firth, Sharon
Firth, Shirley
Fontaine, Nicolas
Fraser, Anna
Gmoser, Hans
Goodman, Russell
Graham, Laurie
Grandi, Thomas
Greene, Nancy
Grinnell, Rae
Groff, Doug
Gudwer, Doug
Haight, Didi
Harvey, Pierre
Heggtveit, Anne
Heggtveit, Halvor
Henderson, Scott
Hewson, Joanne
Hilzinger, Karl
Holloway, Sue
Hunter, Jim
Hunter, Malcolm
Huser, Cathy
Irwin, Bert
Irwin, Dave
Jacobs, Dave
Jacobsen, George

Johnson, Don
Keenan, Bill
Kent, Chris
Kirby, Peter
Klettl, Loni
Konantz, Gordon
Kreiner, Kathy
Kreiner, Laurie
Lalonde, Bernie
Langlois, Lloyd
Laroche, Alain
Laroche, Philippe
Laroche, Yves
Lee-Gartner, Kerrin
Lyon, Don
McCleery, Alan
McLeish, Robin
McMahon, Davic
Meloche, Lise
Midgley, Arnold
Miller, Esther
Monod, Peter
Mullen, Gary
Murray, Dave
Nemesvary, Mike
Nesbitt, Keith
Olivier, Caroline
Omholt-Jensen, Jarl
Pace, Kate
Pangman, Arthur
Pelchat, Ann_Marie
Percy, Karen
Pilcher, Al
Podborski, Steve
Podivinsky, Edi
Poscente, Vincent
Raine, Al
Ramage, Pat
Read, Ken
Rees, David
Ritchie, John
Rochon, Stephane
Ryan, Peter
Schmidt-Foster, Angela
Servold, Clarence
Servold, Irvin
Simboli, Chris
Smith-Johannsen, Herman
Sorensen, Gerry
Stemmle, Brian
Taylor, John
Thomas, Bronwen
Thompson, William
Tindale, Bill
Tommy, Andy Jr.
Tommy, Art
Tommy, Fred
Townsend, Stephanie
Turgeon, Melanie
Weber, Richard
Wheeler, Lucile
Wurtele, Rhoda
Wurtele, Rhona

SKI JUMPING
Bagguley, Howard
Bulau, Horst
Charland, Jacques

Collins, Steve
Gravelle, Gérard
Graves, Richard
Hunt, Ted
Laferte, Lucien
Morris, Fred
Servold, Irvin
Wilson, Peter

SNOWBOARDING
Anderson, Jasey Jay
Andrew, Trevor
Fawcett, Mark
Glazier, Lori
Rebagliati, Ross
Ricker, Maelle

SNOWMOBILING
Duhamel, Yvon
Villeneuve, Gilles
Villeneuve, Jacques

SNOWSHOES
Ball, Jim
Buddo, Don
Grenda, Ed
Montabone, Monty
Young, Walter

SOARING
Audette, Julien

SOCCER
Albrecht, J.I.
Anderson, Dave
Anderson, George
Brewster, Ken
Bunbury, Alex
Caithness, Charlie
Capozzi, Herb
Chursky, Tony
Corazzin, Carlo
Cowan, Jack
Dasovic, Nick
David, Tracy
Deacon, Tom
Denoncourt, Sonia
Dolan, Paul
Draffin, Ernie
Etchegary, Gus
Fitzpatrick, Allan
Forrest, Craig
Forsyth, David
Fraser, Iain
Fryatt, Dave
Gray, Gerry
Grenda, Ed
Hayes, John
Hershfield, Leible
Hooper, Charmaine
Hooper, Lyndon
Hume, Fred
Kouzmanis, Tom
Kulai, Dan
Lenarduzzi, Bob
Lenarduzzi, Sam
Letteri, Tony
Limniatis, John

Mayers, Wallace
McKee, Walt
McMahon, John
Miller, Colin
Mobilio, Domenic
Morris, Jim
Newsham, David
Nicholl, Jimmy
Peschisolido, Paul
Pomfret, Jack
Reid, Bobby
Robertson, Sandy
Ruys, Henk
Samuel, Randy
Sanford, Aubrey
Simpson, Bill
Skinner, Larry Sr.
Spencer, Jim
Spring, Harry
Steele, David
Stronge, Stan
Thorburn, Cliff
Turner, Dave
Watson, Mark
Whitton, John
Wilson, Bruce
Yallop, Frank

SOFTBALL
Abbott, Colin
Anderson, Andy
Bagnell, Norm
Baker, Brad
Baker, Mary
Bath, Doc
Baytor, Terry
Bend, Olive
Bitz, Ed
Bodashefsky, Larry
Bottoms, Lynn
Branchaud, Mike
Burrows, Bob
Casselman, Bruce
Challis, Terry
Chiarelli, John
Clayton, Juanita
Coben, Muriel
Coggles, Susan
Cooke, Myrtle
Cooperband, Mary
Corbett, Ed
Cowdrey, Jim
Desabrais, Paul
Deschamps, Claude
Domik, Bob
Durnan, Bill
Fedoruk, Sylvia
Fletcher, Doug
Foster, Red
Fox, Fred
French, Joan
Fuller, Rose
Gibbons, Pops
Gibson, Doug
Gillett, George
Guzzo, Patrick
Hershfield, Leible
Holness, Bob

Lay, Marion
Leach, Al
Leuszler, Winnie Roach
Limpert, Marianne
Loaring, John
Lockhart, Gene
Lumsdon, Cliff
Lumsdon, Kim
Lyle, Dulcie
MacDonald, Byron
MacDonald, Gary
MacPherson, Michelle
Mady, Levente
Mahony, Bill
Malar, Joanne
Mason, Susan
Mayers, Wallace
McArton, Cheryl
McBain, Barb
McKinnon, Archie
McNamee, Kathleen
Meraw, Ann
Merklinger, Anne
Michel, Yvette
Miles, Kay
Mindorff, Philip
Moore, Marie
Myden, Curtis
Nagy, George
New, Maureen
Nicholas, Cindy
Norman, Percy
Nugent, Andrea
Ottenbrite, Anne
Oxenbury, Noel
Parenti, Eddie
Pickell, Stephen
Pomfret, Jack
Ponting, Tom
Pound, Richard
Priestley, Gladys
Puddy, Bill
Quirk, Wendy
Reid, Cam
Renaud, Chris
Richardson, Kathy
Richardson, Stephanie
Ritchie, Andy
Robertson, Bruce
Rogers, Bruce
Rogers, Danny
Ross, Marie Claire
Ryder, Gus
Sawchuk, Bill
Schootman, Teddy
Shakespeare, Shannon
Sheehan, Jeff
Shockey-Milanese, Barbara
Slater, Bill
Sloan, Susan
Smith, Becky
Smith, George
Smith, Graham
Smith, Gwen
Smith, Sandra
Smith, Shannon
Smith, Sue
Snelling, Deryk

Stewart, Mary
Stratten, Gaye
Stulac, George
Sweetnam, Nancy
Szmidt, Peter
Tanner, Elaine
Tapp, Jay
Tapp, Larry
Tewksbury, Mark
Thierry, Nick
Thomas, Ted
Thompson, Dan
Tihanyi, Jeno
Versfeld, Mark
Walker, Dennis
Walker, Elisabeth
Wallenius, Rob
Ward, Peter
Watson, Whipper Billy
Welbourn, Graham
West, Mike
Wheaton, Robert
Whittall, Beth
Wu, Walter
Wurtele, Rhona
Young, George

SYNCHRONIZED SWIMMING
Alexander, Lisa
Barber, Wendy
Bedard, Nancy
Bremner, Janice
Calkins, Michelle
Cameron, Michelle
Carrier, Lyna
Carrier, Lyne
Clark, Karen
Cody, Della
Eon, Suzanne
Fonteyne, Karen
Forbes, Pansy
Fortier, Sylvie
Frechette, Sylvie
Glen, Kathy
Hambrook, Sharon
Hartzell, Irene
Hermanson, Myrna
Hould-Marchand, Valerie
Kryczka, Kelly
Kuleza, Kasia
Larsen, Christine
Laviolette, Chantal
Muir, Debbie
Oxenbury, Noel
Paradis, Renéé
Read, Cari
Seller, Peggy
Simard, Martine
Thivierge, Jojo
Vanderburg, Helen
Vilagos, Penny
Vilagos, Vicky
Waldo, Carolyn
Woodley, Erin

TABLE TENNIS
Barton, Julie

Bauld, Donald
Bédard, Hélène
Cada, Petra
Caetano, Errol
Chiu, Barbara
Domonkos, Mariann
Geng, Lijuan
Heap, Alan
Hsu, Gloria
Huang, Johnny
Joe, Peter
Johnson, Julia
Kosanovic, Zoran
Marinko, Max
McKnight, Becky
Nesukaitis, Violetta
Ng, Gideon Joe
Normandin, Pierre
Pintea, Horatio
Polisois, Alex
Wong, Chi Chong

TAEKWON-DO
Norman, Clint

TENNIS
Babbitt, Ethel
Babbitt, John
Barclay, Ann
Bardsley, Jim
Barlow, Wendy
Bassett, Carling
Bauld, Donald
Bedard, Bob
Belkin, Mike
Blackwood, Marjorie
Blais, Thérèse
Bonneau, Bonny
Bonneau, Stéphane
Boyce, Jim
Brabenec, Hana
Brabenec, Josef Jr.
Brabenec, Josef Sr.
Brockway, Dot
Brown, Louise
Butt, Susan
Carpenter, Keith
Chang, Albert
Condon, Eddie
Connell, Grant
Crocker, Willard
Dewis, Karen
Dufresne, Christian
Ebbels, Bill
Fairs, Jack
Fauquier, Harry
Fontana, Don
Genois, Réjean
Godbout, François
Halder, Wally
Harris, Lesley
Hetherington, Jill
Howson, Barry
Hy, Patricia
Januskova, Eva
Kelesi, Helen
Lareau, Sebastien
Leeming, Marjorie

Lovett, Claire
Macken, Brendan
Macken, Jim
Macken, Patricia
Main, Lorne
Martell, Henry
Matthews, John
Mayers, Wallace
McDiarmid, Don
Michibata, Glenn
Mikowetz, Rudy
Nestor, Daniel
Nunns, Brenda
Nunns, Gilbert
O'Hara, Jane
Ouellette, Bert
Percival, Lloyd
Phinney, Gertrude
Power, Dale
Pridham, Chris
Purdy, Margaret
Rainville, Marcel
Richman, Joey
Robillard, Gene
Rochon, Henri
Rosenfeld, Bobbie
Rubes, Jan
Rusedski, Greg
Schwengers, Bernie
Simpson, Rene
Sinclair, Ken
Steele, Don
Strong, Lawrence
Sznajder, Andrew
Tindle, Janice
Urban, Faye
Walton, Dorothy
Watt, Laird
Watt, R.N.
White, Al
Wilson, Ruth
Wostenholme, Martin
Wright, Jack

TOUCH FOOTBALL
Belsher, Don
Huband, Deb
Robinson, Bill

TRACK & FIELD
Acoose, Paul
Adams, Jeff
Adams, Robert
Andersen, Roxy
Anderson, Kate
Andrusyshyn, Zenon
Apps, Syl Sr.
Armstrong, Brian
Babits, Laslo
Baert, Jean-Paul
Bailey, Angela
Bailey, Dave
Bailey, Donovan
Bailey, Marjorie
Baker, Alison
Ball, James
Bannon, Paul
Barnes, Rolph

Bath, Doc
Bauck, Dean
Beaton, Bob
Beers, John
Bell, Jane
Berrett, Tim
Binns, Hilda
Blackman, Craig
Bogue, Glenn
Boileau, Art
Boldt, Arnold
Bond-Mills, Catherine
Bordeleau, Alain
Boucher, Alain
Bourdeau, Yvan
Bourgeois, Joel
Bowen, Stacy
Boychuk, Andy
Boyd, Barry
Bradley-Kameli, Sue
Branch, Cecilia
Bricker, Cal
Brill, Debbie
Brothers, Tanya
Brown, Hal
Brown, Larry
Brown, Wally
Buddo, Don
Burns, Leo
Butler, Kathy
Caffery, Jack
Cameron, Fred
Campbell, Debbie
Campbell, Rachelle
Campbell, R.D.
Casanova, Willie
Catherwood, Ethel
Chalmers, Angela
Chambers, Carlton
Chambul, Borys
Charette, Richard
Cheater, Millie
Christie, Alan
Clark, Paul
Clark, Ranza
Clarke, Karen
Clement, Diane
Clement, Doug
Coaffee, Cyril
Cohen, Laurie
Colistro, Peter
Cook, Myrtle
Cooperband, Mary
Corazza, John
Coté, Gérard
Courtwright, Jim
Coy, Eric
Craig, John
Craig, Paul
Crooks, Charmaine
Crothers, Bill
Crowley, Maureen
Crummer, Keith
Daniels, Danny
Davies, Jack
Deacon, Bruce
Desmarteau, Etienne
Devonish, Nicole

Dickson, Gordon
Docherty, Alexander
Dolegiewicz, Bishop
Donahue, Jake
Dowds, Maureen
Drayton, Jerome
Duffy, James
Duhaime, Greg
Duprey, Donalda
Eckel, Shirley
Edeh, Rosey
Edge, Dave
Edwards, Phil
Egerton, Stan
Elliott, Geoff
Elmer, Ken
Enright, Jim
Esmie, Robert
Estwick, Leslie
Eville, Vern
Fabre, Edouard
Farrell, Neil
Fedoruk, Sylvia
Fee, Earl
Fell, Graeme
Ferguson, Rich
Ferguson, Tracey
Finlay, Robert
Fisher, Joan
Fitzgerald, Mel
Floreal, Edrick
Fonseca, Peter
Foot, Fred
Fournier, Lionel
Fox, Fred
Fox, Terry
Fraser, Bud
Fraser, Hugh
Fritz, Bill
Frost, Barclay
Gairdner, Bill
Gallant, Georgie
Gareau, Jacqueline
Garvie, Clarence
Gavillucci, Angelo
Gendron, Francine
Gilbert, Glenroy
Gillis, Duncan
Good, Norah
Goulding, George
Gowan, Geoff
Graham, John
Gray, George
Gray, Rob
Greenidge, Ricardo
Griffiths, Joe
Haist, Jane
Halvorsen, John
Hammond, Alvin
Harding, Dick
Harper, George
Haslam, Eleanor
Hauch, Rosemarie
Hawkins, John
Haydenluck, Greg
Heikkila, Bill
Hendry, Joan
Hershfield, Leible

Higgins, Robina
Highbaugh, Larry
Hinds, Sterling
Histed, Jack
Hoffman, Abby
Hood, Graham
Hoogewerf, Simon
Howard, Tom
Howie, Al
Hudson, John
Humber, Bruce
Hume, Ian
Issajenko, Angella Taylor
Jackes, Arthur
Jerome, Harry
Jerome, Valerie
Jobin, Marcel
Johnson, Ben
Johnson, Don
Joy, Greg
Keating, Murray
Keeper, Joe
Kern, Laurie
Kerr, Bobby
Kerr, Dave
Kidd, Bruce
Killingbeck, Molly
King, Donald
Knox, Walter
Komonen, Dave
Konihowski, Diane
Konihowski, John
Krause, Willi
Kroeker, Tim
Kyle, Doug
Landry, Denis
Lane, Sharon
Lapointe, Francois
Latulippe, Phil
LeBlanc, Guillaume
Lee, Scott
Lefrancois, Charles
Lenover, Max
Lewington, Nancy
Lewis, Ray
Loaring, John
Lockett, Donna
Longboat, Tom
Lord, Hervé
Lord, Tom
Loverock, Patty
Lyle, Dulcie
Lyon, George
MacBeth, Fred
MacDonald, Jackie
MacGowan, Margaret
Mach, Gerard
Mackie-Morelli, Anne
Maddin, Janet
Mah, Sy
Maher, Peter
Mahorn, Atlee
Makolosky, Randy
Malcolm, Andrew
Manning, Peter
Marquette, Ulla
Martin, Carol
Martin, Robert

Mather, Eddie
Matthias, Brendan
Maughan, George
Maynes, Billy
McBlain, Liz
McCaffrey, Janice
McCloy, Paul
McCredie, Nancy
McEwen, Don
McFarlane, Bob
McFarlane, Don
McGee, Doug
McGill, Frank
McGillivray, David
McInnis, Andy
McKay, Willie
McKinnon, Archie
McKinnon, Frank
McKoy, Mark
McLaren, Grant
McLaren, Robert
McLeod, Barbara
McNaughton, Duncan
McNie, Murray
McRoberts, Brit
Meagher, Aileen
Meagher, Robyn
Meldrum, Jenny
Michel, Yvette
Miles, Johnny
Miller, Leigh
Miller, Zan
Minor, Ron
Money, Ken
Montabone, Monty
Moore, Bob
Moreau, Lucette
Mullins, Joe
Neilson, Scott
Newhouse, Ian
Nicks, Frank
Oakley, Alex
O'Connor, Larry
Ogden, Steve
Ogilvie, Peter
Olafsson, Shirley
Olesen, Marc
Oliver, Roy
Olsen, Phil
Olson, Betty
Orton, George
Ottey, Milt
Palmason, Diane
Palmer, Lillian
Parnell, Bill
Parry, Jack
Patrick, Muzz
Pauletto, Bruno
Payne, Marita
Peden, Doug
Peel, Ann
Pells, Leah
Percival, Lloyd
Petitclerc, Chantal
Phibbs, Bob
Phinney, Gertrude
Pickard, Vic
Pidskalny, Diane

Pilon, Jacques
Piotrowski, Irene
Pirnie, Bruce
Poce, Paul
Poitras, Tina
Porter, Ken
Pugh, Lionel
Pullen, Tom
Puntous, Patricia
Puntous, Sylviane
Pyzer, Doug
Quessy, Marc
Radmore, Joey
Raike, Stan
Rankine, Scotty
Rau, Richard
Reed, Georgette
Reid, Brigitte
Reid, Patrick
Reiser, Glenda
Richardson, Jillian
Richman, Joey
Robinson, Bobby
Rock, Richard
Roe, Lot
Rogin, Bill
Roost, Ain
Rosenfeld, Bobbie
Ross-Giffen, Jill
Ruegger, Silvia
Ryan, Doreen
Salmond, Gary
Sanderson, Lyle
Saunders, Bryan
Sax, Joe
Schnurr, Paula
Scorrar, Doug
Scott, Debbie
Seller, Peggy
Seltzer, Sheila
Shannon, Carver
Sharpe, Tony
Shepherd, George
Sherring, William
Short, George
Shrubb, Alf
Sigfusson, Svein
Simpson, Bruce
Singleton, Harvey
Slythe, Christine
Smith, Ethel
Smith, Michael
Smylie, Rod Sr.
Smyth, Jack
Snyder, Brad
Sovran, Gino
Sparling, Jean
Spir, Peter
Spooner, Hugh
Spowage, Cheryl
Sprague, Dave
Springstead, Velma
St. Pierre, Martin
Steen, Dave
Steen, Dave
Stevenson, Art
Stewart, Gordon
Storey, Irene

Stride, Bryan
Strike, Hilda
Sullivan, Kevin
Surin, Bruny
Takacs, Ed
Tashlin, Lesley
Taylor, Betty
Thomson, Earl
Tobacco, Terry
Town, Tom
Trelle, Herman
Turner, John
Van Kiekebelt, Debbie
Vandervliet, Mary
Van Vliet, Maury
Vigars, Bob
Viger, Andre
Vince, Anthony
Vine, Bill
Walker, Louise
Wall, Gwen
Wallingford, Ron
Walsh, Brenda
Warren, Harry
Washburn, Leroy
Watt, David
Wedmann, Wilf
Wendling, Wendy
Wenzel, Joan
Werthner, Penny
White, Al
White, Betty
White, Julie
Wiley, Alison
Williams, Desai
Williams, Freddie
Williams, Lynn
Williams, Paul
Williams, Percy
Wilson, Doug Sr.
Wilson, Murray
Wolff, Doreen
Woods, Maggie
Worrall, Jim
Wright, Harold
Wright, Joe Sr.
Wright, Thelma
Yakubowich, Joyce
Yetman, Wayne
York, Patrick
Young, Joe
Young, Walter

TRAMPOLINE
Blais, Ginette
Nemesvary, Mike
Ross, John

TRIATHLON
Bates, Mark
Bermel, Lynne
Donnelly, Sharon
Fuhr, Heather
Hellard, Rick
MacMartin, Andrew
McNicoll, Bruce
Montgomery, Carol

Ritchie, Jo-Anne

VOLLEYBALL
Anderson, Randy
Baydock, Donna
Bigras, Sylvie
Bishop, Carole
Bridle, Wezer
Buchberger, Kerri Ann
Child, John
Danyluk, Terry
Davis, Pat
Drakich, Ed
Dunn, Marc
Eisler, Laurie
Gratton, Paul
Heese, Mark
Hitchcock, Dean
Hitchcock, Monica
Hunt, Helen
Kelly, Janis
Nord, Dennis
Pischke, Garth
Sawula, Lorne
Tennant, Mark
Wigston, Fran

WATER POLO
Bol, René
Gifford, Heather
Gilbey, Janice
Gross, George Jr.
Gunell, Roy
Hart, David
McCleery, Alan
McGill, Frank
Meyer, Bill
Pugliese, Rick
Richardson, John
Seller, Peggy

WATER SKIING
Allan, Liz
Athans, Gary
Athans, George Jr.
Athans, Greg
Clifford, John
Crutchfield, Linda
Gregoire, Hélène
Hazzard, Elmer
Llewellyn, Jaret
McClintock, Joel
McClintock, Judy
Messner, Joe
Messner, Pat
Reid, Bruce
Reid, Ian
Ward, Clint

WEIGHTLIFTING
Allan, Maurice
Bilodeau, Alain
Blinn, Moya
Bratty, Gary
Burke, Larry
Cardinal, Marc
Cyr, Louis
Delamarre, Victor

Demers, Jacques
Flynn, Clarke
Gilchrist, Jack
Hadlow, Terry
Hepburn, Doug
Hill, Harvey
Legace, Francois
Lipari, Michel
Mercier, Michel
Morris, Price
Nesbitt, Keith
Parente, Mario
Pietracupa, Michel
Prior, Russ
Robertson, Doug
Robitaille, Daniel
Roy, Aldo
Roy, Kevin
Salter, Allen
Smith, Rosaire
Smith, Wayne
Squires, Bert
Sylvain, Jules
Varaleau, Jack
Woo, Wes

**WHEELCHAIR BASKET-
BALL**
Benoit, Chantal
Enright, Jim
Ferguson, Tracey
Gavillucci, Angelo
Griffin, Pat
Hansen, Rick
Kutrowski, Linda
Lapalme, Denis
Lord, Hervé
McClellan, Reg
Minor, Ron
Pidskalny, Diane
Tonello, Jerry
Wright, Doug

WRESTLING
Abdou, Justin
Anderson, Dave
Beiler, Egon
Bergey, Kim
Bertie, Gordon
Bianco, Scott
Boese, Kurt
Bohay, Gary
Bolger, Pat
Borodow, Andy
Calder, Marty
Conacher, Lionel Sr.
Cox, Doug
Cummings, Dave
Daniar, Stephen
Davis, Clark
DeBenedetti, Tania
Deschatelets, Richard
Donison, Butch
Donison, Danny
Donison, Lee
Flanagan, Pat
Garvie, Clarence
Garvie, Gord

Geris, Harry
Hart, Bret
Hohl, David
Hope, Gord
Iacovelli, Orlando
Johl, Yogi
Kallos, Garry
Kawasaki, Mitch
Kiniski, Gene
Ladik, Oleg
Lappage, Ron
Layton, Lord Athol
Leyshon, Glynn
Matheson, Dan
McCready, Earl
Michienzi, Peter
Mitchell, Doug
Molle, Bob
Mosca, Angelo
Nordhagen, Christine
Nye, Barry
Oberlander, Fred
Oberlander, Phil
Pettigrew, Vern
Pilon, Claude
Pyle, Dave
Renken, Brian
Renken, Lloyd
Rinke, Chris
Robinson, Bob
Rokosh, Greg
Schleimer, Joseph
Sissaouri, Guivi
Sorensen, Ole
Steckle, Bob
Stockton, Donald
Stuebbing, Jeff
Stupp, Howard
Takahashi, Ray
Tam, Selwyn
Thomas, Howard
Trelle, Herman
Trifunov, Jim
Watson, Whipper Billy
Wilson, Chris
Wishart, Wyatt
Woodcroft, Greg
Wright, Joe Sr.
Wurr, Alfred
Yeats, Doug
York, Patrick
Zilberman, Victor

WHO'S WHO IN CANADIAN SPORT

The Guide to Canadian Sport
Written by Bob Ferguson

Additional copies of this book may be purchased for $35.00 plus GST (7%). No PST is charged on books. HST (15%) is charged for residents of Nova Scotia, New Brunswick and Newfoundland. Shipping and handling are additional. Please allow 3 weeks for delivery.

Please send me _____ copy (ies) of **Who's Who in Canadian Sport.**

All orders must be accompanied by one of the following:

❑ Cheque enclosed (make payable to "Who's Who in Canadian Sport")
❑ Purchase order enclosed
❑ VISA _____ Expiry date _____ Signature _____

Ship to: (please include a street address)

Name: _____

Address: _____

City: _____ Province: _____ Postal Code: _____

Tel: (   ) _____ Fax: (   ) _____

Quantity	Price	Total
	$35.00	
Subtotal 1		
Shipping and handling ($5.00 per book)		
* Subtotal 2		
(870812583RT0001) GST (7%) or HST (15%)		
Grand Total		

* International orders add 15% to Subtotal 2
Orders placed from outside Canada must be prepaid by VISA or by cheque/money order converted to Canadian funds. Taxes **DO NOT** apply. Allow additional time (beyond 3 to 4 weeks) for delivery.

Send orders to:
Bob Ferguson,
Who's Who in Canadian Sport
112 Banchory Crescent
Kanata, Ontario K2K 2V5

Future Projects

Who's Who in Canadian Sport is the first in a series of publications planned by **Sporting Facts,** a subsidiary of **Harlas Inc.**

Next year we plan to publish the **Book of Canadian Sports Lists**, a comprehensive compilation of champions in virtually all sport categories through the years. Also included are the names of major national award winners and members of Canadian international Games teams.

Further along the track a Halls of Fame registry and massive sports trivia book are in the works.

If you have any suggestions, information or general observations you wish to pass along contact **Bob Ferguson, 112 Banchory Cresc., Kanata, ON, K2K 2V5, phone/fax (613) 271-8690 or e-mail:** HYPERLINK mailto:Fergwho@home.com Fergwho@home.com.